tions, and a separately-searchable database of more than 1,500 full-text online government publications in the crime and justice area. Full-text articles, many of which are available in both HTML and PDF format, can be easily downloaded or printed. The site links to many sources of information on other U.S. Department of Justice Web sites including the Bureau of Justice Assistance (BJA http://www.ojp.usdoj.gov/bja) and the Bureau of Justice Statistics (BJS http://www.ojp.usdoj.gov/bjs).
URL: http://www.ncjrs.org

SITE NAME: NIJ International Center
SITE DESCRIPTION: Home page of the National Institute of Justice's International Center. The Center was created in 1997 as a response to the increasing globalization of crime.
FEATURES: The International Center seeks to stimulate, facilitate, evaluate, and disseminate both national and international criminal justice research and information. A key feature of the site is the Center's fully-searchable Virtual Library—a repository of information related to comparative, international, and transnational crime and justice issues.
URL: http://www.ojp.usdoj.gov/nij/international

SITE NAME: Partnerships Against Violence Network (PAVNET)
SITE DESCRIPTION: PAVNET describes itself as a virtual library of information about violence and youth-at-risk, representing data from several different federal agencies.
FEATURES: A research database, funding opportunities for researchers, a PAVNET mailgroup for violence-prevention profession-als, and an overview of PAVNET-sponsored programs. The PAVNET research database is an online, searchable source of information about current federally-funded research on violence.
URL: http://www.pavnet.org

SITE NAME: RAND Criminal Justice
SITE DESCRIPTION: RAND Criminal Justice shares in a tradition of innovative and quality research that goes back over 50 years.
FEATURES: Many full-text RAND publications in the area of crime causation, crime prevention, and crime control policy are available online. Sentencing and corrections, drug policy and drug control, and violence prevention are just a few of RAND's many interests.
URL: http://www.rand.org/crim

SITE NAME: Sourcebook of Criminal Justice Statistics
SITE DESCRIPTION: The Sourcebook of Criminal Justice Statistics online brings together data from more than 100 sources about all aspects of crime and justice in the United States. The site is fully searchable and offers more than 600 viewable tables.
FEATURES: Covers criminal offending, characteristics of persons arrested, victimization, judicial processing, imprisonment, capital punishment, public opinion, and justice system statistics.
URL: http://www.albany.edu/sourcebook

SITE NAME: Western Criminology Review
SITE DESCRIPTION: Run by the Western Society of Criminology, this site provides access to the society's online journal, the Western Criminology Review. Visit the Society's homepage at http://www.sonoma.edu/cja/wsc/wscmain.html.
FEATURES: Full-text articles on a wealth of topics in the field of criminology from the journal. Past and current issues are available, and a complete table of contents for each issue is provided.
URL: http://wcr.sonoma.edu

Sites Maintained by Individuals

SITE NAME: Crime Theory
SITE DESCRIPTION: Maintained by Bruce Hoffman (the University of Washington), this site offers many great insights into the field of criminology!
FEATURES: Descriptions of major theories and significant theorists; criminology timeline; glossary; bibliographies; teaching forum; and games. A criminology forum allows visitors to post questions and announcements, and to engage in a conversational give-and-take with other users. An archive of early criminological texts contains the original writings of historically influential criminologists.
URL: http://www.crimetheory.com

SITE NAME: Crime Theory Readings
SITE DESCRIPTION: Maintained by Professor Cecil Greek and stu-dents in the School of Criminology at Florida State University, this site was developed in support of an online course offering in crimi-nological theory.
FEATURES: Detailed lecture notes describing various criminological perspectives, including the Classical School, Positivism, biological theories, ecological approaches, learning theory, labeling theory, and more!
URL: http://www.criminology.fsu.edu/crimtheory/lectures.htm

SITE NAME: Criminological Theory
SITE DESCRIPTION: Maintained by Professor Matthew Robinson (Appalachian State University), this site focuses on the kinds of the-ories described in this textbook.
FEATURES: Lots of links to other sites, links to searchable databas-es, and a poll that you can take to submit your vote on what you think causes crime.
URL: http://www.appstate.edu/~robinsnmb/theorylinks.htm

SITE NAME: Dr. Frank Schmalleger's Cybrary
SITE DESCRIPTION: Known on the Internet as "The World's Crime and Justice Directory."
FEATURES: Provides a fully-searchable database of more than 12,000 links to sites in criminology and criminal justice. The data-base also contains links to all federal documents available through the National Institute of Justice and the National Criminal Justice Reference Service. Message boards dealing with all aspects of crime and justice are available at the site (http://talkjustice.com), and the full-text of the American Society of Criminology's Task Force Reports is available in PDF format (http://talkjustice.com/task.pdf). Remember to check the Cybrary for updates on any of the sites list-ed here.
URL: http://talkjustice.com/cybrary.asp

SITE NAME: Mega Links in Criminal Justice
SITE DESCRIPTION: Operated by Professor Tom O'Connor (North Carolina Wesleyan College) Mega Links provides an incredibly comprehensive resource for anyone interested in the field of crimi-nology.
FEATURES: Section headings include criminology, crime analysis, law, juvenile justice, prisons, current events, reform, technology, and more! The site also offers a Beginner's Guide to Understanding Criminological Theory, and an Advanced Guide to Understanding Criminology Theory—both developed by the site's creator.
URL: http://faculty.ncwc.edu/toconnor

CRIMINOLOGY TODAY

AN INTEGRATIVE INTRODUCTION

The publisher and the author of this book
jointly donate a portion of sales proceeds
to research and education
in the field of crime and justice.

CRIMINOLOGY TODAY

AN INTEGRATIVE INTRODUCTION

THIRD EDITION

FRANK SCHMALLEGER, PH.D.

Professor Emeritus, The University of North Carolina at Pembroke

Prentice
Hall

Upper Saddle River, New Jersey 07458

Library of Congress Cataloging-in-Publication Data
Schmalleger, Frank.
    Criminology today : an integrative introduction/Frank Schmalleger.—3rd ed.
        p. cm.
    Includes index.
    ISBN 0-13-091795-8
    1. Criminology. 2. Criminology—United States. I. Title
HV6025 .S346 2002
364—dc21

2001021304

Publisher: Jeff Johnston
Executive Acquisitions Editor: Kim Davies
Assistant Editor: Sarah Holle
Production Editor: Janet Bolton
In-house Liaison: Adele M. Kupchik
Director of Manufacturing and Production: Bruce Johnson
Managing Editor: Mary Carnis
Manufacturing Manager: Ilene Sanford
Creative Director: Cheryl Asherman
Marketing Manager: Ramona Sherman
Director of Marketing Communication & New Media: Frank I. Mortimer, Jr.
Photo Researcher: Julie Tesser
Front Cover Photograph: Tristan Paviot © Tony Stone
Back Cover Photograph: Paul Edmundson © Tony Stone
Cover Photo/Illustration & Design: Blair Brown
Senior Design Coordinator: Miguel Ortiz
Interior Design: Lorraine Castellano
Composition: Carlisle Communications Ltd., Dubuque, Iowa
Printing and Binding: RR Donnelley & Sons Company, Willard, OH

Photo Credits
Chapter 1: Stephen Agricola, Stock Boston; Chapter 2: Bob Daemmrich, Stock Boston/PNI; Chapter 3: Pictor; Chapter 4: The Granger Collection; Chapter 5: Ian Turner, Spooner, Liaison Agency, Inc.; Chapter 6: Photofest; Chapter 7: Springer, Liaison Agency, Inc.; Chapter 8: PictureQuest Vienna; Chapter 9: AP/Wide World Photos; Chapter 10: David R. Swanson, Liaison Agency, Inc.: Chapter 11: John Griffin, The Image Works; Chapter 12: Photofest; Chapter 13: Joel Stettenheim, SABA Press Photos, Inc.; Chapter 14: Marc Yankus; Chapter 15: Allan Tannenbaum, Corbis/Sygma; Chapter 16: Photofest

Pearson Education LTD.
Pearson Education Australia PTY, Limited
Pearson Education Singapore, Pte. Ltd.
Pearson Education North Asia Ltd.
Pearson Education Canada, Ltd.
Pearson Educación de Mexico, S.A. de C.V.
Pearson Education—Japan
Pearson Education Malaysia, Pte. Ltd.

Prentice Hall

10 9 8 7 6 5 4 3 2 1
ISBN 0-13-091795-8

For Peggy, Nicole, and Malia

Brief Contents

Contents

CHAPTER 6

PSYCHOLOGICAL AND PSYCHIATRIC FOUNDATIONS OF CRIMINAL BEHAVIOR 169

CHAPTER 7   **SOCIOLOGICAL THEORIES I: SOCIAL STRUCTURE**   **201**

| CHAPTER 8 | SOCIOLOGICAL THEORIES II: SOCIAL PROCESS AND SOCIAL DEVELOPMENT | 227 |

CHAPTER 12   WHITE-COLLAR AND ORGANIZED CRIME   357

CHAPTER 13   DRUG ABUSE AND CRIME   387

Foreword

The United States is currently experiencing a decline in levels of violent crime. Unfortunately, however, the decline may be short-lived. Acts of violence continue to occur at levels far higher than the historical norm. They have become more random, more brutal, and targeted toward more vulnerable victims—for example, children and innocent bystanders.

When seen in historical context, today's statistics may evidence only a brief respite from the extraordinarily high crime levels that have plagued our nation for decades. Experts predict another crime wave within the next ten years because of a projected increase in the number of teenagers in America—teenagers who are twice as violent as today's adults. The next generation of children is also more likely to be born to a single mother, to experience poverty, and to be unemployed than previous generations—all factors known to relate to later criminality. When James Q. Wilson, a foremost authority on crime, wrote recently about what advice he would give to Americans struggling with the crime problem, he offered only two words: "Get ready."[1]

It is this sense of urgency, combined with what may be an unwarranted complacency among today's policymakers that the crime "problem" is finally under control, that creates a daunting challenge for today's criminology students, who must, above all, learn criminology so that they can contribute to much needed future solutions. In short, criminology students must seek to become relevant. We have become too detached from applied criminology, and as a result, current crime policies are overly bureaucratic and highly political. We must strive to change the perception that "criminologists . . . are insular and detached types who fiddle with equations while the cities burn."[2]

Criminology is the only academic discipline devoted exclusively to the scientific study of crime causation and control. When the public puts pressure on government officials to "do something" about the crime problem, surely criminologists have an obligation to assist in identifying key issues, proposing policy and program solutions, and evaluating the results.

But learning criminology is not easy. In fact, it is hard to imagine a more difficult subject matter than criminology. At its core, criminology requires an understanding of the vagaries of human behavior, with an appreciation of their biological, cultural, and sociological foundations. Each contributes a partial explanation for crime, but none is comprehensive, and all are fraught with controversy. Understanding crime is made even more complex because the behavior is defined and controlled by a justice system that consists of many diverse organizations, such as the police and corrections, and each is governed by a separate system of complex laws and philosophies. How can a person make sense of all these competing theories and contradictory data?

Thank goodness for Frank Schmalleger's *Criminology Today!* In writing it, he has done the hard work for us. He succeeds in making this complex social problem clearly understandable. He begins by describing, in an easy-to-understand manner, the nature and diversity of the crime problem today. He critically reviews the nation's divergent crime indicators and suggests what recent patterns portend about the crime problem—ever changing, potentially more threatening. He then advances our understanding of the causes of crime by synthesizing criminology's most salient theories, grounding his review in current as well as historical traditions. Students can flounder in crime data and theory without a good and objective guide. Dr. Schmalleger serves as an authoritative and compassionate guide.

The uniqueness of this book, and its biggest strength, derives from Schmalleger's orientation: It is always practical and socially relevant. He teaches the student how to relate criminology facts and theories to the everyday world. Discussions of the death penalty, for example, are illustrated with real-life stories of recent executions; and the material covered in the text is particularly up-to-date. Events like New York's subway-pusher murder, the Rae Carruth trial, the Columbine High School shootings, the use of DNA evidence in O. J. Simpson's criminal and civil trials, recent federal

---

[1]James Q. Wilson and Joan Petersilia, *Crime* (San Francisco: Institute for Contemporary Studies, 1995).

[2]Elliott Currie, "Shifting the Balance: On Social Action and the Future of Criminological Research," *Journal of Research in Crime and Delinquency,* Vol. 30, No. 4 (1993).

crime control legislation, and the Oklahoma City bombing are all discussed. Including such material not only makes the connection between academic criminology and real-world practice patently obvious, but it also provides an immediate attention getter for students, who are more likely to become fully engaged by such timely material. In a sense, it makes criminology come alive.

This book synthesizes and interprets the best available evidence on crime and crime control, but it goes still further. In his final chapter, Dr. Schmalleger encourages us to consider our future and to work toward promoting better crime pre-vention and control practices. In the end, mastering the material in *Criminology Today* should enable us to do much more than simply sit passively and "get ready" for the next crime wave, for what we understand, we can often change. Dr. Schmalleger's text provides an excellent road map for increasing that understanding.

Joan Petersilia, Ph.D.
Professor of Criminology, Law, and Society
University of California, Irvine
Former President of the American Society of Criminology

Preface

The field of criminology is far deeper, and much broader intellectually, than the 600-or-so pages of information that any printed textbook can fit between its covers. Moreover, the field is changing daily, as new theories of causation are proposed; as novel forms of crime take their place alongside traditional ones; and as policymakers strive to embrace ever more effective crime control techniques in legislative debates, social programs, and innovative media campaigns.

Echoing these sentiments, it's been said that an introductory textbook like this one must be a mile long, but it can only be an inch thick. In other words, any introduction to criminology must cover the history of the field and the important theorists and theories of the past and present. It must also provide a solid overview of the crime picture in contemporary society, and it must offer some insight into the crime control policies of yesterday and today. Most such books are also expected to include a description of different types of crime, along with an explanation of the complex social and individual nexus that leads to crime. As an author of a number of books in the field of crime and justice, I can attest to the fact that this is a tall order. Because of its physical limits, an introductory text cannot spend too much time describing any one perspective, theory, law, or offense.

Thankfully, in writing the third edition of *Criminology Today* I no longer found myself bound by the traditional limits of print media. This new edition, for the first time, makes extensive use of educational technologies that were only in their infancy when the first edition of this book appeared. Even though the first edition was accompanied by a Web site (the first criminology text to have reached such a milestone, I am told), and the second edition built that site into a comprehensive and interactive learning tool, it is with this new edition that the true possibilities of the Internet have been fully embraced. Sprinkled throughout the pages of this book you will find icons pointing to new learning possibilities. Among them are

- *Web Quests!*, which challenge you to work your way through comprehensive Web-based chapter projects.

Web Quests! make studying enjoyable and open the door to a wealth of electronic information.

- *Web Extras!*, which take you to sites that are closely related to the materials you are reading about. Web Extras! provide a "virtual criminology" tour of the Internet, with visits to sites too numerous to mention in this brief preface.
- *Audio Extras!*, which allow you to listen to the author introduce each chapter of your text
- *Library Extras!*, which provide a list of readily accessible Web-based reading assignments that round out chapter materials

All are new to this edition, and each has been closely integrated with the text to provide a wealth of freely available materials that add substantial value to the learning experience. Web Quests!, Web Extras!, Audio Extras!, and Library Extras! finally allow me, as an author, to offer you a textbook that is far more than the proverbial "inch-thick" book would be.

Other special features of *Criminology Today* make this book substantially different from all the other available texts which deal with the same subject matter. The following list highlights what I see as the important differences:

- *Criminology Today* makes use of the latest-available instructional technologies and offers students the opportunity to learn from the Internet, from videos, and from print media.
- *Criminology Today* emphasizes the wide and interdisciplinary variety of academic perspectives that contribute to a thorough and well-informed understanding of the crime problem— hence the book's subtitle, *An Integrative Introduction.*
- *Criminology Today* is up-to-date. It addresses the latest social issues and discusses innovative criminological perspectives within a well-grounded and traditional theoretical framework.
- *Criminology Today* is socially relevant. It contrasts contemporary issues of crime and social order with existing and proposed crime control policies.

- *Criminology Today* is interesting and easy to read. Written for today's student, it makes use of attention-getting stories, news briefs, images, and charts and graphs to capture student attention.
- *Criminology Today* is policy oriented. Unlike many existing texts, it stresses the consequences of criminological thought for social policy and describes the practical issues associated with understanding and controlling crime. Social policies focusing on prevention, treatment, rehabilitation, and victim restoration are all discussed.
- *Criminology Today* is thematic. It builds upon the divergence between the social problems viewpoint and the social responsibility perspective. In so doing, it highlights the central issue facing criminologists today: whether crime should be addressed as a matter of individual responsibility and accountability or treated as a symptom of a dysfunctional society.
- *Criminology Today* provides instructors and students with a wealth of resources for studying crime and society's response to it, including an award-winning World Wide Web site (http://www.prenhall.com/schmalleger), an annotated instructor's edition, a video library, full-color transparencies, an excellent student study guide, and other supplements.

The thematic approach of *Criminology Today* is dualistic. On the one hand, it presents a social problems framework, which holds that crime may be a manifestation of underlying cultural issues like poverty, discrimination, and the breakdown of traditional social institutions. It contrasts the social problems approach with a social responsibility perspective, which claims that individuals are fundamentally responsible for their own behavior and which maintains that they choose crime over other, more law-abiding, courses of action. The thematic contrast is an important one, for it provides students with a useful framework for integrating the voluminous material contained within the field of criminology. Contrasting the two perspectives, as this book does, provides fertile ground for a dialectical process whereby students can better understand the central issues defining contemporary criminology and come to their own conclusions about the value of criminological theorizing.

As an author, I have tried to ensure that today's students will find *Criminology Today* relevant, interesting, informative, *and* useful. It is my fondest hope that this book and its Internet extensions will assist students in drawing their own conclusions about the American crime problem, that it will help prepare them for the future, and that it will allow them to make informed decisions about public crime control policy.

Acknowledgments

A book like *Criminology Today* draws upon the talents and resources of many people and is the end result of much previous effort. This text could not have been written without the groundwork laid by previous criminologists, academics, and researchers; hence a hearty thank-you is due everyone who has contributed to the development of the field of criminology throughout the years, and especially to those theorists, authors, and social commentators who are cited in this book. Without their work, the field would be that much poorer. I would like to thank, as well, all the adopters—professors and students alike—of my previous textbooks, for they have given me the encouragement and fostered the steadfastness required to write this new edition of *Criminology Today*.

The Prentice Hall team, whom I have come to know so well and who have worked so professionally with me on this and other projects, deserves a special thanks. The team includes Robin Baliszewski, Kim Davies, Cheryl Asherman, Juanita Griffin, Sarah Holle, Craig Marcus, Frank Mortimer, Miguel Ortiz, Ramona Sherman, Santos Shih, and Mary Carnis. I would especially like to thank Janet Bolton and Adele Kupchik at Prentice Hall for their commitment and attention to this project. My thanks also to cover designer Blair Brown, interior designer Lorraine Castellano, and photo researcher Julie Tesser, whose efforts have helped make *Criminology Today* both attractive and visually appealing. The keen eye of copy editor Judith Mara Riotto is beyond compare, and this book is much richer for her efforts.

My new friends and professional colleagues, Debra Kelly at Virginia's Longwood College and Karel Kurst-Swanger at Oswego State University helped in many ways. Dr. Kelley's assistance in developing content for two new chapters in this edition showed her to be a true scholar who is very much in touch with the field of criminology. Dr. Kurst-Swanger helped develop the detailed conceptual poster that graphically describes criminological thought and which is bundled with this text. Her efforts are greatly appreciated.

Manuscript reviewers Reed Adams, Mount Olive College; Michael P. Brown, Ball State University; Bryan D. Byers, Ball State University; Dianne Carmody, Western Washington University; Myrna Cintron, Sam Houston State University; Ellen G. Cohn, Florida International University; Mark L. Dantzker, Loyola University; Taylor Davis, Georgia Southern University; Patrick G. Donnelly, University of Dayton; Martin E. Heischmidt, Rend Lake College; Ronald D. Hunter, Jacksonville State University; Debra Kelley, Longwood College; John Kirkpatrick, University of New Hampshire; Joan Luxenburg, University of Central Oklahoma; M. Joan McDermott, Southern Illinois University; Robert Mutchnick, Indiana University of Pennsylvania; Glen E. Sapp, Central Carolina Community College; Tamson L. Six, Virginia Commonwealth University; and Anthony W. Zumpetta, West Chester University are due a special thank-you for helping me stick to important themes when I might otherwise have strayed and for their guidance in matters of detail. I am especially thankful to supplements author Ellen Cohn for the quality products she has created and for her exceptional ability to build intuitively upon concepts in the text. Thanks also to Bob Winslow at California State University—San Diego for insight and encouragement on a number of important issues, and to Richard Guymon at Maplewoods Community College, to Jack Humphrey at UNC-G, and to Stephen J. Schoenthaler for their valuable suggestions in the preparation of this new edition.

This book has benefited greatly from the quick availability of information and other resources through online services and in various locations on the Internet's World Wide Web. I am grateful to the many information providers who, although they are too numerous to list, have helped establish such useful resources.

I am thankful as well for the assistance of Bill Tafoya and Nancy Carnes, both with the Federal Bureau of Investigation (Bill is now retired); William Ballweber at the National Institute of Justice; David Beatty, Director of Public Affairs with the National Victim Center; Kris Rose at the National Criminal Justice Reference Service; Marilyn Marbrook and Michael Rand at the Office of Justice Programs; Mark Reading at the Drug Enforcement Administration; and Barbara Maxwell at *USA Today*.

Finally, but by no means least, I am indebted to a small but very special group of contemporary criminologists who have laid the foundation for our discipline's presence on the

Internet. Among them are Cecil Greek at Florida State University, whose online lecture notes (http://www.criminology.fsu.edu/crimtheory) are massively informative; Tom O'Connor of North Carolina Wesleyan College, whose Megalinks in Criminal Justice (http://faculty.ncwc.edu/toconnor) provide an amazingly comprehensive resource; Matthew Robinson at Appalachian State University, whose Crime Theory Links (http://www.appstate.edu/~robinsnmb/theorylinks.htm) allow visitors to vote on what they think are the causes of crime; Bruce Hoffman, whose Crime Theory site (http://crimetheory.com) at the University of Washington offers many great insights into the field; T. R. Young, Garth Massey, and others at the Red Feather Institute (http://www.tryoung.com), whose excellent and far-reaching collection of online postmodern works, including the *Red Feather Journal of Postmodern Criminology*, adds much to available Web-based resources; and Regina Schekall, volunteer Webmaster for the Santa Clara Police Department, whose organized crime page (www.crime.org) provides a valuable resource for both students and educators. All of these excellent resources are referred to throughout this book—and it is to these modern day visionaries that *Criminology Today* owes much of its technological depth.

About the Author

Frank Schmalleger, Ph.D., is Professor Emeritus at The University of North Carolina at Pembroke. He is also director of the Justice Research Association (JRA), a private consulting firm and think tank focusing on issues of crime and justice. The Justice Research Association, which is based in Hilton Head Island, South Carolina, serves the needs of the nation's civil and criminal justice planners and administrators through workshops, conferences, and grant-writing and program-evaluation support. JRA also supports the Criminal Justice Distance Learning Consortium (CJDLC), which can be found on the Web at http://cjcentral.com/cjdlc, Talk Justice (http://talkjustice.com), and the Cybrary—also known as "the world's criminal justice directory" (http://talkjustice.com/cybrary.asp).

Dr. Schmalleger holds degrees from the University of Notre Dame and Ohio State University, having earned both a master's (1970) and a doctorate in sociology (1974) from Ohio State University with a special emphasis in criminology. From 1976 to 1994, he taught criminal justice courses at the University of North Carolina at Pembroke. For the last 16 of those years he chaired the university's Department of Sociology, Social Work, and Criminal Justice. As an adjunct professor with Webster University in St. Louis, Missouri, Schmalleger helped develop the university's graduate program in security administration and loss prevention. He taught courses in that curriculum for more than a decade. Schmalleger has also taught in the New School for Social Research's online graduate program, helping build the world's first electronic classrooms in support of distance learning through computer telecommunications. An avid Web surfer and site builder, Schmalleger is also the creator of award-winning World Wide Web sites, including one which supports this textbook (http://www.prenhall.com/schmalleger).

Frank Schmalleger is the author of numerous articles and many books, including the widely used *Criminal Justice Today: An Introductory Text for the 21st Century* (Prentice Hall, 2001), now in its sixth edition; *Criminal Justice: A Brief Introduction,* Fourth Edition Update (Prentice Hall, 2002); *Criminal Law Today* (Prentice Hall, 2002); with John Smykla, *Corrections in the 21st Century* (Glencoe/McGraw-Hill, 2001); *Crime and the Justice System in America: An Encyclopedia* (Greenwood Publishing Group, 1997); *Trial of the Century: People of the State of California vs. Orenthal James Simpson* (Prentice Hall, 1996); *Career Paths: A Guide to Jobs in Federal Law Enforcement* (Regents/Prentice Hall, 1994); *Computers in Criminal Justice* (Wyndham Hall Press, 1991); *Criminal Justice Ethics* (Greenwood Press, 1991); *Finding Criminal Justice in the Library* (Wyndham Hall Press, 1991); *Ethics in Criminal Justice* (Wyndham Hall Press, 1990); *A History of Corrections* (Foundations Press of Notre Dame, 1983); and *The Social Basis of Criminal Justice* (University Press of America, 1981). Schmalleger is also founding editor of the journal *The Justice Professional.*

Schmalleger's philosophy of both teaching and writing can be summed up in these words: "In order to communicate knowledge we must first catch, then hold, a person's interest—be it student, colleague, or policymaker. Our writing, our speaking, and our teaching must be relevant to the problems facing people today, and they must—in some way—help solve those problems."

Criminology Today is supported by a widely acclaimed award-winning Web site accessible at http://www.prenhall.com/schmalleger. Once you arrive at the site, click on the cover of your book to enter. The feature-rich third edition Web site builds upon a strong tradition of standard-setting excellence in Web-based media. It offers the following special features:

Electronic syllabus. Check here to see if your instructor has created an online syllabus. If so, refer to it to keep track of reading assignments, test dates, term papers, and other coursework. The electronic syllabus posted by your instructor may also contain links to Web-based media, such as online lectures, and to sites chosen by your instructor for you to view.

Audio Extras! Hear the author introduce each chapter. Audio chapter introductions require Real Player™ or Windows Media Player™ software.

Chapter learning objectives. Set your study goals for each chapter with chapter-specific learning objectives. Use these objectives to maintain your focus on important materials as you read the text.

Practice review questions. Prepare for tests and assess your knowledge of critical content with online review questions. Use these true-false and multiple-choice questions to test yourself as often as you want—and watch your scores improve.

Electronic homework. Respond to online essay questions, and e-mail your answers to your instructor for grading. Electronic homework makes it possible for you to demonstrate your knowledge of core concepts while it helps save trees!

Chapter summaries. Review chapter materials with online summaries of key points. Bulleted summaries allow for quick and easy access to critical content and can help you remember important chapter information.

Web Quests. Work your way through comprehensive Web-based chapter projects, and learn how to do criminology research on the Internet. Web Quests! make studying enjoyable and open the door to a wealth of electronic information.

Web Extras Visit sites that are closely related to the materials you are reading about. Web Extras! provide a virtual criminology tour of the Internet and add depth to textbook material.

Library Extras! Read carefully selected documents from the American Society of Criminology, the Bureau of Justice Statistics, the National Institute of Justice, the Bureau of Justice Assistance, the Federal Bureau of Investigation, and many other sources at the *Criminology Today* electronic library. Library Extras! are constantly updated to bring you the latest in criminological research and data.

Crime and justice news. Stay up-to-the-minute with late-breaking crime and justice news. Continually updated stories provide complete coverage of current events in the crime and justice field.

E-mail announcements of late-breaking crime news. Sign up for e-mail announcements, and have the latest in breaking crime news delivered right to your desktop every day. E-mail announcements are a convenient and easy way of keeping abreast of events in the justice field.

Careers Center. Use the Careers Center to find the best-paying jobs in the justice profession. If you aren't sure that you want to work in the justice system, this feature can help you decide your future.

Message boards. Discuss crime and justice issues with students and professors from across the country and around the world. Our boards allow you to read and post messages whenever you are connected to the Internet.

E-mail discussion list. Join our e-mail discussion list, and stay abreast of what other students are talking about. E-mail discussions are a handy way to stay current on crime and justice issues and to share your thoughts with others. You can also begin an e-mail study group to review text materials with students at other colleges. Visit http://crimtoday.listbot.com to sign up quickly.

Dr. Frank Schmalleger's Cybrary. Find what you're looking for on the Web with Dr. Frank Schmalleger's cyber-library of crime and justice links. Containing over 12,000 criminology-related sites in its fully searchable database, the Cybrary is well known on the Internet as "the world's crime and justice directory."

Electronic glossary. Use this Web-based glossary as a ready-made study aid to help you understand Key Terms and other text materials. Our glossary includes standardized terminology from the criminal justice, criminology, law, and corrections fields.

The U.S. Constitution. Review the full text of the U.S. Constitution, including all amendments. Use this feature to research the constitutionally protected rights of those facing processing by the justice system.

CRIMINOLOGY TODAY

AN INTEGRATIVE INTRODUCTION

the crime picture

PART

Over the years, social commentators have observed that people are simultaneously attracted to and repulsed by crime—especially gruesome crimes involving personal violence. The popularity of today's TV crime shows, Hollywood-produced crime movies, true-crime books and magazines, and Web sites devoted exclusively to the coverage of crime news supports that observation. One of the things that fascinates people about crime is that it sometimes seems so inexplicable. How can the actions of Dylan Klebold and Eric Harris, the Columbine High School students who shot 12 of their fellow students and a teacher, be explained? Could the Columbine tragedy have been prevented? Why would a mother, like South Carolina's Susan Smith, murder her young children? Why did Cherica Adams, the 24-year-old pregnant girlfriend of former Carolina Panthers football star Rae Carruth, have to die?

But people wonder not only about murder. Even "everyday" crimes like robbery, drug use, assault, vandalism, and computer intrusion need explaining. Why do people fight? Does it matter to a robber that he may end up in prison? How can so many people sacrifice love, money, careers, and even their lives, for access to illegal drugs? What motivates a terrorist to give up his own life to take others? Why do gifted techno-savvy teens and preteens feel the need to devote themselves to cracking secure sites on the Internet?

While this text may not answer all of these questions, it will examine the multitude of causative factors that come into play when a crime is committed, and it will help you appreciate the challenges of crafting effective crime control policy. In the first two chapters of this book, however, we will focus primarily on examining the nature and extent of crime and deviance, and in Chapter 3 we will explore the historical basis for the scientific study of crime and will attempt to understand the research methods that criminologists use today.

If only we could have reached them sooner or found this tape. If only we would have searched their room. If only we would have asked the right questions.

—Eric Harris, one of the Columbine High School shooters, in a videotaped prediction (made before the shooting) of his parents' anticipated reaction[i]

Society secretly wants crime, needs crime, and gains definite satisfactions from the present mishandling of it! We condemn crime; we punish offenders for it; but we need it. The crime and punishment ritual is part of our lives!

—Karl Menninger[ii]

---

[i]Mental Health Infosource. Web posted at http://www.mhsource.com/pt/p000201a.html. Accessed January 5, 2001.

[ii]Karl Menninger, *The Crime of Punishment* (New York: Viking, 1968).

<table>
<table><thead><tr><th>CHAPTER 1</th><th>CHAPTER 2</th><th>CHAPTER 3</th></tr></thead><tbody><tr><td>What Is Criminology?</td><td>Patterns of Crime</td><td>Research Methods and Theory Development</td></tr></tbody></table>
</table>

Crime is the only way to get ahead, Duke. You'll never have anything if you live your life within the law.

—Dialogue from the NBC-TV Movie *Beyond Suspicion*[1]

Much is already known about the phenomenon of crime. Further development in theoretical criminology will result primarily from making sense out of what we already know.

—George B. Vold and Thomas J. Bernard[2]

what is criminology?

CHAPTER 1

The objective of criminology is the development
of a body of general verified principles.

—Edwin Sutherland and Donald Cressey[3]

The whole paraphernalia of the criminal law
and the criminal courts is based on the need
of the upper class to keep the lower class in its place.

—Jay Frost[4]

OUTCOMES

LEARNING

After reading this chapter, you should be able to
- ◆ Understand what criminology is and what criminologists do
- ◆ Define crime
- ◆ Recognize the difference between criminal and deviant acts, and appreciate the complexity of this distinction
- ◆ Understand the legalistic approach to the study of crime, and know why it is limiting
- ◆ Know what a theory is, and explain the role of theorizing in the study of criminal behavior
- ◆ Understand the distinction between the social problems and social responsibility perspectives on crime causation

Hear the author discuss this chapter at *crimtoday.com*

INTRODUCTION

On May 5, 2000, 30-year-old Andrew Goldstein was sentenced to 25 years to life in prison after being convicted of murder for pushing 32-year-old Kendra Ann Webdale to her death in front of a speeding New York City subway train more than a year earlier.[5] Webdale, a music company receptionist, was decapitated and her body badly mangled as it was dragged along the tracks by a train pulling into the 23rd Street and Broadway station in Manhattan. Goldstein, a paranoid schizophrenic who had been in and out of mental institutions for years, had randomly chosen Webdale from among the commuters waiting on the Long Island Railroad platform. When the police arrived, Goldstein told officers he was "crazy" and asked them to take him to a hospital. Goldstein apologized to the Webdale family before he was sentenced, and he blamed the killing on his failure to take doctor-ordered antipsychotic medication.[6]

Shortly after Goldstein entered prison, another random attack grabbed the attention of New Yorkers. Around noon on July 9, 2000, in what was an apparent robbery attempt, 25-year-old Tiffany F. Goldberg was struck from behind by a man wielding a cantaloupe-sized piece of concrete as she walked from church to a subway station on busy 42nd Street.[7] Goldberg, an aspiring Broadway actress, had just attended services at Marble Collegiate Church, two blocks from the scene of the attack. Stunned, and with her skull fractured by the blow, Goldstein reflexively held on to her purse while her attacker attempted to pry it from her hands. An off-duty fireman who was driving through the area yelled at the man until he ran off. Following the attack, Goldberg was rushed to the emergency room at Bellevue Hospital and eventually recovered. Her assailant was never found.

The attack on Goldberg was similar to one eight months earlier in which Nicole Barrett, a 27-year-old woman from Texas, suffered serious head injuries when a homeless man ran up behind her at midday and smashed her skull with a six-pound brick as she walked along Madison Avenue in New York. Paris Drake, 34, was arrested shortly after the attack and was charged with attempted murder, assault, and criminal possession of a weapon.[8] Drake, an ex-con, had served a total of six years in prison for a variety of convictions going back to 1982. Drake has not yet been tried as this book goes to press,

Andrew Goldstein (left) was sentenced to 25 years to life in prison after being convicted of murder for pushing 32-year-old Kendra Ann Webdale (right) to her death in front of a speeding New York City subway train. What do crimes like Goldstein's tell us about American society today? *(Marty Lederhandler, AP/Wide World Photos (left) and Kevin M. Polowy, AP/Wide World Photos (right)*

and he claims he was arrested in a case of mistaken identity. His police record includes 21 arrests for robbery, burglary, felony assault, and drug sales and possession. Barrett, who remained unconscious for days after being hit on the head, underwent a series of operations to relieve swelling around her brain and eventually recovered the use of most of her faculties.[9]

Random violent attacks perpetrated by strangers are the kinds of crime that people fear most. Although attacks like those on Kendra Webdale, Tiffany Goldberg and Nicole Barrett are relatively uncommon, they are widely reported in the media and appear to lead to a heightened sense of insecurity among members of the public. This is true even though crime rates have declined in recent years to levels not seen in nearly three decades.

WHAT IS CRIME?

Americans and the American mass media show an unabashed penchant for closely following gruesome and spectacular crimes and for thoroughly documenting crimes and transgressions involving celebrities, athletes, and other well-known people. During the 1990s, for example, the murders of Nicole Brown Simpson (for which football star O. J. Simpson was tried and acquitted), Gianni Versace (internationally known fashion designer), Ennis Cosby (son of entertainer Bill Cosby), James Jordan (father of basketball great Michael Jordan), gangsta rappers Tupac Shakur and Christopher Wallace (known to fans as Notorious B.I.G. or Biggie Smalls), and 6-year-old beauty queen JonBenet Ramsey all received much press coverage. The alleged misdeeds of other celebrities, such as boxer Michael Tyson (who bit off parts of an opponent's ear in the ring), rappers Sean "Puff Daddy" Combs (arrested on assault charges, along with friend Jennifer Lopez) and Snoop Doggy Dogg[10] (acquitted of murder charges), for-

mer Carolina Panthers wide receiver Rae Carruth (convicted in 2001 of conspiracy in the shooting death of his pregnant girlfriend), actor Robert Downey, Jr. (who repeatedly served time for drug possession), Dennis Rodman (convicted in California of DUI and driving without a valid license), and Brad Renfro (arrested for allegedly trying to steal a yacht)—to name just a few—attracted considerable attention. Keep up-to-date with the latest crime news at Web Extra! 1-1.

Web Extra! 1-1 at crimtoday.com

Of course, not all wrongdoing is crime. Crime can be defined in a variety of ways, and some scholars have suggested that at least four definitional perspectives can be found in contemporary criminology.[11] These diverse perspectives see crime from (1) legalistic, (2) political, (3) sociological, and (4) psychological viewpoints. How we see any phenomenon is crucial because it determines the assumptions that we make about how that phenomenon should be studied. The perspective that we choose to employ when viewing crime determines the kinds of questions we ask, the nature of the research we conduct, and the type of answers that we expect to receive. Those answers, in turn, influence our conclusions about the kinds of crime control policies that might be effective. Hence when we study crime, it is vital to keep in mind that there are differing viewpoints within the field of criminology as to the fundamental nature of the subject matter itself.

Seen from a legalistic perspective, **crime** is *human conduct in violation of the criminal laws of a state, the federal government, or a local jurisdiction that has the power to make such laws.* This is the definition of crime that we will use in this textbook because without a law that circumscribes a particu-

CRIME IN THE NEWS
Brick Victim's Family Finds "Miracle" in NYC

The family of an Athens, Texas, woman who was hit in the head with a brick on a busy midtown Manhattan street last week says they asked for a miracle when they learned of the brutal attack—and that's what they're getting.

Speaking to the public Monday for the first time since an unknown homeless man struck down Nicole Barrett in an apparent random act of violence near Grand Central Terminal, the 27-year-old temp worker's family said they visited with her in the morning, and she was able to smile.

"We asked for a miracle to start with, and we haven't expected anything less," said Sharon Barrett, flanked by her son, Scott, with New York City Mayor Rudolph Giuliani and Police Commissioner Howard Safir at a news conference at Bellevue Hospital.

"One of the first people to get to Nikki was a priest—so we know she was prayed for from the very beginning—that means very much to us," said the devout Southern Baptist who arrived from Texas with her son and her husband, Arlen, at her daughter's bedside. Barrett said that her daughter doesn't know what happened to her and was told by her boyfriend that she suffered an accident.

"She smiled at us this morning, which is very encouraging for us," said Scott Barrett, 24.

CHEERED BY OUTPOURING OF SUPPORT

Nicole Barrett was hit in the head with a brick while walking on Madison Avenue near 42nd Street on Nov. 16 and remains in critical condition in the neurosurgical intensive care unit since undergoing brain surgery at Bellevue.

The family said they were also cheered by the outpouring of support they've gotten from New Yorkers and said they didn't blame the big city for harming their Nicole.

"We in no way look at New York City in a bad light," said the victim's brother. "It's gorgeous."

"This was an act of one man. It could have happened in Athens," said Sharon Barrett. "Look at Columbine—no one expected that. We just can't believe there are so many kind people in the world, much less in one city—perfect strangers letting us know their thoughts are with us. We appreciate that."

PLENTY OF TIPS, BUT NO ARREST

Scott Barrett said that Nicole had been to the city before moving here, performing in New York's Thanksgiving Day Parade with a drill team from the community college in her hometown. He said her family is hoping that she will improve enough by Thursday to enjoy the holiday again.

"We have had several offers, but our wishes are just for a nice turkey meal by her bedside," he said.

Police have followed up on hundreds of tips but have so far been unsuccessful in finding a suspect, said Safir, holding a police artist's sketch of the attacker.

He asked the public, particularly anyone riding the Lexington Avenue subway the day of the attack, to come forward. "We are just covering all the bases," he said. "At this point we don't know, but since the brick weighs 6½ pounds, perhaps he got on the subway or a bus."

CITY TO CRACK DOWN ON HOMELESS

The attack on Barrett has prompted a controversial crackdown on homeless people in the city, with the mayor ordering police to prevent them from sleeping on the streets.

"They will be told to go—you can't sleep in the street, they're not going to have the choice to sleep in the street," said Giuliani, adding that he doesn't believe the Constitution gives anyone the right to sleep in alcoves and doorways. "The ones that wind up in jail probably have warrants for their arrest."

Source: Howard Stier, "Daughter Smiles as They Visit Her Bedside," APB News, November 23, 1999. Reprinted with permission.

lar form of behavior, there can be no crime, no matter how deviant or socially repugnant the behavior in question may be.

A recent case from Down Under well illustrates the principle that without a law defining an activity as illegal, there can be no crime. A few years ago, an Australian court acquitted Aboriginal activist John Kelly of "making a demand with menaces"—an offense under Australian law that is similar to the crime of extortion. Kelly was charged by prosecutors with trying to extort $10,000 (Australian) by threatening to "point the bone," or place a death curse, on a well-known Australian comedian. Northern Territory Supreme Court Judge Steven Bailey directed a jury to acquit Kelly after a three-day trial, saying that "there was no evidence of unlawful conduct" in

the Aboriginal activity of "pointing the bone" and that any threat made on the basis of such activity was essentially meaningless.[12] Had Kelly threatened to kill the comedian with a gun, the judge would have probably found otherwise. As in this case, however, the laws of most states would make it difficult or impossible to convict someone of assault charges for putting a voodoo curse on another person or for burning an effigy of the person in a "black magic" ritual.

The notion of crime as behavior[13] that violates the law derives from earlier work by criminologists like Paul W. Tappan, who defined *crime* as "an intentional act in violation of the criminal law . . . committed without defense or excuse, and penalized by the state as a felony or misdemeanor."[14] Edwin Sutherland, regarded by many as a founding figure in American criminology, said of crime that its "essential characteristic . . . is that it is behavior which is prohibited by the State as an injury to the State and against which the State may react . . . by punishment."[15]

Although we have chosen to adopt the legalistic approach to crime in this textbook, it is important to realize that while such an approach is useful in the study of criminology, it is also limiting. Many times, those who adhere to a legalistic perspective insist that the nature of crime cannot be separated from the nature of law, as the one explicitly defines the other. Not easily recognized by any legalistic definition of crime, however, is the social, moral, and individual significance of fundamentally immoral forms of behavior. Simply put, some activities not contravened by **statute** nonetheless still call out for a societal response, sometimes leading commentators to proclaim, "That ought to be a crime!" or "There ought to be a law against that!"

Another serious shortcoming of the legalistic approach to crime is that it yields the moral high ground to powerful individuals who are able to influence the making of laws and the imposition of criminal definitions on lawbreakers. By making their own laws, powerful but immoral individuals may escape the label "criminal." Although democratic societies like the United States would seem to be immune from such abuses of the legislative process, history demonstrates otherwise. In Chapter 9 we will explore this issue further and will focus on the process of criminalization, which is the method used to **criminalize** some forms of behavior—or make them illegal—while other forms remain legitimate.

The legalistic definition of crime also suffers from its seeming lack of recognition of the fact that formalized laws have not always existed. Undoubtedly, much immoral behavior occurred even in dimly remembered historical epochs, and contemporary laws probably now regulate most such behavior. English common law, for example, upon which much American **statutory law** is based, judged behavior in terms of traditional practice and customs and did not make use of written statutes. Although all American jurisdictions have enacted comprehensive legal codes, many states still adhere to a common law tradition. In such "common law states," individuals may be prosecuted for violating traditional notions of right and wrong, even though no violation of written law took place. Needless to say, such prosecutions rarely occur, and when they do they are not often successful.[16] Common law is discussed in more detail in Chapter 4. Learn more about common law at Web Extra! 1-2.

Web Extra! 1-2 at crimtoday.com

Changes in the law will undoubtedly continue to occur, perhaps even legitimizing former so-called crimes or recognizing that fundamentally moral forms of behavior have been unduly criminalized. Over the last decade, for example, state legislatures along with members of the general public have debated the pros and cons of euthanasia. Until recently, Dr. Jack Kevorkian, perhaps the best-known pro-euthanasia activist of modern times, had been waging a crusade to legalize doctor-assisted suicide for terminally ill individuals. Kevorkian ad-mitted assisting many seriously ill people who took their own lives, mostly in the state of Michigan. Although tried under Michigan common law, which prosecutors claimed criminalized assisted suicide, he was acquitted. In 1999, however, after Michigan enacted statutory provisions outlawing physician-assisted suicide, Kevorkian was rearrested, tried, and convicted of a number of crimes and was sentenced to 10 to 25 years in prison. Evidence against Kevorkian came mostly from a videotape aired on CBS's *60 Minutes*, showing the doctor giving a lethal injection to 52-year-old Thomas Youk, who suffered from Lou Gehrig's disease. Learn more about Kevorkian, the ideology that motivated him, and the criminal trials that eventually led to his imprisonment at Web Extra! 1-3.

Web Extra! 1-3 at crimtoday.com

A second perspective on crime is the political one. From a political point of view, crime is the result of criteria that have been built into the law by powerful groups, which are then used to label selected undesirable forms of behavior as illegal. Those who adhere to this point of view say that crime is a definition of human conduct that is created by authorized agents in a politically organized society. Seen this way, laws serve the interests of the politically powerful, and crimes are merely forms of behavior that are perceived by those in power as direct or indirect threats to their interests. Thus the political perspective defines crime in terms of the power structures that exist in society and asserts that criminal laws do not necessarily bear any inherent relationship to popular notions of right and wrong.

The political processes that create criminal definitions, however, are generally easier to comprehend in totalitarian societies than in democratic ones. Nonetheless, the political perspective, as we shall see in Chapter 15, can also be meaningfully applied to American society. John F. Galliher, a contemporary criminologist, summarizes the political perspective on crime when he writes, "One can best understand crime in a class-structured society such as the United States as the end product of a chain of interactions involving powerful groups that use their power to establish criminal laws and sanctions against less powerful persons and groups that may pose a threat to the group in power."[17] It is important to realize, Galliher points out, that since legal definitions of criminality are arrived at through a political process, the subject matter of criminality will be artificially limited if we insist on seeing crime solely as a violation of the criminal law.

Some criminologists insist that the field of criminology must broaden its concerns and go beyond those behaviors that are defined as crimes through the political process. Not doing so, they say, restricts rather than encourages inquiry into relevant forms of human behavior.[18] Adherents of our third perspective, the sociological one, would likely agree with this statement. Also called the "sociolegal viewpoint," the sociological perspective sees crime as "an antisocial act of such a nature that its repression is necessary or is supposed to be necessary to the preservation of the existing system of society."[19] Some criminologists have gone so far as to claim that any definition of

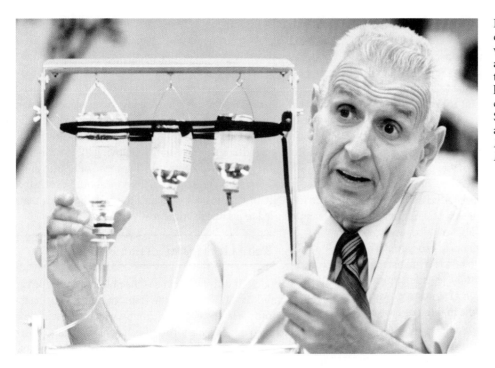

Dr. Jack Kevorkian prior to being convicted and imprisoned for violating Michigan's statute against assisted suicide. How does the debate over assisted suicide highlight the changing nature of criminal activity in the United States? Do you think that doctor-assisted suicide should be a crime? *Detroit News, Gary Porter/Gamma-Liaison, Inc.*

crime must include all forms of antisocial behavior.[20] Ron Claassen, a modern-day champion of restorative justice (discussed in more detail in Chapter 9), suggests, for example, that "crime is primarily an offense against human relationships, and secondarily a violation of a law—since laws are written to protect safety and fairness in human relationships."[21] A more comprehensive sociological definition of crime was offered by Julia Schwendinger and Herman Schwendinger in 1975. It says that crime encompasses "any harmful acts," including violations of "the fundamental prerequisites for well-being, [such as] food, shelter, clothing, medical services, challenging work and recreational experiences, as well as security from predatory individuals or repressive and imperialistic elites."[22] The Schwendingers have challenged criminologists to be less constrained in what they see as the subject matter of their field, saying that violations of human rights may be more relevant to criminological inquiry than many acts that have been politically or legally defined as crime. "Isn't it time to raise serious questions about the assumptions underlying the definitions of the field of criminology," ask the Schwendingers, "when a man who steals a paltry sum can be called a criminal while agents of the State can, with impunity, legally reward men who destroy food so that price levels can be maintained whilst a sizable portion of the population suffers from malnutrition?"[23] Jeffrey H. Reiman, another contemporary criminologist, asks similar questions. "The fact is that the label 'crime' is not used in America to name all or the worst of the actions that cause misery and suffering to Americans," says Reiman. "It is primarily reserved for the dangerous actions of the poor." Writing about unhealthy and unsafe workplaces, Reiman asks, "Doesn't a crime by any other name still cause misery and suffering? What's in a name?"[24] While a sociolegal approach to understanding crime is attractive to many, others claim that it suffers from wanting to crim-

inalize activities that cause only indirect harm. In other words, it is easier for most people to appreciate the criminality involved in, say, a holdup, a rape, or a murder, than in cost-cutting efforts made by a businessperson, even when those efforts result in injuries to workers or consumers.

Finally, from a psychological (or maladaptive) perspective, "crime is a form of social maladjustment which can be designated as a more or less pronounced difficulty that the individual has in reacting to the stimuli of his environment in such a way as to remain in harmony with that environment."[25] Seen this way, crime is problem behavior, especially human activity that contravenes the criminal law and results in difficulties in living within a framework of generally acceptable social arrangements. According to Matthew B. Robinson, "The maladaptive view of crime does not require any of the [traditional] elements ...in order for an act to be a crime: no actual harm to others; no prohibition by law before the act is committed; no arrest; and no conviction in a court of law. Any behavior which is maladaptive—i.e., which stands in the way of an individual developing to his or her fullest potential—would be considered crime. If criminologists adopted this view of crime," says Robinson, "the scope of criminology would be greatly expanded beyond its current state. All actually or even potentially harmful behaviors could be examined, analyzed, and documented for the purpose of gaining knowledge about potentially harmful behaviors and developing strategies to protect people from all harmful acts, not just those that are called 'crime' today."[26]

As this discussion shows, a unified or simple definition of crime is difficult to achieve. The four points of view that we have discussed here form a kind of continuum, bound on one end by strict legalistic interpretations of crime, and on the other by much more fluid behavioral and moralistic definitions.

THEORY VERSUS REALITY
Should Doctor-Assisted Suicide Remain Illegal?

On June 26, 1997, the U.S. Supreme Court upheld the constitutionality of two laws prohibiting assisted suicide. In *Vacco* v. *Quill*,[1] the plaintiffs claimed that a New York law banning physician-assisted suicide violated the Fourteenth Amendment's equal protection clause because state law allows those wishing to hasten their own deaths to do so by directing the removal of life-support systems but does not permit terminally ill people to self-administer prescribed lethal drugs to end their lives. The Court disagreed and upheld the New York ban.

The other 1997 case was that of *Washington* v. *Glucksberg*.[2] In *Glucksberg,* the Court upheld a Washington State law that makes "[p]romoting a suicide attempt" a felony, and provides, "A person is guilty of [that crime] when he knowingly causes or aids another person to attempt suicide." Respondents in the case were four Washington physicians who occasionally treated terminally ill, suffering patients. The physicians declared that they would assist such patients in ending their lives were it not for the state's assisted-suicide ban. They, along with three gravely ill plaintiffs and a nonprofit organization that counsels people considering physician-assisted suicide, filed suit against the state of Washington, seeking a declaration that the ban is unconstitutional. The basis of their action resided in the claim that the Fourteenth Amendment's due process clause establishes a liberty interest which extends to a personal choice by a mentally competent, terminally ill adult to commit physician-assisted suicide. The Supreme Court disagreed, ruling that Washington's prohibition against causing or aiding a suicide does not violate the due process clause. In the words of the Court:

An examination of our Nation's history, legal traditions, and practices demonstrates that Anglo-American common law has punished or otherwise disapproved of assisting suicide for over 700 years; that rendering such assistance is still a crime in almost every State; that such prohibitions have never contained exceptions for those who were near death; that the prohibitions have in recent years been reexamined and, for the most part, reaffirmed in a number of States; and that the President recently signed the Federal Assisted Suicide Funding Restriction Act of 1997, which prohibits the use of federal funds in support of physician assisted suicide.

The Court concluded, "In light of that history, this Court's decisions led to the conclusion that respondents' asserted 'right' to assistance in committing suicide is not a fundamental liberty interest protected by the Due Process Clause."

Although the Court ruled that terminally ill people do not have a constitutionally protected right to doctor-assisted suicide, it did nothing to bar states from legalizing the process. Now, inspired by a growing right-to-die movement, some jurisdictions appear ready to lift the traditional ban on such activity.

In 1994, Oregon became the first state to legalize doctor-assisted suicide under prescribed conditions. Although a state judge blocked the Oregon law from taking immediate effect,[3] the statute represented a complete about-face in the legal status of medically assisted suicide. In 1997, following a new initiative under which Oregon voters again approved physician-assisted suicide, the U.S. Ninth Circuit Court of Appeals reversed the lower court's ruling and allowed assisted suicides to proceed.

Oregon law allows a terminally ill patient, defined as a person having no more than six months to live, to request a prescription for a fatal dose of medication. The patient must make the request three times—both in writing and verbally. A 15-day waiting period is mandated before the second request can be made. Moreover, two doctors must agree that the patient is terminally ill, and witnesses have to attest that the patient's desire to die is voluntary. If the patient appears depressed, a psychologist must be called, and the patient, not the doctor, must self-administer the lethal medication. Lethal injections are prohibited.[4]

In 1998, the first year the pioneering law was operational, 16 patients took their lives with the assistance of Oregon physicians. In 1999, the number climbed to 27. Still, Oregon's assisted-suicide law continues to face many challenges. As of this writing, opponents of the law are attempting to gain a hearing before the U.S. Supreme Court, and the U.S. Congress has been considering a bill that would make it a crime for any doctor to prescribe controlled substances with the intention of hastening death. As long as the Oregon law remains on the books, however, it provides an example of the fact that what may be a crime in one jurisdiction or location may not be criminal in another.[5]

DISCUSSION QUESTIONS

1. What is crime? Is doctor-assisted suicide a crime? Why or why not?
2. Who is Dr. Jack Kevorkian (discussed elsewhere in this chapter)? Do you agree with the state of Michigan that he is a criminal? Why or why not?

(continued on the next page)

(continued from previous page)

3. Are there any activities that are not presently against the law that you think should be criminal? If so, what are they?

4. Are there any activities that are against the law but that you think should be legal? If so, what are they?

Sources: Carol M. Ostrom, "Caregivers Torn over Oregon's Assisted-Suicide Law," *Seattle Times,* March 20, 2000. Web posted at http://seattletimes.nwsource.com/news/local/html98/hosp_20000320.html. Accessed October 17, 2000. Alissa J. Rubin, "House Taking Aim at Oregon Law on Assisted Suicide," *Los Angeles Times,* October 22, 1999. Web posted at http://www.dallasnews.com/national/1022nat6suicide.htm. Accessed October 17, 2000.

1. *Vacco* v. *Quill,* 117 S. Ct. 2293 (1997).
2. *Washington* v. *Glucksberg,* 117 S. Ct. 2258 (1997).
3. Carrie Dowling, "Assisted-Suicide Law Blocked," *USA Today,* December 8, 1994, p. 3A.
4. Carey Goldberg, "Oregon Braces for New Fight on Helping the Dying to Die," *New York Times,* June 17, 1997, p. 1A.
5. See William McCall, "Oregon Assisted Suicide Law in Limbo," Associated Press wire service, June 27, 1997.

CRIME AND DEVIANCE

Sociologically speaking, many crimes can be regarded as deviant forms of behavior—that is, as behaviors which are in some way abnormal. Piers Beirne and James Messerschmidt, two contemporary criminologists, define deviance as "any social behavior or social characteristic that departs from the conventional norms and standards of a community or society and for which the deviant is sanctioned."[27] Their definition is flawed, however, in that it does not count as deviant sanctionable behavior that is not punished, nor does it explicitly include the notion of statistical deviance—or those forms of behavior which are neither sanctioned nor disapproved but which are, nonetheless, highly peculiar. Hence we prefer another approach to defining deviance. The definition of **deviant behavior** that we will use in this book is as follows: *Deviant behavior is human activity that violates social norms or is statistically different from the average.*

Abnormality, deviance, and crime are concepts that do not always easily mesh. Some forms of deviance are not violations of the criminal law, and the reverse is equally true (see Figure 1-1). Deviant styles of dress, for example, although perhaps outlandish to the majority, are not circumscribed by criminal law unless (perhaps) decency statutes are violated by a lack of clothing. Even in such cases, laws are subject to interpretation and may be modified as social norms change over time.

A decade ago, for example, Patricia Marks, a New York State county judge, overturned the convictions of ten women who had been arrested for publicly displaying their breasts. The women, known as the Topfree Ten, had been arrested after baring their chests during a picnic in a city park. At the time, New York law forbade women from displaying their breasts in public—unless they were breast-feeding or performing onstage. The women claimed that the law discriminated against them and argued that if men have the right to appear in public without a shirt, then the same right should apply to women. Judge Marks agreed and, in reversing the convictions, ruled that the New York statute was sexist and gender biased because "male and female breasts are physiologically similar except for lactation capability."[28] The judge relied in part on the testimony of experts who articulated their belief that "community standards have changed and women's breasts are no longer considered a private or intimate part of the body."

The Topfree movement soon spread across the country and into Canada. In 1999, the Florida public nudity conviction of Kayla Sosnow was overturned by Florida's 8th Circuit Court of Appeals. Sosnow, who had been arrested for not wearing a shirt in the Osceola National Forest in 1996, is a member of the Florida Topfree Ten. She was supported in her appeal by the National Organization for Women, the American Civil Liberties Union (ACLU), the Human Rights Council of North Central Florida, the Florida Coalition for Peace and Justice, and the Gainesville (Florida) Women's Health Center. After the court's ruling, Sosnow spoke with reporters, telling them that the court's action removed one more obstacle to equal rights for women. "Who decides that women's breasts are more obscene than men's?" she asked. "By going topfree, we are rejecting the criminalization of our breasts and reclaiming control of our bodies."[29]

On May 16, 2000, the Brevard Chapter of the ACLU of Florida filed suit in Brevard County Court challenging county and state laws which prohibit women from exposing their chests in public except while breast-feeding. The suit is predicated upon an equal rights amendment to the Florida Constitution passed by state voters in November 1998. The amendment states that all "natural persons, female and male alike, are equal before the law."

The Topfree movement highlights the role that societal interpretation plays in defining a criminal offense. Even if appellate courts are correct, and no noteworthy physiological differences exist between the breasts of men and women, American society nonetheless appears to have turned relatively minor differences of size and shape into a major distinguishing factor between the sexes. In other words, a relatively insignifi-

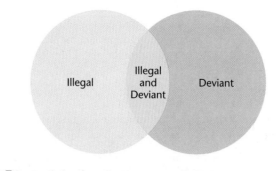

■ **FIGURE 1-1**   THE OVERLAP BETWEEN DEVIANCE AND CRIME.

cant biological difference has traditionally been endowed with a great deal of social significance, and laws regulating various styles of dress (or undress) have evolved based on subjective perceptions rather than objective considerations.

Some types of behavior, although quite common, are still against the law. Speeding on interstate highways, for example, although probably something that most motorists engage in at least from time to time, is illegal. Complicating matters still further is the fact that certain forms of behavior are illegal in some jurisdictions but not in others. Adult homosexual behavior, for example, is regarded as a matter of personal choice in many states but is a criminal offense in others. Similarly, some common forms of adult heterosexual activity continue to be criminalized in a number of jurisdictions under the rubric of "crimes against nature," while a growing number of states have rescinded laws originally intended to regulate such activity.

WHAT SHOULD BE CRIMINAL?

As you have probably realized by now, the question "What is crime?" is quite different from the question "What should be criminal?" Although most people agree that certain forms of behavior, such as murder, rape, burglary, and theft, should be against the law, there is far less agreement about the appropriate legal status of things like drug use, abortion (including the use of "abortion pills" like RU-486 or Mifeprex®), gambling, and "deviant" forms of consensual adult sexual behavior (including homosexuality).

While the question "What should be criminal?" can be answered in many different ways, the social and intellectual processes by which an answer is reached can be found in two contrasting points of view: (1) the consensus perspective, and (2) the pluralist perspective. The consensus viewpoint holds that laws should be enacted to criminalize given forms of behavior when members of society generally agree that such laws are necessary. The consensus perspective (described in greater detail in Chapter 9) is most applicable to homogeneous societies, or those characterized by shared values, norms, and belief systems. In a multicultural and diverse society like the United States, however, a shared consensus may be difficult to achieve. In such a society, even relatively minor matters may lead to complex debates over the issues involved. Not long ago, for example, a Chicago municipal ordinance banned giving wine to a dog and provided that anyone who did so could be arrested and jailed.[30] While the ordinance may have seemed reasonable to those who enacted it (after all, dogs sometimes need to be shielded from their owners' indiscretions, and there are plenty of precedents in the form of laws already on the books that are intended to protect animals), others felt that the law was silly and unnecessary. Still others insisted that dogs should have a right to imbibe just as do humans who are of drinking age. The ordinance pitted wine connoisseurs, collectors, growers, and sellers, as well as animal rights activists, against animal protectionists and some city council members. Those favoring repeal of the ordinance argued that it was old-fashioned and reflected badly on an acceptable consumer product which was also a staple of certain ethnic diets (i.e., the French and Italians frequently drink wine with meals, and their descendants living in Chicago, because of the "bad press" associated with the law, might find their lifestyles negatively affected). Eventually, the ordinance was repealed, and the hubbub it had inspired ended. The debate, however, shows just how difficult it is to achieve a consensus over even relatively minor matters in a society as complex as our own.

The second perspective, the pluralist view of crime (described in more detail in Chapter 9), recognizes the importance

Deviance is relevant to the social context within which it occurs, as these licensed "sex workers" in Amsterdam show. Why is sex-for-hire against the law in most American jurisdictions? *Todd Haimann, Corbis*

of diversity in societies like ours. It says that behaviors are typically criminalized through a political process only after debate over the appropriate course of action. The political process usually takes the form of legislation and appellate court action. On August, 29, 2000, for example, the U.S. Supreme Court issued an emergency order barring distribution of marijuana to people in California whose doctors recommended it for medicinal purposes.[31] The Court's action reflected the conflict between federal narcotics laws and a 1996 California voter initiative known as Proposition 215, which allows seriously ill patients to grow and use marijuana for pain relief with a doctor's recommendation. The 9th U.S. Circuit Court of Appeals had earlier ruled in support of Proposition 215, holding that "medical necessity is a legally cognizable defense" to a federal charge of illegally distributing drugs. Reflecting the plurality of perspectives on the issue, not even the Supreme Court justices who heard the case could agree on the appropriate course of action. Justice John Paul Stevens, for example, wrote that the government "has failed to demonstrate that the denial of necessary medicine to seriously ill and dying patients will advance the public interest or that the failure to enjoin the distribution of such medicine will impair the orderly enforcement of federal criminal statutes."

In 2001, the Supreme Court case of *U.S. v. Oakland Cannabis Buyers' Cooperative* (No. 00-151) may have closed the door on any kind of state-support for medical marijuana. In *Oakland*, the Court held that there is no recognizable medical necessity exception to the federal Controlled Substances Act's prohibitions on the distribution or manufacturing of marijuana. Learn more about the medical marijuana movement via Web Extra! 1-4.

Web EXTRA!   Web Extra! 1-4 at crimtoday.com

WHAT DO CRIMINOLOGISTS DO?

A typical dictionary definition of a **criminologist** is "one who studies crime, criminals, and criminal behavior."[32] Occasionally, the term *criminologist* is used broadly to describe almost anyone who works in the criminal justice field, regardless of formal training. There is a growing tendency, however, to reserve application of the term *criminologist* to academics, researchers, and policy analysts with advanced degrees who are involved in the study of crime and crime trends and in the analysis of societal reactions to crime. Hence, it is more appropriate today to describe specially skilled investigators, crime laboratory technicians, fingerprint experts, crime scene photographers, ballistics experts, and others who work to solve particular crimes as criminalists. A **criminalist** is "a specialist in the collection and examination of the physical evidence of crime."[33] Police officers, corrections professionals, probation and parole officers, judges, district attorneys, criminal defense at-

torneys, and others who do the day-to-day work of the criminal justice system are best referred to as criminal justice professionals.

Academic criminologists and research criminologists generally hold doctoral degrees (Ph.D.'s) in the field of criminology or criminal justice from an accredited university. Some criminologists hold degrees in related fields like sociology and political science but have specialized in the study and control of crime and deviance. Most Ph.D. criminologists teach either criminology or criminology-related subjects in institutions of higher learning, including universities and two- and four-year colleges. Nearly all criminology professors are involved in research or writing projects by which they strive to advance criminological knowledge. Some Ph.D. criminologists are strictly researchers and work for federal agencies like the National Institute of Justice (NIJ), the Bureau of Justice Statistics (BJS), and the National Criminal Justice Reference Service (NCJRS) or for private (albeit often government-funded) organizations with such names as RAND and the Search Group, Inc.

The results of criminological research in the United States are generally published in journals like *Criminology* (the official publication of the American Society of Criminology), *Theoretical Criminology, Justice Quarterly* (the Academy of Criminal Justice Sciences), *Crime and Delinquency,* the *American Journal of Criminal Justice* (the Southern Criminal Justice Association), the *Journal of Qualitative Criminology, Social Problems,* and *Victimology.*[34] International English-language journals are numerous and include the *Canadian Journal of Criminology,* the *Australian and New Zealand Journal of Criminology,* and the *British Journal of Criminology.* Read some of these journals and visit the organizations that sponsor them at Web Extra! 1-5.

Web EXTRA!   Web Extra! 1-5 at crimtoday.com

People who have earned master of arts, master of science, and bachelor's degrees in the field of criminology often find easy entrance into police investigative or support work, probation and parole agencies, court-support activities, and correctional (prison) work. Criminologists also work for government agencies interested in the development of effective social policies intended to deter or combat crime. Many criminologists with master's degrees also teach at two- and four-year colleges and schools.

Private security provides another career track for individuals interested in criminology and criminal justice. The number of personnel employed by private security agencies today is twice that of public law enforcement agencies, and the gap is widening. Many upper- and mid-level private managers working for private security firms hold criminology or criminal justice degrees. The same may soon be true for the majority of law enforcement personnel, especially those in managerial positions.

Anyone trained in criminology has many alternatives (See Table 1-1). Some people with undergraduate degrees in criminology or criminal justice decide to go on to law school. Some

TABLE 1-1 ■ What Do Criminologists Do?

The term criminologist *is usually applied to credentialed individuals, such as those holding advanced degrees in the field, who engage in the study of crime, criminal behavior, and crime trends. The word* criminalist *is used to describe people who specialize in the collection and examination of the physical evidence associated with specific crimes. Others working in the criminal justice system are called* criminal justice professionals. *This table lists the activities of all three.*

The activities of criminologists include, but are not limited to

Data gathering
Data analysis
Theory construction
Hypothesis testing
Social policy creation
Public advocacy
Public service
Analysis of crime patterns and trends
Scholarly presentations and publications
Education and training
Threat assessment and risk analysis

Jobs in the field of criminalistics include, but are not limited to

Forensics examiner
Crime laboratory technician
Ballistics expert

Crime scene investigator
Crime scene photographer
Polygraph operator
Fingerprint examiner

Jobs in the field of criminal justice include, but are not limited to

Law enforcement officer
Probation or parole officer
Correctional officer
Prison program director
Computer crime investigator
Juvenile justice worker
Judge
Defense attorney
Prosecutor
Jailer
Private security officer
Victims' advocate

teach high school, while others become private investigators. Many criminologists provide civic organizations (such as victims' assistance and justice advocacy groups) with much needed expertise, a few work for politicians and legislative bodies, and some appear on talk shows to debate the pros and cons of various kinds of social policies designed to "fight" crime. Some criminologists even write books like this one!

WHAT IS CRIMINOLOGY?

The attempt to understand crime predates written history. Prehistoric evidence, including skeletal remains showing signs of primitive cranial surgery, seems to indicate that preliterate people explained deviant behavior by reference to spirit possession. Primitive surgery was an attempt to release unwanted spiritual influences. In the thousands of years since, many other theoretical perspectives on crime have been advanced. This book describes various criminological theories and covers some of the more popular ones in detail.

Before beginning any earnest discussion, however, it is necessary to define the term *criminology*. As our earlier discussion of the nature of crime and deviance indicates, not only must criminologists deal with a complex subject matter—consisting of a broad range of illegal behaviors committed by frequently unknown or uncooperative individuals—but they also must manage their work under changing conditions mandated by ongoing revisions of

A criminalist at work. Crime scene investigators, like the person shown here, can provide crucial clues needed to solve crimes. How does the work of a criminologist differ from that of a criminalist? *Corbis, Sygma*

the law and fluctuating social policy. In addition, as we have already seen, a wide variety of perspectives on the nature of crime abounds. All this leads to considerable difficulties in defining the subject matter under study.

There is some evidence that the term *criminology* was coined in 1889[35] by a Frenchman, Paul Topinard, who used it to differentiate the study of criminal body types within the field of anthropology from other biometric pursuits.[36] Topinard, while he may have coined the term, did little to help define it. As with the concept of crime, various definitions of *criminology* can be found in the literature today. A little more than a decade ago, criminologist Joseph F. Sheley wrote, "There seem to be nearly as many definitions of *contemporary criminology* as there are criminologists."[37]

One straightforward definition can be had from a linguistic analysis of the word *criminology*. As most people know, *ology* means "the study of something," and the word *crimen* comes from the Latin, meaning "accusation," "charge," or "guilt." Hence, linguistically speaking, the term *criminology* literally means "the study of crime." In addition to this fundamental kind of linguistic definition, three other important types of definitions can be found in the literature. They are (1) disciplinary, (2) causative, and (3) scientific. Each type of definition is distinguished by its focus. Disciplinary definitions are those which, as their name implies, focus on criminology as a discipline. Seen from this viewpoint, criminology is a field of study or a body of knowledge. Some of the earliest criminologists of the past century, including Edwin H. Sutherland, who is often referred to as the "dean of American criminology," offered definitions of their field that emphasized its importance as a discipline of study. Sutherland, for example, wrote in the first edition of his textbook *Criminology* in 1924 that "criminology is the body of knowledge regarding the social

problem of crime."[38] Sutherland's text was to set the stage for much of American criminology throughout the rest of the twentieth century. Reprinted in 1934 with the title *Principles of Criminology,* it was to become the most influential textbook ever written in the field of criminology.[39] Although Sutherland died in 1950, his revered text was revised for many years by Donald R. Cressey and later by David F. Luckenbill. By 1974, Sutherland's classic definition of *criminology* had been modified by Cressey to read, "Criminology is the body of knowledge regarding delinquency and crime as a social phenomenon. It includes within its scope the processes of making laws, of breaking laws, and of reacting toward the breaking of laws."[40]

Causative definitions emphasize criminology's role in uncovering the underlying causes of crime. In keeping with such an emphasis, contemporary criminologists Gennaro F. Vito and Ronald M. Holmes say that "criminology is the study of the causes of crime."[41]

Finally, there are those who point to the scientific nature of contemporary criminology as its distinguishing characteristic. According to Clemens Bartollas and Simon Dinitz, for example, "Criminology is the scientific study of crime."[42] Writing in 1989, Bartollas and Dinitz seemed to be echoing an earlier definition of criminology offered by Marvin E. Wolfgang and Franco Ferracuti, who wrote in 1967 that "criminology is the scientific study of crime, criminals, and criminal behavior."[43]

Sutherland suggested that criminology consists of three "principal divisions": (1) the sociology of law, (2) scientific analysis of the causes of crime, and (3) crime control.[44] Another well-known criminologist, Clarence Ray Jeffery, similarly sees three components of the field: (1) detection (of the offender), (2) treatment, and (3) explaining crime and criminal behavior.[45] In like manner, contemporary criminologist Gregg Barak writes that criminology is "an in-

Criminology examines the causes of crime and seeks ways to prevent or control it. Criminal justice examines the criminal justice system, including police, courts, and corrections. How do the two disciplines complement one another? *D. Greco, The Image Works.*

terdisciplinary study of the various bodies of knowledge, which focuses on the etiology of crime, the behavior of criminals, and the policies and practices of crime control."[46]

For our purposes, we will use a definition that brings together the works of previous writers but that also recognizes the increasingly professional status of the criminological enterprise. Throughout this book, then, we will view **criminology** as *an interdisciplinary profession built around the scientific study of crime and criminal behavior, including their manifestations, causes, legal aspects, and control.* As this definition indicates, criminology includes consideration of possible solutions to the problem of crime. Hence, this text (in later chapters) describes treatment strategies and social policy initiatives that have grown out of the existing array of theoretical explanations for crime.

Our definition is in keeping with the work of Jack P. Gibbs, an outstanding criminologist of the twentieth century, who wrote that the purpose of criminology is to offer well-researched and objective answers to four basic questions: (1) "Why do crime rates vary?" (2) "Why do individuals differ as to **criminality**?" (3) "Why is there variation in reactions to crime?" and (4) "What are the possible means of controlling criminality?"[47]

As a field of study, criminology in its present form is primarily a social scientific discipline. Contemporary criminologists generally recognize, however, that their field is interdisciplinary—that is, it draws upon other disciplines to provide an integrated approach to understanding the problem of crime in contemporary society and to advance solutions to the problems crime creates. Hence anthropology (especially cultural anthropology or ethnology), biology, sociology, political science, psychology, psychiatry, economics, ethology (the study of character), medicine, law, philosophy, ethics, and numerous other fields all have something to offer the student of criminology, as do the tools provided by statistics, computer science, and other forms of scientific and data analysis (See Figure 1-2).

The interdisciplinary nature of criminology was well stated by Jim Short, past President of the American Society of Criminology, who recently said, "The organization of knowledge by traditional disciplines has become increasingly anachronistic, as the generation of knowledge has become more interdisciplinary. From its earliest beginnings, when philosophers grappled with relationships between human nature and behavior and biologists sought to relate human physiology to behavior, criminology's concerns have reached across virtually all disciplines that focus on the human condition. Additionally, much of the impetus for criminology has come from concerns that crime be controlled. Criminology thus cuts across professions as well as disciplines."[48]

It is important to note that although criminology may be interdisciplinary as well as cross-professional, few existing explanations for criminal behavior have been successfully or fully integrated. Just as physicists today are seeking a unified field theory to explain the wide variety of observable forms of

■ **FIGURE 1-2** CRIMINOLOGY'S MANY ROOTS.

matter and energy, criminologists have yet to develop a generally accepted integrated approach to crime and criminal behavior that can explain the many diverse forms of criminality while also leading to effective social policies in the area of crime control. The attempt to construct criminological theories of relevance is made all the more difficult because, as discussed earlier, the phenomenon under study—crime—is very wide ranging and is subject to arbitrary and sometimes unpredictable legalistic and definitional changes.

Not only must a successfully integrated criminology bring together the contributions of various theoretical perspectives and disciplines, it must also—if it is to have any relevance—blend the practical requirements of our nation's judicial system with emotional and rational calls for morality and justice. Is the death penalty, for example, justified? If so, on what basis? Is it because it is a type of vengeance and therefore deserved? Can we say that it is unjustified because many sociological studies have shown that it does little to reduce the rate of serious crime, such as murder? Just what do we mean by "justice," and what can criminological studies tell us—if anything—about what is just and what is unjust?

The editors of the relatively new journal, *Theoretical Criminology*,[49] which began publication in 1997, wrote in the inaugural issue that "criminology has always been somewhat of a haphazardly-assembled umbrella-like structure which nevertheless usefully shelters a variety of theoretical interests that are espoused and employed by different disciplinary, methodological and political traditions." Such a structure, they said, "has obvious advantages, notably that it facilitates an interdisciplinary and inclusivist formation rather than supposing an exclusive but contentious 'core.' But one of its weaknesses is that its inhabitants, many of whom shuttle backwards and forwards between it and their parent disciplines, tend to communicate

THEORY VERSUS REALITY
Varying Perspectives on Crime and Criminology

What is crime? What is criminology? Throughout the years, writers have offered contrasting definitions of these terms. This box contains a number of definitions of both terms. Note that the definitions used in this book appear at the beginning of the table.

CRIME

Our Definition
"Human conduct in violation of the criminal laws of a state, the federal government, or a local jurisdiction that has the power to make such laws."

Legalistic Definition
"Crime is a violation of law."
—Edwin H. Sutherland, *Criminology* (Philadelphia: Lippincott, 1924), p. 18
Crime is "an intentional act in violation of the criminal law (statutory and case law), committed without defense or excuse, and penalized by the state as a felony or misdemeanor."
—Paul W. Tappan, "Who Is the Criminal?" *American Sociological Review*, Vol. 12 (1947), pp. 96–102

Political Definition
"Crimes are acts perceived by those in power as direct or indirect threats to their interests" and which are defined as criminal through a political process.
—Joseph F. Sheley, *Criminology: A Contemporary Handbook* (Belmont, CA: Wadsworth, 1991), p. 40

Sociological Definition
Crime is "an anti-social act of such a nature that its repression is necessary or is supposed to be necessary to the preservation of the existing system of society."
—Ezzat Fattah, *Introduction to Criminology* (Burnaby, British Columbia: School of Criminology, Simon Fraser University, 1989)

Psychological Definition
"Crime is a form of social maladjustment which can be designated as a more or less pronounced difficulty that the individual has in reacting to the stimuli of his environment in such a way as to remain in harmony with that environment."
—Ezzat Fattah, *Introduction to Criminology* (Burnaby, British Columbia: School of Criminology, Simon) Fraser University, 1989)

CRIMINOLOGY

Our Definition
"An interdisciplinary profession built around the scientific study of crime and criminal behavior, including their manifestations, causes, legal aspects, and control."

Linguistic Definition
"The study of (*ology*) crime (*crimen*)."
Note: The Latin term *crimen* literally means "accusation," "charge," or "guilt."

Disciplinary Definition
"Criminology is the body of knowledge regarding the social problem of crime."
—Edwin H. Sutherland, *Criminology* (Philadelphia: Lippincott, 1924), p. 11
"Criminology is the body of knowledge regarding delinquency and crime as a social phenomenon. It includes within its scope the processes of making laws, of breaking laws, and of reacting toward the breaking of laws."
—Edwin H. Sutherland and Donald R. Cressey, *Criminology*, 9th ed. (Philadelphia: Lippincott, 1974), p. 3
"Criminology ...is the study of crimes, criminals, and victims."
—Stephen Schafer, *Introduction to Criminology* (Reston, VA: Reston Publishing, 1976), p. 3

Causative Definition
"Criminology is the study of the causes of crime."
—Gennaro F. Vito and Ronald M. Holmes, *Criminology: Theory, Research, and Policy* (Belmont, CA: Wadsworth,1994), p. 3

Scientific Definition
"Criminology is the scientific study of crime."
—Clemens Bartollas and Simon Dinitz, *Introduction to Criminology: Order and Disorder* (New York: Harper & Row, 1989), p. 548
"Criminology is the scientific study of crime, criminals, and criminal behavior."
—Marvin A. Wolfgang and Franco Ferracuti, *The Subculture of Violence* (London: Tavistock, 1967)

(continued on next page)

(continued from previous page)

DISCUSSION QUESTIONS

1. Which definition of *crime* most appeals to you? Why?
2. Which definition of *criminology* seems most useful? Why?
3. Why might varying definitions such as those shown here be useful?

honestly and meaningfully only with those who speak the same theoretical language."[50] In other words, while the field of criminology can benefit from the wide variety of ideas available via a multiplicity of perspectives, all of which seek to understand the phenomenon we call crime, successful cross-disciplinary collaboration can be quite difficult.

As the earlier definition of *criminology* indicates, however, it is more than a field of study or a collection of theories; it is also a profession.[51] In his 1996 presidential address to the American Society of Criminology, Charles F. Wellford identified the "primary purposes" of the criminology profession. Wellford said, "Controlling crime through prevention, rehabilitation, and deterrence and ensuring that the criminal justice system reflects the high aspiration we have as a society of 'justice for all,' characterize the principal goals that in my judgment motivate the work of our field."[52]

Notably, criminology also contributes to the discipline of **criminal justice,** which emphasizes application of the criminal law and study of the components of the justice system, especially the police, courts, and corrections. As one author stated, "Criminology gives prominence to questions about the *causes of criminality,* while the *control of lawbreaking* is at the heart of criminal justice."[53] Learn more about the interdisciplinary nature of criminology from the *Encyclopedia Britannica* via Web Extra! 1-6.

Web EXTRA! Web Extra! 1-6 at crimtoday.com

Theoretical Criminology

Theoretical criminology, a subfield of general criminology, is the type of criminology most often found in colleges and universities. Theoretical criminology, rather than simply describing crime and its occurrence, posits explanations for criminal behavior. As Edwin Sutherland stated, "The problem in criminology is to explain the criminality of behavior. ...However, an explanation of criminal behavior should be a specific part of [a] general theory of behavior and its task should be to differentiate criminal from noncriminal behavior."[54]

To explain and understand crime, criminologists have developed many theories. A **theory**, at least in its ideal form, is made up of clearly stated propositions that posit relationships, often of a causal sort, between events and things under study. An old Roman theory, for example, proposed that in-

sanity is caused by the influence of the moon and may even follow its cycles—hence the term *lunacy.*

Theories attempt to provide us with explanatory power and help us understand the phenomenon under study. The more applicable a theory is found to be, the more generalizable it is from one specific instance to others—in other words, the more it can be applied to other situations. A **general theory** of crime is one that attempts to explain all (or at least most) forms of criminal conduct through a single, overarching approach. Unfortunately, as Don M. Gottfredson, past President of the American Society of Criminology, observes, "theories in criminology tend to be unclear and lacking in justifiable generality."[55] When we consider the wide range of behaviors regarded as criminal—from murder, to drug use, to white-collar and computer crime—it seems difficult to imagine one theory that can explain them all or that might even explain the same type of behavior under varying circumstances. Still, many past theoretical approaches to crime causation were **unicausal** while attempting to be all-inclusive. That is, the approaches posited a single, identifiable source for all serious deviant and criminal behavior.

An **integrated theory**, in contrast to a general theory, does not necessarily attempt to explain all criminality but is distinguishable by the fact that it merges (or attempts to merge) concepts drawn from different sources. As Gregg Barak states, "An integrative criminology . . . seeks to bring together the diverse bodies of knowledge that represent the full array of disciplines that study crime."[56] Hence, integrated theories provide potentially wider explanatory power than narrower formulations. Don C. Gibbons, Professor of Sociology at Portland State University, notes, "The basic idea of theoretical integration is straightforward; it concerns the combinations of single theories or elements of those theories into a more comprehensive argument. At the same time, it would be well to note that in practice, integration is a matter of degree: some theorists have combined or integrated more concepts or theoretical elements than have others."[57]

Both theoretical integration and the general applicability of criminological theories to a wide variety of law-violating behavior are intuitively appealing concepts. Even far more limited attempts at criminological theorizing, however, often face daunting challenges. "As we shall see," notes Gibbons, "criminologists have not managed to articulate a large collection of relatively formalized arguments in a general or integrated form."[58] Hence although we will use the word *theory* in describing the many explanations for crime covered by this book, it should be recognized that the word is only loosely applicable to some of the perspectives we will discuss.

As we shall learn in Chapter 3, many social scientists insist that to be considered theories, explanations must consist of sets of clearly stated, logically interrelated, and measurable propositions. The fact that only a few of the theories described in this book rise above the level of organized conjecture—and those offer only limited generalizability and have rarely been integrated—is one of the greatest challenges facing criminology today.

CRIMINOLOGY AND SOCIAL POLICY

Of potentially broader importance than theory testing are **social policies** based on research findings. In the mid-1990s, for example, the U.S. Senate heard testimony from then-Attorney General Janet Reno, Senator Paul Simon, and television studio executives over the claim that television is responsible for encouraging violent acts among young people. The hearing grew, in part, from an Ohio mother's claim that the Music Television (MTV) cartoon *Beavis and Butt-Head* led her 5-year-old son to set a fire that killed his 2-year-old sister. The show had featured a lead character chanting, "Fire is good." As the investigation revealed, experts who study televised cartoons have found that violent episodes average nearly one every two minutes.[59]

In a report presented to the attorney general, the Citizens Task Force on TV Violence recommended, among other things, restricting violence on television between 6 A.M. and 10 P.M.—the time when children are most likely to be watching.[60] The task force told Reno that networks and cable companies should voluntarily agree to the restrictive period or face regulation through government action.

Copycat violence has also been attributed to films. Touchstone Pictures, for example, reedited the movie *The Program,* cutting scenes in which drunken football players test their nerve by lying end to end in the middle of a highway. Several young men who apparently copied the stunt were either killed or critically injured. Commenting on the incidents, a Touchstone spokesperson said, "While the scene in the movie in no way advocates this irresponsible activity, it is impossible for us to ignore that someone may have recklessly chosen to imitate it."[61]

In July 2000, a number of professional groups—including the American Medical Association, the American Academy of Pediatrics, the American Psychological Association, and the American Academy of Child and Adolescent Psychiatry—issued a joint statement saying that violence in television, music, video games, and movies leads to increased levels of violent behavior among children.[62] The effects of violence in the media "are measurable and long-lasting," said the statement. The groups reached the conclusion "based on over 30 years of re-

search . . . that viewing entertainment violence can lead to increases in aggressive attitudes, values and behaviors, particularly in children." Moreover, they said, "prolonged viewing of media violence can lead to emotional desensitization toward violence in real life." The statement was prompted by a spate of school shootings that marred the 1990s and by public fears of growing levels of violence among American teenagers.

A few weeks later, the U.S. Senate's Judiciary Committee issued a special report charging media violence with contributing to violent episodes nationwide.[63] The report concluded that parents must take the lead in shielding their children against violent images in the mass media and included recommendations for the entertainment industry.

Finally, in late 2000, the Federal Trade Commission (FTC) issued a report on teenage violence that had been commissioned by the President in the wake of the 1999 shooting at Columbine High School in Littleton, Colorado.[64] The FTC concluded that "Hollywood aggressively markets violent movies, music and electronic games to children even when they have been labeled as appropriate only for adults."[65] The complete 116-page FTC report *Marketing Violent Entertainment to Children* is available at Web Extra! 1-7.

Web EXTRA!   Web Extra! 1-7 at crimtoday.com

Both the FTC and the Judiciary Committee reports came amidst arguments in Congress over a proposed new juvenile justice bill that would toughen penalties for violent juvenile offenders and would provide states with $1 billion a year to fight juvenile crime. As this book goes to press, the Senate is still debating what, if anything, to do about violence in the media and how to reduce its impact on children. It seems, however, that—First Amendment issues aside—legislation can soon be expected to regulate programming if the television, movie, and gaming industries do not do more to regulate themselves and their products. In the words of Senator Simon, "TV is a powerful sales medium, and too often what it sells is violence."[66]

Professional criminologists are acutely aware of the need to link sound social policy to the objective findings of well-conducted criminological research. A recent meeting of the American Society of Criminology (ASC), for example, focused on the need to forge just such a link. At the meeting, ASC President Alfred Blumstein, of Carnegie Mellon University, told criminologists gathered there that "an important mission of the ASC and its members involves the generation of knowledge that is useful in dealing with crime and the operation of the criminal justice system, and then helping public officials to use that knowledge intelligently and effectively."[67] Blumstein added, "So little is known about the causes of crime and about the effects of criminal justice policy on crime that new insights about the criminal justice system can often be extremely revealing and can eventually change the way people think about the crime problem or about the criminal justice system."[68]

Social Policy and Public Crime Concerns

Although American crime rates have been declining steadily for almost a decade, concern over crime remains pervasive in the United States today. Two decades ago, crime was the number one concern of Americans voicing opinions in public polls. In the interim, concern over crime came to be replaced with cold war and, later, economic worries. Following a spate of seemingly random violence, however, including well-publicized shootings of foreign tourists in Florida, cult-based violence in Texas and elsewhere, gang-related drive-by shootings, terrorist bombings, and highly visible inner-city violence, fear of crime once again moved to the forefront of national concerns.

A Gallup poll conducted in mid-2000 found concerns about crime topping the list of the worst problems facing local communities.[69] When asked to identify important issues in their area, more than a quarter of the public (27%) mentioned crime, including related problems of gangs, drugs, and guns. Education ranked second on the list, cited by 17%, followed by economic issues (15%), development issues (7%), and poverty (3%). Gallup poll officials noted that "trends on this question date back to 1959, and suggest that the more things change, the more they stay the same. While some issues, such as racial integration and Vietnam, have come and gone from the list of concerns, others—including crime, education, and the economy—appear to be enduring worries. Crime and education are as high on the list today as ever, while concern over the economy is low relative to other years."[70]

A separate study found that workplace homicide is the fastest-growing type of murder in the United States today and that it is the leading cause of workplace death for women.[71] Experts explained the rise in on-the-job homicides as the outgrowth of the recession years of the early 1990s, which led to corporate downsizing and increased job-related stresses.[72] Substance abuse and the ready availability of guns were cited as other contributing factors. Robbery is another. Of all workers, taxi drivers are most at risk of being murdered on the job. A recent National Institute for Occupational Safety and Health study showed that during the past decade, 26.9 of every 100,000 taxi drivers and dispatchers were murdered on the job—nearly 40 times the overall 0.7 per 100,000 job-related homicide rate for all workers.[73]

Concern over crime is not necessarily related to the actual incidence of crime, however, as crime rates (discussed in detail in Chapter 2) have declined substantially in recent years. Moreover, Americans are feeling as safe today as at any time in the last 40 years. Only 34% of Americans say that they would be afraid of walking alone at night close to their homes, the lowest level since 1965.[74] Only 15% of those polled say that they frequently worry about the possibility of being murdered—down from 10% in 1993.[75] See Web Extra! 1-8 for recent public opinion poll releases about crime, concerns about crime, and fear of crime.

Web Extra! 1-8 at crimtoday.com

Even if fear of crime has recently declined, concern over crime remains an important determinant of public policy. Hence political agendas promising to lower crime rates or to keep them low, as well as those that call for changes in the conditions that produce crime, can be quite successful for candidates or incumbents who promote them in an environment where concern over crime is high.[76]

THE THEME OF THIS BOOK

This book builds on a social policy theme by contrasting two perspectives now popular in American society and in much of the rest of the world (see Figure 1-3). One point of view, termed the **social problems perspective**, holds that crime is a manifestation of underlying social problems like poverty, discrimination, inequality of opportunity, the breakdown of traditional social institutions, the poor quality of formal education in some parts of the country, pervasive family violence experienced during the formative years, and inadequate socialization practices that leave young people without the fundamental values necessary to contribute meaningfully to the society in which they live. Advocates of the social problems perspective, while generally agreeing that crime and violence are serious social problems, advance solutions based on what is, in effect, a public health model. Adherents of that model says that crime must be addressed in much the same way as public health concerns like AIDS, herpes, and tobacco addiction.

Proponents of the social problems perspective typically foresee solutions to the crime problem as coming in the form of large-scale government expenditures in support of social programs designed to address the issues that are perceived to

According to pollsters, crime is one of the American public's top concerns. Given recent statistics showing falling crime rates, is such concern justified? *H. Darr Beisner, USA Today*

Social
Problems

Social
Responsibility

■ **FIGURE 1-3** THE THEME OF THIS BOOK: SOCIAL PROBLEMS
VERSUS SOCIAL RESPONSIBILITY. AT THE CORE OF TODAY'S
THINKING ABOUT CRIME EXISTS A CRUCIAL DISTINCTION
BETWEEN THOSE WHO BELIEVE THAT *CRIME IS A MATTER OF
INDIVIDUAL RESPONSIBILITY* (THE SOCIAL RESPONSIBILITY
PERSPECTIVE) AND THOSE WHO EMPHASIZE THAT *CRIME IS A
MANIFESTATION OF UNDERLYING SOCIAL PROBLEMS* BEYOND THE
CONTROL OF INDIVIDUALS (THE SOCIAL PROBLEMS VIEWPOINT).

lie at the root of crime. Government-funded initiatives, designed to enhance social, educational, occupational, and
other opportunities are perceived as offering programmatic
solutions to ameliorate most causes of crime.

During the 2000 presidential campaign, for example, a
section of the Democratic National Platform advocated "stopping crime before it starts." That section, which exemplified a
social problems approach to crime control, read, "Democrats
also know that all Americans are better off if we stop crime before it claims new victims, rather than focusing single-mind-
edly on pursuing perpetrators after the harm is done. That is
why we are firmly committed to sound and proven crime-pre-
vention strategies that are good for all Americans. Solid investments in children and youth, in job creation, and in skills
development are powerful antidotes to crime."[77]

The social problems approach to crime is characteristic
of what social scientists term a *macro* approach because it
portrays instances of individual behavior (crimes) as arising
out of widespread and contributory social conditions which
enmesh unwitting individuals in a causal nexus of uncontrollable social forces.

A contrasting perspective lays the cause of crime squarely
at the feet of individual perpetrators. This point of view holds
that individuals are fundamentally responsible for their own
behavior and maintains that they choose crime over other,
more law-abiding courses of action. Perpetrators may choose
crime, advocates of this perspective say, because it is exciting,
because it offers illicit pleasures and the companionship of
like-minded thrill seekers, or because it is simply less demanding than conformity. This viewpoint, which we shall call
the **social responsibility perspective,** has a close affiliation

with what is known in criminology as rational choice theory
(discussed in detail in Chapter 4). Advocates of the social responsibility perspective, with their emphasis on individual
choice, tend to believe that social programs do little to solve
the problem of crime because, they say, a certain number of
crime-prone individuals, for a variety of personalized reasons,
will always make irresponsible choices. Hence advocates of the
social responsibility approach suggest crime reduction strategies based on firm punishments, imprisonment, individualized rehabilitation, increased security, and a wider use of police
powers. The social responsibility perspective characteristically
emphasizes a form of *micro* analysis that tends to focus on individual offenders and their unique biology, psychology, background, and immediate life experiences.

The social responsibility perspective came to the fore
during the 2000 presidential campaign, when then-Governor
George W. Bush of Texas called for ushering in "the
Responsibility Era." Bush's message, said the Republican
National Committee, "tells children that there are right
choices in life and wrong choices in life."[78] The committee
went on to explain that "[President] Bush believes the laws
should be fully enforced and that criminal conduct should
have serious consequences. In his two terms as Governor he
has advocated and signed comprehensive reforms toughen-
ing the juvenile justice code, abolishing a mandatory release
law for certain violent offenders, effectively ending parole for
violent repeat offenders, passing some of the toughest sex offender laws in the country, and restoring a provision making
it a felony to assault a police officer. "As a result," the committee claimed, "overall crime in Texas decreased 14 percent
and violent crime decreased 20 percent."

The contrast between the social problems and the social responsibility perspectives was spotlighted in the 1997 trial of
Jesse Timmendequas, a previously convicted sex offender and
admitted killer of 7-year-old Megan Kanka.[79] The defense for
Timmendequas centered on his claims of repeated sexual abuse
by his father as he was growing up—an experience his attorneys
said left him helplessly attracted sexually to young children.
The jury hearing the case rejected Timmendequas's abuse defense, found him guilty of killing Kanka, and recommended
that he be sentenced to die. In summing up the feelings of
many of those present, prosecutor Kathryn Flicker noted that
"Timmendequas's childhood was not a bed of roses." But, she
asked, "where does individual responsibility fit into the whole
scheme? He was responsible as an adult, as we all are."[80]

In recent years, the social responsibility perspective has substantially influenced national crime control policy. Examples of conservatism in our nation's approach to
criminals abound. The Violent Crime Control and Law
Enforcement Act of 1994, for example, which is discussed in
detail in Chapter 15, expanded the number of capital crimes
under federal law from a handful of offenses to 52.[81] The law
also made $8.8 billion available to municipalities to put
100,000 new police officers on the streets, and it allocated $7.9
billion for states to build and operate prisons and incarceration alternatives like boot camps. Prison funding was

THEORY VERSUS REALITY
A Public Health Model of Crime Control

This book builds upon a theme that contrasts the *social problems* perspective on crime with another approach called *social responsibility*. An example of the social problems perspective can be found in the growing popularity of the public health model of crime control. According to the National Institute of Justice (NIJ), "Looking at violence only as a criminal justice issue has limited crime prevention strategies." But now, says NIJ, "policymakers are recognizing that violence is a health issue as well." Excerpts from a recent NIJ report, which are contained in this box, detail how the public health approach can be applied to the study of crime and justice.

Treating violence as a major problem in criminal justice and health suggests some new strategies for prevention. Public health campaigns to induce people to take responsibility for avoiding illness have led many to change their daily behavior. Safer sex practices are a dramatic and widespread personal response to the AIDS epidemic. Although it is decidedly harder to protect oneself against violence than against a virus, the public health approach offers useful lessons in preventing and controlling violence. Three public health concepts that are especially germane to preventing violence are public education, control of contagion, and early detection.

Public Education

Education forms the backbone of public health efforts. Over the past 20 years, full-scale public education campaigns have increased the use of seat belts and have reduced the use of tobacco. Antismoking education has been successful not only in getting a large part of the smoking population to quit, but also in preventing many young people from starting to smoke. An antiviolence campaign even half as effective as the antismoking campaign would dramatically reduce violent behavior. Such a campaign could target youth, could get at the roots of violent behavior (such as a lack of respect for women, in cases of sexual and domestic assault), and could teach alternative ways to solve disputes (for example, conflict resolution and communication skills).

Control of Contagion

The health care model stresses control of epidemics by targeting people at risk for disease, such as those living in crowded or unsanitary conditions. Who is at risk for violence? Through new research and anecdotal evidence, some profiles of at-risk populations are emerging. For instance, increasing evidence suggests that a predilection toward violence can be transmitted from generation to generation. One research study found that youths who have been abused or neglected are 38% more likely to be arrested for a violent crime by the time they are adults than those who have not been mistreated.

In addition, data indicate that a person who has been shot is more likely to be victimized again than someone who has not. And yet another recent study found that women who were raped or were victims of attempted rape as adolescents were more than twice as likely as other women to be the victim of rape or attempted rape during their first year in college.

How do we inoculate those at risk? Counseling can provide victims of violence with support and constructive ways to channel their rage, which would reduce the likelihood they would lash out at someone else, seek retribution, or continue to feel vulnerable. Counseling can also provide new coping and crime prevention skills to reduce fear as well as the chance of a repeat victimization. When a person comes to the emergency room with a gunshot or knife wound, the hospital staff must report the incident to the police so that the criminal justice system can intervene. Funding is needed for counseling to help victims prevent repeat victimization and to guide them from becoming victimizers themselves.

Early Detection

To treat people at risk for violence, the system must first identify them. The public health model teaches that the earlier an ailment can be detected, the better the chance of curing it. In cases of violence between strangers, detection is usually straightforward: The victim turns to the criminal justice system. When the victim and the offender have a prior relationship, the criminal justice system may not be involved until the violence escalates into serious assault or murder. In these cases, early detection and intervention can be especially important.

Promise for the Future

An opportunity exists to screen for violence by a medical community that increasingly emphasizes prevention and the family doctor approach to health care. Family doctors are well positioned to notice patterns that suggest that a patient is at risk of violence. Twenty years ago, doctors rarely asked patients about their sexual and drinking habits, but now most doctors routinely ask such questions. Asking, "Do you have trouble controlling your temper? What happens when you lose it?" could be just as routine. If a patient replies that he occasionally "takes a swipe" at his partner or "breaks furniture," the physician could tell him that this is a health problem and that he needs help.

Treating violence as both a health issue and a criminal justice issue opens the door to more resources. Researchers sponsored by the National Institute of Justice are studying violence, but a vast amount of information still needs to be collected. Computerized records of reasons for injuries and sophisticated studies about prevalence will offer a better grasp of patterns. With data in hand, stronger arguments can be made for increased allocation of limited resources. A better balance is needed: The federal government spends on research about $794 per year per life lost because of cancer, but only $31 per year per life lost to violence.

The value of the public health approach is that investing in detection, education, and counseling is cost effective. It is less expensive to incorporate early identification into the health care system and to provide services than to face the burden of escalating emergency room, law enforcement, court, child welfare, and prison costs. But what is truly unbearable is the cost in human lives that the nation will pay if efforts

(continued on next page)

(continued from previous page)

to prevent violence fail. Ultimately, early intervention and treatment by the health care system, combined with criminal justice efforts, will start giving the victims of violence what they deserve: for the crime not to have happened.

DISCUSSION QUESTIONS

1. What are the major differences between the social problems and the social responsibility perspectives on crime?

2. Which perspective do you find most appealing? Why?

3. Which perspective is closest to the public health model of crime prevention discussed here?

4. Do you believe that the public health model is applicable to the crime problem? Can crime be effectively prevented or reduced using the public health model? Why or why not?

Source: Lucy N. Friedman, "Adopting the Health Care Model to Prevent Victimization," *National Institute of Justice Journal* (November 1994).

---

intended to ensure that additional prison cells would be available to put—and keep—violent offenders behind bars. A subchapter of the 1994 Violent Crime Control Act created a federal "Three Strikes and You're Out" law, mandating life imprisonment for criminals convicted of three violent federal felonies or drug offenses. Similarly, the law increased or created new penalties for over 70 federal criminal offenses, primarily covering violent crimes, drug trafficking, and gun crimes.

Since the 1994 federal legislation was passed, many states have moved to toughen their own laws against violent criminals. Violent juveniles and repeat offenders have been especially targeted. As the number of people behind bars has soared, legislatures in a number of states have also moved to reduce inmate privileges, such as removing television sets, exercise equipment, and free magazines and reducing the number of hours of visitation and recreation permitted for inmates.

A note about wording is in order: Although the social responsibility perspective might also be termed the *individual responsibility perspective* because it stresses individual responsibility above all else, we've chosen to use the term *social responsibility perspective* instead, as it holds that individuals must be ultimately responsible to the social group of which they are a part and that they should be held accountable by group standards if they are not. In short, this perspective is characterized by societal demands for the exercise of individual responsibility.

THE SOCIAL CONTEXT OF CRIME

Crime does not occur in a vacuum. Every crime has a unique set of causes, consequences, and participants. Crime affects some people more than others, having a special impact on those who are direct participants in the act itself—offenders, victims, police officers, witnesses, and so on. Crime, in general, provokes reactions from the individuals it victimizes, from concerned groups of citizens, from the criminal justice system, and sometimes from society as a whole, which manifests its concerns via the creation of new social policy. Reactions to crime, from the everyday to the precedent setting, may color the course of future criminal events.[82]

In this book, we shall attempt to identify and examine some of the many social, psychological, economic, biological, and other causes of crime, while simultaneously expounding on the many differing perspectives that have been advanced to explain both crime and criminality. An example of differing perspectives can be found in the Theory versus Reality box in this chapter entitled "The Murder of John Lennon." The box provides insight into the motivation of Mark David Chapman (Lennon's killer) and shows that the assumptions we, as outsiders to the event itself, make about the genesis of criminal purpose are not always correct. As the box reveals, popular conceptions of criminal motivation are typically shaped by media portrayals of offender motivation, which often fail to take into consideration the felt experiences of the law violator. By identifying and studying this diversity of perspectives on criminality, we will discover the characteristic disjuncture among victims, offenders, the justice system, and society as to the significance that each assigns to the behavior in question—and often to its motivation. It will not be unusual to find, for example, that sociological or psychological initiatives with which the offenders themselves do not identify are assigned to offenders by theorists and others.

Another example of misattribution can be seen in the decade-old case of Damian Williams, the black man sentenced in December 1993 to ten years in prison for beating white truck driver Reginald Denny during the Los Angeles riots. Most reporters and many attorneys assumed that Williams was motivated during the beating by his knowledge of verdicts of innocence that had been returned earlier that day in the state trial of California police officers accused of beating black motorist Rodney King—an incident captured on videotape that galvanized the nation. An infuriated Williams, the media supposed (and reported), attacked Denny in response to frustrations he felt at a justice system that seemed to protect whites at the expense of blacks. Williams, however, told a reporter at his sentencing that he knew nothing about the verdicts at the time he attacked Denny and that he was just caught up in the riots. "Maybe other people knew about [the King verdict], but I wasn't aware of it until later. ...I was just caught up in the rapture," Williams said.[83] Williams served three years in prison and was released. In an interesting footnote to the Denny beating, however, Williams was arrested again in 2000 and charged with the murder of 43-year-old Grover Tinner, a South Central

Los Angeles resident who died after being shot in an alley in a dispute that apparently involved drugs.[84]

Making Sense of Crime: The Causes and Consequences of the Criminal Event

This book recognizes that criminal activity is diversely created and variously interpreted. In other words, this book depicts crime not as an isolated individual activity, but as a *social event.*[85] Like other social events, crime is fundamentally a social construction.[86] To say that crime is a social construction is not to lessen the impact of the victimization experiences which all too many people undergo in our society every day. Nor does such a statement trivialize the significance of crime prevention efforts or the activities of members of the criminal justice system. Likewise, it does not underplay the costs of crime to individual victims and to society as a whole. It does, however, recognize that although a given instance of criminal behavior may have many causes, it also carries with it many different kinds of meanings—at least one for offenders, another (generally quite different meaning, of course) for victims, and still another for agents of the criminal justice system. Similarly, a plethora of social interest groups, from victims' advocates to prisoner "rights" and gun control organizations, all interpret the significance of lawbreaking behavior from unique points of view, and each arrives at different conclusions as to what should be done about the so-called crime problem.

For these reasons, we have chosen to apply the concept of **social relativity** to the study of criminality.[87] Social relativity means that social events are differently interpreted according to the cultural experiences and personal interests of the initiator, the observer, or the recipient of that behavior. Hence, as a social phenomenon, crime means different things to the offender, to the criminologist who studies it, to the police officer who investigates it, and to the victim who experiences it firsthand.

Figure 1-4 illustrates both the causes and the consequences of crime in rudimentary diagrammatic form. In keeping with the theme of this textbook, it depicts crime as a social event. The figure consists of a foreground, describing those features which immediately determine the nature of the criminal event (including responses to the event as it is transpiring), and a background, in which generic contributions to crime can be seen along with interpretations of the event after it has taken place. We call the background causes of crime *contributions,* and use the word *inputs* to signify the more immediate propensities and predispositions of the actors involved in the situation. Inputs also include the physical features of the setting in which a specific crime takes place. Both background contributions and immediate inputs contribute to and shape the criminal event. The more or less immediate results or consequences of crime are termed *outputs,* while the term *interpretations* appears in the diagram to indicate that any crime has a lasting impact both on surviving participants and on society.

As Figure 1-4 shows, the criminal event is ultimately a result of the coming together of inputs provided by the

- offender
- victim
- society
- justice system

Offenders bring with them certain background features, such as personal life experiences, a peculiar biology (insofar as they are unique organisms), a distinct personality, personal values and beliefs, and various kinds of skills and knowledge (some of which may be useful in the commission of crime). Background contributions to crime can be vitally important. Recent research, for example, tends to cement the existence of a link between child-rearing practices and criminality in later life. Joan McCord, reporting on a 30-year study of family relationships and crime, found that self-confident, nonpunitive, and affectionate mothers tend to insulate their male

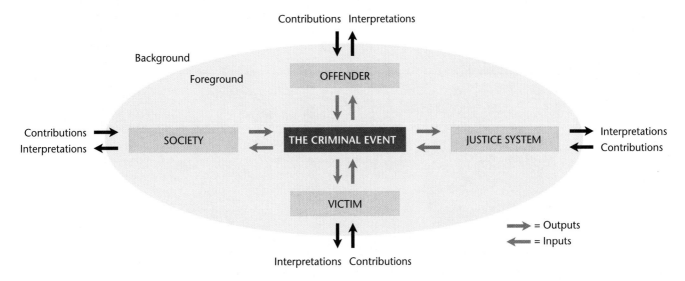

■ **FIGURE 1-4**   THE CAUSES AND CONSEQUENCES OF CRIME.

THEORY VERSUS REALITY
The Murder of John Lennon

At 10:50 P.M. on December 8, 1980, Mark David Chapman, 25, killed famous musician and former Beatle John Lennon. Lennon, who was returning home from a recording session with his wife, Yoko Ono, died in a hail of bullets fired from Chapman's .38-caliber pistol. As a musical luminary, John Lennon was well known to the world. Even his private life—from his residence in the exclusive Dakota Apartments in New York City to his dietary preferences and investment portfolios—was the subject of popular news stories and media exposés.

Following Lennon's death, the public generally assumed that Chapman had chosen his murderous course of action due to innate, albeit perverted, needs fed by a twisted rationale—specifically, to become famous by killing a celebrity. In similar assassination attempts involving Gerald Ford, Ronald Reagan, and others, the media has assumed much the same type of motivation. News stories have

communicated to the public the image of would-be assassins sparked by the desire to make headlines and to see their names become household words. To assign such motivation to the killers of famous people is understandable from the media's perspective. Many of the people encountered by newscasters and writers in their daily work have an obvious interest in seeing their names in print. Constant experiences with such people do much to convince byline authors and narrators that the drive for glory is a major motivator of human behavior.

Such "pop psychology," however, probably does not provide an accurate assessment of the motivation of most assassins. We know from recent conversations with Chapman that he, at least, was driven by a different mind-set. In an interview ten years after the killing (the first one he gave since the shooting), Chapman related a story of twisted emotions and evil whisperings inside his own head. Just before the shooting, the

unemployed Chapman, living in Hawaii, had gotten married. Faced with a difficult financial situation and rising debts, he became enraged by what he perceived as Lennon's "phoniness." Lennon, he reasoned, had become rich singing about the virtues of the common person, yet Lennon himself lived in luxury made possible by wealth far beyond the reach of Chapman and others like him. According to Chapman, "He [Lennon] had told us to imagine. ...He had told us not to be greedy. And I had believed!" In effect, Chapman shifted responsibility for his own failure onto Lennon. For that, he reasoned, Lennon must pay. In preparation for the killing, Chapman recorded his own voice over Lennon's songs, screaming such things as, "John Lennon must die! John Lennon is a phony." Once a born-again Christian, Chapman turned to Satanism and prayed for demons to enter his body so that he could have the strength to carry out the mission he had set for himself.

(continued on next page)

Mark David Chapman (left) killed well-known musician John Lennon (right) in 1980. In 2000, Chapman's bid for parole was denied. What can crimes like Chapman's tell us about criminal motivation? *A. Hill, SIPA Press (left) and Sunset Boulevard, Corbis/Sygma (right)*

(continued from previous page)

Today, says Chapman, he has changed. Much of his time behind bars is spent writing religious tracts and other stories, with inspiration drawn from verses Lennon made famous. In an interview that Chapman gave shortly before his first parole eligibility date in September 2000, the now-repentant killer indulged in psychological self-analysis and blamed the killing on a father who never showed love. "I think the main problem," said Chapman, "was

that my father never talked about life or problems . . . and I guess the more I look back on it, I didn't feel any love from him. Perhaps I was getting back, killing John Lennon, ruining my life as well." Parole officials were unimpressed with Chapman's self-assessment and denied his bid for parole.

DISCUSSION QUESTIONS

1. Why did Chapman kill Lennon? Will we ever be sure of his true

motivation? How can we know when we have uncovered it?
2. Was Chapman insane at the time of the killing? What does insanity mean in this context? How can it be determined?
3. Should Chapman be paroled? Why or why not?

Sources: Jack Jones, "Decade Later, Killer Prays to be Forgiven," *USA Today*, December 3, 1990, p. 1a. "John Lennon's Killer Blames His Own Father," Reuters wire service, September 26, 2000.

children from delinquency and, consequently, later criminal activity.[88] Difficulties associated with the birthing process have also been linked to crime in adulthood.[89] Birth trauma and negative familial relationships are but two of the literally thousands of kinds of experiences individuals may have. Whether individuals who undergo trauma at birth and are deprived of positive maternal experiences will turn to crime depends on many other things, including their own mixture of other experiences and characteristics, the appearance of a suitable victim, the failure of the justice system to prevent crime, and the evolution of a social environment in which criminal behavior is somehow encouraged or valued.

Each of the parties identified in Figure 1-4 contributes immediate inputs to the criminal event. Foreground contributions by the offender may consist of a particular motivation, a specific intent (in many cases), or a drug-induced state of mind.

Some crimes are especially difficult to understand, no matter how they are viewed. In 1995, for example, the town of Union, South Carolina, was devastated by the trial of Susan Smith. Smith, who originally claimed that a carjacker had forced her from her car and had driven off with her two young sons still in the vehicle, confessed to the murders of both Alex, 1, and Michael, 3. Smith admitted she drove the car, with her sons still strapped into child safety seats, off a pier and into a nearby lake. An exhaustive ten-day nationwide search for the boys had failed to turn up any significant leads, and the case might have gone unsolved until investigators discovered a letter from Smith's lover saying that he felt unable to accept both her and the children. An autopsy revealed that the children were still alive as the car went into the lake but that both drowned as the car flipped onto its roof and sank. Smith again made headlines in 2000 when a sexual affair she was having with a correctional officer at Women's Correctional Institution in Columbia, South Carolina, came to light. Smith had been serving a life sentence at the facility.[90] The officer, 50-year-old Lieutenant Houston Cagle, was fired, and the incident prompted investigations in women's prisons nationwide.

Like the offender, the **criminal justice system** also contributes to the criminal event, albeit unwillingly, through its failure to (1) prevent criminal activity, (2) adequately identify and inhibit specific offenders prior to their involvement in

crime, and (3) prevent the release of convicted criminals who later become repeat offenders. Such background contributions can be seen in prisons (a central component of the justice system) that serve as "schools for crime," fostering anger against society and building a propensity for continued criminality in inmates who have been "turned out." Similarly, the failure of system-sponsored crime prevention programs—ranging from the patrol activities of local police departments to educational and diversionary programs intended to redirect budding offenders—helps set the stage for the criminal event. On the other hand, proper system response may reduce crime. A recent study by Carol W. Kohfeld and John Sprague, for example, found that police response (especially arrest) could, under certain demographic conditions, dramatically reduce the incidence of criminal behavior.[91] Additionally, Kohfeld and Sprague found that arrest "constitutes communication to criminals in general," further supporting the notion that inputs provided by the justice system have the power to either enhance or reduce the likelihood of criminal occurrences. Immediate inputs provided by the justice system typically consist of such features of the situation as the presence or absence of police officers, the ready availability (or lack thereof) of official assistance, the willingness of police officers to intervene in precrime situations, and the response time required for officers to arrive at a crime scene.

Few crimes can occur without a victim. Sometimes the victim is a passive participant in the crime, such as an innocent person killed on the street outside of his or her home by random gunfire from a drive-by shooting. In such cases, the victim is simply in the proverbial wrong place at the wrong time. Even then, however, merely by being present the victim contributes his or her person to the event, thereby increasing the severity of the incident (that is, the random shooting that injures no one may still be against the law, but it is a far less serious crime than a similar incident in which somebody is killed). Sometimes, however, victims more actively contribute to their own victimization through the appearance of defenselessness (perhaps because of old age, drunkenness, or disability), by failing to take appropriate defensive measures (leaving doors unlocked or forgetting to remove the key from a car's ignition), through an unwise display of wealth (flashing large-denomination bills in a public place), or simply by

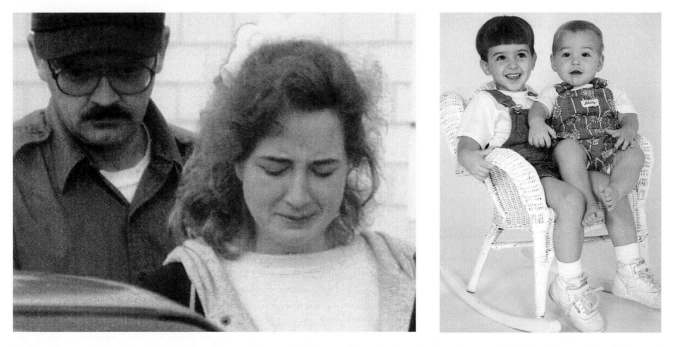

Some crimes are especially difficult to understand. Susan Smith, of Union, South Carolina, confessed to drowning her two young sons, Alex, 1, and Michael, 3, in 1994. The boys are shown in happier times in the photo on the right. *Spartan Herald Journal, Corbis/Sygma (left) and American Fast Photo, SABA Press Photos, Inc. (right)*

making other unwise choices (walking down a dark alley off of Times Square at 2 or 3 A.M., for example). In a recent study of Canadian victimization, Leslie W. Kennedy and David R. Forde found that violent personal victimization "is contingent on the exposure that comes from following certain lifestyles."[92] This was especially true, they found, "for certain demographic groups, particularly young males."

Although lifestyles may provide the background that fosters victimization, a more active form of victimization characterizes "victims" who initiate criminal activity, such as the barroom brawler who picks a fight but ends up on the receiving end of the ensuing physical violence. Victim-precipitated offenses are those that involve active victim participation in the initial stages of a criminal event and that take place when the soon-to-be victim instigates the chain of events which ultimately results in the victimization.

Finally, the general public (termed *society* in Figure 1-4) contributes to the criminal event both formally and informally. Society's formal contributions sometimes take the form of legislation, whereby crime itself is defined. Hence as we shall discuss in considerable detail in Chapter 15, society structures the criminal event in a most fundamental way by delineating (through legislation and via statute) which forms of activity are to be thought of as criminal.

Society's less formal contributions to crime arise out of generic social practices and conditions like poverty, poor and informal education, various forms of discrimination by which pathways to success are blocked, and the **socialization** process. Socialization has an especially important impact on crime causation because it provides the interpretative foundation used to define and understand the significance of particular situations in which we find ourselves, and it is upon those interpre-

tations that we may (or may not) decide to act. Date rape, for example, can occur when a man concludes that his date "owes" him something for the money he has spent on her. That feeling, however inappropriate from the point of view of the victim and the justice system, probably has its roots in early learned experiences—including values communicated from television, the movies, and popular music—about gender-related roles under such circumstances. In other words, society, through the divergent values and expectations it places upon people, property, and behavior under particular conditions, may provide the motivational basis for many offenses.

The contributions society makes to the backgrounds of both offender and victim and to the structure of the justice system, and the influences each in turn have upon the general social order, provide for a kind of "feedback loop" in our vision of crime (even though the loop is not shown in Figure 1-4 for fear of unnecessarily complicating it). Through socialization, for example, individuals learn about the dangers of criminal victimization; but when victimization occurs and is publicized, it reinforces the socialization process, leading to an increased wariness of others, and so on. An example can be seen in the fact that children throughout the United States are routinely taught to avoid strangers and to be suspicious of people they do not know. A few decades ago, stranger avoidance was not ordinarily communicated to children; it entered cultural awareness following a number of horrendous and well-publicized crimes involving child victims. It is now a shared part of the socialization process experienced by countless children every day throughout the United States.

The contributions made by society to crime are complex and far reaching. Some say that the content of the mass media (television, movies, newspapers, popular music, etc.) can lead to crime by exposing young people to inappropriate role models and to the kinds of activity—violence and unbridled sexuality, for example—that encourage criminality.

Society's foreground contributions to crime largely emanate from the distribution of resources and the accessibility of services, which are often the direct result of economic conditions. In a study of the availability of medical resources (especially quality hospital emergency services), William G. Doerner found that serious assaults may "become" homicides when such resources are lacking but that homicides can be prevented through the effective utilization of capable medical technology.[93] Hence societal decisions leading to the distribution and placement of advanced medical support equipment and personnel can effectively lower homicide rates in selected geographic areas. Of course, homicide rates will be higher in areas where such equipment is not readily available. In Doerner's words, "The causes of homicide transcend the mere social world of the combatants."[94]

The moments that immediately precede any crime are ripe with possibilities. When all the inputs brought to the situation by all those present coalesce into activity which violates the criminal law, a crime occurs. Together, the elements, experiences, and propensities brought to the situation by the offender and the victim, and those that are contributed to the pending event by society and the justice system, precipitate and decide the nature, course, and eventual outcome of the criminal event. As one well-known criminologist recently explained, "An understanding of crime and criminality as constructed from the immediate interactions of criminals, control agents, victims, and others, and therefore as emerging from a tangled experiential web of situated dangers and situated pleasures, certainly refocuses theories of criminal causality on the criminal moment."[95] While focused on the criminal event as it unfolds, however, it is important to note that some of the inputs brought to the situation may be inhibiting; that is, they may tend to reduce the likelihood or severity of criminal behavior.

As mentioned earlier, the causes of crime, however well documented, tell only half the criminological story. Each and every crime has consequences. Although the immediate consequences of crime may be relatively obvious for those parties directly involved (for example, the offender and the victim), crime also indirectly impacts society and the justice system over the longer term. Figure 1-4 terms the immediate effects of crime *outputs*. As with the causes of crime, however, the real impact of such outputs is mediated by perceptual filters, resulting in what the figure terms *interpretations*. After a crime has taken place, each party to the event must make sense out of what has transpired. Such interpretations consist of cognitive, emotional, and (ultimately) behavioral reactions to the criminal event.

Interpretations are ongoing. They happen before, during, and after the criminal event and are undertaken by all those associated with it. In an interesting and detailed study of the interpretative activity of criminal justice system personnel, James F. Gilsinan has documented what happens when callers reach the 911 operator on police emergency lines.[96] Because many prank calls and calls for information are made to 911

operators, the operator must judge the seriousness of every call that comes through. What the caller says was found to be only a small part of the informational cues that the operator seeks to interpret before assigning the call to a particular response (or nonresponse) category. Honest calls for help may go unanswered if the operator misinterprets the call. Hence quite early on in the criminal event, the potential exists for a crucial representative of the justice system to misinterpret important cues and to conclude that no crime is taking place.

Other interpretative activities may occur long after the crime has transpired, but they are at least as significant. The justice system, taken as a whole, must decide guilt or innocence and must attempt to deal effectively with convicted offenders. Victims must attempt to make sense of their victimizations in such a way as to allow them to testify in court (if need be) and to pick up the pieces of their crime-shattered lives. Offenders must come to terms with themselves and decide whether to avoid prosecution (if escape, for example, is possible), accept blame, or deny responsibility. Whatever the outcome of these more narrowly focused interpretative activities, society—because of the cumulative impact of individual instances of criminal behavior—will also face tough decisions through its courts and lawmaking agencies. Society-level decision making may revolve around the implementation of policies designed to stem future instances of criminal behavior, the revision of criminal codes, or the elimination of unpopular laws.

Our perspective takes a three-dimensional integrative view of the social event called *crime*. We will (1) attempt to identify and understand the multiple causes that give rise to criminal behavior, (2) highlight the processes involved in the criminal event as it unfolds, and (3) analyze the interpretation of the crime phenomenon, including societal responses to it. From this perspective, crime can be viewed along a temporal continuum as an emergent activity that (1) arises out of past complex causes; (2) assumes a course that builds upon immediate interrelationships between victim, offender, and the social order that exist at the time of the offense; and which, after it has occurred, (3) elicits a formal response from the justice system, shapes public perceptions, and (possibly) gives rise to changes in social policy.

The advantages of an integrative perspective can be found in the completeness of the picture that it provides. The integrative point of view results in a comprehensive and inclusive view of crime because it emphasizes the personal and social underpinnings as well as the consequences of crime. The chapters that follow employ the integrative perspective advocated here to analyze criminal events and to show how various theoretical approaches can be woven into a consistent perspective on crime.

THE PRIMACY OF SOCIOLOGY?

This book recognizes the contributions made by numerous disciplines to the study of crime and crime causation including biology, economics, psychology, psychiatry, physiology, and political science. It is important to recognize, however, that the primary perspective from which many contemporary criminologists operate is a sociological one. Hence, a large number of today's theoretical explanations of criminal behavior are routinely couched in the language of social science and fall within the framework of sociological theory. The social problems versus social responsibility theme, around which this book is built, is in keeping with such a tradition.

Many, however, would disagree with those who claim that the sociological perspective should be accorded heightened importance in today's criminological enterprise. Those who argue in favor of the primacy of sociology emphasize the fact that crime, as a subject of study, is a social phenomenon. Central to any study of crime, they say, must be the social context of the criminal event because it is the social context that brings victims and criminals together.[97] Moreover, much of contemporary criminology rests upon a tradition of social scientific investigation into the nature of crime and criminal behavior that is rooted in European and American sociological traditions that are now well over 200 years old.[98]

One of sociology's problems, however, has been its apparent reluctance to accept the significance of findings from other fields, as well as its frequent inability to integrate such findings into existing sociological understandings of crime. Another has been its seeming inability to demonstrate conclusively effective means of controlling violent (as well as other forms of) crime. As Diana Fishbein, Professor of Criminology at the University of Baltimore, says, "Sociological factors play a role. But they have not been able to explain why one person becomes violent and another doesn't."[99]

While sociological theories continue to develop, new and emerging perspectives ask to be recognized. The role of biology in explaining criminal tendencies, for example, appears to be gaining strength as investigations into the mapping of human DNA continue. Charles F. Wellford, past President of the American Society of Criminology, explained the current state of affairs, saying, "I strongly believe that the future development of causal theory is dependent upon our movement toward integrated theories that involve biological, social, and cultural dimensions. Our failure to achieve much in the way of understanding the causal sequences of crime is in part a reflection of our slowness in moving toward multidisciplinary, integrated theoretical structures. The fact is that for two-thirds of this century, as criminology developed, we remained committed to a small number of sociological models for which there is extensive proof of their important but limited value. Fortunately in the last 20 years, this has begun to change. Today we see under way substantial research efforts that are based upon models of explanation that far exceed the traditional sociological approaches."[100]

Nonetheless, whatever new insights may develop over the coming years, it is likely that the sociological perspective will continue to dominate the field of criminology for some time to come. Such dominance is rooted in the fact that crime—regardless of all the causative nuances that may be identified in its development—occurs within the context of the social world. As such, the primary significance of crime and of criminal behavior is fundamentally social in nature, and any control over crime must stem from effective social policy.

SUMMARY

At the start of this chapter, the term *crime* was simply defined as a violation of the criminal law. Near the end of this chapter, we recognized the complexity of crime, calling it an "emergent phenomenon." In the process, crime was effectively redefined as a lawbreaking event whose significance arises out of an intricate social nexus involving a rather wide variety of participants. As we enter the twenty-first century, contemporary criminologists face the daunting task of reconciling an extensive and diverse collection of theoretical explanations for criminal behav-

ior. All these perspectives aim to assist in understanding the social phenomenon of crime—a phenomenon that is itself open to interpretation and that runs the gamut from petty offenses to major infractions of the criminal law. At the very least, we should recognize that explanations for criminal behavior rest on shaky ground insofar as the subject matter they seek to interpret contains many different forms of behavior, each of which is subject to personal, political, and definitional vagaries.

DISCUSSION QUESTIONS

1. This book emphasizes a social problems versus social responsibility theme. Describe both perspectives. How might social policy decisions based on these perspectives vary?
2. What is *crime*? What is the difference between crime and deviance? How might the notion of crime change over time? What impact does the changing nature of crime hold for criminology?
3. Do you believe that doctor-assisted suicide should be legalized? Why or why not? What do such crimes as doc-

tor-assisted suicide have to tell us about the nature of the law and about crime in general?
4. Do you think that policymakers should address crime as a matter of individual responsibility and accountability, or do you think that crime is truly a symptom of a dysfunctional society? Why?
5. Describe the various participants in a criminal event. How does each contribute to an understanding of the event?

6. What do criminologists do? Do you think you might want to become a criminologist? Why or why not?

7. Why is the sociological perspective especially important in studying crime? What other perspectives might be relevant? Why?

WEB QUEST!

Learn what criminologists do by visiting some of the professional associations they have formed. The American Society of Criminology (http://www.asc41.com) and the Academy of Criminal Justice Sciences (http://www.acjs.org)—each with over 2,000 members—are among the oldest and most established of such organizations and are easily accessible via the Internet. Regional associations include the Midwestern Criminal Justice Association (http://mcja.nmu.edu), the Northeastern Association of Criminal Justice Sciences (http://www.neacjs.org), the Southern Criminal Justice Association (http://www.scja.net), and the Western Society of Criminology (http://www.sonoma.edu/cja/wsc/wscmain.html). Many state organizations exist as well, and most can be found on the Internet.

You might also want to visit some forensic Web sites, including the American Academy of Forensic Sciences (http://www.aafs.org), the American College of Forensic Examiners (http://www.acfe.com), and the British Forensic Science Society (http://www.forensic-science-society.org.uk). Hundreds of other criminology-related professional associations can be found by searching Dr. Frank Schmalleger's Criminal Justice Cybrary (http://talkjustice.com/cybrary.asp) and using search terms like "association," "academy," "society," and so on. The Cybrary also contains an "Associations" category that you can use to speed your search.

If asked to do so by your instructor, visit the Web sites listed here, and write a brief description of what each contains. Include in your descriptions the mission statement for each organization that you visit.

LIBRARY EXTRAS!

The Library Extras! listed here complement the Web Extras! found throughout this chapter. Library Extras! may be accessed on the web at **crimtoday.com.**

Library Extra! 1-1. Elliott Currie, "Reflections on Crime and Criminology at the Millennium," *Western Criminology Review,* Vol. 2, No. 1 (1999).

Library Extra! 1-2. Richard Hil, "Toward a More 'Progressive' Criminology? A Rejoinder to Elliott Currie," *Western Criminology Review,* Vol. 2, No. 2 (2000).

Library Extra! 1-3. Elliott Currie, "Response to Richard Hil," *Western Criminology Review,* Vol. 2, No. 2 (2000).

Library Extra! 1-4. Matthew B. Robinson, "What You Don't Know Can Hurt You: Perceptions and Misconceptions of Harmful Behaviors among Criminology and Criminal Justice Students," *Western Criminology* Review, Vol. 2, No. 1 (1999).

Library Extra! 1-5. Frank P. Williams, Marilyn D. McShane, and Ronald L. Akers, "Worry about Victimization: An Alternative and Reliable Measure for Fear of Crime," *Western Criminology Review,* Vol. 2, No. 2 (2000).

NOTES

[1] Air date: November 22, 1993.

[2] George B. Vold and Thomas J. Bernard, *Theoretical Criminology,* 3rd ed. (New York: Oxford University Press, 1986).

[3] Edwin Sutherland and Donald Cressey, *Principles of Criminology,* 9th ed (Philidelphia: J. B. Lippincott, 1973), p. 3.

[4] Jay Frost, *The English* (London: Avon Press, 1968).

[5] "Subway Pusher Gets 25 Years to Life," APB News, May 5, 2000. Web posted at http://apbnews.com/newscenter/breakingnews/2000/05/05/subwaypush0505_01.html. Accessed February 18, 2001.

[6] The case resulted in passage of a New York State statute called "Kendra's Law," which allows violent mental patients to be medicated by force.

[7] "Robber Bashes Woman with Concrete Block," Associated Press, July 10, 2000.

[8] "Woman Fights for Life after Brick Attack," APB News, November 18, 1999. Web posted at http://www.apbnews.com/newscenter/breakingnews/1999/11/18/brick1118_01.html. Accessed February 18, 2001.

[9] "Homeless Man Charged in NYC Brick Assault," APB News, December 1, 1999. Web posted at http://www.apbnews.com/newscenter/breakingnews/1999/12/01/brick1201_01.html. Accessed February 18, 2001; and Katheline E. Finkelstein, "A Year after Brick Attack, She's Vowing She Won't 'Tiptoe Around Life,'" *New York Times,* December 24, 2000, p. 23.

[10] His real name is Calvin Broadus.

[11] See, for example, Ezzat Fattah, *Introduction to Criminology* (Burnaby, British Columbia: School of Criminology, Simon Fraser University, 1989).

[12] "Aborigine Cleared of Death Curse Extortion," Reuters wire service, February 20, 1997.

[13] From the standpoint of the law, the proper word is *conduct* rather than *behavior*, because the term *conduct* implies intentional and willful activity, whereas *behavior* refers to any human activity—even that which occurs while a person is unconscious, as well as that which is unintended.

[14] Paul W. Tappan, "Who Is the Criminal?" *American Sociological Review*, Vol. 12 (1947), pp. 96–102.

[15] Edwin Sutherland, *Principles of Criminology*, 4th ed. (New York: J. B. Lippincott, 1947).

[16] In 1996, for example, euthanasia advocate Dr. Jack Kevorkian was arrested and unsuccessfully prosecuted in Michigan on charges of violating the state's common law against suicide.

[17] John F. Galliher, *Criminology: Human Rights, Criminal Law, and Crime* (Englewood Cliffs, NJ: Prentice Hall, 1989), p. 2.

[18] C. D. Shearing, "Criminologists Must Broaden Their Field of Study beyond Crime and Criminals," in R. Boostrom, ed., *Enduring Issues in Criminology* (San Diego: Greenhaven, 1995).

[19] Fattah, *Introduction to Criminology*.

[20] Hermann Mannheim, *Comparative Criminology* (Boston: Houghton-Mifflin, 1965).

[21] Ron Claassen, "Restorative Justice: Fundamental Principles." Web posted at http://www.fresno.edu/pacs/rjprinc.htm. Accessed May 5, 2000.

[22] H. Schwendinger and J. Schwendinger, "Defenders of Order or Guardians of Human Rights?" in I. Taylor, P. Walton, and J. Young, eds., *Critical Criminology* (London: Routledge and Kegan Paul, 1975).

[23] Ibid.

[24] Jeffrey H. Reiman, "A Crime by Any Other Name," in Jeffrey Reiman, *The Rich Get Richer and the Poor Get Prison*, 4th ed. (Boston: Allyn and Bacon, 1997).

[25] Fattah, *Introduction to Criminology*.

[26] Matthew Robinson, "Defining 'Crime.'" Web posted at http://www.appstate.edu/~robinsnmb/smokeharms.htm. Accessed November 4, 2000.

[27] Piers Beirne and James W. Messerschmidt, *Criminology* (San Diego, CA: Harcourt Brace Jovanovich, 1991), p. 20.

[28] "Topless Standard," *Fayetteville* (N.C.) *Observer-Times*, November 14, 1991, p. 7A.

[29] "Bare Breasts Not Illegal Says Judge," Air Capital Naturist Society. Web posted at http://www.aircapital.org/mainsite/topfree.htm. Accessed February 18, 2001.

[30] See The Wineman online at http://www.thewineman.com/strangelaw.htm. Accessed March 1, 2001.

[31] *U.S. v. Oakland Cannabis Buyers' Cooperative*, A-145 (August 29, 2000).

[32] *The American Heritage Dictionary on CD-ROM*, (Boston: Houghton Mifflin, 1992).

[33] *The American Heritage Dictionary of the English Language*, 3rd ed. (Boston: Houghton Mifflin, 1996).

[34] This list is not meant to be exclusive. There are many other journals in the field; too many to list here.

[35] Piers Beirne, *Inventing Criminology* (Albany: State University of New York Press, 1993).

[36] See also Paul Topinard, *Anthropology* (London: Chapman and Hall, 1894).

[37] Joseph F. Sheley, *Criminology: A Contemporary Handbook* (Belmont, CA: Wadsworth, 1991), p. xxiii.

[38] Edwin H. Sutherland, *Criminology* (Philadelphia: J. B. Lippincott, 1924), p. 11.

[39] "Sutherland, Edwin, H.," *Encyclopedia of Criminology*. Web posted at http://www.fitzroydearborn.com/chicago/criminology/sample-sutherland-edwin.asp. Accessed November 5, 2000.

[40] Edwin H. Sutherland and Donald R. Cressy, *Criminology*, 9th ed. (Philadelphia: J.B. Lippincott, 1974), p. 3.

[41] Gennaro F. Vito and Ronald M. Holmes, *Criminology: Theory, Research, and Policy* (Belmont, CA: Wadsworth, 1994), p. 3.

[42] Clemens Bartollas and Simon Dinitz, *Introduction to Criminology: Order and Disorder* (New York: Harper and Row, 1989), p. 548.

[43] Marvin E. Wolfgang and Franco Ferracuti, *The Subculture of Violence: Towards an Integrated Theory in Criminology* (London: Tavistock, 1967).

[44] Sutherland, *Principles of Criminology*, p. 1.

[45] Clarence Ray Jeffery, "The Historical Development of Criminology," in Herman Mannheim, ed., *Pioneers in Criminology* (Montclair, NJ: Paterson Smith, 1972), p. 458.

[46] Gregg Barak, *Integrating Criminologies* (Boston: Allyn and Bacon, 1998), p. 303.

[47] Jack P. Gibbs, "The State of Criminological Theory," *Criminology*, Vol. 25, No. 4 (November 1987), pp. 822–823.

[48] Jim Short, "President's Message: On Communicating, Crossing Boundaries and Building Bridges," *The Criminologist*, Vol. 22, No. 5 (September/October 1997), p. 1.

[49] Available through Sage Publications, Thousand Oaks, California.

[50] Piers Beirne and Colin Sumner, "Editorial Statement," *Theoretical Criminology*, Vol. 1, No. 1 (February 1997), pp. 5–11.

[51] There are, however, those who deny that criminology deserves the name "discipline." See, for example, Don C. Gibbons, *Talking about Crime and Criminals: Problems and Issues in Theory Development in Criminology* (Englewood Cliffs, NJ: Prentice Hall, 1994), p. 3.

[52] Charles F. Wellford, "Controlling Crime and Achieving Justice: The American Society of Criminology 1996 Presidential Address," *Criminology*, Vol. 35, No. 1 (1997), p. 1.

[53] Gibbons, *Talking about Crime and Criminals*, p. 4.

[54] Sutherland, *Principles of Criminology*.

[55] Don M. Gottfredson, "Criminological Theories: The Truth as Told by Mark Twain," in William S. Laufer and Freda Adler, eds., *Advances in Criminological Theory*, Vol. 1 (New Brunswick, NJ: Transaction, 1989), p. 1.

[56] Barak, *Integrating Criminologies*, p. 5.

[57] Don C. Gibbons, "Talking about Crime: Observations on the Prospects for Causal Theory in Criminology," *Criminal Justice Research Bulletin*, Vol. 7, No. 6 (Sam Houston State University, 1992).

58 Ibid.

59 "Fanning the Fire over Beavis," *USA Today,* October 15, 1993, p. D1.

60 "Networks Turn Thumbs Down on TV-Violence Report," United Press wire service, Northeastern edition, December 17, 1993.

61 "Film Scene to Be Cut after Fatal Imitation," *USA Today,* October 20, 1993, p. 1A.

62 Congressional Public Health Summit, *Joint Statement on the Impact of Entertainment Violence on Children,* July 26, 2000.

63 Judiciary Committee of the U.S. Senate, *Children, Violence, and the Media* (Washington, D.C.: U.S. Government Printing Office, 2000).

64 Federal Trade Commission, *Marketing Violent Entertainment to Children* (Washington, D.C.: U.S. Government Printing Office, 2000).

65 Sue Pleming, "U.S. Report Says Hollywood Aims Violence at Kids," Reuters Wire Service, September 11, 2000.

66 "Fanning the Fire over Beavis."

67 Alfred Blumstein, "Making Rationality Relevant: The American Society of Criminology 1992 Presidential Address," *Criminology,* Vol. 31, No. 1 (February 1993), p. 1.

68 Ibid.

69 Lydia Saad, "Crime Tops List of Americans' Local Concerns," Gallup Organization, June 21, 2000. Web posted at http://www.gallup.com/poll/releases/pr000621.asp. Accessed February 20, 2001.

70 Ibid.

71 Northwestern National Life Company, *Fear and Violence in the Workplace,* research report, October 18, 1993.

72 "Survey: Homicides at Work on the Rise," *USA Today,* October 18, 1993, p. 3B.

73 "Cab Drivers Face High Death Risk," *Fayetteville* (N.C.) *Observer-Times,* October 31, 1993, p. 8A.

74 "Gallup Poll Topics: Crime Issues," Gallup Organization. Web posted at http://www.gallup.com/poll/indicators/indcrime.asp. Accessed March 10, 2001.

75 "As Confidence in Police Rises, American's Fear of Crime Diminishes," Gallup Organization. Web posted at http://www.gallup.com/poll/releases/pr981124.asp. Accessed March 10, 2001.

76 For an especially good discussion of this issue, see Theodore Sasson, *Crime Talk: How Citizens Construct a Social Problem* (Hawthorne, NY: Aldine de Gruyter, 1995).

77 Democratic National Committee Web site at http://www.democrats.org/hq/resources/platform/platform.html. Accessed November 4, 2000.

78 Republican National Committee Web site at http://www.georgewbush.com/issues/crime.html. Accessed November 4, 2000.

79 Megan's death led most states and the federal government to pass "Megan's Law," requiring community notification when released sex offenders move into an area.

80 Melanie Burney, "Megan's Law," Associated Press wire service, June 21, 1997.

81 Public Law 103–322.

82 For a good overview of this issue, see Wesley G. Skogan, ed., *Reactions to Crime and Violence: The Annals of the American Academy of Political and Social Science* (Thousand Oaks, CA: Sage, 1995).

83 "Denny Beating," Associated Press wire service, December 8, 1993.

84 Randy Dortinga, "Rodney King Rioter Charged with Murder," APB News, July 20, 2000. Web posted at http://apbnews.com/newscenter/breakingnews/2000/07/20/surrender0720_01.html. Accessed March 10, 2001.

85 For an excellent discussion of crime as a social event, see Leslie W. Kennedy and Vincent F. Sacco, *Crime Counts: A Criminal Event Analysis* (Toronto: Nelson Canada, 1996).

86 For a good discussion of the social construction of crime, see Leslie T. Wilkins, "On Crime and Its Social Construction: Observations on the Social Construction of Crime," *Social Pathology,* Vol. 1, No. 1 (January 1995), pp. 1–11.

87 For a parallel approach, see Terance D. Miethe and Robert F. Meier, *Crime and Its Social Context: Toward an Integrated Theory of Offenders, Victims, and Situations* (Albany: State University of New York Press, 1995).

88 Joan McCord, "Family Relationships, Juvenile Delinquency, and Adult Criminality," *Criminology,* Vol. 29, No. 3 (August 1991), pp. 397–417.

89 Elizabeth Candle and Sarnoff A. Mednick, "Perinatal Complications Predict Violent Offending," *Criminology,* Vol. 29, No. 3 (August 1991), pp. 519–529.

90 "Susan Smith Prison Guard Fired," Associated Press Wire service, September 1, 2000.

91 Carol W. Kohfeld and John Sprague, "Demography, Police Behavior, and Deterrence," *Criminology,* Vol. 28, No. 1 (February 1990), pp. 111–136.

92 Leslie W. Kennedy and David R. Forde, "Routine Activities and Crime: An Analysis of Victimization in Canada," *Criminology,* Vol. 28, No. 1 (February 1990), pp. 137.

93 William G. Doerner, "The Impact of Medical Resources on Criminally Induced Lethality: A Further Examination," *Criminology,* Vol. 26, No. 1 (February 1988), pp. 171–177.

94 Ibid., p. 177.

95 Jeff Ferrell, "Criminological *Verstehen:* Inside the Immediacy of Crime," *Justice Quarterly,* Vol. 14, No. 1 (1997), p. 11.

96 James F. Gilsinan, "They Is Clowning Tough: 911 and the Social Construction of Reality," *Criminology,* Vol. 27, No. 2 (May 1989), pp. 329–344.

97 See, for example, Miethe and Meier, *Crime and Its Social Context.*

98 For a good discussion of the historical development of criminology, see Leon Radzinowicz, *In Search of Criminology* (Cambridge: Harvard University Press, 1962).

99 As quoted in W. Wayt Gibbs, "Trends in Behavioral Science: Seeking the Criminal Element," *Scientific American,* Vol. 272, No. 3 (March 1995), pp. 100–107.

100 Wellford, "Controlling Crime and Achieving Justice" p. 4.

"I had," said he, "come to an entirely erroneous conclusion which shows, my dear Watson, how dangerous it always is to reason from insufficient data."

—Arthur Conan Doyle,[1]

If you wish to make a big difference in crime, you must make fundamental changes in society.

—James Q. Wilson[2]

patterns of crime

CHAPTER 2

Once I've done a crime, I just forget it. I go from crime to crime.

—Serial killer Henry Lee Lucas, 1984

[Rape] is the only crime in which the victim becomes the accused.

—Freda Adler, 1975[3]

I hate this "crime doesn't pay" stuff. Crime in the United States is perhaps one of the biggest businesses in the world today.

—Peter Kirk, Professor of Criminalistics, University of California, 1960

KEY CONCEPTS

IMPORTANT TERMS

aggravated assault	first-degree murder	negligent homicide
arson	forcible rape	Part I offenses
burglary	hate crime	Part II offenses
carjacking	household crimes	rape
clearance rate	larceny-theft	robbery
cohort	latent crime rate	second-degree murder
correlation	mass murder	self-report surveys
criminal homicide	Monitoring the Future	serial murder
criminality index	motor vehicle theft	simple assault
dark figure of crime	National Crime Victimization	statistical school
date rape	Survey (NCVS)	superpredators
demographics	National Incident-Based Reporting	Uniform Crime Reporting
desistance phenomenon	System (NIBRS)	Program
felony murder	National Youth Survey (NYS)	

IMPORTANT NAMES

Alfred Blumstein	James A. Fox	Joan Petersilia
John Braithwaite	André Michel Guerry	Adolphe Quételet
Elliott Currie	Thomas Robert Malthus	William Wilbanks
John J. DiIulio, Jr.	Coramae Richey Mann	James Q. Wilson

OUTCOMES

LEARNING

After reading this chapter, you should be able to
- ◆ Explain the history of statistical crime data collection and analysis, and understand the usefulness and limitations of crime data
- ◆ Recognize the various methods currently used to collect and disseminate crime data
- ◆ Describe and explain the major sources of crime data in the United States, including the UCR, NIBRS, and NCVS
- ◆ Define and discuss the social dimensions of crime, including key demographic factors
- ◆ Discuss the economic costs of crime

 Hear the author discuss this chapter at *crimtoday.com*

INTRODUCTION

Wesley "Pop" Honeywood, 94, knows little about statistics, but he is familiar with crime. Over the years, Honeywood, who lives in Jacksonville, Florida, has been arrested 46 times. Five of those arrests were for felonies. Honeywood has been imprisoned on eight occasions since 1946, serving sentences in Philadelphia, Baltimore, Tampa, Orlando, and Jacksonville.

Honeywood's troubles with the law began at the close of World War II, when he and a couple of friends stole a bomber and flew it over Italy for fun. After landing, Honeywood was arrested by military police, did a brief stint in jail, and received a dishonorable discharge from the army.

Not long ago, the geriatric career criminal stood before a Florida judge, awaiting sentencing after pleading guilty to charges of armed assault and possession of a firearm by a convicted felon. The incident grew out of Honeywood's liking for grapes, which he had watched ripen in his neighbor's yard at the end of the summer. Finally, unable to resist the temptation any longer, Honeywood helped himself to bunches of the fruit. When confronted by the neighbor, Honeywood pulled a gun and threatened the man.

Because of all the crimes he's committed, Honeywood now faces sentencing as a habitual offender and could be sent to prison for 60 years. Making matters worse is the fact that Honeywood was on probation for the attempted sexual battery of a 7-year-old girl when he was arrested for the grape theft. And age hasn't mellowed him. Honeywood admits shooting a man in the buttocks in 1989 but claims self-defense. The case never went to trial.

Honeywood says he is not afraid of a prison sentence. "I can do it," he smiles. "I've been locked up a whole lot of times here, but they turn me loose every time."

Circuit Judge R. Hudson Olliff, who will soon sentence Honeywood, worries about his age and the fact that he probably won't survive a long prison stay. But, he says, "the first duty is to protect the public. If he is a 94-year-old that is a danger to the public and he has to go to jail, so be it."

Honeywood, however, wishes he had plea-bargained. "I wish they would give me house arrest," he says. "I don't go nowhere, but stay home. My lawyer says he [the judge] might put me in an old folks home." Even if he goes to prison, Honeywood figures he may beat the odds. His father lived to be 113.

A HISTORY OF CRIME STATISTICS

Pop Honeywood is a statistical anomaly. Few people are involved in crime past middle age. Fewer still ever reach Honeywood's stage in life. Statistical data from the *Sourcebook of Criminal Justice Statistics*[4] show that the likelihood of crime commission declines with age. People 65 years of age and older, for example, commit fewer than 1% of all crimes, and the proportion of crimes committed by those over age 90 is so small that it cannot be meaningfully expressed as a percentage of total crime.

Although the gathering of crime statistics is a relatively new phenomenon, population statistics have been collected periodically since pre-Roman times. Old Testament accounts of enumerations of the Hebrews, for example, provide evidence of Middle Eastern census taking thousands of years ago. In like manner, the New Testament describes how the family of Jesus had to return home to be counted during an official census, providing evidence of routine census taking during the time of Christ. The *lustrum,* which was a ceremonial purification of the entire ancient Roman population after census taking, leads historians to conclude that Roman population counts were made every five years. Centuries later, the *Doomsday Book,* created by order of William the Conqueror in 1085 to 1086, provided a written survey of English landowners and their property. Other evidence shows that

primitive societies around the world also took periodic counts of their members. The Incas, for example, a pre-Columbian Indian empire in western South America, required successive census reports to be recorded on knotted strings called *quipas.*

Although census taking has occurred throughout history, inferences based on statistical **demographics** appear to be a product of the last 200 years. In 1798, English economist **Thomas Robert Malthus** (1766–1834) published his *Essay on the Principle of Population as It Affects the Future Improvement of Society,* in which he described a worldwide future of warfare, crime, and starvation. The human population, Malthus predicted, would grow exponentially over the following decades or centuries, leading to a shortage of needed resources, especially food. Conflict on both the interpersonal and international levels would be the result, Malthus claimed, as individuals and groups competed for survival.

View contemporary U.S. demographic data from the U.S. Census Bureau at Web Extra! 2-1.

Web EXTRA! **Web Extra! 2-1 at crimtoday.com**

Adolphe Quételet and André Michel Guerry

As a direct result of Malthusian thought, investigators throughout Europe began to gather "moral statistics," or social enumerations which they thought would prove useful in measuring the degree to which crime and conflict existed in societies of the period. Such statistics were scrutinized in hopes of gauging "the moral health of nations"—a phrase commonly used throughout the period. One of the first such investigators was **André Michel Guerry** (1802–1866), who calculated per capita crime rates throughout various French provinces in the early 1800s.

In 1835, Belgian astronomer and mathematician **Adolphe Quételet** (1796–1864) published a statistical analysis of crime in a number of European countries, including Belgium, France, and Holland. Quételet set for himself the goal of assessing the degree to which crime rates vary with climate, sex, and age. He noticed what is still obvious to criminal statisticians today—that crime changes with the seasons, with many violent crimes showing an increase during the hot summer months, and property crimes increasing in frequency during colder parts of the year. As a consequence of these observations, Quételet proposed what he called the "thermic law." According to the thermic law, Quételet claimed, morality undergoes seasonal variation—a proposal that stimulated widespread debate in its day.[5]

The first officially published crime statistics appeared in London's *Gazette* beginning in 1828 and in France's *Compte generale* in 1825. Soon comparisons (or what contemporary statisticians call 'correlations') began to be calculated between economic conditions and the rates of various types of crime. From a study of English statistical data covering the years 1810 to 1847, Joseph Fletcher concluded that prison commitments increased as the price of wheat rose. In like fashion, German writer Gerog von Mayr, whose data covered the years 1836 to 1861, discovered that the rate of theft increased with the price of rye in Bavaria.

The work of statisticians like Guerry and Quételet formed the historical basis for what has been called the **statistical school** of criminology. The statistical school foreshadowed the development of both sociological criminology and the ecological school, perspectives which are discussed in considerable detail later in this book. Learn more about early social statisticians and the effect their work has had upon developments in the social sciences at Web Extra! 2-2.

Web Extra! 2-2 at crimtoday.com

CRIME STATISTICS TODAY

The gathering of crime statistics has continued apace ever since crime-related data collection officially began well over a century ago. Today's U.S. crime statistics come from the Bureau of Justice Statistics (BJS) and the Federal Bureau of Investigation (FBI). BJS conducts the annual **National Crime Victimization Survey (NCVS),** while the FBI publishes yearly data under its summary-based **Uniform Crime Reporting Program,** and its incident-driven **National Incident Based Reporting System (NIBRS).**

NCVS data appears in a number of annual reports, the most important of which is *Criminal Victimization in the United States.* FBI data take the form of the annual publication *Crime in the United States.* Numerous other surveys and reports are made available through the Bureau of Justice Statistics. Such surveys not only cover the incidence of crime and criminal activity in the United States, but also extend to many other aspects of the criminal justice profession, including justice system expenditures, prisons and correctional data, probation and parole populations, jail inmate information, statistics on law enforcement agencies and personnel, and information on the activities of state and federal courts. These and other reports are generally made available free of charge to interested parties through the National Criminal Justice Reference Service (NCJRS), which is located in Rockville, Maryland.[6] Visit the Bureau of Justice Statistics via Web Extra! 2-3.

Web Extra! 2-3 at crimtoday.com

NCJRS is available via Web Extra! 2-4.

Web Extra! 2-4 at crimtoday.com

The largest annual statistical compilation of printed data on crime and criminal justice in one source is BJS's *Sourcebook of Criminal Justice Statistics,* which is printed yearly by the U.S. Government Printing Office. The *Sourcebook* consists of approximately 800 tables, covering all aspects of criminal justice in the United States. *Sourcebook* information is a compilation of statistics from many different places and includes much of the data found in the aforementioned publications, *Crime in the United States* and *Criminal Victimization in the United States.* Available on the World Wide Web, as well as in print, the Web-based *Sourcebook* is continually updated. Access the online *Sourcebook* via Web Extra! 2-5.

Web Extra! 2-5 at crimtoday.com

Other crime-related and criminal justice information sources include the National Archive of Criminal Justice Data, operated by the Interuniversity Consortium for Political and Social Research (ICPSR) at Ann Arbor,

Americans are especially fearful of random acts of violence. Here a man with a knife threatens Washington, D.C., police outside the U.S. Supreme Court building. What are the root causes of violent crime? *Dennis Cook, AP/Wide World Photos.*

Michigan (which is described in greater detail in the Web Quest! section at the end of Chapter 3); the Justice Statistics Clearinghouse (part of BJS); the Justice Research and Statistics Association; the Bureau of Justice Assistance Clearinghouse; the Police Executive Research Forum (PERF); the Police Foundation; the Data Resources Program of the National Criminal Justice Reference Service; and the SEARCH Group, Inc. These and other sites can be easily located on the Web via the Criminal Justice Cybrary at http://talkjustice.com/cybrary.asp.

Programmatic Problems with Available Data

This chapter will describe crime in the United States, or what some authors call "the crime picture" in America, using information derived from the latest BJS and FBI reports. It is important to realize at the outset, however, that the nature of the information provided by these two agencies differs significantly. In recognition of these difficulties, a Uniform Crime Reports (UCR) release begins with these words: "Data users are cautioned against comparisons of crime trends presented in this report and those estimated by the National Crime Victimization Survey (NCVS), administered by the Bureau of Justice Statistics. Because of differences in methodology and crime coverage, the two programs examine the Nation's crime problem from somewhat different perspectives, and their results are not strictly comparable. The definitional and procedural differences can account for many of the apparent discrepancies in results from the two programs."[7]

Each crime-reporting program uses its own specialized definitions in deciding which events should be scored as crimes. Sometimes the definitions vary considerably between programs, and none of the definitions used by the reporting agencies are strictly based on federal or state statutory crime classifications. Contrast, for example, the following definitions of rape, one of which represents the summary-based UCR definition, another the NIBRS definition, still another the NCVS definition, and a fourth, which is taken from the U.S. Code:

Forcible Rape (UCR)
The carnal knowledge of a female forcibly and against her will. Included are rapes by force and attempts or assaults to rape. Statutory offenses (where no force is used but the victim is under the age of legal consent) are excluded.

Rape (NIBRS)
The carnal knowledge of a person, forcibly and/or against that person's will; or not forcibly or against the person's will where the victim is incapable of giving consent because of his/her temporary or permanent mental or physical incapacity or because of his/her youth.

Rape (NCVS)
Carnal knowledge through the use of force or the threat of force, including attempts. Statutory rape (without force) is excluded. Both heterosexual and homosexual rape are included.

Aggravated Sexual Abuse (U.S. Code: Title 18, Chapter 109A, Section 2241)
(a) By force or threat. Whoever, in the special maritime and territorial jurisdiction of the United States or in a Federal prison, knowingly causes another person to engage in a sexual act—
  (1) by using force against that other person; or
  (2) by threatening or placing that other person in fear that any person will be subjected to death, serious bodily injury, or kidnapping; or attempts to do so, shall be fined under this title, imprisoned for any term of years or life, or both.

As the definitions reveal, the summary-based UCR only counts as rape the forced "carnal knowledge" of a *female* person and excludes homosexual rape from the count. Even more significantly, the traditional UCR program counts attempts to commit rape as though the crime had actually been accomplished—even though the woman may have fought off her assailant. The NIBRS and the NCVS, on the other hand, count homosexual rape (the rape of a person by another person of the same gender) within their tally of rape statistics but, as discussed in more detail shortly, the NCVS does not include rapes perpetrated on individuals under the age of 12. Federal law is the most inclusive of all, since a 1986 law against "sexual abuse" replaced previous federal rape statutes. Under the new federal statute, which avoids use of the term *rape* entirely, the crime of "sexual abuse" encompasses both heterosexual and homosexual forms of rape, as well as rape within marriage and many other forms of forced sexual activity. With these caveats in mind, we shall now briefly describe each of the nation's major crime data-gathering programs.

The UCR Program

The Uniform Crime Reporting Program was begun by the FBI in 1929 in response to a national initiative undertaken by the International Association of Chiefs of Police (IACP). The IACP's goal was to develop a set of uniform crime statistics for use by police agencies and policymakers throughout the country. In 1930, the U.S. Congress enacted Title 28, Section 534, of the U.S. Code, which authorized the attorney general of the United States to begin gathering crime information. The attorney general designated the FBI to serve as a national clearinghouse on crime statistics, and police agencies around the country began submitting data under the UCR Program. In its initial year of operation, 400 police departments, representing cities and towns in 43 states, participated in the program.

Initial UCR data was structured in terms of seven major offense categories: murder, rape, robbery, aggravated assault, burglary, larceny, and motor vehicle theft. These crimes, called **Part I offenses,** when averaged together and compared with the country's population, formed the FBI's Crime Index. The *Crime Index* provides a crime rate that can be compared over time and from one geographic location to another. Rates of crime under the UCR Program are generally expressed as "*x* number of offenses per 100,000 people." The 1999 rate of criminal homicide, for example, was 5.7 murders for every 100,000 people in the U.S. population.

In 1979, Congress mandated that arson be added to the list of index offenses. Unfortunately, the inclusion of arson as an eighth index offense has made it more difficult to compare pre- and post-1979 Crime Indexes. Such comparisons now often require a separate tabulation to factor arson out of the index.

Part I offenses are subdivided into two categories: violent personal crimes (consisting of murder, rape, robbery, and aggravated assault) and property crimes (consisting of burglary, larceny, motor vehicle theft, and arson). Part I offenses, showing the number of crimes reported to the police in 1999, are listed in Table 2-1 and shown diagrammatically in Figure 2-1, the FBI's "Crime Clock." UCR trend data since 1960 are shown graphically in Figure 2-2.

Each year, when the FBI issues the UCR, it includes information within each Part I offense category on the percentage of crimes that have been "cleared." *Cleared crimes* are those for which an arrest has been made or for which the perpetrator is known but an arrest is not possible (as when the offender is deceased or is out of the country). Cleared crimes are also referred to as "solved," although clearances as counted by the FBI have nothing to do with successful in-court prosecution. Hence, those charged with a crime that is scored as cleared by the FBI may not yet have been adjudicated. In official UCR terminology, a Part I offense is regarded as cleared or solved when (1) "a law enforcement agency has charged at least one person with the offense" or (2) "a suspect has been identified and located and an arrest is justified, but action is prevented by circumstances outside law enforcement control." Clearance rates are reported in the UCR for each Part I crime category. A **clearance rate** refers to

■ **FIGURE 2-1** THE FBI's "CRIME CLOCK" FOR 1999.
Source: FBI, *Crime in the United States, 1999* (Washington, D.C.: U.S. Government Printing Office, 2000).

the proportion of reported or discovered crimes within a given offense category that are solved.

Problems with the UCR

The most significant methodological feature of the Uniform Crime Reporting Program is indicated by its name. It is a *re-*

TABLE 2-1 ■ Major Crimes Known to the Police, 1999 (UCR Part I Offenses)

OFFENSE	NUMBER	RATE PER 100,000	CLEARANCE RATE (%)
Personal/Violent Crimes			
Murder	15,533	5.7	69
Forcible rape	89,107	32.7	49
Robbery	409,670	150.2	29
Aggravated assault	916,383	336.1	59
Property Crimes			
Burglary	2,099,739	770.0	14
Larceny	6,957,412	2,551.4	19
Motor vehicle theft	1,147,305	420.7	15
Arson	66,321	35.0	17
U.S. total	**11,701,470**	**4,303.8**	**21**

Note: Totals include arson, an offense not normally shown in official FBI totals of Part I offenses.

Source: Federal Bureau of Investigation, *Crime in the United States, 1999* (Washington, D.C.: U.S. Government Printing Office, 2000).

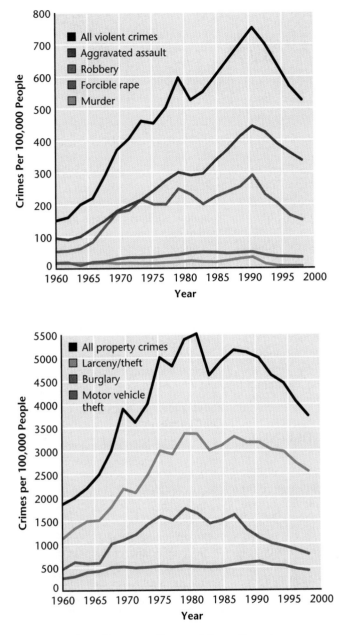

■ **FIGURE 2-2**   RECORDED RATES OF MAJOR CRIMES, 1960–1999 (UCR).
Source: Federal Bureau of Investigation, *Crime in the United States* (Washington, D.C.: U.S. Government Printing Office, various years).

porting program. In other words, only crimes that are reported to the police (or which are discovered by them or by others who then report them) are included in the statistics compiled by the program. Unless someone complains to the police about a criminal incident, it will go unreported and will not appear in the UCR. Most complaints, of course, are made by victims.

Because UCR data are based on *reported* crime, the program has been criticized for seriously underestimating the true incidence of criminal activity within the United States—a measurement that would also include unreported crimes. Unreported and underreported criminal activity has been

called the **dark figure of crime.** Some experts say, for example, that rape is the most underreported crime in the UCR, with four to five times as many rapes occurring each year as are reported. Reasons for not reporting a crime like rape are numerous and include (1) fear of the perpetrator; (2) shame, which may carry over from traditional attitudes about sexual behavior and a woman's role in sexual encounters; (3) fears the victim may have of not being believed; and (4) fear of further participation in the justice system, such as the possibility of the victim's being required to go to court and testify against the offender, thereby exposing herself to potentially embarrassing cross-examination and public scrutiny.

Although rape is indeed seriously underreported (a conclusion drawn from comparison of NCVS and UCR rape statistics), many other crimes are underreported as well. The most seriously underreported crime may be larceny, because the theft of small items may never make it into official police reports.

NIBRS: The New UCR

Recently, the UCR has undergone a number of significant changes, and more are scheduled to be implemented shortly as a new, enhanced, incident-driven crime-reporting program, funded in part by the federal Crime Identification Technology Act of 1998,[8] is phased in. The new program, the National Incident-Based Reporting System, will revise the definitions of a number of index offenses, but its incident-driven nature will be its most important feature. "Incident-driven" means that in the future the FBI will collect detailed data on the circumstances surrounding each serious criminal incident. The new data-collection format will focus on each single incident and arrest within 22 crime categories, with incident, victim, property, offender, and arrestee information being gathered when available. The 22 NIBRS crime categories are in turn made up of 46 specific crimes called "Group A offenses" (as compared with only eight major offenses on which the "old" UCR gathered data). In addition to Group A offenses, there are 11 Group B offense categories for which only arrest data are reported. The goal of NIBRS, to which the UCR is slowly being converted, is to make data on reported crime more useful by relating it more completely than the old system did to other available information, such as victim and offender characteristics.

NIBRS moves beyond the aggregate statistics and raw counts of crimes and arrests that composed the old summary-style UCR Program and develops individual records for each reported crime incident and its associated arrest. In doing so, NIBRS gathers detailed data on weapons or force used; injuries received; relationships between victims and offenders; crime locations; victim, offender, and arrestee age, sex, and race; victim and arrestee residency and ethnicity; victim type (such as individual, business, government, religious, and financial institutions); use of alcohol, drugs, and computers by offenders; and the circumstances of aggravated assaults and homicides. Specialized crime information can be developed

CRIME IN THE NEWS
Crime Hits 20-Year Low, FBI Says

America was safer in 1999 than at any time since Jimmy Carter was president, the FBI showed in its annual release of nationwide crime data.

The FBI's Uniform Crime Reports, which were released this weekend, indicate that from 1998 to 1999, serious crime fell 7 percent to its lowest per capita level since the late 1970s.

The data, drawn from 17,000 police agencies nationwide, reported that killings and robberies fell 8 percent each, the FBI said. Aggravated assault dropped 6 percent, rape by 4 percent and several categories of theft also dropped again in 1999.

1.4 MILLION VIOLENT CRIMES

The FBI said there were 1.4 million violent crimes last year, or 525 offenses per 100,000 inhabitants. Aggravated assaults accounted for most violent crimes, at 64 percent. Robberies represented 29 percent and murder 1 percent.

The weapon of choice for robberies and assaults, both deadly and nonlethal, were hands, fists and feet one-third of the time. Firearms were used in one-quarter of violent crimes and knives and other weapons for 15 percent and 27 percent of the cases, respectively.

Property crimes fell 7 percent from 1998, to 10.2 million offenses.

NOT ALL AREAS BENEFIT

Most states benefited from the crime drop, but some saw a rise. Crime went up in Montana, South Dakota, Texas and Vermont. Crime in West Virginia shot up over 40 percent from 1998.

The areas with the most significant drop in crime included Arkansas, Indiana, Ohio, Mississippi, New Mexico and Puerto Rico. It went down more than 25 percent in North Dakota.

Eric Sterling, president of the Criminal Justice Policy Foundation, said the eight-year decline in the U.S. crime rate is good news, but, "for serious criminologists, why crime is going down is by no means obvious."

He listed possible contributing factors, such as modern police methods, a decreasing number of drug users and dealers, the incarceration boom and America's strongest economy in decades.

ACQUAINTANCE KILLINGS

Overall, arguments were the cause in 30 percent of homicides last year. Victims knew their assailants in 48 percent of the cases. A third of all homicide victims were killed by a male spouse.

Clearances—the rate of cases being solved or otherwise resolved—are the highest for homicide cases, however, with 69 percent cleared in 1999. Robbery and property crime cases were solved at a relatively lower rate, by comparison, at 14 percent and 22 percent, respectively.

Drug arrests are still high, at 1.5 million in 1999. Arrests for driving under the influence of alcohol or drugs matched the number of drug busts last year. But there were 100,000 more DUI arrests than the year before.

Mothers Against Drunk Driving national president Millie Webb told APBnews.com that law enforcement needs the continued support from the public as it tried to keep highways safe.

Congress is set to approve the lowering of blood-alcohol limits in states from 0.10 to 0.08 percent. As states enact the lower standard in coming years, DUI arrests will likely climb, but Webb said she hoped the new laws would act as a deterrent to drinking and driving.

"We don't want to arrest more people." she said. "We want to save more lives."

CAR THEFT, ARSON DECLINE

Other findings included the lowest rate of vehicle theft since 1985. The average value of stolen cars was $6,104, the FBI said. Older-model cars are most often stolen for their parts.

Arsons also declined 4 percent, to 76,000 offenses in 1999.

Geographically, crime was highest per capita in the South and lowest in the Northeast, which also had the highest number of sworn officers for its population density, at 2.9 per 1,000 inhabitants.

Source: James Gordon Meek, "Figures Show Drop in Killings, Rapes and Thefts," APB News, October 16, 2000. Reprinted with permission.

from this data, including information on crimes against the elderly, crimes against women, domestic violence, and so on.[9] Additionally, state and local agencies can add other data-gathering categories to the NIBRS format to address issues of importance to them.

The following offense categories, the Group A offenses, are those for which extensive crime data are collected under NIBRS:[10]

1. Arson
2. Assault offenses, including aggravated assault, simple assault, intimidation
3. Bribery
4. Burglary/breaking and entering
5. Counterfeiting/forgery
6. Destruction/damage/vandalism of property
7. Drug/narcotic offenses, including drug/narcotic violations, drug equipment violations
8. Embezzlement
9. Extortion/blackmail
10. Fraud offenses, including false pretenses/swindles/confidence games, credit card/automatic teller machine fraud, impersonation, welfare fraud, wire fraud

11. Gambling offenses, including betting/wagering, operating/promoting/assisting gambling, gambling equipment violations, sports tampering
12. Homicide offenses, including murder and nonnegligent manslaughter, negligent manslaughter, justifiable homicide
13. Kidnapping/abduction
14. Larceny/theft offenses, including pocket picking, purse snatching, shoplifting, theft from building, theft from coin-operated machine or device, theft from motor vehicle, theft of motor vehicle parts or accessories, and all other forms of larceny
15. Motor vehicle theft
16. Pornography/obscene material
17. Prostitution offenses, including prostitution, assisting or promoting prostitution
18. Robbery
19. Forcible sex offenses, including forcible rape, forcible sodomy, sexual assault with an object, forcible fondling
20. Nonforcible sex offenses, including incest, statutory rape
21. Stolen property offenses, including receiving stolen property
22. Weapon law violations

The following eleven additional offense categories, the Group B offenses, are those for which only arrest data are reported under NIBRS:

1. Bad checks
2. Curfew/loitering/vagrancy violations
3. Disorderly conduct
4. Driving under the influence
5. Drunkenness
6. Nonviolent family offenses
7. Liquor law violations
8. Peeping Tom
9. Runaway
10. Trespass of real property
11. All other offenses

NIBRS reports are much more detailed than those developed under the UCR Program. Under the summary-based UCR, for example, whenever an aggravated assault occurred, the police department under whose jurisdiction it came merely recorded one instance of aggravated assault. Under NIBRS, however, that same department is required to collect (1) information about the offense (including the type of location where it occurred, whether a weapon was involved or used, whether the perpetrator was under the influence of drugs or alcohol, and whether there was a racial, religious, or gender-based motivation behind the offense), (2) information about the parties involved (including such demographics as sex, age, and race of both victim and offender; any known relationship between victim and offender; and circumstances that might have motivated the crime, such as an argument), and (3) information about the property (if any) involved (including the value of any property damaged, seized, or stolen as a consequence of the offense).

The Justice Research and Statistics Association (JRSA) has identified the many advantages of incident-based crime-reporting systems over summary-based crime-reporting systems:[11]

- Data collection is not restricted to a limited number of offense categories.
- Offense definitions can meet local, state, and national reporting needs.
- Detail on individual crime incidents (offenses, offenders, victims, property, and arrests) can be collected and analyzed.
- Arrests and clearances can be linked to specific incidents or offenses.
- All offenses in an incident can be recorded and counted, unlike the current situation with the hierarchy rule in the FBI Uniform Crime Reports, where only the most serious offense that occurs during a criminal incident is counted—regardless of what other crimes may have been committed.
- Additional crime-scoring categories, such as crimes against society, can be created.
- Distinctions can be made between attempted and completed crimes.
- Linkages can be established between variables for examining interrelationships between offenses, offenders, victims, property, and arrestees.
- Detailed crime analyses can be made within and across law enforcement jurisdictions.
- Regional law enforcement agencies can share information easily.
- Strategic and tactical crime analyses can be made at the local and regional levels.

Learn more by visiting JRSA at Web Extra! 2-6.

Web Extra! 2-6 at crimtoday.com

Although the FBI began accepting crime incident data from state reporting agencies in NIBRS format in 1989, the transition process is not moving as quickly as planned. NIBRS was originally scheduled to be fully in place by 1999. However, delays continue to occur in some areas. According to the FBI, NIBRS will be implemented "at a pace commensurate with the resources, abilities, and limitations of the contributing law enforcement agencies."

A sample of NIBRS data can be viewed at Web Extra! 2-7.

Web Extra! 2-7 at crimtoday.com

To learn more about the effects of NIBRS on crime statistics, including comparisons of FBI UCR data with NIBRS data, see Web Extra! 2-8.

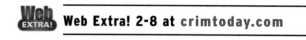

Web Extra! 2-8 at crimtoday.com

Table 2-2 shows how NIBRS offense definitions differ from traditional UCR definitions, and you can learn more about such definitional differences at Web Extra! 2-9.

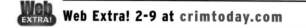

Web Extra! 2-9 at crimtoday.com

Finally, the Bureau of Justice Statistics provides a NIBRS information Web page, which is accessible via Web Extra! 2-10.

Web Extra! 2-10 at crimtoday.com

Hate Crimes

An important recent change in the UCR Program involves the collection of **hate crime** statistics, which was mandated by the U.S. Congress with passage of the Hate Crime Statistics Act of 1990.[12] Under the law, the FBI is required to serve as a repository for data collected on crimes motivated by religious, ethnic, racial, or sexual orientation prejudice. The Violent Crime Control and Law Enforcement Act of 1994[13] mandated the addition to the hate crimes category of crimes motivated by biases against people with disabilities, and the UCR Program began reporting such crimes in 1997.

According to the Bureau of Justice Statistics, hate crimes, also called "bias crimes," are crimes characterized by "manifest evidence of prejudice based on race, religion, sexual orientation, or ethnicity, including where appropriate the crimes of murder, non-negligent manslaughter, forcible rape, aggravated assault, simple assault, intimidation, arson, and destruction, damage, or vandalism of property."[14]

Based on FBI statistics on hate crimes, 7,876 hate crime incidents were reported in 1999.[15] These incidents involved 9,807 victims, with 70% of the incidents involving a single victim. Since a single incident may involve multiple offenses, it is important to state also that the 7,876 reported incidents accounted for a total of 9,301 chargeable offenses. Slightly more than one-half of these incidents were motivated by racial bias (56%), 16.5% were motivated by religious bias, 16% by bias based on sexual orientation, and 11% by bias based on ethnicity or national origin. Crimes against the person represented 67% of all reported offenses, with intimidation being the most commonly reported personal offense at 35%, followed by simple assault at 19%. In the crimes-against-property category, vandalism or destruction of property was the most frequently occurring type of hate offense. Since the term *victim* in the FBI classification of hate crimes can refer to "a person, business, in-

stitution, or a society as a whole," it is important to note that eight of every 10 reported victims was an individual. Murder accounted for only 0.2% of all hate crimes, or a total of 17 people who were killed in 1999 because the offender was motivated by hate.

The Role of Hate Groups

Hate groups like the Ku Klux Klan (KKK), the Aryan Nations, the National Alliance, and the Identity church movement have existed for many years and have long been associated with acts of violence. It is easy to classify groups within the hate-group category when their fundamental purpose is grounded in prejudice. In the case of some other groups, however, classification is not as easy. Are all militia groups hate groups? Given its anti-Semitic position, for example, does the Nation of Islam, led by Louis Farrakhan, qualify as a hate group? The Anti-Defamation League seemed to think so when it officially protested Farrakhan's October 18, 1998 appearance on the TV show *Meet the Press*. In an interview with NBC's Tim Russert, Farrakhan blamed Jews for controlling and oppressing blacks, saying, "They are the greatest controllers of Black minds, Black intelligence." Following the interview, Abraham H. Foxman, National Director of the Anti-Defamation League, wrote a letter to Bob Wright, President of the National Broadcasting Corporation, complaining that "interviews such as yesterday's give unwarranted status to Farrakhan as a Black leader while offering him an opportunity to propagate his message of hate which we have all heard before."[16]

We might ask, however, whether hate groups are a necessary feature of hate crimes. Citing a wide array of research studies, James B. Jacobs and Kimberly A. Potter found that "the vast majority of reported hate crimes are not committed by organized hate groups and their members, but by teenagers, primarily white males, acting alone or in a group."[17] Visit the National Criminal Justice Reference Service's "Hate Crime Resources" page via Web Extra! 2-11 and the Anti-Defamation League's "Combating Hate" page at Web Extra! 2-12 to learn more about hate crimes.

Web Extras! 2-11 and 2-12 at crimtoday.com

Data Gathering under the NCVS

Another major national crime statistics-gathering program, the NCVS, began collecting data in 1972. It differs from FBI-supported programs in one especially significant way: Rather than depending on reports of crimes to the police, the data contained in the NCVS consists of information elicited through interviews with members of randomly selected households throughout the nation. Hence the NCVS uncovers a large number of crimes that may not have been reported, and it is therefore regarded by many researchers as a more

TABLE 2-2 ■ Definitional Differences between the UCR, NIBRS, and NCVS			
OFFENSE	**UCR**	**NIBRS**	**NCVS**
Murder and nonnegligent manslaughter	The willful (nonnegligent) killing of one human being by another.	The willful (nonnelignet) killing of one human being by another.	NA
Forcible sex offense	NA	Any sexual act directed against another person, forcibly and/or against that person's will; or not forcibly or against the person's will where the victim is incapable of giving consent. Forcible rape, forcible sodomy, sexual assault with an object, and forcible fondling are included in this category.	NA
Forcible rape	The carnal knowledge of a female, forcibly and against her will.	The carnal knowledge of a person, forcibly and/or against that person's will; or not forcibly or against the person's will where the victim is incapable of giving consent because of his/her temporary or permanent mental or physical incapacity or because of his/her youth.	Carnal knowledge through the use of force or threat of force, including attempts. Rape includes victimization of both males and females.
Sexual assault	NA	NA	A wide range of victimizations, separate from rape or attempted rape. These crimes include attacks or attempted attacks generally involving unwanted sexual contact between victim and offender. Sexual assaults may or may not involve force and include such things as grabbing or fondling. Sexual assault also includes verbal threats.
Robbery	The unlawful taking or attempted taking of property that is in the immediate possession of another by force or threat of force or violence and/or by putting the victim in fear.	The taking of or attempting to take anything of value under confrontational circumstances from the control, custody, or care of another person by force or threat of force or violence and/or by putting the victim in fear of immediate harm.	Completed or attempted theft, directly from a person, of property or cash by force or threat of force, with or without a weapon.

(continued on the next page)

TABLE 2-2 ■ Definitional Differences between the UCR, NIBRS, and NCVS (*continued*)			
OFFENSE	UCR	NIBRS	NCVS
Assault	The unlawful attack by one person upon another.	The unlawful attack by one person upon another.	The unlawful physical attack, whether aggravated or simple, on a person. It includes attempted assaults with or without a weapon, but excludes rape, attempted rape, and attacks involving theft or attempted theft (which are classified as robbery).
Aggravated assault	The unlawful attack by one person upon another for the purpose of inflicting severe or aggravated bodily injury; this type of assault usually is accompanied by the use of a weapon or by means likely to produce death or great bodily harm.	The unlawful attack by one person upon another wherein the offender uses a weapon or displays it in a threatening manner, or the victim suffers obvious severe or aggravated bodily injury involving apparent broken bones, loss of teeth, possible internal injury, severe laceration, or loss of consciousness. This also includes assault with disease (as in cases when the offender is aware that he/she is infected with a deadly disease and deliberately attempts to inflict the disease by biting, spitting, etc.).	NA
Burglary	The unlawful entry of a structure to commit a felony or a theft (excludes tents, trailers, and other mobile units used for recreational purposes).	The unlawful entry of a structure with intent to commit a felony or a theft (excludes tents, trailers, and other mobile units used for recreational purposes).	The unlawful or forcible entry or attempted entry of a residence, garage, shed, or other structure on the premises, usually but not always involving theft.
Larceny-theft	The unlawful taking, carrying, leading, or riding away of property from the possession or constructive possession of another (including attempts). Motor vehicles are excluded.	The unlawful taking, carrying, leading, or riding away of property from the possession or constructive possession of another (including attempts). Motor vehicles are excluded.	The completed or attempted theft of property or cash without personal contact.
Motor vehicle theft	The theft or attempted theft of a motor vehicle. *Motor vehicle* is defined as a self-propelled vehicle that runs on land surface and not on rails. This offense category includes the stealing of automobiles, trucks, buses, motorcycles,	The theft of a motor vehicle, *Motor vehicle* is defined as a self-propelled vehicle that runs on land surface and not on rails. This offense category includes the stealing of auto-mobiles, trucks, buses, motorcycles, motor scooters,	NA

(continued on the next page)

OFFENSE	UCR	NIBRS	NCVS
	motor scooters, snowmobiles, etc. It does not include farm equipment, bulldozers, airplanes, construction equipment, or motorboats.	snowmobiles, etc. It does not include farm equipment, bulldozers, airplanes, construction equipment, or motorboats.	
Arson	The burning or attempted burning of property with or without intent to defraud.		

TABLE 2-2 ◼ Definitional Differences between the UCR, NIBRS, and NCVS (*continued*)

NA = Not Applicable

Source: Ramona R. Rantala, *Effects of NIBRS on Crime Statistics* (Washington, D.C.: Bureau of Justice Statistics, 2000).

accurate measure of the actual incidence of crime in the United States than either the UCR or NIBRS. NCVS data is gathered by U.S. Census Bureau personnel who survey approximately 49,000 households consisting of about 101,000 people. Interviews are conducted at six-month intervals, with individual households rotating out of the sample every three years. New households are continually added to the sample to replace those which have been dropped.

NCVS interviewers collect individual and household victimization data from anyone 12 years old or older at residences within the sample. Questions are about the incidence of rape, personal robbery, aggravated and simple assault, household burglary, personal and household theft, and motor vehicle theft as they have affected household members during the past six months. Information is gathered on victims (including sex, age, race, ethnicity, marital status, income, and educational level), offenders (sex, age,

Convicted killers John William King (front in left photo) and Lawrence Russell Brewer (rear) are escorted from the Jasper County, Texas, Courthouse in 1998. King and Brewer, along with Shawn Allen Berry (not shown), were convicted of the pickup truck dragging death of James Byrd, Jr. (right). What is the central feature of "hate crime"? *Gamma-Liaison, Inc. (right) and David J. Phillip, AP/Wide World Photos (left)*

race, and relationship to the victim), and crimes (time and place of occurrence, use of weapons, nature of injury, and economic consequences of the criminal activity for the victim). Questions also cover self-protective measures employed by victims, the possibility of substance abuse by offenders, and the level of previous experience victims may have had with the criminal justice system. Finally, interviewed victims are asked to describe and assess law enforcement response to victimizations that were reported to the police. Unlike the UCR and NIBRS, the NCVS does not measure criminal homicide, arson, or crimes against businesses (such as shoplifting, burglaries of stores, robberies of gas stations and convenience stores, and credit card and commercial fraud). Similarly, the NCVS does not attempt to uncover, nor does it report, crimes against children under 12 years of age.

The NCVS survey instrument is well designed, and data gatherers are thoroughly schooled in interviewing techniques. NCVS interviewers are trained, for example, not to inadvertently lead or "coach" respondents into supplying doubtful information and not to spend an excess amount of time making small talk with respondents. Questions used by the survey, however, are designed to elicit information about crimes that may not be in the forefront of the respondent's mind. Following are a few typical survey questions:

- Was anything stolen from you while you were away from home, for instance at work, in a theater or restaurant, or while traveling? (If "yes," how many times?)
- (Other than any incidents you've already mentioned) was anything (else) at all stolen from you during the last 6 months? (If "yes," how many times?)
- Did you find any evidence that someone *Attempted* to steal something that belonged to you (other than any incidents already mentioned)? (If "yes," how many times?)
- Did you call the police during the last 6 months to report something that happened to *you* which you thought was a crime? (Do not count any calls made to the police concerning the incidents you have just told me about.) (If "yes," what happened?)
- Did anything happen to *you* during the last 6 months which you thought was a crime but did *not* report to the police (other than incidents already mentioned)? (If "yes," what happened?)

The number of victimizations counted by the NCVS for any single reported criminal occurrence is based on the number of people victimized by the event. Hence, a robbery may have more than one victim and will be so reported in NCVS data. Although this distinction is applied to personal crimes, households are treated as individual units, and all household crimes are counted only once, no matter how many members the household contains.

NCVS Findings

The next few sections of this chapter present data from the UCR, NIBRS, and NCVS in narrative form. Some of the more general findings from NCVS reports for the 1990s, however, reveal a number of consistent and interesting patterns:

- Nearly 30 million victimizations are reported to the NCVS annually, including about 21 million property crimes and 7.5 million violent crimes.
- Approximately 23 million American households (25% of the total) report being touched by crime in any given year.
- City residents are twice as likely as rural residents to be criminally victimized.
- About one-half of all violent crimes, two-fifths of all **household crimes,** and slightly more than one-quarter of all personal thefts are reported to the police.
- Men are more likely to be victimized than women.
- Young people are more likely to be victimized than older people.
- Blacks are more likely to be victimized than members of any other racial group.
- Members of lower-income families are more likely to become victims of violent crimes than members of middle- and upper-income families.
- Young men display the greatest likelihood of violent victimization, whereas elderly women display the lowest.
- The chance of violent criminal victimization is much higher among young black men than among any other segment of the population.

It is important to note that NCVS-reported rates of violent victimization declined significantly in all categories beginning around the mid-1990s and that rates of property crime began declining even earlier. NCVS victimization rates for both violent crimes and property crimes throughout the United States for the years 1973 through 1999 are shown in Figure 2-3.

The decline in victimization rates noted by the NCVS in recent years is especially noteworthy because it contrasts with continuing high concern about crime among the general public, as reported in Chapter 1. Increased levels of public concern about crime may, however, be explained by four factors: (1) a persistent media focus on stranger-precipitated violent crime, especially school shootings and random acts of violence, and the seeming inability of the criminal justice system to protect innocent victims, (2) a continuation of the "war on drugs" and the ongoing publicity associated with drug arrests involving huge sums of money, (3) the sense that crime rates are just "taking a breather" and that they retain explosive potential which could manifest should American neighborhoods drop their guard, and (4) increased reporting by victims of all crime, especially violent crime.

Increased reporting may, in turn, be the result of a nationwide growth in crime awareness. In 1973, for example, only about 33% of all crimes were reported to the police.[18] Today, nearly 40% of all crimes are reported. Similarly, while

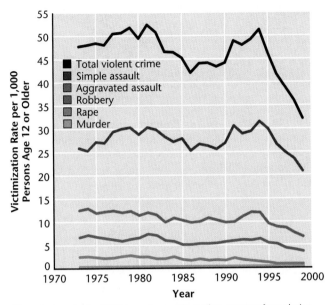

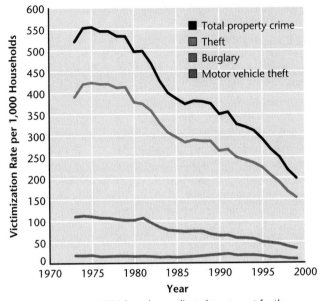

Note: Data prior to 1991 have been adjusted to account for redesign of the NCVS that occurred in that year. Homicide data, which are not reported by the NCVS, were calculated from the FBI's Uniform Crime Reports.

■ **FIGURE 2-3**   MAJOR CRIMES RATES FROM THE NCVS, 1973–1999.

Note: Data prior to 1991 have been adjusted to account for the redesign of the NCVS that occurred in that year.

Source: Bureau of Justice Statistics, National Crime Victimization Survey, 1973–1999.

approximately 20% of personal thefts were reported to the police in 1973, the rate of reporting for such crimes now stands at approximately 30%.

Critique of the NCVS

Just as the UCR and NIBRS have been criticized for underestimating the actual incidence of criminal activity within the United States, the NCVS can be criticized for possible overreporting. No attempt is made to verify the actual occurrence of any of the crimes reported to NCVS interviewers. Hence no measure exists of the number of crimes falsely reported or of the number of crimes that might be underreported in NCVS data. Although the proportion is not known, it is likely that some individuals, when approached by NCVS interviewers, may be unable to resist embellishing crime reports pertaining to their households and may even concoct criminal incidence data for purposes of self-aggrandizement or because of attempts to please interviewers by providing copious amounts of data.

As previously noted, NCVS data-gathering efforts began in 1972. Hence the program is much newer than the FBI's UCR Program, and comparisons of officially reported crimes with levels of self-reported victimization are unavailable for the years before 1973. As with the UCR and NIBRS, definitions of crimes measured by the NCVS do not necessarily correspond to any federal or state statutes or to definitions used for other purposes, making comparisons with other state and federal crime records difficult. Complicating matters still further, recent changes in NCVS categories have re-

sulted in the inability to easily compare NCVS findings of even a few years ago with current NCVS data.[19]

PATTERNS OF CHANGE

Since official crime statistics were first gathered beginning around 1930, there have been three major shifts in crime rates. The first occurred during the early 1940s and was due to the outbreak of the Second World War. This was a time when crime decreased sharply due to the large number of young men who entered military service. Young males make up the most "crime-prone" segment of the population, and their removal to the European and Pacific theaters of war did much to lower crime rates at home. From 1933 to 1941, the Crime Index declined from 770 to 508 offenses per every 100,000 members of the American population.[20]

The second significant shift in offense statistics was a dramatic increase in most forms of crime that began in the 1960s and ended in the 1990s. Many criminologists believe that this shift also had a link to World War II. With the end of the war and the return of millions of young men to civilian life, birth rates skyrocketed between 1945 and 1955, creating a postwar baby boom. By 1960, baby boomers were entering their teenage years. A disproportionate number of young people in the U.S. population produced a dramatic increase in most major crimes.

Other factors contributed to the increase in reported crime during the same period. Modified reporting requirements, which reduced victims' stress associated with filing

CRIME IN THE NEWS
Crowded Prisons, Plummeting Crime Rates

As America's crime rate has dropped to its lowest level in a decade and the prison population has risen to a historic high, authorities are debating if and how these two trends are connected.

The discussion was further energized this week by the release of the latest national prison population figures from the federal Bureau of Justice Statistics (BJS). That report, which indicated there are nearly 2 million people currently incarcerated, also begs this question: Is the crime rate down *because* a record number of criminals are locked up?

"They absolutely have to be related," said University of Chicago economist Steven Levitt. "It would be startling if locking up almost 2 million people didn't reduce crime."

"If you've got the bad guys chained to a bench, they can't be out there in public doing their mayhem," added Morgan Reynolds, director of the Criminal Justice Center of the Dallas-based National Center for Policy Analysis.

While he noted there is no hard and fast link between the jail population and crime in the outside world, Allen Beck, chief statistician for corrections at the BJS, agreed that incarceration does prevent a certain amount of crime. This is particularly true of crimes such as domestic assault, armed robbery, serial murder and rape.

"I don't think there's any doubt we would have more crime if some of those high-rate offenders were out in the community," said Beck.

PRISON HAVING SOME SUCCESS

Since most of the prison population is in the over-30 age range, most of the crime reduced would have been committed by older offenders, said Alfred Blumstein, criminology professor at Carnegie-Mellon University. Blumstein said the steady decline since 1985 in offenses committed by those over 30 shows that prison is having some success.

For crimes committed by those younger than 30—the most crime-prone years—Blumstein said prison's effect is less dramatic because fewer young offenders are in prison.

Beck co-authored the BJS *Prisoners in 1998* report that describes the steady increase in the prison population to just under 1.9 million by the end of 1998.

Beck said an increase in prison sentences also deters certain types of crimes, especially economic and property crimes such as fraud, burglary and auto theft. But in other areas—particularly so-called crimes of opportunity like drug trafficking—prison has been shown to be ineffective, Beck said.

BACK ON THE STREETS

Forty percent of prisoners today will be back on the streets within 12 months, said Beck. The U.S. prison system experiences a turnover of 500,000 prisoners a year—with a half-million flowing in and slightly less flowing out each year, he said.

After the crime wave of the 1980s, criminologists at Carnegie-Mellon issued a study that found that, despite a 200 percent increase in the number of violent felons jailed that decade, violent crime dropped only 9 percent.

Another study, authored by Levitt, found a closer correlation: a 10 percent increase in the prison population reduces crime by 1 to 3 percent.

"Long sentences focused on violent, repeat offenders are extremely effective," Levitt said. But he also pointed out that sending small-time or nonviolent criminals to jail may give society little public safety payback for the expense involved.

POLICING, PROBATION, PAROLE, PRISON

But in individual communities, jailing a robbery-prone crack head or violent juvenile has made a big difference in safety, said William Bratton, former police chief of New York City and Boston. Bratton is widely credited for reducing crime in those cities through police tactics that target crime hot spots and jail repeat offenders.

"Studies show a small proportion of the criminals commit a large portion of the crime," said Bratton.

But besides a simple jail term, Bratton believes that aggressive policing and tightly controlled parole and probation programs can control the behavior of those prone to trouble.

"We know for a fact that in New York, we changed the gun-carrying habits of people on the streets," he said. That, in turn, cut the number of shootings and murders, he said.

Beyond prison, other developments helped cut crime, experts say. New policing methods worked, as did a prolonged economic expansion, stricter parole and probation monitoring and greater street-level vigilance by neighbors, said Jean O'Neil of the National Crime Prevention Council.

"As there are no single causes for crime, there are no single causes for the drop in crime," O'Neil said.

LONGER SENTENCES FOR THE SAME CROWD

Paradoxically, the decrease in crime and rise in the prison population doesn't mean that more people are winding up in prison, said Beck. Convicts that enter prison these days just stay longer, he said.

Beck's study found three factors are responsible for a large portion of the increase in prisoners:
• Longer sentences
• More cautions and restrictive parole releases
• More parole violators returned to prison

DRUG CRIME NOT CHARTED

Another issue in the crime-prison connection has to do with which offenses are

(continued on the next page)

(continued from previous page)

counted in the nation's recognized crime rate, calculated by the FBI's Uniform Crime Report (UCR).

The UCR measures a string of violent crimes and three property crimes: burglary, larceny-theft and motor vehicle theft. Although drug offenders are one of the largest groups of criminals in the prison system, drug crime isn't measured in the FBI statistics.

VIOLENT CRIME SWINGS

In the 1980s, violent crime and drug crime rose sharply. The number of adults arrested shot up 45 percent and the prison population more than doubled, said Beck.

When violent crime—and the crime rate—began dropping in the 1990s, drug crime kept climbing, with drug law violations rising by 35 percent between 1990 and 1997, Beck said. These drug crimes didn't show up in the crime rate, but the jailing of tens of thousands of offenders increased the prison population.

At the same time, arrests plunged in cases of murder, rape, robbery and bur-glary—crimes that often draw prison time, said Beck.

"So even though violent crime is down, the likelihood of going to prison is going up," said Beck.

In recent years, parole violations caused the biggest increase in prison numbers. From 1990 to 1997, the increase in new convicts entering prison grew only 4 percent, while the number of offenders returned to prison on parole violations grew almost 40 percent, the BJS found.

INMATE NUMBERS PEAKING

The number of U.S. prisoners is finally beginning to stabilize, with the plunging crime rate beginning to pull down the number of inmates, said Beck. Predictions by sentencing reform groups that the United States will incarcerate 2 million inmates by the year 2000 will probably not materialize, he said.

"In the next 12 months we'll see some leveling off," Beck said.

Levitt agreed, saying that with the diminishing returns of locking up small-time offenders, states need to rethink their prison construction plans.

"As crime falls, you need fewer cells to punish criminals to the same extent," he said. "If that's the case, it doesn't make sense to keep adding to prison capacity."

ANOTHER UPSWING AHEAD?

But the effects of ballooning numbers of prisoners may, in the future, breed more crime, when angry ex-cons without viable skills emerge from prison.

"In the short term, we're incapacitating offenders and reducing crime." said James Fox, professor of Criminal Justice at Northeastern University, "We're really not prepared for what the impact may be down the road."

Source: Jim Krane, "Is There a Connection between the Two?" APB News, August. 20, 1999. Reprinted with permission.

police reports, and the publicity associated with the rise in crime sensitized victims to the importance of reporting. Crimes which may have gone undetected in the past began to figure more prominently in official statistics. Similarly, the growing professionalization of some police departments resulted in more accurate and increased data collection, making some of the most progressive departments appear to be associated with the largest crime increases.[21] Finally, the 1960s were tumultuous years, punctuated as they were by the Vietnam War, a vibrant civil rights struggle, the heady growth of secularism, dramatic increases in the divorce rate, diverse forms of "liberation," and the influx of psychedelic and other drugs. As a consequence, social norms were blurred, and group control over individual behavior declined substantially. The "normless" quality of American society in the 1960s contributed greatly to the rise in crime. From 1960 to 1980, crime rates rose from 1,887 to 5,950 offenses per every 100,000 members of the U.S. population.

Crime rates continued their upward swing, with the exception of a brief decline in the early 1980s, when postwar boomers began to "age out" of the crime-prone years and American society emerged from the cultural drift which had characterized the previous 20 years. About the same time, however, an increase in drug-related criminal activity led crime rates to soar once again, especially in the area of violent crime. Crime rates peaked about 1991 and have since begun to show a third major shift, with decreases in the rate of most major crimes being re-ported since that time. Between 1991 and 1999, the Crime Index decreased from 5,897 to 4,304 offenses per every 100,000 citizens, sending it down to levels not seen since 1975. James Fox, Dean of Criminal Justice at Northeastern University, referred to the 1990s drop in crime as Newton's Law of Criminology. "What goes up," said Fox, "must come down."[22]

Recent decreases in crime may be largely due to an "aging out" of the post–World War II baby-boomer generation, members of which are now too old to continue active criminal lifestyles, as well as to the advent (and widespread implementation) of family-planning practices beginning around 1960. Such practices include development of the birth control pill and the legalization of abortion, which kept birth rates relatively low among members of the boomer generation and may have especially affected birth rates among members of economically disadvantaged groups.[23] Economists John J. Donohue and Steven D. Levitt, in a detailed study of the effects of legalized abortion on rates of offending, found that legalized abortion contributed significantly to recently observed reductions in crime.[24] Donohue and Levitt note that "crime began to fall roughly 18 years after abortion legalization." They found that "the 5 states that allowed abortion in 1970 experienced declines earlier than the rest of the nation, which legalized in 1973 with *Roe* v. *Wade*. States with high abortion rates in the 1970s and 1980s experienced greater crime reductions in the 1990s. In high abortion states, only arrests of those born after abortion legalization fall relative to low abortion states." According to Donohue and Levitt, "Legalized abortion appears to account for as much as 50 percent of the recent drop in crime." Not surprisingly, these findings are disputed by some who find them suggestive of a conspiracy of oppression targeted at the socially disadvantaged.

However, while recent declines in the crime rate are noteworthy, they do not even begin to bring the overall rate of crime in this country anywhere close to the low crime rates characteristic of the early 1940s and the 1950s. From a long-term perspective, even with recent declines, crime rates in this country remain more than seven times what they were in 1940.

A fourth (and coming) shift in crime rates may be discernible on the horizon, as the size of an increasingly violent teenage population is anticipated to grow over the next decade or two. University of Pennsylvania Professor John J. DiIulio, Jr., for example, warns of a coming generation of **superpredators**—young violent offenders bereft of any moral sense and steeped in violent traditions. Superpredators, according to DiIulio, are juveniles "who are coming of age in actual and 'moral poverty' without the benefits of parents, teachers, coaches, or clergy to teach them right from wrong and show them 'unconditional love.'"[25] Although some criminologists dispute his conclusion, DiIulio predicts that the coming crime wave will peak around 2010. "By the year 2010," says DiIulio, "there will be approximately 270,000 more juvenile superpredators on the streets than there were in 1990."[26]

THE CRIME PROBLEM

Some people find it more meaningful to speak of the crime *problem* rather than the crime *rate*. They ask, Do crime rates provide an accurate measure of the extent of the crime problem in the United States? To answer this question, we might ask another one: Are U.S. crime rates really on the decline? While official statistics would seem to say "yes," it is important to realize that official rates are based only on a highly select group of crimes chosen by the FBI and the Bureau of Justice Statistics. Drug offenses, for which arrests continue to increase (see Figure 2-4), are not included in the FBI's crime index calculations and play no direct role in NCVS-reported victimization rates. A significant and ongoing increase in drug-related arrests, combined with widely popular "get tough on crime" initiatives (discussed in Chapter 15) have accounted for a substantial increase in our country's correctional populations (see Figure 2-5). This increase in correctional populations has been all the more surprising for many because it has occurred in the face of officially declining rates of crime. As a consequence, some criminologists question whether the size of our nation's correctional population, rather than our traditional emphasis on crime rates, might not provide a truer picture of the crime problem in the United States.

There are other indications that crime rates, no matter how they are figured, might not provide an accurate assess-

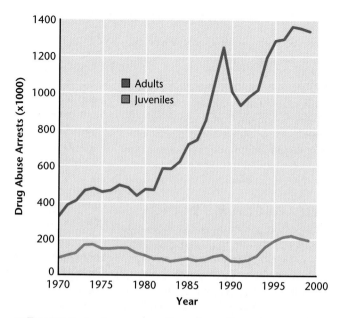

■ **FIGURE 2-4** ARRESTS FOR DRUG ABUSE VIOLATIONS BY AGE, 1970–1999.
Source: Federal Bureau of Investigation, *Crime in the United States* (Washington, D.C.: U.S. Government Printing Office, various years).

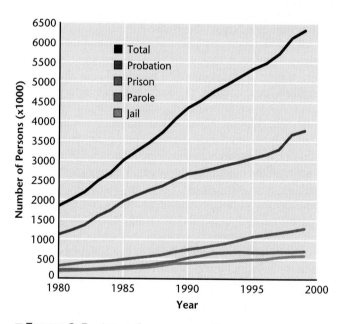

■ **FIGURE 2-5** ADULT CORRECTIONAL POPULATIONS IN THE U.S., 1980–1999.
Source: Bureau of Justice Statistics, *Correctional Populations in the United States, 1980–99* (Washington, D.C.: U.S. Government Printing Office, 2000).

ment of the actual extent of the crime problem in any society, especially if rates are computed without regard to an international context. Noted criminologist **Elliott Currie,** for example, says that while Americans seem smugly satisfied that crime rates are going down, a close examination of international crime rates reveals that the United States remains a "far more violent place than the rest of the advanced industrial world."[27] Moreover, says Currie, America's rate of violent crime "is still out of the ballpark by comparison with every other industrial democracy." Even when measured against our own historical standards, Currie points out, "the recent declines [in crime rates] are not exactly what they are sometimes described as being." While the media often portray crime's decline as "a sudden fall from a plateau, which appears quite spectacular," Currie says, the fact is that the data merely "represent a falling-off from an extraordinary peak." Levels of violence, in the United States, he argues, despite recent declines, are still unreasonably high. The decline of the last decade, Currie notes, "merely puts us back at close to the very high endemic levels of violence we've been suffering for thirty-odd years."

According to Currie, we Americans have hidden our crime problem, not beaten it. The real issue, says Currie, is that "public discourse about crime rarely counts the people behind bars as part of our crime problem. Instead they are usually counted as part of the solution, if they are counted at all." Hence when we assess the degree of the crime problem in the United States, we usually do so by looking at crime rates, and "we fail to include that part of the problem that's represented by the people currently behind bars." Says Currie, the "problem is that we measure our crime rate without factoring in the reality that we've simply shifted some of the total 'pool' of criminals in our society from one place to another. We haven't stopped producing. We've just moved them." Instead of measuring the crime rate, suggests Currie, we should be measuring the criminality problem in our society. This error, concludes Currie, is "like measuring the extent of some physical illness in our society while systematically excluding from the count all those people who are so sick we've had to put them in the hospital." While nobody would do that in the public health field, Currie says, "we do it all the time in the field of criminology." Currie's ideas can be summarized by a formula representing the **criminality index** (that is, the actual extent of the crime problem) in any society, as follows:

criminality index = actual crime rate + latent crime rate

where the **latent crime rate** refers to a rate of crime calculated on the basis of crimes that would likely be committed by those who are in prison or jail or otherwise incapacitated by the justice system. It is important to note that the latent crime rate does not count the criminal activity of anyone on probation or parole since probationers and parolees, by virtue of the fact that they are not behind bars, are capable of committing crimes that contribute to the actual crime rate.

The formula shown here permits calculation not only of a general index of criminality, but also of criminality indexes for specific crimes. The criminality index for robbery, for example, can be computed by adding the reported rate of robberies with the estimated robbery rate that would have been generated by incarcerated individuals had they been free. In 1999, for example, approximately 409,000 robberies were reported. If 140,000 persons were in prison in 1999 for robbery, and if the average number of robberies committed by a "typical" robber in any given year is known to be around 5,[28] we can then calculate that 700,000 were prevented by imprisonment. On this basis, we can conclude that the total number of potential robberies in the U.S. in 1999 would have been 1,109,000—for a composite robbery index of approximately 400 robberies per 100,000 residents. Such calculations reveal a potential U.S. robbery *problem* that is more than twice that shown in official crime statistics, which count only the actual number of robberies reported to the police or to survey interviewers. With this caveat in mind, it is to official counts of crime that we now turn our attention.

MAJOR CRIMES

Criminal Homicide

A few years ago, in a dispute turned violent over grades, Charles R. Mize, Jr., 24, repeatedly knifed and killed his father, a popular Georgia high school football coach, and then stabbed his mother 12 times before she persuaded him to call the police.[29] Mize, a student at Georgia State University who was described as a stable, fun-loving young man by friends and neighbors, pleaded guilty under Georgia law to "murder with malice." As a result of his cooperation, prosecutors dropped their plans to seek the death penalty, and Mize was sentenced to life in prison plus five years. Mize's mother recovered and has indicated that, in time, she may be able to forgive her son for what he did. Charles Mize will be eligible for parole in as few as seven years.

The terms *homicide* and *murder* are often used interchangeably, although they are not the same. Homicide refers to the willful killing of one human being by another, whereas murder is an unlawful homicide. Some homicides, such as those committed in defense of one's self or family, may be justifiable and therefore legal. The term used by most courts and law enforcement agencies to describe murder is **criminal homicide**. In legal parlance, criminal homicide means the causing of the death of another person without legal justification or excuse.

Jurisdictions generally distinguish between various types of murder. Among the distinctions made are **first-degree murder,** also called "premeditated murder;" **second-degree murder;** and third-degree murder, or **negligent homicide.** First-degree murder differs from the other two types of murder in that it is planned. It involves what some statutes call "malice aforethought," which may become evident by someone "lying in wait" for the victim but can also be proved by a murderer's simple action of going into an adjacent room to find a weapon and returning with it to kill. In effect, any activity in preparation to kill that demonstrates the passage of time, however brief, between formation of the intent to kill and the act of killing itself is technically sufficient to establish the legal requirements needed for a first-degree murder prosecution.

Second-degree murder, on the other hand, is legally regarded as a true crime of passion. It is an unlawful killing in which the intent to kill and the killing itself arise almost simultaneously. Hence, a person who kills in a fit of anger is likely to be charged with second-degree murder, as is one who is provoked into killing by insults, physical abuse, and the like. For a murder to be second degree, however, the killing must follow immediately upon the abuse. Time that elapses between abuse or insults and the murder itself allows the opportunity for thought to occur and hence for premeditation.

Both first- and second-degree murderers intend to kill. Third-degree murder is different. It is a term that varies in meaning between jurisdictions but often refers to homicides that are the result of some other action which is unlawful or negligent. Hence it is frequently called "negligent homicide," "negligent manslaughter," "manslaughter," or "involuntary manslaughter." Under negligent homicide statutes, for example, a drunk driver who causes a fatal accident may be charged with third-degree murder, even though that person had not the slightest intent to kill.

Serial murder and **mass murder** are two varieties of what is usually first-degree murder.[30] Although most murderers only kill once in their lives, serial and mass murderers kill more than one person. Serial killers continue to murder over a long time, perhaps even years.[31] Serial killer John Wayne Gacy, for example, who was put to death in Illinois in 1994 and whose execution is described in a Theory versus Reality box in this chapter, was the highly publicized killer of thirty-three young men and boys. Gacy's sale of prison paintings to curious collectors earned him thousands of dollars.[32]

Jeffrey Dahmer, another serial killer, was convicted a decade ago of the homosexual dismemberment slayings of 15 young men and was sentenced to 936 years in prison. Dahmer was himself murdered in prison in 1994. Other serial killers of the past few decades include David Berkowitz, better known as the infamous "Son of Sam," who killed young men and women in New York; Charles Manson, who ordered his followers to kill seven Californians, including famed actress Sharon Tate; Henry Lee Lucas, the Texas killer convicted of 11 murders but linked to as many as 140 more;[33] Ted Bundy, who killed many college-age women; and Aileen Carol Wuornos, charged with the murders of six men who picked her up as she hitchhiked through Florida. For record-keeping purposes, serial murder has been defined as criminal homicide that "involves the killing of several victims in three or more separate events."[34]

Similar to the serial killer is the spree killer, who kills a number of victims over a relatively short time in what has often been called a "killing spree." Andrew Cunanan, who killed fashion designer Gianni Versace and others in 1997, provides an example of a spree killer. Cunanan's killing spree lasted three months and claimed five victims.[35] He was put on the FBI's "Ten Most Wanted" list before committing suicide aboard a Miami yacht where he had hidden.

Mass murderers are different. They kill a number of people at one time. Mass murder has been defined by the Bureau of Justice Statistics as "the killing of four or more victims at one location, within one event."[36] The April 20, 1999, Columbine High School shooting—in which 13 people died and 23 others were wounded—was one such event. Likewise, terrorist attacks, as in the 1993 World Trade Center bombing in which five people died or the 2000 attack on the U.S. guided missile cruiser *Cole,* can also result in mass murder. Robberies, too, may result in multiple homicide victims, and revenge-seeking gunmen sometimes claim many lives. There has been a spate of mass killings in the United States in recent years, including a number of school shootings. Similarly, 87 people died in 1990 at the Happy Land social club in the Bronx, New York, in a fire started by an arsonist who was upset that his girlfriend, a hat checker at the club, had left him. Other instances of mass murder include 31 people killed in 1991 when a gunman smashed a pickup truck through the front window of a Kileen, Texas, cafeteria and shot lunchgoers to death; 21 killed at a McDonald's restaurant in San Ysidro, California, in 1984 by an out-of-work security guard named James Huberty; and 13 killed at the University of Texas by sniper Charles Whitman, who was holed up in a clock tower.

Serial killer John Wayne Gacy sometimes dressed as a clown to disarm his victims. This painting by Gacy shows his fascination with clowns. Do you agree that Gacy should have been executed? *Brad Elterman, SIPA Press*

THEORY VERSUS REALITY
Serial Killer John Wayne Gacy's Execution

On May 10, 1994, serial killer John Wayne Gacy was put to death by lethal injection at Statesville Correctional Center, a maximum-security facility in Joliet, Illinois. Gacy, once known as an affable remodeling contractor, had been convicted a decade and a half earlier of the sex-linked slayings of 33 young men and boys. His execution was originally set for June 1980, but dozens of appeals kept him alive on death row for 14 years.

According to prosecutors, Gacy often dressed as a clown, handcuffing his victims and looping a rope around their necks on the pretext that he was about to perform a clever stunt. Others may have participated willingly in the sexual sadism that preceded their deaths. Most ended up being horribly tortured and mutilated before dying. Bodies of some of Gacy's victims were discovered in the muddy basement crawl space of his home near O'Hare International Airport. Others were dumped into a nearby river.

As Gacy was strapped to a gurney in preparation for execution, revelers out- side shouted, "Kill the clown!" Others yelled, "John-nee, the devil's waiting for you!" Vendors sold $10 T-shirts bearing slogans that read, "No Tears for the Clown." Death penalty opponents, however, continued to file appeals and to seek clemency for Gacy right up until the time of execution. Seth Donnelly, Executive Director of the Illinois Coalition against the Death Penalty, explained his group's delaying tactics this way: "The crimes for which he [Gacy] has been convicted are heinous. But we're opposed to the death penalty as an institution, not on the basis of who may be scheduled to be executed."

Following the procedure, relatives of Gacy's victims expressed relief that he was dead. "I don't think anything he has gone through has been the smallest part of what he has put us and our families through. He got off easy," said Vito Mazzara, whose 20-year-old brother, James, was killed by Gacy. "He got a much easier death than any of his victims," said William Kunkle, who prosecuted Gacy and witnessed the execution.

According to State Corrections Director Howard Peters, Gacy's last statement was that "taking his life would not compensate for the loss of the others and that this was the state murdering him."

DISCUSSION QUESTIONS

1. What is the difference between mass murder and serial killing? Between first-and second-degree murder? Which categories best fit Gacy? Why?

2. Why would someone like Gacy kill? What might have motivated him? How could you investigate such a question so that you could have confidence that your answers would reflect Gacy's true motivation?

3. Are you in favor of the death penalty or opposed to it? Defend your position.

Sources: Lindsey Tanner, "Gacy Execution," the Associated Press online, May 10, 1994; "State Team Preparing for Gacy Killing," United Press online, Central edition, April 11, 1994.

Some jurisdictions have created a special category of **felony murder,** whereby an offender who commits a crime during which someone dies (or which causes someone to die) can be found guilty of first-degree murder, even though the person committing the crime had no intention of killing anyone. Bank robberies in which one of the robbers is shot to death by police, for example, or in which a bank patron succumbs to a fear-induced heart attack may leave a surviving robber subject to the death penalty under the felony murder rule. Hence felony murder is a special class of criminal homicide whereby an offender may be charged with first-degree murder when that person's criminal activity results in another person's death.

Murder Statistics

Statistics discussed in this section are derived from the FBI's Uniform Crime Reporting Program, because the NCVS does not gather information on criminal homicide. UCR statistics count only the number of murders committed, not attempts to murder, because attempts are scored as aggravated as- saults. Likewise, the UCR program does not count cases of negligent manslaughter among murder statistics.

According to the UCR, 15,533 murders were committed throughout the United States in 1999.[37] The 1999 rate of criminal homicide was 5.7 people murdered for every 100,000 individuals in the U.S. population.

Age is no barrier to murder. In 1999, for example, 205 murder victims were under the age of 1, while 281 were 75 years old or older. Seventy-three murders were committed by offenders over 75, while four murders were committed by those aged 5 to 8. Of the murder victims in 1999, 76% were male, and 46% were black (50% were white, and the remainder were of other races).

The most populous region of the country, the southern states, accounted for the most murders—43% of the total. However, although the UCR divides the country into four regions (the Northeast, South, Midwest, and West), each region varies significantly by population. Hence cross-regional comparisons, other than rates or changes in reported rates, must be interpreted with caution. While all regions of the country showed a decrease of 9% in the murder rate from 1998 to 1999, the nation's cities showed a 7% decrease. Metropolitan murder rates were 50% greater than that of rural areas—approximately 6 per every 100,000 city residents.

As in other recent years, the typical murder offender in 1999 was a young black man. Of all those offenders for whom gender was reported, 79% were male. Seventy-two percent of all murder arrestees in 1999 were between the ages of 17 and 34 years old, and 52% were black (46% were white, and the remainder were of other races). Significantly, although blacks make up only 13% of the American population, they typically account for more than half of all people arrested for murder.

FBI statistics reveal a plethora of other information about the crime of murder. Approximately one-half of all murder victims in 1999, for example, were either related to (14%) or acquainted with (34%) their assailants. Only 12% of murders were committed by strangers, and the relationship between killer and victim was undetermined for 40% of all reported murders.

Murder is primarily an intraracial crime. In 1999, 85% of white victims were killed by other whites, whereas 94% of black victims died at the hands of black killers. As in other years, handguns were the weapon of choice in most murders, with 51% of all murder victims dying of handgun-inflicted injuries. Another 4% were killed with shotguns, and 3% with rifles. Knives (or other sharp instruments) were used in 13% of murders, and blunt instruments (clubs, hammers, and so on) in 6%. Hands, fists, and feet were listed as murder weapons in those 7% of all murder cases in which victims were punched and kicked to death.

Various circumstances lead to murder, although in 1999 arguments were the most common cause of such crime. Thirty percent of all murders resulted from arguments, and 17% were the consequence of other felonious activity like robbery, rape, and arson. Murderous arguments may arise over sexual claims, jealousy, money, personal honor, or anything else that may lead to anger or bring offense.

Of all reported or discovered criminal homicides in 1999, 69% were cleared—the highest rate of clearance for any of the index offenses. Rural counties reported the highest clearance rates (75%), while large cities had the lowest rates of clearance (67%).

Forcible Rape

Former world heavyweight boxing champion Mike Tyson may be the most famous person in recent memory to have served prison time for **forcible rape.** In 1991, Tyson was convicted of the hotel room rape of 18-year-old Desiree Washington and was sentenced to six years in prison. Washington was participating in the 1991 Miss Black America pageant when she met Tyson and accompanied him to his room. Tyson was released from prison in 1995 and reentered the world of professional boxing—only to be tem-

porarily banned from the sport by the Nevada State Athletic Commission after he bit off part of Evander Holyfield's ear during a World Boxing Association heavyweight title rematch in Las Vegas in 1997.

The UCR, as currently reported, distinguishes between three categories of **rape:** (1) forcible rape, (2) statutory rape, and (3) attempted forcible rape. Some jurisdictions draw a distinction between forcible rape with the use of a weapon and forcible rape without the use of a weapon. Although the UCR (unlike NIBRS) does not make such a distinction, it does, however, record statistics on the use of weapons associated with the crime of rape.

Other types of rape include spousal rape, gang rape, date rape, and homosexual rape. Spousal rape, or the rape of one's spouse, is a relatively new concept, having entered the law of many state jurisdictions only in recent years. Just a few decades ago it was believed that a woman entering into marriage implicitly gave her consent to sexual intercourse at the behest of her husband. In today's more enlightened times, wives may prosecute their spouses under rape statutes if their husbands force them to have nonconsensual intercourse.

Date rape, which is often defined as unlawful forced sexual intercourse with a woman against her will that occurs within the context of a dating relationship, has also received much attention in recent times, although it is undoubtedly a phenomenon that has existed as long as the institution of dating. According to recent studies, date rape is much more common than previously believed. Some authors suggest that date rape may occur when the male partner concludes that his date "owes" him something for the money he has spent on her.[38] Many women apparently do not report the crime, and their hesitancy exists for a variety of reasons. Sometimes they feel responsible for some aspect of the social relationship which led to the rape; in other instances they may feel some concern for the offender and not wish to have him become the target of a criminal prosecution—even one that is deserved.

Same-sex rape, although not punishable as rape in all jurisdictions, is coming to be more widely recognized. Many states and a number of foreign countries now provide for the prosecution of men who force other men to have sex with them, as happens especially in prison. In 1994, the English House of Lords, for example, passed an amendment to the British Criminal Justice Bill[39] replacing the offense of "nonconsensual buggery of men," which carried a ten-year sentence, with the crime of "male rape," which is punishable by life imprisonment.

Although rape statutes have evolved to the point where many jurisdictions prosecute cases of homosexual rape, gender bias still characterizes most rape laws. No jurisdictions, for example, effectively prosecute husbands raped by their wives, and lesbian rape (the rape of one woman by another) is never prosecuted as such. On very rare occasions, however, a female individual may be charged with the rape of a male individual. In 1993, for example, Jean-Michelle Whitiak, 24, a Fairfax County, Virginia, swimming coach, pleaded guilty to one count of statutory rape resulting from an affair with a 13-year-old boy.[40] Whitiak also admitted to having sex with two of the boy's friends.

The motivation of rapists has been the subject of frequent study. Contemporary social scientific wisdom, supported by the research of scholars like A. Nicholas Groth,[41] holds that rape is primarily a crime of power and that most rapists seek self-aggrandizement via the degradation of another human being. Rapists, this school of thought maintains, demean their victims in order to feel important and powerful. Hence, the rape of elderly and physically unattractive women by virile and powerful young men can be explained as a crime of power rather than one of sex. Some scholars, however, have recently begun to cast doubt on power as the primary motivation of rapists, returning to an emphasis on sexual gratification as the root cause of sexual assault.[42]

Rape Statistics

UCR statistics on rape, as currently reported, include both forcible rape and attempted forcible rape. Statutory rape and other sex offenses are excluded from the count of rape crimes. In 1999, 89,107 rapes were reported nationwide under the UCR Program, a decrease of 4.3% over the previous year. The rate of reported forcible rape was officially put at 32.7 rapes per 100,000 people. However, the rape rate for females is effectively twice that figure, because any realistic tally of such crimes should compare the number of women raped with the number of female individuals in the overall population (rather than to a count of the entire population, which includes males). When such a comparison is made, the rate of reported rape is 67 per 100,000 for women in large cities, 66 per 100,000 for women in small towns, and 45 per 100,000 for women in rural counties. The hot summer months generally show the highest rate of reported forcible rape. The year 1999 was no exception, with the month of July showing the largest number of reports.

Substantial regional variation exists in UCR statistics on forcible rape. In 1999, the highest rape rate was recorded at 70 victims per 100,000 females in the South, with 66 per 100,000 in the West, 68 per 100,000 in the Midwest, and a low of 44 per 100,000 in the Northeast. Although the FBI reports that rapes in the southern part of the United States occur with almost twice the frequency of such crimes in the northeastern part of the nation, it makes no attempt to explain the observed variation.

In 1999, 49% of all reported forcible rapes were cleared by arrest or exceptional means (such as the death of the suspected offender) with rural and suburban county law enforcement agencies reporting slightly higher clearance rates than city law enforcement agencies. The nationwide number of reported rapes decreased four percent over the previous year.

NCVS data paint a somewhat different picture of rape than the UCR statistics. According to the NCVS, 141,000 rapes occurred in 1999, while 60,000 were attempted—giving a total rape count of 201,000 cases.[43] The NCVS calculates a rape rate of 180 per 100,000 females, a rate substantially higher than that found in FBI data.

The NCVS reports that rapes by strangers are almost twice as common as those by nonstrangers. Of rapes involving strangers, 50% occur between 6 P.M. and midnight, while only 38% of nonstranger rapes occur during those hours. The NCVS also records the location of criminal events to include parking lots or garages, commercial buildings, school property, school buildings, apartments, yards and parks, public transportation, and so forth. Most rapes (17.9%) are described as occurring "on the street not near own or friend's home." However, of the rapes involving nonstrangers, 50% occur within the victim's home. Only 17.2% of rapes recorded by the NCVS involved the use of weapons, although weapons were employed in 34.6% of all rapes committed by strangers.

The NCVS also collects data on self-protective measures taken by victims. Of the rape victims responding to NCVS interviewers, 80% reported the use of some type of self-protective measure. These measures included "resisting" (20.8% of all such measures reported), persuading or appeasing the offender (18.7%), running away or hiding (13%), scaring or warning the offender (13%), raising an alarm (11%), and screaming (8.9%). Only 6% of rape victims reported attacking their victimizers, and fewer than one in 100 attacked the offender with weapons.

Many rape victims (51%) reported that the self-protective measures that were taken helped the situation, although 17% believed the measures made their situation worse. Another 14% said such measures had no effect on the situation. Twenty percent of rape victims reported economic costs due to time lost from work as a result of victimization.

As mentioned earlier, NCVS data score only victimizations of household residents who are 12 years of age or older. Recent BJS studies, however, have found that many victims of rape are quite young. A 1994 study, for example, of eleven states and the District of Columbia, found that 10,000 girls under the age of 18 were raped in reporting jurisdictions—about half of all the rapes that were reported in those areas.[44] Investigators found that at least 3,800 victims were children under the age of 12. As a result of these figures, the study's authors concluded that "the rape of young girls is alarmingly commonplace." When young women and girls are raped, however, the crimes often go unreported because they frequently involve family members or friends. The survey found that although girls under the age of 18 make up 25% of the nation's female population, they account for 51% of all rape victims.

Even researchers were surprised by the number of young girls who reported having been raped. As Patrick A. Langan, one of the report's authors, said, "The [finding] that one in six of the reported rapes were girls under 12 was startling. You would think that the number would have been minute. But it's not tiny. . . . It's a substantial part of the picture."

Robbery

The crime of robbery is regarded as a personal crime because it is committed in the presence of the victim. **Robbery** is defined by the UCR/NIBRS Program as "the unlawful taking or attempted taking of property that is in the immediate possession of another by force or threat of force or violence and/or by putting the victim in fear." The NCVS definition is similar and also involves *attempts*. Although some individuals mistakenly use the terms *robbery* and *burglary* interchangeably (as in the phrase "my house was robbed"), it should be remembered that robbery is a personal crime and that individuals are robbed, not houses (which are burglarized).[45]

A number of terms are used to describe subtypes of robbery. *Highway robbery*, for example, simply refers to any robbery that occurs in a public place, generally out-of-doors. It is also called "street robbery" by the FBI. *Strong-arm robbery* means that the robber or robbers were unarmed and took the victim's possessions through intimidation or brute physical force. Strong-arm robbery is often perpetrated by a group of robbers working in consort, as when a gang preys upon one or two unwary victims. The

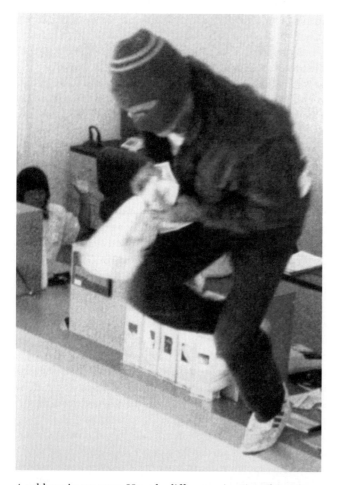

A robbery in progress. How do differences in crime data-gathering programs influence our perceptions of the extent of crime in American society? *Bill Nation, Corbis/Sygma*

term *armed robbery* signifies that a weapon was used—most often a gun. Armed robberies usually occur when banks, service stations, convenience stores, and other commercial establishments are robbed.

Robbery Statistics

The 1999 UCR reports that 409,670 robberies came to the attention of authorities across the nation that year, meaning that the rate of robbery was 150 per every 100,000 people in the United States. Cities are the places where most robberies occur, with large metropolitan areas recording a robbery rate of 477 per 100,000 inhabitants in 1999, while rural areas reported a mere 15 robberies per 100,000.

In 1999, according to the UCR, 42% of robberies were committed using strong-arm tactics, and firearms were the weapon of choice in 40% more. Knives were used in 8%, and a variety of other dangerous weapons in the remainder.

Robberies occur most frequently in December, probably reflecting an increased need for money and other goods around the holiday season. Most robbery (approximately 48%) takes the form of highway robbery, and robberies of businesses account for approximately 24% of all such crimes, while 2% of robberies are bank robberies.

Estimated losses due to robberies throughout the United States in 1999 totaled $463 million. However, as the FBI concludes, "The impact of this violent crime on its victims cannot be measured in terms of monetary loss alone. While the object of a robbery is to obtain money or property, the crime always involves force or threat of force, and many victims suffer serious personal injury."[46] In addition to monetary loss and possible physical injury, many robbery victims suffer lasting psychological trauma.

The nationwide clearance rate for robberies reported by the UCR in 1999 was 29%. The highest clearance rate was 39% in rural counties, and the lowest rate of clearance for robberies was found in the nation's cities. Youths under the age of 18 accounted for offenders arrested in 15% of all robberies counted as cleared, and 62% of all people apprehended for robbery were under 25 years of age. The offenders were males in 90% of all robberies, and blacks accounted for 54% of those arrested (44% were white, and the remainder were members of other racial groups).

NCVS statistics show a much higher number of robberies than do UCR data. NCVS interviewers uncovered approximately 810,000 robberies in 1999, which the BJS report broke down as 530,000 completed and 280,000 attempted. NCVS data show that 1 in every 2 completed robberies (and 1 out of every 3 attempted robberies) resulted in injuries to the victim. By far the most robbery-prone segment of the population is the 12- to 15-year-old age group, and males are robbed almost twice as frequently as females. Blacks report a robbery victimization rate three times higher than that of whites, and the incidence of robbery declines as family income rises. Members of the poorest families interviewed by NCVS field researchers (families with incomes of less than $7,500) were the most frequently robbed (8.1 per 1,000 people), while members of families with yearly incomes above $75,000 reported the lowest incidence of robbery (1.8 per 1,000 people). Of course, income and educational levels tend to be correlated. Hence, as the NCVS report concluded, the more educated a person is, the less their chance of being robbed.

NCVS data reveal that victims took some type of protective action in 63% of all robberies and that "a robbery ...committed by an offender who was known to the victim was significantly more likely to result in physical injury than a robbery . . . that was committed by a stranger."[47] Eleven percent of all robbery victims incurred medical expenses as a direct result of victimization, and 12% of all robberies caused the victim to miss time at work.

NCVS survey data reveal that only 50.1% of all robberies are reported to the police. Women are far more likely to report robberies (64%) than are men (42%), although men are only slightly more likely to resist robbery than are women.

Aggravated Assault

On July 14, 1996, rapper Luther Campbell, the former front man of 2 Live Crew, was charged with injuring a woman by throwing her into the crowd during a concert.[48] Campbell, whose stage name is Luke Skywalker, allegedly held the woman down with help from members of his dance troupe, then picked her up and launched her into the audience. The victim was knocked unconscious and Campbell was arrested by police who charged him with assault and battery. If it could have been shown that Campbell intended to harm the woman he might have been charged with aggravated assault. Chargers against the rapper were eventually dropped.

The UCR Program defines **aggravated assault** as "the unlawful attack by one person upon another for the purpose of inflicting severe or aggravated bodily injury." If a weapon is used or if serious bodily injury requiring hospitalization results, the UCR/NIBRS is likely to count the offense as an aggravated assault. The NCVS definition of aggravated assault is essentially the same, although the NCVS also reports on the crime of **simple assault,** which it defines as an "attack without a weapon resulting either in minor injury or in undetermined injury requiring less than two days of hospitalization." Hence under both the NCVS and the UCR/NIBRS, an assault with a deadly weapon would be scored as aggravated assault, although UCR/NIBRS data are far more likely to score any assault that results in hospitalization as "aggravated." Under all programs, assaults that cause serious bodily injury are also scored as aggravated assaults, even without the use of a weapon. If an assault results in death, however, the offense would become a homicide rather than an assault, for statistical-reporting purposes.

Assault Statistics

According to the UCR, 916,383 aggravated assaults were reported to police agencies across the nation in 1999, pro-

ducing an aggravated assault rate of 336.1 for every 100,000 people in the country. A total of 1,503,000 aggravated assaults were reported to NCVS interviewers in 1999, which translates into an aggravated assault rate of 670 per every 100,000 people aged 12 or over. Rates of aggravated assault were highest in metropolitan areas and lowest in rural areas.

The greatest number of aggravated assaults are usually recorded during the hot summer months, and 1999 was no exception, with July showing the highest incidence of such crimes. When cross-regional comparisons are made (always difficult as populations vary between regions), the southern states accounted for the most aggravated assaults (42%), the western states provided 23% of the total, the midwestern region 19%, and the Northeast 15%. Assault rates were higher in the South than elsewhere in the country.

During 1999, 35% of aggravated assaults reported to the police were committed with blunt objects, meaning that the offender probably grabbed whatever was at hand to commence or continue the attack. Hands, feet, and fists were used in 30% of all aggravated assaults, firearms were employed in 18%, and knives or other cutting or stabbing instruments were used in 18%.[49] Like most other index offenses, aggravated assault has shown a steady yearly decrease. The number of aggravated assaults reported nationwide has decreased by 20% over the past five years.

Because victims often know the people who assault them, the clearance rate for aggravated assault (which stood at 59% in 1999) is relatively high. As with most crimes, city police agencies report a lower rate of clearance for aggravated assault than other law enforcement departments, while rural areas have the highest rate of clearance.

Burglary

Burglary is a property crime, although it can have tragic consequences. In January 1994, Paxton, Massachusetts, Police Chief Robert Mortell, 38, was shot in the chest and died while involved in a foot chase with burglary suspects. A small town of only 4,100 residents, Paxton is unaccustomed to violence. Chief Mortell, a husband and father of three children, who were at the time aged 7 to 12, was quite popular with townspeople. "He was more than an authority figure. He was a security figure. When you lose a security figure, it sends shock waves through the community," said Joseph W. McKay, Paxton's Chief Selectman.[50]

The UCR defines **burglary** as "the unlawful entry of a structure to commit a felony or a theft." The definition goes on to say that "the use of force to gain entry is not required to classify an offense as burglary." Burglaries, as scored by the NCVS and the UCR/NIBRS, generally fall into three subclassifications: (1) forcible entry, (2) attempted forcible entry, and (3) unlawful entry where no force is used. Forcible entries are those burglaries in which some evidence of breakage, prying, or other evidence of forceful entry is found. A broken window, a jimmied door, a loosened air-conditioning duct—all may provide evidence of forcible entry. Attempted forcible entries (that is, attempted burglaries) are another form of burglary reported by the UCR and NIBRS. Attempted forcible entry also shows evidence of force, although the perpetrator may not have achieved actual entry. The third type of burglary, unlawful entry where no force is used, occurs when a burglar enters an unlocked residence uninvited, stealing items found there.

Although most burglaries are, strictly speaking, property crimes, the potential for personal violence is inherent in many such crimes. Nighttime burglary, for example, which is more severely punished in some jurisdictions than daytime burglary, holds the possibility of violent confrontation between offender and homeowner. Assault, rape, and even murder may be the outcome of such encounters. On the other hand, sometimes burglars themselves are injured or killed by irate residents.

According to the laws of most jurisdictions and to the UCR/NIBRS and NCVS definitional categories, burglary has not occurred unless it was the intent of the unlawful entrant to commit a felony or a theft once inside the burglarized location. Other forms of illegal entry may simply be counted as trespass.

Burglary Statistics

The FBI recorded 2,099,739 reported burglaries in 1999, a decrease of 10% over the previous year. Burglary has shown a steady decrease over the past decade, with the 1999 burglary rate approximately 22% lower than five years earlier. The UCR rate of reported burglary in 1999 was 770 per 100,000 inhabitants. As with most other Part I offenses, cities had the highest rate of burglary (802 per 100,000), whereas rural areas had the lowest (551 per 100,000).

Of reported burglaries in 1999, 64% involved forcible entry, 29% were the result of unlawful entries in which no force was used, and 7% were attempts. Two of every three reported burglaries were of residences (the remainder were commercial burglaries or burglaries committed on government property).

The average amount lost per burglary in 1999 was set at $1,458 by the FBI, although the loss was slightly lower for residential property (on average $1,441 per incident) than for nonresidential property ($1,490 per incident). The total loss suffered by all burglary victims in 1999 was estimated at approximately $3.1 billion.

Of all arrestees for the crime of burglary in 1999, 87% were men, 63% were under the age of 25, and 69% were white. Blacks accounted for 29% of burglary arrestees, and members of other races made up the remaining 2%.

Because burglaries are typically property crimes, the clearance rate for burglaries is quite low. Only 14% of all burglaries were cleared in 1999. As with other crimes, rural law enforcement agencies cleared a higher proportion of burglaries (16%) than city departments (13%).

In contrast to the UCR, NCVS statistics on burglary paint quite a different picture. In 1999, the NCVS reported 3,652,000 household burglaries and attempted burglaries—nearly 90% more than UCR/NIBRS estimates.[51] Rates of burglary were generally higher for black households than for white, regardless of family income levels, although wealthy black families had far lower burglary rates than did low-income white families. The same was true for locality. Hence black people living in cities were more likely than whites to have their houses burglarized, while blacks living in rural areas were also more likely than their white neighbors to become burglary victims, although wealthy blacks in either locale were less likely than poor whites to experience burglary. NCVS data also show that the longer a respondent lives at a particular residence, the less likely that person will be to report having been burglarized. Hence a residence of six months or less was associated with a burglary rate of 151 per 1,000 households versus a rate of only 38 per 1,000 households when those living at the reporting address had been there for five years or more.

Larceny

Larceny is another name for theft. Sometimes the word *larceny* is used by itself in published crime reports, and at other times *larceny-theft* is used. Both mean the same thing. The UCR/NIBRS defines **larceny-theft** as "the unlawful taking, carrying, leading, or riding away by stealth of property, other than a motor vehicle, from the possession or constructive possession of another" person, including attempts. The NCVS definition is similar, except that it further subdivides larceny into categories of "household larceny" and "personal larceny." Crimes of larceny do not involve force, nor do those who commit larceny intentionally put their victims in fear, as do robbers.

Differences exist between the NCVS and the UCR in the way subtypes of larceny are categorized. The UCR, for example, scores both purse snatching and pocket picking as larceny-theft, whereas the NCVS calls such crimes "personal larceny with contact." Similarly, the UCR scores shoplifting and thefts from coin-operated machines as larceny, but the NCVS does not gather data on commercial thefts and so excludes all such incidents from larceny counts. With these provisos in mind, larceny data in the NCVS and the UCR can be compared.

Larceny Statistics

The UCR Program counted 6,957,412 reports of larceny in 1999, for a rate of 2,551 such crimes per every 100,000 people in the population. The larceny rate decreased 6.5% from the previous year, but as in other years, reported larcenies were most common during July and August. Most items reported stolen had been taken from motor vehicles (26%), meaning that packages, money, and other goods were stolen from parked cars. Of all larcenies reported,

10% were of motor vehicle accessories like tires, "mag" wheels, cellular phones, CD players, and radar detectors. Another 14% of the total reported number of larcenies were from buildings, 14% were due to shoplifting, and 5% were of bicycles. Purse snatching, pocket picking, and thefts from coin-operated machines each accounted for less than 1% of the total number of larcenies reported to the police in 1999.

The average reported value of property stolen per larceny incident was $678 in 1999. This figure, however, is open to interpretation because reports to the police which estimate the dollar value of stolen or destroyed property are likely to be exaggerated. Some victims hope to receive a high return from insurance companies for stolen goods (even though such hope may be unfounded), some are unsure of the value of missing items, and others honestly overestimate the worth of lost goods because they do not realistically allow for depreciation. In addition, false claims are sometimes filed by people seeking to bilk insurance companies. Hence in instances of larceny, burglary, auto theft, and arson, it is difficult to know with certainty the true value of lost or stolen items.

NCVS data on larceny estimate 16,495,000 cases of larceny in 1999, with the majority (5,789,000 cases) involving the theft of items worth between $50 and $249. NCVS estimates put the figure for larceny far above the number of thefts officially reported to the police and recorded by the UCR. NCVS trend data, however, show that all forms of larceny have been on the decline since peaking around 1978 and 1979.

Motor Vehicle Theft

Motor vehicle theft is defined by the UCR simply as "the theft or attempted theft of a motor vehicle." The FBI adds that "this offense category includes the stealing of automobiles, trucks, buses, motorcycles, motorscooters, snowmobiles, etc." Excluded from the UCR/NIBRS count of motor vehicle theft is the stealing of vehicles like airplanes, boats, trains, and spacecraft (which would be counted as larcenies). The taking of a motor vehicle by a person having lawful access to that vehicle is similarly excluded. This designation often includes spouses, who are sometimes reported as having stolen a vehicle owned by their marriage partners. In most jurisdictions, however, married people effectively own most types of property jointly, even though titles, deeds, receipts, and so forth may not specifically list both parties. Hence a wife who tells her husband that he may not drive her car will not be taken seriously if she calls the police when he disobeys.

Carjacking, a much more serious crime than motor vehicle theft, involves the stealing of a car while it is occupied. Hence although carjacking involves theft, it is akin to robbery or kidnapping. Often the theft occurs at gunpoint, and in many carjacking cases, the victim is either injured or killed.

Carjacking, almost unheard of a decade ago, increased rapidly in the early 1990s when thieves targeted vehicles that could be sold easily for valuable parts.

Motor Vehicle Theft Statistics

The NCVS definition of a *motor vehicle* is quite concise: "an automobile, truck, motorcycle, or any other motorized vehicle legally allowed on public roads and highways." Both the NCVS and the UCR/NIBRS include attempts in counts of motor vehicle theft. Because of the similarity of definitions and because most motor vehicle thefts are reported for insurance purposes, NCVS and UCR statistics on motor vehicle theft are in close agreement. A total of 1,147,305 vehicles were reported stolen in 1999 by the FBI, while NCVS data estimate that 1,068,000 were illegally taken. The rate of motor vehicle theft in 1999 was 421 vehicles per 100,000 people, according to the FBI, and the value of motor vehicles stolen that year totaled more than $7 billion nationwide.

August is usually the prime month for motor vehicle thefts, and most thefts in any given month occur in the nation's cities. As a result, the UCR calls motor vehicle theft "primarily a large-city problem."

Law enforcement agencies reported a 15% clearance rate for motor vehicle thefts nationwide in 1999, although 67% of all stolen vehicles were recovered. Hence although many stolen vehicles were eventually returned to their rightful owners, relatively few arrests of car thieves were made.

Arson

More than a decade ago, William Krause and Kenneth Hayward were convicted under a federal antiarson statute of burning two large wooden crosses in the yard of a home owned by a white couple who had entertained black guests over the Labor Day weekend in 1989. Each was sentenced to a number of years in prison but appealed to the U.S. Supreme Court, claiming that their cross-burning conviction violated their constitutional right of freedom of expression. In 1994, however, the Supreme Court upheld both convictions without comment.[52]

The UCR defines **arson** as "any willful or malicious burning or attempt to burn, with or without intent to defraud, a dwelling house, public building, motor vehicle or aircraft, personal property of another, etc." The FBI adds that "only fires determined through investigation to have been willfully or maliciously set are classified as arsons." The NCVS does not report arson statistics.

Arson may occur for a variety of reasons. Some arsonists are thrill seekers who set fires for the excitement it brings. Others are vandals, wanting only to accomplish a random sort of destruction. Such people, sometimes called "pyromaniacs," may suffer from psychological problems which contribute to their fire-setting activities. Sometimes arson is a vengeful act, in which a former employee may strike back at

An arson fire. Arson causes millions of dollars' worth of property damage yearly. Are UCR statistics on arson accurate? *Lester Sloan, Woodfin Camp & Associates*

an employer, or an aggrieved former spouse may attempt to settle past scores. A few arsonists are called "vanity pyromaniacs." They are people, often in some official or responsible role, who place themselves in position to take credit for putting out fires which they secretly start. A handful of security guards, firefighters, and others in similar positions of trust have been involved in this kind of behavior.

In many other instances, arson is used to disguise other felonies, like murder or burglary. Buildings containing the bodies of murder victims, for example, may be burned to cover the evidence of homicide or to make the victim's death appear to have been caused by the fire itself. Most instances of arson, however, appear to be intended to defraud insurance companies into paying for property that the owners no longer want but which they haven't been able to dispose of legally (through sale, transfer, or other means).

Arson Statistics

Although nearly 16,000 law enforcement agencies contributed data to the FBI for use in 1999 UCR tabulations,

only 11,617 agencies forwarded any kind of arson information. Much of the arson data received by the FBI during 1999 was incomplete, consisting of less than 12 months of information or lacking in the kind of detail needed for FBI composites. Only 11,550 agencies provided complete arson information for any part of the year, and 8,061 agencies reported such data for all 12 months of 1999. Hence, UCR arson data remain incomplete. As the FBI warns, "Caution is recommended when viewing arson trend information. The percent change figures may have been influenced by improved arson reporting procedures during the collection's relatively limited timespan. It is expected that year-to-year statistical comparability will improve as collection continues."[53]

With these provisos in mind, it is safe to say that 66,321 instances of arson were reported under the UCR Program in 1999, with an average property loss per instance of approximately $10,882. Of the total number of arsons reported, 27% involved residences, 30% were of motor vehicles, 6% were of commercial buildings, and nearly 3.5% involved storage facilities of one sort or another. Public buildings were targeted by approximately 5% of all reported arsons.

Nationally, the clearance rate for arson was only 17%, with the highest rates of clearance being reported in small towns (those with populations of less than 10,000). Of all arson arrests in 1999, 54% involved juveniles—a higher percentage than for any other index crime. Seventy-four percent of arson arrestees were white, and 86% were men.

PART II OFFENSES

The traditional UCR also contains a report on arrests made by police for various crimes referred to as **Part II offenses.** Part II offenses are generally less serious than Part I offenses, and some are classified as misdemeanors in many jurisdictions. Only arrests are recorded because many Part II offenses, by virtue of both their semisecret nature (some might be regarded as "victimless" or "social-order" offenses) and their lesser degree of seriousness, are not reported to the police and are discovered only when an arrest occurs.

A list of Part II offenses and the 1999 incidence of each is provided in Table 2-3. Total arrests for Part II offenses in 1999 were estimated at 11.7 million, with arrests for driving under the influence (1.5 million), simple assault (1.3 million), and drug-abuse violations (1.5 million) leading the list. When Part I offenses are added to the total, the overall arrest rate for the United States in 1999 was measured at 5,317 arrests per 100,000 people, with arrests of residents of small cities (6,741 per 100,000) showing the highest rate.

Part II offenses reported in the UCR do not identify arrestees and make no attempt to distinguish offenders arrested once from those who have been arrested many times. Hence some frequently arrested individuals may have contributed significantly to the overall incidence of Part II crime statistics.

TABLE 2-3 ▪ UCR Part II Offenses, 1999	
OFFENSE CATEGORY	NUMBER OF ARRESTS
Simple assault	1,294,400
Forgery and counterfeiting	106,900
Fraud	363,800
Embezzlement	17,100
Stolen property (receiving)	121,900
Vandalism	278,200
Weapons (carrying)	172,400
Prostitution and related offenses	92,100
Sex offenses (statutory rape, etc.)	92,400
Drug-law violations	1,532,200
Gambling	10,400
Offenses against the family (nonsupport, etc.)	151,200
Driving under the influence	1,511,300
Liquor law violations	657,900
Public drunkenness	656,100
Disorderly conduct	633,100
Vagrancy	30,000
Curfew/loitering	167,200
Runaways	148,300
All other violations of state and local laws (except traffic-law violations)	3,728,100
Total	**11,765,000**

Source: Federal Bureau of Investigation, *Crime in the United States, 1999* (Washington, D.C.: U.S. Government Printing Office, 2000).

OTHER SOURCES OF DATA

Many other programs and surveys provide crime data on a regular basis. Of special interest to students of criminology might be campus crime statistics, which colleges are required to report to the federal Department of Education under the Crime Awareness and Campus Security Act of 1990.[54] Congress enacted the law following the brutal rape and murder of 19-year-old Jeanne Cleary in her dormitory room at Lehigh University in Bethlehem, Pennsylvania, in 1986. It was only after Cleary died that her parents learned that 38 violent crimes had occurred on the Lehigh campus in the previous three years but had not been made public.[55]

The Campus Security Act amended Section 485 of the Higher Education Act (HEA) of 1965 by adding campus crime statistics- and security-reporting requirements for all colleges and universities that receive any form of federal funding. The security provisions were amended in 1992 by the Campus Sexual Assault Victims' Bill of Rights to require that schools develop policies to deal with sexual assault on campus and that they provide certain assurances to victims. Under the provisions of the act, all prospective students and employees are entitled to a copy of a school's crime statistics

for the three most recent calendar years and a copy of the school's security policies. Current students and employees are to be given this information automatically.

Under a 1998 amendment to the HEA,[56] the federal Office of Postsecondary Education was authorized and funded by Congress to create the Campus Security Statistics Web site (CSSW). The site provides a direct link to reported criminal offenses for over 6,700 colleges and universities in the United States. Colleges and universities are required to report their crime statistics to the Office of Postsecondary Education for posting by October 1 of each year. Schools can be fined up to $25,000 for each crime they fail to report. Visit the CSSW via Web Extra! 2-13.

Web Extra! 2-13 at crimtoday.com

UNREPORTED CRIME

Many crimes are not reported, leading criminologists to talk about the, "dark figure of crime."[57] As we learned earlier in this chapter, this term refers to the large number of unreported crimes that never make it into official crime statistics. Crime's dark figure is sometimes glimpsed through offender self-reports, also known as offender **self-report surveys,** in which anonymous respondents without fear of disclosure or arrest are asked to report confidentially any violations of the criminal law that they have committed. Unfortunately for researchers, self-reports of crime are too often limited to asking questions only about petty offenses (such as shoplifting or simple theft), are usually conducted among young people like high school or college students (and hence may not provide results that are representative of the wider population), typically focus on juvenile delinquency rather than adult criminality, and cannot guarantee that respondents have told the truth. Limitations aside, some criminologists believe that "the development and widespread use of the self-report method of collecting data on delinquent and criminal behavior is one of the most important innovations in criminological research in the 20th century."[58]

Early self-report surveys were conducted in the 1940s, and researchers found that respondents were often ready and willing to make self-reports of their delinquency and criminal behavior.[59] In 1943, Austin Lo Porterfield provided the first published results from a self-report survey on crime.[60] Porterfield analyzed the juvenile court records of 2,049 delinquents from the Fort Worth, Texas, area and identified 55 offenses for which those juveniles had been adjudicated delinquent. He then surveyed 200 men and 137 women from three colleges in northern Texas to determine if and how frequently they had committed any of the same kinds of offenses. He found that every one of the college students had committed at least one such offense. The offenses committed by the college students were equally as serious as those committed by the adjudicated delinquents, although not as frequent; yet few of the college students had come into contact with legal authorities.[61]

Young men displaying signs of gang membership. Self-report surveys of cross-sections of the American population provide an alternative to the data-gathering techniques used by many other crime-reporting programs. What kinds of offenses might self-report surveys be especially adept at uncovering?
A. Lichtenstein, Corbis/Sygma

Inspired by Porterfield's methodology, James S. Wallerstein and Clement J. Wylie sampled a group of 1,698 adult men and women in 1947 via mailed questionnaires containing 49 offense categories.[62] The researchers requested self-reports of delinquent behavior committed before the age of 16. Almost all respondents reported committing at least one delinquent act, and 64% of the men and 29% of the women admitted committing at least 1 of the 14 felonies that had been included on the checklist.

Although the contributions of Porterfield and Wallerstein and Wylie were significant developments in the self-report methodology, the work of James F. Short and F. Ivan Nye[63] revolutionized ideas about the feasibility of using survey procedures with a hitherto taboo topic and changed thinking about delinquent behavior itself. What distinguished Short and Nye's research from previous self-report methods was their attention to methodological issues and their clear focus on the substantive relationship between social class and delinquent behavior.[64]

Short and Nye collected self-report data from high school students in three western communities varying in size from 10,000 to 40,000 people; from three midwestern communities varying across rural, rural-urban fringe, and suburban areas; and from a training school for delinquents in a western state. A 21-item list of criminal and antisocial behaviors was used to measure delinquency. Focusing on the relationship between delinquent behavior and the socioeconomic status of the adolescents' parents, Nye, Short, and Virgil Olson found that among the different socioeconomic groups, relatively few differences in delinquent behavior were statistically significant.[65]

Some of the more recent and best-known self-report surveys include the **National Youth Survey (NYS)** and the **Monitoring the Future** study. Begun by Delbert S. Elliott, David Huizinga, and Suzanne S. Ageton in 1976, the NYS surveyed a national sample of 1,725 youths between the ages of 11 and 17.[66] Members of the group (or "panel") were in-

terviewed each year for 5 years between 1977 and 81 and later at 3-year intervals. The survey, which was last conducted in 1993, followed the original respondents into their thirties. Self-report data were compared with official data over time, and data were gathered on a wide variety of variables, including the demographic and socioeconomic status of respondents, parents, and friends, neighborhood problems, education, employment, skills, aspirations, encouragement, normlessness, attitudes toward deviance, exposure to delinquent peers, self-reported depression, delinquency, drug and alcohol use, victimization, pregnancy, abortion, use of mental health and outpatient services, violence by respondent and acquaintances, use of controlled drugs, and sexual activity. Among other things, researchers found that (1) females were involved in a much higher proportion of crime than previously thought, (2) race differentials in crime were smaller than traditional data sources (that is, the UCR) indicated, and (3) violent offenders begin lives of crime much earlier than previous estimates provided by official statistics indicated. The NYS also found a consistent progression from less serious to more serious acts of delinquency over time.

Monitoring the Future[67] is an ongoing national self-report study of the behaviors, attitudes, and values of American secondary school students, college students, and young adults. The study began in 1975, and each year, a total of 50,000 8th-, 10th-, and 12th-grade students are surveyed. (12th graders have been surveyed since 1975, and 8th and 10th graders since 1991.) In addition, annual follow-up questionnaires are mailed to a sample of each graduating class for a number of years after their initial participation.

Findings from the Monitoring the Future survey have provided a primary source of information on trends in drug use among young people in this country for the last 25 years. For 1998, for example, the Monitoring the Future study found that substance abuse among young teens continues to increase—especially the use of cocaine and marijuana—and that alcohol use remains unacceptably high. The 1998 survey found that 23% of high school seniors reported using marijuana within the past month (versus 12% in 1992), 19% of tenth graders reported such use (versus 8% in 1992), and past-month marijuana use rose from 4% of eighth graders in 1992 to 10% in 1998. Even though it is based on self-reports, the survey may underestimate the amount of drug use among teens because it is unable to poll school dropouts and because students completing the survey may fear official reprisals even in the face of assurances to the contrary. Learn more about the Monitoring the Future study via Web Extra! 2-14.

Web EXTRA! **Web Extra! 2-14 at crimtoday.com**

The dark figure of crime can be at least partially estimated through analysis of data from the NCVS. According to NCVS analysts, the majority of crimes measured by the NCVS were not reported to the police.[68] More specifically, according to the NCVS:[69]

- Only 38% of all victimizations, 48% of violent victimizations, 29% of personal thefts, and 41% of all household crimes were reported to the police. In fact, household crimes and personal thefts were more likely to not be reported to the police than to be reported.
- Of the three major crime categories, violent crimes were most likely to be reported to the police, followed by household crimes. Personal thefts were the least likely crimes to be reported.
- Three of four motor vehicle thefts were reported to the police, making this the most highly reported of crimes. Personal larcenies without contact between victim and offender and household larcenies were least likely to be reported (at 28% and 27%, respectively).
- Women were more likely to report violent victimizations to the police than were men, and some evidence suggests that this was also the case for crimes of theft.
- White victims were somewhat more likely than black victims to report thefts to the police. The reporting rates for violent crimes committed against whites and blacks were similar.
- Violent crimes committed by strangers were no more likely to be reported to the police than violent crimes committed by someone who was known to the victim.
- The youngest victims of violent crimes and thefts— youths between 12 and 19 years of age—were less likely than people in any other age group to report crimes to the police.
- Homeowners were significantly more likely than those who rented to report household crimes to the police (44% versus 38%).
- Families with an annual income of $25,000 a year or more were more likely to report victimizations of their households than those earning under $10,000 a year.
- Generally, as the value of loss increased, so did the likelihood that a household crime would be reported.

Victims have many reasons for not reporting crimes:

- Fear of future victimization by the same offender
- Embarrassment over the type of victimization (as with some sex crimes) or over the fact of victimization (as with some cases of fraud where the victim is embarrassed to admit having fallen for a fraudulent scheme)
- The view that the police are likely to be ineffective in solving the crime
- Feelings of hostility toward the police and the justice system
- The belief that the matter is a private affair, perhaps one that should be settled personally without police involvement
- The view that the incident is too trivial or too common to require reporting
- The fear that involvement in court proceedings may entail a considerable degree of personal inconvenience

- The belief that the incident is not, or should not be, a crime (as might be the case in some drug offenses, employee thefts, and traffic violations)

An interest in recovering property or in receiving insurance payments motivates most victims of property crimes who reported their victimization to the police. The two most common reasons for not reporting violent victimizations were that the crime was a personal or private matter (20%) or that the offender was unsuccessful and the crime was only attempted (17%).

THE SOCIAL DIMENSIONS OF CRIME

What Are "Social Dimensions"?

Crime does not occur in a vacuum. It involves real people— human perpetrators and victims, just like you and me. Because society defines certain personal characteristics as especially important, however, it is possible to speak of the "social dimensions of crime," that is, aspects of crime and victimization as they relate to socially significant attributes by which groups are defined and according to which individuals are assigned group membership. Socially significant attributes include gender, ethnicity or race, age, income or wealth, profession, and social class or standing within society. Such personal characteristics provide criteria by which individuals can be assigned to groups like "the rich," "the poor," "male," "female," "young," "old," "black," "white," "white-collar worker," "manual laborer," and so on.[70]

We have already alluded briefly to the fact that the UCR, NIBRS, and NCVS structure the data they gather in ways that reflect socially significant characteristics. The UCR, for example, provides information on reported crimes which reveals the sex, age, and race of both victims and perpetrators. NCVS statistics document the race, age, and sex of crime victims and the incomes of households reporting victimizations.

The social dimensions of crime are said by statisticians to reveal relationships or correlations. A **correlation** is simply a connection or association which is observed to exist between two measurable variables. Correlations are of two types: positive and negative. If one measurement increases when another, with which it is correlated, does the same, then a positive correlation, or a positive relationship, is said to exist between the two. When one measurement decreases in value as another rises, a negative, or inverse, correlation has been discovered. NCVS data, for example, show a negative relationship between age and victimization. As people age, victimization rates decline. Hence although some elderly people do become crime victims, older people as a group tend to be less victimized than younger people. UCR data, on the other hand, show a positive relationship between youth and the likelihood of arrest—specifically, between young adulthood and arrest. Young adults, it appears, commit the most crimes.

Hence as people age, they tend to be both less likely to be victimized and less likely to become involved in criminal activity.

A word of caution is in order, however. Correlation does not necessarily imply causation. Because two variables appear to be correlated does not mean that they have any influence on each other or that one causes the other to either increase or decrease. Correlations that involve no causal relationship are said to be "spurious." A study of crime rates, for example, shows that many crimes seem to occur with greater frequency in the summer. Similarly, industry groups tell us that food retailers sell more ice cream in the summer than at any other time. Are we to conclude, then, from the observed correlation between crime rates and ice cream sales, that one in some way causes the other? To do so on the basis of an observed correlation alone would obviously be foolish.

Even if two variables appear to be related, it may be difficult to determine the actual nature of the relationship. Some criminologists have observed, for example, that in the past, as the number of prison cells increased, so did the crime rate. While this relationship no longer seems to hold, the implication at the time was that building more prisons would somehow cause more crime. Others have noted how the rather remarkable growth in the number of criminal defense attorneys over the past three or four decades has almost precisely paralleled the observed rate of increase in violent crime—with similar implications. Of course, it would seem logical to conclude that swelling crime rates have led to increases in the number of both attorneys and prison cells.

Some observed correlations do appear to shed at least a little light on either the root causes of crime or the nature of criminal activity. It is to these that our discussion now turns.

Age and Crime

If arrest records are any guide, criminal activity is associated more with youth than with any other stage of life. Every year, UCR data consistently show that young people, from their late teens to their early and mid-twenties, account for the bulk of street, property, and predatory crime (that is, Part I offenses) reported in this country. Although young people between their 13th and 18th birthdays make up about 6% of the population, they account for approximately 30% of all arrests for major crimes and 18% of total arrests in the United States in a given year.

During the 1990s, a number of well-known criminologists, among them **Alfred Blumstein**,[71] **John J. DiIulio, Jr.**,[72] **James Alan Fox**,[73] **Joan Petersilia**,[74] and **James Q. Wilson**,[75] alerted policymakers to a coming demographic shift that they believed would combine with an increased level of youth violence to produce alarming rates of violent crime by 2010. James Fox, for example, noted that within a few years, "the number of teens, ages 14–17, will increase by 20 percent, with a larger increase among blacks in this age group (26 percent)."[76] This fact, said Fox, is especially worrisome because

over the past ten years, "the rate of murder committed by teens, ages 14–17, [has] increased 172 percent." Indicative of what he saw as a significant trend, Fox said that "black males aged 14–24," although comprising only 1 percent of the population, "now constitute 17 percent of the victims of homicide and over 30 percent of the perpetrators." Also, claimed Fox, "the differential trends by age of offender observed for homicide generalize to other violent offenses." During the five years prior to his sounding the alarm, Fox noted that "the arrest rate for violent crimes (murder, rape, robbery and aggravated assault) rose over 46% among teenagers, but only 12% among adults." Joan Petersilia, a former American Society of Criminology (ASC) president (who also wrote the foreword to this textbook), lent her weight to the belief that an avalanche of youth-spawned violence would soon inundate American society. Petersilia believed that there was very little that anyone can do to avert it. She cited James Q. Wilson's sage advice: "Get ready."[77]

The predicted tidal wave of criminal violence has yet to materialize, causing policymakers and others to question the factual basis of such fears. Although shifting demographics may soon result in an increase in the percentage of the American population that is made up of young people in the "crime prone years,"[78] contemporary FBI statistics show that many forms of juvenile crime are declining. James Fox, however, says the problem is far from solved. The recent drop in juvenile crime, says Fox, is good news, but "it hardly means the problem [has been] solved. It's like a 500-pound man losing 50 pounds. It doesn't mean he's thin."[79]

Like other writers who have warned of a coming crime wave, Alfred Blumstein, another past president of the ASC, notes that "[p]articularly relevant to future crime, and to consideration of prevention and intervention strategies, is the size of the current teenage population. The age **cohort** responsible for much of the recent youth violence is the smallest it has been in recent years. By contrast, the cohort of children ages 5 to 15, who will be moving into the crime-prone ages in the near future, is larger."[80]

Crime waves, however, come and go—and no one stays young forever. Involvement in crime appears to decrease consistently, beginning at approximately age 25. The same is true for Part II offenses, with the exception of vagrancy, public drunkenness, gambling, and certain sex crimes—declines in these types of criminal involvement are more likely to begin around age 30. Even though crimes of all kinds appear to decline with age, and even though chronic repeat offenders commit fewer crimes as they grow older, criminologists have found that differences in offense rates remain much the same throughout the life cycle.[81] In other words, proportionate differences in rates of offending are unchanged between social groups like males and females, the rich and the poor, whites and blacks, and so on, even as members of those groups age.

Although most forms of criminality decrease with age, which is sometimes referred to as the **desistance phenomenon**, even old age is no bar to criminal involvement.

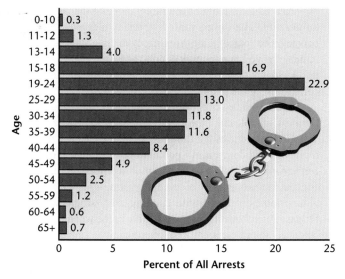

■ **FIGURE 2-6** ARRESTS BY AGE FOR PART I OFFENSES, 1999.
Source: Federal Bureau of Investigation, *Crime in the United States, 1999* (Washington, D.C.: U.S. Government Printing Office, 2000).

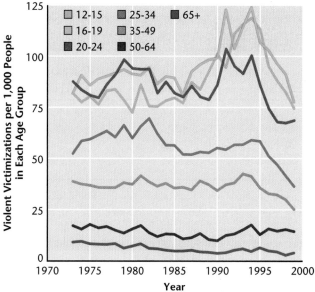

Note: Because of changes made to the victimization survey, data prior to 1992 are adjusted to make them comparable to data collected under the redesigned methodology. Estimates for 1993 and beyond are based on collection year while earlier estimates are based on data year. Due to changes in the methods used, these data differ from earlier versions. Violent crimes included are homicide, rape, robbery, and both simple and aggravated assault.

■ **FIGURE 2-7** VIOLENT VICTIMIZATION RATES BY AGE OF VICTIM, 1973–1999.
Source: Bureau of Justice Statistics.

According to UCR statistics, around 450,000 people aged 50 or over are arrested every year throughout the country. Of those, nearly 60,000 are past the age of 65. Figure 2-6 provides a graphic comparison of people arrested by age for all reported Part I offenses, and Figure 2-7 shows violent crime victimization rates by age.

Recently, crimes of the elderly, or geriatric criminality, have sparked much interest among criminologists and the popular media. Movies like *The Over the Hill Gang* have depicted the exploits of aged criminals. Although in the minority, real-life elderly criminals are not hard to find. The case of Edward Cook, 68, who still remains a fugitive, is illustrative. Cook usually works with an elderly female companion, and the two are known for showing up in swank jewelry stores, posing as casually dressed tourists. The couple travels with a video camera casually slung over Cook's shoulder. Cook, however, keeps the camera running—recording security devices and showcased valuables throughout the targeted stores. Cook returns after closing hours, deactivates store alarms, and helps himself to the choicest jewels.

Why do older people commit crimes? One author explains it this way: "The reasons older people turn to crime are varied. Some people never retire—from trouble. Others find that retirement gets them into trouble. Boredom and unstructured leisure, fear of the future, frustration over limited finances, family neglect or stress—the same conditions that contribute to teenage crime—can lead seniors to commit desperate or foolish acts."[82]

Some older criminals use their age to advantage. Few people, for example, suspect older people of criminal intent. Hence potential victims are less likely to be on their guard against crime in the presence of an older offender. Similarly, experience gained from previous criminality,

and from life in general, can be turned into assets in the criminal arena. As the old adage goes, "Knowledge is power," and whereas social convention holds that wisdom comes with age, so does increased criminal opportunity for those so inclined.

Although street crime may be the bailiwick of the young, the indications are that older offenders are overrepresented in other forms of crime, including those that require special skills and knowledge. Many of these crimes are job related and involve fraud, deception, or business activities which are criminal. Such crimes are discussed in detail in Chapter 12.

Although the elderly are less likely to be victimized than other groups, statistics show many more elderly victims than geriatric criminals. The NCVS defines *elderly* to include everyone aged 65 or older living in the United States.[83] NCVS data show that "persons age 65 or older are the least likely of all age groups in the nation to experience crime,"[84] and victimization rates among the elderly have been declining since 1974—about the time NCVS data gathering began. According to the NCVS, "The rates for personal theft and household crime among the elderly in 1996 were the lowest ever recorded in the 20 year history of NCVS."[85]

Even so, approximately 2 million criminal victimizations of the elderly occur in the United States every year.[86] Table 2-4 shows NCVS victimization rates for various age

TABLE 2-4 ■ Number of Victimizations by Age (Per 1,000 People)		
AGE	**VIOLENT CRIME**	**PERSONAL THEFT**
12–24	64.6	112.7
25–49	27.2	71.2
50–64	8.5	38.3
65 and over	4.0	19.5

Source: U.S. Department of Justice, *Elderly Crime Victims* (Washington, D.C.: Bureau of Justice Statistics, March 1994); and BJS, *Age Patterns of Victims of Serious Violent Crime* (Washington, D.C.: BJS, September 1997).

groups. A recent report by the NCVS makes the following observations about elderly crime victims:[87]

- The violent crime rate is nearly sixteen times higher for people under 25 than for people over age 65 (64.6 victimizations versus 4 victimizations per 1,000 people in each age group).
- As with personal crime victimizations, people over the age of 65 are significantly less likely to become victims of all forms of household crime than are members of younger age groups.
- Personal larceny with contact (purse snatching and pocket picking) is an exception. Those who are 65 or older were about as likely as those under age 65 to be victims of personal larceny with contact.
- Injured elderly victims of violent crime are more likely than younger victims to suffer a serious injury.
- Elderly victims of violent crime are more likely than younger victims to face assailants who are strangers.
- Elderly victims of violent crime are almost twice as likely as younger victims to be raped, robbed, or assaulted at or near their homes.
- Elderly victims act to protect themselves during a violent crime less often than do younger victims.
- Elderly victims of robbery and personal theft are more likely than younger victims to report those crimes to the police.

One crime against the elderly which is often not reported is elder abuse. The physical and emotional abuse of the elderly by family members, caregivers, and others has been called a "national tragedy,"[88] involving as it does an estimated 1.5 million cases per year. Recent hearings before the House Subcommittee on Human Services, Select Committee on Aging, revealed that one of every twenty-five Americans over the age of 65 suffers from some form of abuse, neglect, or exploitation.[89] Subcommittee members also concluded that elder abuse is increasing. Unfortunately,

however, cases of elder abuse rarely come to the attention of authorities. The desire shared by many elderly citizens for privacy, the fear of embarrassment at having abuse at the hands of loved ones revealed, and the relatively limited ability of elderly citizens to access law enforcement services all contribute to the problem.

To address the concerns of the elderly, the 1994 Violent Crime Control and Law Enforcement Act provides, under Title 24, Protections for the Elderly, monies for the development of local community partnerships between senior citizen groups and law enforcement agencies designed to combat crimes against older Americans. The act also provides monies to assist with funding a Missing Alzheimer's Disease Patient Alert Program, which, in the words of the legislation, "shall be a locally based, proactive program to protect and locate missing patients with Alzheimer's disease and related dementias." Finally, the act increases penalties for telemarketing fraud directed against the elderly and requires criminal justice agencies to assist in providing background information on caregivers with felony convictions who are being considered for employment in nursing homes and long-term-care facilities.

Gender and Crime

Gender appears to be so closely linked to most forms of criminal activity that it has been called "the best single predictor of criminality."[90] Table 2-5 shows the degree of involvement in each of the major crimes by gender. The columns in the table do not show the total number of crimes reported, but rather represent the proportion of male-female involvement in each Part I offense. For example, of all murders in this country in a given year, approximately 90% are committed by men and 10% by women.

The apparently low rate of female criminality has been explained by some as primarily due to cultural factors, including early socialization, role expectations, and a reluctance among criminal justice officials to arrest and prosecute women. Others have assumed a biological propensity toward crime and aggression among men which may be lacking in women. Although these and other issues are addressed in later chapters, it is important here to note that the rate of female criminality has changed very little over time—a fact much in contrast to assumptions made years ago by some criminologists who insisted that the degree of female involvement in crime would increase as women assumed more powerful roles in society.

Even when women commit crimes, they are more often followers than leaders. A recent study of women in correctional settings, for example, found that women are far more likely to assume "secondary follower roles during criminal events" than "dominant leadership roles."[91] Only 14% of women surveyed played primary roles, but those who did "felt that men had little influence in initiating or leading them into crime." African-American women were found to be more likely to play "primary and equal crime roles" with

TABLE 2-5 ■ **Male-Female Involvement in Crime**

UCR INDEX CRIME	PERCENTAGE OF ARRESTS BY GENDER	
	MALES (%)	FEMALES (%)
Murder and nonnegligent manslaughter	88.6	11.4
Rape	98.7	1.3
Robbery	89.9	10.1
Aggravated assault	80.3	19.7
Burglary	87.1	12.9
Larceny-theft	64.5	35.5
Motor vehicle theft	84.4	15.6
Arson	85.6	14.4
Average, all crimes	**78.2**	**21.8**

Source: Federal Bureau of Investigation, *Crime in the United States, 1999* (Washington, D.C.: U.S. Government Printing Office, 2000).

men or with female accomplices than were white or Hispanic women. Statistics like these dispel the myth that the female criminal in America has taken her place alongside male offenders—in terms of either leadership roles or the absolute number of crimes committed.

Turning to victimization as it is associated with gender, women are victimized far less frequently than men in most crime categories. NCVS data show that crimes of violence reported by American women reflect victimization rates of 34.6 per 1,000 female individuals aged 12 or older, versus 49.9 for males. As with the population in general, the rate of female victimization for all crimes decreases with age, leading NCVS authors to conclude that (1) white women aged 65 or older have the lowest violent crime rates, and

(2) black women aged 65 or older have the lowest personal theft rates.[92] Two significant exceptions are rape and spousal abuse. Rape is a crime of special concern to many people because official reports to the police of rape have continued to show relatively stable rates of victimization, even as reports of many other types of crimes have declined substantially.[93]

Chapter 10 provides a detailed description of the victimization of women in general and of the crime of rape in particular. That chapter also provides recent information from the annual National Violence against Women (NVAW) survey. The NVAW survey is supported under the 1994 Violence against Women Act (VAWA)[94] and is sponsored by the National Institute of Justice and the Centers for Disease

Female gang members fighting. Although much female criminality has long been overlooked, criminologists are now increasingly aware of gender issues. How does the criminality of men and women appear to differ? *Copaken/Gamma-Liaison, Inc.*

THEORY VERSUS REALITY
Adolescent Motherhood and Crime

A 1997 study by the Office of Juvenile Justice and Delinquency Prevention identified a significant relationship between adolescent motherhood and crime. The study found that children born to teenage mothers had a considerably higher likelihood of turning to crime than those born to older mothers. Following are edited excerpts from the study.

Nearly 1 million American teenagers (about 10% of all 15- to 19-year-old girls) become pregnant each year. About 33% abort their pregnancies, 14% miscarry, and 52% bear children—72% of them out of wedlock. Of the half million teens who give birth, approximately 75% are first-time mothers. More than 175,000 are 17 years old or younger.

These young mothers and their offspring are especially vulnerable to severe adverse social and economic consequences. More than 80% of these young mothers end up in poverty and on welfare, many for the majority of their children's critically important development years.

One recent study looked at the higher engagement in crime by male children of adolescent mothers and found that the sons of adolescent mothers are 2.7 times more likely to be incarcerated than the sons of mothers who delayed childbearing until their early twenties. Nationally, about 5% of all young men were behind bars over a thirteen-year period. This is well below the 10.3% rate of observed incarceration for young men born to adolescent mothers and slightly above the 3.8% rate for young men born to mothers who began their families at age 20 or 21.

Roughly half of the observed difference for young men born to adolescent versus older childbearers is accounted for by observable differences in the demographic and background characteristics of offspring of both groups of mothers. Still, if these adolescents postponed childbearing until age 20 or 21, it would, by itself, reduce the incarceration rate for the affected children by 13% (from 10.3% to 9.1%).

Even the relatively small fraction of the higher incarceration rate that is directly

attributable to adolescent childbearing costs society dearly. A delay in childbearing until the age of 20.5 would reduce the national average incarceration rate by 3.5%, for an annual savings of about $1 billion in correctional costs and a potential savings of nearly $3 billion in total law enforcement costs. These results are, of course, long range. Even if all prospective adolescent mothers were to delay their childbearing as of tomorrow, the incarceration rates would not fall as predicted for approximately twenty years—the earliest age at which young offenders start going to jail in any substantial numbers.

Thus policies that successfully address adolescent childbearing could lead to additional cost savings for the nation.

Source: Rebecca A. Maynard, Ph.D., and Eileen M. Garry, *Adolescent Motherhood: Implications for the Juvenile Justice System* (Washington, D.C.: Office of Juvenile Justice and Delinquency Prevention, January 1997), citing "Crime: The Influence of Early Childbearing on the Cost of Incarceration," in Rebecca A. Maynard, ed., *Kids Having Kids: Economic Costs and Social Consequences of Teen Pregnancy* (Washington, D.C.: Urban Institute Press, 1996).

Control and Prevention. The first NVAW survey solicited telephone responses from 8,000 women and 8,000 men throughout the United States. Selected survey results released in July 2000 showed that nearly 25% of women and 7.5% of men were raped and/or physically assaulted by a current or former spouse, cohabiting partner, or date at some time over the course of their life.[95] Women, however, bore the brunt of the violence, with the NVAW survey finding that women are significantly more likely than men to report being victims of rape, physical assault, or stalking. The survey also found that rates of intimate partner violence vary significantly among women according to ethnicity. Asian and Pacific Islander women and men reported lower rates of intimate partner violence than did men and women from other minority backgrounds. Similarly, socioeconomic status was associated with violence, with poor women experiencing the highest rates of violence.

Violence among intimates may lead to other forms of crime. The National Clearinghouse for the Defense of Battered Women, one of the few national organizations that

collect data on the relationship between violence against women and women's involvement in illegal activity, reports that more than half of all women in detention had been battered or raped before being incarcerated. Other studies have similarly uncovered a link between the victimization of women and their criminal behavior.[96]

Ethnicity and Crime

Several years ago, Professor Lani Guinier of the University of Pennsylvania School of Law was interviewed on *Think Tank*, a PBS show. Guinier was asked by Ben Wattenberg, the program's moderator, "When we talk about crime, crime, crime, are we really using a code for black, black, black?" Guinier responded this way: "To a great extent, yes, and I think that's a problem, not because we shouldn't deal with the disproportionate number of crimes that young black men may be committing, but because if we can't talk about race, then when we talk about crime, we're really talking about other things, and it means that we're not being honest in terms of acknowledging what the problem is and then trying to deal with it. It's a way of distancing ourselves from the real problem, which is the terrible rise in urban violence."[97]

Crimes, of course, are committed by individuals of all races. The link between crime—especially violent, street, and predatory crimes—and race, however, shows a pattern that is striking in terms of its racial dimensions. In some crime categories arrests of black offenders equal or exceed arrests of whites. In 1999, for example, 52% of all murder arrestees in the United States were black, and 46% were white.

Although these simple numbers may be surprising to some, more significant still are calculations of crime rates based on race. Such rates, which take into consideration the relative proportion of racial groups in the U.S. population and assess the extent to which criminal activity is associated with each, are quite revealing. The U.S. Bureau of Census, for example, says that 12.8% of the population identify themselves as black, and 82.2% count themselves as white.[98] Hispanics make up most of the remainder of the population. Arrest rates by race are shown in Figure 2-8. The figure shows, for example, that although blacks are arrested for approximately 52% of all murders committed in a given year, the murder rate among blacks is seven times that of whites because blacks account for only one-eighth of the population. Similar rate comparisons are shown in the figure for a number of other crimes. The figure diagrammatically represents relative rates of arrest by race that are numerically presented in Table 2-6.

Some authors maintain that racial differences in arrest and imprisonment rates are due to the differential treatment of blacks and other minorities at the hands of a discriminatory criminal justice system.[99] In a recent book, for example,

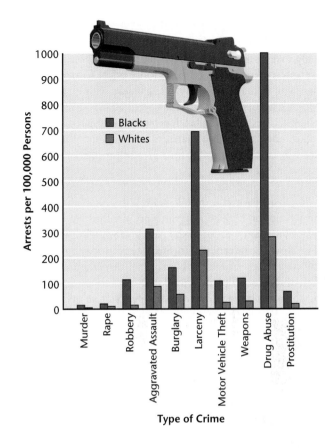

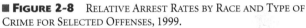

■ **FIGURE 2-8** RELATIVE ARREST RATES BY RACE AND TYPE OF CRIME FOR SELECTED OFFENSES, 1999.
Source: Derived from FBI, *Crime in the United States, 1999* (Washington, D.C.: U.S. Government Printing Office, 2000); and Population Estimates Program, Population Division of the U.S. Census Bureau, *Resident Population Estimates of the U.S.,* January 1, 2000.

TABLE 2-6 ■ Arrest Rates by Race (per 100,000 People) and Relative Rates of Arrest for Selected Offenses, 1999			
OFFENSE	BLACKS	WHITES	RATE OF ARREST, BLACK VS. WHITE
Murder	14	2	7.0:1
Rape	19	5	3.8:1
Robbery	115	14	8.2:1
Aggravated assault	312	88	3.5:1
Burglary	159	58	2.7:1
Larceny	690	231	2.9:1
Motor vehicle theft	112	22	5.0:1
Weapons	120	30	4.0:1
Drug abuse	1,002	282	3.5:1
Prostitution	69	17	4.0:1

Source: Derived from FBI, *Crime in the United States, 1999* (Washington, D.C.: U.S. Government Printing Office, 2000); and Population Estimates Program, Population Division of the U.S. Census Bureau, *Resident Population Estimates of the U.S.,* January 1, 2000.

Marvin D. Free, Jr., claims that the fact that blacks are under-represented as criminal justice professionals results in their being overrepresented in arrest statistics.[100] Some police officers, according to Free, may be more prone to arrest blacks than whites, may frequently arrest blacks without sufficient evidence to support criminal charges, and may overcharge in criminal cases involving black defendants, which may lead to unfair and misleading statistical tabulations that depict blacks as being responsible for a greater proportion of crime than is in fact the case.

Other writers disagree. In *The Myth of a Racist Criminal Justice System,* for example, **William Wilbanks** claims that although the practice of American criminal justice may have been significantly racist in the past, and while some vestiges of racism may indeed remain, the system is today by and large objective in its processing of criminal defendants.[101] Using statistical data, Wilbanks shows that "at every point from arrest to parole there is little or no evidence of an overall racial effect, in that the percentage outcomes for blacks and whites are not very different."[102] Wilbanks claims to have reviewed "all the available studies that have examined the possible existence of racial discrimination from arrest to parole." In essence, he says, "this examination of the available evidence indicates that support for the 'discrimination thesis' is sparse, inconsistent, and frequently contradictory."[103]

Practically speaking, a nonracist criminal justice system is not necessarily the result of a total absence of racism, because some individual actors within the system will inevitably act in a racially biased fashion. Rather, it may be the result of a series of actions, some of which may be racially motivated, that, when taken together, collectively balance. Hence, says Wilbanks, the net result is a system that is today not observably racist in its results.

Wilbanks is careful to counter arguments advanced by those who continue to suggest that the system is racist. He writes, for example, "Perhaps the black/white gap at arrest is a product of racial bias by the police in that the police are more likely to select and arrest black than white offenders. The best evidence on this question comes from the National Crime Survey which interviews 130,000 Americans each year about crime victimization. . . . The percent of offenders described by victims as being black is generally consistent with the percent of offenders who are black according to arrest figures."[104] Such data are complemented by annual surveys conducted by the Centers for Disease Control and Prevention (CDC), which consistently find that people treated at hospital emergency rooms for nonfatal gunshot wounds related to crime are mainly male, black, and young. The most recent CDC study, for example, found that men comprise almost 90% of those treated for firearm injuries connected to crimes and that 59% of those treated are black. According to the CDC, "The racial breakdown for crime-related [gunshot] wounds [is] 59% black, 19% white, and 14% Hispanic."[105]

However, observes Wilbanks, "the assertion that the criminal justice system is not racist does not address the reasons why blacks appear to offend at higher rates than whites

before coming into contact with the criminal justice system. . . . It may be," he suggests, "that racial discrimination in American society has been responsible for conditions (e.g., discrimination in employment, housing, and education) that lead to higher rates of offending by blacks, but that possibility does not bear on the question of whether the criminal justice system discriminates against blacks."[106] Marvin Free, Jr., agrees, suggesting that blacks are still systematically denied equal access to societal resources which would allow for full participation in American society, resulting in a higher rate of law violation.[107] In a recent work that considers such issues in great detail, John Hagan and Ruth D. Peterson attribute higher crime rates among ethnic minorities to (1) concentrated poverty, (2) joblessness, (3) family disruption, and (4) racial segregation.[108]

A more fundamental critique of Wilbanks's thesis comes from **Coramae Richey Mann,** who says that his overreliance on quantitative or statistical data fails to capture the reality of racial discrimination within the justice system.[109] White victims, says Mann, tend to overreport being victimized by black offenders because they often misperceive Hispanic and other minority offenders as black. Similarly, says Mann, black victims are sometimes reluctant to report victimization—especially at the hands of whites. Moreover, says Mann, statistics on specific crimes like rape may include false accusations by white women to hide their involvement with black lovers. And, says Mann, a greater integration of black neighborhoods (in the sense that whites are less reluctant to enter such neighborhoods than blacks are to enter white neighborhoods) may result in a disproportionate but misleading number of reports of white victims. Finally, the fact that far more whites than blacks live in the United States means that they will naturally account for a greater percentage of victims, which explains the seeming overvictimization of whites by blacks.

Although Mann cites the need for the greater use of qualitative measures, most available data on race and crime are statistical. And so speaking, African-Americans not only appear to commit street crimes at a rate disproportionate to their representation in the population, but they are also disproportionately victimized by such crimes. One author recently asserted that "black-on-black crime is the true face of crime in America."[110] No less a figure than American civil rights leader Jesse Jackson has identified black-on-black crime as "the most important issue of the civil rights movement today."[111] If such assertions are even partially correct, although unpopular, then, many suggest, it is incumbent upon policymakers to admit and realistically assess the degree of overinvolvement in street crime that characterizes a disproportionately large segment of the black population in America today—for such an admission is the first step toward realistically addressing the problem.

Such overinvolvement may be a sign of a sinister form of racism. U.S. District Judge Robert L. Carter, for example, points out that although American society seems prepared to tolerate the conditions that produce high crime rates among blacks, it is unlikely that it would if whites were

CRIME IN THE NEWS
Violence Hits Blacks Hardest

If you are a black man in the United States, you are more likely to be killed than any other race or gender, according to a new FBI study.

If you are a white woman, you are the least likely to be the victim of a homicide, according to the findings, which were released during the weekend.

FBI researchers compared crime-reporting data from 1978 to 1997 and found that the victim pool has grown slightly younger. Twenty years ago, people in their mid- to late-20s had a higher homicide rate than other age groups in the country.

But in the past decade the demographic changed significantly. Homicide victims are mostly in their early- to mid-20s now.

The study, which was included in the FBI's 1999 Uniform Crime Reports, is the most comprehensive survey done by the FBI in 20 years.

1 IN 40 BLACK MEN A LIKELY VICTIM

In 1997, one out of 40 black males could expect to become a homicide victim. Black females were the next most likely victims, with an anticipated homicide rate of one out of 199 people, the FBI said.

That year, one out of 288 white males were expected to be murdered in their lifetimes; one out of 794 white females were likely to become homicide victims.

Still, the FBI reported that homicide rates declined for the last eight years leading to 1999. There were fewer homicides in 1997 (18,210) than there were in 1973 (19,640).

BLACK-ON-BLACK VIOLENCE

Robert J. Castelli, a scholar at John Jay College of Criminal Justice at the City University of New York, said drug fights can take much of the credit for the killings. Drugs have ravaged users and sellers alike, particularly in the crack cocaine and heroin turf wars of the late 1980s and early 1990s.

Drug offenders also have gotten younger over the past few decades, he said, and their propensity for violence has evolved to unprecedented brutality when money and power on the streets are at stake.

Castelli, a retired 22-year veteran of the New York State Police, noted that much of the violence occurs in urban areas, where blacks are the majority.

"Just like blacks are the probable victims, they also are the probable committers of those crimes" in their communities, Castelli said.

Blacks accounted for a slim majority of killers in the United States, at 50 percent, according to the FBI. Whites were the offenders in 45 percent of killings last year, and the rest were of other races.

The FBI report said 94 percent of black victims were slain by black offenders, and 85 percent of white victims were killed by whites.

RACIAL DISPARITY?

Eric Sterling, president of the Criminal Justice Policy Foundation, said that of the 14 million arrests made last year, 70 percent of those taken into police custody were white and under 25 years of age. But Department of Justice statistics for 1999 showed that roughly half of those in state and federal lockup were black, disproportionate to the racial makeup of the United States.

"White people are being arrested, but they are not going to prison at the rate that black people are going to prison," Sterling said.

Source: James Gordon Meek, "Murder Victims Getting Younger, Report Says," APB News, October 16, 2000. Reprinted with permission.

committing as many crimes. During a recent speech, Judge Carter said that two of every three black men in the United States aged 20 to 29 are either in prison, awaiting trial, or on probation, and he noted that "everyone in this room knows that if white men were in this situation or in danger of being so placed, there would be a nationwide howl of protest."[112] The fact that no such protest can be heard, said Carter, "is outrageous and constitutes unmitigated racism. Instead of seeking remedies," observed the judge, "the nation is spending billions of dollars for new prison facilities, apparently gearing up to be able to soon house half the 20 to 29-year-old black men."

At the very least, it would seem that the existing relationship between race and most forms of street crime is one source of continuing divisiveness in American society. In a recent report, the National Criminal Justice Commission, a project of the National Center on Institutions and Alternatives (NCIA), noted that "the fact that so many minority men are in the criminal justice system raises profoundly disturbing questions." The commission concluded, "To the extent that racial disparities in prison are the result of racial bias, then that bias must be rooted out of the criminal justice system. To the extent that they are the result of higher African-American crime, then the underlying causes of that crime must be addressed. Failure to do so puts the nation at risk of social catastrophe."[113]

High rates of crime and of criminal victimization within the black community have led to a heightened fear of crime among black Americans. A recent report by the Bureau of Justice Statistics, which was based on data from the American Housing Survey (conducted by the Department of Housing and Urban Development), found that "black households are nearly three times more likely than white ones to fear crime in their neighborhoods and that black fear is growing faster than white fear."[114] The survey shows that fear of neighborhood crime has risen almost twice as much among blacks as whites since the mid-1980s. In black central-city households, neighborhood crime was cited as residents' primary concern. Study findings are said to "mirror the incidence of violent crime, which victimizes blacks more than whites and central city residents more than those in suburbs or rural areas."[115] The BJS report noted that a separate survey of state prison inmates found that 43% were serving time for crimes committed in their own neighborhoods.

Finally, in any discussion of race and crime, one caveat that was alluded to earlier needs to be stressed. It has to do with the fact that racial identity is not always well defined and is frequently subject to personal and social interpretation. This appears to be especially true in the case of mixed-race individuals, for whom the concept of "race" itself may have lost all meaning. Hence as the American population becomes more biologically and culturally homogeneous, categorizing offenders on the basis of race may prove far less meaningful for analytical purposes.

Social Class and Crime

Prior to 1960, criminologists generally assumed that a correlation existed between social class and crime. They believed that members of lower social classes were more prone to commit crime, and they thought that this propensity applied to all types of criminal activity. In the early 1960s, however, studies of the relationship between social class and crime, which made use of offender self-reports, seemed to show that the relationship between social class and criminality was an artifact of discretionary practices within the criminal justice system.[116] Such studies, especially of teenagers, found that rates of self-reported delinquency and criminality were fairly consistent across various social classes within American society. Similar studies of white-collar criminality (which is discussed in more detail in Chapter 12) seemed to show that although the nature of criminal activity may vary between classes, members of all social classes have nearly equal tendencies toward criminality. Hence the apparent penchant for crime among members of the lower social classes was explained away as a consequence of discretionary decisions by police officers, prosecutors, and judges—decisions that discriminated against those with lower social status and that resulted in such individuals being arrested, found guilty, and sentenced to imprisonment much more frequently than members of other classes.

In 1978, a comprehensive reevaluation of 35 previous studies of the relationship between social class and crime concluded that previously claimed links were nonexistent.[117] Publication of the 1978 report fueled further study of the relationship between social class and crime, and in 1981, a seminal article by Australian criminologist **John Braithwaite**—who summarized the results of 224 previous studies on the subject—concluded rather convincingly that members of lower social classes were indeed more prone to commit crime.[118] In contrast to earlier studies, Braithwaite found that "socioeconomic status is one of the very few correlates of criminality which can be taken, on balance, as persuasively supported by a large body of empirical evidence."

Many of the difficulties surrounding research into the relationship between social class and crime appear to stem from a lack of definitional clarity. In the many different studies evaluated by Braithwaite, for example, neither crime nor class were uniformly defined. Margaret Farnworth, Terence P. Thornberry, Marvin D. Krohn,[119] and others have similarly suggested that earlier studies may have been seriously flawed by their near-exclusive focus on young people and by their conceptualization of crime in terms of relatively minor offenses (truancy, vandalism, and so on). Hence a lack of concise definitions of the subject matter, combined with inadequate measurement techniques, may have led to misleading results.

More recent data provided by the National Youth Survey[120] and analytical techniques which define *class* based on a status-attainment model using indicators of sustained underclass status[121] and which define *delinquency* as repeated involvement in more serious street crimes[122] have led researchers to conclude that a fairly significant correlation between criminality and social class exists.[123] Therefore, although it would be grossly unfair to conclude that all, or even most, members of lower social classes are criminals, careful statistical analysis of available information appears to show that street crimes, including crimes of violence, theft, and drug abuse, are more likely to be perpetrated by individuals with low socioeconomic status.[124] Such findings have led to the introduction of the "underclass" concept as a way of helping to explain the criminality of those with low social standing.

THE COSTS OF CRIME

Fear of crime and the changes it forces us to make in our lives are important aspects of the overall cost of crime. The total impact of crime on American society, however, is difficult to measure because crime can affect its victims in many ways. Some victims are physically injured and may require medical treatment or hospitalization. Others suffer the loss of valued property or are psychologically traumatized. Still others will miss time from work as they strive to repair lives shattered by crime. The Bureau of Justice Statistics, using NCVS data, attempts to measure the economic costs of crime by assessing two dimensions of total cost: the value of property lost to criminal activity and medical expenses associated with victimization. As BJS points out, however, such data are not all-inclusive. "Medical costs may continue to accumulate for months or years after a victimization," says the bureau.[125] "The victim is not specifically asked about psychological counseling, although some victims may have included this as

TABLE 2-7 ■ **Estimated Economic Losses Due to Crime**

OFFENSE	AVERAGE LOSS PER INCIDENT	TOTAL LOSSES FOR ALL INCIDENTS
Personal Crimes	$218	$4,110,000,000
Rape	234	33,000,000
Robbery	555	680,000,000
Assault	124	649,000,000
Personal larceny	NA	2,748,000,000
Household Crimes	914	13,536,000,000
Household larceny	221	1,750,000,000
Burglary	834	3,970,000,000
Motor vehicle theft	3,990	7,816,000,000
Mean loss, all crimes	**$524**	**$17,646,000,000**

NA—Not available.

Source: Patsy A. Klaus, "The Costs of Crime to Victims of Crime," Bureau of Justice Statistics *Crime Data Brief* (February 1994).

a medical cost. Increases to insurance premiums as a result of filing claims, decreased productivity at work, moving costs incurred when moving as a result of victimization, intangible costs of pain and suffering, and other similar costs are also not included."[126]

According to BJS, victims of major crimes (rape, robbery, assault, personal and household theft, burglary, and motor vehicle theft) lost $17.6 billion in direct costs in 1992. These costs included "losses from property theft or damage, cash losses, medical expenses, and amount of pay lost because of injury or activities related to . . . crime." Estimated economic losses for crimes recorded by the NCVS in 1992 are shown in Table 2-7. A more comprehensive review of the costs associated with all types of crime was conducted by the National Institute of Justice (NIJ) and was reported in 1996.[127] According to NIJ, "Victimizations generate $105 billion annually in property and productivity losses and outlays for medical expenses. This amounts to an annual 'crime tax' of roughly $425 per man, woman, and child in the United States." When the values of pain, long-term emotional trauma, disability, and risk of death are put

in dollar terms, the costs rise to $450 billion annually (or $1,800 per person).

The bureau also notes:

- Economic loss of some type occurs in 71% of all personal crimes, which include rape, robbery, assault, and personal theft.
- In crimes of violence (rape, robbery, assault), economic losses occur in 23% of victimizations.
- Household crimes of burglary, theft, and motor vehicle theft involve economic loss in 91% of all victimizations.
- Lost property is not recovered in 89% of personal crimes and 85% of household crimes.
- Approximately 31% of all victims of crimes of violence (robbery and assault) sustain some physical injury.
- For crimes of violence involving injuries in which medical expenses are known, 65% involve costs of $250 or more.
- As a result of crime, 1.8 million victims lose 6.1 million days from work each year, which translates into an average of 3.4 days of lost work per victimization.

SUMMARY

Crime statistics have been gathered in one form or another for at least 150 years. Although early data about crime may have been used to assess the moral health of nations, modern-day crime statistics programs provide a fairly objective picture of crime in the United States and elsewhere. Statistics often form the basis for social policy, and innovative strategies like the "three strikes and you're out" initiative of the 1990s are frequently based on an understanding of crime patterns provided by such information.

Today, two large-scale government programs collect crime data in the United States. One, the National Crime Victimization Survey, is run by the Bureau of Justice Statistics and provides yearly reports on the criminal victimization of households and individuals. The other, the Uniform Crime Reporting Program (which is undergoing modification via the incorporation of data from the National Incident Based Reporting System, or NIBRS), is administered by the Federal Bureau of Investigation and collects information annually on crimes reported to the police and on arrests throughout the country.

As discussed, the social correlates of crime in the United States include age, gender, ethnicity, and social class. Although crime statistics do not tell the whole story and other forms of crime need to be recognized, it appears from the best information available that young black men are especially overrepresented in American street crime statistics. While some people see this as an indictment of American society, a number of criminologists feel that recognizing the reality of such involvement could help our society secure a safer future for all of its citizens and could enhance effective crime prevention efforts.

Other than age, gender, and ethnicity, social class can be a significant indicator of the likelihood of criminal involvement. Suffice it here to say that crimes are committed by members of all social classes. As we will see in later chapters, however, powerful classes make the laws and are therefore less apt to have need of breaking them, while at the same time they are probably more committed to preserving the status quo. Hence many offenders, especially those arrested for street, property, and predatory crimes, come from the lower social classes.

Some people argue that crime statistics do not justify the degree of concern that Americans express about crime. Others suggest that statistics are misleading and that they do not provide a true measure of the extent of the crime problem in America. Nonetheless, even though the actual incidence of crime is difficult to measure, crime statistics can provide us with an appreciation for the extent of the problems facing victims of crime, social policymakers, and the criminal justice system today.

DISCUSSION QUESTIONS

1. This book emphasizes a social problems versus social responsibility theme. Which perspective is best supported by a realistic appraisal of the "social dimensions" of crime discussed in this chapter? Explain.
2. What are the major differences between the NCVS, UCR, and NIBRS? Can useful comparisons be made among these programs? If so, what comparisons?
3. What does it mean to say that the UCR is summary based while NIBRS is incident based? When NIBRS is fully operational, what kinds of data will it contribute to the UCR Program? How will this information be useful?
4. What is a crime rate? How are rates useful? How might the NCVS, UCR, and NIBRS make better use of rates?
5. Why don't victims report crimes to the police? Which crimes appear to be the least frequently reported? Why are those crimes so rarely reported? Which crimes appear to be the most frequently reported? Why are they so often reported?
6. Is the extent of the crime problem in this country accurately assessed by the statistical data available through the UCR/NIBRS and the NCVS? Why or why not?
7. This chapter discusses losses due to crime. Can you think of any ways in which losses due to crime might be measured other than those discussed here? If so, how?
8. This chapter says that black people appear to be overrepresented in many categories of criminal activity. Do you believe that the statistics cited in this chapter accurately reflect the degree of black-white involvement in crime? Why or why not? How might they be inaccurate?

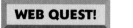

A rich repository of crime and justice information on the World Wide Web can be found at the National Criminal Justice Reference Service (NCJRS). NCJRS makes an excellent starting point for Web exploration in the field of criminology because it is essentially a collection of clearinghouses supporting all bureaus of the U.S. Department of Justice, the Office of Justice Programs and its programs offices, the National Institute of Justice, the Office of Juvenile Justice and Delinquency Prevention, the Bureau of Justice Statistics, the Bureau of Justice Assistance, and the Office for Victims of Crime. It also provides direct links to the Office of National Drug Control Policy, the home of our nation's cabinet-level "drug czar." The NCJRS documents database is one of the most extensive sources available anywhere of online information about crime statistics, crime prevention, and research and evaluation in the area of crime control. The database is fully searchable, and the complete text of many documents is directly available on the Web.

NCJRS provides a wealth of services to an international community of policymakers and professionals in the criminology field. You can be among them by pointing your browser to the NCJRS home page: http://www.ncjrs.org. When you arrive at the NCJRS home page, you will find it arranged by topical areas, each of which is "clickable." The site contains links organized under the following key headings:

- Corrections
- Courts
- Drugs and Crime
- International
- Juvenile Justice
- Law Enforcement
- Victims of Crime
- Statistics
- More Issues in Criminal Justice
- In the Spotlight

Choices listed in the right-hand margin of the page allow users to conduct keyword search of all topics on the site, to review NCJRS catalogs, to see a listing of upcoming conferences in the crime and justice field and to review currently available crime and justice grants.

If your instructor asks you to, explore some of NCJR's features. Conduct a document search on a topic of interest to you, and create an annotated bibliography of selected documents available from NCJRS. Enhance the bibliography with the Internet addresses of Web sites related to the topic you selected.

LIBRARY EXTRAS!

The Library Extras! listed here complement the Web Extras! found throughout this chapter. Library Extras! may be accessed on the Web at crimtoday.com.

Library Extra! 2-1. Bureau of Justice Statistics, *Crime and Victim Statistics* (latest update).

Library Extra! 2-2. David Cantor and James P. Lynch, "Self-Report Surveys as Measures of Crime and Criminal Victimization," *Criminal Justice 2000* (Washington, D.C.: National Institute of Justice, 2000).

Library Extra! 2-3. Federal Bureau of Investigation, *Crime in the United States* (latest update).

Library Extra! 2-4. Federal Bureau of Investigation, *Hate Crime Statistics* (latest update).

Library Extra! 2-5. Beth E. Richie, Kay Tsenin, and Cathy Spatz Widom, *Research on Women and Girls in the Justice*

System: Plenary Papers of the 1999 Conference on Criminal Justice Research and Evaluation—Enhancing Policy and Practice through Research, Vol. 3 (Washington, D.C.: National Institute of Justice, 2000).

Library Extra! 2-6. Terence P. Thornberry and Marvin D. Krohn, "The Self-Report Method for Measuring Delinquency and Crime," *Criminal Justice 2000* (Washington, D.C.: National Institute of Justice, 2000).

Library Extra! 2-7. United Nations Crime and Justice Information Network, *United Nations Surveys on Crime Trends and the Operations of Criminal Justice Systems* (Vienna: UNCJIN, 2000).

NOTES

[1] Arthur Conan Doyle, "The Adventure of the Speckled Band" *The Strand,* February 1892.
[2] James Q. Wilson, *Thinking about Crime* (New York: Basic Books, 1983), p. 251.
[3] Freda Adler, *Sisters in Crime* (New York: McGraw-Hill, 1975).
[4] Ann L. Pastore and Kathleen Maguire, eds., *Sourcebook of Criminal Justice Statistics, 2000.* Web posted at http://www.albany.edu/sourcebook. Accessed January 5, 2001.
[5] A number of contemporary criminologists continue to study the effect of weather on crime. See, for example, Ellen G. Cohn, "The Effect of Weather and Temporal Variations on Calls for Police Service," *American Journal of Police,* Vol. 15, No. 1 (1996), pp. 23–43; Ellen G. Cohn, "The Prediction of Police Calls for Service: The Influence of Weather and Temporal Variables on Rape and Domestic Violence," *Environmental Psychology,* Vol. 13 (1993), pp. 71–83; Ellen G. Cohn, "Weather and Crime,"
British Journal of Criminology, Vol. 30, No. 1 (1990), pp. 51–64; and Derral Cheatwood, "Is There a Season for Homicide?" *Criminology,* Vol. 26, No. 2 (May 1988), pp. 287–306.
[6] NCJRS may be reached at 800-851-3420, or write to National Institute of Justice, National Criminal Justice Reference Service, Box 6000, Rockville, MD 20850.
[7] Federal Bureau of Investigation, *Crime in the United States, 1992* (Washington, D.C.: U.S. Government Printing Office, 1993), p. vi.
[8] Public Law 105-251.
[9] See Association of State UCR Programs, "NIBRS News." Web posted at http://www.asucrp.org/news/index.html. Accessed March 30, 2001.
[10] Federal Bureau of Investigation, *National Incident Reporting System: Volume 1, Data Collection Guidelines* (Washington, D.C.: U.S. Government Printing Office, 1998).

11. JRSA Incident-Based Reporting Resource Center. Web posted at http://www.jrsa.org/ibrrc/more_about/index.html. Accessed March 22, 2001.

12. 28 U.S.C.A. 534.

13. Public Law 103-322.

14. Bureau of Justice Assistance, *Addressing Hate Crimes: Six Initiatives That Are Enhancing the Efforts of Criminal Justice Practitioners* (Washington, D.C.: U.S. Department of Justice, 2000).

15. FBI, *Crime in the United States, 1999* (Washington, D.C.: U.S. Government Printing Office, 2000), p. 59.

16. Web posted at http://www.adl.org/frames/front_islam.html. Accessed December 5, 2000.

17. James B. Jacobs and Kimberly A. Potter, "Hate Crimes: A Critical Perspective," in Michael Tonry, ed., *Crime and Justice: A Review of Research* (Chicago: University of Chicago Press, 1997), p. 19.

18. Bureau of Justice Statistics, *Criminal Victimization in the United States, 1973–92 Trends* (Washington, D.C.: U.S. Department of Justice, 1994), p. 5.

19. For further information, see Ronet Bachman and Bruce Taylor, "The Measurement of Family Violence and Rape by the Redesigned National Crime Victimization Survey," *Justice Quarterly*, Vol. 11, No. 3 (September 1994); Bureau of Justice Statistics, "National Crime Victimization Survey Redesign," *BJS Fact Sheet* (October 19, 1994); and BJS, "Questions and Answers about the Redesign" (October 30, 1994).

20. The President's Commission on Law Enforcement and Administration of Justice, *The Challenge of Crime in a Free Society* (Washington, D.C.: U.S. Government Printing Office, 1967). The President's Commission relied on Uniform Crime Reports data, and the other crime statistics reported in this section come from UCRs for various years.

21. Frank E. Hagan, *Research Methods in Criminal Justice and Criminology*, 5th ed. (Boston, MA: Allyn & Bacon, 2000).

22. As quoted by George Cantor, "The Young and the Ruthless? Predicted Wave of 'Predators' Fuels Debate on Stricter Juvenile Penalties," *Detroit News*, May 18, 1997.

23. See, for example, Jackie Cissell, "Health Commentary: When Birth Control Could Lead to Race Control," *Milwaukee Times Internet Edition*, Sept. 16, 1999. Web posted at http://www.milwtimes.com/articles/oped/09031999/oped25409031999.htm. Accessed December 5, 2000.

24. John J. Donohue and Steven D. Levitt, "Legalized Abortion and Crime," Stanford Law School, Public Law and Legal Theory Working Paper No. 1 (2000). Web posted at http://papers.ssrn.com/paper.taf?abstract_id=174508. Accessed January 10, 2001.

25. John J. DiIulio, Jr., "The Question of Black Crime," *Public Interest* (fall 1994), pp. 3–12.

26. John DiIulio, *How to Stop the Coming Crime Wave* (New York: Manhattan Institute, 1996), p. 1.

27. All of the references to the work of Elliott Currie in this section are from Elliott Currie, "Reflections on Crime and Criminology at the Millennium," *Western Criminology Review*, Vol. 2, No. 1 (1999). Web posted at http://wcr.sonoma.edu/v2n1/currie.html. Accessed February 13, 2001.

28. Some researchers have attempted to estimate the number of crimes that would otherwise be committed by incarcerated individuals. See, for example, Jose A. Canela-Cacho, Alfred Blumstein, and Jacqueline Cohen, "Relationship between the Offending Frequency of Imprisoned and Free Offenders," *Criminology*, Vol. 35, No. 1 (1997), pp. 133–175.

29. "Son Pleads Guilty to Killing Father, Wounding Mother," United Press wire service, Northern edition, February 21, 1994.

30. Although, technically speaking, mass murder could be classified as second-degree murder depending on the circumstances under which it occurs, no cases of second-degree mass murder are documented.

31. For excellent coverage of serial killers, see Steven Egger, *The Killers among Us: An Examination of Serial Murder and Its Investigation* (Upper Saddle River, NJ: Prentice Hall, 1998); Steven A. Egger, *Serial Murder: An Elusive Phenomenon* (Westport, CT: Praeger, 1990); Stephen J. Giannangelo, *The Psychopathology of Serial Murder: A Theory of Violence* (New York: Praeger, 1996); and Philip Jenkins, *Using Murder: The Social Construction of Serial Homicide* (Hawthorne, NY: Aldine de Gruyter, 1994).

32. The state of Illinois later sued Gacy's estate to recoup the money made on his paintings. For additional information, see "State Wants Gacy's Money, Even If He's Dead," United Press wire service, Southeast edition, May 18, 1994.

33. A few years ago, Lucas recanted all of his confessions, saying he never killed anyone—except possibly his mother (a killing he said he didn't remember). See "Condemned Killer Admits Lying, Denies Slayings," *Washington Post*, October 1, 1995.

34. Bureau of Justice Statistics, *Report to the Nation on Crime and Justice*, 2nd ed. (Washington, D.C.: U.S. Government Printing Office, 1988), p. 4.

35. There is no definitive cutoff between serial killing and spree killing in terms of time. Cunanan's three-month spree may qualify him as a serial killer in the minds of some criminologists. Nonetheless, renowned homicide investigators Robert Ressler (a former FBI criminal profiler) and Vernon Geberth (a retired New York commander of homicide investigations and a noted forensic expert) both classify him as a spree killer. (See Michael Grunwald, "Cunanan Leaves Experts at Loss," *Boston Globe* via Simon and Schuster Newslink, July 28, 1997.

36. BJS, *Report to the Nation on Crime and Justice*, 2nd ed.

37. This and other UCR statistics in this chapter are taken from FBI, *Crime in the United States, 1999*.

38. Frank Schmalleger and Ted Alleman, "The Collective Reality of Crime: An Integrative Approach to the Causes

and Consequences of the Criminal Event," in Gregg Barak, *Varieties of Criminology: Readings from a Dynamic Discipline* (New York: Praeger, 1994).

39 "British Law Lords Recognize Male Rape," United Press wire service, Northern edition, July 12, 1994.

40 "Swim Coach Guilty of Statutory Rape," *USA Today*, August 13, 1993, p. 3A.

41 A. Nicholas Groth, *Men Who Rape: The Psychology of the Offender* (New York: Plenum, 1979).

42 See, for example, Schmalleger and Alleman, "The Collective Reality of Crime."

43 This and most other NCVS data are taken from the Bureau of Justice Statistics, *Criminal Victimization in the United States, 1999* (Washington, D.C.: U.S. Department of Justice, 2000).

44 Patrick A. Langan and Caroline Wolf Harlow, "Child Rape Victims, 1992" (Washington, D.C.: Bureau of Justice Statistics, 1994); and Pierre Thomas, "Rape of Girls Too Common, Study Finds; Half of All Victims Are under Age 18," *Washington Post* wire service, June 23, 1994.

45 The occupants of houses may be robbed, of course, by someone who comes to their door. Hence, household robbery is a crime distinguishable from household burglary.

46 FBI, *Crime in the United States, 1992*, p. 27.

47 BJS, *Criminal Victimization in the United States, 1990*, (Washington, D.C.: U.S. Department of Justice, 1991), p. 68.

48 "Luther Campbell Charged for Throwing Woman into Audience," September 12, 1996. Associated press. Web posted at http://www.canoe.ca/JamMusicArtistsT/ 2livecrew.html. Accessed February 13, 2001.

49 Numbers do not total 100% because of rounding.

50 Trudy Tynan, "Chief Killed," Associated Press wire service, February 2, 1994.

51 This is true even though the NCVS does not record burglaries of businesses or commercial properties.

52 Richard Carelli, "Scotus-Cross Burning," Associated Press wire service, March 28, 1994.

53 FBI, *Crime in the United States, 1992*, p. 54.

54 20 USC §1092.

55 Diana Jean Schemo, "Colleges Rushing to Compile Crime Statistics for the Web," *New York Times* online, October 18, 2000. Web posted at http://www.nytimes.com/2000/ 10/19/national/19CRIM.html. Accessed March 1, 2001.

56 H.R. 6. Higher Education Amendments of 1998, Public Law 105-244.

57 The coining of the term "dark figure of crime" is sometimes attributed to Michael Gottfredson. See Michael Gottfredson, "Substantive Contributions of Victimization Surveys," in Michael Tonry and Norval Morris, eds., *Crime and Justice: An Annual Review of Research*, Vol. 7 (Chicago: University of Chicago Press, 1986).

58 Terence P. Thornberry and Marvin D. Krohn, "The Self-Report Method for Measuring Delinquency and Crime," *Criminal Justice 2000* (Washington, D.C.: National Institute of Justice, 2000).

59 See Austin L. Porterfield, "Delinquency and Outcome in Court and College," *American Journal of Sociology*, Vol. 49 (November 1943), pp. 199–208; and J. S. Wallerstein and C. J. Wylie, "Our Law-Abiding Law-Breakers," *Probation*, Vol. 25 (1947), pp. 107–112.

60 Porterfield, "Delinquency and Outcome in Court and College."

61 Some of the wording in this section is adapted from Thornberry and Krohn, "The Self-Report Method for Measuring Delinquency and Crimes."

62 Wallerstein and Wylie, "Our Law-Abiding Law-Breakers."

63 J. F. Short, Jr., and F. I. Nye, "Reported Behavior as a Criterion of Deviant Behavior," *Social Problems*, Vol. 5 (1957), pp. 207–213; and J. F. Short, Jr., and F. I. Nye, "Extent of Unrecorded Juvenile Delinquency: Tentative Conclusions," *Journal of Criminal Law and Criminology*, Vol. 49 (1958), pp. 296–302.

64 Some of the wording in this section is adapted from Thornberry and Krohn, "The Self-Report Method for Measuring Delinquency and Crime."

65 F. Ivan Nye, James F. Short, Jr., and Virgil Olson, "Socioeconomic Status and Delinquent Behavior." *American Journal of Sociology* Vol. 63 (January 1958), pp. 381–389.

66 See, for example, Delbert S. Elliott, David Huizinga, and Suzanne S. Ageton, *Explaining Delinquency and Drug Use* (Newbury Park, CA: Sage, 1985).

67 Lloyd D. Johnston, Patrick M. O'Malley and Jerald G. Bachman, *National Survey Results on Drug Use from the Monitoring the Future Study, 1975–1995* (Rockville, MD: U.S. Department of Health and Human Services, 1996).

68 BJS, *Criminal Victimization in the United States, 1990*, p. 100.

69 Ibid., pp. 100–101.

70 For an excellent overview of the social dimensions of crime, see John Hagan and Ruth D. Peterson, *Crime and Inequality* (Stanford, CA: Stanford University Press, 1995); and James W. Messerschmidt, *Crime as Structured Action: Gender, Race, Class and Crime in the Making* (Thousand Oaks, CA: Sage, 1997).

71 Alfred Blumstein, "Violence by Young People: Why the Deadly Nexus?" *National Institute of Justice Journal*, No. 229 (August 1995).

72 John J. DiIulio, Jr., "The Question of Black Crime," *Public Interest* (fall 1994), pp. 3–12.

73 James Alan Fox, *Trends in Juvenile Violence: A Report to the United States Attorney General on Current and Future Rates of Juvenile Offending* (Boston: Northeastern University Press, 1996); and Gary Fields, "Youth Violent Crime Falls 9.2%," *USA Today*, October 3–5, 1997, p. 1A (quoting James Fox).

74 James Q. Wilson and Joan Petersilia, *Crime* (San Francisco, CA: Institute for Contemporary Studies Press, 1995).

75 Ibid.

76 Fox, *Trends in Juvenile Violence*.

77 Wilson and Petersilia, *Crime*.

[78] Council on Crime in America, *The State of Violent Crime in America: A First Report of the Council on Crime in America* (Washington, D.C.: New Citizenship Project, 1996).

[79] Fox, *Trends in Juvenile Violence.*

[80] Blumstein, "Violence by Young People."

[81] Travis Hirschi and Michael Gottfredson, "Age and the Explanation of Crime," *American Journal of Sociology,* Vol. 89 (1983), pp. 552–84.

[82] Edna Buchanan, "You're Under Arrest," *New Choices for Retirement Living,* June 1994, p. 61.

[83] U.S. Department of Justice, *Elderly Crime Victims* (Washington, D.C.: Bureau of Justice Statistics, March 1994).

[84] Ibid.

[85] BJS, *Age Patterns of Serious Violent Crime* (Washington, D.C.: U.S. Department of Justice, September 1997).

[86] For an excellent review of homicide and the elderly, see James Alan Fox and Jack Levin, "Homicide against the Elderly: A Research Note," *Criminology,* Vol. 29, No. 2 (May 1994), pp. 317–327.

[87] U.S. Department of Justice, *Elderly Crime Victims.*

[88] Mel E. Weith, "Elder Abuse: A National Tragedy," *FBI Law Enforcement Bulletin,* February 1994, pp. 24–26.

[89] U.S. Congress, House Subcommittee on Human Services, Select Committee on Aging, *Elder Abuse: An Assessment of the Federal Response,* 101st Congress, 1st Session, June 7, 1989.

[90] Stephen E. Brown, Finn-Aage Esbensen, and Gilbert Geis, *Criminology: Explaining Crime and Its Context,* 2nd ed. (Cincinnati: Anderson, 1996), p. 198.

[91] Leanne Fiftal Alarid et al., "Women's Roles in Serious Offenses: A Study of Adult Felons," *Justice Quarterly,* Vol. 13, No. 3 (September 1996), p. 431.

[92] U.S. Department of Justice, *Elderly Crime Victims,* p. 4.

[93] NCVS data show that the rate of rape has dropped somewhat over the past two decades even though the number of such crimes reported to the police has increased. Generally, UCR data are probably more reliable than NCVS data where rape is concerned because the NCVS's use of a redesigned questionnaire has thrown the reliability of NCVS rape data into question. In fact, for 1992, the number of rapes reported to the police (UCR data) exceeded the number of estimated rape victimizations (NCVS data) for the first time since recordkeeping began. See Kathleen Maguire and Ann L. Pastore, eds., *Sourcebook of Criminal Justice Statistics, 1993* (Washington, D.C.: U.S. Superintendent of Documents, 1994), Table 3.26, for additional information.

[94] The Violence against Women Act (VAWA) is Title IV of the Violent Crime Control and Law Enforcement Act of 1994 (Public Law 103-322).

[95] Patricia Tjaden and Nancy Thoennes, *Extent, Nature, and Consequences of Intimate Partner Violence: Findings from the National Violence against Women Survey* (Washington, D.C.: National Institute of Justice, July 2000).

[96] Beth E. Richie, Kay Tsenin, and Cathy Spatz Widom, *Research on Women and Girls in the Justice System* (Washington, D.C.: National Institute of Justice, September 2000).

[97] Reprinted in "For the Record," *Washington Post* wire service, March 3, 1994.

[98] Population Estimates Program, Population Division of the U.S. Census Bureau, *Resident Population Estimates of the U.S.,* January 1, 2000. Web posted at http://www.census.gov/population/www/estimates/uspop.html. Accessed February 23, 2001.

[99] For a good overview of the issues, see Dee Cook and Barbara Hudson, *Racism and Criminology* (Thousand Oaks, CA: Sage, 1993).

[100] Marvin D. Free, Jr., *African-Americans and the Criminal Justice System* (New York: Garland, 1996).

[101] William Wilbanks, *The Myth of a Racist Criminal Justice System* (Monterey, CA: Brooks/Cole, 1987).

[102] William Wilbanks, "The Myth of a Racist Criminal Justice System," *Criminal Justice Research Bulletin,* Vol. 3, No. 5 (Huntsville, TX: Sam Houston State University, 1987), p. 2.

[103] Ibid., p. 5.

[104] Ibid., p. 3.

[105] Jim Abrams, "Gun Crimes," Associated Press wire service, April 12, 1997.

[106] Wilbanks, "The Myth of a Racist Criminal Justice System," p. 2.

[107] *African-Americans and the Criminal Justice System.*

[108] John Hagan and Ruth D. Peterson, *Crime and Inequality* (Stanford, CA: Stanford University Press, 1995).

[109] Coramae Richey Mann, "The Reality of a Racist Criminal Justice System," in Barry W. Hancock and Paul M. Sharp, eds., *Criminal Justice in America: Theory, Practice and Policy* (Upper Saddle River, NJ: Prentice Hall, 1996), pp. 51–59.

[110] Paul Glastris and Jeannye Thornton, "A New Civil Rights Frontier: After His Own Home and Neighborhood Were Invaded by Street Punks, Jesse Jackson Dedicated Himself to Battling Black-on-Black Crime," *U.S. News and World Report,* January 17, 1994, p. 38.

[111] Ibid.

[112] Robert L. Carter, "The Criminal Justice System Is Infected with Racism," *Vital Speeches of the Day,* Vol. 62, No. 10 (March 1, 1996), pp. 290–293.

[113] Steven R. Doonziger, ed., *The Real War on Crime: The Report of the National Criminal Justice Commission* (New York: Harper Perennial, 1996), p. 128.

[114] Michael J. Sniffen, "Crime Fear," Associated Press wire service, Northern edition, June 20, 1994.

[115] Ibid.

[116] For a good review of the issues involved, see John Hagan, *Structural Criminology* (New Brunswick, NJ: Rutgers University Press, 1989).

[117] Charles R. Tittle, Wayne Villemez, and Douglas Smith, "The Myth of Social Class and Criminality: An Empirical

Assessment of the Empirical Evidence," *American Sociological Review*, Vol. 43, No. 5 (1978), pp. 643–656; see also Charles R. Tittle, "Social Class and Criminality," *Social Forces*, Vol. 56, No. 2 (1977), pp. 474–502.

[118] John Braithwaite, "The Myth of Social Class and Criminality Reconsidered," *American Sociological Review*, Vol. 46, No. 1 (1981), pp. 36–57.

[119] Margaret Farnworth, Terence P. Thornberry, and Marvin D. Krohn, "Measurement in the Study of Class and Delinquency: Integrating Theory and Research," *Journal of Research in Crime and Delinquency*, Vol. 31, No. 1 (1994), pp. 32–61.

[120] The National Youth Survey (NYS) begun in 1976, first reported results in 1977. It is headquartered at the University of Colorado.

[121] See, for example, Delbert S. Elliott, "Serious Violent Offenders: Onset, Developmental Course, and Termination—The American Society of Criminology 1993 Presidential Address," *Criminology*, Vol. 32, No. 1 (1994), pp. 1–21; and Delbert S. Elliott and Suzanne S. Ageton, "Reconciling Race and Class Differences in Self-Reported and Official Estimates of Delinquency," *American Sociological Review*, Vol. 45, No. 1 (1980), pp. 95–100.

[122] Such as research conducted by Farnworth, Thornberry, and Krohn, "Measurement in the Study of Class and Delinquency."

[123] International studies are similarly supportive. See, for example, Per Olof H. Wikstrom, "Housing Tenure, Social Class and Offending: The Individual-Level Relationship in Childhood and Youth," *Criminal Behaviour and Mental Health*, Vol. 1, No. 1 (1991), pp. 69–89; and William R. Smith, *Social Structure, Family Structure, Child Rearing, and Delinquency: Another Look* (Stockholm: University of Stockholm, 1991).

[124] See also Nicole H. Rafter, "Crime and the Family," *Women and Criminal Justice*, Vol. 1, No. 2 (1990), pp. 73–86; and Margaret Farnworth, *Social Background and the Early Onset of Delinquency: Exploring the Utility of Various Indicators of Social Class Background* (Albany, NY: Hindelang Criminal Justice Research Center, 1990).

[125] Patsy A. Klaus, "The Costs of Crime to Victims of Crime," Bureau of Justice Statistics Crime Data Brief, February 1994.

[126] Ibid.

[127] National Institute of Justice, "The Extent and Costs of Crime Victimization: A New Look," January 1996.

Criminological research is most frequently concerned with the discovery of the causes of crime and the effect of various methods of treatment.

—Hermann Mannheim[1]

Researchers always say that more money is needed for research. But let me point out that the nation's budget for research on violence is considerably less than one-half what the federal government will spend this year on mohair price subsidies. Nothing against goats, but a shortage of fuzzy sweaters is not what is keeping people behind locked doors at night.

—John Monahan[2]

research methods and theory development

CHAPTER 3

The cardinal principle of experimentation is that we must accept the outcome whether or not it is to our liking.

—Abraham Kaplan[3]

It is . . . pathetic to observe how many statistical refinements are wasted on utterly inadequate basic material.

—Hermann Mannheim[4]

KEY CONCEPTS

IMPORTANT TERMS

applied research	internal validity	randomization
confounding effects	intersubjectivity	replicability
control group	meta-analysis	research
controlled experiments	operationalization	research designs
data confidentiality	participant observation	secondary research
descriptive statistics	primary research	survey research
external validity	pure research	tests of significance
hypothesis	qualitative methods	theory
inferential statistics	quantitative methods	variable
informed consent	quasi-experimental designs	*verstehen*

LEARNING OUTCOMES

After reading this chapter, you should be able to
- ◆ Appreciate the relevance of criminological theory to the study of crime and criminals
- ◆ Recognize the role of criminological research in theory development, and display an understanding of various types of research designs
- ◆ Identify research limitations, including problems in data collection and analysis
- ◆ Recognize the ethical considerations involved in conducting criminological research
- ◆ Describe the process of writing a research report, and identify common sources for publishing research findings
- ◆ Identify the impact of criminological research on the creation of social policy

Hear the author discuss this chapter at *crimtoday.com*

INTRODUCTION

On July 11, 2000, a 38-year-old Indiana man named Jay Scott Ballinger, who called himself a "missionary of Lucifer," pleaded guilty to setting 26 church fires over a five-year period that ended in 1999.[5] Ballinger was sentenced to more than 42 years in prison. Ballinger's claim that he was in league with the devil is a perspective popularized in recent years by shows like the *X-Files* and movies like *The Blair Witch Project* and its successors.

Ballinger's self-professed demonic allegiance reminds me of the first criminology class that I taught years ago at a small southern college in the heart of what was then referred to as the Bible Belt. Many of my students were devoutly religious and thoroughly churched in such hallowed concepts as good and evil, sin, salvation, and redemption. When the three-month course was nearly over, and a detailed discussion of biological, psychological, and sociological theories of crime causation had ended, I decided to take a survey. I wanted to see which of the theories we had discussed most appealed to

the majority of my students. On the last day of class, I took a brief survey. After explaining what I was about to do, I started with the question, "How many of you think that most criminal behavior can be explained by the biological theories of crime causation we've studied?" Only one or two students raised their hands. This was a very small number, for the class, a popular one, held 131 students and was taught in a small auditorium. "How many of you," I continued, "think psychological theories explain most crime?" Again, only a handful of students responded. "Well, then, how many of you feel sociological theories offer the best explanation for crime?" I asked. A few more hands went up. Still, the majority of students had not voted one way or the other. Fearing that my teaching had been for naught and not knowing what else to ask, I blurted out, "How many of you believe that 'the devil made him do it' is the best explanation for crime that we can offer?" At that, almost all the students raised their hands.

I realized then that an entire semester spent trying to communicate the best thoughts of generations of criminologists had had little impact on most students in the class. They had listened to what I had to say, they had considered each of the theories I presented, and then they had dismissed all of them out of hand as so much idle conjecture—assigning them the status of ruminations sadly out of touch with the true character of human nature and lacking in appreciation for the true cosmic temper of human activity.

That class held a lesson for me greater than any which the students had learned. It taught me that criminological theory cannot be fully appreciated until and unless its fundamental assumptions are comprehended. Until students can be brought to see the value of criminological theorizing, unless they can be shown why criminologists think and believe the way they do, it is impossible to ever convince them that the criminological enterprise is worthy of serious attention.

This chapter describes how criminologists make use of contemporary social scientific research methods in the development of criminological theories. It is my way of showing to those now embarking upon the study of criminology why the modern-day science of criminology has both validity and purpose—that is, to show how it is applicable to the realities of today's world. Were it not, the study of criminology would be pointless, and criminological theorizing would be fruitless and irrelevant. Happily, because contemporary criminology is built on a social scientific approach to the subject matter of crime, criminology has much to offer as we attempt to grapple with the crime problems now facing us. For criminology to bear the fruit of which it is capable, however, it must do more than use good social scientific techniques. To realize its ultimate promise, criminology must become accepted as a policy-making tool, consulted by lawmakers and social planners alike, and respected for what it can tell us about both crime and its prevention. Learn more about research methods in the social sciences at Web Extra! 3-1.

Web EXTRA! Web Extra! 3-1 at crimtoday.com

THE SCIENCE OF CRIMINOLOGY

Over the past century, criminologists have undertaken the task of building a "scientific criminology," as distinguished from what had been the "armchair criminology" of earlier years. Armchair criminologists offered their ideas to one another as conjecture—fascinating "theories" that could be debated (and sometimes were) ad nauseam. Although the ruminations of armchair criminologists may have achieved a considerable degree of popular acclaim through (1) the involvement of distinguished lecturers, (2) the association of such ideas with celebrated bastions of higher learning, and (3) their publication in prestigious essays, they were rarely founded on anything other than mere speculation.

The ideas of armchair criminologists followed in the intellectual tradition of Medieval Christian Theologians who sometimes busied themselves with debates over questions like how many angels could fit on the head of a pin or whether Noah had forgotten to take certain types of insects aboard the ark. They were the kinds of things one could probably never know with certainty, no matter how much the ideas were debated. Under such circumstances, one person's theory was another's fact and still another's wishful thinking.[6]

Although it is easy to dispense with armchair criminology as the relaxed musings of carefree intellectuals undertaken almost as sport, it is far more difficult to agree on the criteria necessary to move any undertaking into the realm of serious scientific endeavor. Present-day criminology is decidedly more scientific, however, than its intellectual predecessor—which means that it is amenable to objective scrutiny and systematic testing. In fact, the drive to make criminology "scientific" has been a conscious one, beginning with many of the approaches discussed in Chapter 5.

A variety of criteria have been advanced for declaring any endeavor "scientific." Among them are these:[7]

- The systematic collection of related facts (as in the building of a database)
- An emphasis on the availability and application of the scientific method
- "The existence of general laws, a field for experiment or observation . . . and control of academic discourse by practical application"
- "The fact that it has been . . . accepted into the scientific tradition"
- An "emphasis on a worthwhile subject in need of independent study even if adequate techniques of study are not yet available" (as in the investigation of paranormal phenomena)

Probably all the foregoing could be said of criminology. For one thing, criminologists do gather facts. The mere gathering of facts, however, although it may lead to a descriptive criminology, falls short of offering satisfactory explanations for crime. Hence most contemporary criminologists are concerned with identifying relationships among the facts they observe and with attempting to understand the many and diverse causes of crime. This emphasis on unveiling causality moves criminology beyond the merely descriptive into the realm of conjecture and theory building. A further emphasis on measurement and objectivity gives contemporary criminology its scientific flavor.

THEORY BUILDING

Ultimately, the goal of research within criminology is the construction of theories or models that allow for a better understanding of criminal behavior and that permit the development of strategies intended to address the problem of crime. Simply put, a theory consists of a set of interrelated propositions which provide a relatively complete form of understanding. Hence even if we find that crime is higher when the moon is full, we must still ask why. Is it because the light from full moons makes it possible for those who want to commit a crime to see better at night? If so, then we would expect crime to be higher in areas where there is no cloud cover than in areas where clouds obliterate the full moon's light. Likewise, cities should show less of a rise in crime during full moons than rural areas and small towns, as city lights effectively minimize the impact of the light of the moon. In any event, a complete lunar theory of crime causation would contain specific propositions about the causal nature of the phenomena involved.

There are many ways to define the word *theory*. One cogent definition comes from Don M. Gottfredson, a well-known criminologist of modern times, who writes, "Theories consist of postulates [assumptions], theoretical constructs, logically derived hypotheses, and definitions. Theories can be improved steadily through **hypothesis** testing, examination of evidence from observations, revisions of the theory, and repetitions of the cycle, repeatedly modifying the theory in light of the evidence."[8] Another well-known methodologist describes theories this way: "A theory is a set of related propositions that suggest why events occur in the manner that they do. The propositions that make up theories are of the same form as hypotheses: they consist of concepts and the linkages or relationships between them."[9]

These definitions both have something to offer; however, the definition of the term *theory* that we choose to use in this book combines aspects of both. For our purposes, then, a **theory** is *a series of interrelated propositions which attempt to describe, explain, predict, and ultimately control some class of events*. Theories gain explanatory power from inherent logical consistency and are "tested" by how well they describe and predict reality. In other words, a good theory provides relatively complete understanding, and it is supported by observations and stands up to continued scrutiny.

Theories serve a number of purposes. For one thing, they give meaning to observations. They explain what we see in a particular setting by relating those observations to other things already understood. Hence a simple example of a theory of physics explains the behavior of light by saying that light has the properties of both waves and particles. Such a theory is immediately useful, for although we may have trouble conceptualizing light's essence, we can easily grasp ideas like wave and particle, both of which we experience in everyday living.

Theories within criminology serve the same purpose as those in the physical sciences, although they are often more difficult to test. Few people, for example, can intuitively understand the motivation of "lust murderers" (a term developed by the Federal Bureau of Investigation and popularized by some recent movies)—that is, men who sexually abuse and kill women, often sadistically. Most people, after all, are not lust murderers and therefore lack an intellectual starting point in striving to understand what goes on in the minds of those who are. Some psychiatric theories (discussed in

Chapter 6) suggest that lust murderers kill because of a deep-seated hatred of women. Hate is something that most minds can grasp, and a vision of lust murder as an extreme example of the age-old battle between the sexes provides an intellectual "handle" that many can appreciate. Hence theory building dispenses of the old adage that "it takes one to know one," instead bringing at least the possibility of understanding within the reach of all. Note, however, that although such limited explanations as the one discussed here may provide a degree of understanding, they must still be tested to determine whether they are true.

Theories provide understanding in a number of ways. Kenneth R. Hoover identifies four "uses of theory in social scientific thinking":[10]

1. Theories provide patterns for the interpretation of data. Population density, for example, tends to be associated with high crime rates, and maps showing high population density tend to be closely associated with diagrams that reflect rates of crime. Hence, some theorists are quick to suggest, overcrowding increases aggression and therefore crime. "People," says Hoover, "like to think in terms of images, analogies, and patterns; this helps to simplify complex realities and to lighten the burden of thought."

2. Theories link one study with another. Some years ago, for example, a case study of women's prisons in California found the existence of artificially constructed "families" around which women's lives centered. A similar but later study of a Chinese prison also found that the female inmates there had created familylike groups, prompting some theorists to suggest that women feel a need to nurture and to be nurtured by aspects of social structure and that they carry this need with them into prison. The fact that cross-cultural support was found for the suggestion provided a linkage between the two studies, which tended to lend further support to the suggestion itself.

3. Theories supply frameworks within which concepts and variables acquire special significance. The death penalty, for example, although especially significant to individuals condemned to die, acquires special significance when seen as a tool employed by the powerful to keep the powerless under their control.

4. Theories allow us to interpret the larger meaning of our findings for ourselves and for others. Hence the death penalty has become a moral issue for many Americans today, shrouded as it is in ethical considerations and images of national identity and ultimate justice.

Learn more about the nature of modern social scientific thought and theory construction at Web Extras! 3-2 and 3-3.

Web EXTRA! **Web Extras! 3-2 and 3-3 at crimtoday.com**

THE ROLE OF RESEARCH

More important than the claims made by theories and by the theorists who create them are findings of fact that either support those claims or leave them without foundation. Hence theories, once proposed, need to be tested against the real world via a variety of research strategies, including experimentation and case studies. This is equally true whether the proposed theory is relatively simple or dauntingly complex.

In late 1998, for example, Kim Rossmo, Ph.D., an inspector with the Vancouver (Canada) Police Department, used a simple hypothesis that he had developed through years of experience to help police capture a serial rapist.[11] The rapist had attacked 11 women and had eluded officials for years. Rossmo's hypothesis involved geographic profiling, which extended the belief that most humans—criminals included—are inherently lazy, and—except for a small buffer zone around their home—tend to commit crimes close to where they live or work. Based on this simple assumption, Rossmo created a computer simulation designed to estimate the location of a suspect's residence by assessing the areas where crimes attributable to him had occurred. When Canadian authorities compared probable locations identified by the computer with suspects whom they had already identified as possible rapists, only one name stood out. A comparison of that man's DNA with DNA found in semen recovered from rape victims convinced them that he was the person they were looking for.

As with Rossmo's geographic profiling hypothesis, any theory gains credence if activity based on it produces results in keeping with what the theory would predict. Bernard P. Cohen, a seminal thinker on the subject of social scientific theory construction, tells us that "scientific knowledge is theoretical knowledge, and the purpose of methods in science is to enable us to choose among alternative theories."[12]

Doretha Crawford, center, and Beverly Johnson, left, were tried for gouging out their sister's eyes. Prosecutors claimed that they blinded their sister, Myra Obasi (shown in photo on right) while literally trying to beat the devil out of her because they thought she was possessed. Obasi, who at first supported prosecutors' version of events, later said that she couldn't remember what happened but that Crawford and Johnson had nothing to do with the loss of her eyes. Research helps to establish the validity of our beliefs about crime. How might claims about demonic influences over human behavior be researched? *Ariane Kadoch, The Dallas Morning News (left and center) and Pat Sullivan, AP/Wide World Photos (right)*

CRIME IN THE NEWS
Geo-Profiling: Potent New Police Technique

Picture a small city in eastern Canada whose residents were rarely touched by violent crime. Then, startlingly, a serial rapist began attacking women, injecting a dose of fear into a normally tranquil community.

By the time the assailant sexually assaulted his 11th victim, police were desperate. They compiled a list of 300 possible suspects and prepared to conduct expensive, laborious DNA tests on each one, hoping to match DNA residue taken from victims.

That's when Det. Kim Rossmo got a call.

Rossmo, a detective inspector with the Vancouver Police Department, developed an investigative technique called geographic profiling. Using geo-profiling, police try to trace a serial criminal to his home or workplace by computing distances with geographic clues he's left—such as dead bodies, sites of attacks and other known locations the lawbreaker visited.

Rossmo explained geographic profiling to attendees at the International Association of Crime Analysts here recently, giving criminal analysts a window into one of law enforcement's newest and least-known investigative techniques.

Rossmo's methodology would come in handy on the serial rapist case and many others.

VALUABLE SEARCH TOOL

As part of his doctoral research at British Columbia's Simon Fraser University, Rossmo developed an algorithm—a mathematical model of repeated calculations—that targets serial criminals by the spatial patterns they produce.

Since then, Rossmo's algorithm has been computerized, allowing it to make hundreds of thousands of calculations that pinpoint a criminal's hideout within a fraction of the crime site area.

PRIORITY: DANGER

Rossmo most often gets a call when a serial criminal is on the loose. Since many

agencies—in Canada, the United States and Europe—seek his services simultaneously, Rossmo said he gauges which community is most at risk.

In the eastern Canadian sexual assault case—Rossmo didn't want to divulge the location—his geographic profile turned out to be remarkably accurate. With 300 suspects on their hands, the local police could only look forward to a lengthy period of laboratory testing.

But Rossmo's geo-profiling technique helped the police get their man much more quickly. The Vancouver detective visited crime scenes, read reports, and talked to victims and investigators. He analyzed the data using his computerized algorithm and found a neighborhood hot spot to focus on.

SEVENTH TIME'S A CHARM

Instead of hauling suspects in alphabetically by last name, police matched suspect's addresses against Rossmo's findings and tested those who lived nearest the hot spot's peak. The seventh suspect lawmen tested was a positive DNA match. Police arrested the man and cracked the case.

"If they didn't have geographic profile prioritization, they might've started with Archer and ended with Young," Rossmo said.

LAZY TO A FAULT

Despite its complicated mathematical calculations, geographic profiling is based on a simple theory. Criminologists say most humans—criminals included—are inherently lazy. Just as a person will shop in the grocery store nearest his or her home, a predatory criminal usually picks his victims in familiar areas—except for a small buffer zone around his home, says Rossmo.

Thus, when an arsonist sets a series of fires, police can estimate his whereabouts (usually a residence) by dumping the addresses of buildings burned into the computer and calculating the location most central to the crime scenes.

CRIME AS TOPOGRAPHY

In reality, Rossmo's crime-busting technique is more complex. He walks through crime scenes, conducts interviews and reads police reports. With years of investigative experience under his belt, Rossmo puts emphasis on certain locations based on his psychological assumptions about the quarry. At the same time, he discards or discounts other locations that he believes might skew his findings.

Rossmo then keys his data into the computer. The machine converts street addresses into latitudinal and longitudinal coordinates and creates a three-dimensional "jeopardy surface" or topographical model of the data. The jeopardy surface looks like a mountain range, with colored bands of peaks and valleys that show where the addresses converge—the peaks—and where they don't—the valleys.

When Rossmo superimposes the jeopardy surface onto a street grid, the result isn't an exact map to the killer's house, but it's something close to it.

METHOD USED IN 80 CASES

Since 1990, Rossmo has used his geo-profiling technique in more than 80 cases, representing 1,800 crime locations. He believes his work helped crack about half of those cases.

But Rossmo doesn't measure his success only by cases cleared. He's interested in geographic accuracy.

In cases where an arrest has been made, Rossmo's been able to estimate the location of the offender's home within the top five percent of the search area. That means, if police believe the offender lives somewhere within a 10-square-mile area, Rossmo can tell investigators which half-square-mile section to search.

In some cases, he's more accurate. In the Canadian rapist investigation described above, Rossmo's suspect lived within the first 2.2 percent of the area searched.

(continued from previous page)

The more a criminal strikes, the more clues Rossmo can enter into his computer. Theoretically, that makes his predictions more accurate. But Rossmo's computer doesn't spit out a name and address. After the computer does its thing, Rossmo writes a report suggesting strategies for capture.

"It's the investigator that solves the case. Our role is to support him or her," Rossmo said.

COPS, MEET RIGEL

Rossmo's algorithm has been incorporated into a software program called Rigel, manufactured by the Vancouver firm Environmental Criminology Research Inc. (ECRI). Rossmo is a member of ECRI's board of directors and acts as the company's chief scientist.

Currently, Rigel runs only on a Sun Microsystems UltraSparc workstation. But ECRI is reprogramming it for use on Windows NT workstations and servers.

The software isn't cheap—ECRI president Barry Dalziel priced a copy at $70,000, which includes some training and help with installation.

Rigel, emphasized Dalziel, isn't perfect. For best results, it should be used by a police investigator or crime analyst who undergoes a year of training, some of it under Rossmo's personal tutelage.

"If it sends them off on a wild goose chase, police investigators aren't likely to use the system again," said Dalziel.

IT'S A CANADIAN THING

Besides Rossmo's Vancouver Police, two other agencies have been trained in geographic profiling with Rigel: The Royal Canadian Mounted Police, Canada's national police force, and the Ontario Provincial Police. Rossmo said the British National Crime Faculty, another national law enforcement agency, will be certified in 1999.

No U.S. law enforcement agencies are on Rossmo's training list—even though he's been invited to help crack dozens of cases in the States.

THE REAL ROBOCOP

If its geo-profiling uses weren't enough, Dalziel said investigators will be able to use a new version of Rigel to predict a serial criminal's next crimes, including dates and crime locations.

And cops will be able to predict and monitor the likely "hunting grounds" of paroled sex offenders by plotting past crime data and behavioral traits into Rigel, said Dalziel.

"Say there were crimes in that area that matched [a parolee's] M.O., his name would pop up," Dalziel said.

Source: Jim Krane, "Cracking the Toughest Serial Criminal Cases," APB News, December 31, 1998. Reprinted with permission.

Knowledge is inevitably built on experience and observation. Hence the crux of scientific research is data collection. Data collection occurs through a variety of techniques, including direct observation, the use of surveys and interviews, participant observation, and the analysis of existing data sets—all of which will be discussed shortly.

Research can be defined as the use of standardized, systematic procedures in the search for knowledge.[13] Some researchers distinguish between applied research and nonapplied, or pure, research. **Applied research** "consists of scientific inquiry that is designed and carried out with practical application in mind."[14] In applied research, the researcher is working toward some more or less practical goal. It may be the reduction of crime, the efficient compensation of victims of crime, or an evaluation of the effectiveness of policies implemented to solve some specific aspect of the crime problem. **Pure research,** on the other hand, is undertaken simply for the sake of advancing scientific knowledge. It "does not carry the promise or expectation of immediate, direct relevance."[15]

Another type of research, secondary research or secondary analysis, can be distinguished from primary research.[16] **Primary research** "is characterized by original and direct investigation,"[17] whereas **secondary research** consists of new evaluations of existing information which has already been collected by other researchers.

Scientific research generally proceeds in stages, which can be divided conceptually among (1) problem identification, (2) the development of a research design, (3) a choice of data-collection techniques, and (4) a review of findings, which often includes statistical analysis.

Problem Identification

Problem identification, the first step in any research, consists of naming a problem or choosing an issue to study. Topics may be selected for a variety of reasons. Larry S. Miller and John T. Whitehead, for example, say that "the choice of what criminologists study is influenced by political decisions,"[18] meaning that the availability of government grant monies frequently determines the focus of much contemporary research in the area of crime. It may also be that private foundation monies have become available to support studies in a specific area. Or perhaps the researcher has a personal interest in a particular issue and wants to learn more, or maybe a professor or teacher has assigned a research project as part of the requirements for a class. Whatever the reason for beginning research, however, the way in which a research problem is stated will help narrow the research focus and will serve as a guide to the formulation of data-gathering strategies.

Although some criminological research undertaken today is purely descriptive, the bulk of research in criminology is intended to explore issues of causality, especially the claims made by theories purporting to explain criminal behavior. As such, much contemporary research is involved with the testing of hypotheses.

The *American Heritage Dictionary* defines the word *hypothesis* in two ways:

1. "An explanation that accounts for a set of facts and that can be tested by further investigation"
2. "Something that is taken to be true for the purpose of argument or investigation"

Within the modern scientific tradition, a hypothesis serves both purposes. Some criminologists, as mentioned earlier, have observed what appears to be a correlation, or relationship, between the phases of the moon and the rate of crime commission. Such observers may propose the following hypothesis: The moon causes crime. Although this is a useful starting hypothesis, it needs to be further refined before it can be tested. Specifically, the concepts contained within the hypothesis must be translated into measurable variables. A **variable** is simply a concept that can undergo measurable changes.

Scientific precedent holds that only measurable items can be satisfactorily tested. The process of turning a simple hypothesis into one that is testable is called **operationalization.** An operationalized hypothesis is one that is stated in such a way as to facilitate measurement. It is specific in its terms and in the linkages it proposes. We might, for example, move a step further toward both measurability and specificity in our hypothesis about the relationship between the moon and crime by restating it as follows: Rates of murder, rape, robbery, and assault rise when the moon's fullness increases and are highest when the moon is fullest. Now we have specified what we mean by crime (that is, murder, rape, robbery, and assault), rates of which can be calculated. The degree of the moon's fullness can also be measured. Once we have operationalized a hypothesis and made the concepts it contains measurable, those concepts have, in effect, become variables.

Now that the concepts within our hypothesis are measurable, we can test the hypothesis itself. That is to say, we can observe what happens to crime rates as the moon approaches fullness, as well as what happens when the moon is full, and see whether our observations support our hypothesis. As our dictionary definition tells us, once a hypothesis has been operationalized, it is assumed to be true for purposes of testing. It is accepted, for study purposes,

until observation proves it untrue, at which point it is said to be rejected. As two renowned research methodologists have stated, "The task of theory-testing . . . is predominantly one of rejecting inadequate hypotheses."[19]

Research Designs

Research designs structure the research process. They provide a kind of road map to the logic inherent in one's approach to a research problem. They also serve as guides to the systematic collection of data. **Research designs** consist of the logic and structure inherent in any particular approach to data gathering.

A simple study, for example, might be designed to test the assertion that the consumption of refined white sugar promotes aggressive or violent tendencies among men. One could imagine researchers approaching prison officials with the proposal that inmate diets be altered to exclude all refined sugar. Under the plan, cafeteria cooks would be instructed to prepare meals without the use of sugar. Noncaloric sweeteners would be substituted for sugar in recipes calling for sugar, and sweetened beverages and carbonated drinks containing sugar would be banned. Likewise, the prison canteen would be prohibited from selling items containing sugar for the duration of the experiment.

To determine whether the forced reduction in sugar consumption actually affected inmates' behavior, researchers might look at the recorded frequency of aggressive incidents (sometimes called "write-ups" in prison jargon) occurring within the confines of the prison before the experiment was initiated and compare such data with similar information on such incidents following the introduction of dietary changes. A research design employing this kind of logic can be diagrammed as follows:

$$O_1 \times O_2$$

A nighttime break-in. Are phases of the moon correlated with changes in the rate of occurrence of certain crimes? It is the job of researchers to determine the validity of such claimed relationships—and of theorists to explain why such relationships hold. *Pictor*

Here "O_1" (termed a *pretest*) refers to the information gathered on inmate aggressiveness prior to the introduction of dietary changes (which themselves are shown as "X," also called the *experimental intervention*), and "O_2" (termed the *posttest*) signifies a second set of observations—those occurring after dietary changes have been implemented. Researchers employing a strategy of this type, which is known as a "one-group pretest-posttest" design, would likely examine differences between the two sets of observations, one made before introduction of the experimental intervention, and the other after. The difference, they may assume, would show changes in behavior resulting from changes in diet—in this case the exclusion of refined white sugar.

Although this basic research design well illustrates the logic behind naive experiments, it does not lend good structure to a research undertaking because it does not eliminate other possible explanations of behavioral change. For example, during the time between the first and second observations, inmates may have been exposed to some other influence which reduced their level of aggression. A new minister may have begun preaching effective sermons filled with messages of love and peace to the prison congregation; television cable service to the prison may have been disrupted, lowering the exposure inmates received to violent programming; a new warden may have taken control of the facility, relaxing prison rules and reducing tensions; a transfer or release of especially troublesome inmates, scheduled at some earlier time, may have occurred; a new program of conjugal visitation may have been initiated, creating newfound sexual outlets and reducing inmate tensions; and so on. In fact, the possibilities for rival explanations (that is, those that rival the explanatory power of the hypothesis under study) are nearly limitless. Rival explanations like these, called by some researchers "competing hypotheses" and by others **confounding effects**, make the results of any single series of observations uncertain.

Achieving Validity in Research Designs

Confounding effects, which may invalidate the results of research, are of two general types: those that affect the **internal validity** of research findings and those that limit the ability of researchers to generalize the research findings to other settings—called **external validity**. Often, when external validity is threatened, researchers do not feel confident that interventions that "worked" under laboratory-like or other special conditions will still be effective when employed in the field. Hence researchers achieving internal validity may be able to demonstrate that diets low in refined white sugar lower the number of instances of overt displays of aggressiveness in a single prison under study. They may not feel confident (for reasons discussed in the paragraphs that follow), however, that similar changes in diet, if implemented in the general nonprison population, would have a similar effect. Most researchers consider internal validity, or the certainty that experimental interventions did indeed cause the changes observed in the study group, the most vi-

tal component of any planned research. Without it, considerations of external validity become irrelevant. Factors that routinely threaten the internal validity of a design for research are said to include[20]

- *History:* specific events that occur between the first and second observations, which may affect measurement. The examples given in the prison study described earlier (the arrival of a new minister or a new warden, for example) are all applicable here.
- *Maturation:* processes occurring within the respondents or subjects that operate as a result of the passage of time. Fatigue and decreases in response time due to age are examples.
- *Testing:* the effects of taking a test upon the scores of a later testing. When respondents are measured in some way that requires them to respond, they tend to do better (that is, their scores increase) the next time they are tested. In effect, they have learned how to take the test or how to be measured, even though they may not have acquired more knowledge about the subject matter which the test intends to measure.
- *Instrumentation:* changes in measuring instruments, or in survey takers, which occur as a result of time. Batteries wear down, instruments need to be recalibrated, interviewers grow tired or are replaced with others, and so on—all of which can change the nature of the observations made.
- *Statistical regression:* a return to more average scores. When respondents have been selected for study on the basis of extreme scores (as may be the case with personality inventories), later testing will tend to show a "regression toward the mean" because some extreme scores are inevitably more the result of accident or luck rather than anything else.
- *Differential selection:* built-in biases that result when more than one group of subjects is involved in a study and when the groups being tested are initially somehow different. The random assignment of subjects to test groups greatly reduces the chances that such significant differences will exist.
- *Experimental mortality:* a differential loss of respondents from comparison groups, which may occur when more than one group is being tested (for example, one group loses members at a greater rate than another group, or certain kinds of members are lost from one group, but not from another).

Threats to external validity include

- *Reactive effects of testing:* sensitizing effects of initial tests. A pretest may sensitize subjects in such a way that they especially respond to the experimental intervention when it is introduced. Nonpretested subjects (such as those in other locations) may not respond in the same way.

- *Self-selection:* a process whereby subjects are allowed to decide whether they want to participate in a study. Self-selected subjects may be more interested in participation than others, and they may respond more readily to the experimental intervention or treatment.
- *Reactive effects of experimental arrangements:* sensitizing effects of the setting. People being surveyed or tested may know that they are part of an experiment and therefore may react differently than if they were in more natural settings. Even if they are not aware of their participation in a study, the presence of some investigative paraphernalia (such as observers, cameras, and tape recorders) might change the way in which they behave.
- *Multiple-treatment interference:* interaction of multiple exposures or treatments. Sometimes more than one study is simultaneously conducted on the same person or group of people. Under such circumstances, "treatments" to which subjects are exposed may interact, changing what would otherwise be the study's results. Multiple-treatment interference may also result from delayed effects, as when a current study is affected by one which has already been completed.

Experimental and Quasi-Experimental Research Designs

To amass greater confidence that the changes intentionally introduced into a situation are the real cause of observed variations, it is necessary to achieve some degree of control over factors that threaten internal validity. In the physical sciences, controlled experiments often provide the needed guarantees. **Controlled experiments** are those that attempt to hold conditions (other than the intentionally introduced experimental intervention) constant. In fact, some researchers have defined the word *experiment* simply as "controlled observation."

Whereas constancy of conditions may be possible to achieve within laboratory settings, it is far more difficult to come by in the social world, which by its very nature is in an ongoing state of flux. Hence although criminologists sometimes employ true experimental designs in the conduct of their research, they are more likely to find it necessary to use quasi-experimental designs, or approaches to research which "are deemed worthy of use where better designs are not feasible."[21] **Quasi-experimental designs** are especially valuable when aspects of the social setting are beyond the control of the researcher. The crucial defining feature of quasi-experimental designs is that they give researchers control over the "when and to whom" of *measurement,* even though others decide the "when and to whom" of exposure to the experimental intervention.

Sometimes, for example, legislators enact new laws intended to address some aspect of the crime problem, specifying the kinds of crime prevention measures to be employed and what segment of the population is to receive them.

Midnight basketball, intended to keep young people off the streets at night, provides an example of a legislatively sponsored intervention. During debate on the 1994 Violent Crime Control and Law Enforcement Act, midnight basketball became a point of contention, with senators asking whether money spent in support of such an activity would actually reduce the incidence of serious street crime in our nation's inner cities. Unfortunately, no good research data that could answer the question were then available. Now, however, federally funded midnight basketball programs, which have existed for a number of years, might be studied by researchers. Hence although criminologists were not politically situated so as to be able to enact midnight basketball legislation, they are able to study the effects of such legislation after it has been enacted.

Whether criminologists decide on experimental or quasi-experimental designs to guide their research, they depend upon well-considered research strategies to eliminate rival explanations for the effects they observe. One relatively powerful research design that criminologists frequently employ can be diagrammed as follows:

$$\text{Experimental group} \quad O_1 \quad X \quad O_2$$
$$\text{Control group} \quad O_3 \quad \quad O_4$$

The meaning of the notation used here is similar to that of the one-shot case study design discussed earlier. This approach, however, called the "pretest-posttest control group design," gains considerable power from the addition of a second group. The second group is called a **control group** because it is not exposed to the experimental intervention.

Critical to the success of a research design like this is the use of randomization in the assignment of subjects to both the experimental and control groups. **Randomization** is the process whereby individuals are assigned to study groups without biases or differences resulting from selection. Self-selection (when some individuals volunteer for membership in either the experimental or control group) is not permitted, nor are researchers allowed to use personal judgment in assigning subjects to groups.

Control over potential threats to internal validity is achieved by the introduction of a properly selected control group because it is assumed that both experimental and control groups are essentially the same at the start and that any threats to internal validity will affect both groups equally as the experiment progresses—effectively canceling out when final differences between the two groups are measured. If some particular historical event, for example, affects the experimental group and modifies the measurable characteristics of that group, that event should have the same impact on the control group. Hence, in the previous design, when O_4 is subtracted from O_2, the remaining observable *net effects* are assumed to be attributable to the experimental intervention.

In the prison study discussed earlier, randomization would require that all inmates be systematically but randomly divided into two groups. Random assignments are typically made by using a table of random numbers. In this simple study, however, something as easy as the flip of a coin should suffice. One group (the experimental group), would no longer receive refined white sugar in their diets, while the other (the control group) would continue eating as before. Because, with this one exception in diet, both groups would continue to be exposed to the same environment, it can be assumed that any other influences on the level of violence within the prison will cancel out when final measurements are taken and that measurable differences in violence between the two groups can be attributed solely to the effects of the experimental variable (in this case, of course, removal of sugar from the diet).

Techniques of Data Collection

It is the combination of (1) hypothesis building, (2) operationalization, and (3) systematic observation in the service of hypothesis testing that has made modern-day criminology scientific and that has facilitated scientific theory building within the field. Hence once a research problem has been identified, concepts have been made measurable, and a research design has been selected, investigators must then decide on the type of data to be gathered and the techniques of data gathering they wish to employ. Ultimately, all research depends on the use of techniques to gather information, or data, for eventual analysis. Like research designs, which structure a researcher's approach to a problem, data-gathering strategies provide approaches to the accumulation of information needed for analysis to occur.

Many first-time researchers select data-gathering techniques on the basis of ease or simplicity. Some choose according to cost or the amount of time the techniques require. The most important question to consider when beginning to gather information, however, is whether the data-gathering strategy selected will produce information in a usable form. The kind of information needed depends, of course, on the questions to be answered. Surveys of public opinion as to the desirability of the death penalty, for example, cannot address issues of the punishment's effectiveness as a crime control strategy.

Five major data-gathering strategies typify research in the field of criminology: surveys, case studies, participant observation, self-reporting, and secondary analysis.

Surveys

Survey research typically involves the use of questionnaires. Respondents may be interviewed in person or over the telephone or queried via e-mail or fax. Mail surveys are common, although they tend to have a lower response rate than other types of social surveys. The information produced through the use of questionnaires is referred to as "survey data." Survey data provide the lifeblood of polling companies like Gallup, CNN, and Roper, which gather data on public opinion, voting preferences, and so forth. Similarly, U.S. Census Bureau data are gathered by survey takers who are trained periodically for that purpose. Survey data also inform the National Crime Victimization Survey (NCVS) and result

in such publications as *Crime and the Nation's Households, Criminal Victimization in the United States,* and other NCVS-related reports produced by the Bureau of Justice Statistics. Surveys have also been used in criminology to assess fear of crime and attitudes toward the police and to discover the extent of unreported crime.

Case Studies

Case studies are built around in-depth investigations into individual cases. The study of one (perhaps notorious) offender, the scrutiny of a particular criminal organization, and the analysis of a prison camp may all qualify as case studies. Case studies are useful for what they can tell us to expect about other, similar cases. If study of a street gang, for example, reveals the central role of a few leaders, then we would expect to find a similar organizational style among other gangs of the same kind.

When one individual (a "single subject") is the focus of a case study, the investigation may take the form of a life history. Life histories involve gathering as much historical data as possible about a given individual and his or her experiences during early socialization and adulthood. Most life histories are quite subjective because they consist primarily of the recounting of events by the participants themselves. Life histories may also be gathered on groups of individuals, and similarities in life experience which are thereby discovered may provide researchers with clues to current behavior or with points at which to begin further investigations.

Case studies, although they may suffer from high levels of subjectivity in which feelings cannot be easily separated from fact, provide the opportunity to investigate individual cases—an element that is lacking in both survey research and participant observation.

Participant Observation

Participant observation "involves a variety of strategies in data gathering in which the researcher observes a group by participating, to varying degrees, in the activities of the group."[22] Some participant researchers operate undercover, without revealing their identity as researchers to those whom they are studying, whereas others make their identity and purpose known from the outset of the research endeavor. As one criminologist states, participant observation "means that criminologists must venture inside the immediacy of crime."[23]

One of the earliest and best-known participant observers in the field of criminology was William Foote Whyte, who described his 1943 study of criminal subcultures in a slum district that he called "Cornerville" this way: "My aim was to gain an intimate view of Cornerville life. My first problem, therefore, was to establish myself as a participant in the society so that I would have a position from which to observe. I began by going to live in Cornerville, finding a room with an Italian family. . . . It was not enough simply to make the acquaintance of various groups of people. The sort of information that I sought required that I establish intimate social relations. . . . This active participation gave me something in common with them so that we had other things to talk about besides the weather. It broke down the social barriers and made it possible for me to be taken into the intimate life of the group."[24]

It is possible to distinguish between at least two additional kinds of participant observation: (1) the participant as observer, and (2) the observer as complete participant. When researchers make their presence known to those whom they are observing, without attempting to influence the outcome of their observations or the activities of the group, they fit the category of participants who are observers. When they become complete participants in the group they are observing, however, researchers run the risk of influencing the group's direction. As Whyte explains, "I made it a rule that I should try to avoid influencing the actions of the group. I wanted to observe what the men did under ordinary circumstances; I did not want to lead them into different activities."[25] Even researchers who make their presence known, however, may inadvertently influence the nature and direction of social interaction because people tend to act differently if they know they are being watched.

Another problem facing the participant observer is that of "going native," or of assuming too close an identification with the subjects or the behavior under study. Like undercover police officers who may at times be tempted to participate in the illegalities they are supposed to be monitoring, participant researchers may begin to experience feelings of kinship with their subjects. When that happens, all sense of the research perspective may be lost, and serious ethical problems may arise.

On the other hand, some researchers may feel disgust for the subjects of their research. Data gatherers with a particular dislike of drug abuse, for example, may be hard put to maintain their objectivity when working as participant observers within the drug subculture. Hence as Frank Hagan observes, "The researcher must avoid not only overidentification with the study group, but also aversion to it."[26]

Self-Reporting

Another subjective data-gathering technique is one that uses self-reports to investigate aspects of a problem not otherwise amenable to study. When official records are lacking, for example, research subjects may be asked to record and report rates of otherwise secretive behavior. Self-reports may prove especially valuable in providing checks on official reports consisting of statistical tabulations gathered through such channels as police departments, hospitals, and social service agencies.

Self-reports may also be requested of subjects in survey research, and it is for that reason that self-reporting is sometimes considered simply another form of survey research. However, many self-reporting techniques require the maintenance of a diary or personal journal and request vigilant and ongoing observations of one's own behavior by the sub-

ject under study. Hence sex researchers may ask subjects to maintain an ongoing record of their frequency of intercourse, the variety of sexual techniques employed, and their preference in partners—items of information that are not easy to come by through other means or that cannot be accurately reconstructed from memory.

Self-reporting enters the realm of the purely subjective when it consists of introspection, or personal reflection. Introspective techniques, or those intended to gather data on secretive feelings and felt motivation, are often used by psychologists seeking to assess the mental status of patients. Criminologists, however, have at times used introspective techniques to categorize criminal offenders into types and to initiate the process of developing concepts more amenable to objective study.

Secondary Analysis

Not all data-gathering techniques produce new data. Secondary analysis, for example, purposefully culls preexisting information from data that has already been gathered and examines it in new ways. Secondary analysis can be thought of as the secondhand analysis of information that was originally collected for another purpose. The secondary analysis of existing data and the use of previously acquired information for new avenues of inquiry are strategies that can save researchers a considerable amount of time and expense.

One important source of data for secondary analysis is the National Archive of Criminal Justice Data located in the Institute for Social Research at the University of Michigan. In the words of the U.S. Department of Justice, the archive's sponsoring agency, "The Archive continually processes the most relevant criminal justice data sets for the research community,"[27] maintaining information on victimization, various aspects of the criminal justice system, and juvenile delinquency. Access to archive data is by request, and data sets are for sale to individual researchers. Visit the archive via Web Extra! 3-4.

Web **EXTRA!** ▌ **Web Extra! 3-4 at crimtoday.com**

Many other important sources of existing information useful in criminological research can be found in the publication *Directory of Criminal Justice Information Sources,*[28] available in a new edition every few years from the National Institute of Justice. The latest edition contains a summary of information services offered, contact names, phone numbers, addresses, a list of publications produced, and more for 158 criminology-related information sources.

The use of secondary data rarely alerts research subjects to the fact that they (or the data they have provided) are being studied, although they may have been so aware when the data were first gathered. Hence secondary analysis, which constitutes one form of unobtrusive research, is said to be "nonreactive." Although unobtrusive measures include other

Social science research within a correctional setting. Inmate surveys may increase our knowledge of crime causation. Specifically, what might such surveys tell us? Rick *Friedman, Black Star*

forms of data collection, the use of archival records in data analysis constitutes a virtual "goldmine of information waiting to be exploited."[29] Nonetheless, it is important to keep in mind that secondary analysis usually involves the use of information that was collected for a purpose outside of the interests of the current researcher.

Problems in Data Collection

Scientific data gathering builds on observations of one sort or another. Observation is, of course, not unique to science. Individuals often make personal observations and draw a plethora of intimate conclusions based on what they see or hear. Scientific observation, however, generally occurs under controlled conditions and must meet the criteria of inter-subjectivity and replicability. **Intersubjectivity** means that, for observations to be valid, independent observers must report seeing the same thing under the same circumstances. "Do you see what I see?" is a question that highlights the central role of intersubjectivity in scientific observation. If observers cannot agree on what they saw, then the raw data necessary for scientific analysis have not been acquired. **Replicability** of observations means that, at least in the field of scientific experimentation, when the same conditions exist, the same results can be expected to follow. Hence valid experiments can be replicated. The same observations made at one time can be made again at a later time if all other conditions are the same.

In the physical sciences, replicability is easy to achieve. Water at sea level, for example, will always boil at 100° Celsius. Anyone can replicate the conditions needed to test such a contention. When replicability cannot be achieved, it casts the validity of the observation into doubt. Some years ago, for example, a few scientists claimed to have achieved nuclear fusion at room temperature. Their supposed ac-

complishment was dubbed "cold fusion" and was hailed as a major breakthrough in the production of nuclear energy. However, when scientists elsewhere attempted to replicate the conditions under which cold fusion was said to occur, they could find no evidence that the initial experimenters were correct. Replicability and intersubjectivity are critical to the scientific enterprise for, as one researcher states, "science rests its claim to authority upon its firm basis in observable evidence."[30]

It is important to recognize, however, that some observations—even those which stand up to the tests of intersubjectivity and replicability—can lead to unwarranted conclusions. For example, spirit possession, an explanation for deviance that was apparently widely held in primitive times, must have appeared to be well validated by the positive behavioral changes which became apparent in those who submitted to the surgery called for by the theory—a craniotomy intended to release offending spirits from the head of the afflicted person. The actual cause of behavioral reformation may have been brain infections resulting from unsanitary surgical conditions, slips of the stone knife, or the intensity of pain endured by those undergoing the procedure without anesthetics. To the uncritical observer, however, the theory of spirit possession as a cause of deviance, and cranial surgery as a treatment technique, would probably appear to have been supported by the evidence of induced behavioral change.

Some methodologists note that "theories are as much involved in the determination of fact as facts are in establishing a theory."[31] Theories are intimately involved in the process of data collection. They determine what kinds of data we choose to gather, what we look for in the data itself, and how we interpret the information we have gathered. In short, theories determine what we see, as well as what we ignore. In the late

1700s, for example, when a meteor shower was reported to the French Academy of Sciences, observers reported that some fragments had struck the ground, causing tremendous explosions. The learned scientists of the academy quickly dismissed these accounts, however, calling them "a superstition unworthy of these enlightened times."[32] Everyone, they said, knows that stones don't fall from the sky.

Data Analysis

Some data, once collected, are simply archived or stored. Most data, however, are subject to some form of analysis. Data analysis generally involves the use of mathematical techniques intended to uncover correlations between variables and to assess the likelihood that research findings can be generalized to other settings. These are statistical techniques, and their use in analyzing data is called "statistical analysis." Some theorists, for example, posit a link between poverty and crime. Hence we might suspect that low-income areas would be high-crime areas. Once we specify what we mean by "low-income" and "crime," so that they become measurable variables, and gather data on income levels and the incidence of crime in various locales, we are ready to begin the job of data analysis.

Statistical techniques provide tools for summarizing data. They also provide quantitative means for identifying patterns within the data and for determining the degree of correlation that exists between variables. Statistical methods can be divided into two types: descriptive and inferential. **Descriptive statistics** are those that describe, summarize, or highlight the relationships within the data which have been gathered. **Inferential statistics**, on the other hand, attempt to generalize findings by specifying how likely they are to be true for other populations or in other locales.

Descriptive statistics include measures of central tendency, commonly called the "mean," "median," and "mode." *Mode* refers to the most frequently occurring score or value in any series of observations. If, for example, we measure the age of all juvenile offenders held in a state training facility, it may be that they range in age from 12 to 16, with 15 being the most commonly found age. Fifteen, then, would be the modal age for the population under study.

Median defines the midpoint of a data series. Half of the scores will be above the mean and the other half will be below. It may be, for example, that in our study of juveniles, we find equal numbers in each age category. The median age for those offenders would then be 14.

The mathematical average of all scores within a given population is the *mean.* The mean is the most commonly used measure of central tendency. It is calculated by simply adding together all the scores (or ages, in our example) and dividing by the total number of observations. Although calculations of the mean, median, and mode will often yield similar results, such will not be the case with populations that are skewed in a particular direction. If our population of ju-

veniles, for example, consisted almost entirely of 16-year-olds, then the mode for that population would inevitably be 16, while other measures of central tendency would yield somewhat lower figures.

Other descriptive statistics provide measures of the standard deviation of a population (that is, the degree of dispersion of scores about the mean) and the degree of correlation or interdependence between variables (that is, the extent of variation in one that can be expected to follow from a measured change in another). As discussed in Chapter 2 (where the term *correlation* is defined), although the degree of correlation may vary, the direction of correlation can also be described. We say, for example, that if one variable increases whenever another, upon which it is dependent, does the same, a positive correlation, or positive relationship, exists between the two. When one variable decreases in value as another rises, a negative, or inverse, correlation exists.

Another statistical technique, one which provides a measure of the likelihood that a study's findings are the results of chance, is commonly found in criminological literature. **Tests of significance** are designed to provide researchers with confidence that their results are, in fact, true, and not the result of sampling error. We may, for example, set out to measure degree of gun ownership. Let's say that the extent of gun ownership in the area under study is actually 50%. (We have no way of knowing this, of course, until our study is complete.) We may decide to use door-to-door surveys of randomly selected households because cost prohibits us from canvassing all households in the study area. Even if we have made our best survey effort, however, some slight probability remains that the households we have chosen to interview may all be populated by gun owners. Although it is very unlikely, we may, by chance, have excluded those without guns. Assuming that everyone interviewed answers truthfully, we would come away with the mistaken impression that 100% of the population in the study area is armed!

The likelihood of faulty findings increases as sample size decreases. Were we to sample only one or two households, we would have little likelihood of determining the actual incidence of gun ownership. The larger the sample size, however, the greater the confidence we can have in our findings. Hence a positive correlation exists between sample size and the degree of confidence we can have in our results. Even so, in most criminological research, it is not possible to study all members of a given population, and so samples must be taken. Statistical tests of significance, expressed as a percentage, assess the likelihood that our study findings are due to chance. Hence a study that reflects a 95% confidence level can be interpreted as having a 5% likelihood that the results it reports are mere happenstance. In other words, for every hundred such studies, five yield misleading results. The problem, of course, is that it would be impossible to know (without further research) which five that would be!

Learn more about statistics and statistical methods from the American Statistical Association and the American Association for the Advancement of Science via Web Extras! 3-5 and 3-6. Read about statistical tools on the World Wide Web via Web Extra! 3-7.

WebEXTRA! Web Extras! 3-5, 3-6, and 3-7 at crimtoday.com

QUANTITATIVE VERSUS QUALITATIVE METHODS

A few years ago, then–U.S. Attorney General Janet Reno addressed researchers, criminologists, and professors gathered at the annual meeting of the American Society of Criminology in Miami, Florida. "Let's stop talking about numbers," Reno exhorted the crowd, "and start talking about crime in human terms." With her admonition, Reno placed herself squarely on the side of those who feel that there has been a tendency in American criminology over the past half century to overemphasize **quantitative methods** or techniques—that is, those that produce measurable results which can be analyzed statistically. To be sure, as such critics would be quick to admit, a considerable degree of intellectual comfort must be achieved in feeling that one is able to reduce complex forms of behavior and interaction to something countable (as, say, the frequency of an offense). Intellectual comfort of this sort derives from the notion that anything expressible in numbers must be somehow more meaningful than that which is not.

It is crucial to realize, however, that numerical expression is mostly a result of how researchers structure their approach to the subject matter and is rarely inherent in the subject matter itself. Such is especially true in the social sciences, where attitudes, feelings, behaviors, and perceptions of all sorts are subject to quantification by researchers who impose upon such subjective phenomena artificial techniques for their quantification.

One recent highly quantitative study, for example, reprinted in the journal *Criminology,* reported on the relationship between personality and crime.[33] The study found that "greater delinquent participation was associated with a personality configuration characterized by high Negative Emotionality and Weak Constraint." It may seem easy to quantify "delinquent participation" by measuring official arrest statistics (even here, however, official statistics may not be a good measure of delinquent behavior, as many law violations go undiscovered), but imagine the conceptual nightmares associated with trying to make measurable such concepts as "negative emotionality" and "weak constraint." In such studies, even those replete with numerical data derived through the use of carefully constructed question-naires, questions still remain of precisely what it is that has been measured.

Not everyone who engages in social science research labors under the delusion that everything can and must be quantified. Those who do, however, are said to suffer from the "mystique of quantity." As some critics point out, "The failure to recognize this instrumentality of measurement makes for a kind of *mystique of quantity;* which responds to numbers as though they were repositories of occult powers. . . . The mystique of quantity is an exaggerated regard for the significance of measurement, just because it is quantitative, without regard either to what has been measured or to what can subsequently be done with the measure."[34] The mystique of quantity treats numbers as having intrinsic scientific value. Unfortunately, this kind of thinking has been popular in the social sciences where researchers, seeking to make clear their intellectual kinship with physical scientists, have been less than cautious in their enthusiasm for quantification.

Qualitative methods, in contrast to those that are quantitative, produce subjective results, or results which are difficult to quantify. Even though their findings are not expressed numerically, qualitative methods provide yet another set of potentially useful criminological research tools. Qualitative methods are important for the insight they provide into the subjective workings of the criminal mind and the processes by which meaning is accorded to human experience. Introspection, life histories, case studies, and participant observation all contain the potential to yield highly qualitative data.[35]

Consider, for example, how the following personal account[36] of homicidal motivation conveys subjective insights into the life of a Los Angeles gang member that would otherwise be difficult to express:

> Wearing my fresh Pendleton shirt, beige khakis, and biscuits [old men's comfort shoes, the first shoe officially dubbed "Crip shoe"], I threw on my black bomber jacket and stepped out into the warm summer night. I walked up Sixty-Ninth Street to Western Avenue and took a car at gunpoint. Still in a state of indecision, I drove toward the hospital.
>
> I intentionally drove through Sixties' hood. Actually, I was hoping to see one of them before I had made it through, and what luck did I have. There was Bank Robber, slippin' [not paying attention, not being vigilant] hard on a side street. I continued past him and turned at the next corner, parked and waited. He would walk right to me.
>
> Sitting in the car alone, waiting to push yet another enemy out of this existence, I reflected deeply about my place in this world, about things that were totally outside the grasp of my comprehension. Thoughts abounded I never knew I could conjure up. In retrospect, I can honestly say that in those moments before Bank Robber got to the car, I felt free. Free, I guess, because I had made a decision about my future.
>
> "Hey," I called out to Robber, leaning over to the passenger side, "got a light?"
>
> "Yeah," he replied, reaching into his pants pocket for a match or lighter. I never found out which.

I guess he felt insecure, because he dipped his head down to window level to see who was asking for a light.

"Say your prayers, muthaf. . . ."

Before he could mount a response I blasted him thrice in the chest, started the car, and drove home to watch "Benny Hill." Bangin' was my life. That was my decision.

The passage was written by Sanyika Shakur, once known as "Monster Kody" to fellow South Central Los Angeles Crips members. Monster, named for his readiness to commit acts of brutality so extreme that they repulsed even other gang members, joined the Crips at age 11. Sent to a maximum security prison while still in his teens, Monster learned to write, took on the name Sanyika Shakur, and joined the black nationalist New Afrikan Independence Movement. Shakur's prison-inspired autobiography, *Monster*, provides a soul-searching account of the life of an L.A. gang member. The purpose of the book, says Shakur, is "to allow my readers the first ever glimpse at South Central from my side of the gun, street, fence, and wall."

Although Shakur's book is a purely personal account and may hold questions of generalizability for researchers, imagine the difficulties inherent in acquiring this kind of data through the use of survey instruments or other traditional research techniques. Autobiographical accounts, introspection, and many forms of participant observation amount to a kind of phenomenological reporting in which description leads to understanding and intuition is a better guide to theory building than volumes of quantifiable data.

In a seminal 1997 article, Jeff Ferrell uses the term **verstehen** to describe the kind of subjective understanding that can be achieved by criminologists who immerse themselves in the everyday world of the criminals they study.

Criminological *verstehen,* a term derived from the early writings of sociologist Max Weber, means, says Ferrell, "a researcher's subjective understandings of crime's situational meanings and emotions—its moments of pleasure and pain, its emergent logic and excitement—within the larger process of research." Ferrell adds, "It further implies that a researcher, through attentiveness and participation, at least can begin to apprehend and appreciate the specific roles and experiences of criminals, crime victims, crime control agents, and others caught up in the day-to-day reality of crime."[37]   Learn more about *verstehen* at "Max Weber's Home Page" via Web Extra! 3-8.

Web EXTRA!   Web Extra! 3-8 at crimtoday.com

A growing number of criminologists believe that qualitative data-gathering strategies represent the future of criminological research. Martin D. Schwartz and David O. Friedrichs say that this initiative is central to postmodern criminology. As discussed in Chapter 16, postmodern criminology builds upon[38]

- A method that can reveal starkly how knowledge is constituted and can uncover pretensions and contradictions of traditional scholarship in the field
- A highlighting of the significance of language and signs in the realm of crime and criminal justice
- A source of metaphors and concepts (such as hyperreality) that capture elements of an emerging reality, and the new context and set of conditions in which crime occurs

An 18-year-old Los Angeles gang member. Some researchers doubt that quantitative methods can adequately assess the subjective experiences of certain kinds of offenders. What is the nature of such "subjective experiences"? *Jim Tynan, Impact Visuals Photo & Graphics, Inc.*

"The guiding premise here," say Schwartz and Friedrichs, "is that a postmodernist approach enables us to comprehend at a more appropriate level [than the more traditional techniques of quantitative criminology] our knowledge of a dynamic and complex human environment."

VALUES AND ETHICS IN THE CONDUCT OF RESEARCH

Research, especially research conducted within the social sciences, does not occur in a vacuum. Values enter into all stages of the research process, from the selection of the problem to be studied to the choice of strategies to address it. In short, research is never entirely free from preconceptions and biases, although much can be done to limit the impact such biases have on the results of research.

The most effective way of controlling the effects of biases is to be aware of them at the outset of the research. If, for example, researchers know that the project they are working on elicits strong personal feelings but necessitates the use of interviewers, then it would be beneficial to strive to hire interviewers who are relatively free of biases or can control the expression of their feelings. Potential data gatherers might themselves be interviewed to determine their values and the likelihood that they might be tempted to interpret the data they gather or to report it in ways that are biased. Similarly, data gatherers who are prejudiced against subgroups of potential respondents can represent a threat to the validity of the research results. The use of such interviewers may "turn off" some respondents, perhaps through racial innuendo, personal style, mannerisms, and so forth.

Of similar importance are ethical issues which, although they may not affect the validity of research results, can have a significant impact on the lives of both researchers and research subjects. The protection of human subjects from harm, privacy, the need for disclosure of research methods, and **data confidentiality**—which embraces the principle of protecting the confidentiality of individual research participants, while simultaneously preserving justified research access to needed information provided by them—are all critical ethical issues.

To address these and other concerns, both the Academy of Criminal Justice Sciences (ACJS) and the American Society of Criminology (ASC) have adopted official codes of ethics. Concerning confidentiality issues, for example, the ACJS Code of Ethics says that researchers "should seek to anticipate potential threats to confidentiality." The code goes on to say, "Techniques such as the removal of direct identifiers, the use of randomized responses, and other statistical solutions to problems of privacy should be used where appropriate. Care should be taken to ensure secure storage, maintenance, and/or destruction of sensitive records."[39]

The ACJS code also says, "Confidential information provided by research participants should be treated as such by members of the Academy, even when this information enjoys no legal protection or privilege and legal force is applied. The obligation to respect confidentiality also applies to members of research organizations (interviewers, coders, clerical staff, etc.) who have access to the information. It is the responsibility of administrators and chief investigators to instruct staff members on this point and to make every effort to insure that access to confidential information is restricted."[40]

Informed consent is a strategy used by researchers to overcome many of the ethical issues inherent in criminological research. **Informed consent** means that research subjects are informed as to the nature of the research about to be conducted, their anticipated role in it, and the uses that will be made of the data they provide. Ethics may also require that data derived from personal interviews or the testing of research subjects be anonymous (not associated with the names of individual subjects) and that raw (unanalyzed) data be destroyed after a specified time interval (often at the completion of the research project).

Federal regulations require a plan for the protection of sensitive information as part of grant proposals submitted to federal agencies. The National Institute of Justice, for example, a major source of grant support for researchers in the area of criminology, has this to say:[41]

Research that examines individuals' traits and experiences plays a vital part in expanding our knowledge about criminal behavior. It is essential, however, that researchers protect subjects from needless risk of harm or embarrassment and proceed with willing and informed cooperation.

NIJ requires that investigators protect information identifiable to research participants. When information is safeguarded, it is protected by statute from being used in legal proceedings: "[S]uch information and copies thereof shall be immune from legal process, and shall not, without the consent of the person furnishing such information, be admitted as evidence or used for any purpose in any action, suit, or other judicial, legislative, or administrative proceedings" (42 United States Code 3789g).

Some universities, research organizations, and government agencies have established institutional review boards tasked with examining research proposals before they are submitted to funding organizations to determine whether expectations of ethical conduct have been met. Institutional review boards often consist of other researchers with special knowledge of the kinds of ethical issues involved in criminological research.

Participant observation sometimes entails an especially thorny ethical issue: Should researchers themselves violate the law if their research participation appears to require it? The very nature of participant observation is such that researchers of adult criminal activity may at times find themselves placed in situations where they are expected to "go along with the group" in violating the law. Those researching gang activity, for example, have sometimes been asked to transmit potentially incriminating information to other gang members, to act as drug couriers, and even to commit crimes of violence to help establish territorial claims important to members of the gang. Researchers who refuse may endanger not only their research, but themselves. Compliance with the expectations of criminal groups, of course, evokes other kinds of dangers, including the danger of apprehension and prosecution for violations of the criminal law. As one criminologist explains, "Criminological (and other) field researchers cannot conveniently distance themselves from their subjects of study, or from the legally uncertain situations in which the subjects may reside, in order to construct safe and 'objective' studies. Instead criminological field research unavoidably entangles those who practice it in complex and ambiguous relations to the subjects and situations of study, to issues of personal and social responsibility, and to law and legality."[42]

Although the dilemma of a participant observer, especially one secretly engaged in research, is a difficult one, some of the best advice on the subject is offered by Frank E. Hagan, who says, "In self-mediating the potential conflicting roles of the criminal justice researcher, it is incumbent on the investigator to enter the setting with eyes wide open. A decision must be made beforehand on the level of commitment to the research endeavor and the analyst's ability to negotiate the likely role conflicts. Although there are no hard and fast rules . . . *the researcher's primary role is that of a scientist.*"[43]

Hagan also suggests that a code of ethics should guide all professional criminologists in their research undertakings.

This code, says Hagan, would require the researcher to take the following personal responsibilities.[44]

■ Avoid procedures that may harm respondents.
■ Honor commitments to respondents, and respect reciprocity.
■ Exercise objectivity and professional integrity in performing and reporting research.
■ Protect confidentiality and the privacy of respondents.

Hagan's admonition to "exercise objectivity and professional integrity" became especially important in the mid–1990s, when supporters of Project D.A.R.E. blocked publication of research results that showed the program to be ineffective.[45] D.A.R.E., a widely popular antidrug program that is common in the nation's schools, is a favorite of educational administrators because of the funding it provides. The study, a review of most prior D.A.R.E. research, was conducted by the Research Triangle Institute, a respected research firm in North Carolina, and was paid for by the National Institute of Justice (NIJ).[46] When results showed that D.A.R.E. programs did not significantly reduce drug use among student participants, however, NIJ decided not to publish the findings. "We're not trying to hide the study," said NIJ's Ann Voit. "We just do not agree with one of the major findings."[47] In contrast, Research Triangle Institute researcher Susan T. Ennett proposed that results of the study should be used to decide how to spend drug-education money. Other studies have since supported the finding that D.A.R.E. does not have a significant impact on actual drug use, drug-related outcomes, or attitudes toward drugs.[48]

Because criminological research can affect social policy, which often involves the expenditure of public funds, the ethical code of the American Society of Criminology mandates

Project D.A.R.E. participants. A few years ago, studies of Project D.A.R.E. questioned its effectiveness, but government officials decided not to publish the results. How can the objectivity of social scientific research be ensured? *Mark Burnett, Stock Boston*

that criminologists must be "committed to enhancing the *general well being* of societies and of the individuals and groups within them." Thus, says the ASC code, "criminologists have an obligation not to recreate forms of social injustice such as discrimination, oppression, or harassment in their own work."[49]

Learn more about ethics in criminological research directly from the American Society of Criminology and the Academy of Criminal Justice Sciences via Web Extras! 3-9 and 3-10. To read a comprehensive code of ethical standards for general survey research, visit the Council of American Survey Research Organizations via Web Extra! 3-11.

Web EXTRA! Web Extras! 3-9, 3-10, and 3-11 at crimtoday.com

SOCIAL POLICY AND CRIMINOLOGICAL RESEARCH

In 1990, Joan Petersilia used the occasion of her presidential address to the American Society of Criminology to identify how research funded by the National Institute of Justice had affected social policy. Petersilia identified five such areas:[50]

1. Research has shaped the way police respond to calls for service and how they are deployed.
2. Research has helped identify career criminals and has provided information about their behavior, along with suggestions on how best to deal with such people.
3. Research has improved the ability of judges, correctional officials, and others to classify offenders and to predict recidivism.
4. Research has provided useful information about the relationship between drug use and crime.
5. Research has confirmed that no particular rehabilitation program "necessarily" reduces recidivism.

Although research in the area of criminology may have much to offer policymakers, publicly elected officials are often either ignorant of current research or do not heed the advice of professional criminologists, seeking instead to create politically expedient policies. Even when excellent research is available to guide policy creation, a realistic appraisal must recognize that criminologists are as much to blame for counterproductive policies as anyone.

As Robert M. Bohm explained in his 1993 presidential address to the Academy of Criminal Justice Sciences, "Besides powerful critiquing of both existing and proposed policies, many of us have the capability of producing rea-

soned analyses and proposals based on historical, theoretical, and cross-cultural understanding. Yet . . . much of our work is simply ignored because it is not politically expedient or does not serve the dominant ideology. At the same time, others among us are more than willing to do the bidding of politicians and criminal justice officials in order to feed at the trough of political largess. I don't know whether these people actually believe in what they are doing, or maybe they still believe in the myth that their work is objective or value-neutral. In either case, these apologists for the status quo legitimize and perpetuate . . . short-sighted, counterproductive, detrimental policies . . . and do a disservice to our discipline."[51]

Three-strikes laws, which became popular with legislatures across the country over the last decade, provide an example of the kind of dilemma facing criminologists who would influence social policy on the basis of statistical evidence. Three-strikes laws require that felons receive lengthy prison sentences (often life without the possibility of parole) following their third felony conviction. Such laws are built on the commonsense notion that "getting tough" on repeat offenders by putting them in prison for long periods should reduce the crime rate. Logic seems to say that lengthy prison sentences for recidivists will reduce crime by removing the most dangerous offenders from society.

A recent study of the three-strikes laws in 22 states, however, concluded that such legislation typically results in clogged court systems and crowded correctional facilities and encourages three-time felons to take dramatic risks to avoid capture.[52] A wider-based study[53], dubbed "the most comprehensive study ever of crime prevention,"[54] found that "much of the research on prisons was inadequate or flawed, making it impossible to measure how much crime was actually prevented or deterred by locking up more criminals." More significantly, the central finding of the massive study, which was sponsored by the federal Office of Justice Programs and was carried out by researchers at the University of Maryland's Department of Criminology and Criminal Justice, was that current government-sponsored crime prevention initiatives—totaling over $3 billion annually—are often poorly evaluated, leading to uncertainty over whether funded programs actually work. The study, a **meta-analysis** (that is, a study of other studies), reviewed more than 500 impact evaluations of local crime prevention programs and practices throughout the nation. Researchers concluded that due to largely ineffective evaluation efforts which are often only loosely tied to funded programs, "the current [government-sponsored research] plan does not . . . provide effective guidance to the nation about what works to prevent crime." Hence, although the three-strikes laws remain popular with the voting public and lawmakers have been quick to seize upon get-tough crime prevention policies in the interest of getting votes, solid and consistent research support showing the efficacy of such laws continues to be elusive.

THEORY VERSUS REALITY
The American Society of Criminology Task Force Reports

At the 1994 annual meeting of the American Society of Criminology, then-Attorney General Janet Reno appealed to the nation's assembled criminologists for urgent assistance in dealing with some of the major crime and criminal justice issues facing the country. Her address to conventioneers identified 12 important problem areas, and she challenged ASC members to translate existing research findings into useful recommendations that could benefit practitioners and policymakers throughout the nation who routinely confront issues of crime and justice.

Following her presentation, the ASC National Policy Committee formed 12 task forces—one to investigate each issue identified by the attorney general. Task force members were asked to distill research findings into policy recommendations that could meaningfully contribute to public debates which were then raging (and are still continuing) over how best to deal with problems of crime, juvenile delinquency, prison overcrowding, and so on.

In 1997, after all 12 task forces had submitted final reports to the attorney general, the reports were published by the National Institute of Justice and were made available through the National Criminal Justice Reference Service under the title *Critical Criminal Justice Issues: Task Force Reports from the American Society of Criminology*. At the time of publication, Freda Adler, a former ASC president, noted, "Many of the[se] findings have already found their way into the policymaking process; others are likely to follow the same path." Jeremy Travis, then–Director of the National Institute of Justice, termed the reports a "remarkable contribution to improving our understanding of the issues of crime and the challenge of justice."

The following individual task force reports are contained in *Critical Criminal Justice Issues*:

■ Early Prevention of and Intervention for Delinquency and Related Problem Behavior
■ Youth Violence

■ A New Vision for Inner-City Schools
■ Drug Policy Options: Lessons from Three Epidemics
■ Drugs and the Community
■ Violence against Women
■ Domestic and International Organized Crime
■ Designing out Crime
■ The State of the Police
■ A Crime Control Rationale for Reinvesting in Community Corrections
■ Three-Strikes Legislation: Prevalence and Definitions
■ American Crime Problems from a Global Perspective

The task force reports are available in text-only, HTML, and Adobe Acrobat® format from the National Criminal Justice Reference Service's World Wide Web site (http://www.ncjrs.org), and they can be viewed at the *Criminology Today* Web site (crimtoday.com), where the 132-page publication, *Critical Criminal Justice Issues*, is available in its entirety.

WRITING THE RESEARCH REPORT

Following the research and the analysis of data, findings are typically presented in the form of a report or paper in which suggestions for further study may be made. Policy issues, or strategies for addressing the problems identified by the researcher, are also frequently discussed. Charts, graphs, and tables may be included in the body of a research report. Most reports are professional-looking documents prepared on a word processor with a grammar and spelling checker and printed on a laser or ink-jet printer. Some are eventually published in professional journals, and a few become staples of the field—frequently cited works that serve to illustrate fundamental criminological or methodological principles.

Most research reports follow a traditional format which has been developed over the years as a generally acceptable

way of presenting research results. Following are the component features of professional reports.

■ *Title page.* The title page contains the names of the report's authors, their institutional or professional affiliations, the date of the report, and, of course, its title. Many report titles consist of a main title and a subtitle. Subtitles generally give additional information about the report's subject matter. Although some report titles seem all-inclusive, such as

"The Impact of Family Structure and Quality on Delinquency: A Comparative Assessment of Structural and Functional Factors,"[55]

others are relatively straightforward and to the point, such as

"Comparing Criminal Career Models."[56]

■ *Acknowledgments.* Often the author wishes to express appreciation to individuals and organizations that facilitated the study or without whose help the study would not have been possible. Sources of grant support, including funding agencies and foundations; individuals and organizations who either participated in the study or were themselves studied; and people who facilitated various aspects of the study or the production of the report are all frequently acknowledged.

■ *Table of contents.* Reports of any length (say, beyond ten pages) often contain a table of contents. A table of contents helps readers quickly find the needed material and provides structure to the report itself. A good table of contents will reflect section headings within the body of the report.

■ *Preface (if desired).* The purpose of a preface is to allow the author to make observations, often of a personal nature, which might not be appropriate within the body of the report. Reasons for choosing the subject of study, observations about the promise held by the field of study, and wide-ranging statements about the future of criminological research are all frequent topics of prefaces found in research reports.

■ *Abstract.* An abstract is a brief (usually one-paragraph) summation of the report's findings, allowing readers to gauge, without reading the entire report, whether the subject matter will be of interest to them. In this day of modern electronic information retrieval, abstracts serve the additional function of providing a quick synopsis that can readily be made available to those searching large databases containing many research articles. Reproduced here is a concise and well-written abstract from John M. Hagedorn's study entitled "Homeboys, Dope Fiends, Legits, and New Jacks," which appeared in the May 1994 issue of *Criminology.*[57] Note that this abstract concludes with a one-sentence policy observation.

Milwaukee research finds that most young male adult gang members cannot be described accurately as "committed long-term participants" in the drug economy. Rather, most adult gang members are involved sporadically with drug sales, moving in and out of conventional labor markets at irregular intervals. Four types of male adult gang members are described; only one type has rejected conventional values. Despite relatively high average earnings from drug sales, most gang members would accept full-time jobs with modest wages. This suggests that severe and mandatory penalties for cocaine use and sales should be ended.

■ *Introduction.* Most authors write an introductory section as part of their research report. The introduction describes the aim and purpose of the study and provides a general statement of the problem studied. It also furnishes a general conceptual framework for the remainder of the report. The introduction may outline issues related to the problem under study and issues which could benefit from further investigation.

■ *Review of existing literature.* Most research builds on existing knowledge and makes use of previous findings. To cite a few proverbial observations, although it is not true that "there is nothing new under the sun" when conducting research, it is also not necessary to "reinvent the wheel." In other words, the relevant works of other researchers should be discussed in any report, and the bearing previous studies have upon the present one should be explained. Sometimes researchers who are engaged in literature reviews discover that the questions they wish to study have already been answered or that someone else has found a more concise way of stating their concerns. Hence, new investigators can avoid concept development that is merely repetitive and even data gathering that has already been undertaken.

■ *Description of existing situation.* Sometimes a description of the existing situation is combined with a report's introduction. If not, then it is appropriate to elaborate on the problem under study by providing details which describe the conditions existing at the beginning of the study.

■ *Statement of the hypothesis.* Research etiquette in criminology frequently requires the statement of a hypothesis to be tested. Most researchers have an idea of what they expect to find. Often they have set out to test a theory or a proposition derived from a theory. Researchers may, for example, wish to test whether the Brady Law, which limits handgun sales, has effectively met its goal of reducing the number of deaths by firearms. A hypothesis should be a clear and concise statement of what the study purports to test. As mentioned previously, hypotheses useful in guiding research are always operationalized, or expressed in terms that are in some way measurable. Descriptive studies, on the other hand, are not designed to prove or disprove assumptions (although they may not be free of them), and such studies may not contain hypotheses.

■ *Description of the research plan.* The research design, data-gathering strategies, and plans for statistical analysis should all be described here. This section, although it may be elaborate and lengthy, simply provides an overview of the methodology employed by the researcher and explains how the problem was investigated and why particular research strategies were chosen.

■ *Disclaimers and limitations.* All research is subject to limitations. Shortages of money, time, personnel, and other resources impose limitations on research undertakings, as do shortcomings in statistical techniques and restrictions on the availability of data. Limitations should be honestly appraised and presented in the research report so that readers will be able to assess their impact on the results that are reported.

■ *Findings or results.* Along with an overview of the research as it was actually conducted, the "findings" section provides a statement of research results. Many regard it as the heart of the report. The manner in which results are presented can be crucial for ease of understanding. Some researchers choose to employ tables containing raw numbers, when pictorial forms of representation like charts and graphs would better facilitate comprehension. Bar charts and pie charts are probably the most commonly employed types of diagrams, although the type of data collected will determine the appropriate format for its presentation.

■ *Analysis and discussion.* Once findings have been presented, they should be discussed and analyzed. Not all analysis need be of a quantitative sort. However, much of today's criminological literature is replete with statistical analyses, some of it quite sophisticated. Unfortunately, however, poorly conceptualized research cannot be helped by later analysis, no matter how sophisticated that analysis may be. It is therefore of crucial importance to the success of any research endeavor that early planning—including conceptual development, strategies for data collection, and research designs—be undertaken with an eye toward producing data that will lend themselves to meaningful analysis after data gathering has been completed. The analysis section should also focus on whether the data, as analyzed, support the study's guiding hypothesis.

■ *Summary and conclusions.* The summation section encapsulates the study's purpose and findings in a few paragraphs. It may also contain discussion of suggested improvements or recommended solutions to the problem studied based on the evidence produced by the report. Policy implications are also discussed (if at all) in the conclusion of the report, because they are simply broad-based solutions to problems which have been identified.

■ *Appendixes.* Not all reports contain appendixes. Those that do may place sample questionnaires, accompanying cover letters, concise exhibits from literature reviews, detailed statistical tables, copies of letters of support, detailed interview information, and so forth near the end of the document. Appendixes should only be used if they serve the purpose of further explicating the report's purpose, methods, or findings. Otherwise, appendixes may appear to "pad" the report and can discredit the researcher's efforts in the eyes of readers.

■ *List of references.* No report is complete without a bibliography or other list of references used in planning the study and in document preparation. Although all items listed in the bibliography may not be referenced within the body of the report, source material should still be listed if it was reviewed and served some purpose in study development. Literature that is examined, for example, may guide the researcher to other material or may provide useful insights during the study's overall conceptual formation.

■ *Endnotes.* Either endnotes or footnotes may be used to reference quoted sources or to refer readers to supporting documents. Sometimes a combination of footnotes and endnotes is employed. Endnotes, as their name implies, appear at the conclusion of a report (often after the summary but before the appendixes), whereas footnotes are found at the bottom of the pages containing the referenced material.

Writing for Publication

Criminologists often seek to publish the results of their research to share them with others working in the field. The primary medium for such publication consists of refereed professional journals. Refereed journals are those that employ the services of peer reviewers to gauge the quality of the manuscripts submitted to them. Although the review process can be time consuming, it is believed to result in the publication of manuscripts that make worthwhile contributions to the field of criminology and in the rejection of those of lesser quality.

Perhaps the best-known professional journals in the field of criminology today are the *American Journal of Criminal Justice, Crime and Delinquency, Crime and Social Justice,* the *Crime Control Digest, Criminal Justice and Behavior, Criminal Justice Ethics,* the *Criminal Justice Policy Review,* the *Criminal Justice Review, Criminology,* the *Journal of Contemporary Criminal Justice,* the *Journal of Crime and Justice,* the *Journal of Criminal Justice Education,* the *Journal of Criminal Law and Criminology,* the *Journal of Research in Crime and Delinquency,* the *Justice Professional, Justice Quarterly,* and *Theoretical Criminology.* For a comprehensive list of journals in the field of criminology, including some that are Web-based, visit Web Extra! 3-12.

Web EXTRA!   Web Extra! 3-12 at crimtoday.com

Each journal has its own requirements for manuscript submission. Some require a single copy of a manuscript; others ask for multiple copies. A few journals request manuscript files on disk along with hard copies, and still others are moving toward electronic submission via the Internet. An increasing number of journals have established submission fees, usually in the $10 to $20 range, to help defray the costs associated with the review process.

Submission etiquette within the field of criminology demands that an article be sent to only one journal at a time. Simultaneous submissions are disliked and create real difficulties for both authors and editors when articles are accepted by more than one publication. Given the complexities of the review and publications processes, it is probably best to write the editor of any journal to which submission is being contemplated to inquire as to that journal's particular expectations.

Most journals require that manuscripts be prepared according to a particular style, meaning that citations, capitalization, footnoting, abstracts, notes, headings, and subheadings are all expected to conform to the style of other articles published in the same journal. Two of the most prevalent styles are the APA style (the style promulgated by the American Psychological Association) and the ASA, or American Sociological Association, style.

Most criminological journals, however, utilize a modification of one of these styles. When considering the submission of a manuscript for publication review, it is advisable to write to the editor of the journal in question requesting a style sheet or general style guidelines. Style guides are also available from the American Psychological Association[58] and the American Sociological Association, with third-party publishers making style guides available through university and special-purpose bookstores.

If a research report is not intended for publication, other styles may be acceptable. Answers to general questions about report writing and style can be found in publications like William Strunk and E. B. White's *The Elements of Style*[59] and Mary-Claire van Leunen's *A Handbook for Scholars.*[60]

SUMMARY

Criminology—like its sister disciplines of sociology, psychology, geography, and political science—is a social science that endeavors to apply the techniques of data collection and hypothesis testing through observation and experimentation. Successful hypothesis testing can lead to theory building and to a more complete understanding of the nature of crime and crime causation. Although the scientific framework and its techniques have largely been inherited from the physical sciences—such as chemistry, astronomy, and physics—in which they have been well established for centuries, criminology has been accepted into the scientific tradition by all but the most hard-nosed purists. Even so, criminologists are still game to study aspects of the field which are in need of study, even where adequate resources (funding) or techniques (for example,

the complete mapping of all human chromosomes) are not yet available.

Another component of scientific criminology, the detailed description of crime and related phenomena even where meaningful hypotheses are lacking, is also very much with us. In one descriptive area alone, that of crime statistics (discussed in Chapter 2), so much data have already been gathered that it is unlikely they will ever be completely analyzed.

The fondest hope of many criminologists today is that effective research into the causes of crime, coupled with meaningful evaluations of crime prevention efforts, will one day significantly influence social policy mandates, resulting in legislation and government-sponsored initiatives built on programs shown to be effective.

DISCUSSION QUESTIONS

1. This book emphasizes a social problems versus social responsibility theme. How might a thorough research agenda allow us to decide which perspective is most fruitful in combating crime?
2. What is a *hypothesis?* What does it mean to operationalize a hypothesis? Why is operationalization necessary?
3. What is a *theory?* Why is the task of criminological theory construction so demanding? How do we know if a theory is any good?
4. Explain experimental research. How might a good research design be diagrammed? What kinds of

threats to the validity of research designs can you identify? How can such threats be controlled or eliminated?
5. List and describe the various types of data-gathering strategies discussed in this chapter. Is any one technique "better" than another? Why or why not? Under what kinds of conditions might certain types of data-gathering strategies be most appropriate?
6. What is the difference between quantitative and qualitative research? What are the advantages and disadvantages of each?

WEB QUEST!

Visit the world's largest archive of computerized social science data at the Interuniversity Consortium for Political and Social Research (ICPSR) at http://www.icpsr.umich. edu. The ICPSR is based at the Institute for Social Research at the University of Michigan. An important part of the ICPSR is the National Archive of Criminal Justice Data, which began operating in 1978 (http://www.icpsr.umich. edu/NACJD). The three goals of ICPSR's criminal justice data archive are to

■ Provide computer-readable data for the quantitative study of crime and the criminal justice system through the development of a central data archive that disseminates computer-readable data

■ Supply technical assistance in selecting data collections and the computer hardware and software for analyzing data efficiently and effectively

■ Offer training in quantitative methods of social science research to facilitate secondary analysis of criminal justice data

ICPSR brings together the data collections of over 370 member colleges and universities in the United States and abroad. It also routinely receives data from the Bureau of Justice Statistics, the National Institute of Justice, the Office for Juvenile Justice and Delinquency Prevention, and the Federal Bureau of Investigation. As a consequence, the consortium is able to provide access to voluminous amounts of information. UCR/NIBRS and NCVS data are available through ICPSR, as is information on capital punishment, adult and juvenile correctional facilities, and jails; state and federal court statistics; expenditure and employment data for the criminal justice system; and surveys of law enforcement and other criminal justice agencies.

Much of ICPSR's available information takes the form of data sets which are ready for analysis through software packages such as the Statistical Package for the Social Sciences (SPSS) and SPSS PC-plus. A link to the National Archive of Criminal Justice Data is available at crimtoday.com. ICPSR can also be accessed directly at http://www.icpsr.umich. edu/index.html.

If your instructor asks you to do so, read the "Frequently Asked Questions" (FAQ) section within the National Archive of Criminal Justice Data, and prepare a summary of each question and answer contained there.

LIBRARY EXTRAS!

The Library Extras! listed here complement the Web Extras! found throughout this chapter. Library Extras! may be accessed on the Web at crimtoday.com.

Library Extra! 3-1. American Society of Criminology, *Code of Ethics* (November 2000).

Library Extra! 3-2. Academy of Criminal Justice Sciences, *Code of Ethics* (March 2000).

Library Extra! 3-3. Donald R. Lynam and Richard Milich, "Project DARE: No Effects at 10-Year Follow-up," *Journal of Consulting and Clinical Psychology,* Vol. 67, No. 4 (August 1999).

Library Extra! 3-4. *Social Research Update* (published quarterly by the Department of Sociology, University of Surrey, England).

Library Extra! 3-5. Lawrence W. Sherman et al., *Preventing Crime: What Works, What Doesn't, What's Promising* (Washington, D.C.: National Institute of Justice, 1997).

NOTES

[1] Hermann Mannheim, *Comparative Criminology* (Boston: Houghton Mifflin, 1967), p. 73.

[2] John Monahan, "The Causes of Violence," *FBI Law Enforcement Bulletin,* January 1994, p. 14.

[3] Abraham Kaplan, *The Conduct of Inquiry: Methodology for Behavioral Science* (San Francisco: Chandler, 1964), p. 145.

[4] Mannheim, *Comparative Criminology.*

[5] "'Missionary of Lucifer' Admits 26 Church Arsons," Associated Press wire service, July 12, 2000. Web posted at http://apbnews.com/newscenter/breakingnews/2000/ 07/12/lucifer0712_01.html. Accessed October 30, 2000.

[6] As discussed by Piers Beirne and Colin Sumner, "Editorial Statement," *Theoretical Criminology: An International Journal,* Vol. 1, No. 1 (February 1997), pp. 5–11.

[7] Mannheim, *Comparative Criminology,* p. 20.

[8] Don M. Gottfredson, "Criminology Theories: The Truth as Told by Mark Twain," in William S. Laufer

and Freda Adler, eds., *Advances in Criminological Theory*, Vol. 1 (New Brunswick, NJ: Transaction, 1989), p. 3.

9 Kenneth R. Hoover, *The Elements of Social Scientific Thinking*, 5th ed. (New York: St. Martin's, 1992), p. 34.

10 Ibid., p. 35.

11 Jim Krane, "Geo-Profiling: A Potent New Police Technique," *APB News*, December 31, 1998. Web posted at http://apbnews.com/cjprofessionals/behindthebadge/1998/12/31/geoprofile1231_01.html. Accessed October 30, 2000.

12 Bernard P. Cohen, *Developing Sociological Knowledge: Theory and Method*, 2nd ed. (Chicago: Nelson-Hall, 1989), p. 13.

13 Ibid., p. 71.

14 Susette M. Talarico, *Criminal Justice Research: Approaches, Problems and Policy* (Cincinnati: Anderson, 1980), p. 3.

15 Ibid.

16 For a good review of secondary research, see J. H. Laub, R. J. Sampson, and K. Kiger, "Assessing the Potential of Secondary Data Analysis: A New Look at the Glueck's Unraveling Juvenile Delinquency Data," in Kimberly L. Kempf, ed., *Measurement Issues in Criminology* (New York: Springer-Verlag, 1990), pp. 241–257; and Robert J. Sampson and John H. Laub, *Crime in the Making* (Cambridge: Harvard University Press, 1993).

17 *Crime in the Making*, p. 3.

18 Larry S. Miller and John T. Whitehead, *Introduction to Criminal Justice Research and Methods* (Cincinnati: Anderson, 1996).

19 Donald T. Campbell and Julian C. Stanley, *Experimental and Quasi-Experimental Designs for Research* (Chicago: Rand McNally, 1966), p. 35.

20 As identified in ibid., p. 5, from which many of the descriptions that follow are adapted.

21 Ibid., p. 34.

22 Frank E. Hagan, *Research Methods in Criminal Justice and Criminology* (New York: Macmillan, 1993), p. 103.

23 Jeff Ferrell, "Criminological *Verstehen*: Inside the Immediacy of Crime," *Justice Quarterly*, Vol. 14, No. 1 (1997), p. 11.

24 William Foote Whyte, *Street Corner Society: The Social Structure of an Italian Slum* (Chicago: University of Chicago Press, 1943), pp. v–vii.

25 Ibid., p. vii.

26 Hagan, *Research Methods in Criminal Justice and Criminology*, p. 192.

27 Nicole Vanden Heuvel, *Directory of Criminal Justice Information Sources*, 8th ed. (Washington, D.C.: National Institute of Justice, 1992), p. 145.

28 Joyce Hutchinson, *Directory of Criminal Justice Information Sources*, 9th ed. (Washington, D.C.: National Institute of Justice, 1994).

29 Hagan, *Research Methods in Criminal Justice and Criminology*, p. 218.

30 Hoover, *The Elements of Social Scientific Thinking*, p. 34.

31 Kaplan, *The Conduct of Inquiry*, p. 134.

32 As reported in ibid.

33 Avshalom Caspim et al., "Are Some People Crime-Prone? Replications of the Personality-Crime Relationship across Countries, Genders, Races, and Methods," *Criminology*, Vol. 32, No. 2 (May 1994), pp. 163–195.

34 Kaplan, *The Conduct of Inquiry*, p. 172.

35 Of course, as with almost anything else, qualitative data can be assigned to categories, and the categories can be numbered. Hence qualitative data can be quantified, although the worth of such effort is subject to debate.

36 Sanyika Shakur, *Monster: The Autobiography of an L.A. Gang Member* (New York: Penguin, 1993), pp. 45–46.

37 Ferrell, "Criminological *Verstehen*," p. 10.

38 Martin D. Schwartz and David O. Friedrichs, "Postmodern Thought and Criminological Discontent: New Metaphors for Understanding Violence," *Criminology*, Vol. 32, No. 2 (May 1994), pp. 221–246.

39 Academy of Criminal Justice Sciences, *Code of Ethics*, Section 18.

40 Ibid., Section 19.

41 National Institute of Justice, *1994–95 NIJ Program Plan* (Washington, D.C.: NIJ, 1993), p. 21.

42 Jeff Ferrell, "Criminological *Verstehen*," p. 8.

43 Hagan, *Research Methods in Criminal Justice and Criminology*, pp. 31–32.

44 Ibid., p. 42.

45 See Dennis Cauchon, "Study Critical of D.A.R.E. Rejected," *USA Today*, October 4, 1994, p. 2A.

46 See Susan T. Ennett et al., "How Effective Is Drug Abuse Resistance Education? A Meta-Analysis of Project DARE Outcome Evaluations," *American Journal of Public Health*, Vol. 84, No. 9 (September 1994), pp. 1394–1401.

47 Susan T. Ennett et al., "Long Term Evaluation of Drug Abuse Resistance Education," *Addictive Behaviors*, Vol. 19, No. 2 (1994), pp. 113–125.

48 Donald R. Lynam and Richard Milich, "Project DARE: No Effects at 10-Year Follow-up," *Journal of Consulting and Clinical Psychology*, Vol. 67, No. 4 (August 1999), pp. 590–593.

49 American Society of Criminology, *Draft Code of Ethics*. Section II, paragraph 7 (unpublished manuscript).

50 Joan Petersilia, "Policy Relevance and the Future of Criminology—The American Society of Criminology, 1990 Presidential Address," *Criminology*, Vol. 29, No. 1 (1991), pp. 1–15.

51 Robert M. Bohm, "On the State of Criminal Justice: 1993 Presidential Address to the Academy of Criminal Justice Sciences," *Justice Quarterly*, Vol. 10, No. 4 (December 1993), p. 537.

52 The Campaign for an Effective Crime Policy, *The Impact of Three Strikes and You're Out Laws: What Have We Learned?* (Washington, D.C.: CECP, 1997).

[53] Lawrence W. Sherman et al., *Preventing Crime: What Works, What Doesn't, What's Promising* (Washington, D.C.: National Institute of Justice, 1997).

[54] Fox Butterfield, no headline, *New York Times News Service* online, April 16, 1997, 7:06 EST.

[55] Patricia Van Voorhis et al., "The Impact of Family Structure and Quality on Delinquency: A Comparative Assessment of Structural and Functional Factors," *Criminology,* Vol. 26, No. 2 (May 1988), pp. 235–261.

[56] David F. Greenberg, "Comparing Criminal Career Models," *Criminology,* Vol. 30, No. 1 (February 1992), pp. 133–140.

[57] John M. Hagedorn, "Homeboys, Dope Fiends, Legits, and New Jacks," *Criminology,* Vol. 32, No. 2 (May 1994), p. 197.

[58] American Psychological Association, *Publication Manual of the American Psychological Association* (Washington, D.C.: APA, 1994).

[59] William Strunk, Jr., and E. B. White, *The Elements of Style,* 4th ed. (New York: Macmillan, 1999).

[60] Mary-Claire van Leunen, *A Handbook for Scholars,* rev. ed. (Oxford: Oxford University Press, 1992).

crime causation

PART

The need to know *why* people commit crimes is central to criminology. Our need to understand criminal *motivation* differs, however, from our ability to describe crime *causation*. The causes of crime may vary substantially from the reasons a particular offender had in mind when breaking the law. Crime causation involves a wide array of factors, including the shaping of personality by early childhood experiences like poor parenting, conscious and unconscious attempts at peer group emulation, the impact of poverty on people whose lives might be destitute were it not for the opportunities provided by crime, the values and lifestyles learned from those around us, and, quite possibly, fundamental and profound genetic influences on the choices that we make.

At the same time, it is important to consider barriers that might prevent crime, even in the face of strong criminal motivation and in situations where the causes of crime seem firmly rooted in social, economic, and other conditions. Barriers to crime are those aspects of a setting that limit criminal opportunity and prevent offending. Barriers cause would-be criminals to reconsider their intention to violate the law. They can extend to internal strictures by which people limit their own freedom of action, even in the face of strong temptation.

In this part, we consider various theoretical approaches to crime causation, including biological theories (Chapter 5), psychological approaches (Chapter 6), and sociological perspectives (Chapters 7, 8, and 9). As we move through these chapters, we will be examining aspects of the human organism and its physical surroundings, as well as the contents of individual consciousness and the nature of the social environment—and we will always be looking for clues as to what leads to crime. We begin our consideration of theoretical perspectives with Chapter 4, "Classical and Neoclassical Thought"—A chapter rich in historical subject matter that takes us back to the early days of criminological theorizing.

Men have always loved to fight. If they didn't love to fight, they wouldn't be men.
—*General George S. Patton, Jr.*[i]

The only way to get out is to die.
—*Eric Norah, 11, after attending the funeral of classmate Robert Sandifer, killed in a gang shooting in Chicago as police sought him on murder charges*[ii]

---

[i]As cited in David Jones, *History of Criminology: A Philosophical Perspective* (Westport, CT: Greenwood Press, 1986), p. 1.

[ii]"So Young to Kill, So Young to Die," *Time*, September 19, 1994, p. 54.

Nature has placed mankind under the governance
of two sovereign masters, pain and pleasure.

—Jeremy Bentham[1]

The more promptly and the more closely punishment
follows upon the commission of a crime, the more just
and useful will it be.

—Cesare Beccaria[2]

classical and neoclassical thought

CHAPTER

4

The criminal element now calculates
that crime really does pay.

—Ronald Reagan[3]

Society is pressed to its ancient defense against the
violent criminal: the fear of swift and severe
punishment. Either we take that road now, or we will
live in the sickly twilight of a soulless people too weak
to drive predators out of their own house.

—Francis T. Murphy, President of the Federation of New York
State Judges[4]

KEY CONCEPTS

IMPORTANT TERMS

capable guardian	individual rights advocates	recidivism
capital punishment	just deserts model	recidivism rate
Classical School	justice model	retribution
Code of Hammurabi	law and order advocates	routine activities theory
common law	lifestyle theory	situational choice theory
dangerousness	*mala in se*	situational crime prevention
determinate sentencing	*mala prohibita*	social contract
deterrence	mores	soft determinism
displacement	natural law	specific deterrence
Enlightenment	natural rights	target hardening
folkways	neoclassical criminology	trephination
general deterrence	nothing-works doctrine	truth in sentencing
hard determinism	Panopticon	Twelve Tables
hedonistic calculus	positivism	utilitarianism
incapacitation	rational choice theory	

IMPORTANT NAMES

Cesare Beccaria	Marcus Felson	Thomas Paine
Jeremy Bentham	Thomas Hobbes	Jean-Jacques Rousseau
Ronald V. Clarke	Jack Katz	William Graham Sumner
Lawrence Cohen	John Locke	
Derek Cornish	Montesquieu	

OUTCOMES

LEARNING

After reading this chapter, you should be able to
◆ Recognize the major principles of the Classical School of criminological thought
◆ Explain the philosophical bases of classical thought
◆ Discuss the Enlightenment, and describe its impact on criminological theorizing
◆ Identify modern-day practices that embody principles of the Classical School
◆ Discuss the policy implications of the Classical School
◆ Assess the shortcomings of the classical approach

Hear the author discuss this chapter at *crimtoday.com*

INTRODUCTION

A few years ago, at a conference sponsored by the *New York Post,* New York Mayor Rudolph W. Giuliani confronted issues of crime and social responsibility head on. In his speech, Giuliani laid the burden of the crime problem at the feet of what he called the tension between personal freedoms and individual responsibilities. We mistakenly look to government and elected officials, Giuliani said, to take on responsibility for solving the problem of crime when, instead, it is each individual citizen who must become accountable for fixing what is wrong with society today. In the mayor's words, "We only see the oppressive side of authority. . . . What we don't see is that freedom is not a concept in which people can do anything they want, be anything they can be. Freedom is about authority. Freedom is about the willingness of every single human being to cede to lawful authority a great deal of discretion about what you do."[5]

"The fact is," the mayor continued, "that we're fooling people if we suggest to them the solutions to these very, very deep-seated problems are going to be found in government. . . . The solutions are going to be found when we figure out as a society what our families are going to be like in the next century, and how maybe they are going to be different. They are going to have to be just as solid and just as strong in teaching every single youngster their responsibility for citizenship. We're going to find the answer when schools once again train citizens. . . . If we don't do that, it's very hard to hold us together as a country, because it's shared values that hold us together. We're going to come through this when we realize that it's all about, ultimately, individual responsibility. That, in fact, the criminal act is about individual responsibility and the building of respect for law and ethics is also a matter of individual responsibility."

Many of the problems facing Guiliani's administration, including what was, at the time, rampant crime and what the mayor perceived as an overemphasis on individual rights at the expense of group responsibility, have roots that go back centuries to the time of the Enlightenment and to the American and French Revolutions. We shall discuss that era shortly, following some additional introductory comments.

MAJOR PRINCIPLES OF THE CLASSICAL SCHOOL

This brief section summarizes the central features of the Classical School of criminological thought. Each of the points listed in this discussion can be found elsewhere in this chapter, where they are discussed in more detail. The present cursory overview is intended to provide more than a summation; it is meant to be a guide to the rest of this chapter.

Most classical theories of crime causation make the following basic assumptions:

- Human beings are fundamentally rational, and most human behavior is the result of free will coupled with rational choice.
- Pain and pleasure are the two central determinants of human behavior.
- Punishment, a necessary evil, is sometimes required to deter law violators and to serve as an example to others who would also violate the law.
- Root principles of right and wrong are inherent in the nature of things and cannot be denied.
- Society exists to provide benefits to individuals which they would not receive in isolation.
- When men and women band together for the protection offered by society, they forfeit some of the benefits which accrue from living in isolation.

- Certain key rights of individuals are inherent in the nature of things, and governments that contravene those rights should be disbanded.
- Crime disparages the quality of the bond that exists between individuals and society and is therefore an immoral form of behavior.

FORERUNNERS OF CLASSICAL THOUGHT

The notion of crime as a violation of established law did not exist in most primitive societies. The lack of lawmaking bodies, the absence of formal written laws, and loose social bonds precluded the concept of crime as law violation. All human societies, however, from the simplest to the most advanced, evidence their own widely held notions of right and wrong. Sociologists call such fundamental concepts of morality and propriety "mores" and "folkways." *Mores, folkways,* and *law* are terms used by **William Graham Sumner** near the start of the twentieth century to describe the three basic forms of behavioral strictures imposed by social groups upon their members.[6] According to Sumner, mores and folkways govern behavior in relatively small primitive societies, whereas in large, complex societies, they are reinforced and formalized through written laws.

Mores consist of proscriptions covering potentially serious violations of a group's values. Murder, rape, and robbery, for example, would probably be repugnant to the mores of any social group. **Folkways,** on the other hand, are simply time-honored customs, and although they carry the force of tradition, their violation is less likely to threaten the survival of the social group. The fact that American men have traditionally worn little jewelry illustrates a folkway which has given way in recent years to various types of male adornment, including earrings, gold chains, and even makeup. Mores and folkways, although they may be powerful determinants of behavior, are nonetheless informal, because only laws, from among Sumner's trinity, have been codified into formal strictures wielded by institutions and created specifically for enforcement purposes.

Another method of categorizing socially proscriptive rules is provided by some criminologists who divide crimes into the dual categories of *mala in se* and *mala prohibita.* Acts that are **mala in se** are said to be fundamentally wrong, regardless of the time or place in which they occur. Forcing someone to have sex against his or her will and the intentional killing of children are sometimes given as examples of behavior thought to be *mala in se.* Those who argue for the existence of *mala in se* offenses as a useful heuristic category usually point to some fundamental rule, such as religious teachings (the Ten Commandments, the Koran, and so on), to support their belief that some acts are inherently wrong. Such a perspective assumes that uncompromisable standards for human behavior rest within the very fabric of lived experience.

Mala prohibita offenses are those acts that are said to be wrong for the simple reason that they are prohibited. So-called victimless or social-order offenses like prostitution, gambling, drug use, and premarital sexual behavior provide examples of *mala prohibita* offenses. The status of such behaviors as *mala prohibita* is further supported by the fact that they are not necessarily crimes in every jurisdiction. Prostitution, for example, is legal in parts of Nevada, as is gambling. Gambling, mainly because of the huge revenue potential it holds, is rapidly being legalized in many areas while it remains illegal in others.

The Demonic Era

Since time began, humankind has been preoccupied with what appears to be an ongoing war between good and evil. Oftentimes, evil has appeared in impersonal guise, as when the great bubonic plague, also known as the "black death," ravaged Europe and Asia in the fourteenth century, leaving as much as three-quarters of the population dead in a mere span of 20 years. At other times, evil has seemed to wear a human face, as when the Nazi Holocaust claimed millions of Jewish lives during World War II.

Whatever its manifestation, the very presence of evil in the world has begged for interpretation, and sage minds throughout human history have advanced many explanations for the evil conditions that individuals and social groups have at times been forced to endure. Some forms of evil, like the plague and the Holocaust, appear cosmically based, whereas others—including personal victimization, criminality, and singular instances of deviance—are the undeniable result of individual behavior. Cosmic-level evil has been explained by ideas as diverse as divine punishment,

karma, fate, and the vengeful activities of offended gods. Early explanations of personal deviance ranged from demonic possession to spiritual influences to temptation by fallen angels—and even led to the positing of commerce between human beings and supernatural entities like demons, werewolves, vampires, and ghosts.

Archaeologists have unearthed skeletal remains which provide evidence that some early human societies believed that outlandish behavior among individuals was a consequence of spirit possession. Carefully unearthed skulls, dated by various techniques to approximately 40,000 years ago, show signs of early cranial surgery, or **trephination**, apparently intended to release evil spirits thought to be residing within the heads of offenders. Such surgical interventions were undoubtedly crude and probably involved fermented anesthetics along with flint cutting implements.

Early Sources of the Criminal Law

The Code of Hammurabi

Modern criminal law is the result of a long evolution of legal principles. The **Code of Hammurabi** is one of the first known bodies of law to survive and be available for study today. King Hammurabi ruled the ancient city of Babylon from 1792 to 1750 B.C. and created a legal code consisting of a set of strictures engraved on stone tablets. The Hammurabi laws were originally intended to establish property and other rights and were crucial to the continued growth of Babylon as a significant commercial center. Hammurabi law spoke to issues of theft, property owner-

Demons torment a man in this historical rendition. Crime and other social evils have always begged for explanation. What would today's criminologists think of the claim that "the devil made him do it"? *Corbis*

ship, sexual relationships, and interpersonal violence. As the well-known criminologist Marvin Wolfgang has observed, "In its day, 1700 B.C., the Hammurabi Code, with its emphasis on **retribution**, amounted to a brilliant advance in penal philosophy mainly because it represented an attempt to keep cruelty within bounds."[7] Prior to the code, captured offenders often faced the most barbarous of punishments, frequently at the hands of revenge-seeking victims, no matter how minor their transgressions had been. Learn more about the Code of Hammurabi at Web Extra! 4-1.

Web Extra! 4-1 at crimtoday.com

Early Roman Law

Of considerable significance for our own legal tradition is early Roman law. Roman legions under Emperor Claudius I (10 B.C.–A.D. 54) conquered England in the middle of the first century, and Roman authority over Britannia was further consolidated by later Roman rulers who built walls and fortifications to keep out the still-hostile Scots. Roman customs, law, and language were forced upon the English population during the succeeding three centuries under the Pax Romana—a peace imposed by the military might of Rome.[8]

Early Roman law derived from the **Twelve Tables**, which were written around 450 B.C. The tables were a collection of basic rules regulating family, religious, and economic life. They appear to have been based on common and fair practices generally accepted among early tribes which existed prior to the establishment of the Roman Republic. Unfortunately, only fragments of the tables survive today.

The best-known legal period in Roman history occurred during the reign of Emperor Justinian I (527–565 A.D.). By the end of the sixth century, the Roman Empire had declined substantially in size and influence and was near the end of its life. In what may have been an effort to preserve Roman values and traditions, Justinian undertook the laborious process of distilling Roman laws into a set of writings. The Justinian Code, as these writings came to be known, actually consisted of three lengthy legal documents: (1) the Institutes, (2) the Digest, and (3) the Code itself. Justinian's code distinguished between two major legal categories: public and private laws. Public laws dealt with the organization of the Roman state, its Senate, and governmental offices. Private law concerned itself with contracts, personal possessions, the legal status of various types of people (citizens, free people, slaves, freedmen, guardians, husbands and wives, and so forth), and injuries to citizens. It contained elements of both our modern civil and criminal law, and it influenced Western legal thought through the Middle Ages. Learn more about early Roman law at Web Extra! 4-2.

Web Extra! 4-2 at crimtoday.com

Common Law

Common law forms the basis for much of our modern statutory and case law. It has often been called *the* major source of modern criminal law. **Common law** refers to a traditional body of unwritten legal precedents created through everyday practice in English society and supported by court decisions during the Middle Ages. Common law is so called because it was based on shared traditions and standards, rather than on those that varied from one locale to another. As novel situations arose and were handled by British justices, their declarations became the start for any similar future deliberation. These decisions generally incorporated the customs of society as it operated at the time.

Common law was given considerable legitimacy in the eleventh century upon the official declaration that it was the law of the land by Edward the Confessor, an English king who ruled from 1042 to 1066. The authority of common law was further reinforced by the decision of William the Conqueror to use popular customs as the basis for judicial action following his subjugation of Britain in 1066 A.D.

Eventually, court decisions were recorded and made available to barristers (English trial lawyers) and judges. As criminologist Howard Abadinsky wrote, "Common law involved the transformation of community rules into a national legal system. The controlling element [was] precedent."[9] Today, common law forms the basis of many of the laws on the books in English-speaking countries around the world. Learn more about common law at Web Extra! 4-3.

Web Extra! 4-3 at crimtoday.com

The Magna Carta

The Magna Carta (literally, "great charter") is another important source of modern laws and legal procedure. The Magna Carta was signed on June 15, 1215, by King John of England at Runnymede, under pressure from British barons who took advantage of John's military defeats at the hands of Pope Innocent III and King Philip Augustus of France. The barons demanded a pledge from the king to respect their traditional rights, and they forced the king to agree to be bound by law.

At the time of its signing, the Magna Carta, although 63 chapters in length, was little more than a feudal document[10] listing specific royal concessions. Its original purpose was to ensure feudal rights and to guarantee that the king could not encroach on the privileges claimed by landowning barons. Additionally, the Magna Carta guaranteed the freedom of the church and ensured respect for the customs of towns. Its wording, however, was later interpreted during a judicial revolt in 1613 to support individual rights and jury trials. Sir Edward Coke, Chief Justice under James I, held that the Magna Carta guaranteed basic liberties for all British citizens and ruled that any acts of Parliament which contravened common law would be void. Some evidence suggests that this famous ruling became the basis for the rise of the U.S.

The Magna Carta, an important source of modern Western laws and legal procedure. What are some other important sources of modern criminal law? *Corbis-Bettmann*

Supreme Court, with its power to nullify laws enacted by Congress.[11] Similarly, one specific provision of the Magna Carta, designed originally to prohibit the king from prosecuting the barons without just cause, was expanded into the concept of due process of law, a fundamental cornerstone of modern legal procedure. Because of these later interpretations, the Magna Carta has been called "the foundation stone of our present liberties."[12]

The Enlightenment

The **Enlightenment**, also called the Age of Reason, was a highly significant social movement which occurred during the seventeenth and eighteenth centuries. The Enlightenment built upon ideas developed by thinkers like Francis Bacon (1561–1626), Thomas Hobbes (1588–1679), John Locke (1632–1704), René Descartes (1596–1650), Jean-Jacques Rousseau (1712–1778), and Baruch Spinoza (1632–1677). Because of their indirect contributions to classical criminological thought, it will be worthwhile to spend a few paragraphs discussing the writings of a few of these important historical figures. Learn more about the Enlightenment and the intellectual figures who gave it life at Web Extra! 4-4.

Web Extra! 4-4 at crimtoday.com

Thomas Hobbes (1588–1679)

English philosopher **Thomas Hobbes** developed what many writers regard as an extremely negative view of human nature and social life, which he described in his momentous work, *Leviathan* (1651). Hobbes described the natural state of men and women as one that is "nasty, brutish, and short." Fear of violent death, he said, forces human beings into a **social contract** with one another to create a state. The state, according to Hobbes, demands the surrender of certain natural rights and submission to the absolute authority of a sovereign, while offering protection and succor to its citizens in return. Although the social contract concept significantly influenced many of Hobbes's contemporaries, much of his writing was condemned for assuming an overly pessimistic view of both human nature and existing governments.

John Locke (1632–1704)

In 1690, English philosopher **John Locke** published his *Essay Concerning Human Understanding*, in which he put forth the idea that the natural human condition at birth is akin to that of a blank slate upon which interpersonal encounters and other experiences indelibly inscribe the traits of personality. In contrast to earlier thinkers, who assumed that people are born with certain innate propensities and even rudimentary intellectual concepts and ideas, Locke ascribed the bulk of adult human qualities to life experiences.

In the area of social and political thought, Locke further developed the Hobbesian notion of the social contract. Locke contended that human beings, through a social contract, abandon their natural state of individual freedom and lack of interpersonal responsibility to join together and form society. Although individuals surrender some freedoms to society, government—once formed—is obligated to assume responsibilities toward its citizens and to provide for their protection and welfare. According to Locke and other writers, governments should be required to guarantee certain inalienable rights to their citizens, including the right to life, health, liberty, and possessions. A product of his times, during which the dictatorial nature of monarchies and the Roman church were being much disparaged, Locke stressed the duties which governments have toward their citizens, while paying very little attention to the inverse—the responsibilities of individuals to the societies of which they are a part. As a natural consequence of such an emphasis, Locke argued that political revolutions, under some circumstances, might become an obligation incumbent upon citizens.

Locke also developed the notion of checks and balances between divisions of government, a doctrine that was elaborated by French jurist and political philosopher Charles-Louis de Secondat **Montesquieu** (1689–1755). In *The Spirit of Laws* (1748), Montesquieu wove Locke's notions into the concept of a separation of powers between divisions of government. Both ideas later found a place in the U.S. Constitution.

Jean-Jacques Rousseau (1712–1778)

Swiss-French philosopher and political theorist **Jean-Jacques Rousseau** further advanced the notion of the social contract in his treatise of that name (*Social Contract*, 1762). According to Rousseau, human beings are basically good and fair in their natural state but historically were corrupted by the introduction of shared concepts and joint activities like property, agriculture, science, and commerce. As a result, the social contract emerged when civilized people agreed to establish governments and systems of education to correct the problems and the inequalities brought on by the rise of civilization.

Rousseau also contributed to the notion of **natural law**, a concept originally formulated by Saint Thomas Aquinas (1225–1274), Baruch Spinoza (1632–1677), and others to provide an intuitive basis for the defense of ethical principles and morality. Natural law was used by early Christian church leaders as a powerful argument in support of their interests. Submissive to the authority of the church, secular rulers were pressed to reinforce church doctrine in any laws they decreed. Thomas Aquinas, a well-known supporter of natural law, wrote in his *Summa Theologica* that any man-made law which contradicts natural law is corrupt in the eyes of God. Religious practice, which strongly reflected natural law conceptions, was central to the life of early British society. Hence natural law, as it was understood at the time, was incorporated into English common law throughout the Middle Ages.

Rousseau agreed with earlier writers that certain immutable laws are fundamental to human nature and can be readily ascertained through reason. Man-made law, in contrast, he claimed, derives from human experience and history—both of which are subject to continual change. Hence man-made law, also termed "positive law," changes from time to time and from epoch to epoch. Rousseau expanded the concept of natural law to support emerging democratic principles, and he claimed that certain fundamental human and personal rights were inalienable because they were based on the natural order of things.

Natural Law and Natural Rights

Thomas Paine (1737–1809), an English-American political theorist and the author of *The Rights of Man* (1791 and 1792), defended the French Revolution, arguing that only democratic institutions could guarantee the **natural rights** of individuals. At the Second Continental Congress, Thomas Jefferson (1743–1826) and other congressional representatives—many of whom were well versed in the writings of Locke and Rousseau—built the Constitution of the United States around an understanding of natural law as they perceived it. Hence when Jefferson wrote of inalienable rights to "life, liberty, property," he was following in the footsteps of his intellectual forebears and meant that such rights were the natural due of all men and women because they were inherent in the social contract between citizens and their government.

Natural law and natural rights have a long intellectual history and are with us today in a number of guises. In a *National Review* article subtitled "If Natural Law Does Not Permit Us to Distinguish between Men and Hogs, What Does?" Harry V. Jaffa, Director of the Claremont Institute's Center for the Study of the Natural Law, called an 1854 speech given by Abraham Lincoln "the most moving and compelling exhibition of natural-law reasoning in all political history."[13] In that speech, Lincoln argued in favor of freedom for slaves by succinctly pointing out that there is no difference between people, whatever their color. In Lincoln's words, "Equal justice to the South, it is said, requires us to consent to the extending of slavery to new countries. That is to say, inasmuch as you do not object to my taking my hog to Nebraska, therefore I must not object to your taking your slave. Now, I admit this is perfectly logical, if there is no difference between hogs and Negroes." Lincoln's point, of course, was that there is a huge difference between human beings and animals by virtue of their nature and that such a difference cannot be denied by logic.

Other commentators have cited the "crimes against humanity" committed by Nazis during World War II as indicative of natural law principles. The chilling testimony of Rudolf Hess,[14] Hitler's deputy, during the 1945 war crimes trial in Nuremberg, Germany, as he recalled the "Fuehrer's" order to exterminate millions of Jews indicates the extent of the planned "final solution." Hess testified, "In the summer of 1941, I was summoned to Berlin to Reichsfuehrer SS Himmler to receive personal orders. He told me something to the effect—I do not remember the exact words—that the Fuehrer had given the order for a final solution of the Jewish question. We, the SS, must carry out that order. If it is not carried out now then the Jews will later on destroy the German people. He had chosen Auschwitz on account of its easy access by rail and also because the extensive site offered space for measures ensuring isolation."[15] Who could argue against the premise, natural law supporters ask, that Hitler's final solution to the Jewish "question" was inherently wrong?

Although the concept of natural law has waned somewhat in influence over the past half century, many people today still hold that the basis for various existing criminal laws can be found in immutable moral principles or in some other identifiable aspect of the natural order. The Ten Commandments, "inborn tendencies," the idea of sin, and perceptions of various forms of order in the universe and in the social world have all provided a basis for the assertion that natural law exists. Modern-day advocates of natural law still claim that it comes from outside the social group and that it is knowable through some form of revelation, intuition, or prophecy.

The present debate over abortion is an example of the modern-day use of natural law arguments to support both sides in the dispute. Antiabortion forces, frequently called "pro-lifers" or "right-to-lifers," claim that an unborn fetus is a person and that he or she is entitled to all the protection that we would give to any other living human being. Such protection, they suggest, is basic and humane and lies in the natural relationship of one human being to another and

Thomas Paine (1737–1809), an important contributor to the concept of natural law. What are the central tenets of natural law? *Corbis*

within the relationship of a society to its children. Right-to-lifers are striving for passage of a law, or a reinterpretation of past Supreme Court precedent, that would support their position. Advocates of the present law (which allows abortion upon request under certain conditions) maintain that abortion is a right of any pregnant woman because she is the only one who should be in control of her body. Such "pro-choice" groups also claim that the legal system must address the abortion question but only by way of offering protection to this natural right of women.

Perhaps the best-known modern instance of natural law debate occurred during confirmation hearings for U.S. Supreme Court Justice Clarence Thomas. Thomas, who was confirmed in 1991, once wrote an opinion in which he argued from a natural law point of view. That opinion was later challenged by Senate Judiciary Committee members who felt that it reflected an unbending judicial attitude. Learn more about natural law at Web Extra! 4-5.

Web Extra! 4-5 at crimtoday.com

THE CLASSICAL SCHOOL

As many authors have pointed out, the Enlightenment fueled the fires of social change, leading eventually to the French and American Revolutions and providing many of the intellectual underpinnings of the U.S. Constitution. The Enlightenment—one of the most powerful intellectual initiatives of the last millennium—also inspired other social movements and freed innovative thinkers from the chains of convention. As a direct consequence of Enlightenment thinking, superstitious beliefs were discarded, and men and women began to be perceived, for the first time, as self-determining entities possessing a fundamental freedom of choice. Following the Enlightenment, many supernatural explanations for human behavior fell by the wayside, and free will and rational thought came to be recognized as the linchpins of all significant human activity. In effect, the Enlightenment inspired the reexamination of existing doctrines of human behavior from the point of view of rationalism.

Within criminology, the Enlightenment led to the development of the **Classical School** of criminological thought. Crime and deviance, which had previously been explained by reference to mythological influences and spiritual shortcomings, took their place in Enlightenment thought alongside other forms of human activity as products of the exercise of free will. Once people were seen as having control over their own lives, crime came to be explained as a particularly individualized form of evil—that is, as moral wrongdoing fed by personal choice.

Cesare Beccaria (1738–1794)

Cesare Beccaria (his Italian name was Cesare Bonesana, but he held the title Marchese di Beccaria) was born in Milan, Italy. The eldest of four children, he was trained at Catholic schools and earned a doctor of laws degree by the time he was 20.

In 1764, Beccaria published his *Essay on Crimes and Punishments*. Although the work appeared originally in Italian, it was translated into English in London in 1767. Beccaria's *Essay* consisted of 42 short chapters covering only a few major themes. Beccaria's purpose in penning the book was not to set forth a theory of crime, but to communicate his observations on the laws and justice system of his time. In the *Essay*, Beccaria distilled the notion of the social contract into the idea that "laws are the conditions under which independent and isolated men united to form a society."[16] More than anything else, however, his writings consisted of a philosophy of punishment. Beccaria claimed, for example, that although most criminals are punished based on an assessment of their criminal intent, they should be punished instead based on the degree of injury they cause. The purpose of punishment, he said, should be deterrence rather than retribution, and punishment should be imposed to prevent offenders from committing additional crimes. Beccaria saw punishment as a tool to an end, not an end in itself, and crime prevention was more important to him than revenge.

To help prevent crimes, Beccaria argued, adjudication and punishment should both be swift, and once punishment is decreed, it should be certain. In his words, "The more promptly and the more closely punishment follows upon the commission of a crime, the more just and useful it will be." Punishment that is imposed immediately following crime commission, claimed Beccaria, is connected with the wrongfulness of the offense, both in the mind of the offender and in the minds of others who might see the punishment imposed and thereby learn of the consequences of involvement in criminal activity.

Beccaria concluded that punishment should be only severe enough to outweigh the personal benefits to be derived from crime commission. Any additional punishment, he argued, would be superfluous. Beccaria's concluding words on punishment are telling. "In order," he said, "for punishment not to be, in every instance, an act of violence of one or of many against a private citizen, it must be essentially public, prompt, necessary, the least possible in the given circumstances, proportionate to the crimes, [and] dictated by the laws."

Beccaria distinguished between three types of crimes: those that threaten the security of the state, those that injure citizens or their property, and those that run contrary to the social order. Punishment should fit the crime, Beccaria wrote, declaring that theft should be punished through fines, personal injury through corporal punishment, and serious crimes against the state (such as inciting revolution) via application of the death penalty. Beccaria was opposed to the death penalty in most other circumstances, seeing it as a kind of warfare waged by society against its citizens.

Beccaria condemned the torture of suspects, a practice still used in the eighteenth century, saying that it was a device which ensured that weak suspects would incriminate themselves, while strong ones would be found innocent. Torture, he argued, was also unjust because it punished individuals before they had been found guilty in a court of law. In Beccaria's words, "No man can be called guilty before a judge has sentenced him, nor can society deprive him of public protection before it has been decided that he has in fact violated the conditions under which such protection was accorded him. What right is it then, if not simply that of might, which empowers a judge to inflict punishment on a citizen while doubt still remains as to his guilt or innocence?"

Beccaria's *Essay* also touched upon a variety of other topics. He distinguished, for example, between two types of proof: "perfect proof," in which there was no possibility of innocence, and "imperfect proof," where some possibility of innocence remained. Beccaria also believed in the efficacy of a jury of one's peers but recommended that half of any jury panel should consist of peers of the victim, whereas the other half should be made up of peers of the accused. Finally, Beccaria wrote that oaths were useless in a court of law because accused individuals will naturally deny their guilt even if they know themselves to be fully culpable.

Beccaria's ideas were widely recognized as progressive by his contemporaries. His principles were incorporated into the French penal code of 1791 and significantly influenced the justice-related activities of European leaders like Catherine the Great of Russia, Frederick the Great of Prussia, and Emperor Joseph II of Austria. Evidence suggests that Beccaria's *Essay* influenced framers of the U.S. Constitution, and some scholars claim that the first ten amendments to the Constitution, known as the Bill of Rights, might not have existed were it not for Beccaria's emphasis on the rights of individuals in the face of state power. Perhaps more than anyone else, Beccaria is responsible for the contemporary belief that criminals have control over their behavior, that they choose to commit crimes, and that they can be deterred by the threat of punishment. Learn more about Cesare Beccaria at Web Extra! 4-6.

Web Extra! 4-6 at crimtoday.com

Jeremy Bentham (1748–1832)

Jeremy Bentham, another founding personality of the Classical School, wrote in his *Introduction to the Principles of Morals and Legislation* (1789) that "nature has placed mankind under the governance of two sovereign masters, pain and pleasure."[17] To reduce crime or, as Bentham put it, "to prevent the happening of mischief," the pain of crime commission must outweigh the pleasure to be derived from criminal activity. Bentham's claim rested upon his belief, spawned by Enlightenment thought, that human beings are fundamentally rational and that criminals will weigh in their minds the pain of punishment against any pleasures thought likely to be derived from crime commission.

Bentham advocated neither extreme nor cruel punishment—only punishment sufficiently distasteful to the offender that the discomfort experienced would outweigh the pleasure to be derived from criminal activity. Generally, Bentham argued, the more serious the offense, the more reward it holds for its perpetrator and therefore the more weighty the official response must be. "Pain and pleasure," said Bentham, "are the instruments the legislator has to work with" in controlling antisocial and criminal behavior.

Bentham's approach has been termed **hedonistic calculus** or **utilitarianism** because of its emphasis on the worth any action holds for an individual undertaking it. As Bentham stated, "By the principle of utility is meant that principle which approves or disapproves of every action whatsoever, according to the tendency which it appears to have to augment or diminish the happiness of the party whose interest is in question; or, what is the same thing . . . to promote or to oppose that happiness." In other words, Bentham believed that individuals could be expected to weigh, at least intuitively, the consequences of their behavior before acting so as to maximize their own pleasure and minimize pain. The value of any pleasure, or the inhibitory tendency of any pain, according to Bentham, could be calculated by its intensity, duration, certainty, and immediacy (or remoteness in time).

Bentham claimed that nothing was really new in his pleasure-pain perspective. "Nor is this a novel and unwarranted, any more than it is a useless theory," he wrote. "In all this there is nothing but what the practice of mankind, wheresoever they have a clear view of their own interest, is perfectly comfortable to. An article of property, an estate in land, for instance, is valuable, on what account? On account of the pleasures of all kinds which it enables a man to produce, and what comes to the same thing the pains of all kinds which it enables him to avert." In fact, Bentham's ideas were not new, but their application to criminology was. In 1739, David Hume distilled the notion of utilitarianism into a philosophical perspective in his book *A Treatise of Human Nature.* Although Hume's central concern was not to explain crime, scholars who followed Hume observed that human behavior is typically motivated more by self-interest than by anything else.

Like Beccaria, Bentham focused on the potential held by punishment to prevent crime and to act as a deterrent for those considering criminal activity. In any criminal legislation, he wrote, "the evils of punishment must . . . be made to exceed the advantage of the offence." Bentham distinguished between 11 different types of punishment:

- *Capital punishment,* or death
- *Afflictive punishment,* which includes whipping and starvation
- *Indelible punishment,* such as branding, amputation, and mutilation
- *Ignominious punishment,* such as public punishment involving use of the stocks or pillory
- *Penitential punishment,* whereby an offender might be censured by his or her community
- *Chronic punishment,* such as banishment, exile, and imprisonment
- *Restrictive punishment,* such as license revocation or administrative sanction
- *Compulsive punishment,* which requires an offender to perform a certain action, such as to make restitution or to keep in touch with a probation officer
- *Pecuniary punishment* involving the use of fines
- *Quasi-pecuniary punishment,* in which the offender is denied services which would otherwise be available to him or her
- *Characteristic punishment,* such as mandating that prison uniforms be worn by incarcerated offenders

Utilitarianism is a practical philosophy, and Bentham was quite practical in his suggestions about crime prevention. Every citizen, he said, should have their first and last names tattooed on their wrists for the purpose of facilitating police identification. He also recommended the creation of a centralized police force focused on crime prevention and control—a recommendation which found life in the English Metropolitan Police Act of 1829, which established London's New Police under the direction of Sir Robert Peel.

Bentham's other major contribution to criminology was his suggestion that prisons be designed along the lines of what he called a "Panopticon House." The **Panopticon**, as

Bentham envisioned it, was to be a circular building with cells along the circumference, each clearly visible from a central location staffed by guards. Bentham recommended that Panopticons should be constructed near or within cities so that they might serve as examples to others of what would happen to them should they commit crimes. He also wrote that prisons should be managed by contractors who could profit from the labor of prisoners and that the contractor should "be bound to insure the lives and safe custody of those entrusted to him." Although a Panopticon was never built in Bentham's England, French officials funded a modified version of such a prison which was eventually built at Lyons, and three prisons modeled after the Panopticon concept were constructed in the United States.

Bentham's critics have been quick to point out that punishments seem often not to work. Even punishments as severe as death appear not to have any effect on the incidence of crimes like murder (a point which we will discuss in greater detail later in this chapter). Such critics forget Bentham's second tenet, however, which is that for punishment to be effective, "it must be swift and certain." For any punishment to have teeth, Bentham said, it not only must mandate a certain degree of

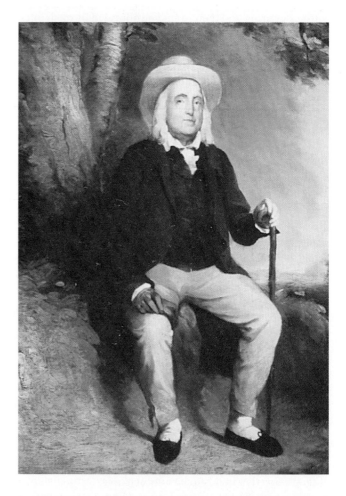

Jeremy Bentham (1748–1832), whose work is closely associated with the Classical School of criminology. What are the key features of the Classical School? *Corbis*

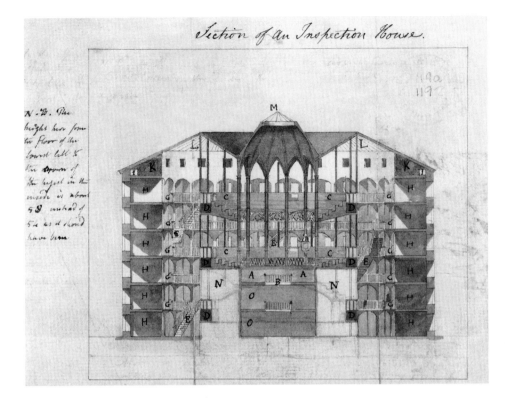

An architect's rendering of Jeremy Bentham's Panopticon design for a prison. *University College, London*

displeasure, but also must follow almost immediately upon its being decided, and there must be no way of avoiding it. Learn more about Jeremy Bentham from the Bentham Project via Web Extra! 4-7.

Web EXTRA! Web Extra! 4-7 at **crimtoday.com**

Heritage of the Classical School

The Classical School was to influence criminological thinking for a long time to come. From the French Revolution and the U.S. Constitution to today's emphasis on deterrence and crime prevention, the Classical School has molded the way in which thinkers on the subject of crime have viewed the topic for more than 200 years. The heritage left by the Classical School is still operative today in the following five principles, each of which is a fundamental constituent of modern-day perspectives on crime and human behavior:

- *Rationality.* Human beings have free will, and the actions they undertake are the result of choice.
- *Hedonism.* Pleasure and pain, or reward and punishment, are the major determinants of choice.
- *Punishment.* Criminal punishment is a deterrent to unlawful behavior, and deterrence is the best justification for punishment.
- *Human Rights.* Society is made possible by individuals cooperating together. Hence society owes to its citizens respect for their rights in the face of government action, and for their autonomy insofar as such autonomy can be secured without endangering others or menacing the greater good.

- *Due Process.* An accused should be presumed innocent until proved otherwise, and an accused should not be subject to punishment before guilt is lawfully established.

NEOCLASSICAL CRIMINOLOGY

By the end of the 1800s, classical criminology, with its emphasis on free will and individual choice as the root causes of crime, gave way to another approach known as "positivism." **Positivism**, which made use of the scientific method in studying criminality, is discussed in much greater detail in Chapter 5. For the purposes of this chapter, however, it is important to realize that positivism, in its original formulation, was based upon an acceptance of **hard determinism**, or the belief that crime results from forces that are beyond the control of the individual. Hence, as we shall see later in this book, the original positivists completely rejected the notion of free will and turned their attention instead to the impact of socialization, genetics, economic conditions, peer group influences, and other factors that might determine criminality. Acceptance of the notion of determinism, of course, implied that offenders were not entirely (if at all) responsible for their crimes and suggested that crime could be prevented by changing the conditions that produced criminality (see Figure 4-1).

While positivism remains an important component of contemporary criminology, many of its assumptions were undermined in the 1970s by studies that seemed to show that offenders could not be rehabilitated no matter what was

Free Will ——— Soft Determinism ——— Hard Determinism

Classical Criminology ——— 19th Century Positivist Criminology

■ **FIGURE 4-1** CLASSICAL CRIMINOLOGY VERSUS POSITIVISM—THE ROLE OF FREE WILL.

tried, by a growing and widespread public fear of crime that led to "get tough on crime" policies, and by a cultural reaffirmation of belief in the rational nature of man. The resulting resurgence of classical ideals, referred to as **neoclassical criminology**, focused on the importance of character (a kind of middle ground between total free will and hard determinism), the dynamics of character development, and the rational choices that people make as they are faced with opportunities for crime. The neoclassical movement appears to have had its start with a number of publications produced in the 1970s. One of these was Robert Martinson's national survey of rehabilitation programs.[18] Martinson found that when it came to the rehabilitation of offenders, nothing seems to work, as most resume their criminal careers after release from prison. The phrase "Nothing Works!" became a rallying cry of conservative policymakers everywhere, and the **nothing-works doctrine** received much public attention. Many conservative politicians and some criminologists began calling existing notions of crime prevention and rehabilitation into question amidst claims that enhanced job skills, increased opportunities for employment, and lessened punishment did nothing to stem what was then a rising tide of crime. In 1975, Harvard political scientist James Q. Wilson wrote *Thinking about Crime,* in which he suggested that crime is not a result of poverty or social conditions and cannot be affected by social programs.[19] Wilson argued, instead, for the lengthy incarceration of offenders and for the elimination of criminal opportunity. Also in 1975, David Fogel, who was then Director of the Illinois Law Enforcement Commission, published a book called *We Are the Living Proof: The Justice Model of Corrections.*[20] Fogel's **justice model**, predicated on the growing belief that prisons do not rehabilitate or cure, was proposed to the Illinois state legislature as a model for prison reform. Fogel argued that for the criminal justice process to work, offenders must be treated "as responsible as well as accountable, that is, volitional."[21]

Rational Choice Theory

Rational choice theory, a product of the late 1970s and early 1980s, mirrors many of the principles found in classical criminology. The theory rests upon the belief that criminals make a conscious, rational, and at least partially informed choice to commit crime. It employs cost-benefit analysis, akin to similar theories in the field of economics which view human behavior as the result of personal choice made after weighing both the costs and the benefits of available alternatives. Rational choice theory is noteworthy for its emphasis on the rational and adaptive aspects of criminal offending. It "predicts that individuals choose to commit crime when the benefits outweigh the costs of disobeying the law. Crime will decrease," according to such theories, "when opportunities are limited, benefits are reduced, and costs are increased."[22]

Two varieties of rational choice theory can be identified. One, which builds on an emerging emphasis on victimization, is called **routine activities theory**. A second, which is largely an extension of the rational choice perspective, is called **situational choice theory**.

Routine activities theory (also called **lifestyle theory**) was proposed by **Lawrence Cohen** and **Marcus Felson** in 1979.[23] Cohen and Felson suggested that lifestyles contribute significantly to both the volume and the type of crime found in any society. The two believed that changes in the nature of American society during the 1960s and 1970s—specifically, increased personal affluence and greater involvement in social activities outside the home—brought about increased rates of household theft and personal victimization by strangers. Central to the routine activities approach is the claim that crime is likely to occur when a motivated offender and a suitable target come together in the absence of a capable guardian. A **capable guardian**, simply put, is one who effectively discourages crime. Hence a person who has taken crime prevention steps is less likely to be victimized. As Cohen and Felson observe, "The risk of criminal victimization varies dramatically among the circumstances and locations in which people place themselves and their property."[24] For example, a person who routinely uses an automated teller machine late at night in an isolated location is far more likely to be preyed upon by robbers than is someone who stays home after dark. Lifestyles that contribute to criminal opportunities are likely to result in crime because they increase the risk of potential victimization.[25] Although noncriminal lifestyles at a given point in one's lifetime are partly the result of unavoidable social roles and assigned social positions, those who participate in a given lifestyle generally make rational decisions about specific behaviors (such as going to a given automated teller machine at a certain time). The same is true of criminal lifestyles. Hence the meshing of choices made by both victims and criminals contributes significantly to both the frequency and the type of criminal activity observed in society.

In a later work, Felson suggested that a number of "situational insights" might combine to elicit a criminal response from individual actors enmeshed in a highly varied social world. Felson pointed out that "individuals vary greatly in their behavior from one situation to another" and said that criminality might flow from temptation, bad company, idleness, or provocation.[26] Convenience stores, for example, create temptations toward theft when they display their merchandise within easy reach of customers. Other authors have defined the term *situation* to mean "the perceptive field of the individual at a given point in time" and have suggested that it can be described "in terms of who is there, what is going on, and where it is taking place."[27]

Situational choice theory provides an example of **soft determinism**. It views criminal behavior "as a function of choices and decisions made within a context of situational constraints and opportunities."[28] The theory holds that "crime is not simply a matter of motivation; it is also a matter of opportunity."[29] Situational choice theory suggests that the probability of criminal activity can be reduced by changing the features of the environment. **Ronald V. Clarke** and **Derek B. Cornish**, collaborators in the development of the situational choice perspective, analyze the choice-structuring properties of a potentially criminal situation. They define *choice-structuring properties* as "the constellation of opportunities, costs, and benefits attaching to particular kinds of crime."[30] Clarke and Cornish suggest the use of situational strategies like "cheque guarantee cards, the control of alcohol sales at football matches, supervision of children's play on public housing estates, vandal resistant materials and designs, 'defensible space' architecture, improved lighting, closed-circuit television surveillance,"[31] and the like as effective crime prevention additions to specific situations—all of which might lower the likelihood of criminal victimization in given instances.

In brief, rational choice theorists concentrate on "the decision-making process of offenders confronted with specific contexts" and have shifted "the focus of the effort to prevent crime . . . from broad social programs to target hardening, environmental design or any impediment that would [dissuade] a motivated offender from offending."[32] Sixteen techniques of situational crime control can be identified, and each can be classified according to the four objectives of situational prevention. The four objectives are to (1) increase the effort involved in crime, (2) increase the risks associated with crime commission, (3) reduce the rewards of crime, and (4) reduce the rationalizations that facilitate criminal activity. Table 4-1 outlines the sixteen techniques and provides examples of each.

Although rational choice theory is similar to classical deterrence theory, earlier approaches focused largely on the balance between pleasure and pain as the primary determinant or preventative of criminal behavior. Rational choice theory tends to place less emphasis on pleasure and emotionality, and more upon rationality and cognition. Some rational choice theorists distinguish among the types of choices offenders make as they move toward criminal involvement. One type of choice, known as "involvement decisions," has been described as "multistage" and is said to "include the initial decision to engage in criminal activity as well as subsequent decisions to continue one's involvement or to desist."[33] Another type of choice, event decisions, *relates* to particular instances of criminal opportunity, such as the decision to rob a particular person or to let him or her pass. Event decisions—in contrast to involvement decisions, which may take months or even years to reach—are usually made quickly. Learn more about rational choice theories via Web Extra! 4-8.

Web Extra! 4-8 at crimtoday.com

The Seductions of Crime

One criminologist who focuses on the relationship between the decision to commit crime and the rewards that such a decision brings is **Jack Katz**. In the book *Seductions of Crime*, Katz explains crime as the result of the "often wonderful attractions

TABLE 4-1 ■ Sixteen Techniques of Situational Crime Control, with Examples

INCREASING PERCEIVED EFFORT	INCREASING PERCEIVED RISKS	REDUCING ANTICIPATED REWARDS	INHIBITING RATIONALIZATIONS
Target hardening	*Entry/exit screening*	*Target removal:*	*Facilitating compliance*
Steering wheel locks	Baggage screening	Removable car radios	Trash bins
Bandit screens	Merchandise tags	Exact change fares	Simplified tax forms
Access control	*Formal surveillance*	*Identifying property*	*Controlling disinhibitors*
Fenced yards	Burglar alarms	Property marking	Ignition interlocks
Entry phones	Security guards	Vehicle licensing	Server intervention
Deflecting offenders	*Surveillance by employees*	*Reducing temptations*	*Rule setting*
Tavern location	Park attendants	Gender-neutral phone lists	Customs declarations
School location	Receptionists	Concealing valuables	Hotel registrations
Controlling facilitators	*Natural surveillance*	*Denying benefits*	*Increasing informal sanctions*
Credit card photos	Defensible spaces	Graffiti cleaning	Prosecuting shoplifters
Ignition interlocks	Neighborhood watches	LoJack auto-recovery systems	Roadside speedometers

Source: Adapted from Ronald V. Clarke, "Situational Crime Prevention—Everybody's Business." Paper presented at the 1995 Australian Crime Prevention Council conference.

within the lived experience of criminality."[34] Crime, Katz says, is often pleasurable for those committing it, and pleasure of one sort or another is the major motivation behind crime. Sometimes, however, the kind of pleasure to be derived from crime is not immediately obvious. Moreover, as Katz points out in the following paragraph, criminologists have often depicted crime as something to be avoided and have failed to understand just how good crime *feels* to those who commit it:[35]

> The social science literature contains only scattered evidence of what it means, feels, sounds, tastes, or looks like to commit a particular crime. Readers of research on homicide and assault do not hear the slaps and curses, see the pushes and shoves, or feel the humiliation and rage that may build toward the attack, sometimes persisting after the victim's death. . . . How adolescents manage to make the shoplifting or vandalism of cheap and commonplace things a thrilling experience has not been intriguing to many students of delinquency. . . . The description of "cold-blooded, senseless murders" has been left to writers outside the social sciences. Neither academic methods nor academic theories seem to be able to grasp . . . how it makes sense to them to kill when only petty cash is at stake. Sociological and psychological studies of robbery rarely focus on the distinctive attractions of robbery, even though research has now clearly documented that alternative forms of criminality are available and familiar to many career robbers.

For criminal offenders, crime is indeed rewarding, Katz says. It feels good, he tells his readers. "The particular seductions and compulsions [which criminals] experience may be unique to crime," he says, "but the sense of being seduced and compelled is not. To grasp the magic in the criminal's sensuality, we must acknowledge our own."[36] Katz describes the almost sexual attraction shoplifting held for one young offender. As the thief said, "The experience was almost orgasmic for me. There was a buildup of tension as I contemplated the danger of a forbidden act, then a rush of excitement at the moment of committing the crime, and finally a delicious sense of release."[37]

Katz's approach, which stresses the sensual dynamics of criminality, says that for many people, crime is sensually compelling. As one writer notes, "Jack Katz argues for a redirection of the criminological gaze—from the traditional focus on background factors such as age, gender, and material conditions to foreground or situational factors that directly precipitate criminal acts and reflect crimes' sensuality."[38] Learn more about the seductions of crime at Web Extra! 4-9.

Web EXTRA!　**Web Extra! 4-9 at crimtoday.com**

Situational Crime Control Policy

Building upon the work of rational and situational choice theorists, Israeli criminologist David Weisburd describes the advantages of a situational approach to crime prevention. Weisburd points out, "Crime prevention research and policy have traditionally been concerned with offenders or potential offenders. Researchers have looked to define strategies that

would deter individuals from involvement in crime or rehabilitate them so they would no longer want to commit criminal acts. In recent years crime prevention efforts have often focused on the incapacitation of high-rate or dangerous offenders so they are not free to victimize law-abiding citizens. In the public debate over crime prevention policies, these strategies are usually defined as competing approaches."[39] However, Weisburd says, "they have in common a central assumption about crime prevention research and policy: that efforts to understand and control crime must begin with the offender. In all of these approaches, the focus of crime prevention is on people and their involvement in criminality."

"Although this assumption continues to dominate crime prevention research and policy," says Weisburd, "it has begun to be challenged by a very different approach that seeks to shift the focus of crime prevention efforts." The new approach developed in large part as a response to the failures of traditional theories and programs. The 1970s, in particular, saw a shattering of traditional assumptions about the effectiveness of crime prevention efforts and led to a reevaluation of research and policy about crime prevention. For many scholars and policymakers, this meant having to rethink assumptions about criminality and how offenders might be prevented from participating in crime. Others suggested that a more radical reorientation of crime prevention efforts was warranted. They argued that the shift must come not in terms of the specific strategies or theories that were used, but in terms of the unit of analysis that formed the basis of crime prevention efforts. This new crime prevention effort called for a focus not on people who commit crime, but on the context in which crime occurs.

This approach, which is called **situational crime prevention**, looks to develop greater understanding of crime and more effective crime prevention strategies through concern with the physical, organizational, and social environments that make crime possible.[40] The situational approach does not ignore offenders; it merely places them as one part of a broader crime prevention equation that is centered on the context of crime. It demands a shift in the approach to crime prevention, however, from one that is concerned primarily with why people commit crime to one that looks primarily at why crime occurs in specific settings. It moves the context of crime into central focus and sees the offender as but one of a number of factors that affect it. Situational crime prevention is closely associated with the idea of a "criminology of place," which is discussed in the Theory versus Reality box in Chapter 7.

Weisburd suggests that a "reorientation of crime prevention research and policy from the causes of criminality to the context of crime provides much promise." Says Weisburd, "At the core of situational prevention is the concept of opportunity." In contrast to offender-based approaches to crime prevention that usually focus on the dispositions of criminals, situational crime prevention begins with the opportunity structure of the crime situation. By "opportunity structure," advocates of this perspective are not referring to sociological concepts like differential opportunity or anomie, but rather to the immediate situational and environmental components of the context of crime. Their approach to crime prevention is to try to reduce the opportunities for crime in specific situations. This may involve efforts as simple and straightforward as **target hardening** or access control.[41]

The value of a situational approach lies in the fact that criminologists have found it difficult to identify who is likely to become a serious offender and to predict the timing and types of future offenses that repeat offenders are likely to commit. And, as Weisburd says, "legal and ethical dilemmas make it difficult to base criminal justice policies on models that still include a substantial degree of statistical error." Moreover, Weisburd adds, "if traditional approaches worked well, of course, there would be little pressure to find new forms of crime prevention. If traditional approaches worked well, few people would possess criminal motivation and fewer still would actually commit crimes."

Situational prevention advocates argue that the context of crime provides a promising alternative to traditional offender-based crime prevention policies.[42] They assume that situations provide a more stable and predictable focus for crime prevention efforts than do people. In part, this assumption develops from commonsense notions of the relationship between opportunities and crime. Shoplifting, for example, is by definition clustered in stores and not residences, and family disputes are unlikely to be a problem outside of the home. High-crime places, in contrast to high-crime people, cannot flee to avoid criminal justice intervention, and crime that develops from the specific characteristics of certain places cannot be easily transferred to other contexts.

Another example can be found in robberies, which are most likely to be found in places where many pedestrians stroll (such as bus stops and business districts), where there are few police or informal guardians (e.g., doormen), and where a supply of motivated offenders can be found nearby or at least within easy public transportation access.[43] Similarly, such places are not likely to be centers for prostitution, which would favor easy access of cars (and little interference by shopkeepers who are likely to object to the obvious nature of street solicitations), nor flashing, which is more likely to be found in the more anonymous environments of public parks.

Situational crime control policy suggests 12 ways in which environments and situations can be changed to reduce crime:[44]

1. Target hardening
2. Access control
3. Offender deflection (e.g., through physical barriers)
4. Facilitator control (e.g., gun controls)
5. Entry/exit screening (e.g., metal detectors)
6. Formal surveillance (e.g., security guards or television monitoring)
7. Employee surveillance (e.g., doormen, clerks)
8. Natural surveillance (e.g., street lighting)
9. Target removal (e.g., removing cash from registers after business hours)
10. Property identification (e.g., etching, tagging)
11. Inducement removal (e.g., rapid repair of disabled vehicles left by the roadside)
12. Rule setting (e.g., "No one allowed beyond this point")

Learn more about situational crime prevention and target hardening via Web Extra! 4-10.

Web Extra! 4-10 at crimtoday.com

Critique of Rational Choice Theory

Rational and situational choice and routine activities theories can be criticized for an overemphasis on individual choice and a relative disregard for the role of social factors in crime causation, such as poverty, poor home environment, and inadequate socialization. In a recent study, for example, Laura J. Moriarty and James E. Williams found that the routine activities approach explained 28% of property crimes committed in socially disorganized (high-crime) areas of a small Virginia city and explained only 11% of offenses committed in low-crime areas.[45] In the words of the authors, "This research demonstrates more support for routine activities theory in socially disorganized areas than in socially organized areas."[46] Hence although one could argue that the kinds of routine activities supportive of criminal activity are more likely to occur in socially disorganized areas, it is also true that the presence (or absence) of certain ecological characteristics (that is, the level of social disorganization), may enhance (or reduce) the likelihood of criminal victimization. As the authors state, "Those areas characterized by low socioeconomic status will have higher unemployment rates, thus creating a larger pool of motivated offenders. Family disruption characterized by more divorced or separated families will result in more unguarded living structures, thus making suitable targets more available. Increased residential mobility will result in more non-occupied housing, which creates a lack of guardianship over the property and increases the number of suitable targets."[47]

Rational choice theory, in particular, seems to assume that everyone is equally capable of making rational decisions when, in fact, such is probably not the case. Some individuals are more logical than others by virtue of temperament, personality, or socialization, whereas others are emotional, hotheaded, and unthinking. Empirical studies of rational choice theory have added scant support for the perspective's underlying assumptions, tending to show instead that criminal offenders are often unrealistic in their appraisals of the relative risks and rewards facing them.[48] Similarly, rational and situational choice theories seem to disregard individual psychology and morality with their emphasis on external situations. Moral individuals, say critics, when faced with easy criminal opportunities, may rein in their desires and turn their backs on temptation.

Finally, the emphasis of rational and situational choice theories upon changing aspects of the immediate situation to reduce crime has been criticized for resulting in the **displacement**

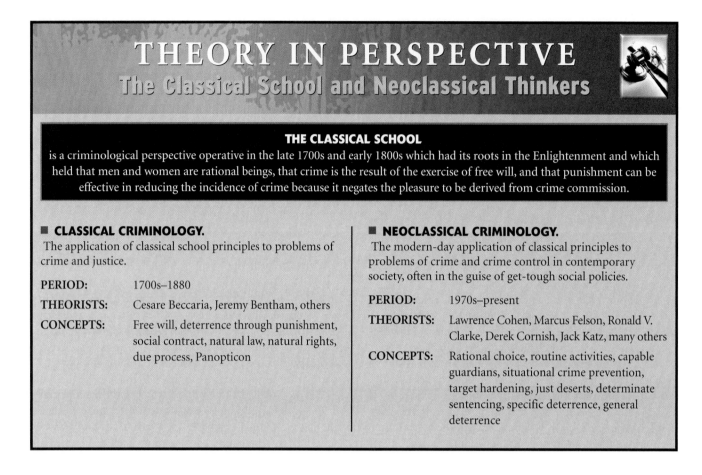

THEORY IN PERSPECTIVE
The Classical School and Neoclassical Thinkers

THE CLASSICAL SCHOOL

is a criminological perspective operative in the late 1700s and early 1800s which had its roots in the Enlightenment and which held that men and women are rational beings, that crime is the result of the exercise of free will, and that punishment can be effective in reducing the incidence of crime because it negates the pleasure to be derived from crime commission.

■ **CLASSICAL CRIMINOLOGY.**
The application of classical school principles to problems of crime and justice.

PERIOD:	1700s–1880
THEORISTS:	Cesare Beccaria, Jeremy Bentham, others
CONCEPTS:	Free will, deterrence through punishment, social contract, natural law, natural rights, due process, Panopticon

■ **NEOCLASSICAL CRIMINOLOGY.**
The modern-day application of classical principles to problems of crime and crime control in contemporary society, often in the guise of get-tough social policies.

PERIOD:	1970s–present
THEORISTS:	Lawrence Cohen, Marcus Felson, Ronald V. Clarke, Derek Cornish, Jack Katz, many others
CONCEPTS:	Rational choice, routine activities, capable guardians, situational crime prevention, target hardening, just deserts, determinate sentencing, specific deterrence, general deterrence

of crime from one area to another.[49] Target hardening,[50] a key crime prevention strategy among such theorists, has sometimes caused criminals to find new targets of opportunity in other areas.[51]

PUNISHMENT AND NEOCLASSICAL THOUGHT

Punishment is a central feature of both classical and neoclassical thought. Whereas punishment served the ends of deterrence in classical thought, its role in neoclassical thinking has been expanded to support the ancient concept of retribution. Those who advocate retribution see the primary utility of punishment as revenge.

If a person is attracted to crime and chooses to violate the law, modern neoclassical thinkers argue, then he or she *deserves* to be punished because the consequences of crime were known to the offender before the crime was committed. Moreover, the criminal *must* be punished, such thinkers propose, so that future criminal behavior can be curtailed.

In 1994, the "caning" of an American teenager in Singapore provided an example of just this kind of thinking. In that year, 18-year-old Michael Fay from Dayton, Ohio, was ordered to receive six lashes from a four-foot-long, half-inch-thick split-bamboo rod called a *rotan*. Fay's caning was to be his punishment for five charges of vandalism, mischief, and keeping stolen property—crimes committed while he lived

in Singapore with his parents and to which he pleaded guilty. Fay, along with other teenagers, had spray-painted and thrown eggs at parked cars. At the time of the offenses, Fay was probably unaware that Singapore law mandates caning in cases of vandalism when an indelible substance is used. The law was originally passed in the 1960s to curtail the use of political graffiti. Caning is no simple punishment. It has been described as making "pieces of skin and flesh fly at each stroke."[52] Singapore law requires that those who faint be revived by a doctor so that the caning can continue.[53]

Before Fay's caning, his parents begged Singapore's courts for leniency, pleaded for intervention from the International Red Cross, beseeched Singapore President Ong Teng Cheong for clemency, and asked then-President Bill Clinton for help—all to no avail. Although many Americans expressed dismay at the severity of the punishment, the Singapore Embassy in Washington, D.C., along with newspapers and television stations throughout the United States, received thousands of letters and phone calls from American citizens supporting the punishment and saying that the U.S. judicial system could learn something from the crime reduction strategies used in Singapore.

Notions of revenge and retribution are morally based. They build on a sense of indignation at criminal behavior and on the sense of righteousness inherent in Judeo-Christian notions of morality and propriety. Both philosophies of punishment turn a blind eye to the mundane and practical consequences of any particular form of punishment. Hence advocates of retributive philosophies of punishment easily dismiss critics of, say, the death penalty, who frequently challenge the efficacy of court-ordered capital punishment on the basis that such sentences do little to deter others. Wider issues, including general deterrence, become irrelevant when a person focuses narrowly on the emotions which crime and victimization engender in a given instance. Simply put, from the neoclassical perspective some crimes cry out for vengeance, while others demand little more than a slap on the wrist or an apology from the offender.

Just Deserts

The old adages, "He got what was coming to him" and "She got her due," well summarize the thinking behind the **just deserts model** of criminal sentencing. Just deserts, a concept inherent in the justice model, refers to the concept that criminal offenders deserve the punishment they receive at the hands of the law and that any punishment which is imposed should be appropriate to the type and severity of crime committed. The idea of just deserts has long been a part of Western thought, dating back at least to Old Testament times. The Old Testament dictum of "an eye for an eye, and a tooth for a tooth" has been cited by many as divine justification for strict punishments. Some scholars believe, however, that in reality the notion of "an eye for an eye" was intended to reduce the barbarism of existing penalties, whereby an aggrieved party might exact the severest of punishments for only minor offenses. Even petty offenses were often punished by whipping, torture, and sometimes death.

One famous modern-day advocate of the just deserts philosophy was Christian apologist C. S. Lewis, who wrote[54]

> The concept of desert is the only connecting link between punishment and justice. It is only as deserved or undeserved that a sentence can be just or unjust. I do not here contend that the question: "is it deserved?" is the only one we can reasonably ask about a punishment. We may very properly ask whether it is

likely to deter others and to reform the criminal. But neither of these two last questions is a question about justice. There is no sense in talking about a "just deterrent" or a "just cure"—we demand of a deterrent not whether it is just but whether it will deter. We demand of a cure not whether it is just but whether it succeeds. Thus when we cease to consider what the criminal deserves and consider only what will cure him or deter others, we have tacitly removed him from the sphere of justice altogether.

According to the neoclassical perspective, doing justice ultimately comes down to an official meting out of what is deserved. Justice for an individual is nothing more nor less than what that individual deserves when all the circumstances surrounding that person's situation and behavior are taken into account.

Deterrence

True to its historical roots, **deterrence** is a hallmark of modern neoclassical thought. In contrast to early thinkers, however, today's neoclassical writers distinguish between deterrence that is specific and that which is general. **Specific deterrence** is a goal of criminal sentencing that seeks to prevent a particular offender from engaging in repeat criminality. **General deterrence**, in contrast, works by way of example and seeks to prevent others from committing crimes similar to the one for which a particular offender is being sentenced.

Following their classical counterparts, modern-day advocates of general deterrence frequently stress that for punishment to be an effective impediment to crime it must be swift, certain, and severe enough to outweigh the rewards which flow from criminal activity. Unfortunately, those who advocate punishment as a deterrent are often frustrated by the complexity of today's criminal justice system and by the slow and circuitous manner in which cases are handled and punishments are meted out. Punishments today, even when imposed by a court, are rarely swift in their imposition. Swift punishments would follow quickly after sentencing. The

Michael Fay, the 18-year-old American teenager who was caned in Singapore in 1994 for spray-painting cars, makes the sign of the cross before entering Singapore's High Court. Just deserts advocates say that Fay got what he deserved. What do you think? *Jonathan Drake, Corbis*

wheels of modern criminal justice, however, are relatively slow to grind to a conclusion given the many delays inherent in judicial proceedings and the numerous opportunities for delay and appeal available to defense counsel. Similarly, certainty of punishment is anything but a reality. Certain punishments are those which cannot be easily avoided. However, even when punishments are ordered, they are frequently not carried out—at least not fully. In contemporary America, offenders sentenced to death, for example, are unlikely to ever have their sentences finalized. For those who do, an average of nearly twelve years passes between the time a sentence of death is imposed and the time it is carried out.[55] Death row inmates and their lawyers typically barrage any court that will hear them with a plethora of appeals designed to delay or derail the process of justice. Often they win new trials. If they are able to wait long enough, some inmates may find their sentences overturned by blanket U.S. Supreme Court rulings that find fault with some aspect of a state's trial process. Those who are able to delay even longer may die of natural causes before the machinery of the state grinds its way to a conclusion.

If the neoclassicists are correct, criminal punishments should ideally prevent a repetition of crime. Unfortunately, as high rates of contemporary recidivism indicate, punishments in America rarely accomplish that goal. **Recidivism** means, quite simply, the repetition of criminal behavior by those already involved in crime. Recidivism can also be used to measure the success of a given approach to the problem of crime. When so employed, it is referred to as a **recidivism rate**, expressed as the percentage of convicted offenders who have been released from prison and who are later rearrested for a new crime, generally within five years following release. Studies show that recidivism rates are high indeed, reaching levels of 80 to 90% in some instances, meaning that eight or nine of every ten criminal offenders released from confinement are rearrested for new lawbreaking activity within five years of being set free. Such studies, however, do not measure the numbers of released offenders who return to crime but who are not caught, and they ignore those who return to crime more than five years after release from prison. Were such numbers available, recidivism rates would likely be even higher.

One reason why American criminal justice seems so ineffectual at preventing crime and reducing recidivism may be that the punishments that contemporary criminal law provides are rarely applied to the majority of offenders. Statistics show that few lawbreakers are ever arrested and that of those who are, fewer still are convicted of the crimes with which they have been charged. After a lengthy court process, most offenders processed by the justice system are released, fined, or placed on probation. Relatively few are sent to prison, although short of capital punishment, prison is the most severe form of punishment available to authorities today. To represent this situation, criminal justice experts often use a diagram known as a "crime funnel." Figure 4-2 shows the crime funnel for 2000. As the figure shows, fewer than 1% of criminal law violators in America can be expected to spend time in prison as punishment for their crimes.

Serious Crimes
Committed Annually
42 Million (Estimate)

Crimes Reported
to the Police
14.4 Million

People Arrested
10 Million

People Sent
to Prison
419,500

■ **FIGURE 4-2** THE CRIME FUNNEL.
Source: Statistics derived from the Bureau of Justice Statistics, *Sourcebook of Criminal Justice Statistics, 2000* (Washington, D.C.: National Institute of Justice, 2001).

Exacerbating the situation is the fact that few people sent to prison ever serve anything close to the sentences that have been imposed on them. Many inmates serve only a small fraction of their sentences due to early release made possible by time off for good behavior, mandated reentry training, and the practical considerations necessitated by prison overcrowding.

The Death Penalty

Notions of deterrence, retribution, and just deserts all come together in **capital punishment**. The many different understandings of crime and crime control, along with arguments over free will and social determinism, combine with varying philosophies of punishment to produce considerable disagreement over the efficacy of death as a form of criminal sanction.

The extent to which the death penalty acts as a general deterrent has been widely studied. Some researchers have compared murder rates between states which have eliminated the death penalty and those which retain it, finding little variation in the rate at which murders are committed.[56] Others have looked at variations in murder rates over time in jurisdictions which have eliminated capital punishment, with similar results.[57] A now-classic 1988 Texas study provided a comprehensive review of capital punishment by correlating homicide rates with the rate of executions within the state between 1930 and 1986.[58] The study, which was especially important because Texas has been quite active in the capital punishment arena, failed to find any support for the use of death as a deterrent.

In 1996, researchers at the Institute for Law and Justice in Alexandria, Virginia, published *Convicted by Juries, Exonerated by Science,* a report funded by the National Institute of Justice.[59] The report provided a detailed review of 28 cases in which postconviction DNA evidence conclusively exonerated defendants who had been sentenced to lengthy prison terms. The 28 cases were selected on the basis of a detailed examination of records which indicated that the convicted defendants might have actually been innocent. The men in the study had served, on average, seven years in prison, and most had been tried and sentenced before the widespread availability of reliable DNA testing—although eyewitness testimony and other forensic evidence had led to their convictions. In each case, the DNA results unequivocally demonstrated that the defendants had been improperly convicted, and each defendant was ultimately set free. Although the study did not specifically involve the death penalty, *Convicted by Juries* showed just how fallible the judicial process can be.

More recent studies have focused on claimed injustices inherent in the sentencing process that leads to the imposition of the death penalty and on the seemingly inequitable application of capital punishment. In 2000, for example, a nonprofit group, the Texas Defender Service, examined hundreds of capital trials and appeals, including every published death penalty decision handed down by the Texas Court of Criminal Appeals (the state's highest criminal court) since 1976.[60] The study found, among other things, that (1) poor clients routinely receive bad representation by court-appointed attorneys, (2) race has a pervasive influence on the administration of capital punishment because prosecutors are far more likely to ask for imposition of the death sentence in cases where the victim is white as opposed to black, and (3) blacks and Hispanics are often excluded from capital juries. The report also identified instances in which prosecutors intentionally distorted the truth to win convictions; cases involving the use of courtroom testimony from disbarred psychiatrists, and examples of the use of unreliable "jailhouse informers" in capital cases.

A 2000 U.S. Department of Justice (DOJ) study found significant racial and geographic disparities in the imposition of federal death sentences.[61] The study revealed that 80% of the 682 defendants who have faced capital charges in federal courts since 1995 have been black. Perhaps even more significantly, U.S. attorneys in only 49 of the nation's 94 judicial districts have prosecuted defendants for capital crimes. Critics of the study noted that such numbers are meaningless unless compared to the actual proportion of minority defendants qualifying for capital prosecution. Similarly, the absence, in some jurisdictions, of crimes that might qualify for prosecution as capital offenses may explain the lack of death penalty prosecutions, rather than the supposed exercise of prosecutorial discretion.

A potentially more significant study, conducted by Columbia University Law School professors James S. Liebman and Jeffrey Fagan, was published at about the same time as the DOJ review.[62] Liebman and Fagan examined 4,578 death penalty appeals from 1973 to 1995 and found that most cases were seriously flawed—with many having to be retried. A state or federal court threw out the conviction or death sentence in 68% of the cases analyzed. This means that appellate courts found serious, reversible errors in almost seven out of every ten cases involving capital sentences. Eighty-two percent of defendants whose death sentences

were overturned by state appellate courts due to serious error were found to deserve a sentence less than death, and 7% were found to be innocent of the capital crime with which they had been charged. According to the study's authors, "Our 23 years worth of findings reveal a capital punishment system collapsing under the weight of its own mistakes."

Studies like the ones cited here have caused official rethinking of the death penalty in some parts of the country. In January 2000, Illinois Governor George Ryan suspended executions in his state after DNA results showed conclusively that 13 death row prisoners were innocent. About the same time, the American Bar Association called upon each capital punishment jurisdiction not to carry out the death penalty until that jurisdiction has had the opportunity to implement policies and procedures (1) to ensure that death penalty cases are administered fairly and impartially and in accordance with due process, and (2) to minimize the risk that innocent parties may be executed.[63] Figure 4-3 shows the number of people released from death row across the United States since 1976 after proof of their innocence became available.

Opponents of capital punishment make ten claims: (1) Capital punishment does not deter crime; (2) the death penalty has, at times, been imposed on innocent people, and no workable system is currently in place to prevent the accidental execution of innocents; (3) human life is sacred, even the life of a murderer; (4) state-imposed death lowers society to the same moral (or immoral) level as the murderer; (5) the death penalty has been (and may still be) imposed in haphazard and seemingly random fashion; (6) the death penalty is imposed disproportionately upon ethnic minorities; (7) capital punishment goes against the fundamental precepts of almost every organized religion; (8) the death penalty is more expensive than imprisonment; (9) capital punishment is widely viewed as inhumane and barbaric around the world; and (10) there is a better alternative (usually said to be life in prison without possibility of parole).

Advocates of capital punishment generally discount each of these claims, countering with the notion that death is *deserved* by those who commit especially heinous acts and that

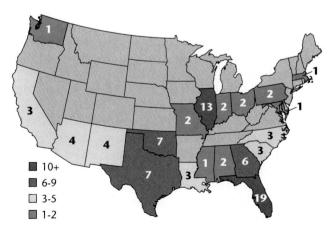

▪ **FIGURE 4-3** DEATH ROW PRISONERS EXONERATED AND FREED SINCE 1976.
Source: Death Penalty Information Center.

anything short of capital punishment under certain circumstances is an injustice in itself. Some people, the claim is made, deserve to die for what they have done. Such arguments evolve from a natural law perspective, are sometimes supported on religious grounds, and are based on the notion of just deserts, as discussed earlier.

Many death penalty advocates are also not convinced that the sanction cannot be an effective deterrent. As with other punishments, a death penalty that is swift and certain, they point out, is likely to deter others. Modern-day capital punishment, however, rarely meets these requirements. In contemporary America, offenders sentenced to death are unlikely to ever have their sentences finalized. For those who do, years often pass between the time the sentence is imposed and the time it is carried out.[64] Even if the threat of death does not effectively deter others, advocates of capital punishment say, it will ensure that those people who are put to death will never commit another crime.

As this book goes to press, a 23-member panel called the National Committee to Prevent Wrongful Executions, an offshoot of the Washington, D.C.–based Constitution Project, is organizing to study the mechanics of the death penalty in America. The committee includes syndicated columnist Ann Landers; former FBI Director William Sessions; former New York Governor Mario Cuomo; Cardinal William H. Keeler, Archbishop of Baltimore; Charles Gruber, former President of the International Association of Chiefs of Police; Beth A. Wilkinson, a lawyer who won a death sentence against Oklahoma City bomber Timothy McVeigh; G. Elaine Smith, past President of the American Baptist Churches, U.S.A.; Paula Kurland, a victims' rights advocate and mother who watched as the killer of her daughter was executed; Rabbi Eric H. Yoffie, President of the Union of American Hebrew Congregations; and others on both sides of the issue. Follow the deliberations of the committee via Web Extra! 4-11.

Web Extra! 4-11 at crimtoday.com

Capital Punishment and Race

According to the Washington, D.C.–based Death Penalty Information Center, the death penalty has been imposed disproportionately on racial minorities throughout American history.[65] Statistics maintained by the center show that "since 1930 nearly 90% of those executed for the crime of rape in this country were African-Americans. Currently, about 50% of those on the nation's death rows are from minority populations representing 20% of the country's population." The center, fervently against capital punishment, claims that "evidence of racial discrimination in the application of capital punishment continues. Nearly 40% of those executed since 1976 have been black, even though blacks constitute only 12% of the population. And in almost every death penalty case, the race of the victim was white." In 1996 alone, according to the center, "89% of the death sentences carried out involved white victims, even though 50% of the homicides in this country have black victims. Of the 229 executions that have occurred since the death penalty was reinstated" in 1972, says the center, "only one has involved a white defendant for the murder of a black person."

A 1994 congressional report by the Subcommittee on Civil and Constitutional Rights[66] reached much the same conclusion. The report, entitled *Racial Disparities in Federal Death Penalty Prosecutions, 1988–1994,* had this to say about race and capital punishment under federal law: "Racial minorities are being prosecuted under federal death penalty law far beyond their proportion in the general population or the population of criminal offenders. Analysis of prosecutions under the federal death penalty provisions of the Anti-Drug Abuse Act of 1988 reveals that 89% of the defendants selected for capital prosecution have been either African-American or Mexican-American. Moreover, the number of prosecutions under this Act has been increasing over the past two years with no decline in racial disparities. All ten of the recently approved federal capital prosecutions have been against black defendants. This pattern of inequality adds to the mounting evidence that race continues to play an unacceptable part in the application of capital punishment in America today."[67] The report was prepared with the assistance of the Death Penalty Information Center.

On the other hand, capital punishment advocates say that the real question is not whether ethnic differences exist in the rate of imposition of the death penalty, but whether the penalty is *fairly* imposed. They argue, for example, that if 50% of all crimes eligible for capital punishment are committed by members of a particular ethnic group, then anyone anticipating fairness in imposition of the death penalty would expect to see 50% of death row populations composed of members of that particular ethnic group—no matter how small the group might be. In like manner, one would also expect to see the same relative ethnicity among those executed. In short, they say, if fairness is to be any guide, those committing capital crimes should be the ones sentenced to death—regardless of race, ethnicity, gender, or other similar social characteristics.

The claim that the death penalty is or is not discriminatory is difficult to investigate. Although evidence may suggest that blacks and other minorities in the United States have in the past been unfairly sentenced to die,[68] the present evidence is not as clear. For an accurate appraisal to be made, any claims of disproportionality must go beyond simple comparisons with racial representation in the larger population and must somehow measure both frequency and seriousness of capital crimes between and within racial groups. Following that line of reasoning, the Supreme Court, in the 1987 case of *McCleskey* v. *Kemp,*[69] held that a simple showing of racial discrepancies in the application of the death penalty does not amount to a constitutional violation. Learn more about the death penalty from the Death Penalty Information Center at Web Extra! 4-12.

Web Extra! 4-12 at crimtoday.com

CRIME IN THE NEWS
Death Row Fashion Ads Spark Outrage

When serial killer Cesar Francesco Barone was 35, he was sentenced to death row for sexually assaulting and killing three women in Oregon.

Sixteen years earlier, police believe he crept into the bedroom of a 73-year-old neighbor in Fort Lauderdale, Fla., raped her and strangled her to death in her bed.

That same year, he was charged but later acquitted of trying to bludgeon to death his grandmother with a rolling pin.

Today, at age 39, Barone is selling sweaters from death row.

Barone appears this month in a 100-page magazine insert published by Benetton, the Italian clothing manufacturer. Benetton says it created the supplement to force Americans to consider the human cost of executing criminals.

But to the murder victims' families, along with prosecutors and police who put the inmates behind bars, the Benetton project presents a dishonest, one-sided view of the inmates that ignores the agony suffered by their victims.

"HE'D BE OUT MURDERING AND RAPING"

The supplement, entitled, "We, On Death Row," consists of photographs and interviews with 26 death row inmates.

An Oregon police officer, who investigated Barone for six years, said Barone's interview is particularly disturbing. At one point, the interviewer asks Barone what he would be doing if he were a free man. Barone, who once worked as an aide in a nursing home—where police say he preyed on elderly women—says he would "probably be doing what I was doing before I came here, working in medicine."

Michael O'Connell, a homicide detective with the Washington County Sheriff's Department, has a different answer.

"He'd be out murdering and raping, I can assure you of that," O'Connell said. "He's a sociopath. He's unable to show any compassion or empathy for anyone. He hasn't ever shown an inkling of remorse."

INMATE PICTURED HOLDING BIBLE

In fact, Benetton prevented the inmates featured in its supplement from expressing remorse or talking about their crimes.

That would have distracted readers from the point of "We, On Death Row," said Speedy Rice, a legal adviser for the supplement and a law professor at Gonzaga University in Spokane, Wash.

"We didn't think it was the right forum to do that," Rice said. "[Benetton] approached us to do a project on the human faces of people on death row."

At least one of the subjects is already dead. Harvey Lee Green, convicted of killing two people during a robbery of a dry cleaners, was executed Sept. 24, 1999. In the Benetton supplement, Green is pictured holding a Bible and talks about his faith in God and his hope for mercy.

"This project took one view: Who is it America is executing at the end of the 20th century?" Rice added.

ASKED ABOUT MONICA LEWINSKY

To accomplish that goal, inmates answer questions about God, their childhoods, their favorite television shows. Others talk about what they'd be doing if they weren't behind bars.

In some cases, the questions verge on the bizarre. Barone is asked for his opinion about Bill Clinton and Monica Lewinsky. Another man talks about his love of sports and then reveals that his favorite athlete is the infamous NFL running back O. J. Simpson.

To Sarah Froemsdorf, this approach humanizes killers at the expense of the victims.

Froemsdorf's husband, Missouri State Trooper James Froemsdorf, had arrested Jerome Mallett in 1985 after stopping him for speeding and learning he was wanted for a Texas robbery. But Mallett, sitting in the back of Froemsdorf's police cruiser, escaped from his handcuffs, beat the trooper and then shot him to death.

"While Jim was unconscious, Jerome Mallett put the last two bullets in his head that took his life," Froemsdorf said. "And they want us to have pity for this man. I have no pity. His life was one of destruction and he took away something good."

CALLS TO BOYCOTT COMPANY

David Hans, whose father was killed three years ago by an inmate featured in the supplement, said he doesn't even want to know what his killer has to say.

In the three years since the killing of Hans' father, a deputy with the Jefferson County, Ky., Sheriff's Department, Hans says he has grown weary of hearing outsiders clamoring to abolish the death penalty.

"Someone on the outside looking in can say, 'We can humanize this, and maybe the death row isn't the best thing,'" Hans said. "But it's totally different once you've lived through it."

Disgusted by the ads, some have called for a boycott of Benetton items.

"Benetton is using the blood of murder victims to promote their commodity," said Dianne Clements, the president of Justice for All, a pro-death penalty group based in Houston. "And that's despicable, actually, and I would hope that the American public reacts by buying even fewer Benetton items."

"These guys wouldn't be on a poster unless they had killed," Clements said. "Let's call a spade a spade. The only reason they are on a poster is because they are capital murderers."

Source: Hans H. Chen, "Survivors Say Inmates Humanized at Victim's Expense," APB News, January 10, 2000. Reprinted with permission.

POLICY IMPLICATIONS OF THE CLASSICAL SCHOOL

Much of the ongoing practice of criminal justice in America today is built around the justice model. During the last quarter of the twentieth century, the justice model led to the advent of determinate sentencing, to truth in sentencing, to a corresponding reduction of emphasis on rehabilitation, and to a rebirth of interest in the use of capital punishment.[70]

Determinate sentencing is a strategy that mandates a specified and fixed amount of time to be served for every offense category. Under determinate sentencing schemes, for example, judges in affected jurisdictions might be required to impose seven-year sentences on armed robbers, but only one-year sentences on strong-armed robbers (who use no weapon). Determinate sentencing schemes build upon the twin notions of classical thought that (1) the pleasure of a given crime can be somewhat accurately assessed, and (2) a fixed amount of punishment necessary for deterrence can be calculated and specified. **Truth in sentencing** requires judges to assess and make public the actual time an offender is likely to serve once sentenced to prison, and many recently enacted truth-in-sentencing laws require that offenders serve a large portion of their sentence (often 80%) before they can be released.

Partially as a result of the widespread implementation of determinate sentencing strategies and the passage of truth-in-sentencing laws during the last quarter century, prison populations today are larger than ever before. By the beginning of 2000, the nation's state and federal prison population (excluding jails) stood at 1,366,721 inmates, a figure that represented an increase of 722% over 1970. Figure 4-4 shows the total U.S. prison population from 1960–2000.

Law and Order Versus Individual Rights

Modern-day heirs of the Classical School see punishment as a central tenet of criminal justice policy and believe it to be a natural and deserved consequence of criminal activity. Such thinkers call for greater prison capacity and new prison construction. They use evidence such as the crime funnel (Figure 4-2) to argue that although punishment is theoretically an effective crime preventative, in today's society few criminals are ever punished. Building on a just deserts model, these **law and order advocates** continue to seek stiffer criminal laws and enhanced penalties for criminal activity. They insist on the importance of individual responsibility and claim that law violators should be held unfailingly responsible for their actions. Law and order advocates generally want to ensure that the sentences imposed by criminal courts are the sentences served by offenders, and they argue against reduced prison time for any reason.

Many just deserts advocates rally around the death penalty because they believe it is either called for as a natural consequence of specific forms of abhorrent behavior or because they believe that if imposed swiftly and with certainty, it will deter

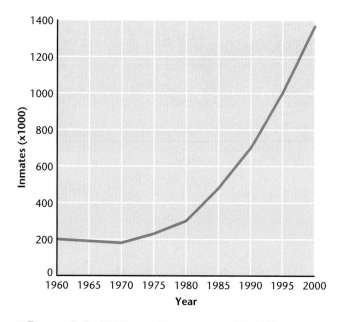

■ **FIGURE 4-4**   U.S. PRISON POPULATION, 1960–2000.
Source: Bureau of Justice Statistics.

others from committing similar crimes in the future. They answer critics who claim that evidence does not support the deterrent value of capital punishment by pointing out that death is at least a specific deterrent, if not a general one. They hasten to add that regardless of concerns about deterrence, some crimes cry out for the ultimate punishment, and that in cases of extreme law violation, death is the offender's due.

Standing in sharp contrast to today's law and order advocates are **individual rights advocates** who emphasize rights rather than punishment. Individual rights advocates defend the prerogatives of individuals against potential government excesses inherent in the social contract. Citing correctional overcrowding, high rates of recidivism, and increased criminal activity in many areas of society, individual rights advocates point out that an increasing emphasis on imprisonment has done little to stem the tide of rising crime. They call for renewed recognition of constitutional and personal rights in the face of criminal prosecution and for reduction in the use of imprisonment as a criminal sanction—suggesting that it be employed as a kind of last resort to deal with only the most dangerous offenders.

Individual rights advocates argue that **dangerousness**, or the likelihood that a given individual will later harm society or others, should be the major determining criterion for government action against the freedom of its citizens. Dangerousness, they suggest, should form the standard against which any need for incapacitation might be judged. **Incapacitation**, simply put, is the use of imprisonment or other means to reduce the likelihood that an offender will be capable of committing future offenses.

Proponents of modern-day incapacitation often distinguish between selective incapacitation, in which crime is controlled via the imprisonment of specific individuals, and collective incapacitation, whereby changes in legislation and/or sentencing patterns lead to the removal from society of

Rahway (New Jersey) State Prison. Today's "law and order" approach has led to dramatically overcrowded prisons. How can overcrowding be reduced? *J. P. Laffont, Corbis/Sygma*

entire groups of individuals judged to be dangerous. Advocates of selective incapacitation as a crime control strategy point to studies which show that the majority of crimes are perpetrated by a small number of hard-core repeat offenders. The most famous of those studies, conducted by University of Pennsylvania Professor Marvin Wolfgang, focused on 9,000 men born in Philadelphia in 1945.[71] By the time this cohort of men had reached age 18, Wolfgang was able to determine that 627 "chronic recidivists" were responsible for the large majority of all serious violent crimes committed by the group. Other, more recent, studies have similarly shown that a small core of criminal perpetrators is probably responsible for most criminal activity in the United States.

Such thinking has led to the development of incapacitation as a modern-day treatment philosophy and to the creation of innovative forms of incapacitation that do not require imprisonment—such as home confinement, the use of halfway houses or career training centers for convicted felons, and psychological and/or chemical treatments designed to reduce the likelihood of future crime commission. Similarly, such thinkers argue, the decriminalization of many offenses and the enhancement of social programs designed to combat what they see as the root causes of crime—including poverty, low educational levels, a general lack of skills, and inherent or active discrimination—will lead to a much reduced incidence of crime in the future, making high rates of imprisonment unnecessary.

A CRITIQUE OF CLASSICAL THEORIES

Classical and neoclassical thought represents more a philosophy of justice than it does a theory of crime causation. As Randy Martin, Robert J. Mutchnick, and W. Timothy Austin have observed, for example, "The true test of Beccaria's essay can be judged by the influence it has had over time on our justice system."[72] The influence of Beccaria, the Enlightenment, and classical thinkers can be found today in the U.S. Constitution, in existing get-tough approaches to crime, and in a continuing emphasis on individual rights. Martin and colleagues conclude that the Classical School "has left behind a legacy that we see in almost every aspect of our present-day justice system."[73]

As we observed in Chapter 3, any perspective gains credence if actions taken on the basis of its assertions appear to bear fruit. Not surprisingly, advocates of today's neoclassical approaches to crime control take much of the credit for the recent drop-off in crime rates. After all, following the implementation of "get tough on crime" policies like the determinate sentencing schemes called for by the just deserts model, official rates of crime have shown substantial declines. As discussed in Chapter 2, however, the extent of crime's decline may not be as substantial as many people think; publicized statistical declines may be largely an artifact of the measuring process or may be due to demographic changes in the American population.

Critics charge that classical and neoclassical thought lacks comprehensive explanatory power over criminal motivation, other than to advance the relatively simple claim that crime is the result of free will, the personal attractions of crime, and individual choice. Such critics point out that classical theory is largely bereft of meaningful explanations as to how a choice for or against criminal activity is made. Similarly, classical theory lacks any appreciation for the deeper fonts of personal motivation, including those represented by aspects of human biology, psychology, and the social environment. Moreover, the Classical School, as originally detailed in the writings of Beccaria and Bentham, lacked any scientific basis for the claims it made. Although neoclassical writers have advanced the scientific foundation of classical claims (via studies like those showing the effectiveness of particular forms of deterrence), many still defend their way of thinking by referring to what are purely philosophical ideals, such as just deserts.

THEORY VERSUS REALITY
Assessing Dangerousness

Dangerousness is a difficult concept to comprehend. Indicators of dangerousness have yet to be well defined in the social scientific literature, and legislators who attempt to codify any assessment of future dangerousness often find themselves frustrated. On the individual level, however, dangerousness might be more easily assessed. What follows is a description of the criteria one judge, Lois G. Forer, used in deciding whether an offender needed to spend a long time away from society.

I had my own criteria or guidelines—very different from those established by most states and the federal government—for deciding on a punishment. My primary concern was public safety. The most important question I asked myself was whether the offender could be deterred from committing other crimes. No one can predict with certainty who will or will not commit a crime, but there are indicators most sensible people recognize as danger signals:

■ First, was this an irrational crime? If an arsonist sets a fire to collect insurance, that is a crime but also a rational act. Such a person can be deterred by being made to pay for the harm done and the costs to the fire department. However, if the arsonist sets fires just because he likes to see them,

it is highly unlikely that he can be stopped from setting others, no matter how high the fine. Imprisonment is advisable even though it may be a first offense.
■ Second, was there wanton cruelty? If a robber maims or slashes the victim, there is little likelihood that he can safely be left in the community. If a robber simply displays a gun but does not fire it or harm the victim, then one should consider his life history, provocation, and other circumstances in deciding whether probation is appropriate.
■ Third, is this a hostile person? Was his crime one of hatred, and does he show any genuine remorse? Most rapes are acts of hostility, and the vast majority of rapists have a record of numerous sexual assaults. I remember one man who raped his mother. I gave him the maximum sentence under the law—20 years—but with good behavior, he got out fairly quickly. He immediately raped another elderly woman.
■ Fourth, is this a person who knows he is doing wrong but cannot control himself? Typical of such offenders are pedophiles. One child abuser who appeared before me had already been convicted of abusing his first wife's child. I got him on the second wife's child and sentenced him to the maximum. Still, he'll get out with good behavior, and I shudder to think about the children around him when he does. This is one case in which justice is not tough enough.

By contrast, some people who have committed homicide present very little danger of further violence—although many more do. Once a young man came before me because he had taken aim at a person half a block away and then shot him in the back, killing him. Why did he do it? "I wanted to get me a body." He should never get out.

DISCUSSION QUESTIONS

1. How are public safety and criminal punishment related?
2. Do you agree that the criteria used by Judge Forer to identify dangerousness are useful? Why or why not?
3. Do you believe that offenders who are identified as "dangerous" should be treated differently from other offenders? If so, how?

Source: Lois G. Forer, "Justice by the Numbers; Mandatory Sentencing Drove Me from the Bench," *Washington Monthly,* April 1992, pp. 12–18. Reprinted with permission from *The Washington Monthly.* Copyright by The Washington Monthly Company, 1611 Connecticut Ave., N.W., Washington, D.C. 20009; 202-462-0128. Web Site: www.washingtonmonthly.com.

SUMMARY

The Enlightenment, a social and cultural renaissance which occurred throughout the late seventeenth and early eighteenth centuries, proved to be a highly liberating force in the Western world. Enlightenment thinkers established many of the democratic principles that formed the conceptual foundations of the American and French Revolutions. Their ideas are still alive today and significantly shape our understanding of human nature and human behavior. The twin conceptual prongs around which

this textbook is built—social responsibility and individual rights—both have their roots in Enlightenment thought and in the belief in free will which it engendered. Notions of deterrence as a goal of the justice system and of punishment as a worthy consequence of crime owe much of their contemporary influence to the Classical School of criminology. As we begin the twenty-first century, we carry with us an intellectual heritage far older than we may realize.

DISCUSSION QUESTIONS

1. This book emphasizes a social problems versus social responsibility theme. Which perspective is most clearly supported by classical and neoclassical thought? Why?
2. Name the various preclassical thinkers identified in this chapter. What ideas did each contribute to Enlightenment philosophy? What form did those ideas take in classical criminological thought?
3. Define *natural law*. Do you believe that natural law exists? If so, what types of behaviors would be contravened by natural law? If not, why not?
4. What is meant by the idea of a social contract? How does the concept of a social contract relate to natural law?
5. What were the central concepts that defined the Classical School of criminological thought? Which of those concepts are still alive? Where do you see evidence for the survival of those concepts?
6. What are the major differences between individual rights advocates and law and order advocates? Which perspective most appeals to you? Why? Which is most closely aligned with classical criminology?
7. Define *recidivism*. What is a recidivism rate? Why are recidivism rates so high today? What can be done to lower them?

WEB QUEST!

Few debates encompass the issues raised in this chapter better than the one now raging over the death penalty. Visit some of the death penalty sites on the Internet to explore arguments on both sides of the debate and to identify the individual rights and law and order issues involved. Here are a few such sites:

ACLU Death Penalty Page (http://www.aclu.org/issues/death/hmdp.html)

Amnesty International Death Penalty Campaign (http://www.amnesty.org/ailib/intcam/dp/index.html)

Campaign to End the Death Penalty (http://www.nodeathpenalty.org)

Cornell Law School Death Penalty Project (http://www.lawschool.cornell.edu/lawlibrary/death/default.htm)

Dead Man Talkin' (http://monkey.hooked.net/monkey/m/hut/deadman/deadman.html)

Death Penalty Net (http://www.deathpenalty.net)

Justice against Crime (http://users.deltanet.com/users/ghc)

Justice for All (http://www.jfa.net)

Pro-Deathpenalty.com (http://www.prodeathpenalty.com)

Other sites representing both sides of the capital punishment debate can be found by searching the Criminal Justice Cybrary (talkjustice.com/cybrary.asp). If your instructor asks you to, visit each of the sites listed here, along with others of your choosing. Then write a brief summary of the philosophy represented by each site that you view.

LIBRARY EXTRAS!

The Library Extras! listed here complement the Web Extras! found throughout this chapter. Library Extras! may be accessed on the Web at crimtoday.com.

Library Extra! 4-1. American Society of Criminology, *Critical Criminal Justice Issues: Task Force Reports from the American Society of Criminology* (Washington, D.C.: National Institute of Justice, 1997).

Library Extra! 4-2. Dan Fleissner and Fred Heinzelmann, *Crime Prevention through Environmental Design and Community Policing* (Washington, D.C.: National Institute of Justice, 1996).

Library Extra! 4-3. Hugo Adam Bedau, *The Case against the Death Penalty* (American Civil Liberties Union, online document, no date).

Library Extra! 4-4. Ronald V. Clarke, "Situational Crime Prevention: Everybody's Business." Paper presented at the 1995 Australian Crime Prevention Council conference.

Library Extra! 4-5. Jennifer C. Honeyman and James R. P. Ogloff, "Capital Punishment: Arguments for Life and for Death," *Canadian Journal of Behavioral Science*, Vol. 28 (1996).

Library Extra! 4-6. Sharon C. Smith, *Capital Punishment in the United States* (Washington, D.C.: Close Up Foundation, 1999).

NOTES

[1] Jeremy Bentham, *An Introduction to the Principles of Morals and Legislation* (London: T. Payne, 1789).

[2] Cesare Beccaria, *Essay on Crimes and Punishments,* translated by Henry Paolucci (New York: Bobbs-Merrill, 1963).

[3] To crime victims invited to the White House, April 18, 1984. Quotation number 2042 in James B. Simpson, *Simpson's Contemporary Quotations* (Boston: Houghton Mifflin, 1988).

[4] *New York Times,* April 23, 1984. Quotation number 1579 in James B. Simpson, *Simpson's Contemporary Quotations* (Boston: Houghton Mifflin, 1988).

[5] *New York Newsday,* April 20, 1998.

[6] William Graham Sumner, *Folkways* (New York: Dover, 1906).

[7] Marvin Wolfgang, "The Key Reporter," *Phi Beta Kappa,* Vol. 52, No. 1.

[8] Roman influence in England had ended by 442 A.D., according to Crane Brinton, John B. Christopher, and Robert L. Wolff, *A History of Civilization,* 3rd ed., Vol. 1 (Englewood Cliffs, NJ: Prentice Hall, 1967), p. 180.

[9] Howard Abadinsky, *Law and Justice* (Chicago: Nelson-Hall, 1988), p. 6.

[10] Edward McNall Burns, *Western Civilization,* 7th ed. (New York: W. W. Norton, 1969), p. 339.

[11] Ibid., p. 533.

[12] Brinton, Christopher, and Wolff, *A History of Civilization,* p. 274.

[13] Harry V. Jaffa and Ernest van den Haag, "Of Men, Hogs, and Law: If Natural Law Does Not Permit Us to Distinguish between Men and Hogs, What Does?" *National Review,* February 3, 1992, p. 40.

[14] Referred to in official transcripts as Rudolf Franz Ferdinand Hoess.

[15] International Military Tribunal, "One Hundred and Eighth Day, Monday, 4/15/1946, Part 03," in *Trial of the Major War Criminals before the International Military Tribunal, Volume XI. Proceedings: 4/8/1946–4/17/1946* (Nuremberg: International Military Tribunal, 1943), pp. 398–400.

[16] The quotations attributed to Beccaria in this section are from Beccaria, *Essay on Crimes and Punishments.*

[17] The quotations attributed to Bentham in this section are from Bentham, *An Introduction to the Principles of Morals and Legislation.*

[18] R. Martinson, "What Works: Questions and Answers about Prison Reform," *Public Interest,* No. 35 (1974), pp. 22–54.

[19] James Q. Wilson, *Thinking about Crime* (New York: Vintage, 1975).

[20] David Fogel, *We Are the Living Proof: The Justice Model of Corrections* (Cincinnati: Anderson, 1975).

[21] Conrad P. Rutkowski, "Fogel's 'Justice Model'" Stop Trying to Reform. Punish, but Treat All Alike," *Illinois Issues,* February 1976.

[22] Felton M. Earls and Albert J. Reiss, *Breaking the Cycle: Predicting and Preventing Crime* (Washington, D.C.: National Institute of Justice, 1994), p. 49.

[23] L. E. Cohen and Marcus Felson, "Social Change and Crime Rate Trends: A Routine Activity Approach," *American Sociological Review,* Vol. 44, No. 4 (August 1979), pp. 588–608. Also see Marcus Felson and L. E. Cohen, "Human Ecology and Crime: A Routine Activity Approach," *Human Ecology,* Vol. 8, No. 4 (1980), pp. 389–406; Marcus Felson, "Linking Criminal Choices, Routine Activities, Informal Control, and Criminal Outcomes," in Derek B. Cornish and Ronald V. Clarke, eds., *The Reasoning Criminal: Rational Choice Perspectives on Offending* (New York: Springer-Verlag, 1986), pp. 119–128; and Ronald V. Clarke and Marcus Felson, eds., *Advances in Criminological Theory: Routine Activity and Rational Choice* (New Brunswick, NJ: Transaction, 1993).

[24] Lawrence E. Cohen and Marcus Felson, "Social Change and Crime Rate Trends: A Routine Activities Approach," *American Sociological Review,* Vol. 44, No. 4 (1979), p. 595.

[25] For a test of routine activities theory as an explanation for victimization in the workplace, see John D. Wooldredge, Francis T. Cullen, and Edward J. Latessa, "Victimization in the Workplace: A Test of Routine Activities Theory," *Justice Quarterly,* Vol. 9, No. 2 (June 1992), pp. 325–335.

[26] Marcus Felson, *Crime and Everyday Life: Insight and Implications for Society* (Thousand Oaks, CA: Pine Forge Press, 1994).

[27] Gary LaFree and Christopher Birkbeck, "The Neglected Situation: A Cross-National Study of the Situational Characteristics of Crime," *Criminology,* Vol. 29, No. 1 (February 1991), p. 75.

[28] Ronald V. Clarke and Derek B. Cornish, eds., *Crime Control in Britain: A Review of Police and Research* (Albany: State University of New York Press, 1985), p. 8.

[29] Ronald V. Clarke, "Situational Crime Prevention—Everybody's Business." Paper presented at the 1995 Australian Crime Prevention Council conference. Web posted at http://barney.webace.com.au/~austcpc/conf95/clarke.htm. Accessed December 2, 2000.

[30] See Derek B. Cornish and Ronald V. Clarke, "Understanding Crime Displacement: An Application of Rational Choice Theory," *Criminology,* Vol. 25, No. 4 (November 1987), p. 933.

[31] Clarke and Cornish, *Crime Control in Britain,* p. 48.

[32] Werner Einstadter and Stuart Henry, *Criminological Theory: An Analysis of Its Underlying Assumptions* (Fort Worth: Harcourt Brace, 1995), p. 70.

[33] Daniel J. Curran and Claire M. Renzetti, *Theories of Crime* (Boston: Allyn and Bacon, 1994), p. 18.

[34] Jack Katz, *Seductions of Crime: Moral and Sensual Attractions in Doing Evil* (New York: Basic Books, 1988), p. 8.

[35] Ibid., p. 3.

[36] Ibid., p. 76.

[37] Ibid., p. 71.

[38] Bill McCarthy, "Not Just 'For the Thrill of It': An Instrumentalist Elaboration of Katz's Explanation of Sneaky

Thrill Property Crimes," *Criminology,* Vol. 33, No. 4 (1995), pp. 519–538.

[39] The quotations attributed to Weisburd in this section are from David Weisburd, "Reorienting Crime Prevention Research and Policy: From the Causes of Criminality to the Context of Crime," *NIJ Research Report* (Washington, D.C.: National Institute of Justice, June 1997).

[40] See P. Brantingham and P. Brantingham, "Situational Crime Prevention in Practice," *Canadian Journal of Criminology* (January 1990), pp. 17–40; and R. V. Clarke, "Situational Crime Prevention: Achievements and Challenges," in M. Tonry and D. Farrington, eds., *Building a Safer Society: Strategic Approaches to Crime Prevention, Crime and Justice: A Review of Research,* Vol. 19 (Chicago: University of Chicago Press, 1995).

[41] Weisburd, "Reorienting Crime Prevention Research and Policy."

[42] See, for example, J. E. Eck and D. Weisburd, eds., *Crime and Place: Crime Prevention Studies,* Vol. 4 (Monsey, NY: Willow Tree Press, 1995).

[43] See L. Sherman, "Hot Spots of Crime and Criminal Careers of Places," in J. E. Eck and D. Weisburd, eds., *Crime and Place: Crime Prevention Studies,* Vol. 4 (Monsey, NY: Willow Tree Press, 1995); and L. Sherman, P. R. Gartin, and M. E. Buerger, "Hot Spots of Predatory Crime: Routine Activities and the Criminology of Place," *Criminology,* Vol. 27, No. 1 (1989), pp. 27–56.

[44] Weisburd, "Reorienting Crime Prevention and Policy."

[45] Laura J. Moriarty and James E. Williams, "Examining the Relationship between Routine Activities Theory and Social Disorganization: An Analysis of Property Crime Victimization," *American Journal of Criminal Justice,* Vol. 21, No. 1, 1996, pp. 43–59.

[46] Ibid., p. 43.

[47] Ibid., p. 46.

[48] Kenneth D. Tunnell, "Choosing Crime: Close Your Eyes and Take Your Chances," *Justice Quarterly,* Vol. 7 (1990), pp. 673–690.

[49] See R. Barr and K. Pease, "Crime Placement, Displacement and Deflection," in M. Tonry and N. Morris, eds., *Crime and Justice: A Review of Research,* Vol. 12 (Chicago: University of Chicago Press, 1990).

[50] For a good summation of target hardening, see Ronald V. Clarke, *Situational Crime Prevention* (New York: Harrow and Heston, 1992).

[51] For a good summation of studies on displacement, see R. Hesseling, "Displacement: A Review of the Empirical Literature," in R. V. Clarke, ed., *Crime Prevention Studies,* Vol. 3 (Monsey, NY: Willow Tree Press, 1994).

[52] Carol J. Castaneda, "Not All Urging Mercy for Teen Facing Flogging," *USA Today,* April 4, 1994, p. 3A.

[53] The number of lashes Fay received was reduced to four, and he spent an additional month imprisoned in Singapore before being released and returning to the United States.

[54] C. S. Lewis, "The Humanitarian Theory of Punishment," *Res Judicatae,* Vol. 6 (1953), pp. 224–225.

[55] Tracey L. Snell, *Capital Punishment, 1999* (Washington, D.C.: Bureau of Justice Statistics, 2000), p. 12.

[56] See, for example, W. C. Bailey, "Deterrence and the Death Penalty for Murders in Utah: A Time Series Analysis," *Journal of Contemporary Law,* Vol. 5, No. 1 (1978), pp. 1–20; and W. C. Bailey, "An Analysis of the Deterrent Effect of the Death Penalty for Murder in California," *Southern California Law Review,* Vol. 52, No. 3 (1979), pp. 743–764.

[57] See, for example, B. E. Forst, "The Deterrent Effect of Capital Punishment: A Cross-State Analysis of the 1960s," *Minnesota Law Review,* Vol. 61 (1977), pp. 743–764.

[58] Scott H. Decker and Carol W. Kohfeld, "Capital Punishment and Executions in the Lone Star State: A Deterrence Study," *Criminal Justice Research Bulletin* (Criminal Justice Center, Sam Houston State University), Vol. 3, No. 12 (1988).

[59] Edward Connors et al., *Convicted by Juries, Exonerated by Science: Case Studies in the Use of DNA Evidence to Establish Innocence after Trial* (Washington, D.C.: National Institute of Justice, 1996).

[60] Texas Defender Service, *A State of Denial: Texas Justice and the Death Penalty* (Houston: Texas Defender Service, 2000). Web posted at http://www.texasdefender.org/study. Accessed January 5, 2001.

[61] U.S. Department of Justice, *The Federal Death Penalty System: A Statistical Survey—1988–2000* (Washington, D.C.: U.S. Department of Justice, 2000).

[62] James S. Liebman, Jeffrey Fagan, and Valerie West, "A Broken System: Error Rates in Capital Cases, 1973–1995," Columbia Law School, 2000. Web posted at http://www.law.columbia.edu/instructionalservices/liebman. Accessed May 2, 2001.

[63] The American Bar Association resolution may be viewed at http://www.abanet.org/irr/rec107.html. Accessed December 12, 2000.

[64] Snell, *Capital Punishment, 1999,* p. 12.

[65] From the Death Penalty Information Center's site on the World Wide Web: http://www.deathpenaltyinfo.org. Accessed December 15, 2000.

[66] A subcommittee of the Committee on the Judiciary.

[67] Death Penalty Information Center, *Racial Disparities in Federal Death Penalty Prosecutions: 1988–1994.* Web posted at http://www.deathpenaltyinfo.org/dpic.r05.html. Accessed March 2, 2001.

[68] As some of the evidence presented before the Supreme Court in *Furman* v. *Georgia* (408 U.S. 238, 1972) suggested.

[69] *McCleskey* v. *Kemp,* 481 U.S. 279, 107 S.Ct. 1756, 95 L. Ed. 2d 262 (1987).

[70] Randy Martin, Robert J. Mutchnick, and W. Timothy Austin, *Criminological Thought: Pioneers Past and Present* (New York: Macmillan, 1990), p. 18.

[71] Marvin Wolfgang, Thorsten Sellin, and Robert Figlio, *Delinquency in a Birth Cohort* (Chicago: University of Chicago Press, 1972).

[72] Martin, Mutchnick, and Austin, *Criminological Thought,* p. 17.

[73] Ibid., p. 18.

The evidence is very firm that there is a genetic factor involved in crime.

—Sarnoff A. Mednick[1]

Investigators of the link between biology and crime find themselves caught in one of the most bitter controversies to hit the scientific community in years.

—*Time*[2]

biological roots of criminal behavior

I share with other behavior geneticists . . . the position that parents in most working- to professional-class families may have little influence on what traits their children will eventually develop as adults. Moreover, I seriously doubt that good child-rearing practices can greatly reduce an undesirable trait's prevalence, whether it be low IQ, criminality, or any other trait of social concern.

—David C. Rowe[3]

Legislative and judicial responses to new genetic discoveries will have a major effect on whether we are about to enter an unprecedented period of behavioral genetic determinism and, with it, social disruption, or the promised enlightened era of genetic marvels.

—Mark A. Rothstein, Cullen Distinguished Professor of Law, University of Houston Law Center[4]

KEY CONCEPTS

IMPORTANT TERMS

atavism	endomorph	monozygotic (MZ) twins
behavioral genetics	eugenic criminology	paradigm
biological theories	eugenics	phrenology
born criminals	genetic determinism	schizoids
constitutional theories	heritability	sociobiology
criminal anthropology	hypoglycemia	somatotyping
criminaloids	Juke family	supermale
cycloid	Kallikak family	testosterone
displastics	masculinity hypothesis	
ectomorph	mesomorph	

IMPORTANT NAMES AND CASES

Buck v. *Bell*	Henry Herbert Goddard	Cesare Lombroso
Charles Darwin	Charles Buckman Goring	Konrad Lorenz
Richard Louis Dugdale	Richard J. Herrnstein	William H. Sheldon
Arthur H. Estabrook	Earnest A. Hooton	Johann Gaspar Spurzheim
Franz Joseph Gall	C. Ray Jeffery	Edward O. Wilson
Sir Francis Galton	Ernst Kretschmer	James Q. Wilson

OUTCOMES

LEARNING

After reading this chapter, you should be able to
- Recognize the importance of biological explanations of criminal behavior
- Identify the fundamental assumptions made by biological theorists of crime causation
- Explain the relationship between human aggression and biological determinants
- Describe the research linking genetics and crime
- Explain the contribution of sociobiology to the study of criminality
- Identify modern day social policies that reflects the biological approach to crime causation
- Assess the shortcomings of biological theories of criminal behavior

Hear the author discuss this chapter at *crimtoday.com*

INTRODUCTION

One of the most vicious murders ever to occur in Arizona was the 1984 mutilation killing of Maude Moormann by her 36-year-old adoptive son, Robert Henry Moormann.[5] Robert's biological mother drowned shortly after his birth in 1948, and he lived with his grandparents for a short while before being turned over to a Catholic social services agency for adoption. At age 2 1/2, a childless couple, Henry and Maude Moormann, adopted the boy. According to popular accounts, Maude was overly protective of her new son, leaving him ill-

prepared for encounters with other children. Robert became a notoriously poor student, frequently failing classes and often running away from home. At age 13, he was sent to the Sun School in Phoenix, a shelter for troubled boys, after having been accused of molesting a little girl. While home for Christmas holidays, he hid a .22-caliber pistol under his pillow and shot his mother in the stomach while she sat by his bed to talk with him. The bullet lodged in her liver, and surgeons feared to remove it. Though she recovered, Maude Moormann always insisted that the shooting had been an accident. Afterward, Robert was in and out of juvenile facilities for a variety of offenses—most centered on sexual malad-justment and the molestation of young girls. By the time he was 18, Moormann had been arrested for accosting yet another girl and had been placed on the drug Mellaril to limit his sexual appetites.

As an adult, Moormann was finally sent to prison for kidnapping and molesting an 8-year-old neighborhood girl in 1972. In 1979, he was paroled but soon went back to prison for a parole violation. By 1984, Moormann had entered the prison's furlough program and, on January 12 of that year, was released to visit with his mother in a local motel. On that fateful night, Moormann demanded that his mother sign papers that would leave him sole heir to her estate. After she refused, Moormann beat her, tied her to the motel room bed, and suffocated her with a pillow. He then made a brief trip to a convenience store where he bought household cleansers and a variety of knives. Upon returning to the motel room, he cut his mother's body into many pieces, stuffing some in a local trash receptacle and flushing her severed fingers down the toilet so that her remains couldn't be easily identified. Then he meticulously cleaned the room to hide any signs of the murder. He was arrested, however, after arousing the suspicions of a prison guard to whom he had offered a box of flesh-covered raw bones for the guard's dogs. It took a jury only two hours to convict him, and he was sentenced to death.

Robert Moormann was a poor physical specimen who had been judged unfit for the military draft. He had poor vision and flat feet and suffered from poor reading skills and learning disabilities. One physician, to whom he had been taken as a boy, diagnosed him as suffering from brain-stem trauma—the result of two traffic accidents in which he had been involved when young.

Did Moormann's crimes have a biological basis? Of that we may never be sure, although many biological theories have been advanced to explain criminality. Abnormalities of the brain, brain damage,[6] genetic predispositions, vitamin deficiencies, an excess of hormones like testosterone, hypoglycemia (low blood sugar), fetal alcohol syndrome (FAS),[7] a relative lack of neurotransmitters like serotonin in the brain, and blood abnormalities are among the many biological explanations of crime available today.

The field of criminology has been slow to give credence to biological theories of human behavior. One reason for this, as noted in Chapter 1, is that contemporary criminology's academic roots are firmly grounded in the social sciences. As well-known biocriminologist **C. Ray Jeffery**, commenting on the historical development of the field, observes, "The term *criminology* was given to a social science approach to crime as developed in sociology. . . . Sutherland's (1924) text *Criminology* was pure sociology without any biology or psychology; beginning with publication of that text, criminology was offered in sociology departments as a part of sociology separate from biology, psychology, psychiatry and law. . . . Many of the academicians who call themselves criminologists are sociologists."[8]

Even today, little doubt exists that biological understandings of criminality are out of vogue. In 1992, for example, a conference sponsored by the National Institutes of Health that was intended to focus on the biological roots of crime was canceled after critics charged that the meeting would, by virtue of its biological focus, be racist and might intentionally exclude sociological perspectives on the subject.[9] Dr. Peter Breggin, Director of the Center for the Study of Psychiatry in Bethesda, Maryland, and leader of the opposition to the conference, argued that "the primary problems that afflict human beings are not due to their bodies or brains, they are due to the environment. Redefining social problems as public health problems is exactly what was done in Nazi Germany."[10] Three years later, when the conference was finally held at a site selected to discourage demonstrations, C. Ray Jeffery pointed out that "when ideology replaces rational thought there is little hope for a better understanding of human problems."[11]

According to Lee Ellis and Anthony Walsh, "one reason why most criminologists are skeptical about genetic influences on criminal behavior is that it seems improbable that behavior that is defined differently in every society could have a genetic foundation."[12] "In other words," ask Ellis and Walsh, "why would genes affect behavior that is

A mother reads to her child. Are the choices that people make determined more by their biology or by what they have learned? This question forms the essence of the "nature versus nurture" controversy. *J. Carini, The Image Works*

circumscribed by laws that vary from one society to another?" The answer, they say, "lies in the fact that in nearly all societies with written criminal statutes, there are a fairly standard set of 'core behavior patterns' that are criminalized." Hence, they conclude, "it is possible to maintain that there is little variation from one society to another in what constitutes criminal behavior."[13]

There are those today who charge that outspoken critics of biological investigation into the root causes of crime fail to recognize that the advance of science has never been impeded by objective consideration of alternative points of view. Narrow-minded criticism, made before all the facts are in, such observers say, does little to advance human understanding. Open inquiry, as C. Ray Jeffery notes, requires objective consideration of all points of view and an unbiased examination of each for its ability to shed light on the subject under study. Hence for an adequate consideration of biological theories as they may relate to crime and crime causation, we need to turn to literature outside of the sociological and psychological mainstream.

MAJOR PRINCIPLES OF BIOLOGICAL THEORIES

This brief section serves to summarize the central features of **biological theories** of crime causation. Each of these points can be found elsewhere in this chapter, where it is discussed in more detail. This cursory overview, however, is intended to provide more than a summary; it is meant to be a guide to the rest of this chapter.

Biological theories of crime causation make certain fundamental assumptions:

- The brain is the organ of the mind and the locus of personality. In the words of well-known biocriminologist Clarence Ray Jeffery, "The brain is the organ of behavior; no theory of behavior can ignore neurology and neurochemistry."[14]
- The basic determinants of human behavior, including criminal tendencies, are, to a considerable degree, constitutionally or genetically based.
- Observed gender and racial differences in rates and types of criminality may be at least partially be the result of biological differences between the sexes and between racially distinct groups.
- The basic determinants of human behavior, including criminality, may be passed on from generation to generation. In other words, a penchant for crime may be inherited.
- Much of human conduct is fundamentally rooted in instinctive behavioral responses characteristic of biological organisms everywhere. Territoriality, condemnation of adultery, and acquisitiveness are but three examples of behavior which may be instinctual to human beings.

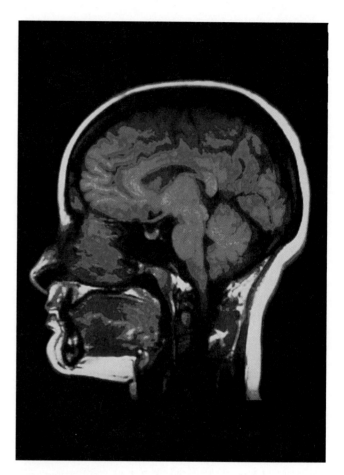

The brain is indeed "the organ of the mind," as early criminologists claimed. Here a computer-enhanced image shows areas of activity within the brain. Do you think biology may play a role in crime? *Scott Camazsine, Photo Researchers, Inc.*

- The biological roots of human conduct have become increasingly disguised, as modern symbolic forms of indirect expressive behavior have replaced more primitive and direct ones.
- At least some human behavior is the result of biological propensities inherited from more primitive developmental stages in the evolutionary process. In other words, some human beings may be farther along the evolutionary ladder than others, and their behavior may reflect that fact.
- The interplay between heredity, biology, and the social environment provides the nexus for any realistic consideration of crime causation.

BIOLOGICAL ROOTS OF HUMAN AGGRESSION

In 1966, **Konrad Lorenz** published his now-famous work, *On Aggression*.[15] It was an English-language translation of a 1963 book entitled *Das Sogenannte Bose: Zur Naturgeschichte der Aggression* (The Nature of Aggression), which had originally appeared in German. In his writing, Lorenz described how aggression permeates the animal kingdom and asked, "What is the value of all this fighting?" He wrote, "In nature, fighting is such an ever-present process, its behavior mechanisms and weapons are so highly developed and have so obviously arisen under the . . . pressure of a species-preserving function, that it is our duty to ask this . . . question."[16]

Lorenz accepted the evolutionary thesis of nineteenth-century biologist **Charles Darwin** that intraspecies aggression favored the strongest and best animals in the reproductive process, but he concluded that aggression served a variety of other purposes as well. Aggression, said Lorenz, ensures an "even distribution of animals of a particular species over an inhabitable area"[17] and provides for a defense of the species from predators. Human aggression, he claimed, meets many of the same purposes but can take on covert forms. Lorenz described the drive to acquire wealth and power, which was so characteristic of Western men at the time of his writing, as part of the human mating ritual whereby a man might "win" a prized woman through displays of more civilized forms of what could otherwise be understood as intraspecies aggression.

In today's enlightened times, such observations may seem to many like mere foolishness. Lorenz's greatest contribution to the study of human behavior, however, may have been his claim that all human behavior is, at least to some degree, "adapted instinctive behavior." In other words, much of human conduct, according to Lorenz, is fundamentally rooted in instinctive behavioral responses characteristic of biological organisms everywhere and present within each of us in the form of a biological inheritance from more primitive times. Even rational human thought, claimed Lorenz, derives its motivation and direction from instinctual aspects of human biology. The highest human virtues, such as the value placed on human life, "could not have been achieved," said Lorenz, "without an instinctive appreciation of life and death."[18]

Building upon the root functions of aggression, Lorenz concluded that much of what we today call "crime" is the result of overcrowded living conditions, such as those experienced by city dwellers, combined with a lack of legitimate opportunity for the effective expression of aggression. Crowding, from this perspective, increases the likelihood of aggression, while contemporary socialization simultaneously works to inhibit it. In the words of Lorenz, "In one sense we are all psychopaths, for each of us suffers from the necessity of self-imposed control for the good of the community."[19] When people break down, said Lorenz, they become neurotic or delinquent, and crime may be the result of stresses that have been found to typically produce aggression throughout the animal kingdom.

At first blush, Lorenz's explanations, like many of the biologically based theories we will encounter in this chapter, appear to be more applicable to violent crime than to other forms of criminal offense. However, it is important to recognize that modern frustrations and concomitant manifestations of aggression may be symbolically, rather than directly,

Charles Darwin (1809–1882), founder of modern evolutionary theory. *Julia Cameron, Corbis-Bettmann*

expressed. Hence the stockbroker who embezzles a client's money, spurred on by the need to provide material goods for an overly acquisitive family, may be just as criminal as the robber who beats his victim and steals her purse to have money to buy liquor.

Early Biological Theories

Numerous perspectives on criminal biology predate Lorenz's work. Some of the perspectives fall into the category of criminal anthropology. **Criminal anthropology** is the scientific study of the relationship between human physical characteristics and criminality. Criminal anthropology probably derives from earlier subjective feelings, prominent for millennia, that unattractiveness, deformity, and disfigurement are somehow associated with evil, spiritual malaise, and general uncleanliness. Physiognomy, or the "science" of reading personality characteristics from facial features, can be traced to ancient Greece. Greek culture espoused the notion that the mind and body were closely interconnected—a belief which implied that a twisted mind would reside in a deformed body. "Aristotle confirmed this view in his *Metaphysics* when he reasoned that the essence of the body is contained in the soul."[20]

One of the earliest criminological anthropologists was **Franz Joseph Gall** (1758–1828). Gall hypothesized, in his theory of **phrenology** (also called "craniology"), that the

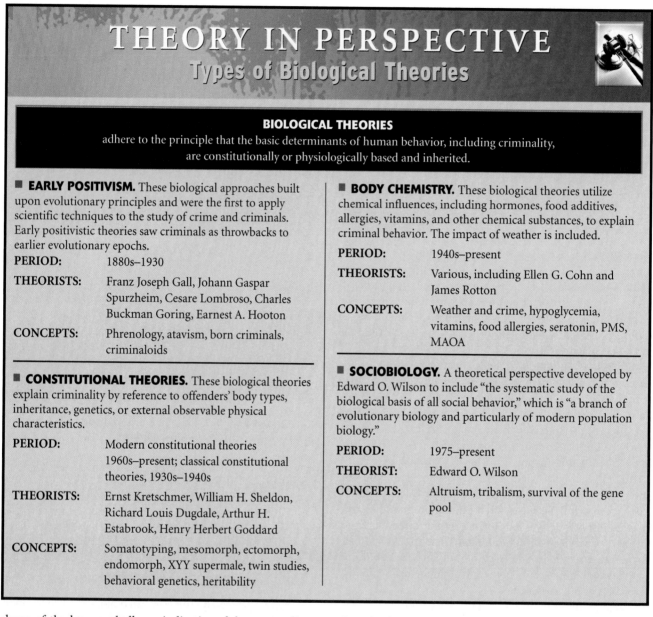

THEORY IN PERSPECTIVE
Types of Biological Theories

BIOLOGICAL THEORIES
adhere to the principle that the basic determinants of human behavior, including criminality, are constitutionally or physiologically based and inherited.

■ **EARLY POSITIVISM.** These biological approaches built upon evolutionary principles and were the first to apply scientific techniques to the study of crime and criminals. Early positivistic theories saw criminals as throwbacks to earlier evolutionary epochs.

PERIOD:	1880s–1930
THEORISTS:	Franz Joseph Gall, Johann Gaspar Spurzheim, Cesare Lombroso, Charles Buckman Goring, Earnest A. Hooton
CONCEPTS:	Phrenology, atavism, born criminals, criminaloids

■ **CONSTITUTIONAL THEORIES.** These biological theories explain criminality by reference to offenders' body types, inheritance, genetics, or external observable physical characteristics.

PERIOD:	Modern constitutional theories 1960s–present; classical constitutional theories, 1930s–1940s
THEORISTS:	Ernst Kretschmer, William H. Sheldon, Richard Louis Dugdale, Arthur H. Estabrook, Henry Herbert Goddard
CONCEPTS:	Somatotyping, mesomorph, ectomorph, endomorph, XYY supermale, twin studies, behavioral genetics, heritability

■ **BODY CHEMISTRY.** These biological theories utilize chemical influences, including hormones, food additives, allergies, vitamins, and other chemical substances, to explain criminal behavior. The impact of weather is included.

PERIOD:	1940s–present
THEORISTS:	Various, including Ellen G. Cohn and James Rotton
CONCEPTS:	Weather and crime, hypoglycemia, vitamins, food allergies, seratonin, PMS, MAOA

■ **SOCIOBIOLOGY.** A theoretical perspective developed by Edward O. Wilson to include "the systematic study of the biological basis of all social behavior," which is "a branch of evolutionary biology and particularly of modern population biology."

PERIOD:	1975–present
THEORIST:	Edward O. Wilson
CONCEPTS:	Altruism, tribalism, survival of the gene pool

shape of the human skull was indicative of the personality and could be used to predict criminality. Gall's approach contained four themes:

■ The brain is the organ of the mind.
■ Particular aspects of personality are associated with specific locations in the brain.
■ Portions of the brain that are well developed will cause personality characteristics associated with them to be more prominent in the individual under study, whereas poorly developed brain areas lead to a lack of associated personality characteristics.
■ The shape of a person's skull corresponds to the shape of the underlying brain and is therefore indicative of the personality.

Gall was one of the first Western writers to firmly locate the roots of personality in the brain. Prior to his time, it was

thought that aspects of personality resided in various organs throughout the body—a fact reflected in linguistic anachronisms which survive into the present day (as, for example, when someone is described as "hard-hearted" or as having "a lot of gall" or as thinking with some organ other than the brain). Greek philosopher Aristotle was said to believe that the brain served no function other than to radiate excess heat from the body. Hence Gall's perspective, although relatively primitive by today's standards, did much to advance physiological understandings of the mind-body connection in Western thought.

Although Gall never tested his theory, it was widely accepted by many of his contemporaries because it represented something of a shift away from the theological perspectives prevalent at the time and a move toward scientific understanding—a trend that was well under way by the time of his writings. Phrenology also provided for systematic evaluation of suspected offenders and was intriguing for its ease of use. One of Gall's students, **Johann Gaspar Spurzheim** (1776–1853), brought phrenological theory to America and, through a series of lectures and publications on the subject, helped to spread its influence. Phrenology's prestige in America extended into the twentieth century, finding a place in classification schemes used to evaluate newly admitted prisoners. Even Arthur Conan Doyle's fictional character Sherlock Holmes was described as using phrenology to solve a number of crimes. It is still popular today among palm readers and fortune-tellers, some of whom offer phrenological "readings"—although a few states have outlawed such activities. Learn more about phrenology at Web Extra! 5-1.

Web Extra! 5-1 at crimtoday.com

The Positivist School

One of the best-known, early scientific biological theorists—nineteenth-century Italian army prison physician **Cesare Lombroso** (1836–1909)—coined the term *atavism* to suggest that criminality was the result of primitive urges which, in modern-day human throwbacks, survived the evolutionary process. He described "the nature of the criminal" as "an atavistic being who reproduces in his person the ferocious instincts of primitive humanity and the inferior animals."[21]

At about this time, Charles Darwin was making a substantial impact on the scientific world with his theory of biological evolution. Darwin proposed that human beings and other contemporary living organisms were the end products of a long evolutionary process governed by such rules as natural selection and survival of the fittest. Lombroso adapted elements of Darwin's theory to suggest that primitive traits survived in present-day human populations and led to heightened criminal tendencies among individuals who harbored them. Darwin himself had proposed this idea when he wrote, "With mankind some of the worst dispositions which occasionally without any assignable cause make their appearance in families, may perhaps be reversions to a savage state, from which we are not removed by very many generations."[22]

The atavistic individual, said Lombroso in his now-classic work, *L'Uomo delinquente* (1876), was essentially a throwback to a more primitive biological state. According to Lombroso, such an individual, by virtue of possessing a relatively undeveloped brain, is incapable of conforming his behavior to the rules and expectations of modern complex society. Lombroso has been called the father of modern criminology because he was the first criminologist of note to employ the scientific method—particularly measurement, observation, and attempts at generalization—in his work. Other writers have referred to him as the "father of the Italian School" of criminology in recognition of the fact that nineteenth-century positivism began in Italy.

Positivism, as mentioned in Chapter 4, built upon two principles: (1) an unflagging acceptance of social determinism, or the belief that human behavior is determined not by the exercise of free choice but by causative factors beyond the control of the individual, and (2) application of scientific techniques to the study of crime and criminology. The term *positivism* had its roots in the writings of Auguste Comte (1798–1857), who proposed use of the scientific method in the study of society in his 1851 work, *A System of Positive Polity*.[23] Comte believed that a new "positive age" was dawning during which both society and human nature would be perfected, and his writings were an attempt to bring that age to fruition. Positivism holds that social phenomena are observable, explainable, and measurable in quantitative terms. For a strict positivist, reality consists of a world of objectively defined facts which can be scientifically measured, and—ultimately—controlled.[24]

Lombroso's scientific work consisted of postmortem studies of the bodies of executed offenders and deceased criminals, measuring the bodies in many different ways. The body of one such well-known criminal, named Vilella, provided Lombroso with many of his findings and reinforced his belief that most offenders were biologically predisposed toward criminality. When he examined Vilella's brain, Lombroso found an unusual depression which he named "the median occipital fossa." Lombroso identified features of Vilella's brain as being similar to those found in lower primates. Study of another offender, an Italian soldier whom Lombroso calls "Misdea" in his writings[25] and who "attacked and killed eight of his superior officers and comrades," supported his conclusions.

In addition to his examination of Vilella, Lombroso conducted autopsies on another 65 executed offenders and examined 832 living prison inmates, comparing physical measurements of their body parts to measurements taken from 390 soldiers. As a result of his work, Lombroso claimed to have found a wide variety of bodily features predictive of criminal behavior. Among them were exceptionally long arms, an index finger as long as the middle finger, fleshy pouches in the cheeks "like those in rodents," eyes that were either abnormally close together or too far apart, large teeth, ears which lacked lobes, prominent cheekbones, a crooked nose, a large amount of body hair, protruding chin, large lips, a nonstandard number of ribs, and eyes of differing colors or hues. Lombroso went so far as to enumerate characteristics of particular types of offenders. Murderers, whom he called "habitual homicides," have, in Lombroso's words, "cold, glassy eyes, immobile and sometimes sanguine and inflamed; the nose, always large, is frequently aquiline or, rather, hooked; the jaws are strong, the cheekbones large, the hair curly, dark, and abundant; the beard is frequently thin, the canine teeth well developed and the lips delicate."[26]

Atavism implies the notion that criminals are born that way. Lombroso was continuously reassessing his estimates of the proportion, from among all offenders, of the born criminal population. At one point, he asserted that fully 90% of offenders committed crimes because of atavistic influences. He later revised the figure downward to 70%, admitting that

THEORY VERSUS REALITY
Positivism: The Historical Statement

In 1901, Enrico Ferri, one of the fathers of positivist criminology, was invited to deliver a series of lectures at the University of Naples. Ferri used the occasion to admonish classical criminologists and to advance the principles of positivism. This box contains excerpts from those lectures.

Let us speak of this new science, which has become known in Italy by the name of the Positive School of Criminology.... The 19th century has won a great victory over mortality and infectious diseases by means of the masterful progress of physiology and natural science. But while contagious diseases have gradually diminished, we see on the other hand that moral diseases are growing more numerous.... While typhoid fever, smallpox, cholera and diptheria retreated before the remedies which enlightened science applied by means of the experimental method, removing their concrete causes, we see on the other hand that insanity, suicide and crime, that painful trinity, are growing apace. And this makes it very evident that the science which is principally, if not exclusively, engaged in studying these phenomena of social disease, should feel the necessity of finding a more exact diagnosis of these moral diseases of society, in order to arrive at some effective and more humane remedy....

The science of positive criminology arose in the last quarter of the 19th century.... [T]he positive school of criminology arises out of the very nature of things, the same as every other line of science. It is based on the conditions of our daily life....

The general opinion of classic criminalists and of the people at large is that crime involves a moral guilt, because it is due to the free will of the individual who leaves the path of virtue and chooses the path of crime, and therefore it must be suppressed by meeting it with a proportionate quantity of punishment.... And the illusion of a free human will (the only miraculous factor in the eternal ocean of cause and effect) leads to the assumption that one can choose freely between virtue and vice. How can you still believe in the existence of a free will, when modern psychology armed with all the instruments of positive modern research, denies that there is any free will and demonstrates that every act of a human being is the result of an interaction between the personality and the environment of man?

And how is it possible to cling to that obsolete idea of moral guilt, according to which every individual is supposed to have the free choice to abandon virtue and give himself up to crime? The positive school of criminology maintains, on the contrary, that it is not the criminal who wills; in order to be a criminal

it is rather necessary that the individual should find himself permanently or transitorily in such personal, physical and moral conditions, and live in such an environment which become for him a chain of cause and effect, externally and internally, that disposes him toward crime. This is our conclusion ... and it constitutes that vastly different and opposite method, which the positive school of criminology employs as compared to the leading principle of the classic school of criminal science.

DISCUSSION QUESTIONS

1. Why does Ferri link control over contagious diseases with the study of crime?
2. If Ferri were asked to define "positive criminology" what kind of definition do you think he would offer?
3. How are notions of moral guilt and free will associated in Ferri's line of thought?

Source: Ernest Unterman, trans., *The Positive School of Criminology: Three Lectures Given at the University of Naples, Italy, on April 22, 23, and 24, 1901 by Enrico Ferri* (Chicago: Charles H. Kerr, 1912).

normal individuals might be pulled into lives of crime. In addition to the category of the born criminal, Lombroso described other categories of offenders, including the insane, "criminaloids," and criminals incited by passion. The insane were said to include mental and moral degenerates, alcoholics, drug addicts, and so forth. **Criminaloids**, also termed "occasional criminals," were described as people who were pulled into breaking the law by virtue of environmental influences. Nevertheless, most criminaloids were seen by Lombroso as exhibiting some degree of atavism and hence were said to "differ from **born criminals** in degree, not in kind." Those who became criminals by virtue of passion were said to have surrendered to intense emotions, including love, jealousy, hatred, or an injured sense of honor.

Although he focused on physical features, Lombroso was not insensitive to behavioral indicators of criminality. In his later writings, he claimed that criminals exhibited acute sight, hearing abilities that were below the norm, an insensitivity to pain, a lack of moral sensibility, cruelty, vin-

dictiveness, impulsiveness, a love of gambling, and a tendency to be tattooed.

In 1893, Lombroso published *The Female Offender*.[27] In that book, he expressed his belief that women exhibit far less anatomical variation than do men, but he insisted that criminal behavior among women, as among men, derived from atavistic foundations. Violence among women, although a rarity in the official statistics of the late 1800s, was explained by the **masculinity hypothesis**, or the belief that criminal women exhibited masculine features and mannerisms. Lombroso saw the quintessential female offender, however, as a prostitute. The prostitute, said Lombroso, is "the genuine typical representative of criminality" among women.[28] Prostitutes, he claimed, act out atavistic yearnings and, in doing so, return to a form of behavior characteristic of humankind's primitive past. Learn more about Lombroso and the theory of atavism via Web Extra! 5-2.

Web Extra! 5-2 at crimtoday.com

Evaluations of Atavism

Following in Lombroso's positivistic footsteps around the turn of the twentieth century, English physician **Charles Buckman Goring** (1870–1919) conducted a well-controlled statistical study of Lombroso's thesis of atavism. Using newly developed but advanced mathematical techniques to measure the degree of correlation between physiological features and criminal history, Goring examined nearly 3,000 inmates at Turin prison beginning in 1901. Enlisting the aid of London's Biometric Laboratory, he concluded that "the whole fabric of Lombrosian doctrine, judged by the standards of science, is fundamentally unsound."[29] Goring compared the prisoners with students at Oxford and Cambridge Universities, British soldiers, and noncriminal hospital patients and published his findings in 1913 in his lengthy treatise *The English Convict: A Statistical Study.*[30] The foreword to Goring's book was written by Karl Pearson, who praised Goring for having no particular perspective of his own to advance. Goring could, Pearson said, therefore objectively evaluate the ideas of others, such as Lombroso.

A similar study was conducted between 1927 and 1939 by **Earnest A. Hooton,** a professor of anthropology at Harvard University. In 1939, Hooton published *Crime and the Man,*[31] in which he reported having evaluated 13,873 inmates from ten states, comparing them along 107 physiological dimensions with 3,203 nonincarcerated individuals who formed a control group. His sample consisted of 10,953 prison inmates, 2,004 county jail prisoners, 743 criminally insane, 173 "defective delinquents," 1,227 "insane civilians," and 1,976 "sane civilians."

Hooton distinguished between regions of the country, saying that "states have favorite crimes, just as they have favorite sons." He reported finding physiological features characteristic of specific criminal types in individual states. For example, "Massachusetts criminals," he said, "are notable for thick beards, red-brown hair, dark brown, green-brown and blue-gray eyes, whites of eyes discolored with yellow or brown pigment flecks, rayed pattern of the iris of the eye, external and median folds of the upper eyelids, broad, high nasal roots and bridges, concave nasal profiles, thick nasal tips, right deflections of the nasal septum, thin integumental lips, thin upper membranous lip and thick lower lip, absence of lip seam, some . . . protrusion of the jaws, pointed or median chins, much dental decay but few teeth lost, small and soldered or attached ear lobes, and right facial asymmetries."[32] He went on to say that through a sufficient degree of statistical manipulation, "we finally emerge with differences between the offense groups which are not due to accidents of sampling, are not due to state variations, and are independent of differences between the ages of the offense groups. Thus, in the case of first-degree murder we find the members of that offense group deficient in persons with abundant head hair, deficient in individuals with narrow nasal bridges, presenting an excess of persons with pointed or median chins, and with compressed cheek

bones."[33] He also found that first-degree murderers were more "square-shouldered" than other criminals and had larger ear lobes. From findings like these, he was drawn to the conclusion that "crime is not an exclusively sociological phenomenon, but is also biological."[34]

In writing "it is impossible to improve and correct environment to a point at which these flawed and degenerate human beings will be able to succeed in honest social competition,"[35] Hooton made it clear that he did not believe that rehabilitation programs could have much effect upon most offenders, and he suggested banishing them to a remote location. Hooton concluded that criminals showed an overall physiological inferiority to the general population and that crime was the result of "the impact of environment upon low grade human organisms."[36] Learn more about the life and work of Earnest Hooton at Web Extra! 5-3.

Web Extra! 5-3 at crimtoday.com

Hooton, an example of whose work is provided in Figure 5-1, was quickly criticized along a number of dimensions. Stephen Schafer, a well-known contemporary criminologist, says, "The major criticisms were that his criminal population was not a representative sample of all criminals, that his control group was a fantastic conglomeration of noncriminal civilians, . . . that he emphasized selected characteristics and disregarded others, that he gave no convincing evidence that the criminal's 'inferiority' was inherited, and that he failed to explore other important data that were available."[37] Perhaps even more significant, Hooton failed to recognize that members of his noncriminal control group may in fact have been involved in crime but had managed to elude capture and processing by the criminal justice system. In other words, it may have been that the most successful criminals did not appear in Hooton's study group of inmates because they had eluded the law, thereby making their way into his supposedly noncriminal control group. His study may have simply demonstrated that "inferior" criminal specimens are the ones who get caught and end up in prison.

Nonetheless, claims that physical abnormalities may be linked to crime persist into the present day. In a study of 170 teenage boys reported in 2000, for example, Canadian researchers L. Arseneault and Richard E. Tremblay conducted hormonal, anthropometric, psychophysiological, neuropsychological, and psychiatric evaluations of 1,037 boys who had attended kindergarten in 1984 in a socially and economically disadvantaged area of Montreal.[38] Using evaluations provided years later by parents, teachers, classmates, and the children themselves, Arseneault and Tremblay concluded that subtle physical abnormalities, including minor abnormalities in the shape of the ears, tongue, and teeth, were associated with an increased risk of behavioral and psychiatric problems. The researchers suggested that such minor physical abnormalities might have resulted from genetic problems or prenatal insults associated with exposure to

OLD AMERICAN CRIMINALS

Mosaic of Cranial, Facial, Metric and Morphological Features

MASSACHUSETTS

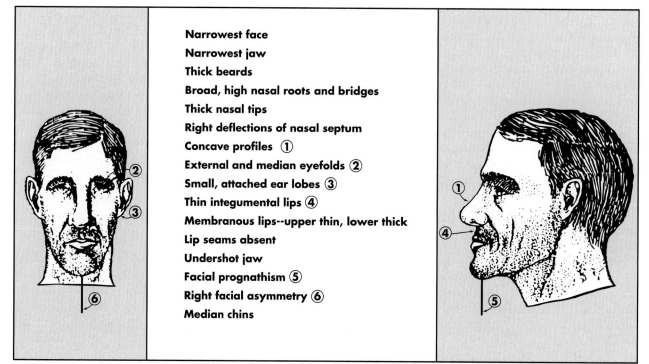

Narrowest face
Narrowest jaw
Thick beards
Broad, high nasal roots and bridges
Thick nasal tips
Right deflections of nasal septum
Concave profiles ①
External and median eyefolds ②
Small, attached ear lobes ③
Thin integumental lips ④
Membranous lips--upper thin, lower thick
Lip seams absent
Undershot jaw
Facial prognathism ⑤
Right facial asymmetry ⑥
Median chins

■ **FIGURE 5-1**   EARNEST A. HOOTON'S "MASSACHUSETTS CRIMINAL."
Source: Reprinted by permission of the publishers from *Crime and the Man* by Earnest Albert Hooton, Cambridge, Mass: Harvard University Press. Copyright © 1939 by the President and Fellows of Harvard College, renewed 1967 by Mary C. Hooton.

toxins. They concluded that "both the total count of minor physical anomalies and the total count of minor physical anomalies of the mouth were significantly associated with an increased risk of violent delinquency in adolescence, beyond the effects of childhood physical aggression and family adversity." Arseneault and Tremblay recognized, however, that abnormalities of the type they identified might be associated with neurological deficits and that abnormalities of the mouth could lead to feeding problems in the first months after birth, which might somehow cause problems in development or socialization.

Body Types

Constitutional theories are those which explain criminality by reference to offenders' body types, genetics, or external observable physical characteristics. A constitutional, or physiological, orientation which found its way into the criminological mainstream during the early and mid-twentieth century was that of body types. Also called **somatotyping**, this perspective was primarily associated with the work of **Ernst Kretschmer** and **William H. Sheldon**. Kretschmer, a professor of psychiatry at the German University of Tubingen, proposed a relationship between body build and

personality type and created a rather detailed "biopsychological constitutional typology." Kretschmer's somatotypology revolved around three basic mental categories: cycloids (also called "cyclothymes"), schizoids (or "schizothymes"), and displastics. The **cycloid** personality, which was associated with a heavyset, soft type of body, according to Kretschmer, vacillated between normality and abnormality. Cycloids were said to lack spontaneity and sophistication and were thought to commit mostly nonviolent property types of offenses. **Schizoids**, who tended to possess athletic, muscular bodies but, according to Kretschmer, could also be thin and lean, were seen as more likely to be schizophrenic and to commit violent types of offenses. **Displastics** were said to be a mixed group described as highly emotional and often unable to control themselves. Hence they were thought to commit mostly sexual offenses and other crimes of passion.

Influenced by Kretschmer, William H. Sheldon utilized measurement techniques to connect body type with personality.[39] Sheldon felt that Kretschmer had erred in including too large an age range in his work. Therefore he chose to limit his study to 200 boys between the ages of 15 and 21 at the Hayden Goodwill Institute in Boston. Sheldon concluded that four basic body types characterized the entire

Endomorphs on the march. A group of would-be actors line up to audition for roles in the movie *Fat Chance.* How might body type relate to criminal activity? *Marty Lederhandler, AP/Wide World Photos*

group. These types, described partly in Sheldon's words, are as follows.

- The **endomorph,** who is soft and round and whose "digestive viscera are massive and highly developed" (i.e., the person is overweight and has a large stomach)
- The **mesomorph,** who is athletic and muscular and whose "somatic structures . . . are in the ascendancy" (i.e., the person has larger bones and considerable muscle mass)
- The **ectomorph,** who is thin and fragile and who has "long, slender, poorly muscled extremities, with delicate, pipestem bones"
- The balanced type, a person of average build, being neither overweight, thin, nor exceedingly muscular

Individuals were ranked along each of the three major dimensions (the balanced type was excluded), using a seven-point scale. A score of 1-1-7, for example, would indicate that a person exhibited few characteristics of endomorphology or mesomorphology but was predominantly ectomorphic. Sheldon claimed that varying types of temperament and personalities were closely associated with each of the body types he identified. Ectomorphs were said to be "cerebrotonic," or restrained, shy, and inhibited. Endomorphs were "viscerotonic," or relaxed and sociable. The mesomorphic, or muscular, body type, however, he said was most likely to be associated with delinquency or "somatotonia," which he described as "a predominance of muscular activity and . . . vigorous bodily assertiveness." Sheldon's work was supported by constitutional studies of juvenile delinquents conducted by Sheldon Glueck and Eleanor Glueck and reported in 1950.[40] The Gluecks compared 500 known delinquents with 500

nondelinquents and matched both groups on age, general intelligence, ethnic-racial background, and place of residence. Like Sheldon, the Gluecks concluded that mesomorphy was associated with delinquency. Learn more about early theories of body types via Web Extra! 5-4.

Web Extra! 5-4 at crimtoday.com

Early biological theorists like Sheldon, Lombroso, and Gall provide an interesting footnote in the history of criminological thought. Today, however, their work is mostly relegated to the dustbins of academic theorizing. Modern biological theories of crime are far more sophisticated than their early predecessors, and it is to these that we now turn.

Chemical and Environmental Precursors of Crime

Recent research in the area of nutrition has produced some limited evidence that the old maxim "You are what you eat!" may contain more than a grain of truth. Biocriminology has made some significant strides in linking violent or disruptive behavior to eating habits, vitamin deficiencies, genetic inheritance, and other conditions which affect the body. Studies of nutrition, endocrinology, and environmental contaminants have all contributed to advances in understanding such behavior.

One of the first studies to focus on chemical imbalances in the body as a cause of crime was reported in the British medical journal *Lancet* in 1943.[41] The authors of the study linked murder to **hypoglycemia,** or low blood sugar. Low blood sugar, produced by too much insulin in the blood or by near-starvation diets, was said to reduce the mind's capacity to effectively reason or to judge the long-term consequences of behavior. More recent studies have linked excess consumption of refined white sugar to hyperactivity and aggressiveness. Popular books like *Sugar Blues* provide guides for individuals seeking to free themselves from the negative effects of excess sugar consumption.[42]

To some degree, even courts have accepted the notion that excess sugar consumption may be linked to crime. In the early 1980s, for example, Dan White, a former San Francisco police officer, was given a reduced sentence after his lawyers convinced the court that their defendant's consumption of massive amounts of refined white sugar had increased his excitability and had lowered his ability to make reasoned decisions. White had been convicted of murdering San Francisco Mayor George Moscone and City Councilman Harvey Milk during a dispute in the mayor's office. The night before the killings, White stayed awake drinking Coca-Cola and eating many Twinkies.

More than ten years later, however, a well-conducted 1994 study reported in the *New England Journal of Medicine* seemed to contradict the notion that sugar may lead to hyperactivity.[43] Similarly, neither sugar nor artificial sweeteners were shown to have any link to an increase in learning disabilities. In the study, researchers at Vanderbilt University and the University of Iowa varied the diets of supposedly sugar-sensitive youngsters from diets high in sugar, to a diet that was low in sugar but contained the artificial sweetener aspartame. A third experimental diet contained very little sugar but had added saccharin. After surveying parents, teachers, and babysitters and testing the study group for changes in memory, concentration, and math skills, the researchers concluded, "We couldn't find any difference in terms of their behavior or their learning on any of the three diets."[44] Hence, to date, the evidence concerning sugar's impact on behavior is less than clear.

While dietary levels of refined sugar may or may not affect behavior, studies done using positron-emission tomography (PET), in which scans of the prefrontal cortex of subjects' brains were analyzed, show interesting results. PET scans can be used to measure the "uptake" of glucose by the brain. In a study conducted by Adrian Raine in 1994, PET scans of the brains of 22 murderers (including some who had only attempted murder) revealed that murderers showed much lower levels of glucose uptake in the prefrontal cortex than did the controls.[45] "The differences were not related to age, gender, handedness, ethnicity, motivation, history of head injury, or presence of schizophrenia. In addition, no subjects were taking psychoactive drugs at the time of the test."[46] Raine and his colleagues say that their data strongly suggest that "deficits localized to the prefrontal cortex may be related to violence" in some offenders. Raine also notes that "frontal damage is associated with impulsivity, loss of self-control, immaturity, lack of tact, inability to modify and inhibit behavior appropriately, and poor social judgment." The researchers explain, however, that prefrontal cortex dysfunc-

tion must be evaluated in terms of how individuals who exhibit the condition interact with environmental conditions, including social and psychological influences. Because prefrontal cortex dysfunction may result in failure in school, the inability to hold a job, problems in relationships, and so forth, it may not be a direct cause of crime but might rather predispose those afflicted with the condition to "a criminal and violent way of life."[47]

Allergic reactions to common foods have been reported as the cause of violence and homicide by a number of investigators.[48] Some foods—including milk, citrus fruit, chocolate, corn, wheat, and eggs—are said to produce allergic reactions in sensitive individuals, leading to a swelling of the brain and the brain stem. Involvement of the central nervous system in such allergies, it has been suggested, reduces the amount of learning which occurs during childhood and may contribute to delinquency as well as to adult criminal behavior. Such swelling is also thought to impede the higher faculties, reducing a person's sense of morality and creating conditions that support impulsive behavior.

Some studies have implicated food additives, such as the flavor enhancer monosodium glutamate, dyes, and artificial flavorings in producing criminal violence.[49] Other research has found that coffee and sugar may trigger antisocial behavior.[50] Researchers were led to these conclusions through finding that inmates consumed considerably greater amounts of coffee, sugar, and processed foods than others.[51] It is unclear, however, whether inmates drink more coffee because of boredom or whether "excitable" personalities feel a need for the kind of stimulation available through coffee consumption. On the other hand, habitual coffee drinkers in nonprison populations have not been linked to crime, and other studies, like the one conducted by Mortimer Gross of the University of Illinois, show no link between the amount of sugar consumed by inmates and hyperactivity.[52] Nonetheless, some prison programs have been designed to limit intake of dietary stimulants through nutritional management and the substitution of artificial sweeteners for refined sugar. Vitamins have also been examined for their impact on delinquency. At least one researcher found that disruptive children consumed far less than optimal levels of vitamins B_3 and B_6 than did nonproblem youths.[53] Some researchers have suggested that the addition of these vitamins to the diets of children who are deficient in them could control unruly behavior and improve school performance.

The role of food and diet in producing criminal behavior, however, has not been well established. The American Dietetic Association and the National Council against Health Fraud have concluded that no convincing scientific relationship between crime and diet has yet been demonstrated.[54] Both groups are becoming concerned that poor nutrition may result from programs intended to have behavioral impacts, such as those that reduce or modify diets in prisons or elsewhere.

In 1997, British researchers Roger D. Masters, Brian Hone, and Anil Doshi published a study purporting to show that industrial and other forms of environmental pollution cause people to commit violent crimes.[55] The study used statistics from the FBI's Uniform Crime Reporting Program and data from the U.S. Environmental Protection Agency's Toxic Release Inventory. A comparison between the two data sets showed a significant correlation between juvenile crime and high environmental levels of both lead and manganese. Masters and his colleagues suggested an explanation based on a neurotoxicity hypothesis. "According to this approach, toxic pollutants—specifically the toxic metals lead and manganese—cause learning disabilities, an increase in aggressive behavior, and—most importantly—loss of control over impulsive behavior. These traits combine with poverty, social stress, alcohol and drug abuse, individual character, and other social and psychological factors to produce individuals who commit violent crimes."[56]

According to Masters, the presence of excess manganese lowers levels of serotonin and dopamine in the brain. Both of these neurotransmitters are associated with impulse control and planning. Masters notes that low brain levels of serotonin are known to cause mood disturbances, poor impulse control, and increases in aggressive behavior.[57] Masters claims that children who are raised from birth on infant formula and who are not breast-fed will absorb five times as much manganese as breast-fed infants. Calcium deficiency is known to increase the absorption of manganese, and, says Masters, "a combination of manganese toxicity and calcium deficiency adds up to 'reverse' Prozac."[58]

In defense of his thesis, Masters cites other studies, the largest of which was an examination of 1,000 black children in Philadelphia that showed that the level of exposure to lead was a reliable predictor of the number of juvenile offenses among the exposed male population, the seriousness of juvenile offenses, and the number of adult offenses. Recent studies, including many of which Masters was unaware, seem to support his thesis.[59]

According to Masters, toxic metals affect individuals in complex ways. Because lead diminishes a person's normal ability to detoxify poisons, he says, it may heighten the effects of alcohol and drugs. Industrial pollution, automobile traffic, lead-based paints, and aging water-delivery systems are all possible sources of contamination. In a recent interview, Masters said, "The presence of pollution is as big a factor [in crime causation] as poverty. . . . It's the breakdown of the inhibition mechanism that's the key to violent behavior."[60] When brain chemistry is altered by exposure to heavy metals and other toxins, he said, people lose the natural restraint that holds their violent tendencies in check.

In 1999, researchers set out to test the hypothesis that enhancing brain levels of serotonin might reduce aggression and impulsivity in aggressive male criminals.[61] In the volunteer-only study, 10 young male offenders were given daily injections of d,l-fenfluramine, a drug that makes serotonin more available to brain cells. Findings showed that "the drug" produced a significant, dose-dependent decrease in aggressive responding . . . 2 to 4.5 hours after dosing." Moreover, "all ten subjects decreased their aggressive responding following the highest 0.8 mg/kg dose." Subjects exhibiting the highest rates of aggression showed the greatest decreases in aggression levels after being treated with d,l-fenfluramine. According to researchers, impulsivity similarly decreased.

In addition to chemical substances that are likely to be ingested and that may impact behavior, other environmental features have also been linked to the likelihood of aggressive behavior. During the early 1980s, for example, Alexander G. Schauss and his followers were able to show that the use of a specific shade of pink could have a calming effect on people experiencing feelings of anger and agitation.[62] Findings indicated that exposure to pink produced an endocrine change which caused a tranquilizing effect on the muscles. This involuntary effect, said researchers, was not subject to conscious control. As a result of such studies, jail cells in a

Davidson County (North Carolina) Sheriff Gerald Hedge shows off his newly redecorated jail. The jail sports pink walls, a color that psychologists think may lower the likelihood of aggressive behavior. The blue teddy bears were the sheriff's idea. How do you think offenders will react?
Sonny Hedgecech

number of locales—including Seattle, San Bernardino, San Mateo County (California), Southbridge (Massachusetts), New Orleans, and Charlotte (North Carolina)—were painted pink in hopes that aggressive tendencies among inmates might be reduced. Researchers supported such measures, saying that "the use of pink color in reducing aggression and causing muscular relaxation of inmates is humane and requires no medication or physical force."[63]

More recent studies have focused on prenatal exposure to substances like marijuana, tobacco smoke, and alcohol. In 2000, for example, L. Goldschmidt and colleagues reported the results of a ten-year study that monitored the development of the children of more than 600 low-income women. The study, which began during pregnancy, found that prenatal marijuana use was significantly related to increased hyperactivity, impulsivity, and inattention symptoms, increased delinquency, and externalizing problems.[64] The findings remained significant even when researchers controlled for other lifestyle features.

Similarly, in 1998, David Fergusson and colleagues, in a study of 1,022 New Zealand children who had been followed for 18 years, found that "children whose mothers smoked one pack of cigarettes or more per day during their pregnancy had mean rates of conduct disorder symptoms that were twice as high as those found among children born to mothers who did not smoke during their pregnancy."[65] The observed relationship was twice as strong among male teens as among females. Similar relationships between prenatal smoking and aggression and hyperactivity in later life have been reported by Dutch researchers.[66]

Prenatal alcohol exposure also seems to be linked to delinquency and psychiatric problems later in life. A 1999 study of 32 children by Tresa M. Roebuck and colleagues found that alcohol-exposed children exhibited greater delinquency and less intelligence than a control group of children who had not suffered from alcohol exposure while in the womb. The researchers concluded that their findings, which are consistent with the work of other researchers,[67] showed that "alcohol-exposed children, although less impaired intellectually, are more likely than children with mental retardation to exhibit antisocial behaviors, lack of consideration for the rights and feelings of others, and resistance to limits and requests of authority figures."[68] Learn more about the role of environmental contaminants, fetal alcohol exposure, and other such factors as they contribute to criminality at Web Extra! 5-5.

WEB EXTRA!   Web Extra! 5-5 at   crimtoday.com

Hormones and Criminality

Hormones have also come under scrutiny as potential behavioral determinants. The male sex hormone **testosterone**, for example, has been linked to aggression. Most studies on the subject have consistently shown a relationship between high blood testosterone levels and increased aggressiveness

in men. More focused studies have unveiled a direct relationship between the amount of the chemical present and the degree of violence used by sex offenders,[69] while other researchers have linked steroid abuse among bodybuilders to destructive urges and psychosis.[70] Contemporary investigations demonstrate a link between testosterone levels and aggression in teenagers,[71] while others show that adolescent problem behavior and teenage violence rise in proportion to the amount of testosterone in the blood of young men.[72] In 1987, for example, a Swedish researcher, Dan Olweus, reported that boys aged 15 to 17 showed levels of both verbal and physical aggression which correlated with the level of testosterone present in their blood.[73] Olweus also found that boys with higher levels of testosterone "tended to be habitually more impatient and irritable than boys with lower testosterone levels." He concluded that high levels of the hormone led to increased frustration and habitual impatience and irritability.

In what may be the definitive work to date on the subject, Alan Booth and D. Wayne Osgood conclude that there is a "moderately strong relationship between testosterone and adult deviance," but they suggest that the relationship "is largely mediated by the influence of testosterone on social integration and on prior involvement in juvenile delinquency."[74] In other words, measurably high levels of testosterone in the blood of young men may have some effect on behavior, but that effect is likely to be moderated by the social environment.

Similar conclusions were reached in 1998 by Swedish researchers who evaluated 61 men undergoing forensic psychiatric examinations for blood levels of free testosterone, total testosterone, and sex hormone–binding globulin (SHBG).[75] SHBG is known to determine the level of testosterone concentration in the blood and in body tissue. The Swedish researchers found that blood levels of total testosterone and SHBG were closely related to the extent of antisocial personality, alcoholism, and criminality exhibited by the subjects under study.

A 1997 study by Paul C. Bernhardt found that testosterone might not act alone in promoting aggression.[76] Bernhardt discovered that aggressive behavior in men may be influenced by high testosterone levels combined with low brain levels of the neurotransmitter serotonin. He postulates that testosterone's true role is to produce dominance-seeking behavior, but not necessarily overt aggression. When individuals are frustrated by their inability to achieve dominance, however, says Bernhardt, serotonin then acts to reduce the negative psychological impact of frustration, producing calmer responses. Men whose brains are lacking in serotonin, however, feel the effects of frustration more acutely and therefore tend to respond to frustrating circumstances more aggressively, especially when testosterone levels are high.

A few limited studies have attempted to measure the effects of testosterone on women. Women's bodies manufacture roughly one-tenth the amount of the hormone secreted by men. Even so, subtle changes in testosterone levels in women have been linked to changes in personality and sexual behavior.[77] One such study showed that relatively high blood levels of testosterone in female inmates were associated with "aggressively dominant behavior" in prison.[78] Few such studies exist, however, and their findings should probably be regarded as inconclusive.

Fluctuations in the level of female hormones may also bear some relationship to law violation. In 1980, a British court exonerated Christine English of charges that she murdered her live-in lover, after English admittedly ran him over with her car after an argument. English's defense rested on the fact that she was suffering from premenstrual syndrome (PMS) at the time of the homicide. An expert witness, Dr. Katharina Dalton, testified at the trial that PMS had caused English to be "irritable, aggressive, . . . and confused, with loss of self-control."[79]

Another case involving PMS was decided in 1991 by a Fairfax, Virginia, judge who dismissed drunk driving and other charges against Dr. Geraldine Richter, an orthopedic surgeon.[80] After being stopped for driving erratically, Richter allegedly kicked and cursed a Virginia state trooper and admitted to having consumed four glasses of wine. A Breathalyzer test showed her blood-alcohol level to be nearly 0.13°—above the 0.10° level Virginia law sets for drunk driving. Charges against Dr. Richter were dismissed after a gynecologist testified on her behalf, saying that the behavior she exhibited was likely to have been due primarily to PMS.

Although evidence linking PMS to violent or criminal behavior is far from clear, some researchers believe that a drop in serotonin levels in the female brain just before menstruation might explain the agitation and irritability sometimes associated with premenstrual syndrome. Serotonin has been called a "behavior-regulating chemical," and animal studies have demonstrated a link between low levels of the neurotransmitter present in the brain and aggressive behavior. For example, monkeys with low serotonin levels in their brains have been found to be more likely to bite, slap, and chase others of their kind. Studies at the National Institute on Alcohol Abuse and Alcoholism have linked low serotonin levels in humans to impulsive crimes. Men convicted of premeditated murder, for example, have been found to have normal serotonin levels, whereas those convicted of crimes of passion had lower levels.[81]

One 1998 study of 781 21-year-old men and women found a clear relationship between elevated *blood* levels of serotonin (which correspond to lower *brain* levels of the chemical) and violence in men.[82] The study controlled for a host of possible intervening factors, including gender, diet, psychiatric medications, illicit drug use, season of the year (during which the blood test was done), plasma levels of tryptophan (the dietary precursor of serotonin), alcohol and tobacco use, psychiatric diagnoses, platelet count, body mass, socioeconomic status, IQ, and history of suicide attempts. The relationship held true when both court records and self-reports of violence were assessed. No relationship between serotonin levels and aggression was seen in female subjects. According to the study's authors, "This is the first study to demonstrate that a possible index of serotonergic function is related to violence in the general population. . . . The epidemiological serotonin effect was not small, [but rather] indicated a moderate effect size in the population."

Other hormones, such as cortisol and the thyroid hormone T3, have also been implicated in delinquency and poor impulse control. In 2000, for example, Keith McBurnett reported the results of a study that evaluated 38 boys between the ages of 7 and 12 who had been referred to a clinic for the management of behavioral problems.[83] The children were studied for four years, using various medical and psychological assessment tools. McBurnett and fellow researchers found that the "meanest" boys had the lowest levels of the hormone cortisol in their saliva. According to McBurnett, "Low cortisol levels were associated with persistence and early onset of aggression. . . . Boys with lower cortisol concentrations . . . exhibited triple the number of aggressive symptoms and were named as most aggressive by peers three times as often as boys who had higher cortisol concentrations." Although McBurnett did not explain why low cortisol levels might be linked to aggression, he suggested that "children with persistent conduct disorder may have genes that predispose them to produce certain hormones differently, or their hormone production may have been altered before or soon after birth."

Sex hormones, such as testosterone, have been linked to aggressive behavior. Testosterone also enhances secondary sexual characteristics like body hair and muscle mass in males. What kinds of crime might be hormonally influenced? *The Kobal Collection*

A few years ago, two separate Swedish studies found evidence suggesting that elevated levels of the thyroid hormone T3 were related to alcoholism, psychopathy, and criminality.[84] Blood serum levels of the thyroid hormone FT4 (thyroxine), on the other hand, were negatively related to antisocial behavior. The researchers concluded that the results of their studies "indicate an intimate relationship between T3 and FT4, and abuse and antisocial behavior. . . . They emphasize the importance of further studies on T3 as a biological marker for abuse, social deviance, and repeated violent behavior."[85] Learn more about the possible role of hormones in criminality at Web Extra! 5-6.

Web EXTRA! Web Extra! 5-6 at crimtoday.com

Weather and Crime

Weather may also have an influence on human behavior. Research on crime and meteorologic variables has looked at everything from sunshine and humidity to wind speed, barometric pressure, and rainfall. After reviewing both published and unpublished research in this area, Ellen G. Cohn and James Rotton of Florida International University concluded that temperature is the only weather variable that is consistently and reliably related to criminal behavior (see Figure 5-2).[86] In general, field research has found a definite positive correlation between temperature and violent crime. As one might expect, more violent crime is reported to the police on warm days than on cold days. However, the rela-

tionship between temperature and criminal behavior is more complex than it first appears. Cohn and Rotton's research incorporates not only temperature, but also a variety of time-based or temporal variables, such as the time of day and the day of the week. Their findings suggest that relationships between temperature and various types of criminal behavior are affected, or moderated, by the time of day, the day of the week, and the season of the year.

In a study of assaults in Minneapolis, Cohn and Rotton found that the relationships between temperature and assaults were strongest during evening and early hours of the night.[87] A replication conducted in Dallas, also found that temperature's correlation with assaults was strongest during evening hours, which are usually the coolest time of day.[88] Other studies conducted in Minneapolis found that temperature was significantly correlated with certain property crimes (burglary, larceny, and robbery),[89] with domestic violence,[90] and with disorderly conduct.[91]

Cohn and Rotton's findings are consistent with predictions that might be derived from routine activities theory (discussed in Chapter 4). They suggest that uncomfortably hot and cold temperatures keep people apart, resulting in less opportunity for victims and motivated offenders to come into contact with one another. Temporal variables, such as time of day and day of week, moderate the relationship between temperature and crime by also affecting opportunity; offenders and victims are more likely to come into contact with each other during evening and weekend hours than during the day, when many people are busy at work or school or are engaged in other routine activities.

GENETICS AND CRIME
Criminal Families

Some scholars have suggested that a penchant for crime may be inherited and that criminal tendencies are genetically based. Beginning in the late 1800s, researchers in the field of criminal anthropology focused on criminal families, or families that appeared to exhibit criminal tendencies through several generations.

In 1877, **Richard Louis Dugdale** (1841–1883) published a study of one such family—the **Juke family**.[92] Dugdale traced the Juke lineage back to a notorious character named Max, a Dutch immigrant who arrived in New York in the early 1700s. Two of Max's sons married into the notorious "Juke family of girls," six sisters, all of whom were said to be illegitimate. Max's male descendants were reputed to be vicious, and one woman named Ada had an especially bad reputation and came to be known as "the mother of criminals." By the time of the study, Dugdale was able to identify approximately 1,200 of Ada's descendants. Included among their numbers were seven murderers, 60 habitual thieves, 90 or so other criminals, 50 prostitutes, and 280 paupers. Dugdale compared the crime-prone Jukes with another family, the pure-blooded progeny of Jonathan Edwards, a Puritan preacher and one-time president

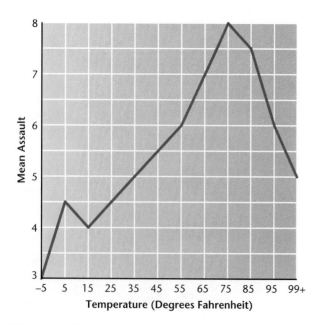

■ **FIGURE 5-2**   Assault as a Function of Temperature.
Source: E. G. Cohn and J. Rotton, "Assault as a Function of Time and Temperature: A Moderator-Variable Time-Series Analysis," *Journal of Personality and Social Psychology,* Vol. 72 (1997), pp. 1322–1334. Data used with permission.

of Princeton University. Descendants of Edwards included American presidents and vice presidents and many successful bankers and businesspeople. No one was identified among the Edwards lineage who had had a run-in with the law. In 1916, **Arthur H. Estabrook** published a follow-up to Dugdale's work, in which he identified an additional 715 Juke descendants, including 378 more prostitutes, 170 additional paupers, and 118 other criminals.[93]

Following in the tradition of family tree researchers, **Henry Herbert Goddard** (1866–1957) published a study of the **Kallikak family** in 1912.[94] Goddard attempted to place the study of deviant families within an acceptable scientific framework via the provision of a kind of control group. For comparison purposes he used two branches of the same family. One branch began as the result of a sexual liaison between Martin Kallikak, a Revolutionary War soldier, and a barmaid whose name is unknown. As a result of this union, an illegitimate son (Martin, Jr.) was born. After the war, Kallikak returned home and married a righteous Quaker girl, and a second line of descent began. Although the second, legitimate branch, produced only a few minor deviants, the illegitimate line resulted in 262 "feebleminded" births and various other epileptic, alcoholic, and criminal descendants. (The term *feebleminded,* which was much in vogue at the time of Goddard's study, was later recast as "mentally retarded," and today people exhibiting similar characteristics might be referred to as "mentally handicapped" or "mentally challenged.") Because feeblemindedness appeared to occur with some predictability in Goddard's study, whereas criminal activity seemed to be only randomly represented among the descendants of both Kallikak lines, Goddard concluded that a tendency toward feeblemindedness was inherited but that criminality was not.

Studies like these, which focused on inherited mental degeneration, led to the **eugenics** movement of the 1920s and early 1930s and to the development of **eugenic criminology**,[95] which held that the root causes of criminality were largely passed from generation to generation in the form of "bad genes." Eugenic criminology replaced the idea of the "feebleminded criminal" with the "defective delinquent," and social policies developed during the eugenics movement called for the sterilization of mentally handicapped women to prevent their bearing additional offspring.[96] Those policies were supported by the federal Eugenics Record Office, which funded studies of "cacogenic" or "bad-gened" families, and were endorsed by the 1927 U.S. Supreme Court case of **Buck v. Bell**.[97] In *Buck,* Justice Oliver Wendell Holmes, Jr., writing in support of a Virginia statute permitting sterilization, said, "It is better for all the world, if instead of waiting to execute degenerate offspring for crime, or to let them starve for their imbecility, society can prevent those persons who are manifestly unfit from continuing their kind." Read the Court's opinion in *Buck* v. *Bell* at Web Extra! 5-7.

 Web Extra! 5-7 at crimtoday.com

The eugenics movement, as it existed in this country before World War II, was largely discredited by intense worldwide condemnation of Nazi genetic research and mass sterilization and eugenics programs, including those which led to the Holocaust. As a consequence, research attempting to ferret out the biological underpinnings of behavioral traits remains suspect in the minds of many today.

The XYY "Supermale"

Recent developments in the field of human genetics have led to the study of the role of chromosomes, and sex-linked chromosomes in particular, in crime causation. The first well-known study of this type was undertaken by Patricia A. Jacobs,[98] a British researcher who in 1965 examined 197 Scottish prisoners for chromosomal abnormalities through a relatively simple blood test known as "karyotyping."[99] Twelve members of the group displayed chromosomes which were unusual, and seven were found to have an XYY chromosome. "Normal" male individuals possess an XY chromosome structure, and "normal" female individuals are XX. Some other unusual combinations might be XXX, wherein a woman's genetic makeup contains an extra X chromosome, or XXY, also called Klinefelter's syndrome, in which a man might carry an extra X, or female, chromosome. Klinefelter's men often have male genitalia but are frequently sterile and evidence breast enlargement and intellectual retardation. The XYY man, however, whose incidence in the prison population was placed at around 3.5% by Jacobs, was quickly identified as potentially violent and was termed a **supermale**.

Following the introduction of the supermale notion into popular consciousness, a number of offenders attempted to offer a chromosome-based defense. In 1969, for example, Lawrence E. Hannell, who was adjudged a supermale, was acquitted of murder in Australia on the grounds of insanity.[100] Such a defense, however, did not work for Richard Speck, who also claimed to be an XYY man and was convicted of killing eight Chicago nursing students in 1966. It was later learned that Speck did not carry the extra Y chromosome.

To date, there have been nearly 200 studies of XYY males. Although not all researchers agree, taken as a group these studies[101] tend to show that supermales

- Are taller than the average male, often standing 6'1" or more
- Suffer from acne or skin disorders
- Have less than average intelligence
- Are overrepresented in prisons and mental hospitals
- Come from families with a lower than average history of crime or mental illness

The supermale phenomenon, also called the "XYY syndrome," may have been more sensationalism than fact. Little evidence suggests that XYY men actually commit crimes of greater violence than do other men, although they may commit somewhat more crimes overall. A 1976 Danish study of 4,000 men, which found precisely that, may have helped put the issue to rest.[102] The Danish survey, conducted of men born in Copenhagen between 1944 and 1947, also found that the incidence of XYY men was less than 1% in the general male population. Other recent researchers have similarly concluded that "studies done thus far are largely in agreement and demonstrate rather conclusively that males of the XYY type are not predictably aggressive."[103]

Chromosomes and Modern-Day Criminal Families

In 1993, Dutch criminologists caught worldwide attention with their claim that they had uncovered a specific gene with links to criminal behavior. Researcher H. Hilger Ropers, geneticist Han Brunner, and collaborators studied what media sources called "the Netherlands' most dysfunctional family."[104] Although the unnamed family displayed IQs in the near-normal range, they seemed unable to control their impulses and often ended up being arrested for violations of the criminal law. The arrests, however, were always of men. Tracing the family back five generations, Brunner found fourteen men whom he classified as genetically given to criminality. None of the women in the family displayed criminal tendencies, although they were often victimized by their crime-prone male siblings. One brother raped a sister and later stabbed a mental hospital staffer in the chest with a pitchfork. Another tried to run over his supervisor with his car. Two brothers repeatedly started fires and were classified as arsonists. Another brother frequently crept into his sisters' rooms and forced them to undress at knifepoint.

According to Ropers and Brunner, because men have only one X chromosome, they are especially vulnerable to any defective gene. Women, with two X chromosomes, have a kind of backup system in which one defective gene may be compensated for by another wholesome and correctly functioning gene carried in the second X chromosome. After a decade of study, which involved the laboratory filtering of a huge quantity of genetic material in a search for the defective gene, Ropers and Brunner announced that they had isolated the specific mutation that caused the family's criminality. The gene, they said, is responsible for the production of an enzyme called monoamine oxidase A (MAOA). MAOA is crucially involved in the process by which signals are transmitted within the brain. Specifically, MAOA breaks down the chemicals serotonin and noradrenaline. Both are substances that have been linked to aggressive behavior in human beings. Because men with the mutated gene do not produce the enzyme necessary to break down chemical transmitters, researchers surmise, their brains are overwhelmed with stimuli—a situation that results in uncontrollable urges and, ultimately, criminal behavior.

Behavioral Genetics

Sir Francis Galton (1822–1911) was the first Western scientist to systematically study heredity and its possible influence upon human behavior.[105] In 1907, Galton wrote that "the perpetuation of the criminal class by heredity is a question difficult to grapple with on many accounts. . . . It is, however, easy to show that the criminal nature tends to be inherited. . . . The true state of the case appears to be that the criminal population receives steady accessions from those who, without having strongly marked criminal natures, do nevertheless belong to a type of humanity that is exceedingly ill suited to play a respectable part in our modern civilization, though it is well suited to flourish under half-savage conditions, being naturally both healthy and prolific."[106] Galton's work contributed to the development of the field of **behavioral genetics**, which is the study of genetic and environmental contributions to individual variations in human behavior.

While Galton might have believed that heredity was in some way related to criminality, he had no opportunity to explore the relationship in depth. More recently, however, studies of the criminal tendencies of fraternal and identical twins have provided a methodologically sophisticated technique for ferreting out the role of heredity in crime causation. Fraternal twins, also called "dizygotic (DZ) twins," develop from different fertilized eggs and share only the genetic material common among siblings. Identical twins, also called **monozygotic (MZ) twins**, develop from the same egg and carry virtually the same genetic material. Hence if human behavior has a substantial heritable component, twins should tend to display similar behavioral characteristics despite variations in their social environment. Similarly, any observed relationship might be expected to be stronger among monozygotic twins than among dizygotic twins.

One of the first studies to link MZ twins to criminality was published in the 1920s by German physician Johannes Lange.[107] Lange examined only 17 pairs of fraternal twins and 13 pairs of identical twins but found that in ten of the 13 identical pairs both twins were criminal, whereas only two of the 17 fraternal pairs exhibited such similarity. Lange's findings drew considerable attention, even though his sample was small and he was unable to adequately separate environmental influences from genetic ones. The title of his book, *Verbrechen als Schicksal* (Crime as Destiny), indicates Lange's firm conviction that criminality has a strong genetic component.

A much larger twin study was begun in 1968 by European researchers Karl O. Christiansen and Sarnoff Mednick, who analyzed all twins (3,586 pairs) born on a selected group of Danish islands between 1881 and 1910.[108] Christiansen and Mednick found significant statistical support for the notion that criminal tendencies are inherited, and they concluded that 52% of identical twins and 22% of fraternal siblings displayed the same degree of criminality within the twin pair. Such similarities remained apparent even among twins who had been separated at birth and who were raised in substantially different environments.

In 1994, Dutch researchers reported finding substantial genetic influences on delinquent and aggressive behavior in a

CRIME IN THE NEWS
"Delinquency Genes" Identified?

Some aspects of juvenile delinquency and Attention Deficit Disorder (ADD) may be genetically influenced and passed on from parents to children, according to a new study presented at the American Society of Criminology (ASC) conference.

Experts cautioned that the link, even if definitively proven, would only be one element influencing such behavior, with environmental and other biological factors playing strong roles as well. Still, the study and related research seem sure to generate controversy.

Speaking before a session of the weeklong gathering of criminologists at the Marriott Wardman Hotel, David C. Rowe, a behavioral geneticist from the University of Arizona, said his study showed that two genes relate to delinquency and Attention Deficit Disorder and that the behavior traits encoded in those genes could be passed from parents to children.

Behavioral genetics is a new and sometimes controversial approach to the study of all aspects of human behavior, including criminal activities. It is based on the belief that genes—the minuscule protein strands that dictate the shape and size of our bodies—may also affect how we think and behave.

PARENT AND CHILD GROUPS STUDIED

Rowe's study, presented at a session entitled "Genetic and Environmental Influences on Antisocial Behavior," involved families who had children in treatment for delinquency and Attention Deficit Disorder (ADD) and a second set of families without children in therapy. Rowe used this second group as a control group. He said he identified two genes shared by the children in therapy that showed a correlation to delinquency and ADD.

Rowe then tried to determine if the same genetic characteristics, along with the corresponding behavioral traits, were shared by the parents. He asked the two groups of parents to fill out questionnaires about their childhoods, answering questions about how often they stole things, got into fights, or had difficulty paying attention in class. Rowe found that the parents who reported the most delinquent experiences and ADD symptoms as teens were more likely to have children who experienced similar problems. And these parents shared the same pattern in the two critical genes that Rowe had identified in the delinquent children.

The scientist noted his study was limited, but predicted it would have implications for the treatment of troubled young people. "There are going to be very many genes linked to behavior, and this is just an early study," Rowe said. "I think that with this knowledge, we can do more in the way of treatment."

"INTELLIGENCE GENES" PREVIOUSLY FOUND

Rowe's initial findings add to a growing body of similar scientific findings. [In 1997], for instance, Robert Plomin, a British scientist, claimed to be the first to identify a gene that controls intelligence. Plomin studied the genetic makeup of a group of child prodigies, looking for a common gene that might control their behavior. He reported that he found one, and called it the IGF2R gene on chromosome 6.

However, both Rowe and Plomin cautioned that human behavior, either delinquent or cerebral, was controlled by many genes *and* a healthy dose of environmental factors as well.

"A single gene like this has only a small effect," Rowe said. "All of these are multi-gene traits."

Rowe said scientists are working to identify all the genes responsible for any given human behavior. "But we're talking about a 20-year enterprise," he said.

Source: Hans H. Chen, "Study Says Behavioral Traits Pass from Parents to Children," APB News, November 14, 1998. Reprinted with permission.

study that compared 221 pairs of biologically unrelated siblings in adoptive families to 111 pairs of biologically related siblings in similar settings.[109] Using a sophisticated study design, the researchers were able to conclude that "genetic influences accounted for 70% of the variance of aggressive behavior," while predicting only 39% of delinquency and 47% of attention-related problems.

In 1996, British researchers who studied 43 monozygotic and 38 dizygotic same-sex twins through the use of self-report questionnaires concluded that "common bad behaviors of the sort admitted to by the majority of adolescents have a substantially heritable component. Additive genetic effects account for most of the variation, with no evidence of a contribution from shared environment."[110] The researchers also determined that genetic effects on behavior appear to increase with age. The British research was supported by the findings of a joint United States–Australian examination of 2,682 adult twin pairs.[111] In that study, researchers found "a substantial genetic influence on risk for conduct disorder" (which was defined to include chronic stealing, lying, bullying, arson, property destruction, weapons use, cruelty to animals or people, fighting, aggression, truancy, and running away from home).

The Human Genome Project

Many of the questions criminologists have raised about the role of genetics in criminal behavior may soon be answered by the results of research undertaken by the Human Genome Project (HGP).[112] HGP is an international research program designed to construct detailed maps of the human genome. Begun in the United States in 1990 through a joint effort of the Department of Energy and the National Institutes of Health, its purpose is to determine the complete nucleotide sequence of human DNA, to localize the estimated 50,000 to 100,000 genes within the human genome, and to determine the sequences of the estimated 3 billion chemical base pairs that make up human DNA. According to the National Human Genome Research Institute, "The scientific products of the HGP will comprise a resource of detailed information about the structure, organization and function of human DNA, information that constitutes the basic set of inherited 'instructions' for the development and functioning of a human being." HGP intends to store the information it develops in databases and to develop tools for the analysis of the data it produces, with the goal of eventually transferring that information and associated technologies to the private sector. The transfer is meant to stimulate the multibillion-dollar U.S. biotechnology industry and to foster the development of new medical treatments and technologies. As this book goes

to press, HGP plans to finish it's work by the end of the year 2003—two years ahead of schedule.[113]

The acquisition and use of the genetic knowledge developed by HGP are likely to have momentous implications for both individuals and society. In the area of crime control policy, HGP-developed information is expected to pose a number of choices for public and professional deliberation. Hence the analysis of the ethical, legal, and social implications of genetic knowledge and the development of policy options for public consideration are central components of the human genome research effort.

Some scientists are confident that future advances in the field of behavioral genetics brought about by HGP will support the idea of behavioral **genetic determinism**, or the belief that genes are the major determining factor in human behavior. Others, however, warn that discoveries in behavioral genetics may need to be interpreted in terms of what is already known about social and psychological influences on behavior.

Early results associated with HGP, however, are interesting. A few years ago, for example, researchers at the University of Texas Health Science Center in San Antonio announced the discovery of a pleasure-seeking gene that, they suspect, plays a role in deviant behavior, addictions, and maybe even murder and violence. The gene, called "DRD2 A1 allele," is normally involved in controlling the flow of dopamine. Dopamine, a powerful brain chemical, gives people a sense of well-being. When defective, however, the DRD2 A1 allele diminishes dopamine function, which may drive a person to take drugs, drink, or engage in activity that provides a dopamine-like experience. "We think they're seeking out ways of fixing the lack of pleasure," says Kenneth Blum, University of Texas Health Science Center, San Antonio. "You might be a pleasure seeker for alcohol, drugs, sex or maybe you get it from violence or murder."[114]

The Human Genome Project not withstanding, behavioral geneticists examining the crime problem face some daunting issues. Among them is the difficulty of coming up with a suitable definition of crime, determining how best to measure criminality once it has been defined, separating out the influences of the environment from what may be genetic influences on behavior, and distinguishing among the multiple and potentially interrelated influences of many genes. In the final analysis, the explanatory power of **heritability**, which is a statistical construct that estimates the amount of variation in a population that is attributable to genetic factors, appears to be limited by the fact that it may apply only to specific environments that existed at the time of a given study. As one noted geneticist says, "If the population or the environment changes, the heritability most likely will change as well. Most important, heritability statements provide no basis for predictions about the expression of the trait in question in any given individual."[115] Learn more about the Human Genome Project by visiting the National Human Genome Research Institute via Web Extra! 5-8.

A genome researcher at work. The National Center for Human Genome Research at the National Institutes of Health supports the international Human Genome Project, a research program to determine the complete nucleotide sequence of human DNA. What ethical, legal, and social implications are inherent in such a project? *Durand Trippett, SIPA Press*

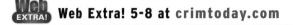

Web Extra! 5-8 at crimtoday.com

You might also want to visit the U.S. Department of Energy's Human Genome Program site at Web Extra! 5-9.

Web Extra! 5-9 at crimtoday.com

Male-Female Differences in Criminality

A number of contemporary writers propose that criminologists must recognize that "the male is much more criminalistic than the female."[116] As Chapter 2 describes, with the exception of crimes like prostitution and shoplifting, the number of crimes committed by men routinely far exceeds the number of crimes committed by women in almost all categories, and when women commit crimes, they are far more likely to assume the role of followers than leaders.[117] The data on the extent of male-female criminality show surprising regularity over time. The proportion of homicides committed by men versus women, for example, has remained more or less constant for decades (see Table 5-1). Similarly, the proportion of men murdered by men versus the proportion of women murdered by women has been consistent, showing a much greater propensity for men to murder one another.

If culture exercises the major role in determining criminality, as many social scientists today suggest, then we would expect to see recognizable increases in the degree and nature of female criminality over time, especially as changes in socialization practices, cultural roles, and other ethnographic patterns increase the opportunity for women to commit what had previously been regarded as traditionally male offenses. With the exception of a few crimes, such as embezzlement, drug abuse, and liquor law violations, however, such has not been the case. Although women comprise 51% of the population of the United States, they are arrested for only 17% of all violent crimes and 30% of property crimes[118]—a proportion that has remained surprisingly constant over the years since the FBI began gathering crime data more than half a century ago. Simply put, even with all the cultural changes which have created new possibilities for women in crime, few women have taken advantage of these newfound freedoms. Such apparent differences not only have existed over time, but also can be seen in cross-cultural studies. Chapter 2 provides additional statistics of this sort.

Such findings are in contrast with the suggestions of authors like Freda Adler, who in her 1975 book, *Sisters in Crime*, proposed that as women entered "nontraditional occupations" and roles, there "would be a movement toward parity with men in the commission of crime in terms of both incidence and type."[119] Darrell J. Steffensmeir, who studied changes in women's criminality following publication of Adler's book, found almost no evidence to support the belief that a new female criminal is emerging or that female criminality is undergoing the kind of increase Adler might have expected.[120] The lack of contemporary validation for Adler's thesis suggests that something else is occurring; that is, some element other than cultural inhibition or equality of opportunity is preventing women from taking their place alongside men as equals in crime. Biological criminologists suggest that the organic correlates of gender provide the needed explanation.

In evaluating the criminality of women based on statistics alone, however, danger prevails of misidentifying causal factors operative in the behavior itself. Although men consistently commit more murders than women, for example, we should not jump to the conclusion that this bit of evidence shows a genetic predisposition toward interpersonal violence in men which is absent in women. To do so would fail to recognize the role of other causal factors. Observable racial variation in crime rates has provided some writers with a basis for claiming that some racial groups are disproportionately violent, while simultaneously attributing such violence to a genetic basis. A look at the statistics, for example, appears to show that in the United States, blacks are seven times as likely as whites to commit murder, three times as likely to commit rape, nine times as likely to rob, and twice as likely, on average, to commit any kind of crime.[121] Chapter 2 provides additional statistics of this sort.

Such statistics, however, can be inherently misleading because—unlike the undeniable and easily observable biological differences that exist between men and women—racial groupings are defined more by convention than by genetics. In fact, some writers suggest that "pure" racial groups no longer exist and that even historical racial distinctions were based more on political convention than on significant genetic differences.

TABLE 5-1 ■ Male and Female Murder Perpetrators as a Percentage of All Arrests for Homicide, 1960-1999									
1960		1975		1980		1990		1999	
Male	Female	Male	Female	Male	Female	Male	Female	Male	Female
82.5%	17.5%	84.7%	15.3%	87.2%	12.8%	89.6%	10.4%	88.6%	11.4%

Source: Adapted from Federal Bureau of Investigation, *Crime in the United States* (Washington, D.C.: U.S. Government Printing Office, 1961, 1976, 1981, 1991, and 2000).

The criminality of women (or relative lack thereof) is, in all likelihood, culturally determined to a considerable degree. Nonetheless, the consistency of data which routinely show that women are far less likely than men to be involved in most property crimes, and less likely still to commit violent crimes, requires recognition. We have already evaluated the role that testosterone may play in increasing the propensity toward violence and aggression among men. A few authors suggest that testosterone is the agent primarily responsible for male criminality and that its relative lack in women leads them to commit fewer crimes. Some evidence supports just such a hypothesis. Studies have shown, for example, that female fetuses exposed to elevated testosterone levels during gestation develop masculine characteristics, including a muscular build and a demonstrably greater tendency toward aggression later in life.[122] Even so, genetically based behavioral differences between men and women are so moderated by aspects of the social environment, including socialization, the learning of culturally prescribed roles, and the expectations of others, that definitive conclusions are difficult to reach.

One recently proposed social-psychological explanation for homicidal behavior among women, for example, suggests that men who kill tend to do so out of a need to control a situation, whereas women who kill tend to do so because they have lost control over themselves.[123] The theory says "that women as a group are more 'controlled' than men, particularly with respect to their experience and expression of anger." Such control is said to emanate from the fact that "men are always the subjects and women the objects in [a] male-centric universe."[124] As a consequence of our culture's overemphasis on a woman's looks rather than on her performance, the theory says, women internalize a "self-image on the basis of appearance rather than substance of character," resulting in low self-esteem and low self-confidence. Low self-esteem, the argument goes, necessitates greater self-control and results in lower criminality among women. Such a perspective suggests that women tend to commit homicides only when driven "past the brink" of self-control, thus offering an explanation for why homicides committed by women are generally spontaneous rather than planned, why they usually involve the killing of intimates, and why they generally occur in the home. "Women generally view themselves as part of a collective of relationships around them," say some theorists, "and evaluate their self-worth based on the value and success of these relationships."[125] Hence when relationships break down, a woman's self-worth may be negated, resulting in a lessening of control—and homicide may ensue.

Sociobiology

In the introduction to his insightful article summarizing sociobiology, Arthur Fisher writes, "Every so often, in the long course of scientific progress, a new set of ideas appears, illuminating and redefining what has gone before like a flare bursting over a darkened landscape."[126] To some, **sociobiology**—a theoretical synthesis of biology, behavior, and evolutionary ecology brought to the scientific community by **Edward O. Wilson** in his seminal 1975 work *Sociobiology: The New Synthesis*[127]— holds the promise of just such a new **paradigm**. In his book, Wilson defined sociobiology as "the systematic study of the biological basis of all social behavior" and as "a branch of evolutionary biology and particularly of modern population biology." Through his entomological study of social insects, especially ants, Wilson demonstrated that particular forms of behavior could contribute to the long-term survival of the social group. Wilson focused on altruism (selfless, helping behavior) and found that contrary to the beliefs of some evolutionary biologists, helping behavior facilitates the continuity of the gene pool among altruistic individuals. Wilson's major focus was to show that the primary determinant of behavior, including human behavior, was the need to ensure the survival and continuity of genetic material from one generation to the next.

Territoriality, another primary tenent of Wilson's writings, was said to explain much of the conflict seen between and among human beings, including homicide, warfare, and other forms of aggression. In Wilson's words, "Part of man's problem is that his intergroup responses are still crude and primitive, and inadequate for the extended extraterritorial relationships that civilization has thrust upon him." The "unhappy result," as Wilson terms it, may be "tribalism," expressed through the contemporary proliferation of street gangs, racial tension, and the hardened encampments of survivalist and separatist groups.

Women's boxing, a relatively new sport, reflects women's changing social roles. Male-female differences in criminality, however, seem to display considerable regularity over time. Does this mean that men and women have inherently different behavioral tendencies? *AFP, Corbis*

The sad results of territoriality, whatever its cause, can be seen in the deadly adventure of 15-year-old Michael Carter and his companions, who ended up in the wrong place at the wrong time. On June 18, 1997, Carter, from Highland Township, Michigan, and two of his friends hopped a CSX Transportation train headed for the town of Holly. The three were looking for a free ten-mile ride on their way to see friends. But they missed their jumping-off point, sailed past the town of Holly, and ended up in a run-down inner-city ghetto in the middle of Flint, Michigan, around midnight. Soon the three were surrounded by gang members, led into a secluded area, and shot. Carter died at the scene, while friend Dustin Kaiser, also 15, survived a gunshot wound to the head. The 14-year-old girl who had accompanied the boys was raped and shot in the face, but lived.[128]

As sociobiologists tell us, the violence and aggressiveness associated with territoriality is often reserved for strangers. The approach of sociobiology can explain intragroup aggression—or the violence that occurs within groups—as well as that which occurs between groups. Wilson writes that his theory suggests that, within the group, "a particularly severe form of aggressiveness should be reserved for actual or suspected adultery. In many human societies," he observes, "where sexual bonding is close and personal knowledge of the behavior of others detailed, adulterers are harshly treated. The sin," he adds, "is regarded to be even worse when offspring are produced."[129] Hence territoriality and acquisitiveness extend, from a sociobiological perspective, to location, possessions, and even other people. Human laws, says Wilson, are designed to protect genetically based relationships which people have with one another, as well as their material possessions and their claimed locations in space. Violations of these intuitive relationships result in crime and in official reactions by the legal system.

Wilson's writing propelled researchers into a flurry of studies intended to test the validity of his assertions. One study, for example, found that Indian adult male Hanuman langurs (a type of monkey) routinely killed the young offspring of female langurs with whom they bonded when those offspring had been sired by other male langurs.[130] A Canadian study of violence in the homes of adoptive children found a human parallel to the langur study, showing that stepchildren run a 70 times greater risk of being killed by their adoptive parents than do children living with their natural parents.[131] Some writers concluded that "murderous behavior, warfare, and even genocide were unavoidable correlates of genetic evolution, controlled by the same genes for territorial behavior that had been selected in primate evolution."[132] Others suggested that biological predispositions developed during earlier stages of human evolution color contemporary criminal activity. Male criminals, for example, tend toward robbery and burglary—crimes in which they can continue to enact their "hunter instincts" developed long ago. The criminality of women, on the other hand, is more typical of "gatherers" when it involves shoplifting, simple theft, and so on.

Human behavioral predilections can be studied in a variety of ways. In the 1989 book *Evolutionary Jurisprudence*, John H. Beckstrom reports on his examination of over 400 legal documents which, he claimed, showed support for Wilson's contentions that humans tend to act so as to preserve territorial claims, the likelihood of successful reproduction, and the continuation of their own particular genetic material.[133] In his analysis, Beckstrom used legal claims and court decisions spanning over 300 years of judicial activity. Other theorists have gone so far as to imply that, among humans, there may be a gene-based tendency to experience guilt and to develop a conscience. Hence notions of right and wrong, whether embodied in laws or in social convention, may flow from such a naturalistic origin. Learn more about sociobiology in general and the sociobiology of sociopathy at Web Extras! 5-10 and 5-11.

Web Extras! 5-10 and 5-11 at crimtoday.com

As sociobiology began to receive expanded recognition from American investigators, some social scientists, believing the basic tenents of their profession to be challenged by the movement, began to treat it as "criminology's anti-discipline."[134] Contemporary criminologist John Madison Memory writes, "By the early 1980s sociobiology presented such a significant threat to American criminology that it could no longer be ignored."[135] Criticisms were quick to come. Memory identifies many such critiques, including these charges:

- Sociobiology fails to convey the overwhelming significance of culture, social learning, and individual experiences in shaping the behavior of individuals and groups.
- Sociobiology is fundamentally wrong in its depiction of the basic nature of man; there is no credible evidence of genetically based or determined tendencies to act in certain ways.
- Sociobiology is just another empirically unsupported rationale for the authoritative labeling and stigmatization of despised, threatening, powerless minorities.
- Man is so thoroughly different from other animal species, even other primates, that there is no rational basis for the application to man of findings from animal studies.

Many such criticisms were advanced by old-guard academics, some of whom still flourish, in an effort to prevent their own discipline's decline in influence in the face of otherwise convincing sociobiological claims. In the words of one observer, "Most criminologists, like most academicians, were wedded to a paradigm, and wedded even to the idea of paradigm, the idea that one great problem solution can permit the explanation of nearly all the unexplained variation in the field."[136] In other words, many criminologists were committed to the idea that one theory (generally

Sociobiologists tell us that certain traits, such as territoriality, are common to both animals and humans. How might territoriality lead to crime? *Paul Lally, Stock Boston*

their own) could explain all that there was to know about crime and its causes. Fortunately, today, many open-minded scholars are beginning to sense the growing need for a new synthesis—for a way in which to integrate the promise of biological theories like sociobiology with other long-accepted perspectives like sociology and psychology. As a result, evidence suggests that the field of criminology is now ripe for a new multicausal approach.

CRIME AND HUMAN NATURE: A CONTEMPORARY SYNTHESIS

A decade ago, Arnold L. Lieber delivered the invited address at the annual meeting of the American Psychological Association in Denver, Colorado.[137] Lieber used the forum to describe his research on biology and crime, which linked phases of the moon to fluctuations in the incidence of violence among human beings. Nights around full moons, according to Lieber, show a significant rise in crime. Although critics found this type of research nonsensical, police officers, hospital personnel, ambulance drivers, and many late-night service providers who heard of Lieber's talk understood what he was describing. Many such individuals, in their own experience, had apparently seen validation of the "full moon thesis."

Shortly after Lieber's presentation, criminologist **James Q. Wilson** and psychologist **Richard J. Herrnstein** teamed up to write *Crime and Human Nature,* a book-length treatise that reiterates many of the arguments proposed by biological

criminologists over the past century.[138] Their purpose, at least in part, was to reopen discussion of biological causes of crime. "We want to show," Herrnstein said, "that the pendulum is beginning to swing away from a totally sociological explanation of crime."[139] Their avowed goal was "not to state a case just for genetic factors, but to state a comprehensive theory of crime that draws together all the different factors that cause criminal behavior."[140]

The constitutional factors that Wilson and Herrnstein cite as contributing to crime include the following:[141]

- *Gender.* "Crime," the authors say, "has been predominantly male behavior."
- *Age.* "In general, the tendency to break the law declines throughout life."
- *Body type.* "A disproportionate number of criminals have a mesomorphic build."
- *Intelligence.* Criminality is said to be clearly and consistently associated with low intelligence.
- *Personality.* Criminals are typically aggressive, impulsive, and cruel.

Although personality, behavioral problems, and intelligence may be related to environment, the authors say that "each involves some genetic inheritance." Wilson and Herrnstein do recognize social factors in the development of personality, but they suggest that constitutional factors predispose a person to specific types of behavior and that societal reactions to such predispositions may determine, to a large degree, the form of continued behavior. Hence the interplay between heredity, biology, and the social environment may be the key nexus in any consideration of crime causation.

POLICY ISSUES

Biological theories of crime causation present unique challenges to policymakers. According to C. Ray Jeffery, a comprehensive biologically based program of crime prevention and crime control would include[142]

- "Pre- and postnatal care for pregnant women and their infants," to monitor and address potentially detrimental developmental conditions which could lead to heightened aggression and crime later in life
- Monitoring of children throughout the early stages of their development to identify "early symptoms of behavioral disorder"
- Monitoring of children in their early years to reduce the risk of exposure to violence-inducing experiences like child abuse and violence committed by other children
- Neurological examinations, including CAT, PET, and MRI scans, "given when the need is evident"
- Biological research, conducted in our nation's prisons and treatment facilities, which might better identify the root causes of aggression and violence. Laws that prevent the experimental use of prison subjects, the analysis of the bodies of executed prisoners, and other similar types of biological investigations must change, says Jeffery.

Jeffery adds that the fundamental orientation of our legal system must also change to acknowledge contributions of biological criminologists. Such a change would replace or supplement our current "right to punishment" doctrine with a "right to treatment" philosophy. Jeffery concludes his analysis by saying, "If legal and political barriers prevent us from regarding antisocial behavior as a medical problem, and if we do not permit medical research on criminal behavior, how can we ever solve the crime problem?"[143]

The dangers of too great a dependence on biological approaches to crime, however, raise the specter of an Orwellian bogeyman in charge of every aspect of human social life, from conception to the grave—and include the possible abortion of defective fetuses, capital punishment in lieu of rehabilitation, and enforced sterilization. Precedent for such fears can be found in cases like *Buck* v. *Bell*,[144] discussed earlier in this chapter, in which the U.S. Supreme Court, influenced by the genetically based perspectives of the times, sanctioned state-enforced sterilization statutes.

Potential links between race and crime, suggested by some researchers, are especially repugnant to many who criticize biological criminology, seeing it as a reemergence of the eugenics movement of the early twentieth century. Ronald Walters, a political scientist at Howard University, for example, observes that "seeking the biological and genetic aspects of violence is dangerous to African-American youth. . . . When you consider the perception that black people have always been the violent people in this society, it is a short step from this stereotype to using this kind of research for social control."[145]

According to University of Maryland Criminologists Gary LaFree and Katheryn K. Russell, "a major reason for moving away from studies of differential crime rates by race, beginning in the 1960s, was to avoid negative associations between race and crime: blacks already were disadvantaged by the economy and the society. Thus, to imply that crime problems were more serious for blacks than for others seemed to be double victimization." Yet, these same authors add, "no group has suffered more than African-Americans by our failure to understand and control street crime."[146]

Although biological theories of crime may have problems, some criminologists believe that to ignore the potential contributions of biological theorists because of hypothetical policy consequences or because of the supposed danger of racial prejudice does a disservice to the science of criminology and denies the opportunity for compassionate and objective researchers to realistically assist in the process of crime reduction. In 1993, for example, the Youth Violence Initiative, begun under President George Bush to study problem behavior among American youth, was canceled by the Clinton administration because indications were that it might identify a disproportionate number of racial and ethnic minorities as delinquent.

In 1997, in an attempt to bring biological theorizing into the criminological mainstream, Lee Ellis and Anthony Walsh expanded on the theme of genetic predispositions, noting that "in the case of behavior, nearly all of the effects of genes are quite indirect because they are mediated through complex chains of events occurring in the brain. This means that

Former New Jersey Police Superintendent Carl Williams. Williams, a 35-year police veteran, was forced to resign when the "racial profiling" practices his officers used to target motorists became public. Possible links between race and crime, suggested by some researchers, are especially repugnant to many who criticize biological criminology. Why might varying rates of arrest and of criminal offending appear to be associated with race? *Charles Rex Arbogast, AP/Wide World Photos*

there are almost certainly no genes for something as complex as criminal behavior. Nevertheless, many genes may affect brain functioning in ways that either increase or reduce the chances of individuals learning various complex behavior patterns, including behavior patterns that happen to be so offensive to others that criminal sanctions have been instituted to minimize their recurrence."[147]

CRITIQUES OF BIOLOGICAL THEORIES

In 1998, in a critique of biological theories of crime, Nicole Hahn Rafter, a noted criminologist at Northeastern University, argued against the possible development of a contemporary eugenics movement based upon the findings of modern-day genetics. In *Creating Born Criminals,* Rafter attempted to demonstrate the need for contemporary researchers and policymakers to know how eugenic reasoning worked in the past so that they would be able to recognize the dangers posed by any theory that interprets social problems in biological terms and that sees what might be innate differences as evidence of biological inferiority.[148] While genetic solutions to human problems may seem to offer a near-future panacea, Rafter warns that policymakers must always be on their guard against the danger of oversimplifying social issues as complex as crime.

A more focused contemporary critique of biological perspectives on crime causation is provided by Glenn D. Walters and Thomas W. White, who contend that "genetic research on crime has been poorly designed, ambiguously reported, and exceedingly inadequate in addressing the relevant issues."[149] Walters and White highlight the following specific shortcomings of studies in the area:

- Few biological studies adequately conceptualize criminality. "Several studies," they say, "have defined criminality on the basis of a single arrest."[150]
- Twin studies, in particular, have sometimes failed to properly establish whether a pair of twins is monozygotic or dizygotic. This is because some MZ twins are not identical in appearance, and only a few twin studies have depended on biological testing rather than on a simple evaluation of appearances.
- Problems in estimating the degree of criminality among sample populations are rife in biological (and in many other) studies of criminality. Interview data are open to interpretation, and existing statistical data on the past criminality of offenders are not always properly appreciated.
- Methodological problems abound in many studies which attempt to evaluate the role of genetics in crime. Walters and White mention, among other things, the lack of control or comparison groups, small sample sizes, the dropping out of subjects from study groups, biased sampling techniques, and the use of inappropriate forms of statistical analysis.
- Results obtained outside the United States may not be applicable within this country. Twin studies conducted in Sweden and Denmark provide an example of this potential lack of generalizability.

Walters and White nonetheless conclude that "genetic factors are undoubtedly correlated with various measures of criminality," but they add that "the large number of methodological flaws and limitations in the research should make one cautious in drawing any causal inferences at this point in time."[151]

SUMMARY

Contemporary criminology, stung in large part by social policy fiascoes engendered by the eugenics movement of 100 years ago, has shown considerable reluctance to adapt the contributions of biological theories to an understanding of criminality. An objective understanding of any social phenomenon, however, requires clear consideration of all available evidence. Modern proponents of biological perspectives on crime and crime causation point out that the link between the social environment and human behavior is continuously mediated by the brain. Human activity flows from the human mind, and the mind is biologically grounded in the brain. The brain itself is apparently subject to influences from other aspects of the body, such as genes, hormones, neurotransmitters, and the levels of various chemicals in the blood. Such realizations require only a small intellectual leap to the realization that biological aspects of the human organism may play similar contributory roles in criminal behavior.

Unfortunately for proponents of biological theories that seek to explain crime, sociological and psychological explanations for human behavior are well entrenched. In addition, studies purporting to have identified biological determinants of behavior have been energetically criticized on methodological and other grounds. As a consequence, many criminologists have concluded that while biology provides both a context for, and specific precursors to, human behavior, biological predispositions for behavior in most instances of human interaction are overshadowed by the role of volition, the mechanisms of human thought, and the undeniable influences of socialization and acculturation. Even so, any honest and comprehensive approach to human behavior must recognize the biological precursors of that behavior.

DISCUSSION QUESTIONS

1. This book emphasizes a social problems versus social responsibility theme. Which perspective is best supported by biological theories of crime causation? Why?
2. What are the central features of biological theories of crime? How do such theories differ from other perspectives that attempt to explain the same phenomena?
3. Why have biological approaches to crime causation been out of vogue lately? Do you agree or disagree with those who are critical of such perspectives? Why?
4. What does the author of this book mean when he writes, "Open inquiry . . . requires objective consideration of all points of view and an unbiased examination of each for its ability to shed light on the subject under study"? Do you agree or disagree with this assertion? Why?
5. What are the social policy implications of biological theories of crime? What U.S. Supreme Court case, discussed in this chapter, might presage a type of policy based on such theories?

WEB QUEST!

Visit *Crime Times* on the World Wide Web at http://crime-times.org. *Crime Times* offers one of the Web's best sources for reviews and information about research on biological causes of criminal, violent, and psychopathic behavior. Hard-copy versions of *Crime Times* in newsletter format are regularly mailed to selected members of Congress, medical schools, psychiatrists, criminologists, psychologists, researchers, foundations, justice system professionals, and media representatives. Both the newsletter and the Web versions of *Crime Times* focus on research concerning the link be-

tween aberrant behavior and neurochemical imbalances, physical injury, drugs, toxic environments, diet, food and chemical sensitivities, birth trauma, and genetic vulnerabilities to such factors.

If your instructor asks you to, review the archive of articles found at the *Crime Times* site, and pay special attention to those dealing with environmental contaminants and crime. Write a paper summarizing the research findings contained in these articles, being sure to provide a complete bibliography of the sources you used.

LIBRARY EXTRAS!

The Library Extras! listed here complement the Web Extras! found throughout this chapter. Library Extras! may be accessed on the Web at crimtoday.com.

Library Extra! 5-1. Greater Boston Physicians for Social Responsibility, *In Harm's Way: Toxic Threats to Child Development* (Boston: 2000).

Library Extra! 5-2. Sally Lehrman, *DNA and Behavior: Is Our Fate in Our Genes?* (The DNA Files online).

Library Extra! 5-3. Joseph D. McInerney, "Genes and Behavior: A Complex Relationship," *Judicature,* Vol. 83, No. 3 (November/December 1999).

Library Extra! 5-4. "New Studies Show Strong Links between Diet, Behavior," *Crime Times,* Vol. 4, No. 1 (1998), pp. 1–4.

Library Extra! 5-5. Mark A. Rothstein, "The Impact of Behavioral Genetics on the Law and the Courts," *Judicature,* Vol. 83, No. 3 (November/December 1999).

Library Extra! 5-6. "Zeroing in on Pollution, Criminality Connection," *Crime Times,* Vol. 3, No. 4 (1997), pp. 1–3.

NOTES

1. Quoted in Karen J. Winkler, "Criminals Are Born as Well as Made, Authors of Controversial Book Assert," *Chronicle of Higher Education,* January 16, 1986, p. 9.
2. Anastasia Toufexis, "Seeking the Roots of Violence," *Time,* April 19, 1993, p. 52.
3. David C. Rowe, *The Limits of Family Influence* (New York: Guilford Press, 1994).
4. Mark A. Rothstein, "The Impact of Behavioral Genetics on the Law and the Courts," *Judicature,* Vol. 83, No. 3 (November–December 1999). Web posted at http://www.

ornl.gov/hgmis/publicat/judicature/article5.html. Accessed March 2, 2001.
5. For a detailed description of Moormann's life, see John C. C'Anna, "Robert Henry Moormann," *Police,* April 1992, pp. 50–54, 86–88.
6. See, for example, Henrik Soderstrom et al., "Reduced Regional Cerebral Blood Flow in Non-psychotic Violent Offenders," *Psychiatry Research,* Vol. 98 (2000), pp. 29–41; and Antoine Bechara et al., "Insensitivity to Future Consequences Following Damage to Human

Prefrontal Cortex," *Cognition*, Vol. 50, No. 7 (1994), pp. 7–15.

[7] See, for example, Ann Pytkowicz Streissguth et al., "Fetal Alcohol Syndrome in Adolescents and Adults," *Journal of the American Medical Association*, Vol. 265, No. 15 (April 17, 1991).

[8] C. Ray Jeffery, "Biological Perspectives," *Journal of Criminal Justice Education*, Vol. 4, No. 2 (fall 1993), pp. 292–293.

[9] C. Ray Jeffery, "Genetics, Crime and the Canceled Conference," *Criminologist*, Vol. 18, No. 1 (January/February 1993), pp. 1–8.

[10] Toufexis, "Seeking the Roots of Violence," p. 53.

[11] C. Ray Jeffery, "The Genetics and Crime Conference Revisited," *Criminologist*, Vol. 21, No. 2 (March/April 1996), p. 3.

[12] Lee Ellis and Anthony Walsh, "Gene-Based Evolutionary Theories in Criminology," *Criminology*, Vol. 35, No. 2 (1997), p. 230.

[13] Ibid., p. 230.

[14] Jeffery, "Biological Perspectives," p. 298.

[15] Konrad Lorenz, *On Aggression* (New York: Harcourt, Brace and World, 1966).

[16] Ibid., p. 23.

[17] Ibid., p. 38.

[18] Ibid., p. 249.

[19] Ibid., p. 249.

[20] "Physical Attractiveness and Criminal Behavior," *The Encyclopedia of Criminology*. Web posted at http://www.fitzroydearborn.com/chicago/criminology/sample-physical.asp. Accessed November 17, 2000.

[21] Cesare Lombroso, "Introduction," in Gina Lombroso-Ferrero, *Criminal Man According to the Classification of Cesare Lombroso*, (1911; reprinted, Montclair, NJ: Patterson Smith, 1972), p. xiv.

[22] Charles Darwin, *Descent of Man: And Selection in Relation to Sex*, rev. ed. (London: John Murray, 1874), p. 137.

[23] Auguste Comte, *A System of Positive Polity*, trans. John Henry Bridges (New York: Franklin, 1875). Originally published in four volumes, 1851–1854.

[24] See K. L. Henwood and N. F. Pidgeon, "Qualitative Research and Psychological Theorising," *British Journal of Psychology*, Vol. 83 (1992), pp. 97–111.

[25] Lombroso, "Introduction," in Lombroso-Ferrero, *Criminal Man According to the Classification of Cesare Lombroso*, p. xv.

[26] Della Fossetta, *Cerebellare Mediana in un Criminale*" (Institute Lombardo di Scienze e Lettere, 1872), pp. 1058–1065, as cited and translated by Thorsten Sellin, "A New Phase of Criminal Anthropology in Italy," *The Annuals of the American Academy of Political and Social Science, Modern Crime*, No. 525 (May 1926), p. 234.

[27] The English-language version appeared in 1895 as Cesare Lombroso, *The Female Offender* (New York: D. Appleton, 1895).

[28] Marvin Wolfgang, "Cesare Lombroso," in Hermann Mannheim, *Pioneers in Criminology*, 2nd ed. (Montclair, NJ: Patterson Smith, 1972), p. 254.

[29] Charles Goring, *The English Convict: A Statistical Study* (London: His Majesty's Stationery Office, 1913; reprint Montclair, NJ: Patterson Smith, 1972), p. 15.

[30] Ibid.

[31] Earnest A. Hooton, *Crime and the Man* (Cambridge: Harvard University Press, 1939; reprint Westport, CT: Greenwood Press, 1972).

[32] Ibid., pp. 57–58.

[33] Ibid., p. 72.

[34] Ibid., p. 75.

[35] Ibid., p. 388.

[36] Earnest A. Hooton, *The American Criminal: An Anthropological Study* (Cambridge: Harvard University Press, 1939).

[37] Stephen Schafer, *Theories in Criminology: Past and Present Philosophies of the Crime Problem* (New York: Random House, 1969), p. 187.

[38] L. Arseneault et al., "Minor Physical Anomalies and Family Adversity as Risk Factors for Violent Delinquency in Adolescence," *American Journal of Psychiatry*, Vol. 157, No. 6 (June 2000), pp. 917–923.

[39] William H. Sheldon, *Varieties of Delinquent Youth* (New York: Harper and Brothers, 1949).

[40] Sheldon Glueck and Eleanor Glueck, *Unraveling Juvenile Delinquency* (Cambridge: Harvard University Press, 1950).

[41] D. Hill and W. Sargent, "A Case of Matricide," *Lancet*, Vol. 244 (1943), pp. 526–527.

[42] William Dufty, *Sugar Blues* (Pandor, PA: Chilton Book Co., 1975).

[43] Nanci Hellmich, "Sweets May Not Be Culprit in Hyper Kids," *USA Today*, February 3, 1994, p. 1A, reporting on a study published in the *New England Journal of Medicine*.

[44] Ibid.

[45] See Adrian Raine et al., "Prefrontal Glucose Deficits in Murderers Lacking Psychosocial Deprivation," *Neuropsychiatry, Neuropsychology, and Behavioral Neurology*, Vol. 11, No. 1 (1998), pp. 1–7; and Adrian Raine et al., "Selective Reductions in Prefrontal Glucose Metabolism in Murderers," *Biological Psychiatry*, Vol. 36 (September 1, 1994), pp. 319–332.

[46] "PET Study: Looking Inside the Minds of Murderers," *Crime Times*, Vol. 1, No. 1–2 (1995). Web posted at http://www.crime-times.org/95a/w95ap1.htm. Accessed November 15, 2000.

[47] Raine et al., "Selective Reductions in Prefrontal Glucose Metabolism in Murderers."

[48] See, for example, A. R. Mawson and K. J. Jacobs, "Corn Consumption, Tryptophan, and Cross National Homicide Rates," *Journal of Orthomolecular Psychiatry*, Vol. 7 (1978), pp. 227–230; and A. Hoffer, "The Relation of Crime to Nutrition," *Humanist in Canada*, Vol. 8 (1975), p. 8.

[49] See, for example, C. Hawley and R. E. Buckley, "Food Dyes and Hyperkinetic Children," *Academy Therapy*, Vol. 10 (1974), pp. 27–32; and Alexander Schauss, *Diet, Crime and Delinquency* (Berkeley, CA: Parker House, 1980).

50 "Special Report: Measuring Your Life with Coffee Spoons," *Tufts University Diet and Nutrition Letter,* Vol. 2, No. 2 (April 1984), pp. 3–6.

51 See, for example, "Special Report: Does What You Eat Affect Your Mood and Actions?" *Tufts University Diet and Nutrition Letter,* Vol. 2, No. 12 (February 1985), pp. 4–6.

52 See *Tufts University Diet and Nutrition Newsletter,* Vol. 2, No. 11 (January 1985), p. 2; and "Special Report: Why Sugar Continues to Concern Nutritionists," *Tufts University Diet and Nutrition Letter,* Vol. 3, No. 3 (May 1985), pp. 3–6.

53 A. Hoffer, "Children with Learning and Behavioral Disorders," *Journal of Orthomolecular Psychiatry,* Vol. 5 (1976), p. 229.

54 "Special Report: Does What You Eat Affect Your Mood and Actions?" p. 4.

55 Roger D. Masters, Brian Hone, and Anil Doshi, "Environmental Pollution, Neurotoxicity, and Criminal Violence," in J. Rose, ed., *Environmental Toxicology* (London and New York: Gordon and Breach, 1997).

56 Peter Montague, "Toxics and Violent Crime," *Rachel's Environment and Health Weekly,* No. 551 (June 19, 1997).

57 See, for example, Jefrey Halperin et al., "Serotonergic Function in Aggressive and Nonaggressive Boys with ADHD," *American Journal of Psychiatry,* Vol. 151, No. 2 (February 1994), pp. 243–248.

58 Masters, Hone, and Doshi, "Environmental Pollution, Neurotoxicity, and Criminal Violence."

59 See, for example, Rick Nevin, "How Lead Exposure Relates to Temporal Changes in IQ, Violent Crime, and Unwed Pregnancy," *Environmental Research,* Vol. 83, No. 1 (May 2000), pp. 1–22.

60 Quoted in Alison Motluck, "Pollution May Lead to a Life of Crime," *New Scientist,* Vol. 154, No. 2084 (May 31, 1997), p. 4.

61 Don Cherek and Scott Lane, "Effects of d,1-fenfluramine on Aggressive and Impulsive Responding in Adult Males with a History of Conduct Disorder," *Psychopharmacology,* Vol. 146 (1999), pp. 473–481.

62 See Alexander G. Schauss, "Tranquilizing Effect of Color Reduces Aggressive Behavior and Potential Violence," *Journal of Orthomolecular Psychiatry,* Vol. 8, No. 4 (1979), pp. 218–221; and David Johnston, "Is It Merely a Fad, or Do Pastel Walls Stop Jail House Brawls?" *Corrections Magazine,* Vol. 7, No. 3 (1981), pp. 28–32.

63 Questions were raised, however, about the long-term effects of confinement in pink cells, and some researchers suggested that extended exposure to the color pink could generate suicidal impulses.

64 L. Goldschmidt, N. L. Day, and G. A. Richardson, "Effects of Prenatal Marijuana Exposure on Child Behavior Problems at Age 10," *Neurotoxicology and Teratology,* Vol. 22, No. 3 (May/June 2000), pp. 325–336.

65 David Fergusson, Lianne Woodward, and L. John Horwood, "Maternal Smoking during Pregnancy and Psychiatric Adjustment in Late Adolescence," *Archives of General Psychiatry,* Vol. 55 (August 1998), pp. 721–727.

66 Jacob F. Orlebeke, Dirk L. Knol, and Frank C. Verhulst, "Increase in Child Behavior Problems Resulting from Maternal Smoking during Pregnancy," *Archives of Environmental Health,* Vol. 52, No. 4 (July/August 1997), pp. 317–321.

67 See, for example, Streissguth et al., "Fetal Alcohol Syndrome in Adolescents and Adults."

68 Tresa M. Roebuck, Sarah N. Mattson, and Edward P. Riley, "Behavioral and Psychosocial Profiles of Alcohol-Exposed Children," *Alcoholism: Clinical and Experimental Research,* Vol. 23, No. 6 (June 1999), pp. 1070–1076.

69 See, for example, R. T. Rada, D. R. Laws, and R. Kellner, "Plasma Testosterone Levels in the Rapist," *Psychosomatic Medicine,* Vol. 38 (1976), pp. 257–268.

70 "The Insanity of Steroid Abuse," *Newsweek,* May 23, 1988, p. 75.

71 Dan Olweus et al., "Testosterone, Aggression, Physical and Personality Dimensions in Normal Adolescent Males," *Psychosomatic Medicine,* Vol. 42 (1980), pp. 253–269.

72 Richard Udry, "Biosocial Models of Adolescent Problem Behaviors," *Social Biology,* Vol. 37 (1990), pp. 1–10.

73 Dan Olweus, "Testosterone and Adrenaline: Aggressive Antisocial Behavior in Normal Adolescent Males," in Sarnoff A. Mednick, Terrie E. Moffitt, and Susan A. Stack, eds., *The Causes of Crime: New Biological Approaches* (Cambridge: Cambridge University Press, 1987), pp. 263–282.

74 Alan Booth and D. Wayne Osgood, "The Influence of Testosterone on Deviance in Adulthood: Assessing and Explaining the Relationship," *Criminology,* Vol. 31, No. 1 (1993), p. 93.

75 E. G. Stalenheim et al., "Testosterone as a Biological Marker in Psychopathy and Alcoholism," *Psychiatry Research,* Vol. 77, No. 2 (February 1998), pp. 79–88.

76 Paul C. Bernhardt, "Influences of Serotonin and Testosterone in Aggression and Dominance: Convergence with Social Psychology," *Current Directions in Psychological Science,* Vol. 6, No. 2 (April 1997), pp. 44–48.

77 Richard Udry, Luther Talbert, and Naomi Morris, "Biosocial Foundations for Adolescent Female Sexuality," *Demography,* Vol. 23 (1986), pp. 217–227.

78 James M. Dabbs, Jr., and Marian F. Hargrove, "Age, Testosterone, and Behavior among Female Prison Inmates," *Psychosomatic Medicine,* Vol. 59 (1997), pp. 447–480.

79 *Regina* v. *English* unreported, Norwich Crown Court, 10 November 1981.

80 "Drunk Driving Charge Dismissed: PMS Cited," *Fayetteville (North Carolina) Observer-Times,* June 7, 1991, p. 3A.

81 Toufexis, "Seeking the Roots of Violence," pp. 52–54.

82 Terrie E. Moffitt et al., "Whole Blood Serotonin Relates to Violence in an Epidemiological Study," *Biological Psychiatry,* Vol. 43, No. 6 (March 15, 1998), pp. 446–457.

[83] Keith McBurnett et al., "Low Salivary Cortisol and Persistent Aggression in Boys Referred for Disruptive Behavior," *Archives of General Psychiatry*, Vol. 57, No. 1 (January 2000), pp. 38–43.

[84] See E. G. Stalenheim, L. von Knorring, and L. Wide, "Serum Levels of Thyroid Hormones as Biological Markers in a Swedish Forensic Psychiatric Population," *Biological Psychiatry*, Vol. 43, No. 10 (May 15, 1998), pp. 755–761; and P. O. Alm et al., "Criminality and Psychopathy as Related to Thyroid Activity in Former Juvenile Delinquents," *Acta Psychiatr Scand*, Vol. 94, No. 2 (August 1996), pp. 112–117.

[85] Stalenheim, von Knorring, and Wide, "Serum Levels of Thyroid Hormones as Biological Markers in a Swedish Forensic Psychiatric Population."

[86] J. Rotton and E. G. Cohn, "Weather, Climate, and Crime," in R. Bechtel and E. Churchman, eds., *New Handbook of Environmental Psychology* (New York: Wiley, forthcoming).

[87] E. G. Cohn and J. Rotton, "Assault as a Function of Time and Temperature: A Moderator-Variable Time-Series Analysis," *Journal of Personality and Social Psychology*, Vol. 72 (1997), pp. 1322–1334.

[88] J. Rotton and E. G. Cohn, "Violence as a Curvilinear Function of Temperature in Dallas: A Replication," *Journal of Personality and Social Psychology*, Vol. 78 (2000), pp. 1074–1081.

[89] E. G. Cohn and J. Rotton, "Weather, Seasonal Trends, and Property Crimes in Minneapolis, 1987–1988: A Moderator-Variable Time-Series Analysis of Routine Activities," *Journal of Environmental Psychology* (in press).

[90] J. Rotton and E. G. Cohn, "Temperature, Routine Activities, and Domestic Violence: A Reanalysis," *Victims and Violence* (in press).

[91] J. Rotton and E. G. Cohn, "Weather, Disorderly Conduct, and Assaults: From Social Contact to Social Avoidance," *Environment and Behavior*, Vol. 32 (2000), pp. 649–671.

[92] Richard Louis Dugdale, *The Jukes: A Study in Crime, Pauperism, Disease, and Heredity*, 3rd ed. (New York: G. P. Putnam's Sons, 1895).

[93] Arthur H. Estabrook, *The Jukes in 1915* (Washington, D.C.: Carnegie Institute of Washington, 1916).

[94] Henry Herbert Goddard, *The Kallikak Family: A Study in the Heredity of Feeblemindedness* (New York: Macmillan, 1912).

[95] See Nicole Hahn Rafter, *Creating Born Criminals* (Champaign: University of Illinois Press, 1997).

[96] See Nicole Hahn Rafter, ed., *White Trash: The Eugenics Family Studies, 1877–1919* (Boston: Northeastern University Press, 1988).

[97] *Buck v. Bell*, 274 U.S. 200, 207 (1927).

[98] P. A. Jacobs, M. Brunton, and M. Melville, "Aggressive Behavior, Mental Subnormality, and the XYY Male," *Nature*, Vol. 208 (1965), p. 1351.

[99] Biologists often define *karyotype* as "a photomicrograph of metaphase chromosomes in a standard array."

[100] See David A. Jones, *History of Criminology: A Philosophical Perspective* (Westport, CT: Greenwood Press, 1986), p. 124.

[101] Many of which have been summarized in J. Katz and W. Chambliss, "Biology and Crime," in J. F. Sheley, ed., *Criminology* (Belmont, CA: Wadsworth, 1991), pp. 245–272.

[102] As reported by S. A. Mednick and J. Volavka, "Biology and Crime," in N. Morris and M. Tonry, *Crime and Justice: An Annual Review of Research*, Vol. 2 (Chicago: University of Chicago Press, 1980), pp. 85–158; and D. A. Andrews and James Bonta, *The Psychology of Criminal Conduct* (Cincinnati: Anderson, 1994), pp. 126–127.

[103] T. Sarbin and J. Miller, "Demonism Revisited: The XYY Chromosomal Anomaly," *Issues in Criminology*, Vol. 5 (1970), p. 199.

[104] Geoffrey Cowley and Carol Hallin, "The Genetics of Bad Behavior: A Study Links Violence to Heredity," *Newsweek*, November 1, 1993, p. 57.

[105] See Joseph D. McInerney, "Genes and Behavior: A Complex Relationship," *Judicature*, Vol. 83, No. 3 (November–December 1999).

[106] Sir Francis Galton, *Inquiry into Human Faculty and Its Development*, 2nd ed. (London: J. M. Dent and Sons, 1907).

[107] Johannes Lange, *Verbrechen als Schicksal* (Leipzig: Georg Thieme, 1929).

[108] Karl O. Christiansen, "A Preliminary Study of Criminality among Twins," in Sarnoff Mednick and Karl Christiansen, eds., *Biosocial Bases of Criminal Behavior* (New York: Gardner Press, 1977).

[109] Edwin J. C. G. van den Oord, Dorret I. Boomsma, and Frank C. Verhulst, "A Study of Problem Behaviors in 10- to 15-Year-Old Biologically Related and Unrelated International Adoptees," *Behavior Genetics*, Vol. 24, No. 3 (1994), pp. 193–205.

[110] Peter McGuffin and Anita Thapar, "Genetic Basis of Bad Behaviour in Adolescents," *Lancet*, Vol. 350 (August 9, 1997), pp. 411–412.

[111] Wendy Slutske et al., "Modeling Genetic and Environmental Influences in the Etiology of Conduct Disorder: A Study of 2,682 Adult Twin Pairs," *Journal of Abnormal Psychology*, Vol. 106, No. 2 (1997), pp. 266–279.

[112] Much of the information and some of the wording in this section come from the National Human Genome Research Institute's World Wide Web page at http://www.nhgri.nih.gov/HGP. Accessed November 16, 2000.

[113] National Human Genome Research Institute, press release, "Genome Project Leaders Announce Intent to Finish Sequencing the Human Genome Two Years Early," no date. Web posted at http://www.nhgri.nih.gov/NEWS/Finish_sequencing_early/Intent_to_finish_sequencing_early.html. Accessed November 16, 2000.

114 Quoted in Tim Friend, "Violence Linked to Gene Defect: Pleasure Deficit May Be the Spark," *USA Today,* May 9, 1996. See the original research at Kenneth Blum et al., "Reward Deficiency Syndrome," *American Scientist,* Vol. 84 (March/April 1996), pp. 132–145. Web posted at http://www.sigmaxi.org/amsci/Articles/96Articles/ Blum-full.html. Accessed January 5, 2001.

115 McInerney, "Genes and Behavior."

116 Jeffery, "Biological Perspectives," p. 300.

117 Leanne Fiftal Alarid et al., "Women's Roles in Serious Offenses: A Study of Adult Felons," *Justice Quarterly,* Vol. 13, No. 3 (September 1996), pp. 432–454.

118 Federal Bureau of Investigation, *Crime in the United States, 1999* (Washington, D.C.: U.S. Government Printing Office, 2000).

119 Freda Adler, *Sisters in Crime: The Rise of the New Female Criminal* (New York: McGraw-Hill, 1975).

120 Darrell J. Steffensmeir, "Sex Differences in Patterns of Adult Crime, 1965–1977: A Review and Assessment," *Social Forces,* Vol. 58 (1980), pp. 1098–1099.

121 FBI, *Crime in the United States, 1999,* as computed by the author.

122 See, for example, D. H. Fishbein, "The Psychobiology of Female Aggression," *Criminal Justice and Behavior,* Vol. 19 (1992), pp. 99–126.

123 Robbin S. Ogle, Daniel Maier-Katin, and Thomas J. Bernard, "A Theory of Homicidal Behavior among Women," *Criminology,* Vol. 33, No. 2 (1995), pp. 173–193.

124 Ibid., p. 177.

125 Ibid., p. 179.

126 Arthur Fisher, "A New Synthesis Comes of Age," *Mosaic,* Vol. 22, No. 1 (spring 1991), pp. 2–9.

127 The quotations attributed to Wilson in this section are from Edward O. Wilson, *Sociobiology: The New Synthesis* (Cambridge: Belknap Press of Harvard University Press, 1975).

128 Janet Zimmerman, "Six Held in Brutal Attack of Mich. Teens," *USA Today,* June 24, 1997, p. 3A.

129 Ibid., p. 327.

130 Sarah Blaffer Hrdy, *The Langurs of Abu: Female and Male Strategies of Reproduction* (Cambridge: Harvard University Press, 1977).

131 Research by Martin Daly and Margo Wilson of McMaster University in Hamilton, Canada, as reported in Arthur Fisher, "A New Synthesis II: How Different Are Humans?" *Mosaic,* Vol. 22, No. 1 (spring 1991), p. 14.

132 Fisher, "A New Synthesis II" p. 11.

133 John H. Beckstrom, *Evolutionary Jurisprudence: Prospects and Limitations on the Youth of Modern Darwinism Throughout the Legal Process* (Urbana: University of Illinois Press, 1989).

134 John Madison Memory, "Sociobiology and the Metamorphoses of Criminology: 1978–2000," unpublished manuscript.

135 Ibid., p. 11.

136 Ibid., p. 33.

137 See also Arnold L. Lieber, *The Lunar Effect: Biological Tides and Human Emotions* (Garden City, NY: Anchor Press, 1978).

138 James Q. Wilson and Richard J. Herrnstein, *Crime and Human Nature* (New York: Simon and Schuster, 1985).

139 Quoted in Winkler, "Criminals Are Born as Well as Made," p. 5.

140 Wilson and Herrnstein, *Crime and Human Nature.*

141 Winkler, "Criminals Are Born as Well as Made," p. 8.

142 Jeffery, "Biological Perspectives," p. 303.

143 Ibid.

144 *Buck v. Bell,* 274 U.S. 200, 207 (1927).

145 Tou Fexis, "Seeking the Roots of Violence," p. 53.

146 Gary LaFree and Katheryn K. Russell, "The Argument for Studying Race and Crime," *Journal of Criminal Justice Education,* Vol. 4, No. 2 (fall 1993), p. 279.

147 Ellis and Walsh, "Gene-Based Evolutionary Theories in Criminology," pp. 229–230.

148 Rafter, *Creating Born Criminals.*

149 Glenn D. Walters and Thomas W. White, "Heredity and Crime: Bad Genes or Bad Research?" *Criminology,* Vol. 27, No. 3 (1989), pp. 455–485. See also P. A. Brennan and S. A. Mednick, "Reply to Walters and White: Heredity and Crime," *Criminology,* Vol. 28, No. 4 (November 1990), pp. 657–661.

150 Ibid., p. 476.

151 Ibid., p. 478.

Question: "When you put the shotgun
up against her left cheek and pulled the trigger,
did you love your mother?"

Answer: "Yes."

—Lyle Menendez, testifying at his trial on charges that he and
his brother killed their parents[1]

We understand today that it is a cruel and ignorant
practice to torture men and women whose mental
disturbance expresses itself in the form of religious or
other eccentricities, but we are still too deep in
darkness to realize that the same is true of those
whose quirks show themselves in criminality.

—Max G. Schlapp and Edward H. Smith[2]

psychological and psychiatric foundations of criminal behavior

CHAPTER 6

Children will watch anything, and when a broadcaster uses crime and violence and other shoddy devices to monopolize a child's attention, it's worse than taking candy from a baby. It is taking precious time from the process of growing up.

—Newton N. Minow, Federal Communications Commission[3]

[The psychopath] lacks those normal human sentiments without which life in common is impossible.

—Gordon Allport[4]

The American dream is, in part, responsible for a great deal of crime and violence because people feel that the country owes them not only a living but a good living.

—David Abrahamsen[5]

KEY CONCEPTS

IMPORTANT TERMS

alloplastic adaptation	forensic psychology	psychopath
antisocial (asocial) personality	guilty but mentally ill (GBMI)	psychopathology
antisocial personality disorder	id	psychosis
attachment theory	insanity	psychotherapy
autoplastic adaptation	irresistible-impulse test	punishments
behavior theory	*M'Naughten* rule	rewards
Brawner rule	modeling theory	schizophrenics
conditioning	neurosis	selective incapacitation
correctional psychology	operant behavior	self-control
criminal psychology	paranoid schizophrenics	sociopath
Durham rule	psychiatric criminology	sublimation
ego	psychoanalysis	substantial-capacity test
electroencephalograms (EEGs)	psychological profiling	superego
forensic psychiatry	psychological theories	Thanatos

IMPORTANT NAMES AND CASES

Albert Bandura	Hans J. Eysenck	Sigmund Freud
Hervey M. Cleckley	*Foucha* v. *Louisiana*	B. F. Skinner

OUTCOMES

LEARNING

After reading this chapter, you should be able to
- ◆ Identify the contributions of psychology and psychiatry to the understanding of criminal behavior
- ◆ Explain the relationship between personality and criminal behavior
- ◆ Recognize the importance of modeling theory to an understanding of criminality
- ◆ Understand the unique characteristics of those found not guilty by reason of insanity
- ◆ Identify current social policy that reflects the psychological approach to criminal behavior

Hear the author discuss this chapter at *crimtoday.com*

INTRODUCTION

Some crimes cry out for explanation. In November 2000, Persephone Elaine Muhammad (AKA Persephone Elaine Simmons), a 30-year-old Huger, South Carolina, resident, was arrested and charged with the murder of her two young children. Muhammad allegedly killed her 18-month-old son, Yusan, by striking him in the head with an ax. She then stabbed her 10-year-old daughter, Ingrid, in the chest and slit her throat with a kitchen knife. An older daughter, Amber, escaped the mobile home where the killings took place and ran to a neighbor's house. By the time police arrived, Muhammad had dumped the bodies of her dead children in a nearby field.

After she was taken into custody, Muhammad fought with officers and was charged with additional counts of assault on a police officer. The murders apparently surprised Elizabeth Goldiner, principal of the school that Amber and Ingrid attended. "She was a mother who loved her children," Goldiner said of Muhammad. "But I don't think she knew how to love them; she was very different and distant but wanted the best for her children."[6] As this book goes to press, Muhammad is undergoing evaluation at a psychiatric hospital.

Ten years before the South Carolina killings, an infamous murderer captivated the nation's attention. Shortly after midnight on July 22, 1991, a handcuffed man flagged down a police car in suburban Milwaukee.[7] Officers soon learned that the man was Tracy Edwards, a 32-year-old city resident. The lurid story of homosexual abuse and physical attack that Edwards told led investigators to the apartment of a 31-year-old loner named Jeffrey Dahmer. Dahmer was quickly arrested, and a search of his apartment revealed the body parts of at least 11 people. In a confession to police, Dahmer told of how he had repeatedly lured men and boys to his apartment, murdered them, and then dismembered their bodies. Soon police investigations implicated Dahmer in a ten-year killing spree which spanned several states and may have reached as far as Europe. Edwards, whom Dahmer had met in a shopping mall, explained that he went to Dahmer's apartment because Dahmer "seemed so normal."[8] Sadly, one of Dahmer's victims, a 15-year-old boy, had earlier been discovered by police dazed and bleeding—and was returned to Dahmer's apartment after officers concluded that the situation involved nothing but a dispute between homosexual lovers.

Dahmer pleaded insane as a defense to charges of murder, but an expert witness at his trial, psychiatrist Park Dietz, testified that although Dahmer suffered from various psychological disorders, he could have chosen not to kill. Comparing Dahmer's sexual desires with someone who wants money but chooses not to rob, Dietz said, "The choice is exactly the same. . . . The freedom to make it is exactly the same."[9] In contrasting testimony, another expert witness claimed that Dahmer "had uncontrollable urges to kill and have sex with dead bodies."[10] Dahmer was sentenced to 15 consecutive life terms—one each for the murders of his 15 victims[11]—but was himself murdered in prison by another inmate in late 1994.

Around the time that Dahmer died, another strange incident was making headlines around the world. In that case, housewife Lorena Bobbitt of Manassas, Virginia, was acquit-

Jeffrey Dahmer, perhaps the most infamous serial killer of the twentieth century. What explains the public's fascination with serial killers? *Milwaukee Journal, SIPA Press*

ted on charges of malicious wounding for admittedly severing her allegedly philandering husband's penis with one stroke from a sharp kitchen knife while he slept. Bobbitt drove away with the severed organ still clutched in her fist, and she threw it out of her car window onto a grassy field some distance from the couple's apartment. Rescue workers recovered the penis in a predawn search, and it was reattached during hours of microvascular surgery.[12] In defense of her actions, she accused her husband, John, of marital rape. At trial, the defense attorney, sounding very much like a pop psychologist, explained Mrs. Bobbitt's actions to the jury in these words: "Why did she cut his penis off? Something happened . . . that drove her over the edge. If this was sheer jealousy, she'd have cut his throat. But what did she attack? . . . The very thing that wounded her." Although John Bobbitt was later arrested and charged with raping his wife, a jury voted 12 to 0 to acquit him of all charges.[13]

What motivates people to kill or maim or to commit other, less serious offenses? How can many killers seem so "normal" before exploding into criminality—giving no hints of the atrocities they are about to commit? How can a mother kill her own children and seemingly feel little or no remorse? For answers to questions like these, many people turn to psychological theories. Psychologists are the pundits of the modern age of behaviorism, offering explanations rooted in determinants that lie within individual actors. Psychological determinants of deviant or criminal behavior may be couched in terms of exploitative personality characteristics, poor impulse control, emotional arousal, an immature personality, and so on. Two contemporary commentators observe that "the major sources of theoretical development in criminology have been—and continue to be—psychological. A theory of criminal conduct is weak indeed if uninformed by a general psychology of human behavior."[14] Other writers go so far as to claim that any criminal behavior is only a symptom of a more fundamental psychiatric disorder.[15]

Before beginning a discussion of psychological theories, however, it is necessary to provide a brief overview of the terminology used to describe the psychological study of crime and criminality. **Forensic psychology**, one of the fastest-growing subfields of psychology, is the application of the science and profession of psychology to questions and issues relating to law and the legal system.[16] Forensic psychology is sometimes referred to as **criminal psychology**, and forensic psychologists are also called "criminal psychologists," "correctional psychologists," and "police psychologists." Unlike forensic psychologists (who generally hold Ph.D.s), forensic psychiatrists are medical doctors, and **forensic psychiatry** is a medical subspecialty that applies psychiatry to the needs of crime prevention and solution, criminal rehabilitation, and issues of the criminal law.[17]

What is the fundamental distinguishing feature of psychological approaches as opposed to other attempts to explain behavior? Criminologists Cathy Spatz Widom and Hans Toch offer the following insight: "Theories are psychological insofar as they focus on the individual as the unit of analysis. Thus

THEORY VERSUS REALITY
What Is Forensic Psychology?

The American Academy of Forensic Psychology defines *forensic psychology* as "the application of the science and profession of psychology to questions and issues relating to law and the legal system." According to the academy, the practice of forensic psychology includes the following elements:

- Psychological evaluation and expert testimony regarding criminal forensic issues like trial competence, waiver of *Miranda* rights, criminal responsibility, death penalty mitigation, battered woman syndrome, domestic violence, drug dependence, and sexual disorders
- Testimony and evaluation regarding civil issues like personal injury, child custody, employment discrimination, mental disability, product liability, professional malpractice, civil commitment, and guardianship
- Assessment, treatment, and consultation regarding individuals with a high risk for aggressive behavior in the community, in the workplace, in treatment settings, and in correctional facilities
- Research, testimony, and consultation on psychological issues affecting the

legal process, such as eyewitness testimony, jury selection, children's testimony, repressed memories, and pretrial publicity
- Specialized treatment service to individuals involved with the legal system
- Consultation to lawmakers about public policy issues with psychological implications
- Consultation and training for law enforcement, criminal justice, and correctional system personnel
- Consultation and training for mental health system practitioners on forensic issues
- Analysis of issues related to human performance, product liability, and safety
- Court-appointed monitoring of compliance with settlements in class-action suits affecting mental health or criminal justice settings
- Mediation and conflict resolution
- Policy and program development in the psychology-law arena
- Teaching, training, and supervision of graduate students, psychology, and

psychiatry interns/residents and law students

Psychologists who already hold Ph.D.s and who are interested in the practice of forensic psychology may apply for certification by the American Board of Professional Psychology (ABPP), which awards a "Diplomate in Forensic Psychology" to those who function "at the highest level of excellence in his or her field of forensic competence." The ABPP diploma is awarded only to applicants who have received at least 100 hours of specialized training in forensic psychology and who have had 1,000 hours of experience in forensic psychology over a minimum of five years, although an LL.B. or J.D. degree may substitute for two of those years. The diploma is generally recognized by the American judicial system as the definitive standard of professional competence in forensic psychology.

Source: Adapted with permission from the American Board of Forensic Psychology's World Wide Web page at http://www.abfp.com/academy.html. Accessed November 29, 2000.

any theory that is concerned with the behavior of individual offenders or which refers to forces or dynamics that motivate individuals to commit crimes would be considered to have a psychological component."[18] Another writer, Curt R. Bartol, defines *psychology* as "the science of behavior and mental processes."[19] Bartol goes on to say that "psychological criminology . . . is the science of the behavior and mental processes of the criminal. Psychological criminology," says Bartol, "focuses on individual criminal behavior—how it is acquired, evoked, maintained, and modified."

MAJOR PRINCIPLES OF PSYCHOLOGICAL THEORIES

This brief section summarizes the central features of **psychological theories** of crime causation.[20] Each of these points can be found elsewhere in this chapter, where it is discussed

in more detail. This cursory overview, however, is intended to provide more than a summary; it is meant to be a guide to the rest of this chapter.

Most psychological theories of crime causation make the following fundamental assumptions:

- The individual is the primary unit of analysis.
- Personality is the major motivational element within individuals because it is the seat of drives and the source of motives.
- Crimes result from abnormal, dysfunctional, or inappropriate mental processes within the personality.
- Criminal behavior, although condemned by the social group, may be purposeful for the individual insofar as it addresses certain felt needs. Behavior can be judged "inappropriate" only when measured against external criteria purporting to establish normality.

Charles Manson achieved notoriety because he seemed so difficult to understand. What do you think motivated his crimes? *Corbis*

- Normality is generally defined by social consensus— that is, what the majority of people in any social group agree is "real," appropriate, or typical.
- Defective, or abnormal, mental processes may have a variety of causes, including a diseased mind, inappropriate learning or improper conditioning, the emulation of inappropriate role models, and adjustment to inner conflicts.

EARLY PSYCHOLOGICAL THEORIES

Twin threads ran through early psychological theories. One strand emphasized behavioral **conditioning**; the other focused mostly on personality disturbances and diseases of the mind. Together, these two foci constituted the early field of psychological criminology. The concept of conditioned behavior was popularized through the work of Russian physiologist Ivan Pavlov (1849–1936), whose work with dogs won the Nobel Prize in physiology and medicine in 1904. The dogs, who salivated when food was presented to them, were always fed in the presence of a ringing bell. Soon, Pavlov found, the dogs would salivate, as if in preparation for eating, when the bell alone was rung, even when no food was present. Hence salivation, an automatic response to the presence of food, could be conditioned to occur in response to some other stimulus, demonstrating that animal behavior could be predictably altered via association with external changes arising from the environment surrounding the organism.

The Psychopath

The other thread wending its way through early psychological theories was that of mental disease, or **psychopathology**. The concept of psychopathology has been called "one of the

most durable, resilient and influential of all criminological ideas."[21] In its original formulation, psychopathology embodied the notion of a diseased mind. It described a particular form of insanity which was thought to have a constitutional, or physiological, basis. The concept is summarized in the words of Nolan D. C. Lewis, who wrote during his tenure as Director of the New York State Psychiatric Institute and Hospital at Columbia University during World War II that "the criminal, like other people, has lived a life of instinctive drives, of desires, of wishes, of feelings, but one in which his intellect has apparently functioned less effectually as a brake upon certain trends. His constitutional makeup deviates toward the abnormal, leading him into conflicts with the laws of society and its cultural patterns."[22]

The term *psychopathy* comes from the Greek words *psyche* (meaning "soul" or "mind") and *pathos* ("suffering" or "illness"). The word, which appears to have been coined by German neurologist Richard von Krafft-Ebing (1840–1902),[23] made its way into English psychiatric literature through the writings of Polish-born American psychiatrist Bernard H. Glueck (1884–1972)[24] and British psychiatrist William Healy (1869–1963).[25] The **psychopath**, also called a **sociopath**, has been historically viewed as perversely cruel, often without thought or feeling for his victims.[26] By the Second World War, the role of the psychopathic personality in crime causation had become central to psychological theorizing. In 1944, for example, well-known psychiatrist David Abrahamsen wrote, "When we seek to explain the riddle of human conduct in general and of antisocial behavior in particular, the solution must be sought in the personality."[27]

The concept of a psychopathic personality, which by its very definition is asocial, was fully developed by Georgian neuropsychiatrist **Hervey M. Cleckley** in his 1941 book, *The Mask of Sanity*[28]—a work that was to have considerable impact on the field of psychology for many years to come. Cleckley described the psychopath as a "moral idiot," or as one who does not feel empathy with others, even though that person may be fully cognizant of what is objectively happening around him or her. The central defining characteristic of a psychopath came to be "poverty of affect," or the inability to accurately imagine how others think and feel. Hence it becomes possible for a psychopath to inflict pain and engage in cruelty without appreciation for the victim's suffering. Charles Manson, for example, whom some regard as a psychopath, once told a television reporter, "I could take this book and beat you to death with it, and I wouldn't feel a thing. It'd be just like walking to the drugstore."

In *The Mask of Sanity*, Cleckley describes numerous characteristics of the psychopathic personality, some of which are listed here:

- Superficial charm and "good intelligence"
- Absence of delusions, hallucinations, or other signs of psychosis
- Absence of nervousness or psychoneurotic manifestations
- Inability to feel guilt or shame
- Unreliability
- Chronic lying
- Ongoing antisocial behavior
- Poor judgment and inability to learn from experience
- Self-centeredness and incapacity to love
- Unresponsiveness in general interpersonal relations
- An impersonal, trivial, and poorly integrated sex life
- Failure to follow any life plan

For Cleckley, "psychopathy was defined by a constellation of dysfunctional psychological processes as opposed to specific behavioral manifestations."[29] Cleckley noted that, in cases he had observed, the behavioral manifestations of psychopathy varied with the person's age, gender, and socioeconomic status.

Even though the psychopath has a seriously flawed personality, he can easily fool others into trusting him—hence the title of Cleckley's book. Cleckley described the good first impression made by a typical psychopath as follows: "More often than not, the typical psychopath will seem particularly agreeable and make a distinctly positive impression when he is first encountered. Alert and friendly in his attitude, he is easy to talk with and seems to have a good many genuine interests. There is nothing at all odd or queer about him, and in every respect he tends to embody the concept of a well-adjusted, happy person. Nor does he, on the other hand, seem to be artificially exerting himself like one who is covering up or who wants to sell you a bill of goods. He would seldom be confused with the professional backslapper or someone who is trying to ingratiate himself for a concealed purpose. Signs of affectation or excessive affability are not characteristic. He looks like the real thing."[30]

According to Cleckley, indicators of psychopathology appear early in life, often in the teenage years. They include lying, fighting, stealing, and vandalism. Even earlier signs may be found, according to some authors, in bed-wetting, cruelty to animals, sleepwalking, and fire setting.[31] Others have described psychopaths as "individuals who display impulsive-

ness, callousness, insincerity, pathological lying and deception, egocentricity, poor judgment, an impersonal sex life, and an unstable life plan."[32] Learn more about the concept of the psychopath as a clinical construct by visiting the Society for Research in Psychopathology via Web Extra! 6-1.

Web EXTRA! **Web Extra! 6-1 at crimtoday.com**

Antisocial Personality Disorder

In recent years, the terms *sociopath* and *psychopath* have fallen into disfavor. In the attempt to identify sociopathic individuals, some psychologists have come to place greater emphasis on the type of *behavior* exhibited, rather than on identifiable personality traits. By 1968, the American Psychiatric Association's (APA's) *Diagnostic and Statistical Manual of Mental Disorders* had completely discontinued using the words *sociopath* and *psychopath,* replacing them with the terms *antisocial* and *asocial personality.*[33] In that year, the APA manual changed to a description of **antisocial (asocial) personality** types as "individuals who are basically unsocialized and whose behavior pattern brings them repeatedly into conflicts with society. They are incapable of significant loyalty to individuals, groups, or social values. They are grossly selfish, callous, irresponsible, impulsive, and unable to feel guilt or to learn from experience and punishment. Frustration tolerance is low. They tend to blame others or offer plausible rationalization for their behavior."[34] In most cases, individuals exhibiting, through their behavioral patterns, an antisocial personality are said to be suffering from **antisocial personality disorder** (sometimes referred to in clinical circles as "APD," "ASPD," or "ANPD").

The World Health Organization, in its *Classification of Mental and Behavioral Disorders,* describes antisocial personality disorder as a "personality disorder usually coming to attention because of a gross disparity between behavior and the prevailing social norms, [which is] characterized by at least three of the following: (a) callous unconcern for the feelings of others; (b) gross and persistent attitude of irresponsibility and disregard for social norms, rules and obligations; (c) incapacity to maintain enduring relationships, though having no difficulty in establishing them; (d) very low tolerance to frustration and a low threshold for discharge of aggression, including violence; (e) incapacity to experience guilt and to profit from experience, particularly punishment; [and] (f) marked proneness to blame others, or to offer plausible rationalizations, for the behavior that has brought the patient into conflict with society."[35] Other features of ASPD have been identified as lack of empathy, inflated and arrogant self-appraisal, and glib, superficial charm.[36]

Individuals manifesting the characteristics of an antisocial personality are, sooner or later, likely to run afoul of the law. As one writer says, "The impulsivity and aggression, the selfishness in achieving one's own immediate needs, and the disregard for society's rules and laws bring these people to the attention of the criminal justice system."[37] Moreover, studies of individuals who score high on psychological inventories designed to measure degree of psychopathy[38] have been found to exhibit high rates of both criminality and recidivism, and psychopaths who have also been diagnosed as schizophrenics display even higher levels of criminality.[39]

The causes of ASPD are unclear. Somatogenic causes, or those based on physiological features of the human organism, are said to include a malfunctioning of the central nervous system characterized by a low state of arousal that drives the sufferer to seek excitement, and brain abnormalities that may have been present in most antisocial personalities since birth. Some studies show that **electroencephalograms (EEGs)** taken of individuals diagnosed as having antisocial personality disorder are frequently abnormal, reflecting "a malfunction of some . . . inhibitory mechanisms" that makes it unlikely that persons characterized by antisocial personality disorder will "learn to inhibit behavior that is likely to lead to punishment."[40] It is difficult, however, to diagnose antisocial personalities through physiological measurements because similar EEG patterns also show up in patients with other types of disorders. Psychogenic causes, or those rooted in early interpersonal experiences, are said to include the inability to form attachments to parents or other caregivers early in life, sudden separation from the mother during the first six months of life, and other forms of insecurity during the first few years of life. In short, a lack of love or the sensed inability to unconditionally depend upon one central loving figure (typically the mother in most psychological literature) immediately following birth is often posited as a major psychogenic factor contributing to the development of antisocial personality disorder. Other psychogenic causes have been identified and include deficiencies in childhood role playing, the inability to identify with one's parents during childhood and adolescence, and severe rejection by others.

Most studies of antisocial personality types have involved male subjects. Only rarely have researchers focused on women with antisocial personalities, and it is believed that only a small proportion of those afflicted with ASPD are women.[41] What little research there is suggests that females with ASPD possess many of the same definitive characteristics as their male counterparts and that they assume their antisocial roles at similarly early ages.[42] The lifestyles of antisocial females, however, appear to emphasize sexual misconduct, including lifestyles involving abnormally high levels of sexual activity. Such research, however, can be misleading because the cultural expectations of female sexual behavior inherent in early studies may not always have been in keeping with reality. That is, early researchers may have had so little accurate information about female sexual activity that the behavior of women judged to possess antisocial personalities may have actually been far closer to the norm than originally believed.

Some recent studies which attempt to classify criminal offenders by type of mental disorder have determined that antisocial personality disorders characterize 46.6% of all inmates, while schizophrenics account for 6.3% of the inmate population, manic-depressives another 1.6%, drug-disordered persons 18.6%, depressed individuals 8.1%, and alcohol abuse–related sufferers another 33.1%.[43] A review of 20 such studies found great variation in the degree and type of disorders said to be prevalent among incarcerated offenders.[44] The studies categorized from 0.5 to 26% of all inmates as psychotic, 2.4 to 28% as mentally subnormal, 5.6 to 70% as antisocial personalities, 2 to 7.9% as neurotic, and 11 to 80% of inmates as suffering from mental disorders induced by alcoholism or excessive drinking. Generally, such studies conclude that few convicted felons are free from mental impairment of one sort or another.

Learn more about antisocial personality disorder at the National Library of Medicine via Web Extra! 6-2. Possible forms of treatment for the disorder can be found at Web Extra! 6-3.

Web Extras! 6-2, and 6-3 at crimtoday.com

Personality Types and Crime

In 1964, **Hans J. Eysenck**, a British psychiatrist, published *Crime and Personality*, a book-length treatise in which he explained crime as the result of fundamental personality characteristics.[45] Eysenck described three personality dimensions, each with links to criminality. Psychoticism, which Eysenck said "is believed to be correlated with criminality at all stages,"[46] is defined by such characteristics as a lack of empathy, creativeness, tough-mindedness, and antisociability. Psychoticism, said Eysenck, is also frequently characterized by hallucinations and delusions. Extroverts were described as carefree, dominant, and venturesome, operating with high levels of energy. "The typical extrovert," Eysenck wrote, "is sociable, likes parties, has many friends, needs to have people to talk to, and does not like reading or studying by himself."[47] Neuroticism, the third of the personality characteristics Eysenck described, was said to be typical of people who are irrational, shy, moody, and emotional.

According to Eysenck, psychotics are the most likely to be criminal because they combine high degrees of emotionalism with similarly high levels of extroversion. Individuals with such characteristics, claimed Eysenck, are especially difficult to socialize and to train. Eysenck cited many studies in which children and others who harbored characteristics of psychoticism, extroversion, and neuroticism performed poorly on conditioning tests designed to measure how quickly they would respond appropriately to external stimuli. Conscience, said Eysenck, is fundamentally a conditioned reflex. Therefore an individual who does not take well to conditioning will not fully develop a

THEORY IN PERSPECTIVE
Types of Psychological and Psychiatric Theories

PSYCHOLOGICAL AND PSYCHIATRIC THEORIES
of criminology are derived from the behavioral sciences and focus on the individual as the unit of analysis.

■ **PSYCHIATRIC CRIMINOLOGY,** also known as FORENSIC PSYCHIATRY. An approach that envisions a complex set of drives and motives operating from recesses deep within the personality to determine behavior.

PERIOD:	1930s–present
THEORISTS:	Hervey M. Cleckley, many others
CONCEPTS:	Psychopath, sociopath, antisocial and asocial personality

■ **PSYCHOANALYTIC CRIMINOLOGY.** A psychiatric approach developed by Austrian psychiatrist Sigmund Freud which emphasizes the role of personality in human behavior and which sees deviant behavior as the result of dysfunctional personalities.

PERIOD:	1920s–present
THEORISTS:	Sigmund Freud, others
CONCEPTS:	Id, ego, superego, sublimation, psychotherapy, Thanatos, neurosis, psychosis, schizophrenia

■ **FRUSTRATION-AGGRESSION THEORY.** A perspective that holds that frustration is a natural consequence of living and a root cause of crime. Criminal behavior can be a form of adaptation when it results in stress reduction.

PERIOD:	1940s–present
THEORISTS:	J. Dollard, Albert Bandura, Richard H. Walters, S. M. Halleck
CONCEPTS:	Frustration, aggression, displacement, catharsis, alloplastic and autoplastic adaptation

■ **MODELING THEORY.** A psychological perspective that says people learn how to behave by modeling themselves after others whom they have the opportunity to observe.

PERIOD:	1950s–present
THEORISTS:	Gabriel Tarde, Albert Bandura, others
CONCEPTS:	Imitation, interpersonal aggression, modeling, disengagement

■ **BEHAVIOR THEORY.** A psychological perspective which posits that individual behavior which is rewarded will increase in frequency, while that which is punished will decrease.

PERIOD:	1940s–present
THEORISTS:	B. F. Skinner, others
CONCEPTS:	Operant behavior, conditioning, stimulus-response, reward, punishment

■ **SELF-CONTROL THEORY.** A perspective that says the root cause of crime can be found in a person's inability to exercise socially appropriate controls over the self.

PERIOD:	1940s-present
THEORISTS:	Michael R. Gottfredson, Travis Hirschi, Harold Grasmick
CONCEPTS:	Self-control, general theory, criminal opportunity

conscience and will continue to exhibit the asocial behavioral traits of a very young child.

Eysenck's approach might be termed *biopsychology* because he claimed that personality traits were fundamentally dependent upon physiology, specifically upon the individual's autonomic nervous system, which Eysenck described as "underlying the behavioral trait of emotionality or neuroticism."[48] Some individuals were said to possess nervous systems that could not handle a great deal of stimulation. Such individuals, like the introvert, shun excitement and are easily trained. They rarely become criminal offenders. However, those who possess nervous systems which need

stimulation, said Eysenck, seek excitement and are far more likely to turn to crime. As support for his thesis, Eysenck cited studies of twins showing that identical twins were much more likely than fraternal twins to perform similarly on simple behavioral tests. In particular, Eysenck quoted from the work of J. B. S. Haldane, who was reputed to be a "world-famous geneticist." Haldane, having studied the criminality of 13 sets of identical twins, concluded, "An analysis of the thirteen cases shows not the faintest evidence of freedom of the will in the ordinary sense of the word. A man of a certain constitution, put in a certain environment, will be a criminal. Taking the record of any criminal, we could predict the behavior of a monozygotic twin placed in the same environment. Crime is destiny."[49] Up to two-thirds of all behavioral variance, claimed Eysenck, could be attributed to "a strong genetic basis."

Early Psychiatric Theories

Psychological criminology, with its historical dual emphasis on (1) early forces that shape personality, and (2) conditioned behavior, can be distinguished from **psychiatric criminology**, also known as "forensic psychiatry," which envisions a complex set of drives and motives operating from hidden recesses deep within the personality to determine behavior. Psychiatrist David Abrahamsen, writing in 1944, explained crime this way: "Antisocial behavior is a direct expression of an aggression or may be a direct or indirect manifestation of a distorted erotic drive. Crime," said Abrahamsen, "may . . . be considered a product of a person's tendencies and the situation of the moment interacting with his mental resistance."[50] The key questions to be answered by psychiatric criminology, according to Abrahamsen, are, "What creates the criminal impulse? What stimulates and gives it direction?" A later forensic psychiatrist answered the question this way: "Every criminal is such by reason of unconscious forces within him."[51] Forensic psychiatry explains crime as being caused by biological and psychological urges mediated through consciousness. Little significance is placed upon the role of the environment external to the individual after the first few formative years of life. Psychiatric theories are derived from the medical sciences, including neurology, and, like other psychological theories, focus on the individual as the unit of analysis.

CRIMINAL BEHAVIOR AS MALADAPTATION

The Psychoanalytic Perspective

Perhaps the best-known psychiatrist of all time is **Sigmund Freud** (1856–1939). Freud coined the term *psychoanalysis* in 1896 and based an entire theory of human behavior on it. From the point of view of psychoanalysis, criminal behavior is maladaptive, or the product of inadequacies inherent in the offender's personality. Significant inadequacies may result in full-blown mental illness, which in itself can be a direct cause of crime. The psychoanalytic perspective encompasses diverse notions like personality, neurosis, and psychosis and more specific concepts like transference, sublimation, and repression. **Psychotherapy**, referred to in its early days as the "talking cure" because it highlighted patient-therapist communication, is the attempt to relieve patients of their mental disorders through the application of psychoanalytic principles and techniques.

According to Freud, the personality is made up of three components—the id, the ego, and the superego—as shown in Figure 6-1. The **id** is the fundamental aspect of the personality from which drives, wishes, urges, and desires emanate. Freud focused primarily on love, aggression, and sex as fundamental drives in any personality. The id is direct and singular in purpose. It operates according to the pleasure principle, seeking full and immediate gratification of its needs. Individuals, however, were said to rarely be fully aware of the urges that percolate up (occasionally into awareness) from the id because it is a largely unconscious region of the mind. Nonetheless, from the Freudian perspective, each of us

Sigmund Freud (1856–1939), examining a manuscript in the office of his Vienna home, circa 1930. *Corbis*

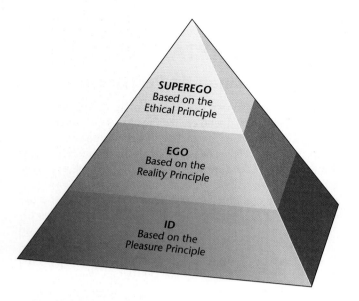

■ **FIGURE 6-1** THE PSYCHOANALYTIC STRUCTURE OF PERSONALITY.

carries within our id the prerequisite motivation for criminal behavior. We are, each one of us, potential murderers, sexual aggressors, and thieves—our drives and urges kept in check only by other, controlling, aspects of our personalities.

A second component of the personality, the **ego**, is primarily charged with reality testing. Freud's use of the word *ego* should not be confused with popular usage, whereby a person might talk about an "inflated ego" or an "egotistical person." For Freud, the ego was primarily concerned with how objectives might be best accomplished. The ego tends to effect strategies for the individual that maximize pleasure and minimize pain. It lays out the various paths of action that can lead to wish fulfillment. The ego inherently recognizes that it may be necessary to delay gratification to achieve a more fulfilling long-term goal.

The **superego**, the last component of the personality, is much like a moral guide to right and wrong. If properly developed, it assays the ego's plans, dismissing some as morally inappropriate while accepting others as ethically viable. The id of a potential rapist, for example, might be filled with lustful drives, and his ego may develop a variety of alternative plans whereby those drives might be fulfilled, some legal and some illegal. His superego will, if the individual's personality is relatively well integrated and the superego is properly developed, turn the individual away from law-violating behavior based on his sensual desires and guide the ego to select a path of action that is in keeping with social convention. When the dictates of the superego are not followed, feelings of guilt may result. The superego is one of the most misunderstood of Freudian concepts. In addition to elements of conscience, the superego also contains what Freud called the "ego-ideal," which is a symbolic representation of what society values. The ego-ideal differs from the conscience in that it is less forceful in controlling behavior in the absence of the likelihood of discovery.

Although Freud wrote little about crime per se, he did spend much of his time attempting to account for a variety of abnormal behaviors, many of which might lead to violations of the criminal law. One way in which a person might be led into crime, according to the perspective of psychoanalysis, is as the result of a poorly developed superego. In the individual without a fully functional superego, the mind is left to fall back on the ego's reality-testing ability. To put it simply, the ego, operating without a moral guide, may select a path of action which, although expedient at the time, violates the law. Individuals suffering from poor superego development are likely to seek immediate gratification without giving a great deal of thought to the long-term consequences of the choices they make.

From the Freudian point of view, inadequate sublimation can be another cause of crime. **Sublimation** is the psychological process whereby one item of consciousness comes to be symbolically substituted for another. Sublimation is often a healthy process. Freud held that many outstanding accomplishments of the human species were due to sublimation, through which powerful sexual and aggressive drives are channeled into socially constructive activity. However, crime can result from improper sublimation. According to Freud, for example, a man may hate his mother, his hatred being perhaps the faulty by-product of the striving for adult independence. He may, however, be unable to give voice to that hatred directly. Perhaps the mother is too powerful or the experience of confronting his mother would be too embarrassing. The man may act out his hatred for his mother by attacking other women whom he symbolically substitutes in his mind for the mother figure. Hence, from the Freudian perspective, men who beat their wives, become rapists, sexually harass coworkers, or otherwise abuse women may be enacting feelings derived from early life experiences that they would be unable to otherwise express.

Sublimation, like many other psychoanalytical concepts, is a slippery idea. Mother hatred, for example, although a plausible explanation for acts of violence by men against women, is difficult to demonstrate, and the link between such hidden feelings and adult action is impossible to prove. Even so, should an offender be so diagnosed, it would do little good for him to deny the psychoanalytical explanation assigned to him, because doing so would only result in the professional reproach, "Yes, but you have hidden the knowledge of your true feelings from yourself. You are not aware of why you act the way you do!"

Freud also postulated the existence of a death instinct, which he called **Thanatos**. According to Freud, all living things, which he referred to as "animate matter," have a fundamental desire to relax back into an inanimate state, or death. Living, said Freud, takes energy and cunning. Hence death, at least at some level, is an easier choice because it releases the organism from the need for continued expenditure of energy. Thanatos was seen as contributing to many of the advances made by the human species and as underlying a large proportion of individual accomplishments. Were it not for a wish to die, operative at some basic instinctual level, said Freud, few people would have the courage to take risks—and without the assumption of risk, precious little progress would be possible in any sphere of life. The notion of an innate death wish has been used to explain why some offenders seem to behave in ways that ensure their eventual capture. Serial killers who send taunting messages to the police, terrorists who tell the media of their planned activities or who take credit for public attacks, rapists who "accidentally" leave their wallets at the scene, and burglars who break into occupied dwellings may all, for the most part unconsciously, be seeking to be stopped, captured, punished, and even killed.

From the Freudian perspective, **neurosis**, a minor form of mental illness, may also lead to crime. Neurotic individuals are well in touch with reality but may find themselves anxious, fearful of certain situations, or unable to help themselves in others. Fear of heights, for example, may be a neurosis, as may be compulsive hand washing or eating disorders. A classic example of the compulsive neurotic can be found in the individual who uses paper towels to open doorknobs, refraining from touching the knob directly for fear of picking up germs. Although such behavior may be unreasonable from the point of view of others, it is reality based (there are germs on doorknobs) and, for the individual demonstrating it, probably unavoidable. Most neuroses do not lead to crime. Some, however, can. A few years ago, for example, Stephen Blumberg of Des Moines, Iowa, was sentenced in federal court to nearly six years in prison and fined $200,000 for the theft of more than 21,000 rare books from hundreds of libraries.[52] Blumberg, whose compulsive interest in rare books began at yard sales and with searches in trash receptacles, may have seen himself as being involved in a messianic mission to preserve recorded history. Compulsive shoplifters may also be manifesting another form of neurosis—one in which a powerful need to steal can drive even well-heeled individuals to risk arrest and jail.

The Psychotic Offender

For many law-abiding citizens, extreme forms of criminal behavior are often difficult to understand, as the gruesome story of Gary Heidnik illustrates.[53] At his double-murder trial in 1988, Heidnik claimed insanity after he admittedly killed two women and tortured four others. All six women had been held captive in the basement of Heidnik's Philadelphia row house for four months, where they had been shackled with chains. One woman, who was chained to a wall and standing in a puddle of water, was electrocuted when Heidnik pushed a live electrical cord against her bare skin. He starved a second woman to death. Heidnik was arrested on March 24, 1987, after one of the captive women escaped and led police to the house. At the scene, police found evidence that Heidnik had mixed the ground flesh of at least one victim with dog food and fed it to the other captives.

A jury rejected Heidnik's claim of insanity and convicted him on two charges of first-degree murder. He was executed

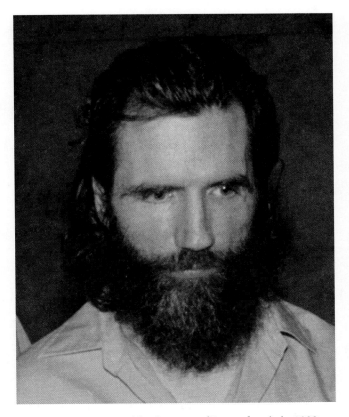

Gary Heidnik, executed by the state of Pennsylvania in 1999. Heidnik *wanted* to die for his crimes. Should he have been executed? *AP/Wide World Photos*

in July 1999. Assistant District Attorney Charles Gallagher, who prosecuted Heidnik, called the case one of the most complicated he has ever taken to court. "He's an evil man and he did evil things. That's what the death penalty is for," Gallagher said.

Some seemingly inexplicable forms of criminality may be the result of **psychosis**. Whereas neurotic individuals often face only relatively minor problems in living, psychotic people, according to psychiatric definitions, are out of touch with reality in some fundamental way. They may suffer from hallucinations, delusions, or other breaks with reality. The classic psychotic thinks he is Napoleon or sees spiders covering what others see only as a bare wall. Individuals suffering from a psychosis are said to be "psychotic." Psychoses may be either organic (that is, caused by physical damage to, or abnormalities in, the brain) or functional (that is, having no known physical cause). Canadian criminologist Gwynn Nettler says, "Thought disorder is the hallmark of psychosis.... People are called crazy when, at some extremity, they cannot 'think straight.'"[54] Nettler identifies three characteristics of psychotic individuals: "(1) a grossly distorted conception of reality, (2) moods, and swings of mood, that seem inappropriate to circumstance, and (3) marked inefficiency in getting along with others and caring for oneself."[55] Psychotics have also been classified as schizophrenic or paranoid schizophrenic.

Westley Alan Dodd, hanged in 1993 for murdering young boys whom he molested. "People need to know it's the only thing that will stop me," he said of his execution. Might there have been some other alternative? Benjamin Benschneider, *Seattle Times/Gamma-Liaison, Inc.*

Schizophrenics are said to be characterized by disordered or disjointed thinking, in which the types of logical associations they make are atypical of other people. **Paranoid schizophrenics** suffer from delusions and hallucinations.

Unfortunately, psychiatrists have not been able to agree on definitive criteria for schizophrenia that would allow for convenient application of the term. One prominent psychiatrist writes of "how varying. . . . schizophrenia may appear, ranging from no striking symptoms at all to conspicuous psychotic features. . . . Thus on the surface," he continues, "the schizophrenic may appear normal and, to some extent, lead a conventional life."[56] The same author later tells us, "Schizophrenia is not a clearly defined disease. . . . It is characterized rather by a . . . kind of alteration of thinking or feeling."[57] At the very least, then, we can safely say that schizophrenia is a disorganization of the personality. In its most extreme form, it may manifest itself by way of hallucinations, delusions, and seemingly irrational behavior.

With these caveats in mind, it is fair to say that psychoses may lead to crime in a number of ways. Following the Vietnam War, for example, a number of instances were reported in which former American soldiers suffering from a kind of battlefield psychosis killed friends and family members thinking they were Vietcong soldiers—that is, the enemy. These men, who had been traumatized by battlefield experiences in Southeast Asia, relived their past on American streets. In other crimes committed by psychotics, thought disorders may be less obvious or may exist only temporarily.

The Link between Frustration and Aggression

In his early writings, Freud suggested that aggressive behavior is a response to frustration. Aggression toward others, Freud said, is a natural response to frustrating limitations imposed upon a person. The frustration-aggression thesis was later developed more fully in the writings of J. Dollard,[58] Albert Bandura, Richard H. Walters, and others. Dollard's frustration-aggression theory held that although frustration can lead to various forms of behavior—including regression, sublimation, and aggressive fantasy—direct aggression toward others is its most likely consequence. Because everyone suffers some form of frustration throughout life, beginning with weaning and toilet training, Dollard argued, aggression is a natural consequence of living. Dollard pointed out, however, that aggression could be manifested in socially acceptable ways (perhaps through contact sports, military or law enforcement careers, or simple verbal attacks) and that it could be engaged in vicariously by observing others who are acting violently (as in movies, on television, through popular fiction, and so on). Dollard applied the psychoanalytical term *displacement* to the type of violence which is vented on something or someone who is not the source of the original frustration and suggested that satisfying one's aggressive urges via observation was a form of "catharsis."

The story of Paul Calden, a former insurance company executive, provides us with an example of the frustration-aggression theory as it applies to real-life crime. In January 1993, the 33-year-old Calden, dressed in a business suit, opened fire with a 9mm semiautomatic handgun on his former bosses in the Island Center Cafe, a Tampa, Florida, cafeteria—killing three people and injuring two others. Calden went up to the table where the five were eating, showed them the gun, shouted, "This is what you get for firing me!" and pulled the trigger.[59] He had been let go from his position as an underwriter with Fireman's Fund Insurance Company in March 1992. Calden then killed himself. He appears to have been acting out of frustrations born of his experience with having been fired.

Some psychologists have tried to identify what it is that causes some individuals to displace aggression or to experience it vicariously (through catharsis), while others respond violently and directly toward the immediate source of their frustrations. Andrew F. Henry and James F. Short, Jr., for example, writing in the 1950s, suggested that child-rearing practices are a major determining factor in such a causal nexus.[60] Restrictive parents who both punish and love their children, said Henry and Short, will engender in their children the ability to suppress outward expressions of aggression. When one parent punishes and the other loves, or when both punish but neither shows love, children can be expected

CRIME IN THE NEWS
Children's Brutal Deaths Stun S.C. Town

A mother charged with hacking and beating two of her children to death made her first court appearance today while a stunned community tried to make sense of the tragedy.

Police said that on Saturday, Persephone Elaine Muhammad, 30, killed two of her children, stabbing one with a knife and hitting the other over the head with an ax. The children were identified as Ingrid Simmons, 10, and her brother, 18-month-old Yusan Muhammad.

Muhammad's oldest child, Amber Simmons, age unknown, escaped the carnage and ran to a neighbor's house for help, authorities said. Police have not disclosed any motive for the slayings.

Berkeley County sheriff's Maj. C.W. Henerey said police believe Muhammad killed the children in her mobile home at 125 Lucky Lane and then dumped the bodies in a nearby field.

"The children were not killed in the field," Henerey said. "I won't go into details other than to say most of the physical evidence—an ax and knife—were seized in the mobile home."

A magistrate today ordered Muhammad sent to a state mental hospital for an emergency evaluation. Jack Sinclaire, assistant solicitor general for the 9th Circuit Solicitor's Office, said the evaluation will probably take about 15 days.

Under South Carolina law, magistrates are not allowed to set a bond in cases where the defendant is facing a possible life sentence in prison.

SCHOOLMATES WRITE LETTERS

Amber and Ingrid Simmons attended the Cainhoy Elementary School with about 250 pre-kindergarten through fourth grade students. Ingrid was a third-grader while Amber is in the fifth grade, the school's principal, Elizabeth Goldiner, said.

"I told the teachers this morning, If you don't teach anything, I'll understand," Goldiner told APBnews.com. "We let [the students] talk; they wrote cards to Ingrid, cards to Amber and even wrote the mother a letter."

Huger is a rural, unincorporated community located about 30 miles northeast of Charleston. Most of the families who live here are poor, with about 95 percent qualifying for a free school lunch for their children.

COUNSELORS BROUGHT IN

Goldiner said that ministers and guidance counselors were brought to the elementary school today to help classmates of the Simmons children cope with the tragedy.

"We had different ways of looking at the whole thing. We're angry, we're mad, we're upset and we're sad," Goldiner said. "All those emotions are running through us. Our main purpose today was to make sure the kids know that we love them and care for them and they feel safe here."

The Rev. Ross Rector, a county chaplain who was meeting and talking with children in the school, said the community is stunned and that many children are looking for answers that are not easy to find.

"It's just an overwhelming tragedy and compounded by the fact that everyone in the school knew them," Rector said. "The main concern of the children is how this can happen. The home is supposed to be a safe place, and this shakes them up a bit when they think it could happen at home."

SOMETHING AMISS AT HOME?

Goldiner described Ingrid Simmons as a "sweet" child.

"She was very shy, very reserved but a beautiful little girl," Goldiner said.

"When you earned her trust, she would melt in your hands. There were days when you would give her a hug and she wouldn't respond."

Goldiner said that the school had suspicions that something was amiss in Ingrid's family life, but she refused to give details.

"She was a mother who loved her children, but I don't think she knew how to love them," Goldiner said. "She was very different and distant but wanted the best for her children."

Police and school officials said they knew nothing about the father or fathers of the three children.

BODIES FOUND IN FIELD

The bodies were discovered shortly after 12:30 P.M. Saturday when the sheriff's department received a telephone call reporting a possible homicide at the mobile home.

When police arrived, Amber Simmons led them to a field near the mobile home where the bodies of her brother and sister were found. Yusan had been beaten and struck in the head with an ax, and Ingrid had been stabbed in the chest and her throat had been cut, authorities said.

Henerey said that Muhammad was in the trailer when police returned. She was charged with the double slaying. She also gave police another name, Persephone Elaine Simmons, authorities said.

After she was taken into custody, Henerey said that Muhammad assaulted several officers. He refused to give details, but said that four officers were slightly injured in the fracas and that Muhammad was charged with numerous counts of assaulting officers.

Source: Robert Anthony Phillips, "Mother Charged With Hacking Daughter, Baby Son," APB News, November 13, 2000. Reprinted with permission.

to show anger directly and perhaps even immediately because they will not be threatened with the loss of love. Physical punishment, explained Henry and Short, rarely threatens the loss of love, and children so punished cannot be expected to refrain from direct displays of anger.

In 1960, Stewart Palmer studied murderers and their siblings to determine the degree of frustration to which they had been exposed as children.[61] He found that male murderers had experienced much more frustration than their brothers. In fact, more than twice as many frustrating experiences, ranging from difficult births to serious illnesses, childhood beatings, severe toilet training, and negative school experiences, were reported by the murderers than by their law-abiding siblings.

CRIME AS ADAPTIVE BEHAVIOR

Some psychiatric perspectives have held that "crime is a compromise, representing for the individual the most satisfactory method of adjustment to inner conflicts which he cannot express otherwise. Thus, his acting out the crime fulfills a certain aim or purpose."[62] One pressing need of many criminals, according to some psychologists, is the need to be punished, which arises, according to psychiatric theory, from a sense of guilt. Psychiatrists who suggest that the need to be punished is a motivating factor in criminal behavior are quick to point out that this need may be a closely guarded secret, unknown even to the offender. Hence, from the psychiatric point of view, many drives, motives, and wishes are unconscious or even repressed by people who harbor them. The concept of repression holds that the human mind may choose to keep certain aspects of itself out of consciousness, possibly because of shame, self-loathing, or a simple lack of adequate introspection. The desire for punishment, however, sometimes comes to the fore. In 1993, for example, Westley Alan Dodd was hanged to death by authorities in Washington State for the kidnapping, rape, and murder of three little boys four years earlier. Dodd, who said he had molested dozens of children over the course of a decade, sought the death penalty after he was convicted, saying he deserved to die and vowing to sue the American Civil Liberties Union or anyone else who sought to save him.[63]

Crime can be adaptive in other ways as well. Some psychiatrists see it as an adaptation to life's stresses. According to Seymour L. Halleck, a psychiatrist and adjunct professor of law at the University of North Carolina at Chapel Hill, turning to crime can provide otherwise disenfranchised individuals with a sense of power and purpose.[64] In Halleck's words, "During the planning and execution of a criminal act the offender is a free man. . . . The value of this brief taste of freedom cannot be overestimated. Many of the criminal's apparently unreasonable actions are efforts to find a moment of autonomy."[65] Halleck says that crime can also provide "excellent rationalizations" for perceived in-

adequacies—especially for those whose lives have been failures when judged against the benchmarks of the wider society. "The criminal is able to say . . . , 'I could have been successful if I had not turned to crime. All my troubles have come to me because I have been bad.'" Hence crime, according to Halleck, provides "a convenient resource for denying, forgetting or ignoring . . . other inadequacies."[66]

Insofar as the choice of crime reduces stresses which the individual faces by producing changes in the environment (empowerment), it is referred to as **alloplastic adaptation**. When crime leads to stress reduction as a result of internal changes in beliefs, value systems, and so forth, it is called **autoplastic adaptation**. The offender who is able to deny responsibility for other failures by turning to crime is said to be seeking autoplastic adaptation. Because other forms of behavior may also meet many of the same needs as does crime, Halleck points out that an individual may select crime over various other behavioral alternatives only when no reasonable alternatives are available or when criminal behavior has inherent advantages—as might be the case under instances of economic or social oppression. (That is, individuals who are actively discriminated against may find personal and political significance in violating the laws of the oppressing society.)

In any case, from Halleck's point of view, crime "has many advantages even when considered independently of the criminal's conscious or unconscious needs for gratification."[67] In other words, even though crime can be immediately rewarding or intensely pleasureful, says Halleck, such rewards are more "fringe benefits" than anything else. The central significance of criminal behavior for most offenders is that it "is an action which helps one survive with dignity."[68] Halleck tells us that "We cannot understand the criminal unless we appreciate that his actions are much more than an effort to find a specific gratification."[69] In the final analysis, criminal behavior is, from Halleck's point of view, a form of adjustment to stress and oppression.

In another approach to stress as a causative agent in crime commission, Arnold S. Linsky, Ronet Bachman, and Murray A. Straus suggest that stress may lead to aggression toward others and toward oneself (that is, self-destructive behavior like suicide, smoking, and abuse of alcohol).[70] Linsky and his colleagues attempt to measure stress at the societal level, arguing that although the relationship between stress and aggression has been studied at the individual level, "the neglect of social stress as an explanation for society-to-society differences in aggression may be partially due to a lack of an objective means of comparing the stressfulness of life in different societies."[71] Concluding that societal stress levels heighten levels of aggression, the authors suggest that social policies should be created to reduce the impact of such stressful events as having to stop work, foreclosing on a mortgage, and dropping out of school.

Finally, we should recognize that perceptions vary, and although criminal behavior may appear to be a valid choice for some individuals who are seeking viable responses to perceived stresses and oppression, their perceptions may not be wholly accurate. In other words, misperceived stress and oppression may still lead to crime, even when far simpler solutions may be found in a more realistic appraisal of the offender's situation.

MODELING THEORY

On December 1, 1997, 14-year-old Michael Carneal walked up to a student prayer group in his Kentucky high school and opened fire with a .22-caliber pistol. Like a trained marksman, he squeezed off eight shots, killing three students and wounding five others. Lieutenant Colonel Dave Grossman, a retired Army Ranger and former West Point assistant professor of psychology, was amazed at the accuracy of Carneal's shooting. "He . . . got eight hits on eight different targets, five of them head shots," says Grossman. It was, Grossman says, a "truly, truly stunning" feat of marksmanship.[72]

Where did Carneal learn to shoot like that? And what made him *want* to shoot? The local sheriff couldn't understand Carneal's motivation and fielded questions about a possible conspiracy or an anti-Christian terror campaign.[73] But no conspiracy ever came to light, and Carneal and his family were churchgoers themselves. Although not a criminologist, Grossman thinks he knows what caused the shootings. The colonel reviewed Carneal's psychiatric records and found that the teenager had spent hundreds of hours playing violent computer games—including Quake, Redneck Rampage, and Resident Evil—for months before the shooting. Grossman calls the games "hypnotic murder simulators" and says that they are surprisingly similar to military combat-training programs. "This boy was doing exactly what he was drilled to do," says Grossman. Some young men, like Carneal, says Grossman, "play these video games not twice a year, but hours every night, and they shoot every living creature in sight until they run out of bullets or run out of targets."

Do violent computer games lead to violent crime? While the jury is still out on that question, the importance of imitation and modeling in shaping behavior has long been studied. One of the earliest attempts to explain crime and deviance as learned behavior can be found in the work of Gabriel Tarde (1843–1904), a French social theorist of the late 1800s. Tarde discounted the biological theories of Lombroso and others, which were so prevalent in his day, and suggested that it was possible to infer certain regularities or laws that appeared to govern the social world. The basis of any society, Tarde believed, was imitation—or, more precisely, the tendency of people to pattern their behavior after the behavior of others. Tarde developed a theory of human behavior that built upon three laws of imitation and suggestion.[74] Tarde's first law held that individuals in close intimate contact with one another tend to imitate each other's behavior. His second law stated that imitation moves from the top down. This means that poor people tend to imitate wealthy people, youngsters tend to emulate those older than themselves, lower-class people tend to imitate members of the upper class, and so on. The third law of imitation is the law of insertion, which says that new acts and behaviors tend to either reinforce or replace old ones. Hence the music of each generation replaces the music of the one that preceded it, the politics of young people eventually becomes the politics of the nation, fadish drugs are substituted for traditional ones, and new forms of crime tend to take the place of older ones (as

Bret Wengeler of Cheney, Washington, displaying the Web site of his computer video game, *Blow Away Your Boss*. Players put a photo of their boss, or of anyone they choose, into the game and then hunt him or her down with a handgun through office corridors and cubicles. Some people claim that such games can produce real crimes through modeling behavior. What do you think? *Jeff T. Green, AP/Wide World Photos*

when, for example, computer criminals become a more serious threat to financial institutions than bank robbers).

More recently, **Albert Bandura** developed a comprehensive **modeling theory** of aggression. Bandura tells us that "a
complete theory of aggression must explain how aggressive
patterns are developed, what provokes people to behave aggressively, and what sustains such actions after they have been
initiated."[75] Although everyone is capable of aggression, he
says, "people are not born with . . . repertories of aggressive
behavior. They must learn them." He goes on to say, "The specific forms that aggressive behavior takes, the frequency with
which it is expressed, the situation in which it is displayed,
and the specific targets selected for attack are largely determined by social learning factors."

Modeling theory, a form of social learning theory, asserts
that people learn how to act by observing others. In some of
his early work, Bandura experimented with children who observed adult role models striking inflatable cartoon characters. When the children were observed following their
encounter with adult behavior, they too exhibited similarly
aggressive behavior. Bandura also studied violence on television and concluded that "television is an effective tutor. Both
laboratory and controlled field studies in which young children and adolescents are repeatedly shown either violent or
nonviolent fare, disclose that exposure to film violence shapes
the form of aggression and typically increases interpersonal
aggressiveness in everyday life."[76] A later study by other researchers showed that even after ten years, the level of violence
engaged in by young adults was directly related to the degree
of violent television they had been exposed to as children.[77]

Bandura explained modeling behavior by referring to the
frequent hijacking of domestic airliners to Cuba, which occurred in the United States in the late 1960s and early 1970s.
Such hijackings, Bandura found, followed immediately on
the heels of similar incidents in Eastern European nations
under Soviet domination. American hijackings, he said, were
simply modeling those in Europe, and hijackers in this country were learning from news accounts of their foreign tutors.

Once aggressive patterns of behavior have been acquired,
it becomes necessary to show how they can be activated.
Aggression can be provoked, Bandura suggests, through
physical assaults and verbal threats and insults, as well as by
thwarting a person's hopes or obstructing his or her goal-
seeking behavior. Deprivation and "adverse reductions in the
conditions of life" (a lowered standard of living, the onset of
disease, a spouse leaving or caught cheating, for example) are
other potential triggers of aggression. Bandura adds, however, that a human being's ability to foresee the future consequences of present behavior infuses another dimension into
the activation of learned patterns of aggression. That is, aggressive behavior can be perceived as holding future benefits
for individuals exhibiting it. In short, it can be seen as a
means to a desired end.

An example of aggression that resulted from thwarted
goal seeking, and that may have been seen as holding future
benefits for the boys involved, occurred on the evening of

February 27, 1995. On that evening, teenage neo-Nazi skinhead brothers Bryan and David Freeman bludgeoned their
parents and younger brother to death in the family's
Allentown, Pennsylvania, home.[78] David was 15 years old at
the time of the killings; Bryan was 17. The first to be killed was
probably their 48-year-old mother, Brenda, who suffered
massive head injuries and stab wounds. Investigators theorize
that Brenda confronted the boys after their noisy late-night
return home and was arguing with them when at least one son
attacked her, smashing her skull with a club. She fell facedown
in the carpeted hallway outside the bedroom her sons shared,
trying to protect her head with her hands. One of the boys
then jumped on his mother and stabbed her repeatedly in the
back. After what may have been a brief conference, the brothers then made their way upstairs to their parents' bedroom,
where their 54-year-old father, Dennis, was sleeping. There,
they cut their father's throat and clubbed him to death before
he could leave the bed. Next, they moved on to the bedroom
of their younger brother, Eric, 11, crushing his skull with a
hammer as he slept. Viewing the murder scene the next day,
Lehigh County Coroner Wayne Snyder called the slayings "the
most savage, brutal, cowardly acts of murder I've ever seen."[79]

By all accounts, the young Freeman brothers had normal
childhoods. Then, about two years before the murders, they
began to change. The changes were gradual at first but soon
became more pronounced. The boys fell in with a rebellious
crowd, took to drinking, and experimented with drugs.[80]
Soon they stopped attending school regularly, shaved their
heads, began bodybuilding, and paid for a series of garish tattoos to cover their arms and torsos. They began attending
white supremacist meetings and collected fascist paraphernalia, including knives. Two weeks before killing their parents, the brothers paid to have their foreheads tattooed:
Bryan with "Berserker" and David with "Seig Heil." Run-ins
with the police had become routine, and, authorities believe,
when their parents took away the boys' car and threatened to
have them reinstitutionalized, the killings took place.

Bandura also says that individuals sometimes become
aggressive because they are rewarded for doing so. The early-
twentieth-century American concept of a "macho"—virile
and masculine—male figure, for example, was often associated with the expectation of substantial reward. The macho
male figure was the one who won the most respect from his
fellows, inevitably came away with the greatest honors (on
the playing field, in school, from the community, and so on),
and eventually married the most desirable woman. Whether
this perception was accurate, it was nonetheless subscribed to
by a significant proportion of American men and, for many
decades, served as a guide to daily behavior.

Another form of reward can flow from aggression.
Bandura called it the "reduction of aversive treatment." By
this he meant that simply standing up for one's self can improve the way one is treated by others. Oftentimes, for example, standing up to a bully is the most effective way of dealing
with the harassment one might otherwise face. Similarly,
there is an old saying that "the squeaky wheel gets the grease,"

and it means, quite simply, that people who are the most demanding will be recognized. Aggressive people often get what they go after.

Bandura recognized that everyone has self-regulatory mechanisms that can ameliorate the tendency toward aggression. People reward or punish themselves, Bandura said, according to internal standards they have for judging their own behavior. Hence aggression may be inhibited in people who, for example, value religious, ethical, or moral standards of conduct like compassion, thoughtfulness, and courtesy. Nonetheless, Bandura concluded, people who devalue aggression may still engage in it via a process he called "disengagement," whereby rationalizations are constructed which overcome internal inhibitions. Disengagement may result from (1) "attributing blame to one's victims," (2) dehumanization through bureaucratization, automation, urbanization, and high social mobility, (3) vindication of aggressive practices by legitimate authorities, and (4) desensitization resulting from repeated exposure to aggression in any of a variety of forms.

Modeling theory has been criticized for lacking comprehensive explanatory power. How, for example, can striking differences in sibling behavior, when early childhood experiences were likely much the same, be explained? Similarly, why do apparent differences exist between the sexes with regard to degree and type of criminality, irrespective of social background and early learning experiences? More recent versions of modeling theory, sometimes called "cognitive social learning theory,"[81] attempt to account for such differences by hypothesizing that reflection and cognition play a significant role in interpreting what one observes and in determining responses. Hence few people are likely to behave precisely as others because they will have their own ideas about what observed behavior means and about the consequences of emulation.

BEHAVIOR THEORY

Behavior theory has sometimes been called the "stimulus-response approach" to human behavior. "At the heart of behavior theory is the notion that behavior is determined by environmental consequences which it produces for the individual concerned."[82] When an individual's behavior results in rewards, or in the receipt of feedback which the individual, for whatever reason, regards as pleasurable and desirable, then it is likely that the behavior will become more frequent. Under such circumstances, the behavior in question is reinforced. Conversely, when punishment follows behavior, chances are that the frequency of that type of behavior will decrease. The individual's responses are termed **operant behavior** because a person's behavioral choices effectively operate on the surrounding environment to produce consequences for the individual. Similarly, stimuli provided by the environment become behavioral cues that serve to elicit conditioned responses from the individual. Responses are said to be conditioned according to the individual's past experi-

ences, wherein behavioral consequences effectively defined some forms of behavior as desirable and others as undesirable. Behavior theory is often employed by parents seeking to control children through a series of **rewards** and **punishments**. Young children may be punished, for example, with spanking, the loss of a favored toy (at least for a period of time), a turned-off television, and so forth. Older children are often told what rules they are expected to obey and what rewards they can anticipate receiving if they adhere to those rules. They also know that punishments will follow if they do not obey the rules.

Rewards and punishments have been further divided into four conceptual categories: (1) positive rewards, which increase the frequency of approved behavior by adding something desirable to the situation—as when a "good" child is given a toy; (2) negative rewards, which increase the frequency of approved behavior by removing something distressful from the situation—as when a "good" child is permitted to skip the morning's chores; (3) positive punishments, which decrease the frequency of unwanted behavior by adding something undesirable to the situation—as when a "bad" child is spanked; and (4) negative punishments, which decrease the frequency of unwanted behavior by removing something desirable from the situation—as when a "bad" child's candy is taken away. According to behavior theory, it is through the application of rewards and punishments that behavior is shaped.

Behavior theory differs from other psychological theories in that the major determinants of behavior are envisioned as existing in the environment surrounding the individual rather than actually in the individual. Perhaps the best-known proponent of behavior theory is **B. F. Skinner** (1904–1990). Skinner, a former Harvard professor, rejected unobservable psychological constructs, focusing instead on patterns of responses to external rewards and stimuli. Skinner did extensive animal research involving behavioral concepts and created the notion of programmed instruction, which allows students to work at their own pace and provides immediate rewards for learning accomplishments.

Although behavior theory has much to say about the reformation of criminal offenders through the imposition of punishment, the approach is equally significant for its contributions to understanding the genesis of such behavior. As one writer states, "It is the balance of reinforcement and punishment in an individual's learning history which will dictate the presence or absence of criminal behavior."[83] According to the behavioral model, crime results when individuals "receive tangible rewards (positive reinforcement) for engaging in delinquent and criminal behavior, particularly when no other attractive alternative is available."[84]

A few years ago, for example, Sundahkeh "Ron" Bethune, 15, shot and killed a 26-year-old pizza deliveryman who gunned his car motor as Bethune attempted to rob him. Ron, who had been dabbling in the drug trade and who could afford high-priced clothing, jewelry, and other accoutrements of apparent wealth, was esteemed by many other young people in his Morganton, North Carolina, community. When the deliveryman tried to run from Ron in front of a group of his friends, Bethune saw no other choice but to kill him. "I just had to show them I wasn't some little punk," he said afterward in a prison interview.[85] Ron Bethune did not think of the long-term consequences of his behavior on the night of the killing. All he wanted was to earn the approval of those who were watching him. The crowd's anticipated awestruck response to murder was all the reward Ron needed to pull the trigger that night. He is now serving five years for second-degree murder.

Behavior theory has been criticized for ignoring the role that cognition plays in human behavior. Martyrs, for example, persist in what may be defined by the wider society as undesirable behavior, even in the face of severe punishment—including the loss of their own lives. No degree of punishment is likely to deter a martyr who answers to some higher call. Similarly, criminals who are punished for official law violations may find that their immediate social group interprets criminal punishment as status enhancing. As an acquaintance of the author said, after being released from prison where he had served time for murder, "You woulda thought I had won a Grammy award or somethin'." Members of his community held him in awe. As he walked down the street, young people would say, "There goes John! You better not mess with John!" From the point of view of behavior theory, criminal punishments are in danger of losing sway over many forms of human behavior in today's diverse society. Our society's fragmented value system leads to various interpretations of criminal punishments, thereby changing the significance of experiences like arrest, conviction, and imprisonment. In times past, criminal offenders were often shunned and became social outcasts. Today, those who have been adjudicated criminal may find that their new status holds many rewards.

ATTACHMENT THEORY

Another psychological approach to explaining crime and delinquency is **attachment theory**. Attachment theory was first proposed in the 1950s by John Bowlby (1907–1990), an English child psychiatrist who observed children during his tenure at the London Child Guidance Clinic after World War II.[86] Bowlby was especially interested in the maladjusted behavior of children who lacked a solid relationship with a mother figure. After years of working with children, Bowlby concluded that for healthy personality development to occur, "the infant and young child should experience a warm, intimate, and continuous relationship with his mother (or permanent mother substitute) in which both find satisfaction and enjoyment."[87]

Bowlby identified three forms of attachment: secure attachment, anxious-avoidant attachment, and anxious-resistant attachment.[88] Only the first, he said, is a healthy form of attachment. It develops when a child is confident that the mother figure will be responsible and available

when needed. The development of healthy attachment, then, is largely dependent upon the availability of a mother figure who is sensitive to signals from the child, who is accessible to the child, and who is lovingly responsive to the child's needs. The successful development of secure attachment between a child and his or her primary caregiver, Bowlby said, provides the basic foundation for all future psychological development. Bowlby believed that secure attachments form early in childhood as the developing infant experiences nurturing and protective care. Hence children develop a secure psychological base if they are "nourished physically and emotionally, comforted if distressed [and] reassured if frightened."[89]

According to attachment theory, delinquent behavior arises whenever nonsecure attachments are created. Anxious-avoidant attachment, for example, develops when children feel rejection and develop a lack of confidence concerning parental support and care. Anxious-resistant attachment develops from similar experiences and results in feelings of uncertainty which cause the child (and, later, the adult) to feel anxious, to become fearful of his or her environment, and to cling to potential caregivers or partners. Bowlby calls delinquents "affectionless," meaning that they have not formed intimate attachments as children and are thus unable to form such attachments later in life. Attachment theory predicts that the most problematic individuals will be those who were abandoned at an early age, who experienced multiple placements (in foster homes, and so on), who had to deal with the early absence of one or both parents, and who faced traumatic conditions in early childhood (physical, sexual, or other abuse).

Recent tests of attachment theory seem to confirm that difficulties in childhood (especially before the age of 8) produce adult criminality later in life.[90] Studies have shown that children who were raised in insecure environments are likely to engage in violent behavior as adults and that childhood insecurity leads to a relative lack of empathy.[91] Some attachment theorists believe that the development of empathy is the most important single factor leading to conformity. When children do not receive empathetic understanding from those around them while being socialized, they appear to become unable to see others around them as deserving of empathy, and they become more likely to inflict injury on those they encounter. Learn more about attachment theory by visiting the Attachment Research Center via Web Extra! 6-4.

Web EXTRA! **Web Extra! 6-4 at crimtoday.com**

SELF-CONTROL THEORY

Many people, regardless of what they have learned and independently of flaws in their personality, are able to exercise self-control sufficient to keep them from getting into trouble with the law, even under the most challenging of circumstances. **Self-control** refers to a person's ability to alter his or her own states and responses.[92] Many psychologists suggest that "the capacity to override and alter the self's responses is a vital characteristic that sets human beings apart from other species."[93] Self-control is most obvious when exercised in the face of adversity, as when people override their own natural tendencies to act or when they act contrary to their preferences and impulses. Hence self-control is both key to adaptive success and central to virtuous behavior, especially insofar as the latter requires conforming to socially desirable standards in place of the pursuit of selfish goals.

In the field of psychology, four types of self-control have been identified. The first type is impulse control, in which people resist temptations and refrain from acting on impulses that they consider to be socially or personally undesirable. Impulses subject to control include those to eat or drink, to take drugs, to act violently or aggressively, to engage in sexual activity, and so forth. A second type of self-control is exercised over the contents of the mind and includes suppressing unwanted thoughts, focusing thoughts or concentrating, reasoning and analysis, and inference and guided intuition. A third type of self-control can be exercised over one's emotional and mood states, and a fourth type involves controlling performance—as when a person persists in the face of adversity or physical challenges. Since self-control permits the changing of the self, it is a premier adaptive skill. Self-control enables people who are able to exercise it to adjust themselves to a much wider range of circumstances than they otherwise could. Psychologists sometimes argue that the majority of today's personal and social problems (which include things like drug abuse, violence, school failure, alcoholism, unwanted pregnancy, venereal disease, irresponsible money management, underachievement, poor eating habits and obesity, lack of exercise, cigarette smoking, and delinquency and criminality) stem from deficiencies or failures in self-control.[94]

A somewhat different perspective on self-control is offered by criminologists Michael R. Gottfredson and Travis Hirschi as part of their general theory of crime, which is discussed in more detail in Chapter 8. "Gottfredson and Hirschi's general theory of crime claims to be *general,* in part, due to its assertion that the operation of a single mechanism, low self-control, accounts for 'all crime, at all times'; acts ranging from vandalism to homicide, from rape to white-collar-crime."[95] Gottfredson and Hirschi define *self-control* as the degree to which a person is vulnerable to temptations of the moment.[96] They propose that self-control is acquired early in life and that low self-control is the premier individual-level cause of crime. Self-control, say Gottfredson and Hirschi, develops by the end of childhood and is fostered through parental emotional investment in the child, which includes monitoring the child's behavior, recognizing deviance when it occurs, and punishing the child. Gottfredson and Hirschi also recognize the sociological dimensions of criminality by noting that the link between self-control and crime depends substantially upon criminal opportunity, which in itself is a function of the struc-

tural or situational circumstances that an individual encounters. Hence these theorists suggest that "the link between self-control and crime is not deterministic, but probabilistic, affected by opportunities and other constraints."[97]

Gottfredson and Hirschi reject the notion that some people have an enduring propensity to commit crime or that any such propensity compels people to do so.[98] Crimes, they say, require "no special capabilities, needs, or motivation; they are, in this sense, available to everyone."[99] Instead, Gottfredson and Hirschi suggest that some people have a lasting tendency to ignore the long-term consequences of their behavior, that such people tend to be impulsive, reckless, and self-centered, and that crime is often the end result of such tendencies.[100]

Building on the work of Gottfredson and Hirschi, Harold G. Grasmick identifies some of the characteristics of individuals with low levels of self-control.[101] According to Grasmick, such people are impulsive and seek immediate gratification. Those with higher levels of self-control are more inclined to defer gratification in favor of long-term gains. People with less self-control lack diligence, tenacity, and persistence, said Grasmick, and prefer simple tasks and want "money without work, sex without courtship, [and] revenge without court delays."[102] Grasmick also believed that risk seeking is an important determinant of self-control, and he said that people with little self-control are drawn to activities that are adventurous and exciting. Similarly, said Grasmick, these people prefer physical activity over contemplation or conversation and tend to be indifferent or insensitive to the needs of others. While those who lack self-control are not necessarily antisocial or malicious, they are predisposed to being self-centered. Finally, according to Grasmick, self-control is inversely associated with a low frustration tolerance and with an inclination to handle conflict through confrontation.

INSANITY AND THE LAW

Unfortunately for criminologists, psychological conceptions of mental illness, antisocial personality, and even psychopathy are not readily applicable to the criminal justice system, which relies instead on the legal concept of **insanity**.[103] Insanity, for purposes of the criminal law, is strictly a legal, not a clinical, determination. Seen this way, *insanity* is a term that refers to a type of defense allowable in criminal courts. While the legal concept of insanity is based upon claims of mental illness, it has no precise counterpart in the jargon of contemporary psychologists or psychiatrists, who speak instead in terms of mental status or, at most, psychosis and personality disorder. As a consequence, legal and psychiatric understandings of mental impairment rarely coincide.

In the 1992 case of *Foucha v. Louisiana,* the U.S. Supreme Court recognized the problem, saying; "It is by now well established that insanity as defined by the criminal law has no direct analog in medicine or science. The divergence between law and psychiatry is caused in part by the legal fiction represented by the words 'insanity' or 'insane,' which are a kind of lawyer's catchall and have no clinical meaning."[104]

Because insanity is a defense to criminal prosecution, a criminal defendant may be found "not guilty by reason of insanity" and avoid punitive sanctions, even when it is clear that he or she committed a legally circumscribed act. The burden of proving a claim of "not guilty by reason of insanity," however, falls upon the defendant.[105] Just as a person is assumed to be innocent at the start of any criminal trial, so too is the person assumed to be sane.

A defendant has a right to the opportunity to prove a claim of insanity in court and cannot be forced to take medications during trial that might control the condition. In 1992, for example, the U.S. Supreme Court, in the case of *Riggins* v. *Nevada*,[106] held that the "forced administration of antipsychotic medication" may have impaired the accused's ability to defend himself and violated due process guarantees.

In 1984, the U.S. Congress enacted the Insanity Defense Reform Act (IDRA), part of the 1984 Crime Control and Prevention Act.[107] Congress had been spurred to action by John Hinckley's attempted assassination of then-President Ronald Reagan. At trial, Hinckley's lawyers claimed that their client's history of schizophrenia left him unable to control his behavior, and Hinckley was acquitted of the criminal charges which had been brought against him. Although Hinckley was institutionalized to prevent him from harming others, his release is mandated by federal law which existed at the time of his trial when (and if) he recovers.

Through the IDRA, Congress intended to prohibit the presentation, at trial, of evidence of mental disease or defect, short of legal insanity, to excuse conduct.[108] Insanity under the act is defined as a condition in which the defendant can be shown to have been suffering under a "severe mental disease or defect" and, as a result, "was unable to appreciate the nature and quality or the wrongfulness of his acts."[109] The IDRA also placed the burden of proving insanity squarely on the defendant—a provision that has been unsuccessfully challenged a number of times since the act was passed.

The IDRA created a special verdict of "not guilty by reason of insanity" (NGRI).[110] Through a comprehensive civil commitment procedure, a defendant found NGRI can be held in custody pending a court hearing. The hearing must occur within 40 days of the verdict. At the conclusion of the hearing, the court determines whether the defendant should be hospitalized or released. In the words of the U.S. Supreme Court, "The Insanity Defense Reform Act of 1984 ensures that a federal criminal defendant found not guilty by reason of insanity will not be released onto the streets."[111]

The IDRA is especially significant because it contains a provision which permits mentally ill individuals to be held for trial in the hopes that they will recover sufficiently to permit their trial to proceed. The law allows for an initial hearing to determine the mental status of the defendant. If the defendant is found incompetent to stand trial, he will be

Insanity can be used as a defense against criminal charges. Lorena Bobbitt sobs on the witness stand before acquittal on charges she severed her husband's penis with a kitchen knife. Bobbitt claimed a kind of irresistible impulse. Should she have been acquitted? *Gary Hershorn, Corbis*

committed to a hospital "for such a reasonable period of time, not to exceed four months, . . . to determine whether there is a substantial probability that in the foreseeable future he will attain the capacity to permit the trial to proceed; and . . . for an additional reasonable period of time until . . . his mental condition is so improved that trial may proceed." The law sets no maximum period of confinement, implying only that the defendant will undergo periodic review while institutionalized "if the court finds that there is a substantial probability that within such additional period of time he will attain the capacity to permit the trial to proceed."[112]

The *M'Naughten* Rule

One of the first instances within the Western legal tradition where insanity was accepted as a defense to criminal liability can be found in the case of Daniel M'Naughten (also spelled "McNaughton" and "M'Naghton"). M'Naughten was accused of the 1843 killing of Edward Drummond, the secretary of British Prime Minister Sir Robert Peel. By all accounts, M'Naughten had intended to kill Peel, but because he was suffering from mental disorganization, he shot Drummond instead, mistaking him for Peel. At his trial, the defense presented information to show that M'Naughten was suffering from delusions, including the belief that Peel's political party was, in some vague way, persecuting him. The court accepted his lawyer's claims, and the defense of insanity was established in Western law. Other jurisdictions were quick to adopt the *M'Naughten* rule, as the judge's decision in the case came to be called. The *M'Naughten* **rule** holds that individuals cannot be held criminally responsible for their actions if at the time of the offense either (1) they did not know what they were doing, or (2) they did not know that what they were doing was wrong.

Today the *M'Naughten* rule is still followed by many states when insanity is at issue in criminal cases. Critics of the *M'Naughten* rule say that although the notion of intent inherent within it appeals greatly to lawyers, "it is . . . so alien to current concepts of human behavior that it has been vigorously attacked by psychiatrists. An obvious difficulty with the *M'Naughten* rule is that practically everyone, regardless of the degree of his criminal disturbance, knows the nature and quality and rightness or wrongness of what he is doing."[113]

The Irresistible-Impulse Test

The *M'Naughten* ruling opened the floodgates for other types of insanity claims offered as defenses to charges of criminal activity. One interesting claim is that of irresistible impulse. The **irresistible-impulse test**—employed by 18 states, some of which also follow the dictates of *M'Naughten*—holds that a defendant is not guilty of a criminal offense if the person, by virtue of his or her mental state or psychological condition, was not able to resist committing the action in question. Some years ago, for example, a television advertisement claimed that a certain brand of potato chip was so good that, once you opened the container, you couldn't eat just one. Friends of the author would test themselves by purchasing the brand in question, opening the pack, and eating a chip. They would then try and resist the temptation to have another, thereby hoping to prove the commercial wrong. Although this may seem a silly exercise in self-assessment, it did prove a point. The commercial, in fact, was right most of the time. Additional chips were almost impossible to avoid for anyone who tried this experiment—especially if they kept the chips around for any length of time! Of course, eating potato chips is not a crime, even if the chips are irresistible.

Commercials aside, it is difficult for anyone to really know whether a given person in a particular situation was able to control his or her behavior. Kleptomania is a disorder in which an individual feels compelled to steal. Kleptomaniacs are often shoplifters but have also been known to be unable to resist the urge to steal while visiting the homes of friends or relatives.

In 1994, Lorena Bobbitt, whose case was described earlier in this chapter, was found not guilty by virtue of temporary insanity of charges of maliciously wounding her husband by cutting off his penis with a kitchen knife. Her attorneys successfully employed the irresistible-impulse defense, convincing the jury that Mrs. Bobbitt acted as a result of irresistible impulse after years of "physical abuse, verbal abuse and sexual abuse" at the hands of her husband. Her attorneys maintained that, while committing the crime, she had a brief psychotic breakdown and could not resist the impulse to maim her husband.

Scientific advances now on the horizon combine with the irresistible-impulse test to open a number of intriguing possibilities. One has to do with new colognes and perfumes rumored to be marketed soon. These scents combine the usual toiletries with pheromones—chemical substances that, at least in insect form, have been shown to produce very predictable, and apparently uncontrollable, behavior. Pheromones, which stimulate the olfactory nerves to produce specific chemicals which then target neuroreceptors in the brain, directly alter brain chemistry. Most uses of pheromones to date have been in the area of pest control, where sexual pheromones that attract specific types of male insects, for example, are released into the atmosphere to confuse the insect's mating behavior or to lure pests into a trap. Clearly at issue, if the new products are marketed, will be claims of uncontrollable sexual desire. Will toiletries containing human pheromones lead to instances of sexual attack? If so, will the attackers be held blameless on claims of irresistible impulse, and what will then be the civil liability of the product makers themselves?

The *Durham* Rule

In 1954, Judge David Bazelon of the U.S. Court of Appeals for the District of Columbia announced a new rule in the case of Monte Durham. In the words of the court, "The rule we now hold is simply that an accused is not criminally responsible if his unlawful act was the product of mental disease or mental defect." Judge Bazelon continued, defining the terms of the court's decision, "We use 'disease' in the sense of a condition which is considered capable of improving or deteriorating. We use 'defect' in the sense of a condition which is not considered capable of either improving or deteriorating and which may be congenital or the result of injury or the residual effect of a physical or mental disease."[114]

Although this new rule was intended to simplify the adjudication of mentally ill offenders, it has resulted in additional confusion. Many criminal defendants suffer from mental diseases or defects. Some show retarded mental development, others are dyslexic, a few are afflicted with Down's syndrome, others have cerebral palsy (which would perhaps meet Judge Bazelon's definition), and a vast number evidence some degree of neurosis or psychosis. The link between any of these conditions and criminal behavior in specific cases, however, is far from clear. Some people struggle with psychological handicaps or mental illnesses all their lives, never violating the criminal law. Others, with similar conditions, are frequent law violators. The **Durham rule** provides no way of separating one group from the other.

Finally, some observers have noted the "danger of circularity" in the *Durham* rule. If a person exhibits unusual behavior during the commission of a crime, the criminal behavior itself may be taken as a sign of mental disease, automatically exonerating the offender of criminal culpability.

The Substantial-Capacity Test

In the determination of insanity for purposes of criminal prosecution, 19 U.S. states adhere to the **substantial-capacity test**, a standard embodied in the Model Penal Code of the

American Law Institute. The substantial-capacity test blends elements of the *M'Naughten* rule with the irresistible-impulse standard. Insanity is said to be present when a person lacks "the [substantial] mental capacity needed to understand the wrongfulness of his act, or to conform his behavior to the requirements of the law."[115] A lack of mental capacity does not require total mental incompetence, nor does it mandate that the behavior in question meet the standard of total irresistibility. The problem, however, of determining just what constitutes "substantial mental capacity," or its lack, has plagued this rule from its inception.

The *Brawner* Rule

The *Brawner* rule, created in 1972 in the case of *U.S.* v. *Brawner*,[116] is rather unique among standards of its type. This rule, in effect, delegates responsibility to the jury to determine what constitutes insanity. The jury is asked to decide whether the defendant could be *justly* held responsible for the criminal act with which he or she stands charged, in the face of any claims of insanity or mental incapacity. Under the *Brawner* rule, which has not seen wide applicability, juries are left with few rules to guide them other than their own sense of fairness.

Guilty but Mentally Ill

Frustrated by the seeming inability of criminal courts to effectively adjudicate mentally ill offenders and by the abuse of insanity claims by offenders seeking to avoid criminal punishments, several states have enacted legislation permitting findings of "guilty but insane" or **guilty but mentally ill** (**GBMI**). In 1997, for example, Pennsylvania multimillionaire John E. du Pont was found guilty but mentally ill in the shooting death of former Olympic gold medalist David Schultz during a delusional episode. Although defense attorneys were able to show that du Pont sometimes thought he saw Nazis in his trees, heard the walls talking, and had cut off pieces of his own skin in efforts to remove bugs from outer space, he was held criminally liable for Schultz's death and was sentenced to 13 to 30 years in confinement.

A GBMI verdict means that a person can be held responsible for a specific criminal act, even though a degree of mental incompetence may be present. In most GBMI jurisdictions, a jury must return a finding of "guilty but mentally ill" if (1) every statutory element necessary for a conviction has been proved beyond a reasonable doubt, (2) the defendant is found to have been *mentally ill* at the time the crime was committed, and (3) the defendant was not found to have been *legally insane* at the time the crime was committed. The difference between mental illness and legal insanity is crucial because a defendant can be mentally ill by standards of the medical profession, but sane for purposes of the law.

Upon return of a GBMI verdict, a judge may impose any sentence possible under the law for the crime in question. Offenders adjudicated GBMI are, in effect, found guilty of the criminal offense with which they are charged but, because of their mental condition, are generally sent to psychiatric hospitals for treatment rather than to prison. Once they have been declared "cured," however, such offenders can be transferred to correctional facilities to serve out their sentences.

Federal Provisions for the Hospitalization of Individuals Found "NGRI"

Federal law provides for confinement in a "suitable facility" of criminal defendants found not guilty by reason of insanity.[117] The law mandates a "psychiatric or psychological examination and report" and a hearing to be held within 40 days after the not guilty verdict. If the hearing court finds that the person's release would "create a substantial risk of bodily injury to another person or serious damage of property of another due to a present mental disease or defect," the statute says, "the court shall commit the person." To be released later, a person committed under the law "has the burden of proving by clear and convincing evidence that his release would not create a substantial risk of bodily injury to another person or serious damage of property of another due to a present mental disease or defect." The person can be discharged "when the director of the facility in which an acquitted person is hospitalized . . . determines that the person has recovered from his mental disease or defect to such an extent that his release, or his conditional release under a prescribed regimen of medical, psychiatric, or psychological care or treatment, would no longer create a substantial risk of bodily injury to another person or serious damage to property of another."

The federal statute has been used as a model by many of the states. A few laws, which differ from the federal model, have been held to be unconstitutional, especially when they permit the continued confinement of offenders who have been declared "well," even though they may still be dangerous. In 1992, for example, the U.S. Supreme Court, in the case of *Foucha* v. *Louisiana,* ordered the release of Terry Foucha, who had been adjudicated "not guilty by reason of insanity" in the state of Louisiana. Although a psychiatrist later found Foucha to have overcome a drug-induced psychosis which had been present at the time of the crime, a state court ordered Foucha returned to the mental institution in which he had been committed, ruling that he was dangerous on the basis of the same doctor's testimony. The psychiatrist found that although Foucha was "in good shape" mentally, he had "an antisocial personality." Foucha's antisocial personality was described as "a condition that is not a mental disease and is untreatable." The doctor, citing the fact that Foucha had been involved in several altercations at the institution, said that he would not "feel comfortable in certifying that [Foucha] would not be a danger to himself or to other people." In effect, the Supreme Court struck down a provision of the Louisiana law which made possible continued confinement of recovered persons who had once been deemed not guilty by reason of insanity, when their continued confinement was predicated solely on the basis of the belief that they might represent a continuing danger to the community.

Insanity became an issue at the 1997 murder trial of multimillionaire John E. du Pont. In 1996, du Pont shot and killed wrestler David Schultz during a delusional episode. Although defense attorneys were able to show that du Pont sometimes saw Nazis in his trees, heard the walls talking, and had cut off pieces of his skin to remove bugs from outer space, he was found guilty but mentally ill and was sentenced to serve 13 to 30 years in confinement. Should he have been absolved of criminal responsibility? *Chris Gardner, AP/Wide World Photos*

SOCIAL POLICY AND FORENSIC PSYCHOLOGY

Psychological theories continue to evolve. For example, recent research in the field has shown a stability of aggressiveness over time. That is, children who display early disruptive or aggressive behavior are, according to studies that follow the same individuals over time, likely to continue their involvement in such behavior as adults.[118] Some researchers have found that aggressiveness appears to stabilize over time.[119] Children who demonstrate aggressive traits early in life often evidence increasingly frequent episodes of such behavior until, finally, such behavior becomes a major component of the adolescent or adult personality. From such research it is possible to conclude that problem children are likely to become problem adults.

Expanding research of this sort holds considerable significance for those who are attempting to assess dangerousness and to identify personal characteristics which would allow for the prediction of dangerousness in individual cases.

The ability to accurately predict future dangerousness is of great concern to today's policymakers. In 1993, for example, Michael Blair, a convicted child molester paroled after serving 18 months of a ten-year prison sentence, was charged with the kidnap-slaying of young Ashley Estell, who disappeared from a soccer match in Plano, Texas. Ashley was found dead the next day.[120] Similarly, in November of that year, Anthony Cook was executed in Huntsville, Texas, for the slaying of law student Dirck VanTassel, Jr.[121] Cook killed VanTassel only 13 days after being paroled, robbing him of his wallet, watch, and wedding ring and shooting him four times in the head. Less than a month later, in what was to be a very sad case, Richard Allen Davis, a twice-convicted kidnapper, was arrested for the kidnap-murder of 12-year-old Polly Klaas.[122] Klaas was abducted from a slumber party in her Petaluma, California, home as her mother slept in the next room. Davis had been paroled only a few months earlier after serving an eight-year prison term for a similar offense.

Can past behavior predict future behavior? Do former instances of criminality presage additional ones? Are there other, identifiable, characteristics which violent offenders might manifest that could serve as warning signs to criminal justice decision makers faced with the dilemma of whether to release convicted felons? This, like many other areas, is one in which criminologists are still learning. One recent study found a strong relationship between childhood behavioral difficulties and later problem behavior.[123] According to the authors of the study, "Early antisocial behavior is the best predictor of later antisocial behavior. It appears that this rule holds even when the antisocial behavior is measured as early as the preschool period." Using children as young as 3 years old, researchers were able to predict later delinquency, leading them to conclude that "some antisocial behavioral characteristics may be components of temperament." A second study, which tracked a sample of male offenders for over 20 years, found that stable but as yet "unmeasured individual differences" account for the positive association which exists between past criminal behavior and the likelihood of future recurrence.[124] A 1996 analysis of recidivism studies by Canadians Paul Gendreau, Tracy Little, and Claire Goggin found that criminal history, a history of preadult antisocial behavior, and "criminogenic needs"—which were defined as measurable antisocial thoughts, values, and behavior—were all predictors of recidivism.[125]

Prediction, however, requires more than generalities. It is one thing to say, for example, that generally speaking 70% of children who evidence aggressive behavior will show violent tendencies later in life, and quite another to be able to predict which specific individuals will engage in future violations of the criminal law. **Selective incapacitation** is a policy based on the notion of career criminality.[126] Career criminals, also termed "habitual offenders," are people who repeatedly violate the criminal law. Research has shown that only a small percentage of all offenders account for most of the crimes reported to the police. Some studies have found that as few as 8% of all offenders commit as many as 60 serious crimes each per year.[127] A recent Wisconsin study found that imprisonment of individuals determined to be career offenders saved the state approximately $14,000 per year per offender when the cost of imprisonment was compared with the estimated cost of new crimes.[128] Researchers in the Wisconsin study concluded that "prison pays" and suggested that the state continue pursuing a policy of aggressive imprisonment of career offenders, even in the face of escalating costs and vastly overcrowded prisons. The strategy of selective incapacitation, however, which depends on accurately identifying potentially dangerous offenders in existing criminal populations, has been criticized by some authors for yielding a rate of "false positives" of over 60%.[129] Potentially violent offenders are not easy to identify, even on the basis of past criminal records, and sentencing individuals to long prison terms simply because they are thought likely to commit crimes in the future would no doubt be unconstitutional.

The federal 1984 Comprehensive Crime Control Act,[130] which established the U.S. Sentencing Commission, targeted career offenders. Guidelines created by the commission contain, as a central feature, a "criminal history" dimension which substantially increases the amount of punishment an offender faces based on his or her history of law violations. The sentencing guidelines originally classified a defendant as a career offender if "(1) the defendant was at least 18 years old at the time of the . . . offense, (2) the . . . offense is a crime of violence or trafficking in a controlled substance, and (3) the defendant has at least two prior felony convictions of either a crime of violence or a controlled substance offense."[131] The definition, however, later came under fire for casting individuals with a history of minor drug trafficking into the same category as serial killers and the like.

Definitions of dangerousness are fraught with difficulty because, as some authors have pointed out, "dangerousness is not an objective quality like obesity or brown eyes, rather it is an ascribed quality like trustworthiness."[132] Dangerousness is not necessarily a personality trait which is stable or easily identifiable. Even if it were, some studies of criminal careers seem to show that involvement in crime decreases with age.[133] Hence, as one author states, if "criminality declines more or less uniformly with age, then many offenders will be 'over the hill' by the time they are old enough to be plausible candidates for preventive incarceration."[134]

No discussion of social policy as it relates to the insights of criminal psychology would be complete without mention of correctional psychology. **Correctional psychology** is concerned with the diagnosis and classification of offenders, the treatment of correctional populations, and the rehabilitation of inmates and other law violators. Perhaps the most commonly used classification instrument in correctional facilities today is the Minnesota Multiphasic Personality Inventory, better known as the MMPI. Based on the results of an MMPI inventory, an offender may be assigned to a security level, a correctional program, or a treatment program. Psychological treatment, when employed, typically takes the form of individual or group counseling. Psychotherapy, guided group interaction, cognitive therapy, behavioral modification, and various forms of interpersonal therapy are representative of the range of techniques used.

Social Policy and the Psychology of Criminal Conduct

A practical synthesis of psychological approaches to criminal behavior is offered by D. A. Andrews and James Bonta in their 1994 book, *The Psychology of Criminal Conduct*.[135] Andrews and Bonta prefer the term *psychology of criminal conduct,* or PCC, to distinguish their point of view from what they call "the weak psychology represented in mainstream sociological criminology and clinical/forensic psychology."[136] Any useful synthesis of contemporary criminal psychology, they claim, should be fundamentally objective and empirical. Clearly, they dislike many currently well-accepted perspectives, which they say have "placed higher value on social theory and political ideology than [on] rationality and/or respect for evidence."[137] Specifically, say Andrews and Bonta, "The majority of perspectives on criminal conduct that are most favored in mainstream criminology reduce people to hypothetical fictions whose only interesting characteristics are their location in the social system. Almost without exception," they write, "the causal significance of social location is presumed to reflect inequality in the distribution of social wealth and power." This kind of theorizing, the authors claim, "is a major preoccupation of mainstream textbook criminology, even though such a focus has failed to significantly advance understanding of criminal conduct."[138]

In *The Psychology of Criminal Conduct*, Andrews and Bonta do not attempt to develop a new behavioral theory, but rather ask for the objective application of what is now understood about the psychology of crime and criminal behavior. Their book is a call for practical coalescence of what is already known of the psychology of criminal offenders. Such coalescence is possible, they say, through the application of readily available, high-quality psychological findings. The authors claim, for example, that from the nearly 500 published reports on "controlled evaluations of community and correctional interventions," it is possible to conclude that treatment reduces recidivism "to at least a mild degree."[139] Further, a detailed consideration of published studies finds that, among other things, targeting higher-risk cases and using treatments outside of formal correctional settings which extend to an offender's family and peers are all elements of the most effective treatment strategies. Similarly, along with objective measures of the success of rehabilitation programs and strategies, Andrews and Bonta say, effective intervention and treatment services based on the use of psychological assessment instruments which have already demonstrated their validity, empirically established risk factors that can be accurately assessed, and accurately measured community crime rates are all ready and waiting to make a practical psychology of criminal conduct available to today's policymakers. In the words of Andrews and Bonta, "There exists now an empirically defensible general psychology of criminal conduct (PCC) that is of practical value. . . . It should speak to policy advisors, policy-makers and legislators who must come to see that . . . human science is not just [a] relic of a positivistic past."[140] The major remaining issue "on which work is only beginning," say the authors, "is how to make use of what works."[141]

CRIMINAL PSYCHOLOGICAL PROFILING

During World War II, the War Department recruited psychologists and psychiatrists in an attempt to predict the future moves that the enemy forces might make. Psychological and psychoanalytic techniques were applied to the study of German leader Adolf Hitler, Italian leader Benito Mussolini, Japanese general and prime minister Hideki Tojo, and other Axis leaders. Such psychological profiling of enemy leaders may have given the allies the edge in battlefield strategy. Hitler, probably because of his heightened sensitivity to symbols, his strong belief in fate, and his German ancestry (Freud was Austrian), became the central figure that profilers analyzed.

Today, criminal **psychological profiling** is used to assist police investigators seeking to better understand individuals wanted for serious offenses. Criminal psychological profiling is also called "criminal profiling" and "behavioral profiling." During a recent interview, famed profiler John Douglas, the retired FBI special agent who became the model for the Scott Glenn character in Thomas Harris's *Silence of the Lambs,* described criminal profiling this way: "It is a behavioral composite put together of the unknown subject after analyzing the crime scene materials, to include the autopsy protocol, autopsy and crime scene photographs, as well as the preliminary police reports. It is also a detailed analysis of the victim and putting that information together. To me, it's very much like an internist in medicine who now attempts to put a diagnosis, say, on an illness; I'm trying to put a diagnosis on this particular case that's relative to motive, as well as the type of person(s) who would perpetrate that type of crime."[142]

Profilers develop a list of typical offender characteristics and other useful principles by analyzing crime scene and autopsy data in conjunction with interviews and other studies of past offenders. In general, the psychological profiling of criminal offenders is based on the belief that almost any form of conscious behavior, including each and every behavior engaged in by the offender during a criminal episode, is symptomatic of the individual's personality. Hence the way in which a kidnapper approaches his victims, for example, the manner of attack used by a killer, and the specific sexual activities of a rapist might all help paint a picture of the offender's motivations, personal characteristics, and likely future behavior. Sometimes psychological profiles can provide clues as to what an offender might do following an attack. Some offenders have been arrested, for example, after returning to the crime scene—a behavior typically predicted by specific behavioral clues left behind. Remorseful types can be expected to visit the victim's grave, permitting fruitful stakeouts of cemeteries.

While criminal profiling is not necessarily useful in every case, it can help narrow the search for an offender when used correctly in repetitive crimes involving an individual offender, such as serial rape or murder. Knowledge gleaned from profiling can also help in the interrogation of suspects and can be used to identify and protect possible victims before the offender has a chance to strike again.

Throughout the 1990s, the American public became enthralled with psychological profiling. A number of retired FBI profilers have written books and novels about their careers. One of the best known of these retired agents is John Douglas, who was mentioned earlier. Douglas's books include exposés of his profiling assignments and include *Mindhunter* (1996), *Journey into Darkness* (1997), and *Obsession* (1998). Another retired FBI profiler who helped popularize the field is Robert K. Ressler. Ressler's 1992 book, *Whoever Fights Monsters,*[143] a tale of his years at the FBI fighting serial killers, is often credited with having created much of the public's contemporary fascination with psychological profiling.

Although psychological profiling is a contemporary favorite of the entertainment media, profilers have also contributed significantly to the scientific literature in criminology. For example, in a well-known study of lust murderers (men who kill and often mutilate victims during or following a forced sexual episode), FBI Special Agents Robert R. Hazelwood and John E. Douglas distinguished between the organized nonsocial and the disorganized asocial types.[144] The organized nonsocial lust murderer was described as exhibiting complete indifference to the interests of society and as being completely self-centered. He was also said to be "methodical

John Douglas, the retired FBI profiler who became the model for the Scott Glenn character in Thomas Harris's *Silence of the Lambs,* shown with co-author Mark Olshanker. How does psychological profiling assist criminal investigators? *Carolyn Olshanker, Scribner Publishing*

The FBI released its long-awaited school threat assessment guide today, but it has sparked as much controversy as the subject it attempts to dissect.

The School Shooter: A Threat Assessment Perspective was authored by FBI behavioral profiler Mary Ellen O'Toole of the National Center for the Analysis of Violent Crime at Quantico, Va., in response to issues magnified by the April 20, 1999, deadly shootings at Columbine High School in Colorado.

O'Toole was unavailable today to comment on the completed report, but said in an extensive interview last year that she did not intend to "profile" the typical teenaged school shooter—an impossible task.

REPORT IDENTIFIES 60 TRAITS

Still, the final 45-page document written for educators, law enforcement and mental health professionals does contain a list of 60 behavioral or personality traits that she advises be considered after a student has made some type of threat. If a majority of the traits hold true, then a threat may be judged serious enough to involve police intervention, she wrote.

Many of the danger signs listed by the FBI imply a student's inability to cope with stress or strong emotions. Other listed traits judge a person's ego and capacity for compassion.

O'Toole further advises that a threat assessment coordinator be appointed by a school's administration. Threats received would be assembled by the coordinator and then presented to a "multidisciplinary team" consisting, she suggests, of school administrators and possibly a mental health professional, such as a school psychologist, and someone from law enforcement.

The team, under O'Toole's plan, would examine the threatener's personality and the dynamics of their family, school and social environments—all in the context of the primarily anti-social behavioral traits she has identified.

'SERIOUSLY FLAWED'

Kevin Dwyer of the National Mental Health Association, an advisor to O'Toole, said her final report is a better aide for law enforcement officers than anything previously published on school threat assessment, but is still seriously flawed. He said the FBI's 60 "descriptors," as he called them, are essentially broad assumptions about potential violent offenders based on FBI research gleaned from a study of 18 school shootings in recent years, including Columbine.

"You should not be making judgments from so few kids," Dwyer told APBnews.com. "If you took all those [school shooting incidents] together and you start making generalizations from those alone, that's an extreme mistake."

However, Dwyer said he approved of the team approach pitched by O'Toole because it reduces the likelihood of biases against a student and opens up possibilities for positive interventions, including mental health counseling or treatment for those who may not be violently inclined.

CLASSIFYING STUDENT THREATS

Once a threat has been received and the student's personality and interpersonal interactions evaluated, the school threat assessment team would then judge the seriousness of the threat itself, under O'Toole's proposal.

Threats would be judged as low, medium or high. An example of a "low" threat level might be a student who threatens the life of a classmate in an e-mail; a "medium" threat could be a student-made video, like the one created by Columbine killers Dylan Klebold and Eric Harris, showing the students dramatizing a mock shooting of classmates; a "high" level threat might be a phoned-in bomb threat, the guide states.

High-level threats should be immediately reported to law enforcement, O'Toole advised, but a medium level threat may not require that action.

"I THINK WE'RE GOING TO ALIENATE PEOPLE"

Montgomery County, Md., Police Capt. Drew Tracy, a recognized national expert in school threat assessment and tactical response, said he has grave concerns about the FBI's proposals, which could unfairly target kids who aren't a danger.

He said he hopes no one uses it as a set guide. In spite of assurances by the FBI and Attorney General Janet Reno, the FBI threat assessment model could stigmatize students, alienate parents and cause some teachers to look at a child who shows some of the traits the FBI lists as a potential legal liability, he said.

"Even if this checklist comes out, are we going to stop violence in the schools? No," Tracy said. "I think we're going to alienate people and run into problems."

He faulted O'Toole's examples of low, medium and high threats, saying a phoned-in bomb threat may not be as serious as a direct threat e-mailed to an individual.

Tracy said he also was concerned that the behavioral traits in the FBI threat assessment guide would have a negative impact when widely publicized by the news media.

"When you come out and label certain things, people throughout the country are going to look at this assessment by this knowledgeable individual and start thinking it's the Bible," Tracy said. "And if these people show three-quarters of these traits, 'Oh my God, this person is going to have problems.' "

"CRIMINALIZING KIDS' WORRIES"

Dwyer said some of Tracy's concerns are warranted, but the FBI guide will still be helpful for educators and cops.

"They'll at least be steered in a better direction than if they were looking at some of the materials that have been put out commercially and otherwise that use

(continued on the next page)

(continued from previous page)

a somewhat structured profiling process," he said.

But Dwyer said the emphasis on threat assessment and threat response fails to address threat prevention—helping to ensure that kids don't get to the point where making violent threats is appealing.

"The report3 doesn't do a good job of reinforcing that we have to teach kids to seek adult help when they're confused or upset," he said. "We're criminalizing kids'

worries and not giving them the vehicle to have that kind of communication."

Source: James Gordon Meek, "Should Educators Try to Identify 'High Threat' Students?," APB News, September 6, 2000. Reprinted with permission.

and cunning," as well as "fully cognizant of the criminality of his act and its impact on society." His counterpart, the disorganized asocial lust murderer, was described this way: "The disorganized asocial lust murderer exhibits primary characteristics of societal aversion. This individual prefers his own company to that of others and would be typified as a loner. He experiences difficulty in negotiating interpersonal relationships and consequently feels rejected and lonely. He lacks the cunning of the nonsocial type and commits the crime in a more frenzied and less methodical manner. The crime is likely to be committed in close proximity to his residence or place of employment, where he feels secure and more at ease."[145]

During the 1980s, the FBI led the movement to develop psychological profiling techniques through its concentration on violent sex offenders and arsonists. Today, much of that work continues at the Behavioral Science Unit (BSU) at the FBI's Training Academy in Quantico, Virginia. The official mission of the BSU is to develop and provide programs of training, research, and consultation in the behavioral and so-

cial sciences for the FBI and the law enforcement community that will improve or enhance their administration, operational effectiveness, and understanding of crime. The BSU's research work focuses on developing new and innovative investigative approaches and techniques to the solution of crime by studying the offender and his or her behavior and motivation. The instructors offer courses on Applied Criminal Psychology, Clinical Forensic Psychology, Community Policing and Problem-Solving Strategies, Crime Analysis, Death Investigation, Gangs and Gang Behavior, Interpersonal Violence, Research Methodology, Stress Management in Law Enforcement, and Violence in America. The BSU also coordinates with and supports other FBI units, such as the National Center for the Analysis of Violent Crime of the Critical Incident Response Group, which provides operational assistance to FBI field offices and law enforcement agencies. Visit the FBI's Behavioral Science Unit via Web Extra! 6-5.

Web Extra! 6-5 at crimtoday.com

SUMMARY

Psychological and psychiatric theories of criminal behavior emphasize individual propensities and characteristics in explanations of criminality. Whether the emphasis is on conditioned behavior, the development of parental attachment, or the psychoanalytic structure of the human personality, these approaches see the wellsprings of human motivation, desire, and behavioral choice as being firmly rooted in the personality. Some theorists now consider the state of psy-

chological criminology to be sufficiently advanced to allow for the development of a consistent and dependable social policy in the prediction of dangerousness and the rehabilitation of offenders. Similarly, the recent development of psychological profiling as a serious crime-fighting undertaking may soon change the nature of localized crime prevention strategies.

DISCUSSION QUESTIONS

1. This book emphasizes a social problems versus social responsibility theme. Which perspective is best supported by psychological theories of crime causation? Why?

2. How do psychological theories of criminal behavior differ from the other types of theories presented in this book? How do the various psychological and psychiatric approaches presented in this chapter differ from one another?

3. How would the perspectives discussed in this chapter suggest that offenders might be prevented from committing additional offenses? How might they be rehabilitated?

4. How can crime be a form of adaptation to one's environment? Why would an individual choose such a form of adaptation over others that might be available?

5. Which of the various standards for judging legal insanity discussed in this chapter do you find the most useful? Why?

WEB QUEST!

Visit *Psychiatric Times* on the World Wide Web at http://www.psychiatrictimes.com. Once there, locate the subject index by clicking on "Articles by Topic." Review the articles to find those that might contribute to your understanding of criminality. If your instructor asks you to, create an annotated bibliography which lists those articles, along with a brief description of each.

Alternatively, you might wish to visit the Attachment Library provided by the Departments of Psychology and Child Psychiatry at the State University of New York at Stony Brook. The library contains a great deal of information on attachment research, along with a gallery of attachment arti-

facts. It is available at http://www.psychology.sunysb.edu/ewaters/menus/online_articles.htm. The site contains an important series of articles concerning attachment theory. Included are documents entitled (1) "Mary Ainsworth Autobiography," (2) "Learning to Love," (3) "Explaining Disorganized Attachment," (4) "Sensitivity and Security in Colombia," (5) "Attachment and Socialization," (6) "Attachment as an Organizational Construct," (7) "Measuring Adult Attachment," (8) "Traits, Behavioral Systems, and Relationships," (9) "Origins of Attachment Theory," and (10) "Note on Security." If your instructor asks you to, review each of these articles, and write a brief summary of each.

LIBRARY EXTRAS!

The Library Extras! Listed here complement the Web Extras! found throughout this chapter. Library Extras! may be accessed on the Web at crimtoday.com.

Library Extra! 6-1. Kristen M. Beystehner, "Psychoanalysis: Freud's Revolutionary Approach to Human Personality" (online article, accessed March 10, 2001).

Library Extra! 6-2. Inge Bretherton, "The Origins of Attachment Theory: John Bowlby and Mary Ainsworth" (online article, accessed March 11, 2001).

Library Extra! 6-3. Michael W. Decaire, "Forensic Psychology: The Misunderstood Beast" (online article, accessed May 28, 2001).

Library Extra! 6-4. Michael Jonathan Grinfeld, "Bridging the Divide: Can Forensic Psychiatrists and Lawyers Just Get Along?" *Psychiatric Times*, Vol. 16, No. 8 (August 1999).

Library Extra! 6-5. Ralph Serin, "Can Criminal Psychopaths Be Identified?" (Correctional Service of Canada, 1999).

NOTES

1. George J. Church, "Sons and Murderers," *Time,* online edition, October 3, 1993.
2. Max G. Schlapp and Edward H. Smith, *The New Criminology* (New York: Boni and Liveright, 1928), p. 36.
3. To U.S. Senate Subcommittee on Juvenile Delinquency, *New York Post,* June 19, 1961. Quotation number 8572 in James B. Simpson, *Simpson's Contemporary Quotations* (Boston: Houghton Mifflin, 1988).
4. Gordon W. Allport, in the foreword to W. McCord & J. McCord, *The Psychopath* (New York: D. Van Nostrand Co., 1964).
5. Quoted in the San Francisco *Examiner & Chronicle,* November 18, 1975. Quotation number 1847 in James B. Simpson, *Simpson's Contemporary Quotations* (Boston: Houghton Mifflin, 1988).
6. Robert Anthony Phillips, "Children's Brutal Deaths Stun S.C. Town: Mother Charged with Hacking Daughter, Baby Son," APB News online, November 13, 2000. Web posted at http://apbnews.com/newscenter/breakingnews/2000/11/13/momkill1113_01.html. Accessed November 18, 2000.
7. "Police Fear Killings Span 10 Years," *USA Today,* July 26, 1991, p. 3A.
8. "Multilator 'Seemed So Natural,'" *Fayetteville* (N.C.) *Observer-Times,* July 28, 1991, p. 7A.
9. "Doctor: Dahmer Wanted to Freeze-Dry a Victim," *Fayetteville* (N.C.) *Observer-Times,* February 13, 1992, p. 7A.
10. "Psychiatrist: Dahmer Lacked Will to Stop," *Fayetteville* (N.C.) *Observer-Times,* February 4, 1992, p. 5A.
11. "Dahmer: 936 Years for 'Holocaust,'" *USA Today,* February 18, 1992, p. 1A.
12. Carlos Sanchez and Marylou Tousignant, "Jury Acquits Bobbitt; Discrepancies, Lack of Evidence Cited," *Washington Post* wire service, November 11, 1993.
13. Ibid.

[14] D. A. Andrews and James Bonta, *The Psychology of Criminal Conduct* (Cincinnati: Anderson, 1994), p. 69.

[15] See Adrian Raine, *The Psychopathology of Crime: Criminal Behavior as a Clinical Disorder* (Orlando, FL: Academic Press, 1993).

[16] American Board of Forensic Psychology, World Wide Web site at http://www.abfp.com/brochure.html. Accessed November 22, 2000.

[17] See the American Academy of Psychiatry and the Law, World Wide Web site at http://www.cc.emory.edu/AAPL. Accessed December 20, 2000.

[18] Cathy Spatz Widom and Hans Toch, "The Contribution of Psychology to Criminal Justice Education," *Journal of Criminal Justice Education,* Vol. 4, No. 2 (fall 1993), p. 253.

[19] Curt R. Bartol, *Criminal Behavior: A Psychosocial Approach,* 3rd ed. (Englewood Cliffs, NJ: Prentice Hall, 1991), p. 16.

[20] For additional information, see S. Giora Shoham and Mark C. Seis, *A Primer in the Psychology of Crime* (New York: Harrow and Heston, 1993); and Frederic L. Faust, "A Review of *A Primer in the Psychology of Crime,*" *Social Pathology,* Vol. 1, No. 1 (January 1995), pp. 48–61.

[21] Nicole Hahn Rafter, "Psychopathy and the Evolution of Criminological Knowledge," *Theoretical Criminology,* Vol. 1, No. 2 (May 1997), p. 236.

[22] Nolan D. C. Lewis, "Foreword," in David Abrahamsen, *Crime and the Human Mind* (1944; reprint, Montclair, NJ: Patterson Smith, 1969), p. vii.

[23] As noted by Rafter, "Psychopathy and the Evolution of Criminological Knowledge." See Richard von Krafft-Ebing, *Psychopathia Sexualis* (1886; reprint, New York: Stein and Day, 1965); and Richard von Krafft-Ebing, *Textbook of Insanity* (Germany, 1879; reprint, Philadelphia: F. A. Davis, 1904).

[24] Bernard H. Glueck, *Studies in Forensic Psychiatry* (Boston: Little, Brown, 1916).

[25] William Healy, *The Individual Delinquent* (Boston: Little, Brown, 1915).

[26] Early writings about the psychopathic personality focused almost exclusively on men, and most psychiatrists appeared to believe that very few women (if any) possessed such traits.

[27] David Abrahamsen, *Crime and the Human Mind* (1944; reprint, Montclair, NJ: Patterson Smith, 1969), p. 23.

[28] Hervey M. Cleckley, *The Mask of Sanity,* 4th ed. (St. Louis: C. V. Mosby, 1964).

[29] Quoted in Joseph P. Newman and Chad A. Brinkley, "Psychopathy: Rediscovering Cleckley's Construct," *Psychopathology Research,* Vol. 9, No. 1 (March 1998).

[30] Ibid.

[31] Gwynn Nettler, *Killing One Another* (Cincinnati: Anderson, 1982), p. 179.

[32] Ralph Serin, "Can Criminal Psychopaths Be Identified?" Correctional Service of Canada, October 22, 1999. Web posted at http://www.csc-scc.gc.ca/text/pblct/forum/e012/e0121.shtml. Accessed December 20, 2000.

[33] American Psychiatric Association, *Diagnostic and Statistical Manual of Mental Disorders,* 2nd ed. (Washington, D.C.: American Psychiatric Association, 1968).

[34] Ibid., p. 43.

[35] See Internet Mental Health, "Disorders: European Description." Web posted at http://www.mentalhealth.com/icd. Accessed January 5, 2001.

[36] Robert D. Hare, "Psychopathy and Antisocial Personality Disorder: A Case of Diagnostic Confusion," *Psychiatric Times,* Vol. 13, No. 2 (February 1996).

[37] Albert I. Rabin, "The Antisocial Personality— Psychopathy and Sociopathy," in Hans Toch, *Psychology of Crime and Criminal Justice* (Prospect Heights, IL: Waveland, 1979), p. 330.

[38] Especially Hare's Revised Psychopathy Checklist, also called the Psychopathy Checklist—Revised (PCL-R). The PCL-R provides a numerical score reflecting the degree to which a person's symptoms match the traditional clinical conception of psychopathy. This score can be statistically analyzed into two factors, one covering attitudes and feelings, the other covering socially deviant behavior.

[39] For recent research in this area, see A. Tengstrom et al., "Psychopathy (PCL-R) as a Predictor of Violent Recidivism among Criminal Offenders with Schizophrenia in Sweden," *Law and Behavior,* Vol. 24, No. 1 (2000), pp. 45–58. For additional information, see V. L. Quinsey et al., *Violent Offenders: Appraising and Managing Risk* (Washington, D.C.: American Psychological Association, 1998); and V. L. Quinsey, M. E. Rice, and G. T. Harris, "Actuarial Prediction of Sexual Recidivism," *Journal of Interpersonal Violence,* Vol. 10, No. 1 (1995), pp. 85–105.

[40] R. D. Hare, *Psychopathy: Theory and Research* (New York: John Wiley and Sons, 1970).

[41] L. N. Robins, *Deviant Children Grow Up* (Baltimore: Williams and Wilkins, 1966).

[42] S. B. Guze, *Criminality and Psychiatric Disorders* (New York: Oxford University Press, 1976).

[43] S. Hodgins and G. Cote, "The Prevalence of Mental Disorders among Penitentiary Inmates in Quebec," *Canada's Mental Health,* Vol. 38 (1990), pp. 1–4.

[44] H. Prins, *Offenders, Deviants or Patients? An Introduction to the Study of Socio-Forensic Problems* (London: Tavistock, 1980).

[45] Hans J. Eysenck, *Crime and Personality* (Boston: Houghton Mifflin, 1964).

[46] Hans J. Eysenck, "Personality and Criminality: A Dispositional Analysis," in William S. Laufer and Freda Adler, eds., *Advances in Criminology Theory,* vol. 1 (New Brunswick, NJ: Transaction, 1989), p. 90.

[47] Eysenck, *Crime and Personality,* pp. 35–36.

[48] Ibid., p. 92.

[49] Ibid., p. 53, citing J. B. S. Haldane, "Foreword," to Johannes Lange, *Crime as Destiny: A Study of Criminal Twins* (London: G. Allen and Unwin, 1931), p. 53.

[50] Abrahamsen, *Crime and the Human Mind,* p. vii.

51 P. Q. Roche, *The Criminal Mind: A Study of Communications between Criminal Law and Psychiatry* (New York: Grove Press, 1958), p. 52.

52 "Nationline: Book Thief," *USA Today,* August 1, 1991, p. 3A.

53 Anne Sciater, "Torturer-Killer Wants to Die Today, as Scheduled," *USA Today,* April 15, 1997, p. 2A.

54 Nettler, *Killing One Another,* p. 159.

55 Ibid., p. 155.

56 Abrahamsen, *Crime and the Human Mind,* p. 99.

57 Ibid., p. 100.

58 J. Dollard et al., *Frustration and Aggression* (New Haven, CT: Yale University Press, 1939).

59 Carl Weiser, "This Is What You Get for Firing Me!" *USA Today,* January 28, 1993, p. 3A.

60 Andrew F. Henry and James F. Short, Jr., *Suicide and Homicide: Economic, Sociological, and Psychological Aspects of Aggression* (Glencoe, IL: Free Press, 1954).

61 Stewart Palmer, *A Study of Murder* (New York: Crowell, 1960).

62 Abrahamsen, *Crime and the Human Mind,* p. 26.

63 Nancy Gibbs, "The Devil's Disciple," *Time,* January 11, 1993, p. 40.

64 Seymour L. Halleck, *Psychiatry and the Dilemmas of Crime: A Study of Causes, Punishment and Treatment* (Berkeley: University of California Press, 1971).

65 Ibid., p. 77.

66 Ibid., p. 78.

67 Ibid., p. 80.

68 Ibid.

69 Ibid.

70 Arnold S. Linsky, Ronet Bachman, and Murray A. Straus, *Stress, Culture, and Aggression* (New Haven, CT: Yale University Press, 1995).

71 Ibid., p. 7.

72 Adapted from Richard Danielson, "Programmed to Kill," *St. Petersburg Times,* March 22, 2000. Web posted at http://www.sptimes.com/News/032200/Floridian/Programmed_to_kill.shtml. Accessed December 5, 2000.

73 "Who Is Michael Carneal?" CNN Interactive, December 3, 1997. Web posted at http://www.cnn.com/US/9712/03/school.shooting.pm. Accessed December 5, 2000.

74 Gabriel Tarde, *The Laws of Imitation,* trans. E. C. Parsons (1890; reprint, Gloucester, MA: Peter Smith, 1962).

75 Albert Bandura, "The Social Learning Perspective: Mechanisms of Aggression," in Hans Toch, *Psychology of Crime and Criminal Justice,* (Prospect Heights, IL: Waveland, 1979), p. 198.

76 Ibid., p. 199.

77 M. M. Lefkowitz et al., "Television Violence and Child Aggression: A Follow-up Study," in G. A. Comstock and E. A. Rubinstein, eds., *Television and Social Behavior,* Vol. 3 (Washington, D.C.: U.S. Government Printing Office, 1972), pp. 35–135.

78 Aminah Franklin, "Brutal, Cowardly Murder: Police Say Threats Preceded Slaying of Salisbury Family," *Morning Call,* March 1, 1995, p. A1.

79 Ibid.

80 David Washburn, "Brothers Cultivated Defiant Attitude," *Morning Call,* March 1, 1995, p. A4.

81 Widom and Toch, "The Contribution of Psychology to Criminal Justice Education."

82 Ibid., p. 253.

83 C. R. Hollin, *Psychology and Crime: An Introduction to Criminological Psychology* (London: Routledge, 1989), p. 42.

84 Widom and Toch, p. 254.

85 "15-Year-Old Killer Feared Being Called a 'Little Punk,'" *Fayetteville* (N.C.) *Observer-Times,* December 26, 1993, p. 1A.

86 See Mary D. Salter Ainsworth, "John Bowlby, 1907–1990," *American Psychologist,* Vol. 47 (1992), p. 668.

87 John Bowlby, "The Nature of the Child's Tie to Its Mother," *International Journal of Psycho-Analysis,* Vol. 39 (1958), pp. 350–373.

88 See John Bowlby, *Maternal Care and Mental Health,* World Health Organization Monograph (1951); and John Bowlby, *A Secure Base* (New York: Basic Books, 1988).

89 Bowlby, *A Secure Base,* p. 11.

90 David P. Farrington and Donald J. West, "Effects of Marriage, Separation, and Children on Offending by Adult Males," *Current Perspectives on Aging and the Life Cycle,* Vol. 4 (1995), pp. 249–281.

91 Stephen A. Cernkovich and Peggy C. Giordano, "Family Relationships and Delinquency," *Criminology,* Vol. 25 (1987), pp. 295–313.

92 Roy F. Baumeister and Julie Juola Exline, "Self-Control, Morality, and Human Strength," *Journal of Social and Clinical Psychology,* Vol. 19, No. 1 (April 2000), pp. 29–42.

93 Ibid.

94 See R. F. Baumeister, T. F. Heatherton, and D. Tice, *Losing Control: How and Why People Fail at Self-Regulation* (San Diego: Academic Press, 1994).

95 Teresa C. LaGrange and Robert A. Silverman, "Low Self-Control and Opportunity: Testing the General Theory of Crime as an Explanation for Gender Differences in Delinquency," *Criminology,* Vol. 37, No. 1 (1999), p. 41.

96 M. R. Gottfredson and Travis Hirschi, *A General Theory of Crime* (Stanford, CA: Stanford University Press, 1990).

97 Ibid.

98 Douglas Longshore, "Self-Control and Criminal Opportunity: A Prospective Test of the General Theory of Crime," *Social Problems,* Vol. 45, No. 1 (February 1998), pp. 102–114.

99 Gottfredson and Hirschi, *A General Theory of Crime,* p. 88.

100 Longshore, "Self-Control and Criminal Opportunity."

101 Harold G. Grasmick et al., "Testing the Core Empirical Implications of Gottfredson and Hirschi's General Theory of Crime," *Journal of Research in Crime and Delinquency,* Vol. 30 (1993), pp. 5–29.

[102] Citing Gottfredson and Hirschi, *A General Theory of Crime*, p. 89.

[103] In civil proceedings, however, the state may confine a mentally ill person if it shows "by clear and convincing evidence that the individual is mentally ill and dangerous." *Jones* v. *U.S.*, 463 U.S. 354 (1983).

[104] *Foucha* v. *Louisiana*, 504 U.S. 71 (1992), Justices Kennedy and Rhenquist's dissenting opinion.

[105] *Leland* v. *Oregon*, 343 U.S. 790 (1952).

[106] *Riggins* v. *Nevada*, 504 U.S. 127 (1992).

[107] 18 U.S.C. § 17.

[108] See, for example, *U.S.* v. *Pohlot*, 827 F.2d 889, 897 (3d Cir. 1987), cert. denied, 484 U.S. 1011, 108 S.Ct. 710, 98 L.Ed.2d 660 (1988).

[109] 18 U.S.C. § 401.

[110] 18 U.S.C. §§ 17 and 4242(b).

[111] *Terrance Frank* v. *U.S.*, no. 91-8230. Decided October 13, 1992.

[112] October 12, 1984, P.L. 98-473, title II, Sec. 403(a), 98 Stat. 2057.

[113] Halleck, *Psychiatry and the Dilemmas of Crime*, p. 213.

[114] *Durham* v. *U.S.*, 214 F.2d 862 (D.C. Cir. 1954).

[115] American Law Institute, *Model Penal Code: Official Draft and Explanatory Notes* (Philadelphia: The Institute, 1985).

[116] *U.S.* v. *Brawner*, 471 F.2d 969 (D.C. Cir. 1972).

[117] June 25, 1948, Ch. 645, 62 Stat. 855; Oct. 12, 1984, P.L. 98-473, title II, § 403(a), 98 Stat. 2059; November 18, 1988, P.L. 100-690, title VII, § 7043, 102 Stat. 4400.

[118] See, for example, D. P. Farrington, "Childhood Aggression and Adult Violence: Early Precursors and Later Life Outcomes," in D. J. Pepler and K. H. Rubin, eds., *The Development and Treatment of Childhood Aggression* (Hillsdale, NJ: Erlbaum, 1990), pp. 2–29; and R. E. Tremblay et al., "Early Disruptive Behavior: Poor School Achievement, Delinquent Behavior and Delinquent Personality: Longitudinal Analyses," *Journal of Consulting and Clinical Psychology*, Vol. 60, No. 1 (1992), pp. 64–72.

[119] R. Loeber, "Questions and Advances in the Study of Developmental Pathways," in D. Cicchetti and S. Toth, eds., *Models and Integration: Rochester Symposium on Developmental Psychopathology* (Rochester, NY: University of Rochester Press, 1991), pp. 97–115.

[120] "State Probing Release of Molester Now Charged with Murder," United Press International wire service, Southwestern edition, September 24, 1993.

[121] "Texas Executes Convicted Killer Who Waived Appeals," Reuters wire service, Western edition, November 10, 1993.

[122] Christine Spolar, "California Town Cries as Polly Klaas Is Found; Twice-Convicted Suspect Faces Murder, Kidnapping Charges in Abduction of 12-Year-Old," *Washington Post* wire service, December 6, 1993.

[123] Jennifer L. White et al., "How Early Can We Tell? Predictors of Childhood Conduct Disorder and Adolescent Delinquency," *Criminology*, Vol. 28, No. 4 (1990), pp. 507–528.

[124] Daniel S. Nagin and David P. Farrington, "The Stability of Criminal Potential from Childhood to Adulthood," *Criminology*, Vol. 30, No. 2 (1992), pp. 235–260.

[125] Paul Gendreau, Tracy Little, and Claire Goggin, "A Meta-Analysis of the Predictors of Adult Offender Recidivism: What Works!" *Criminology*, Vol. 34, No. 4 (November 1996), pp. 575–607.

[126] For one of the first and still definitive works in the area of selective incapacitation, see Peter Greenwood and Allan Abrahamsen, *Selective Incapacitation* (Santa Monica, CA: Rand, 1982).

[127] M. A. Peterson, H. B. Braiker, and S. M. Polich, *Who Commits Crimes?* (Cambridge: Oelgeschlager, Gunn and Hain, 1981).

[128] Jeremy Travis, "But They All Come Back," papers from the Executive Session on Sentencing and Corrections, No. 7 (Washington, D.C.: National Institute of Justice, 2000).

[129] J. Monahan, *Predicting Violent Behavior: An Assessment of Clinical Techniques* (Beverly Hills, CA: Sage, 1981).

[130] The 1984 Amendment to § 200 of Title II (Sec. 200-2304) of P.L. 98-473 is popularly referred to as the "1984 Comprehensive Crime Control Act."

[131] U.S. Sentencing Commission, *Federal Sentencing Guidelines Manual* (Washington, DC: U.S. Government Printing Office, 1987), p. 10.

[132] Jill Peay, "Dangerousness—Ascription or Description," in M. P. Feldman, ed., *Developments in the Study of Criminal Behavior*, Vol. 2, *Violence* (New York: John Wiley and Sons, 1982), p. 211, citing N. Walker, "Dangerous People," *International Journal of Law and Psychiatry*, Vol. 1 (1978), pp. 37–50.

[133] See, for example, Michael Gottfredson and Travis Hirschi, *A General Theory of Crime* (Stanford, CA: Stanford University Press, 1990); and Travis Hirschi and Michael Gottfredson, "Age and the Explanation of Crime," *American Journal of Sociology*, Vol. 89 (1983), pp. 552–584.

[134] David F. Greenberg, "Modeling Criminal Careers," *Criminology*, Vol. 29, No. 1 (1991), p. 39.

[135] Andrews and Bonta, *The Psychology of Criminal Conduct*.

[136] Ibid., p. 1.

[137] Ibid.

[138] Ibid., pp. 20–21.

[139] Ibid., p. 227.

[140] Ibid., p. 227.

[141] Ibid., p. 236.

[142] Interviewed by Amy Goldman, February 27, 1998. Web posted at http://www.serialkillers.net/interviews/jdouglas2bak.html. Accessed December 20, 2000.

[143] Robert K. Ressler and Tom Shachtman, *Whoever Fights Monsters* (New York: St. Martin's Press, 1992).

[144] Robert R. Hazelwood and John E. Douglas, "The Lust Murderer," *FBI Law Enforcement Bulletin* (Washington, D.C.: U.S. Department of Justice, April 1980).

[145] Ibid.

If we would change the amount of crime in the community, we must change the community.

—Frank Tannenbaum[1]

Society prepares the crime; the criminal commits it.

—Chinese Proverb

sociological theories I: social structure

CHAPTER 7

> I got a 14-shot Beretta, and I ain't worried about no
> police or anybody else.
>
> —Broadway Gangster Crip Member "Antoine"[2]

KEY CONCEPTS

IMPORTANT TERMS

anomie	ecological theories	social pathology
broken windows thesis	environmental criminology	social processes
Chicago Area Project	focal concerns	social structure
Chicago School of criminology	illegitimate opportunity structure	social structure theories
conduct norms	reaction formation	sociological theories
criminology of place	relative deprivation	strain theory
cultural transmission	social disorganization	subcultural theory
culture conflict theory	social disorganization theory	subculture
defensible space	social ecology	techniques of neutralization
distributive justice	social life	

IMPORTANT NAMES

Robert Agnew	Robert K. Merton	W. I. Thomas
Ernest Burgess	Walter B. Miller	Frederic M. Thrasher
Richard A. Cloward	Lloyd E. Ohlin	William F. Whyte
Albert Cohen	Robert Park	Marvin Wolfgang
Franco Ferracuti	Thorsten Sellin	Florian Znaniecki
David Matza	Clifford Shaw	
Henry McKay	Gresham Sykes	

OUTCOMES

LEARNING

After reading this chapter, you should be able to

- ◆ Explain how the organization and structure of society may contribute to criminality
- ◆ Identify the role that cultural differences play in crime causation
- ◆ Distinguish between a number of social structure theories of criminal behavior
- ◆ Identify modern-day social policy that reflects the social structure approach
- ◆ Assess the shortcomings of the social structure approach

Hear the author discuss this chapter at *crimtoday.com*

INTRODUCTION

In late July 1993, a tourist traveling home to Mint Hill, North Carolina, from the state's seacoast city of Wilmington, a couple of hundred miles away, was robbed and shot while he napped during a rest period on the shoulder of state Route 74. The murder, like the 22 others committed that year in rural Robeson County, North Carolina, would have attracted little attention outside of the local area had it not been for the fact that the dead tourist was 57-year-old James Jordan, father of Chicago Bulls basketball superstar Michael Jordan. After Jordan was killed, his body was dumped 25 miles away

in South Carolina's Gum Swamp Creek. The new red Lexus sport coupe that Jordan had been driving showed up later, apparently stripped by teenagers acquainted with the killers.

Two local 18-year-olds, Larry Martin Demery and Daniel Andre Green (AKA Lord D.A.A.S. U'allah), were quickly arrested and charged with Jordan's murder. Both had long records of trouble with the law. Demery, a lanky native American with a Guns N' Roses tattoo on his right forearm, was out of work and on parole for check forgery at the time of the murder. In the year preceding the crime, Demery had been charged with four other felonies, ranging from armed robbery to breaking and entering.[3] In one crime attributed to Demery, the robbery of a convenience store, a 61-year-old clerk was struck on the head with a cinder block and seriously injured. When Demery was arrested in the Jordan case, police were already looking for him on four other warrants, all issued for failure to appear for trial on more than a dozen occasions.

Daniel Green's record of law violations was even more serious. In the ninth grade, the semiliterate Green was suspended for assaulting the school's principal. He promptly dropped out of school. Shortly afterward, in 1991, Green was convicted of assault with intent to kill after he pleaded guilty to charges of beating a friend with the blunt side of an axe. The friend, Robert Ellison, 18, was in a coma for months, and Green spent two and one-half years in prison for assault. Shortly before Jordan was killed, Demery and Green robbed a convenience store. Green shot store clerk Clewis Demory three times for no apparent reason. Demery and Green's life of crime came to an abrupt halt when Demery pleaded guilty to first-degree murder and nine other felonies and then turned state's witness in a plea bargain which helped prosecutors build a case against Green. Even without a plea bargain, the evidence against the two was strong. A confiscated home video made shortly after Jordan's death showed Green dancing and rapping while wearing Michael Jordan's NBA ring and watch and using his golf equipment—items that had been in James Jordan's car when he was slain. Trial testimony revealed that Green and Demery drove around in Jordan's Lexus for four days after the killing, picking up dates and talking on the dead man's cellular phone. Green even wore the victim's pants, which had been stolen from the Lexus, to court during trial.[4] In 1996, Green was convicted of murdering Jordan and was sentenced to life plus ten years in prison. Demery received a life sentence. A year after going to prison, Demery was back in court, where he was sentenced to another 40 years in prison for a string of robberies and assaults committed before the Jordan slaying.

Although features of individual personality can always be identified as contributing factors in almost any crime, the motivation behind the killing of James Jordan may have arisen out of social and economic deprivation. Both Green and Demery were born into relative poverty. Both came from families lacking in educational achievement and in the basic skills needed for success in the modern world. Advocates of a social structure approach to explaining crime might well argue that poverty, academic failure, and subcultural values that focused on greed and excitement dictated the direction that the lives of Green and Demery would take—and all but ensured their fateful encounter with James Jordan that sultry July afternoon.

MAJOR PRINCIPLES OF SOCIOLOGICAL THEORIES

Theories that explain crime by reference to social structure are only one of three major sociological approaches to crime causation. (We will describe the other two in Chapters 8 and 9.) Before proceeding, however, it seems best to discuss some of the general features of the sociological viewpoint. Although sociological perspectives on crime causation are quite diverse, most build upon the following assumptions:

- Social groups, social institutions, the arrangements of society, and social roles all provide the proper focus for criminological study.
- Group dynamics, group organization, and subgroup relationships form the causal nexus out of which crime develops.
- The structure of society and its relative degree of organization or disorganization are important factors contributing to the prevalence of criminal behavior.
- Although it may be impossible to predict the specific behavior of a given individual, statistical estimates of group characteristics are possible. Hence the probability that a member of a given group will engage in a specific type of crime can be estimated.

Ecological theories suggest that crime shows an unequal geographic distribution. Why might certain geographic areas be associated with specific patterns of crime? *Peter Turnley, Corbis*

Sociological theories examine institutional arrangements within society (that is, **social structure**) and the interaction between and among social institutions, individuals, and groups (that is, **social processes**) as they affect socialization and have an impact on social behavior (that is, **social life**). Sociological theories are keenly interested in the nature of existing power relationships between social groups and in the influences that various social phenomena bring to bear on the types of behaviors that tend to characterize *groups* of people. In contrast to more individualized psychological theories, which have what is called a "micro" focus, sociological approaches utilize a "macro" perspective, stressing the type of behavior likely to be exhibited by group members rather than attempting to predict the behavior of specific individuals.

As noted in Chapter 1, sociological thought has influenced criminological theory construction more significantly than any other perspective during the past half century. This has probably been due, at least in part, to a widespread American concern with social problems, including civil rights, the women's movement, issues of poverty, and the decline in influence experienced by many traditional social institutions, such as the family, government, organized religion, and educational institutions.

Although all sociological perspectives on crime share the characteristics identified in this section, particular theories give greater or lesser weight to selected components of social life. Hence we can identify three key sociological explanations for crime:

- Crime is the result of an individual's location within the structure of society. This approach focuses on the social and economic conditions of life, including poverty, alienation, social disorganization, weak social control, personal frustration, relative deprivation, differential opportunity, alternative means to success, and deviant subcultures and subcultural values that conflict with conventional values. (These are the primary features of *social structure theories*, which are discussed in this chapter.)
- Crime is the end product of various social processes, especially inappropriate socialization and social learning. This approach stresses the role of interpersonal relationships, the strength of the social bond, a lack of self-control, and the personal and group consequences of societal reactions to deviance as they contribute to crime. (These are the primary characteristics of *social process theories* and *social development theories*, which are discussed in Chapter 8.)
- Crime is the product of class struggle. This perspective emphasizes the nature of existing power relationships between social groups, the distribution of wealth within society, the ownership of the means of production, and the economic and social structure of society as it relates to social class and social control. (These are the primary features of *conflict theories*, which are discussed in Chapter 9.)

SOCIAL STRUCTURE THEORIES

The theories in this chapter are termed **social structure theories** because they explain crime by reference to the institutional structure of society. They name the various formal and informal arrangements between social groups as the root causes of crime and deviance. Although different kinds of social structure theories have been advanced to explain crime, they all have one thing in common: They highlight those aspects of society that contribute to the low socioeconomic status of identifiable groups as significant causes of crime. Social structure theorists view members of socially and economically disadvantaged groups as being more likely to commit crime, and they see economic and social disenfranchisement as fundamental causes of crime. Poverty, lack of education, an absence of salable skills, and subcultural values conducive to crime are all thought to be predicated on the social conditions surrounding early life experiences, and they provide the causal underpinnings of social structure theories. Environmental influences, socialization, and traditional and accepted patterns of behavior are all used by social structuralists to portray the criminal as a product of his or her social environment and to depict criminality as a form of acquired behavior. Social injustice, racism, and feelings of disenfranchisement may play important roles in crime by perpetuating the conditions that cause it. From a social structure perspective, crime is seen largely as a lower-class phenomenon, while the criminality of the middle and upper classes is generally discounted as less serious, less frequent, and less dangerous.

TYPES OF SOCIAL STRUCTURE THEORIES

This chapter describes three major types of social structure theories: (1) social disorganization theories (also called "ecological approaches"), (2) strain theories, and (3) culture conflict perspectives (also called "cultural deviance" theories). All share a number of elements in common, and the classification of a theory into one subcategory or another is often a matter of which aspects a writer chooses to emphasize rather than the result of any clear-cut definitional elements inherent in the perspectives themselves.

Social Disorganization Theory

The first type of social structure approach discussed in this chapter, **social disorganization theory**, is closely associated with the ecological school of criminology. Much early criminology in the United States is rooted in the study of urban settlements and communities[5] and in the human ecology movement of the early twentieth century. The idea of the community as a functional whole which directly determines the quality of life for its members was developed and ex-

THEORY IN PERSPECTIVE
Types of Social Structure Theories

SOCIAL STRUCTURE APPROACHES

emphasize the role of poverty, lack of education, absence of marketable skills, and subcultural values as fundamental causes of crime. Social structure approaches portray crime as the result of an individual's location within the structure of society and focus on the social and economic conditions of life.

■ **SOCIAL DISORGANIZATION.** Depicts social change, social conflict, and the lack of social consensus as the root causes of crime and deviance. An offshoot, social ecology, sees society as a kind of organism and crime and deviance as a kind of disease or social pathology.

PERIOD:	1920s–1930s
THEORISTS:	Robert Park, Ernest Burgess, W. I. Thomas, Florian Znaniecki, Clifford Shaw, Henry McKay
CONCEPTS:	Social ecology, ecological theories, social pathology, social disorganization, Chicago School of criminology, Chicago Area Project, demographics, concentric zones, delinquency areas, cultural transmission (Criminology of place, environmental criminology, defensible space, and the broken windows thesis represent, at least in part, a contemporary reinterpretation of early ecological notions.)

■ **STRAIN THEORY.** Points to a lack of fit between socially approved success goals and the availability of socially approved means to achieve those goals. As a consequence, according to the perspective of strain theory, individuals who are unable to succeed through legitimate means turn to other avenues that promise economic and social recognition.

PERIOD:	1930s–present
THEORISTS:	Robert K. Merton, Steven F. Messner, Richard Rosenfeld, Peter Blau and Judith Blau, Robert Agnew
CONCEPTS:	Anomie, goals, means, innovation, retreatism, ritualism, rebellion, differential opportunity, relative deprivation, distributive justice, general strain theory (GST)

■ **CULTURE CONFLICT.** Sees the root cause of crime in a clash of values between variously socialized groups over what is acceptable or proper behavior.

PERIOD:	1920s–present
THEORISTS:	Thorsten Sellin, Frederic M. Thrasher, William F. Whyte, Walter Miller, Gresham Sykes, David Matza, Franco Ferracuti, Marvin Wolfgang, Richard A. Cloward, Lloyd E. Ohlin, Albert Cohen, many others
CONCEPTS:	Subculture, violent subcultures, socialization, focal concerns, delinquency and drift, techniques of neutralization, illegitimate opportunity structures, reaction formation, conduct norms

plored around the beginning of the twentieth century by sociologists like Emile Durkheim (1858–1917),[6] Ferdinand Toennies (1855–1936),[7] and Georg Simmel (1858–1918).[8] Durkheim believed that crime was a normal part of all societies and that law was a symbol of social solidarity. Hence, for Durkheim, an act is "criminal when it offends strong and defined states of the collective conscience."[9]

Some of the earliest sociologists to study American communities were **W. I. Thomas** and **Florian Znaniecki**. In *The Polish Peasant in Europe and America,* Thomas and Znaniecki described the problems Polish immigrants faced

in the early 1900s when they left their homeland and moved to American cities.[10] The authors noted how rates of crime rose among people who had been so displaced, and they hypothesized that the cause was the **social disorganization** which resulted from immigrants' inability to successfully transplant guiding norms and values from their home cultures into the new one. Learn more about early social disorganization perspectives via Web Extra! 7-1.

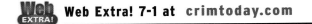

Web Extra! 7-1 at **crimtoday.com**

Read more about classical sociological theory at Web Extra! 7-2.

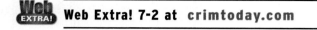

Web Extra! 7-2 at crimtoday.com

The Chicago School

Some of the earliest sociological theories to receive widespread recognition can be found in the writings of **Robert Park** and **Ernest Burgess.**[11] In the 1920s and 1930s, Park and Burgess, through their work at the University of Chicago, developed what became known as **social ecology,** or the ecological school of criminology. The social ecology movement, which was influenced by the work of biologists on the interaction of organisms with their environments, concerned itself with how the structure of society adapts to the quality of natural resources and to the existence of other human groups.[12] As one writer puts it, social ecology is "the attempt to link the structure and organization of any human community to interactions with its localized environment."[13] Because ecological models build upon an organic analogy, it is easy to portray social disorganization as disease or pathology.[14] Hence social ecologists who studied crime developed a disease model built around the concept of **social pathology.** In its initial statement, social pathology was defined as "those human actions which run contrary to the ideals of residential stability, property ownership, sobriety, thrift, habituation to work, small business enterprise, sexual discretion, family solidarity, neighborliness, and discipline of will."[15] The term referred simply to behavior not in keeping with the prevalent norms and values of the social group. Over time, however, the concept of social pathology changed, and it came to represent the idea that aspects of society may be somehow pathological, or "sick," and may produce deviant behavior among individuals and groups who live under or are exposed to such social conditions.

Social disorganization and, therefore, social pathology may arise when a group is faced with "social change, uneven development of culture, maladaptiveness, disharmony, conflict, and lack of consensus."[16] Due to the rapid influx of immigrant populations at the beginning of the twentieth century, American cities were caught up in swift social change, and Park and Burgess saw in them an ideal focus for the study of social disorganization. Park and Burgess viewed cities in terms of concentric zones, which were envisioned much like the circles on a target (see Figure 7-1). Each zone had its unique characteristics wherein unique populations and typical forms of behavior could be found. Park and Burgess referred to the central business zone as Zone I, or the "loop," in which retail businesses and light manufacturing were typically located. Zone II, surrounding the city center, was home to recent immigrant groups and was characterized by deteriorated housing, factories, and abandoned buildings. It was portrayed as being in transition from residential to business uses. Zone III contained mostly working-class tenements, while Zone IV was occupied by middle-class citizens

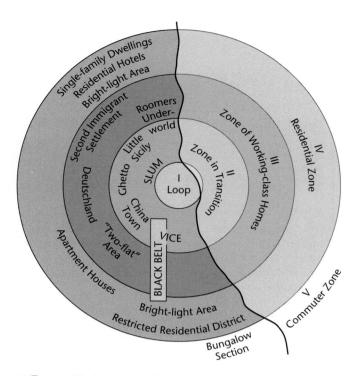

■ **FIGURE 7-1** CHICAGO'S CONCENTRIC ZONES.
Source: Robert E. Park, Ernest W. Burgess, and R. D. McKenzie, *The City* (Chicago: University of Chicago Press, 1925), p. 55. Copyright © University of Chicago Press. Reprinted with permission.

with single-family homes, each with their own yards and garages. Zone V, consisting largely of suburbs, was called the "commuter zone." Significantly, Park and Burgess noticed that residents of inner-city zones tend to migrate to outer zones as their economic positions improve.

Clifford Shaw and **Henry McKay,** other early advocates of the ecological approach, applied the concentric zone model to the study of juvenile delinquency. They conducted empirical studies of arrest rates for juveniles in Chicago during the years 1900–1906, 1917–1923, and 1927–1933. These years were associated with high rates of neighborhood transition, during which one immigrant group after another moved in rapid succession from the inner city toward the suburbs—a process that was repeated with the arrival of each new wave of immigrants. Shaw and McKay found that rates of offending remained relatively constant over time within zones of transition, and they concluded, therefore, that delinquency was caused by the nature of the environment in which immigrants lived rather than by some characteristic of the immigrant groups themselves.[17] Shaw and McKay saw social disorganization as the inability of local communities to solve common problems, and they believed that the degree of disorganization in a community was largely predicated upon the extent of residential mobility and racial heterogeneity present in that community. In effect, as a new immigrant group, like the Polish, replaced an old immigrant group, like the Irish, and became dominant in a particular location, the process of succession was complete. As a result of their studies, they developed the idea of **cultural transmission,** which held that traditions of delinquency are transmitted through successive generations of the same zone in the same way that language, roles, and attitudes are communicated.

Because early **ecological theories,** including those of Park and Burgess, were developed through a close focus on selected geographic locals, the methodology upon which they were predicated came to be known as "area studies;" and because 1920s Chicago served as the model for most such studies, they were soon collectively referred to as the **Chicago School of criminology.** Although the applicability of these early studies to other cities or to other time periods was questionable, it was generally accepted that the Chicago School had demonstrated the tendency for criminal activity to be associated with urban transition zones which, because of the turmoil or social disorganization that characterized them, were typified by lower property values, impoverished lifestyles, and a general lack of privacy.

Even at the height of its popularity, the ecological school recognized that American crime patterns might be different from those found elsewhere in the world and that crime zones might exist in city areas other than those surrounding the core. Early comparisons of American, European, and Asian data, for instance, found higher crime rates at the so-called city gates (near-suburban areas providing access to downtown) in Europe and Asia.

The greatest contribution the ecological school made to criminological literature can be found in its claim that society, in the form of the community, wields a major influence on human behavior.[18] Similarly, ecological theorists of the Chicago School formalized the use of two sources of information: (1) official crime and population statistics, and (2) ethnographic data. Population statistics, or demographic data, when combined with crime information, provided empirical material that gave scientific weight to ecological investigations. Ethnographic information, gathered in the form of life stories, or ethnographies, described the lives of city inhabitants. By comparing one set of data with the other—demographics with ethnographies—ecological investigators were able to show that life experience varied from one location to another and that personal involvement in crime had a strong tendency to be associated with place of residence. Learn more about the Chicago School of criminology at Web Extra! 7-3.

Web Extra! 7-3 at **crimtoday.com**

The Criminology of Place

Ecological approaches to crime causation have found a modern rebirth in the **criminology of place.** The criminology of place, also called **environmental criminology,** is an emerging perspective within the contemporary body of criminological theory that builds upon the contributions of routine activities theory, situational crime prevention (both of which

were discussed in Chapter 4), and ecological approaches. It emphasizes the importance of geographic location and architectural features as they are associated with the prevalence of victimization. Such "hot spots" of crime, including neighborhoods, specific streets, and even individual houses and businesses, have been identified by recent writers. Lawrence W. Sherman, for example, tells of a study that revealed that 3% of places (addresses and intersections) in Minneapolis produce 50% of all calls to the police.[19] Crime, noted Sherman, although relatively rare in Minneapolis and similar urban areas, is geographically concentrated.

Reflecting the questions first addressed by Shaw and McKay, another contemporary researcher, Rodney Stark, asks, "How is it that neighborhoods can remain the site of high crime and deviance rates despite a complete turnover in their populations? . . . There must be something about places as such that sustains crime."[20] Stark has developed a theory of deviant neighborhoods. It consists of thirty propositions, including the following:[21]

- To the extent that neighborhoods are dense and poor, homes will be crowded.
- Where homes are more crowded, there will be a greater tendency to congregate outside the home in places and circumstances that raise levels of temptation and offer opportunity to deviate.
- Where homes are more crowded, there will be lower levels of supervision of children.
- Reduced levels of child supervision will result in poor school achievement, with a consequent reduction in stakes in conformity and an increase in deviant behavior.
- Poor, dense neighborhoods tend to be mixed-use neighborhoods.
- Mixed use increases familiarity with and easy access to places offering the opportunity for deviance.

Central to the criminology of place is the **broken windows thesis,** which holds that physical deterioration and an increase in unrepaired buildings leads to increased concerns for personal safety among area residents.[22] Heightened concerns, in turn, lead to further decreases in maintenance and repair and to increased delinquency, vandalism, and crime among local residents, which spawn even further deterioration in both a sense of safety and the physical environment. Offenders from other neighborhoods are then increasingly attracted by the area's perceived vulnerability.

Even within so-called high-crime neighborhoods, however, crimes tend to be concentrated at specific locations, such as street blocks or multiple-family dwellings. This kind of microlevel analysis has also shown, for example, that some units within specific apartment buildings are much more likely to be the site of criminal occurrences than others. Apartments near complex or building entrances appear to be more criminally dangerous, especially if they are not facing other buildings or apartments. Likewise, pedestrian tunnels, unattended parking lots, and convenience stores

Monitoring security cameras. Defensible space can be defined in terms of barriers to crime commission and preventative surveillance opportunities. How might such features be enhanced in high-crime areas? *Remi Benali, Liaison Agency, Inc.*

with clerks stationed in less visible areas are often targeted by criminal offenders.

The criminology of place employs the concept of **defensible space,** a term which evolved out of a conference in 1964 at Washington University in Saint Louis, Missouri.[23] *Defensible space* has been defined as "a surrogate term for the range of mechanisms—real and symbolic barriers, strongly defined areas of influence, and improved opportunities for surveillance—that combine to bring an environment under the control of its residents."[24] The Saint Louis conference, which brought criminologists, police officers, and architects face-to-face, focused on crime problems characteristic of public housing areas. Findings demonstrated that specific architectural changes which enhanced barriers, defined boundaries, and removed criminal opportunity could do much to reduce the risk of crime—even in the midst of high-crime neighborhoods.

The criminology of place holds that location can be as predictive of criminal activity as the lifestyles of victimized individuals or the social features of victimized households. (*Place* has been defined by researchers as "a fixed physical environment that can be seen completely and simultaneously, at least on its surface, by one's naked eyes."[25]) Places can be criminogenic due to the routine activities associated with them. On the other hand, some places host crime because they provide the characteristics that facilitate its commission. In Sherman's study, for example, Minneapolis parks drew exhibitionists because they provided "opportunities for concealment" up until the moment when the "flasher" struck. Making changes to the parks, such as moving walkways some distance from trees and shrubbery, would reduce criminal opportunity.

Recognizing the importance of criminology of place, New York City police developed a program a few years ago designed to close businesses with repeated crime problems. Called Operation Padlock, the program appeared to be successful in reducing the incidence of certain kinds of crime. As Sherman points out, "neither capital punishment of places (as in arson of crack houses) nor incapacitation of the routine activities of criminal hot spots (as in revocation of liquor licenses) seems likely to eliminate crime. But since the routine activities of places may be regulated far more easily than the routine activities of persons, a criminology of place would seem to offer substantial promise for public policy as well as theory."[26]

Some crime prevention programs are combining ideas derived from the criminology of place with spatial mapping techniques to fight crime. The Theory versus Reality box in this chapter provides information about crime mapping techniques. Visit the Crime Mapping Research Center via Web Extra! 7-4 to learn more about crime mapping.

Web EXTRA! Web Extra! 7-4 at crimtoday.com

Strain Theory

The second type of social structure theory discussed in this chapter is strain theory. Strain theories depict delinquency as a form of adaptive, problem-solving behavior, usually committed in response to problems involving frustrating and undesirable social environments. The classic statement of strain theory was offered in 1938 by **Robert K. Merton,** who developed the concept of anomie. *Anomie,* a French word meaning "normlessness," was popularized by Emile Durkheim in his 1897 book, *Suicide.*[27] Durkheim used the term to explain how a breakdown of predictable social conditions can lead to feelings of personal loss and dissolution.

Merton's use of the term *anomie* was somewhat different. In Merton's writings, **anomie** came to mean a disjunction between socially approved means to success and legitimate goals.[28] Merton maintained that legitimate goals, involving such things as wealth, status, and personal happiness, are generally portrayed as desirable for everyone. The widely acceptable means to these goals, however, including education, hard work, financial savings, and so on, are not equally available to all members of society. As a consequence, crime and deviance tend to arise as alternative means to success when individuals feel the strain of being pressed to succeed in socially approved ways but find that the tools necessary for such success are not available to them. Merton's emphasis on the felt strain resulting from a lack of fit between goals and means led to his approach being called **strain theory.**

Complicating the picture further, Merton maintained, was the fact that not everyone accepts the legitimacy of socially approved goals. Merton diagrammed possible combinations of goals and means as shown in Table 7-1, referring to each combination as a mode of adaptation.

THEORY VERSUS REALITY
The Criminology of Place, Routine Activities, and Crime Mapping

Today's law enforcement agencies are using routine activities theory (discussed in Chapter 4) along with the criminology of place to develop situational crime prevention techniques that combine technology with the spatial analysis of crime. One proponent of this approach is the Crime Mapping Research Center run by the U.S. Department of Justice. Crime mapping, used in conjunction with geographic information systems (GIS), allows for the effective use of law enforcement resources by helping police administrators direct patrols to places where they are most needed. This box contains excerpts from a National Institute of Justice report on crime mapping.

In the routine activities interpretation, crimes are seen as needing three ingredients: a *likely offender*, a *suitable target*, and the *absence of a guardian* capable of preventing the criminal act. *Guardian* is broadly interpreted to mean anyone capable of discouraging, if only through his or her mere presence, or interceding in, criminal acts. The mention of guardians begs discussion of the *density paradox*. This refers to the idea that, on the one hand, high population densities create a high potential for crime because people and property are crowded in small spaces. There are many likely offenders and suitable targets. On the other hand, surveillance is plentiful, and criminal acts in public spaces are likely to be observed by others, who, however unwittingly, take on the role of guardians. Crime can be prevented or reduced by making people less likely to offend (by increasing guilt and fostering development of the "inner policeman" who tames criminal impulses), by making targets less available, and by making guardians more numerous or effective. The process of making targets less available in various ways has become known by the generic term *situational crime prevention*.

Putting the routine activities approach and its sibling, situational crime prevention, into a geographic context involves asking how each element is distributed in geographic space. Where are the likely offenders? (What is the geography of the youthful male population?) Where are the suitable targets? (What is the geography of convenience stores, malls, automated teller machines, poorly illuminated pedestrian areas?) Where are the guardians? (What is the potential for surveillance, both formal and informal, of targets or areas that may contain targets? Where are the public or quasi-public spaces that lack surveillance and are ripe for graffiti and other incivilities?)

The perspective that focuses on criminal spatial behavior develops a scenario in which the motivated (potential) criminal uses cues, or environmental signals, to assess victims or targets. Cues, or clusters of cues, and sequences of cues relating to the social and physical aspects of the environment are seen as a *template* that the offender uses to evaluate victims or targets. Intimately tied to this process is the concept of *activity space*, the area in which the offender customarily moves about and that is familiar to him or her.

At the micro level of analysis, these concepts are useful in that it is known that activity spaces vary with demographics. For example, younger persons tend to

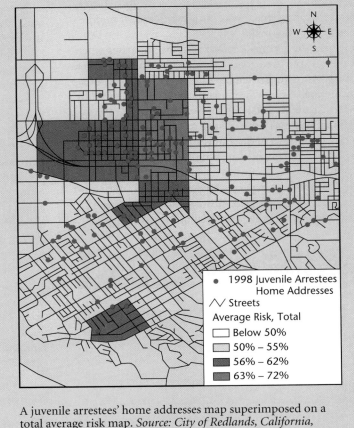

A juvenile arrestees' home addresses map superimposed on a total average risk map. *Source: City of Redlands, California, 1999. Reproduced with permission.*

(continued on the next page)

(continued from previous page)

have constricted activity spaces. They do not usually have the resources to travel far. Historically, women have had more geographically limited activity spaces than men due to the higher probability that men would work farther from home and that their jobs would be more likely to give them greater mobility. This is less true today but is still valid to some degree.

Analysts considering crime patterns from a theoretical perspective might think in terms of putting the crimes of interest through a series of "filter" questions. The most obvious is the question, How important is geography in explaining this pattern? (Is the pattern random, or not? If not, why not?) Can routine activity theory or criminal spatial behavior theory help explain this pattern? Is this pattern normal or unusual for this area? If the pattern is an anomaly, why is this? What resources can be brought to bear to better understand the social and other environmental dynamics of the area of interest? Analysts can take their intimate knowledge of the local environment and develop their own set of diagnostic questions, which could be the foundation of an analytic model.

For a list of Web sites displaying active crime maps, see Web Extra! 7-5.

Web Extra! 7-5 at crimtoday.com

DISCUSSION QUESTIONS

1. How does routine activities theory support the concepts involved in the spatial analysis of crime?
2. What is the density paradox? What implications does it have for crime prevention?
3. What "filter questions" are discussed in this box? Can you think of any other filter questions that might be asked?

Source: Keith Harries, *Mapping Crime: Principles and Practice* (Washington, D.C.: National Institute of Justice, 1999). Web posted at http://www.ojp.usdoj.gov/cmrc. Accessed December 5, 2000.

The initial row in Table 7-1 signifies acceptance of the goals that society holds as legitimate for everyone, with ready availability of the means approved for achieving those goals. The mode of adaptation associated with this combination of goals and means, *conformity,* typifies most middle- and upper-class individuals.

Innovation, the second form of adaptation, arises when an emphasis on approved goal achievement combines with a lack of opportunity to participate fully in socially acceptable means to success. This form of adaptation is experienced by many lower-class individuals who have been socialized to desire traditional success symbols, such as expensive cars, large homes, and big bank accounts, but who do not have ready access to approved means of acquiring them, such as educational opportunity. Innovative behavioral responses, including crime, can be expected to develop when individuals find themselves so deprived. However, in Merton's words, "poverty as such, and consequent limitation of opportunity, are not sufficient to induce a conspicuously high rate of criminal behavior. Even the often mentioned 'poverty in the midst of plenty' will not necessarily lead to this result." It is only insofar as those who find themselves in poverty are pressured to achieve material success and the acquisition of other associated symbols of status that innovation results.

Third, *ritualism* describes the form of behavior that arises when members of society participate in socially desirable means but show little interest in goal achievement. A ritualist may get a good education, work every day in an acceptable occupation, and appear outwardly to be leading a solid middle-class lifestyle. Yet that person may care little for the symbols of success, choosing to live an otherwise independent lifestyle.

Retreatism describes the behavior of those who reject both the socially approved goals and means. They may become dropouts, drug abusers, or homeless or participate in alternative lifestyles like communal living. Such individuals are often socially and psychologically quite separate from the larger society around them.

Merton's last category, *rebellion,* signifies a person, or rebel, who wishes to replace socially approved goals and means with some other system. Political radicals, revolutionaries, and antiestablishment agitators may fit into this category. Merton believed that conformity was the most common mode of adaptation prevalent in society, whereas retreatism was least common.

Relative Deprivation

A contemporary version of Merton's anomie theory has been proposed by Steven F. Messner and Richard Rosenfeld, who suggest that inconsistencies in the American Dream are to be blamed for most criminal activity. Messner and Rosenfeld

TABLE 7-1 ■ Goals and Means Disjuncture		
	GOALS	MEANS
Conformity	+	+
Innovation	+	−
Ritualism	−	+
Retreatism	−	−
Rebellion	±	±

Source: Robert K. Merton, *Social Theory and Social Structure,* 1968 enlarged edition. Copyright 1967, 1968 by Robert K. Merton. Adapted with permission of the Free Press, a division of Macmillan, Inc.

write, "Our thesis is that the American Dream itself exerts pressures toward crime by encouraging an anomic cultural environment, an environment in which people are encouraged to adopt an 'anything goes' mentality in the pursuit of personal goals."[29]

It is often said that Americans are the richest people on earth and that even the poorest Americans are far richer in terms of material possessions than the average citizen of many third world nations. Even if such an assertion is true, however, it means little to someone who is poor when judged in terms of the relatively affluent standards of the United States. Hence deprivation has an important psychological component, which means that it cannot be accurately assessed in absolute terms. **Relative deprivation** refers to the economic and social gap that exists between rich and poor who live in close proximity to one another.

According to sociologists Peter Blau and Judith Blau, two proponents of the relative deprivation concept, people assess their position in life by way of comparison with things and people they already know.[30] Hence inner-city inhabitants develop an increasing sense of relative deprivation when growing up in impoverished communities with the opportunity to witness well-to-do lifestyles in nearby neighborhoods. According to the Blaus, relative deprivation creates feelings of anger, frustration, hostility, and social injustice on the part of those who experience it. Relative deprivation is also related to the notion of **distributive justice,** which refers to an individual's perception of his or her rightful place in the reward structure of society. Thus, according to the principle of distributive justice, even wealthy and socially privileged individuals may feel slighted or shortchanged if they feel they have been inadequately rewarded for their behavior or their accomplishments. The perception of what amounts to the rightful distribution of rewards, however, appears to be highly dependent upon cultural expectations. Hence while even the most successful Americans may feel that they deserve more, studies show that Japanese society has been able to accommodate rapid socioeconomic growth without generating a felt sense of economic injustice, even among its least successful members, and without a substantial increase in crime.[31]

Recent surveys provide evidence for distinguishing between two types of relative deprivation: personal and group.[32] Personal relative deprivation is characteristic of individuals who feel deprived compared to other people. Group relative deprivation, on the other hand, refers to a communal sense of injustice that is shared by members of the same group. Hence while people who experience personal deprivation are likely to feel socially isolated and personally stressed, those who believe the entire social group to which they belong is deprived relative to other groups are more prone to participate in social movements and may actively attempt to change the social system. Group relative deprivation can be a powerful force for social change. In fact, some political analysts have suggested that the strain produced by relative deprivation with the West played an important role in

the downfall of the Soviet Union and of communism in Eastern Europe.[33]

General Strain Theory

In 1992, strain theory was reformulated by **Robert Agnew** and others and was changed into a comprehensive perspective called "general strain theory" (GST).[34] GST suggests that delinquent behavior is a coping mechanism that enables adolescents to deal with the socioemotional problems generated by negative social relations. GST expands on traditional strain theory in several ways. First, it significantly widens the focus of strain theory to include all types of negative relations between an individual and others. Second, GST maintains that strain is likely to have a cumulative effect on delinquency after reaching a certain threshold. Third, general strain theory provides a more comprehensive account of the cognitive, behavioral, and emotional adaptations to strain than traditional strain approaches. Finally, GST more fully describes the wide variety of factors affecting the choice of delinquent adaptations to strain.

According to GST, strain occurs when others do the following: (1) prevent or threaten to prevent an individual from achieving positively valued goals; (2) remove or threaten to remove positively valued stimuli that a person possesses; or (3) present or threaten to present someone with noxious or negatively valued stimuli. Agnew sees the crime-producing effects of strain as cumulative and concludes that whatever form it takes, "strain creates a predisposition for delinquency in those cases in which it is chronic or repetitive."[35] Nonetheless, according to Agnew, several factors determine whether a person will respond to the experience of strain in a criminal or conforming manner. These factors include temperament, intelligence, interpersonal skills, self-efficacy, association with criminal peers, and conventional social support.

An analysis by Agnew of other strain theories found that all such theories share at least two central explanatory features.[36] Strain theories, Agnew said, (1) focus "explicitly on negative relationships with others, relationships in which the individual is not treated as he or she wants to be treated," and (2) argue that "adolescents are pressured into delinquency by the negative affective states—most notably anger and related emotions—that often result from negative relationships."[37]

In 1994, Raymond Paternoster and Paul Mazerolle tested some of the assumptions underlying GST through an analysis of data from the National Youth Survey.[38] They found partial support for GST and discovered that negative relations with adults, feelings of dissatisfaction with friends and school life, and the experience of stressful events (for example, family dissolution) were positively related to delinquency, as was living in an unpleasant neighborhood (one beset by social problems and physical deterioration). When conceived of more broadly as exposure to negative stimuli, general strain was found to be significantly related to delinquency.

Contrary to Agnew's hypothesis, however, Paternoster and Mazerolle found no evidence that the effects of strain were enhanced when they were experienced for longer periods of time or that they were diminished when adolescents classified the dimension of their life in which they experienced strain as "unimportant." Consistent with earlier findings,[39] Paternoster and Mazerolle found that feelings of general strain were positively related to later delinquency, regardless of the number of delinquent peers, moral beliefs, self-efficacy, and level of conventional social support. Some support was found for the belief that general strain leads to delinquency by weakening the conventional social bond and by strengthening the unconventional bond with delinquent peers.

Learn more about strain theory via Web Extra! 7-6.

Web Extra! 7-6 at crimtoday.com

Culture Conflict Theory

The third type of social structure theory discussed in this chapter can be found in the culture conflict approach to explaining crime. **Culture conflict theory** (also called "cultural deviance theory") suggests that the root cause of criminality can be found in a clash of values between differently socialized groups over what is acceptable or proper behavior. The culture conflict concept is inherent in ecological criminology (which was discussed in the first part of this chapter) and its belief that zones of transition, because they tend to be in flux, harbor groups of people whose values are often at odds with those of the larger, surrounding society.

The culture conflict perspective found its clearest expression in the writings of **Thorsten Sellin** in his 1938 book, *Culture Conflict and Crime.*[40] Sellin maintained that the root cause of crime could be found in different values about what is acceptable or proper behavior. According to Sellin, **conduct norms,** which provide the valuative basis for human behavior, are acquired early in life through childhood socialization. It is the clash of norms between variously socialized groups that results in crime. Because crime is a violation of laws established by legislative decree, the criminal event itself, from this point of view, is nothing other than a disagreement over what should be acceptable behavior. For some social groups, what we tend to call "crime" is simply part of the landscape—something that can be expected to happen to you unless you take steps to protect yourself. From this point of view, those to whom crime happens are not so much victimized as they are simply ill-prepared.

In 1997, Danish actress Annette Sorensen was arrested after leaving her toddler in a stroller outside of a Manhattan restaurant while she sat inside, drinking margaritas with the child's father. Sorensen was charged with endangering the welfare of a child. Her 14-month-old daughter, Liv, was placed in temporary foster care. Sorensen, who was in tears following her arrest, could not understand what had happened. "We do this in Denmark all the time," the Copenhagen resident told police.[41] Her daughter was soon ordered re-

turned by a city judge, and Sorensen and the child flew home to Denmark, where children are routinely left in strollers outside of restaurants and other public places.[42]

Sellin described two types of culture conflict. The first type, *primary conflict,* arises when a fundamental clash of cultures occurs. Sellin's classic example was that of an immigrant father who kills his daughter's lover following an old-world tradition which demands that a family's honor be kept intact. In Sellin's words, "A few years ago, a Sicilian father in New Jersey killed the sixteen-year-old seducer of his daughter, expressing surprise at his arrest since he had merely defended his family honor in a traditional way. In this case . . . [t]he conflict was external and occurred between cultural codes or norms. We may assume that where such conflicts occur . . . norms of one cultural group or area migrate to another and that such conflict will continue so long as the acculturation process has not been completed."[43]

The other type of conflict, *secondary conflict,* arose, according to Sellin, when smaller cultures within the primary one clashed. So it is that middle-class values, upon which most criminal laws are based, may find fault with inner-city or lower-class norms, resulting in the social phenomenon we call "crime."

In Sellin's day, prostitution and gambling provided plentiful examples of secondary conflict. Many lower-class inner-city groups accepted gambling and prostitution as a way of life—if not for individual members of those groups, then at least as forms of behavior which were rarely condemned for those choosing to participate in them. Today, drug use and abuse provide more readily understandable examples. For some segments of contemporary society, drug sales have become a source of substantial income, and the conduct norms which typify such groups support at least the relative legitimacy of lives built around the drug trade. In other words, in some parts of America, drug dealing is an acceptable form of business. To those who make the laws, however, it is not. It is from the clash of these two opposing viewpoints that conflict, and crime, emerge.

Subcultural Theory

Fundamental to the notion of culture conflict is the idea of subcultures. Like the larger culture of which it is a part, a **subculture** is a collection of values and preferences which is communicated to subcultural participants through a process of socialization. Subcultures differ from the larger culture in that they claim the allegiance of smaller groups of people. Whereas the wider American culture, for example, may proclaim that hard work and individuality are valuable, a particular subculture may espouse the virtues of deer hunting, male bonding, and recreational alcohol consumption. Although it is fair to say that most subcultures are not at odds with the surrounding culture, some subcultures do not readily conform to the parameters of national culture. Countercultures, which tend to reject and invert the values of the surrounding culture, and criminal subcultures, which may actively espouse deviant activity, represent the other extreme. **Subcultural theory** is a sociological perspective that emphasizes the contribution made by variously socialized cultural groups to the phenomenon of crime.

Some of the earliest writings on subcultures can be found in **Frederic M. Thrasher**'s 1927 book, *The Gang*.[44] Thrasher studied 1,313 gangs in Chicago. His work, primarily descriptive in nature, led to a typology in which he described different types of gangs. In 1943, **William F. Whyte,** drawing on Thrasher's work, published *Street Corner Society*.[45] Whyte, in describing his three-year study of the Italian slum he called "Cornerville," further developed the subcultural thesis, showing that lower-class residents of a typical slum could achieve success through the opportunities afforded by slum culture—including racketeering and bookmaking.

Focal Concerns

In 1958, **Walter Miller** attempted to detail the values that drive members of lower-class subcultures into delinquent pursuits. Miller described *lower-class culture* as "a long established, distinctively patterned tradition with an integrity of its own."[46] In Miller's words, "A large body of systematically interrelated attitudes, practices, behaviors, and values characteristic of lower-class culture are designed to support and maintain the basic features of the lower-class way of life. In areas where these differ from features of middle-class culture, action oriented to the achievement and maintenance of the lower-class system may violate norms of the middle class and be perceived as deliberately nonconforming. . . . This does not mean, however, that violation of the middle-class norm is the dominant component of motivation; it is a byproduct of action primarily oriented to the lower-class system."

In the same article, entitled "Lower Class Culture as a Generating Milieu of Gang Delinquency," Miller outlined what he termed the **focal concerns** or key values, of delinquent subcultures. Such concerns included trouble, toughness, smartness, excitement, fate, and autonomy. Miller concluded that subcultural crime and deviance are not the direct consequences of poverty and lack of opportunity, but emanate, rather, from specific values characteristic of such subcultures. Just as middle-class concerns with achievement, hard work, and delayed gratification lead to socially acceptable forms of success, said Miller, so too do lower-class concerns provide a path to subculturally recognized success for lower-class youth.

Miller found that trouble is a dominant feature of lower-class culture. Getting into trouble, staying out of trouble, and dealing with trouble when it arises become focal points in the lives of many members of lower-class culture. Miller recognized that getting into trouble was not necessarily valued in and of itself but was seen as an oftentimes necessary means to valued ends. In Miller's words, "[For] men, 'trouble' frequently involves fighting or sexual adventures while drinking; for women, sexual involvement with disadvantageous consequences."

Like many theorists of the time, Miller was primarily concerned with the criminality of men. The lower-class masculine concern with toughness which he identified, Miller admitted, may have been a product of the fact that many men in the groups he examined were raised in female-headed families. Miller's "toughness," then, may reflect an almost obsessive concern with masculinity as a reaction to the perceived threat of overidentification with female role models. In words that sound as applicable today as when they were written, Miller tells us, "The genesis of the intense concern over 'toughness' in lower-class culture is probably related to the fact that a significant proportion of lower-class males are reared in a predominantly female household and lack a consistently present male figure with whom to identify and from whom to learn essential components of a 'male' role. Since women serve as a primary object of identification during the pre-adolescent years, the almost obsessive lower-class concern with 'masculinity' probably resembles a type of compulsive reaction-formation."

Miller described "smartness" as the "capacity to outsmart, outfox, outwit, dupe, take, [or] con another or others and the concomitant capacity to avoid being outwitted, taken or duped oneself. . . . In its essence," said Miller, "smartness involves the capacity to achieve a valued entity—material goods, personal status—through a maximum use of mental agility and a minimum of physical effort."

Excitement was seen as a search for thrills—often necessary to overcome the boredom inherent in lower-class lifestyles. Fights, gambling, picking up women, and making the rounds were all described as derivative aspects of the lower-class concern with excitement. "The quest for excitement," said Miller, "finds . . . its most vivid expression in the . . . recurrent 'night on the town' . . . a patterned set of activities in which alcohol, music, and sexual adventuring are major components."

Fate is related to the quest for excitement and to the concept of luck or of being lucky. As Miller stated; "Many lower-class persons feel that their lives are subject to a set of forces over which they have relatively little control. These are not . . . supernatural forces or . . . organized religion . . . but relate more to a concept of 'destiny' or man as a pawn. . . . This often implicit world view is associated with a conception of the ultimate futility of directed effort toward a goal."

Autonomy, as a focal concern, manifests itself in statements like, "I can take care of myself" or "No one's going to push me around." Autonomy produces behavioral problems from the perspective of middle-class expectations when it surfaces in work environments, public schools, or other social institutions built on expectations of conformity.

Miller's work derived almost entirely from his study of black inner-city delinquents in the Boston area in the 1950s. As such, it may have less relevance to members of lower-class subcultures in other places or at other times.

Delinquency and Drift

Members of delinquent subcultures are, to at least some degree, participants in the larger culture that surrounds them. How is it, then, that subcultural participants may choose behavioral alternatives which seemingly negate the norms and values of the larger society? In other words, how can a person give allegiance to two seemingly different sets of values—those of the larger culture and those of a subculture—at the same time?

Gresham Sykes and **David Matza** provided an answer to this question in their 1957 article "Techniques of Neutralization."[47] Sykes and Matza suggested that offenders can overcome feelings of responsibility when involved in crime commission through the use of five types of justifications:

- *Denying responsibility,* by pointing to one's background of poverty, abuse, lack of opportunity, and so on. Example: "The trouble I get into is not my fault."
- *Denying injury,* by explaining how insurance companies, for example, cover losses. Claims that "everyone does it" or that the specific victim could "afford it" fall into this category. Example: "They're so rich, they'll never miss it."
- *Denying the victim,* or justifying the harm done by claiming that the victim, for whatever reason, deserved the victimization. Example: "I only beat up drunks."
- *Condemning the condemners,* by asserting that authorities are corrupt or responsible for their own victimization. Offenders may also claim that society has made them into what they are and must now suffer the consequences. Example: "They're worse than we are. They're all on the take."
- *Appealing to higher loyalties,* as in defense of one's family honor, gang, girlfriend, or neighborhood. Example: "We have to protect ourselves."

In the words of Sykes and Matza, "It is our argument that much delinquency is based on what is essentially an unrecognized extension of defenses to crimes, in the form of justifications for deviance that are seen as valid by the delinquent but not by the legal system or society at large."[48]

A few years later, Matza went on to suggest that delinquents tended to drift into crime when available **techniques of neutralization** combined with weak or ineffective values espoused by the controlling elements in society. In effect, said Matza, the delinquent "drifts between criminal and conventional action," choosing whichever is the more expedient at the time. By employing techniques of neutralization, delinquents need not be fully alienated from the larger society. When opportunities for crime present themselves, such techniques provide an effective way of overcoming feelings of guilt and of allowing for ease of action. Matza used the phrase "soft determinism" to describe drift, saying that delinquents were neither forced to make choices because of fateful experiences early in life, nor were they entirely free to make choices unencumbered by the realities of their situation.

More recent studies have found that whereas "only a small percentage of adolescents generally approve of violence or express indifference to violence . . . [a] large percentage of adolescents . . . accept neutralizations justifying

the use of violence in particular situations."[49] The acceptance of such justifications by many young people today is seen as supporting high levels of adolescent violence. Studies have also found that young people who disapprove of violence but associate with delinquent peers will often use neutralization techniques as justifications for violence in which they personally engage.[50]

Violent Subcultures

Some subcultures are decidedly violent and are built around violent themes and around values supporting violent activities. In 1967, **Franco Ferracuti** and **Marvin Wolfgang** published their seminal work, *The Subculture of Violence: Toward an Integrated Theory of Criminology,*[51] which drew together many of the sociological perspectives previously advanced to explain delinquency and crime. According to some writers, the work of Wolfgang and Ferracuti "was substantively different from the other subculture theories, perhaps because it was developed almost a decade after delinquent-subculture theories and criminology had developed new concerns."[52] Ferracuti and Wolfgang's main thesis was that violence is a learned form of adaptation to certain problematic life circumstances and that learning to be violent takes place within the context of a subcultural milieu which emphasizes the advantages of violence over other forms of adaptation. Such subcultures are characterized by songs and stories that glorify violence, by gun ownership, and by rituals which tend to stress macho models. They are likely to teach that a quick and decisive response to insults is necessary to preserve one's prestige within the group. Subcultural group members have a proclivity for fighting as a means of settling disputes. Subcultures of violence both expect violence from their members and legitimize it when it occurs. In the words of Ferracuti and Wolfgang, "The use of violence . . . is not necessarily viewed as illicit conduct, and the users do not have to deal with feelings of guilt about their aggression."[53] In other words, for participants in violent subcultures, violence can be a way of life.

Wolfgang and Ferracuti based their conclusions on an analysis of data which showed substantial differences in the rate of homicides between racial groups in the Philadelphia area. At the time of their study, nonwhite men had a homicide rate of 41.7 per 100,000 versus a homicide rate of only 3.4 for white men. Statistics on nonwhite women showed a homicide rate of 9.3 versus 0.4 for white women. Explaining these findings, Wolfgang and Ferracuti tell us, "Homicide is most prevalent, or the highest rates of homicide occur, among a relatively homogeneous subcultural group in any large urban community. . . . The value system of this group, as we are contending, constitutes a subculture of violence. From a psychological viewpoint, we might hypothesize that the greater the degree of integration of the individual into this subculture, the higher the probability that his behavior will be violent in a variety of situations."[54]

Wolfgang and Ferracuti extend their theory of subcultural violence with the following "corollary propositions":[55]

- No subculture can be totally different from or totally in conflict with the society of which it is a part.
- To establish the existence of a subculture of violence does not require that the actors sharing in these basic value elements should express violence in all situations.
- The potential resort or willingness to resort to violence in a variety of situations emphasizes the penetrating and diffusive character of this culture theme.
- The subcultural ethos of violence may be shared by all ages in a subsociety, but this ethos is most prominent in a limited age group, ranging from late adolescence to middle age.
- The counternorm is nonviolence.
- The development of favorable attitudes toward violence and its use in a subculture usually involves learned behavior and a process of differential learning, association, or identification.
- The use of violence in a subculture is not necessarily viewed as illicit conduct, and the users therefore do not have to deal with feelings of guilt about their aggression.

Other writers have commented on geographic distinctions between violent subcultures in different parts of the

Violent subcultures produce violent acts. Eighteen spent cartridges lay around the body of this New Orleans murder victim. Why are some subcultures "violent" while others are not? *Bryce Lankard*

United States. A body of criminological literature exists, for example, which claims that certain forms of criminal violence are more acceptable in the southern United States than in northern portions of the country.[56] Some writers have also referred to variability in the degree to which interpersonal violence has been accepted in the South over time, whereas others have suggested that violence in the South might be a traditional tool in the service of social order.[57] Without at least a modicum of expressive violence, such as lynchings, dueling, and outright fighting, these authors suggest, southern social solidarity following the Civil War might have been seriously threatened. In short, the notion of a "southern violence construct" holds that an "infernal trinity of Southerner, violence and weaponry"[58] may make crimes like homicide and assault more culturally acceptable in the South than in other parts of the country.

In 1999, James W. Clarke, a political science professor at the University of Arizona, advanced the notion that the high rate of black underclass homicide in the United States flows from a black subculture of violence created by generations of white-on-black violence that first emerged with the "generation of black males that came of age after emancipation."[59] According to Clarke, many black males learn from earlier generations to seek status through their ability to "harm, intimidate, and dominate others."[60]

Clarke traces the roots of white-on-black violence to the arrival of the first African slaves in America in the seventeenth century. He draws up slave narratives, plantation documents, interviews with former slaves conducted by the Works Progress Administration, the Tuskegee Institute—NAACP files on lynching, historical state documents on convict labor, the testimony of victims of the Ku Klux Klan, and the Department of Justice's Peonage Files to document the black experience with violence in the United States. Clarke concludes that reforms built around social programs intent on alleviating joblessness and improving education cannot eliminate the violent subculture of the black underclass because the subculture shared by members of that group lacks the conventional values needed for such reforms to succeed. The culture of violence, Clarke argues, can only be eliminated through an emphasis on discipline and family structure.

In an interesting aside that relates to the chapter-opening story and further illustrates how violent subcultural norms are transmitted from generation to generation, Virginia Demery, 41, the mother of Larry Martin Demery, one of the men arrested and charged with killing Michael Jordan's father, was convicted on September 28, 1993, of using a shotgun in an assault on reporters who came to her mobile home following her son's arrest. Although no one was injured in the incident, reporters who brought criminal charges against her later said that members of the news media should be able to "expect a general amount of civility when they go to interview someone."[61] Ms. Demery gave reporters until the count of five to leave her property, but the gun discharged, accidentally she claimed, at the count of two.

The wider culture often recognizes, sometimes begrudgingly and sometimes matter-of-factly, a violent subculture's internal rules. Hence when one member of such a subculture kills another, the wider society may take the killing less "seriously" than if someone outside the subculture had been killed. As a consequence of this realization, Franklin Zimring and his associates described what they called "wholesale" and "retail" costs for homicide, in which killings that are perceived to occur within a subculture of violence (when both the victim and the perpetrator are seen as members of a violent subculture) generally result in a less harsh punishment than do killings which occur outside of the subculture.[62] Punishments, said Zimring, relate to the perceived seriousness of the offense, and if members of the subculture within which a crime occurs accept the offense as part of the landscape, so too will members of the wider culture which imposes official sanctions on the perpetrator.

Differential Opportunity Theory

In 1960, **Richard A. Cloward** and **Lloyd E. Ohlin** published *Delinquency and Opportunity*.[63] Their book, a report on the nature and activities of juvenile gangs, blended the subcultural thesis with ideas derived from strain theory. Cloward and Ohlin identified two types of socially structured opportunities for success: illegitimate and legitimate. They observed that whereas legitimate opportunities were generally available to individuals born into middle-class culture, participants in lower-class subcultures were often denied access to them. As a consequence, illegitimate opportunities for success were often seen as quite acceptable by participants in so-called illegitimate subcultures.

Cloward and Ohlin used the term **illegitimate opportunity structure** to describe preexisting subcultural paths to success which are not approved of by the wider culture. Where illegitimate paths to success are not already in place, alienated individuals may undertake a process of ideational evolution through which "a collective delinquent solution" or a "delinquent means of achieving success" may be decided upon by members of a gang. Because the two paths to success, legitimate and illegitimate, differ in their availability to members of society, Cloward and Ohlin's perspective has been termed "differential opportunity."

According to Cloward and Ohlin, delinquent behavior may result from the ready availability of illegitimate opportunities and the effective replacement of the norms of the wider culture with expedient subcultural rules. Hence delinquency and criminality may become "all right," or legitimate, in the eyes of gang members and may even form the criteria used by other subcultural participants to judge successful accomplishments. In the words of Cloward and Ohlin, "A delinquent subculture is one in which certain forms of delinquent activity are essential requirements for the performance of the dominant roles supported by the subculture."[64] Its "most crucial elements" are the "prescriptions, norms, or rules of conduct that define the activities required of a full-fledged member."[65] "A person attributes legitimacy to a system of rules and corresponding models of behavior," wrote Cloward and Ohlin, "when he accepts them as binding on his conduct."[66] "Delinquents have withdrawn their support from established norms and invested officially forbidden forms of conduct with a claim to legitimacy.[67]

Cloward and Ohlin noted that a delinquent act can be "defined by two essential elements: it is behavior that violates basic norms of the society, and, when officially known, it evokes a judgment by agents of criminal justice that such norms have been violated."[68] For Cloward and Ohlin, however, crime and deviance were just as normal as any other form of behavior supported by group socialization. In their words, "Deviance and conformity generally result from the same kinds of social conditions," and "deviance ordinarily represents a search for solutions to problems of adjustment." In their view, deviance is just as much an effort to conform, albeit to subcultural norms and expectations, as is conformity to the norms of the wider society. They added, however, that "it has been our experience that most persons who participate in delinquent subcultures, if not lone offenders, are fully aware of the difference between right and wrong, between conventional behavior and rule-violating behavior. They may not care about the difference, or they may enjoy flouting the rules of the game, or they may have decided that illegitimate practices get them what they want more efficiently than legitimate practices."[69]

Cloward and Ohlin described three types of delinquent subcultures: (1) criminal subcultures, in which criminal role models are readily available for adoption by those being socialized into the subculture; (2) conflict subcultures, in which participants seek status through violence; and (3) retreatist subcultures, where drug use and withdrawal from the wider society predominate. Each subculture was thought to emerge from a larger, all-encompassing "parent" subculture of delinquent values. According to Cloward and Ohlin, delinquent subcultures had at least three identifiable features: (1) "Acts of delinquency that reflect subcultural support are likely to recur with great frequency," (2) "access to a successful adult criminal career sometimes results from participation in a delinquent subculture," and (3) "the delinquent subculture imparts to the conduct of its members a high degree of stability and resistance to control or change."[70]

Cloward and Ohlin divided lower-class youth into four types, according to their degree of commitment to middle-class values and material achievement. Type I youths were said to desire entry to the middle class via improvement in their economic position. Type II youths were seen as desiring entry to the middle class but not improvement in their economic position. Type III youths were portrayed as desiring wealth without entry to the middle class. As a consequence, Type III youths were seen as the most crime prone. Type IV youths were described as dropouts who retreated from the cultural mainstream through drug and alcohol use.

Cloward and Ohlin had substantial impact on American social policy through the sponsorship of David Hackett, President John F. Kennedy's head of the newly created

Committee on Juvenile Delinquency and Youth Crime. Out of the relationship between the theorists and Hackett, the Mobilization for Youth program, established under the auspices of the 1961 Juvenile Delinquency Prevention and Control Act, was begun in 1962 with $12.5 million in initial funding.[71] Mobilization for Youth, a delinquency prevention program based on Cloward and Ohlin's opportunity theory, created employment and educational opportunities for deprived youths.

Reaction Formation

Another criminologist whose work is often associated with both strain theory and the subcultural perspective is **Albert Cohen.** Like Cloward and Ohlin, Cohen's work focused primarily on the gang behavior of delinquent youth. In Cohen's words, "When we speak of a delinquent subculture, we speak of a way of life that has somehow become traditional among certain groups in American society. These groups are the boys' gangs that flourish most conspicuously in the 'delinquency neighborhoods' of our larger American cities. The members of these gangs grow up, some to become law-abiding citizens and others to graduate to more professional and adult forms of criminality, but the delinquent tradition is kept alive by the age-groups that succeed them."[72]

Cohen argued that youngsters from all backgrounds are generally held accountable to the norms of the wider society through a "middle-class measuring rod" of expectations related to school performance, language proficiency, cleanliness, punctuality, neatness, nonviolent behavior, and allegiance to other similar standards. Like strain theorists, Cohen noted that unfortunately not everyone is prepared, by virtue of the circumstances surrounding his or her birth and subsequent socialization, for effectively meeting such expectations.

In an examination of vandalism, Cohen found that "nonutilitarian" delinquency, in which things of value are destroyed rather than stolen or otherwise used for financial gain, is the result of middle-class values turned upside down.[73] Delinquent youths, argued Cohen, who are often alienated from middle-class values and lifestyles through deprivation and limited opportunities, can achieve status among their subcultural peers via vandalism and other forms of delinquent behavior.

Children, especially those from deprived backgrounds, turn to delinquency, Cohen claimed, because they experience status frustration when judged by adults and others according to middle-class standards and goals which they are unable to achieve. Because it is nearly impossible for nonmainstream children to succeed in middle-class terms, they may overcome anxiety through the process of reaction formation, in which hostility toward middle-class values develops. Cohen adapted **reaction formation** from psychiatric perspectives and used it to mean "the process in which a person openly rejects that which he wants, or aspires to, but cannot obtain or achieve."[74]

Cohen discovered the roots of delinquent subcultures in what he termed the "collective solution to the problem of status."[75] When youths who experience the same kind of alienation from middle-class ideals band together, they achieve a collective and independent solution and create a delinquent subculture. Cohen wrote, "The delinquent subculture, we suggest, is a way of dealing with the problems of adjustment. . . . These problems are chiefly status problems: certain children are denied status in the respectable society because they cannot meet the criteria of the respectable status system. The delinquent subculture deals with these problems by providing criteria of status which these children can meet."[76]

Cohen's approach is effectively summarized in a "theoretical scenario" offered by Donald J. Shoemaker, who says that lower-class youths undergo a working-class socialization that combines lower-class values and habits with middle-class success values.[77] Lower-class youth then experience failure in school because they cannot live up to the middle-class norms operative in American educational institutions. They suffer a consequent loss of self-esteem and increased feelings of rejection, leading to their dropping out of school and associating with delinquent peers. Hostility and resentment toward middle-class standards grow through reaction formation. Finally, such alienated youths achieve status and a sense of improved self-worth through participation in a gang of like-minded peers. Delinquency and crime are the result.

Gangs Today

Gangs have become a major source of concern in contemporary American society. Although the writings of investigators like Cohen, Thrasher, and Cloward and Ohlin focused on the illicit activities of juvenile gangs in the nation's inner cities, most gang-related crimes of the period involved vandalism, petty theft, and battles over turf. The ethnic distinctions which gave rise to gang culture in the 1920s through the 1950s are today largely forgotten. Italian, Hungarian, Polish, and Jewish immigrants, whose children made up many of the early gangs, have been, for the most part, successfully integrated into the society that is modern America.

Today's gangs are quite different from the gangs of the first half of the twentieth century. The 1998 National Youth Gang Survey was the fourth national survey of gang activity and membership to be conducted by the National Youth Gang Center (NYGC).[78] The 1998 survey sample consisted of (1) 1,216 police departments serving cities with populations of 25,000 or more, (2) 660 suburban county police and sheriff's departments, (3) a randomly selected sample of 339 police departments serving small towns, and (4) a randomly selected sample of 743 rural county police and sheriff's departments. Although the police departments were able to come up with their own definition of a "youth gang," motorcycle gangs, hate or ideology groups, prison gangs, and gangs comprised exclusively of adults were intentionally excluded from the survey.

Forty-eight percent of the responding departments reported active youth gangs in their jurisdictions in 1998, and

CRIME IN THE NEWS
D.C. Gang Blamed for 31 Killings

A gang leader and his cohorts built a reputation as one of the most bloodthirsty factions in this city known for its violent drug gangs, authorities charge.

Now, Kevin Gray and 16 of his alleged associates, including chief lieutenant Rodney Moore, are facing charges that their gang, dubbed Murder Inc. by authorities, were responsible for 31 slayings and 10 attempted murders, including one botched hit that Gray allegedly ordered from a Washington jail cell, federal prosecutors say.

The allegations of murder and violence that occurred during the past decade are contained in a 158-page racketeering indictment handed up Monday by a federal grand jury in Washington, said Channing Phillips, a spokesman for the U.S. attorney's office in Washington.

The sweeping indictment—and the record number of murder allegations it contains—replaces an earlier federal case filed against the 29-year-old Gray, Moore and six of their alleged associates

last May, Phillips said. The previous indictment charged the members of the gang with 16 counts of murder and various other acts of violence and intimidation, most against customers or rivals, Phillips said.

"A MURDER-FOR-HIRE GROUP"

The new indictment goes much further, linking Gray and his gang to 15 other homicides and 10 attempted murders dating back to 1989. Some of the killings were done on a contract basis for other local drug organizations, Phillips said. In all, authorities said, Gray had a hand in 22 of the 31 slayings. Moore took part in a dozen of them, authorities allege.

"Toward the end, they were operating as kind of a murder-for-hire group," Phillips said.

Gray's lawyer, Francis D. Carter, declined to comment on the indictment. Moore's lawyer, Barry Coburn, said today: "We have every intention of defending against these charges vigorously."

All but one of the suspects named in the new indictment—a man whom authorities identified as Wilford Oliver—were in custody today, either on charges stemming from the original indictment or on unrelated charges. Bail information was not immediately available.

JAIL NO DETERRENT

Authorities say that jail has been no deterrent to the gang. Even though Gray has been jailed since his October 1999 arrest on unrelated drug charges, the reign of terror continued, authorities allege.

According to the new indictment, Gray last year ordered a hit on a man he believed was cooperating with authorities. The victim survived the attack and is confined to a wheelchair, authorities said.

Gray has since been transferred from a jail in Washington to a more secure facility in Virginia, where his telephone privileges have been curtailed, Phillips said.

Source: Seamus McGraw, "Federal Indictment Targets Drug, 'Murder for Hire' Groups," APB News, November 21, 2000. Reprinted with permission.

an estimated 4,464 jurisdictions in the United States experienced gang activity during 1998. Respondents estimated that 28,700 gangs and 780,000 gang members were active in the United States in 1998. Forty-two percent of the responding police departments reported that the gang problem in their jurisdiction in 1998 was "staying about the same" as in previous surveys, 28% that it was "getting worse," and 30% that it was "getting better." In other words, more than two-thirds responded that their gang problem was either "staying about the same" or "getting worse."

Respondents were asked to estimate the proportion of their youth gang members who engaged in specific types of serious and violent crimes. Twenty-seven percent of respondents said "most or all" gang members (75–100%) were involved in drug sales, and 3% said most or all gang members were involved in robbery. Twelve percent of respondents said most or all of their gang members were involved in aggravated assault. Twenty-eight percent of youth gangs were identified as drug gangs (that is, gangs organized specifically for the purpose of trafficking in drugs).

Survey respondents in 1998 were also asked to estimate how often gang members used firearms in assaults in their ju-

risdictions. The results were as follows: "often" (19%), "sometimes" (30%), "rarely" (29%), "not used" (15%), and "did not know" or did not answer the question (7%).

Nationally, 92% of gang members were estimated to be male, and 8% were estimated to be female. Only 1.5% of gangs were female dominated (more than 50% female). The 1998 age distribution of gang members was as follows: under age 15 (11%), 15 to 17 (29%), 18 to 24 (46%), and over 24 (14%).

The distribution of gang members by race/ethnicity in 1998 was as follows: Hispanic/Latino (46%), African American (34%), Caucasian (12%), Asian (6%), and other races (2%). About 33% of gangs were reported to have a significant mixture of two or more racial/ethnic groups.

The 1998 survey confirmed previous findings that gang members are often involved in a variety of serious and violent crimes. Almost half of the law enforcement agencies reporting gang problems are involved in collaborative efforts with other law enforcement and criminal justice agencies to combat youth gangs and the serious and violent crimes they commit.

In addition to conducting the National Youth Gang Surveys, the National Youth Gang Center provides a compilation of gang-related legislation, maintains a repository of gang-related literature, analyzes gang-related data and statistics, and coordinates the activities of the Youth Gang Consortium. You can visit the NYGC via Web Extra! 7-7.

Web Extra! 7-7 at crimtoday.com

Another group of special interest to anyone wanting to know more about gangs is the National Alliance of Gang Investigators Associations. Visit the alliance via Web Extra! 7-8.

Web Extra! 7-8 at crimtoday.com

Although its data is a couple of years older than that available through the NYGC, the National Gang Crime Research Center's Project Gangfact provides a profile of gangs and gang members nationwide. The 1996 Gangfact report, based on data collected by 28 researchers in 17 states, found the following:[79]

- The average age for joining a gang, nationally, is 12.8 years of age.
- Over half who joined gangs have tried to quit.
- More than two-thirds of gangs have written rules for members to follow.
- Over half of all gangs hold regular weekly meetings.
- Nearly 30% of gangs require their members to pay dues.
- Approximately 55% of gang members were recruited by other gang members, while the remainder sought out gang membership.

- Most gang members (79%) said they would leave the gang if given a "second chance in life."
- Four-fifths of gang members reported that their gangs sold crack cocaine.
- Most gangs (70%) are not racially exclusive and consist of members drawn from a variety of ethnic groups.
- One-third of gang members report that they have been able to conceal their gang membership from their parents.
- Most gangs (83%) report having female members, but few allow female members to assume leadership roles.
- Many gang members (40%) report knowing male members of their gangs who had raped females.

Members of modern youth gangs generally identify with a name (such as the "Crips" and "Bloods," which are well-known Los Angeles–area gangs), a particular style of clothing, symbols, tattoos, jewelry, haircut, and hand symbols.

Gangs can be big business. In addition to traditional criminal activities like burglary, extortion, vandalism, and protection rackets, drug dealing has become a mainstay of many inner-city gangs. Los Angeles police estimate that at least four city gangs earn over $1 million each per week through cocaine sales.[80] The potential for huge drug-based profits appears to have changed the nature of gangs themselves, making them more prone toward violence and cutthroat tactics. Gang killings, including the now-infamous drive-by shootings, have become commonplace in our nation's cities.

Rodney Dailey, a self-avowed former Boston-area drug dealer and gun-wielding gang member, says that in today's gang world, "shoot before you get shot is the rule." According

Los Angeles gang members under arrest. Gangs have become a major source of concern in today's society. Why have gangs become such a prominent feature of contemporary society? *Douglas C. Pizac, AP/Wide World Photos*

to Dailey, "Things that normally people would have had fist-fights about can get you shot or stabbed" today.[81] Dailey is the founder of Gang Peace, an outreach group which tries to reduce gang-related violence.

Guns have become a way of life for many young gang members. As a young man named Jamaal, hanging around with friends outside Boston's Orchard Park housing project, recently put it, "We don't fight, we shoot." Police in the area describe how values among youth have changed over the past decade or two. Today they "think it's fun to pop someone," they say.[82]

Contemporary researchers, however, are drawing some new distinctions between gangs and violence. A few years ago, G. David Curry and Irving A. Spergel, in a study of Chicago communities, distinguished between juvenile delinquency and gang-related homicide.[83] They found that communities characterized by high rates of delinquency do not necessarily experience exceptionally high rates of crime or of gang-related homicides. They concluded that although gang activity may be associated with homicide, "gang homicide rates and delinquency rates are ecologically distinct community problems." Gang-related homicide, they found, seems to be well explained by classical theories of social disorganization and is especially prevalent in areas of the city characterized by in-migration and by the "settlement of new immigrant groups." In their study, high rates of juvenile delinquency seemed to correlate more with poverty, which the researchers defined as "social adaptation to chronic deprivation." According to Curry and Spergel, "Social disorganization and poverty rather than criminal organization and conspiracy may better explain the recent growth and spread of youth gangs to many parts of the country. Moreover, community organization and social opportunity in conjunction with suppression, rather than simply suppression and incapacitation, may be more effective policies in dealing with the social problem."[84] In proposing a national gang strategy, Finn-Aage Esbensen reminds policymakers that many gang members are delinquent before they become associated with gangs.[85] Esbensen says that "concerns with gang suppression should not supplant efforts to implement effective delinquency intervention and prevention strategies."[86]

POLICY IMPLICATIONS OF SOCIAL STRUCTURE THEORIES

Theoretical approaches which fault social structure as the root cause of crime point in the direction of social action as a panacea. In the 1930s, for example, Clifford Shaw, in an effort to put his theories into practice, established the **Chicago Area Project.** Through the Chicago Area Project, Shaw sought to reduce delinquency in transitional neighborhoods. Shaw analyzed oral histories gathered from neighborhood citizens to determine that delinquents were essentially normal youngsters who entered into illegal activities at early ages, often through street play. Hence he worked to increase opportunities for young people to embark on successful work careers.

The Chicago Area Project attempted to reduce social disorganization in slum neighborhoods through the creation of community committees. Shaw staffed these committees with local residents rather than professional social workers. The project had three broad objectives: (1) improving the physical appearance of poor neighborhoods, (2) providing recreational opportunities for youth, and (3) involving project members directly in the lives of troubled youth through school and courtroom mediation. The program also made use of "curbside counselors," streetwise workers who could serve as positive role models for inner-city youth. Although no effective assessment programs were established to evaluate the Chicago Area Project during the program's tenure, in 1984 Rand Corporation reviewers published a 50-year review of the program, declaring it "effective in reducing rates of juvenile delinquency."[87]

Similarly, Mobilization for Youth, cited earlier in this chapter as an outgrowth of Cloward and Ohlin's theory of differential opportunity, provides a bold example of the treatment implications of social structure theories. Mobilization for Youth sought not only to provide new opportunities, but also through direct social action to change the fundamental arrangements of society and thereby address the root causes of crime and deviance. Leaders of Mobilization for Youth decided that "what was needed to overcome . . . formidable barriers to opportunity . . . was not community organization but community action" that attacked entrenched political interests. Accordingly, the program promoted "boycotts against schools, protests against welfare policies, rent strikes against 'slum landlords,' lawsuits to ensure poor people's rights, and voter registration."[88] A truly unusual government-sponsored program for its time, Mobilization for Youth was eventually disbanded amid protests that "the mandate of the President's Committee was to reduce delinquency, not to reform urban society or to try out sociological theories on American youths."[89]

The War on Poverty declared by the Kennedy and Johnson administrations during the 1960s and subsequent federal and state-run welfare programs that provide supplemental income assistance have been cited[90] as examples of programs that at least held the potential to reduce crime rates by redistributing wealth in American society.[91] Such programs, however, have come under increasing fire recently, and the federal Welfare Reform Reconciliation Act of 1996[92] reduced or eliminated long-term benefits that had previously been available through avenues like the federal Aid to Families with Dependent Children (AFDC) program. The 1996 legislation also established stricter work requirements for welfare recipients through a new Welfare-to-Work program under the Personal Responsibility and Work Opportunity Reconciliation Act of 1996.[93]

CRITIQUE OF SOCIAL STRUCTURE THEORIES

The fundamental assumption of social structure approaches is that social injustice, racism, and poverty are the root causes of crime. Hence the social structure perspective is intimately associated with the first prong of this textbook's theme, the social problems approach, which was described in Chapter 1. If the assumptions that inform social structure theories are true, they largely negate the claims of those who advocate our theme's other prong, the social responsibility perspective.

Social structure explanations for criminality received an enormous boost during the 1960s with the report of President Lyndon B. Johnson's Commission on Law Enforcement and Administration of Justice, a widely disseminated and highly influential document that portrayed social inequality and stifled opportunity as fundamental causes of crime. Recently, however, a number of social commentators have begun to question the nature of the relationship between poverty, apparent social inequities, and crime.[94] Some now argue the inverse of the "root causes" argument, saying that poverty and what appear to be social injustices are produced by crime, rather than the other way around. Disorder, fear, and crime, they suggest, undermine positive social and economic institutions. Families, schools, churches, businesses, and other institutions cannot function properly in social settings where crime is a taken-for-granted part of the social landscape. If this proposed inverse relationship is even partially true, then addressing poverty and social inequality as the "root causes" of crime is not only an ineffective crime prevention strategy, but an unnecessarily costly one as well.

This chapter has identified three types of social structure theory, and each can be uniquely critiqued. Some authors have suggested, for example, that ecological theories give too much credence to the notion that spatial location determines crime and delinquency. The nature of any given location changes over time, they say, and evolutions in land-use patterns, such as a movement away from homeownership and toward rental or low-income housing, may seriously affect the nature of a neighborhood and the concomitant quality of social organization found there. Similarly, rates of neighborhood crime and delinquency may be "an artifact of police decision-making practices"[95] and may bear little objective relationship to the actual degree of law violation in an area. Such police bias (that is, enforcement efforts focused on low-income inner-city areas), should it exist, may seriously mislead researchers into categorizing certain areas as high in crime when enforcement decisions made by police administrators merely make them appear that way.

Another critique of the ecological school can be found in its seeming inability to differentiate between the condition of social disorganization and the things such a condition is said to cause. What, for example, is the difference between social disorganization and high rates of delinquency? Isn't delinquency a form of the very thing said to cause it? As Stephen J. Pfohl has observed, early ecological writers sometimes used the incidence of delinquency as "both an example of disorganization and something caused by disorganization,"[96] making it difficult to gauge the efficacy of their explanatory approach.

Similarly, those who criticize the ecological approach note that many crimes occur outside of geographic areas said to be characterized by social disorganization. Murder, rape, burglary, incidents of drug use, assault, and so on, all occur in affluent, "well-established" neighborhoods as well as in other parts of a community. Likewise, white-collar, computer, environmental, and other types of crime may actually occur with a greater frequency in socially well-established neighborhoods than elsewhere. Hence the ecological approach is clearly not an adequate explanation for all crime, nor for all types of crime.

From a social responsibility perspective, those who criticize strain theory note that Merton's original formulation of strain theory is probably less applicable to American society today than it was in the 1930s. That's because in the last few decades considerable effort has been made toward improving success opportunities for all Americans, regardless of ethnic heritage, race, or gender. Hence it is less likely that individuals today will find themselves without the opportunity for choice, as was the case decades ago. Travis Hirschi criticizes contemporary strain theory for its inability "to locate people suffering from discrepancy" and notes that human beings are naturally optimistic—a fact, he says, which "overrides . . . aspiration-expectation disjunction." Hirschi concludes that "expectations appear to affect delinquency, but they do so regardless of aspirations, and strain notions are neither consistent with nor required by the data."[97] Similarly, recent studies have found that, contrary to what might be expected on the basis of strain theory, "delinquents do not report being more distressed than other youth."[98] In fact, delinquent youth who are not afforded the opportunities for success that are available to others appear to be well shielded from sources of stress and despair through their participation in delinquency. Hence "although strain theorists often have portrayed the lives of delinquents in grim terms . . . this depiction does not square well with the lived world of delinquency."[99]

Subcultural approaches, which constitute the last of the three types of social structure explanations for crime discussed in this chapter, have been questioned by some criminologists who see them as lacking in explanatory power. Canadian criminologist Gwynn Nettler, for example, criticizes the notion of violent subcultures by insisting that it is tautological, or circular. Nettler argues that saying that people fight because they are violent or that "they are murderous because they live violently" does little to explain their behavior. Attributing fighting to "other spheres of violence," he says, may be true, but it is fundamentally "uninformative."[100]

The subcultural approach has also been criticized for being racist because many so-called violent subcultures are said to be populated primarily by minorities. Margaret Anderson says that "the problem with this explanation is that it turns attention away from the relationship of black communities to the larger society and it recreates dominant stereotypes about blacks as violent, aggressive, and fearful. Although it may be true that rates of violence are higher in black communities, this observation does not explain the fact."[101] In sociological jargon, one might say that an observed correlation between race and violence does not necessarily provide a workable explanation for the relationship.

There are other problems with social structure theories which routinely link low levels of socioeconomic status (SES) to high levels of delinquency. A fundamental problem can be found in the fact that empirical studies have consistently found weak or nonexistent correlations between an individual's SES and his or her self-reported delinquency.[102] Moreover, such studies have shown that while low SES may promote delinquency by increasing social alienation and financial strain and by decreasing educational opportunity and occupational aspiration, high SES may also promote delinquency by increasing a person's willingness to take risks and by decreasing the influence of conventional values. Other studies have found parental monitoring (defined as knowing where the child is and what he is doing) and discipline to be far more effective predictors of the degree of delinquent involvement than low SES.[103]

Social structure theories suffer from another shortcoming that generally affects most other sociological perspectives on crime causation. In the words of Nettler, "The conceptual bias of social scientists emphasizes environments—cultures and structures—as the powerful causes of differential conduct. This bias places an intellectual taboo on looking elsewhere for possible causes as, for example, in physiologies. This taboo is . . . strongly applied against the possibility that ethnic groups may have genetically transmitted differential physiologies that have relevance for social behavior."[104] In this critique, Nettler is telling us that social scientists unnecessarily downplay the causative role of nonsociological factors. Many outside of sociology believe that such factors are important, but since sociological theorizing has captured the lion's share of academic attention over the past few decades, the role of other causative factors in the etiology of criminal behavior is in danger of being shortchanged.

Finally, some see the inability of social structure theories to predict which individuals—or at least what proportion of a given population—will turn to crime as a crucial failure of such perspectives. Although the large majority of people growing up in inner-city poverty-ridden areas, for example, probably experience an inequitable opportunity structure firsthand, only a relatively small number of those people become criminal. It is true that substantially more people living under such conditions may become criminal than those living in other types of social environments. Nonetheless, a large proportion of people experiencing strain, as well as a large number of people raised in deviant subcultures, will still embrace noncriminal lifestyles—but social structure theories cannot tell us which ones. In his book *The Moral Sense,* James Q. Wilson suggests that most people—regardless of socialization experiences and the structural aspects of their social circumstances—may still carry within them an inherent sense of fairness and interpersonal morality.[105] If what Wilson suggests is even partially true, then the explanatory power of social structure theories will inevitably be limited by human nature itself.

SUMMARY

Sociological theories explore relationships between and among groups and institutions and envision crime as the result of social processes, as the natural consequence of aspects of social structure, or as the result of economic and class struggle. Social structure theories, with which this chapter has mostly been concerned, are only one of three types of sociological explanations for crime. Social structure theories emphasize poverty, lack of education, absence of marketable skills, and subcultural values as fundamental causes of crime.

Three subtypes of social structure theories can be identified: social disorganization theory, strain theory, and culture conflict theory. Social disorganization theory encompasses the notion of social pathology, which sees society as a kind of organism and crime and deviance as a kind of disease or social pathology. Theories of social disorganization are often associated with the perspective of social ecology and with the Chicago School of criminology, which developed during the 1920s and 1930s. Strain theory points to a lack of fit between socially approved success goals and the availability of socially approved means to achieve those goals. As a consequence, according to the perspective of strain theory, individuals unable to succeed through legitimate means turn to other avenues that promise economic and social recognition. Culture conflict theory suggests that the root cause of criminality can be found in a clash of values between differently socialized groups over what is acceptable or proper behavior.

Because theories of social structure look to the organization of society for their explanatory power, intervention strategies based on them typically seek to alleviate the social conditions that are thought to produce crime. Social programs based on social structure assumptions frequently seek to enhance socially acceptable opportunities for success and to increase the availability of meaningful employment.

DISCUSSION QUESTIONS

1. What is the nature of sociological theorizing? What are the assumptions upon which sociological perspectives on crime causation rest?
2. What are the three key sociological explanations for crime that are discussed at the beginning of this chapter? How do they differ from one another?
3. What are the three types of social structure theories that this chapter describes? What are the major differences between them?
4. Do you believe ecological approaches have a valid place in contemporary criminological thinking? Why or why not?

5. How, if at all, does the notion of a "criminology of place" differ from more traditional ecological theories? Do you see the "criminology of place" approach as capable of offering anything new over traditional approaches? If so, what?

6. What is a violent subculture? Why do some subcultures stress violence? How might participants in a subculture of violence be turned toward less aggressive ways?

7. This book emphasizes a social problems versus social responsibility theme. Which of the theoretical perspectives discussed in this chapter best support the social problems approach? Which support the social responsibility approach? Why?

8. What are the policy implications of the theories discussed in this chapter? What kinds of changes in society and in government policy might be based on the theories discussed here? Would they be likely to bring about a reduction in crime?

WEB QUEST!

A number of highly useful crime theory Web sites are maintained by professors who are actively engaged in scholarship in the criminology and criminal justice fields. Some of the best known of these sites include Cecil Greek's online lecture notes (http://www.criminology.fsu.edu/crimtheory) at Florida State University; Tom O'Connor's Megalinks in Criminal Justice (http://faculty.ncwc.edu/toconnor) at North Carolina Wesleyan College; Matthew Robinson's Crime Theory Links (http://www.appstate.edu/~robinsnmb/theorylinks.htm) at Appalachian State University; and Bruce Hoffman's Crime Theory site (http://crimetheory.com) at the University of Washington. Visit each of these sites, and discover what they have to offer. If your instructor asks you to, write a summary of the materials describing social structure theories that you find at each site. Remember to check this textbook's site at crimtoday.com for updated URLs.

LIBRARY EXTRAS!

The Library Extras! listed here complement the Web Extras! found throughout this chapter. Library Extras! may be accessed on the Web at crimtoday.com.

Library Extra! 7-1. David Hollenbach, "The Common Good and Urban Poverty," *America,* June 5, 1999, pp. 8–11.

Library Extra! 7-2. Rebecca S. Katz, "Building the Foundation for a Side-by-Side Explanatory Model: A General Theory of Crime, the Age-Graded Life Course Theory, and Attachment Theory," *Western Criminology Review,* Vol. 1, No. 2 (1999).

Library Extra! 7-3. George L. Kelling, *Crime Control, the Police, and Culture Wars: Broken Windows and Cultural Pluralism.* National Institute of Justice 1997–1998 Lecture Series.

Library Extra! 7-4. Suresh K. Lodha and Arvind Verma, "Animations of Crime Maps Using Virtual Reality Modeling Language," *Western Criminology Review,* Vol. 1, No. 2 (1999).

NOTES

[1] Frank Tannenbaum, *Crime and the Community* (Boston: Ginn, 1938), p. 25.

[2] "L.A.: Waiting on a Razor's Edge," *Newsweek,* March 29, 1993, p. 28.

[3] "Nation, Town 'Shocked' by Slaying," *USA Today,* August 18, 1993, p. 1A.

[4] "Ex-convict Convicted in Jordan's Murder Trial," Associated Press, no date. Web posted at http://collegian.ksu.edu/ISSUES/v100/SP/n105/ap-JordansFather—19.3.html. Accessed January 5, 1998.

[5] Charles R. Tittle, "Theoretical Developments in Criminology," *Criminal Justice 2000* (Washington, D.C.: National Institute of Justice, 2000), p. 70.

[6] Emile Durkheim, *The Division of Labor in Society,* trans. George Simpson (1893; reprint, New York: Free Press, 1947).

[7] Ferdinand Toennies, *Community and Society,* trans. Charles P. Loomis (1887; reprint, East Lansing: Michigan State University Press, 1957).

[8] Georg Simmel, "The Metropolis and Mental Life," in Donald N. Levine, ed., *On Individuality and Social Forms* (Chicago: University of Chicago Press, 1903).

[9] Durkheim, *The Division of Labor in Society,* p. 80.

[10] W. I. Thomas and Florian Znaniecki, *The Polish Peasant in Europe and America* (Boston: Gorham, 1920).

[11] Robert Park and Ernest Burgess, *The City* (Chicago: University of Chicago Press, 1925).

[12] "Human Ecology," *Encyclopedia Britannica* online (britannica.com). Accessed March 7, 2001.

[13] Peter Haggett, "Human Ecology," in Alan Bullock and Oliver Stallybrass, eds., *The Fontana Dictionary of Modern Social Thought* (London: Fontana, 1977), p. 187.

[14]For an excellent contemporary review of measuring the extent of social disorganization, see Barbara D. Warner and Glenn L. Pierce, "Reexamining Social Disorganization Theory Using Calls to the Police as a Measure of Crime," *Criminology,* Vol. 31, No. 4 (November 1993), pp. 493–513.

[15]Edwin M. Lemert, *Social Pathology* (New York: McGraw-Hill, 1951), p. 3.

[16]Ibid., p. 7.

[17]Clifford R. Shaw et al., *Delinquency Areas* (Chicago: University of Chicago Press, 1929).

[18]David Matza, *Becoming Deviant* (Englewood Cliffs, NJ: Prentice Hall, 1969).

[19]Lawrence W. Sherman, Patrick R. Gartin, and Michael E. Buerger, "Hot Spots of Predatory Crime: Routine Activities and the Criminology of Place," *Criminology,* Vol. 27, No. 1 (1989), pp. 27–55.

[20]Rodney Stark, "Deviant Places: A Theory of the Ecology of Crime," *Criminology,* Vol. 25, No. 4 (1987), p. 893.

[21]Ibid., pp. 895–899.

[22]James Q. Wilson and George Kelling, "Broken Windows," *Atlantic Monthly,* March 1982, pp. 1–11.

[23]Oscar Newman, *Architectural Design for Crime Prevention* (Washington, D.C.: U.S. Department of Justice, 1973). See also Oscar Newman, *Creating Defensible Space* (Washington, D.C.: Office of Housing and Urban Development, 1996).

[24]Oscar Newman, *Defensible Space: Crime Prevention through Urban Design* (New York: Macmillan, 1972), p. 3. See also Ralph B. Taylor and Adele V. Harrell, "Physical Environment and Crime," National Institute of Justice, May 1996.

[25]Sherman, Gartin, and Buerger, "Hot Spots of Predatory Crime," p. 31.

[26]Ibid., p. 49.

[27]Emile Durkheim, *Suicide: A Study in Sociology* (New York: Free Press, 1897).

[28]Robert K. Merton, "Social Structure and Anomie," *American Sociological Review,* Vol. 3 (October 1938), pp. 672–682; and Robert K. Merton, *Social Theory and Social Structure,* rev. ed. (New York: Free Press, 1957).

[29]Steven F. Messner and Richard Rosenfeld, *Crime and the American Dream* (Belmont, CA: Wadsworth, 1994), p. 68.

[30]J. Blau and P. Blau, "The Cost of Inequality: Metropolitan Structure and Violent Crime." *American Sociological Review,* Vol. 147 (1982), pp. 114–129.

[31]Masahiro Tsushima, "Economic Structure and Crime: The Case of Japan," *Journal of Socio-Economics,* Vol. 25, No. 4 (Winter 1996), p. 497.

[32]Thomas F. Pettigrew, "Applying Social Psychology to International Social Issues," *Journal of Social Issues* (winter 1998).

[33]Fatos Tarifa, "The Quest for Legitimacy and the Withering Away of Utopia," *Social Forces,* Vol. 76, No. 2 (December 1997), p. 437.

[34]Robert Agnew, "Foundation for a General Strain Theory of Crime and Delinquency," *Criminology,* Vol. 30, No. 1 (February 1992), pp. 47–87.

[35]Ibid., p. 60.

[36]Agnew, "Foundation for a General Strain Theory of Crime and Delinquency."

[37]Ibid., p. 48.

[38]Raymond Paternoster and Paul Mazerolle, "General Strain Theory and Delinquency: A Replication and Extension," *Journal of Research in Crime and Delinquency,* Vol. 31, No. 3 (1994), pp. 235–263.

[39]Robert Agnew and Helene Raskin White, "An Empirical Test of General Strain Theory," *Criminology,* Vol. 30, No. 4 (1992), pp. 475–499.

[40]Thorsten Sellin, *Culture Conflict and Crime* (New York: Social Science Research Council, 1938).

[41]Rick Hampson, "Danish Mom Finds New York Doesn't Kid Around," *USA Today,* May 14, 1997, p. 3A.

[42]Although the practice may seem strange to Americans, the author, while teaching in Iceland, saw firsthand lines of un-attended infants bundled into strollers awaiting their parents outside of restaurants and sports centers. The practice seems especially prevalent in Scandinavian countries, where the threat of child abduction is virtually unknown.

[43]Sellin, *Culture Conflict and Crime,* p. 68.

[44]Frederic M. Thrasher, *The Gang* (Chicago: University of Chicago Press, 1927).

[45]William F. Whyte, *Street Corner Society: The Social Structure of an Italian Slum* (Chicago: University of Chicago Press, 1943).

[46]The quotations attributed to Miller in this section are from Walter Miller, "Lower Class Culture as a Generating Milieu of Gang Delinquency," *Journal of Social Issues,* Vol. 14, No. 3 (1958), pp. 5–19.

[47]Gresham Sykes and David Matza, "Techniques of Neutralization: A Theory of Delinquency," *American Sociological Review,* Vol. 22 (December 1957), pp. 664–670.

[48]Ibid.

[49]Robert Agnew, "The Techniques of Neutralization and Violence," *Criminology,* Vol. 32, No. 4 (1994), pp. 555.

[50]Ibid.

[51]Franco Ferracuti and Marvin Wolfgang, *The Subculture of Violence: Toward an Integrated Theory of Criminology* (London: Tavistock, 1967).

[52]Frank P. Williams III and Marilyn D. McShane, *Criminological Theory* (Englewood Cliffs, NJ: Prentice Hall, 1988), p. 79.

[53]Ferracuti and Wolfgang, *The Subculture of Violence.*

[54]Ferracuti and Wolfgang, *The Subculture of Violence,* p. 151.

[55]Ibid.

[56]For an excellent review of the literature, see F. Frederick Hawley, "The Southern Violence Construct: A Skeleton in the Criminological Closet," paper presented at the annual meeting of the American Society of Criminology, 1988.

[57]Bertram Wyatt-Brown, *Southern Honor: Ethics and Behavior in the Old South* (Oxford: Oxford University Press, 1983).

58Hawley, "The Southern Violence Construct," p. 27.

59James W. Clarke, *The Lineaments of Wrath: Race, Violent Crime, and American Culture* (New Brunswick, NJ: Transaction, 1998), p. 4.

60Ibid., p. 4.

61"Suspect's Mom Convicted of Shooting at Reporters," *Fayetteville* (N.C.) *Observer-Times,* September 29, 1993, p. 1A.

62Franklin Zimring et. al., "Punishing Homicide in Philadelphia: Perspectives on the Death Penalty," *University of Chicago Law Review,* Vol. 43 (1976), pp. 227–252.

63Richard A. Cloward and Lloyd E. Ohlin, *Delinquency and Opportunity: A Theory of Delinquent Gangs* (Glencoe, IL: Free Press, 1960).

64Ibid., p. 7.

65Ibid., p. 13.

66Ibid., p. 16.

67Ibid., p. 19.

68Ibid., p. 3.

69Ibid., p. 37.

70Ibid., pp. 12–13.

71Stephen J. Pfohl, *Images of Deviance and Social Control,* 2ed (New York: McGraw Hill, 1994), pp. 224–225.

72Albert Cohen, *Delinquent Boys: The Culture of the Gang* (New York: Free Press, 1955), p. 13.

73Ibid., p. 13.

74Donald J. Shoemaker, *Theories of Delinquency: An Examination of Explanations of Delinquent Behavior* (New York: Oxford University Press, 1984), p. 102, citing Cohen.

75Cohen, *Delinquent Boys,* p. 76.

76Cohen, *Delinquent Boys,* p. 121.

77Shoemaker, *Theories of Delinquency,* p. 105.

78This section draws heavily upon John P. Moore and Ivan L. Cook, *Highlights of the 1998 National Youth Gang Survey* (Washington, D.C.: Office of Juvenile Justice and Delinquency Prevention, 1999), from which much of the wording has been adapted.

79National Gang Crime Research Center, *Achieving Justice and Reversing the Problem of Gang Crime and Gang Violence in America Today: Preliminary Results of the Project Gangfact Study* (Chicago: National Gang Crime Research Center, 1996).

80Carl Rogers, "Children in Gangs," *Criminal Justice, 1993–94* (Guilford, CT: Dushkin, 1993), pp. 197–199.

81"Youths Match Power, Fear, Guns," *Fayetteville* (N.C.) *Observer-Times,* September 6, 1993, p. 2A.

82Ibid.

83The quotations attributed to Curry and Spergel in this section are from G. David Curry and Irving A. Spergel, "Gang Homicide, Delinquency, and Community," *Criminology,* Vol. 26, No. 3 (1988), pp. 381–405.

84Ibid., p. 401.

85Finn-Aage Esbensen, "A National Gang Strategy," in J. Mitchell Miller and Jeffrey P. Rush, eds., *Gangs: A Criminal Justice Approach* (Cincinnati: Anderson, 1996).

86Cited in Mary H. Glazier, review of J. Mitchell Miller and Jeffrey P. Rush, eds., *Gangs: A Criminal Justice Approach* (Cincinnati: Anderson, 1996), in *The Criminologist,* July/August 1996, p. 29.

87Steven Schlossman et al., *Delinquency Prevention in South Chicago: A Fifty-Year Assessment of the Chicago Area Project* (Santa Monica, CA: Rand Corporation, 1984).

88J. Robert Lilly, Francis T. Cullen, and Richard A. Ball, *Criminological Theory: Context and Consequences* (Newbury Park, CA: Sage, 1989), p. 80.

89Lamar T. Empey, *American Delinquency: Its Meaning and Construction* (Homewood, IL: Dorsey, 1982), p. 243.

90See James DeFronzo, "Welfare and Burglary," *Crime and Delinquency,* Vol. 42 (1996), pp. 223–230.

91Since overall rates of crime rose throughout much of the 1970s and 1980s, the effectiveness of such programs remains very much in doubt.

92Public Law 104–193 (August 22, 1996).

93Sec. 103 of the Welfare Reform Act of 1996.

94See, for example, George L. Kelling, "Crime Control, the Police, and Culture Wars: Broken Windows and Cultural Pluralism," in National Institute of Justice, *Perspectives on Crime and Justice: 1997–1998 Lecture Series* (Washington, D.C.: National Institute of Justice, 1998).

95Robert J. Bursik, "Social Disorganization and Theories of Crime and Delinquency: Problems and Prospects," *Criminology,* Vol. 26, No. 4 (1988), p. 519.

96Stephen J. Pfohl, *Images of Deviance and Social Control* (New York: McGraw-Hill, 1985), p. 167.

97Travis Hirschi, review of Delbert S. Elliott, David Huizinga, and Suzanne S. Ageton, *Explaining Delinquency and Drug Use* (Beverly Hills, CA: Sage, 1985), in *Criminology,* Vol. 25, No. 1 (February 1987), p. 195.

98John Hagan, "Defiance and Despair: Subcultural and Structural Linkages between Delinquency and Despair in Life Course," *Social Forces,* Vol. 76, No. 1 (September 1997), p. 119.

99Ibid.

100Gwynn Nettler, *Killing One Another* (Cincinnati: Anderson, 1982), p. 67.

101Margaret Anderson, "Review Essay: Rape Theories, Myths, and Social Change," *Contemporary Crises,* Vol. 5 (1983), p. 237.

102Bradley R. Entner Wright et al., "Reconsidering the Relationship between SES and Delinquency: Causation but Not Correlation," *Criminology,* Vol. 37, No. 1 (February 1999), pp. 175–194.

103R. Larzelre and G. R. Patterson, "Parental Management: Mediator of the Effect of Socioeconomic Status on Early Delinquency," *Criminology,* Vol. 28 (1990), pp. 301–323.

104Nettler, *Killing One Another,* p. 54.

105James Q. Wilson, *The Moral Sense* (New York: Free Press, 1993).

Children learn to become delinquents by becoming members of groups in which delinquent conduct is already established.

—Albert K. Cohen[1]

It's like it ain't so much what a fellow does, but it's the way the majority of folks is looking at him when he does it.

—William Faulkner[2]

sociological theories II: social process and social development

CHAPTER 8

> If the child who "steps off on the wrong foot" remains on an ill-starred path, subsequent stepping-stone experiences may culminate in life-course-persistent antisocial behavior.
>
> —Terrie E. Moffitt[3]

KEY CONCEPTS

IMPORTANT TERMS

Cambridge Study in Delinquent Development	evolutionary ecology	reintegrative shaming
cohort analysis	human development	secondary deviance
containment	impression management	social bond
containment theory	interactionist perspectives	social capital
control ratio	labeling	social control theories
criminal career	learning theory	social development perspective
desistance	life course	social process theories
differential association	moral enterprise	stigmatic shaming
differential identification theory	persistence	tagging
discrediting information	primary deviance	total institutions
dramaturgical perspective	Project on Human Development in Chicago Neighborhoods (PHDCN)	

IMPORTANT NAMES

Ronald L. Akers	Sheldon Glueck	Terrie E. Moffitt
Howard Becker	Erving Goffman	Walter C. Reckless
John Braithwaite	Michael Gottfredson	Robert J. Sampson
Robert Burgess	Travis Hirschi	Edwin Sutherland
Lawrence E. Cohen	Howard B. Kaplan	Frank Tannenbaum
David P. Farrington	John H. Laub	Charles R. Tittle
Daniel Glaser	Edwin M. Lemert	Donald J. West
Eleanor Glueck	Richard Machalek	Marvin Wolfgang

◆ OUTCOMES

After reading this chapter, you should be able to
- ◆ Recognize how the process of social interaction between people contributes to criminal behavior
- ◆ Identify and distinguish between a number of social process and social development perspectives
- ◆ Identify current social policy initiatives that reflect the social development approach
- ◆ Assess the shotcomings of the social process and social development perspectives

LEARNING

Hear the author discuss this chapter at *crimtoday.com*

INTRODUCTION

In late 1993, James Hamm found himself at the center of a vicious controversy. Hamm, a convicted murderer, had served 18 years in prison for shooting a man in the head over a drug deal gone bad and was about to enter the Arizona State University School of Law. Hamm had been paroled in June 1992 after Arizona's parole board judged him "rehabilitated." While in prison, Hamm, a former divinity student, earned a bachelor's degree in sociology and had been active in Middle Ground, a prisoners' rights group. While the 45-year-old Hamm worked on getting an education, students at the university were challenging his access to law school, saying that a convicted murderer did not deserve to be admitted. Mark Killian, the Arizona Republican House Speaker, claimed, "There are a lot of hard-working young people out there who could not get into law school because he did."[4] Members of the Arizona Board of Regents, which runs the state's public universities, called for a review of policies on admitting ex-convicts to the schools. Hamm, who scored in the top 5% of all applicants taking the law school admissions test nationwide, was eventually admitted and received a juris doctorate in 1997. The state's parole board, however, refused to terminate Hamm's parole, and he remains ineligible to practice law. In Hamm's words, the controversy surrounding him "touches on feelings about crime, criminals, recidivism, the failure of the criminal justice system. . . . I'm a lightning rod for those feelings," he said.[5]

The case of James Hamm provides an example of how society's continued reaction to what it defines as criminal behavior can change the course of an offender's life—often for the worst—even after he has paid his "dues." As a certain professor liked to say, while there are plenty of ex-cons, there is no such thing as an "ex-ex-con"—or "once a con, always a con." Society, it seems, never forgets.

THE SOCIAL PROCESS PERSPECTIVE

The theories discussed in the first part of this chapter are called **social process theories**, or **interactionist perspectives**, because they depend on the process of interaction between individuals and society for their explanatory power. Social process theories of crime causation assume that everyone has the potential to violate the law and that criminality is not an innate human characteristic. According to social process theories, criminal behavior is learned in interaction with others, and the socialization process that occurs as the result of group membership is

seen as the primary route through which learning occurs. Among the most important groups contributing to the process of socialization are the family, peers, work groups, and reference groups with which one identifies. Such groups instill values and norms in their members and communicate what are (for their members) acceptable worldviews and patterns of behavior.

Social process perspectives hold that the process through which criminality is acquired, deviant self-concepts are established, and criminal behavior results is active, open-ended, and ongoing throughout a person's life. They suggest that individuals who have weak stakes in conformity are more likely to be influenced by the social processes and contingent experiences that lead to crime, and they believe that criminal choices, once made, tend to persist because they are reinforced by the reaction of society to those whom it has identified as deviant.

TYPES OF SOCIAL PROCESS APPROACHES

A number of theories can be classified under the social process umbrella. Among them are social learning theory, social control theory, labeling theory, reintegrative shaming, and dramaturgy. Learning theories place primary emphasis upon the role of communication and socialization in the acquisition of learned patterns of criminal behavior and the

The Trenchcoat Mafia as they appeared in the Columbine High School yearbook in 1998. Two members of the group went on a shooting spree at the Littleton, Colorado, high school in 1999.

Which social process theory might best explain their behavior?
Sygma, Corbis

SOCIAL PROCESS THEORIES, ALSO KNOWN AS INTERACTIONIST PERSPECTIVES, depend on the process of interaction between individuals and society for their explanatory power. Social process theories of crime causation assume that everyone has the potential to violate the law and that criminality is not an innate human characteristic. According to social process theories, criminal behavior is learned in interaction with others, and the socialization process that occurs as the result of group membership is seen as the primary route through which learning occurs.

■ **SOCIAL LEARNING THEORY.** Says that all behavior is learned in much the same way and that crime, like other forms of behavior, is also learned. Places primary emphasis upon the role of communication and socialization in the acquisition of learned patterns of criminal behavior and the values that support that behavior.

PERIOD: 1930s–present

THEORISTS: Edwin Sutherland, Robert Burgess, Ronald L. Akers, Daniel Glaser

CONCEPTS: Differential association, differential association–reinforcement (including operant conditioning), differential identification

■ **SOCIAL CONTROL THEORY.** Focuses on the strength of the bond that people share with the institutions and individuals around them, especially as those relationships shape their behavior. Seeks to identify those features of the personality and of the environment that keep people from committing crimes.

PERIOD: 1950s–Present

THEORISTS: Walter C. Reckless, Howard B. Kaplan, Travis Hirschi, Michael Gottfredson, Charles R. Tittle, others

CONCEPTS: Inner and outer containment, self-derogation, social bond, control-balance

■ **LABELING THEORY (OR SOCIETAL REACTION THEORY).** Points to the special significance of society's response to the criminal, and sees continued crime as a consequence of limited opportunities for acceptable behavior which follow from the negative responses of society to those defined as offenders.

PERIOD: 1938–1940, 1960s–1980s, 1990s revival

THEORISTS: Frank Tannenbaum, Edwin M. Lemert, Howard Becker, John Braithwaite, others

CONCEPTS: Tagging, labeling, outsiders, moral enterprise, primary and secondary deviance, reintegrative shaming, stigmatic shaming

■ **DRAMATURGY.** Depicts human behavior as centered around the purposeful management of impressions, and seeks explanatory power in the analysis of social performances.

PERIOD: 1960s–present

THEORISTS: Erving Goffman, others

CONCEPTS: Total institutions, impression management, back and front regions, performances, discrediting information, stigma, spoiled identity

values that support that behavior. Control theories focus on the strength of the bond that people share with institutions and individuals around them, especially as those relationships shape their behavior. Labeling theory, also known as "societal reaction theory," points to the special significance of society's response to the criminal. It sees the process through which a person comes to be defined as a criminal, along with society's formal imposition of the label "criminal" upon that person, as a significant contributory factor in determining future criminality. Reintegrative shaming, a contemporary offshoot of labeling theory, emphasizes possible positive outcomes of the labeling process, while dramaturgy demonstrates how people can effectively manage the impressions they make on others. It is to learning theories that we now turn our attention.

Learning Theory

Social **learning theory** says that all behavior is learned in much the same way and that crime, like other forms of behavior, is also learned. People learn to commit crime from others, and such learning includes the acquisition of norms, values, and patterns of behaviors conducive to crime. Hence, according to learning theory, criminal behavior is a product of the social environment and not an innate characteristic of particular people.

Differential Association

One of the earliest and most influential forms of learning theory was advanced by **Edwin Sutherland** in 1939. Sutherland's thesis was that criminality is learned through a process of **differential association** with others who communicate criminal values and who advocate the commission of crimes.[6] Sutherland emphasized the role of social learning as an explanation for crime because he believed that many of the concepts popular in the field of criminology at the time—including social pathology, genetic inheritance, biological characteristics, and personality flaws—were inadequate to explain the process by which an otherwise normal individual turns to crime. Sutherland was the first well-known criminologist to suggest that all significant human behavior is learned and that crime, therefore, is not substantively different from any other form of behavior.

Although Sutherland died in 1950, the tenth edition of his famous book, *Criminology,* was published in 1978 under the authorship of Donald R. Cressey, a professor at the University of California at Santa Barbara. The 1978 edition of *Criminology* contained the finalized principles of differential association (which, for all practical purposes, were complete as early as 1947). Nine in number, the principles read as follows:[7]

1. Criminal behavior is learned.
2. Criminal behavior is learned in interaction with others in a process of communication.
3. The principal part of the learning of criminal behavior occurs within intimate personal groups.
4. When criminal behavior is learned, the learning includes (a) techniques of committing the crime, which are sometimes very complicated, sometimes very simple, and (b) the specific direction of motives, drives, rationalizations, and attitudes.
5. The specific direction of motives and drives is learned from definitions of the legal codes as favorable or unfavorable.
6. A person becomes delinquent because of an excess of definitions favorable to law violation over definitions unfavorable to law violation.
7. Differential associations may vary in frequency, duration, priority, and intensity.
8. The process of learning criminal behavior by association with criminal and anticriminal patterns involves all of the mechanisms that are involved in any other learning.
9. While criminal behavior is an expression of general needs and values, it is not explained by those general needs and values, since noncriminal behavior is an expression of the same needs and values.

Differential association found considerable acceptance among mid-twentieth-century theorists because it combined then-prevalent psychological and sociological principles into a coherent perspective on criminality. Crime as a form of learned behavior became the catchword of mid-twentieth-century criminology, and biological and other perspectives were largely abandoned by those involved in the process of theory testing.

Differential Association–Reinforcement Theory

In 1966, **Robert Burgess** and **Ronald L. Akers** published an article outlining what they called "a differential association–reinforcement theory of criminal behavior."[8] The perspective, which is often referred to as "differential reinforcement theory" or "sociological learning theory," expands on Sutherland's original idea of differential association by adding the idea of reinforcement. Reinforcement, a concept drawn from psychology, was discussed earlier in this textbook under the heading "Behavior Theory" in Chapter 6. In that chapter, we pointed out the power of punishments and rewards to shape behavior. In developing their perspective, Burgess and Akers integrated psychological principles of operant conditioning with sociological notions of differential association, and they reorganized Sutherland's nine principles into seven. The flavor of their approach is obvious in the first of these statements, which says, "Criminal behavior is learned according to the principles of operant conditioning."[9] Fundamental to this perspective is the belief that human beings learn to define behaviors that are rewarded as positive and that an individual's criminal behavior is rewarded at least sometimes by individuals and groups that value such activity.

Although the 1966 Burgess-Akers article only alluded to the term *social learning,* Akers began to apply that term to differential association–reinforcement theory with the 1973 publication of his book *Deviant Behavior: A Social Learning Approach.*[10] According to Akers, "The basic assumption in social learning theory is that the same learning process, operating in a context of social structure, interaction, and situation, produces both conforming and deviant behavior."[11] Akers identified two primary learning mechanisms. The first is differential reinforcement (also called "instrumental conditioning"), in which behavior is a function of the frequency, amount, and probability of experienced and perceived contingent rewards and punishments. The second is imitation, in which the behavior of others and its consequences are observed and modeled. These learning mechanisms, said Akers, operate in a process of differential association involving direct and indirect, verbal and nonverbal, communication, interaction, and identification with others. As with Sutherland's theory of differential association, the relative frequency, intensity, duration, and priority of associations remains important because it determines the amount, frequency, and probability of reinforcement of behavior that is either conforming or deviant. Interpersonal association also plays an important role because, as with Sutherland's theory, it can expose individuals to deviant or conforming norms and role models.

Akers has continued to develop learning theory, and in 1998 he published the book *Social Learning and Social Structure,* in which he explained crime rates as a function of social learning that occurs within a social structure.[12] He termed this explanation the "social structure–social learning"

CRIME IN THE NEWS
Kids Likely to Follow Parents to Prison

Across the United States, more than 1.5 million children go through life with at least one parent in prison.

An estimated 60 percent of the country's 1.8 million state and federal prisoners are parents. Since men make up 94 percent of the prison population, most are fathers.

And according to speakers at a U.S. Bureau of Justice Assistance law enforcement conference here, those figures are a harbinger of the prison population of the future.

CYCLE THREATENS TO SNOWBALL

Statistics show that children whose parents are locked away in prison are likely to be jailed themselves. And with corrections systems now sequestering Americans at an unprecedented pace, the parent-child inmate cycle threatens to snowball.

With more parents behind bars today, more children will follow tomorrow, speakers said.

In fact, a child with an incarcerated parent is five times more likely to be jailed than a child who grows up with parents who manage to stay out of jail, said Ann Jacobs, director of the Women's Prison Association, a group which develops programs for incarcerated women.

One in 10 of those children will be jailed before adulthood, said Jacobs.

"Children with an incarcerated parent are much more susceptible to a bad activity such as gang involvement, early pregnancy and early crime activity," said Jacobs.

LOCKING UP MOTHERS HURTS

And when a mother goes to jail, the effect on a child is particularly bad, said Jacobs.

Jacobs pointed to a recent federal law, the Adoption and Safe Families Act of 1997, as worsening the situation. Instead of seeking to reunify children with their parents—who may have reformed after leaving jail—the law makes it easier for authorities to strip away parental rights and place a child with relatives or in foster care.

The majority of women prisoners are nonviolent offenders, often locked up on drug charges, said Jacobs. Since many states now employ strict sentencing guidelines—and since women are generally low-level offenders with little information that might entice a prosecutor to bargain for a lesser plea—women offenders often draw long prison sentences, said Jacobs.

"I personally find this devastating," she said. "I can't tell you how many women I know who've lost their kids, and then turned out to be good moms."

Those children, she said, are more likely to be headed for trouble—and jail—without their mother's support.

VISITATION ENCOURAGED

Jacobs and others who spoke at the workshop on incarcerated parents said children should be encouraged to visit parents in prison, to strengthen family bonds and give the jailed parents incentive to turn their lives around.

"Now, can we actively involve the family, instead of sending out ambulances to repair the damage that's being done to them?" asked Jim Mustin, founder of the Family Corrections Network, a group that seeks to strengthen ties between family members inside prison and out.

Currently, roughly half of incarcerated mothers receive visits from their children, Jacobs said.

VALUE SYSTEMS TAUGHT IN PRISON

Inside the prison, too, more should be done to teach inmates how to be better parents, said Garry Mendez, director of the National Trust for the Development of African-American Men.

Mendez said he was less interested in reforming the system than those inside it.

"How come, when we have this captive audience of males, we can't try to teach them how to be responsible fathers?" Mendez asked.

Mendez's group works inside prisons to change the value systems of prisoners, teaching them to take care of their own mental and physical health, and to respect their families.

"We demand that they take care of themselves. We tell them, 'Don't call anyone home collect and tell them what to do,' " said Mendez. "Instead, when you call, ask them if there's anything you can do."

Source: Jim Krane, "Experts Warn of Trouble With Growing Incarceration Rate," APB News, April 8, 1999. Reprinted with permission.

(SSSL) theory of crime. Like Sutherland, Akers has summarized his approach in several concise propositions:[13]

1. Deviant behavior is learned according to the principles of operant conditioning.
2. Deviant behavior is learned both in nonsocial situations that are reinforcing or discriminating and through social interaction in which the behavior of others is reinforcing or discriminating for such behavior.
3. The principal part of the learning of deviant behavior occurs in those groups which comprise or control the individual's major source of reinforcements.
4. The learning of deviant behavior, including specific techniques, attitudes, and avoidance procedures, is a function of the effective and available reinforcers and the existing reinforcement contingencies.
5. The specific class of behavior learned and its frequency of occurrence are a function of the effective and available reinforcers and the deviant or nondeviant direc-

A child watches his mother smoking a cigarette. Social learning theory says that social behavior is learned. Will this child grow up to be a smoker? *James King-Holmes, Science Photo Library/Photo Researchers, Inc.*

tion of the norms, rules, and definitions which in the past have accompanied the reinforcement.

6. The probability that a person will commit deviant behavior is increased in the presence of normative statements, definitions, and verbalizations which, in the process of differential reinforcement of such behavior over conforming behavior, have acquired discriminative value.

7. The strength of deviant behavior is a direct function of the amount, frequency, and probability of its reinforcement. The modalities of association with deviant patterns are important insofar as they affect the source, amount, and scheduling of reinforcement.

Differential Identification Theory

Like the approach of Ronald Akers, **Daniel Glaser's differential identification theory** builds upon Sutherland's notion of differential association.[14] The central tenet of Glaser's differential identification theory is that "a person pursues criminal behavior to the extent that he identifies himself with real or imaginary persons from whose perspective his criminal behavior seems acceptable."[15] In effect, Glaser proposed that the process of differential association leads to an intimate personal identification with lawbreakers, resulting in criminal or delinquent acts. Glaser recognized that people will identify with various others and that some of these identifications will be relatively strong and

others will be weak—hence the term *differential* identification. According to Glaser, however, it is not the frequency or the intensity of association that, as Sutherland believed, determines behavior, but the symbolic process of identification. Identification with a person, or with an abstract understanding of what that person might be like, can be more important than actual associations with real people. Hence role models can consist of abstract ideas rather than actual people, and an individual might selectively identify with, say, a serial killer or a terrorist bomber, even though he or she has never met such a person. Glaser also recognized the role of economic conditions, frustrations with one's place in the social structure, learned moral creeds, and group participation in producing differential identifications. Alternatively, according to Glaser, identification with noncriminals offers the possibility of rehabilitation.

Social Control Theory

According to Charles R. Tittle, a prominent sociologist at Washington State University with a specialty in crime and deviance, **social control theories** emphasize "the inhibiting effect of social and psychological integration with others whose potential negative response, surveillance, and expectations regulate or constrain criminal impulses."[16] In other words, social control theorists seek to identify those features of the personality and the environment that keep people from committing crimes. Controlling features of personality and the physical environment were identified earlier in Chapters 6 and 7, respectively. As Tittle observes, however, social control theorists take a step beyond static aspects of the personality and physical features of the environment in order to focus on the *process* through which social integration develops. It is the extent of a person's integration with positive social institutions and with significant others that determines that person's resistance to criminal temptations; social control theorists focus on the process through which such integration develops. Rather than stressing causative factors in criminal behavior, however, social control theories tend to ask why people actually obey rules instead of breaking them.[17]

Containment Theory

In the 1950s, a student of the Chicago School, **Walter C. Reckless,** wrote *The Crime Problem.*[18] Reckless tackled head-on the realization that most sociological theories, although conceptually enlightening, offered less than perfect predictability. That is, they lacked the ability to predict precisely which individuals, even those exposed to various "causes" of crime, would become criminal. Reckless thought that the sociological perspectives prevalent at the time offered only half of a comprehensive theoretical framework. Crime, Reckless wrote, was the consequence of social pressures to involve oneself in violations of the law, as well as of failure to resist such pressures. Reckless called his approach **containment theory,** and he compared it with a biological immune response, saying that only some people exposed to a disease actually come down with it. Sickness, like crime, Reckless avowed, results from the failure of control mechanisms—some internal to the person, and others external. In the case of sickness, external failures might include unsanitary conditions, the failure of the public health service, the unavailability of preventative medicine, or the lack of knowledge necessary to make such medicine effective. Still, disease will not result unless the individual's resistance to disease-causing organisms is low or unless the individual is in some other way weak or susceptible to the disease.

In the case of crime, Reckless wrote, *external containment* consists of "the holding power of the group."[19] Under most circumstances, Reckless said, "the society, the state, the tribe, the village, the family, and other nuclear groups are able to hold the individual within the bounds of the accepted norms and expectations."[20] In addition to setting limits, Reckless saw society as providing individuals with meaningful roles and activities. He saw such roles as an important factor of *external containment.*

Inner containment, said Reckless, "represents the ability of the person to follow the expected norms, to direct himself."[21] Such ability was said to be enhanced by a positive self-image, a focus on socially approved goals, personal aspirations that are in line with reality, a good tolerance for frustration, and a general adherence to the norms and values of society. A person with a positive self-image can avoid the temptations of crime simply by thinking, "I'm not that kind of person." A focus on socially approved goals helps keep people on the proverbial straight and narrow path. "Aspirations that are in line with reality" are simply realistic desires. In other words, if a person seriously desires to be the richest person in the world, disappointment will probably result. Even when aspirations are reasonable, however, disappointments will occur—hence the need for a good tolerance for frustration.

Reckless's containment theory is diagrammed in Figure 8-1. "Pushes toward crime" represents those factors in an individual's background that might propel him or her into criminal behavior. They include a criminogenic background or upbringing that involves participation in a delinquent

subculture, deprivation, biological propensities toward deviant behavior, and psychological maladjustment. "Pulls toward crime" signifies all the perceived rewards crime may offer, including financial gain, sexual satisfaction, and higher status. "**Containment**" is a stabilizing force and, if effective, blocks such pushes and pulls from leading the individual toward crime.

Reckless believed that inner containment was far more effective than external containment in preventing law violations. In his words, "As social relations become more impersonal, as society becomes more diverse and alienated, as people participate more and more for longer periods of time away from a home base, the self becomes more and more important as a controlling agent."[22]

Delinquency and Self-Esteem

As mentioned at the start of this section, social control theory predicts that when social constraints on antisocial behavior are weakened or absent, delinquent behavior will emerge. An innovative perspective on social control was offered by **Howard B. Kaplan** in the mid-1970s.[23] Kaplan proposed that people who are ridiculed by their peers suffer a loss of self-esteem, assess themselves poorly, and (thereby) abandon the motivation to conform. This approach has come to be known as the "self-derogation theory of delinquency."

A number of studies appear to support the idea that low self-esteem fosters delinquent behavior.[24] At the same time, however, it appears that delinquency can also enhance self-esteem, at least for some delinquents.[25] At least one study has found that delinquent behavior enhances self-esteem in adolescents whose self-esteem is already very low.[26]

Some researchers have examined ethnic identification as a factor in low self-esteem and as a precursor to delinquent behavior. In 1986, K. Leung and F. Drasgow tested Kaplan's self-derogation theory using white, black, and Hispanic youth groups.[27] They concluded that while all three groups reported low self-esteem, only among white youngsters were low levels of self-esteem related to delinquent behavior. Other researchers, however, found no differences in self-

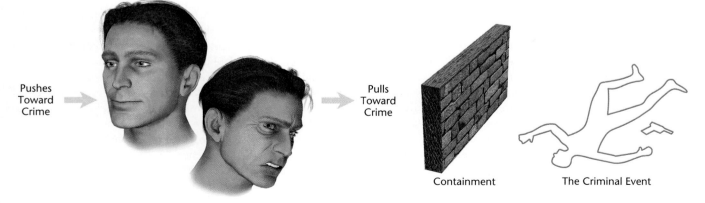

Pushes Toward Crime

Pulls Toward Crime

Containment

The Criminal Event

■ **FIGURE 8-1** A DIAGRAMMATIC REPRESENTATION OF CONTAINMENT THEORY.

esteem and delinquency between black and white delinquents and nondelinquents.[28]

In 1990, in an effort to explain some of the contradictory findings of self-derogation research, Daphna Oyserman and Hazel Rose Markus proposed that "possible selves," rather than self-esteem, might be a major explanatory factor in delinquency.[29] According to the self-esteem approach of Oyserman and Markus, the degree of disjuncture between what a person wants to be and what they fear they might become is a good potential predictor of delinquency.[30] Hence an adolescent who is confused about what he or she wants to be or fears becoming may resort to delinquency in order to resolve the conflict. Oyserman and Markus suggest that the highest levels of delinquency can be found among youth who lack balance between their expected selves ("Someday I'll be happily married and have a good job and a nice family") and their feared selves ("I could fail in school, be arrested, and end up in prison").

Social Bond Theory

An important form of control theory was popularized by **Travis Hirschi** in his 1969 book, *Causes of Delinquency.*[31] Hirschi's approach was well received by criminologists and "has epitomized social control theorizing for nearly three decades."[32] Hirschi argued that through successful socialization, a bond forms between individuals and the social group. When that bond is weakened or broken, deviance and crime may result. Hirschi described four components of the **social bond**:

■ Attachment: a person's shared interests with others
■ Commitment: the amount of energy and effort put into activities with others
■ Involvement: the amount of time spent with others in shared activities
■ Belief: a shared value and moral system

In his writings, Hirschi cites the psychopath as an example of the kind of person whose attachment to society is nearly nonexistent.[33] Other relatively normal individuals may find their attachment to society loosened through "the process of becoming alienated from others [which] often involves or is based on active interpersonal conflict," says Hirschi. "Such conflict could easily supply a reservoir of socially derived hostility sufficient to account for the aggressiveness of those whose attachments to others have been weakened."[34]

The second component of the social bond—commitment—reflects a person's investment of time and energies into conforming behavior and the potential loss of the rewards that he or she has already gained from that behavior. In Hirschi's words, "The idea, then, is that the person invests time, energy, himself, in a certain line of activity—say, getting an education, building up a business, acquiring a reputation for virtue. Whenever he considers deviant behavior, he must consider the costs of this deviant behavior, the risk he runs of losing the investment he has made in conventional behavior."[35] For such a traditionally successful person, says Hirschi, "a ten-dollar-holdup is stupidity" because the potential for losing what has already been acquired through commitment to social norms far exceeds what stands to be gained. Recognizing that his approach applies primarily to individuals who have been successfully socialized into conventional society, Hirschi adds, "The concept of commitment assumes that the organization of society is such that the interests of most persons would be endangered if they were to engage in criminal acts."[36]

Involvement, for Hirschi, means "engrossment in conventional activities"[37] and is similar to Reckless's concept of meaningful roles. In explaining the importance of involvement in determining conformity, Hirschi cites the colloquial saying that "idle hands are the devil's workshop." Time and energy, he says, are limited, and if a person is busy at legitimate pursuits, he or she will have little opportunity for crime and deviance.

Belief, the last of Hirschi's four aspects of the social bond, sets his control theory apart from subcultural approaches. Hirschi says that unlike subcultural theory, "control theory assumes the existence of a common value system within the society or group whose norms are being violated. . . . We not only assume the deviant has believed the rules, we assume he believes the rules even as he violates them."[38] How can a person simultaneously believe it is wrong to commit a crime and still commit it? Hirschi's answer is that "many persons do not have an attitude of respect toward the rules of society."[39] That is, although they know the rules exist, they basically do not care. They invest little of their sense of self in moral standards.

In 1990, Hirschi, in collaboration with **Michael Gottfredson**, proposed a general theory of crime based on the concepts advanced earlier in control theory.[40] (Control theory was briefly discussed in Chapter 6.) Gottfredson and Hirschi began by asking, "What is crime?" Nearly all crimes, they concluded, are mundane, simple, trivial, easy acts aimed at satisfying desires of the moment. Hence their general theory is built on a classical or rational choice perspective—that is, the belief that crime is a natural consequence of unrestrained human tendencies to seek pleasure and avoid pain. Crime, said Gottfredson and Hirschi, is little more than a subset of general deviant behavior. Hence, they concluded, crime bears little resemblance to the explanations offered in the media, by law enforcement officials, or by most academic thinkers on the subject.

According to Gottfredson and Hirschi, the offender is neither the diabolical genius of fiction nor the ambitious seeker of the American Dream often portrayed by other social scientists. On the contrary, offenders appear to have little control over their own desires. When personal desires conflict with long-term interests, those who lack self-control often opt for the desires of the moment, thus contravening legal restrictions and becoming involved in crime.[41] Central to Gottfredson and Hirschi's thesis is the belief that

The social bond forms early in life. What might this child be learning? *Steve Rubin, The Image Works*

a well-developed social bond will result in the creation of effective mechanisms of self-control. As others have noted, "For Gottfredson and Hirschi, self-control is the key concept in the explanation of all forms of crime as well as other types of behavior. Indeed, they believe that all current differences in rates of crime between groups and categories may be explained by differences in the management of self-control."[42]

Control-Balance Theory

Traditional control theories posit that deviance and crime result from either weak social bonds or low levels of self-control. A novel form of control theory can be found in **Charles R. Tittle**'s control-balance perspective.[43] Tittle's control-balance approach results from a blending of the social bond and containment perspectives. Tittle argues that too much control can be just as dangerous as too little. The crucial concept in Tittle's approach is what he calls the **control ratio**. The control ratio is the amount of control to which a person is subject versus the amount of control that person exerts over others. The control ratio is said to not only predict the probability that one will engage in deviance, but also the specific form that deviance will take.

High levels of control, or overcontrol, are termed "control surplus," while low levels are called "control deficit." Individuals with control surpluses are able to exercise a great deal of control over others and will work to extend their degree of control even further. Their efforts lead to deviant actions involving exploitation, plunder, and decadence.[44] A control deficit exists for people unable to exercise much control over others (and who are, hence, overly controlled). Control deficits result in deviance as an attempt to escape repressive controls. Deviance engendered by control deficit takes the form of predation (physical violence, theft, sexual assault, robbery, and so on), defiance (challenges to conventional norms, including vandalism, curfew violations, and sullenness), or submission (which Tittle describes as "passive, unthinking, slavish obedience to the expectations, commands, or anticipated desires of others"[45]). According to Tittle, however, control imbalance only sets the stage for deviance. Deviance ultimately occurs once a person realizes, at some level, that acts of deviance can reset the control ratio in a favorable way. Finally, opportunity also plays a significant role in Tittle's theory. "No matter how favorable the motivational and constraint configuration," says Tittle, "the actual likelihood of deviance occurring depends on there being an opportunity for it to happen."[46]

Labeling Theory

Another social process perspective is based on the study of societal reactions to deviance. Society's response to known or suspected offenders is important not only because it determines the individual futures of those who are labeled as criminals, but also because it may contribute to a heightened incidence of criminality by reducing the behavioral options available to labeled offenders.

An early description of societal reaction to deviance can be found in the work of **Frank Tannenbaum**. Tannenbaum's book *Crime and the Community,* published in 1938, popularized the term **tagging** to explain what happens to offenders following arrest, conviction, and sentencing. Tannenbaum told his readers that crime was essentially the result of "two opposing definitions of the situation"—those of the delinquent and the community at large. "This conflict over the situation," he said, "is one that arises out of a divergence of values. As the problem develops, the situation gradually becomes redefined. The attitude of the community hardens definitely into a demand for suppression. There is a gradual shift from the definition of the specific acts as evil to a definition of the individual as evil, so that all his acts come to be looked upon with suspicion. . . . From the community's point of view, the individual who used to do bad and mischievous things has now become a bad and unredeemable human being. . . . The young delinquent becomes bad because he is defined as bad and because he is not believed if he is good. There is a persistent demand for consistency in character. The community cannot deal with people whom it cannot define."[47]

Tannenbaum used the phrase "dramatization of evil" to explain the process whereby an offender comes to be seen as ultimately and irrevocably "bad." After the process has been completed, Tannenbaum said, the offender "now lives in a different world. He has been tagged. . . . The process of making the criminal, therefore, is a process of tagging."[48] Once a person has been defined as bad, few legitimate opportunities remain open to him or her. As a consequence, the offender finds that only other people who have been similarly defined by society as bad are available to associate with him or her. This continued association with negatively defined others leads to continued crime.

Using terminology developed by **Edwin M. Lemert,** it became fashionable to call an offender's initial acts of deviance "primary deviance" and the offender's continued acts of deviance, especially those resulting from forced association with other offenders, "secondary deviance." **Primary deviance,** Lemert pointed out, may be undertaken to solve some immediate problem or to meet the expectations of one's subcultural group. Hence the robbery of a convenience store by a college student temporarily desperate for tuition money, although not a wise undertaking, may be the first serious criminal offense ever committed by the student. The student may well intend for it to be the last, but if arrest ensues and the student is "tagged" with the status of a criminal, then secondary deviance may occur as a means of adjustment to the negative status. In Lemert's words, "When a person begins to employ his deviant behavior or a role based upon it as a means of defense, attack, or adjustment to the overt and covert problems created by the consequent societal reaction to him, his deviation is secondary."[49]

Secondary deviance becomes especially important because of the forceful role it plays in causing tagged individuals to internalize the negative labels which have been applied to them. Through such a process, labeled individuals assume the role of the deviant. According to Lemert, "Objective evidences of this change will be found in the symbolic appurtenances of the new role, in clothes, speech, posture, and mannerisms, which in some cases heighten social visibility, and which in some cases serve as symbolic cues to professionalization."[50]

The name most often associated with labeling theory is that of **Howard Becker.** In 1963, Becker published *Outsiders: Studies in the Sociology of Deviance,*[51] the work in which the **labeling** perspective found its fullest development. In *Outsiders,* Becker described the deviant subculture of jazz musicians and the process by which an individual becomes a marijuana user, among other things. His primary focus, however, was to explain how a person becomes labeled an outsider, as "a special kind of person, one who cannot be trusted to live by the rules agreed on by the group."[52] The central fact about deviance, says Becker, is that it is a social product, that "it is created by society." Society creates both deviance and the deviant person by responding to circumscribed behaviors. The person who engages in sanctioned behavior is, as part of the process, labeled a deviant. In Becker's words, "Social groups create deviance by making the rules whose infraction constitutes deviance, and by applying those rules to particular people and labeling them as outsiders. From this point of view, deviance is not a quality of the act the person commits, but rather a consequence of the application by others of rules and sanctions. . . . The deviant is one to whom that label has been successfully applied."[53] For Becker, as for other labeling theorists, no act is intrinsically deviant or criminal but must be defined as such by others. Becoming deviant, Becker noted, involves a sequence of steps that eventually lead to commitment to a deviant identity and participation in a deviant career.

In developing labeling theory, Becker attempted to explain how some rules come to carry the force of law, while others have less weight or apply only within the context of marginal subcultures. His explanation centered on the concept of **moral enterprise,** a term which he used to encompass all the efforts a particular interest group makes to have its sense of propriety embodied in law. "Rules are the products of someone's initiative," said Becker, "and we can think of the people who exhibit such enterprise as moral entrepreneurs."[54]

An early example of moral enterprise can be found in the Women's Christian Temperance Union (WCTU), a group devoted to the prohibition of alcohol. From 1881–1919 the WCTU was highly visible in its nationwide fight against alcohol—holding marches and demonstrations, closing drinking establishments, and lobbying legislators. Press coverage of the WCTU's activities swayed many politicians into believing that the lawful prohibition of alcoholic beverages was inevitable, and an amendment to the U.S. Constitution soon followed, ushering in the age of prohibition. Moral enterprise is similarly used, Becker claimed, by other groups seeking to support their own interests with the weight of law. Often the group that is successful at moral enterprise does not represent a popular point of view. The group is simply more effective than others at maneuvering through the formal bureaucracy that attends the creation of legislation.

Becker was especially interested in describing deviant careers—the processes by which individuals become members of deviant subcultures and take on the attributes associated with the deviant role. Becker argued that most deviance, when it first occurs, is likely to be transitory. That is, it is unlikely to occur again. However, transitory deviance can be effectively stabilized in a person's behavioral repertoire through the labeling process. Once a person is labeled "deviant," opportunities for conforming behavior are seriously reduced. Behavioral opportunities that remain open are primarily deviant ones. Hence throughout the person's career, the budding deviant increasingly exhibits deviant behavior, not so much out of choice, but rather because his or her choices are restricted by society. Additionally, successful deviants must acquire the techniques and resources necessary to undertake the deviant act (be it drug use or bank robbery) and must develop the mind-set characteristic of others like them. Near the completion of a deviant career, the person who has been labeled a deviant internalizes society's negative label, assumes a deviant self-concept, and is likely to become a member of a deviant subgroup. Becker says, "A drug addict once told me that the moment she felt she was really 'hooked' was when she realized she no longer had any friends who were not drug addicts."[55] In this way, says Becker, deviance finally becomes a "self-fulfilling prophecy." Labeling, then, is a cause of crime insofar as the actions of society in defining the rule breaker as deviant push the person further in the direction of continued deviance.

Labeling theory contributed a number of unique ideas to the criminological literature, including the following:

■ Deviance is the result of social processes involving the imposition of definitions, rather than the consequence of any quality inherent in human activity itself.

■ Deviant individuals achieve their status by virtue of social definition, rather than because of inborn traits.

■ The reaction of society to deviant behavior and to those who engage in such behavior is the major element in determining the criminality of the person and of the behavior in question.

■ Negative self-images follow from processing by the formal criminal justice system, rather than precede delinquency.

■ Labeling by society and handling by the justice system tend to perpetuate crime and delinquency, rather than reduce it.

Becker's typology of delinquents helped explain the labeling approach. It consisted of (1) the pure deviant, (2) the falsely accused deviant, and (3) the secret deviant. The pure deviant is one who commits norm-breaking behavior and whose behavior is accurately appraised as such by society. An example might be the burglar who is caught in the act of burglary, then tried and convicted. Such a person, we might say, has gotten what he deserves. The falsely accused individual is one who, in fact, is not guilty, but is labeled "deviant" nonetheless. The falsely accused category in Becker's typology demonstrates the power of social definition. Innocent people sometimes end up in prison, and one can imagine that the impact of conviction and of the experiences which attend prison life can leave the falsely accused with a negative self-concept and with group associations practically indistinguishable from those of the true deviant. In effect, the life of the falsely accused is changed just as thoroughly as is the life of the pure deviant by the process of labeling. Finally, the secret deviant violates social norms, but his or her behavior is not noticed, and negative societal reactions do not follow. The secret deviant again demonstrates the power of societal reaction—in this case by the very lack of consequences.

Recently, Mike S. Adams proposed a general sociological learning theory of crime and deviance that incorporates components of labeling theory and differential association.[56] Adams contends that "labeling effects are mediated by associations with delinquent peers." He concludes that labeling is not a direct cause of delinquency and crime but "appears to cause delinquency indirectly via the effects of associations with delinquent peer groups." In other words, "the causal chain linking primary to secondary deviance must incorporate links that account for the effects of associations with delinquent [peers]."[57] Learn more about labeling theory at Web Extra! 8-1.

Web Extra! 8-1 at crimtoday.com

Reintegrative Shaming

In a contemporary offshoot of labeling theory, **John Braithwaite** and colleagues at the Australian National University (ANU) reported initial results of studies on reintegrative shaming in 1997.[58] In contrast to traditional labeling theory, which emphasizes stigmatization and the resulting amplification of deviance, reintegrative shaming describes processes by which a deviant is labeled and sanctioned but then brought back into a community of conformity through words, gestures, or rituals.

Braithwaite, along with Lawrence W. Sherman of the University of Maryland and Heather Strang at ANU, compared the effectiveness of traditional court processing of criminal offenders with a restorative justice approach operating in Canberra, Australia, known as "diversionary conferencing." The diversionary conferencing approach "consists of an emotionally intense meeting, led by a police officer, between admitted offenders and their supporters, usually family and friends, and the victim of the offense, together with their supporters. In the absence of a direct victim, a representative of the community in which the offence occurred expresses the victim perspective on the events. The group discusses the consequences of the offense for all the parties and then determines what restitution the offenders must comply with to repair the harm for which they are responsible and so avoid going to court."[59]

Called RISE, for Reintegrative Shaming Experiments, the project assessed the efficacy of each approach using criteria like these: (1) prevalence and frequency of repeat offending, (2) victim satisfaction with the process, (3) estimated cost savings within the justice process, (4) changes in drinking or drug use behavior among offenders, and (5) perceptions of procedural justice, fairness, and protection of rights.[60]

At the core of the study was Braithwaite's belief that two different kinds of shame exist. One is called "stigmatic shaming." **Stigmatic shaming** is thought to destroy the moral bond between the offender and the community. The other type of shame, **reintegrative shaming**, is thought to strengthen the moral bond between the offender and the community. According to Braithwaite, "Stigmatic shaming is what American judges employ when they make an offender post a sign on his property saying 'a violent felon lives here,' or a bumper sticker on his car saying 'I am a drunk driver.' Stigmatic shaming sets the offender apart as an outcast—often for the rest of the offender's life. By labeling him or her as someone who cannot be trusted to obey the law, stigmatic shaming says the offender is expected to commit more crimes."[61]

Braithwaite's alternative to stigmatic humiliation is "to condemn the crime, not the criminal."[62] Through carefully monitored diversionary conferences, Braithwaite hopes to give offenders the opportunity to rejoin the community as law-abiding citizens. To earn the right to a fresh start, says Braithwaite, offenders must express remorse for their past conduct, apologize to any victims, and repair the harm caused by the crime.

Minor offenders perform court-ordered duties in public view. Some people believe that shaming can be an effective rehabilitative tool. What different kinds of shaming can you identify? *L. Delevingne, Stock Boston*

Preliminary results from the RISE studies support the claimed value of reintegrative shaming. To date, however, most such results have been measured through interviews with offenders following diversionary conferences and consist primarily of anecdotal evidence based on the reported feelings of respondents. Findings show that offenders are far more likely to feel ashamed of their crimes if handled through conferences rather than through formal court processing. Moreover, both offenders and victims report finding conferences more fair than official court proceedings. Learn more about the reintegrative shaming experiments at Web Extra! 8-2.

Web EXTRA! Web Extra! 8-2 at crimtoday.com

Dramaturgy

Another social process approach to the study of criminology can be found in the work of **Erving Goffman**. Goffman's 1959 book, *The Presentation of Self in Everyday Life*, introduced students of criminology to the concept of dramaturgy.[63] The **dramaturgical perspective** says that individuals play a variety of nearly simultaneous social roles—such as mother, teacher, daughter, wife, and part-time real estate agent—and that such roles must be sustained in interaction with others. Shakespeare's famous claim that "all the world's a stage, and all the men and women merely players: They have their exits and their entrances; and one man in his time plays many parts"[64] provides a good summation of Goffman's dramaturgical approach.

Goffman argued that social actors present themselves more or less effectively when acting out a particular role and that role performances basically consist of managed impressions. Through communications, both verbal and nonverbal, social actors define the situations in which they are involved. A medical doctor, for example, may wear a lab coat and a name tag with her title emblazoned on it, carry a stethoscope and other medical accoutrements, and introduce herself as "Dr. Smith." Each choice the doctor makes, in what she wears or says or how she acts, is intended to convey, according to Goffman, medical authority—and to thereby establish certain rules of interpersonal interaction, that is, to demand a certain appropriate kind of subservience from specified others, including patients, nurses, and laboratory technicians. Medical doctors may, by way of their esoteric knowledge and the awe they inspire in patients and their families, mystify their audiences and thereby gain compliance with their wishes, which makes their jobs easier. Criminals, through a similar process of managed impressions and by way of the fear they engender in their victims, may likewise achieve cooperation.

Impression management, according to Goffman, is a complex process involving a never-ending give-and-take of information. Back regions (such as dressing rooms) in which actors prepare for their roles, front regions (such as offices) where furniture, degrees, and plaques are carefully placed, and personal displays of status or role occupancy all play a part in the management of impressions. When impression management has been successful, said Goffman, dramatic realization has occurred. "Together," he said, "the participants contribute to a single overall definition of the situation which involves not so much a real agreement as to what exists but rather a real agreement as to whose claims concerning what issues will be temporarily honored."[65]

Goffman also claimed that a performer can "be completely taken in by his own act," or on the other hand, "the performer may not be taken in at all by his own routine"[66] and may not be the person he represents himself as being. When the performer is not duped but others are, then the performance is a sham or a fraud. In such cases of misrepresentation, he said, "we may take a harsh view of performers such as confidence men who knowingly misrepresent every fact about their lives, [but] we may have some sympathy for those who have but one fatal flaw and who attempt to conceal the fact that they are, for example, ex-convicts."[67]

Deviant behavior finds its place in the dramaturgical perspective through the concept of discreditable disclosure. Some actors, said Goffman, may find themselves discredited by the introduction of new information, especially by information they have sought to hide. When such **discrediting information** is revealed, the flow of interaction is disrupted, and the nature of the performance may be altered substantially. In an example from real life, which was made into a play and the 1993 movie *M. Butterfly,* a French diplomat in China spent twenty years living with a Beijing opera singer, never knowing that "she" was really a he.[68] Such an interpersonal relationship must have required nothing less than heroic impression management, with the potential for discrediting information always close at hand.

Goffman would say that "to be a given kind of person" requires the dramatic realization of one's claimed status. What one is depends on how successful one is at acquiring the abilities necessary to convince others of one's claims. In his words, "A status, a position, a social place is not a material thing. . . . It is a pattern of appropriate conduct, coherent, embellished, and well articulated. . . . It is . . . something that must be enacted and portrayed, something that must be realized."[69]

Goffman's work takes on considerable relevance for criminology in his later writings, especially his book *Stigma: Notes on the Management of Spoiled Identity*.[70] In *Stigma*, Goffman advanced the notion that discredited, or stigmatized, individuals differ significantly from "normals" in the way that society responds to them. "By definition . . .," he said, "we believe that a person with a stigma is not quite human. On this assumption we exercise varieties of discrimination, through which we effectively, if often unthinkingly, reduce his life chances. We construct a stigma-theory, an ideology to explain his inferiority and account for the danger he represents. . . . We tend to impute a wide range of imperfections on the basis of the original one."[71] Stigmata (the plural of stigma) may be physical (such as birthmarks), behavioral (such as theft), or ideational (such as a low rank in the proverbial pecking order).

In *Stigma*, Goffman is primarily concerned with how "normals" and stigmatized individuals interact. At times, says Goffman, discredited individuals are known to others before they come into contact with them. When that happens, normal people approach the stigmatized with expectations of encountering further stigmatizing behavior. When discrediting information does not precede interpersonal encounters, the stigmatized individual may attempt to "pass" as normal using various techniques of concealment, including aliases and misrepresentation.

According to Goffman, societal reactions, although they may forcibly create social identities, are also instrumental in the formation of group identities. When similarly discredited individuals come together in like-minded groups, they may align themselves against the larger society. In so reacting, they may justify their own deviant or criminal behavior. At the conclusion of *Stigma*, Goffman reminded us, "The normal and the stigmatized are not persons, but rather perspectives. These are generated in social situations during mixed contacts by virtue of the unrealized norms that are likely to play upon the encounter."[72]

In another book, *Asylums*, Goffman described **total institutions**—facilities from which individuals can rarely come and go and in which communal life is intense and circumscribed.[73] Individuals in total institutions tend to eat, sleep, play, learn, and worship (if at all) together. Military camps, seminaries, convents, prisons, rest homes, and mental hospitals are all types of asylums, according to Goffman. Goffman believed that residents of total institutions bring "presenting cultures" with them to their respective facilities. In the case of prisons, for example, some inmates carry street culture into correctional facilities, whereas others, from different walks of life, bring a variety of other cultural baggage. However, said Goffman, residents undergo a period of "disculturation," during which they drop aspects of the presenting culture that are not consistent with existing institutional culture—a culture they must acquire.

POLICY IMPLICATIONS OF SOCIAL PROCESS THEORIES

Social process theories suggest that crime prevention programs should work to enhance self-control and to build social bonds. One program that seeks to build strong social bonds while attempting to teach positive values to young people is the Juvenile Mentoring Program (JUMP) of the Office of Juvenile Justice and Delinquency Prevention

The Taming of the Shrew, performed in Tucson, Arizona. Some criminologists suggest that people, like actors on a stage, intentionally present themselves to others in ways calculated to produce predictable social responses. How might criminals manipulate impressions? *First Image, The Image Works*

(OJJDP). Fundamentally a social control initiative, JUMP was funded by Congress in 1992 under an amendment to the Juvenile Justice and Delinquency Prevention Act of 1974.[74] OJJDP-sponsored JUMP programs commenced operation in 1996. JUMP places at-risk youth in a one-on-one relationship with favorable adult role models. At-risk youth are defined as those who are at risk of delinquency, gang involvement, educational failure, or dropping out of school. General demographic information is used in conjunction with scores on a standardized risk-assessment instrument known as the Problem Oriented Screening Instrument for Teens in order to identify potential JUMP participants.

As of September 2000, 7,422 youths were enrolled in more than 100 JUMP programs nationwide (see Figure 8-2). The average age at the time of enrollment was just under 12 years. Although evaluation data are just beginning to come in on the project, both youth and mentors were very positive when rating various aspects of their mentoring experiences. Learn more about JUMP at Web Extra! 8-3.

Web EXTRA! Web Extra! 8-3 at crimtoday.com

Another social control–based program is Preparing for the Drug Free Years (PDFY).[75] PDFY is designed to increase effective parenting and is part of the Strengthening America's Families Project. OJJDP, which runs the program, says, "The PDFY curriculum is guided theoretically by the social development model, which emphasizes the role of bonding to family, school, and peers in healthy adolescent development. The model specifies that strong bonding to positive influences reduces the probability of delinquency and other problem behaviors."[76]

PDFY works with parents of children in grades 4 to 8 in an effort to reduce drug abuse and behavioral problems in

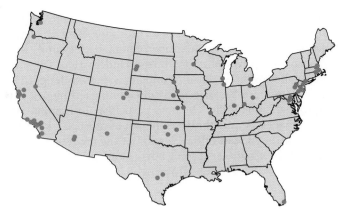

■ FIGURE 8-2 JUVENILE MENTORING PROGRAMS NATIONWIDE.
Source: Office of Juvenile Justice and Delinquency Prevention.

adolescents. It seeks to teach effective parenting skills as a way to decrease the risks that juveniles face. PDFY incorporates both behavioral skills training and communication-centered approaches into parent training. Through a series of ten one-hour sessions, parents learn to (1) increase their children's opportunities for family involvement, (2) teach needed family-participation and social skills, and (3) provide reinforcement for positive behavior and appropriate consequences for misbehavior. Early studies show that program participation (session attendance) tends to be high and that the program is effective at improving general child-management skills among parents.[77] Learn more about PDFY at Web Extra! 8-4.

Web EXTRA! Web Extra! 8-4 at crimtoday.com

People in total institutions share all aspects of their lives—such as these monks in a Buddhist monastery. How is a prison like a monastery? *Woodfin Camp & Associates*

A program that emphasizes the development of self-control is the Montreal Preventive Treatment Program.[78] It addresses early childhood risk factors for gang involvement by targeting boys from poor socioeconomic backgrounds who display disruptive behavior while in kindergarten. The program offers training sessions for parents that are designed to teach family crisis management, disciplining techniques, and other parenting skills. The boys participate in training sessions that emphasize the development of prosocial skills and self-control. At least one evaluation of the program showed that it was effective at keeping boys from joining gangs.[79]

CRITIQUE OF SOCIAL PROCESS THEORIES

Criticisms of social process theories are many and varied. Perhaps the most potent criticism of association theory is the claim that Sutherland's initial formulation of differential association is not applicable at the individual level because even people who experience an excess of definitions favorable to law violation may still not become criminal. Likewise, those who rarely associate with recognized deviants may still turn to crime. In addition, the theory is untestable because most people experience a multitude of definitions—both favorable and unfavorable to law violation—and it is up to them to interpret just what those experiences mean. Hence classifying experiences as either favorable or unfavorable to crime commission is difficult at best.

Other critics suggest that differential association alone is not a sufficient explanation for crime. If it were, then we might expect correctional officers, for example, to become criminals by virtue of their constant and continued association with prison inmates. Similarly, wrongly imprisoned people might be expected to turn to crime upon release from confinement. Little evidence suggests that either of these scenarios actually occurs. In effect, association theory does not seem to provide for free choice in individual circumstances, nor does it explain why some individuals, even when surrounded by associates who are committed to lives of crime, are still able to hold onto other, noncriminal, values. Finally, association theory fails to account for the emergence of criminal values, addressing only the communication of those values.

Similarly, the labeling approach, although it successfully points to the labeling process as a reason for continued deviance and as a cause of stabilization in deviant identities, does little to explain the origin of crime and deviance. In addition, few, if any, studies seem to support the basic tenets of the theory. Critics of labeling have pointed to its "lack of firm empirical support for the notion of secondary deviance," and "many studies have not found that delinquents or criminals have a delinquent or criminal self-image."[80] There is also a lack of unequivocal empirical support for the claim that contact with the justice system is fundamentally detrimental to the personal lives of criminal perpetrators. Even if that supposition were true, however, one must ask whether it would ultimately be

better if offenders were not caught and forced to undergo the rigors of processing by the justice system. Although labeling theory hints that official processing makes a significant contribution to continued criminality, it seems unreasonable to expect that offenders untouched by the system would forego the rewards of future criminality. Finally, labeling theory has little to say about *secret deviants,* or people who engage in criminality but are never caught. An important question about secret deviants, for example, asks whether they can be expected to continue in lives of deviance if never caught.

Goffman's work has been criticized as providing a set of "linked concepts" rather than a consistent theoretical framework.[81] Other critics have faulted Goffman for failing to offer suggestions for institutional change or for not proposing treatment modalities based on his assumptions. Goffman's greatest failing may be in taking the analogy of the theater too far and convincing readers that real life is but a form of playacting. According to George Psathas, one of Goffman's critics, "Performing and being are not identical."[82]

THE SOCIAL DEVELOPMENT PERSPECTIVE

Over the past 25 years, an emerging appreciation for the process of **human development** has played an increasingly important role in understanding criminality.[83] *Human development* refers to the relationship between the maturing individual and his or her changing environment and to the social processes that relationship entails. Students of human development recognize that the process of development occurs through reciprocal and dynamic interactions that take place between individuals and various aspects of their environment. The **social development perspective** understands that development, which begins at birth (and perhaps even earlier), occurs primarily within a social context. Unlike learning theory (discussed earlier in this chapter), however, social development theories see socialization as only one feature of that context. If socialization were the primary determinant of criminality, development theorists point out, then we might expect that all problem children would become criminals as adults. Since that doesn't happen, there must be other aspects to the development process that social learning theories don't fully appreciate.

According to the social development perspective, human development occurs on many levels simultaneously, including psychological, biological, familial, interpersonal, cultural, societal, and ecological. Hence social development theories tend to be integrated theories, or theories that combine various points of view on the process of development. The rest of this chapter describes different kinds of social development theories. You can also learn more about such perspectives at Web Extra! 8-5.

Web Extra! 8-5 at crimtoday.com

CONCEPTS IN SOCIAL DEVELOPMENT THEORIES

Most sociological explanations for crime involve the study of groups and the identification of differences among groups of offenders. In contrast, social development theories focus more on individual rates of offending and seek to understand both increases and decreases in rates of offending over the individual's lifetime. Social development theories generally employ longitudinal (over time) measurements of delinquency and offending, and they pay special attention to the transitions that people face as they move through the life cycle.

Most theories of social development recognize that a critical transitional period occurs as a person moves from childhood to adulthood. Life course theorists have identified at least seven developmental tasks that American adolescents must confront: (1) establishing identity, (2) cultivating symbiotic relationships, (3) defining physical attractiveness, (4) investing in a value system, (5) obtaining an education, (6) separating from family and achieving independence, and (7) obtaining and maintaining gainful employment.[84] It is generally recognized that youth are confronted with many obstacles, or risks,

in their attempts to resolve these issues as they work to make a successful transition to adulthood. Figure 8-3 provides a conceptual model of the developmental processes that a maturing child experiences during adolescence. Learn more about the transitional process leading to adulthood at Web Extra! 8-6.

Web EXTRA! Web Extra! 8-6 at *crimtoday.com*

The Life Course Perspective

Traditional explanations for crime and delinquency often lack a developmental perspective.[85] They ignore developmental changes throughout the life course and frequently fail to distinguish between different phases of criminal careers. In contrast, developmental theories draw attention to the fact that criminal behavior tends to follow a distinct pattern across the life cycle. Criminality is relatively uncommon during childhood; it tends to begin as sporadic instances of delinquency during late adolescence and early adulthood and then diminishes and sometimes completely disappears from a person's behavioral repertoire by age 30 or 40. Of course,

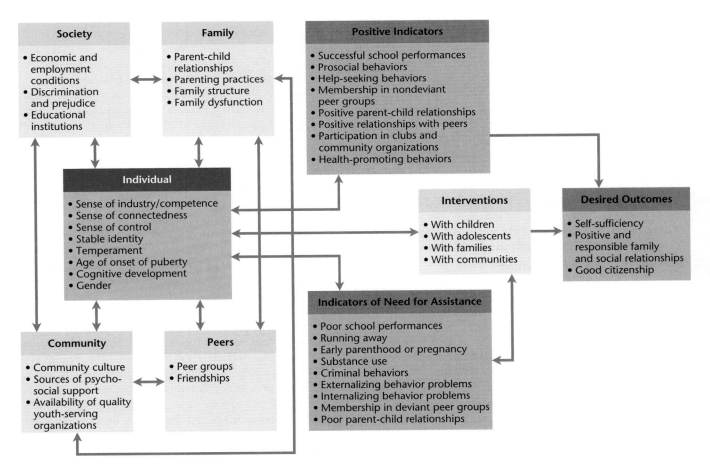

■ **FIGURE 8-3** A CONCEPTUAL MODEL OF ADOLESCENT DEVELOPMENT.
Source: Family and Youth Services Bureau, *Understanding Youth Development: Promoting Positive Pathways of Growth* (Washington, D.C.: U.S. Department of Health and Human Services, 2000).

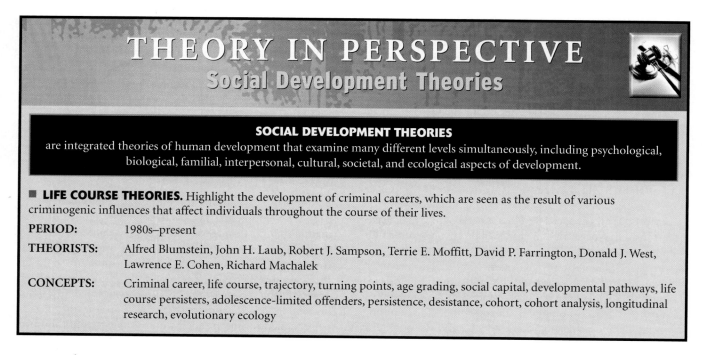

THEORY IN PERSPECTIVE
Social Development Theories

SOCIAL DEVELOPMENT THEORIES
are integrated theories of human development that examine many different levels simultaneously, including psychological, biological, familial, interpersonal, cultural, societal, and ecological aspects of development.

■ **LIFE COURSE THEORIES.** Highlight the development of criminal careers, which are seen as the result of various criminogenic influences that affect individuals throughout the course of their lives.

PERIOD: 1980s–present

THEORISTS: Alfred Blumstein, John H. Laub, Robert J. Sampson, Terrie E. Moffitt, David P. Farrington, Donald J. West, Lawrence E. Cohen, Richard Machalek

CONCEPTS: Criminal career, life course, trajectory, turning points, age grading, social capital, developmental pathways, life course persisters, adolescence-limited offenders, persistence, desistance, cohort, cohort analysis, longitudinal research, evolutionary ecology

some people never commit crimes or do so only rarely, while others become career criminals and persist in lives of crime.

Contemporary life course theory had its roots in a 1986 National Academy of Sciences (NAS) panel report prepared by Alfred Blumstein, Jacqueline Cohen, Jeffrey Roth, and Christy Visher.[86] The NAS report emphasized the importance of the study of criminal careers and of crime over the life course. The NAS panel defined a **criminal career** as "the longitudinal sequence of crimes committed by an individual offender."[87] The report was especially important for its analysis of "offending development," a concept that underlies the life course perspective.

The panel noted that criminal careers could be described in terms of four dimensions: participation, frequency, duration, and seriousness. *Participation,* which refers to the fraction of a population that is criminally active, depends on the scope of criminal acts considered and the length of the observation period.[88] *Frequency* refers to the number of crimes committed by an individual offender per unit of time. Hence a burglar who commits one burglary a year has a much lower frequency than one who is active monthly or weekly. Of course, frequency is generally not constant and varies over the life course—even for habitual offenders. *Duration* refers to the length of the criminal career. A criminal career can be very short, consisting of only one offense, or it can be quite long, as in the case of habitual or chronic criminals. *Seriousness* is relatively self-explanatory, although it is worthwhile to note that some offenders with long criminal careers commit only petty crimes, while others are serious habitual offenders, and still others commit offenses with a mixed degree of seriousness.

Life course criminology was given its name in a seminal book written by **Robert J. Sampson** and **John H. Laub** in 1993.[89] Earlier, the **life course** concept had already been defined as "pathways through the life span involving a sequence of culturally defined, age-graded roles and social transitions enacted over time."[90] Life course theories, which build on social learn-

ing and social control principles, recognize that criminal careers may develop as the result of various criminogenic influences which affect individuals over the course of their lives.

Researchers who focus on the life course as it leads to delinquency, crime, and criminal identities are interested in evaluating the prevalence, frequency, and onset of offending, as well as identifying different developmental pathways to delinquency. Life course researchers ask a variety of questions: How do early childhood characteristics (for example, antisocial behavior) lead to adult behavioral processes and outcomes? How do life transitions (for example, shifts in relationships from parents to peers, transitions from same-sex peers to opposite-sex peers, transitions from attending school to beginning work, marriage, divorce, and so on) influence behavior and behavioral choices? How do offending and victimization interact over the life cycle?[91]

Life course researchers examine "trajectories and transitions through the age-differentiated life span."[92] A trajectory is a pathway or line of development through life which is marked by a sequence of transitions in such areas as work, marriage, parenthood, and criminal behavior. "Trajectories refer to longer-term patterns and sequences of behavior, whereas transitions are marked by specific life events (e.g., first job or the onset of crime) that are embedded in trajectories and evolve over shorter time spans."[93] The concept of age differentiation (or age grading) recognizes the fact that certain forms of behavior and some experiences are more appropriate (in terms of their social consequences) in parts of the life cycle than in others. Having a baby, for example, is more manageable when a woman is married, has a spouse with a dependable job and income, is covered by health insurance, and so on, than during adolescence (when marital and employment transitions have yet to be successfully made). Life course theorists search for evidence of continuity between childhood or adolescent experiences and adult outcomes or lifestyles.

Three sets of dynamic concepts are important to the life course perspective: (1) activation, (2) aggravation, and (3) desistance.[94] *Activation* refers to the ways that delinquent behaviors, once initiated, are stimulated and the processes by which the continuity, frequency, and diversity of delinquency are shaped. Three types of activation are possible: (1) acceleration, or increased frequency of offending over time, (2) stabilization, or increased continuity over time, and (3) diversification, or the propensity of individuals to become involved in more diverse delinquent activities. *Aggravation,* the second dynamic process, refers to the existence of a developmental sequence of activities that escalate or increase in seriousness over time. *Desistance,* the third process, describes a slowing down in the frequency of offending (deceleration), a reduction in its variety (specialization), or a reduction in its seriousness (deescalation).[95] Desistance is discussed in greater detail later in this chapter.

Another central organizing principle of life course theories is linked lives. The concept of linked lives refers to the fact that human lives "are typically embedded in social relationships with kin and friends across the life span."[96] Family, friends, and coworkers exercise considerable influence on the life course of most people.

Life course theories are supported by research dating back more than half a century. During the 1930s, for example, **Sheldon Glueck** and **Eleanor Glueck** studied the life cycles of delinquent boys.[97] The Gluecks followed the careers of 500 nondelinquents and 500 known delinquents in an effort to identify the causes of delinquency. Study group participants were matched on age, intelligence, ethnicity, and neighborhood residence. Data were originally collected through psychiatric interviews with subjects, parent and teacher reports, and official records obtained from police, court, and correctional files. Surviving subjects were interviewed again between 1949 and 1965.

Significantly, the Gluecks investigated possible contributions to crime causation on four levels: sociocultural (socioeconomic), somatic (physical), intellectual, and emotional-temperamental. They concluded that family dynamics played an especially significant role in the development of criminality, and they observed that "the deeper the roots of childhood maladjustment, the smaller the chance of adult adjustment."[98] Delinquent careers, said the Gluecks, tend to carry over into adulthood and frequently lead to criminal careers.

Laub and Sampson's Age-Graded Theory

A few years ago, John H. Laub and Robert J. Sampson dusted off 60 cartons of nearly forgotten data that had been collected by the Gluecks and was stored in the basement of the Harvard Law School.[99] Upon reanalysis of the data, Laub and Sampson found that children who turned to delinquency were frequently those who had trouble at school and at home and who had friends who were already involved in delinquency. They also found that two events in

the life course—marriage and job stability—seemed to be especially important in reducing the frequency of offending in later life.

Using a sophisticated computerized analysis of the Gluecks' original data, Laub and Sampson developed an "age-graded theory of informal social control."[100] Like Hirschi (discussed earlier), Laub and Sampson suggest that delinquency is more likely to occur when an individual's bond to society is weak or broken. Their theory, however, also recognizes "that social ties embedded in adult transitions (e.g. marital attachment, job stability) explain variations in crime unaccounted for by childhood deviance."[101] Hence although it incorporates elements of social bond theory, Laub and Sampson's perspective also emphasizes the significance of continuity and change over the life course.

Central to Laub and Sampson's approach is the idea of turning points in a criminal career. The idea of turning points was first identified by G. B. Trasler in 1980. Trasler wrote, "As they grow older, most young men gain access to other sources of achievement and social satisfaction—a job, a girlfriend, a wife, a home and eventually children—and in doing so become gradually less dependent upon peer-group support."[102] Given the importance of turning points—which may turn a person either toward or away from criminality and delinquency—a clear-cut relationship between early delinquency and criminality later in life cannot be assumed. Turning points can occur at any time in the life course, although, like Trasler, Sampson and Laub identified two especially significant turning points: employment and marriage. Employers who are willing to give "troublemakers" a chance and marriage partners who insist on conventional lifestyles seem to be able to successfully redirect the course of a budding offender's life. Other important turning points can occur in association with leaving home, having children, getting divorced, graduating from school, receiving a financial windfall, and so on. According to Laub and Sampson, even chronic offenders can be reformed when they experience the requisite turning points, while individuals with histories of conventionality can begin offending in response to events and circumstances that undermine previously restraining social bonds.[103]

Because transitions in the life course are typically associated with age, and because transitional events (like marriage) either enhance or weaken the social bond, Sampson and Laub contend that "age-graded changes in social bonds explain changes in crime." Since these events are not the result of "purposeful efforts to control," they are dubbed "informal social controls."[104]

Another important concept in Laub and Sampson's theory is **social capital**. Laub and Sampson use the concept of social capital to refer to the degree of positive relationships, with other people and with social institutions, that individuals build up over the course of their lives.[105] Social capital can be enhanced by education, a consistent employment background, enriching personal connections, a "clean" record, and so on. The greater a person's social capital, the less the chance of criminal activity.[106]

Moffitt's Dual Taxonomic Theory

Criminologists have long noted that although adult criminality is almost always preceded by antisocial behavior during adolescence, most antisocial children do not become adult criminals. In what has been called "the most innovative approach to age-crime relationships and lifecourse patterns,"[107] psychologist **Terrie E. Moffitt** developed a two-path (dual taxonomic) theory of criminality that helps to explain this observation.[108] Moffitt's two-path theory contends that, as a result of neuropsychological deficits (specifically, early brain damage or chemical imbalances) combined with poverty and family dysfunction, some people come to display more or less constant patterns of misbehavior throughout life.[109] These people are termed "life-course-persistent offenders" or "life course persisters." Life course persisters tend to fail in school and become involved in delinquency at an early age. As a consequence, their opportunities for legitimate success are increasingly limited with the passage of time.

Other teenagers, says Moffitt, go through limited periods where they exhibit high probabilities of offending. Probabilities of offending are generally highest for these people, says Moffitt, during the midteen years. This second group, called "adolescence-limited offenders," is led to offending primarily by structural disadvantages, according to two-path theory. The most significant of these disadvantages is the status anxiety of teenagers that stems from modern society's inadequacy at easing the transition from adolescence to adulthood for significant numbers of young people. Moffitt hypothesizes that a significant source of adolescent strain arises from the fact that biological maturity occurs at a relatively early age (perhaps as early as age 12) and brings with it the desire for sexual and emotional relationships, as well as personal autonomy.[110] Society, however, does not permit the assumption of autonomous adult roles until far later (around age 18). As adolescents begin to desire autonomy, says Moffitt, they are prevented from achieving it because of preexisting societal expectations and societally limited opportunities, resulting in what Moffitt calls a "maturity gap." They might be told, "You're too young for that," or "Wait until you grow up." Lacking the resources to achieve autonomy on their own, they are drawn into delinquent roles by lifelong deviants who have already achieved autonomy and who serve as role models for others seeking early independence. At least an appearance of autonomy is achievable for adolescence-limited offenders by engaging in actions that mimic those routinely undertaken by life-course-persistent offenders. Once adolescence-limited offenders realize the substantial costs of continuing misbehavior, however, they abandon such social mimicry and the participation in delinquent acts that characterizes it. As they mature, they begin to aspire toward achieving legitimate autonomy. Those who fail to successfully make the transition add to the ranks of the life-course-persistent population.

Moffitt notes that adolescence-limited offenders display inconsistencies in antisocial behavior, from one place to another. They might, for example, participate in illicit drug use with friends or shoplift in stores. They might also experiment sexually. Still, their school behavior is likely to remain within socially acceptable bounds, and they will probably act with respect toward teachers, employers, and adults. Life-course-persistent offenders, on the other hand, consistently engage in antisocial behavior across a wide spectrum of social situations.

Research findings indicate that positive developmental pathways are fostered when adolescents are able to develop (1) a sense of industry and competency, (2) a feeling of connectedness to others and to society, (3) a belief in their ability to control their future; and (4) a stable identity.[111] Adolescents who develop these characteristics appear more likely than others to engage in prosocial behaviors, exhibit positive school performances, and be members of nondeviant peer groups. Competency, connectedness, control, and identity are outcomes of the developmental process. They develop through a person's interactions with his or her community, family, school, and peers. The following kinds of interactions appear to promote development of these characteristics:

- Interactions in which children engage in productive activities and win recognition for their productivity
- Interactions in which parents and other adults control and monitor adolescents' behaviors in a consistent and caring manner while allowing them a substantial degree of psychological and emotional independence
- Interactions in which parents and other adults provide emotional support, encouragement, and practical advice to adolescents
- Interactions in which adolescents are accepted as individuals with unique experiences based on their temperament, gender, biosocial development, and family, cultural, and societal factors

Farrington's Delinquent Development Theory

Life course theorists use the term **persistence** to describe continuity in crime, or continual involvement in offending. **Desistance**, on the other hand, refers to the cessation of criminal activity or to the termination of a period of involvement in offending behavior (that is, abandoning a criminal career). Desistance (which was mentioned briefly earlier in this chapter) can be of two forms: unaided and aided. *Unaided desistance* refers to desistance that occurs without the formal intervention or assistance of criminal justice agencies like probation or parole agencies, the courts, or prison or jail. *Aided desistance*, which does involve agencies of the justice system, is generally referred to as "rehabilitation." As noted earlier in our discussion of adolescence-limited offenders, delinquents often mature successfully and grow out of offending. Even older persistent offenders, however, may tire of justice system interventions or lose the personal energy required for continued offending. Such offenders are said to have "burned out."

A number of early criminologists noted the desistance phenomenon, whereby offenders appear to undergo relatively intense periods of criminal involvement during the teenage years, with continued involvement extended into their 20s and even 30s. By age 35 or so, however, a kind of spontaneous desistance seems to occur. Marvin Wolfgang described the process as one of "spontaneous remission," although it was recognized far earlier. In 1833, Adolphe Quetelet argued that the penchant for crime diminished with age "due to the enfeeblement of physical vitality and the passions."[112] The Gluecks later developed the concept of maturational reform to explain the phenomenon and suggested that the "sheer passage of time" caused delinquents to "grow out" of this transitory phase and to "burn out" physiologically. "Ageing is the only factor," they concluded, "which emerges as significant in the reformative process."[113]

In 1985, Walter R. Grove proposed a maturational theory of biopsychosocial desistance which sees the desistance phenomenon as a natural or normal consequence of the aging process.[114] Grove wrote, "As persons . . . move through the life cycle, (1) they will shift from self-absorption to concern for others; (2) they will increasingly accept societal values and behave in socially appropriate ways; (3) they will become more comfortable with social relations; (4) their activities will increasingly reflect a concern for others in their community; and (5) they will become increasingly concerned with the issue of the meaning of life."[115]

Some criminologists argue, however, that the claim that aging causes desistance is meaningless because it doesn't explain the actual mechanisms involved in the desistance phenomenon. In other words, the claim that an offender "ages out" of crime offers no more explanatory power than the claim that turning 16 causes delinquency.

Longitudinal studies of crime in the life course conducted by **David P. Farrington** and **Donald J. West** have shown far greater diversity in the ages of desistance than in the ages of onset of criminal behavior.[116] In 1982, in an effort to explain the considerable heterogeneity of developmental pathways, Farrington and West began tracking a cohort of 411 boys born in London in 1953. The study, known as the **Cambridge Study in Delinquent Development**, is ongoing. It uses self-reports of delinquency as well as psychological tests and in-depth interviews. To date, participants have been interviewed eight times, with the earliest interviews being conducted at age 8.

The Cambridge study reveals that life course patterns found in the United States are also characteristic of English delinquents. Farrington found that the study's persistent offenders suffered from "hyperactivity, poor concentration, low achievement, an antisocial father, large family size, low family income, a broken family, poor parental supervision, and parental disharmony."[117] Other risk factors for delinquency included harsh discipline, negative peer influences, and parents with offense histories of their own. Chronic offenders were found to have friends and peers who were also offenders, and offending was found to begin with early antisocial behavior, including aggressiveness, dishonesty, prob-

lems in school, truancy, hyperactivity, impulsiveness, and restlessness. Consistent with other desistance studies, Farrington found that offending tends to peak around the age of 17 or 18 and then declines. By age 35, many subjects were found to have assumed conforming lifestyles, although they were often separated or divorced with poor employment records and patterns of residential instability. Many former offenders were also substance abusers and consequently served as very poor role models for their children.

While studies of desistance are becoming increasingly common, one of the main methodological problems for researchers is determining when desistance has occurred. Some theorists conceptualize desistance as the complete or absolute stopping of criminal behavior of any kind, while others see it as the gradual cessation of criminal involvement.[118]

Evolutionary Ecology

Because life course theory uses a developmental perspective in the study of criminal careers, life course researchers typically use longitudinal research designs involving cohort analysis. **Cohort analysis** usually begins at birth and traces the development of a population whose members share common characteristics, until they reach a certain age. One well-known analysis of a birth cohort, undertaken by **Marvin Wolfgang** during the 1960s, found that a small nucleus of chronic juvenile offenders accounted for a disproportionately large share of all juvenile arrests.[119] Wolfgang studied male individuals born in Philadelphia in 1945 until they reached age 18. He concluded that a small number of violent offenders were responsible for most of the crimes committed by the cohort. Six percent of cohort members accounted for 52% of all arrests. A follow-up study found that the seriousness of the offenses among the cohort increased in adulthood but that the actual number of offenses decreased as the cohort aged.[120] Wolfgang's analysis has since been criticized for its lack of a second cohort, or control group, against which the experiences of the cohort under study could be compared.[121] More recently, Wolfgang published a cohort analysis of 5,000 individuals born in the Wuchang district of the city of Wuhan in China. The study, from which preliminary results were published in 1996, used Chinese-supplied data to compare delinquents with nondelinquents. It found "striking differences in school deportment, achieved level of education, school dropout rate, type of employment, and unemployment rate" between the two groups.[122]

The ecological perspective on crime control, pioneered by **Lawrence E. Cohen** and **Richard Machalek**, provides a contemporary example of a life course approach.[123] Like other life course theories, **evolutionary ecology** blends elements of previous perspectives—in this case building upon the approach of social ecology—while emphasizing developmental pathways encountered early in life. According to University of Wyoming criminologist Bryan Vila, "the evolutionary ecological approach . . . draws attention to the ways people develop over the course of their lives. Experiences and environment

THEORY VERSUS REALITY
Social Influences on Developmental Pathways

A recent report by the Family and Youth Services Bureau (an agency of the U.S. Department of Health and Human Services) identified five "aspects of the social context" that can either promote or block the development of prosocial behavior among adolescents. These aspects include the following:

■ *Biophysical aspects of the individual.* Biophysical characteristics that have been found to influence developmental pathways during adolescence include temperament, gender, cognitive development, and the age of onset of puberty. The influence of these factors on development depends to a large extent on how others in the social context react to them. Individuals bring these aspects of self to the interactions in which they are engaged, and the reaction of the social context to these aspects determines the quality and nature of the interactions.

■ *Aspects of the society.* Society may be understood as the economic and institutional structures, values, and mores that constitute a national identity. Some of the aspects of society that influence the development of a sense of competency, connectedness, control, and identity are current economic and employment conditions, discrimination and prejudice, and educational institutions. Societal factors influence adolescent development directly and also indirectly through their effects on communities and families. The societal factors of prejudice and discrimination often present barriers to positive developmental pathways for minority and economically disadvantaged youths. For these youths, community and family contexts are particularly important for moderating the potentially negative influences of societal factors.

■ *Aspects of the community.* The community context (neighborhood or town) incorporates where individuals spend their time and with whom they spend it. The aspects of the community context that have been studied with respect to their effects on adolescent development include community culture, availability of sources of support to parents and youths, and availability of quality community institutional or organizational resources for children and youths. As with societal factors, community factors have both direct and indirect influences on developmental pathways during adolescence. Formal and informal broad-based community institutions and organizations, in particular, influence adolescent development directly by teaching and encouraging prosocial behaviors and indirectly by supporting parents in their parenting efforts.

■ *Aspects of the family.* The following aspects of the family context have received considerable research attention with respect to their influences on developmental pathways: the quality of the parent-child relationship, parenting styles or practices, family structure, and family dysfunction. In general, family practices that serve to monitor and control adolescents' behaviors in a caring and consistent manner, provide support and encouragement to adolescents, and allow them psychological and emotional independence appear to be most effective in fostering the development of a sense of competency, connectedness, control over one's fate in life, and identity.

■ *Aspects of peer relationships.* Research findings do not support the popular notion that adolescent problem behaviors are the result of peer pressure. In fact, current research suggests that peers do not direct adolescents to new behaviors as much as they reinforce existing dispositions that helped direct the adolescent to a particular peer group in the first place. Close friendships with peers during adolescence have been found to promote positive growth because they foster the development of conceptions of fairness, mutual respect, empathy, and intimacy. Through these conceptions, youths are able to develop a sense of connectedness to others and a stable sense of identity.

The information in this report suggests that interventions designed to assist youths in making successful transitions to adulthood will need to provide adolescents, either directly or through parents and community resources, with opportunities to engage in interactions that foster the development of a sense of competency, connectedness, control, and identity. The research also suggests that interventions must address children, families, and communities as a unit if they are to be effective for large numbers of children and their families.

DISCUSSION QUESTIONS

1. How might the five "aspects of the social context" identified in this box as impacting the development of prosocial behavior among adolescents interact?

2. How would you rank the five aspects of the social context identified in this box in order of relative importance? Why would you choose such a ranking?

3. Are there other important "aspects of the social context" that can be identified? If so, what might they be?

Source: Family and Youth Services Bureau, *Understanding Youth Development: Promoting Positive Pathways of Growth* (Washington, D.C.: U.S. Department of Health and Human Services, January 1997).

early in life, especially those that affect child development and the transmission of biological traits and family management practices across generations, seem particularly important."[124] According to Vila, evolutionary ecology "attempts to explain how people acquire criminality—a predisposition that disproportionately favors criminal behavior—when and why they express it as crime, how individuals and groups respond to those crimes, and how all these phenomena interact as a dynamic self-reinforcing system that evolves over time."[125]

Developmental Pathways

Researchers have found that manifestations of disruptive behaviors in childhood and adolescence are often age dependent, reflecting a developing capability to display different behaviors with age.[126] Budding behavioral problems can often be detected at an early age. In 1994, for example, Rolf Loeber and Dale F. Hay described the emergence of opposition to parents and aggression toward siblings and peers as a natural developmental occurrence during the first two years of life.[127] Loeber and Hay found, however, that as toddlers develop the ability to speak, they become increasingly likely to use words to resolve conflicts. As a consequence, oppositional behaviors decline between ages 3 and 6, as children acquire greater verbal skills for expressing their needs and for dealing with conflict. Children who are unable, for whatever reason, to develop adequate verbal coping skills, however, distinguish themselves from the norm by committing acts of intense aggression, initiating hostile conflict, and being characterized by parents as having a difficult temperament.[128] Figure 8-4 shows the order in which disruptive and antisocial childhood behaviors tend to manifest between birth and late adolescence. Figure 8-5, in contrast, shows the order of development of skills and attitudes deemed necessary for successful prosocial development during childhood and adolescence.

One of the most comprehensive studies to date that has attempted to detail life pathways leading to criminality began in 1986. The study, called the Program of Research on the Causes and Correlates of Delinquency, is sponsored by the U.S. Department of Justice's Office of Juvenile Justice and Delinquency Prevention. The program, a longitudinal study that is producing ongoing results, intends to improve the understanding of serious delinquency, violence, and drug use by examining how youths develop within the context of family, school, peers, and community.[129] It has compiled data on 4,500 youths from three distinct but coordinated projects: the Denver Youth Survey, conducted by the University of Colorado; the Pittsburgh Youth Study, undertaken by University of Pittsburgh researchers; and the Rochester Youth Development Study, fielded by professors at the State University of New York at Albany.

The Causes and Correlates projects all use a similar research design. All of the projects are longitudinal investigations involving repeated contacts with youths during a substantial portion of their developmental years. In each project, researchers conduct individual, face-to-face inter-

views with inner-city youths considered to be at high risk for involvement in delinquency and drug abuse. Multiple perspectives on each child's development and behavior are obtained through interviews with the child's primary caretakers and in interviews with teachers. In addition to interview data, the studies collect extensive information from official agencies, including police, courts, schools, and social services.[130]

Program results show that (1) delinquency is related to individual risk factors like impulsivity; (2) the more seriously involved in drugs a youth is, the more seriously that juvenile will be involved in delinquency; (3) children who are more attached to and involved with their parents are less involved in delinquency; (4) greater risks exist for violent offending when a child is physically abused or neglected early in life; (5) students who are not highly committed to school have higher rates of delinquency, and delinquency involvement reduces commitment to

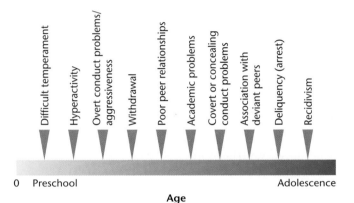

■ FIGURE 8-4 MANIFESTATIONS OF DISRUPTIVE AND ANTISOCIAL BEHAVIORS IN CHILDHOOD AND ADOLESCENCE. *Source:* Barbara Tatem Kelley et al., *Developmental Pathways in Boys' Disruptive and Delinquent Behavior* (Washington, D.C.: Office of Juvenile Justice and Delinquency Prevention, December 1997).

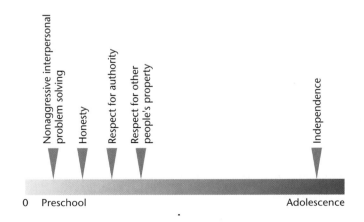

■ FIGURE 8-5 DEVELOPMENTAL TASKS NECESSARY FOR PROSOCIAL DEVELOPMENT DURING CHILDHOOD AND ADOLESCENCE. *Source:* Barbara Tatem Kelley et al., *Developmental Pathways in Boys' Disruptive and Delinquent Behavior* (Washington, D.C.: Office of Juvenile Justice and Delinquency Prevention, December 1997).

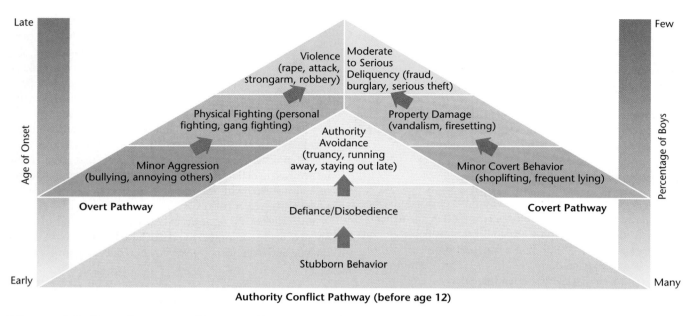

■ **FIGURE 8-6** THREE PATHWAYS TO DISRUPTIVE BEHAVIOR AND DELINQUENCY.
Source: Barbara Tatem Kelley et al., *Developmental Pathways in Boys' Disruptive and Delinquent Behavior* (Washington, D.C.: Office of Juvenile Justice and Delinquency Prevention, December 1997).

school; (6) poor family life, and especially poor parental supervision, exacerbates delinquency and drug use; (7) affiliation with street gangs and illegal gun ownership are both predictive of delinquency; (8) living in a "bad" neighborhood doubles the risk for delinquency; and (9) family receipt of public assistance (welfare) is associated with the highest risk of delinquency (followed by low socioeconomic status).[131] Results also showed that "peers who were delinquent or used drugs had a great impact on [other] youth." In terms of desistance, program results show that "the best predictors of success were having conventional friends, having a stable family and good parental monitoring, having positive expectations for the future, and not having delinquent peers."[132]

Perhaps the most significant result of the Causes and Correlates study is the finding that three separate developmental pathways to delinquency exist. The pathways identified by the study are shown in Figure 8-6. They are[133]

- The *authority conflict pathway,* on which subjects appear to begin quite young (as early as 3 or 4 years of age). "The first step," said the study authors, "was stubborn behavior, followed by defiance around age 11, and authority avoidance—truancy, staying out late at night, or running away."
- The *covert pathway,* which begins with "minor covert acts such as frequent lying and shoplifting, usually around age 10." Delinquents following this path quickly progress "to acts of property damage, such as firestarting or vandalism, around age 11 or 12, followed by moderate and serious forms of delinquency."
- The *overt pathway,* in which the first step is marked by minor aggression such as "annoying others and bullying—around age 11 or 12." Bullying was found to escalate into "physical fighting and violence as the juvenile pro-

gressed along this pathway." The overt pathway eventually leads to violent crimes like rape, robbery, and assault.

Researchers have found that these three different pathways are not necessarily mutually exclusive and can at times converge (see Figure 8-7). Self-report data show that simultaneous progression along two or more pathways leads to higher rates of delinquency than would otherwise occur.[134] Learn more about the Causes and Correlates study, and view results from each study site, at Web Extra! 8-7.

Web EXTRA! **Web Extra! 8-7 at crimtoday.com**

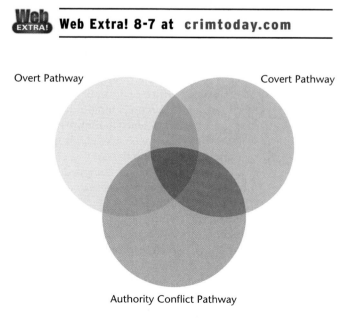

■ **FIGURE 8-7** SINGLE OR MULTIPLE DISRUPTIVE PATHWAYS.
Source: Barbara Tatem Kelley et al., *Developmental Pathways in Boys' Disruptive and Delinquent Behavior* (Washington, D.C.: Office of Juvenile Justice and Delinquency Prevention, December 1997).

The Project on Human Development in Chicago Neighborhoods uses this drawing as its masthead. The multidisciplinary project, which consists of a longitudinal analysis of how individuals, families, institutions, and communities evolve together, is jointly sponsored by the National Institute of Justice and the John D. and Catherine T. MacArthur Foundation. *Hyde Park Bank Foundation*

The Chicago Human Development Project

Another recent study that could produce substantially significant results began in 1990. The **Project on Human Development in Chicago Neighborhoods (PHDCN)** is jointly sponsored by the National Institute of Justice and the John D. and Catherine T. MacArthur Foundation.[135] PHDCN is directed by physician Felton J. Earls, Professor of Human Behavior and Development at Harvard University's School of Public Health. Also involved in the project are Robert Sampson, Professor of Sociology at the University of Chicago, and Stephen Raudenbush, Professor of Education at Michigan State University. Earls and Reiss describe the ongoing research as "the major criminologic investigation of this century."[136]

PHDCN, which consists of a longitudinal analysis of how individuals, families, institutions, and communities evolve together, is now "tracing how criminal behavior develops from birth to age 32."[137] It involves experts from a wide range of disciplines, including psychiatry, developmental and clinical psychology, sociology, criminology, public health and medicine, education, human behavior, and statistics.

The project is actually two studies combined into a single, comprehensive design. The first is an intensive study of Chicago's neighborhoods. This aspect of the project is evaluating the social, economic, organizational, political, and cultural components of each neighborhood. It seeks to identify changes that take place in the neighborhoods over the study's eight-year period. The second project component consists of a series of coordinated longitudinal evaluations of 7,000 randomly selected children, adolescents, and young adults. This aspect of the study is looking at the changing circumstances of people's lives and is attempting to identify personal characteristics that may lead toward or away from antisocial behavior. Researchers are exploring a wide range of variables—from prenatal drug exposure, lead poisoning, and nutrition to adolescent growth patterns, temperament, and self-image—as they try to identify which individuals might be most at risk for crime and delinquency. Additional features of the project include a study of children's exposure to violence and its consequences and an evaluation of child care and its impact on early childhood development. A variety of study methodologies are being used, including self-reports, individualized tests and examinations, direct observation, the examination of existing records, and reports by informants. The questions being explored can be described as follows:[138]

- *Communities.* Why do some communities experience high rates of antisocial behavior while other, apparently similar, communities are relatively safe?
- *School.* Some children have achievement problems early in school. Others have behavior or truancy problems. Some exhibit both kinds of problems, and others neither. Why do these differences exist? What are their causes and effects?
- *Peers.* Delinquent youths tend to associate with delinquent peers and usually act in groups. Does this association *lead* to delinquency, or is it simply a case of "like finding like"? Are the influences of peers equally important for girls and for boys, or are their developmental pathways entirely different?
- *Families.* Poor parenting practices are strongly associated with substance abuse and delinquency, but are they the cause of such behavior? If so, then social programs in parenting skills could make a difference. But what if there are underlying factors, such as temperamental characteristics or social isolation, that cause problems in both parents and children?
- *Individual differences.* What health-related, cognitive, intellectual, and emotional factors in children promote positive social development? What factors put them at risk of developing antisocial behaviors?

PHDCN is already producing results and has led to targeted interventions intended to lower rates of offending. According to Sampson, "Instead of external actions (for example, a police crackdown), we stress in this study the effectiveness of 'informal' mechanisms by which residents themselves achieve public order. In particular, we believe that collective expectations for intervening on behalf of neighborhood children is a crucial dimension of the public life of neighborhoods."[139] Life course perspectives, like the perspective that informs PHDCN, often point to the need for early intervention with nurturant strategies that build self-control through positive socialization. As Bryan Vila points out, "There are two main types of nurturant strategies: those that improve early life experiences to forestall the development of strategic styles based on criminality, and those that channel child and adolescent development in an effort to improve the match between individuals and their environment."[140] Nurturant crime control strategies are discussed in more detail in Chapter 15. Learn more about the Project on Human Development in Chicago Neighborhoods at Web Extra! 8-8.

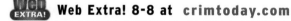

Web Extra! 8-8 at crimtoday.com

POLICY IMPLICATIONS OF SOCIAL DEVELOPMENT THEORIES

Social development strategies have been widely applied to juvenile justice and human services settings. The Office of Juvenile Justice and Delinquency Prevention has adopted the social development model as the foundation for its Comprehensive Strategy for Serious, Violent, and Chronic Juvenile Offenders program. The Comprehensive Strategy Program provides participating communities with a framework for preventing delinquency, intervening in early delinquent behavior, and responding to serious, violent, and chronic offending. It assists communities in establishing or modifying a juvenile justice "continuum of care" through risk-focused prevention, risk and needs assessment, structured decision making, and graduated sanctions training and technical assistance. OJJDP's Comprehensive Strategy Program centers around the following six components:

- Strengthening families in their role of providing guidance and discipline and instilling sound values as the first and primary teacher of children
- Supporting core social institutions, including schools, churches, and other community organizations, so that they can reduce risk factors and help children develop their full potential
- Promoting prevention strategies that enhance protective factors and reduce the impact of negative risk factors affecting the lives of young people at risk for high delinquency

- Intervening immediately and constructively when delinquent behavior first occurs
- Identifying and controlling a small segment of violent and chronic juvenile offenders
- Establishing a broad spectrum of *sanctions* that ensure accountability and a continuum of services

OJJDP recently began a national evaluation of the Comprehensive Strategy Program, with results to be reported in 2001 or later. Learn more about the program via Web Extra! 8-9 where you can keep abreast of the ongoing evaluation.

Web Extra! 8-9 at crimtoday.com

Another contemporary example of social intervention efforts tied to a developmental model is Targeted Outreach, a program operated by Boys and Girls Clubs of America.[141] The program had its origins in the 1972 implementation of a youth development strategy based on studies undertaken at the University of Colorado which showed that at-risk youths could be effectively diverted from the juvenile justice system through the provision of positive alternatives. Using a wide referral network made up of local schools, police departments, and various youth service agencies, club officials work to end what they call the "inappropriate detention of juveniles."[142]

The program's primary goal is to provide a positive, productive alternative to gangs for the youths who are most vulnerable to their influences or are already entrenched in gang activity. Currently, the program recruits at-risk youngsters—many as young as 7 years old—and diverts them into activities that are intended to promote a sense of belonging, competence, usefulness, and self-control. A sense of belonging is fostered through clubs that provide familiar settings where each child is accepted. Competence and usefulness are developed through opportunities for meaningful activities which young people in the club program can successfully undertake. Finally, Targeted Outreach provides its youthful participants with a chance to be heard and, consequently, with the opportunity to influence decisions affecting their future. To date, Targeted Outreach has served more than 10,000 at-risk youths, although it currently operates through only three local clubs. Organizers hope that Targeted Outreach will eventually involve more than 1.5 million youngsters between the ages of 7 and 17. Mobilization for Youth and Targeted Outreach both stand as examples of the kinds of programs that theorists who focus on the social structure typically seek to implement.

CRITIQUE OF SOCIAL DEVELOPMENT THEORIES

Social development theories have been criticized for, among other things, definitional issues. What, for example, do life course concepts like turning point, pathway, risk factor, persistence, desistance, and criminal career really mean? Precise definitions of such concepts are necessary if hypotheses derived from life course theories are to be tested. Some writers have identified "associated problems of how to develop risk/needs assessment devices and how to use these both in fundamental research (to maximize the yield of serious offenders while still making it possible to draw conclusions about the general population) and in applied research (to decide which populations should be targeted by interventions)."[143]

Like the social structural approaches discussed in Chapter 7, social development theories are intimately associated with the first prong of this textbook's theme—the social problems approach, which was described in Chapter 1. For policymakers, an important question is what role individual choice plays, if any, in human development. Do people actively select components of the life course? Do they influence their own trajectories? Since so many important life course determinants are set in motion in early childhood and during adolescence, should those who make wrong choices be held accountable?

SUMMARY

In this chapter, we discussed both social process and social development explanations for crime and criminality. Social process approaches include social learning theory, social control theory, labeling theory, reintegrative shaming, and dramaturgy. Social development theories, in contrast, focus on the life course and emphasize contingent events that affect the transitions that people make as they move through the life cycle.

While all of these perspectives assume that everyone has the potential to violate the law, and while they all stress the important role of social interaction in crime causation, social development theories are the most comprehensive. They evaluate all aspects of the life experience, from birth through adolescence and into adulthood, for clues to the social conditions, individual circumstances, and life experiences that lead to crime and deviance. Crucial to the social development perspective is the idea that human development occurs simultaneously on many levels. Because they examine offending over the life course, theories of social development tend to make use of longitudinal studies, or the analysis of cohorts over time.

DISCUSSION QUESTIONS

1. This chapter describes both social process and social development perspectives. What are the significant differences between these two perspectives? What kinds of theories characterize each?
2. This textbook emphasizes a social problems versus social responsibility theme. Which of the perspectives discussed in this chapter (if any) best support the social problems approach? Which (if any) support the social responsibility approach? Why?
3. This chapter contains a discussion of the labeling process. Give a few examples of the everyday imposition of positive, rather than negative, labels. Why is it so difficult to impose positive labels on individuals who were previously labeled negatively?
4. Do you believe that Erving Goffman's dramaturgical approach, which sees the world as a stage and individuals as actors upon that stage, provides any valuable insights into crime and criminality? If so, what are they?
5. What kinds of social policy initiatives might be suggested by social process theories? By social development theories? Which do you think might be most effective? Why?
6. What are the shortcomings of the social process perspective? Of the social development perspective?

WEB QUEST!

Visit the Office of Juvenile Justice and Delinquency Prevention on the World Wide Web at http://ojjdp.ncjrs.org. Browse the site to learn about the programs and initiatives supported by OJJDP. The programs listed, for example, include the Causes and Correlates of Delinquency Program, the Drug-Free Communities Support Program, the Juvenile Mentoring Program, the Safe Futures Program, and the Strengthening America's Families initiative. Select at least five of these programs or initiatives, and study the underlying philosophy associated with each. Which of these programs appears to be based on social process principles? On social development concepts? Are there any programs listed on the OJJDP site that seem to be built on assumptions drawn from social structural approaches? If so, which programs? After you have listed and described at least five programs or initiatives, classify each according to its theoretical underpinnings, and submit your findings to your instructor if asked to do so.

LIBRARY EXTRAS!

The Library Extras! listed here complement the Web Extras! found throughout this chapter. Library Extras! may be accessed on the Web at crimtoday.com.

Library Extra! 8-1. David Asma, *Welcome to Jail: Some Dramaturgical Notes on Admission to a Total Institution* (online article, accessed March 12, 2001).

Library Extra! 8-2. Philip W. Harris, Wayne N. Welsh, and Frank Butler, "A Century of Juvenile Justice," *Criminal Justice 2000,* Vol. 1 (Washington, D.C.: National Institute of Justice, 2000).

Library Extra! 8-3. Richard M. Lerner, "Adolescent Development: Challenges and Opportunities for Research, Programs, and Policies," *Annual Review of Psychology,* Vol. 49 (1998), pp. 413–446.

Library Extra! 8-4. Shadd Maruna, "Desistance and Development: The Psychosocial Process of 'Going Straight,'" in Mike Bragden, ed., *The British Criminology Conferences: Selected Proceedings,* Vol. 2 (online Journal, posted March, 1999).

Library Extra! 8-5. Coordinating Council on Juvenile Justice and Delinquency Prevention, *Combating Violence and Delinquency: The National Juvenile Justice Action Plan* (Washington, D.C.: Office of Juvenile Justice and Delinquency Prevention 1996).

Library Extra! 8-6. Testimony of Mr. John Wilson, Acting Administrator of the Office of Juvenile Justice and Delinquency Prevention, before the U.S. House of Representatives, Committee on the Judiciary (online article, posted October 3, 2000).

Library Extra! 8-7. James Q. Wilson, "Thinking About Crime: The Debate over Deterrence," *Atlantic Monthly,* September 1983, pp. 72–88.

NOTES

[1] Albert K. Cohen, *Delinquent Boys: The Culture of the Gang* (Glencoe, IL: Free Press, 1955), p. 11.

[2] William Faulkner, *As I Lay Dying* (New York: Random House, 1964).

[3] Terrie E. Moffitt, "Adolescence-Limited and Life-Course-Persistent Antisocial Behavior: A Developmental Taxonomy," *Psychological Review,* Vol. 100, No. 4 (1993), pp. 674–701.

[4] "Killer's Admission to Law School Criticized," *Fayetteville* (N.C.) *Observer-Times,* September 12, 1993, p. 14A.

[5] Ibid.

[6] Edwin Sutherland, *Principles of Criminology,* 3rd ed. (New York: Lippincott, 1939).

[7] Edwin H. Sutherland and Donald R. Cressey, *Criminology* (New York: Lippincott, 1978).

[8] Robert Burgess and Ronald L. Akers, "A Differential Association–Reinforcement Theory of Criminal Behavior," *Social Problems,* Vol. 14 (1966), pp. 363–383.

[9] Ibid., p. 364.

[10] Ronald L. Akers, *Deviant Behavior: A Social Learning Approach* (Belmont, CA: Wadsworth, 1973).

[11] Ibid.

[12] Ronald L. Akers, *Social Learning and Social Structure: A General Theory of Crime and Deviance* (Boston: Northeastern University Press, 1998).

[13] Ronald L. Akers, *Deviant Behavior: A Social Learning Approach,* 3rd ed. (Belmont, CA: Wadsworth, 1985), pp. 40–41.

[14] Daniel Glaser, "Differential Association and Criminological Prediction," *Social Problems,* Vol. 8 (1960), pp. 6–14.

[15] Daniel Glaser, "Differential Identification," in Henry N. Pontel, *Social Deviance: Readings in Theory and Research,* 3rd ed. (Upper Saddle River, NJ: Prentice Hall 1999), p. 146.

[16] Charles R. Tittle, "Theoretical Developments in Criminology," in National Institute of Justice, *Criminal Justice 2000, Vol. 1: The Nature of Crime: Continuity and Change* (Washington, D.C.: National Institute of Justice, 2000), p. 65.

[17] For a good overview of social control approaches, see George S. Bridges and Martha Myers, eds., *Inequality, Crime, and Social Control* (Boulder, CO: Westview Press, 1994).

[18] Walter C. Reckless, *The Crime Problem,* 4th ed. (New York: Appleton-Century-Crofts, 1967).

[19] Ibid., p. 470.

[20] Ibid., p. 470.

[21] Ibid., p. 475.

[22] Ibid., p. 475.

[23] Howard B. Kaplan, "Self-Derogation and Violence." Paper presented at the first meeting of the International Society for Research on Aggression, Toronto, August 1974. See also Howard B. Kaplan and A. D. Pokorny, "Self-Derogation as an Antecedent of Suicidal Responses." Paper presented at the Eighth International Congress on Suicide Prevention and Crisis Intervention, Jerusalem, October 19–22, 1975.

[24] Howard B. Kaplan, *Deviant Behavior in Defense of Self* (New York: Academic Press, 1980).

[25] M. Rosenberg, C. Schooler, and C. Schoenbach, "Self-Esteem and Adolescent Problems: Modeling Reciprocal Effects," *American Sociological Review,* Vol. 54 (1989), pp. 1004–1018.

26 L. E. Wells, "Self-Enhancement through Delinquency: A Conditional Test of Self-Derogation Theory," *Journal of Research in Crime and Delinquency,* Vol. 26, No. 3 (1989), pp. 226–252.

27 K. Leung and F. Drasgow, "Relation between Self-Esteem and Delinquent Behavior in Three Ethnic Groups: An Application of Item Response Theory," *Journal of Cross-Cultural Psychology,* Vol. 17, No. 2 (1986), pp. 151–167.

28 G. Calhoun, Jr., S. Connley, and J. A. Bolton, "Comparison of Delinquents and Non-delinquents in Ethnicity, Ordinal Position and Self-Perception," *Journal of Clinical Psychology,* Vol. 40, No. 1 (1984), pp. 323–328.

29 D. Oyserman and H. R. Markus, "Possible Selves in Balance: Implications for Delinquency," *Journal of Social Issues,* Vol. 46, No. 2 (1990), pp. 141–157.

30 Daphna Oyserman and Hazel Markus, "The Sociocultural Self," in J. Suls, ed., *Psychological Perspectives on the Self,* Vol. 4 (Hillsdale, NJ: Lawrence Erlbaum Associates, 1993), pp. 187–220.

31 Travis Hirschi, *Causes of Delinquency* (Berkeley: University of California Press, 1969).

32 Tittle, "Theoretical Developments in Criminology," p. 65.

33 Hirschi, *Causes of Delinquency.*

34 Ibid.

35 Ibid.

36 Ibid.

37 Ibid.

38 Ibid.

39 Ibid.

40 Michael Gottfredson and Travis Hirschi, *A General Theory of Crime* (Stanford, CA: Stanford University Press, 1990).

41 See also Michael R. Gottfredson and Travis Hirschi, "Criminality and Low Self-Control," in John E. Conklin, ed., *New Perspectives in Criminology* (Boston: Allyn and Bacon, 1996).

42 Werner Einstadter and Stuart Henry, *Criminological Theory: An Analysis of Its Underlying Assumptions* (Fort Worth: Harcourt Brace, 1995), p. 189.

43 Charles R. Tittle, *Control Balance: Toward a General Theory of Deviance* (Boulder, CO: Westview Press, 1995).

44 For an excellent summation of control-balance theory, see Alex R. Piquero and Matthew Hickman, "An Empirical Test of Tittle's Control Balance Theory," *Criminology,* Vol. 37, No. 2 (1999), pp. 319–341.

45 Ibid., p. 327.

46 Tittle, *Control Balance,* p. 95. For a good critique of control-balance theory, see Joachim J. Savelsberg, "Human Nature and Social Control in Complex Society: A Critique of Charles Tittle's Control Balance," *Theoretical Criminology,* Vol. 3 No. 3 (August 1999), pp. 331–338.

47 Frank Tannenbaum, *Crime and the Community* (New York: Atheneum Press, 1938), pp. 17–18.

48 Ibid., p. 19.

49 Edwin M. Lemert, *Social Pathology: A Systematic Approach to the Theory of Sociopathic Behavior* (New York: McGraw-Hill, 1951), p. 76.

50 Ibid.

51 Howard Becker, *Outsiders: Studies in the Sociology of Deviance* (New York: Free Press, 1963).

52 Ibid., p. 1.

53 Ibid., p. 9.

54 Ibid., p. 147.

55 Ibid., pp. 37–38.

56 Mike S. Adams, "Labeling and Differential Association: Towards a General Social Learning Theory of Crime and Deviance," *American Journal of Criminal Justice,* Vol. 20, No. 2 (1996), pp. 147–164.

57 Ibid., p. 160.

58 John Braithwaite and Heather Strang, "The Right Kind of Shame for Crime Prevention," *RISE Working Papers, Number 1* (Australian National University, 1997). Web posted at http://www.aic.gov.au/rjustice/rise/working/risepap1.html. Accessed March 11, 2001.

59 *RISE Working Papers: Introduction* (Canberra: Australian National University, 1997).

60 A number of papers have been released in the Reintegrative Shining Experiments (RISE) series. They include Lawrence W. Sherman and Heather Strang, *The Right Kind of Shame for Crime Prevention* (Canberra: Australian National University, 1997); Heather Strang and Lawrence W. Sherman, *The Victim's Perspective* (Canberra: Australian National University, 1997); Lawrence W. Sherman and Geoffrey C. Barnes, *Restorative Justice and Offenders' Respect for the Law* (Canberra: Australian National University, 1997); and Lawrence W. Sherman and Heather Strang, *Restorative Justice and Deterring Crime* (Canberra: Australian National University, 1997).

61 John Braithwaite and Heather Strang, "Restorative Justice and Offenders' Respect for the Law," *RISE Working Papers, Number 3* (Australian National University, 1997). Web posted at http://www.aic.gov.au/rjustice/rise/working/risepap3.html. Accessed March 11, 2001.

62 Ibid.

63 Erving Goffman, *The Presentation of Self in Everyday Life* (Garden City, NY: Doubleday, 1959), p. 135.

64 William Shakespeare, *As You Like It* [1598–1600], Act II, Scene 7, line 139.

65 Goffman, *The Presentation of Self in Everyday Life,* pp. 9–10.

66 Ibid., p. 17.

67 Ibid., p. 60.

68 "People," *USA Today,* September 13, 1993, p. 2D.

69 Goffman, *The Presentation of Self in Everyday Life,* p. 75.

70 Erving Goffman, *Stigma: Notes on the Management of Spoiled Identity* (Englewood Cliffs, NJ: Prentice Hall, 1963).

71 Ibid., p. 5.

72 Ibid., p. 138.

73 Erving Goffman, *Asylums: Essays on the Social Situation of Mental Patients and Other Inmates* (Garden City, NY: Anchor, 1961).

74 P.L. 93-415; 42 U.S.C. 5667e.

75 See Kevin Haggerty, et al., *Preparing for the Drug Free Years* (Washington, D.C.: Office of Juvenile Justice and

Delinquency Prevention, 1999). Web posted at http://www. ncjrs.org/html/jjbulletin/9907/theo.html. Accessed March 11, 2001.

[76] Ibid., at http://www.ncjrs.org/html/jjbulletin/9907/theo.html. Accessed March 11, 2001.

[77] Haggerty et al., *Preparing for the Drug Free Years.*

[78] Material in this paragraph is adapted from Finn-Aage Esbensen, "Preventing Adolescent Gang Involvement," *OJJDP Juvenile Justice Bulletin* (Washington, D.C.: Office of Juvenile Justice and Delinquency Prevention, September 2000).

[79] See R. E. Tremblay et al., "From Childhood Physical Aggression to Adolescent Maladjustment: The Montreal Prevention Experiment," in R. D. Peters and R. J. McMahon, *Preventing Childhood Disorders, Substance Abuse, and Delinquency* (Thousand Oaks, CA: Sage, 1996), pp. 268–298.

[80] Randy Martin, Robert J. Mutchnick, and W. Timothy Austin, *Criminological Thought: Pioneers Past and Present* (New York: Macmillan, 1990), p. 368.

[81] Laurie Taylor, "Erving Goffman," *New Society,* December 1968, p. 836.

[82] George Psathas, "Ethnomethods and Phenomenology," in Donald McQuarie, ed., *Readings in Contemporary Sociological Theory: From Modernity to Post-Modernity* (Toronto: Prentice Hall Canada, 1999).

[83] For some influential writings of the period, see K. F. Riegel, "Toward a Dialectical Theory of Development," *Human Development,* Vol. 18 (1975), pp. 50–64; and U. Bronfenbrenner, *The Ecology of Human Development* (Cambridge: Harvard University Press, 1979).

[84] R. M. Lerner, "Early Adolescence: Towards an Agenda for the Integration of Research, Policy and Intervention," in R.M. Lerner, ed., *Early Adolescence: Perspectives on Research, Policy, and Intervention* (Hillsdale, NJ: Erlbaum, 1993), pp. 1–13.

[85] See T. P. Thornberry, *Developmental Theories of Crime and Delinquency* (Piscataway, NJ: Transaction, 1997).

[86] A. Blumstein et al., eds., *Criminal Careers and Career Criminals* (Washington, D.C.: National Academy Press, 1986).

[87] See Alfred Blumstein et al., "Introduction: Studying Criminal Careers," in A. Blumstein et al., eds., *Criminal Careers and Career Criminals* (Washington, D.C.: National Academy Press), p. 12.

[88] Blumstein et al., *Criminal Careers and Career Criminals,* pp. 12–30.

[89] Robert J. Sampson and John H. Laub, *Crime in the Making: Pathways and Turning Points through the Life Course* (Cambridge: Harvard University Press, 1993).

[90] G. H. Edler, Jr. "Perspectives on the Life-Course," in G. Elder, ed., *Life-Course Dynamics* (Ithaca, NY: Cornell University Press, 1985).

[91] Philip W. Harris, Wayne N. Welsh, and Frank Butler, "A Century of Juvenile Justice," *Criminal Justice 2000,* Vol. 1 (Washington, D.C.: National Institute of Justice, 2000).

[92] G. H. Elder, Jr., ed., *Life-Course Dynamics* (Ithaca, NY: Cornell University Press, 1985).

[93] Robert J. Sampson and John H. Laub, "Understanding Variability in Lives Through Time: Contributions of Life-Course Criminology," in Alex Piquero and Paul Mazerolle, *Life-Course Criminology: Contemporary and Classic Readings* (Belmont, CA: Wadsworth, 2001), p. 243.

[94] Marc LeBlanc and Rolf Loeber, "Developmental Criminology Updated," in Michael Tonry, ed., *Crime and Justice: A Review of Research,* Vol. 23 (Chicago: University of Chicago Press, 1998).

[95] Adapted from Harris, Welsh, and Butler, "A Century of Juvenile Justice," p. 379.

[96] Glen H. Elder, Jr., "Time, Human Agency, and Social Change: Perspectives on the Life Course," *Social Psychology Quarterly,* Vol. 57, No. 1 (1994), pp. 4–15.

[97] See, for example, the collected papers of Sheldon Glueck, 1916–1972, which are part of the David L. Bazelon collection at Harvard University Law School (Cambridge, MA). Results of the Gluecks' work was reported in S. Glueck and E. Glueck, *Unraveling Juvenile Delinquency* (New York: The Commonwealth Fund, 1950).

[98] Sheldon Glueck and Eleanor Glueck, *Delinquents and Nondelinquents in Perspective* (Cambridge: Harvard University Press, 1968).

[99] John H. Laub and Robert J. Sampson, "Urban Poverty and the Family Context of Delinquency: A New Look at Structure and Process in a Classic Study," *Child Development,* Vol. 65 (1994), pp. 523–540. See also John H. Laub and Robert J. Sampson, "Turning Points in the Life Course: Why Change Matters to the Study of Crime," *Criminology,* Vol. 31, No. 3 (1993), pp. 301–325; and Robert J. Sampson and John H. Laub, "Crime and Deviance in the Life Course," *Annual Review of Sociology,* Vol. 18 (1992), pp. 63–84.

[100] See John H. Laub and Leana C. Allen, "Life Course Criminology and Community Corrections," *Perspectives,* Vol. 24, No. 2 (spring 2000), pp. 20–29.

[101] Sampson and Laub, "Crime and Deviance in the Life Course," pp. 63–84.

[102] G. B. Trasler, "Aspects of Causality, Culture, and Crime." Paper presented at the Fourth International Seminar at the International Centre of Sociological, Penal and Penitentiary Research and Studies, Messina, Italy, 1980.

[103] Laub and Sampson, "Turning Points in the Life Course."

[104] Ibid.

[105] See Laub and Allen, "Life Course Criminology and Community Corrections," pp. 20–29.

[106] Sampson and Laub, *Crime in the Making.*

[107] Tittle, "Theoretical Developments in Criminology," p. 68.

[108] Moffitt, "Adolescence-Limited and Life-Course-Persistent Antisocial Behavior," pp. 674–701.

[109] Adapted from Tittle, "Theoretical Developments in Criminology."

[110] Moffitt, "Adolescence-Limited and Life-Course-Persistent Antisocial Behavior."

[111] Family and Youth Services Bureau, *Understanding Youth Development: Promoting Positive Pathways of Growth* (Washington, D.C.: U.S. Department of Health and Human Services, 2000).

[112] A. Quetelet, *A Treatise on Man and the Development of His Facilities* (Gainesville, Florida: Scholars Facsimiles and Reprints, 1969).

[113] Sheldon and Eleanor Glueck, *Later Criminal Careers* (New York: The Commonwealth Fund, 1937), p. 105.

[114] Walter R. Gove, "The Effect of Age and Gender on Deviant Behavior: A Biopsychosocial Perspective," in Alice S. Rossi, ed., *Gender and the Life Course* (New York: Aldine, 1985).

[115] Ibid., p. 128.

[116] David P. Farrington, "The Twelfth Jack Tizard Memorial Lecture: The Development of Offending and Antisocial Behavior from Childhood—Key Findings from the Cambridge Study in Delinquent Development," *Journal of Child Psychology and Psychiatry,* Vol. 360 (1995), pp. 929–964.

[117] David P. Farrington, "Explaining and Preventing Crime: The Globalization of Knowledge—The American Society of Criminology 1999 Presidential Address," *Criminology,* Vol. 38, No. 1 (February 2000), pp. 1–24.

[118] Alex Piquero and Paul Mazerolle, *Life-Course Criminology,* p. xv.

[119] Marvin Wolfgang, Robert Figlio, and Thorsten Sellin, *Delinquency in a Birth Cohort* (Chicago: University of Chicago Press, 1972).

[120] Marvin Wolfgang, Terence Thornberry, and Robert Figlio, *From Boy to Man, from Delinquency to Crime* (Chicago: University of Chicago Press, 1987).

[121] Steven P. Lab, "Analyzing Change in Crime and Delinquency Rates: The Case for Cohort Analysis," *Criminal Justice Research Bulletin,* Vol. 3, No. 10 (Huntsville, TX: Sam Houston State University, 1988), p. 2.

[122] Marvin Wolfgang, "Delinquency in China: Study of a Birth Cohort," National Institute of Justice Research Preview, May 1996.

[123] Lawrence E. Cohen and Richard Machalek, "A General Theory of Expropriative Crime: An Evolutionary Ecological Approach," *American Journal of Sociology,* Vol. 94, No. 3 (1988), pp. 465–501; and Lawrence E. Cohen and Richard Machalek, "The Normalcy of Crime: From Durkheim to Evolutionary Ecology," *Rationality and Society,* Vol. 6 (1994), pp. 286–308.

[124] Bryan Vila, "Human Nature and Crime Control: Improving the Feasibility of Nurturant Strategies," *Politics and the Life Sciences* (March 1997), pp. 3–21.

[125] Ibid.

[126] Barbara Tatem Kelley et al., *Developmental Pathways in Boys' Disruptive and Delinquent Behavior* (Washington, D.C.: Office of Juvenile Justice and Delinquency Prevention, December 1997).

[127] R. Loeber and D. F. Hay, "Developmental Approaches to Aggression and Conduct Problems," in M. Rutter and D. F. Hay, eds., *Development through Life: A Handbook for Clinicians* (Oxford: Blackwell Scientific, 1994).

[128] Ibid.

[129] The Causes and Correlates of Delinquency study is being conducted by Terence P. Thornberry of the Rochester Youth Development Study at the University of Albany, New York, Rolf Loeber of the Pittsburgh Youth Study at the University of Pittsburgh, and David Huizinga of the Denver Youth Survey at the University of Colorado.

[130] Adapted from Katharine Browning et al., "Causes and Correlates of Delinquency Program," *OJJDP Fact Sheet* (Washington, D.C.: U.S. Department of Justice, April 1999).

[131] Compiled from Katharine Browning and Rolf Loeber, "Highlights of Findings from the Pittsburgh Youth Study," *OJJDP Fact Sheet* (Washington, D.C.: U.S. Department of Justice, February 1999); Katharine Browning, Terence P. Thornberry, and Pamela K. Porter, "Highlights of Findings from the Rochester Youth Development Study," *OJJDP Fact Sheet* (Washington, D.C.: U.S. Department of Justice, April 1999); and Katharine Browning and David Huizinga, "Highlights of Findings from the Denver Youth Survey," *OJJDP Fact Sheet* (Washington, D.C.: U.S. Department of Justice, April 1999).

[132] Browning and Huizinga, "Highlights of Findings from the Denver Youth Survey."

[133] Barbara Tatem Kelley et al., *Developmental Pathways in Boys' Disruptive and Delinquent Behavior* (Washington, D.C.: Office of Juvenile Justice and Delinquency Prevention, December 1997).

[134] Kelley, et al., *Developmental Pathways in Boys' Disruptive and Delinquent Behavior,* p. 14.

[135] See Felton J. Earls and Albert J. Reiss, *Breaking the Cycle: Predicting and Preventing Crime* (Washington, D.C.: National Institute of Justice, 1994).

[136] Ibid. Available online at http://www.ncjrs.org/txtfiles/break.txt. Accessed March 12, 2001.

[137] Ibid.

[138] Adapted from the MacArthur Foundation, "The Project on Human Development in Chicago Neighborhoods." Web posted at http://www.macfound.org/research/hcd/hcd_5.htm. Accessed January 5, 2001.

[139] Project on Human Development in Chicago Neighborhoods press release, "Study of Chicago Finds Neighborhood Efficacy Explains Reductions in Violence." No date. Web posted at http://phdcn.harvard.edu/press/index.htm. Accessed January 5, 2001.

[140] Vila, "Human Nature and Crime Control," p. 10.

[141] Robert W. Sweet, Jr., "Preserving Families to Prevent Delinquency," *Office of Juvenile Justice and Delinquency Prevention Model Programs, 1990* (Washington, D.C.: U.S. Department of Justice, April 1992).

[142] Ibid.

[143] Farrington, "The Twelfth Jack Tizard Memorial Lecture," p. 16.

Social stratification breeds envy. And that leads to crime.

—Natalya Lemesheva, Russian Schoolteacher[1]

To move beyond criminal justice is to move beyond capitalism.

—Richard Quinney[2]

Gender differences in crime suggest that crime may not be so normal after all.

—Kathleen Daly and Meda Chesney-Lind[3]

sociological theories III: social conflict

CHAPTER

9

[I] attribute the social and psychological problems of modern society to the fact that society requires people to live under conditions radically different from those under which the human race evolved.

—The Unabomber[4]

The influence of the postmodern agenda on the social analysis of crime has taken several forms. Most obvious during the 1980s and 1990s was the increasing incoherence both of forms of deviance theory that had done battle with orthodox criminology and of orthodox forms of social criticism like Marxism.

—Ian Taylor[5]

KEY CONCEPTS

IMPORTANT TERMS

androcentricity	left realism	postmodern criminology
bourgeoisie	left-realist criminology	power-control theory
conflict perspective	liberal feminists	proletariat
consensus model	Marxist criminology	radical criminology
critical criminology	partcipatory justice	radical feminism
deconstructionist theories	patriarchy	restorative justice
feminist criminology	peacemaking criminology	social class
gender gap	peace model	socialist feminists
instrumental Marxism	pluralist perspective	structural Marxism

IMPORTANT NAMES

Freda Adler	John Hagan	Richard Quinney
Willem Bonger	Stuart Henry	Jeffrey H. Reiman
William J. Chambliss	Karl Marx	Rita J. Simon
Meda Chesney-Lind	Raymond J. Michalowski	Austin Turk
Ralf Dahrendorf	Dragan Milovanovic	George B. Vold
Kathleen Daly	Harold E. Pepinsky	Jock Young
Walter DeKeseredy	Roscoe Pound	

OUTCOMES

LEARNING

After reading this chapter, you should be able to
- ◆ Recognize the ways in which power conflict between social groups contributes to crime and criminal activity
- ◆ Understand the distinctions between a number of social conflict theories
- ◆ Identify those social policy initiatives that reflect the social conflict approach
- ◆ Assess the shortcomings of the social conflict perspective

Hear the author discuss this chapter at *crimtoday.com*

INTRODUCTION

In April 1996, Harvard-educated Theodore Kaczynski, 52, a Lincoln, Montana, recluse, was arrested and charged with the infamous Unabomber terrorist bombings. Kaczynski admitted responsibility for the bombings in early 1998 and was sentenced to life in prison without parole.

The Unabomber's 18-year-long mail bomb campaign had targeted universities, airlines, and researchers. The attacks killed three people and injured 23 others in 16 separate bombing incidents. Prior to Kaczynski's arrest, a 56-page, 35,000-word "manifesto" was mailed to the offices of the *New York Times,* the *Washington Post,* and *Penthouse* magazine. Titled "Industrial Society and Its Future," the Unabomber manifesto

was a rambling thesis condemning American social institutions and high technology—and calling for a new social order based on a return to simpler times. It blamed many of the world's existing problems on the Industrial Revolution and forecast an Orwellian future in which helpless humans would be controlled by computers. Excerpts from the manifesto were widely published and helped lead to Kaczynski's capture. The manifesto's introductory paragraphs (which use the word *we* in referring to the bomber) are reproduced in the Theory versus Reality box in this chapter. Read the Unabomber's entire manifesto online at Web Extra! 9-1.

Web Extra! 9-1 at crimtoday.com

THEORY VERSUS REALITY
The Unabomber and Domestic Terrorism

This box contains the introductory paragraphs of the Unabomber's rambling 56-page manifesto. The manifesto, entitled "Industrial Society and Its Future," was mailed to the *New York Times,* the *Washington Post,* and *Penthouse* magazine prior to Unabomber Ted Kaczynski's arrest. Kaczynski's misplaced idealism demonstrates how social conflict, and the ideologies borne of it, can lead to crime.

The Industrial Revolution and its consequences have been a disaster for the human race. They have greatly increased the life-expectancy of those of us who live in "advanced" countries, but they have destabilized society, have made life unfulfilling, have subjected human beings to indignities, have led to widespread psychological suffering (in the Third World to physical suffering as well) and have inflicted severe damage on the natural world. The continued development of technology will worsen the situation. It will certainly subject human beings to greater indignities and inflict greater damage on the natural world, it will probably lead to greater social disruption and psychological suffering, and it may lead to increased physical suffering even in "advanced" countries.

The industrial-technological system may survive or it may break down. If it survives, it MAY eventually achieve a low level of physical and psychological suffering, but only after passing through a long and very painful period of adjustment and only at the cost of permanently reducing human beings and many other living organisms to engineered products and mere cogs in the social machine. Furthermore, if the system survives, the consequences will be inevitable: There is no way of reforming or modifying the system so as to prevent it from depriving people of dignity and autonomy.

If the system breaks down the consequences will still be very painful. But the bigger the system grows the more disastrous the results of its breakdown will be, so if it is to break down it had best break down sooner rather than later.

We therefore advocate a revolution against the industrial system. This revolution may or may not make use of violence; it may be sudden or it may be a relatively gradual process spanning a few decades. We can't predict any of that. But we do outline in a very general way the measures that those who hate the industrial system should take in order to prepare the way for a revolution against that form of society.

DISCUSSION QUESTIONS

1. What motivated the Unabomber? Why did he advocate "a revolution against the industrial system"?
2. Do you think that the Unabomber really believed his bombings would create a better world? If so, how did he think they would bring about such change?

Ted Kaczynski, the self-confessed "Unabomber." Kaczynski admitted responsibility for 16 bombings over an 18-year period. The bombings resulted in three deaths and 23 injuries. In 1998, Kaczynski was sentenced to life in prison without the possibility of parole. What motivates criminals like the Unabomber? *John Youngbear, AP/Wide World Photos*

LAW AND SOCIAL ORDER PERSPECTIVES

Kaczynski's idealism is reminiscent of the kind of thinking that characterized much of Europe during the mid to late 1800s. Among the most important thinkers of that period, for the purposes of this chapter, were Karl Marx and Friedrich Engels. In 1848, in *The Communist Manifesto,* Marx and Engels advanced the idea that communism would inevitably replace capitalism as the result of a natural historical process or dialectic. The egalitarian ideals of these early writers fed the communist ideology that led to the Marxist-inspired Bolshevik Revolution of 1917, the fall of the Romanov dynasty in Russia, the coming to power of Vladimir Lenin and (later) Joseph Stalin in Russia, and the rise of the Soviet Union. Communism soon came to denote a totalitarian system in which a single political party controls the government, which in turn owns the means of production and distributes wealth with the professed aim of establishing a classless society.[6]

The decline of European monarchies during the first half of the twentieth century, the rise of socialist ideals, and the advent of Marxist-inspired revolutions all conspired to change laws and create new kinds of criminal activity. Hence an understanding of the interplay between law and social order is critical to any study of social change and to theories of criminology that emphasize the role of social conflict as it underlies criminality. Three analytical perspectives shed some light on this subject:

- The consensus perspective
- The pluralist perspective
- The conflict perspective

The Consensus Perspective

The **consensus model** of social organization (described briefly in Chapter 1) is built around the notion that most members of society agree on what is right and wrong and that the various elements of society—including institutions like churches, schools, government agencies, and businesses—work together toward a common and shared vision of the greater good. According to **Raymond J. Michalowski,** whose work is used to describe each of the three major approaches discussed in this section, the consensus perspective is characterized by four principles:[7]

- A belief in the existence of core values. The consensus perspective holds that commonly shared notions of right and wrong characterize the majority of society's members.
- The notion that laws reflect the collective will of the people. Law is seen as the result of a consensus, achieved through legislative action, and represents a kind of social conscience.
- The assumption that the law serves all people equally. From the consensus point of view, the law not only embodies a shared view of justice, but is itself perceived to be just in its application.
- The idea that those who violate the law represent a unique subgroup with some distinguishing features. The consensus approach holds that law violators must somehow be improperly socialized or psychologically defective or must suffer from some other lapse which leaves them unable to participate in what is otherwise widespread agreement on values and behavior.

The consensus perspective was operative in American politics and characterized social scientific thought in this country throughout much of the early 1900s. It found its greatest champion in **Roscoe Pound,** former Dean of the Harvard School of Law and one of the greatest legal scholars of modern times. Pound developed the notion that the law is a tool for engineering society. The law, Pound said, meets the needs of men and women living together in society and can be used to fashion society's characteristics and major features. Pound distilled his ideas into a set of jural postulates. Such postulates, Pound claimed, explain the existence and form of all laws insofar as laws reflect shared needs. Pound's postulates read as follows:[8]

- In civilized society men and women[9] must be able to assume that others will commit no intentional aggressions upon them.
- In civilized society men and women must be able to assume that they may control for beneficial purposes what they have discovered and appropriated to their own use, what they have created by their own labor, and what they have acquired under the existing social and economic order.
- In civilized society men and women must be able to assume that those with whom they deal in the general intercourse of society will act in good faith and hence
  1. Will make good reasonable expectations that their promises or other conduct will reasonably create.
  2. Will carry out their undertakings according to the expectations which the moral sentiment of the community attaches thereto.
  3. Will restore specifically or by equivalent what comes to them by mistake or [by an] unanticipated or not fully intended situation whereby they receive at another's expense what they could not reasonably have expected to receive under the circumstances.
- In civilized society men and women must be able to assume that those who are engaged in some course of conduct will act with due care not to cause an unreasonable risk of injury upon others.
- In civilized society men and women must be able to assume that those who maintain things likely to get out of hand or to escape and do damage will restrain them or keep them within their proper bounds.

The Pluralist Perspective

Contrary to the assumptions made by consensus thinkers, however, it has become quite plain to most observers of the contemporary social scene that not everyone agrees on what the law should say. Society today is rife with examples of conflicting values and ideals. Consensus is hard to find. Modern debates center on issues like abortion, euthanasia, the death penalty, the purpose of criminal justice agencies in a diverse society, social justice, the rights and responsibilities of minorities and other underrepresented groups, women's issues, the proper role of education, economic policy, social welfare, the function of the military in a changing world, environmental concerns, and appropriate uses of high technology. As many contemporary public forums would indicate, there exists within America today a great diversity of social groups, each with its own point of view regarding what is right and what is wrong, and each with its own agenda. Add to that the plethora of self-proclaimed individual experts busily touting their own points of view, and anything but a consensus of values seems characteristic of society today.

Such a situation is described by some writers as "pluralist." A **pluralistic perspective** (described briefly in Chapter 1) mirrors the thought that a multiplicity of values and beliefs exists in any complex society and that different social groups will each have their own set of beliefs, interests, and values. A crucial element of this perspective, however, is the assumption that although different viewpoints exist, most individuals agree on the usefulness of law as a formal means of dispute resolution. Hence from a pluralist perspective, the law, rather than reflecting common values, exists as a peacekeeping tool that allows officials and agencies within the government to settle disputes effectively between individuals and among groups. It also assumes that whatever settlement is reached will be acceptable to all parties because of their agreement on the fundamental role of law in dispute settlement. The basic principles of the pluralist perspective include the following notions:[10]

- Society consists of many and diverse social groups. Differences in age, gender, sexual preference, ethnicity, and the like often provide the basis for much naturally occurring diversity.
- Each group has its own characteristic set of values, beliefs, and interests. Variety in gender, sexual orientation, economic status, ethnicity, and other forms of diversity produce interests which may unite like-minded individuals but which may also place them in natural opposition to other social groups.
- A general agreement exists on the usefulness of formalized laws as a mechanism for dispute resolution. People and groups accept the role of law in the settlement of disputes, and they accord decisions reached within the legal framework at least a modicum of respect.
- The legal system is value neutral. That is, the legal system is itself thought to be free of petty disputes and above the level of general contentiousness which may characterize relationships between groups.
- The legal system is concerned with the best interests of society. Legislators, judges, prosecutors, attorneys, police officers, and correctional officials are assumed to perform idealized functions that are beyond the reach of the everyday interests of self-serving groups. Hence such official functionaries can be trusted to act in accordance with the greater good, to remain unbiased, and to maintain a value-free system for the enforcement of laws.

Paul Hill, sentenced to die for the murders of a Florida abortion clinic doctor and the doctor's security escort. Hill's self-righteous attitude reflects the plurality of values characteristic of society today. Why did some people see Hill as a martyr? *Steve Mawyer, Corbis*

According to the pluralist perspective, conflict is essentially resolved through the peacekeeping activities of unbiased government officials exercising objective legal authority.

The Conflict Perspective

A third point of view, the **conflict perspective**, maintains that conflict is a fundamental aspect of social life itself that can never be fully resolved. At best, according to this perspective, formal agencies of social control merely coerce the unempowered or the disenfranchised to comply with the rules established by those in power. From the conflict point of view, laws become a tool of the powerful, useful in keeping others from wresting control over important social institutions. Social order, rather than being the result of any consensus or process of dispute resolution, rests upon the exercise of power through law. Those in power must work ceaselessly to remain there, although the structure which they impose on society—including patterns of wealth building that they define as acceptable and circumstances under which they authorize the exercise of legal power and military might—gives them all the advantages they are likely to need.

Conflict theory in the social sciences has a long history. In 1905, the writings of **Willem Bonger** echoed Marxist principles by describing the ongoing struggle between the haves and the have-nots as a natural consequence of capitalist society.[11] Bonger advanced the notion that in such societies only those who lack power are routinely subject to the criminal law. Georg Simmel's 1908 text, *Conflict and the Web of Group Affiliations* highlighted the role of social conflict in two- and three-person groups, which Simmel called diads and triads.[12] Thorsten Sellin's notion of culture conflict, proposed in 1938 (and discussed in Chapter 7), also incorporated the notion of social conflict. Since Sellin's day, many other thinkers have contributed to the development of conflict theory. Before discussing specific ideas, however, it is important to understand the six key elements of the conflict perspective.[13]

- Society is made up of diverse social groups. As in the pluralist perspective, diversity is thought to be based on distinctions which people hold to be significant, such as gender, sexual orientation, and social class.
- Each group holds to differing definitions of right and wrong. Moralistic conceptions and behavioral standards vary from group to group.
- Conflict between groups is unavoidable. Conflict is based on differences held to be socially significant (such as ethnicity, gender, and social class) and is unavoidable because groups defined on the basis of these characteristics compete for power, wealth, and other forms of recognition.

- The fundamental nature of group conflict centers on the exercise of political power. Political power is the key to the accumulation of wealth and to other forms of power.
- Law is a tool of power and furthers the interests of those powerful enough to make it. Laws allow those in control to gain what they define (through the law) as legitimate access to scarce resources and to deny (through the law) such access to the politically disenfranchised.
- Those in power are inevitably interested in maintaining their power against those who would usurp it.

RADICAL-CRITICAL CRIMINOLOGY

The conflict perspective is thoroughly entrenched in **radical criminology**, which is also diversely known as, or related to, schools of thought referred to as "new," "critical," or **Marxist criminology**. Radical criminology, which appeared on the

The tomb of Karl Marx, in Highgate Cemetery, London. Marxist thought underpins the writings of many radical criminologists. How did Marxism influence criminology? *Rex Features USA Ltd.*

THEORY IN PERSPECTIVE
Social Conflict Theories

SOCIAL CONFLICT THEORIES
emphasize the power of conflict within society, which is thought to be based largely on inequities between social classes.

■ **RADICAL CRIMINOLOGY.** Holds that the causes of crime are rooted in social conditions which empower the wealthy and the politically well organized but disenfranchise those who are less fortunate.

PERIOD:	1960s–present
THEORISTS:	Karl Marx, Ralf Dahrendorf, George B. Vold, Richard Quinney, William J. Chambliss, Raymond J. Michalowski, Austin Turk
CONCEPTS:	Social class, bourgeoisie, proletariat

■ **LEFT-REALIST CRIMINOLOGY.** A branch of radical criminology that holds that crime is a "real" social problem experienced by the lower classes.

PERIOD:	1980s–present
THEORISTS:	Walter DeKeseredy, Jock Young
CONCEPTS:	Radical realism, critical realism, street crime, social justice, crime control

■ **FEMINIST CRIMINOLOGY.** A radical criminological approach to the explanation of crime that sees the conflict and inequality present in society as being based primarily on gender.

PERIOD:	1970s–present
THEORISTS:	Freda Adler, Rita J. Simon, Kathleen Daly, Meda Chesney-Lind, John Hagan
CONCEPTS:	Power-control, gender socialization, empowerment

■ **PEACEMAKING CRIMINOLOGY.** Holds that crime control agencies and citizens must work together to alleviate social problems, including crime.

PERIOD:	1980s–present
THEORISTS:	Harold E. Pepinsky, Richard Quinney
CONCEPTS:	Compassionate criminology, restorative justice

American scene in the 1970s, has its roots in the writings of nineteenth-century social utopian thinkers. Primary among them is **Karl Marx**, whose writings on the conflicts inherent in capitalism led to the formulation of communist ideals and, many would say, to the rise of communist societies the world over.

According to Marx, two fundamental social classes exist within any capitalist society: the haves and the have-nots. Marx termed these two groups the "bourgeoisie" and the "proletariat." The **proletariat** encompasses the large mass of people, those who are relatively uneducated and who are without power. In short, the proletariat are the workers. The **bourgeoisie** are the capitalists—the wealthy owners of the means of production (for example, the factories, businesses, land, and natural resources). Although Marx was German, the terms *proletariat* and *bourgeoisie* were taken from Marx's knowledge of the French language and are in turn derived from Latin. In ancient Rome, for example, members of that city's lowest class were propertyless and were individually referred to as *proletarius*.

According to Marx, the proletariat, since they possess neither capital nor the means of production, must earn their living by selling their labor. The bourgeoisie, by nature of their very position within society, stand opposed to the proletariat in ongoing class struggle. Marx saw such struggle between classes as inevitable to the evolution of any capitalist society, and he believed that the natural outcome of such struggle would be the overthrow of capitalist social order and the birth of a truly classless, or communist, society. Learn more about the life and writings of Karl Marx at Web Extras! 9-2 and 9-3.

Web Extras! 9-2 and 9-3 at crimtoday.com

Early Radical Criminology

Radical criminology is the intellectual child of three important historical circumstances: (1) the ruminations of nineteenth-century social utopian thinkers, including Karl Marx, Friedrich Engels, Georg Wilhelm, Friedrich Hegel, George Simmel, Willem Bonger, and Max Weber; (2) the rise of conflict theory in the social sciences; and (3) the dramatic radicalization of American academia in the 1960s and 1970s.

Central to the perspective of radical criminology is the notion of social class. Some authors maintain that "class is nothing but an abbreviation to describe a way of living, thinking, and feeling."[14] For most sociologists, however, the concept of **social class** entails distinctions made between individuals on the basis of significant defining characteristics, such as race, religion, education, profession, income, wealth, family background, housing, artistic tastes, aspirations, cultural pursuits, child-rearing habits, speech, accent, and so forth. Individuals are assigned to classes by others and by themselves on the basis of characteristics which are both ascribed and achieved. Ascribed characteristics are those with which a person is born, such as race or gender, while achieved characteristics are acquired through personal effort or chance over the course of one's life and include such things as level of education, income, place of residence, and profession.

Although Marx concerned himself with only two social classes, most social scientists today talk in terms of at least three groups: the upper, middle, and lower classes. Some, such as Vance Packard, have distinguished between five hierarchically arranged classes (the real upper, semiupper, limited-success, working, and real lower classes), while further subdividing classes "horizontally" according to ascribed characteristics like race and religion.[15]

Within the discipline of criminology, **George B. Vold** helped to create the field of radical criminology. In his 1958 book, *Theoretical Criminology,* Vold described crime as the product of political conflict between groups, seeing it as a natural expression of the ongoing struggle for power, control, and material well-being.[16] According to Vold, conflict is "a universal form of interaction," and groups are naturally in conflict because their interests and purposes "overlap, encroach on one another and [tend to] be competitive."[17] Vold also addressed the issue of social cohesion, noting that as intergroup conflict intensifies, the loyalty of individual members to their groups increases. "It has long been realized that conflict between groups tends to develop and intensify the loyalty of group members to their respective groups," Vold wrote.[18] Vold's most succinct observation of the role conflict plays in contributing to crime was expressed in these words: "The whole political process of law making, law breaking, and law enforcement becomes a direct reflection of deep-seated and fundamental conflicts between interest groups. . . . Those who produce legislative majorities win control over the power and dominate the policies that decide who is likely to be involved in violation of the law."[19]

From Vold's point of view, powerful groups make laws, and those laws express and protect their interests. Hence the body of laws that characterize any society is a political statement, and crime is a political definition imposed largely upon those whose interests lie outside of that which the powerful, through the law, define as acceptable. In his writings about conflict, Vold went so far as to compare the criminal with a soldier, fighting, through crime commission, for the very survival of the group whose values he or she represents.

In Vold's words, "The individual criminal is then viewed as essentially a soldier under conditions of warfare: his behavior may not be 'normal' or 'happy' or 'adjusted'—it is the behavior of the soldier doing what is to be done in wartime."[20] Vold's analogy, probably influenced by World War II, was meant to express the idea that crime is a manifestation of denied needs and values—that is, the cultural heritage of disenfranchised groups who are powerless to enact their interests in legitimate fashion. Hence theft becomes necessary for many poor people, especially those left unemployed or unemployable by the socially acceptable forms of wealth distribution defined by law.

Conflict theorists of the early and mid-1900s saw in the concept of social class the rudimentary ingredients of other important concepts like authority, power, and conflict. **Ralf Dahrendorf,** for example, wrote that "classes are social conflict groups the determinant of which can be found in the participation in or exclusion from the exercise of authority."[21] For Dahrendorf, conflict was ubiquitous, a fundamental part of and coextensive with any society. "Not the presence but the absence of conflict is surprising and abnormal," he wrote, "and we have good reason to be suspicious if we find a society or social organization that displays no evidence of conflict. To be sure, we do not have to assume that conflict is always violent and uncontrolled . . . We must never lose sight of the underlying assumption that conflict can be temporarily suppressed, regulated, channeled, and controlled but that neither a philosopher-king nor a modern dictator can abolish it once and for all."[22]

From Dahrendorf's perspective, it was power and authority which were most at issue between groups and over which class conflicts arose. Dahrendorf also recognized that situations characterized by conflict are rarely static and that it is out of conflict that change arises. For Dahrendorf, change could be either destructive or constructive. Destructive change brings about a lessening of social order, whereas constructive change increases cohesiveness within society. Dahrendorf's 1959 book, *Class and Class Conflict in Industrial Society,* set the stage for the radical writers of the 1960s and 1970s.

Another mid-twentieth-century conflict theorist, **Austin Turk,** said that in the search for an explanation of criminality, "one is led to investigate the tendency of laws to penalize persons whose behavior is more characteristic of the less powerful than of the more powerful and the extent to which some persons and groups can and do use legal processes and agencies to maintain and enhance their power position vis-à-vis other persons and groups."[23] In his 1969 seminal work, *Criminality and Legal Order,* Turk wrote that in any attempt to explain criminality, "it is more useful to view the social order as mainly a pattern of conflict" rather than to offer explanations for crime based on behavioral or psychological approaches.[24] Turk, like most other conflict criminologists, saw the law as a powerful tool in the service

Deteriorating factories in Knovokuznetsk, Siberia. Radical criminology has its origins in the writings of Karl Marx, whose thinking was strongly influenced by the social conditions of the industrial era. *Peter Turnley, Corbis*

of prominent social groups seeking continued control over others. Crime was the natural consequence of such inter-group struggle because it resulted from the definitions imposed by the laws of the powerful upon the disapproved strivings of the unempowered.

Radical Criminology Today

Radical criminologists of today are considerably more sophisticated than their Marxist forebears. Contemporary radical criminology holds that the causes of crime are rooted in social conditions which empower the wealthy and the politically well organized but disenfranchise those who are less fortunate. **William J. Chambliss**, a well-known spokesperson for radical thinkers, succinctly summarizes the modern perspective in these words: "What makes the behavior of some criminal is the coercive power of the state to enforce the will of the ruling class."[25]

In 1971, Chambliss, along with Robert T. Seidman, published a critically acclaimed volume entitled *Law, Order, and Power*. Their work represented something of a bridge between earlier conflict theorists and the more radical approach of the Marxists. Through its emphasis on social class, class interests, and class conflict, *Law, Order, and Power* presented a Marxist perspective stripped of any overt references to capitalism as the root cause of crime. "The more economically stratified a society becomes," Chambliss and Seidman wrote, "the more it becomes necessary for the dominant groups in the society to enforce through coercion the norms of conduct which guarantee their supremacy."[26] Chambliss and Seidman outlined their position in four propositions:[27]

■ The conditions of one's life affect one's values and norms. Complex societies are composed of groups with widely different life conditions.
■ Complex societies are therefore composed of highly disparate and conflicting sets of norms.
■ The probability of a given group's having its particular normative system embodied in law is not distributed equally but is closely related to the political and economic position of that group.
■ The higher a group's political or economic position, the greater the probability that its views will be reflected in laws.

Chambliss also believed that middle- and upper-class criminals are more apt to escape apprehension and punishment by the criminal justice system, not because they are any smarter or more capable of hiding their crimes than are lower-class offenders, but because of a "very rational choice on the part of the legal system to pursue those violators that the community will reward them for pursuing and to ignore those violators who have the capability for causing trouble for the agencies."[28]

By the 1970s, Chambliss's writings assumed a much more Marxist flavor. In an article published in 1975, Chambliss once again recognized the huge power gap separating the haves from the have-nots.[29] Crime, he said, is created by actions of the ruling class which define as criminal such things as undertakings and activities that contravene the interests of the rulers. At the same time, he said, members of the ruling class will inevitably be able to continue to violate the criminal law with impunity because it is their own creation.

Soon the Marxist flavor of Chambliss's writing had become undeniable. He began using Marxist terminology. "As capitalist societies industrialize and the gap between the bourgeoisie and the proletariat widens," he wrote, "penal law will expand in an effort to coerce the proletariat into submission."[30] For Chambliss, the economic consequences of crime within a capitalist society were partially what perpetuated it. "Crime reduces surplus labor," he wrote, "by creating employment not only for the criminals but for law enforcers, welfare workers, professors of criminology, and a horde of people who live off the fact that crime exists."[31] Socialist societies, claimed Chambliss, should reflect much lower crime rates than capitalist societies because a "less intense class struggle should reduce the forces leading to and the functions of crime."[32] Learn more about the writings of William J. Chambliss at Web Extra! 9-4.

Web Extra! 9-4 at crimtoday.com

Although Chambliss provides much of the intellectual bedrock of contemporary radical criminology, that school of thought found its most eloquent expression in the writings of **Richard Quinney.** In 1974, Quinney, in an attempt to challenge and change American social life for the better, set forth his six Marxist propositions for an understanding of crime:[33]

- American society is based on an advanced capitalist economy.
- The state is organized to serve the interests of the dominant economic class—that is, the capitalist ruling class.
- Criminal law is an instrument of the state and ruling class to maintain and perpetuate the existing social and economic order.
- Crime control in capitalist society is accomplished through a variety of institutions and agencies established and administered by a governmental elite, representing ruling-class interests, for the purpose of establishing domestic order.
- The contradictions of advanced capitalism—the disjunction between existence and essence—require that the subordinate classes remain oppressed by whatever means necessary, especially through the coercion and violence of the legal system.
- Only with the collapse of capitalist society and the creation of a new society, based on socialist principles, will there be a solution to the crime problem.

A few years later, Quinney published *Class, State, and Crime,* in which he argued that almost all crimes committed by members of the lower classes are necessary for the survival of individual members of those classes. Crimes, said Quinney—in fashion reminiscent of Vold's notion of the criminal as a soldier—are actually an attempt by the socially disenfranchised "to exist in a society where *survival* is not assured by other, collective means."[34] He concludes, "Crime is

inevitable under capitalist conditions" because crime is "a response to the material conditions of life. Permanent unemployment—and the acceptance of that condition—can result in a form of life where criminality is an appropriate and consistent response."[35] The solution offered by Quinney to the problem of crime is the development of a socialist society. "The *ultimate meaning* of crime in the development of capitalism," he writes, "is the need for a socialist society."[36]

Contemporary radical criminology attributes much of the existing propensity toward criminality to differences in social class, and in particular to those arrangements within society which maintain class differences. As Quinney puts it, "Classes are an expression of the underlying forces of the capitalist mode of production."[37] "Within the class structure of advanced capitalism," he writes, "is the dialectic that increases class struggle and the movement for socialist revolution."[38] Table 9-1 depicts the class structure of the United States as Quinney portrayed it.

TABLE 9-1 ■ Class Structure of the United States, with Estimated Percentages of the Adult Population	
Capitalist Class 1.5%	Those who own and control production and wield state power
Petty Bourgeoisie 18.5%	Professionals, middle management, bureaucrats
Working Class 80%	Technical and skilled working class, 25%
	Technical, 10%
	Teachers
	Nurses
	Medical technicians
	Skilled, 15%
	Craftsmen
	Clerical workers
	Salespeople
	Transportation workers
	Industrial workers
	Reserve army, 15%
	Unskilled working class, 55%
	Unskilled, 30%
	Industrial labor
	Service workers
	Office workers
	Salespeople
	Clerical workers
	Unemployed (percentage varies)
	Pauperized poor, 10%

Source: Adapted from Richard Quinney, *Class, State, and Crime: On the Theory and Practice of Criminal Justice* (New York: David McKay, 1977), p. 77. Reprinted with permission.

Today's radical criminologies can be divided into two schools: structuralist and instrumentalist. **Structural Marxism** sees capitalism as a self-maintaining system in which the law and the justice system work to perpetuate the existing system of power relationships. Hence according to structural Marxism, even the rich are subject to certain laws designed to prevent them from engaging in forms of behavior that might undermine the system of which they are a part. Laws regulating trade practices and monopolies, for example, regulate the behavior of the powerful and serve to ensure survival of the capitalist system. **Instrumental Marxism**, on the other hand, sees the criminal law and the justice system as tools that the powerful use to control the poor and to keep them disenfranchised. Hence according to instrumental Marxism, the legal system serves not only to perpetuate the power relationships that exist within society, but also to keep control in the hands of those who are already powerful. A recently popular book by **Jeffrey H. Reiman** builds upon this premise. Entitled *The Rich Get Richer and the Poor Get Prison*, Reiman's work contends that the criminal justice system is biased against the poor from start to finish and that well-to-do members of society control the criminal justice system—from the definition of crime through the process of arrest, trial, and sentencing.[39] Reiman also claims that many of the actions undertaken by well-off people should be defined as criminal, but they aren't. Such actions include the refusal to make workplaces safe, the refusal to curtail deadly industrial pollution, the promotion of unnecessary surgery, and the prescription of unnecessary drugs. This kind of self-serving behavior, says Reiman, creates occupational and environmental hazards for the poor and for those who are less well-off than the rule makers themselves. These conditions, claims Reiman, produce as much death, destruction, and financial loss as the so-called crimes of the poor. Learn more about radical criminology at Web Extra! 9-5.

Web EXTRA! Web Extra! 9-5 at crimtoday.com

Critical Criminology

Some writers distinguish between critical criminology and radical criminology, saying that the former is simply a way of critiquing social relationships that lead to crime, whereas the latter constitutes a proactive call for a radical change in the social conditions which lead to crime.

Gresham M. Sykes explains **critical criminology** this way: "It forces an inquiry into precisely how the normative content of the criminal law is internalized in different segments of society, and how norm-holding is actually related to behavior."[40] As David A. Jones states in his insightful *History of Criminology*, however, "Sometimes, it may be difficult to distinguish 'critical' from a truly Marxist criminology. One basis, advanced by Marvin Wolfgang, is that 'critical' criminology is 'more reactive than proactive,' meaning that 'criti-

cal' criminology does not aim to overthrow the 'ruling class' so much as it may criticize the way it believes such a group dominates society."[41]

A cogent example of the critical perspective in contemporary criminology can be had in the work of Elliott Currie. Currie claims that " 'market societies'—those in which the pursuit of private gain becomes the dominant organizing principle of social and economic life—are especially likely to breed high levels of violent crime."[42] Market societies, says Currie, are characterized by more than free enterprise and a free market economy. They are societies in which the striving after personal economic gain runs rampant and becomes the hallmark of social life. The conditions endemic to market societies lead to high crime rates because they undercut and overwhelm more traditional principles that "have historically sustained individuals, families and communities." The United States is the world's premier market society, says Currie, and its culture provides "a particularly fertile breeding ground for serious violent crime." Similarly, the recent and dramatic rise in crime rates in former communist countries throughout Europe can be explained by the burgeoning development of new market societies in those nations. According to Currie, seven "profoundly criminogenic and closely intertwined mechanisms" operate in a market society to produce crime:

- "The progressive destruction of livelihood," which results from the long-term absence of opportunities for stable and rewarding work—a consequence of the fact that market societies view labor "simply as a cost to be reduced" rather than as an asset with intrinsic value.
- "The growth of extremes of economic inequality and material deprivation," which causes many children to spend their developmental years in poverty.
- "The withdrawal of public services and supports, especially for families and children," resulting from the fact that "it is a basic operating principle of market society to keep the public sector small."
- "The erosion of informal and communal networks of mutual support, supervision, and care," brought about by the high mobility of the workforce that is characteristic of market societies.
- "The spread of a materialistic, neglectful, and 'hard' culture," which exalts brutal forms of individualized competition.
- "The unregulated marketing of the technology of violence," including the ready availability of guns, an emphasis on advancing technologies of destruction (such as the military), and mass-marketed violence on television and in the media.
- "The weakening of social and political alternatives," leaving people unable to cope effectively with the forces of the market society which undermine their communities and destroy valuable interpersonal relationships.

Currie suggests that as more nations emulate the "market society" culture of the United States, crime rates throughout the world will rise. An increasing emphasis on punishment and the growth of huge prison systems, says Currie, will consequently characterize most of the world's nations in the twenty-first century.

Radical-Critical Criminology and Policy Issues

Some contemporary writers on radical criminology tell us that "Marxist criminology was once dismissed as a utopian perspective with no relevant policy implication except revolution. At best, revolution was considered an impractical approach to the problems at hand. Recently, however, many radicals have attempted to address the issues of what can be done under our current system."[43]

Most radical-critical criminologists of today have had to come to terms with the collapse of the Soviet Union, a society that represented utopian Marxism in practice. They have also had to recognize that a sudden and total reversal of existing political arrangements within the United States is highly unlikely. As a consequence, such theorists have begun to focus, instead, on promoting a gradual transition to socialism and to socialized forms of government activity. These middle-range policy alternatives include "equal justice in the bail system, the abolition of mandatory sentences, prosecution of corporate crimes, increased employment opportunities, and promoting community alternatives to imprisonment."[44] Likewise, programs to reduce prison overcrowding, efforts to highlight injustices within the current system, the elimination of racism and other forms of inequality in the handling of both victims and offenders, increased equality in criminal justice system employment, and the like are all frequently mentioned as midrange strategies for bringing about a justice system that is more fair and closer to the radical ideal.

Raymond J. Michalowski summarizes well the policy directions envisioned by today's radical-critical criminologists when he says, "We cannot be free from the crimes of the poor until there are no more poor; we cannot be free from domination of the powerful until we reduce the inequalities that make domination possible; and we cannot live in harmony with others until we begin to limit the competition for material advantage over others that alienates us from one another."[45]

Even so, few radical-critical criminologists seem to expect to see dramatic changes in the near future. As Michael J. Lynch and W. Byron Groves explain, "In the end, the criminal justice system has failed as an agent of social change because its efforts are directed at an individual as opposed to social remedies. . . . For these reasons, radicals suggest that we put our efforts into the creation of economic equality or employment opportunities to combat crime."[46]

Critique of Radical-Critical Criminology

Radical-critical criminology has been criticized for its nearly exclusive emphasis on methods of social change at the expense of well-developed theory. As William V. Pelfrey explains, "It is in the Radical School of Criminology that theory is almost totally disregarded, except as something to criticize, and radical methods are seen as optimum."[47]

Radical-critical criminology can also be criticized for failing to recognize what appears to be at least a fair degree of public consensus about the nature of crime, that is, that crime is undesirable and that criminal activity is to be controlled. Were criminal activity in fact a true expression of the sentiments of the politically and economically disenfranchised, as some radical criminologists claim, then public opinion might be expected to offer support for at least certain forms of crime. Even the sale of illicit drugs, however— a type of crime which may provide an alternative path to riches for the otherwise disenfranchised—is frequently condemned by residents of working-class communities.[48]

An effective criticism of Marxist criminology, in particular, centers on the fact that Marxist thinkers appear to confuse issues of personal politics with social reality. As a consequence of allowing personal values and political leanings to enter the criminological arena, Marxist criminologists have frequently appeared to sacrifice their objectivity. Jackson Toby, for example, claims that Marxist and radical thinkers are simply building upon an "old tradition of sentimentality toward those who break social rules."[49] Such sentimentality can be easily discounted, he says, when we realize that "color television sets and automobiles are stolen more often than food and blankets."[50]

Marxist criminology has also been refuted by contemporary thinkers who find that it falls short in appreciating the multiplicity of problems that contribute to the problem of crime. Some years ago, for example, the astute criminologist Hermann Mannheim critiqued Marxian assumptions by showing how "subsequent developments" have shown that "Marx was wrong in thinking" (1) "that there could be only two classes in a capitalist society," (2) that "class struggle was entirely concerned with the question of private property in the means of production," (3) "that the only way in which fundamental social changes could be effected was by violent social revolution," and (4) "that all conflicts were class conflicts and all social change could be explained in terms of class conflicts."[51]

Mannheim went on to point out that the development of a semiskilled workforce along with the advent of highly skilled and well-educated workers has led to the creation of a multiplicity of classes within contemporary capitalist societies. The growth of such classes, said Mannheim, effectively spreads the available wealth in those societies where such workers are employed and reduces the likelihood of revolution.

A now-classic critique of radical criminology was offered in 1979 by Carl Klockars.[52] Klockars charged that Marxists are unable to explain low crime rates in some capitalist countries, such as Japan, and that they seem equally unwilling to acknowledge or address the problems of communist countries, which often have terrible human rights records. Writing more than 20 years ago, Klockars claimed that Marxist criminologists behaved more like "true believers" in a "new religion" who were unwilling to objectively evaluate their beliefs.[53]

Marxist criminology has suffered a considerable loss of prestige among many would-be followers in the wake of the collapse of the former Soviet Union and its client states in Eastern Europe and other parts of the world. With the death of Marxist political organizations and their agendas, Marxist criminology seems to have lost some of its impetus. Many would argue that, in fact, the work of writers like Quinney and Chambliss presaged the decline of Soviet influence and had already moved Marxist and radical criminology into new areas, effectively shedding the reigns of world communism and ending any association with its institutional embodiment in specific parts of the world. The work of Elliott Currie (discussed earlier in this chapter) and others has since led in a post-Marxist direction while retaining a critical emphasis on the principles out of which radical criminology was fashioned. Consequently, today's radical criminologists have largely rescinded calls for revolutionary change while simultaneously escalating their demands for the eradication of gender, racial, and other inequalities in the criminal justice system; for the elimination of prisons; for the abolition of capital punishment; and for an end to police misconduct.

EMERGING CONFLICT THEORIES

The radical ideas associated with mid-twentieth-century Marxist criminology contributed to the formation of a number of new and innovative approaches to crime and criminology. Among them are emerging conflict criminologies, such as left-realist criminology, feminist criminology, postmodern criminology, and peacemaking criminology. It is to these perspectives that we now turn our attention.

Left-Realist Criminology

Left-realist criminology, a recent addition to the criminological landscape, is a natural outgrowth of practical concerns with street crime, the fear of crime, and everyday victimization. Realist criminology faults radical-critical criminologists for romanticizing street crime and the criminals who commit it. Radical-critical criminologists, they charge, falsely imagine street criminals as political resisters in an oppressive capitalist society. While realist criminology does not reject the conflict perspective inherent in radical-critical criminology, it shifts the center of focus onto a pragmatic assessment of crime and the needs of crime victims. Realist criminology seeks to portray crime in terms understandable to those most often affected by it: victims and their families, offenders, and criminal justice personnel. The test insisted upon by realist criminology is not whether a particular perspective on crime control or an explanation of crime causation complies with rigorous academic criteria, but whether the perspective speaks meaningfully to those faced

with crime on a routine basis. As one contemporary source states, "For realists crime is no less harmful to its victims because of its socially constructed origins."[54]

Realist criminology is generally considered synonymous with **left realism.** Left realism, also called "radical realism" or "critical realism," builds on many of the concepts inherent in radical and Marxist criminology while simultaneously claiming greater relevance than either of its two parent perspectives. Left realism also tends to distance itself from some of the more visionary claims of early radical and Marxist theory.[55] Daniel J. Curran and Claire M. Renzetti portray left realism as a natural consequence of increasingly conservative attitudes toward crime and criminals in both Europe and North America. "Though not successful in converting many radicals to the right," they claim, "this new conservatism did lead a number of radical criminologists to temper their views a bit and to take what some might call a less romanticized look at street crime."[56]

Some authors credit **Walter DeKeseredy**[57] with popularizing left-realist notions in North America, and **Jock Young**[58] is identified as a major source of left-realist writings in England. Prior to the writings of DeKeseredy and Young, radical criminology, with its emphasis upon the crime-inducing consequences of existing power structures, tended to portray the ruling class as the "real criminals" and saw street criminals as social rebels who were acting out of felt deprivation. In contrast, DeKeseredy and Young were successful in refocusing leftist theories onto the serious consequences of street crime and upon the crimes of the lower classes. Left realists argue that victims of crime are often the poor and disenfranchised who fall prey to criminals with similar backgrounds. They do not see the criminal justice system and its agents as pawns of the powerful, but rather as institutions that could offer useful services if modifications were made to reduce their use of force and to increase their sensitivity toward the public.

A central tenet of left realism is that radical ideas must be translated into realistic social policies if contemporary criminology is to have any practical relevance. In a recent review of left realism in Australia and England, concrete suggestions with respect to community policing models, for example, are indicative of the direction left realists are headed. Instead of seeing the police as oppressors working on behalf of the state, left realists recommend that the police work with, and answer to, the communities they serve.[59] The major goal of left realism is therefore to achieve "a fair and orderly society" through a practical emphasis on social justice.[60] Hence left realists are concerned with the reality of crime and the damage it does to the most vulnerable segments of the population.

Critique of Left-Realist Criminology

Left-realist criminology has been convincingly criticized for representing more of an ideological emphasis than a theory. As Don C. Gibbons explains, "Left realism can best be described as a general perspective centered on injunctions to 'take crime seriously' and to 'take crime control seriously' rather than as a well-developed criminological perspective."[61]

Realist criminologists appear to build upon preexisting theoretical frameworks but rarely offer new propositions or hypotheses that are testable. They do, however, frequently suggest crime control approaches which are in keeping with the needs of the victimized. Policies promulgated by left realists understandably include an emphasis on community policing, neighborhood justice centers, and dispute resolution mechanisms, whereas right realists are more punitive in their policy suggestions. Piers Beirne and James W. Messerschmidt summarize the situation this way: "What left realists have essentially accomplished is an attempt to theorize about conventional crime realistically while simultaneously developing a 'radical law and order' program for curbing such behavior."[62]

Feminist Criminology

As some have observed, "Women have been virtually invisible in criminological analysis until recently and much theorizing has proceeded as though criminality is restricted to men."[63] Others put it this way: "Criminological theory assumes a woman is like a man."[64] Beginning in the 1970s, however, advances in feminist theory were applied to criminology, resulting in what has been called a **feminist criminology**. Other strands of feminist thought inform feminist criminology, including liberal feminism, radical feminism, socialist feminism, and Marxist feminism. Each of these perspectives argues that conflict in society is based on inequalities due primarily to gender, although they may vary on the degree to which inequality exists.

Feminist criminology is a self-conscious corrective model intended to redirect the thinking of mainstream criminologists to include gender awareness. It points out the inequities inherent in patriarchal forms of thought. **Patriarchy** refers to male dominance. James W. Messerschmidt offers a definition of patriarchy that is in keeping with the traditions of Marxist criminology. Messerschmidt says that patriarchy is a "set of social relations of power in which the male gender appropriates the labor power of women and controls their sexuality."[65] Evidence of patriarchy can be found in many different places. The fact that crime is often seen as an act of aggression, for example, contributes to the perpetuation of a male-centered criminology in which men are biologically characterized as having an aggressive nature that needs to be channeled and controlled. Society's acceptance of the belief that men are predisposed to aggression, however, led to the socialization of women as passive actors, which has excluded them from criminological study and made them more susceptible to continued victimization by men. In other words, traditional criminology, like the society of which it has been a part, has been male-centered, and women have been largely ignored by criminologists, heightening their sense of powerlessness and dependence upon men.

Early works in the field of feminist criminology include **Freda Adler**'s *Sisters in Crime*[66] and **Rita J. Simon**'s *Women and Crime*,[67] both published in 1975. In these books, the authors attempted to explain existing divergences in crime rates between men and women as being due primarily to socialization rather than biology. Women, claimed these authors, were

taught to believe in personal limitations; they faced reduced socioeconomic opportunities and, as a result, suffered from lowered aspirations. As gender equality increased, they said, it could be expected that male and female criminality would take on similar characteristics. As Chapter 2 points out, however, such has not been the case to date, and the approach of Adler and Simon has not been validated by observations surrounding increased gender equality over the past few decades. Another early work, *Women, Crime and Criminology* was published in 1977 by British sociologist Carol Smart.[68] Smart's book did much to sensitize criminologists to sexist traditions within the field and led to recognition of women's issues. Smart pointed out that men and women experience and perceive the world in different ways. She showed how important it is for women to have a voice in interpreting the behavior of other women, as opposed to having the behavior of women interpreted from a man's standpoint—a perspective that does not include women's experience.

Early feminist theorizing may not have borne the fruit that some researchers anticipated, but it has led to a heightened awareness of gender issues within criminology. Two of the most insightful contemporary proponents of the need to apply feminist thinking to criminological analysis are **Kathleen Daly** and **Meda Chesney-Lind**. Daly and Chesney-Lind are concerned about the existence of **androcentricity** in criminology, and they point out that "gender differences in crime suggest that crime may not be so normal after all."[69] In other words, traditional understandings of what is "typical" about crime are derived from a study of men only, or, more precisely, from that relatively small group of men who commit most crimes. The relative lack of criminality exhibited by women, however, which is rarely acknowledged as having criminological significance, calls into question many traditional assumptions about crime—and especially the assumption that crime is somehow a "normal" part of social life. In general terms, Daly and Chesney-Lind have identified the following five elements of feminist thought that "distinguish it from other types of social and political thought:"[70]

- Gender is not a natural fact but a complex social, historical, and cultural product; it is related to, but not simply derived from, biological sex difference and reproductive capacities.
- Gender and gender relations order social life and social institutions in fundamental ways.
- Gender relations and constructs of masculinity and femininity are not symmetrical but are based on an organizing principle of men's superiority and social, political, and economic dominance over women.
- Systems of knowledge reflect men's views of the natural and social world; the production of knowledge is gendered.
- Women should be at the center, not the periphery, of intellectual inquiry; they should not be invisible or treated as appendages to men.

In a similar, but more recent, analysis of feminist criminology, Susan Caulfield and Nancy Wonders describe "five major contributions that have been made by feminist scholarship and practice" to criminological thinking: (1) a focus on gender as a central organizing principle of contemporary life; (2) an awareness of the importance of power in shaping social relationships; (3) a heightened sensitivity to the way in which social context helps shape human relationships; (4) the recognition that social reality must be understood as a process, and the development of research methods which take this into account; and (5) a commitment to social change as a crucial part of feminist scholarship and practice.[71] As is the case with most feminist writing in the area of criminology today, Caulfield and Wonders hold that these five contributions of feminist scholarship "can help to guide research and practice within criminology."[72]

Feminism is a way of seeing the world. It is not strictly a sexual orientation. To be a feminist is to "combine a female mental perspective with a sensitivity for those social issues that influence primarily women."[73] Central to understanding feminist thought in both its historical and its contemporary modes is the realization that feminism views gender in terms of power relationships. In other words, according to feminist approaches, men have traditionally held much more power in society than have women. Male dominance has long been reflected in the patriarchal structure of Western society, a structure which has excluded women from much decision making in socially significant areas. Sexist attitudes—deeply ingrained notions of male superiority—have perpetuated inequality between the sexes. The consequences of sexism and of the unequal gender-based distribution of power have been far reaching, affecting fundamental aspects of social roles and personal expectation at all levels.

Various schools of feminist thought exist, with liberal and radical feminism envisioning a power-based and traditional domination of women's bodies and minds by men throughout history. **Radical feminism** depicts men as fundamentally brutish, aggressive, and violent and sees men as controlling women through sexuality by taking advantage of women's biological dependence during child bearing years and their inherent lack of physical strength relative to men. Radical feminists believe, for example, that the sexual victimization of girls is a learned behavior, as young males are socialized to be aggressive, resulting in male domination over females. They view society as patriarchal and believe that because men control the law, women are defined as subjects. Those young women who are sexually and physically exploited may run away or abuse substances, thereby becoming criminalized. Hence from the point of view of radical feminism, the exploitation of women by men triggers women's deviant behavior. The elimination of male domination should therefore reduce crime rates for women and "even precipitate a decrease in male violence against women."[74]

Liberal feminists, although they want the same gender equality as other feminists, lay the blame for present inequalities on the development within culture and society of "separate and distinct spheres of influence and traditional attitudes about the appropriate role of men and women."[75] A recent book by Alida V. Merlo and Joycelyn M. Pollock, for example, points out that feminists are often blamed in today's political atmosphere for the recent upsurge in crime because many, by entering or creating innovative family structures, have lowered what might otherwise be the positive effect of traditional family values on crime control.[76] Liberal feminists call for elimination of traditional divisions of power and labor between the sexes as a way of eliminating inequality and promoting social harmony.

Socialist feminists, who provide a third perspective, see gender oppression as a consequence of the economic structure of society and as a natural outgrowth of capitalist forms of social organization. Egalitarian societies, from the socialist point of view, would be built around socialist or Marxist principles with the aim of creating a society that is free of gender and class divisions. The present, capitalist social structure, sees men committing violent street crimes, with women more likely to commit property and vice crimes.[77]

A fourth and complementary feminist perspective has been identified by Sally S. Simpson, who refers to it as an alternative framework developed by women of color. In Simpson's words, "The alternative frameworks developed by women of color heighten feminism's sensitivity to the complex interplay of gender, class, and race oppression."[78]

John Hagan built upon defining features of power relationships in his book *Structural Criminology,* in which he explained that power relationships existing in the wider society are effectively "brought home" to domestic settings and are reflected in everyday relationships between men, women, and children within the context of family life.[79] Hagan writes, "Work relations structure family relations, particularly relations between fathers and mothers and, in turn, relations between parents and their children, especially mothers and their daughters."[80] Hagan's approach, which has been termed **power-control theory**, suggests that "family class structure shapes the social reproduction of gender relations, and in turn the social distribution of delinquency."[81] In most middle- and upper-middle-class families, says Hagan, a paternalistic model, in which the father works and the mother supervises the children, is the norm. Under the paternalistic model, girls are controlled by both parents—through male domination and by female role modeling. Boys, however, are less closely controlled and are relatively free to deviate from social norms, resulting in higher levels of delinquency among males. In lower- and lower-middle-class families, however, the paternalistic model is frequently absent. Hence in such families there is less "gender socialization and less maternal supervision of girls," resulting in higher levels of female delinquency.[82]

In a work supportive of Hagan's thesis, Evelyn K. Sommers recently conducted a series of four hour-long interviews with 14 female inmates in a Canadian medium-security prison.[83] Focusing on what led to violations of the criminal law, Sommers identified four common themes to explain the criminality of the women she interviewed: (1) financial need, (2) drug involvement, (3) personal anger rooted in sexual and physical abuse or a sense of loss, and (4) fear. Because "need" was identified as the cause of lawbreaking behavior by four of five women interviewed, Sommers concluded that women's criminality is based on two underlying issues: the effort to maintain connection within relationships (such as between mother and child) and a personal quest for empowerment (as single mothers are expected to be independent and capable of providing for themselves and their children).

In a cogent analysis which encompasses much of contemporary feminist theory, Daly and Chesney-Lind suggest that feminist thought is more important for the way it informs and challenges existing criminology than for the new theories it offers. Much current feminist thought within criminology emphasizes the need for gender awareness. Theories of crime causation and prevention, it is suggested, must include women, and more research on gender-related issues in the field is badly needed. Additionally, say Daly and Chesney-Lind, "criminologists should begin to appreciate that their discipline and its questions are a product of white, economically privileged men's experiences"[84] and that rates of female criminality, which are lower than those of males, may highlight the fact that criminal behavior is not as "normal" as once thought. Because modern-day criminological perspectives were mostly developed by white middle-class men, the propositions and theories they advance fail to take into consideration women's "ways of knowing."[85] Hence the fundamental challenge posed by feminist criminology is, Do existing theories of crime causation apply as well to women as they do to men? Or, as Daly and Chesney-Lind ask, given the current situation in theory development, "do theories of men's crime apply to women?"[86]

Other feminists have analyzed the process by which laws are created and legislation passed and have concluded that modern-day statutes frequently represent characteristically masculine modes of thought. Such analysts have concluded that existing criminal laws are overly rational and hierarchically structured, reflecting traditionally male ways of organizing the social world.[87]

Until recently, for example, many jurisdictions viewed assault victims differently based on the gendered relationships involved in the offense. Assault (or, more precisely, battery), for example, is defined as an attack by one person upon another. Until the last few decades of the twentieth century, however, domestic violence statutes tended to downplay the seriousness of the attacks involved, giving the impression that because they occurred within the home and the victims were typically women, they weren't as important to the justice system as other forms of assault. Hence cases of domestic assault were often handled informally by responding officers, and offenders were rarely arrested or removed from the home.[88] Similarly, some would argue, legal definitions of prostitution, pornography, and rape are determined primarily by men's understanding of the behavior in question and not by the experiences of women. Hence in traditional criminology, women receive special protection because they are considered vulnerable to crime, but the experiences of women do not define the nature of the law or of the justice system's response. Consequently, some analysts suggest, existing laws need to be replaced by, or complemented with, "a system of justice based upon . . . the specifically feminine principles of care, connection and community."[89]

In the area of social policy, feminist thinkers have pointed to the need for increased controls over men's violence toward women, the creation of alternatives (to supplement the home and traditional family structures) for women facing abuse, and the protection of children. They have also questioned the role of government, culture, and the mass media in promulgating pornography, prostitution, and rape and have generally portrayed ongoing crimes against women as characteristic of continuing traditions in which women are undervalued and controlled. Many radical feminists have suggested the replacement of men with women in positions of power, especially within justice system and government organizations, while others have

Aileen Wuornos, accused serial killer. Although some women are moving into areas of traditional male criminality, the number of women committing most forms of crime is still far lower than that of men. How does the criminality of women appear to differ from that of men? *Daytona Beach News, Corbis/Sygma*

CRIME IN THE NEWS
Women Cops Less Prone to Violence, Report Says

When it comes to misconduct claims against police officers in the nation's second-largest city, it's a man's world.

A study by a feminist organization found that the city paid out $63.4 million to settle lawsuits alleging misconduct against male officers during the 1990s. In contrast, only $2.8 million was paid in cases targeting female officers, even though they make up 18 percent of the force's officers.

Proponents of female police officers said the study, released Monday, shows that women are better equipped to avoid violent confrontations than their male counterparts.

"Hopefully this will be an impetus for police chiefs who want to hire more women, and cities that want to save money," said Penny Harrington, director of the National Center for Women and Policing and former chief of police of Portland, Oregon.

127 LAWSUIT PAYMENTS

The center and the Feminist Majority Foundation commissioned the study, which analyzed 127 Los Angeles Police Department lawsuit payments of more than $100,000 from 1990 to 1999. Of those, 78 met the criteria for inclusion in the study because the gender of the officers could be determined and the cases involved allegations of excessive force, sexual assault or domestic violence.

The study includes 255 male officers and 27 female officers.

Spokesmen for the LAPD were unavailable to comment on the report's findings. An official with the mayor's office said he has not seen the report and could not comment on it.

$10 MILLION IN SEX ASSAULT CLAIMS

The study found that male officers were responsible for $10.4 million in lawsuit payments involving charges of sexual assault, sexual molestation and domestic violence.

Male officers on the force outnumbered female officers by 4-to-1 during the period measured. But the amount paid out in cases of brutality and misconduct involving male officers outweighed those of female officers by 23-to-1, the study said.

Payments for killings by male officers outweighed those by female officers by a ratio of 43-to-1.

MINORS ALLEGEDLY MOLESTED

No women officers were targeted in the lawsuits alleging sexual misconduct and domestic violence by officers. Eight lawsuits targeted men for alleged sexual assault, sexual abuse, molestation, and domestic violence.

The largest sex-related settlement, $6.3 million, was in a lawsuit involving a male

officer who sexually battered a minor in her home while responding to a police call. In another case, a sergeant allegedly molested four minors in a police car while he was on duty.

In another case, the city paid $1.5 million after an officer killed his ex-wife, her boyfriend and then himself. According to the study, the LAPD was aware of his violent domestic history.

WOMEN "DE-ESCALATE" VIOLENCE

Harrington, who served as police chief of Portland from 1985 to 1986, said the study confirms her belief that women officers know how to defuse violence.

"Studies have shown that women get the same kinds of calls that men get, it's just that from the time we're young we learn how to de-escalate violence," she said. "We're taught as young girls that when we're around people who are getting angry, what we need to do is calm them down. Women don't have their ego invested in winning a confrontation with someone. It's OK for us to back down or not come out as the strong person."

Despite their qualities, women make up only 14 percent of police departments nationwide, Harrington said.

Source: Randy Dortinga, "Study of LAPD Shows Fewer Claims Against Female Officers," APB News, September 20, 2000. Reprinted with permission.

---

noted that replacement still would not address needed changes in the structure of the system itself, which is gender biased due to years of male domination. Centrists, on the other hand, suggest a more balanced approach, believing that individuals of both genders have much to contribute to a workable justice system.[90] The Crime in the News box above describes some of the benefits women officers bring to policing. Learn more about feminist criminology at Web Extras! 9-6 and 9-7.

 Web Extras! 9-6 and 9-7 at crimtoday.com

Critique of Feminist Criminology

Some would argue that in the area of theoretical development, feminist criminology has yet to live up to its promise. Throughout the late 1970s and 1980s, few comprehensive feminist theories of crime were proposed; feminist criminology focused instead on descriptive studies of female involvement in crime.[91] Although such data gathering may have laid the groundwork for theory building which is yet to come, few descriptive studies attempted to link their findings to existing feminist theory in any comprehensive way. Theory development suffered again in the late 1980s and early 1990s as an increased concern with women's victimization, especially the victimization of women at the hands of men, led to further descriptive studies with a somewhat different focus. Male violence against women was seen as adding support to the central tenet of feminist criminology that the relationship between the sexes is primarily characterized by the exercise of power (or lack thereof). Such singularity of focus, however, did not make for broad theory building. As one writer explains the current state of feminist criminology, "Feminist theory is a theory in formation."[92] To date, feminist researchers have continued to amass descriptive studies, while feminist analysis has hardly advanced beyond a framework for the "deconstruction" of existing theories—that is, for their reevaluation in light of feminist insights.[93] A fair assessment of the current situation would probably conclude that the greatest contributions of feminist thought to criminological theory building are yet to come.

Feminist criminology has faced criticism from many other directions. As mentioned previously, predicted increases in female crime rates have failed to materialize as social opportunities available to both genders have become more balanced. The **gender gap** in crime—with males accounting for much more law violation than females—continues to exist. As modern-day criminologist Karen Heimer, notes, the gender gap is "virtually a truism in criminology." Says Heimer, "The relationship holds, regardless of whether the data analyzed are arrest rates, victimization incidence reports on characteristics of offenders, or self-reports of criminal behavior." And, Heimer notes, "as far as we can tell, males have always been more criminal than females, and gender differences emerge in every society that has been studied systematically."[94] Other critics have pointed to fundamental flaws in feminist thought, asking such questions as, "If men have more power than women, then why are so many more men arrested?"[95] Gender disparities in arrest (unrelated to reported rates of crime) are rarely found,[96] however, nor do sentencing practices seem to favor women.[97] The chivalry hypothesis of many years ago, under which it was proposed that women are apt to be treated more leniently by the justice system because of their gender, does not appear to operate today.[98]

Some critics even argue that a feminist criminology is impossible. Daly and Chesney-Lind, for example, agree that although feminist thought may inform criminology, "a feminist criminology cannot exist because neither feminism nor criminology is a unified set of principles and practices."[99] In other words, according to these authors, a criminology built solely on feminist principles is unlikely because neither feminist thought nor criminology meets the strict requirements of formal theory building. Even with such a caveat in mind, however, it should still be possible to construct a gender-aware criminology—that is, one which is informed by issues of gender and that takes into consideration the concerns of feminist writers. A "feminist-oriented criminology," say Caulfield and Wonders, is one that will transgress traditional criminology. "This transgression, or 'going beyond boundaries,'" they write, "must occur at a number of levels across a number of areas covered within criminology" and will eventually move us toward a more just world.[100]

Postmodern Criminology

Some significant, new approaches now emerging within criminology are largely the result of postmodernist social thought. Most such theories can be lumped together under the rubric "postmodern criminology." **Postmodern criminology** applies understandings of social change that are inherent in postmodern philosophy to criminological theorizing and to issues of crime control.

Postmodern thought, which developed primarily in Europe after World War II, represents "a rejection of the enlightenment belief in scientific rationality as the main vehicle to knowledge and progress."[101] One important aspect of postmodern social thought can be found in its efforts to demonstrate the systematic intrusion of sexist, racist, capitalist, colonialist, and professional interests into the very content of science. Contemporary feminist scholar Joycelyn M. Pollock puts it this way: "Post-modernism questions whether we can ever 'know' something objectively; so-called neutral science is considered a sham and criminology's search for causes is bankrupt because even the question is framed by androcentric, sexist, classist, and racist definitions of crime, criminals, and cause."[102]

Postmodern criminology is not so much a theory as it is a group of new and emerging criminological perspectives that are all informed by the tone of postmodernism. At the cutting edge of postmodern criminology can be found novel paradigms with such intriguing names as "chaos theory," "discourse analysis," "topology theory," "catastrophe theory," "Lacanian thought," "Godel's theorem," "constitutive theory," and "anarchic criminology."[103]

All postmodern criminologies build on the feeling that past criminological approaches have failed to realistically assess the true causes of crime and have therefore failed to offer workable solutions for crime control—or if they have, that such theories and solutions may have been appropriate at one time, but that they are no longer applicable to the postmodern era. Hence much postmodern criminology is deconstructionist, and such theories are sometimes called "deconstructionist theories."

Deconstructionist theories are approaches that challenge—often quite effectively—existing criminological perspectives to debunk them and to work toward replacing them with approaches more relevant to the postmodern era. They intend to offer freedom from oppressive forms of thought by deconstructing and pulling apart the foundations of existing thought, knowledge, and belief in modern Western culture. Bruce DiCristina, for example, proposes one form of postmodern criminology that he calls "anarchic criminology."[104] Anarchic criminology is "a criminology which embraces alternative methods and epistemologies, encourages imaginative solutions to social and criminal problems, and in the process continually undermines encrusted hierarchies of certainty, truth, and power."[105]

Two especially notable authors in the field of postmodern criminology are **Stuart Henry** and **Dragan Milovanovic**,[106] whose constitutive criminology, which is rooted in phenomenology, claims that crime and crime control are not "object-like entities," but rather constructions produced through a social process in which offender, victim, and society are all involved.[107]

A central feature of constitutive criminology is its assertion that individuals shape their world while also being shaped by it. Hence the behaviors of those who offend and victimize others cannot be understood in isolation from the society of which they are a part. Individuals, however, tend to remain unaware of the role they play in the social construction of their subjective worlds, and they fail to realize that, at least to some degree, they are able to create new meanings while freeing themselves from old biases.

One area that demonstrates well constructionist notions is the sociology of law, which highlights the inherent interrelatedness between law and social structure. Milovanovic, for example, suggests the application of semiotics to the study of law.[108] *Semiotics* is a term akin to *semantics,* and both words derive from the Greek word *sēma,* meaning "sign." Milovanovic sees semiotics as being especially useful in the study of law and criminology because everything we know, say, do, think, and feel is mediated through signs—a sign being anything that stands for something else. Hence language, gestures, sensations, objects, and events are all interpreted by the human mind through the use of signs. A semiotic criminology is concerned, therefore, with identifying how language systems (for example, those of medicine, law, education, gangs, sports, prison communities, criminal justice practitioners, and criminologists) communicate uniquely encoded values. Such values are said to "oppress those who do not communicate meaning from within the particular language system in use" because they may prevent effective discourse with those in power.[109]

The application of semiotics to the study of law can be illustrated by the term *mental illness.* As a sign, this term is imbued with multiple—perhaps even contradictory—meanings. Possible interpretations for what this sign represents include a disease in need of treatment and a person needing psychiatric services. Moreover, *mental illness* means something different in the law (wherein the proper phrase is *legal insanity*) than it does in medicine or in the lay community. Different interpretations reflect different values, and these values can be traced to divergent interest groups. Moreover, as Milovanovic notes, the meaning of *mental illness* has changed over time—and continues to change.

Semiotics can also be applied directly to the notion of crime, as crime itself is a "socially constructed category," or sign. In the words of Henry and Milovanovic, crime "is a categorization of the diversity of human conflicts and transgressions into a single category 'crime,' as though these were somehow all the same. It is a melting of differences reflecting the multitude of variously motivated acts of personal injury into a single entity."[110] Such a statement, to the minds of constitutive criminologists, lays bare the true meaning of the word *crime,* effectively "deconstructing" it.

Crime should be understood, say Henry and Milovanovic, as an integral part of society—not as something separate and apart from it. From this perspective, a kind of false consciousness, or lack of awareness, gives rise to criminal activity.

According to Werner Einstadter and Stuart Henry, crime is seen to be the culmination of certain processes that allow persons to believe that they are somehow not connected to other humans and society. These processes place others into categories or stereotypes and make them different or alien, denying them their humanity. These processes result in the denial of responsibility for other people and to other people.[111] Hence from a constitutive point of view, crime is simply "the power to deny others," and crime is caused by "the structure, ideology and invocation of discursive practices that divide human relations into categories, that divide responsibility from others and to others into hierarchy and authority relations." Learn more about postmodern criminology at Web Extra! 9-8.

Web Extra! 9-8 at crimtoday.com

Critique of Postmodern Criminology

Ian Taylor, a British sociologist who lent focus to radical-critical criminology in the 1970s with the publication of two well-received books,[112] criticizes postmodern approaches to crime and deviance for their "increasing incoherence."[113] Not only do postmodern criminologists employ terminology that is only vaguely defined, but, Taylor seems to say, the "battle with orthodox criminology" has led postmodern approaches to increasingly obfuscate their most basic claims. A second result of the postmodern influence on criminology, says Taylor, "has been the development of a social account of crime that entirely lacks a value or ethical foundation."[114] Deconstructionism, for example, may challenge traditional theories, but unless it offers viable alternatives for crime control and prevention, it does little good. Taylor criticizes what he calls "privileged academic commentators working within the postmodern tradition" for being "nihilistic," and he says that "the idea of a critical criminology organized only around the libertarian idea of 'radical nonintervention' seem[s] entirely unhelpful as a point of departure."[115]

Peacemaking Criminology

Throughout much of history, formal agencies of social control, especially the police, officials of the courts, and correctional personnel, have been seen as pitted against criminal perpetrators and would-be wrongdoers. Crime control has been traditionally depicted in terms of a kind of epic struggle in which diametrically opposed antagonists continuously engage one another, but in which only one side can emerge as victorious. Recently, however, a new point of view known as **peacemaking criminology** has come to the fore. Criminology as peacemaking is a form of postmodern criminology that has its roots in Christian and Eastern philosophies. Peacemaking criminology advances the notion that social control agencies and the citizens they serve should work together to alleviate social problems and human suffering and thus reduce crime.[116] Peacemaking criminology, which includes the notion of service, and has also been called "compassionate criminology," suggests that "compassion, wisdom, and love are essential for understanding the suffering of which we are all a part and for practicing a criminology of nonviolence."[117]

Peacemaking criminology is a relatively new undertaking, popularized by the works of **Harold E. Pepinsky**[118] and Richard Quinney[119] beginning in 1986. Both Pepinsky and Quinney restate the problem of crime control from one of "how to stop crime" to one of "how to make peace" within society and between citizens and criminal justice agencies. Peacemaking criminology draws attention to many issues, among them (1) the perpetuation of violence through the continuation of social policies based on dominant forms of criminological theory, (2) the role of education in peacemaking, (3) "commonsense theories of crime," (4) crime control as human rights enforcement, and (5) conflict resolution within community settings.[120]

Commonsense theories of crime are derived from everyday experience and beliefs and are characteristic of the "person in the street." Unfortunately, say peacemaking criminologists, fanciful commonsense theories all too often provide the basis for criminological investigations, which in turn offer support for the naive theories themselves. One commonsense theory criticized by peacemaking criminologists is the "black-male-as-savage theory,"[121] which holds that African-American men are far more crime prone than their white counterparts. Such a perspective, frequently given added credence by official interpretations of criminal incidence data, only increases the crime control problem by further distancing black Americans from government-sponsored crime control policies. A genuine concern for the problems facing all citizens, say peacemaking criminologists, would more effectively serve the ends of crime control.

Richard Quinney and John Wildeman summarize well the underpinnings of peacemaking criminology with these words: "(1) Thought of the Western rational mode is conditional, limiting knowledge primarily to what is already known; (2) each life is a spiritual journey into the unknown and the unknowable, beyond the ego-centered self; (3) human existence is characterized by suffering; crime is suffering; and the sources of suffering are within each of us; (4) through love and compassion, beyond the ego-centered self, we can end suffering and live in peace, personally and collectively; (5) crime can be ended only with the ending of suffering, only when there is peace and social justice; and (6) understanding, service, justice—all these—flow naturally from love and compassion, from mindful attention to the reality of all that is, here and now. A criminology of peacemaking—a nonviolent criminology of compassion and service—seeks to end suffering and thereby eliminate crime."[122]

Elsewhere Quinney writes, "A society of meanness, competition, greed, and injustice is created by minds that are greedy, selfish, fearful, hateful, and crave power over others. Suffering on the social level can be ended only with the ending of suffering on the personal level. Wisdom brings the awareness that divisions between people and groups are not between the bad and the good or between the criminal and the noncriminal. Wisdom teaches interbeing. We must become one with all who suffer from lives of crime and from the sources that produce crime. Public policy must then flow from this wisdom."[123]

Other recent contributors to the peacemaking movement include Bo Lozoff, Michael Braswell, and Clemens Bartollas. In *Inner Corrections,* Lozoff and Braswell claim that "we are fully aware by now that the criminal justice system in this country is founded on violence. It is a system which assumes that violence can be overcome by violence, evil by evil. Criminal justice at home and warfare abroad are of the same principle of violence. This principle sadly dominates much of our criminology."[124] *Inner Corrections,* which is primarily a compilation of previous works on compassion and prison experience, provides meditative techniques and prayers for those seeking to become more compassionate, and includes a number of letters from convicts who demonstrate the book's philosophy.

In another recent work entitled "Correctional Treatment, Peacemaking, and the New Age Movement," Bartollas and Braswell apply New Age principles to correctional treatment.[125] "Most offenders suffered abusive and deprived childhoods," they write. "Treatment that focuses on the inner child and such qualities as forgiveness and self-esteem could benefit offenders. Some New Age teachings tempered by the ancient spiritual traditions may offer offenders the hope they can create a future that brings greater fulfillment than their past. This changed future may include growing out of the fear of victimization, becoming more positive and open to possibilities, viewing one's self with more confidence and humility, understanding the futility of violence, and attaining emotional and financial sufficiency."[126]

In a fundamental sense, peacemaking criminologists exhort their colleagues to transcend personal dichotomies to end the political and ideological divisiveness that separates people. "If we ourselves cannot know peace . . . how will our acts disarm hatred and violence?" they ask.[127] Lozoff and Braswell express the same sentiments this way: "Human transformation takes place as we change our social, economic and political structure. And the message is clear: without peace within us and in our actions, there can be no peace in our results. Peace is the way."[128]

Restorative Justice

Peacemaking criminology suggests that effective crime control can best be achieved by the adoption of a peace model based on cooperation rather than retribution. The **peace model** of crime control focuses on effective ways for developing a shared consensus on critical issues that could seriously affect the quality of life. These issues include major crimes like murder and rape but may also extend to property rights, rights to the use of new technologies, the ownership of information, and so on. Relatively minor issues, including sexual preference, nonviolent sexual deviance, gambling, drug use, noise, simple child custody claims, and publicly offensive behavior can be dealt with in ways that

A homeless man in New York City. Peacemaking criminology holds that the alleviation of social problems and the reduction of human suffering will lead to a truly just world and will thus reduce crime. What do you think? *Susan Tannenbaum, Impact Visuals Photo & Graphics, Inc.*

require few resources beyond those immediately available in the community.

Alternative dispute-resolution mechanisms play an important role in peacemaking perspectives.[129] Mediation programs, such as modern-day dispute-resolution centers and neighborhood justice centers, are characterized by cooperative efforts to reach dispute resolution, rather than by the adversarial-like proceedings now characteristic of most American courts. Dispute-resolution programs are based on the principle of **participatory justice**, in which all parties to a dispute accept a kind of binding arbitration by neutral parties. Now operating in over 200 areas throughout the country, dispute-resolution centers often utilize administrative hearings and ombudsmen and are staffed by volunteers who work to resolve disputes without assigning blame.

The Community Dispute Settlement Program, which began in Philadelphia in the 1970s, was one of the earliest of modern-day community mediation programs in the country and has been well studied.[130] Mediation in America, however, has a long and varied history. For many years, Native American tribes have routinely employed dispute-resolution mechanisms in dealing with behavioral problems and even crime. Perhaps the best-known dispute-settlement mechanism among Native Americans today is the Navajo Peacemaker Court, which serves as an adjunct to the tribal court.[131]

Miami's "drug court," a local judicial initiative, provides an example of another kind of dispute resolution program. The drug court program, which began in 1989, diverts nonviolent drug users from the traditional path of streets to court to jail and is one of the first of its kind in the nation. Officially called the Dade County Diversion and Treatment Program, the drug court "channels almost all nonviolent defendants arrested on drug possession charges into an inno-

vative court-operated rehabilitation program as an alternative to prosecution. . . . The program expands on the traditional concept of diversion to provide a year or more of treatment and case management services that include counseling, acupuncture, fellowship meetings, education courses, and vocational services along with strict monitoring through periodic urine tests and court appearances. Defendants who succeed in the program have their criminal cases dismissed."[132] Drug court processing appears to be successful at reducing the incidence of repeat offenses, does not result in a criminal record for those who complete the program, and offers drug-dependent offenders a second chance at gaining control over substance abuse problems.

Alternative dispute resolution strategies are not without their critics, who charge that such programs are often staffed by poorly qualified individuals who are ill-prepared to mediate disputes effectively. Nonetheless, as case-processing expenses continue to rise and as minor cases continue to flood justice system agencies, we can expect that an emphasis on alternative means of dispute resolution will continue.

Many alternative dispute-resolution strategies are really a form of restorative justice. Postmodern writers describe **restorative justice** as "a new system based on remedies and restoration rather than on prison, punishment and victim neglect."[133] They see it as "a system rooted in the concept of a caring community"[134] and hope that it will lead to social and economic justice and increased concern and respect for both victims and victimizers in the not-too-distant future. Restorative justice is more than a system, however; it is a modern social movement meant to reform the criminal justice system. The restorative justice movement, which stresses healing rather than retribution, is based upon three principles. The first is a view of crime "as more than simply law-breaking, an offense against governmental authority; [instead] crime is understood to cause multiple injuries to victims, the community and even the offender. Second, proponents argue that the criminal justice process should help repair those injuries. Third, they protest the government's apparent monopoly over society's response to crime,"[135] insisting that victims, offenders, and their communities must also be involved in a concerted effort to heal the harm caused by crime.

Critique of Peacemaking Criminology

Peacemaking criminology has been criticized as being naive and utopian, as well as for failing to recognize the realities of crime control and law enforcement. Few victims, for example, would expect to gain much from attempting to make peace with their victimizers (although such strategies do occasionally work). Such criticisms, however, may be improperly directed at a level of analysis which peacemaking criminologists have not assumed. In other words, peacemaking criminology, while it involves work with individual of-

fenders, envisions positive change on the societal and institutional level and does not suggest to victims that they attempt to effect personal changes in offenders.

POLICY IMPLICATIONS

The policy implications of social conflict theory are fairly clear: Reduce conflict, and crime rates will fall. At one extreme, radical-Marxist criminologists argue that the only effective way of reducing conflict is through a total dismantling of the existing capitalist system in the United States and its replacement by a socialist economic structure. At the other extreme are the calls of peacemaking criminologists for a practical application of the principles of conflict resolution. Between these two extremes lie left-realism and feminist criminology, although the solutions they offer vary from the reduction of paternalism in all its forms to a practical recognition of the consequences of crime to victims.

SUMMARY

This chapter has described social conflict theories. Conflict theories hold that social conflict is the root cause of crime. For some conflict theorists, social order rests upon the exercise of coercive power rather than an agreed-upon consensus. Radical criminologists hold that the ongoing battle between the haves and the have-nots in capitalist societies leads to crime and to definitions of crime that unfairly criminalize the activities of the disenfranchised. They believe that criminal law is a tool of the powerful, who use it to perpetuate their control over the less fortunate.

Radical criminology and its contemporary offshoots, including feminist criminology, critical criminology, postmodernism, and peacemaking criminology, seek to redress injustices in society as a way of ending the marginalization of the politically and economically disentitled. Feminist criminology believes that the consequences of sexism and of the traditionally unequal gender-based distribution of power within our patriarchal society have been far reach-

ing, affecting fundamental aspects of social roles and personal expectation at all levels, including crime and the field of criminology. Postmodernists doubt that an objective study of crime is even possible; they believe that criminology's search for the causes of crime is implicitly doomed because the questions it raises are framed by sexist, class-specific, and racist assumptions. Hence postmodernists attempt to deconstruct existing theories in hopes of revealing the fallacies inherent in traditional perspectives.

Unfortunately for social conflict theorists, not many of their predictions have come true. Conflict theorists, especially those of the more radical persuasion, have been criticized for being overly idealistic and for lacking an appreciation for the everyday problems of crime victims. The demise of the Soviet Union in the 1990s and the associated decline of world communism have further questioned the wisdom of some of the most fundamental concepts inherent in radical criminology and its intellectual descendants.

DISCUSSION QUESTIONS

1. This book emphasizes a social problems versus social responsibility theme. Which of the theoretical perspectives discussed in this chapter (if any) support the social problems approach? Which (if any) support the social responsibility approach? Why?
2. Explain the difference between the consensus, pluralist, and conflict perspectives. Which comes closest to your way of understanding society? Why?
3. What is Marxist criminology? How, if at all, does it differ from radical criminology? From critical criminology?
4. Does the Marxist perspective hold any significance for contemporary American society? Why or why not?
5. What are the fundamental propositions of feminist criminology? How would feminists change the study of crime?
6. What does it mean to say that traditional theories of crime need to be "deconstructed"? What role does deconstructionist thinking play in postmodern criminology?

WEB QUEST!

This Web Quest! requires you to visit four sites on the Web: (1) the Critical Criminology Division of the American Society of Criminology (ASC) at http://sun.soci.niu.edu/~critcrim, (2) the Critical Criminologist (the newsletter of ASC's Critical Criminology Division) at http://sun.soci.niu.edu/~critcrim/other/newslet.html, (3) the Newsletter of the Marxist Section of the American Sociological Association (ASA) at http://www.tryoung.com/fromleft/winter97.htm, and (4) the Red Feather Institute's Journal of Postmodern Criminology at http://www.tryoung.com/journal-pomocrim/pomocrimindex.html. First familiarize yourself with the availability of materials at each site, and get a general feel for the differences between them. Then read some of the electronic manuscripts and other postings at each site. Which of those e-papers relate directly to the concepts discussed in this chapter? How do those materials expand upon the content of this chapter? Submit your answers to your instructor if asked to do so. Be sure to check the Web Quest! section of crimtoday.com in case the URLs listed here change.

LIBRARY EXTRAS!

The Library Extras! listed here complement the Web Extras! found throughout this chapter. Library Extras! may be accessed on the Web at crimtoday.com.

Library Extra! 9-1. Lance Hannon, *Still Just the Study of Men and Crime? A Content Analysis* (online publication, accessed March 20, 2001).

Library Extra! 9-2. Karen Heimer, *Changes in the Gender Gap in Crime and Women's Economic Marginalization* (online publication, accessed March 20, 2001).

Library Extra! 9-3. Meda Chesney-Lind, *Critical Criminology: Toward a Feminist Praxis* (online publication, accessed March 20, 2001).

Library Extra! 9-4. Dragan Milovanovic, *Dueling Paradigms: Modernist versus Postmodernist Thought* (online publication, accessed March 20, 2001).

Library Extra! 9-5. *The Red Feather Dictionary of Critical Social Science* (online publication, accessed March 21, 2001).

Library Extra! 9-6. T. R. Young, *Socialist Proposition on Crime in Capitalist Society* (online publication, accessed March 21, 2001).

NOTES

[1] Natasha Alova, "Russia—Juvenile Crime," Associated Press wire service, Northern Edition, February 9, 1994.

[2] Richard Quinney, *Class, State, and Crime: On the Theory and Practice of Criminal Justice* (New York: David McKay, 1977), p. 145.

[3] Kathleen Daly and Meda Chesney-Lind, "Feminism and Criminology," *Justice Quarterly,* Vol. 5, No. 5 (December 1988), p. 527.

[4] The Unabomber, *Manifesto*. Web posted at http://www.thecourier.com/manifest.htm. Accessed March 16, 2001.

[5] Ian Taylor, "Crime and Social Criticism," *Social Justice,* Vol. 26, No. 2 (summer 1999), p. 150.

[6] "Communism," *Encyclopedia Britannica* online. Web posted at britannica.com. Accessed January 3, 2001.

[7] Raymond J. Michalowski, "Perspectives and Paradigm: Structuring Criminological Thought," in Robert F. Meier, ed., *Theory in Criminology* (Beverly Hills, CA: Sage, 1977), pp. 17–39.

[8] Roscoe Pound, *Social Control through the Law: The Powell Lectures* (Hamden, CT: Archon, 1968), pp. 113–114.

[9] Although Pound's postulates originally referred only to men, we have here used the now-conventional phrase "men and women" throughout the postulates to indicate that Pound was speaking of everyone within the social group. No other changes to the original postulates have been made.

[10] Adapted from Michalowski, "Perspectives and Paradigm."

[11] Georg Simmel, *Conflict and the Web of Group Affiliations* (New York: The Free Press, 1964). Originally published in 1908.

[12] William Bonger, *Criminality and Economic Conditions* (Bloomington: Indiana University Press, 1969). Originally published in Amsterdam as *Criminalite et Conditions Economiques* (1905); translated into English in 1916.

[13] Adapted from Michalowski, "Perspectives and Paradigm."

[14] Quinney. *Class, State, and Crime.*

[15] Vance Packard, *The Status Seekers* (London: Harmondsworth, 1961).

[16] George B. Vold, *Theoretical Criminology* (New York: Oxford University Press, 1958).

[17] Ibid., p. 205.

[18] Ibid., p. 206.

[19] Ibid., pp. 208–209.

[20] Ibid., p. 309.

[21] Ralf Dahrendorf, *Class and Class Conflict in Industrial Society* (Stanford, CA: Stanford University Press, 1959).

[22] Ralf Dahrendorf, "Out of Utopia: Toward a Reorientation of Sociological Analysis," *American Journal of Sociology,* Vol. 64 (1958), pp. 115–127.

[23] Austin Turk, *Criminality and Legal Order* (Chicago: Rand McNally, 1969), p. vii.

[24] Ibid.

[25] William J. Chambliss, "Toward a Political Economy of Crime," in C. Reasons and R. Rich, eds., *The Sociology of Law* (Toronto: Butterworth, 1978), p. 193.

[26] William Chambliss and Robert T. Seidman, *Law, Order, and Power* (Reading, MA: Addison-Wesley, 1971), p. 33.

[27] Adapted from ibid., pp. 473–474.

[28] William J. Chambliss, *Crime and the Legal Process* (New York: McGraw-Hill, 1969), p. 88.

[29] Chambliss, "Toward a Political Economy of Crime."

[30] Ibid.

[31] Ibid., p. 152.

[32] Ibid.

[33] Richard Quinney, *Critique of the Legal Order: Crime Control in Capitalist Society* (Boston: Little, Brown, 1974), p. 16.

[34] Quinney, *Class, State, and Crime,* p. 58.

[35] Ibid.

[36] Ibid., p. 61.

[37] Ibid., p. 65.

[38] Quinney, *Class, State, and Crime,* p. 77.

[39] Jeffrey H. Reiman, *The Rich Get Richer and the Poor Get Prison: Ideology, Class and Criminal Justice,* 6th ed. (Boston: Allyn and Bacon, 2000).

[40] Gresham M. Sykes, "Critical Criminology," *Journal of Criminal Law and Criminology,* Vol. 65 (1974), pp. 206–213.

[41] David A. Jones, *History of Criminology: A Philosophical Perspective* (Westport, CT: Greenwood, 1986), p. 200.

[42] The quotations attributed to Currie in this section are from Elliott Currie, "Market, Crime, and Community," *Theoretical Criminology,* Vol. 1, No. 2 (May 1997), pp. 147–172.

[43] Michael J. Lynch and W. Byron Groves, *A Primer in Radical Criminology,* 2nd ed. (Albany: Harrow and Heston, 1989), p. 126.

[44] Ibid., p. 128.

[45] Raymond J. Michalowski, *Order, Law, and Crime: An Introduction to Criminology* (New York: Random House, 1985), p. 410.

[46] Lynch and Groves, *A Primer in Radical Criminology,* p. 130.

[47] William V. Pelfrey, *The Evolution of Criminology* (Cincinnati, Ohio: Anderson, 1980), p. 86.

[48] For a good overview of critiques of radical criminology, see J. F. Galliher, "Life and Death of Liberal Criminology," *Contemporary Crisis,* Vol. 2, No. 3 (July 1978), pp. 245–263.

[49] Jackson Toby, "The New Criminology Is the Old Sentimentality," *Criminology,* Vol. 16 (1979), pp. 516–526.

[50] Ibid.

[51] Hermann Mannheim, *Comparative Criminology* (Boston: Houghton Mifflin, 1965), p. 445.

[52] Carl Klockars, "The Contemporary Crisis of Marxist Criminology," *Criminology,* Vol. 16 (1979), pp. 477–515.

[53] Ibid.

[54] Einstadter and Henry, *Criminological Theory: An Analysis of Its Underlying Assumptions* (Toronto: Harcourt, 1995), p. 233.

[55] For an excellent review of critical realism in a Canadian context, see John Lowman and Brian D. MacLean, eds., *Realist Criminology: Crime Control and Policing in the 1990s* (Toronto: University of Toronto Press, 1994).

[56] Daniel J. Curran and Claire M. Renzetti, *Theories of Crime* (Boston: Allyn and Bacon, 1994), p. 283.

[57] See M. D. Schwartz and W. S. DeKeseredy, "Left Realist Criminology: Strengths, Weaknesses, and the Feminist Critique," *Crime, Law, and Social Change,* Vol. 15, No. 1 (January 1991), pp. 51–72; W. S. DeKeseredy and B. D. MacLean, "Exploring the Gender, Race, and Class Dimensions of Victimization: A Left Realist Critique of the Canadian Urban Victimization Survey," *International Journal of Offender Therapy and Comparative Criminology,* Vol. 35, No. 2 (summer 1991), pp. 143–161; and W. S. DeKeseredy and M. D. Schwartz, "British and U.S. Left Realism: A Critical Comparison," *International Journal of Offender Therapy and Comparative Criminology,* Vol. 35, No. 3 (fall 1991), pp. 248–262.

[58] See Jock Young, "The Failure of Criminology: The Need for a Radical Realism," in R. Matthews and J. Young, eds., *Confronting Crime* (Beverly Hills, CA: Sage, 1986), pp. 4–30; Jock Young, "The Tasks of a Realist Criminology," *Contemporary Crisis,* Vol. 11, No. 4 (1987), pp. 337–356; and Jock Young, "Radical Criminology in Britain: The Emergence of a Competing Paradigm," *British Journal of Criminology,* Vol. 28 (1988), pp. 159–183.

[59] D. Brown and R. Hogg, "Essentialism, Racial Criminology, and Left Realism," *Australian and New Zealand Journal of Criminology,* Vol. 25 (1992), pp. 195–230.

[60] Roger Matthews and Jock Young, "Reflections on Realism," in Jock Young and Roger Matthews, eds., *Rethinking Criminology: The Realist Debate* (Newbury Park, CA: Sage, 1992).

[61] Don C. Gibbons, *Talking about Crime and Criminals: Problems and Issues in Theory Development in Criminology* (Englewood Cliffs, NJ: Prentice Hall, 1994), p. 170.

[62] Piers Beirne and James W. Messerschmidt, *Criminology* (New York: Harcourt Brace Jovanovich, 1991), p. 501.

[63] Gibbons, *Talking about Crime and Criminals,* p. 165, citing Loraine Gelsthorpe and Alison Morris, "Feminism and Criminology in Britain," *British Journal of Criminology* (spring 1988), pp. 93–110.

[64] Sally S. Simpson, "Feminist Theory, Crime and Justice," *Criminology,* Vol. 27, No. 4 (1989), p. 605.

[65] James W. Messerschmidt, *Capitalism, Patriarchy and Crime: Toward a Socialist Feminist Criminology* (Totowa, NJ: Rowman and Littlefield, 1986).

66 Freda Adler, *Sisters in Crime: The Rise of the New Female Criminal* (New York: McGraw-Hill, 1975).

67 Rita J. Simon, *Women and Crime* (Lexington, MA: Lexington Books, 1975).

68 Carol Smart, *Women, Crime and Criminology: A Feminist Critique* (London: Routledge, 1977).

69 Daly and Chesney-Lind, "Feminism and Criminology," p. 527.

70 Ibid., pp. 497–535.

71 Susan Caulfield and Nancy Wonders, "Gender and Justice: Feminist Contributions to Criminology," in Gregg Barak, ed., *Varieties of Criminology: Readings from a Dynamic Discipline* (Westport, CT: Praeger, 1994), pp. 213–229.

72 Ibid.

73 Roslyn Muraskin and Ted Alleman, eds., *It's a Crime: Women and Justice* (Englewood Cliffs, NJ: Prentice Hall, 1993), p. 1.

74 F. P. Williams III and M. D. McShane, *Criminological Theory* (Englewood Cliffs, NJ: Prentice Hall, 1994), p. 238.

75 Carol Pateman, "Feminist Critiques of the Public/Private Dichotomy," in Anne Phillips, ed., *Feminism and Equality* (Oxford: Basil Blackwell, 1987).

76 Alida V. Merlo and Joycelyn M. Pollock, eds., *Women, Law and Social Control* (Needham Heights, MA: Allyn and Bacon, 1995).

77 Williams and McShane, *Criminological Theory,* p. 238.

78 Simpson, "Feminist Theory, Crime and Justice."

79 John Hagan, *Structural Criminology* (New Brunswick, NJ: Rutgers University Press, 1989), p. 130.

80 Ibid., p. 13.

81 Ibid.

82 Ibid.

83 Evelyn K. Sommers, *Voices from Within: Women Who Have Broken the Law* (Toronto: University of Toronto Press, 1995).

84 Daly and Chesney-Lind, "Feminism and Criminology," p. 506.

85 Ibid.

86 Ibid., p. 514.

87 For an intriguing analysis of how existing laws tend to criminalize women and their reproductive activities, see Susan O. Reed, "The Criminalization of Pregnancy: Drugs, Alcohol, and AIDS," in Muraskin and Alleman, eds., *It's a Crime,* pp. 92–117; and Drew Humphries, "Mothers and Children, Drugs and Crack: Reactions to Maternal Drug Dependency," in Muraskin and Alleman, eds., *It's a Crime,* pp. 131–145.

88 Ngaire Naffine, *Feminism and Criminology* (Philadelphia: Temple University Press, 1996).

89 Dawn H. Currie, "Feminist Encounters with Postmodernism: Exploring the Impasse of the Debates on Patriarchy and Law," *Canadian Journal of Women and Law,* Vol. 5, No. 1 (1992), p. 10.

90 For an excellent overview of feminist theory in criminology and for a comprehensive review of research regarding female offenders, see Joanne Belknap, *The Invisible Woman: Gender, Crime and Justice* (Belmont, CA: Wadsworth, 1996).

91 Such studies are still ongoing and continue to add to the descriptive literature of feminist criminology. See, for example, Deborah R. Baskin and Ira Sommers, "Female Initiation into Violent Street Crime," *Justice Quarterly,* Vol. 10, No. 4 (December 1993), pp. 559–583; Scott Decker et al., "A Woman's Place Is in the Home: Females and Residential Burglary," *Justice Quarterly,* Vol. 10, No. 1 (March 1993), pp. 143–162; and Jill L. Rosenbaum, "The Female Delinquent: Another Look at the Role of the Family," in Muraskin and Alleman, eds., *It's a Crime,* pp. 399–420.

92 Ronald L. Akers, *Criminological Theories: Introduction and Evaluation* (Los Angeles: Roxbury, 1994), p. 39.

93 For additional insight into the notion of deconstruction as it applies to feminist thought within criminology, see Carol Smart, *Feminism and the Power of Law* (New York: Routledge, 1989).

94 Karen Heimer, "Changes in the Gender Gap in Crime and Women's Economic Marginalization," in *The Nature of Crime: Continuity and Change—Criminal Justice 2000,* Vol. 1 (Washington, D.C.: National Institute of Justice, 2000), p. 428.

95 Daly and Chesney-Lind, "Feminism and Criminology," p. 512.

96 See, for example, Darrell J. Steffensmeier and Emile Andersen Allan, "Sex Disparities in Arrests by Residence, Race, and Age: An Assessment of the Gender Convergence/Crime Hypothesis," *Justice Quarterly,* Vol. 5, No. 1 (March 1988), pp. 53–80.

97 Darrell Steffensmeier, John Kramer, and Cathy Streifel, "Gender and Imprisonment Decisions," *Criminology,* Vol. 31, No. 3 (August 1993), pp. 411–446. Gender-based differences, however, have been discovered in some instances of probation- and parole-related decision making. See Edna Erez, "Gender, Rehabilitation, and Probation Decisions," *Criminology,* Vol. 27, No. 2 (1989), pp. 307–327; and Edna Erez, "Dangerous Men, Evil Women: Gender and Parole Decision-Making," *Justice Quarterly,* Vol. 9, No. 1 (March 1992), pp. 106–126.

98 See, for example, Kathleen Daly, "Neither Conflict nor Labeling nor Paternalism Will Suffice: Intersections of Race, Ethnicity, Gender, and Family in Criminal Court Decisions," *Crime and Delinquency,* Vol. 35, No. 1 (January 1989), pp. 136–168.

99 Citing Allison Morris, *Women, Crime and Criminal Justice* (New York: Blackwell, 1987).

100 Caulfield and Wonders, "Gender and Justice," p. 229.

101 Gregg Barak, "Introduction: Criminological Theory in the 'Postmodernist' Era," in Gregg Barak, ed., *Varieties of Criminology: Readings from a Dynamic Discipline* (Westport, CT: Praeger, 1994), pp. 1–11.

102 Joycelyn M. Pollock, *Criminal Women* (Cincinnati: Anderson, 1999), p. 146.

103 For an excellent and detailed discussion of many of these approaches, see Dragan Milovanovic, *Postmodern Criminology* (Hamden, CT: Garland, 1997).

104 Bruce DiCristina, *Methods in Criminology: A Philosophical Primer* (New York: Harrow and Heston, 1995).

105 Jeff Ferrell, "Anarchy against the Discipline," a review of Bruce DiCristina's *Methods in Criminology: A Philosophical Primer* (New York: Harrow and Heston, 1995), in the *Journal of Criminal Justice and Popular Culture*, Vol. 3, No. 4 (August 15, 1995).

106 See, for example, Stuart Henry and Dragan Milovanovic, *Constitutive Criminology: Beyond Postmodernism* (London: Sage, 1995); and Milovanovic, *Postmodern Criminology.*

107 Milovanovic, *Postmodern Criminology.*

108 Dragan Milovanovic, *Primer in the Sociology of Law*, 2nd ed. (New York: Harrow and Heston, 1994).

109 Ibid.

110 Henry and Milovanovic, *Constitutive Criminology*, p. 118.

111 Werner Einstadter and Stuart Henry, *Criminological Theory: An Analysis of Its Underlying Assumptions* (Fort Worth, TX: Harcourt Brace, 1995), p. 291.

112 Ian Taylor, Paul Walton, and Jock Young, *The New Criminology: For a Social Theory of Deviance* (London: Routledge, 1973); and Ian Taylor, Paul Walton, and Jock Young, *Critical Criminology* (London: Routledge, 1975).

113 Ian Taylor, "Crime and Social Criticism," *Social Justice*, Vol. 26, No. 2 (1999), p. 150.

114 Ibid.

115 Ibid.

116 For examples of how this might be accomplished, see F. H. Knopp, "Community Solutions to Sexual Violence: Feminist/Abolitionist Perspectives," in Harold E. Pepinsky and Richard Quinney, eds., *Criminology as Peacemaking* (Bloomington: Indiana University Press), pp. 181–193; and S. Caringella-MacDonald and D. Humphries, "Sexual Assault, Women, and the Community: Organizing to Prevent Sexual Violence," in Pepinsky and Quinney, eds., *Criminology as Peacemaking*, pp. 98–113.

117 Richard Quinney, "Life of Crime; Criminology and Public Policy as Peacemaking," *Journal of Crime and Justice*, Vol. 16, No. 2 (1993), pp. 3–9.

118 See, for example, Harold E. Pepinsky, "This Can't Be Peace: A Pessimist Looks at Punishment," in W. B. Groves and G. Newman, eds., *Punishment and Privilege* (Albany: Harrow and Heston, 1986); Harold E. Pepinsky, "Violence as Unresponsiveness: Toward a New Conception of Crime," *Justice Quarterly*, Vol. 5 (1988), pp. 539–563; and Pepinsky and Quinney, eds., *Criminology as Peacemaking.*

119 See, for example, Richard Quinney, "Crime, Suffering, Service: Toward a Criminology of Peacemaking," *Quest*, Vol. 1 (1988), pp. 66–75; Richard Quinney, "The Theory and Practice of Peacemaking in the Development of Radical Criminology," *Critical Criminologist*, Vol. 1, No. 5

(1989), p. 5; and Richard Quinney and John Wildeman, *The Problem of Crime: A Peace and Social Justice Perspective*, 3rd ed. (Mayfield, CA: Mountain View Press, 1991)—originally published as *The Problem of Crime: A Critical Introduction to Criminology* (New York: Bantam, 1977).

120 All of these themes are addressed, for example, in Pepinsky and Quinney, eds., *Criminology as Peacemaking.*

121 For a good discussion of this "theory," see John F. Galliher, "Willie Horton: Fact, Faith, and Commonsense Theory of Crime," in ibid., pp. 245–250.

122 Quinney and Wildeman, *The Problem of Crime: A Peace and Social Justice Perspective*, pp. vii–viii.

123 Richard Quinney, "Life of Crime: Criminology and Public Policy as Peacemaking," *Journal of Crime and Justice*, Vol. 16, No. 2 (1993), abstract.

124 Bo Lozoff and Michael Braswell, *Inner Corrections: Finding Peace and Peace Making* (Cincinnati: Anderson, 1989).

125 Clemens Bartollas and Michael Braswell, "Correctional Treatment, Peacemaking, and the New Age Movement," *Journal of Crime and Justice*, Vol. 16, No. 2 (1993), pp. 43–58.

126 Ibid.

127 Ram Dass and Gorman, *How Can I Help? Stories and Reflections on Service* (New York: Alfred A. Knopf, 1985), p. 165, as cited in Quinney and Wildeman, *The Problem of Crime: A Peace and Social Justice Perspective*, p. 116.

128 Lozoff and Braswell, *Inner Corrections*, p. vii.

129 For a good overview of such programs, see Thomas E. Carbonneau, *Alternative Dispute Resolution: Melting the Lances and Dismounting the Steeds* (Chicago: University of Illinois Press, 1989).

130 See, for example, J. E. Beer, *Peacemaking in Your Neighborhood: Reflections on an Experiment in Community Mediation* (Philadelphia: New Society Publishers, 1986); and J. Beer, E. Steif, and C. Walker, *Peacemaking in Your Neighborhood: Mediator's Handbook* (Philadelphia: Friends Mediation Service, 1987).

131 For an excellent review of alternative dispute mechanisms among Native American groups, see D. LeResche, "Native American Perspectives on Peacemaking," *Mediation Quarterly*, Vol. 10, No. 4 (summer 1993), complete issue.

132 Peter Finn and Andrea K. Newlyn, *Miami's "Drug Court": A Different Approach* (Washington, D.C.: National Institute of Justice, June 1993), p. 2.

133 Fay Honey Knopp, "Community Solutions to Sexual Violence: Feminist-Abolitionist Perspectives," in Pepinsky and Quinney, eds., *Criminology as Peacemaking*, p. 183.

134 Ibid.

135 Daniel Van Ness and Karen Heetderks Strong, *Restoring Justice* (Cincinnati: Anderson, 1997), p. 31.

crime in the modern world

PART

In the first section of this book, specifically in Chapter 2, we provide a brief overview of crime statistics and of the different kinds of crimes with which the American criminal justice system is typically concerned. In the five chapters that constitute this section, we will describe specific kinds of crimes and the offenders who commit them in considerably more detail.

Chapter 10 concerns itself with violent crimes, also known as "crimes against persons." Included here are brutal acts like murder, rape, and assault. Other violent crimes, like terrorism, are also discussed, as are the situations and circumstances within contemporary American society that are thought to contribute to violence. Chapter 11 looks at property crimes, including theft, burglary, and arson. The activities of fences in buying and disposing of stolen goods are explored, and the relationship of property crimes to other forms of crime is examined. Chapter 12 describes white-collar and organized crime, while Chapter 13 looks at drug crimes and Chapter 14 analyzes the impact that high-technology crimes are having on our society and on efforts to enforce the law.

I'm the big man, I got the gun. Why does she have this attitude?

—Statement made to police by a 16-year-old boy charged with killing 38-year-old Christine Schweiger with a sawed-off shotgun while her 10-year-old daughter watched. Schweiger had told the boy she had no money.[i]

**I wouldn't be in a legitimate business
for all the . . . money in the world.**

—Gennaro Anguilo, Boston Organized Crime Boss[ii]

**You bring me a select group of hackers, and within 90 days
I'll bring this country to its knees.**

—Jim Settle, retired director of the FBI's computer crime squad[iii]

---

[i]Jon D. Hull, "In Milwaukee, a Rash of Murders Provokes a Drive to Ban Handguns," *Time,* December 20, 1993.

[ii]From a compilation of FBI tapes in "Anguilo's Republic," *New England Monthly,* July 1986.

[iii]Jim Settle, as quoted in Andrew Noel, "Unlocking the Door to Security," *Government Technology,* March 1999. Web posted at http://www.govtech.net/ publications/gt/1999/mar/westby/westby.phtml. Accessed March 31, 2001.

In some 200 years of national sovereignty, Americans have been preoccupied repeatedly with trying to understand and control one form of violence or another.

—Albert J. Reiss, Jr., and Jeffrey A. Roth[1]

For years it was fashionable to explain that economic deprivation was the main source of crime and violence. . . . In fact, crime and violence have *increased* with economic prosperity and progress.

—Branko Bokun[2]

Although collective acts of violence and terrorist acts are more visible and receive greater media attention, most violence in this country lacks an ideological motivation and involves a dispute between a single victim and offender.

—Terance D. Miethe and Richard C. McCorkle[3]

crimes against persons

CHAPTER 10

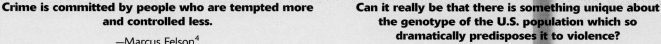

Crime is committed by people who are tempted more and controlled less.

—Marcus Felson[4]

Can it really be that there is something unique about the genotype of the U.S. population which so dramatically predisposes it to violence?

—Steven Rose[5]

KEY CONCEPTS

IMPORTANT TERMS

acquaintance rape
crime typology
cyberstalking
exposure-reduction theory
expressive crimes
institutional robbery
instrumental crimes
intimate-partner assault
National Violence against Women
  (NVAW) Survey

nonprimary homicides
personal robbery
primary homicides
rape myths
rape shield laws
selective disinhibition
separation assault
sibling offense
spousal rape

stalking
terrorism
victim precipitation
Violence against Women Act
  (VAWA)
Violent Criminal Apprehension
  Program (VICAP)

IMPORTANT NAMES

Larry Baron
Ann Burgess
Andrea Dworkin
James Alan Fox
Nicholas Groth
Robert R. Hazelwood
Julie Horney

Mary P. Koss
Jack Levin
Catherine MacKinnon
Jody Miller
Craig T. Palmer
Robert Nash Parker
James Ptacek

Diana E. H. Russell
Diana Scully
Cassia Spohn
Murray A. Straus
Randy Thornhill
Neil Websdale

OUTCOMES

LEARNING

After reading this chapter, you should be able to
  ◆ Describe typologies of violent crime
  ◆ Understand the key issues in explaining patterns of homicide
  ◆ Understand the key issues in explaining patterns of violent crime
  ◆ Explain why the context of familial assault is so important
  ◆ Explain the major patterns of stalking
  ◆ Identify the major characteristics of terrorism

Hear the author discuss this chapter at *crimtoday.com*

INTRODUCTION

On November 3, 2000, Texas millionaire Allen Blackthorne was sentenced to two life terms for taking part in a murder conspiracy. Blackthorne was convicted of arranging the murder of his ex-wife, Shelia Bellush, in order to gain custody of their two daughters. At the time that she was shot and her throat slit, Bellush was in her Florida home with her toddler quadruplets. Bellush had remarried after the divorce from Blackthorne and had moved from Texas to Florida, where she lived with her current husband, their four toddlers, and her

two daughters by Blackthorne. When police discovered Bellush's body, her two-year-old children had been crawling in her blood.

As you will discover in this chapter, the Bellush killing has some characteristics that make it a typical violent crime and some that do not. While many people who are involved in homicide are known to each other, a murder-for-hire is not a typical homicide. Most homicides are both local and situational in nature. In contrast, Blackthorne was convicted of interstate conspiracy to commit murder-for-hire and interstate domestic violence—federal crimes that carry a life

Allen Blackthorne, the Texas millionaire who was convicted in 2000 of the murder-for-hire of his ex-wife, who was the mother of quadruplets. What motivates such criminals? *San Antonio Express, Liaison Agency, Inc.*

sentence. Because they occur locally, most homicides do not fall under federal jurisdiction, and most do not involve the type of planning typical of murder-for-hire. While no one social class has an exclusive claim on violent offending, there are identifiable patterns in offending, and social class determines some of those patterns.

This chapter discusses violent criminal offending by focusing on homicide, rape, robbery, assault, stalking, and terrorism. These offenses, especially the first four, have long been identified as violent because they involve interpersonal harm or threat of harm. The range of possible harm varies from death, as is the case with homicide, to the loss of property, as is the case with robbery. As we have said in earlier chapters, there are many different theories that attempt to explain involvement in crime. Many focus on particular kinds of crimes, and all identify a variety of factors as important in explaining crime. While there is no such thing as the typical crime, criminologists use crime typologies to make sense of the patterns that characterize criminal offending.

VIOLENT CRIME TYPOLOGIES

A **crime typology** categorizes offenses against persons using a particular dimension, such as legal categories, offender motivation, victim behavior, situational aspects of the criminal event, and offender characteristics. Statutory definitions of crimes provide a typology based on legal categories. While this chapter will rely on legal categories as the basis on which to distinguish among types of violent crimes, we will also discuss some of the

explanatory factors associated with violent offending. Crime typologies "are designed primarily to simplify social reality by identifying homogeneous groups of crime behaviors that are different from other clusters of crime behaviors."[6] To be useful, the basis around which a typology is organized should serve a particular purpose. Some typologies use a single variable as the primary explanation for variation in criminal offending, while other typologies offer a number of variables that are thought to interact to produce certain patterns in violent offending. An example of a single-variable typology can be found in the general theory of crime advanced by Michael R. Gottfredson and Travis Hirschi (see Chapter 8), where the authors emphasize low self-control as the crucial determinant of variations in offending. Other theories, such as developmental and life course theories, focus on different explanatory variables or on a combination of factors. No one typology can perfectly capture all violent offending, and a given set of factors may explain better one type or facet of offending. For example, the individual-level factors that give rise to violent offending may not be the same factors that contribute to an increased frequency of offending, especially in terms of criminal careers.[7]

HOMICIDE

State and federal statutes on criminal homicide distinguish between several different forms of this offense based on intent, circumstances, age, and other considerations discussed in Chapter 2. As we noted in that chapter, homicide represents a small fraction of all violent crimes reported to the police in any given year—less than 0.1% in 1999.[8] Only about 12% of all homicides involve strangers, and the most frequent circumstance that precedes a homicide is an argument.[9] Approximately 17% of homicides occur during the commission of another felony, with robbery being the most common.[10] While homicide offenders include men and women, young and old, rich and poor; homicide offending is very much patterned according to certain sociodemographics, with some groups being disproportionately involved as offenders. Distinctive patterns of homicide emerge based on such factors as individual sociodemographics, cultural norms, community characteristics, geographic region, weapons, gangs, and the victim-offender relationship. All of these have been used to further our understanding of homicide patterns and to create typologies surrounding homicide. Much research within criminology has centered around two competing theoretical frameworks, subcultural and structural explanations, which have been offered to explain variation in homicide offending both at the individual level, by focusing on the sociodemographic characteristics of offenders, and at the community level, by focusing on neighborhood and regional variations in homicide. Learn more about the crime of homicide at Web Extra! 10-1.

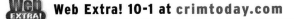
Web Extra! 10-1 at crimtoday.com

The Subculture of Violence Thesis and Structural Explanations

Within the United States, there has been strong research interest in the subculture of violence thesis originally formulated by Marvin Wolfgang and Franco Ferracuti,[11] which was discussed in Chapter 7. These authors stressed the role of norms and values characteristic of certain groups in lifestyles of violence. Ethnic and racial differences in criminal activity reflect distinctive patterns of interaction with others, which are characterized by a shared sense of history, language, values, and beliefs. The existence of a subculture necessitates a sufficient number of people who share not only values and beliefs, but also a forum which expresses membership. Such a forum may be something as elusive as a street corner. It is primarily this subtlety associated with subcultural theory that makes it difficult to test empirically. The subculture of violence thesis has been the primary theoretical perspective used to explain the similarity between homicide victims and offenders. First, homicide statistics reveal that victims and offenders share similar sociodemographic characteristics, such as age, gender, and race. African-Americans are disproportionately represented in the homicide statistics as both victims and offenders.[12] Second, victims and offenders who are intimately known to each other are disproportionately represented in homicide statistics. An analysis of supplemental homicide reports shows that approximately 60% of victims and offenders have some prior relationship.[13]

The subculture of violence thesis has also been explored at the community level, where the emphasis is on the importance of "critical masses" as support for the existence of subcultures.[14] Early research argued that the disproportionate rate at which African-Americans commit homicide is associated with the presence of a large black population, the "critical mass" necessary for the "transmission of violence-related models" and subcultural behavior patterns.[15] However, most of the research that found higher homicide rates to be associated with higher percentages of African-Americans in the population did not take into consideration things like socioeconomic status, level of education, and so on.[16] Research by Robert Sampson using more sophisticated measures and stronger research designs revealed that the racial composition of an area alone did not have a significant effect on the homicide rates for either whites or blacks.[17]

Regional Variations in Subcultural Patterns

Other researchers employing subcultural perspectives have focused on regional variations in patterns of violent crimes, particularly in the South. The South has a long history of high homicide rates.[18] Subcultural theorists have proposed that the high rate of violent crime in the South reflects adherence to a set of violence-related norms that were generally accepted in earlier times but that have since become outdated in other regions.[19] While some researchers found that Southern origin had a significant effect on the production of high homicide rates in particular areas,[20] other researchers

challenge subcultural theories for their inability to control for noncultural factors that might explain the findings.[21] Specifically, Colin Loftin and R. H. Hill conclude that the influence of structural variables, especially poverty, must be considered as alternative explanations for regional differences in homicide rates.[22] While no definitive answers exist on whether the high rates of violence in the South are attributable to a specific subculture of violence or to structural factors, there still remains evidence (that is, arrest statistics) that the South differs from other regions in terms of the frequency of homicides.

The Victim-Offender Relationship

Several researchers have expanded upon Emile Durkheim's original insight that "while family life has a moderating effect upon suicide, it rather stimulates murder."[23] Wolfgang's 1958 study of homicides in Philadelphia revealed that approximately 25% of all homicides were between family members and that women were far more likely than men to be both offenders and victims within this category than within any other.[24] Males were more likely to be killed by friends and strangers than by their family members. However, when a male was killed by a female, the offender was most likely to be his spouse.[25] Other researchers have emphasized qualitative differences in the pattern of homicide within the victim-offender relationship. The work of W. Dwayne Smith and Robert Nash Parker represented the first systematic research which focused on differentiating homicide according to the victim-offender relationship.[26] Their work used two classifications of homicide: primary and nonprimary. **Primary homicides** are the most frequent and involve family members, friends, and acquaintances. These are usually characterized as **expressive crimes**[27] because they often result from interpersonal hostility, based on jealousy, revenge, romantic triangles, and minor disagreements. **Nonprimary homicides** involve victims and offenders who have no prior relationship and usually occur in the course of another crime such as robbery. These crimes are referred to as **instrumental crimes** because they involve some degree of premeditation by the offender and are less likely to be precipitated by the victim. The difference between instrumental and expressive motives for homicide continues to be important in criminological research, and we will return to more research on this shortly.

Parker and Smith hypothesized that because of these qualitative distinctions in homicides, the effects of subcultural and structural measures could be very different once the distinction between the type of homicide was taken into account.[28] Using state homicide rates, these researchers found that structural variables like poverty and the percentage of the population age 20 to 34 are important predictors of differences in primary homicide but are insignificant predictors for non-primary homicide rates.[29]

Further attention to the heterogeneous nature of homicide is found within the work of K. R. Williams and R. L. Flewelling.[30] They disaggregated homicide rates according to

CRIME IN THE NEWS
Most Female Violent Criminals Knew Their Victims

Two out of three violent female offenders in the United States know their victims, and half the time they assaulted victims at home or near a school, according to a report released today by the Department of Justice.

Annually, about 2.1 million women are identified as violent criminals, according to the results of the National Crime Victimization Survey by the Bureau of Justice Statistics.

Some criminologists say this indicates domestic violence is a more serious problem than ever before.

But in an interview Friday, Deputy Attorney General Eric Holder cautioned against overreaction to the findings, which measure victimizations between 1993 and 1997.

CRIME STILL A MAN'S WORLD

"Although the number of women engaged in violent crime has gone up, the number of women compared to men who commit violent crimes is still very small," he said.

Women make up only 14 percent of all violent criminals. Of those, 60 percent said they had been sexually or physically abused prior to their incarceration, the report stated.

"Women are victimized, then they victimize others," said Mary Lee Allen of the Children's Defense Fund. "All of it goes back to child abuse and neglect, which isn't paid enough attention in this country."

The Justice report said 950,000 women were in the care of federal, state or local corrections officials in 1998. These women had an estimated 1.3 million children.

Years before he was nominated as the number two authority at the Justice Department, Holder served the District of Columbia as a superior court judge from 1988–93.

Reflecting back on the women who appeared before his criminal court then, he recalled that their pasts seemed to distinguish them from male defendants.

"The women I saw before me who were charged with violent crimes had really bad histories," Holder said. Sexual and physical abuse going back years was common, as was drug and alcohol abuse. "These were people who, even physically, were in bad shape."

WOMEN ARE FASTEST-GROWING PRISON POPULATION

Eleanor Pam, a professor at New York's John Jay College of Criminal Justice, agreed that histories of childhood abuse and neglect are typical of female offenders.

"Women and girls are sexually molested at much larger rates than boys," she said, noting that women are the fastest-growing prison population in America.

Holder cited research indicating that abuse or neglect during childhood increases the likelihood of arrest as a

juvenile by 53 percent and the likelihood of arrest for a violent crime as an adult by 38 percent.

Once abused or neglected kids reach their teenage years they cannot be easily turned around and persuaded to avoid lashing out with violent or criminal activity.

"It might sound like this is not the sort of area that law enforcement ought to be involved in," Holder said. "The reality is, unless we get intimately involved in this prevention and intervention effort, you never really solve the problems."

That means getting to kids while they're still young, he said.

MENTAL HEALTH IMPORTANT TO LAW ENFORCERS

Some experts believe that children exposed to violence are susceptible to its lure in adulthood. For that reason, a few police departments now bring mental health professionals to crime scenes where children are witnesses or participants.

As a judge, Holder said he sympathized more often with women defendants than men.

"When I looked at the women, and looked at their histories and what they had endured before they got to me in court, it was sad," Holder said.

Source: James Gordon Meek, "Histories of Abuse Common Among Women in Jail," APB News, December 5, 1999. Reprinted by permission.

two criteria: (1) the nature of the circumstances surrounding the homicide, which included whether there was some indicator of a fight or argument precipitating the homicide, and (2) the victim-offender relationship, distinguishing between victims and offenders who were family members, acquaintances, or strangers. By comparing how factors like poverty and population size have different effects on different types of homicide, Williams and Flewelling found that certain factors are more important in explaining one form of homicide over another. Poverty is a stronger predictor of family homicide, and population size is more important in explaining stranger homicide. Both the victim-offender relationship

and the context of the homicide (for example, as the end result of a robbery) are crucial factors to take into account in explaining patterns of homicide.

Beginning in the 1980s, the intimate-partner homicide rate began to decline, a decline that has continued to the present day. Using homicide data from a sample of 29 large cities within the United States from 1976 to 1992, Laura Dugan, Daniel S. Nagin, and Richard Rosenfeld offer an **exposure-reduction theory** of intimate-partner homicide.[31] These researchers examined the ability of the "decline in domesticity, improved economic status of women, and growth in domestic violence resources" to explain decreases in intimate-partner homicide in urban areas.[32] These three factors, they argued, reduced intimate-partner homicides by reducing exposure to the on-going violent dynamics that conventionally precede this form of homicide. Declining domesticity was measured by a decrease in marriage rates and by an increase in divorce rates, with divorces being one means by which individuals can peacefully exit a violent relationship. As women gain equality, more opportunities are available to them that may relieve their economic dependence on men. Finally, the greater the availability of domestic violence resources, such as advocacy, shelters, and other services, the lower the rate of intimate-partner homicide. These resources provide support and offer a way to relieve violence before it escalates to the point of homicide. Given the fact that intimate-partner homicide is often the final outcome of an ongoing violent relationship, "factors which facilitate exit from a violent relationship or inhibit the development of such relationships should reduce the rate of intimate partner homicide by a simple mechanism—the reduction of exposure to a violent partner."[33] Analysis of the data did support the major hypotheses offered by Dugan, Nagin, and Rosenfeld. Generally, as resources supporting dissolution or a nonviolent exit from a violent relationship increased, rates of intimate-partner homicide decreased.

Instrumental and Expressive Homicide

Not all homicide offenders intend to kill their victims. This may be the case when the incident begins as a robbery motivated by instrumental ends, such as getting money. An argument may also precede a homicide, but this circumstance is expressive rather than instrumental because "the dominant motivation is the violence itself," even if lethal violence is not planned in advance.[34] The importance of instigating incidents is explored in research by Carolyn Rebecca Block and Richard Block, who use the instrumental-expressive continuum to formulate a discussion of homicide syndromes, or mechanisms that serve to "link lethal violence to nonlethal sibling offenses . . . [and that can] provide a mechanism by which the explanation and prevention of homicide can be organized."[35] The Blocks use the term **sibling offense** to refer to the incident that begins the homicide. A sibling offense may be a crime, such as robbery, or another incident, such as a lovers' quarrel. It is crucial to take these sibling offenses into account because they help explain why some robberies end in murder while others do not. The Blocks developed a rather elaborate typology of homicide to illustrate how an understanding of the patterns of nonlethal violence can assist in the prevention of lethal violence. For example, there are a great many incidents of street gang violence, most of which do not end in death, and understanding those nonlethal incidents can assist in preventing homicides. An ongoing project in Chicago aimed at reducing street gang violence is an example of how homicide syndromes can be used to reduce the escalation of events that lead to death. As the Blocks state, the purpose behind the street gang violence project in Chicago "is to develop an early warning system for identifying potential street gang–related and competitive confrontational violence crisis areas."[36]

Victim Precipitation

When discussing homicide, the concept of **victim precipitation** focuses on the characteristics of victims which may have precipitated their victimization. Victim precipitation unfortunately seems to blame the victim, and the concept has been quite controversial at times. From a scholarly point of view, however, the thrust of the concept of victim precipitation is not to blame the victim for the event but to examine both individual and situational factors that may have contributed to

Purse snatchers in action. Why do victimologists suggest that some people contribute to their own victimization? *Buu-Turpin, Liaison Agency, Inc.*

and initiated the crime. This is especially important in studying patterns of homicide because quite often a homicide begins as a fight or an argument between people who know each other. The circumstances of the particular encounter determine whether the event will end as some type of assault or as a homicide. In his classic 1958 work on homicide, Marvin E. Wolfgang designated as many as 60% of cases where women had killed their husbands as victim precipitated, but only 9% of incidents where men had killed their wives as victim precipitated.[37] The gendered patterns of victim precipitation have not changed significantly since Wolfgang's investigation. Based on data on intimate-partner homicides in St. Louis, Missouri, Richard Rosenfeld analyzed data from 1980 to 1993 and designated slightly more than one-half of all homicides committed by women and only 12% of those committed by men as victim precipitated.[38]

Wolfgang also identified alcohol use as a factor in homicide cases where the "victim is a direct, positive precipitator in the crime."[39] He concluded that the positive and significant association between alcohol and victim-precipitated homicides may be explained by the fact that the victim was the "first to slap, punch, stab, or in some other manner commit an assault" and that if the victim had not been drinking, he or she would have been less violent.[40] Wolfgang's research on homicide revealed that most victims of spousal homicide had been drinking at the time of the incident, a situation that did not apply to homicide offenders.[41] Learn more about victim precipitation at the Howard League for Penal Reform via Web Extra! 10-2.

Web Extra! 10-2 at crimtoday.com

Weapon Use

As previously noted, there are different perspectives on the role that weapons play in crime, with most of the discussion centering on the role of firearms in homicide. In examining the relationship between guns and homicide, Philip J. Cook and Mark H. Moore differentiate between instrumentality and availability. *Instrumentality* refers to the fact that the type of weapon used in a particular encounter has an effect on whether the encounter ends in death. For example, the involvement of a gun may mean the difference between a criminal event ending as an assault or as a homicide. When guns are used in robberies, the fatality rate is "three times as high as for robberies with knives and 10 times as high as for robberies with other weapons."[42] However, Cook and Moore warn, an examination of fatality rates in isolation does not necessarily support the idea that the involvement of a gun caused the fatality. Other factors must be considered, such as the intent of the offender. Offenders may select a weapon on the basis of their intent; those who bring more lethal weapons to a crime may be more prepared to use deadly force.

Availability refers to issues surrounding how access to guns may increase their presence in all types of interactions, including criminal ones. As Cook and Moore argue, "Availability can be thought of relative to time, expense, and other costs."[43] The ease of availability is important given the relative spontaneity of some violent encounters. The availability of guns is important at the individual level as well as the community level because the greater the presence of guns in a particular neighborhood, the easier the access for individuals beyond their immediate households. Cook and Moore argue that gun availability is a much stronger factor in explaining lethal violence than gun instrumentality. Specifically, Cook and Moore recommend that "rather than a general effort to get guns off the streets, a more focused effort can be directed at prohibiting guns in particularly dangerous locations such as homes with histories of domestic violence, bars with histories of drunken brawls, parks in which gang fights tend to break out, and schools in which teachers and students have been assaulted."[44]

Alcohol and Drug Use

An important conceptual typology detailing the relationship between drugs and crime was developed by Paul J. Goldstein in an article first published in 1985.[45] According to Goldstein, the association of alcohol and illicit drugs with violent offending generally takes one of three forms. Drugs may be linked to violent offending through a *psychopharmacological* model, whereby either infrequent or chronic use of certain drugs produces violent behavior by lowering inhibitions or elevating aggressive tendencies. However, not all drugs produce such effects and the relationship appears to hold only for people with certain types of personalities, using certain substances, in certain settings.

When crimes are committed to support a drug habit, Goldstein says that the concept of *economic compulsion* best describes the relationship between crime and drug use. Finally, he uses the idea of *systemic violence* to describe the connection between drugs and trafficking. Systemic violence can take several forms, ranging from rival drug wars to robberies of drug dealers.

Although distinct types of relationships between drugs and violence can be described, these relationships are not necessarily mutually exclusive. Thus, one or more of the kinds of relationships Goldstein describes may be present in a single criminal incident.

Goldstein and his colleagues attempted to apply this typology to a sample of 414 homicides in New York City during the 1980s. More than half of the homicide cases in the sample involved drugs, with the vast majority of these being classified as systemic. Most of these cases involved drugs other than alcohol, and all of the homicides where alcohol was present were classified as psychopharmacological.[46]

Researchers from the Drug Relationships in Murder Project (DREIM), which analyzed incarcerated homicide offenders in New York State, found that in the majority of homicide cases involving both alcohol and illicit drugs, the primary basis for the connection with the crime was psychopharmacological, which is not in line with Goldstein's research in New York.[47] Furthermore, there appears to be a bias in Goldstein's typology that favors the classification of incidents as systemic. Because the categories of the typology are not mutually exclusive, the same incident may fit in more than one category, and common incidents like robbing a drug dealer are often classified as systemic even though they clearly involve an economic motivation.[48]

One theoretical approach focused on explaining the role that alcohol plays in homicide is **selective disinhibition,** advanced by **Robert Nash Parker** and others.[49] According to this perspective, the "disinhibiting" effect of alcohol is social in nature rather than biochemical. In particular situations or interactions, the presence of alcohol may operate to suspend certain factors that could restrain the occurrence of violence and may operate to put into play certain factors that could increase the occurrence or lethal nature of violence. This perspective relies on the existence of norms that operate both to prohibit and to proscribe the use of violence in particular situations. According to Kathleen Auerhahn and Robert Nash Parker, "Norms that have the least institutional support are more likely to be disinhibited in a particular situation—that is, to lose their effectiveness in discouraging or inhibiting violence."[50] When violence is easily and readily recognized as being inappropriate in a particular situation, this is referred to as "passive constraint." In other violent encounters, "it takes active constraint—a proactive and conscious decision not to use violence to solve the dispute—to constrain or preclude violence."[51] Because alcohol can reduce both of these forms of constraint, "the selective nature of alcohol-related homicide is dependent on the interaction of an impaired rationality and the nature of the social situation."[52] Parker and his colleagues tested this model by analyzing data on homicides in several cities in 1980, in several cities between 1960 and 1980, and in several states from 1976 to 1983. One of the key findings from this research was the ability of alcohol as a variable to significantly predict primary homicide. In relationships between individuals who are known to each other, alcohol may operate to disinhibit restraints against violence, they found. The norms that operate to govern interactions between strangers are more rigid in terms of the type of conduct that is proscribed, whereas relationships between individuals who are known to each other exist on a broader continuum. Just as we can physically embrace our friends and loved ones in a way that is not deemed appropriate with a stranger, the use of violence against those who are known to us is treated with greater tolerance—a tolerance that can be increased even further in the presence of alcohol.[53]

In his research using state-level data, Parker tested several hypotheses derived from competing theoretical perspectives about the effect of alcohol on homicide.[54] Five types of homicides were identified, based on the victim-offender relationship: "robbery, other felony, family intimate, family other, and primary nonintimate."[55] The theoretical perspectives that Parker compared were the economic deprivation, subcultural, social control, and routine activity theories. Concerning the power of variables derived from the economic deprivation approach, poverty had a stronger effect on both robbery and other felony homicides in states with "above average rates of alcohol consumption."[56] Alcohol consumption had direct effects on two of the three types of primary homicide.

Gangs

Gang membership may influence homicide in a number of ways. Analyzing data from Los Angeles, researchers found several differences between homicides involving gang mem-

Los Angeles gang members show off their weapons. Scott Decker applies Colin Loftin's theory of violence as a contagion to the processes that are set into play as more gang members begin to carry guns. How does Loftin view assaultive violence as a contagious social process? *Daniel Laine, Corbis*

bers and nongang members. They found that gang homicides were more likely to involve minority males, to make use of guns, to occur in public places, and to involve victims and offenders with no prior relationship.[57] Richard Rosenfeld and colleagues state that the association of gangs and homicide may be one of two general types: (1) gang-motivated violence, in which violent crime is the direct result of gang activity, and (2) gang-affiliated violence, in which individual gang members are involved in crime but not as a purposeful result of gang activity.[58] Using data from St. Louis, these researchers compared cases of gang-motivated homicide with gang-affiliated homicide and nongang youth homicide. Across all three homicide types, black males were more likely to be participants, and there was very little difference in the neighborhood context. All three types of homicides clustered in disadvantaged communities—communities whose populations were predominantly black. While gang-motivated homicides declined in the early 1990s, gang-affiliated homicides rose, leading the researchers to conclude that their continued increase "results from increased involvement of gang members—not gangs—in the drug trade."[59] This finding supports the work of other researchers who argue that youth gangs are primarily not organized enough to allow for a role in organized drug trade.

Serial Murder

As defined in Chapter 2, serial murder is criminal homicide that "involves the killing of several victims in three or more separate events."[60] Serial killers are both a source of fascination and horror in our culture. Our fascination with serial killers is based on our disbelief that seemingly ordinary individuals could commit such atrocities. While seedy losers are found among serial killers, so too are charismatic, charming, and handsome college men like Ted Bundy. Across the continuum of types who are serial killers, "there is one trait that appears to separate serial killers from the norm: many are exceptionally skillful in their presentation of self so that they are beyond suspicion and thus are difficult to apprehend."[61] One factor that makes it difficult to identify serial killers, even with modern technology, is that these individuals often change the pattern of their offending, including their method of killing.[62]

James Alan Fox and **Jack Levin** have written extensively on both serial killing and mass murder. They offer ten myths of serial murder: (1) serial murder is at epidemic proportions, (2) serial killers have a distinct appearance, (3) all serial killers are insane, (4) all serial killers are sociopaths, (5) serial killers are primarily motivated by pornography, (6) traumatic childhoods are at the root of most serial killers' problems, (7) identification of serial killers prior to killing occurs is a straightforward task, (8) serial killers are primarily sexual sadists, (9) the victim's resemblance to a family member, (usually the killer's mother) is the primary source of victim selection, and (10) serial killers want to be apprehended.[63] While annual figures as high as 5,000 victims of serial killers have been cited, this figure was based on the erroneous assumption that killings without a motive were attributable to serial killers, and it was also based on an accumulation of cases over time.[64] More reasonable estimates suggest that perhaps 100 murders each year are the result of serial killings.[65] While serial killers have been found among various age groups, different races, and both genders, the more typical serial killer is "a white male in his late twenties or thirties who targets strangers at or near his place of residence or work."[66] While acknowledging that the motivations for serial homicide are numerous, Fox and Levin contend that "murder is a form of expressive, rather than instrumental violence."[67] Unlike homicide generally, serial killing is more likely to involve strangers and rarely involves the use of guns.

The vast majority of serial killers are not legally insane or medically psychotic. "They are more cruel than crazy," according to Fox and Levin. "Their crimes may be sickening but their minds are not necessarily sick."[68] Many serial killers are diagnosed as sociopaths, a term for those with antisocial personalities. As discussed in Chapter 6, since they lack a conscience, sociopaths do not consider the needs or basic humanity of others in their decision making or their view of the world. They do not see themselves as being bound by conventional rules or by the expectations of others. Sociopaths view other people as "tools to be manipulated for the purpose of maximizing their personal pleasure."[69] However, many sociopaths are neither serial killers nor involved in violent crime, even though "they may lie, cheat, or steal."[70]

Although not an exclusive characteristic of serial killers, sexual sadism is a strong pattern. In many of the typologies developed by researchers, this characteristic forms the basis for a type of serial killer. Typologies of serial killers are organized around different, but generally related, themes. Ronald Holmes and J. DeBurger developed a taxonomy based on an analysis of 400 cases. Their four different types of serial killers are differentiated by offender motivation, selection of victim, expected gain, and method of murder.[71] *Visionary serial killers* hear voices and have visions that are the basis for a compulsion to murder. *Comfort serial killers* are motivated by financial or material gain. *Hedonistic serial killers* murder because they find it enjoyable and derive psychological pleasure from killing. *Power seekers* operate from some position of authority over others, and their killings usually involve a period where the killer plays a kind of cat-and-mouse game with the victim. The nurse who poisons a patient, restores his health, and continues to repeat the cycle until the patient finally dies is an example of this kind of serial killer. Through the game, the killer gains attention or a boost in self-esteem.[72]

Refining the typology of Holmes and DeBurger, James Fox and Jack Levin offer a three-part typology. They classify serial murderers as either thrill motivated, mission oriented, or expedience directed. *Thrill-motivated killers,* the most common type of serial killer, may be of two types: the sexual sadist and the dominance killer. *Mission-oriented killers* are not as common and generally have either a reformist or a visionary orientation. Reformists want to rid the world of evil, and visionaries hear voices commanding them to do certain activities. Visionary killers are quite rare and tend to be genuinely psychotic. *Expedience-directed serial killers* are either driven by profit or protection. Profit-driven killers may kill for financial or material gain, and protection-oriented killers commit murder to mask other crimes, such as robbery.[73]

Female Serial Killers

Although the vast majority of serial killers are male, there have been female serial killers, and the patterns of their activities are sometimes distinct from those of male serialists.[74] The serial killer typology of Holmes and DeBurger, presented earlier, applies to women as well as men, except that women are rarely hedonistic serial killers.[75] Female serial killers typically select their victims from among people who are known to them, unlike male serial killers, who tend to target strangers.[76] A type of serial killer found primarily among women is the *disciple killer,* who murders as the result of the influence of a charismatic personality. The women who killed at the behest of Charles Manson were of this type. The geographic area in which serial killers operate may be either stable or transient, with no clear preference among male serial killers. However, geographic stability characterizes almost all of the known female serial killers.[77]

Michael D. Kelleher and C. L. Kelleher researched female serial killers from a historical perspective and developed a typology based on motivation. Arguing that there are two broad categories of female serial killers—those who act alone and those who work in partnership with others—Kelleher and Kelleher present a typology based on distinct motivation, selection of victim, and method of killing.[78] The categories include the *black widow,* who generally kills spouses and usually for economic profit, and the *angel of death,* who generally kills "those in her care or who rely on her for some form of medical attention or similar support."[79] The typical career of a female serial killer is longer than that of her male counterpart. Other than women who commit their crimes with others, usually men, female serial killers tend to approach their crimes in a systematic fashion—a characteristic that may explain their longer careers.[80]

Apprehending Serial Killers

Fox and Levin contend that it is extremely difficult to identify and apprehend serial killers because of the cautiousness and skill with which they operate. Ironically, it is these very factors that allow them to operate long enough to be labeled serial killers. Individuals who are less skillful or cautious are generally apprehended because of physical evidence at the crime scene or the selection of a familiar victim. The Federal Bureau of Investigation (FBI) established the **Violent Criminal Apprehension Program (VICAP)** in 1985 to increase the efficiency and effectiveness of serial killer apprehension. Although Fox and Levin call VICAP an "excellent

concept in theory," they note several practical problems with the program.[81] First, the complexity of the data and the associated record keeping have limited the degree of compliance by law enforcement officials, seriously affecting VICAP's potential usefulness. Second, the recognition of patterns among serial killers, even with the assistance of powerful computers, is not easily achieved. Finally, VICAP functions more as a detection tool than as an apprehension tool.

In addition to VICAP, the FBI employs profilers who assist local law enforcement. According to Fox and Levin, "The FBI has done more to advance the art and science of offender profiling than any other organization."[82] Employing a primary classification system based on two prongs, FBI profiling theory distinguishes between *organized nonsocial killers* and *disorganized asocial killers.* Organized killers have a higher level of intelligence, better social skills, and a greater ability to function in all areas of life than do disorganized killers. These two types differ in the method of killing. Although variation certainly exists among them, the "organized/disorganized continuum is used as an overall guideline for drawing inferences from the crime scene to the behavioral characteristics of the killer."[83] Profiles typically do not yield high success rates in terms of actually leading law enforcement to apprehend a killer, but they are not intended to be the primary tool for apprehension. More recent attempts to identify serial killers rely on "geomapping" techniques to approximate the killer's probable location.[84] Most categorizations are based on the case histories and activities of known serial killers after apprehension. While we know a great deal about the patterns of serial murder, this does not necessarily translate into the ability to identify these killers easily before they have committed enough murders to come to the attention of the FBI—a rarity in itself since only the "unsolvable" cases receive FBI attention. Learn more about serial killers from the FBI's Behavioral Analysis Unit via Web Extra! 10-3.

Web EXTRA! **Web Extra! 10-3 at crimtoday.com**

Mass Murder

As defined in Chapter 2, *mass murder* refers to the killing of more than three individuals at a single time.[85] Mass murder can follow the political motivations of the offenders, as was the case with the 1995 Oklahoma City bombing in which 168 individuals, including children, were killed. Other mass murderers kill for more personal reasons. The mass killing at L'Ecole Polytechnique in Montreal, Canada, on December 6, 1989, by Marc Lepine was motivated by a hatred of women; feminists in particular. Lepine, who blamed feminists because he was denied admission to the engineering program at the school, shot and killed 14 female students. Lepine entered a classroom and ordered the male students and the professor to leave the room. Before he began firing, Lepine shouted, "I want the women! You're all a bunch of f-ing feminists! I hate feminists!"[86] He began firing, killing six of the nine women in the room. Lepine then went down the halls and into other parts of the university, killing women as he came across them, before finally turning the gun on himself. Mass murders are usually a shock because they often occur in everyday locales that are thought of as safe and because they erupt spontaneously. Although mass murders do not occur with great frequency, they cause great concern because they shatter the sense of safety that characterizes everyday life.

Jack Levin and James Alan Fox offer a four-part typology of mass murder that differentiates these crimes by motive and then further subdivides them by "victim-offender relationship, degree of planning, and randomness and state of mind of the perpetrator."[87] The four motive categories are revenge, love, profit, and terror. Mass murders that are motivated by *revenge* represent the largest category of such killings and may be against either particular individuals or groups of individuals, as was the case with Marc Lepine in Canada. Other revenge-motivated murderers may be less specific in the selection of a target, as in the case of George Hennard, who hated "all of the residents of the county in which he lived." In 1991, Hennard drove his truck through the front window of Luby's Cafeteria in Killeen, Texas, and then "indiscriminately opened fire on customers as they ate their lunch, killing 23."[88]

Some mass murders are motivated by *love*, Levin and Fox contend, though not in the way that most individuals would conventionally define actions that reflect love. Mass murders motivated by *profit* may result when the killer wants to eliminate witnesses to a crime. Mass murders motivated by *terror* include the killings by the Charles Manson family. Levin and Fox argue that mass murders motivated by anger or love are expressive in nature and that those motivated by profit and terror are more instrumental because there is some concrete goal to be achieved through the killings.[89]

Although most mass murders strike the public as senseless acts of a crazy person, Levin and Fox contend that "most massacrers are not madmen."[90] Yet why would someone like James Huberty, a former security guard, walk calmly into a fast-food restaurant in 1984 and fatally shoot 21 victims at random, most of whom were children? Why would Patrick Edward Purdy shoot and kill five children and wound 30 others at Cleveland Elementary School in Stockton, California, in 1989?[91] Levin and Fox argue that factors like frustration, isolation, blame, loss, and failure and other external and internal motivations and situational elements help make sense of these mass murders. They delineate three types of contributing factors: "*predisposers,* long-term and stable preconditions that become incorporated into the personality of the killer, which are nearly always present in his biography; *precipitants,* short-term and acute triggers, i.e., catalysts; and *facilitators,* conditions, usually situational, which increase the likelihood of a violent outburst but are not necessary to produce that response."[92] Using this typology to explain why, for example, most mass murderers are middle-aged, Levin and Fox contend that it takes a long time to accumulate the kind of rage and frustration that sets off some mass murderers.

Mass murderers often select targets that have some significance for them, such as workers at a site of former employment. As Fox and Levin state, "A majority of mass killers target victims who are specially chosen, not just in the wrong place at the wrong time. The indiscriminate slaughter of strangers by a 'crazed' killer is the exception to the rule."[93] Unlike serial murderers, mass murderers are easy to apprehend because they rarely leave the scene of their crime, either because they commit suicide after the killings or because they stay long enough to be detected.

RAPE

The violent crime of rape has generated much discussion and controversy over the years. To understand why, we must examine the changing legal definitions of rape, our societal understanding of rape, variations in the ways in which theoretical explanations of rape have evolved, and the development of rapist typologies. Concerns with improving the social, legal, medical, and social service response to rape were at the forefront of changes that have brought greater awareness of the extent and nature of violence against women. The significant evolution of this awareness is evidenced by federal legislation first enacted in 1994 and known as the **Violence against Women Act (VAWA)**. VAWA was reauthorized in October 2000. Additional information on VAWA is available in Chapter 15.

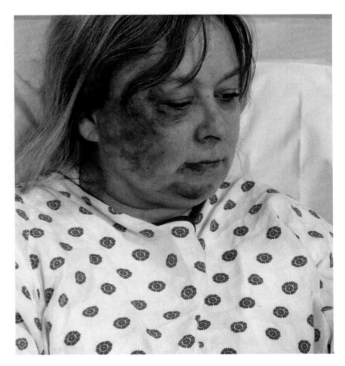

A battered woman in a domestic violence shelter. Crimes against women have come under close scrutiny since Congress passed the Violence against Women Act (VAWA) in 1994. Should these crimes receive special attention from criminologists? *Mark Burnett, Stock Boston*

CRIME IN THE NEWS
All Men Potential Rapists, Claim Authors

A storm of controversy is brewing around an upcoming book by two evolutionary biologists who argue that rape is rooted in sex, not violence, occurring as part of a "natural biological phenomenon."

In *A Natural History of Rape: Biological Bases of Sexual Coercion,* scheduled for release by MIT Press in March, authors Randy Thornhill and Craig Palmer state that until society accepts science as the basis for sexual crimes, prevention programs are "doomed to failure."

"Rape is, in its very essence, a sexual act . . . which has evolved over millennia of human history along with courtship, sexual attraction and other behaviors related to the production of offspring," writes Thornhill, a professor at the University of New Mexico, and Palmer, an instructor at the University of Colorado.

BOOK: POTENTIAL EXISTS IN ALL MEN

At the heart of their controversial argument is the idea that all men—under the right circumstances—could be potential rapists, Thornhill told APBnews.com.

"It has to do with conditions under which men are raised that influence their proneness [to rape], like the characteristics of men's upbringings, boys who are raised in poverty or conditions where social relationships are not enduring. Those things are important conditions for influencing rape proneness," said Thornhill.

But there are certain conditions, he said, such as being isolated with a woman, or in the context of warfare, which may influence "rape proneness."

"A guy, regardless of how he has been raised . . . finding a female in a real vulnerable situation . . . in some conditions rapes her," Thornhill said.

REJECTS "AGGRESSION" MOTIVE

The authors reject the position of many social scientists who see rape primarily as an act of aggression. They say for 25 years, the course of rape treatment and prevention has been steered by feminist ideology, an argument being vociferously challenged by social historians.

Social theorists see rape as an "unnatural behavior that has nothing to do with sex" and a "symptom of an unhealthy society," write Thornhill and Palmer in an article about their book in the journal *The Sciences.*

The theory that rape is a violent crime motivated by the urge to exert power and control was put forth by Susan Brownmiller in her highly-acclaimed 1975 work, *Against Our Will: Men, Women and Rape.*

Brownmiller's book debunked the Freudian idea that "no woman could be raped against [her] will" and prompted new laws shifting the burden of proof away from the victim.

FEMINISTS INCENSED

She said the publication of *A Natural History* shows that women are being forced to once more fight the "Victorian notion that men can't help themselves."

Brownmiller and others are incensed by Thornhill and Palmer's position, fearing that by characterizing rape as a biological imperative, they are turning back the clock on society's thinking.

"We are an evolved society. Why didn't they choose to look at burglary? They did it on rape because they have this theory that women should be blamed," Brownmiller said.

"I accept there is some evolutionary influence on rape, but it's a complex problem with a multitude of causes," said Mary Koss, a psychology professor at the University of Arizona, who co-chaired the American Psychological Association's Task Force on Violence Against Women.

ACADEMICS: BOOK IS "CONFUSED"

Other scientists and academics feel the book's premise is based on sloppy science, dismisses the important contributions of social science to rape prevention and could have potentially harmful consequences.

"It's confused, scientifically weak and naïve," said Jerry Coyne, a professor of evolutionary biology at the University of Chicago. "The big question is, is it nature or are we responsible? I don't believe that [it is nature]. It's a pathology, a byproduct of aggression. If they say that men will rape if they think they can get away with it, why are the vast majority of men incapable of rape?"

Thornhill said most men do not rape because of the costs involved. "Men's sexual psychology pays attention to the costs of their actions. Studies show those who expect to live a long life don't engage in risky behavior. Men in the ghetto or in war are willing to accept more costs because they don't think they're going to live very long."

AUTHORS: SUFFERED DISCRIMINATION

The ideas in the book are not new but Thornhill and others contend they have suffered discrimination and hostility within academia and outside for their views.

Thornhill's theories about rape have appeared in scientific publications for almost 20 years. But with his first book on the topic for a mainstream audience, Thornhill is finding out just how provocative his views are as he tries to tackle a deluge of media inquiries and requests to appear for debates on network television.

Critics say the suggestion that rape is mostly a threat to women of childbearing age neglects the high number of sexual assaults on children and older women, as well as sexual assaults on men.

The authors say current prevention methods based on the existing theory are "doomed to fail."

"DARWINIAN SELECTION" IS BLAMED

In the authors' view, a young man should take into account that it's "Darwinian selection" motivating him to demand sex

(continued on the next page)

(continued from previous page)

even if he knows that his date truly doesn't want it. And again, it's "Darwinian selection" causing him to "mistake a woman's friendly comment or tight blouse as an invitation to sex." They recommend young women be taught that "the way they dress can put them at risk."

But many others disagree strongly. "It's harmful and inconsistent with the American way of life. Not to go out or wear provocative clothing takes away constitutional freedoms to move about, freely associate and self-expression," said Koss. Rapists have been acquitted when defense attorneys argued the woman was "provocatively dressed in a turtleneck and knee-length skirt," she said.

CONTROVERSY COULD AFFECT RAPE CASES

Some fear use of an "evolution defense" could further reduce the number of rape convictions. Brownmiller said that expert witnesses could argue such a defense in high-profile cases, and "it's hard enough to get a conviction in a rape case."

"Nothing in our book says that just because rape is biological it is justified, including in the courtroom," Thornhill said. "Rape is as rape is. Science has no opinion about what is right and wrong."

Koss said she is afraid the controversy could damage progress that has been made in the past 25 years toward combating rape.

"I view sexual violence as a unifying issue," said Koss. "It's not a conservative or liberal issue. Any attempts to create polarization are unwelcome."

Source: Amy Worden, "New Book Says Rape About Sex, Not Violence," APB News, January 28, 2000. Reprinted with permission.

Attempts to measure the extent of rape have occupied a number of different researchers across various disciplines. The diversity of the scholars who have investigated the prevalence and incidence of rape partially explains why findings vary across research studies. There is no agreement on the number of women who are raped each year.[94] What is on the surface a simple matter is very difficult to pinpoint. The final number derived is determined by how rapes are counted and what data sources are used. According to the Uniform Crime Reports (UCR), 89,107 completed or attempted rapes were reported to the police in 1999, and "an estimated 65 of every 100,000 females in the country were reported victims of forcible rape."[95] However, the ability of official statistics to accurately assess the incidence of rape is hampered by victim reporting; most rapes are not reported to the police. Information reported from victims in the National Crime Victimization Survey (NCVS) reveals 183,440 rape incidents during 1999, or almost two attempted or completed rapes for every 1,000 residents age 12 or older.[96] Other problems with both measurement of rape and disclosure to researchers by victims also characterize the NCVS data and have led several researchers to question the accuracy of rape incidence based on these data.[97] The best current measure of the prevalence of rape comes from the **National Violence against Women (NVAW) Survey.** According to estimates from the NVAW survey, 17.6% of women reported either a completed or attempted rape at some point during their lifetime. The prevalence rate for one year was 0.3% for attempted and completed rapes combined, which translates to slightly more than 300,000 rape victims and 876,064 rape incidents annually in the population.[98] The lifetime likelihood of being the victim of a violent crime or the victim of a particular violent crime is higher because risk accumulates over time.

Rape Myths

The ability to capture the extent of sexual violence against women remains hampered by sociocultural factors that contribute to underreporting. **Rape myths** are false assumptions about rape that continue to characterize much of the discourse surrounding sexual violence. Rape myths include notions that women bring false rape charges to "get even" with men, that women bring rape upon themselves by wearing provocative clothing, that women are "asking for it" by going to bars alone, and that women say "no" when they really mean yes. Since 1980, when Martha R. Burt first began researching rape myth ideology,[99] numerous other studies have supported widespread acceptance of these myths.[100] Rape myths serve to undermine the traumatic nature of this offense and to compartmentalize women into "good girls" and "bad girls," only one of whom is seen as a credible or sympathetic rape victim. Rape myths are culturally based and reflect attitudes toward women and their proper role and place in society. As feminists have long argued, rape myths serve to discount the experiences of women by placing stereotypical parameters around who can and who cannot be raped. Rape myths inhibit the reporting of rape and also serve to normalize rape as a crime of violence.[101] Largely as a result of such myths women continue to report that agents of the criminal justice system do not respond with sensitivity and compassion toward their victimization. To argue that sexual violence is associated with rape myth ideology to the same extent that existed 20 years ago is just as naive as to argue that rape myths do not continue to play a role in minimizing societal accountability for the level and acceptance of violence against women.

The Common Law Definition of Rape

Rape myths both fueled and supported the common law understanding of rape. Until the 1970s in the United States and the 1980s in Canada, rape was a common law offense. By this definition, rape was "carnal knowledge of a woman not one's wife by force or against her will." Although rape was clearly understood as a crime under the common law, it was a crime in which the legitimacy of the victim as a victim was challenged. Rape was construed quite narrowly, and the experience of many individuals regarding rape was not represented within this understanding because laws restricted the range of eligible rape victims. Specifically, the common law did not recognize men as victims, did not recognize rape within marriage, did not allow for acts of sexual penetration other than vaginal penetration by a penis, and did not allow for various means by which force could occur. Moreover, the rules of evidence required that the victim who brought forth a rape charge must demonstrate physical resistance to the attack and must have some form of corroboration that the rape occurred. The victim's previous sexual history could be admitted as relevant information. Furthermore, the sociocultural understanding of rape that predominated in the criminal justice system and in the wider society relied on gender stereotypes in which only certain kinds of women were deemed to be credible victims and only certain kinds of men were regarded as possible offenders. The sexual aspect of rape dominated both the legal construction of rape as a crime and the handling of rape cases by institutions.

Rape Law Reform

Rape law reform aimed to make the legal understanding of rape compatible with other violent crimes. Characterized as the second rape, rape investigations, especially at the trial stage, too often forced the victim through further trauma rather than focusing on assessing offender culpability.[102] Feminist groups, at the forefront of organized efforts to bring about rape law reform, were joined by law enforcement officials and prosecutors who supported efforts "to remove obstacles to the apprehension and conviction of offenders."[103] In 1975, Michigan became the first state to dramatically redefine rape to encompass a broader range of sexually assaultive behaviors, and circumstances and a greater variety of victims. Other states followed Michigan's lead, and by 1992, all states had made significant statutory changes to the common law offense of rape.[104] **Cassia Spohn** and **Julie Horney**, two of the most prolific researchers in the area of rape law reform, identify four common themes in all rape law reforms:[105]

- Redefining rape and replacing the single crime of rape with a series of graded offenses defined by the presence or absence of aggravating conditions
- Changing the consent standard by eliminating the requirement that the victim physically resist the attacker
- Eliminating the requirement that the victim's testimony be corroborated
- Placing restrictions on the introduction of evidence of the victim's prior sexual conduct

In some states, broad and sweeping changes were made to existing rape statutes.[106] This was certainly the case in Michigan, which for a time was considered the model for rape law reform. In other states, legal reform was more grad-

ual, with slight changes being made to statutes in a step-by-step fashion. In Texas, for example, only very minor changes were made to existing rape statutes at any one time. Jurisdictions also varied in how the legal redefinition of rape occurred, with many states adopting a tiered approach, renaming the offense *sexual assault* of varying levels, similar to other crimes of assault. The change in terminology from *rape* to *sexual assault* was intended at a symbolic level to more fully capture the violent nature of the crime. Because of the history of sexism surrounding conventional rape laws and the processing of cases, it was argued, the term *rape* implied that the crime was fundamentally a sexual one. The more the sexual aspect of the crime was emphasized, the less the crime was seen as violent.

In one key way, individual rape law reform in states and at the federal level proceeded in different routes: the **rape shield laws**. These laws, first introduced in the 1970s as part of the legal reforms then underway, were intended to protect rape victims by ensuring that defendants did not introduce irrelevant facts about the victim's sexual past into evidence. Previously, no guidelines prevented the defense from bringing into evidence the victim's past sexual history as a way to discredit her and to play to rape myth ideology. The rape shield laws varied in the amount of discretion left with the judge in terms of the type of evidence that could be introduced. However, these laws were quite necessary and sent the message that the courts would no longer be a party to a "second assault" on the victim.[107]

A number of expectations attached to rape law reform. Spohn and Horney identify four general changes that were anticipated in the wake of rape law reform. First, an increase in the reporting of rapes was expected because legal reforms would mean that victims would receive more sympathetic and effective treatment within the criminal justice system. Second, the reforms were expected to produce symbolic change that would emphasize the violent nature of rape. Third, legal reforms were expected to alter the decision-making structure of the criminal justice system by eliminating the consideration of extralegal evidence (for example, what the victim was wearing). Finally, reform was expected to remove the barriers preventing more effective prosecution and higher conviction rates for rape.[108] Learn more about rape law reform at Web Extra! 10-4.

Web EXTRA! Web Extra! 10-4 at crimtoday.com

The Effects of Rape Law Reform

What have been the effects of rape law reform? Have the reforms changed the way rape cases are handled by the criminal justice system? Have legal changes altered the social landscape enough to affect the reporting behavior of rape victims? Questions like these, which highlight some of the goals of rape law reform, have been addressed in research by Spohn and Horney in the most thorough empirical assessment of rape law reform to date.[109] The researchers selected six urban jurisdictions in which to evaluate rape law reforms. Three jurisdictions represented areas of strong legal reform, and three represented areas of weaker reform. This distinction was important because Spohn and Horney expected that the effects of rape law reform would be the most dramatic in areas where reforms had been comprehensive and strong. Strong reforms were represented by jurisdictions in which the entire rape statute had been revised and where elements of reform, such as the rape shield laws, offered little discretion to judges. Spohn and Horney analyzed data from court records of all processed rape cases in the six jurisdictions from 1970 through 1984. They also collected all police reports of rape during this period. To assess the impact of legal reform, the researchers looked at several outcome measures, such as whether there was a change in the reporting of rapes to the police, in the indictment of rape cases by prosecutors, and in the conviction rates for offenders. In addition to statistical analysis of cases and reports, the researchers conducted interviews with a sample of more than 150 judges, prosecutors, and defense attorneys.[110]

As previously noted, Spohn and Horney hypothesized that the impact of rape law reform would be the most pronounced in jurisdictions characterized by strong reforms. While their findings supported this hypothesis in some ways, there was far from uniform support. Detroit, Michigan was one of the three jurisdictions they included with strong reforms. The reforms in Michigan did accomplish some of the expected ends, such as an increase in reports, indictments, and convictions. However, other expected outcomes of reform, such as a greater percentage of convicted rape offenders being sentenced to incarceration, did not materialize. In jurisdictions like Illinois, where reform efforts were less comprehensive, the effects of reform were weak to nonexistent on all of the outcome measures used. Jurisdictions with weak reforms, like Houston, saw significant increases in reports of rape following reform implementation—an effect not seen in Philadelphia, a jurisdiction implementing stronger reforms.[111]

One of the common findings of studies of this type is that new legislation has only a limited effect on changing the behavior of courtroom work groups unless they embrace the reforms or unless the reforms actually force instrumental changes. Spohn and Horney used interviews with criminal justice officials to place their statistical analysis within the context of the legal environment in which rape cases are processed. One of the explicit goals of legal reform was to change the way in which agents of the criminal justice system respond both to the crime of rape and to the victim. Similar to other legal changes that emerge from grassroots activism, the reforms had to be "interpreted and applied by decision makers who may not share the goals of those who championed their enactment and who therefore may not be committed to their implementation."[112] The officials that Spohn and Horney interviewed expressed strong support for the legal changes in their jurisdictions and claimed that the treat-

ment of rape victims had improved significantly. While the statistical analysis revealed no dramatic changes in how officials handled rape cases as the result of legal reforms, the interviews helped interpret this. Some changes, such as more serious attention being given to simple rape cases (that is, cases without aggravating characteristics like the presence of a weapon), were already occurring in jurisdictions prior to rape law reforms. Case law in several jurisdictions had already produced changes such that "a scintilla of corroboration" to a rape charge was sufficient in many rape cases.[113] The researchers stated that "reformers should find encouragement in some evidence for the effectiveness of rape shield laws. Officials in all jurisdictions rated evidence relating to a complainant's sexual history low in importance."[114] Spohn and Horney conclude with the key observation that legal reforms take time to produce large-scale change and that rape law reforms must be continually evaluated for more evidence of how change is occurring.

The Social Context of Rape

Although rape can occur in almost any social context, certain social situations are characterized by a higher prevalence of rape and by a difference in the offender's motivation. A number of contexts within which the crime of rape occurs are described in this section.

Acquaintance Rape

The vast majority of rapes occur when the victim and the offender have some prior relationship—though not necessarily an intimate or familial one. Some researchers and activists who work with rape victims have stated that **acquaintance rape** is the most common scenario for rapes. Acquaintance rape has been referred to as a "hidden crime" because it represents a type of sexual assault that is not reported to the police and that is quite susceptible to rape myth ideology. Among adults, acquaintance rape usually occurs within the context of a dating relationship. For this reason, a great deal of the empirical research on acquaintance rape has focused on the college setting, where dating is a salient characteristic of the social life of undergraduate students.

Rape on College Campuses

Researchers have identified college campuses as places that typically have a high incidence of rape. Although E. J. Kanin had reported in a 1957 *American Journal of Sociology* article that as many as 20% of college women had experienced either a completed or an attempted rape,[115] societal awareness and concern for rape on college campuses did not emerge until the 1980s. Helping to publicize the problem have been a number of high-profile rape cases on college campuses in which the victims not only went public with their experiences but grabbed headlines and the covers of major publications like *Time, Newsweek,* and *People.*[116] Some of these cases include the rape of Katie Koestner at the College of

William and Mary, the rape of Kristen Buxton at Colgate University, and the rape of Christy Brzonkala at the Virginia Polytechnic Institute and State University. In the last case, the victim filed for civil relief under the Violence against Women Act. The case ultimately went before the U.S. Supreme Court, which affirmed the rulings of lower courts that invalidated a VAWA provision that provided a federal civil remedy for the victims of gender-motivated violence. The Court held that the clause could not withstand constitutional scrutiny.[117] Not only has media publicity emphasized the reality of the college setting as a site of rape, but in 1992 the Campus Sexual Assault Victims' Bill of Rights Act became law.[118] It requires campus authorities to "conduct appropriate disciplinary hearings, treat sexual assault victims and defendants with respect, making their rights and legal options clear, and cooperate with them in fully exercising those rights."[119]

One of the most prolific researchers on rape, especially of rape among college students, is **Mary P. Koss**. Koss found that approximately 28% of women reported having experienced an attempted or completed rape since the age of 14.[120] Based on incidents occurring in the last 12 months, Koss calculated an incidence rate of 76 per 1,000 women. Based on comparable estimates from the National Crime Survey (NCS), Koss's estimate was 10 to 15 times the rate obtained with NCS data.[121] Approximately 57% of the rapes involved dating partners, and 73% of the rape victims reported that the offender was drinking. Other studies on college campuses have found similarly high levels of rape and sexual assault.[122]

A great deal of the research on rape in college settings has focused on identifying the unique factors of campus life that may be conducive to rape. Some researchers contend that college fraternities "create a sociocultural context in which the use of coercion in sexual relations with women is normative and in which the mechanisms to keep this pattern of behavior in check are minimal at best and absent at worst."[123] Rather than focusing on the pathological nature of individual males in fraternities, these researchers have identified characteristics of the social organization of fraternities that contribute to the formation of attitudes and behaviors which objectify women and normalize sexual coercion. These characteristics include "a preoccupation with loyalty, group protection and security, use of alcohol as a weapon, involvement in violence and physical force, and an emphasis on competition and superiority."[124] Learn more about campus rape at Web Extra! 10-5.

Web Extra! 10-5 at crimtoday.com

While social organizations like fraternities may reinforce rape myth ideology, other social organizations exist on college campuses around the country that challenge this ideology. The increased awareness of campus rape has led to the development of services and programs that assist victims of sexual violence and that present information that challenges rape myths. State and federal funding has produced a variety of programs that aim to alter the atmosphere surrounding sexual violence on college campuses. Initially, most of these programs either were aimed at women or focused on rape as primarily a women's issue, but newer programs treat rape as an issue for men. Groups like Men against Rape at Tulane University and Men Overcoming Violence (MOVE), which is active throughout New England, were organized to develop programs and initiatives that involve men in the effort to stop rape. Programs range from anger-management groups to male mentoring. For more information about some of these groups, you can visit the National Coalition against Violent Athletes via Web Extra! 10-6 or Mentors in Violence Prevention via Web Extra! 10-7.

Web Extra! 10-6 and 10-7 at crimtoday.com

Marital Rape

As previously mentioned, under common law there was no such crime as **spousal rape**. One of the most challenging aspects of rape law reform was the elimination of the marital exemption for rape. In 1978, one year after Oregon removed the marital exemption from its rape statutes, John Rideout became the first American husband indicted for raping his wife.[125] The Rideout case captured media attention not only because it was the first case of its kind, but also because of the sensational nature of the back-and-forth relationship between the Rideouts. A made-for-television movie of this case was even produced in 1980. In her analysis of rape cases that received enormous media attention, Lisa M. Cuklanz examined the Rideout case and argued that the central issue in this case was the credibility of the new law.[126] The first case that goes to court under any new law should be as strong as possible, but the Rideout case did not fit this scenario because "the preponderance of damaging personal information about Greta Rideout suggested a verdict of 'not guilty' for John even at the very beginning of the trial."[127] At the time of the Rideout case, evidence of the victim's sexual history was allowed. Such evidence damaged Greta Rideout's credibility as a rape victim and illustrated that "she was on trial as much as her husband." Cuklanz notes that in this case, the victim was tried first, "the law second, and the defendant third."[128] At the trial's conclusion, John Rideout was acquitted, and the Rideouts briefly reconciled before finally divorcing.

As Cuklanz notes in her analysis, the media coverage of the Rideout case did not include commentary about the nature of marital rape that could have helped the audience understand the interactional dynamics of the case. In the absence of such information, "character evidence underscored the validity of the traditional interpretation that posited confusion, manipulation, and personal gain as motives."[129] In research on judicial treatment of battered women, James Ptacek highlights the crucial role that such information can play in how criminal justice personnel understand the motivations and situations of both the victims and offenders who come before them in the courtroom. Judges that Ptacek interviewed in his research commented that an understanding of the dynamics of battering greatly assisted them in responding to victims because this understanding "challenged the prevailing 'commonsense' understandings embodied in both written law and judicial practice that dismiss woman battering as 'trivial' and enforce the barrier of 'family privacy' on behalf of violent men."[130]

In an article published in 1982, David Finkelhor and Kersti Yllo said that "the marriage license is a raping license."[131] The first research to systematically examine spousal rape was **Diana E. H. Russell**'s random sample of 930 women in San Francisco in 1990.[132] Approximately 14% of women who had ever been married reported at least one attempted or completed rape by their husbands. Based on an analysis of the interview data, Russell developed a four-part typology of men who rape their wives:[133]

- Husbands who prefer raping their wives to having consensual sex with them
- Husbands who are able to enjoy both rape and consensual sex with their wives or who are indifferent to which it is
- Husbands who would prefer consensual sex with their wives but are willing to rape them when their sexual advances are refused
- Husbands who might like to rape their wives but do not act out these desires

Thus rather than being one-dimensional, rape within marriage has several forms that reflect the various nuances of motivation on the part of offenders.

Rape in Prison

Correctional institutions provide a setting in which same-sex rape can be common. Charles Crawford, Professor of Sociology at Western Michigan University, refers to males who are sexually assaulted in prison as the "forgotten victims."[134] While the high prevalence of rape within prisons has been documented by prison researchers for some time, the victimization of prisoners does not raise the type of societal outrage that is reserved for crimes against "law-abiding" victims. Rape has been documented in both men's and women's prisons, but the patterns differ. Based on published research, rape within women's prisons primarily takes the form of male staff attacking female inmates, whereas in men's prisons, the assaults involve only inmates. While precise estimates of the extent of rape in prison are difficult to develop because of a lack of data, researchers who studied three prisons in Nebraska found that 22% of respondents reported to have been sexually assaulted.[135]

Theoretical Perspectives on Rape

Several theoretical perspectives have been offered to explain individual motivations for rape, why rape is more prevalent in particular contexts, and how certain cultural values may reinforce rape. Many of these perspectives attempt to explain how rape is patterned according to the context, the victim-offender relationship, and the motivations of the rapist.

Feminist Perspectives

There is no one feminist perspective on rape, but for the sake of simplicity we will discuss the common elements that run through the various feminist perspectives. As discussed in Chapter 9, feminists view gender as a social construct rather than as a biological given, and they regard as problematic the way in which gender is used to structure social relations and institutions. The patriarchal relations and structures within our society that contribute to the privileged status of men are inseparable from rape itself because rape serves as a social control mechanism, some feminists argue. Rape is viewed as an act of power or domination in which the "tool" used to subordinate is sexual. Rape is a crime of violence that is sexual in nature, but this aspect is considered to be secondary to the power dynamics that occur in rapes.[136]

Socialization patterns, cultural practices, structural arrangements, media images, norms surrounding sexuality, and women's status in society all combine to create a rape culture in which both men and women come to view male aggression as normal, even in sexual relations.[137] Within this culture, women are blamed for their own rape by virtue of the fact that males are naturally incapable of controlling their sexual desire. For feminists like **Catherine MacKinnon**[138] and **Andrea Dworkin**,[139] rape and sex are not easily distinguishable under patriarchy because the male dominance that characterizes patriarchy is inherent in both the act of rape and the social construction of sex. Who women are and what women choose for themselves become problematic in the perspectives of these feminists because heterosexuality is "compulsory" under patriarchy. The views of feminists like MacKinnon and Dworkin are often met with resistance by others and are misunderstood as "male bashing." MacKinnon and Dworkin do not focus on individual males as somehow being either "good" or "bad." Rather, they focus on the construction of gender and all that flows from it under patriarchy. Patriarchal relations construct male and female to be opposite poles of social existence and being, with *male* defined by dominance and *female* defined by that which is not male—and is generally inferior and subordinate. Under such constructions, MacKinnon and Dworkin ask, how can anyone ever freely choose any kinds of relationships, sexual or otherwise?

The work of Dworkin, MacKinnon, and others also stresses the existence of a rape culture that has the effect of equating sex with violence and objectifying women to the point that they lack an identity separate from that which is defined by men. Pornography is often thought to contribute to the manner in which women are objectified. In pornography, violence and sex are combined in a manner that makes the association normative. In an essay first published in 1974, Robin Morgan asserted that "pornography is the theory, and rape the practice."[140] Susan Brownmiller also discussed both pornography and prostitution as institutions that encourage and support social patterns and responses to rape.[141] While not everyone shares the same view of the role of pornography in supporting the inequality of women and in justifying violence against women, pornography is frequently associated with rape in the writings and research of many prominent feminists.

James W. Messerschmidt acknowledges the positive contributions of feminist thought but critiques these perspectives for their often one-dimensional view of masculinity.[142] Ngaire Naffine also shares Messerschmidt's positive evaluation of this body of work and says that "Dworkin is trying to shatter our complacency about everyday life for women, to get us to see the daily criminal violence and injustice done to women that has been rendered utterly ordinary and so invisible."[143] In his critique of feminist perspectives, Messerschmidt analyzes the various expressions of masculinity that are constructed within particular situations and as a response to particular social conditions. He says, "Middle-class, working-class, and lower-working class young men exhibit unique types of public masculinities that are situationally accomplished by drawing on different forms of youth crime."[144] Just as there is no one single strain of femininity, so too with masculinity. Messerschmidt also contends that the response of the state to violence against women is not monolithic. While there are limits to how the state will respond in behalf of women, the state is viable as a site for positive change in terms of women and feminist ideals. The emergence of rape crisis centers, changes in institutional protocol regarding rape victims, and other similar strategies illustrate that a state that is basically patriarchal in nature can be pushed to respond to women in ways that are positive and that increase women's autonomy. **Neil Websdale** echoes these sentiments in his research on rural woman battering by stating that "organizations set up by the state to further women's interests have played a significant role in improving the status of women."[145] Websdale maintains that some settings, such as those within rural areas, display stronger adherence to patriarchal relations than others; this distinction is crucial to understand that any setting contains many individuals and groups that do not use violence against women and that do not view rape as normative.

The Psychopathological Perspective

The psychopathological perspective on rape is based on two assumptions: (1) Rape is the "result of idiosyncratic mental disease," and (2) "it often includes an uncontrollable sexual impulse."[146] **Diana Scully** contends that, while acknowledging that rape is connected to issues like power and anger, the frequently cited work of **Nicholas Groth**,[147] contains elements of this psychopathological perspective.[148] Groth's

work was based on an analysis of 348 imprisoned convicted rapists. Approximately half of the rapists had attacked young and middle-aged women, while the other half had attacked children, elderly women, or other men. For rapists who had attacked women, 55% reported that the rape was committed to exert control over the women—a type of crime Groth labeled *power rape*. Power rapists, unlike anger rapists, did not purposefully set out to harm the victim. Power rapes are generally planned, Groth said, "although the actual assault may be opportunistic in origin."[149] In the attacks that Groth labeled *anger rapes,* which totaled about 40% of the sample, the men attacked their victims in anger, usually an attack that was impulsive and involved no prior planning on the part of the offender. These assaults were often quite brutal, and following the rape, the offender felt relief because he was able to relieve his anger. The remaining 5% Groth called *sadistic rapes;* these involved a combination of power and anger motives.[150] According to Groth, in sadistic rape, "aggression itself is eroticized," and these rapes frequently involve torture.[151] While not denying that these types of rapists exist, some researchers claim that Groth's model does not appear to successfully characterize the majority of men who rape, and yet this model has been applied as if that were the case.[152] However, Diana E. H. Russell did find elements of Groth's model to be useful in developing her own typology for men who rape within marriage.[153] Several of the factors that Groth identifies as important to understanding the motivation and pattern of rapes are found in other typologies of rapists.

An Integrated Theory of Rape

Larry Baron and **Murray A. Straus** offer what they term "an integrated theory of rape."[154] They combine elements from other theoretical explanations of rape into one model that argues that higher levels of gender inequality, social disorganization, and support for legitimate violence combine to produce higher rape rates at the state level.

"Support for legitimate violence" refers to norms and institutional arrangements that serve to justify the expression of violence in certain contexts as normative. The norms need not directly relate to a particular crime. As Baron and Straus note, there is a "cultural spillover" effect in which "cultural support for rape may not be limited to beliefs and attitudes that directly condone rape and other criminal violence."[155] Rather, when a community legitimizes the use of violence to resolve any kind of situation, this creates a type of spillover effect in which other types of interactions and dynamics come to be governed by similar norms and understandings. Thus one would expect to see high rates of rape associated with high rates of other violent crime.

Gender inequality is related to rates of rape because as women's status in society improves, rape is challenged as a mechanism of social control over women. This occurs as socialization patterns change and as women attain positions of power within society. The connection between gender inequality and rape is supported in cross-cultural and anthropological research.[156] "Social disorganization" refers to the inability of communities to sustain viable social institutions—institutions which serve as a buffer to all sorts of social ills, including criminal activity. Poverty alone is not enough to directly produce crime. However, in the absence of other factors that strengthen institutional structures within communities, poverty is linked to crime by virtue of its association with other factors.

In a test of their theory at the state level, Baron and Straus found support for the direct effect of gender inequality on rape rates. The higher the level of gender inequality—a combination of several measures relating to economic indicators—the higher a state's rape rate. They also examined the direct effect of pornography and found that higher rates of pornography, as measured by things like circulation rates for certain magazines, were associated with higher rates of rape within the state. High levels of social disorganization, measured by such things as residential mobility, percentage of female-headed households, and divorce rates, were also tied to increased rates of rape. While Baron and Straus found no direct support for the relationship between legitimate violence and rape, they argue that there is an indirect effect in which states with higher rates of gender inequality have higher rates of legitimate violence. This association between legitimate violence and gender inequality also has the effect of increasing rape rates such that in states with greater economic inequality the status of women is lower; and where the status of women is lower, the rate of rape tends to be higher.[157]

Evolutionary/Biological Perspectives

Within the evolutionary perspective, "humanity is a product of evolution in which both physical and social traits conducive to survival are selected and survive through a process of natural selection. Propagation is the key to survival of a trait, as a genetic predisposition can be passed on only through offspring."[158] Natural selection favors those traits that are most adaptive and over several generations, it is these traits that survive. An evolutionary perspective does not identify rape per se as an adaptation but rather focuses on certain motives and ends that are conducive to rape. The environment is also thought to play a role because "genes cannot make traits without environmental causes acting in concert."[159] According to **Randy Thornhill** and **Craig T. Palmer**, "selection favored different traits in females and males, especially when the traits were directly related to mating. Although some of these differences could have arisen from what Darwin called natural selection, most of them are now believed to have evolved through sexual selection."[160] *Sexual selection* refers to the observation that some traits appear to survive, not because they are related to survival, but because they further the attainment of mates or defense against competition over mates. This is said to apply primarily to males because "male fitness is limited by access to the opposite sex much more directly than is female fitness, with the result that females compete for mates much less than do males."[161] The specialized jargon and knowledge that in-

forms evolutionary perspectives makes it difficult to understand how they apply to social behaviors like rape, and these perspectives have been severely criticized for justifying rape as "natural." Proponents of the usefulness of evolutionary perspectives on rape contend that evolutionary perspectives can explain why rape is so prevalent and why it takes the forms that it does, and they argue that "biology provides understanding, not justification, of human behavior."[162] The conceptualization of rape as sex is not meant to carry only negative connotations because "the view that rape is always motivated at least in part by sexual desire and that sexual desire may be sufficient motivation to produce rape behavior in some situations implies nothing about what people should do. Also, the view that differences in sexual desire between males and females are evolved and biological implies nothing about the ease or difficulty with which these differences can be changed."[163] Evolutionary perspectives contend that the feminist position on rape that equates it primarily with expressions of violence diminishes the fact that there is a biologically based sexual motivation and that ignoring this eliminates one avenue by which rape may be understood and prevented. Rather than being counter to the agenda of feminists, evolutionary psychologists offer their perspective as another avenue through which rape can be approached, understood, and thereby prevented.

Typologies of Rapists

Several researchers have attempted to develop typologies of rapists. Nicholas Groth's work represents one of the first systematic attempts to do this based on empirical evidence, which he gathered in his capacity as a prison psychologist. **Robert R. Hazelwood** and **Ann Burgess** developed a four-part typology of rapists based on the motivation of the offender.[164] Like Groth's, their typology revolves around the themes of power, anger, and sadism. The four types of rapists they identified are power-assertive, power-reassurance, anger-retaliatory, and anger-excitation rapists. *Power-assertive rapists* plan their crimes and use a great deal of force to subdue the victim. This type of rapist acts out of a hypermasculinity in which the rapist is "simply exercising his prerogative as a male to commit rape."[165] These rapists often employ a type of seduction to subdue their victims initially, and they generally attack their victims several times during the same incident. *Power-reassurance rapists,* the most common type among rapists who attack strangers, generally act out of a sense of social and sexual inadequacy. Robert Hazelwood contends that these are the rapists who are referred to in popular jargon as the "gentleman rapists." They select their victims in advance through stalking and may even attempt to contact the victim after the rape. These rapists generally do not set out to consciously degrade their victims, and they generally target victims of their own age. *Anger-retaliatory rapists* are clearly motivated by anger, and rape becomes the means by which the anger is expressed. These rapists may attack either the actual source of their anger or a representative. Hazelwood contends that this type of rapist "uses the *blitz approach,* subduing the victim with the immediate application of direct and physical force, thereby denying her any opportunity to defend herself."[166] *Anger-excitation rapists* are "sexually stimulated and/or gratified by the victim's response to the infliction of physical and emotional pain."[167] These are generally the rapists whose crimes involve the most planning and the most careful execution, even though the victim selected is generally a stranger. These rapists are "most likely to record activities with the victim," and the nature of the rape is definitely intended to "create pain, humiliation, and degradation for the victim."[168]

Based on interviews with 61 serial rapists, Dennis J. Stevens offers a typology of his own based on motivations. At the time of the interview, the rapists were all incarcerated in a South Carolina maximum-security prison for the crime of rape. Using Nicholas Groth's "Protocol for the Clinical Assessment of the Offender's Sexual Behaviors" to structure the interview, Stevens explored the areas of premeditation, victim selection, style of attack, degree of violence associated with the rape, accompanying fantasies, role of aggression, and other topics. One of the major findings that emerged from Stevens's research was the role of lust as a primary motive among a large proportion of the rapists (42%). While acknowledging that "lust is not a new idea concerning predatory rape,"[169] Stevens believes it to be a primary rather than a secondary motive for rapists. With those Stevens identified as *lust rapists,* a minimal amount of force accompanied the rape. These men selected victims based on the most available target. *Righteous rape* motives formed the primary element for 15% of the rapists. This group viewed their victims as responsible for the attack because these offenders believed that in some "silent deal" the "sex" had already been negotiated and consented to by the victim. Stevens contends that these men saw themselves as "not guilty by reason of circumstance," and they spent a great deal of energy justifying the rape. Like the lust rapists, they "characterized sexual intimacy as their primary objective."[170] *Peer rape* motives, present in 3% of the rapists, took the form of holding friendship responsible for the rape. The rapists claimed, "I had no choice, I ran with bad company."[171] *Control and anger rapes* were committed by 6% of the rapists. These cases included more "violence than necessary to accomplish rape," and the rape itself was described by the rapists as "secondary to the violence powered by their anger."[172] *Supremacy rape* motives were held by 13% of rapists and were characterized by more violence than necessary to subdue the victim during all stages of the attack. Stevens stated that with these rapists, sexual contact was insignificant compared to the punishment given to the victim during and after the attack. *Fantasy rape* motives, primary among 16% of the serial rapists, were characterized by individuals "trying to regain some imaginary goal that had been part of their past."[173] The sex act involved in the rape was less important to these men than the ideas in their heads—ideas that were sometimes quite violent in nature. Stevens classified the motives of 3% of the rapists he inter-

viewed as unclear.[174] A constant theme that emerged throughout Stevens's interviews with the rapists was that for most of them, the amount of force that accompanied the rape was just enough to accomplish the victim's submission. In cases in which extreme violence accompanied all stages of the rape, the violence would have been present regardless of the level of victim resistance. Therefore, one of the conclusions made by Stevens is that advocating the idea that women should not resist their attackers is ill-advised.

Another way to approach a typology of men who rape is represented in the work of Diana Scully, a professor at Virginia Commonwealth University.[175] Scully's research involved intensive interviews with 114 convicted rapists in seven prisons, all of whom volunteered to be interviewed. Scully rejects the psychopathological perspective on rape and instead employs a feminist sociocultural perspective premised on several assumptions. First, rape is "socially learned behavior," involving "not only behavioral techniques, but also a host of values and beliefs, like rape myths, that are compatible with sexual aggression against women."[176] This premise is based on the assumption that both positive and negative forms of social behavior are learned "socially through direct association with others as well as indirectly through cultural context."[177] Second, Scully does not view rape as a reflection of pathology but as a reflection of a continuum of normality in which it is important to understand "how sexual violence is made possible in a society" and "what men who rape gain from their sexually violent behavior."[178] Scully thus approached these interviews with convicted rapists from the feminist perspective of wanting to understand the explanations given by the rapists and also their sociocultural beliefs about women and sexual violence.

Scully identified several patterns to the rationalizations used by men who rape, and she organized these according to two broad types of rapists: admitters and deniers. *Admitters,* the largest category of rapists, included those men who acknowledged that their offense constituted a rape and who provided information that largely corresponded to official records. Even though acknowledging their offense as a rape, admitters purposefully downplayed the amount of force used or other key facts about their offense. Scully uses as an example a rapist who appeared to be quite traumatized during the interview as he discussed his offense but who also failed to mention that the 70-year-old woman he had raped was his grandmother. *Deniers* contended that the sexual relations with their victims was consensual and that the rape offense for which they had been convicted was erroneous. With this group, there were more obvious discrepancies between the information they provided and the official records than with the group of admitters. Several of those whom Scully designated as deniers had in fact used weapons in their offense yet still believed that the sexual relations did not involve force or coercion.

In the interviews, Scully explored how these two groups could operate from an understanding of reality that justified their behavior and tended to normalize it, as well as what they gained from such behavior. While some of the rapists in the admitter group relied on rape myth ideology, this was a more prevalent pattern among the deniers. The rape myths' definition of a very narrow group of individuals as legitimate rape victims was a common theme in the interviews given by these rapists. While variations existed, the majority of rapists in both groups expressed little guilt or empathy for their victims. Scully states, "Sexually violent men identify with traditional images of masculinity and male gender role privilege; they believe very strongly in rape stereotypes, and for them, being male carries the right to discipline and punish women."[179] While men who rape may not all operate from the same level of adherence to definitions of masculinity, they all benefit by the societal assignment of such characteristics as power, force, and the sexual double standard implicit in such definitions. As Scully states, "Hierarchical gender relations and the corresponding values that devalue women and diminish them to exploitable objects or property are the factors that render feeling rules inoperative and empower men to rape."[180] When the status of women in our society, both economically and socially, is considered along with cultural depictions of women found in everything from seemingly benign advertisements to more shocking pornography, women emerge as a group that can in some ways still be victimized with relative impunity. In a society that equates sex and violence and where gender is socially constructed as a hierarchy of difference, we send messages that provide justifications for rape and sexual coercion. The strength of these messages does not require that all men be rapists; it is enough that the potential for rape is established as well as the ideology that excuses the violence of those who do rape.

ROBBERY

Robbery is classified as a violent crime because it involves the threat or use of force. It is also a property crime in that the express purpose of robbery is to take the property of another.[181] Robberies can occur in different locations and are quite often categorized in this manner by both law enforcement agencies and social science researchers. Robberies that occur on the highway or street are often referred to as "muggings." Muggings and robberies that occur in residences are types of **personal robbery.** While residential robberies are most certainly deterred by the presence of security precautions, this effect depends on the type of neighborhood in which the residence is located. Terance D. Miethe and David McDowall found that the security precautions that are effective in neighborhoods characterized by a viable social control structure are ineffective in socially disorganized neighborhoods.[182] Such security precautions as not leaving the home unoccupied are not enough in socially disorganized neighborhoods to compensate for the strong effect of neighborhood context on increasing the likelihood of robbery. The level of precaution at the individual level must be greater if the threat at the neighborhood level is significant. Our homes and persons do not exist as potential targets to motivated offenders in a vacuum; they take this form based as much on their individual vulnerability as on their neighborhood context.

Robberies that occur in commercial settings, such as convenience stores, gas stations, and banks, are termed **institutional robbery.**[183] Several research studies have found that institutional robberies may be prevented through environmental and policy changes. As Scott A. Hendricks and his colleagues found in a study of convenience store robberies, "The robber chooses a target based on various situational crime prevention factors."[184] These factors include staffing, hours of operation, cash-handling policy, and characteristics of the surrounding neighborhood. For example, the researchers found that "the odds of convenience store robbery were twice as high for older neighborhoods than newer neighborhoods."[185] Many of the precautions that lower the risk of robbery, are costly, however, and not all businesses can afford them. As Richard T. Wright and Scott H. Decker note, "This puts businesses located in high-crime neighborhoods in a no-win situation because their clientele frequently are too poor to bear increased prices to support crime prevention measures."[186] Additionally, if the business fails as a result of robberies, the community loses again because the exodus of businesses that are forced to relocate makes the community less viable. Most of the robbers interviewed by Wright and Decker in their ethnographic study of robbers who selected commercial targets generally selected liquor stores, taverns, and pawnshops because of the large amount of cash available. They also targeted businesses with low levels of customer activity because they viewed customers as an unpredictable risk factor. The robbers interviewed as part of Floyd Feeney's research in California during the 1970s reported very little planning overall, but those who engaged in commercial robbery were much more likely to report planning than those who engaged in personal robberies (60% compared to 30%).[187]

The Lethal Potential of Robbery

Robbery offenses carry the threat of injury for the victim—and too often lethal injury. Injuries of at least a minor nature were found among one in every three robbery victims based on an analysis using the National Incident Based Reporting System.[188] Overall, robbery is the context in which 8% of all homicides occur. In 1999, approximately 17% of all homicides occurred during the commission of another felony. Among these cases, robbery was the most likely felony to result in homicide, accounting for almost one-half (47%) of all felony murders.[189] The weapon most often used in robbery homicides is a firearm, accounting for 73% of all cases; the type of firearm used in the vast majority of cases (85%) is a handgun.[190]

Criminal Careers of Robbers

Are robbers specialists or generalists? This distinction refers to whether individuals who engage in robbery specialize in only this crime or whether they vary the types of crimes they commit. The majority of robbery offenders are generalists who have a fairly lengthy but varied criminal career.[191] Research on a sample of inmates in California prisons found that less than 10% of convicted robbers could be labeled specialists who engaged solely in robbery to the exclusion of other offenses.[192] In a survey of inmates sponsored by Rand Corporation, approximately 18% of offenders were primarily involved in only one type of offense.[193] James Q. Wilson and Allan Abrahamse used data from a Rand survey of inmates in 1978 to explore the type of monetary returns offenders earned from their crimes.[194] For the purposes of this analysis, Wilson and Abrahamse decided to group offenders according to offense type—a task that proved problematic because specialization among offenders was not the norm. The typologies developed by these researchers had to be made on the basis of the percentage of certain offenses engaged in by offenders. Diversity in offense type and selection appears to be the norm for the vast majority of offenders, based on both ethnographic and survey data.

Robbery and Public Transportation

One setting in which crime prevention strategies may be quite effective is public transportation. According to Martha J. Smith and Ronald V. Clarke, "Robbery on mass transit is a rare event, even in systems with relatively high numbers of incidents such as New York City."[195] Viewing the prevalence of robbery on public transportation as reflecting a "lack of supervision," Smith and Clarke contend that the majority of these robberies follow one of three scenarios. First, offenders will purposefully select their victims from among passengers in isolated areas of large subway stations, especially when the station is not crowded. Security measures, such as using closed-circuit television monitoring and closing off unused parts of the station, may serve to effectively deter these type of offenders.[196] Second, offenders will select their victims outside the station at particular locales and times that are relatively isolated. Finally, offenders will often "lie in wait" for passengers leaving public transportation.[197] Prevention strategies to deter these types of robberies include a variety of surveillance techniques. In addition to targeting public transportation customers, robbers also target the staff in order to steal the fare money. Smith and Clarke state that policies such as exact fare collection and other similar changes "led to a dramatic fall in the number of bus robberies in New York City."[198]

According to Smith and Clarke, "Transit workers with perhaps the greatest risk of robbery are taxicab drivers, who carry cash, travel by themselves around cities with strangers, and do not choose their destinations."[199] Derek Cornish offers several strategies that taxicab drivers can use to prevent robberies.[200] These tactics range from having a weapon to screening passengers for potential threats. While "drivers can use informal passenger screen practices such as refusing to pick up fares at certain locations," such screening practices "can discriminate against those who live in poorer ar-

eas or are from certain racial or age groups, making it difficult for them to use the service."[201] In fact, these very practices have recently been the subject of debate because of claims of discrimination.

Other strategies, such as the installation of protection partitions between the driver and passenger, can be quite effective in deterring crime. In New York City, such partitions are "required on all yellow cabs and livery cars operated by more than one driver, but individual drivers who own their cars say the partitions are too expensive."[202] In response to the high number of killings of cab drivers in robbery incidents, New York City Mayor Rudolph Guiliani created a $5 million grant program to assist livery cab companies with the cost of installing the protective partitions. A pilot program begun in August 1999 installed digital surveillance cameras in cabs.[203] Under the New York City Police Department's special Taxi-Livery Task Force, created in 1992, police in unmarked cars stop taxis in particular neighborhoods, often according to some strategy, such as every fifth taxi. A similar strategy was also adopted in Boston, again as a response to the substantial number of violent crimes, especially robberies, experienced by cab drivers. While the Boston statute withstood court review, the New York Court of Appeals ruled in December 1999 that the policy of the police department "gave officers too much discretion to stop taxis carrying passengers when they had no reason to suspect any crime was afoot."[204] The U.S. Supreme Court was asked to review both rulings and declined, allowing the rulings of the lower courts to stand.

Policies like those in Boston and New York clearly illustrate the tension involved in policing a democratic society; measures that might prevent certain forms of crime must be weighed against the potential violation of individual liberties. This issue becomes even more complex when a high risk of victimization is experienced by members of a particular occupational group who must function within criminogenic settings or who must interact frequently with strangers.

The Motivation of Robbers

Research tends to support the idea that most robberies, of both people and places, involve very little planning on the part of the offender. Floyd Feeney's research in California during the early 1970s found little evidence that the majority of bank robbers had even been in the bank before the robbery.[205] Most of the robbers Feeney studied did very little planning, no matter what the target, and the planning that did occur was minor and "generally took place the same day as the robbery and frequently within a few hours of it."[206] The motivation and decision making of street robbers have recently been evaluated in a series of research studies conducted by Bruce A. Jacobs, Richard Wright, and others at the University of Missouri at St. Louis. We will examine several of the most important pieces of this large qualitative study involving 86 currently active robbers in St. Louis. To be considered an active robber for the purpose of the research study, "the individual had committed a robbery in the recent past, defined him- or herself as currently active, and was regarded as active by other offenders."[207] Jacobs and Wright found that the decision to offend, like other decisions, occurs as part of ongoing social action that is "mediated by prevailing situations and subcultural conditions."[208] "Fast cash" was the direct need that robbery satisfied, but this need can only be properly understood against the backdrop of street culture. Jacobs and Wright hypothesized that street culture was the intervening force that connected background factors (such as low self-esteem, deviant peer relations, and weak social bonds) to the motivation to offend. They found that the majority of robbers gave little thought to planning robberies until they found themselves needing money. For less than half of the robbers, the financial need was for basic necessities; mostly it was connected to a fairly hedonistic lifestyle. The daily activity of most street robbers was characterized as a "quest for excitement and sensory stimulation" with a "general lack of social stability" in terms of residence or ties to conventional activities or institutions.[209]

Jacobs and Wright considered three alternatives that these individuals could have employed for money: (1) perform legitimate work, (2) borrowing, and (3) committing other crimes. Legitimate employment was not a viable option for these individuals for several reasons. Most of the robbers

Some robbers seem to give little thought to planning their crimes until they need "fast cash." Might this person be an attractive target for such robbers? *Ed Bailey, AP/WideWorld Photos*

had neither the skills nor the education to obtain decent wage jobs, and even if they did have such resources, their perceived need for cash was too immediate for legitimate work to satisfy. Additionally, legitimate work was viewed as an impediment to their "every night is a Saturday night" lifestyle. Borrowing money was not a viable route because many had no one to turn to for a loan, and for those who did, borrowing was not part of the self-sufficient code of the streets. Robbery was preferable to other crimes because it was perceived to be safer than crimes like burglary and quicker than other crimes requiring the translation of stolen goods into cash. Other research has found that some robberies do in fact begin as another crime, such as burglary, and become robberies more by accident than design.[210] Jacobs and Wright conclude that the economic motivation behind robbery should not be interpreted as "genuine financial hardship," but rather as a constant, ongoing crisis situation experienced as a result of the logic of the street context of robbers' daily lives.[211] For the individuals that Jacobs and Wright interviewed, "being a street robber . . . is a way of behaving, a way of thinking, an approach to life."[212] Such individuals are unlikely to be easily deterred by legal sanctions, and the rationality of their decision making is unlikely to be adequately explained outside the context of street culture participation.

Drug Robberies

In their ethnographic research on armed robbers, Richard T. Wright and Scott H. Decker found that "six out of every ten offenders who specialized in street robbery—forty-three of seventy-three—said that they usually preyed on individuals who themselves were involved in lawbreaking."[213] These are generally the cases that are not reflected in official statistics on crime because the victims do not report their victimization to the police. Due to their involvement in illegal behavior, these individuals can be victimized with relative impunity. Because an overriding motivation behind the robberies for many of the offenders in Wright and Decker's research was to get high, it follows that drug dealers would be an obvious target. Among offenders who stated that they selected victims involved in crime, the vast majority targeted drug dealers, though rarely major drug dealers. According to Wright and Decker, "Almost all of these offenders targeted young, street-level dealers who sold quantities of crack cocaine directly to consumers."[214] According to one robber, the attraction of robbing drug dealers was two-fold because drug dealers carry drugs as well as cash: "It satisfies two things for me; my thirst for drugs and the financial aspect."[215] The neighborhoods in which these robbers lived and conducted their routine activities were generally characterized by an abundance of drug dealers, which increased their suitability as targets. Because they were also unlikely to report their victimization to the police, drug customers were also perceived as ideal targets. Wright and Decker further state that within the neighborhoods that these offenders operate, "an ability to mind one's own business is regarded as a crucial survival

A drug dealer shows his wares. Based on research with active robbers, Richard Wright and Scott Decker found that some armed robbers purposefully target drug dealers for robbery. Why would such individuals make good targets? *Hugh Patrick Brown, Corbis/Sygma*

skill."[216] Thus, "from the offenders' perspective, this made such settings ideal for stickups; bystanders are disinclined to get involved and witnesses are reluctant to make a police report."[217] Additionally, the offenders were well aware that the police did not take drug robberies seriously. However, these factors do not consider the one element that makes robbery of drug dealers very risky: "There always is a possibility of violent retaliation" by the drug dealer.[218]

Further analysis of the ethnographic research on the armed robbers in St. Louis by Bruce A. Jacobs, Volkan Topalli, and Richard Wright explored the issue of retaliation by asking, "Why should offenders elect to reduce their chances of getting arrested at the cost of increasing their odds of being killed?"[219] To answer this, the researchers looked at the findings from 25 in-depth interviews with active drug robbers, which were conducted as part of the larger study of robbers in St. Louis. The researchers conceptualized retaliation as an informal sanction "capable of deterrence in its own right; to be sure, it may be the sole sanction offenders face."[220] Drug dealers who are victimized are cut off from one avenue of redress, the formal sanctions provided by police, and hence they "have a strong incentive to retaliate."[221]

The drug robbers interviewed in the St. Louis study were completely aware of the risk involved in targeting drug dealers. They sought to minimize this risk by selecting one of three strategies: intimidation, anonymity maintenance, and hypervigilance. As a general guideline, drug robbers primarily targeted dealers "whose retributive potential was weak."[222] These targets were street corner dealers who were fairly inexperienced, sold drugs in small quantities, and held very little if any status in the organized drug trade. Additionally, the drug robbers used "verbal and physical tactics" in their encounters with these dealers that were purposefully designed to intimidate the dealer to the point that the thought of retaliation was almost eliminated. One offender claimed that he approached drug dealers in a way that left no doubt that "I'm gonna retaliate first."[223] In fact, some of the offenders stated that "some street corner dealer simply dismissed robberies as an occupational hazard and accepted their losses with equanimity."[224] The second strategy used by robbers who targeted drug dealers, anonymity maintenance, involved robbing only those dealers with whom they were totally unfamiliar. In this way, "retaliation becomes moot" because the victim does not know the robber.[225] "Hypervigilance," the third strategy, refers to how offenders consciously "devoted a significant portion of their day-to-day cognitive resources to minimizing the prospect of postoffense victim contact."[226] For offenders engaged in a substantial volume of robberies, the chances of running into a victim were increased, even if the victim was initially unknown to them. Offenders avoided the sites of previous robberies until they could be fairly sure that the threat of recognition or retaliation had subsided. The nomadic lifestyle of the drug robbers, involving movement from place to place, allowed them to easily avoid such places.

Even so, the street lifestyle was "an encapsulated social world" and the "streets enmesh participation in an expansive web of relations."[227] To a large extent, circumstances and situations bring offenders and victims together in unexpected ways, such that "the more members of a network there are, and the denser that network is, the more likely run-ins become. Bus stops, mini-malls, grocery stores, bars, theaters, and fast-food restaurants emerge as contexts fraught with potential risk."[228] These features of the environment not only hinder the offender's ability to manage the risk of retaliation, but also increase the potential for violence within the entire community itself, based on the extent of drug robberies. As Jacobs and his colleagues conclude, this community effect represents the "contagion-like processes through which violence is contracted and contained,"[229] and if "street justice" is stronger than the formal justice represented by law enforcement, the community becomes increasingly unstable. "The more entrenched informal justice becomes, and the more likely formal authorities will 'look the other way,'"[230] the more the community becomes disorganized and violence spreads beyond robbers and their victims. This becomes one set of dynamics that creates and sustains the "tangled web of violence we see in so many high-crime urban locales across the country."[231]

The Gendered Nature of Robbery

According to **Jody Miller**, "with the exception of forcible rape, robbery is perhaps the most gender differentiated serious crime in the United States."[232] Women represent robbery offenders in approximately 10 percent of all incidents.[233]

James W. Messerschmidt contends that the "robbery setting provides the ideal opportunity to construct an 'essential' toughness and 'maleness'. . . . Within the social context that ghetto and barrio boys find themselves, then, robbery is a rational practice for 'doing gender' and for getting money."[234]

Miller's research goal was to assess the extent to which gender organizes robbery offending. To accomplish this, she analyzed a subset of the interviews with active robbers from the research data used by Jacobs and Wright. The sample that Miller used consisted of 37 robbers, 14 of whom were women and 23 of whom were men. The two groups were matched on the characteristics of current age and age at first robbery. In her examination of motivations for robbery, Miller found that economic incentives were the primary motivation among both men and women. There were, however, significant differences in the way in which men and women carried out street robberies. Men exhibited a fairly uniform pattern. Their robberies were characterized by "using physical violence and/or a gun placed on or at close proximity to the victim in a confrontational manner."[235] The presence of a gun was almost a constant in robberies conducted by men. While perceiving women to be easier targets, male robbers tended to rob other men rather than women because of another perception, that men tended to carry more money. The majority of the males targeted as victims were those involved in "street life."

Female robbers, on the other hand, did not exhibit one clear style but instead tended to fall into one of three patterns. The robbery of other women in a "physically confrontational manner" was the most prevalent way in which female robbers worked, but also present were the strategies of using their sexuality to attract male victims and acting as accomplices to male robbers in offenses against other men.[236] Except when robbing men, female robbers as a general rule did not use guns. Miller concludes that, rather than reflecting different motivations, the different strategies for robbery selected by men and women "reflect practical choices made in the context of a gender-stratified environment—one in which, on the whole, men are perceived as strong and women are perceived as weak."[237] While similar cultural and structural forces can drive the offending of men and women in the same way, gender continues to exert an influence on shaping the nature of these interactions in robbery incidents. Learn more about the crime of robbery at Web Extra! 10-8.

Web Extra! 10-8 at crimtoday.com

ASSAULT

Assault is the "prototype of violent crime."[238] Not only is assault the most common violent crime, but it is also the starting point for more serious incidents of interpersonal violence. While there is a tremendous legal difference between assault and homicide, James Garbarino states that this legal difference has "very limited psychological significance" in that many assaults represent "potentially lethal violence." It is important to understand, he says, that assaults can kill, "even if they don't actually end a human life."[239] Garbarino supports his point by stating that social scientists have a difficult time predicting which person will end up taking a life, and thus it is "more practical to identify [those] who are at greatest risk for engaging in potentially lethal violence."[240]

The profile of a typical offender in aggravated assault mirrors that of homicide, with disproportionate involvement of males, African-Americans, 15- to 34-year-olds, those of lower socioeconomic status, those with prior arrest records, and offenders demonstrating little evidence of offense specialization.[241] Also consistent with most homicides, aggravated assaults are "spontaneous, triggered by a trivial altercation or argument that quickly escalates in the heat of passion."[242]

Based on statistics from the National Crime Victimization Survey (NCVS), the overall decline in the crime rate between 1993 and 1999 is primarily due to decreases in the rate of simple assault. In 1999, victims reported 6,164,000 victimizations, a rate of 27.4 per 1,000 residents age 12 or older. The majority of assaults reported by victims are simple rather than aggravated assault. The definition of *aggravated assault* used by the NCVS is "attack or attempted attack with a weapon, regardless of whether or not an injury occurred and attack without a weapon when serious injury results."[243] Aggravated assaults are detailed according to those involving injury and those without injury. The victims and offenders in aggravated assault are for the most part equally likely to be strangers or nonstrangers to each other. When you look at the gender of the victim, a pattern emerges. A slight majority of male victims are assaulted by a stranger, whereas slightly more than one-third (39%) of female victims are assaulted by a stranger in aggravated assaults. Simple assaults, by contrast, are more likely in general to involve nonstrangers (58%). Almost one-half (47%) of male victims are assaulted by nonstrangers, whereas 71% of female victims are assaulted by nonstrangers in these cases. Whether it is an aggravated or simple assault, the largest category of nonstranger offenders of female victims is represented by friends and acquaintances, followed by intimate partners. Weapons are present in less than one-fourth (23%) of all assaults, and when a weapon is present, it is most likely to be something other than a gun or a knife.[244]

Stranger Assault

The possibility of stranger violence elicits a great deal of fear and concern among most members of the population. Based on research using victimization data in both the United States and Great Britain, "the probability of suffering a serious personal crime by strangers is very low,"[245] with this likelihood varying by demographic characteristics like gender, age, marital status, and lifestyle. For example, individuals who have an active social life away from home and in the evening are far more likely to be victimized by strangers, but this effect depends very much on the community context in which the individuals engage in their leisure pursuits.

Marc Riedel and Roger K. Przybylski propose that stranger violence consists of two primary types of stranger relationships.[246] One type of violence between strangers results from the "exploitation of a setting" as is often the case in robberies in which the offenders case the store in advance.[247] Some encounters between strangers, however, are less calculated, and violence can "emerge from more spontaneous encounters between strangers in routine settings such as bars or sporting events."[248] Generally, this is the situation of the typical assault, where something as benign as an offensive remark escalates into violence. Because "confrontational stranger violence occurs in [certain types of] public settings," there is a strong likelihood that assault victims and offenders will be about the same age. Settings in which assaults frequently occur, such as bars, are generally restricted on the basis of age, and they also "acquire local reputations that attract a clientele that is usually homogeneous in age."[249] Thus, compared to assaults within the family, stranger assaults are more likely to involve victims and offenders of similar ages.

Assault within Families

As the statistics from several sources reveal, the majority of assaults involve victims and offenders who are known to each other, quite often in a familial or intimate relationship. In the sections that follow, the familial context of assault is examined, with a special emphasis on how key variables like weapons, alcohol, and other factors help us understand the patterns of these crimes.

Invading the Castle

The current societal awareness of issues surrounding violence among family members did not arise primarily from within criminology. While the statistics on homicide have long supported the violent potential of families, criminologists were not the pioneers in studies centered on the violent aspects of our society's most basic institution. Richard J. Gelles, a leading family-violence researcher, correctly asserted in the 1970s that violence within the family only concerned criminologists when someone was killed.[250] Criminology as a discipline began to give more attention to violent behavior within the family just as societal attention turned to viewing the halo of privacy that has long surrounded the family with a bit more scrutiny. Empirical research concerning the phenomenon of family violence encounters several problems due to the nature of the issue itself. The family as a social institution is intensely private. The discussion of physical, emotional, and sexual violence among family members violates this privacy. These types of abuse also represent extremely sensitive parts of a person's experience which individuals may be reluctant to discuss. The very terrain of family violence invades the "image of the castle [which] implies freedom from interference from outsiders."[251] This image was corroborated in the late 1970s

when Michael Hindelang conducted research on crime-reporting behavior. Two of the most common reasons for not reporting crimes to the police were that it was a "private matter" and that there might be reprisal from the offender. Current research shows that such rationales supporting nonreporting continue to characterize incidents involving violence among family members.[252]

Early Studies of Family Violence

The initial research on violence within the family came from official records and small clinical studies. Official records consistently revealed that women were more likely than men to become victims of domestic violence. Based on an examination of emergency room victims in the late 1970s, Evan Stark and colleagues found that approximately 25% of all women who had been injured had been the victim of a spousal attack.[253] Murray Straus and colleagues at the University of New Hampshire were the first to develop a survey methodology for the study of family violence nationally. They conducted the first National Survey on Family Violence (NSFV) in 1975 with a representative sample of 2,146 families. The second NSFV was conducted in 1985 with a sample of 4,032 households.[254] In both surveys, the key tool developed for measuring family violence was the Conflict Tactics Scale. This scale contains a series of 18 items that range from calm discussion to the use of a potentially lethal weapon. The questions using this measure are presented in the context of disagreements with family members and how such disagreements are resolved. The questions initially ask about positive techniques, such as calmly discussing an issue, and gradually proceed to more coercive tactics, such as using a knife on a family member. The sequence in which questions are asked serves to legitimate response. The questions begin with parent-child relationships, where the use of physical force, such as spanking, is widely viewed as legitimate, and then proceeds to husband-wife relationships. By the time respondents reach the questions concerning spousal behavior, Strauss reasoned that familiarity with the questions would diminish the respondent's uneasiness about answering whether he or she had ever hit a spouse.[255] The rate of violence between spouses in the 1985 National Survey on Family Violence was 161 per 1,000 couples.[256] While this rate was lower than that reported in 1975, it still remained higher than estimates produced from other studies not specifically directed at family violence, such as the National Crime Victimization Survey.

Current Survey Information on Family Violence

In the years since survey research was first used to estimate violence against family members, other surveys have emerged to assess this phenomenon, and existing data sources have been improved to better measure family violence. The FBI has started to prepare specialized reports based on available National Incident Based Reporting System

(NIBRS) data. As explained in Chapter 2, NIBRS is the official reporting system that will replace the FBI's Uniform Crime Reports (UCR) Program. The old UCR Program did not include information on victims and offenders for offenses other than homicide, so there was no way in which to analyze nonlethal criminal behavior within the family. NIBRS will provide such information and will allow for more specialized data analysis. Fourteen states submitted NIBRS data during 1998, and the FBI compiled a special report on these data based on an analysis of family incidents. Using a measure of violent crime that includes murder, rape, robbery, and assault, NIBRS data for 1998 reveal that 27% of violent crimes involve victims and offenders who are related. Among all offenses involving family members that came to the attention of the police, the overwhelming majority (94%) were assaults, a percentage that is "4 points higher than the frequency of assault offenses in overall crimes of violence."[257] Thus while assault is the most frequently occurring violent crime both among the general population and within the family, the percentage is even higher within the family. While aggravated assault accounted for 18% of all violent offenses, the percentage of all family violence offenses involving aggravated assaults is slightly smaller at 15%.[258]

Compared to aggravated assaults generally, firearms are less likely to be used within the family, where fists, hands, and knives are more common. A slight majority of aggravated assault offenses involve some type of injury both in the general population (57.5%) and within the family (60.8%). Women are more likely to be the victims of both aggravated assaults and simple assaults within the family than in the general population (60% versus 41% and 72% versus 60%, respectively).[259] Learn more about family violence and the crimes it entails via Web Extra! 10-9.

Web Extra! 10-9 at crimtoday.com

Intimate-Partner Assault

Intimate-partner assault is one of several terms used to characterize assaultive behavior that takes place between individuals involved in an intimate relationship. Several researchers have noted that terms like *spouse assault* are inappropriate because they give the misleading impression that male and female spouses are equally likely to be victims.[260] Based on research using various data sources, the overwhelming majority of victims of marital violence within heterosexual relationships are women. This empirical reality does not deny that men can be the victims of violence at the hands of their wives; it merely states that based on official records, self-reports, hospital emergency room records, and small clinical samples, it is women who emerge as victims. It is in line with this empirical reality that Neil Websdale entitles his ethnographic exploration of violence in rural areas of Kentucky *Rural Woman Battering and the Justice System*.[261] However, the terms *woman battering* and *wife assault* are biased in terms of heterosexual relationships, and hence some researchers now use the term *intimate-partner assault* because it avoids this bias. We will use this term in our discussion because it now frequently appears in the literature on assault among intimates and because it reflects the changing nature of most sexual assault laws and mandatory arrest laws, which are both gender-neutral and moving away from the legal relationship as the criterion that defines an intimate relationship.

For many individuals, the notion of assault among intimate partners gives rise to the response, "If I was hit, I would leave." This type of response places the burden on the victim to justify why she stayed and takes the burden off of the offending behavior of her partner. More crucially, this type of response ignores the reality that most women do leave violent relationships, a behavior that may trigger a particularly violent response by the male partner, labeled **separation assault** by Martha R. Mahoney.[262] Separation assault clearly illustrates what feminists like Liz Kelly mean when they state that "the use of explicit force/violence is in fact a response to the failure of, or resistance to, other forms of control."[263] A woman who attempts to leave a violent relationship is seen as violating the right of her husband to control her, and even if she does manage to leave, many times the husband will follow her and attempt to bring her back. Neil Websdale offers a dramatic example of separation assault from the ethnographic research that he conducted in the early nineties. Glenda Greer worked as a secretary in a local elementary school in Waynesburg, Kentucky, for 11 years. She was a respected member of the community and had come to have an important place in the lives of many children at her school. Glenda had filed for divorce from her husband, Shannon Greer, based on a pattern of abuse within the marriage. On May 11, 1990, Shannon Greer walked into his soon-to-be-former wife's place of employment and shot her with a 12-gauge shotgun, killing her. He then left the school, drove down a back road, and killed himself. When the police found Shannon Greer's body, the divorce papers were in the car, and scribbled on the papers was a note written by Shannon Greer that said, "There was not a divorce."[264] While not all assaults upon women by their male partners end in homicide, the reality is that some most certainly have,[265] and the dynamics which leaving often set into motion should be remembered. According to a judge interviewed by James Ptacek in a study on judicial treatment of women applying for restraining orders, the increased awareness among the judiciary concerning the seriousness of assaults among intimate partners means that "no judge wants to be the one who didn't grant a restraining order to the woman found face down in the morning."[266]

Violent relationships between intimate partners are characterized by a cycle of violence in which numerous forms of social control may be used. Neil Websdale maintains that in rural communities, the relative geographic isolation of most families makes it easy for men who batter their wives to also control their movement and everyday activities. Men in

Websdale's research disconnected telephone lines, disabled cars, and threatened women at their place of work. These actions narrowed the abused partner's options to leave, especially in the case of women in rural settings where powerful notions of family loyalty and gender roles work against leaving as an option. As Websdale notes in his research, many women who are battered by their husbands must face the fact that if they leave their husbands, they will in effect be leaving their communities. Physical assaults often involve other tactics of abuse, such as emotional abuse and attacks or threats against children. This is especially salient in that most women who have reported abuse by intimate partners also had dependent children.[267]

In analyzing the cases of women in two counties in Massachusetts who applied for restraining orders during 1992 and 1993, as well as observations in the courtroom, **James Ptacek** developed a typology of the type of strategies that men used to control women in violent relationships.[268] Ptacek analyzed both the types of abuse that women reported in their petitions for restraining orders and the rationales that the women provided in their affidavits that "gave some indication of the objectives behind the men's violence and abuse."[269] In 18% of the cases, the woman reported that her male partner had used violence to prevent her from leaving, and in 22% of the cases the woman reported that violence was used to get back at her for leaving. Ptacek argues that women are assaulted in the process of leaving their abusers, and some of the incidents of separation assault had occurred for more than a year following legal separation or divorce. Another tactic used by men was "punishment, coercion, and retaliation against women's actions concerning children,"[270] which could take several forms. Some men attacked their wives during pregnancy, others attacked the woman if she challenged his parental authority over the children, and still others attacked partners who had requested child support through the courts. In about 12% of the cases, the affidavits of women revealed that men used violence in response to other types of legal action. Ptacek labeled this "retaliation or coercion against women's pursuit of court or police remedies" in which the men responded with violence to actions that women were thought to have taken, whether those actions were real or imaginary. The final motivation for the violence of males was "retaliation for other perceived challenges to authority." These challenges included comments that the woman made concerning her male partner's behavior, ranging from drinking behavior to financial matters. As with the other motivational categories, the challenge to male authority was viewed as actionable, and violence was considered a justified course of action.[271] Ethnographic research like that of Neil Websdale and James Ptacek is an important avenue for increasing our knowledge of intimate-partner violence. Another recent source of information comes from survey research, specifically the National Violence against Women Survey, which was mentioned earlier in this chapter.

One goal of the NVAW Survey was to estimate both the extent and the nature of physical abuse among intimate partners. At some point during their lifetime, 22% of women and slightly more than 7% of men report having been physically assaulted by an intimate partner. During the past year, slightly more than 1% of women and less than 1% of men reported physical assault by an intimate partner. The vast majority of the specific behaviors considered to be physical assault were acts like grabbing and shoving, rather than more serious acts involving a gun or knife. Among both same-sex and opposite-sex relationships, males most often perpetrate intimate-partner violence. "Same-sex cohabiting women were nearly three times more likely to report being victimized by a male partner than by a female partner."[272] The increased risk of assault for both men and women who are separated from intimate partners was also confirmed in the NVAW. Both men and women who were separated from their partners were more likely to report physical assault than those currently living with their partners. This supports Ptacek's findings, as well as other research that establishes that leaving an abusive partner is common, as is the violence that follows.[273]

On the extent of injury in intimate-partner assaults, the NVAW reveals that women are more likely than men to report injuries and that most of the injuries received are minor in nature. More findings from the NVAW are presented in the next section of this chapter, which examines stalking. Learn more about intimate-partner violence via Web Extra! 10-10.

Web Extra! 10-10 at crimtoday.com

STALKING

While **stalking** behavior is not new, the labeling of this behavior as one worthy of societal concern, and hence undesirable enough to be criminalized, is relatively new. Several high-profile cases have illustrated the dangerous potential of **stalking** behavior. John Hinkley was obsessed with actress Jodie Foster and thought to capture her attention and admiration by shooting then-President Ronald Reagan in 1981. Mark David Chapman, the man who shot John Lennon in 1980, considered himself to be "one of Lennon's biggest fans." Talk-show host David Letterman was stalked from 1988 to 1993 by a woman who professed her love for him by breaking into his house repeatedly, trespassing on his property, and stealing his car. While the high-profile cases may capture media attention because they involve celebrities, stalking often involves average individuals as they go about their lives.

The first antistalking statute was passed in 1990 in California.[274] At present, all states and the federal government have antistalking laws. Rather than being an offense that occurs once, stalking is conceptualized as a pattern of behavior that causes victims to fear for their personal safety. The definition used in the Model Antistalking Code for States, developed by the National Institute of Justice, is "a course of conduct directed at a specific person that involves repeated visual or physical proximity, nonconsensual communication, or verbal, written or implied threats, or a combination thereof, that would cause a reasonable person fear."[275] *Repeated* is defined to mean at least two occasions. Individual antistalking laws vary in terms of the type of definition given to the term *repeated* and in terms of the requirements connected to threats by the perpetrator and fear by the victim. While the majority of states require that the perpetrator make a "credible threat," some states include threats against family members. Other states demand that the conduct of the perpetrator constitute an implied threat, and they evaluate this in relation to the level of fear expressed by the victim.[276]

Statutory definitions of stalking encompass a number of diverse but interrelated behaviors, such as making phone calls, following the victim, sending letters, making threats in some manner, vandalizing property, and watching the victim. Rather than viewing these behaviors in isolation from one another, antistalking laws take into account the totality of the circumstances so that seemingly benign behaviors are seen in light of how they are connected to other behaviors. This acknowledges that while sending unwanted letters might be seen as innocuous behavior, when this activity is combined with following the victim and standing outside his or her place of work or residence, the behavior takes on a more threatening tone and may be the precursor for more serious offenses like assault, rape, and murder.[277]

The Extent of Stalking

The only national-level data on the nature and extent of stalking come from the National Violence against Women Survey. The survey data are used in several of the sections that follow to identify and characterize a number of the key issues concerning stalking. The definition of stalking used in the NVAW closely follows the Model Antistalking Code for States.[278] For the behaviors in their totality to satisfy the definition of stalking used in the NVAW, the respondents had to have reported victimization on more than one occasion and also that they were "very frightened or feared bodily harm."[279]

The same definition of stalking was used to ask individuals to report the relevant experiences both over their lifetime and during the past 12 months. In the late nineties, approximately 8% of women and 2% of men reported being stalked at some point during their life. Using the survey data to generate estimates for the general population, this means that about one in every 12 women (8.2 million) and one in every 45 men (2 million) are stalked at some point in their life. The annual prevalence rate was 1% of all women surveyed and 0.4% of all men, translating to roughly 1,006,970 women and 370,990 men every year. An overwhelming majority (90%) of individuals surveyed reported being stalked by only one individual during their life.[280] These estimates were based on the strictest definition of stalking, which required that in addition to repeated behaviors that fall within the scope of stalking, the survey respondent had to report a high level of fear. When a lower threshold of fear is used to construct the measure, the estimates are even higher; 12% of women and 4% of men reported being stalked at some point in their life, and 6% of women and 1.5% of men reported being stalked annually.[281]

Upon examination of the type of behaviors that stalkers engaged in, Patricia Tjaden and Nancy Thoennes, the principal investigators for the NVAW survey, conclude that antistalking laws that require an overt threat be made against the victim are ill-advised. While victims reported high levels of fear, stalkers in less than half of the cases made overt threats. In the case of both male and female victims, the vast majority repeated being followed or spied on in some way; many received unwanted telephone calls, and similar percentages reported receiving unwanted items through the mail and being victims of vandalism.[282]

Victim-Offender Relationships in Stalking

The majority of stalking victims identified in the NVAW survey are women (78%, or four out of every five victims). The majority of individuals who stalk are men; 94% of women and 60% of men identified a male as the stalker. The majority of stalking victims are young, with 52% between the ages of 18 and 29 years and 22% between the ages of 30 and 39. Results from the NVAW survey confirmed previous research that showed that the majority of victims know their stalker. A stranger was identified as the stalker in only 23% of the cases where a woman was stalked and 36% of the cases where a man was stalked. For women who are stalked, the majority (59%) are more likely to be stalked by an intimate partner than by a stranger, acquaintance, or relative other than the spouse. On the other hand, the majority of men are stalked by strangers or acquaintances (70%), usually a male in both cases (90%). Tjaden and Thoennes state that while there is no clear explanation for this finding, it may be related to a greater risk of stalking among homosexual as opposed to heterosexual men. The survey found that stalking was more likely to be experienced by male respondents who indicated that they had lived as a couple with another male. According to Tjaden and Thoennes, "In some stalking cases involving male victims and stranger or acquaintance perpetrators, the perpetrator may be motivated by hatred toward homosexuals, while in others the perpetrator may be motivated by sexual attraction."[283] The belief that stalkers suffer from mental illness or personality disorder was not confirmed by the survey findings, as only 7% of the victims stated that they were stalked by offenders who were "mentally ill or abusing drugs or alcohol."[284]

Stalking in Intimate-Partner Relationships

Almost one-fourth (21%) of female respondents in the NVAW survey who had been stalked by an intimate partner, stated that they were stalked before the end of the relationship; 43% indicated that the stalking occurred after the relationship had ended, and slightly over one-third (36%) reported that they were stalked both before and after the end of the relationship with their partner.[285] The survey found that other forms of violence often accompany stalking. For women stalked by an intimate partner, 81% were also physically assaulted and almost one-third were sexually assaulted by their stalker. The percentage of women experiencing assault of either kind by a current or former intimate partner who stalked them was higher than the percentage experiencing some form of assault but no stalking (20% of women who had ever married or lived with a male partner had experienced physical assault by that partner and 5% had experienced sexual assault).[286] Men who stalked their former wives were "significantly more likely than ex-husbands who did not stalk to engage in emotionally abusive and controlling behavior toward their wife."[287]

Consequences of Stalking

Respondents in the NVAW Survey reported a number of diverse consequences of stalking that affected their life negatively. Women who had been stalked reported a significantly higher level of concern for their personal safety than those who had not been stalked. Almost one-third reported seeking counseling, and slightly more than one-fourth lost time from work due to the stalking incidents. Women took a variety of extra self-protective measures as a response to the stalking, with 17% stating that they bought a gun, 11% stating that they changed residences, and 11% moving out of state. Women who had been stalked were more likely than the men to have obtained a protective order against their stalker (23% versus 10%, respectively).[288]

Since the definition used in the NVAW survey to assess stalking required high levels of fear on the part of victims, it is worthwhile to explore the data on whether the victims reported these activities to the police. A higher percentage of women than men reported the stalking to police (55% versus 48%, respectively). When asked reasons for not reporting to the police, the responses of stalking victims were consistent with the more general reasons often given for not reporting crimes to the police: 20% defined it as not a police matter, 17% did not believe the police could do anything, 16% were afraid of reprisal from the stalker, 12% resolved it on their own, and smaller percentages reported that the police would not believe them or that it was a private matter.[289] Responses to questions on satisfaction with law enforcement's handling of the case indicated that about half of respondents approved of police procedure. In cases where an arrest was made in the stalking, three-fourths of the victims in those cases were satisfied with the police handling of the case.[290] Learn more about the crime of stalking at Web Extra! 10-11.

Web Extra! 10-11 at crimtoday.com

Cyberstalking

Another type of stalking, **cyberstalking,** has received attention as efforts progress to better understand the consequences of our increased reliance on electronic communication and the Internet.[291] While no standard definition of cyberstalking exists, this term refers to the use of electronic communication like e-mail or the Internet to harass individuals. A 1999 report from then– U.S. Attorney General Janet Reno made the following recommendations to help control cyberstalking:[292]

- A review of all stalking laws at the state level is needed to ensure that provisions for cyberstalking are included.
- An amendment to federal law is needed to make transmission of communication in specified forms of commerce actionable if the intent involves threatening behavior or causes the recipient fear.
- Training on cyberstalking should be offered at all levels of law enforcement.
- The creation of a Web site with information on cyberstalking should be made available to the public.

TERRORISM

The Federal Bureau of Investigation defines **terrorism** as "a violent act or an act dangerous to human life in violation of the criminal laws of the United States or of any state to intimidate or coerce a government, the civilian population, or any segment thereof, in furtherance of political or social objectives."[293]

The primary distinction between violent criminal acts and terrorist acts has to do with the political motivation or ideology of the offender.[294] Hence bombings, hostage taking, and other similar terroristlike acts which are undertaken for mere individual or pecuniary gain, when no political or social objectives are sought by the perpetrators, would not qualify as acts of terrorism. Politically motivated terrorists, however, probably do not think of themselves as "criminal," preferring instead the "revolutionary" label.

Today, the United States is faced with two types of terrorism: international and domestic. Although the number of terrorist attacks on U.S. interests around the world has shown an overall decline in recent years, it would be a mistake to assume that international terrorism is no longer a serious threat. As one observer on the subject states, "While the number of terrorist attacks generally is declining, the audacity of terrorists and their choice of targets . . . are in some ways more alarming than ever. As long as the United States remains actively engaged in the world, as it clearly must, there will be governments and groups committed to the use of violence to attack U.S. interests and further their own political goals."[295]

In 1996, the horrific truck bombing of U.S. military barracks in Dhahran, Saudi Arabia, validated that observation. Nineteen U.S. Air Force personnel were killed and more than 250 others were injured in the blast, which destroyed the

Khobar Towers housing complex. A 40-person Pentagon task force headed by retired U.S. Army General Wayne Downing later concluded that the Pentagon had failed to take terrorist threats seriously.

Truck bombs pale in comparison with the destructive power of nuclear weapons, the availability of which appears to be rapidly increasing in today's black market. In 1997, for example, two Lithuanian nationals, Alexander Porgrebeshski, 28, and Alexander Darichev, 36, were arrested in Miami and charged with trying to sell Soviet-era nuclear weapons to federal agents posing as arms brokers for drug dealers. The two were caught on videotape negotiating the sale of Bulgarian-made tactical nuclear weapons. Dennis Fagan, chief agent at the U.S. Customs Service's Miami office, said that the incident "shows there are people out there who have the ability to move weapons—strategic weapons—around the world."[296] Today's loose control over nuclear weapons and weapons-grade fissionable materials is the direct result of the collapse of the Soviet Union at the close of the 1980s. That country's dissolution seriously lessened the ability of Russian and former Eastern bloc authorities to retain control over cold war stockpiles of nuclear weapons.

In a 1997 press briefing,[297] Ambassador Philip C. Wilcox, Jr.,[298] who at the time had primary responsibility within the U.S. government for developing, coordinating, and implementing American counterterrorism policy, said, "Terrorists appear to be using much more lethal explosives against mass noncombatant targets." Ambassador Wilcox noted that "American businesses have been singled out for scores of terrorist attacks overseas," and he added, "Terrorism is also a more lethal threat than it has ever been in the past because of growing access of terrorists to technology." He provided an interesting analogy, saying, "In the year 1605, a would-be terrorist named Guy Fawkes tried to blow up the British House of Commons. He used 29 barrels of gunpowder. Fortunately, the plot was foiled. Today, that job could have been done with a small plastic charge concealed in a briefcase. Now, conventional explosives are readily available and the technology to make them and, worse yet, terrorists have increasing access to materials of mass destruction—nuclear, chemical, and biological." Ambassador Wilcox also noted that "in today's volatile mix of religious fanaticism, pathological terrorists . . . and their access to modern technology increases the danger of terrorism tremendously. Terrorists not only have access to these materials of technological resources, another form of technology—the expansion of international media and communications—gives them a much, much broader stage upon which to perform, to intimidate, and to terrorize."

According to the U.S. State Department, 392 international terrorist acts took place in 1999—an increase of 43% over the previous year.[299] As a result of these attacks, 223 people were killed, and 706 were wounded. View the latest government statistics on terrorism at Web Extra! 10-12.

Web **Web Extra! 10-12 at crimtoday.com**
EXTRA!

A more accurate measure of terrorism may be that produced by Pinkerton Risk Assessment Services, which uses a much broader definition of terrorism (one that counts politically motivated violence committed inside a country by its own citizens) than does the State Department. Pinkerton says that terrorist attacks worldwide have increased to record levels and claims that the number of people killed yearly in worldwide terrorist attacks recently rose above 10,000 for the first time since the company began keeping records.[300]

The possibility of terrorism within U.S. borders was highlighted by the 1993 bombing of the World Trade Center in New York City. The ensuing fire and smoke caused six deaths and nearly 1,000 injuries. The bombing, which left a five-story crater under the building, was the only externally directed terrorist incident in 1993 that claimed American lives. One year and six days after the explosion, Nidal Ayyad, Ahmad Ajaj, Mohammad Salameh, and Mahmud Abouhalima—all Islamic fundamentalists who had entered the United States from the Middle East—were convicted of

Pipe bomb damage at the 1996 Olympics in Atlanta, Georgia. How might criminologists explain acts of terrorism? *McDermid, SIPA Press*

all charges that the U.S. government had brought against them, including conspiracy to bomb buildings, explosive destruction of property, and assault on a federal officer. After the bombing, it was discovered, however, that plotters had targeted other vital city areas, including the United Nations and the Holland and Lincoln Tunnels. Had those plots been successfully implemented, many more lives would have been lost, and an untold amount of social disruption would have occurred within the northeastern United States. In 1995, Sheikh Oma Abdel-Rahman, the mastermind behind the Trade Center bombing, and eight other Muslim fundamentalists were convicted in a federal court on charges related to the bombing. Evidence showed that they plotted to start a holy war and conspired to commit assassinations within the United States and to bomb the United Nations.[301] The sheikh was sentenced to life in prison.

The United States may soon experience more international terrorism. As one terrorism expert recently put it, "The U.S. and its Arab allies are losing steadily to Islamic forces energized by several new trends in the Middle East. . . . It is tempting to dismiss the fundamentalists accused of bombing the World Trade Center and planning a host of other violent actions in New York as deranged fanatics, and amateurish ones at that. Yet, to do so is to ignore the fact that radical Islamists, in the U.S. and the Middle East, are pursuing an ambitious political agenda. It also is tempting to characterize the fundamentalists as a fringe group on the periphery of Middle Eastern politics, when, actually, their destabilizing activities are at the center of the region's troubles. Without illusions, Washington must recognize that the slow triumph of militant Islam in the Middle East not only will pose a major threat to the U.S.'s position in the region, but also will bring terrorism to American shores."[302]

The 1995 terrorist bombing of the Alfred P. Murrah federal building in downtown Oklahoma City, Oklahoma, in which 168 people died and hundreds more were wounded, demonstrated just how vulnerable the United States is to terrorist attack from domestic sources. The nine-story building, which included offices of the Social Security Administration, the Drug Enforcement Administration, the Secret Service, and the Bureau of Alcohol, Tobacco, and Firearms, as well as a day-care center called America's Kids, was devastated by a homemade bomb. The fertilizer and diesel fuel device used in the attack was estimated to have weighed approximately 1,200 pounds. It was left in a parked rental truck on the fifth Street side of the building. The blast left a crater 30 feet wide and eight feet deep and spread debris over a ten-block area.

In June 1997, a federal jury found 29-year-old Timothy McVeigh guilty of 11 counts ranging from conspiracy to first-degree murder in the bombing. Jurors concluded that McVeigh had conspired with Terry Nichols, a friend he had met while both were in the army, and with unknown others to use a truck bomb to destroy the Murrah Building. Prosecutors argued that the attack was intended to revenge the 1993 assault on David Koresh's Branch Davidian complex in Waco, Texas, which left 78 cult members dead. The Waco incident happened two years to the day before the Oklahoma City attack. Following the guilty verdicts, McVeigh was sentenced to death.[303] In late 1999, he requested that all appeals on his behalf be dropped and he was executed on June 11, 2001. Although the execution had been stymied by the discovery of case-related documents that the FBI had inadvertently failed to share with McVeigh's defense attorneys, McVeigh became the first person under federal jurisdiction to be put to death since 1963. McVeigh's co-conspirator, Terry Nichols, was convicted of eight counts of involuntary manslaughter but escaped the death penalty.

Terrorist bombings can be devastating. Here an Israeli soldier examines the aftermath of a terrorist bombing of a Tel Aviv bus. Is the United States adequately prepared to deal with the threat of international terrorism? *Shaul Golan and Yedioth Aharonoth, Corbis Sygma*

CRIME IN THE NEWS
Study: Hate Groups Merge, Get More Dangerous

While the number of smaller hate factions may be declining in the United States, larger hard-line groups are gaining in power, according to a report released today by a hate crimes monitoring group.

"The smaller groups that were less active are joining the more serious and potentially dangerous groups," said Mark Potok, spokesman for the Southern Poverty Law Center, an Alabama-based nonprofit group.

The report identified 457 hate groups operating in the United States last year, a 15 percent decline over 1998. The groups, ranging from Ku Klux Klan chapters to neo-Nazi and black separatist organizations, are centered primarily in the eastern United States with the heaviest concentrations in Florida, Ohio and California.

In order to be included in the survey, hard-line groups had to engage in clearly racist behavior such as crime marches, leaflet distribution or rallies, the center said.

VIOLENT WTO PROTESTS CITED

Potok pointed to the neo-Nazi National Alliance and Hammerskin Nation, a skinhead organization, as groups that have the greatest potential for violence.

He said the National Alliance, led by *The Turner Diaries* author William Pierce, who is believed to have provided the blueprint for the Oklahoma City bombing, is increasing its presence in the youth market.

"Pierce brought Resistance Records [a radical right-wing record label] back to life and is positioning himself to reach out to younger people," Potok said.

The study also cites the violent protests at the World Trade Organization meeting in Seattle last November as evidence of a growing convergence of right- and left-wing groups.

"THE SAME ENEMY: GLOBALIZATION"

While many blamed the violence on anarchists, neo-Nazis also were involved in the rioting, Potok said.

"I'm not saying the left is moving into the arms of the Nazis," he said. "But the hard left and the hard right have seen, in effect, the same enemy: globalization."

Potok cited the rise of Web sites devoted to "Third Position" ideology, which includes a mix of left- and right-wing ideas, as another example of efforts to attract generally disenfranchised people, rather than those who espouse a particular political viewpoint.

"They are younger, more Nazified and less Christian," he said. "It's the wave of the future."

BIGGEST DANGERS ARE LONE EXTREMISTS

But some scholars disagree, saying the extremist groups are far less dangerous today as a whole than they were in almost any decade in the last century.

"Hate groups had greater influence in the past," said Brian Levin, a criminology professor at California State San Bernadino. "The movement today has not coalesced in any meaningful way."

Levin said he feels the most potentially dangerous force are the "freelancers," independent individuals who do not belong to a particular group, but draw inspiration from different groups.

"Look at Timothy McVeigh—he wasn't a member of a group," he said. "With the exception of some well-known shootings, the people committing the most violent crimes are not members of hate groups. My fear is not hate groups themselves, but their ability to influence the 'ticking time bombs' and their ability to do damage."

Source: Amy Worden, "Left, Right Ideologies Mesh in Violent Cliques," APB News, March 15, 2000. Reprinted with permission.

Countering the Terrorist Threat

In the mid-1990s, Timothy E. Wirth, U.S. Undersecretary of State for Global Affairs under the Clinton Administration, testified before Congress on the growing threat of international terrorism. "Working in close consultation with the Congress," Wirth said, "successive Administrations have developed a set of principles that continue to guide us as we counter the threat posed by terrorists."[304] According to Wirth, these principles dictate that the U.S. government must

- Make no concessions to terrorists
- Continue to apply increasing pressure to state sponsors of terrorism

- Forcefully apply the rule of law to international terrorists
- Help other governments improve their capabilities to counter the threats posed by international terrorists

"Our counter-terrorism strategy," testified Wirth, "has three key elements—to implement our policy of 'no concessions,' to keep pressure on state sponsors, and to apply the rule of law. These basic policies," Wirth added, "have served us well in the past, and will do so in the future." They apply "equally well to groups such as the Abu Nidal Organization, or a small and unnamed group that may come together to undertake only a single attack."

SUMMARY

Violent offending is a very diverse activity that ranges from cold-blooded, calculated murder to simple assaults that result in little to no injury. Biosocial factors, weapon availability, developmental factors, and the victim-offender relationship have all influenced the violent crime typologies developed by different researchers. Homicide represents the rarest form of violent crime and can take many forms, ranging from the terror caused by serial killing and mass murder to the shock and confusion associated with murder in intimate settings.

Patterns of murder have been found to vary along subcultural dimensions and along social structural dimensions, such as economic inequality and community social disorganization. The unique motivational context of homicide has been the subject of extensive research for some time. Most recently, attention has focused on extending the public health approach to all forms of violent offending and exploring ways in which response to nonlethal violence may more effectively control the level of lethal violence.

DISCUSSION QUESTIONS

1. Why are crime typologies useful for understanding violent crime patterns?
2. What are the most common forms of violent crime? What characterizes these types of crimes?
3. What are the least common forms of violent crime? What characterizes these types of crimes?

4. Why was rape law reform necessary? What have been the beneficial aspects of this reform for rape victims?
5. Is robbery primarily a rational activity? Why or why not?

WEB QUEST!

Visit the FBI's National Center for the Analysis of Violent Crime (NCAVC) on the Web at http://www.fbi.gov/programs/cirg/ncavc.htm. NCAVC, part of the FBI's Critical Incident Response Group, investigates and researches unusual and repetitive violent crimes in this country and abroad.

Describe in your own words the three major organizational components of NCAVC and explain the mission of each. Submit your completed assignment to your instructor if asked to do so.

LIBRARY EXTRAS!

The Library Extras! listed here complement the Web Extras! found throughout this chapter. Library Extras! may be accessed on the Web at crimtoday.com.

Library Extra! 10-1. Attorney General of the United States, *Cyberstalking: A New Challenge for Law Enforcement and Industry* (online document, 1999).

Library Extra! 10-2. Bureau of Justice Statistics, *Female Victims of Violent Crime* (Washington, D.C.: BJS 1996).

Library Extra! 10-3. Bureau of Justice Statistics, *Four Measures of Serious Violent Crime* (online document, 2000).

Library Extra! 10-4. Bureau of Justice Statistics, *Serious Violent Crime Victimization Rates by Race, 1973-1996* (online document, 2000).

Library Extra! 10-5. Bureau of Justice Statistics, *Violent Crime* (Washington, D.C.: BJS, 1994).

Library Extra! 10-6. Patricia Tjaden and Nancy Thoennes, *Extent, Nature, and Consequences of Intimate Partner Violence: Findings from the National Violence against Women Survey* (Washington, D.C.: National Institute of Justice, 2000).

Library Extra! 10-7. Barbara Tatem Kelley et al., *Epidemiology of Serious Violence* (Washington, D.C.: Office of Juvenile Justice and Delinquency Prevention, 1997).

NOTES

[1] Albert J. Reiss, Jr. and Jeffrey A. Roth, eds., *Understanding and Preventing Violence* (Washington, D.C.: National Academy Press, 1993), p. xi.

[2] Branko Bokun, *Stress-Addiction* (London: Vita Books, 1989).

[3] Terance D. Miethe and Richard C. McCorkle, *Crime Profiles: The Anatomy of Dangerous Persons, Places, and Situations* (Los Angeles: Roxbury, 1998), p. 19.

[4] Marcus Felson, *Crime and Everyday Life* (Thousand Oaks, CA: Pine Forge, 1998), p. 34.

[5] Steven Ross, *Times Higher Education Supplement,* Vol. 10 (1995), p. ii.

[6] Miethe and McCorkle, *Crime Profiles;* p. 2.

[7] Neil Alan Weiner and Marvin E. Wolfgang, eds., *Violent Crime, Violent Criminals* (Thousand Oaks, CA: Sage, 1989).

[8] Federal Bureau of Investigations, *Crime in the United States, 1999,* (Washington, D.C.: U.S. Government Printing Office, 2000), pp. 5, 13.

[9] Ibid., p. 17.

[10] Ibid., p. 22.

[11] Marvin Wolfgang and Franco Ferracuti, *The Subculture of Violence: Towards an Integrated Theory in Criminology* (1967; reprint, Beverly Hills, CA: Sage, 1982).

[12] Marc Reidel and Margaret A. Zahn, *The Nature and Patterns of American Homicide* (Washington, D.C.: U.S. Government Printing Office, 1985). See also Margaret A. Zahn and P. C. Sagi, "Stranger Homicide in Nine American Cities," *Journal of Criminal Law and Criminology,* Vol. 78, No. 2 (1987), pp. 377–397.

[13] Kirk R. Williams and Robert L. Flewelling, "The Social Production of Criminal Homicide: A Comparative Study of Disaggregated Rates in American Cities," *American Sociological Review,* Vol. 53, No 3. (1988), pp. 421–431.

[14] Lynne A. Curtis, *American Violence and Public Policy* (New Haven, CT: Yale University Press, 1985); and Lynne A. Curtis, *Violence, Race and Culture* (Lexington, MA: Lexington Books, 1975).

[15] Claude S. Fisher, "Toward a Subcultural Theory of Urbanism," *American Journal of Sociology,* Vol. 80 (1975), p. 1335.

[16] Steven Messner, "Poverty, Inequality and Urban Homicide Rate," *Criminology,* Vol. 20 (1982), pp. 103–114; Steven Messner, "Regional and Racial Effects on the Urban Homicide Rate," *American Journal of Sociology,* Vol. 88 (1983), pp. 997–1007.

[17] Robert Sampson, "Neighborhood Family Structure and the Risk of Personal Victimization," in James Byrne and Robert J. Sampson, eds., *The Social Ecology of Crime* (New York: Springer-Verlag, 1985); and Robert J. Sampson, "Structural Sources in Variation in Race-Age Specific Rates of Offending Across Major U.S. Cities," *Criminology,* Vol. 23, No. 4 (1985), pp. 647–673.

[18] S. Hackney, "Southern Violence," in H.D. Graham and T.R. Gurr, eds. *History of Violence in America: Report of the Task Force on Historical and Comparative Perspectives to the National Commission on the Causes and Prevention of Violence* (New York: Bantam, 1960), pp. 505–528 and L. W. Shannon, "The Spatial Distribution of Criminal Offenses by States," *Journal of Criminal Law, Criminology, and Police Science,* Vol. 45 (1954), pp. 264–273.

[19] Hackey, "Southern Violence"; and Wolfgang and Ferracuti, *The Subculture of Violence.*

[20] R. D. Gastil, "Homicides and a Regional Culture of Violence," *American Sociological Review,* Vol. 36 (1971), pp. 412–427, and Hackney, "Southern Violence."

[21] Colin Loftin and R. H. Hill, "Regional Subculture and Homicide: A Comparison of the Gastil-Hackney Thesis," *American Sociological Review,* Vol 39 (1974), pp. 714–724.

[22] Ibid.

[23] Emile Durkheim, *Suicide: A Study in Sociology* (1951; reprint, Glencoe, IL: Free Press, 1967), p. 354.

[24] Marvin E. Wolfgang, *Patterns in Criminal Homicide* (New York: Wiley, 1958).

[25] Ibid.

[26] Parker and Smith, "Deterrence, Poverty and Type of Homicide"; and Dwayne M. Smith and Robert Nash Parker, "Types of Homicide and Variation in Regional Rates," *Social Forces,* Vol. 59 (1980), pp. 136–147.

[27] The distinction between expressive and instrumental crimes has been incorporated into much research on different crimes. This approach originated in the work of Richard Block and Franklin Zimring, "Homicide in Chicago, 1965–1970," *Journal of Research in Crime and Delinquency,* Vol. 10 (1973), pp. 1–12.

[28] Parker and Smith, "Deterrence, Poverty and Type of Homicide."

[29] Ibid.

[30] Williams and Flewelling, "The Social Production of Criminal Homicide."

[31] Laura Dugan, Daniel S. Nagin, and Richard Rosenfeld, "Explaining the Decline in Intimate Partner Homicide," *Homicide Studies,* Vol. 3, No. 3 (1999), p. 189.

[32] Ibid., p. 208.

[33] Ibid., p. 190

[34] Terance D. Miethe and Kriss A. Drass, "Exploring the Social Context of Instrumental and Expressive Homicides: An Application of Qualitative Comparative Analysis," *Journal of Quantitative Criminology,* Vol. 15, No. 1 (1999), p. 3.

[35] Carolyn Rebecca Block and Richard Block, "Beginning with Wolfgang: An Agenda for Homicide Research," *Journal of Crime and Justice,* Vol. 24, No. 2 (1991), p. 42.

[36] Ibid., p. 54.

[37] Wolfgang, *Patterns in Criminal Homicide.*

38 Richard Rosenfeld, "Changing Relationships between Men and Women: A Note on the Decline in Intimate Partner Homicide," *Homicide Studies,* Vol. 1, No. 1 (1997), pp. 72–83.

39 Wolfgang, *Patterns in Criminal Homicide,* p. 2

40 Ibid., p. 9.

41 Ibid.

42 Philip J. Cook and Mark H. Moore, "Guns, Gun Control, and Homicide," in M. Dwayne Smith and Margaret A. Zahn, eds., *Studying and Preventing Homicide: Issues and Challenges* (Thousand Oaks, CA: Sage, 1999), p 252.

43 Ibid., p. 254.

44 Ibid., p. 266

45 Reprinted as Paul J. Goldstein, "The Drugs/Violence Nexus: A Tripartite Conceptual Framework," in James A. Inciardi and Karen McElrath, eds., *The American Drug Scene* (Los Angeles, CA: Roxbury, 1995).

46 Paul Goldstein et al., "Crack and Homicide in New York City, 1988: A Conceptually Based Event Analysis," *Contemporary Drug Problems,* Vol. 16, cited in Kathleen Auerhahn and Robert Nash parker, "Drugs, Alcohol, and Homicide," in M. Dwayne Smith and Margaret A. Zahn, eds., *Studying and Preventing Homicide: Issues and Challenges* (Thousand Oaks, CA: Sage, 1999).

47 Auerhahn and Parker, "Drugs, Alcohol, and Homicide."

48 Ibid.

49 Ibid.

50 Ibid., p. 107.

51 Ibid., pp. 107–108.

52 Ibid., p. 108

53 Ibid.

54 Robert Nash Parker, "Bringing 'Booze' Back In: The Relationship between Alcohol and Homicide," *Journal of Research in Crime and Delinquency,* Vol. 32, No. 1 (1995), pp. 3–38.

55 Ibid., p. 4.

56 Ibid., p. 25.

57 Cheryl L. Maxsong, M. A. Gordon, and Malcolm W. Klein, "Differences between Gang and Nongang Homicides," *Criminology,* Vol. 23, No. 2 (1985), pp. 209–222.

58 Richard Rosenfeld, Timothy M. Bray, and Arlen Egley, "Facilitating Violence: A Comparison of Gang-Motivated, Gang-Affiliated, and Nongang Youth Homicides," *Journal of Quantitative Criminology,* Vol. 15, No. 4 (1999), pp. 495–516.

59 Ibid., p. 513.

60 Bureau of Justice Statistics, *Report to the Nation on Crime and Justice,* 2nd ed. (Washington, D.C.: U.S. Government Printing Office, 1988), p. 4.

61 James Alan Fox and Jack Levin, "Multiple Homicide: Patterns of Serial and Mass Murder," in Michael Tonry, ed., *Crime and Justice: A Review of Research,* Vol. 23 (1998), p. 413.

62 Ibid.

63 James Alan Fox and Jack Levin, "Serial Murder: Myths and Realities," in M. Dwayne Smith and Margaret A. Zahn, eds., *Studying and Preventing Homicide: Issues and Challenges* (Thousand Oaks, CA: Sage, 1999), pp. 79–96.

64 Ibid.

65 Fox and Levin, "Multiple Homicide," p. 412.

66 Ibid., p. 413.

67 Ibid., p. 415.

68 Fox and Levin, "Serial Murder," p. 84.

69 Ibid.

70 Ibid.

71 Ronald Holmes and J. DeBurger, "Profiles in Terror: The Serial Murderer," *Federal Probation,* Vol. 49, No. 3 (1985), pp. 29–34.

72 Ibid.

73 Fox and Levin, "Serial Murder."

74 Stephen T. Holmes, Eric Hickey, and Ronald M. Holmes, "Female Serial Murderesses: Constructing Different Typologies," *Journal of Contemporary Criminal Justice,* Vol. 7, No. 4 (1991), pp. 245–256.

75 Ibid.

76 Ibid.

77 Ibid.

78 Michael D. Kelleher and C. L. Kelleher, *Murder Most Rare: The Female Serial Killer* (Westport, CT: Praeger, 1998).

79 Ibid., p. 11.

80 Ibid., p. 7.

81 Fox and Levin, "Multiple Homicide," p. 427.

82 Ibid.

83 Ibid., p. 428.

84 Ibid., p. 429.

85 Thomas O'Reilly-Fleming, "The Evolution of Multiple Murder in Historical Perspective," in Thomas O'Reilly-Fleming, ed., *Serial and Mass Murder: Theory, Research, and Policy* (Toronto: Canadian Scholars' Press, 1996).

86 Cited in James Alan Fox and Jack Levin, *Overkill: Mass Murder and Serial Killing Exposed* (New York: Plenum, 1994), p. 202.

87 Jack Levin and James Alan Fox, "A Psycho-Social Analysis of Mass Murder," in Thomas O'Reilly-Fleming, ed., *Serial and Mass Murder: Theory, Research, and Policy* (Toronto: Canadian Scholars' Press, 1996), p. 65.

88 Ibid. p. 66.

89 Ibid.

90 Ibid., p. 69.

91 Ibid., p. 71.

92 Ibid., p. 69.

93 Fox and Levin, *Overkill,* p. 149.

94 For an overview of the measurement of rape in national surveys, see Debra S. Kelley, "The Measurement of Rape," in James F. Hodgson and Debra S. Kelley eds., *Sexual Assault: Policies, Practices, and Challenges* (New York: Praeger, forthcoming). For a more detailed exploration of this topic, see Bonnie S. Fisher and Francis T. Cullen,

"Measuring the Sexual Victimization of Women: Evolution, Current Controversies, and Future Research," in *Criminal Justice 2000: Measurement and Analysis of Crime and Justice* (Washington, D.C.: U.S. Department of Justice, Office of Justice Programs, 2000).

95 FBI, *Crime in the United States,* 1999, p. 25.

96 Bureau of Justice Statistics, *Criminal Victimization in the United States,* (Washington, D.C.: U.S. Department of Justice, Office of Justice Programs, 2000).

97 Diana E. H. Russell and Rebecca M. Bolen, *The Epidemic of Rape and Child Sexual Abuse in the United States* (Thousand Oaks, CA: Sage, 2000). See also Mary P. Koss, "The Underdetection of Rape: Methodological Choices Influence Incidence Estimates," *Journal of Social Issues,* Vol. 48, No. 1 (1992), pp. 61–75; and Mary P. Koss, "The Measurement of Rape Victimization in Crime Surveys," *Criminal Justice and Behavior,* Vol. 23, (1996), pp. 55–69.

98 Patricia Tjaden and Nancy Thoennes. *Prevalence, Incidence, and Consequences of Violence Against Women: Findings from the National Violence against Women Survey* (Washington, D.C.: National Institute of Justice and Centers for Disease Control and Prevention, 1991).

99 Martha R. Burt, "Cultural Myths and Supports for Rape," *Journal of Personality and Social Psychology,* Vol. 38 (1980), pp. 217–230.

100 For example, see Mary P. Koss et al., "Nonstranger Sexual Aggression: A Discriminat Analysis of the Psychological Characteristics of Undetected Offenders," *Sex Roles,* Vol. 12, (1985), pp. 981–992.

101 Martha R. Burt, "Rape Myths," In Andrea Parrot and Laurie Bechhofer, eds., *Acquaintance Rape: The Hidden Crime* (New York: John Wiley and Sons, 1991).

102 Gary LaFree, *Rape and Criminal Justice: The Social Construction of Sexual Assault* (Belmont, CA: Wadsworth, 1989). See also Jeanne C. Marsh, Alison Geist, and Nathan Caplan, *Rape and the Limits of Law Reform* (Boston: Auburn, 1982).

103 Harriet R. Galvin, "Shielding Rape Victims in the State and Federal Courts: A Proposal for the Second Decade," *Minnesota Law Review,* Vol. 70 (1986), pp. 763–916.

104 Cassia Spohn and Julie Horney, *Rape Law Reform: A Grassroots Revolution and Its Impact,* (New York: Plenum, 1992).

105 Ibid., p. 21.

106 Ibid., p. 129.

107 Ibid., p. 129.

108 Ibid., pp. 20–21.

109 Ibid.

110 Julie Horney and Cassia Spohn, "Rape Law Reform and Instrumental Change in Six Urban Jurisdictions," *Law and Society Review,* Vol. 25, No. 1 (1991), pp. 117–153.

111 Spohn and Horney, *Rape Law Reform.*

112 Ibid., p. 167.

113 Ibid., p. 162.

114 Ibid., p. 129.

115 E. J. Kanin, "Male Aggression in Dating-Courtship Relations," *American Journal of Sociology,* Vol. 63 (1957), cited in Martin D. Schwartz and Molly S. Leggett, "Bad Dates or Emotional Trauma? The Aftermath of Campus Sexual Assault," *Violence Against Women,* Vol. 5, No. 3 (1999), pp. 197–204.

116 See Frances P. Bernat, "Rape Law Reform", In James F. Hodgson and Debra S. Kelley, eds., *Sexual Assault: Policies, Practices, and Challenges* (New Brunswick, CT: Praeger, forthcoming).

117 *U.S. v. Morrison,* U.S. Supreme Court, No. 99-5 (May 15, 2000).

118 Public Law 102-325, section 486(c).

119 Carol Bohmer and Andrea Parrot, *Sexual Assault on Campus: The Problem and the Solution* (New York: Lexington Books, 1993), pp. 15–16.

120 Mary P. Koss, C. J. Gidycz, and N. Wisniewski, "The Scope of Rape: Sexual Aggression and Victimization in a National Sample of Students in Higher Education," *Journal of Consulting and Clinical Psychology,* Vol. 55 (1987), pp. 162–170.

121 Mary P. Koss, "Hidden Rape: Sexual Aggression and Victimization in a National Sample of Students in Higher Education," in Patricia Searles and Ronald J. Berger, eds., *Rape and Society: Readings on the Problem of Sexual Assault* (Boulder, CO: Westview Press, 1995).

122 B. L. Yegidis, "Date Rape and other Forced Sexual Encounters among College Students," *Journal of Sex Education and Therapy,* Vol. 12. (1986), pp. 51–54.

123 Patricia Yancey Martin and Robert A. Hummer, "Fraternities and Rape on Campus," *Gender and Society,* Vol. 3, No. 4, (1989), p. 462.

124 Ibid., p. 462.

125 Diana E. H. Russell, *Rape in Marriage* (Bloomington: Indiana University Press, 1990), p. 18.

126 Lisa M. Cuklanz, *Rape on Trial: How the Mass Media Construct Legal Reform and Social Change,* (Philadelphia: University of Pennsylvania Press, 1996).

127 Ibid., p. 49.

128 Ibid., p. 53.

129 Ibid., p. 62.

130 James Ptacek, *Battered Women in the Courtroom: The Power of Judicial Responses* (Boston: Northeastern University Press, 1999), p. 119.

131 David Finkelhor and Kersti Yllo, "Forced Sex in Marriage," *Crime and Delinquency,* Vol. 28, (1980), pp. 459–478.

132 Russell, *Rape in Marriage.*

133 Ibid., p. 133.

134 Charles Crawford, "Sexual Assault behind Bars: The Forgotten Victims," in James F. Hodgson and Debra S. Kelley, eds., *Sexual Assault: Policies, Practices, and Challenges* (New Brunswick, CT: Praeger, forthcoming).

135 Cindy Struckman-Johnson et al., "Sexual Coercion Reported by Men and Women in Prison," *Journal of Sex Research,* Vol. 33, No. 1 (1996), pp. 67–76.

136 Susan Brownmiller, *Against Our Will: Men, Women, and Rape* (New York: Simon and Schuster, 1975).

137 Dianne Herman, "The Rape Culture," in Jo Freeman, ed., *Women: A Feminist Perspective* (Palo Alto, CA: Mayfield, 1984).

138 Catherine MacKinnon, *Toward a Feminist Theory of the State* (Cambridge: Harvard University Press, 1989); and Catherine MacKinnon, *Only Words* (Cambridge: Harvard University Press, 1993).

139 See Andrea Dworkin, *Pornography: Men Possessing Women* (New York: Plenum, 1981); Andrea Dworkin, "Questions and Answers," in Diana E. H. Russell, ed., *Making Violence Sexy: Feminist Views on Pornography* (New York: Teachers College Press, 1993); and Andrea Dworkin, "Against the Male Flood: Censorship, Pornography, and Equality," in Patricia Smith, *Feminist Jurisprudence* (New York: Oxford University Press, 1993).

140 Robin Morgan, *The Word of a Woman: Feminist Dispatches, 1968–1992,* (New York: W. W. Norton, 1992), p. 88.

141 Brownmiller, *Against Our Will.*

142 James W. Messerschmidt, *Masculinities and Crime: Critique and Reconceptualization of Theory* (Lanham, MD: Rowman and Littlefield, 1993).

143 Ngaire Naffine, *Feminism and Criminology* (Philadelphia: Temple University Press, 1996), p. 101.

144 Messerschmidt, *Masculinities and Crime,* p. 119.

145 Neil Websdale, *Rural Woman Battering and the Justice System: An Ethnography* (Thousand Oaks, CA: Sage, 1998), p. 208.

146 Diana Scully and Joseph Marolla, "Riding the Bull at Gilley's: Convicted Rapists Describe the Rewards of Rape," *Social Problems,* Vol. 32, No. 2 (1985), p. 252.

147 Nicholas Groth, *Men Who Rape: The Psychology of the Offender,* (New York: Plenum, 1979).

148 Scully and Marolla, "Riding the Bull at Gilley's."

149 Nicholas Groth, "Rape and Sexual Offenses," in Neil Alan Weiner, Margaret A. Zahn, and Rita J. Sagi, eds., *Violence: Patterns, Causes, Public Policy,* (New York: Harcourt Brace Jovanovich, 1990), p. 76.

150 Groth, *Men Who Rape.*

151 Groth, "Rape and Sexual Offenses," p. 76.

152 Scully and Marolla, "Riding the Bull at Gilley's."

153 Russell, *Rape in Marriage.*

154 Larry Baron and Murray A. Straus, *Four Theories of Rape in American Society: A State-Level Analysis* (New Haven, CT: Yale University Press, 1989).

155 Baron and Straus, *Four Theories of Rape in American Society,* p. 147.

156 For examples, see Peggy Reeves Sanday, "The Sociocultural Context of Rape: A Cross-cultural Study," *Journal of Social Issues* Vol. 37 (1981), pp. 5–27.

157 Ibid., p. 184.

158 Robert T. Sigler, Ida M. Johnson, and Etta F. Morgan, "Forced Sexual Intercourse: Contemporary Views," in

Roslyn Muraskin, ed., *It's a Crime: Women and Justice* (Upper Saddle River, NJ: Prentice Hall, 2000), p. 352.

159 Randy Thornhill, "The Biology of Human Rape," *Jurimetrics,* Vol. 39, No. 2 (1999), p. 138.

160 Randy Thornhill and Craig T. Palmer, *A Natural History of Rape,* (Cambridge: MIT Press, 2000), p. 53.

161 Martin Daly and Margo Wilson, *Homicide* (New York: Aldine De Gruyter, 1988), p. 140.

162 Thornhill and Palmer, *A Natural History of Rape,* p. 199. See also Katharine K. Baker, "What Rape Is and What It Ought Not To Be," *Jurimetrics,* Vol. 30, No. 3 (1999) p. 233.

163 Craig T. Palmer, David N. DiBari, and Scott A. Wright, "Is It Sex Yet? Theoretical and Practical Implications of the Debate over Rapists' Motives," *Jurimetrics,* Vol. 39, No. 3 (1999), pp. 281–282.

164 R. R. Hazelwood and A. N. Burgess, eds., *Practical Aspects of Rape Investigation: A Multidisciplinary Approach* (New York: CRC Press, 1995).

165 Robert R. Hazelwood, "Analyzing the Rape and Profiling the Offender," in Robert R. Hazelwood and Ann Wolbert Burgess, eds., *Practical Aspects of Rape Investigation: A Multidisciplinary Approach* (New York: CRC Press, 1995), p. 162.

166 Ibid., p. 163.

167 Ibid., p. 164.

168 Ibid., p. 165.

169 Dennis J. Stevens, *Inside the Mind of a Serial Rapist* (San Francisco: Austin and Winfield, 1999), p. 39.

170 Ibid., p. 42.

171 Ibid., p. 41.

172 Ibid., p. 47.

173 Ibid., p. 50.

174 Ibid., p. 51.

175 Diana Scully, *Understanding Sexual Violence: A Study of Convicted Rapists* (New York: Routledge, 1990).

176 Ibid., p. 59.

177 Ibid.

178 Ibid.

179 Ibid., p. 165.

180 Ibid., p. 166.

181 Note that while purse snatching and pocket picking involve the express goal of taking someone's property, they are classified as property crimes because they do not involve the same type of direct contact with the victim as does robbery.

182 Terance D. Miethe and David McDowall, "Contextual Effects in Models of Criminal Victimization," *Social Forces,* Vol. 71, No. 3 (1993), pp. 741–760.

183 Miethe and McCorkle, *Crime Profiles,* p. 87.

184 Scott A. Hendricks et al., "A Matched Case-Control Study of Convenience Store Robbery Risk Factors," *Journal of Occupational and Environmental Medicine,* Vol. 41, No. 11 (1999), p. 995.

185 Ibid., p. 1003.

[186] Richard T. Wright and Scott H. Decker, *Armed Robbers in Action: Stickups and Street Culture,* (Boston: Northeastern University Press, 1997), p. 88.

[187] Floyd Feeney, "Robbers as Decision Makers," in Derek B. Cornish and Ronald V. Clarke, eds., *The Reasoning Criminal* (New York: Springer-Verlag, 1986).

[188] Brian A. Reaves, *Using NIBRS Data to Analyze Violent Crime* (Washington, D.C.: U.S. Department of Justice, Office of Justice Programs, Bureau of Justice Statistics, 1993).

[189] Federal Bureau of Investigation, *Crime in the United States, 1999,* p. 22.

[190] Ibid., p. 21.

[191] Thomas Gabor et al., *Armed Robbery: Cops, Robbers, and Victims* (Springfield, IL: Charles C. Thomas, 1987).

[192] Mark A. Peterson and Harriet B. Braiker, *Doing Crime: A Survey of California Prison Inmates* (Santa Monica, CA: Rand Corporation, 1980).

[193] Mark A. Peterson and Harriet B. Braiker, *Who Commits Crimes: A Survey of Prison Inmates* (Cambridge: Oelgeschlager, Gunn, and Hain, 1981).

[194] James Q. Wilson and Allan Abrahamse, "Does Crime Pay?" *Justice Quarterly,* Vol. 9 (1992), pp. 359–377.

[195] Martha J. Smith and Ronald V. Clarke, "Crime and Public Transport," in Michael Tonry ed., *Crime and Justice: A Review of Research,* Vol. 27 (Chicago: University of Chicago Press, 2000), p. 169–234.

[196] Ibid., p. 179.

[197] Ibid., p. 180.

[198] Ibid., p. 181.

[199] Ibid., p. 182.

[200] Derek Cornish, "The Procedural Analysis of Offending and Its Relevance for Situational Prevention," in Ronald V. Clarke, ed., *Crime Prevention Studies,* Vol. 3 (Monsey, NY: Criminal Justice Press, 1994), cited in Martha J. Smith and Ronald V. Clarke, "Crime and Public Transport," in Michael Tonry ed., *Crime and Justice: A Review of Research,* Vol. 27 (Chicago: University of Chicago Press, 2000), p. 181.

[201] Smith and Clarke, "Crime and Public Transport," p. 181.

[202] "Another NYC Cabbie Slain: Seventh Livery Driver Killed This Year," APBnews.com, April 15, 2000. Web posted at http://www.apbnews.com/newscenter/breakingnews/2000/04/15/cabs0415_01.html. Accessed January 14, 2001.

[203] Amy Worden, "NYC Taxis Get Anti-Crime Cabby Cams," APBnews.com, November 17, 1999. Web posted at http://www.apbnews.com/safetycenter/transport/1999/11/17/cabcam117_01.html. Accessed January 14, 2001.

[204] "Supreme Court Lets Taxi-Stop Rulings Stand: NYC Searchers Too Intrusive, but Boston Sweeps Legal," APBnews.com, December 4, 2000. Web posted at http://www.apbnews.com/newscenter/breakingnews/2000/12/04/taxi1204_01.html. Accessed January 14, 2001.

[205] Feeney, "Robbers as Decision Makers."

[206] Ibid., p. 59.

[207] Jody Miller, "Up It Up: Gender and the Accomplishment of Street Robbery," *Criminology,* Vol. 36, No. 1 (1998), p. 43.

[208] Bruce A. Jacobs and Richard Wright, "Stick-Up, Street Culture, and Offender Motivation," *Criminology,* Vol. 37, No. 1 (1999), p. 150.

[209] Ibid., p. 155.

[210] S. Morrison and I. O'Donnell, "An Analysis of the Decision Making Processes of Armed Robbers," in R. Homel, ed., *Crime Prevention Studies;* Vol. 5. *The Politics and Practice of Situational Crime Prevention* (Monsey, NY: Criminal Justice Press, 1996). See also Gabor et al., *Armed Robbery.*

[211] Jacobs and Wright, "Stick-Up, Street Culture, and Offender Motivation," p. 163.

[212] Ibid., pp. 167–168.

[213] Richard T. Wright and Scott H. Decker, *Armed Robbers in Action: Stickups and Street Culture* (Boston: Northeastern University Press, 1997), p. 62.

[214] Ibid., p. 63.

[215] Ibid.

[216] Ibid., p. 65.

[217] Ibid.

[218] Ibid., p. 66.

[219] Bruce A. Jacobs, Volkan Topalli, and Richard Wright, "Managing Retaliation: Drug Robbery and Informal Sanction Threats," *Criminology,* Vol. 38, No. 1 (2000), p. 173.

[220] Ibid., p. 173.

[221] Ibid., p. 177.

[222] Ibid.

[223] Ibid., p. 179.

[224] Wright and Decker, *Armed Robbers in Action,* p. 67

[225] Jacobs, Topalli, and Wright, "Managing Retaliation," p. 180.

[226] Ibid., p. 185.

[227] Ibid., p. 188.

[228] Ibid.

[229] Ibid., p. 172.

[230] Ibid., p. 194.

[231] Ibid.

[232] Miller, "Up It Up," p. 37.

[233] Federal Bureau of Investigation, *Crime in the United States, 1999* (Washington, D.C.: U.S. Government Printing Office, 2000).

[234] James W. Messerschmidt, *Masculinities and Crime: Critique and Reconceptualization of Theory* (Lanham, MD: Rowman and Littlefield, 1993), p. 107. Also cited in Miller, "Up It Up," p. 38.

[235] Miller, "Up It Up," p. 47.

[236] Ibid., p. 51.

[237] Ibid., p. 61.

[238] Reiss and Roth, eds., *Understanding and Preventing Violence,* p. 3.

[239] James Garbarino, *Lost Boys: Why Our Sons Turn Violent and How We Can Save Them* (New York: Free Press, 1999), p. 25.

240 Ibid.

241 Miethe and McCorkle, *Crime Profiles*, p. 25.

242 Ibid., p. 27.

243 Bureau of Justice Statistics, *Criminal Victimization in the United States* (Washington, D.C.: U.S. Department of Justice, Office of Justice Programs, 2000), p. 172.

244 Callie Marie Rennison, *Criminal Victimization, 1999: Changes 1998–1999 with Trends 1993–1999,* (Washington, D.C.: U.S. Department of Justice, Office of Justice Programs, 2000).

245 Robert J. Sampson, "Personal Violence by Strangers: An Extension and Test of Predatory Victimization," *Journal of Criminal Law and Criminology,* Vol. 78, No. 2 (1987), p. 342.

246 Marc Riedel and Roger K. Przybylski, "Stranger Murders and Assault: A Study of a Neglected Form of Stranger Violence," in Anna Victoria Wilson, ed., *Homicide: The Victim/Offender Connection* (Cincinnati: Anderson, 1993).

247 Ibid., p. 376.

248 Ibid.

249 Ibid.

250 Richard J. Gelles, *The Violent Home: A Study of Physical Aggression between Husbands and Wives* (Beverly Hills, CA: Sage, 1974).

251 Murray A. Strauss, Richard J. Gelles, and S. K. Steinmetz, *Behind Closed Doors: Violence in the American Family* (New York: Anchor Books, 1980), p. 31.

252 Michael Hindelang, *Criminal Victimization in Eight American Cities* (Cambridge, MA: Ballinger, 1976).

253 Evan Stark, A. Flitcraft, and W. Frazier, "Medicine and Patriarchical Violence: The Social Construction of a Private Event," *International Journal of Health Service,* Vol. 9, No. 3 (1979), pp. 461–493.

254 Murray A. Strauss, "The National Family Violence Surveys," in Murray A. Strauss and Richard J. Gelles, *Physical Violence in American Families: Risk Factors and Adaptations to Violence in 8,145 Families* (New Brunswick, NJ: Transaction, 1990).

255 Murray A. Strauss, "The Conflict Tactics Scales and Its Critics: An Evaluation and New Data on Validity and Reliability," in Murray A. Strauss and Richard J. Gelles, *Physical Violence in American Families: Risk Factors and Adaptations to Violence in 8,145 Families* (New Brunswick, NJ: Transaction, 1990).

256 Murray A. Strauss and Richard J. Gelles, "How Violent Are American Families? Estimates from the National Family Violence Research and Other Studies," In G. Hotaling, ed., *New Directions in Family Violence Research* (Newbury Park, CA: Sage, 1988).

257 Federal Bureau of Investigation, *Crime in the United States, 1998,* (Washington, D.C.: U.S. Government Printing Office, 1999), p. 280.

258 Ibid.

259 Ibid.

260 For representative examples of this, see R. E. Dobash et al., "The Myth of Sexual Symmetry in Marital Violence," *Social Problems,* Vol. 39, No. 1 (1992), pp. 71–91; and R. E. Dobash and R. Dobash, *Women, Violence, and Social Change,* (New York: Routledge, 1992).

261 Neil Websdale, *Rural Woman Battering and the Justice System: An Ethnography* (Thousand Oaks, CA: Sage, 1998).

262 Martha R. Mahoney, "Legal Issues of Battered Women: Redefining the Issue of Separation," *Michigan Law Review,* Vol., 90, No. 1 (1991), p. 6.

263 Liz Kelly, *Surviving Sexual Violence* (Minneapolis: University of Minnesota Press, 1988), p. 23.

264 Websdale, *Rural Woman Battering and the Justice System;* p. 32.

265 See M. W. Zawit, *Violence between Intimates* (Washington, D.C.: U.S. Department of Justice, Bureau of Justice Statistics, 1994).

266 James Ptacek, *Battered Women in the Courtroom: The Power of Judicial Responses* (Boston: Northeastern University Press, 1990), p. 6.

267 Ibid.

268 Ibid.

269 Ibid., p. 29.

270 Ibid., p. 82.

271 Ibid., pp. 86–87.

272 Patricia Tjaden and Nancy Thoennes, *Extent, Nature, and Consequences of Intimate Partner Violence* (Washington, D.C.: National Institute of Justice, 2000), p. 30.

273 M. L. Bernard and J. L. Bernard, "Violent Intimacy: The Family as a Model for Love Relationships," *Family Relations,* Vol. 32 (1983), pp. 283–286.

274 Violence against Women Grants Office, *Stalking and Domestic Violence: The Third Annual Report to Congress under the Violence against Women Act* (Washington, D.C.: Violence against Women Grants Office, 1998).

275 Ibid., p. 6.

276 Ibid.

277 Ibid.

278 Patricia Tjaden and Nancy Thoennes, *Stalking in America: Findings from the National Violence against Women Survey* (Washington, D.C.: National Institute of Justice, 1998), p. 7.

279 Ibid.

280 Ibid.

281 Ibid.

282 Ibid., p. 7.

283 Ibid., p. 6.

284 Ibid., p. 8.

285 Ibid. See also Tjaden and Thoennes, *Extent, Nature, and Consequences of Intimate Partner Violence.*

286 Tjaden and Thoennes, *Stalking in America.*

287 Ibid., p. 8.

288 Ibid., p. 10.

289 Ibid.

290 Ibid.

291 T. Gregorie, *Cyberstalking: Dangers on the Information Highway* (Arlington, VA: National Center for Victims of Crime, 2000).

292 Janet Reno, *Cyberstalking: A New Challenge for Law Enforcement and Industry—A Report from the U.S. Attorney General to the Vice President* (Washington, D.C.: U.S. Department of Justice, 1999).

293 Federal Bureau of Investigation, Counterterrorism Section, *Terrorism in the United States,* 1987 (Washington, D.C.: FBI, December 1987).

294 See Michael J. Lynch and W. Byron Groves, *A Primer in Radical Criminology* (Monsey, NY: Willow Tree Press, 1990), p. 39; and Michael J. Lynch et al., *The New Primer in Radical Criminology: Critical Perspectives on Crime, Power and Identity* (Monsey, NY: Willow Tree Press, 2000).

295 Peter Flory, "Terrorism Must Continue to Be a Top Priority," *Insight on the News,* Vol. 10, No. 21 (May 23, 1994), pp. 37–38.

296 Catherine Wilson, "Two Accused in Nuke Sale Sting," Associated Press wire service, June 30, 1997.

297 Available on the World Wide Web at http://www.state.gov/www/global/terrorism/1996report/970430.html, accessed July 2, 1997.

298 Ambassador Wilcox was formerly the State Department's coordinator for counterterrorism.

299 U.S. Department of State, *Patterns of Global Terrorism, 1999* (Washington, D.C.: U.S. Government Printing Office, 2000).

300 As cited in George J. Church and Sophfronia Scott Gregory, "The Terror Within," *Time,* July 5, 1993, p. 22.

301 Bruce Frankel, "Sheik Guilty in Terror Plot," *USA Today,* October 2, 1995, p. 1A. Sheikh Abdel-Rahman and co-defendant El Sayyid Nosair were both sentenced to life in prison. Other defendants received sentences of between 25 and 57 years in prison. See Sascha Brodsky, "Terror Verdicts Denounced," United Press International wire service, January 17, 1996.

302 Bradford R. McGuinn, "Should We Fear Islamic Fundamentalists?" *USA Today* magazine, Vol. 122, No. 2582 (November 1993), pp. 34–35.

303 The death penalty was imposed for the first-degree murders of eight federal law enforcement agents who were at work in the Murrah Building at the time of the bombing. While the killings violated Oklahoma law, only the killings of the federal agents fell under federal law, which makes such murders capital offenses.

304 Timothy E. Wirth, *Meeting the Challenge of International Terrorism,* U.S. Department of State Dispatch, Vol. 4, No. 29 (July 19, 1993), pp. 516–520.

The professional thief does not regard society in general as an enemy or perpetrate crimes against society because of hatred toward society. Rather than hate society, the professional thief rejoices in the welfare of the public. He would like to see society enjoy continuous prosperity, for then his own touches will naturally be greater.

—Edwin Sutherland[1]

Although few people have the talent to become professional fences and fewer still actually do so, anybody can buy stolen property and an unknown, but probably quite large, number of people in the United States do.

—Carl B. Klockers[2]

crimes against property

CHAPTER

11

We are all waiting to become victims of a burglar whose intuition about time coincides with our routine.

—George Rengert and John Wasilchick[3]

Like physics and physiology, criminogenesis derives from a movement of physically bounded and identifiable entities about the physical world—movements that can be tracked according to map, clock, and calendar.

—Marcus Felson[4]

KEY CONCEPTS

IMPORTANT TERMS

boosters	joyriding	professional criminals
fence	occasional offenders	snitches
gateway offense	offense specialization	
jockey	persistent thieves	

IMPORTANT NAMES

Mary Owen Cameron	Lloyd W. Klemke	Magnus Seng
Paul F. Cromwell	Carl Klockers	Neil Shover
Laura Dugan	Mike Maguire	Darrell J. Steffensmeier
Mark S. Fleisher	Frank J. McShane	Kenneth D. Tunnell
John R. Hepburn	Richard H. Moore	
Malcolm W. Klein	Barrie A. Noonan	

OUTCOMES

LEARNING

After reading this chapter, you should be able to
◆ Understand the distinction between professional criminals and other kinds of property offenders
◆ Identify the major forms of property crime
◆ Explain the rationalizations and motivations characteristic of property offenders
◆ Understand the application of various typologies to property offenses
◆ Describe how stolen goods are distributed

Hear the author discuss this chapter at *crimtoday.com*

INTRODUCTION

On the evening of December 5, 1980, Dr. Michael Halberstam, a prominent cardiologist and brother of famed author David Halberstam, was returning home with his wife. The Halberstams lived in Great Falls, Virginia, an affluent suburb of Washington, D.C. When Dr. Halberstam entered his residence, he confronted a burglar, who shot him and then fled. Though seriously wounded, Halberstam pursued the burglar and ran him down with his car. Although Halberstam died, the burglar, Bernard Welch, lived. Welch was found to have been a very active thief and a fugitive from another state. Since escaping from a New York prison several years before the Halberstam burglary, Welch had been pursuing a lucrative career as a burglar—so profitable, in fact, that he had driven a new Mercedes to the crime scene. A search of Welch's residence revealed millions of dollars in stolen goods. Details of Welch's career as a burglar, along with photos of the merchandise found in his home, soon filled the front pages of local newspapers.[5] Welch's criminal career was unique not only for a burglar, but for almost any offender. As a professional thief, Welch was far from typical, and his success and skill level placed him in a category shared by few.

Professional criminals are rare in the world of theft, whether the target selected is someone's residence or the "high-brow" world of art museums. The March 18, 1990, theft of several valuable paintings worth more than $300 million from the Stewart Gardner Museum in Boston remains "the unsolved art crime of the century."[6] Two people disguised as Boston police officers entered the museum, incapacitated security guards, and made off with the paintings as well as the surveillance tapes. The Boston art theft was far from typical for several reasons. According to Lynne Chafinch, an expert in art crime theft with the Federal Bureau of Investigation (FBI), the vast majority of "stolen art is lower value" and hence represents works that will not be easily recognized.[7] Even though the FBI maintains a listing of stolen art and cultural property in its National Stolen Art File, the bureau only investigates the theft if it occurred in a "museum as defined by federal statute, [and then] a stolen artwork has to be either more than 100 years old and worth more than $5,000 or less than 100 years old and worth more than $100,000."[8] According to Don Hrycyk, who leads the art theft unit of the Los Angeles Police Department, one of the few of its kind nationally, many of the people involved in art theft are basic burglars who steal art along with any other goods available. Other art thieves do not fit a conventional criminal profile and instead come from the ranks of college professors, gallery owners, and individuals involved in insurance fraud.[9] In more than a decade of such investigation, Hrycyk noted that "about the only type of crook that he hasn't come across is the sophisticated, debonair thief" portrayed in recent movies like *Entrapment* and *The Thomas Crown Affair*.[10] Learn more about art theft at Web Extra! 11-1.

EXTRA! **Web Extra! 11-1 at crimtoday.com**

PERSISTENT AND PROFESSIONAL THIEVES

While legal distinctions separate the offenses of larceny and burglary, both are basically property crimes of theft, and hence in some way all such offenders are thieves. Before discussing the specific legal classifications of these property crimes, some basic differences between persistent thieves and professional thieves are examined. While many thieves are persistent, this does not make them professionals. Willie Sutton, a famous bank robber, saw himself as a professional and defined a professional thief quite simply as "a man who wakes up every morning thinking about committing a crime, the same way another man gets up and goes to his job."[11] In a classic study of the professional thief, Edwin H. Sutherland defines this offender as one who "makes a regular business of stealing," plans carefully, possesses "technical skills and methods which are different from those of other professional criminals," and moves from locale to locale in offending pursuits.[12] **Neil Shover** defines **professional criminals** as those "who commit crime with some degree of skill, earn reasonably well from their crimes, and despite stealing over long periods of time, spend rather little time incarcerated."[13] This is certainly not the profile of most offenders, who continue to commit crimes but never exhibit signs of a professional approach to crime. Rather than being viewed as professional, they are best understood as persistent.

Persistent thieves are those who continue in "common-law property crimes despite their, at best, ordinary level of success."[14] Rather than specializing to any significant degree, the vast majority of persistent thieves alternate between a variety of crimes like burglary, robbery, car theft, and confidence games. Even though they exhibit a generalist approach

to offending, persistent thieves may have "crime preferences" that take the form of characteristics like "whether to avoid or to confront their victim(s)."[15]

Similarly, **offense specialization**, a preference for a certain type of offense, is quite limited among property offenders and does not allow for the classification of most offenders who engage in particular property crimes as professionals or specialists. A significant number of property offenders are fully immersed in a street culture and lifestyle characterized by a hedonistic approach to life and a disregard for conventional pursuits. Their everyday lives are characterized quite often by a wide array of petty crimes, including confidence games like three-card monte, a kind of shell game where the goal is to guess the correct card. Shell games always seem deceptively simple, and hence the deception begins or in other words, the "shaking of the red card."[16]

Malcolm W. Klein used the term *cafeteria-style offending* in his research to refer to the heterogeneous and unplanned nature of offending among gang members.[17] In analyzing offending among gang members for possible patterns, Klein was "reminded of a cafeteria display with [several] choices of food. Imagine the gang member walking along the display, choosing to try a little petty theft,

A burglary in progress. Burglary is a property crime that can turn violent if victims encounter the perpetrator. What are the characteristics of a professional burglar? *David Simson, Stock Boston*

then a group assault, then some truancy, then two varieties of malicious mischief, and so on."[18] Other researchers have used Klein's term to refer to the style of offending found among both violent offenders and property offenders. Research using data sources ranging from official crime statistics to self-reports of offenders to ethnographies confirms that a minimal level of specialization exists among property offenders.[19] Shover, who has studied burglary and professional thieves over the last two decades, suggests that designations like "burglar" have little utility if conceived of in a strict sense of exclusive offending within that crime type but that they can be understood to reflect a preference for offending that is more short term in nature. Many offenders engaged in burglary prefer this type of offending to offenses like robbery because burglary does not involve direct contact with victims, among other reasons. These individuals may engage in other types of offenses, even occasional robbery, but for the most part, their offending is characterized primarily by burglaries of the same type.[20]

Because of the short-term and sporadic nature of their offending, property offenders are also known as **occasional offenders.**[21] The label "occasional" refers not to the frequency of offending, but to the nature and character of offending. **John R. Hepburn** defines occasional property offenders as those whose crimes "occur on those occasions in which there is an opportunity or situational inducement to commit the crime."[22] This observation has been confirmed in subsequent research, most recently in the work of Richard T. Wright and Scott H. Decker, who state that the burglars they interviewed are not a "continually motivated group of criminals; the motivation for them to offend is closely tied to their assessment of current circumstances and prospects."[23]

Criminal Careers of Property Offenders

Criminologists have long studied the criminal careers of offenders, both violent offenders and property offenders. Neil Alan Weiner defines a criminal career as "criminal behavior as an integrated, dynamic structure of sequential unlawful acts that advances within a wider context of causal and correlative influences, including among others, those of biological, psychological, and informal social and formal criminal justice origins."[24] As this definition illustrates, the concept of a career implies a rational progression through defined stages, with some type of planning or formalized logic to the progression. An assumption long attached to criminal careers was the idea that offending becomes more serious and more frequent over time, an assumption strongly challenged by Michael R. Gottfredson and Travis Hirschi.[25] While the idea of deviance and crime as an orderly process similar to the rationality of conventional activities may be appealing for social policy pur-

poses, evidence on offense specialization and the trajectories associated with chronic offending offers more support for crime as a fragmented pursuit than as a "career." Does it then make sense to use the metaphor of a career to apply to the path of criminal offending? While there exists a certain logic to the lifestyle of most offenders, it is not one that easily complies with "a concept appropriate in a distinctly different culture (lawful society)."[26] While conventional society is marked by life events like going to school, seeking employment, and getting married, and by a transformation in lifestyle as a result of these stages as well as maturation, the life cycle of the street is quite different.

Based on ethnographic research on street criminals in urban settings, **Mark S. Fleisher** argues that the "social maturation" of the street life cycle "allows hustlers at any age to speak and act like adolescents and never acquire responsibilities similar to those marking social maturation in lawful society. In the sociocultural world of hustlers, youth is marked by gang membership, 'kids crimes,' the onset of drug and alcohol addictions, and juvenile detention."[27] From the cradle to the grave, the lifestyle of street criminals is "created less by design than by default."[28] This finding, repeatedly confirmed in ethnographic research, does not lessen the responsibility of offenders for their offenses, but rather calls into question the usefulness of concepts borrowed from conventional society. Street criminals do not have careers, and thinking of their offenses or the pattern of their lives as following from a series of life events similar to those outside this sociocultural environment will do little to increase understanding of the patterns of property offending. There is too little planning in how the street criminal approaches life and crime to constitute a career. As will be explored throughout this chapter, the type of offense specialization existing among property offenders is a loosely based preference for certain types of offending but not necessarily for a particular offense.

Property Offenders and Rational Choice

Research on property crimes is often investigated from the perspective of rational choice theories, discussed in Chapter 4. One definition of rationality is offered by Dermot Walsh: "activities identified by their impersonal, methodical, efficient, and logical components."[29] While the decision making, motivation, and target selection of property offenders will be explored throughout this chapter, it is crucial to understand now that the rationality of the typical criminal offender is not the same as "the rationality used by the civil engineer."[30] In line with the research of Thomas Bennett and Richard Wright on the rationality surrounding decision making by burglars,[31] Walsh's research concludes that offenders employ a "limited, temporal rationality." Walsh says, "Not all these men are highly intelligent, and few are equipped to calculate

Bentham-style, even supposing the information were available. Yet it is very common for rationality to be used. Of course it is partial and limited rather than total, but at the time, the actor feels he has planned enough and weighed enough data."[32] This is in many ways no different in spirit from the type of rationality that many conventional individuals employ in their daily activities. While some offenders, certainly those closer to the end of the continuum marked professional, will use a higher degree of rationality and still others will at times exhibit behavior that is totally senseless, most expressions of rationality are not as dramatically clear. As Neil Shover and David Honaker state, "Rationality is not a dichotomous variable," and given the extent to which it is shaped by the social context of offender's lives, research must "learn more about the daily worlds that comprise the immediate contexts of criminal decision making behavior."[33]

This chapter concerns itself with both the professional thief and the persistent, occasional thief. The extent to which property crimes are rational pursuits for either expressive or instrumental gains is a question that will be addressed by examining a wide variety of research on typologies of property crime offending. The major property crimes in the legal classifications of larceny/theft, motor vehicle theft, burglary, and arson will be discussed within this chapter. These offenses were introduced in Chapter 2, which provided offense definitions from several sources, along with statistical information on prevalence. Although some of the earlier material is repeated in this chapter, you should refer back to Chapter 2 for more detail.

LARCENY/THEFT

As noted in Chapter 2, the Uniform Crime Reports (UCR) and the National Incident Based Reporting System (NIBRS) define larceny/theft as "the unlawful taking, carrying, leading, or riding away of property from the possession, or constructive possession, of another."[34] As a form of theft, larceny (as opposed to burglary) does not involve the use of force or other means of illegal entry. For this reason as well as others, larceny is a crime "less frightening than burglary because to a large, perhaps even to a preponderant extent, it is a crime of opportunity, a matter of making off with whatever happens to be lying around loose: Christmas presents in an unlocked car, merchandise on a store counter, a bicycle in a front yard."[35] Just about anything can be stolen in a manner consistent with larceny. In California during November 2000, thieves stole "more than 1,200 young orange trees during nightly raids at the San Joaquin Valley, heartland of the state's citrus crop."[36] The volume and specialized focus of crimes like this are clearly the province of professional thieves; 1,200 orange trees are not the kind of item easily bartered on the street corner or the local pawn shop.

Prevalence and Profile of Larceny/Theft

Larceny is the most frequently occurring property offense, according to both official data compiled by the FBI and data from the National Crime Victimization Survey (NCVS). Within the offenses subsumed under the category of larceny in UCR data, the largest category is theft from motor vehicles, followed by shoplifting and theft from buildings.[37] Offenses like pocket picking and purse snatching are a quite small percentage of all larcenies, less than 1% each. Just as rates of different offenses within the category of larceny differ, so too do estimated losses to victims. As discussed in Chapter 2, data from both the UCR and NCVS provide some basis to estimate the value of loss due to property crimes. Generally, thefts from large structures like buildings generate greater losses than do petty-level personal thefts. While the aggregate economic loss is quite high, slightly more than one-third of all losses individually are under $50. Personal items like jewelry and camera equipment, the largest category of stolen items, constitute almost one-fourth of all stolen goods. The NCVS category of theft covers items taken from motor vehicles, and these account for almost 13% of all items stolen. Firearms and cash constitute smaller percentages, ranging from less than 1% for firearms and 7% for cash.[38]

Theft on College Campuses

Any locale can be the setting for theft. As Marcus Felson notes, "A college campus is a giant delivery system. It funnels students, faculty, staff, and various products into one general location and moves them from building to building to deliver education. It also delivers crime opportunities."[39] Felson, who developed the routine activities perspective, states that "crime feeds off the physical form of local life," a form "organized by how people and things move about in everyday life. In the ways that they move around, people often prevent crime, whether they are aware of it or not, and both people and things sometimes contribute to crime in their presences or their absences."[40]

Larceny is not only the most common index offense throughout the general population, but also the most frequent on college campuses. While the Crime Awareness and Campus Security Act of 1990 (described in Chapter 2) mandates that institutions of higher learning compile and make public data on certain index offenses, crimes of theft are exempt from the requirement. **Magnus Seng**, a researcher who has investigated theft on college campuses, notes that "to omit theft is to present a misleading picture of crime on campus."[41]

Some researchers have conducted independent investigations of theft on college campuses. Seng, for example, gathered data from incident reports at two campuses of Loyola University in Chicago during 1993. The two campuses had different characteristics; for example, one was located in an area with higher theft rates in the general population. Seng wanted to investigate whether the nature and prevalence of crime in the areas surrounding the campuses affected the nature of crime on campus. He found that reported thefts were lower on campus than in the surrounding areas. There was some diversity in the type of stolen items, with purses and wallets being the largest category (22%), followed by cash (14%), bicycles (10%), and about equal percentages of audiovisual and lab/office equipment. Consistent with the value of stolen property in the general population, "over three quarters (77%) of these thefts were classified as involving items worth $300 or less."[42] Members of the university staff had the highest victimization rates for thefts, followed by members of the faculty. Students had the lowest rates. Seng investigated exactly where the thefts occurred and focused on the type of buildings, as this was another factor that distinguished the two campuses. Seng classified all buildings by type, such as classroom, office, multipurpose use, student residence, and so forth. He found that the difference in the design of the campuses was a major determinant of differences in theft rates—a factor more important than the theft rates in surrounding areas. Thefts were more frequent on the campus with the largest number of buildings and the largest population of students, faculty, and staff. Approaching theft as primarily a crime of opportunity, Seng states that the larger campus afforded "more targets of opportunity" for theft.[43]

Research by Elizabeth Ehrhardt Mustaine and Richard Tewksbury using a probability sample of college students in eight states examined the importance of both individual lifestyle and community characteristics on the likelihood of being the victim of a larceny.[44] Similar to other more sophisticated tests of routine activity theory, the research revealed that both measures of individual lifestyle, such as the way in which an individual spends leisure time, and characteristics of the community where the individual resides are predictors of victimization. Mustaine and Tewksbury emphasize that an individual's lifestyle need not be "unhealthy" to constitute risk in terms of victimization. College students who spend a significant amount of time studying away from their residence or who are involved in numerous organizations on campus have an increased risk of major theft victimization. Self-protective measures, such as installing additional door locks and owning a dog, were quite effective deterrents to victimization and resulted in a lower likelihood of suffering either a minor or major theft. The authors conclude that, as in the general population, the "specifics of where you are, what your behaviors are, and what you are doing to protect yourself are the more important aspects of lifestyle influencing victimization risk."[45] Learn more about theft on college campuses at Web Extra! 11-2.

Web Extra! 11-2 at crimtoday.com

Motor Vehicle Theft

As noted in Chapter 2, the UCR defines motor vehicle theft as "the theft or attempted theft of a motor vehicle," where the term *motor vehicle* refers to various means of transportation including automobiles, buses, motorcycles, and snowmobiles.[46] Automobiles, of course, are the type of vehicle most often stolen. Data are compiled and analyzed separately for motor vehicle thefts for several reasons. The frequency with which thefts of motor vehicles occur and the cultural association of automobiles with status warrant special focus. Cars represent more than merely a possession; for many Americans, they are an extension of identity. The type of car one drives reflects social status. It is well known that a Lexus is more expensive than a Volkswagon, and a minivan is not a car that any self-respecting teenager would take for a joyride.

Similar to home-invasion robbery or residential burglary, the theft of a car violates the victim in a way that goes well beyond the financial loss. As well as representing an invasion of the victim's possessions and near residence, auto theft represents a significant inconvenience. The theft of a car makes it difficult for many people to get to work and sometimes requires them to take time away from work to take care of the incident. In fact, motor vehicle theft is the offense in which the highest percentage of victims report that the incident required them to miss some time at work. In 22% of all motor vehicle thefts, the victim reports losing time at work, compared to about 7% for household burglary and 12% for violent crimes like robbery. As with other offenses, approximately one-third of the victims of motor vehicle theft miss work for less than one day, and about one-half for anywhere from one to five days.[47]

Prevalence and Profile of Motor Vehicle Theft

As noted in Chapter 2, approximately 1.15 million vehicles were reported stolen in 1999, with an estimated total value in excess of $7 billion. The largest percentage of stolen vehicles were in a parking lot or garage at the time of the theft (32.1%).[48] A significant percentage of motor vehicle thefts take place either at or quite near the victim's residence (29.5%), with approximately 17% taking place on a street near the home.[49] If a broader definition of "near" is used, the percentage of auto thefts taking place near the victim's residence increases. Depending on the neighborhood in which the victim resides, "near home" can mean different things, and the same distance from the residence in urban communities may be more of a risk for motor vehicle theft than in other communities. Marcus Felson contends that the risks posed by where one parks are related to population density. "In low-density areas, one finds more personal garages and opportunities to park right near the home or office. Those living or working in high-density areas are more likely to have street parking and higher risk of auto theft."[50] The most common activity that victims were engaged in at the time of the motor vehicle theft was sleeping (41%), followed by leisure activities away from the home (15%), activities at home (14%), and employment (10%).[51]

Based on data from NCVS for 1999, on average 84% of all motor vehicle thefts, both attempted and completed, are reported to the police. As is seen with other offenses, the reporting percentage is higher (90%) for completed motor vehicle thefts than for attempted incidents (54%).[52] While the rate of motor vehicle victimization is the same for the lowest income households (under $7,500) as for the highest income households ($75,000 or more), the rate of reporting increases with the income level of the household.[53] Based on available data, approximately 62% of stolen cars are recovered.[54] Both law enforcement agencies and insurance companies keep records of recovered vehicles, but each employs its own definition of recovery. No matter what the condition of the vehicle, law enforcement agencies will consider any found vehicle to be recovered. Insurance companies use definitions that are based on how much damage was done to the vehicle relative to its market value. Even if the 62% recovery rate is a conservative estimate, it must be kept in mind that recovery of a stolen vehicle does not guarantee that the auto is in its original state. In fact, almost "one-third of the recovered stolen vehicles are completely stripped at 'chop shops' and another third are stripped of easy-to-sell accessories like radios, air bags, and seats."[55] Stripping cars for parts has increased since the 1970s, as has the variety of venues for such activities. We will return to this issue shortly.

Cars are stolen for a variety of reasons, including joyriding, temporary transportation needs, use in a crime, and stripping. As we will discuss later, each of these rationales is representative of a fairly distinctive offender profile, with teenagers, for example, most likely to take cars for joyriding. Given the wide variety of rationales supporting automobile theft, almost any type of car is potentially a target. However, thieves tend to prefer certain cars. For the past several years, Honda Accords and Toyota Camrys have been two of the favorite models preferred by thieves.[56] According to Robert Bryant, Chief Executive Officer of the National Insurance Crime Bureau, "Vehicle thieves follow market trends and target the most popular vehicles because they provide the best market for stolen vehicle parts and illegal export to other countries."[57]

Theft of Car Parts

The theft of car parts may be motivated by diverse reasons. Some car parts are worth a significant sum on the illegal market and can be easily sold by even the most inexperienced of thieves. Novice thieves especially often do not have access to the type of network required to sell "hot cars." Also, stolen car parts are more difficult to identify than are entire cars.[58]

In the United States, the Motor Vehicle Theft Law Enforcement Act,[59] passed by Congress in 1984, "called for the marking of the major sheet metal parts of high-theft automobiles with Vehicle Identification Numbers (VINs). The point

of the law was to enable detection of persons engaged in the presumably widespread sale of stolen parts to the auto body repair industry."[60] While previous legislation had required the marking of the transmission, engine, and frame, the requirement to mark additional parts reflected a presumption "that chopping accounts for the theft of a very high proportion of automobiles, particularly those lines which exhibit high theft rates."[61] While data on how many car thefts are carried out for stripping are scarce, some research has been conducted in this regard both in the United States and elsewhere.

Some researchers report that while theft from vehicles constitutes most automobile crime, the exact nature of what is taken from the car has not been the subject of extensive research.[62] Conventional wisdom held that stereo equipment was the primary target. Using data from the 1998 British Crime Survey, Joanna Sallybanks and Nerys Thomas found that "the most frequently stolen items were external parts of the vehicle, such as body panels, windshield wipers, mirrors, luggage racks, antennas, and tires and wheels, followed by stereo equipment and 'other' items (bags, briefcases, cameras, clothing, etc.)."[63] Over the past few years, the theft of stereo equipment has held constant, but the theft of external parts has increased significantly. When parts are the objects of theft from vehicles, these incidents are even less likely to be reported to the police than with other types of thefts. In 1997,

A Philadelphia police officer carries parts of stolen cars out of a chop shop during a raid. A chop shop is a place where stolen cars are disassembled and their parts sold. Why is the sale of parts often more profitable for criminals than the sale of stolen vehicles? *George Widman, AP/Wide World Photos*

for example, 20% of thefts involving car parts and 72% of thefts of stereo equipment were reported to the police. Sallybanks and Thomas offer four reasons why car parts are stolen: "expense of replacing car parts," "lack of availability of car parts for older models," "the demand for license plates," and "youth crazes, e.g. the fashion for wearing VW badges."[64] Further analysis of data on the type of cars stolen supports the first two of these explanations. Concerning fashion trend crazes that drive theft of external parts, VW "redesigned their car badges in order to halt" this theft, "but this proved only a temporary palliative—in the 1980s the Beastie Boys, a rap-rock group, re-introduced the fashion."[65]

Joyriders: Car Theft for Fun

A certain percentage of car thefts are opportunistic in nature, committed by teenagers, usually in groups, for the purpose of fun or thrills. These offenses are referred to as **joyriding.** Because such thefts generally involve the temporary appropriation of the vehicle primarily to satisfy needs ranging from excitement to personal autonomy, joyriding is often characterized as an "expressive act with little or no extrinsic value."[66] This motivation for auto theft is not characterized by planning and quite often resembles the following scenario provided by Michael Gottfredson and Travis Hirschi: "The typical auto theft [involves] a car left unlocked on a public street or in a public parking lot with the keys in the ignition or in plain view [which] is entered by a 16-year-old male or group of males and is driven until it runs out of gas or until the offenders must attend to other obligations."[67]

Most vehicles stolen for purposes of joyriding are recovered, usually found abandoned and often after they have been crashed. The type of vehicles stolen for joyriding are distinct from those stolen for other purposes. Joyriders favor sports cars, particularly American-made cars.[68] While the majority of auto thefts involve victims and offenders who are unknown to each other, cars stolen for joyriding are one of the exceptions to this pattern. While adolescents may select a vehicle for joyriding that belongs to strangers, they are more likely to select the car of a known owner.[69]

Available research offers no definite answer as to whether there is a distinctive social class profile of the joyriding offender. Following the early work of William W. Wattenberg and James Balliestri,[70] the "favored-group hypothesis" associates higher social class with greater involvement in auto theft because of greater access to cars and an earlier association of cars as status symbols. On the other hand, the "disadvantaged-group hypothesis" contends that youths from lower socioeconomic classes are more likely to be involved in car thefts because conventional means of acquiring status symbols like cars are blocked, and they are left with only the avenue of illegitimate acquisition.[71] Although some support has been found for each of these perspectives, other research has failed to find a link between social class and involvement in auto theft among adolescents.[72]

Jockeys: Car Theft for Profit

Jockey is a slang term for car thieves who are regularly involved in "steal-to-order jobs."[73] In horse racing, the value of a jockey lies in how quickly he or she can ride a horse to the finish line; for professional car thieves, "the quicker the ride, the more productive the race, and the more races are made, the more productive the jockey."[74] This type of car theft was recently characterized in American movies like *Gone in 60 Seconds,* in which the lead character, a former jockey, must once again take the reins and successfully steal 50 designated cars in a 24-hour-period to save his brother from death by unscrupulous characters.

While representing the most costly and most serious form of auto theft, professional thefts are not as common as thefts for other uses, such as joyriding. Like joyriders, professional auto thieves operate in groups, but their groups are characterized by a great deal more planning and calculation in target selection. The cars targeted by professional thieves are luxury cars that may be driven across national borders or shipped overseas. These professional thefts have the lowest recovery rates. Still, professionals are only a small part of the vehicle theft problem. Hence, Ronald V. Clark and Patricia M. Harris contend that "successful action against professional theft [would] have less effect on the scale of the overall problem than against thefts for temporary use and much less than against thefts from the vehicle."[75] Learn more about motor vehicle theft at Web Extra! 11-3.

Web Extra! 11-3 at crimtoday.com

A man takes advantage of an opportunity for theft. What will be the impact of this crime on the victim? *Mark C. Burnett, Stock Boston*

Shoplifting and Employee Theft

According to the National Retail Security Survey (NRSS), an annual survey by the University of Florida, "Theft cost U.S. retailers a staggering $25 billion" in 1999.[76] Each incident of shoplifting was estimated to cost the retailer on average $212.68, and thefts by employees averaged $1,058.20 per incident. The largest category of loss is employee theft; 42% of loss results from employee theft, compared to 34% from shoplifting. While the survey shows that both employee theft and shoplifting have increased over time, employee theft has grown at a faster rate. "The theft of merchandise by employees can range from the simple act of walking out the door with stolen goods to complex schemes requiring the manipulation of documents and/or involving several employees."[77] Most of the employees engaging in theft of either cash or merchandise are short-term workers. They are typically found in retail establishments with higher-than-average sales and a significant degree of turnover in management. The threat presented by employee theft means that many retailers perceive the issue of internal theft to be much more serious than the economic loss caused by customer shoplifting.

Another factor for retailers to consider in confronting shoplifting is that efforts to combat shoplifting might impact sales. This concern is reflected by a marketing director who commented, "You don't want to hinder sales by intimidating the shopper. We used to think just about stopping shoplifting. We didn't think enough about selling more merchandise."[78]

Technology represents one of the best ways to address both shoplifting and employee theft. The use of computerized inventory counts to track merchandise is quite useful in quickly identifying thefts by employees. As will be discussed shortly, the widespread prevalence of shoplifting among youths means that increased security personnel in stores are less successful at detection than are electronic and other devices. Personnel must know whom to target to be successful, while security systems make shoplifting more difficult for everyone.[79] Because the efforts of in-store security personnel are not necessarily directed at employees, it should not be surprising that the National Retail Security Survey found that "retailers' loss prevention budget averaged only 0.57 percent of annual retail sales."[80] The very technological developments that make managing inventory lists easier will also be the same techniques that most effectively manage the greatest loss to retailers—employee theft—without seriously undermining the attractiveness of the store to shoppers. While the majority of shoppers are not thieves, all shoppers will be exposed to the same techniques used to safeguard against the actions of a few, and hence these particular strategies may adversely affect the attractiveness of the environment for honest shoppers. Most of us are so familiar with antitheft devices attached to goods that we do not interpret this as a strange part of the shopping experience. The effectiveness of these technological marvels is touted by Don Taylor, Director of Market Planning for Sensormatic, a leading electronic security provider, who says that "when you're in a retail store environment, antitheft tags are worth their weight in gold."[81]

The theft of merchandise from a commercial establishment represents a common and prevalent crime today as in the past. Historically, shoplifting "was most likely a concern that plagued the first merchants who placed their goods out in a public market place."[82] In cities like New York during the late 1800s and early 1900s, shoplifting was pervasive among middle-class women. While previous periods had seen the involvement of the disadvantaged, especially youths, in shoplifting, the involvement of the middle class was seen as especially troubling. One explanation for middle-class involvement cites a change in the production, distribution, and marketing of goods. Women who once created goods for their families now went shopping for those goods in a new venue, the department store. Among other things, "department stores were designed to heighten sensory stimulation and create a desire for the merchandise."[83] Some authors of the early twentieth century suggested that "this new level of temptation and the assignment of shopping to weak-willed and sexually disordered females inevitably led to more shoplifting."[84] Another explanation offered for shoplifting among middle-class women was kleptomania. Because public officials of the early 1900s had no strong inclination to bring members of the middle class into court, kleptomania became a way to minimize the offenses of this group, "thus legitimatizing the actions of the stores and the courts to dismiss or acquit those afflicted with this women's sickness."[85]

Shoplifting continues to be an offense that crosses class lines, although it is not an offense committed primarily by women. The dominant motivation used today to explain shoplifting does not rely on the application of medical labels. Even though "respectable" people continue to be found among those who commit this offense, there is no evidence that these individuals constitute a significant segment of offenders.

Who Shoplifts?

Typically, shoplifting is a crime that the public associates with adolescents—an association that has some basis in empirical reality. In self-reports of offending, official arrest data, and store records, juveniles are overrepresented in statistics on offending.[86] While variation exists in the frequency of offending among adolescents, most offending patterns are fairly sporadic and characterized by a greater prevalence among younger adolescents. The sporadic nature of shoplifting among adolescents is typical across all social classes, even though the most serious and chronic forms are found among the economically disadvantaged. While females represent the majority of offenders in some sources of data on shoplifting, this finding has been seriously challenged in research since the 1970s.[87]

Lloyd W. Klemke's research, which used self-report techniques to assess juvenile shoplifting, revealed that almost two-thirds of the sample had shoplifted at some point in their lifetime.[88] Klemke's sample consisted of high school students from four different schools in the Pacific Northwest. A significantly higher percentage of males compared to females reported shoplifting during the past year. Although previous research by **Mary Owen Cameron** using department store records had revealed that females were more likely than males to be apprehended for shoplifting,[89] Klemke found the reverse to be true. The difference in these findings may be attributed to the fact that Klemke's research included only adolescents, whereas Cameron's research also included adults. In line with Cameron's findings, Klemke "found petty theft to be the dominant pattern for shoplifting," and described such theft as infrequent enough to correspond to the "sporadic pilfering" Cameron reported.[90] Klemke found the frequency of shoplifting to vary by the social class of the offender.

Youths from lower-income households are more likely to shoplift than their higher-income counterparts. However, this relationship is a moderate one at best, and the fact remains that shoplifting is reported by a solid majority of youth in several self-report studies. The relationship between social class and likelihood of shoplifting is stronger among adults. While research in this area is sparse, JoAnn Ray's study of shoppers in Spokane, Washington, revealed that out of a random sample, those in lower income groups were three times more likely to shoplift as those in higher income brackets.[91]

Among Klemke's other findings was a "maturing out" pattern, whereby the high point of "shoplifting activity peaked in the under ten age category" and decreased considerably as the youths entered adolescence.[92] These findings are contrary to other research that supports escalation during late adolescence.

An Adolescent Phase?

No one type of youth is most likely to shoplift. That a majority of youths report such activity makes shoplifting one of the largest categories of unofficial delinquency—that is, delinquency which is not detected by formal authorities. This finding has been observed in research outside the United States. Shoplifting was so prevalent in Janne Kivivuori's research on Finnish adolescents that she concluded that it was "culturally paradigmatic" and that the adolescents themselves viewed it as a normal phase of adolescence.[93] This observation is in line with other research purporting that given its prevalence across a wide variety of individuals, "juvenile delinquency is almost by definition a period in a person's life."[94] Shoplifting that assumes the form of "adolescence-limited phasic behavior can be seen as normal for at least three reasons: because of its relatively high prevalence, because adolescents are expected to loosen their ties to social control, and because our culture is full of descriptions under which periodical crises and phases make sense."[95] Adolescence-limited offenders, discussed in Chapter 8, are the largest group of those engaged in delinquency for whom the onset and desistance from deviance can be fairly well predicted.[96] Using a large

and randomly selected sample of Finnish adolescents, Kivivuori estimated the extent to which shoplifting could be characterized as episodic in nature and looked for identifiable periods of intense activity. The typical phase of shoplifting for the Finnish adolescents began around age 13 and ended by age 14. As in other research, 26% of the adolescents reported a lack of money as the primary rationale for shoplifting, with the same percentage reporting excitement as the primary reason. Equally revealing were the findings on why the adolescents ceased to shoplift. Almost one-third of the sample reported boredom as the reason, followed by 21% who were apprehended and 11% who cited wisdom as their primary rationale for desistance. While Kivivuori concludes that juveniles who engage in phases of intense shoplifting may steal more than juveniles whose shoplifting is not characterized by such phases, there is still no evidence that intense shoplifting reflects significant psychological problems. Shoplifting appears to be one of several forms of deviant behavior during adolescence, and "a shoplifting phase is one of the many cafeteria items selected by juveniles whose ties to sources of social control have been weakened."[97]

Shoplifting as a Gateway Offense

Evidence has long supported the notion that shoplifting is part of the early offense history of a certain segment of property offenders. Hence shoplifting may be a kind of **gateway offense**—an offense that represents a starting point leading to more serious and chronic types of offending. Frederick M. Thrasher's classic study of gangs in Chicago, published in 1927, detailed how various forms of property crime were found among boys in gangs.[98] Although shoplifting was quite prevalent, there was no indication that it served as a starting point for more serious offending, at least in any formal sense. Shoplifting is not an offense limited in any systematic way by the age of the offender; in its simplest form, it requires little skill or training and is accomplished within several different venues. It is less likely that shoplifting forms an impetus for increasing levels of involvement in more serious forms of property crime, as it is likely that shoplifting satisfies material and sensational needs among a group who are fairly nonspecialized in their offending.

Other research has offered more support for shoplifting as a gateway to more serious offending. In interviews with 60 repeat property offenders in a Tennessee prison, **Kenneth D. Tunnell** found that some offenders had begun with shoplifting and that late offenses reflected a calculated move to more serious property crimes. Tunnell found that among the majority of persistent property offenders, their careers "consisted of progressive steps, with each step representing a different crime type of specialty."[99] Tunnell offers no direct research, however, that supports the idea that offenders move systematically from lesser to more serious forms of property offending. Additionally, offenders often fall back on lesser offenses like shoplifting if the occasion presents itself or if such offenses appear to be attractive and profitable. Thus offenders do not clearly move in a linear fashion from one type of property offense to another; it is more like a feedback loop that is sporadic and fragmented in its progression forward.

Meaningful Typologies for Shoplifting

When a behavior is quite prevalent, the usefulness of typologies of offending within a particular offense category is called into question. Several researchers have attempted to use research findings to formulate typologies that focus on the motivation and frequency of offending as the primary means of distinguishing among the quite heterogeneous group that shoplifts. Mary Owen Cameron distinguished between those who engaged professionally in shoplifting and those who were novices. The former group, the **boosters**, were a small percentage of all those apprehended for shoplifting. Boosters usually sold the items that they stole rather than engaging in shoplifting primarily for their own personal consumption. The large group of novice shoplifters, the **snitches**, was characterized by a tendency to steal for their own personal gratification, quite often stealing items of small monetary value.[100]

Richard H. Moore's typology of shoplifters goes beyond the preliminary categorization offered by Cameron and further delves into the motivational variation among these offenders. *Impulsive shoplifters* were inexperienced, rarely planned the offense in advance, and were quite remorseful upon apprehension. *Occasional shoplifters* made up about 15% of Moore's sample, representation similar to the impulsive group. The offending of the occasional group was more frequent than that of the impulsive group and was primarily motivated by peer pressure. The smallest group was the *episodic shoplifters,* who generally had psychological problems. *Amateur shoplifters* were the largest type, making up slightly more than one-half of the sample. Shoplifting was a fairly regular activity for this group, and their offending incidents were calculated to maximize profit and minimize risk. *Semiprofessional shoplifters,* making up almost 12% of the sample, were the group for whom shoplifting was an integral part of their everyday lives. Members of this group possessed the greatest degree of skill and expertise in their offending and showed a clear preference for more expensive items. Moore found that it was only the semiprofessional shoplifters who, like the boosters in Cameron's research, stole merchandise for resale to others.[101] Because Moore's sample consisted entirely of convicted shoplifters, the extent to which the typology he developed is applicable to the majority of shoplifters, those who are never apprehended, is unclear.

In another attempt to develop a typology, **Frank J. McShane** and **Barrie A. Noonan** used a sophisticated statistical technique called "cluster analysis" to sort shoplifters into groups, taking into account relevant demographic characteristics, prior offending history, psychological factors, and measures of life purpose.[102] Using data on 75 subjects who had been apprehended for shoplifting in a variety of retail stores, McShane and Noonan identified four clusters of shoplifters. *Rebels,* accounting for almost 19% of the sample, were primarily composed of younger females with a significant prior history of offending. *Reactionaries* were slightly more than 27% of the sample and were similar to the rebels in that they often had the economic means to pay for the stolen merchandise. Members of this group were older, had higher levels of education, and were more likely to be married and to be male compared to members of other groups. A "distinguishing characteristic of these shoplifters was that occupational pressure was found to be the exclusively reported psychosocial stressor."[103] *Enigmas* were almost one-half of the sample (41.43%), and these offenders, like reactionaries, were older and slightly more likely to be male than most other groups, with a low likelihood of prior criminal offending. Members of this group "were characterized by a notable lack of apparent psychosocial stressors preceding apprehension."[104] The final group, the *infirm,* were more likely to be female than male, and this category was most likely to contain the elderly. Perhaps this latter finding explains another defining characteristic of this group, their tendency to have "experienced more previous episodes of chronic illness."[105]

The Thrill of It All

Many shoplifters have the means to afford the items they steal; in fact, many have the money on them at the time of the offense. Hence there must be some motivation that drives shoplifters other than financial need. Is shoplifting a thrill-seeking activity? Jack Katz, whose work was discussed in Chapter 4, argues that many property crimes, including shoplifting, represent "sneaky thrills"—in other words, it is not a desire for the object that leads to the crime but the crime that makes the object desirable.[106] Referring to adolescents in particular, Katz states that "quite apart from what is taken, they may regard 'getting away with it' as a thrilling demonstration of personal competence, especially if it is accomplished under the eyes of adults."[107] Using self-report data from college students in his classes over a three-year period, Katz concludes that many individuals, once they are apprehended for shoplifting, report feelings of profound degradation, reflecting their basic awareness that shoplifting is wrong. The sense of thrill does not last, as further evidenced by the Finnish adolescents in Kivivuori's research who cited boredom as a reason for desistance from shoplifting. Learn more about the crime of shoplifting at Web Extra! 11-4.

Web EXTRA! Web Extra! 11-4 at crimtoday.com

CRIME IN THE NEWS
Boys, 7 and 10, Busted for Burglary

The arrest of three children, one only 7 years old, on burglary charges has stumped police officers in this Atlanta suburb.

Investigators say none of the boys seem to feel any remorse, and police worry that apparent crimes by youngsters still in elementary school is a sign of things to come.

"We don't know why they do it," Kennesaw police Detective Terry Bishop told APBnews.com. "Maybe its just to shock people. It could be because they're exposed to so much."

THE YOUNGEST EVER

Indeed, police thought the arrest of a 13-year-old boy last week in connection with a burglary would be one of their youngest apprehensions ever for such a crime.

But on Monday, two Kennesaw Elementary School students were caught allegedly vandalizing a home in the high-priced Hillsborough Chase area of Kennesaw.

Police said the boys, ages 7 and 10, were ransacking the house and had smashed a telephone and a ceramic pedestal with a baseball bat. The pair allegedly grabbed

about $1,000 worth of jewelry, a Samurai sword and some ammunition for a handgun, police said.

The 10-year-old is becoming familiar with the criminal justice system. Police said he also faces charges in connection with a burglary two weeks ago and is awaiting a hearing on still more burglary charges in nearby Cherokee County.

Source: Randy Wyles, "Pair Caught Ransacking Home, Police Say," APB News, November 1, 2000. Reprinted with permission.

BURGLARY

In 1967, the President's Commission on Law Enforcement and Administration of Justice noted that the high prevalence of burglaries and the numerous costs incurred by victims make this offense one of the "major reasons for America's alarm about crime."[108] Burglary continues to be a highly prevalent crime. Based on a recent examination of victimization data, 72% of households within the United States are burglarized at least once over the average lifetime.[109] The risk of burglary within any given year is much lower, but even so burglary is accompanied by fear because the offense invades the sanctity and privacy of the home and threatens the existence of businesses. Who are the offenders? Are they primarily professionals who plan their offenses with great care and carry out their tasks with precision and finesse? While the professional burglar is part of our popular culture, this image is far removed from the reality of how most burglars operate. The overwhelming majority of burglars are not charismatic figures who silently steal into a dwelling and make off with the contents of the safe. Bernard Welch, described at the beginning of this chapter, does not represent the typical burglar, either historically or currently.

As discussed in Chapter 2, burglary involves unlawful entry into a structure for the purpose of felony commission, generally a theft. The structure may be a business, a residence, or some other type of building. Force is not a necessary ingredient of burglary, but burglaries are differentiated by whether force is used. In its collection of crime data, the FBI distinguishes between burglaries involving forcible entry, unlawful entry, and attempted forcible entry.[110] According to UCR data for 1999, the majority of burglaries involved

forcible entry, followed in prevalence by unlawful entry and then by attempted forcible entry. In 1999, as in previous years, a slight majority of all burglaries occurred during the day; however, residential burglaries are more likely to occur during the evening.[111] In contrast to robbery, burglary is generally "a victim-avoiding crime."[112] Most residential burglars commit their offenses at a time when residents are unlikely to be home, and the knowledge of such information is important in target selection.

The consequences of both residential and commercial burglary can be quite profound for the victim. Residential burglaries, by definition, do not involve direct confrontation between the victim and the offender; however, the fear left in the aftermath of the offense can have lasting effects on the victim. The invasion of one's home produces a level of fear and apprehension beyond the dollar loss of the property taken. In cases of commercial burglary, because the targets are likely to be smaller, more economically precarious businesses, the loss from burglaries can seriously affect the business's continued viability.[113]

The Social Ecology of Burglary

Just as the propensity for property crime offending varies among individuals, so too do rates of property crime across large aggregate units like states, cities, and communities. Burglary rates are higher in large metropolitan areas and in particular regions of the country, such as the Midwest. Most research on variations in property crime at the aggregate level has examined how economics influences rates of crime. Lifestyle theory[114] and routine activities theory[115] (described in Chapter 4) have had a significant impact on explanations of how the nature and level of property crime offending have altered in response to changes in the routine activities and structures of daily activity. Basically, both of these theoretical perspectives emphasize how the opportunity structure of crime is affected by the everyday activities and environments of victims and offenders. For a criminal act to occur, three ingredients are necessary: (1) someone who wants something (a motivated offender) coming into direct contact with, (2) someone who has that thing (a suitable target), and (3) the lack of anything or anyone to inhibit the crime (a capable guardian). Individuals, families, and communities all change in response to changes in technology, changes in the production and distribution of services and goods, and changes in the social structure of the population. For example, advance in technology have made television sets, radios, stereo systems, and other electronic devices lighter and smaller in the post–World War II United States and hence more suitable targets because they are easier to steal.[116] The changes in crime rate trends since World War II are related not to an increase in the supply of motivated offenders, but to changes in the patterns of routine activities. The basic contention of both lifestyle theory and routine activities theory is that what people do, where they do it, how often they do it, and with whom they do it all influence criminal victimization risk. The concern is to explore not why people commit crimes but rather "how the structure of social life makes it easy or difficult for people to carry out these inclinations," which are taken as a given.[117] The structure of everyday life in one's city, neighborhood, home, workplace, and so forth not only constrains the opportunity for individuals to act on inclinations to commit crimes, but also limits the ability of people to avoid victimization. As Marcus Felson states, "To attack other people or their property, you usually need to gain direct access to them. You have to find or stumble upon them, or they may stumble upon you. . . . The criminal event is a systematic result of the convergence of people and things over space and time. Routine activities provide choices to individuals, including criminals, and set the stage for subsequent events determining the success of the offender in carrying out the crime, or of the potential victim in avoiding victimization."[118]

In a study of residential burglary, Lawrence E. Cohen and David Cantor were interested in testing Michael Hindelang's hypothesis that the affluence of a household was a more important factor in its selection as a target than was ease of access to the household.[119] This hypothesis was offered as a means to resolve the often contradictory findings of previous research on the relationship between the impact of income and race on burglary victimization. Research by P. H. Ennis in the late 1960s found that while burglary rates were higher for blacks than for whites, there is an interaction between race and income.[120] The lowest income groups for whites and the highest income groups for blacks had the highest victimization risk. Cohen and

Cantor sought to test Hindelang's assertion by developing a measure of guardianship that distinguished between homes as more occupied (that is, someone in the home at least 15 hours during the week) and less occupied. The findings largely confirmed Hindelang's hypothesis in that the type of area was found to be the strongest predictor of burglary victimization; however, the relationship between income and victimization risk is not linear. The highest income households and the lowest income households in areas both within and outside the central city had the highest victimization risk.

Using data from the British Crime Survey, Robert J. Sampson and John D. Wooldredge estimated the risk for crimes like burglary and personal theft.[121] Given the specific implications of two components of opportunity theory for victimization risk—the proximity of suitable targets and motivated offenders and the spatial structure of community organization—these researchers were concerned with the impact of community context on lifestyle. For example, opportunity theory hypothesizes that single-adult households are associated with a decrease in guardianship and a corresponding greater risk of victimization than are two-adult households. The proportion of such households may vary between communities; "regardless of one's household composition and even proximity to offenders, living in a community with low guardianship and surveillance may increase victimization risk."[122] The ability of an individual's living arrangement to predict victimization risk may not be a significant factor in victimization risk once relevant structural factors are considered. The influence may be more of where the household is located and the nature of the surrounding households than that of a particular household. The findings from Sampson and Wooldredge's research reveal that the highest victimization risk for burglary is found within single-adult households compared to households with at least two adults. Also younger heads of households and those households left unguarded had the highest victimization risk. Of the seven community-level variables included in the analysis, all but one had moderate to strong effects. The highest victimization risks were for residents in areas characterized by high unemployment, high building density, primary individual households, and single-parent households with children. Thus, even controlling for the individual-level factor of single-person households, the community measure of percentage of single-adult households continues to have a significant effect on increasing the risk of burglary victimization.

In looking at personal theft, Sampson and Wooldredge found that victimization risk for this offense is less for those who are married, older, and male.[123] Victimization risk was higher for individuals with more education and for women. Sampson and Wooldredge explain that these findings are consistent with the predictions of opportunity theory upon consideration of the fact that people of higher socioeconomic status are attractive targets and that the association of purse snatching with personal theft helps to

THEORY VERSUS REALITY
Ethnographic Research on Active Burglars

Ethnographic research purports to understand the nature of burglary by getting as close as possible to the everyday social world of burglars. Rather than focusing on a very large group of burglars, such as those represented by arrest statistics, ethnographic research (discussed in Chapter 2) attempts to understand burglars' way of life and hence offers a depth rarely achieved in survey research or research using official data. However, the information solicited in ethnographic research is taken from a small group of research subjects—as small as one if a case study approach is used. Ethnographic research is often dangerous, costly, and time consuming. The question arises, then, of whether it is worthwhile. Commenting on his own use of this approach in early work on burglars, Neil Shover acknowledged, "A great deal of time and leg work was required to set up and conduct these free-world interviews, and on balance I am not certain they were worth it. I elicited virtually nothing in them which had not been obtained in the earlier stages of the study when I was concentrating upon prison inmates and reading autobiographies."[1]

Do criminologists learn anything special about burglars by focusing on active burglars who are not currently incarcerated? This question is especially important because imprisoned burglars may be quite different from those still on the streets. The incarcerated offenders represent failure, while those who are free are relatively successful burglars who have avoided apprehension. This distinction, however, may be more myth than reality for the vast majority of burglars. The professionalized nature of burglary is quite minimal at best and hence not really the primary rationale for the usefulness of ethnographic data. The true benefit is related to an essential methodological issue common to all research endeavors; it is the classic issue of how individuals behave when they know they are being studied. In the case of studying burglars who are active versus those who are incarcerated, Richard T. Wright and Scott H. Decker note that individuals behave differently "in the wild" than in the jailhouse. The researchers rely on statements made by two of the pioneers in criminology, Edwin Sutherland and Donald Cressey, more than 30 years ago: "Those who have had intimate contacts with criminals in the open know that criminals are not 'natural' in police stations, courts, and prisons, and that they must be studied in their everyday life outside of institutions if they are to be understood."[2] It is this concern for getting as close as possible to the social world one is studying that marks the tradition of ethnography. A further benefit in studying offenders outside institutional settings is the elimination of any bias or distortions that the setting may have on the subject's ability or willingness to be open with the interviewer. Offenders who are currently incarcerated may feel that even in the face of assurances of confidentiality, they can "affect their chances of being released" by what they say or do not say to the researchers. As Wright and Decker state, "Assurances of confidentiality notwithstanding, many prisoners remain convinced that what they say will affect their chances of being released and, therefore, they portray themselves in the best possible light."[3]

Ethnographic research has already been described in Chapter 10, where research by Richard Wright and Scott Decker on armed robbers was discussed. This chapter presents further ethnographic research by Wright and Decker, this time on residential burglars. During 1989, the researchers located and interviewed 105 active residential burglars in St. Louis, Missouri. To qualify for inclusion in Wright and Decker's research, the offenders had to meet one of three criteria: they had to (1) have committed a residential burglary within two weeks prior to contact, (2) define themselves as residential burglars, or (3) be labeled as residential burglars by other offenders so identified. Research subjects were identified by the field workers whom Wright and Decker employed, most of whom were ex-offenders. The interviews with the subjects were all conducted in the field. Building on previous research on active offenders not currently incarcerated, Wright and Decker provide insight into various facets of the offending of burglars, including an examination of their motivation, target selection, entry method, search for valuable goods, and disposal of goods. In addition to answering questions, the offenders were asked to reconstruct their most recent residential burglary offense.

Defining the eligibility of subjects for research and using field workers are common practices in ethnographic research. Similar strategies were followed in the other ethnographic research projects discussed in this chapter. They include research on 30 active burglars in an urban Texas setting by Paul F. Cromwell and his colleagues[4] and research on the professional fence by Darrell J. Stoffensmeier.[5] As you read through the discussion of research in this chapter, keep in mind the strengths of ethnographic research and the insights to be gained by studying criminal offenders within their social and cultural contexts.

DISCUSSION QUESTIONS

1. What is ethnographic research? How does it differ from other types of research in the field of criminology?

(continued on the next page)

(continued from previous page)

2. Can criminologists learn anything special about burglary by focusing on active burglars who are not currently incarcerated?
3. What does the ethnographic research on residential burglars that has been conducted by Richard Wright and Scott Decker

add to our knowledge about burglary?

1. Neil Shover, "Structures and Careers in Burglary," *Journal of Criminal Law, Criminology, and Police Science*, Vol. 63, No. 4 (1972), p. 541.
2. Edwin Sutherland and Donald Cressey, *Criminology*, 8th ed. (Philadelphia: Lippincott, 1970), p. 68, cited in Richard T. Wright and Scott H. Decker, *Burglars on*

the Job: Streetlife and Residential Break-ins (Boston: Northeastern University Press, 1994), p. 5.
3. Wright and Decker, *Burglars on the Job*, p. 5.
4. Paul F. Cromwell, James N. Olson, and D'Aunn Wester Avary, *Breaking and Entering: An Ethnographic Analysis of Burglary* (Newbury Park, CA: Sage, 1991).
5. Darrell J. Steffensmeier, *The Fence: In the Shadow of Two Worlds* (Savage, MD: Rowman and Littlefield, 1986).

explain the greater victimization risk for women. The community factors of the percentage of single adults with children, social cohesion, and street activity were significantly related to victimization risk. Areas characterized by a high degree of family disruption, low social cohesion, and a large amount of street activity had higher victimization risks for personal theft. Sampson and Wooldredge conclude that an overemphasis on individual patterns and lifestyle masks the more substantial effect that neighborhood context has on victimization risks for property crimes like burglary and personal theft. You can learn more about burglary trends by visiting the Bureau of Justice Statistics via Web Extra! 11-5.

Web Extra! 11-5 at crimtoday.com

Types of Burglars

Professional burglars exist, but they are not simply the end of a crude continuum. Building on **Mike Maguire**'s three-part typology of burglary types, Neil Shover analyzes how the social organization of burglary may vary. Maguire offered three basic categories of burglars; low-level, middle-range, and high-level.[124] *Low-level burglars,* primarily found among juveniles, often do their crimes "on the spur of the moment," usually work with others, and are easily dissuaded from a particular target by sound locks, alarms, and or other such security devices. The rewards gained from offending for this group are generally not significant, and many desist from burglary as they get older and as they feel "the pull of conventional relationships and fear of more severe adult sanctions."[125] Members of this group do not develop connections that allow them to move large volumes of stolen goods.

Middle-range burglars are generally a bit older, though they may have begun their offending in burglary as juveniles. These offenders quite often go back and forth between legitimate pursuits and involvement in crime. The use of alcohol and other drugs is more common among middle-range offenders than among the other three groups of burglars. These offenders select targets that take into ac-

count both potential payoff and the risk involved; however, this group is not as easily dissuaded by security devices as are the low-level burglars. While their take from their crimes may be substantial at times, they lack the type of connections that would permit dealing in stolen goods on a large scale.

High-level burglars are professionals. Burglary is an offense characterized by a large prevalence of co-offending, and high-level burglars work in organized crews and "are connected with reliable sources of information about targets."[126] Members of this group earn a good living from the proceeds of their crimes, which are carefully planned, including target selection, generally with the assistance of outside sources. Shover characterizes members of this group as "misfits in a world that values precise schedules, punctuality, and disciplined subordination to authority. High-level thieves value the autonomy to structure life and work as they wish."[127] Professional burglars may be known to the police, but due to their "task-force approach to organization," their activities remain largely concealed from detection.[128] It is only high-level burglars who would attempt such large-scale thefts as the art theft described at the beginning of this chapter.

Burglary Locales

Burglaries at any level may take place within residences or commercial buildings. Although most research has been devoted to residential burglary, many of the findings on patterns of offenders apply to both types. Police reports generally detail the time of the burglary; nighttime residential burglary and daytime commercial burglary are considered the most serious. Evening hours are considered the time burglars are most likely to face homeowners, and daytime hours are the time considered to present the greatest risk of confrontation between offenders and customers or workers.[129] According to NCVS data from 1998, a slightly larger percentage of residential burglaries takes place during the daytime (36.4%) than during the evening hours (29.6%). One-third of burglary reports do not contain information on when the burglary occurred, so those incidents could significantly change the temporal pattern of occurrence.[130]

Burglary is known as a "cold" crime because there is usually very little physical evidence to link the offender to the offense, and by the time that the victims realize that they have been burglarized and called the police, the burglar is usually long gone. This is more true of residential than commercial burglaries, as the latter are more likely to involve alarms or other security devices. Data from the 1998 NCVS also reveal that approximately 44% of victims were working or engaged in leisure activities away from home when their residence was burglarized. Approximately 13% of victims reported being asleep during the burglary.[131]

The Motivation of Burglars

Rational choice perspectives have guided a great deal of research on decision making among property offenders. As discussed in Chapter 4, rational choice perspectives do not necessarily contend that the decision-making process that individuals use is defined by one objective view of rationality. Quite simply, decision making is thought to be guided by some sense of logic from the offender's perspective—one that counters claims of decision making as spontaneous and impulsive. The way in which offenders work out the logic of their decisions may not make sense objectively, but their decisions have their own internal logic from the standpoint of the offenders' social world and based on the understanding that many classes of decision makers are "limited information processors with various simplifying strategies for resolving decisions."[132] These limitations and assumptions must be kept in mind when considering why individuals commit residential burglary.

Across several research studies on active offenders, the most prevalent rationale behind the offense of residential burglary is economic in nature: a need for fast cash.[133] However, this need for cash is not necessarily characterized by the demand to satisfy the basic necessities of life or to maintain a conventional lifestyle. Based on ethnographic research conducted in Texas[134] and in St. Louis,[135] it is safe to say that active burglars do not as a whole have a conventional lifestyle; most of their everyday concerns revolve around maintaining their street status and supporting a lifestyle of self-indulgence and often gratuitous consumption of drugs. Wright and Decker contend that the need to maintain a party lifestyle, to "keep up appearances," and to provide basic necessities for themselves and their families are all key factors that drive the decision of offenders to commit a burglary.[136]

As in the ethnographic research on the lifestyle of armed robbers, discussed in Chapter 10, Wright and Decker found that the vast majority of the residential burglars they interviewed were committed to an "every night is a Saturday night" lifestyle. Thus when offenders discussed their offending as a means of survival, it had to be interpreted against the backdrop of this lifestyle, for it was only within this context that what they meant by "survival" emerged. The vast majority of offenders were committed to the street culture, and almost three-fourths of the money they obtained from burglary pursuits went to support their party lifestyle—a lifestyle that included illicit drugs, alcohol, and sexual pursuits. Keeping up appearances, another crucial part of street culture, resulted in the "need" to buy things that assisted in maintaining street status such as the right clothes. Just as in the conventional world, particular lifestyles are accompanied by signs of status: the right car, the right house, the right address, and so on. While some of the offenders interviewed by Wright and Decker did use the proceeds from their burglaries to pay the bills, the researchers also note that "the bills were badly delinquent because the offenders avoided paying them for as long as possible—even when they had the cash—in favor of buying, most typically, drugs."[137] The lifestyle of these offenders all but guaranteed that "the crimes they commit will be economically motivated," but it is not an economic motivation that results from a desire to satisfy needs as opposed to wants.[138]

Burglaries of commercial establishments are generally thought to be associated even more with instrumental ends, usually economic gain, than are residential burglaries. The same is true of professional burglars who invest more planning and strategy into their offenses. Far from operating from a standpoint of limited rationality, these offenders are calculated and carefully weigh risks and benefits. As Shover details in his work on burglars, professionals use quite sophisticated planning because they are motivated by finding targets with high payoffs, and hence they plan accordingly.[139]

What motivates offenders to focus on burglary as their crime of choice? Some offenders selected burglary quite simply because "they regarded burglary as their 'main line.' "[140] Because most of the offenders interviewed by Wright and Decker regarded themselves as hustlers, "people who were always looking to get over by making some fast cash," they would commit offenses other than burglary if a chance opportunity presented itself.[141] Otherwise, they stayed with the familiar, which was burglary. For many, burglary was not as risky as selling drugs, which has increasingly carried penalties that offenders fear. Robbery was perceived as too risky because it involves direct confrontation with the victim and hence a higher likelihood of being injured. Some offenders stated that they did not own the necessary equipment for robberies—namely guns. Because guns can be easily translated into cash in the street economy, "offenders who are in need of immediate cash often are tempted to sell their weapon instead of resorting to a difficult or risky crime."[142]

A small number of offenders in Wright and Decker's research in St. Louis indicated that "they did not typically commit burglaries as much for the money as for the psychic rewards."[143] This is consistent with Jack Katz's concept of sneaky thrills. As Katz contends, "If we looked more closely at how [offenders] define material needs, we might get a different image of these "serious thieves."[144] Based on his ethnographic research with property offenders, Kenneth D. Tunnell concluded that "excitement was present but only as a latent benefit—a byproduct of the criminal act."[145]

Target Selection

The sites for commercial burglaries are usually selected on the basis of the suitability of the target. Retail establishments are four times as likely to be burglarized than are other types of establishments, such as wholesale or service businesses. Based on a study of commercial burglaries in Philadelphia, Simon Hakim and Yochanan Shachmurove offer three reasons for the dominance of retail stores as burglary targets: "The merchandise is exposed so that the burglar knows precisely what his expected loot is, the merchandise is new and enjoys a high resale value to a fence, and burglars do not need to spend intrusion time searching for the loot."[146] Because burglars can "survey the facility while legitimately shopping or browsing through the store," retail establishments, especially those located away from major thoroughfares in places police response time will be slower, are prime targets.[147]

How do residential burglars select their targets? According to Wright and Decker, most residential burglars already have potential targets in mind before committing their offenses. This does not mean that the targets have been extensively observed or the burglaries carefully planned. Generally, burglars select a target through their knowledge of the occupants, "through receiving a tip," or "through observing a potential target."[148]

While a prior relationship between victims and offenders has long characterized many violent crimes, property crimes are generally not thought of as involving known victims. Certainly, the pattern of the victim-offender relationship in property crimes does not mirror that found within violent crimes, but there are some interesting dynamics in the case of residential burglaries. While the residential burglars interviewed by Wright and Decker rarely selected residences of close friends or relatives as targets, they did quite often purposefully select as targets residences of individuals otherwise known to them.[149] This finding supported earlier research by Neil Shover showing that close to one-half of all burglary offenders targeted a residence of someone known to them.[150] Offenders may target known drug offenders because they know they can be victimized with relative impunity. The context of a job also provided offenders the opportunity to get to know the occupants of the household and the daily routine as well as target suitability. The use of this strategy was common among offenders who discussed repeatedly victimizing the same household. While offenders did occasionally target residences of friends and loved ones, it was generally only in two scenarios. The first scenario occurred when an argument or some type of wrongdoing on the victim's part had occurred; in this case, the burglary was as much for revenge as for economic gain. The other scenario involved the offender being in such a desperate situation for money that anyone was fair game. While many offenders expressed remorse over having burglarized the homes of close family members, this was not universally the case, and burglars' expressions of remorse must be interpreted with the knowledge that "their allegiances seemed forever to be shifting to suit their own ends."[151]

Burglars may also select a target based on information from "tipsters," those who "regularly pass on intelligence about good burglary opportunities for a fee or a cut of the take."[152] This is not a very common method for most burglars, who generally lack such connections. Those who are able to use tipsters may do so in a variety of ways. Some offenders use individuals who work in service capacities within households and businesses, while others are in collusion with insurance agents or other middle-class people who feed the offender information in exchange for money or for some of the stolen merchandise.

The ethnographic research that Wright and Decker conducted in St. Louis made clear that only very rarely was a burglary target chosen on the "spur of the moment," but the type of observation that went into the selection was quite fragmented. However, fragmented observation may sometimes be all that is required. Given the lackadaisical nature of much household security and the fact that approximately one-fourth of burglaries do not involve any type of forced entry, "the world affords abundant poorly protected opportunities for burglars."[153] However, this does not mean that burglars are primarily opportunistic; in fact, such a designation runs counter to the primary concerns of most residential burglars. An open door or window is viewed less as an opportunity to commit burglary and more as a sign that the residence is occupied and hence an undesirable target. Opportunistic burglaries did in fact occur, but they did not fit the scenario of an open window inviting access. More commonly, by chance alone the offender happened to be in a place to observe the resident of a household departing. Because of the precarious nature of these kinds of opportunities presenting themselves, motivated offenders "usually relied on a more proactive strategy to locate potential burglary sites."[154] While offenders do not go out actively searching for potential targets as a general rule, they are "continually 'half looking' for targets."[155]

Target selection is also influenced by other key elements. One of the most important is signs of occupancy because "most offenders are reluctant to burglarize occupied dwellings." This finding, according to Wright and Decker, is "beyond dispute."[156] Burglars have reported that they avoid occupied homes because they want to avoid injury to their victims and to themselves. For some offenders, the fear of their own injury was greater than the fear of apprehension. As one offender claimed in Wright and Decker's research, "I'd rather for the police to catch me versus a person catching me breaking in their house because the person will kill you."[157] To ensure that a residence was unoccupied, offenders would knock on the door, offering some excuse if someone actually answered, phone the residence, or even phone the householder at work.

Most residential burglars also avoid residences with complex security devices because they generally lack the expertise to bypass the system. Even the offenders who engaged targets with alarms would only do so with certain alarms, again because of their lack of expertise. Only a small fraction of the offenders had anything like a sophisticated understanding of alarm security systems. Dogs also will deter an offender from a potential target. Dogs could injure the offender, and even small dogs make noise. Generally, a particular target was selected after the area, and generally offenders tended to stay within the same areas, sometimes within walking distance, because of a lack of access to cars. As one offender in Wright and Decker's research noted, "It's hard as hell getting on a bus carrying a big picture or a vase."[158]

Costs of Burglary

While the economic loss associated with burglary is difficult to estimate with any degree of accuracy, burglary is associated with several types of losses for the individual and the community. According to NCVS data for 1998, well over three-fourths (86%) of all household burglaries involve some type of economic loss. Approximately 20% of household burglaries involve losses exceeding $1,000, with 21% involving loss amounts between $250 and $1,000, 24% involving loss amounts between $50 and $249, and slightly more than 14% involving losses under $50.[159] Remaining categories, not described here, total another 21%. What do offenders steal from homes? According to self-reports of victims of household burglary in 1998, 29% of items stolen from homes are personal in nature, with the largest category being jewelry or clothing. Household furnishings represent 11% of all stolen items, and tools and cash represent the items most likely to be stolen in about 6% each of incidents. Another type of crime cost can be gauged by looking at whether victims lose time from work as a result of their victimization. Among all victims of household burglaries, approximately 7% lose some time from work. Of this group, one-third lose less than one day, slightly over one-half lose anywhere from one to five days, with the remaining 7% losing six days or more.[160]

Using NCVS data to test the relationship between criminal victimization and a household's decision to move, **Laura Dugan**'s research reveals that property crimes like burglary have a greater effect on the decision to move than do violent crimes.[161] Dugan had hypothesized that experi-

encing a violent crime rather than a property crime would have the greater effect on the decision to move—a hypothesis that was not supported by the data she analyzed. Instead, she found that a household's likelihood of moving increases after experiencing a criminal victimization near the home, an effect that was significant and strong for property crime but not for violent crime. Why might this be? Dugan states, "With property crimes like burglary, the anonymity of the offender makes it more likely that the victim blames the entire neighborhood [and] once the neighborhood is a focus for blame, a move is deemed the most effective prevention."[162] Victims do not simply move after one victimization but after several such victimizations, suggesting that it is repeated property victimization near the home that makes people move. The association of property crime victimization and a household's decision to move is a "particularly costly form of precautionary behavior"[163] in that individuals incur costs associated with unplanned relocation. Communities are also affected because the more affluent households are the ones that are the most likely to relocate after experiencing victimization.

The Burglary-Drug Connection

During the 1980s, the once parallel rates of robbery and burglary began to diverge, with robbery increasing and burglary decreasing. Using city-level data from 1984 to 1992, research by Eric Baumer and colleagues linked these changes to the effects that an increased demand for crack cocaine had on altering structures of offending.[164] As a stimulant, crack use is characterized by short highs that are then "followed by an intense desire for more crack."[165] If users are funding their drug habit through criminal pursuits, they need to rely on offenses that complement the demands of their drug of choice. This means that offenses like robbery, which can net cash quickly, directly, and at any time, are better suited to the habits and needs of crack users than is burglary, which is more likely to net stolen goods than cash. As crack use spread throughout inner-city communities, it had the effect over time of "flooding the informal economy with guns, jewelry, and consumer electronic goods" to such an extent that "there is little money to be made through burglary in these neighborhoods."[166] As the illicit market for crack drove down the street value of stolen property, "dramatically enhancing the attractiveness of cash,"[167] burglary became an offense with diminishing rewards. Ethnographic research on active burglars supports the claim that in areas characterized by a strong crack cocaine trade, there is also a "preference for cash-intensive crimes like robbery and a corresponding reduced preference for burglary."[168] The decision making of offenders basically changed as a response to the illicit drug market, but the change was not necessarily associated with a motivational change in the commission of the offense. Certain users of crack are committing crime as a means of supporting their habit, and this individual-level need comes to change the nature of the informal economy in certain communities. Stolen goods lose their street value, and offenders must change their choices in response to this, even though their motivation has not changed; they instead shift to another offense that gets them what they need. This is consistent with research previously discussed that emphasizes that rather than being strictly committed to one type of property offense, most property offenders are generalists.

The Sexualized Context of Burglary

Although economic gain is the primary motive for the vast majority of burglaries, there does exist a category of burglaries with "hidden sexual forces lying at their root."[169] According to Louis B. Schlesinger and Eugene Revitch, the sexual dynamics associated with burglaries may be of two general and interrelated types. One is expressed as fetishes in which the offender steals particular items, not for their material value, but because they provide an outlet for sexual gratification. Another type, voyeuristic burglaries, have a more subtle sexual dynamic in which the goal may be only to "look around, to inspect the drawers,"[170] but not to actually take anything. Schlesinger and Revitch analyzed the clinical records of 52 sexual murderers and found that the majority of these offenders had a history of burglaries. Burglary may serve as a precursor for more serious offenses to come and may constitute part of a pattern of sexual offending. The possible underlying sexual dynamics of burglary may be overlooked in routine investigations of burglary in the absence of a conscious mandate to look for such signs. The importance of this link is that a certain number of sexually motivated homicides begin as other offenses, such as burglary, and the ability to link the two early in the investigation can be important for forensic assessment. Several details of burglary should be more purposefully evaluated as they could be related to a progression of events that could culminate in homicide.

Mark Warr has investigated the connection of sexual offenses with property crimes from a different perspective.[171] Not only can sexual motives underlie property crimes, Warr argues, but the theoretical perspective of opportunity theory, discussed in Chapter 7, can explain patterns of rape and burglary. In Warr's conceptualization, "residential rape and burglary can be viewed as crimes of stealth that involve the unlawful entry of a structure" and hence "have very similar opportunity structures."[172] Using city-level arrest data, Warr finds support for his contention that both the type of residences and the type of people victimized are similar enough in certain rape and burglary incidents to call into question the idea that rape shares a criminal etiology exclusively with violent offending. Warr does not question the violent nature of rape but instead pursues another aspect of the heterogeneity of criminal etiology. Just as the label of violent crime encompasses a great number of diverse criminal behaviors more or less

similar to each other, so too do these incidents share attributes of nonviolent or property crimes. For a certain category of rape termed "home-intrusion rape," "the traditional distinction between violent crime and property crime may not apply," and such incidents represent a "hybrid offense"; they are "a violent crime with the opportunity structure of a property crime."[173] The correspondence in the opportunity structure of rape and burglary warrants consideration if research and investigative procedures are to identify the "proximate causes of rape."[174]

STOLEN PROPERTY

According to **Darrell J. Steffensmeier,** "the 1827 English statute—'a person receiving stolen property knowing the same to be stolen is deemed guilty of a felony'—is the prototype of subsequent American law. The exact wording may vary from one state to another, but the basic elements of the crime—'buying and receiving,' 'stolen property,' and 'knowing it to be stolen'—have remained essentially intact."[175] As previously discussed, a small number of thieves steal for their own consumption and also directly steal cash. In these cases, there is no need to translate the goods into cash. But as these are the exceptions, it is necessary to consider how stolen goods are translated into cash for most offenders? There are several answers to this question because "there are many paths that stolen property may take from thieves to eventual customers."[176] Receiving stolen property is engaged in for various levels of profit by individuals and groups with varying skill levels. Some burglars commit their offenses specifically to get something they know someone wants. In this case, the burglar sells the merchandise directly to the customer.[177] Burglars also may sell to people who are known to them or may take the stolen goods to places like flea markets or auctions. Other paths to disposing of stolen goods "involve the thief and dabbling 'middlemen' who buy and sell stolen property under the cover of a bar, a luncheonette, or an auto service station with the encouragement, if not the active participation, of the proprietor."[178] Some burglars also sell their merchandise to merchants and represent it as legal goods. The most complicated path from the thief to customers is through a **fence.** The use of a professional fence is the least common method of disposing of stolen goods for the majority of thieves but the most common method for professional burglars.

Steffensmeier links the rise of the fence to the availability of mass-produced goods made possible by industrialization.[179] Although there were certainly individuals who dealt in stolen goods before industrialization, it was only with mass-production techniques that it actually became profitable enough for great numbers of people to serve as fences. Steffensmeier used the case study method to research the fence just as **Carl Klockers** did in his classic work.[180] Klockers detailed the career of Vincent Swaggi, who had been a successful fence for more than 20 years. Steffensmeier profiled Sam Goodman, a white male almost 60 years old, whom he began interviewing in early 1980.[181] Building on Klockers's definition, Steffensmeier defines a *fence* as one who "purchases stolen goods both on a regular basis, and for resale."[182] The most crucial defining characteristics of the professional fence are that he or she has "direct contact with thieves," "buys and resells stolen goods regularly and persistently," and thus is a "public dealer—recognized as a fence by thieves, the police, and others acquainted with the criminal community."[183] Steffensmeier and other researchers have recognized variations among fences. Some fences are "occasional" in that their receipt of stolen goods is infrequent. Still other variations and distinguishing characteristics exist among the wide variety of those who in some way are part of the puzzle of how stolen goods move from original owner to the open market.

The Role of Criminal Receivers

In their ethnographic research on residential burglars, **Paul F. Cromwell** and his colleagues offer a three-part typology of criminal receivers: professional receivers, avocational receivers, and amateur receivers.[184] *Professional receivers* are those who fit the definition provided by Steffensmeier. The use of a professional fence to dispose of stolen goods is uncommon among the majority of residential burglars, who lack "sophisticated under-world connections."[185] Such connections often distinguish "high-level burglars" from the more typical and prevalent residential burglars.[186] Burglars and other thieves who develop access to fences cite a number of advantages to their use in disposing of stolen goods. The professional fence offers a safe and quick means of disposing of goods. This is especially the case with burglars who have committed a high-visibility crime, stealing goods that are easily recognizable. In Wright and Decker's ethnographic research on residential burglars, one burglar who had stolen from a local celebrity's house stated, "We couldn't just sell [the jewelry] on the street, it was like too hot to handle."[187] Fences are also the best outlet for a large volume of stolen goods, as this is one factor that distinguishes professional fences from other types. Some professional fences are "generalists" who deal in a wide variety of stolen goods, and others are "specialists" who deal only in certain types of goods. Goodman, the professional fence described in Steffensmeier's research, had started as a specialist but evolved into a generalist as a "function of greater capital and a growing knowledge of varied merchandise."[188] The vast majority of professional fences are involved in a legitimate business that serves as a cover for their criminal activity and facilitates it. Goodman operated a secondhand store whose inventory partially matched the stolen goods he received, a characteristic that made him a "partly covered fence." Fences who were "fully covered" did not deal in stolen goods that were outside their inventory in the legitimate business. "Noncovered" fences were those whose "illicit lines of goods

A Las Vegas pawn shop. Could this shop serve as a front for a fencing operation? *Buddy Mays, Corbis*

are distinct from the legitimate commerce."[189] The more a fence is able to cover his illicit activities by incorporating them into his legitimate enterprises, the safer he is from criminal detection and prosecution.

There is a great deal of variety in the businesses that fences use as a front for their criminal activity. They generally range from those viewed by the "community-at-large as strictly clean," like restaurants, to businesses that "are perceived as clean but somewhat suspect," like auto parts shops and antique shops, to businesses that are viewed as "quasi-legitimate or marginal," like pawnshops.[190] Goodwin's business, a secondhand store, was quasi-legitimate.

Some of the residential burglars interviewed by Wright and Decker stated that they avoided marginal businesses like pawnshops to dispose of stolen goods because, given the increasingly strict regulations of pawnshops, owners must often demand identification, take photos of those selling to them, and also have "hot sheets" of recently stolen goods. In addition, pawnshops generally do not provide the greatest return on the merchandise. Given the fact that many residential burglars commit their offenses for fast cash, "pawnshops almost always had the upper hand in negotiations."[191] The residential burglars who did regularly use pawnshops reported having an established relationship with the owner that enabled them "to pawn stolen property 'off camera'" because they had made transactions with the owner previously that had not resulted in "bringing additional police pressure to bear on his business."[192]

A second type of fence found in the ethnographic research is the *avocational receiver*. For this group, the buying of stolen property is a part-time endeavor "secondary to, but usually associated with, their primary business activity."[193] This is a fairly diverse group that can include individuals involved in respectable occupations, such as the lawyers or bail bondsmen who "provide legitimate professional services to property offenders who cannot pay for these services within anything but stolen property."[194] Others involved in illegitimate occupations, such as drug dealers, may also accept stolen goods. As opposed to the professional fence, the avocational receiver is distinguished by the "frequency of purchase, volume of activity, and level of commitment to the criminal enterprise."[195] Wright and Decker stated that "many of the tough inner-city neighborhoods of St. Louis have an informal economy that operates in part on the sale of stolen property" and that "drug dealers often play a prominent role in this economy, both as buyers and sellers."[196]

Amateur receivers are those "otherwise honest citizens who buy stolen property on a relatively small scale, primarily, but not exclusively, for personal consumption. Crime is peripheral rather than central to their lives."[197] These individuals are quite sporadic in their involvement in activities that generate stolen goods. Cromwell and colleagues cite as an example a "public-school teacher who began her part-time fencing when she was approached by a student who offered her a 'really good deal' on certain items."[198] While these individuals do not engage in receiving stolen property at the same level as professional or avocational fences, "they represent a large market for stolen goods" because they "compensate for lack of volume with their sheer numbers."[199] Stuart Henry's study of property crime among ordinary people, which he termed "hidden-economy crime," supported the involvement of ordinary citizens in a wide variety of property offenses, including receiving stolen property.[200] Learn more about how fences operate at Web Extra! 11-6.

Web Extra! 11-6 at crimtoday.com

ARSON

As noted in Chapter 2, the FBI defines arson as "any willful or malicious burning or attempt to burn, with or without intent to defraud, a dwelling, house, public building, motor vehicle or aircraft, personal property of another, etc."[201] It is only after a fire has been investigated and officially classified as arson by the proper investigative authorities that the FBI records the incident as an arson. Fires that are suspicious or of unknown origins are not included in the FBI's arson statistics.[202] Several diverse motives may underlie arson, from profit to thrill seeking.

Between 1989 and 1996, a wave of arsons at predominantly African-American churches throughout the United States caused enormous concern that these arsons were the result of hate crimes. Some people even contended that they were part of an organized effort for "members of various hate groups to start an all-out war between the races."[203] The level of concern about church arsons resulted in President Clinton's signing of the Church Arson Prevention Act of 1996,[204] legislation designed to increase penalties for church arsons and to accomplish other objectives, such as the rebuilding of destroyed churches. The National Church Arson Task Force had arrested 199 suspects in 150 of the 429 arsons under investigation and had concluded that most of the arsons were the result of individuals acting alone rather than an organized conspiracy.[205] While members of hate groups were certainly among the suspects arrested, so too were religious zealots, Satanists, and those motivated by revenge and greed. In fact, in November 1999, a minister and his accomplices were arrested for setting fire to their church; the suspected motive was a $270,000 insurance policy.[206] Another high-profile case of church arson involved Jay Scott Ballinger, who pleaded guilty in July 2000 to federal charges of setting fire to 26 churches across eight states over a five-year period. Federal prosecutors argue that Ballinger is the "most prolific church arsonist" apprehended since the work of the National Church Arson Task Force began. Ballinger was not a white supremacist but instead someone who considered himself to be a "missionary of Lucifer"; he attempted to make converts by signing people to contracts with the devil.[207] Ballinger was facing the death penalty because of the death of a firefighter killed during one of the fires, but his plea negotiation means that he will spend 42 years in prison.

Fire Setters

The scenario that comes to mind when most people think of arson is of "some crooked businessman torching his establishment in order to collect the insurance money." This is also the image that comes to property claims adjusters, argues Ken Brownlee in a recent article in *Claims* magazine.[208] While representing one part of the reality of arson, he says, arson for profit "has been only a minor part of the loss due to arson for more than a decade."[209] The crooked businessperson may represent one type of arsonist, but not the majority.

Whatever the motive, the vast majority of those involved in arson are juveniles. This pattern has been the case for some time. According to UCR data, juveniles represent the offenders in arson incidents at a much higher rate than is found in any other index offense; 48% of all arsons that are cleared are found to have involved a juvenile offender. Juveniles are a bit more likely to be involved in arsons in cities (52%) than in suburbs (44%) or rural areas (31%). Overall, "among the arson types, juveniles accounted for 26 percent of the clearances for arsons of mobile property, 47 percent of structural arson clearances, and 60 percent of those for arsons of all other property."[210] Juveniles are quite often the culprits in both residential and commercial fires. According to Jay K. Bradish, editor of *Firehouse* magazine, "Arson is the third leading cause of residential fires and the second-leading cause of residential fire deaths nationwide. Arson is the leading cause of deaths and injuries and accounts for the highest dollar loss in commercial fires."[211] In both residential and commercial arson, juveniles are involved more often than adults.

According to Eileen M. Garry, there are three general groups of juvenile fire setters.[212] The first consists of children younger than 7 who generally start fires either accidentally or out of curiosity. The second group are children between the ages of 8 and 12 who may start fires out of curiosity, but "a greater proportion of their fire setting represents underlying psychosocial conflicts."[213] The final group, youths between the ages of 13 and 18, have had a history of fire setting, usually undetected. It is believed that many of the fires started by juveniles may go undetected by official law enforcement because they are started on school property, perhaps even accidentally, and are discovered early by janitors or other school staff who do not report the incident. In response to a growing awareness of the problem created by juvenile fire setters, several agencies and organizations, including the U.S. Fire Administration, have developed model programs to mobilize community agencies across the nation to deal more effectively with juvenile fire setters. For more information on the problem of fire setting among juveniles, as well as the prevalence and issues surrounding arson in the United States, visit the National Fire Data Center online via Web Extra! 11-7.

Web **Web Extra 11-7 at crimtoday.com**
EXTRA!

SUMMARY

Property crimes vary along a continuum from crimes that are so petty in nature that they are not even noticed by the victim, to crimes on a scale so large that the associated economic loss can be vast. The property crimes of professional thieves are characterized by greater planning and financial reward than are those of the vast majority of thieves, who are referred to as "persistent" or "occasional." Strict specialization is rarely found among property offenders, who more typically move back and forth between similar types of property crimes, with infrequent involvement in violent offenses like robbery. While a certain degree of rationality characterizes the crimes and actions of the majority of thieves, despite their level of sophistication, it is a limited or bounded rationality that must be interpreted and understood within the social and cultural context of the everyday lives, situations, and choices of offenders.

The prototypical property crime is a larceny, usually petty in nature. The legal boundaries of larceny are determined by the value of the merchandise taken. One of the most frequent larcenies is shoplifting, a crime that is quite prevalent, especially among adolescents. As with all property crimes, shoplifting may be carried out by professionals, but generally this is not the case.

One of the most serious forms of property crime is burglary, which is distinguished legally by the amount of force used to gain entry into the structure. Both residences and commercial establishments are victimized by burglars. Other factors, such as the time of day, characterize the offense of burglary. As a property crime, burglary can often cross the line to more serious violent crimes like homicide, rape, and robbery. Even in the absence of violent crime, the social costs of burglary to the victim and to society are numerous.

Property crimes usually involve stolen goods that need to be translated into cash. The movement of stolen goods, a criminal offense, has been studied from several perspectives. The professionalization of those who move stolen goods ranges from that of the professional fence, whose business is buying and selling stolen goods in volume, to that of the amateur receiver of stolen goods, who quite often resembles an ordinary, honest citizen.

Arson, like the other property crimes examined in this chapter, has the potential to result in both great economic loss and loss of life. Although arson for profit certainly occurs, the majority of arsons involve adolescents who bring a variety of motives to fire setting.

DISCUSSION QUESTIONS

1. Explain the differences between professional property offenders and persistent property offenders.
2. To what extent are property offenders rational actors? Use examples from larceny, burglary, and receiving stolen property to illustrate your answer.
3. Why is so much attention given to shoplifting among adolescents?
4. How are drugs involved in the offending patterns of burglars?

5. What does it mean to talk about the "sexualized context" of burglary?
6. How are "honest" citizens and professional criminal receivers connected?

7. To what extent is "thrill seeking" a motivation behind several types of property offenses?

WEB QUEST!

Visit the Art Theft Recovery Project on the Web at http://www.saztv.com. Gather information on the types of resources available at the site, the personnel associated with the art theft recovery program, and the site's "major cases."

What does the site list as the "world's most wanted art" for the current year? Submit this information to your instructor if asked to do so.

LIBRARY EXTRAS!

The Library Extras! listed here complement the Web Extras! found throughout this chapter. Library Extras! may be accessed on the Web at crimtoday.com.

Library Extra! 11-1.   Bureau of Justice Statistics, *National Crime Victimization Survey Property Crime Trends, 1973–1999* (online document. Accessed March 25, 2001.)

Library Extra! 11–2.   Central Insurance Companies, *The Top 25 on the Burglary List!* (online document. Accessed March 25, 2001).

Library Extra! 11-3.   Bureau of Justice Statistics, *Violence and Theft in the Workplace: National Crime Victimization Survey* (Washington, D.C.: BJS, 1994).

Library Extra! 11-4.   Eileen M. Garry, *Juvenile Firesetting and Arson* (Office of Juvenile Justice and Delinquency Prevention, 1997).

NOTES

[1] Edwin Sutherland, *The Professional Thief* (Chicago: University of Chicago Press, 1956), p. 172.
[2] Carl B. Klockers, *The Professional Fence* (NY: Free Press, 1974).
[3] George Rengert and John Wasilchick, *Suburban Burglary: A Time and a Place for Everything* (Springfield, IL: Charles C. Thomas, 1985), p. 52.
[4] Marcus Felson, "Linking Criminal Choices, Routine Activities, Informal Control, and Criminal Outcomes," in Derek B. Cornish and Ronald V. Clarke, eds., *The Reasoning Criminal: Rational Choice Perspectives on Offending* (New York: Springer-Verlag, 1986), p. 127.
[5] Neil Shover, *Great Pretenders: Pursuits and Careers of Persistent Thieves* (Boulder: Westview Press, 1996).
[6] William Spain, "Art Crime of the Century Still Frustrates: Empty Frames Still Hang in Boston Museum," APB News, June 16, 2000. Accessed December 1, 2000. http://apbnews.com/newscenter/breakingnews/2000/06/16/artcrime_gardner0161_01.html
[7] William Spain, "Inside the World of Art Theft: Trade Ranks Third After Drugs, Arms Sales," APB News, June 16, 2000. Accessed December 1, 2000.
[8] Ibid. http://apbnews.com/newscenter/breakingnews/2000/06/16/artcrime0616_01.html
[9] Ibid.
[10] Ibid.
[11] Cited in Thomas Gabor, *Everybody Does It!: Crime by the Public* (Toronto: University of Toronto Press, 1994), p. 11.
[12] Edwin H. Sutherland, *The Professional Thief* (Chicago: University of Chicago Press, 1937), p. 3.
[13] Shover, *Great Pretenders*, p. xiii.
[14] Ibid., pp. xii–xiii.
[15] Ibid., p. 63.
[16] Mark S. Fleisher, *Beggars and Thieves: Lives of Urban Street Criminals* (Madison: University of Wisconsin Press, 1995), p. 29.
[17] Malcolm W. Klein, "Offense Specialization and Versatility among Juveniles," *British Journal of Criminology,* Vol. 24 (1984), pp. 185–194.
[18] Ibid., p. 186.
[19] Neil Shover, "Burglary," in Michael Tonry, ed., *Crime and Justice: A Review of Research* (Chicago: University of Chicago Press, 1991).
[20] See Shover, *Great Pretenders;* and Shover, "Burglary."

[21] John R. Hepburn, "Occasional Property Crime," in Robert F. Meier, ed., *Major Forms of Crime* (Beverly Hills, CA: Sage, 1984).

[22] Ibid., p. 76.

[23] Richard T. Wright and Scott H. Decker, *Burglars on the Job: Streetlife and Residential Break-ins* (Boston: Northeastern University Press, 1994), p. 35.

[24] Neil Alan Weiner, "Violent Criminal Careers and 'Violent Career Criminals': An Overview of the Research Literature," in Neil Alan Weiner and Marvin E. Wolfgang, eds., *Violent Crime, Violent Criminals* (Newbury Park, CA: Sage, 1989), p. 39.

[25] Michael R. Gottfredson and Travis Hirschi, "Science, Public Policy, and the Career Paradigm," *Criminology,* Vol. 26 (1988), pp. 37–55.

[26] Fleisher, *Beggars and Thieves,* p. 11.

[27] Ibid., p. 10.

[28] Ibid., p. 11.

[29] Dermot Walsh, "Victim Selection Procedures among Economic Criminals: The Rational Choice Perspective," in Derek B. Cornish and Ronald V. Clarke, eds., *The Reasoning Criminal: Rational Choice Perspectives on Offending* (New York: Springer-Verlag, 1986), p. 40.

[30] Ibid., p. 50.

[31] Thomas Bennett and Richard Wright, *Burglars on Burglary* (Aldershot, Hants, England: Gower, 1984).

[32] Walsh, "Victim Selection Procedures among Economic Criminals," p. 50.

[33] Neil Shover and David Honaker, "The Socially Bounded Decision Making of Persistent Property Offenders," *Howard Journal,* Vol. 31, No. 4 (1992), p. 290.

[34] Ramona R. Rantala and Thomas J. Edwards, *Effects of NIBRS on Crime Statistics* (Washington, D.C.: Office of Justice Programs, 2000), p. 12.

[35] President's Commission on Law Enforcement and Administration of Justice, *The Challenge of Crime in a Free Society* (New York: Avon, 1968), p. 64.

[36] David Barry, "Thieves Peel Off with 1,200 Orange Trees: Culprits Strike California Groves at Night," APB News, November 27, 2000. Web posted at http://www.apbnews.com/newscenter/breakingnews/2000/11/27/trees1127_01.html. Accessed December 1, 2000.

[37] Federal Bureau of Investigation, *Crime in the United States, 1999,* (Washington, D.C.: U.S. Government Printing Office, 2000), p. 45.

[38] Bureau of Justice Statistics, *Criminal Victimization in the United States,* (Washington, D.C.: Bureau of Justice Statistics, 2000), Table 84.

[39] Marcus Felson, *Crime and Everyday Life* (Thousand Oaks, CA: Pine Forge, 1998), p. 75.

[40] Ibid.

[41] Magnus Seng, "Theft on Campus: An Analysis of Larceny-Theft at an Urban University," *Journal of Crime and Justice,* Vol. 19, No. 1 (1996), p. 34.

[42] Ibid., p. 36.

[43] Ibid., p. 40.

[44] Elizabeth Ehrhardt Mustaine and Richard Tewksbury, "Predicting Risks of Larceny Theft Victimization: A Routine Activity Analysis Using Refined Lifestyle Measures," *Criminology,* Vol. 36, No. 4 (1998), pp. 829–858.

[45] Ibid., p. 852.

[46] Federal Bureau of Investigation, *Crime in the United States, 1999,* p. 51.

[47] Bureau of Justice Statistics, *Criminal Victimization in the United States,* Tables 87 and 89.

[48] Ibid., Table 61.

[49] Ibid.

[50] Felson, *Crime and Everyday Life,* p. 32.

[51] Bureau of Justice Statistics, *Criminal Victimization in the United States,* Table 64.

[52] Bureau of Justice Statistics, *Criminal Victimization 1999.* Web posted at http://www.ojp.usdoj.gov/bjs/pub/ascii/cv99.txt. Accessed March 30, 2001.

[53] Ibid.

[54] Caroline Wolf Harlow, *Motor Vehicle Theft* (Washington, D.C.: Bureau of Justice Statistics, 1988).

[55] Kevin Blake, "What You Should Know about Car Theft," *Consumer's Research,* October 1995, cited in Terence D. Miethe and Richard McCorkle, *Crime Profiles: The Anatomy of Dangerous Persons, Places, and Situations* (Los Angeles: Roxbury, 1998), p. 156.

[56] "Japanese Cars Top Thieves' Wish Lists," APB News, November 14, 2000. Web posted at http://www.apbnews.com/newscenter/breakingnews/2000/11/14/cartheft/1114_01.htm. Accessed December 1, 2000.

[57] Ibid.

[58] Miethe and McCorkle, *Crime Profiles.*

[59] Public Law No. 98–547, 98 Stat. 2754 (1984).

[60] Patricia M. Harris and Ronald V. Clarke, "Car Chopping, Parts Marking and the Motor Vehicle Theft Law Enforcement Act of 1984," *Sociology and Social Research,* Vol. 75 (1991).

[61] Ibid., p. 228.

[62] Joanna Sallybanks and Nerys Thomas, "Thefts of External Vehicle Parts: An Emerging Problem," *Crime Prevention and Community Safety: An International Journal,* Vol. 2 (2000), pp. 17–22.

[63] Ibid., p. 18.

[64] Ibid., p. 19.

[65] Ibid., p. 20.

[66] Miethe and McCorkle, *Crime Profiles,* p. 156.

[67] Michael Gottfredson and Travis Hirschi, *"A General Theory of Crime"* (Stanford, CA: Stanford University Press, 1990), p. 35.

[68] Ronald V. Clarke and Patricia M. Harris, "Auto Theft and Its Prevention," in Michael Tonry, ed., *Crime and Justice: A Review of Research* (Chicago: University of Chicago Press, 1992).

[69] Miethe and McCorkle, *Crime Profiles;* and Clarke and Harris, "Auto Theft and Its Prevention."

70 William W. Wattenberg and James Balliestri, "Automobile Theft: A Favored Group Delinquency," *American Journal of Sociology,* Vol. 57 (1952).

71 Miethe and McCorkle, *Crime Profiles.*

72 For research reporting no effect of social class, see Charles H. McCaghy, Peggy C. Giordano, and Trudy Knicely Henson, "Auto Theft: Offender and Offense Characteristics," *Criminology,* Vol. 15 (1977), pp. 367–385.

73 Pierre Tremblay, Yvan Clermont, and Maurice Cusson, "Jockeys and Joyriders: Changing Patterns in Car Theft Opportunity Structures," *British Journal of Criminology,* Vol. 34, No. 3 (1994), p. 314.

74 Ibid.

75 Clarke and Harris, "Auto Theft and Its Prevention," p. 23.

76 Dick Silverman, "Crime and Punishment: With Shoplifting and Employee Theft on the Rise, New Measures Are Being Taken to Stem the Losses," *New York Times,* August 8, 2000, p. x.

77 Gabor, *Everybody Does It!,* p. 80.

78 Dick Silverman, "Crime and Punishment: With Shoplifting and Employee Theft on the Rise, New Measures Are Being Taken to Stem the Losses," *New York Times,* August 8, 2000.

79 Lloyd W. Klemke, *The Sociology of Shoplifting: Boosters and Snitches Today* (Westport, CT: Praeger, 1992).

80 Silverman, "Crime and Punishment."

81 Ibid.

82 Klemke, *The Sociology of Shoplifting,* p. 16.

83 Ibid., p. 20.

84 Ibid.

85 Ibid., p. 19.

86 Ibid.

87 Ibid.

88 Lloyd W. Klemke, "Exploring Juvenile Shoplifting," *Sociology and Social Research,* Vol. 67, No. 1 (1982), pp. 59–75.

89 Mary Owen Cameron, *The Booster and the Snitch: Department Store Shoplifting* (New York: Free Press of Glencoe, 1964).

90 Klemke, "Exploring Juvenile Shoplifting," p. 62.

91 JoAnn Ray, "Every Twelfth Shopper: Who Shoplifts and Why?" *Social Casework,* Vol. 68 (1987).

92 Klemke, "Exploring Juvenile Shoplifting," p. 71.

93 Janne Kivivuori, "The Case of Temporally Intensified Shoplifting," *British Journal of Criminology,* Vol. 38, No. 4 (1998), p. 663.

94 Ibid. For support for this point, see also Robert Sampson and John Laub, "Crime and Deviance over the Life Course: The Salience of Adult Social Bonds," *American Sociological Review,* Vol. 55, No. 5 (1990), pp. 609–627; and David Farrington, "Age and Crime," in Michael Tonry and Norval Morris, eds., *Crime and Justice: An Annual Review of Research,* Vol. 7 (Chicago: University of Chicago Press, 1986).

95 Kivivuori, "The Case of Temporally Intensified Shoplifting," p. 678.

96 Terrie Moffitt, "Adolescence-Limited and Life-Course Persistent Antisocial Behavior: A Developmental Taxonomy," *Psychological Review,* Vol. 100, No. 4 (1993), pp. 674–701.

97 Kivivuori, "The Case of Temporally Intensified Shoplifting."

98 Frederick M. Thrasher, *The Gang: A Study of 1,313 Gangs in Chicago* (Chicago: University of Chicago Press, 1927).

99 Kenneth D. Tunnell, *Choosing Crime: The Criminal Calculus of Property Offenders* (Chicago: Nelson-Hall, 1992), p. 122.

100 Cameron, *The Booster and the Snitch.*

101 Richard H. Moore, "Shoplifting in Middle America: Patterns and Motivational Correlates," *International Journal of Offender Therapy and Comparative Criminology,* Vol. 23, No. 1 (1984), pp. 55–64.

102 Frank J. McShane and Barrie A. Noonan, "Classification of Shoplifters by Cluster Analysis," *International Journal of Offender Therapy and Comparative Criminology,* Vol. 37, No. 1 (1993), pp. 29–40.

103 Ibid., p. 35.

104 Ibid., p. 36.

105 Ibid.

106 Jack Katz, *Seductions of Crime: Moral and Sensual Attractions in Doing Evil* (New York: Basic Books, 1988).

107 Ibid., p. 9.

108 President's Commission, *The Challenge of Crime in a Free Society,* p. 64.

109 Koppel 1987

110 Federal Bureau of Investigation, *Crime in the United States, 1999,* p. 39.

111 Ibid.

112 Shover, *Great Pretenders,* p. 64.

113 Shover, "Burglary."

114 For representative examples of this perspective, see Michael J. Hindelang, *Criminal Victimization in Eight American Cities* (Cambridge, MA: Ballinger, 1978); and Michael J. Hindelang, Michael R. Gottfredson, and James Garolfalo, *Victims of Personal Crime: An Empirical Foundation for a Theory of Personal Victimization* (Cambridge, MA: Ballinger, 1978).

115 For representative discussions of this perspective, see Lawrence E. Cohen and Marcus Felson, "Social Change and Crime Rate Trends: A Routine Activity Approach," *American Sociological Review,* Vol. 44 (1979), pp. 588–607; and Marcus Felson and Lawrence E. Cohen, "Human Ecology and Crime: A Routine Activity Approach," *Human Ecology,* Vol. 8 (1980), pp. 398–405.

116 Felson and Cohen, "Human Ecology and Crime."

117 Marcus Felson, "Linking Criminal Choices."

118 Ibid., p. 120.

119 Lawrence E. Cohen and David Cantor, "Residential Burglary in the United States: Life-style and

Demographic Factors Associated with the Probability of Victimization," *Journal of Research in Crime and Delinquency,* Vol. 18, No. 1 (1981), pp. 113–127.

[120] P. H. Ennis, *Criminal Victimization in the United States: A Report of the National Survey, Field Surveys II: President's Commission on Law Enforcement and Administration of Justice* (Washington, D.C.: U.S. Government Printing Office, 1967).

[121] Robert J. Sampson and John D. Wooldredge, "Linking the Micro- and Macro-Level Dimensions of Lifestyle-Routine Activity and Opportunity Models of Predatory Victimization," *Journal of Quantitative Criminology,* Vol. 3 (1987), pp. 371–393.

[122] Ibid., p. 373.

[123] Ibid.

[124] Mike Maguire, *Burglary in a Dwelling* (London: Heinemann, 1982), cited in Shover, "Burglary," p. 89.

[125] Shover, "Burglary," p. 90.

[126] Ibid., p. 91.

[127] Ibid., p. 92.

[128] Ibid.

[129] Miethe and McCorkle, *Crime Profiles.*

[130] Bureau of Justice Statistics, *Criminal Victimization in the United States,* Table 59.

[131] Ibid., Table 64.

[132] Tunnell, *Choosing Crime,* p. 5.

[133] See Paul F. Cromwell, James N. Olson, and D'Aunn Wester Avary, *Breaking and Entering: An Ethnographic Analysis of Burglary* (Newbury Park, CA: Sage, 1991); and Wright and Decker, *Burglars on the Job.*

[134] Cromwell, Olson, and Avary, *Breaking and Entering.*

[135] Wright and Decker, *Burglars on the Job.*

[136] Ibid., p. 38.

[137] Ibid., pp. 45–46.

[138] Ibid., p. 47.

[139] See Shover, *Great Pretenders.*

[140] Wright and Decker, *Burglars on the Job,* p. 51.

[141] Ibid., p. 52.

[142] Ibid., p. 56.

[143] Ibid.

[144] Katz, *Seductions of Crime,* p. 79.

[145] Tunnell, *Choosing Crime,* p. 41.

[146] Simon Hakim and Yochanan Shachmurove, "Spatial and Temporal Patterns of Commercial Burglaries: The Evidence Examined," *American Journal of Economics and Sociology,* Vol. 55, No. 4 (1996), p. 445.

[147] Ibid., p. 452.

[148] Wright and Decker, *Burglars on the Job,* p. 63.

[149] Ibid.

[150] Shover, "Burglary."

[151] Wright and Decker, *Burglars on the Job,* p. 72.

[152] Ibid., p. 73.

[153] Shover, "Burglary," p. 83.

[154] Wright and Decker, *Burglars on the Job,* p. 100.

[155] Ibid., p. 80.

[156] Ibid., p. 110.

[157] Ibid., p. 113.

[158] Ibid., p. 86.

[159] Bureau of Justice Statistics, *Criminal Victimization in the United States,* Tables 81 and 83.

[160] Ibid., Tables 87 and 89.

[161] Laura Dugan, "The Effect of Criminal Victimization on a Household's Moving Decision," *Criminology,* Vol. 37, No. 4 (1999), pp. 903–930.

[162] Ibid., p. 924.

[163] Ibid., p. 905.

[164] Eric Baumer et al., "The Influence of Crack Cocaine on Robbery, Burglary, and Homicide Rates: A Cross-City, Longitudinal Analysis," *Journal of Research in Crime and Delinquency,* Vol. 35, No. 3 (1998), pp. 316–340.

[165] Ibid., p. 317.

[166] Ibid.

[167] Ibid.

[168] Ibid., p. 319.

[169] Louis B. Schlesinger and Eugene Revitch, "Sexual Burglaries and Sexual Homicide: Clinical, Forensic, and Investigative Considerations," *Journal of the American Academy of Psychiatry and the Law,* Vol. 27, No. 2 (1999), p. 228.

[170] Ibid., p. 232.

[171] Mark Warr, "Rape, Burglary, and Opportunity," *Journal of Quantitative Criminology,* Vol. 4, No. 3 (1988), pp. 275–288.

[172] Ibid., pp. 277–278.

[173] Ibid., p. 287.

[174] Ibid., p. 286.

[175] Darrell J. Steffensmeier, *The Fence: In the Shadow of Two Worlds* (Savage, MD: Rowman and Littlefield, 1986), p. 10.

[176] Ibid., p. 9.

[177] Ibid. See also Wright and Decker, *Burglars on the Job.*

[178] Steffensmeier, *The Fence,* p. 9.

[179] Ibid.

[180] Klockers, *The Professional Fence.*

[181] Steffensmeier, *The Fence.*

[182] Ibid., p. 13.

[183] Ibid.

[184] Cromwell, Olson, and Avary, *Breaking and Entering.*

[185] Wright and Decker, *Burglars on the Job,* p. 167.

[186] Shover, "Burglary," p. 103.

[187] Wright and Decker, *Burglars on the Job,* p. 169.

[188] Steffensmeier, *The Fence,* p. 25.

[189] Ibid., p. 23.

[190] Ibid., p. 21.

[191] Wright and Decker, *Burglars on the Job,* p. 179.

[192] Ibid., pp. 175–176.

[193] Cromwell, Olson, and Avary, *Breaking and Entering,* p. 74.

[194] Ibid., p. 75.

[195] Ibid., p. 76.

[196] Wright and Decker, *Burglars on the Job,* p. 181.

[197] Cromwell, Olson, and Avary, *Breaking and Entering,* p. 76.

[198] Ibid., p. 77.

[199] Ibid.

[200] Stuart Henry, *The Hidden Economy: The Context and Control of Borderline Crime* (Oxford: Martin Robertson, 1978).

[201] Federal Bureau of Investigation, *Uniform Crime Reports* (Washington, D.C.: U.S. Government Printing Office, 1999), p. 54.

[202] Ibid.

[203] Sarah A. Soule and Nella Van Dyke, "Black Church Arson in the United States, 1989–1996" *Ethnic and Racial Studies,* Vol. 22, No. 4 (1999), p. 725.

[204] Public Law 104–155.

[205] "Report Issued on Church Burnings," *Christian Century,* Vol. 114, No. 19 (June 18, 1997).

[206] Angie Cannon and Chitra Ragavan, "Another Look at the Church Fire Epidemic," *U.S. News and World Report,* November 22, 1999, p. x.

[207] Ibid.

[208] Ken Brownlee, "Ignoring Juvenile Arson Is Like Playing with Fire," *Claims,* Vol. 48, No. 3 (March 2000), p. 106.

[209] Ibid.

[210] FBI, *Uniform Crime Reports,* p. 56.

[211] Brownlee, "Ignoring Juvenile Arson Is Like Playing with Fire," p. 106.

[212] Eileen M. Garry, *Juvenile Firesetting and Arson,* Office of Juvenile Justice and Delinquency Prevention Fact Sheet 51 (Washington, D.C.: Office of Juvenile Justice and Delinquency Prevention, 1997).

[213] Ibid., p. 1.

More money has been stolen at the point of a pen than at the point of a gun.

—Woody Guthrie[1]

Organized crime will be a defining issue of the 21st century as the cold war was for the 20th century and colonialism was for the 19th century. Transnational crime will proliferate because crime groups are the major beneficiaries of globalization.

—Professor Louise Shelley, American University[2]

white-collar and organized crime

CHAPTER 12

I hate this crime doesn't pay stuff.
Crime in the United States is
perhaps one of the biggest
businesses in the world today.

—Peter Kirk, Professor of Criminalistics,
University of California[3]

Two men can keep a secret, as long
as one of them is dead.

—Organized Crime Proverb

"Do you know what the Mafia is?"
"The what?"
"The Mafia? M-a-f-i-a?"
"I'm sorry. I don't know what
you're talking about."

—Crime Boss Salvatore Moretti[4]

KEY CONCEPTS

IMPORTANT TERMS

asset forfeiture	Kefauver Committee	organized crime
corporate crime	Mafia	Racketeer Influenced and Corrupt
La Cosa Nostra	money laundering	Organizations (RICO)
environmental crimes	occupational crime	transnational organized crime
ethnic succession	*omerta*	white-collar crime

IMPORTANT NAMES

John Braithwaite	Gilbert Geis	Travis Hirschi
James William Coleman	Michael Gottfredson	Edwin H. Sutherland
Herbert Edelhertz	Gary S. Green	

OUTCOMES

LEARNING

After reading this chapter, you should be able to
- ◆ Discuss white-collar crime and its etiology
- ◆ Describe the nature of corporate crime
- ◆ Explain the history of organized crime in the United States, including La Cosa Nostra
- ◆ Identify new and emerging organized criminal groups within the United States
- ◆ Discuss the relationship between organized crime and the law

Hear the author discuss this chapter at *crimtoday.com*

INTRODUCTION

A few years ago, retiree George Salmon read an advertisement in a local newspaper calling for investors to support a new concept in wireless cable television transmissions. Wireless cable systems, which send television programs to homes using microwaves, serve around 500,000 subscribers nationwide.[5] Salmon called the company's representative and was told he could make as much as a 300% return on his investment in a short time. Attracted by the promise of quick riches, Salmon sent $10,000 to Broadcast Holdings in Costa Mesa, California. Broadcast Holdings promised to develop wireless cable systems in Missouri, Tennessee, and Oregon. Two years later, however, Broadcast Holdings closed after state regulators, charging that the company was trading unregistered securities, raided its offices. In all likelihood, Salmon will never see any part of his investment again.

According to a recent issue of *Worth* magazine, wireless cable is the "fraud du jour"—or the scam of the day. Since 1992, says the magazine, "unscrupulous promoters have raised over $300 million in questionable deals to set up wireless systems."[6] Similar promotions, touting other products, have been common for decades. In the 1960s and 1970s, many rushed to invest in shares of fake gold-mining and energy companies, spurred in part by the Arab oil embargo of 1973, which caused long "gas lines" to form in America's cities and towns. During the 1980s and early 1990s, fraudulent securities dealers hawked international, telecommunications, and biomedical stocks and other sometimes worthless equities almost with impunity, advertising in some of the country's most widely read financial journals and newspapers.

Financial scandals have a long and ubiquitous history in the United States, sometimes involving government regulators themselves. In 1929, for example, the Teapot Dome scandal embroiled the administration of President Warren Harding. The scandal began in 1921, when Secretary of the Interior Albert B. Fall secretly leased naval oil reserves at Teapot Dome, Wyoming, and Elk Hills, California, to developers without asking for competitive bids. A Senate investigation later revealed that large sums of federal money had been loaned to developers without interest. Fall was eventually fined and sent to prison, and a 1927 U.S. Supreme Court decision ordered the fields restored to the U.S. government.

WHITE-COLLAR CRIME

In 1939, famed criminologist **Edwin H. Sutherland** defined *white-collar crime* during his presidential address to the American Sociological Society. **White-collar crime**, said Sutherland, consists of violations of the criminal law "committed by a person of respectability and high social status in the course of his occupation."[7] Many criminologists do not properly understand crime, Sutherland claimed, because they fail to recognize that the secretive violations of public and corporate trust by those in positions of authority are, in fact, just as criminal as predatory acts committed by people of lower social standing.

As Sutherland told those gathered for the address: My thesis is that the traditional "conception(s) and explanations of crime [are] misleading and incorrect; that crime is in fact not closely correlated with poverty or with the psychopathic and sociopathic conditions associated with poverty, and that an adequate explanation of criminal behavior must proceed along quite different lines. The conventional explanations are invalid principally because they are derived from biased samples. The samples are biased in that they have not included vast areas of criminal behavior of persons not in the lower class."[8]

The criminality of upper-class persons "has been demonstrated again and again in the investigations of land offices, railways, insurance, munitions, banking, public utilities, stock exchanges, the oil industry, real estate, reorganization committees, receiverships, bankruptcies and politics," said Sutherland.[9] For still other examples, Sutherland pointed to those he called "the robber barons" of the nineteenth century, citing Cornelius Vanderbilt's famous response to inquiries about his sometimes flagrantly illegal activities. "You don't suppose you can run a railroad in accordance with the statutes, do you?" the wealthy Vanderbilt reportedly quipped.

In a later study that is still widely cited by criminologists, Sutherland reported on the frequency with which the nation's 70 largest corporations violated the law.[10] He found that each of the corporations he studied had been sanctioned by courts or by administrative commissions and that the typical corporation had an average of 14 decisions against it. Ninety-eight percent of corporations are recidivists, or commit crime after crime, Sutherland said, while 90% could be called "habitual criminals" under the habitual offender statutes which existed at the time of his study. "Sixty of the corporations (had) decisions against them for restraint of trade, fifty-four for infringements (generally, of patents), forty-four for unfair labor practices, twenty-seven for misrepresentation in advertising, twenty-six for (illegal) rebates,

and forty-three for miscellaneous offenses," wrote Sutherland.[11] He also found that of the 70 largest corporations studied, "thirty were either illegal in their origin or began illegal activities immediately after their origin."[12] Such businesses may have been built upon price-fixing or unregulated commodities offerings or via unlawful and clandestine negotiations with government regulators.

The only real difference between modern-day white-collar criminals and those of the past, Sutherland claimed, is that today's criminals are more sophisticated. Although no hard-and-fast figures were available to Sutherland, he estimated that the "financial cost of white-collar crime is probably several times as great as the financial cost of all the crimes which are customarily regarded as the 'crime problem.'"[13]

Sutherland also noted that white-collar criminals are far less likely to be investigated, arrested, or prosecuted than are other types of offenders. When they are—on rare occasions—convicted, white-collar criminals are far less likely to receive active prison terms than are "common criminals." If they are sent to prison, the amount of time they are ordered to serve is far less than one would expect given the amount of damage their crimes inflict on society. The deference shown to white-collar criminals, according to Sutherland, is due primarily to their social standing. Many white-collar criminals are well respected in their communities, and many take part in national affairs. Few are perceived as mean-spirited or even ill-intentioned. Private citizens who do not fully understand business affairs sometimes assume that those charged with white-collar crimes were unwittingly caught up in obscure government regulations or that government agencies chose to make examples of a few unfortunate, but typical, businesspeople.

Given these kinds of sentiments, criminologists felt compelled for years to address the question, "Is white-collar crime, crime?" As recently as 1987, writers on the subject were still asking, "Do persons of high standing commit crimes?"[14] Although most criminologists today would answer the question with a resounding "yes," members of the public have been far slower to accept the notion that violations of the criminal law by businesspeople share conceptual similarities with street crime. Attitudes, however, are changing as more headline-making charges are being filed against corporations and their representatives for illegal activities.

Examples of contemporary white-collar crime abound. The insider trading scam of stock market tycoon Ivan Boesky and the securities fraud conviction of junk bond king Michael Milken a few years ago show how fortunes can be amassed through white-collar law violations. Boesky was estimated to have netted a profit of $250 million for himself and a few close friends, while Milken paid a $600 million fine—far less than the amount he is estimated to have reaped from illegal trading.

The nationwide savings and loan (S&L) disaster of the 1980s, which some have called the "biggest white-collar crime in history," serves as another modern-day example of white-collar crime. The savings and loan fiasco was the result of years of intentional mismanagement and personal appropriation of funds by institutional executives. Although the actual amount of money lost or stolen during the scandal may never be known, it is estimated to run into the hundreds of billions of dollars. The collapse of just one such institution, Charles Keating's California-based Lincoln Savings and Loan Association, cost taxpayers—who were left to redeem the insolvent institution—approximately $2.5 billion, while the collapse of Neil Bush's Silverado Banking S&L in Denver cost nearly $1 billion. Some experts say that the final "bailout" of S&Ls nationwide will cost American taxpayers $500 billion[15]—much more than has ever been stolen in all bank robberies throughout the history of our country.

Another type of white-collar crime sprang from the low interest rates characteristic of the early and mid-1990s. Sham banking operations, often with high-sounding names and seemingly prestigious addresses, flourished—offering high interest rates and double-digit rates of return on investments held by the bank. Unfortunately, such "phantom banks," as they were dubbed by the federal comptroller of the currency, evaporated as quickly as they were formed, leaving investors stunned and sometimes penniless. Some of the schemes involved the sale of certificates of deposit in offshore banks, like those in the Caribbean; others bilked investors into buying millions of dollars of what was supposed to be newly privatized Russian stock; and still more offered the seemingly irresistible chance to earn exorbitant returns through sophisticated overseas investments. Recently, the Federal Deposit Insurance Corporation (FDIC) issued a list of 60 unregulated business entities illegally conducting banking businesses within the United States. Canadian officials added another 200 suspects to the list. As one expert on illegal banking operations explained, "It's difficult to prosecute the criminals who run phantom banks because many times the victims are unwilling to press charges or the schemes take months to unravel."[16]

An even more recent white-collar crime appears to have been involved in the 1997 bankruptcy of Canadian gold prospector Bre-X Minerals Ltd. In the mid-1990s, Bre-X officials claimed that assayed ore from the company's Busang mine in Indonesia proved that it owned what was likely to be the world's largest gold reserve. In what some have called "the greatest stock fraud of the century," shares of the company's stock soared from pennies to a value of $206 each. After a number of debacles, including the suspicious death of the company's chief geologist, who fell from a helicopter over the Indonesian jungle, the company admitted the truth of an independent report which showed that the company's claims were based on falsified data.[17] Bre-X shareholders were left with worthless stock certificates while the company's vice president of exploration filed for residency status in the Cayman Islands, where he owned approximately $6 million worth of beachfront homes.[18] Although shareholders sued to recover a portion of their money, David Walsh, Bre-X's President and Chief Executive Officer, died of a brain aneurysm at his home in the Bahamas in 1998. His $100 million estate was frozen, and in November 2000, shareholders reached a $10 million settlement with Bresea Resources, Ltd., a large Bre-X shareholder. The amount of the settlement, however, was far less than the estimated $6 billion that investors lost in the swindle.[19] Learn more about white-collar crime and law enforcement's response from the National White Collar Crime Center via Web Extra 12-1.

Web EXTRA! **Web Extra! 12-1 at crimtoday.com**

Miami businessman David Paul after his conviction on 68 counts of bank fraud. Paul was chairman of south Florida's CenTrust Bank, one of the nation's largest savings and loans. Should white-collar criminals be punished the same as other offenders? *Miami Herald Publishing Co.*

THEORY VERSUS REALITY
White-Collar Crime: The Initial Statement

At least one eminent criminologist has called the concept of white-collar crime "the most significant . . . development in criminology, especially since World War II."[1] The roots of the concept go back to 1939, when Edwin Sutherland first coined the term *white-collar crime* in his presidential address to the American Sociological Society. Details of that address are discussed elsewhere in this chapter. His speech concluded with the following five points:

1. White-collar criminality is real criminality, being in all cases in violation of the criminal law.
2. White-collar criminality differs from lower-class criminality principally in

an implementation of the criminal law, which segregates white-collar criminals administratively from other criminals.
3. The theories of the criminologists that crime is due to poverty or to psychopathic and sociopathic conditions statistically associated with poverty are invalid because, first, they are derived from samples which are grossly biased with respect to socioeconomic status; second, they do not apply to the white-collar criminals; and third, they do not even explain the criminality of the lower class, since the factors are not related to a general process characteristic of all criminality.
4. A theory of criminal behavior which will explain both white-collar criminality and lower-class criminality is needed.

5. A hypothesis of this nature is suggested in terms of differential association and social disorganization.

DISCUSSION QUESTIONS

1. Why is white-collar crime possibly the most significant development in criminology since World War II?
2. Why did Sutherland have to remind people that "white-collar criminality is real criminality"? Why might some have thought otherwise?

[1]Donald J. Newman, "White-Collar Crime: An Overview and Analysis," *Law and Contemporary Problems*, Vol. 23, No. 4 (Autumn 1958).

Source: Edwin Sutherland, "White-Collar Criminality," *American Sociological Review*, Vol. 5 (February 1940), pp. 1–12.

Definitional Evolution of White-Collar Crime

One early writer on white-collar crime explained, "The chief criterion for a crime to be 'white-collar' is that it occurs as a part of, or a deviation from, the violator's occupational role."[20] This focus on the violator, rather than on the offense, in deciding whether to classify a crime as "white-collar" was accepted by the 1967 Presidential Commission on Law Enforcement and Administration of Justice. In its classic report, *The Challenge of Crime in a Free Society,* members of the commission wrote, "The 'white-collar' criminal is the broker who distributes fraudulent securities, the builder who deliberately uses defective material, the corporation executive who conspires to fix prices, the legislator who peddles his influence and votes for private gain, or the banker who misappropriates funds in his keeping."[21]

Over the past few decades, however, the concept of white-collar crime has undergone considerable refinement.[22] The reason, according to the U.S. Department of Justice, is that "the focus [in cases of white-collar crime] . . . has shifted to the nature of the crime instead of the persons or occupations involved."[23] The methods used to commit white-collar crime, such as the use of a computer, and the special skills and knowledge necessary for attempted law violation, have resulted in a contemporary understanding of white-collar crime that emphasizes the type of offense being committed, rather than the social standing or occupational role of the person committing it. Some reasons for this shift are due to

changes in the work environment and in the business world itself. Others are pragmatic. In the words of the Justice Department, "The categorization of 'white-collar crime' as crime having a particular modus operandi [committed in a manner that utilizes deception and special knowledge of business practices and committed in a particular kind of economic environment] is of use in coordinating the resources of the appropriate agencies for purposes of investigation and prosecution."[24]

Between the early definitions of white-collar crime and those which came later, many other investigators refined the conceptual boundaries surrounding the term. **Herbert Edelhertz**, for example, defined *white-collar crime* as any "illegal act or series of illegal acts committed by nonphysical means and by concealment or guile, to obtain money or property, to avoid the payment or loss of money or property, or to obtain business or personal advantages."[25] **Gilbert Geis**, another early writer on the subject, grappled with the notion of "upperworld crime," which he called "a label designed to call attention to the violation of a variety of criminal statutes by persons who at the moment are generally not considered, in connection with such violations, to be the 'usual' kind of underworld and/or psychologically aberrant offenders."[26] Many writers, however, were quick to realize that upperworld, or white-collar, crime might have its counterpart in certain forms of blue-collar crime committed by members of less prestigious occupational groups. Hence the term *blue-collar crime* emerged as a way of classifying the law-violating behavior of people involved in appliance and automobile repair, yard maintenance, house cleaning, and general installation services.

Finally, in an effort to bring closure to the concept of work-related crime, the term *occupational crime* emerged as a kind of catchall category. **Occupational crime** can be defined as "any act punishable by law that is committed through opportunity created in the course of an occupation which is legal."[27] Occupational crimes include the job-related law violations of both white- and blue-collar workers. One of the best typologies of occupational crime to emerge in recent years is that offered by **Gary S. Green** in his book *Occupational Crime*. Green identifies four categories of occupational crime:[28]

- *Organizational occupational crime:* crimes committed for the benefit of an employing organization. In such instances, only the organization or the employer benefits, not individual employees.
- *State authority occupational crime:* crimes by officials through the exercise of their state-based authority. Such crime is occupation specific and can only be committed by officials in public office or by those working for them.

- *Professional occupational crime:* crimes by professionals in their capacity as professionals. The crimes of physicians, attorneys, psychologists, and the like are included here.
- *Individual occupational crime:* crimes by individuals as individuals. This is a kind of catchall category that includes personal income tax evasion, the theft of goods and services by employees, the filing of false expense reports, and the like.

For an interesting presentation of white-collar and occupational crime typologies, visit the National Check Fraud Center and Dr. Tom O'Connor's white-collar crime page via Web Extras! 12-2 and 12-3.

Web Extras! 12-2 and 12-3 at crimtoday.com

Corporate Crime

Corporate malfeasance, another form of white-collar crime, has been dubbed "corporate crime." **Corporate crime** can be defined as "a violation of a criminal statute either by a corporate entity or by its executives, employees, or agents acting on behalf of and for the benefit of the corporation, partnership, or other form of business entity."[29] Corporate crimes come in many forms, ranging from prior knowledge about exploding gas tanks on Pinto automobiles and GM pickup trucks to price-fixing and insider securities trading. Culpability, which often results in civil suits against the corporation along with possible criminal prosecutions, is greatest where company officials can be shown to have had advance knowledge about product defects, dangerous conditions, or illegal behavior on the part of employees.

In a somewhat unusual case, aircraft maintenance company SabreTech was convicted in 1999 in federal court in Miami of eight counts of causing the air transportation of hazardous materials and of one count of failing to provide training in the handling of hazardous materials. The charges resulted from the actions of company employees in improperly packaging oxygen canisters blamed for the 1996 crash of a Valujet airplane in the Florida Everglades. In that disaster, 110 people died. The case marked the first time that a maintenance company had faced criminal charges in connection with an air disaster in the United States. The company, which went out of business, was also charged in state court with numerous counts of murder and manslaughter in the crash. "This is the first criminal homicide prosecution involving a passenger aircraft tragedy in the United States," said Florida State Attorney Katherine Fernandez-Rundle.[30]

Two of the most massive corporate liability issues in U.S. history were settled in September 1994. In one case, U.S. District Court Judge Sam Pointer gave final approval to a

Susan and Jim McDougal, accused of conspiring with former President Bill Clinton in the Whitewater fiasco. What was Whitewater? Danny Johnson, *AP/Wide World Photos*

class action suit against makers and sellers of silicon gel breast implants.[31] The decision, which had taken years to reach, cleared the way for implant recipients to be paid $4.25 billion over 30 years. Of the 2 million American women who have had breast implants, approximately 90,000 filed claims under the action. Women whose claims are approved could each receive between $105,000 and $1.4 million, depending on age, health, and medical condition. Claimants had argued that many of the parties involved in the manufacture and surgical implantation of the implants were aware of the dangers represented by their products but had opted to market them anyway.

In an interesting aside, which many claimed was a continuing effort to cover up critical issues in the case, Mayo Clinic researchers reported in the prestigious *New England Journal of Medicine* at the time of the implant settlement that no link could be found between implants and autoimmune and other disorders reportedly suffered by women claiming to be negatively affected by the implants. It was later revealed that financial support for the study had come from precisely those groups with the most to lose in the financial settlement. Among the contributors were the American Society of Plastic and Reconstructive Surgeons ($500,000), Plastic Surgery Education Foundation ($300,000), American Society of Aesthetic Plastic Surgeons ($210,000), Dow Corning ($500,000), and Bristol-Myers Squibb ($100,000).[32]

The second corporate liability case settled in 1994 involved Union Carbide Corporation, which agreed to sell its entire remaining holdings in Union Carbide India Limited to the Indian company McLeod Russel India.[33] McLeod Russel was the highest bidder in a closed-door auction ordered by India's Supreme Court as part of the American company's punishment for a chemical leak at its storage facilities in Bhopal, India, on December 3, 1984. The tragedy in Bhopal, which many claim was due to criminal negligence, caused more than 3,000 deaths and disabled thousands of residents. Union Carbide had originally been ordered by Indian state courts to pay $81 million to the government as compensation for disaster victims. The country's Supreme Court later ordered the company to pay $470 million as final compensation. Another court then required the seizure of Union Carbide's remaining Indian assets and ordered that they be sold to the highest bidder. Union Carbide officials, who were threatened with murder charges, left the country.

In November 1999, the largest product liability settlement in history was reached between state attorneys general and representatives of the tobacco industry.[34] According to the terms of the agreement, tobacco companies agreed to pay $206 billion to 46 states over 25 years in compensation for the harmful health effects of tobacco and to reimburse the states and the federal government for monies spent on medical problems associated with tobacco use. Under the terms of the agreement, tobacco companies will spend another $1.7 billion to study youth smoking and to finance antismoking advertising. The four other states had reached their own settlements for an additional $40 billion before the federally endorsed settlement was reached.

Product liability cases, such as that involving the tobacco companies, are not necessarily based on violations of the criminal law. A relatively new area of corporate and white-collar criminality, which is defined solely in terms of violations of the criminal law, is that of crimes against the environment.[35] **Environmental crimes** are violations of the criminal law which, although typically committed by businesses or by business officials, may also be committed by

Crimes against the environment have recently become an area of special concern to criminologists. Why have such offenses only recently been recognized as crimes? *J. Muir Hamilton, Stock Boston*

other individuals or organizational entities, and which damage some protected or otherwise significant aspect of the natural environment.

Whaling in violation of international conventions, for example, constitutes a form of environmental crime. So, too, does intentional pollution, especially when state or federal law contravenes the practice. Sometimes negligence may contribute to environmental criminality, as in the case of the 1,000-foot *Valdez* supertanker owned by Exxon Corporation, which ran aground off the coast of Alaska in 1989, spilling 11 million gallons of crude oil over 1,700 miles of pristine coastline. In September 1994, an Alaskan jury ordered Exxon to pay $5 billion in punitive damages to 14,000 people affected by the 1989 spill and another $287 million in actual damages to commercial fishermen in the region. Exxon also agreed to pay $100 million in criminal fines.

Other acts against the environment violate more conventional statutes, although their environmental impact may be obvious. The devastating fires set in oil fields throughout Kuwait by retreating Iraqi Army troops during the Gulf War provide an example of arson which resulted in global pollution while negatively affecting fossil fuel reserves throughout much of the Middle East. These intentional fires, while properly classified as environmental criminality, also serve as an example of ecological terrorism because they were set for the purpose of political intimidation.

Learn more about environmental crimes from the *Villanova Environmental Law Journal* and the Federal Bureau of Investigation (FBI) at Web Extras! 12-4 and 12-5.

 Web Extras! 12-4 and 12-5 at
crimtoday.com

Causes of White-Collar Crime

When Edwin H. Sutherland first coined the term *white-collar crime,* he wrote, "A hypothesis is needed that will explain both white-collar criminality and lower-class criminality."[36] The answer Sutherland gave to his own challenge was that "white-collar criminality, just as other systematic criminality, is learned."[37] He went on to apply elements of his famous theory of differential association theory (discussed in Chapter 8) to white-collar crime, saying that "it is learned in direct or indirect association with those who already practice the behavior."[38]

Other authors have since offered similar integrative perspectives. **Travis Hirschi** and **Michael Gottfredson** (whose work was discussed in Chapters 6 and 8), for example, in an issue of the journal *Criminology* published half a century after Sutherland's initial work, wrote, "In this paper we outline a general theory of crime capable of organizing the facts about white-collar crime at the same time it is capable of organizing the facts about all forms of crime."[39] Their analysis of white-collar crime focuses squarely on the

development of the concept itself. Hirschi and Gottfredson suggest that if we were not aware of the fact that the concept of white-collar crime arose "as a reaction to the idea that crime is concentrated in the lower class, there would be nothing to distinguish it from other" forms of crime.[40] "It may be, then," they write, "that the discovery of white-collar criminals is important only in a context in which their existence is denied by theory or policy."[41] In other words, nothing is unusual about the idea of white-collar crime other than the fact that many people are loath to admit that high-status individuals commit crimes just as do those of lower status.

In fact, say Hirschi and Gottfredson, white-collar criminals are motivated by the same forces that drive other criminals: self-interest, the pursuit of pleasure, and the avoidance of pain. White-collar crimes certainly have special characteristics. They are not as dangerous as other "common" forms of crime; they provide relatively large rewards; the rewards they produce may follow quickly from their commission; sanctions associated with them may be vague or only rarely imposed; and they may require only minimal effort from those with the requisite skills to engage in them.

Hirschi and Gottfredson conclude, however, that criminologists err in assuming that white-collar criminality is common or that it is as common as the forms of criminality found among the lower classes. They reason that the personal characteristics of most white-collar workers are precisely those which we would expect to produce conformity in behavior. High educational levels, a commitment to the status quo, personal motivation to succeed, deference to others, attention to conventional appearance, and other inherent aspects of social conformity—all of which tend to characterize those who operate at the white-collar level—are not the kinds of personal characteristics associated with crime commission. "In other words," say Hirschi and Gottfredson, "selection processes inherent to the high end of the occupational structure tend to recruit people with relatively low propensity to crime."[42]

One other reason most criminologists are mistaken about the assumed high rate of white-collar criminality, Hirschi and Gottfredson tell us, is because "white-collar researchers often take organizations as the unit of analysis" and confuse the crimes committed by organizational entities with those of individuals within those organizations.[43] Similarly, rates of white-collar offending tend to lump together the crimes of corporations with crimes committed by individual representatives of those organizations when making comparisons with the rate of criminal activity among blue-collar and other groups.

A complementary perspective by Australian criminologist **John Braithwaite** says that white-collar criminals are frequently motivated by a disparity between corporate goals and the limited opportunities available to businesspeople through conventional business practices.[44] When pressured to achieve goals which may be unattainable within the existing framework of laws and regulations surrounding their business's area of endeavor, innovative corporate officers may turn to crime to meet organizational demands.[45]

Braithwaite believes that a general theory covering both white-collar and other forms of crime can be developed by focusing on inequality as the central explanatory variable in all criminal activity.[46] Although alienation from legitimate paths to success may lead lower-class offenders to criminal activity in an effort to acquire the material possessions necessary for survival, greed can similarly motivate relatively successful individuals to violate the law in order to acquire even more power and more wealth.[47] New types of criminal opportunities and new paths to immunity from accountability arise from inequitable concentrations of wealth and power. Inequality thus worsens both crimes of poverty motivated by the need to survive and crimes of wealth motivated by greed.

Braithwaite also suggests that corporate culture socializes budding executives into clandestine and frequently illegal behavioral modalities, making it easier for them to violate the law when pressures to perform mount. The hostile relationship that frequently exists between businesses and the government agencies that regulate them may further spur corporate officers to evade the law. Braithwaite emphasizes his belief that the potential for shame associated with discovery—whether by enforcement agencies, the public, or internal corporate regulators—can have a powerful deterrent effect on most corporate executives because they are fundamentally conservative individuals who are otherwise seeking success through legitimate means.[48]

Braithwaite also recommends implementation of an "accountability model," which would hold all those responsible for corporate crimes accountable.[49] Rather than merely punishing corporations through fines, personal punishment meted out to corporate lawbreakers, says Braithwaite, should have the potential to substantially reduce white-collar offending.[50]

In sum, Braithwaite contends that an integrated theory of organizational crime would include insights garnered from (1) strain theories, as to the distribution of legitimate and illegitimate opportunities; (2) subcultural theory, as applied to business subcultures; (3) labeling theory, on the way stigmatization can foster criminal subculture formation, and (4) control theory, as to how potential white-collar offenders can be made accountable.[51]

Dealing with White-Collar Crime

Certain forms of occupational crime may be easier to address than others. Individual occupational crimes especially may be reduced by concerted enforcement and protective efforts, including enhanced Internal Revenue Service auditing programs, theft-deterrent systems, and good internal financial procedures. Consumer information services can help eliminate fraudulent business practices, and increases in both victim awareness and reporting can help target both businesses and individuals responsible for various forms of white-collar or occupational crime.

However, as Donald J. Newman has observed, "if white-collar crime is intrinsic to and normative within the value structure of our society, then no punishment or treatment program will effectively eradicate it."[52] Similarly, Gary S. Green points out that "professional occupational criminals will probably continue to enjoy immunity from prosecution. Hence, they are unlikely to be deterred by sanction or threat and are unlikely to be formally disqualified by their professional organizations. They will therefore feel free and be free to continue or begin their criminal activities."[53]

In the book *The Criminal Elite: The Sociology of White-Collar Crime,* **James William Coleman** suggests four areas of reform through which white-collar crime might be effectively addressed:[54]

- *Ethical.* Ethical reforms include such things as working to establish stronger and more persuasive codes of business ethics. Courses on ethical business might be offered in universities, and corporations could school their employees in right livelihood, or ethical ways of conducting business.
- *Enforcement.* Enforcement reforms center on the belief that white-collar criminals must be more severely punished, but they also include such things as better funding for enforcement agencies dealing with white-collar crime, larger research budgets for regulatory investigators, and the insulation of enforcement personnel from undue political influence.
- *Structural.* Structural reforms "involve basic changes in corporate structure" to make white-collar crime more difficult to commit. Coleman suggests adding members of the public to corporate boards of directors; changing the process whereby corporations are chartered to include control over white-collar crime; enhancing the flow of information between businesses, the public, and administrative bodies; and the "selective nationalization of firms that have long records of criminal violations."[55]
- *Political.* Political reforms, according to Coleman, center on eliminating campaign contributions from corporations and businesses but also include increasing the level of fairness in determining government grants, government purchases, and government contracts. The government, says Coleman, must also police itself. Although this includes enforcing current laws which are intended to regulate the activities of elected officials and administrative personnel, Coleman concludes that "there is some question about how effectively the government can ever police itself."[56]

Learn about the enforcement of laws curtailing white-collar crime from the FBI at WebExtra! 12-6.

WebEXTRA! 12-6 at crimtoday.com

ORGANIZED CRIME

Organized criminal groups have always existed. An early written account of **organized crime** describes the activities of Jonathan Wild, a notorious brigand of the early 1700s.[57] Wild was born in Wolverhampton, Staffordshire, England, in 1682 to "persons of decent character and station." He received a formal education, which was unusual for the times, and at age 15 was apprenticed to a buckle maker. Married at 22, Wild left his wife and new son a year later for the excitement of nearby London. Not long after his arrival in the city, Wild was arrested for nonpayment of debts and thrown into Wood-street Compter, a prison which held debtors and other prisoners, both male and female. During the four years he spent in prison, Wild became intimate with a female inmate by the name of Mary Milliner, who was described as "one of the most abandoned prostitutes and pickpockets on the town." Wild later said that he also used his time in prison to "learn the secrets of the criminals there under confinement." Upon release he shared a home with Milliner, calling her his wife.

Milliner ran a bar on what was then known as Cock Alley in Cripplegate, one of the most notorious parts of London. Soon the bar became a hangout for thieves and other criminals. Wild capitalized on the situation and began purchasing all types of stolen goods and fencing them to merchants and the general public. As one writer of the times observed, "He was at first at little trouble to dispose of the articles brought to him by thieves at something less than their real value, no law existing for the punishment of the receivers of stolen goods." However, the authorities, hearing of Wild's organized criminal activity, soon passed a law forbidding the receipt and sale of stolen items. As a consequence, the value of stolen goods plummeted. Soon, however, Wild discovered a way around the new law. One commentator described his solution this way: Wild called a meeting of thieves in the city and proposed "that when they made prize of anything, they should deliver it to him . . . saying that he would restore the goods to the owners by which means greater sums might be raised, while the thieves would remain perfectly secure from detection." Soon Wild was running the largest criminal organization in England and evading the law by returning stolen goods to their rightful owners in exchange for handsome rewards.

As he rose in both power and wealth, Wild displayed ruthless organizational skills. If a thief or burglar in Wild's gang demanded too much money or threatened to unmask the operation, Wild would have him apprehended and hung—collecting whatever official reward had been offered for the felon's capture. As Wild's organization grew, he hired ships to transport excess inventory to France, the Netherlands, and Belgium. Soon he was trading internationally in stolen goods and living in grand style. Because of his ability to gather intelligence throughout the criminal underworld as well as in the ghettos of London, Wild gained the confidence of advisers to George I—a relationship that kept

him out of harm's way for many years. With the death of George I, however, and increasing British hostility to criminal activity, Wild was finally arrested and charged with running a criminal organization. Sentenced to hang, Wild was executed at Tyburn Prison on May 24, 1725.

History of Organized Crime in the United States

Much of what most Americans traditionally think of today as organized crime—the **Mafia** or **La Cosa Nostra**—has roots which predate the establishment of the United States as a sovereign power. For hundreds of years, secret societies—the products of extreme poverty, feudalism, a traditional disregard for the law, and (some would say) national temperament—have flourished in Italy.[58] During the nineteenth century, the Italian Camorra, based in Naples, became infamous for extortion and murder. The Camorrian code demanded total silence, and the organization issued to its members printed licenses to kill. Italian criminal organizations that came to the United States with the wave of European immigrants during the late nineteenth and early twentieth centuries included the Mafia and the Black Hand. The Black Hand (in Italian, *La Mano Negro*) "specialized in the intimidation of Italian immigrants,"[59] typically extorting protection money and valuables. The Black Hand became especially powerful in Detroit, St. Louis, Kansas City, and New Orleans.

The Mafia, with roots in Sicily, worked to become a quasi-police organization in the Italian ghetto areas of the burgeoning American cities of the industrial era—often enforcing its own set of laws or codes when official intervention was lacking. One of the first well-documented conflicts between the Mafia and American law enforcement came on March 13, 1909, when New York City police officials learned that NYPD Lieutenant Joseph Petrosino had been assassinated upon his arrival in Palermo, Italy. Petrosino had gone to Palermo to investigate allegations that Mafia bosses in New York City were importing Black Hand assassins from the "old country" to do their dirty work. As Petrosino visited the Palermo Court of Justice, he was killed by a single bullet allegedly fired by Mafia boss Vito Cascio Ferro. Although Ferro was arrested and charged with the crime, local deputies provided him with an alibi, and he was never convicted.

Secret societies in Italy were all but expunged during the 1930s and early 1940s under Fascist dictator Benito Mussolini. Surviving Mafia members became vehemently anti-Fascist, sentiments that endeared them to American and allied intelligence services during World War II. Following the war, mafioso leaders resumed their traditional positions of power within Italian society, and links grew between American criminal organizations and those in Italy.

In his comprehensive book, *Organized Crime*, Howard Abadinsky reports that the first mention of the Mafia in New York can be found in a *New York Times* article dated October 21, 1888.[60] The article quotes police inspector Thomas Byrnes

CRIME IN THE NEWS
Are "The Sopranos" the Real Deal?

Do real mobsters cry? Would a wiseguy ever visit a shrink to deal with the everyday stresses in his life—you know, things like whacking a mook or hijacking a cigarette truck?

In the fictional world of HBO's new critically acclaimed series *The Sopranos* (Sundays; 9 P.M. EST), these things happen. The show stars James Gandolfini as modern-day mob boss Anthony "Tony" Soprano, whose bouts of depression and anxiety over the problems in his family and "family" are so severe that he starts seeing a shrink and even taking Prozac.

But what about the real world? APB asked two people who know mob life—from different sides of the coin—to watch the show and tell us if art indeed imitates life in *The Sopranos*.

Georgia Durante is one of the only women to have lived with and left the mob—and survived to tell about it. As a mob wife, mother and, at one time, getaway driver for the wiseguys, she saw their violence and survived their internal wars. Her new book, *The Company She Keeps* (Celebrity Books, October 1998), details her remarkable life.

Ironically, after more than 20 years as a mob moll, Durante met and fell in love with her past adversary, the former head of the Justice Department's Los Angeles organized crime division. Jim Henderson spent 17 years hunting wiseguys and, in his career, convicted more organized-crime figures than any other U.S. attorney in history. The mob actually feared this man, who succeeded in breaking up the West Coast family by turning Jimmy "The Weasel" Fratianno into a government witness against boss Dominic Brooklier.

While both Durante and Henderson gave *The Sopranos* enthusiastic thumbs up, they shared some differing opinions on the show's portrayal of the mob underworld.

APB: How realistic did you find Tony Soprano's *blood* family relationships?

Jim: This is probably the area that I know the least about, but I felt it was realistic about those kind of problems at home and Tony's trying to make a normal home life. I've seen that a number of times. I could see a guy who really cared about his family, maybe hesitating about what the effect [of his lifestyle] might be on the family.

Whoever put this thing together and wrote this stuff has a good feel for it. I really enjoyed this a lot more than a lot of this Mafia crap that's on TV. It shows you the whole person.

Georgia: I don't know if the family life would have been all that normal. I'm just going by my family life, but I was more or less walking on eggshells all the time, afraid that I'd upset [my husband] or I'd get him going and he'd get violent. Tony [of *The Sopranos*] seemed like such a wimpy kind of guy in his family. They do have two sides to them—they absolutely do—but I would see more of a macho guy in the home.

My family life wasn't like that at all. I knew things, but nothing was ever told to me. I saw what was going on, heard conversations, and put two and two together. I'd seen people being beaten to death. [Tony's] wife, Carmela, really was so removed from all of that. She never saw any of that.

APB: How realistic did you find Tony's other "family"?

Jim: I thought it was good, for instance, the way [the mobsters] meet in front of restaurants rather than inside so that they're not bugged. And the loose relationship, but a real relationship, as to who's in charge, who the capo was, who the acting boss was, I thought that was right on.

Georgia: I thought that was pretty realistic. I thought the acting was pretty good. There were a lot of times it made me laugh because it was so real. The [real guys] were a funny group and had a sense of humor. Like the guy in front of the mir-

ror in *The Sopranos* saying (quoting the *Godfather III*), "Just when I thought I was out, they pull me back in." They love to live that glamour. They saw it in the *Godfather* movies, and that's the way they like to see themselves.

APB: Do real goodfellas model their personalities from movies they've seen, or do the movies get it all from them? Which came first, the chicken or the egg?

Georgia: The movies glamorize those guys. I mean, it is the way they act. But when they see themselves on the screen like that, it gives them that John Gotti, kind of, "I'm great" [attitude]. They like to see their names in the paper. They like to see themselves portrayed on TV.

Jim: I do know a lot of guys who saw a lot of movies and think that's how you're supposed to act. But there are also a lot of guys who don't act that way at all. Everything's a lot more subtle.

APB: Would a mob boss ever go to a shrink?

Georgia: No chance. They just keep everything amongst themselves. That's like somebody knowing what they're doing. That's very dangerous. He could get killed for doing that. That is one of the rules. There are certain things that if they say or do, they know that they could die for—and that's one of them. I couldn't see one of those guys actually going to a therapist and talking about what he does for a living, but that's what made the show different and interesting. That's what kept you watching.

Jim: It's not likely at all because you can't really tell them anything that would be of help in dealing with psychological problems. Because nobody is going to make those kind of admissions—that they're in the mob or they're doing illegal activities, especially serious ones involving beating people up and breaking their legs with cars. They'd be afraid that somehow the conversation might be overheard or that they couldn't trust the therapist, who might wind up

(continued on the next page)

(continued from previous page)

being a source to the FBI. It just wouldn't happen.

At the rituals when they make guys, that's one of the rules that you agree not to break. You don't sleep with made guys' wives, you don't kill anybody in a family without permission, you don't talk to the FBI, and you don't say anything about "our thing." That's one of the rules, and you could get killed for violating it.

APB: So, if they can't go to a shrink, how do Mafia men solve their problems?

Georgia: That's something I always wondered about. How could they kill people and live a normal life? They must have a black-and-white, too. That's how I survived it all. The things I couldn't deal with I just gave to that other personality to deal with and just didn't think about it. I think they look at it as a business. I don't know if they have a conscience about it.

Jim: I guess a lot of times they solve them on the street. I remember Jimmy Fratianno, one of the highest-ranking guys to become a government witness. We found out that one of the Marx Brothers had been making some moves on Jimmy's girlfriend. Now here's a guy that's one of the most notorious hit men in the country—you gotta be crazy to be messing around with his girlfriend. I asked him about this. I said, "Is this guy nuts? Does he have a death wish?" And Jimmy said, "No, he's probably pretty safe. I consider that personal business. We never would have hit a guy like that." Now I'm not going to say everyone was like this, but there was this mode of thinking out there.

APB: In the first episode, one of the mob guys cried after his restaurant was blown up. Do wiseguys cry in front of each other?

Georgia: That is so unlike those guys. They're manly amongst each other. They don't cry. I've never seen them break down in front of each other. They have to be macho around each other.

Jim: I've never overheard or been involved in cases where guys were crying, but the side I saw was not human. I can't remember a "crying scene" on any of the wiretaps.

I remember Dominic Brooklier was crying during his trial in Los Angeles when stuff came up about his family. But some of these guys are psychopaths. It's a macho thing. You get into it when you're young, and you can't get out. Some of them *are* real people. It can destroy your life, but it doesn't necessarily destroy every feeling that you have.

APB: What did you think about Nancy Marchand's portrayal of Tony's mother, Livia?

Jim: I thought she was wonderful. I loved that. But I don't really know because I never dealt with [any mobster's] mother—and I did this for 17 years.

Georgia: The mother was not your typical Italian mother. She didn't look Italian and act Italian. They're always feeding you. She didn't do any of that. Italian mothers, their kids are God, their kids can't do anything wrong. They're everything. This guy couldn't do anything right. I think she's a great actress, though, and again, that's what made it interesting.

APB: Tony owns a "waste management" company. Is that an appropriate line of work for a Mafia man?

Jim: Remember the Gambinos ran that garbage business that they got trouble from years ago? Even Sammy "The Bull"

Gravano had that construction firm. That's right on. That's a good cover.

Georgia: They all have titles of some sort—like security consultant. They have something they can put down on paper if they're asked what they do for a living. Maybe a union guy gives them a title. They don't actually go to work.

APB: Was Tony right when he said, depressed, the best Mafia years are over and done with?

Georgia: Definitely. It's no longer the way it is at all. So many of these guys in these positions are turning state's evidence, and nobody can trust each other anymore.

Jim: Yeah, absolutely—starting with Bobby Kennedy, when they put the strike force together. They passed all the wiretap legislation and the immunity statutes which can force people to testify. [And there's] the witness relocation program. All these things were tools that when put together in one package enabled the government to effectively fight these families. There's virtually no family that hasn't had their boss in an upper echelon sent to jail in the last 20 years. The secrets don't work anymore. It's not the same as the old days. I think it's gradually disappearing, with the exception of Chicago and New York. They still have very strong families there, but even that's not the same. People aren't afraid [of the mob]. They know [the mobsters will] go to jail and that the government can protect them. The culture and the government efforts have just diluted it. It's no longer the major criminal problem in this country it was years ago.

Source: Deborah Baer, "An Ex-Mob Moll and Ex-Mob Buster Debate the Accuracy of TV's New Favorite 'Family,'" APB News, January 22, 1999. Reprinted with permission.

as saying that a murder victim named Antonio Flaccomio was "an Italian fruit dealer and a member of a secret society." The society, said Byrnes, was called the Mafia; its members were fugitives from Sicily, an island in the south of Italy.

A Rose By Any Other Name— La Cosa Nostra

Other organized criminal groups, including Jewish and Irish gangs, flourished in New York City prior to the arrival of large numbers of Italian immigrants in the late 1800s. Ethnic succession has been as much a reality in organized crime as in most other aspects of American life. **Ethnic succession** refers to the continuing process whereby one immigrant or ethnic group succeeds another through assumption of a particular position in society.

Throughout the late nineteenth and early twentieth centuries, for example, Jewish gangsters like Meyer Lansky, Benjamin "Bugsy" Siegel, "Dutch" Schultz, and Lepke Buchalter ran many of the "rackets" in New York City, only to have their places taken by Italian immigrants who arrived a few years later. Almost forgotten today is Arnold Rothstein, a famous Jewish gangster who was able to translate many ill-gotten gains into real estate holdings and other legitimate commercial ventures. Among those who remember, Rothstein has been called the "most important organizer and innovator"[61] among Jewish criminal operatives in turn-of-the-century New York and the "Godfather" of organized crime in the city. Italian-American organized criminals are themselves not immune to ethnic succession, which has continued into the present day, with gangs of African-Americans, Hispanics, and Asian-Americans now running significant aspects of the drug trade and controlling other illicit activities in many parts of the country.

Even so, organized criminal activity in the United States throughout the last half century has largely been the domain of Italian-American immigrants and their descendants, especially those of Sicilian descent. As one observer notes, "To beat rival organizations, criminals of Sicilian descent reproduced the kind of illegal groups they had belonged to in the old country and employed the same rules to make them invincible."[62] Hence it was not long before American Mafia leaders had taken over from their criminal predecessors, many of whom were either killed or forced to turn to more legitimate forms of enterprise.

As a consequence of historical events that are well documented, it is both realistic and useful to discuss American organized crime primarily in terms of Sicilian-American involvement. A few caveats must be stated, however. For one thing, although many Sicilians who emigrated to this country either had ties to, or experience with, Mafia organizations in the old country, most did not. Many Sicilian-Americans, in fact, emigrated to America to escape Mafia despotism at home, and most became productive members of their adopted society. Relatively few involved themselves in organized crime. Those who did created an organization known variously as the Mafia, the Outfit, the Mob, La Cosa Nostra (our thing), the syndicate, or simply the organization. Other terms applied to Sicilian-American organized crime include *crime cartel* and the *confederation.*

Joseph Valachi is generally credited with popularizing the term La Cosa Nostra. In 1963, Valachi, a member of the Genovese crime family, used the term while testifying before the McClellan Committee, which was holding hearings into organized crime. Following the hearings, the name Cosa Nostra became increasingly popular with both the American press and the public and has at least partially replaced the term *Mafia* as the *nom du jour* of Italian-American criminal organizations.

The term *Mafia*, however, is still in widespread use. Hence in the paragraphs that follow, Sicilian-American organized criminal groups are referred to as both Mafia and La Cosa Nostra—terms which have been used interchangeably by police investigators, the press, the public, and government commissions over the years.

Prohibition and Official Corruption

By the 1920s, Mafia influence extended to most American cities. But it was the advent of Prohibition that gave organized crime its vital financial wherewithal. In 1919, the U.S. Congress passed the Eighteenth Amendment to the U.S. Constitution, ushering in an age of prohibition on the manufacture, transportation, and sale of alcoholic beverages. The Eighteenth Amendment reads as follows:

> Section 1. After one year from the ratification of this article the manufacture, sale, or transportation of intoxicating liquors within, the importation thereof into, or the exportation thereof from the United States and all territory subject to the jurisdiction thereof for beverage purposes is hereby prohibited.

> —U.S. Constitution, Eighteenth Amendment 1919

In many ways, the advent of Prohibition was a godsend for Mafia leaders. Prior to Prohibition, Mafia operations in American cities were "small time," concerned mostly with gambling, protection rackets, and loan-sharking. Many mafiosi, however, also belonged to a fraternal brotherhood called Unione Siciliana, whose members were well versed in the manufacture of low-cost high-proof untaxed alcohol,[63] an expertise which had been brought from their native country. In addition, the existing infrastructure of organized crime permitted easy and efficient entry into the running and sale of contraband liquor. As one writer explained, "By its nature, bootlegging required national (even international) organization. The liquor came from Canada or Europe, necessitating an extranational arrangement. It rode at anchor outside the territorial limits in bottoms belonging to the underworld. It had to be picked up by small craft to be smuggled ashore. The contraband had to get by the Coast Guard,

Much of what the public believes about organized crime comes from images like this one of Humphrey Bogart starring in the 1951 movie *The Enforcer*. Has the government won the war against organized crime? *Archive Photos*

Customs, and cops. The cargo had to be loaded on trucks, carried across bridges and highways, protected against hijackers, delivered to warehouses, [and] redistributed to retailers. And somewhere, somehow, there had to be collectors, bookkeepers, accountants, enforcers, personnel men, and masterminds to make the rum-running pay."[64]

Prohibition gave existing Mafia families the opportunity to accumulate unheralded wealth. As Abadinsky puts it, "Prohibition enabled men who had been street thugs to become crime overlords."[65] Others describe it this way: "Prohibition proved to be the catalyst that established the wealth and power of modern organized crime syndicates."[66]

The huge profits to be had from bootlegging led to the wholesale bribery of government officials and to the quick corruption of many law enforcement officers throughout the country. Nowhere was corruption more complete than in Chicago, where runners working for organized crime distributed illegal alcohol under police protection[67] and corrupt city government officials received regular payoffs from criminal cartels.

In 1929, President Herbert Hoover appointed the National Commission on Law Observance and Enforcement, better known as the Wickersham Commission after its chairman, George Wickersham. The commission produced a series of 14 reports. Three of them, *Observance and Enforcement of Prohibition, Lawlessness in Law Enforcement,* and *The Police,* either mentioned or decried the corrupting influence Prohibition was having on professional law enforcement in America. Fourteen years after it had been passed, the Eighteenth Amendment was repealed, and with it Prohibition ended.

Section 1. The eighteenth article of amendment to the Constitution of the United States is hereby repealed.

—U.S. Constitution, Twenty-first Amendment 1933

Unfortunately, the heritage of Prohibition-associated corruption is still with us. Official corruption has become an institutionalized part of American life in some parts of the country. As one writer explains, "American cities have a long history of corrupt relations between some illegal enterprises and local police or politicians. For criminal entrepreneurs, payments to politicians or police can be viewed either as normal business expenses in return for services to the enterprise or as extortionate demands that eat into the profits of the enterprise. For police and politicians, levying regular assessments on illegal entrepreneurs has provided a source of extra income as well as a way to oversee neighborhood enterprises that could not be legally controlled. Historically, oversight by local political organizations (or the police) has been the most important source of coordination for illegal enterprises in American cities."[68]

In 1967, the Task Force on Organized Crime, part of President Johnson's Commission on Law Enforcement and Administration of Justice, concluded that "all available data indicate that organized crime flourishes only where it has

corrupted local officials."[69] Sometimes the roots of corruption reach far deeper. As one writer notes, "The line between organized crime and corrupt officials is often unclear, at times nonexistent. . . . In both Chicago and New York those who ran organized criminal activities, gambling and prostitution, were political figures and often elected officials."[70]

The Centralization of Organized Crime

The Prohibition era was a tumultuous time for American organized crime. While its leaders grappled for the huge profits to be reaped from the sale of illegal alcohol, they simultaneously worked to consolidate their power. Gang warfare—not unlike the drive-by shootings and execution-style slayings which now characterize inner-city youth gangs—was the order of the day.

One of the most infamous gangland wars of all time erupted in Chicago in the mid-1920s when Alphonse "Al" Capone, an up-and-coming thug, decided to make a citywide grab for power. Following a number of spectacular killings (dubbed "massacres" by the press), Capone was successful in forging a crime syndicate, and he declared himself the leader of all of Chicago's organized crime families. For a time, his claim remained disputed, primarily by George "Bugs" Moran who had inherited the leadership of a local gang. In a bid to end competition, Capone lured Moran's men to a garage on Chicago's East Side on the ruse that a truckload of bootleg liquor was soon to arrive. Once inside the garage, Moran's men were surprised by five of Capone's executioners. Three were dressed as police officers, while the other two wore plainclothes. The uniformed men ordered the Moran gang against the garage wall, where the plainclothes killers machine-gunned them to death. The killings, which became known as the Saint Valentine's Day massacre, established Capone as undisputed ruler of organized crime in Chicago.

Similar efforts at consolidation were being made nationwide. On April 15, 1931, influential New York City crime figure Giuseppe "Joe the Boss" Masseria was gunned down in a restaurant in the Coney Island section of Brooklyn. His killing, part of what has been called the Castellammarese War, appears to have been ordered by another of the city's bosses, Salvatore Maranzano. Following Masseria's death, Maranzano declared himself the "boss of bosses" over all of New York's crime families. Maranzano, however, soon lost favor with more "Americanized" Mafia figures and was himself killed in September 1931 by armed men who entered his office disguised as immigration officials.

During the next two days, 30 Mafia leaders died in similar gang-ordered executions across the country. By the close of 1931, when the smoke settled and the killings stopped, the Mafia had become an integrated, coordinated criminal organization able to settle most disputes internally and capable of shielding its activities from the prying eyes of investigators. A 1939 exposé written by J. Richard Davis, former attorney for one of New York's crime families, credited the centralization of control to the rise of Charles "Charlie Lucky" Luciano, also known as "Lucky Luciano," who "became leader of the *Unione Siciliani* in 1931.... The 'greasers' in the *Unione,*" wrote Davis, "were killed off, and the organization was no longer a loose, fraternal order of Sicilian blackhanders and alcohol cookers, but rather the framework for a system of alliances which were to govern the underworld."[71] Another author described it this way: "In 1931 organized crime units across the United States formed into monopolistic corporations, and those corporations, in turn, linked themselves together in a monopolistic cartel."[72]

Following 1931, Mafia activity went underground. The Mafia's success at hiding its operations was so great that one expert was able to write, "There is a considerable body of police opinion in the United States which holds that the Mafia in America died in September 1931, on 'Purge Day.'"[73]

As the 1967 President's Commission on Law Enforcement and Administration of Justice observed, Mafia activity remained nearly invisible and investigations of Mafia operations lay dormant until the 1950s. In the words of the commission; "After World War II there was little national interest in the problem [of organized crime] until 1950, when the U.S. Attorney General convened a national conference on organized crime."[74]

Organized crime reemerged into the national spotlight in 1951 when the federal Special Committee to Investigate Organized Crime in Interstate Commerce[75] (better known as the **Kefauver Committee** after its chairman, Estes Kefauver) reported that "a nationwide crime syndicate known as the Mafia operate[s] in many large [American] cities, and the leaders of the Mafia usually control the most lucrative rackets in their cities."[76] Although the Kefauver Committee, which interviewed hundreds of witnesses, noted that it had "found it difficult to obtain reliable data concerning the extent of Mafia operation, the nature of Mafia organization, and the way it presently operates,"[77] it was able to reach the following conclusions:

- A nationwide crime syndicate exists, known as the Mafia, whose tentacles are found in many large cities.
- The American Mafia has international linkages that appear most clearly in connection with narcotics traffic.
- Mafia leaders are usually found in control of the most lucrative rackets in their cities.
- Indications suggest centralized direction and control in these rackets, but leadership appears to be in a group rather than in a single individual.

Public interest in organized crime was again roused when authorities learned of a national meeting of at least 75 leaders of criminal cartels scheduled for November 1957. The purpose of the meeting, held at the home of Joseph Barbara in the small New York town of Apalachin, was never uncovered. Some speculate that syndicate leaders may have met to split up the empire of the recently murdered Albert Anastasia, who was himself reputed to have been a ruthless killer. Barbara, born in Castellammarese del Golfo, Italy, was boss of a northeastern Pennsylvania crime family and died two years after the meeting.

The 1957 meeting resulted in raids on Barbara's house and the arrest of many well-known organized crime figures. In 1959, Joseph Bonanno and 26 others were convicted of obstruction of justice for their refusal to reveal the meeting's purpose. Their convictions, however, were overturned in 1960 by the U.S. Supreme Court, which reasoned in *U.S.* v. *Bufalino*[78] that the suspects had been arrested without probable cause.

The picture that eventually emerged from years of federal investigations into Italian-American organized criminal groups was of 24 crime families operating in the United States under the direction of a "commission," whose membership consisted of the bosses of the nation's most powerful families. The following, taken directly from the 1967 President's Commission report, summarizes what was believed to be true of organized crime at the time of the report: "Today the core of organized crime in the United States consists of 24 groups operating as criminal cartels in large cities across the nation. Their membership is exclusively Italian, they are in frequent communication with each other, and their smooth functioning is insured by a national body of overseers. . . . The wealthiest and most influential core groups," the report concluded, "operate in States including New York, New Jersey, Illinois, Florida, Louisiana, Nevada, Michigan, and Rhode Island."[79] The report placed membership in organized crime at 5,000 nationwide and said that "each of the 24 groups is known as a 'family' with membership varying from as many as 700 men to as few as 20."

Family organization was said to consist of (1) a boss, whose primary functions were described as "maintaining order and maximizing profits," (2) an underboss, who was said to collect information for the boss and to relay messages to and from him, (3) the counselor, or consigliere, who serves as an adviser, (4) numerous lieutenants, or *caporegime,* some of whom "serve as chiefs of operating units," and (5) soldiers, or *soldati,* representing the lowest level of family membership, who "operate a particular illicit enterprise," such as a loan-sharking operation, a lottery, or a smuggling operation. "Beneath the soldiers," the commission found, "are large numbers of employees and . . . agents who are not members of the family and not necessarily of Italian descent. These are people who do most of the actual work in the various enterprises." Unlike the family members who give them orders, "they have no buffers or other insulation from law enforcement." The structure of a typical Sicilian-American organized crime family is shown in Figure 12-1.

The President's Commission also found that organized crime members swear allegiance to a code of conduct which "stipulates that underlings should not interfere with the leaders' interests and should not seek protection from the police. They should be 'standup guys' who go to prison in order that the bosses may amass fortunes. The code gives leaders exploitative authoritarian power over everyone in the

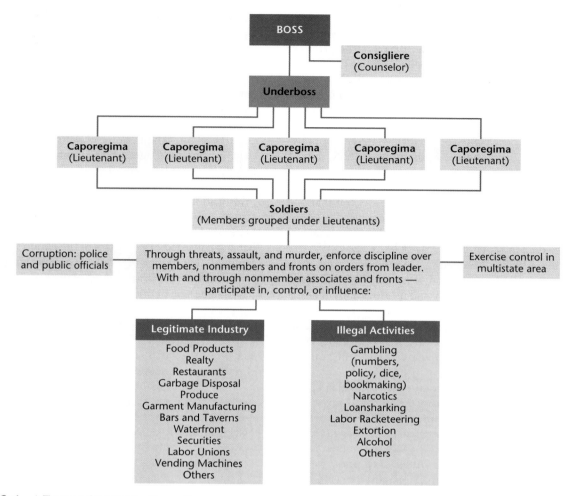

■ FIGURE 12-1 A TYPICAL ORGANIZED CRIME FAMILY.
Source: President's Commission on Law Enforcement and Administration of Justice, *The Challenge of Crime in a Free Society* (Washington, D.C.: U.S. Government Printing Office, 1967), p. 47.

organization. Loyalty, honor, respect, absolute obedience—these are inculcated in family members through ritualistic initiation and customs within the organization, through material rewards, and through violence."

La Cosa Nostra Today

Some writers maintain that at least 24 organized crime families of Sicilian-American heritage continue to operate throughout the United States today. Of these, five operate out of New York:[80]

Luciano/Genovese family (300–400 core members)
Mineo/Gambino family (400–500 core members)
Reina/Lucchese family (125 core members)
Profaci/Colombo family (100 core members)
Bonanno family (75 core members)

Chicago is home to other influential Cosa Nostra families, including the Carlisi family (sometimes called the "Outfit").

The Scarfo organization (run by Nicodemo "Little Nicky" Scarfo) and the Stanfa organization operate in Philadelphia. New Orleans serves as headquarters for the Marcello gang (headed by Carlos Marcello), organized crime in New England is controlled by Ray Patriarca, Jr., and his henchmen, and the Civella mob runs racketeering activities in Kansas City, Missouri. Learn more about Cosa Nostra families now operating in the United States at Web Extra! 12-7.

Web EXTRA! Web Extra! 12-7 at crimtoday.com

Activities of Organized Crime

The 1976 federal Task Force on Organized Crime identified five types of activity which may qualify as organized crime: racketeering, vice operations, theft/fence rings, gangs, and terrorism. Whatever its source, however, money is the centerpiece of, and primary motivation for, all organized criminal activity. Near the start of the Great Depression, notorious

Chicago gangster Al Capone achieved the distinction of being listed in the *Guiness Book of World Records* as having the highest income of any individual in a single year—more than $105 million in 1927.[81]

Things haven't changed much since Capone's day. As one expert on organized crime explains, "It is cash that dominates every aspect of the mob machines. . . . The mobsters' working days are spent worrying about and scheming over money, and finally, quarreling and killing for money, almost all of it derived illegitimately."[82] The same expert gives the example of Philadelphia crime boss Nicky Scarfo, who "even considered killing his own wife, Domenica, over money when he learned that 'little by little, she had robbed him of around four hundred thousand' for her gambling sprees at Trump Plaza in Atlantic City."[83] No amount of money seems too small for concern, and—as in much of the wider society—money often becomes a way of keeping score as to who has been the most successful at what they have done.

Throughout the past half century, Sicilian-American criminal cartels have continued to be involved in (1) the establishment and control of both legalized and illicit forms of gambling, including lotteries, bookmaking, horse-race wagering, and bets on athletic contests; (2) loan-sharking, which involves the lending of money at rates far higher than legally prescribed limits; (3) large-scale drug trafficking; (4) the fencing of stolen goods, including securities; (5) infiltration of legitimate businesses, including labor unions and corporations that can be used as quasi-legitimate fronts for money laundering and other activities; and (6) labor union racketeering via which legitimate businesses are intimidated through threats of strikes, walkouts, and sabotage.

In some states, where lotteries are now run by state government, the organized crime's "take" from illegal gambling has been reduced. Not to be outdone, however, Sicilian-American operatives have moved into legitimate gambling, reportedly buying stakes in casinos in Nevada, New Jersey, and elsewhere. The Flamingo Hotel, the first elaborate hotel-casino in Las Vegas, was said to have been built by crime boss "Bugsy" Siegel and funded by organized crime leaders throughout the country.[84] Cleveland syndicate leader Moe Dalitz is reputed to have financed the Stardust Hotel, and federal officials claim that at least $14 million was illegally skimmed from the hotel's operations between 1973 and 1983.[85] Although New Jersey has made herculean efforts to keep organized crime from influencing casino operations in Atlantic City, some writers point out that "Local 54 of the Hotel Employees and Restaurant Employees Union . . . which represents 22,000 casino hotel employees, has long been dominated by the Bruno family of Philadelphia."[86]

Organized crime is involved in many other kinds of rackets besides gambling. Some evidence suggests, for example, that organized crime today is becoming increasingly active in the illegal copying and distribution of copyrighted software, music, and other forms of recorded media, including videotapes, compact discs, and cassette tapes. The provision of elaborately staged videotaped pornographic productions, including "snuff movies" (in which a sex "star" is actually killed on screen), and elements of child pornography can also be traced to organized criminal activity.

Some sense of the profit derived from the activities of organized crime can be gained from official estimates of the money being collected by Scarfo's gang at the time of his indictment in 1986 on charges of first-degree murder. Scarfo operated illegitimate businesses throughout Philadelphia and southern New Jersey. When he was arrested, his gang was estimated to be taking in "$25,000,000 to $30,000,000 annu-

Mob informant Joseph Valachi testifying before Senate investigators in 1963. How has organized crime changed since Valachi's time? *Locs Mags (UPI), Corbis*

ally from illegal gambling (numbers, video poker, sports betting), and millions more from loansharking, shakedowns of drug dealers and labor union racketeering. Even bigger deals were in the making: Scarfo was preparing to control more than $200,000,000 in Philadelphia waterfront-development projects, as well as to infiltrate the union benefits plans of Atlantic City's bartenders and waitresses."[87]

Code of Conduct

A strict code of conduct governs behavior among members of organized Sicilian-American criminal groups. This code, sometimes called *omerta* (or "manliness"), is unwritten. Members are formally introduced to the code through an initiation ritual which has changed little since it was brought to American shores by Sicilian immigrants well over a hundred years ago. The code of **omerta** functions to concentrate power in the hands of crime bosses while ensuring their protection. As officials with one federal task force stated, "Those aspects of the code which prohibit appealing to outside authorities for justice while at the same time advocating great loyalty, respect and honor are probably most essential to the concentration of power in the hands of a few, and hence to exploitation of lower-status men by their leaders."[88]

A few years ago, the FBI electronically eavesdropped on a house in Medford, Massachusetts, in which Joseph Russo, a New England Cosa Nostra consigliere, conducted an initiation ritual for four new family members. Twenty-one men attended the candlelight ceremony. This was the first time authorities had ever captured a Cosa Nostra induction on tape. As each young man swore to uphold *omerta* and took a vow of silence never to betray the organization or tell its secrets, he held a burning picture of a Catholic saint and prayed; "Come si brucia questa santa, cosi si brucera la mia anima" (As burns this saint, so will burn my soul), a reference to the death awaiting anyone who violates the code.[89]

Another initiate described his induction into Philadelphia's Scarfo gang this way: "I was driven to this million-dollar house in Philadelphia, with a big swimming pool and a big table laid out with food—shrimp, steaks, meatballs, peppers, olives, spaghetti—and about forty chairs. I was on cloud nine. Scarfo is at the head of this long table and says, 'Nick, do you know why you're here?' I said, 'No.' You're supposed to say no. . . . So next, he says, 'We want you to be one of us. Now, look around this table and tell me if there is anyone you have bad feelings with.' I look around and say 'no.' . . . So he makes a speech about how much I've done for the family and then says that I have the freedom to leave now and that I'll always be their friend. There would be no hard feelings if I didn't want to join. I said, 'No, I want to be one of you.' . . . Scarfo points to a gun and a knife on a table and asks if I'd use these for any of these friends around the table. Then he lights a small piece of tissue paper in my hand while I say, 'May I burn like the saints in hell if I ever betray any of my friends.' He also pricks my trigger finger. Then you go around the table and kiss everyone. Then we have a

feast and then you're told the rules. In the days that follow, you go around and meet the guys who weren't at the ceremony. Then word just seems to spread everywhere you go. And everywhere you go, the respect that you receive from nonmembers is enormous."[90]

The rules of the Scarfo family, said this inductee, included the following: "The family doesn't fool with kidnapping, counterfeit money or bonds. You can shake down or rob drug dealers, but you can't protect them, lend them money or deal drugs yourself. No fooling with a member's wife. You can't even look at another guy's wife. That's automatic death. Even hitting another member is automatic death. He can ask for your life. You're supposed to report once a week to your capo, unless there's a good excuse. You can't go out of town without telling him. You always have to touch base. You're also told that silence is the code and this thing comes first. It comes before your mother, your father, your sister, your brother."[91]

Federal investigators and others studying organized crime have identified seven general features characteristic of the code that family members everywhere swear to:[92]

- Do not be an informer. Do not "rat" on others, and do not sell out.
- Be a member of the team. Be loyal to members of the organization.
- Do not interfere with the interests of others. Do not rock the boat.
- Be rational. Do not engage in battle if you cannot win.
- Be a man of honor. Have class. Be independent.
- Respect women and your elders.
- Be a "stand-up" guy (stand-up guys take the "rap," shielding others). Keep your eyes and ears open and your mouth shut.

Like any informal unwritten code, *omerta* has many other implicit rules and is fraught with nuances fully understood only to those raised within its traditions. The code, however, imposes two clear and indisputable requirements on all family members: (1) obey your superiors, and (2) keep silent. Failure to adhere closely to either rule means death. The 1967 President's Commission report stated it this way, "The basic principle of justice in the Sicilian Mafia, as in American organized crime, is deterrence from deviation by means of the threat of certain, swift, uniform and severe punishment."[93]

An example is provided by the recent FBI investigation focusing on New York City crime boss John Gotti (then head of the Gambino family), which yielded a wealth of secretly recorded conversations between Gotti and other organized crime figures. This is what Gotti told his underboss, Frank "Frankie Loc" LoCascio, about why a subordinate had to die: "Anytime you got a partner who don't agree with us, we kill him," Gotti explained. "He didn't rob nothin'. Know why he's dying?" Gotti continued. "He's gonna die because he refused to come in when I called. He didn't do nothing else wrong."[94]

Anthony Accetturo (center), an alleged leader of the Lucchese crime family, celebrating after his acquittal on federal racketeering charges. The trial lasted nearly two years. How does the "code" of organized crime protect its members? *Peter Cannata, AP/Wide World Photos*

The code of *omerta* is similar to the values found among career criminals everywhere. As one federal report stated, "There is a striking similarity between both the code of conduct and the enforcement machinery used in the confederation of organized criminals and the code of conduct and enforcement machinery which governs the behavior of prisoners."[95] Learn more about the Cosa Nostra at Web Extra! 12-8.

Web EXTRA! Web Extra! 12-8 at crimtoday.com

Other Organized Criminal Groups

According to Howard Abadinsky, a hallmark of true criminal organizations is that they function independently of any of their members, including their leaders, and have a continuity over time as personnel within them change.[96] Abadinsky describes the James Gang, which dissolved with the death of its leader, Jesse James. In contrast, says Abadinsky, "when Al Capone was imprisoned fifty years later, the 'Capone Organization' continued, and in its more modern form (the 'Outfit') it continues to operate in Chicago."[97]

Although, until now, we have restricted our discussion of organized crime to Sicilian-American criminal enterprise, it is both useful and realistic to mention the existence of other organized criminal groups in the United States—each characterized by some degree of organizational continuity which is independent of its membership. Among such criminal associations are groups which have been diversely referred to as the Black Mafia, the Cuban Mafia, the Haitian Mafia, the Colombian cartels, the Russian Mafia, Asian criminals (Chinese Tongs and street gangs, Japanese Yakuza, Vietnamese gangs, and Taiwan's Triads), and others. Included

here, as well, might be inner-city gangs (the most well known of which are probably the Los Angeles Crips and Bloods and the Chicago Vice Lords), international drug rings, outlaw motorcycle gangs (such as the Hell's Angels and the Pagans), and other looser associations of small-time thugs, prison gangs, and drug dealers.

Noteworthy among these groups are the Latino organized bands, including Dominican, Colombian, Mexican, and Cuban importers of cocaine and other drugs. Although it is not known precisely how much cocaine has entered this country illegally, much of it has been handled by the Medellín and Cali Cartels, headquartered in Colombia, South America. The Medellín and Cali Cartels consist of approximately 35 organized groups that often cooperate with one another and that have financed their own small armies for protection of both their operations and their personnel. Although recent arrests and some deaths have cut into the cartels' influence, it is believed that they are still responsible for the majority of cocaine entering the United States.

Although it is difficult to categorize such a diversity of groups with any consistency, it is impossible to discuss each of them in a volume of this size. Whether the principle of ethnic succession (discussed earlier) will continue to apply to organized criminal activity is open to debate—although in some American cities Cosa Nostra operatives have already begun to be replaced by Puerto Rican, African-American, and even Russian gangs. In part, such replacement is due to federal and state law enforcement efforts which have seriously affected activities of the mob in some areas of the United States.

Where Sicilian-American organized criminal activity continues to flourish, connections with the "old country" sometimes still remain. In late 1994, for example, New York

City police, in conjunction with federal authorities, announced the arrest of 79 suspects in New York and Italy, all charged with drug conspiracy. Drug-running activities were said to have centered on New York City's Famous Original Ray's Pizza Restaurant on Third Avenue near Forty-third Street. Authorities alleged that the pizza parlor was used as a halfway point in an international drug ring whose ultimate aim was to provide cocaine to "three long-standing organized crime groups in Italy, where cocaine sells for three times what it costs in New York."[98] Among those arrested were Aniello, Francesco, and Roberto Ambrosio—brothers of Italian-American descent who ran the pizzeria.

Transnational Organized Crime

While the focus of most organized crime scholars in this country has been on big-city crime families, transnational organized crime is emerging as one of the most pressing challenges of the early twenty-first century. **Transnational organized crime** refers to unlawful activity undertaken and supported by organized criminal groups operating across national boundaries.

In a recent conference in Seoul, Korea, former Assistant U.S. Attorney General Laurie Robinson discussed transnational organized crime, saying, "The United States recognizes that we cannot confront crime in isolation. With criminals' ability to cross international borders in a few hours, and the advances of our modern age, such as the Internet and telecommunications, crime can no longer be viewed as just a national issue. It is clear crime does not respect international boundaries. It is clear crime is global. As recent economic trends demonstrate, what happens in one part of the world impacts all the rest. And crime problems and trends are no different."[99]

Similarly, in 1995, delegates to the Ninth United Nations Congress on the Prevention of Crime and the Treatment of Offenders in Cairo, Egypt, agreed that transnational organized crime is now a "major force in world finance, able to alter the destinies of countries at critical stages of their economic development." Participants in the conference identified the world's major crime clans as the (1) Hong Kong–based Triads, (2) South American cocaine cartels, (3) Italian Mafia, (4) Japanese Yakuza, (5) Russian *Mafiya,* and (6) West African crime groups—each of which extends its reach well beyond its home country.

Russian organized crime is of special interest, both because it has grown quickly following the collapse of the Soviet Union and because it has taken root in the United States and in other countries outside of the former Soviet sphere of influence. Within Russia itself, "rampant, unchecked organized crime has laid waste to noteworthy democratic reforms and contributed to an economic and moral meltdown within the 15 newly independent republics. Intelligence reports emanating out of Russia peg the numerical size of the Russian Mafia (*Mafiya*) at 100,000 members owing allegiance to 8,000 stratified crime groups who control 70–80% of all private business and 40% of the nation's wealth."[100] The 5,000-

member drug-running organization *Solntsevskaya,* based in the Moscow suburb of Solntsevo, may be the largest organized crime faction currently operating in Russia. Mafia leaders, or "made guys," are referred to as *vory y zakone,* which can be translated as "thieves in law," the Russian word for godfather is *krestnii otets,* and soldiers are known as *boyevik.*

With the dissolution of Soviet-style controls between 1992 and 1994, the Russian mafia quickly seized control of the country's banking system through the investment of ill-gotten gains, money laundering, intimidation, fraud, murder, and the outright purchase of financial institutions. Ninety-five Russian bankers were murdered by *Mafiya* operatives between 1995 and 2000, and hundreds of reform-minded business leaders and investigative journalists have been assassinated or kidnapped.[101] The Analytical Center for Social and Economic Policies, a Russian think tank, estimates that four out of every five Russian businesses pay protection money to the mob.[102] In response to the wave of organized crime that Russia is currently experiencing, more than 25,000 private security firms have sprung up throughout the country. Analysts say, however, that few of these firms are legitimate, with many being fronts for Russian gangsters.[103]

Russian organized criminals differ from their counterparts in the United States because their ranks consist largely of ex-KGB officers, veterans of the war in Afghanistan, underpaid military officers, and former Communist Party operatives who formed powerful economic alliances with traditional gangsters and black marketeers years ago. As some observers note, Russian organized crime seems to be a natural outgrowth of the corrupt practices of officials who operated in the days of strict Soviet control, combined with a huge underground criminal black market that had already developed a complex organizational structure long before the Soviet Union fell apart.[104]

While Russian organized crime profits from American-style activities like narcotics, prostitution, racketeering, and illicit gambling, it is also heavily involved in product diversion and counterfeiting of popular Western goods, software and music duplication, and illicit arms sales and smuggling on a massive scale.

Over the last decade or two, hundreds of thousands of Russian citizens have emigrated to the United States. As U.S. officials are only now discovering, many of these people were former black market profiteers and hard-core offenders who had been released by the KGB from the Soviet gulag.[105] Among them was Marat Balagula, a black market criminal from Odessa who quickly formed alliances between the Russian *Mafiya* and the American Cosa Nostra. Balagula was responsible for the creation of a large-scale East Coast gasoline-tax scam that earned him millions of dollars in a short period of time.

Russian organized criminal groups today operate out of 17 American cities in 14 states. According to one source "The FBI believes there are 15 separate organized crime groups and 4,000 hard-core Mafia criminals from the former Soviet Union at work in the U.S. They are engaged in money laun-

Georgiy Gleyzer being escorted from the federal building in New York City. Gleyzer was arrested in connection with Russian mob activities and charged with terrorizing citizens of Russian communities in New York. What is the future of Russian organized crime in the United States? *Suzanne Plunkett, AP/Wide World Photos*

dering, automobile theft, smuggling, contract murder, loan sharking, medical insurance fraud, narcotics, and credit card and telecommunications fraud. The theft of electronic serial numbers from cellular phones and the duplication (cloning) of these PIN numbers have grown into a multi-million-dollar industry."[106]

The globalization of crime has necessitated the enhanced coordination of law enforcement efforts in different parts of the world and the expansion of American law enforcement activities beyond national borders. U.S. police agencies routinely send agents to assist law enforcement officers in other countries who are involved in transnational investigations. For additional information on transnational organized crime, see Web Extra! 12-9.

Web Extra! 12-9 at crimtoday.com

Organized Crime and the Law

For many years, American law enforcement agencies had few special weapons in the fight against organized crime. Instead, they prosecuted organized criminal operatives under statutes directed at solitary offenders, using laws like those against theft, robbery, assault, gambling, prostitution, drug abuse, and murder. Innovative prosecutors at times drew upon other statutory resources in the drive to indict leaders of organized crime. On October 17, 1931, for example, Al Capone was convicted on various charges of income tax evasion after federal investigators were able to show that he had paid no taxes on an income in excess of $1 million. Laws regulating the sale of alcohol and drugs and statutes circumscribing acts of prostitution have also been used against organized criminals, although with varying degrees of success.

The first federal legislation aimed specifically at curtailing the activities of organized crime is known as the Hobbs Act, a term that encompasses a series of statutes that were passed beginning in 1946. In essence, the Hobbs Act made it a violation of federal law to engage in any form of criminal behavior that interferes with interstate commerce. It also criminalized interstate or foreign travel in furtherance of criminal activity and made it a crime to use the highways, telephone, or mail in support of activities like gambling, drug trafficking, loan-sharking, and other forms of racketeering.

The single most important piece of federal legislation ever passed which specifically targets the activities of organized crime is the **Racketeer Influenced and Corrupt Organizations (RICO)** statute, which was part of the federal Organized Crime Control Act of 1970. The Organized Crime Control Act defines *organized crime* as "the unlawful activities of the members of a highly organized, disciplined association engaged in supplying illegal goods and services, including but not limited to gambling, prostitution, loan-sharking, narcotics, labor racketeering, and other unlawful activities of members of such organizations." The RICO portion of the act brought together under one single piece of legislation the many and diverse activities of American organized crime and made each punishable in a variety of new ways. RICO did not make racketeering itself illegal, but rather focused on the ill-gotten gains derived from such activity, specifying that it shall be unlawful for anyone involved in a pattern of racketeering to derive any income or proceeds from that activity. RICO's definition of *racketeering activity* includes

(A) any act or threat involving murder, kidnapping, gambling, arson, robbery, bribery, extortion, dealing in obscene matter, or dealing in narcotic or other dangerous drugs, which is chargeable under State law and punishable by imprisonment for more than one year;

(B) any act that is indictable under any of the following provisions of title 18, United States Code: section 201 (relating to bribery), section 224 (relating to sports bribery), sections 471, 472, and 473 (relating to counterfeiting), section 659 (relating to theft from interstate shipment) . . . section 664 (relating to embezzlement from pension and welfare funds), sections 891–894 (relating to extortionate credit transactions), section 1029 (relating to fraud and related activity in connection with access devices), section 1084 (relating to the transmission of gambling information), section 1341 (relating to mail fraud), section 1343 (relating to wire fraud), section 1344 (relating to financial institution fraud), sections 1461–1465 (relating to obscene matter), section 1503 (relating to obstruction of justice), section 1510 (relating to obstruction of criminal investigations), section 1511 (relating to the obstruction of State or local law enforcement), section 1512 (relating to tampering with a witness, victim, or an informant), section 1513 (relating to retaliating against a witness, victim, or an informant), section 1951 (relating to interference with commerce, robbery, or extortion), section 1952 (relating to racketeering), section 1953 (relating to interstate transportation of wagering paraphernalia), section 1954 (relating to unlawful welfare fund payments), section 1955 (relating to the prohibition of illegal gambling businesses), section 1956 (relating to the laundering of monetary instruments), section 1957 (relating to engaging in monetary transactions in property derived from specified unlawful activity), section 1958 (relating to use of interstate commerce facilities in the commission of murder-for-hire), sections 2251–2252 (relating to sexual exploitation of children), sections 2312 and 2313 (relating to interstate transportation of stolen motor vehicles), sections 2314 and 2315 (relating to interstate transportation of stolen property), section 2321 (relating to trafficking in certain motor vehicles or motor vehicle parts), sections 2341–2346 (relating to trafficking in contraband cigarettes), sections 2421–2424 (relating to white slave traffic),

(C) any act that is indictable under title 29, United States Code, section 186 (dealing with restrictions on payments and loans to labor organizations) or section 501(c) (relating to embezzlement from union funds),

(D) any offense involving fraud connected with a case under title 11, fraud in the sale of securities, or the felonious manufacture, importation, receiving, concealment, buying, selling, or otherwise dealing in narcotics or other dangerous drugs, punishable under any law of the United States, or

(E) any act that is indictable under the Currency and Foreign Transactions Reporting Act.

Punishments provided for under RICO include **asset forfeiture**, which makes it possible for federal officials to seize the proceeds of those involved in racketeering. In the words of the statute, "Whoever violates any provision of . . . this chapter shall be fined . . . or imprisoned not more than 20 years (or for life if the violation is based on a racketeering activity for which the maximum penalty includes life imprisonment), or both, and shall forfeit to the United States, irrespective of any provision of State law . . . any property . . . derived from any proceeds that the person obtained, directly or indirectly, from racketeering activity or unlawful debt collection." Hence, as a result of RICO, federal agents are empowered to seize the financial and other tangible fruits of organized criminal activity, including businesses, real estate, money, equities, gold and other commodities, vehicles including airplanes and boats, and just about anything else that can be shown to have been acquired through a pattern of racketeering activity.

Money Laundering

Money laundering refers to the process by which illegal gains are disguised as legal income. A more formal definition is offered by the National Institute of Justice, which says that money laundering is "the process of converting illegally earned assets, originating as cash, to one or more alternative forms to conceal such incriminating factors as illegal origin and true ownership."[107]

Title 18, Section 1956 of the U.S. Criminal Code specifically prohibits what it calls the "laundering of monetary instruments" and defines *money laundering* as efforts "to conceal or disguise the nature, the location, the source, the ownership, or the control of the proceeds of specified unlawful activity." To assist in the identification of money launderers, a provision

Attorney General Robert Kennedy describing a link between the Teamsters and organized crime. How influential is organized crime in American society today? *UPI, Corbis*

of the 1986 federal Money Laundering Control Act requires that banks report to the government all currency transactions in excess of $10,000. This requirement is, of course, well known to high-end money launderers who routinely evade it by dealing in commodities like gold, by using foreign banks, or by making a series of smaller deposits and transfers.

Reliable official estimates of the amount of money laundered in the United States are hard to establish. In 1984, however, the President's Commission on Organized Crime estimated that approximately $15 billion of illicit U.S. drug proceeds move illegally every year into international financial channels.[108] Of that amount, $5 billion was thought to be taken out of the country as currency.

A few years ago, the most notorious of foreign banks set up to serve the needs of money launderers, drug dealers, terrorists, and other assorted ne'er-do-wells was closed when banking regulators in the United States, England, and several other countries seized branch assets and arrested many of the bank's officers. The Bank of Credit and Commerce International (BCCI) was chartered in Luxembourg and opened branches throughout the world, including at least one in the Bahamas—islands already known for their role in providing infamous "offshore" banking services which, while trading in currencies internationally, offer customers considerable secrecy and very limited reporting requirements.

BCCI soon grew into one of the largest banks in the world and opened offices in 72 countries. Its friends in America included former President Jimmy Carter, Washington lawyer Clifford Clark, and Orrin Hatch, a powerful senator.[109] Although evidence suggests that BCCI may have provided assistance to U.S. Central Intelligence Agency (CIA) operatives, it also "served to smuggle arms to Syria, Iran, and Libya, and to launder money for the Medellín cartel and Golden Triangle drug warlord Khun Sa."[110] After repeated indictments of top officials, BCCI closed its doors in 1991. During the decade or so that it was in existence, however, it is estimated that many billions of dollars flowed through its numerous branch offices, the majority of it from drug cartels and terrorist organizations seeking to hide the source of their revenues.

In December 1993, the bipartisan President's Commission on Model State Drug Laws released its report, which included a comprehensive package of 44 model state laws designed to crack down on drug and alcohol abuse throughout the country. "Money and property are the economic lifeblood of the illegal drug industry,"[111] the report concluded, and the commission suggested that asset forfeiture—including expedited property seizure, evictions, and strict controls on money laundering—was the best means available for fighting the problem.

If anything, however, the money laundering problem appears to be getting worse. A 1994 report by the Senate Permanent Subcommittee on Investigations found, for example, that "billions of dollars are now leaving our country every year to be put into the flow of commerce and returned to this country as laundered capital."[112]

In that same year, however, in what many experts saw as contrary to the trend in enforcement activities needed to curb organized crime and drug trafficking, the U.S. Supreme Court made money laundering convictions harder to obtain. The case involved Waldemar and Loretta Ratzlaf, high-stakes gamblers from Oregon with lines of credit at fifteen casinos in New Jersey and Nevada.[113] In 1988, in an apparent attempt to hide $160,000 in gambling losses from the Internal Revenue Service (IRS), the Ratzlafs went to several banks in Nevada and California and bought cashier's checks of less than $10,000 each to pay the debt. Their check purchases came under IRS scrutiny as a result of an investigation into the couple's 1986 tax return. In that year, casino records showed that the couple had engaged in large cash transactions with a number of casinos, but they had reported no gambling income on their tax return.

Authorities accused the Ratzlafs of "organizing financial transactions" to evade the currency-reporting requirement of the 1986 federal Money Laundering Control Act. Both Ratzlafs were convicted in federal court in Nevada on charges of conspiracy and interstate travel in aid of racketeering. Waldemar Ratzlaf was sentenced to 15 years in prison and fined $26,300, while Loretta Ratzlaf was sentenced to ten months of home detention and fined $7,900.

The couple's lawyers appealed through the Ninth U.S. Circuit Court of Appeals and finally to the U.S. Supreme Court. The Court, in a 5 to 4 decision, found in favor of the Ratzlafs, saying that federal authorities had failed to prove that the couple knew they were violating the law.[114] The words of Justice Ruth Bader Ginsburg summarize the opinion of the majority: "Not all currency structuring serves an illegal goal. . . . Under the government's construction an individual would commit a felony against the United States by making cash deposits in small doses, fearful that the bank's reports would increase the likelihood of burglary, or in an endeavor to keep a former spouse unaware of his wealth."

In a separate dissenting opinion, however, Justice Harry A. Blackmun criticized the Court's majority, writing, "Waldemar Ratzlaf—to use an old phrase—will be laughing all the way to the bank." Ratzlaf, said Blackmun, "was anything but uncomprehending as he traveled from bank to bank converting his bag of cash to cashier's checks in $9,500 bundles" to pay the debt.

POLICY ISSUES: THE CONTROL OF ORGANIZED CRIME

In a cogent analysis of organized crime, Gary W. Potter tells us that "the question of what we [should] do about organized crime is largely predicated on how we conceptualize organized crime."[115] Potter criticizes current policies for focusing "almost exclusively on *criminal* aspects of organized crime." It is, says Potter, "the *organized* aspects of organized crime which offer the most useful data for formulating future policy."[116]

To understand organized crime and to deal effectively with it, according to Potter, we must study the social context within which it occurs. Such study reveals "that organized crime is simply an integral part of the social, political, and economic system," says Potter.[117] Any effective attack on organized crime, therefore, would involve meeting the demands of the consumers of organized crime's products and services. Potter suggests this can be accomplished either by punishing the consumers more effectively or by educating them about the perils of their own behavior.

Fighting corruption in politics and among law enforcement personnel and administrators is another track Potter suggests in the battle against organized crime. If organized crime has been successful at least partially because it has been able to corrupt local politicians and enforcement agents, then, Potter asks, why not work to reduce corruption at the local level?

Howard Abadinsky recommends four approaches to the control of organized crime, each involving changes at the policy-making level:[118]

- Increasing the risk of involvement in organized crime by increasing the resources available to law enforcement agencies that are useful in fighting organized crime. A greater proportion of tax revenues, for example, might be moved into the fight against organized crime. The 1994 Violent Crime Control and Enforcement Act, which puts more law enforcement officers on the streets, should be helpful in freeing up others to investigate organized crime.
- Increasing law enforcement authority so as to increase the risks of involvement in organized crime. Money laundering statutes that expand the scope of law enforcement authority, racketeering laws, and forfeiture statutes all may be helpful in this regard. Abadinsky also suggests providing a special "good faith" exception "to the exclusionary rule in prosecutions involving RICO violations."[119]
- Reducing the economic lure of involvement in organized crime by making legitimate opportunities more readily available. Educational programs, scholarships, job-training initiatives, and so on might all play a role in such a strategy.
- Decreasing organized criminal opportunity through decriminalization or legalization. This last strategy is perhaps the most controversial. It would decriminalize or legalize many of the activities from which organized crime now draws income. State-run gambling and the ready and legitimate availability of narcotics and other substances, provide examples of the kinds of policy changes necessary to achieve this goal.

Strict enforcement of existing laws is another option. It is a strategy that has recently been used with considerable suc-

cess by a number of federal and state law enforcement operations which have targeted organized crime. In 1987, for example, Nicholas "The Crow" Caramandi agreed to testify in 11 criminal trials against organized crime figures, resulting in more than 52 convictions, mostly in the Pennsylvania and New Jersey areas. Caramandi had bargained for lessened sentences in his own convictions on murder, racketeering, and extortion charges. A few years ago, Caramandi was released from prison and now lives far from Philadelphia under the federal witness relocation program with a new identity and a mob-ordered sentence of death hanging over him.

One of the most spectacular mob trials in recent years was that of John "Dapper Dan" Gotti, who took over control of New York's Gambino crime family after orchestrating the murder of "Big Paul" Castellano in 1985. Over the years, Gotti had been arrested on many occasions and had been prosecuted at least five times for various offenses. His ability to escape conviction earned him the title "the Teflon don." That changed on April 2, 1992, when Gotti was convicted on 13 federal charges, including murder and racketeering. Following the trial, Gotti was sentenced to life in prison without possibility of parole. Gotti's major mistake appears to have been to participate personally in several executions, including that of Castellano. Gotti and his underboss, Frank "Frankie Loc" LoCascio, are now both in federal prison. After Gotti went to prison, his son, John, Jr., took over control of the family. In 1999, however, the younger Gotti pleaded guilty to charges of bribery, extortion, gambling, fraud, tax evasion, and loan-sharking and was sentenced to six and a half years in prison.[120]

The senior Gotti's downfall came at the hands of Salvatore "Sammy the Bull" Gravano, a former underboss in the Gambino crime family. Gravano, who admitted to 19 murders, shared family secrets with federal investigators in return for leniency and succor through the federal witness protection program. Gravano also spent days on the witness stand testifying against his former boss. Federal prosecutor Zachary Carter later called Gravano "the most significant witness in the history of organized crime."[121] In 1997, Gravano again assumed center stage when he testified in federal district court in Brooklyn as the star prosecution witness in the murder and racketeering trial of Vincent Gigante, reputed head of the powerful Genovese crime family. Gravano was assailed by defense lawyers for being a notorious liar and for leading "a life of lies," facts he largely admitted in his best-selling book, *Underboss*.[122] Although Gravano was sent to Phoenix, Arizona, under the witness protection program, he found it hard to lead a straight life, and in 2000 he was arrested on three separate occasions on drug-running and money-laundering charges. As this book goes to press, Gravano is being held in the Maricopa County jail awaiting trial. He has also been indicted by a New York federal grand jury and charged with financing and running a major ecstasy drug ring in conjunction with an Israeli organized crime syndicate.[123]

Some say that in the face of increased law enforcement pressure, the Cosa Nostra is doomed. According to the FBI, most major crime families have now been decimated by enhanced investigation efforts, often supplemented by wire-taps and informant testimony. The FBI claims that a total of 1,173 Cosa Nostra bosses, soldiers, and associates through-out the country have been convicted during the last six years alone. Imprisoned bosses now include not only New York's John Gotti and his son, but Los Angeles's Peter Milano and the leaders of Kansas City's Civella family. Also, a few years ago, 13 members of New England's Patriarca family were convicted of murdering Billy Grasso, one of their underbosses, and were sent to prison. In 1999, federal authorities issued indictments charging 39 reputed mem-bers of five different New York City–area Mafia families with racketeering, murder, extortion, robbery, mail fraud, loan-sharking, illegal gambling, and trafficking in stolen property and counterfeit goods. Among those targeted was 54-year-old Vincent "Vinny Ocean" Palermo, reputed to be the acting head of the New Jersey–based DeCavalcante fam-ily. If convicted, Palermo faces up to 125 years in prison. Others arrested were said to be members of the Gambino, Luchese-Bonanno, and Colombo crime families. Read the indictments in the case at Web Extra! 12-10.

Salvatore "Sammy the Bull" Gravano, who admitted to 19 murders, has been called the "most significant witness in the history of organized crime." Do witnesses like Gravano spell doom for La Cosa Nostra? *J. Markowitz, Sygma*

 Web Extra! 12-10 at crimtoday.com

Can La Cosa Nostra survive such pressure? Nicholas Caramandi says "yes." "It's such a bureaucracy . . . this thing of ours," says Caramandi. "You can't kill it. . . . It's the second government. . . . We serve needs. People come to us when they can't get justice, or to borrow money that they can't get from the bank. . . . It never dies. It's as powerful today as it ever was.

It's just more glorified and more out in the open."[124] The Mob, says Caramandi, reaches all the way to the highest lev-els of political power. Survival is ensured through well-placed friends in America's highest elected offices. Just before going to prison, John Gotti, Sr., told his underbosses, "This is gonna be Cosa Nostra till I die. . . . Be it an hour from now or be it tonight or a hundred years from now, it's gonna be Cosa Nostra."[125]

SUMMARY

This chapter discusses white-collar and organized crime. Unfortunately, observations made about both forms of crime, as valid and useful as they may be, rarely rise above the level of organized conjecture. Hence it is impossible at this point to describe a theory of white-collar crime or a theory of organized crime, except insofar as those concepts can be contained within other theoretical perspectives—as was the case with Edwin H. Sutherland's attempt to ex-plain white-collar crime in terms of differential associa-tion. John Braithwaite's attempt to integrate a variety of theoretical approaches into a general theory which ex-plains all forms of crime, including white-collar crime, may be the most comprehensive theory of organized and white-collar crime to date.

Although both white-collar and organized crime appear to be prevalent in the United States today, and organized and white-collar criminals often share similar goals, such as acquiring wealth and social position, there appears to be considerable variation in commitment between the two types of offenders. Many organized criminals evidence a

long tradition of criminal involvement, often in the form of racketeering, which is largely unknown to most white-col-lar offenders. Similarly, organized crime wraps its members in a kind of deviant subculture with a detailed code of con-duct which affects them throughout their lives. White-col-lar criminals, on the other hand, have typically achieved positions of power and social respectability through con-formity and approved forms of achievement. They often come from cultural backgrounds that support adherence to the law. Hence most white-collar offenders are probably drawn to criminal activity for the immediate financial re-wards it offers, whereas organized criminals are more apt to see crime as a way of life and to condemn the conformist activities of others.

If such differences are true, then white-collar crime may be effectively prevented by strict enforcement efforts which, by their very example, serve as a strong general deterrent to other would-be offenders. Organized criminal groups, on the other hand, given their long-standing commitment to crimi-nal activities, are unlikely to be affected by such threats.

DISCUSSION QUESTIONS

1. What is the difference between white-collar crime and organized crime? What linkages, if any, might exist between the two?
2. What types of white-collar crime has this chapter identified? Is corporate crime a form of white-collar crime? Is occupational crime a form of white-collar crime?
3. Describe a typical organized crime family, as outlined in this chapter. Why does a crime family contain so many different "levels"?

4. What is money laundering? How might money laundering be reduced or prevented? Can you think of any strategies this chapter does not discuss for the reduction of money-laundering activities in the United States? If so, what are they?
5. What strategies does this chapter discuss for combating the activities of organized crime? Which seem best to you? Why? Can you think of any other strategies that might be effective? If so, what are they?

WEB QUEST!

Visit the National White Collar Crime Center (NW3C) at http://www.nw3c.org/home.htm. Explore the center's Web site to learn what NW3C does and to see which agencies are members of the center. Be sure to click on the "What's New,"

"Careers," and "Initiatives" options on the NW3C home page. Describe what you learn in a brief document, and submit it to your instructor if asked to do so.

LIBRARY EXTRAS!

The Library Extras! listed here complement the Web Extras! found throughout this chapter. Library Extras! may be accessed on the Web at crimtoday.com.

Library Extra! 12-1. Lala Camerer, *White Collar Crime in South Africa: An Initial Overview* (online document, accessed April 4, 2001).

Library Extra! 12-2. Tanya Frisby, "The Rise of Organized Crime in Russia: Its Roots and Social Significance," *Europe-Asia Studies,* January, 1998.

Library Extra! 12-3. Richard Lindberg and Vesna Markovic, *Organized Crime Outlook in the New Russia* (online document, accessed April 4, 2001).

Library Extra! 12-4. *The Organized Crime Glossary* (online document, accessed April 5, 2001).

Library Extra! 12-5. U.S. Department of Justice, *Idaho Man Given Longest-Ever Sentence for Environmental Crime* (online document, accessed April 5, 2001).

NOTES

1. As cited on the Woody Guthrie Web page at http://asms.k12.ar.us/classes/humanities/amstud/96-97/wguthrie/influence.htm. Accessed April 2, 2001.
2. John Lloyd, "The Godfathers Go Global," *New Statesman,* December 20, 1999. Web posted at http://www.findarticles.com/cf_0/m0FQP/4467_128/59134979/p1/article.jhtml. Accessed March 2, 2001.
3. *Wall Street Journal,* February 16, 1960. Quotation number 1984 in James B. Simpson, *Simpson's Contemporary Quotations,* (Boston: Houghton Mifflin, 1988).
4. U.S. Senate, Testimony before the Kefauver committee on organized crime, 1951.
5. Kathleen Murray, "The Fraud du Jour Is Wireless Cable," *Worth,* October 1994, p. 118.

6. Ibid., pp. 118–120.
7. Edwin H. Sutherland, "White-Collar Criminality," *American Sociological Review,* Vol. 5, No. 1 (February 1940), pp. 2–10.
8. Ibid.
9. Ibid.
10. Edwin H. Sutherland, "Crime of Corporations," in Albert Cohen, Alfred Lindesmith, and Karl Schuessler, eds., *The Sutherland Papers* (Bloomington: Indiana University Press, 1956), pp. 78–96.
11. Ibid.
12. Ibid.
13. Sutherland, "White-Collar Criminality."
14. Travis Hirschi and Michael Gottfredson, "Causes of White-Collar Crime," *Criminology,* Vol. 25, No. 4 (1987), p. 952.

[15] *USA Today,* April 2, 1991, pp. B1–2.

[16] Karen Gullo, " 'Phantom' Banks across the Country Bilking Investors," Associated Press wire service, September 11, 1994.

[17] James Cox, "Gold Dust or Bust," *USA Today,* April 17, 1997, p. 1B.

[18] In 1998, those assets were frozen in a lawsuit filed by Deloitte and Touche, Inc. See Paul Bagnell, "Felderhof's Caymans Assets Frozen in $3 Billion Negligence Suit," *Financial Post,* January 2, 1998. Web posted at http://www.canoe.ca/MoneyBreXSaga/jan2_felderhofs.html. Accessed January 2, 2001.

[19] See "Bre-X Trial to Go Ahead, Judge Rules," Canada's Internet Network, November 15, 2000. Web posted at http://www.canoe.ca/MoneyBreXSaga/nov15_brextrial-cp.html. Accessed January 2, 2001.

[20] Donald J. Newman, "White-Collar Crime: An Overview and Analysis," *Law and Contemporary Problems,* Vol. 23, No. 4 (autumn 1958).

[21] President's Commission on Law Enforcement and Administration of Justice, *The Challenge of Crime in a Free Society* (Washington, D.C.: U.S. Government Printing Office, 1967), p. 47.

[22] For excellent reviews of the evolution of the concept of white-collar crime, see K. Schlegel and D. Weisburd, "White-Collar Crime: the Parallax View," in Kip Schlegel and David Weisburd, eds., *White-Collar Crime Reconsidered* (Boston: Northeastern University Press, 1992), pp. 3–27; and K. Schlegel and D. Weisburd, "Returning to the Mainstream: Reflections on Past and Future White-Collar Crime Study," in Schlegel and Weisburd, eds., *White-Collar Crime Reconsidered,* pp. 352–365.

[23] Task Force on Organized Crime, *Organized Crime* (Washington, D.C.: U.S. Government Printing Office, 1976),

[24] Ibid.

[25] Herbert Edelhertz, *The Nature, Impact and Prosecution of White-Collar Crime* (Washington, D.C.: National Institute of Law Enforcement and Criminal Justice, 1970).

[26] Gilbert Geis, "Upperworld Crime," in Abraham S. Blumberg, ed., *Current Perspectives on Criminal Behavior: Original Essays on Criminology* (New York: Alfred A. Knopf, 1974).

[27] Gary S. Green, *Occupational Crime* (Chicago: Nelson-Hall, 1990), p. 12.

[28] Ibid., p. 16.

[29] Michael L. Benson, Francis T. Cullen, and William J. Maakestad, *Local Prosecutors and Corporate Crime* (Washington, D.C.: National Institute of Justice, 1993).

[30] "SabreTech Charged with Murder in ValuJet Crash," CNN.com, July 13, 1999. Web posted at http://fyi.cnn.com/US/9907/13/valujet.indictments.03. Accessed March 28, 2001.

[31] Michael Clements, "Breast Implant Pact OK'd: $4.25 Billion Is Available to Claimants," *USA Today,* September 2, 1994, p. 1A.

[32] "Plastic Surgeons, Manufacturers Helped Finance Breast-Implant Study," *USA Today,* September 2, 1994, p. 10A.

[33] Rahul Sharma, "Union Carbide Quits India a Decade after Bhopal," Reuters wire service, September 9, 1994.

[34] Details of the Attorneys General Master Settlement Agreement (MSA) and associated court filings can be accessed at http://www.tobaccoresolution.com.

[35] Of course, environmental damage inflicted by corporations can result in civil liability as well as violate criminal statutes.

[36] Edwin H. Sutherland, "White-Collar Criminality."

[37] Ibid.

[38] Ibid.

[39] Hirschi and Gottfredson, "Causes of White-Collar Crime," p. 949.

[40] Ibid., p. 951.

[41] Ibid., p. 956.

[42] Ibid., p. 960.

[43] Ibid., p. 960.

[44] Braithwaite began many of his studies of white-collar crime with investigations into the criminal activities of pharmaceutical company executives. See, for example, John Braithwaite, *Corporate Crime in the Pharmaceutical Industry* (London: Routledge and Kegan Paul, 1984).

[45] For a test of this thesis, see Anne Jenkins and John Braithwaite, "Profits, Pressure and Corporate Lawbreaking," *Crime, Law, and Social Change,* Vol. 20, No. 3 (1993), pp. 221–232.

[46] John Braithwaite, "Poverty, Power, White-Collar Crime and the Paradoxes of Criminological Theory," *Australian and New Zealand Journal of Criminology,* Vol. 24, No. 1 (1991), pp. 40–48.

[47] Toni Makkai and John Braithwaite, "Criminological Theories and Regulatory Compliance," *Criminology,* Vol. 29, No. 2 (1991), pp. 191–217.

[48] John Braithwaite and Gilbert Geis, "On Theory and Action for Corporate Crime Control," *Crime and Delinquency,* Vol. 28, No. 2 (1982), pp. 292–314. See also Brent Fisse and John Braithwaite, *The Impact of Publicity on Corporate Offenders* (Albany: State University of New York Press, 1983).

[49] Brent Fisse and John Braithwaite, "Accountability and the Control of Corporate Crime: Making the Buck Stop," in Mark Findlay and Russell Hogg, eds., *Understanding Crime and Criminal Justice* (North Ryde, Australia: Law, 1988), pp. 93–127.

[50] Brent Fisse and John Braithwaite, *Corporations, Crime and Accountability* (New York: Cambridge University Press, 1994).

[51] John Braithwaite, "Criminological Theory and Organizational Crime," *Justice Quarterly,* Vol. 6, No. 3 (1989), pp. 333–358.

[52] Newman, "White-Collar Crime."

[53] Green, *Occupational Crime,* p. 256.

[54] James William Coleman, *The Criminal Elite: The Sociology of White-Collar Crime,* 3 ed. (New York: St. Martin's Press, 1994).

[55] Ibid., p. 250.

56 Ibid., p. 252.

57 The details of this account are taken from Camden Pelham, *The Chronicles of Crime: The Newgate Calendar—A Series of Memoirs and Anecdotes of Notorious Characters* (London: T. Miles, 1887), pp. 57–65.

58 Much of the information in this section comes from Julian Symons, *A Pictorial History of Crime* (New York: Bonanza, 1966).

59 Ibid.

60 Howard Abadinsky, *Organized Crime,* 4th ed. (Chicago: Nelson-Hall, 1994).

61 Ibid., p. 112.

62 Luigi Barzini, *The Italians* (New York: Atheneum, 1965).

63 Abadinsky, *Organized Crime,* p. 132.

64 Gus Tyler, "The Crime Corporation," in Abraham S. Blumberg, ed., *Current Perspectives on Criminal Behavior: Original Essays on Criminology* (New York: Alfred A. Knopf, 1974), p. 197, citing Hank Messick, *The Silent Syndicate* (New York: Macmillan, 1966), pp. vii–xii.

65 Abadinsky, *Organized Crime,* p. 173.

66 Ibid.

67 John Kilber, *Capone: The Life and World of Al Capone* (Greenwich, CT: Fawcett, 1971).

68 Mark H. Haller, "Illegal Enterprise: A Theoretical and Historical Interpretation," *Criminology,* Vol. 28, No. 2 (May 1990), p. 209.

69 President's Commission, *Task Force Report: Organized Crime,* Appendix A.

70 Anthony E. Simpson, *The Literature of Police Corruption* (New York: John Jay Press, 1977).

71 J. Richard Davis, "Things I Couldn't Tell Till Now," *Collier's,* August 19, 1939, p. 35.

72 Robert W. Ferguson, *The Nature of Vice Control in the Administration of Justice* (St. Paul: West, 1974), p. 379.

73 Symons, *A Pictorial History of Crime,* p. 226.

74 President's Commission, *The Challenge of Crime in a Free Society,* p. 196.

75 Special Committee to Investigate Organized Crime in Interstate Commerce, U.S. Senate, 82nd Congress, 1951.

76 President's Commission, *The Challenge of Crime in a Free Society,* p. 192, citing the Kefauver Committee report.

77 Ibid.

78 *U.S. v. Bufalino,* 285 G.2d. 408 (1960).

79 The quotations attributed to the 1967 President's Commission report in this section are from President's Commission, *The Challenge of Crime in a Free Society,* p. 195.

80 As identified by Abadinsky in *Organized Crime.*

81 As cited in ibid., pp. 186–187.

82 William Sherman, "Kingpins of the Underworld," *Cosmopolitan,* Vol. 212, No. 3 (March 1992), pp. 158–162.

83 Ibid.

84 Abadinsky, *Organized Crime,* pp. 311–312.

85 Ibid., p. 313.

86 Ibid.

87 Richard Behar, "In the Grip of Treachery," *Playboy,* Vol. 38, No. 11 (November 1991), p. 92.

88 President's Commission on Law Enforcement and Administration of Justice, *Task Force Report: Organized Crime.* (Washington, D.C.: U.S. Government Printing Office, 1967).

89 Sherman, "Kingpins of the Underworld."

90 Behar, "In the Grip of Treachery."

91 Ibid.

92 See, for example, "Corleone Family Rules," Web posted at http://www.webmaze.com/memberpages/doncorleone/rules.html. Accessed April 2, 2001; and "Santino's Mafia Code," Web posted at http://organizedcrime.about.com/newsissues/organizedcrime/blsantino_1.htm. Accessed April 2, 2001.

93 President's Commission on Law Enforcement And Administration of Justice, *The Challenge of Crime in a Free Society.*

94 Secretly tape-recorded conversations played at the 1992 racketeering trial of John Gotti. Web posted at http://ganglandnews.com/locascio.htm. Accessed April 2, 2001.

95 President's Commission, *Task Force Report: Organized Crime,* p. 41.

96 Abadinsky, *Organized Crime.*

97 Abadinsky, *Organized Crime,* p. 5.

98 Joseph B. Treaster, "In Pizza Connection II, 79 Seized in Raids in New York and Italy," *New York Times,* September 16, 1994, p. 1A.

99 Laurie Robinson, address given at the Twelfth International Congress on Criminology, Seoul, Korea, August 28, 1998.

100 Richard Lindberg and Vesna Markovic, *Organized Crime Outlook in the New Russia: Russia Is Paying the Price of a Market Economy in Blood,* Search International, no date. Web posted at http://www.search-international.com/Articles/crime/russiacrime.htm. Accessed January 4, 2001.

101 Ibid.

102 Gary T. Dempsey, "Is Russia Controlled by Organized Crime?" *USA Today* magazine, May 1999.

103 Lindberg and Markovic, *Organized Crime Outlook in the New Russia.*

104 Dempsey, "Is Russia Controlled by Organized Crime?"

105 Lindberg and Markovic, *Organized Crime Outlook in the New Russia.*

106 Lindberg and Markovic, *Organized Crime Outlook in the New Russia.*

107 Clifford Karchmer and Douglas Ruch, "State and Local Money Laundering Control Strategies," *NIJ Research in Brief* (Washington, D.C.: National Institute of Justice, 1992), p. 1.

108 President's Commission on Organized Crime, *The Cash Connection: Organized Crime, Financial Institutions, and Money Laundering* (Washington, D.C.: U.S. Government Printing Office, 1984).

109 According to Abadinsky, *Organized Crime*, p. 427.

110 Ibid.

111 "Presidential Commission Presents Recommendation on Drug Control," United Press wire service, Northern Edition, December 13, 1993.

112 Carolyn Skorneck, "Money Laundering," Associated Press wire service, Northern Edition, April 7, 1994.

113 Laurie Asseo, "Scotus-Money Reporting," Associated Press wire service, Northern Edition, January 11, 1994.

114 *Ratzlaf v. U.S.*, 114 S.Ct. 655, 126 L.Ed. 2d 615 (1994).

115 Gary W. Potter, *Criminal Organizations: Vice, Racketeering, and Politics in an American City* (Prospect Heights, IL: Waveland, 1994), p. 183.

116 Ibid.

117 Ibid.

118 Abadinsky, *Organized Crime*, p. 507.

119 Ibid., p. 508.

120 "'Junior' Gotti Gets Nearly 6 1/2 Years," Associated Press wire service, September 3, 1999.

121 "5-Year Prison Term for Mafia Turncoat," *USA Today*, September 27, 1994, p. 3A.

122 Peter Maas, *Underboss: Sammy the Bull Gravano's Story of Life in the Mafia* (New York: Harper Collins, 1997). According to Ronald Kuby, an attorney suing Gravano to reclaim book royalties under New York's "Son of Sam" law, a roundabout method had been used to pay Gravano in order to avoid the provisions of the law. Kuby claimed that documents would show that author Peter Maas, Gravano, Harper Collins, and International Creative Management, the agent for the book, had conspired to hide payments made to Gravano. To learn more about the case, which remains undecided as this book goes to press, visit http://www.crimelibrary.com/gangsters2/gravano/24.htm.

123 "'Sammy the Bull' Faces More Drug Charges," Associated Press wire service, December 21, 2000.

124 Behar, "In the Grip of Treachery."

125 Bonnie Angelo, "Wanted: A New Godfather," *Time*, April 13, 1992, p. 30.

I believe that the struggle between East and West has been replaced by the world's struggle against drugs.

—Interpol Secretary-General Raymond Kendall[1]

Drug dealers no longer count their money. They weigh it.

—Houston, Texas, Police Lieutenant[2]

drug abuse and crime

CHAPTER 13

There is no moral middle ground. Indifference is not an option. . . . For the sake of our children, I implore each of you to be unyielding and inflexible in your opposition to drugs.

—Nancy Reagan[3]

Alcohol didn't cause the high crime rates of the '20s and '30s; Prohibition did. And drugs do not cause today's alarming crime rates, but drug prohibition does.

—U.S. District Judge James C. Paine[4]

IMPORTANT TERMS

Arrestee Drug Abuse Monitoring
  (ADAM) Program
dangerous drugs
decriminalization
designer drugs
drug-defined crimes

drug-related crimes
drug trafficking
heroin signature program (HSP)
interdiction
legalization

National Household Survey on
  Drug Abuse (NHSDA)
Office of National Drug Control
  Policy (ONDCP)
pharmaceutical diversion
psychoactive substances

OUTCOMES

LEARNING

After reading this chapter, you should be able to
  ◆ Discuss drug-defined and drug-related crimes
  ◆ Define dangerous drugs, and identify the characteristics of psychoactive substances
  ◆ Describe drug trafficking and government efforts to curtail it
  ◆ Identify the pros and cons of various drug-control strategies
  ◆ Explain arguments for and against drug legalization and decriminalization

Hear the author discuss this chapter at *crimtoday.com*

INTRODUCTION

In early July 1997, the childhood home of Mexico's top drug lord, Amado Carrillo Fuentes, was prepared for his funeral.[5] Dirty blankets lay over an open crypt, and candles burned in the home's small chapel, which was adorned with figures of Jesus, the Virgin of Guadalupe, and Jesus Malverde—claimed by drug dealers as their patron saint. Five-foot rose wreaths lined the pathway to the house, where hundreds of wooden chairs stood stacked against walls.

Although mourners gathered to pay respects to Carrillo's mother and sisters, there could be no funeral. Carrillo's body was in the possession of Mexican authorities, who were busy studying and cataloging the corpse. Carrillo, the authorities said, had died two days earlier in a botched attempt by plastic surgeons to change his appearance.

Before his death, Carrillo, the 42-year-old son of Mexican peasants, had replaced the Medellín Cartel's Pablo Escobar as the biggest shipper of cocaine to U.S. cities, earning an estimated $100 million a month in the illicit drug trade. Much of the money was used to pay off thousands of local, state, and federal officials (both in Mexico and in the United States). Carrillo earned the nickname "Lord of the Skies" after arranging to ferry Colombian cocaine into the United States. At one time he was said to have brought jumbo jet loads of cocaine from Colombia to Mexico, smuggling it across the Mexican-Texas border. At the time

of his death, Carrillo's organization had nearly displaced Colombian drug merchants in New York and other American cities, and Carrillo's net worth was estimated to have reached an astounding $25 billion![6]

Carrillo had been very open in his drug dealing until the arrest in February 1997 of General Jesus Gutierrez Rebollo, former head of Mexico's federal antidrug agency. It was reputed that Carrillo would even stroll around the plazas in Juarez, Mexico, to show that he was above the law. On the run from the Mexican national police (the *Federales*) since the general's arrest, Carrillo died in a desperate attempt to escape a closing dragnet of law enforcement officials. U.S. drug agents were told that Carrillo succumbed to heart failure at a Mexico City hospital following ten hours of extensive plastic surgery. Doctors who had performed the operation—for which Carrillo had rented an entire floor of the hospital, cordoning it off with heavily armed guards—fled after his death. Prior to surgery, Carrillo had just returned from Russia, where he had been trying to arrange a safe haven for his family and his money. In an interesting footnote to this story, rumors started circulating throughout Mexico following Carrillo's death that he had been secretly assassinated by Drug Enforcement Administration (DEA) agents who slipped lethal drugs into the medications used during the drug lord's plastic surgery. Many Mexicans believed the rumors because Carrillo died on the Fourth of July—American Independence Day. His death on that date, said the rumor mill, was a silent message to other drug runners, putting them on notice that they might be next.[7]

HISTORY OF DRUG ABUSE IN THE UNITED STATES

Carrillo's death illustrates the desperation that today often characterizes the lives of those involved with illegal drugs—from the highest level "dealers" to the saddest and most addicted of users. The widespread use of illegal drugs affects all segments of society. Even more problematic still is the fact that almost all forms of illicit drug use in America are associated with other forms of criminality. Drugs, and their relationship to crime, provide one of the most significant policy issues of our time. Famed *Washington Monthly* columnist Paul Savoy once reported polls showing that Americans "are so fearful about the drug-driven crime epidemic that more than half of those polled . . . expressed an opinion [which] favored cutting back the constitutional rights of criminal defendants and overruling Supreme Court decisions that limit police conduct in gathering evidence."[8]

The rampant and widespread use and abuse of mind- and mood-altering drugs, so commonplace in the United States today, is of relatively recent origin. Throughout the 1800s and early 1900s, the use of illegal drugs in America was mostly associated with artistic individuals and fringe groups. One hundred years ago, drug abuse, as we understand it today, was almost exclusively confined to a small group of musicians, painters, poets, and other highly imaginative individuals seeking to enhance their creativity. Although it is true that medicinal elixirs of the period contained a variety of potent substances, including cocaine, alcohol, and opium, the lives of relatively few Americans were seriously affected at the time by any drug other than alcohol. One significant exception existed in the form of "opium dens," which flourished in West Coast cities and eventually made their way across the country as a result of increased Asian immigration. Some Chinese immigrants brought opium products with them and introduced other segments of the American population to opium smoking.

Psychoactive substances gained widespread acceptance during the hippie movement, a period of newfound freedoms embraced by a large number of American youth during the late 1960s and early 1970s. The movement, which was characterized by slogans like "If it feels good, do it" and "Tune in, turn on, drop out," promoted free love, personal freedom, experimentation with subjective states of consciousness, and "mind expansion." Cheech and Chong movies, "flower power," paisley clothes, bell-bottom jeans, long hair on men, and Eastern religions all flourished within the context of a drug-fed countercultural movement.

One influential figure in the drug-inspired movement of the times was Harvard professor Timothy Leary. Leary formed the League of Spiritual Discovery in the mid-1960s, describing it as "an orthodox, psychedelic religion that permits the use of LSD and marijuana as sacraments by League members."[9] With the advent of the hippie era, marijuana, LSD, hashish, psilocybin, and peyote burst upon the national scene as an ever-growing number of individuals began to view drugs as recreational substances and as more and more young people identified with the tenor of the period.

Smoker in an opium den in Chinatown, San Francisco, circa 1925. Why did American attitudes toward drugs change? *UPI, Corbis*

Extent of Abuse

Current data on drug abuse in the United States are available through a variety of sources, such as the Monitoring the Future study, conducted by the University of Michigan's Institute for Social Research with funding from the National Institute on Drug Abuse at the National Institutes of Health; the **National Household Survey on Drug Abuse (NHSDA)**, conducted annually by the Substance Abuse and Mental Health Services Administration (SAMHSA); the National Narcotics Intelligence Consumers Committee's *NNICC Report,* published in conjunction with the Drug Enforcement Administration; the National Institute of Justice's quarterly Arrestee Drug Abuse Monitoring Program report; the **Office of National Drug Control Policy's (ONDCP)** *Pulse Check: National Trends in Drug Abuse,* which reports at least once a year on drug-use trends; and annual reports published by the SAMHSA's Drug Abuse Warning Network.

According to NHSDA survey data that were released in 2000, an estimated 14.8 million Americans aged 12 and older were current users of illicit drugs in 1999, meaning that they used an illicit drug at least once during the 30 days prior to being interviewed.[10] In 1999, as in prior years, men had higher rates of current illicit drug use than women (8.7% versus 4.9%). However, rates of nonmedical psychotherapeutic drug use were similar for males (1.9%) and females (1.7%).

Marijuana, the most commonly used illicit drug in 1999, was used by 75% of those reporting drug use. Approximately 57% of illicit drug users consumed only marijuana, 18% used marijuana and another illicit drug, and the remaining 25% used an illicit drug but not marijuana in the past month. Hence overall, about 43% of current illicit drug users in 1999 (an estimated 6.4 million Americans) were users of illicit drugs other than marijuana and hashish, with or without the use of marijuana (see Figure 13-1).

Of the 6.4 million users of illicit drugs other than marijuana, 4 million were using psychotherapeutics nonmedically. This represents 1.8% of the population aged 12 and older. Psychotherapeutics include pain relievers (2.6 million users), tranquilizers (1.1 million users), stimulants (0.9 million users), and sedatives (0.2 million users).

In 1999, an estimated 1.5 million Americans (0.7% of the population aged 12 and older) were current cocaine users. The estimated number of current crack users was 413,000 in 1999, and an estimated 900,000 Americans (or 0.4% of the population) were current hallucinogen users. Survey results showed that an estimated 200,000 Americans (or 0.1% of the population) were current heroin users.

Eleven percent of youths (ages 12 to 17) reported current use of illicit drugs in 1999, with marijuana reported as the most common illicit drug. Almost 8% of youths were current users of marijuana in 1999. The percentage using illicit drugs in the 30 days prior to being interviewed was slightly higher for boys (11.3%) than for girls (10.5%). In this age group, boys had a slightly higher rate of marijuana use than girls (8.4% versus 7.1%), but girls were somewhat more likely to

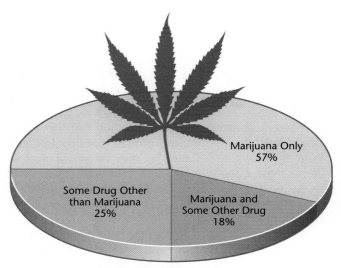

14.8 Million Illicit Drug Users

■ **Figure 13-1** Types of Drugs Used in Past Month by Illicit Drug Users, Age 12 and Older, 1999. *Source:* Substance Abuse and Mental Health Services Administration, *1999 National Household Survey on Drug Abuse* (Washington, D.C.: U.S. Government Printing Office, 2000).

use psychotherapeutics nonmedically than boys (3.2% versus 2.6%). The use of illicit substances by young people aged 12 to 14 is shown graphically in Figure 13-2.

The highest rate of illicit drug use was found among people aged 18 to 20 years, with rates of current use of between 20% and 21%. For these older youths, use is dominated by

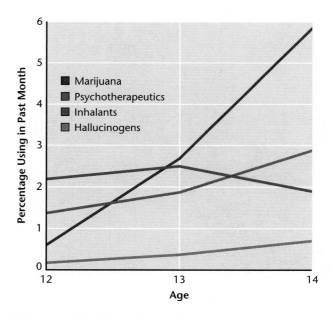

■ **Figure 13-2** Illicit Drug Use among Youths Aged 12–14, 1999. *Source:* Substance Abuse and Mental Health Services Administration, *1999 National Household Survey on Drug Abuse* (Washington, D.C.: U.S. Government Printing Office, 2000).

marijuana, with 18% reporting current marijuana use in 1999. As Figure 13-3 shows, rates of use generally decline in each successively older age group, with only 1.7% of people aged 50 to 64 and 0.6% of those aged 65 and older reporting current illicit use. An exception to this pattern of declining rates is the 40 to 44-year-old age group, which had a rate of 8.6%, somewhat higher than the rate for people aged 30 to 39 years. Members of this cohort were teenagers during the 1970s, the period when drug use incidence and prevalence rates were rising dramatically.

The NHSDA reported that rates of illicit drug use for major racial and ethnic groups in 1999 were 6.6% for whites, 6.8% for Hispanics, and 7.7% for blacks. The rate was highest among the American Indian/Alaska Native population (10.6%) and among people reporting multiple race (11.2%). Asians had the lowest rate (3.2%).

The rate of illicit drug use in metropolitan areas was higher than the rate in nonmetropolitan areas: 7.1% in large metropolitan areas, 7.0% in small metropolitan areas, and 5.2% in nonmetropolitan areas. Rural nonmetropolitan counties had a lower rate of illicit drug use (4.2%) than other counties.

The National Household Survey and the Monitoring the Future study show a leveling or declining national trend in illicit drug use, marijuana use, and cigarette use among adolescents since 1997, following a period of significant increases in the early 1990s.

As in previous NHSDA surveys, the 1999 survey found that illicit drug use rates remain highly correlated with educational status. Among young adults 18 years and older, those who have not completed high school have the highest rate of use (7.1%), whereas college graduates have the lowest rate of use (4.8%). This is despite the fact that adults who had completed four years of college were more likely to have tried illicit drugs in their lifetime than adults who had not completed high school (45.6% versus 30.0%). Hence the more education a person receives, the more likely that person is to discontinue using drugs with age.

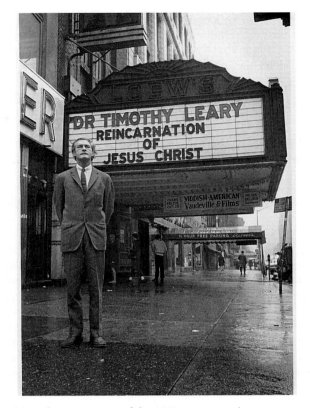

Dr. Timothy Leary, guru of the 1960s new consciousness movement, shown here in New York in 1966. Leary died in 1996, and his ashes were shot into space a year later. What was Leary's message? *UPI, Corbis*

Current employment status was also found to be highly correlated with rates of illicit drug use. The NHSDA found that 14.3% of unemployed adults (aged 18 and older) were illicit drug users, compared with 5.5% of adults employed full-time. Of all current illicit drug users aged 18 and older (7.3 million adults), 71% were employed, including 5.4 million full-time workers and 1.9 million part-time workers.

If NHSDA survey results are accurate, they would seem to indicate that drug abuse is now substantially less of a problem than it was two decades ago. In 1979, the number of current illicit drug users was at its highest level, when estimates of current users reached 25 million. The largest ever annual estimate of marijuana use put routine users at 22.5 million in 1979, while the largest cocaine use estimate was 5.3 million in 1985—figures far greater than those of today. Growth of the American population in the meantime gives the estimated decline even greater weight.

There are, of course, some methodological problems associated with any nationwide survey. In recognition of these problems, NHSDA authors write; "Sample size, coverage, and validity problems are likely to be more pronounced for NHSDA estimates of heavy users than for other measures generated by the survey. Therefore, estimates of heavy use are considered conservative, and changes over time are generally not statistically significant. For example, the NHSDA has produced estimates of about 600,000 frequent cocaine users with

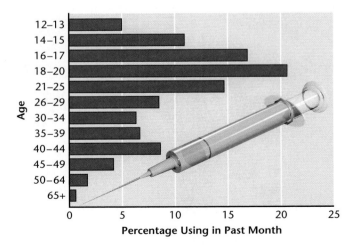

■ **FIGURE 13-3**   ILLICIT DRUG USE BY AGE, 1999.
Source: Substance Abuse and Mental Health Services Administration, *1999 National Household Survey on Drug Abuse* (Washington, D.C.: U.S. Government Printing Office, 2000).

no significant changes in the size of this population since 1985. By using various other data sources and making a number of assumptions (many of which are of uncertain validity), researchers have estimated that there are over 2 million frequent cocaine users in the U.S. . . . Clearly there is considerable uncertainty about the size of the heavy drug-using population."[11] Read the latest NHSDA report at Web Extra! 13-1.

Web Extra! 13-1 at crimtoday.com

Whereas the use of illicit drugs provides one measure of the drug problem facing our country, the ready availability of such drugs provides another. Data from the National Crime Victimization Survey show that two of three students aged 12 to 19 report ready availability of illegal drugs at their school.[12] Students in public schools report a wider availability of drugs than do those in private schools, and students in higher grades (ninth through twelfth) report more drugs available to them than do those in the lower grades. Similar rates of availability were reported by white students (69% of whom said drugs were available to them at school) and black students (67%), and by students living in cities (66%), suburban areas (67%), and rural areas (71%).

Young People and Drugs

While NHSDA data provide a picture of drug abuse among those 12 years of age and older, the National Institute on Drug Abuse's Monitoring the Future (MTF) study provides data on drug abuse among junior high school and high school students. It has tracked twelfth graders' illicit drug use and attitudes toward drugs since 1975. In 1991, eighth and tenth graders were added to the survey. The year 2000 survey gathered responses from over 45,000 students in 435 schools across the nation about lifetime use, past year use, past month use, and daily use of drugs, alcohol, and cigarettes and smokeless tobacco.

Year 2000 data from the Monitoring the Future study show that past year use of any illicit drug by eighth graders declined significantly since 1997—from 22.1% in 1997 to 19.5% in 2000.[13] Drug use among tenth graders was down from 38.5% in 1997 to 36.4% in 2000. For seniors, past year use of any illicit drug remained relatively stable, from 42.4% in 1997 to 40.9% in 2000.

Past year use of marijuana was 15.6% for eighth graders, 32.2% for tenth graders, and 36.5% for twelfth graders. Use of several specific illicit drugs, including PCP, narcotics other than heroin, methamphetamine, crystal methamphetamine ("ice"), barbiturates, tranquilizers, and Rohypnol, remained stable for all teenagers in all categories (lifetime, past year, past month, and daily use) from 1999 to 2000.

Cocaine use by seniors decreased from 1999 to 2000 in several categories. Overall, past year use of cocaine decreased from 6.2% to 5.0%, while past year crack use declined from 2.7% to 2.2%, and past year use of other cocaine decreased from 5.8% to 4.5%. Past year crack use by eighth graders decreased from a ten-year high of 2.1% in 1998 to 1.8% in 1999 and 2000.

Among seniors, heroin use in the past year increased from 1.1% in 1999 to 1.5% in 2000. Among eighth graders, past year heroin use decreased from 1.4% in 1999 to 1.1% in 2000. This decline in heroin use among eighth graders was the first noted since 1997.

Among eighth graders, lifetime use of inhalants decreased from 19.7% in 1999 to 17.9% in 2000. The MTF study found that inhalant use continues to be generally more prevalent among eighth graders than among students in the other two grades. Among twelfth graders, past year use of hallucinogens declined from 9.4% in 1999 to 8.1% in 2000.

Photo illustration of a high school student snorting cocaine. In a typical American classroom, three of 25 students use drugs. What accounts for the recent resurgence in teen drug use? *Matt Mendelsohn Photography*

THEORY VERSUS REALITY
The Harvard Alcohol Study

In 1993, the Harvard School of Public Health conducted its first College Alcohol Study (CAS). The study surveyed a random sample of students at 140 colleges in 39 states and the District of Columbia. The study was the first national examination of the drinking patterns of college students.

The original CAS identified a style of drinking that study authors called "binge drinking." *Binge drinking* was defined as the consumption of five or more drinks in a row for men, and four or more for women at least once in the two weeks preceding the survey. The CAS, with its emphasis on binge drinking, focused media attention on alcohol-related college deaths, including deaths from acute alcohol poisoning, falls, drownings, automobile accidents, fires, and hypothermia resulting from exposure to the elements. The study also led to passage of a congressional resolution to address binge drinking as a national problem and to the appointment of a National Institute on Alcoholism and Alcohol Abuse special task force on college drinking.

The CAS was repeated in 1997 and again in 1999. The 1999 CAS resurveyed 128 schools in 39 states and the District of Columbia. The study reported on the drinking behavior of four categories of students: (1) frequent binge drinkers—defined as those students who had binged three or more times in the past two weeks; (2) occasional binge drinkers—those students who had binged one or two times in the same period; (3) nonbinge drinkers—those students who had consumed alcohol in the past year but who had not binged in the previous two weeks; and (4) abstainers—those students who had not consumed alcohol in the past year.

The CAS found that two of every five students were binge drinkers in 1999. This was the same reported by the 1993 study. However, both abstention and frequent binge-drinking rates increased significantly between 1993 and 1999. The 1999 study found 19% of surveyed students to be abstainers and 23% to be frequent binge drinkers. As in the earlier studies, binge drinkers, and particularly frequent binge drinkers, were more likely than other students to experience alcohol-related problems. At colleges with high binge-drinking rates, students who did not binge drink were at high risk of experiencing the secondhand effects of others' heavy drinking. These secondhand effects included having study patterns interrupted, being kept awake at night, being insulted or humiliated, being subjected to unwanted sexual advances, and having to take care of drunken fellow students.

DISCUSSION QUESTIONS

1. Do you know students who consume alcohol on or off campus? If so, do you think that the College Alcohol Study categories provide a useful way of classifying the different kinds of drinking patterns among members of the student body?
2. What percentage of the student body at your school would you assign to each of the CAS categories?
3. Why might such categories be useful to policymakers?

Source: Henry Weschsler et al., "College Binge Drinking in the 1990s: A Continuing Problem; Results of the Harvard School of Public Health 1999 College Alcohol Study." Web posted at http://www.hsph.harvard.edu/cas/rpt2000/CAS2000rpt.shtml. Accessed January 15, 2001.

Similarly, past year use of LSD among seniors decreased from 8.1% in 1999 to 6.6% in 2000.

Past year use of steroids rose from 1.7% to 2.2% among tenth graders. From 1999 to 2000, use of steroids remained stable among eighth and twelfth graders. Among teenage males, the heaviest users of steroids, past year use was reported by 2.2% of eighth graders, 3.6% of tenth graders, and 2.5% of twelfth graders.

For the second year in a row, the MTF study found an increase in the use of MDMA (ecstasy) among tenth and twelfth graders, and for the first time, the study reported an increase in use among eighth graders. Past year use increased significantly among eighth graders (from 1.7% to 3.1%) and among twelfth graders (from 5.6% to 8.2%). Past year use increased among tenth graders, from 4.4% in 1999 to 5.4% in 2000.

Among eighth graders, disapproval rates for trying marijuana once or twice increased for the second year in a row to 72.5%. Disapproval rates among twelfth graders also increased, with 52.5% of seniors disapproving of trying marijuana once or twice.

Long-term trends are more significant than changes over one year, of course. The MTF study found that self-reported marijuana use by seniors peaked at 50.8% in 1979 and then declined to a low of 21.9% in 1992. Past year marijuana use then increased steadily to 38.5% in 1997. Since then it has declined, although not significantly, to 36.5% in 2000. Visit Web Extra! 13-2 for the latest MTF data.

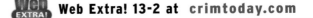 **Web Extra! 13-2 at crimtoday.com**

Costs of Abuse

ONDCP estimates that in 2000, Americans spent $62.3 billion to purchase illegal drugs (see Figure 13-4).[14] The true costs of drug abuse, however, are difficult to measure. Included among them would be measurable expenditures such as those for law enforcement activities intended to prevent drug growing, importation, and use; criminal justice case processing; drug-treatment programs; money laundering; and time lost from work as a result of drug involvement. More difficult to quantify, but equally real, are other costs related to drug abuse, such as death and sickness resulting from exposure to controlled substances, drug-related crime, the fragmentation of families and other relationships caused by illegal drug use, changes in attitudes and worldview among the American population due to drug-crime fear, lost human potential, and the image of the United States on the world stage. In 1997, for example, the latest year for which death certificate data are available, there were 15,973 drug-induced deaths (that is, deaths resulting directly from drug consumption, primarily overdose) in America.[15]

Similarly, acquired immunodeficiency syndrome (AIDS), many cases of which can be traced to intravenous drug use, has proved to be a costly disease in social terms. Researchers at the Centers for Disease Control and Prevention (CDC) say that AIDS is already the leading cause of death of black and Hispanic men aged 25 to 44. And AIDS, says the CDC, "has become the second leading cause of death among black women aged 25 to 44."[16] Homicide is the second leading cause of death for black and Hispanic men in that age group. The CDC finds 73 AIDS cases for every 100,000 black women, but only five per 100,000 white women. Of AIDS cases among minority women, 47% are traceable to intravenous drug use, while 37% appear to be due to heterosexual intercourse. ONDCP estimates that in 1995 there were a total of 52,624 drug-related deaths (that is, deaths due partially to drug abuse) from all causes other than overdose.[17]

Other costs, such as lost productivity due to drug abuse, are estimated to total $77.6 billion annually.[18] More than half of the total, or $43.8 billion, is estimated lost earnings due to drug-related crime victimization, while the remainder of the total is estimated to be suffered by drug abusers themselves.

Tables 13-1 and 13-2 show the estimated financial and social costs of illegal drug use in the United States per year. Table 13-1 includes dollar amounts spent on systemwide efforts at drug control, and Table 13-2 lists types of costs that are much more difficult to quantify.

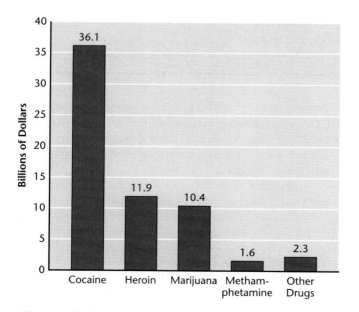

■ **FIGURE 13-4** AMOUNT SPENT ON ILLEGAL DRUGS IN THE UNITED STATES, 2000.
Source: Office of National Drug Control Policy, *What American Users Spend on Illegal Drugs* (Washington, D.C.: ONDCP, 2000).

TABLE 13-1 ■ Direct Costs of Illegal Drug Use	
Type of Cost	*Millions*
Federal drug expenditures (FY 2001 request)	$19,215
All law enforcement[a]	7,398
Interdiction	2,213
International	590
Corrections	2,072
Intelligence	305
Drug prevention	2,122
Drug treatment	3,382
State and local drug-crime expenditures	5,240
Enforcement of drug laws	2,007
Adjudication of drug-law violators	123
Correction of drug-law violators	3,071
State prisons	1,158
Local jails	890
Juveniles	224
Probation, pardon, and parole	677
Other corrections	122
Other criminal justice–related expenditures	38
Health care costs for illegal drug users	2,272
Short-stay hospitals	1,242
Specialty institutions	570
Office-based physicians	52
Support services	201
Other professional services	17
Medical care for drug-related AIDS cases	126
Support services for drug-related AIDS cases	64
Total	$26,727

[a]Not all law enforcement categories are shown.

Note: Figures are the author's estimates from a variety of sources, including Office of National Drug Control Policy, *The National Drug Control Strategy, 2000: FY 2001 Budget Summary* (Washington, D.C.: ONDCP, 2000); and Bureau of Justice Statistics, *Drugs, Crime and the Justice System: A National Report* (Washington, D.C.: U.S. Government Printing Office, 1993).

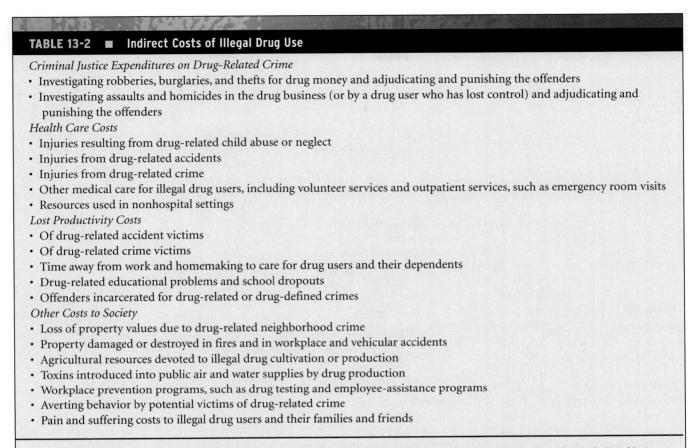

TABLE 13-2 ■ Indirect Costs of Illegal Drug Use

Criminal Justice Expenditures on Drug-Related Crime
- Investigating robberies, burglaries, and thefts for drug money and adjudicating and punishing the offenders
- Investigating assaults and homicides in the drug business (or by a drug user who has lost control) and adjudicating and punishing the offenders

Health Care Costs
- Injuries resulting from drug-related child abuse or neglect
- Injuries from drug-related accidents
- Injuries from drug-related crime
- Other medical care for illegal drug users, including volunteer services and outpatient services, such as emergency room visits
- Resources used in nonhospital settings

Lost Productivity Costs
- Of drug-related accident victims
- Of drug-related crime victims
- Time away from work and homemaking to care for drug users and their dependents
- Drug-related educational problems and school dropouts
- Offenders incarcerated for drug-related or drug-defined crimes

Other Costs to Society
- Loss of property values due to drug-related neighborhood crime
- Property damaged or destroyed in fires and in workplace and vehicular accidents
- Agricultural resources devoted to illegal drug cultivation or production
- Toxins introduced into public air and water supplies by drug production
- Workplace prevention programs, such as drug testing and employee-assistance programs
- Averting behavior by potential victims of drug-related crime
- Pain and suffering costs to illegal drug users and their families and friends

Source: National Institute on Drug Abuse and National Institute on Alcohol Abuse and Alcoholism, *The Economic Costs of Alcohol and Drug Abuse in the United States, 1992* (Washington, D.C.: U.S. Government Printing Office, 1998); and Bureau of Justice Statistics, *Drugs, Crime and the Justice System: A National Report from the Bureau of Justice Statistics* (Washington, D.C.: U.S. Government Printing Office, December 1992).

TYPES OF ILLEGAL DRUGS

By convention, controlled substances are generally grouped according to both pharmacological and legal criteria into the following seven categories: stimulants, depressants, cannabis, narcotics, hallucinogens, anabolic steroids, and inhalants. A separate eighth category, that of dangerous drugs, provides a kind of legal and definitional catchall. The Drug Enforcement Administration uses the term **dangerous drugs** to refer to "broad categories or classes of controlled substances other than cocaine, opiates, and cannabis products."[19] Each category, and some of the drugs it contains, is described in the following paragraphs.[20] Table 13-3 summarizes the differences between the drug categories. Learn more about each type of drug at Web Extra! 13-3.

Web EXTRA! Web Extra! 13-3 at crimtoday.com

Stimulants

Stimulants include cocaine and crack cocaine, amphetamines like Dexedrine and Benzedrine, and methamphetamine. Stimulants act as their name implies: They stimulate the central nervous system and result in higher heart rate, elevated blood pressure, and increased mental activity. Legitimate uses of stimulants include increased alertness, reduced fatigue, weight control, and topical analgesic (pain-killing) action. Such drugs are used illegally, however, by those seeking to produce states of excitability and feelings of competence and power.

Cocaine, the use of which has spread rapidly through American population centers, is available in powdered form or as small "rocks" of crack. Crack cocaine, which is much less expensive than powdered cocaine, is made by mixing cocaine powder with water and baking soda or ammonia. It is usually smoked in a "crack pipe" and is named for the fact that it makes crackling sounds when burned.

Powdered cocaine is inhaled or snorted, but it may also be mixed with volatile chemicals and "freebased" or smoked or injected. Cocaine produces effects similar to other stimulants—euphoria, a sense of intense stimulation, psychic and physical well-being, and what may seem like boundless energy—although cocaine "highs" are generally both more intense and more immediate than those produced by other

TABLE 13-3 ■ **Differences in Drug Categories and Characteristic Controlled Substances**

DRUGS	FEDERAL SCHEDULE	NAMES	PHYSICAL DEPENDENCE	PSYCHOLOGICAL DEPENDENCE
Stimulants				
Cocaine	II	Coke, flake, snow	Possible	High
Amphetamines	II, III	Benzedrine, Dexedrine, ice	Possible	High
Methylphenidate	II	Ritalin	Possible	High
Depressants				
Cloral hydrate	IV	Noctec, Somnos	Moderate	Moderate
Barbiturates	II, III, IV	Amobarbital, Phenobarbital, secobarbital	High–Moderate	High–Moderate
Methaqualone	II	Optimil, Parest, Quaalude, Sopor	High	High
Benzodiazepines	IV	Ativan, Azene, Clonopin, Dalmane, diazepam, Librium, Valium	Low	Low
Cannabis				
Marijuana	I	Pot, Acapulco gold, grass, reefer, weed	Unknown	Moderate
Hashish	I	Hash, hash oil	Unknown	Moderate
Narcotics				
Opium	II, III, V	Dover's Powder, paregoric	High	High
Morphine	II, III	Pectoral syrup	High	High
Codeine	II, III, V	Robitussin A–C	Moderate	Moderate
Heroin	I	Diacetylmorphine, horse, smack	High	High
Methadone	II	Dolophine, Methadose	High	High
Hallucinogens				
LSD	I	Acid, microdot	None	Unknown
Mescaline, peyote	I	Mesc, buttons, cactus	None	Unknown
Amphetamine variants	I	2, 5-DMA, PMA, STP, MDA, MDMA, TMA	Unknown	Unknown
Phencyclidine	II	PCP, angel dust, hog	Unknown	High
Steroids				
Anabolic steroids	III	Anabolin, Androlone, Durabolin, Kabolin	Low	High
Inhalants				
Various common substances		Laughing gas, nitrous oxide, gasoline, Freon, toluene, amyl nitrite, butyl nitrite, acetate	Low	High

drugs. Prolonged cocaine use can cause delusions, hallucinations, weight loss, and overall physical deterioration.

Cocaine sells in Colombia for $1,350 to $3,900 per pound and in the United States for $6,600 to $11,350 (80% pure) at the wholesale level. Once cut and diluted (cocaine is often mixed with sugar and other substances), the American retail price of powdered cocaine skyrockets to between $36,300 and $136,000 per pound. Crack cocaine sells for $3 to $40 per vial, each of which contains several small "rocks."

The Office of National Drug Control Policy estimates that the total annual amount spent on illegal cocaine in the United States is $36.1 billion.

Other stimulants include amphetamines with street names like "bennies," "speed," and "uppers." Amphetamines act to produce mental alertness and increase the ability to concentrate. They are used medically to treat narcolepsy, obesity, and some forms of brain dysfunction. They also cause talkativeness, reduce fatigue, and result in wakefulness.

Fans in Seattle mourn the death of Kurt Cobain, after Nirvana's lead singer committed suicide. Drugs were once called "the love of Cobain's brief life." How could drugs be so attractive? *Grant M. Haller, Corbis Sygma*

Abuse produces irritability, overexhaustion, and—in cases of prolonged abuse—psychosis and death from cardiac arrest.

One drug now catching the attention of many is methamphetamine, a stimulant chemically related to other amphetamines but with stronger effects on the central nervous system. Street names for the drug include "speed," "meth," and "crank." Methamphetamine is used in pill form or in powdered form for snorting or injecting.[21] Crystallized methamphetamine, known as "ice," "crystal," or "glass," is a smokable and still more powerful form of the drug. The effects of methamphetamine use include increased heart rate and blood pressure, increased wakefulness, insomnia, increased physical activity, decreased appetite, and anxiety, paranoia, or violent behavior. The drug is easily made in simple home "laboratories" from readily available chemicals, and recipes describing how to produce the substance circulate on the Internet. Methamphetamine appeals to the abuser because it increases the body's metabolism produces euphoria and alertness, and gives the user a sense of increased energy. Methamphetamine, an increasingly popular drug at "raves" (all-night dancing parties), is not physically addictive but can be psychologically addictive. High doses or chronic use of the drug increases nervousness, irritability, and paranoia.

In 1996, the growing popularity of methamphetamine led to passage of the federal Comprehensive Methamphetamine Control Act. The act is discussed in more detail later in this chapter.

Depressants

The depressant family includes barbiturates, sedatives, and tranquilizers like Nembutal®, Seconal®, Phenobarbital®, quaalude, sopor, Valium®, Librium®, Thorazine®, and Equanil®. Depressants are used legitimately to obtain release

from anxiety, for the treatment of psychological problems, and as mood elevators. Illegitimate users employ these substances to produce intoxication, to counter the effects of other drugs, or in the self-treatment of drug withdrawal.

Depressants are often prescribed by physicians seeking to control patients' stress-related symptoms and to induce relaxed states and even sleep. Individuals who have experienced recent traumatic events, for example, may find that the temporary use of prescribed depressants helps to alleviate the psychic distress that they would otherwise feel. If abused, however, depressants may lead to psychological dependence and to addiction.

Cannabis

The cannabis category includes marijuana, hashish, cannabis plants, sinsemilla, and hashish oil—all of which are collectively referred to as "marijuana." Marijuana is a relatively mild, nonaddictive drug with limited hallucinogenic properties. The primary active chemical in marijuana is tetrahydrocannabinol. Although legitimate uses for cannabis have not been fully recognized, some research suggests that the substance can be used in the treatment of pain and glaucoma and as a supplement to cancer treatments (cannabis appears to control the nausea associated with chemotherapy). Marijuana is used illegitimately to induce states of euphoria, gaiety, detachment, relaxation, intoxication, and focused awareness. Time distortion, increased sex drive, enhanced appetite, uncontrollable giddiness, and short-term memory loss tend to accompany its use.

Street names for marijuana include "pot," "grass," and "weed." Most marijuana is smoked in the form of dried leaves, stems, and flowers of the marijuana plant (or, more accurately, the Indian hemp plant), although processed marijuana "oil" and the cake form of hashish are also widely available. Hashish is made from resins found on the surface of the female marijuana plant and is considerably more potent than other forms of cannabis.

Most of the marijuana consumed in the United States is either grown within the country or comes from Mexico. Although one marijuana plant produces between one and two pounds of dried leaves and stems, marijuana is generally sold to consumers in one-ounce bags. One pound of dried marijuana costs dealers $450 to $2,700, while users pay $25 to $1,000 per one-ounce bag, depending on the reputed potency of the particular variety they are purchasing. Single marijuana cigarettes, sometimes called "joints" or "reefers," sell for $1 to $5. Overall, the Office of National Drug Control Policy estimates that the total amount spent on illegal marijuana in the United States is $10.4 billion annually.

Narcotics

Narcotics, including such drugs as opium, morphine, heroin, methadone, codeine, and Dilaudid, have a number of legitimate uses, including pain relief, antidiarrheal action, and cough suppression. Street use of these drugs is intended to induce pleasure, euphoria, a lack of concern, and general feelings of well-being. The use of narcotics produces drowsiness and relaxation, accompanied by a dreamlike state of reverie. Narcotics are thought to mimic or enhance the activity of endorphins, which are proteins produced by the brain that control pain and influence other subjective experiences.

Heroin and morphine, which are generally sold as a white powder, are derived from opium and are usually injected into the body, although they may also be smoked or eaten. Sometimes users inject these drugs under the skin, a practice called "skin-popping," but most addicts prefer direct intravenous injection for the strong and immediate effects it produces.

One pound of 70% to 90% pure heroin sells in Southeast Asia for $2,700 to $5,000. At the wholesale level in the United States, the same substance brings $40,000 to $110,000 per pound, while mid-level dealers pay up to $270,000 for that amount. Dealers "cut" the drug, effectively diluting it with a variety of other substances. One writer describes it this way: "Once in the United States, heroin may be stepped on (diluted) as many as seven to ten times. What started out in some remote Asian laboratory as 99 percent pure heroin is cut with lactose (milk sugar, a by-product of milk processing), quinine, cornstarch, or almost any other powdery substance that will dissolve when heated. . . . Ultimately, the heroin sold on the street is less than 10 percent pure and sometimes as little as 1 percent to 4 percent pure."[22] Street-level dealers sell diluted heroin in 0.1-gram single-dose bags for as much as $46 each, which translates into an effective retail price of more than $2 million per pound for imported heroin. ONDCP estimates that the to-

tal amount spent on heroin in the United States is $11.9 billion annually.

Although narcotics, including heroin, tend to be highly toxic when taken in large doses, frequent users build up tolerances and require ever larger doses for the desired effects to be induced. Physical addiction may result in drug dependence, and symptoms of withdrawal may appear if the drug is not available. Withdrawal symptoms include nervousness, restlessness, severe abdominal cramps, watery eyes, nasal discharge, and—in later stages—vomiting, diarrhea, weight loss, and pain in the large muscles of the body, especially the back and legs.

Hallucinogens

Hallucinogens, which include drugs like LSD (lysergic acid diethylamide), PCP, peyote, mescaline, psilocybin, MDA, MDMA, belladonna, and mandrake, have no official legitimate use. Street use of these drugs is intended to produce "mind expansion," hallucinations, creative mental states, and perceptual distortions—all of which have been popularly called "psychedelic experiences" or "trips."

The exact process by which hallucinogens act upon the mind is not known, and the effects of these drugs may be unpredictable. LSD "trips," for example, may produce pleasurable hallucinations and sensations or may result in frightening experiences for the user. During such episodes, uncontrollable nightmarish phantasms may appear to users who are no longer able to distinguish external reality from their own subjective states.

Anabolic Steroids

Anabolic steroids include the substances nandrolene, oxandrolene, oxymetholone, and stanozolol. Steroids are used legitimately for weight gain; for the treatment of arthritis, anemia, and connective tissue disorder; and in the battle against certain forms of cancer. Some bodybuilders, professional athletes, and others seeking to build body bulk and to increase strength have created a secondary market in steroids that has resulted in their ready availability through illegal channels of distribution.

Inhalants

Inhalants include a wide variety of psychotropic substances like nitrous oxide, carbon tetrachloride, amyl nitrite, butyl nitrite, chloroform, freon, acetate, and toluene. They are highly volatile substances which generally act as central nervous system depressants. Inhalants are found in fast-drying glues, nail polish remover, room and car deodorizers, lighter fluid, paint thinner, kerosene, cleaning fluids, household sealants, and gasoline. Although some of these substances, such as ether, nitrous oxide, amyl nitrate, and chloroform, have legitimate medical uses, others are employed only to produce a sense of light-headedness often described in colloquial terms as a "rush." The use of inhalants "can disturb vision, impair judgment, and reduce muscle and reflex control."[23]

Inhalants have been called "gateway drugs," or substances that initiate young people into illicit drug use. Easy access to these chemicals is ensured by the fact that few inhalants are subject to legislative control beyond simple administrative regulations. In fact, most inhalants are easily available, being found on household shelves, in hardware stores, and on the shelves of general merchandisers.

Based on self-reports from members of surveyed households who are 12 years or older, an estimated 23.8 million Americans have used inhalants at some point in their lives, and 2.4 million have used these drugs within the past month.[24] Among high school seniors, only marijuana use is more widespread than the use of inhalants.[25] Sixteen percent of high school seniors report having experimented with some form of inhalant. Learn more about inhalants at the National Inhalant Prevention Coalition's Web site via Web Extra! 13-4.

 Web Extra! 13-4 at crimtoday.com

Pharmaceutical Diversion and Designer Drugs

The pharmaceutical diversion and subsequent abuse of legitimately manufactured controlled substances is a major source of drug-related addiction or dependence, medical emergencies, and death. **Pharmaceutical diversion** occurs through illegal prescribing by physicians and illegal dispensing by pharmacists and their assistants. "Doctor shopping," the process of finding a physician who is overly liberal in the type and amount of drug prescribed, and visits to numerous physicians for the purpose of collecting large quantities of prescribed medicines are practices which exacerbate the problem. Depressants, including sedatives, tranquilizers, and antianxiety drugs (especially Xanax® and Valium®), along with stimulants and anabolic steroids, constitute the types of drugs most often diverted.

A number of drugs, especially those which fall into the "designer" category, are manufactured in clandestine drug facilities, which are sometimes called "basement laboratories" because they are operated by individuals out of their homes. As the National Institute of Justice notes, "Clandestine laboratories range from small crude operations in sheds, bathtubs, mobile homes, boats, and motel rooms to highly sophisticated operations with professional quality laboratory glassware and equipment."[26] **Designer drugs** are so named because "they are new substances designed by slightly altering the chemical makeup of other illegal or tightly controlled drugs."[27] Designer drugs like Nexus, a new reputed aphro-

disiac, usually fall under the rubric "synthetic narcotic" or "synthetic hallucinogen."

Designer drugs require the use of a number of specifically identifiable chemicals in their production. Similarly, opium, cocaine, and other naturally occurring psychoactive substances require the use of chemicals in step-by-step processes to make them ready for street-level distribution and consumption. The Chemical Diversion and Trafficking Act (CDTA) of 1988 placed the distribution of eight essential chemicals used in the production of illicit drugs, as well as 12 "precursor chemicals" (from which drugs could be made), under federal control. The CDTA also regulates the distribution of machines which can produce pharmaceutical capsules and tablets. In 1994, the Domestic Chemical Diversion Control Act[28] added 32 other chemicals to the list, bringing the total number of drug-related chemical substances under federal control to 52.

DRUG TRAFFICKING

In everyday usage, the phrase *drug trafficking* can have a variety of meanings. On the one hand, it can refer to smuggling—that is, the illegal shipment of controlled substances across state and national boundaries. On the other, it can mean the sale of controlled substances. Hence in colloquial usage, a person who "traffics" in drugs may simply sell them. Technically speaking, **drug trafficking** includes manufacturing, distributing, dispensing, importing, and exporting (or possession with intent to do the same) a controlled substance or a counterfeit substance.[29] Federal law enforcement agencies, in their effort to reduce trafficking, focus largely on the prevention of smuggling and on the apprehension of smugglers.

Drugs like cocaine, heroin, and LSD are especially easy to smuggle because relatively small quantities of these drugs can be adulterated with other substances to provide large amounts of illicit commodities for sale on the street. Figures 13-5 and 13-6 provide maps of major cocaine and heroin trafficking routes (sometimes called "pipelines") worldwide. Most cocaine that enters the United States originates in the Western Hemisphere, especially in the South American nations of Colombia, Peru, and Bolivia. Transportation routes into the United States include (1) shipment overland from South America through Central America, (2) direct shipments to U.S. ports concealed in containers or packed with legitimate products, (3) flights into the United States via commercial airplanes or in private aircraft, and (4) airdrops to vessels waiting offshore for smuggling into the United States.

Most cocaine entering the United States is smuggled aboard maritime vessels. Fishing vessels with hidden compartments, cargo ships plying international waters, and even private submersibles have all been used in smuggling operations. In 2000, for example, Colombian authorities, with help

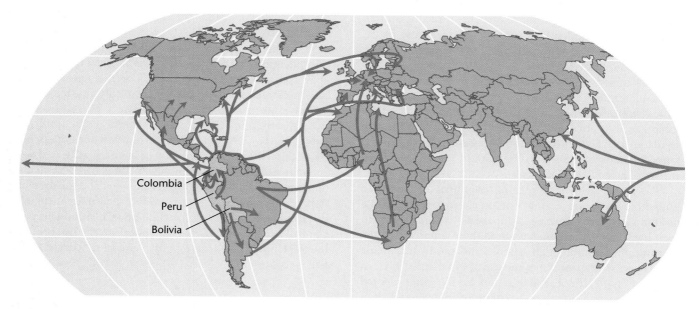

■ **FIGURE 13-5** GLOBAL COCAINE TRAFFICKING: MAJOR COUNTRIES OF ORIGIN AND ROUTES OF TRANSPORTATION.
Source: Adapted from Office of National Drug Control Policy, *The National Drug Control Strategy: 2000 Annual Report* (Washington, D.C.: U.S. Government Printing Office, 2000), p. 78.

from the DEA, seized a sophisticated 90-foot-long submarine that was under construction by drug traffickers in a warehouse in Bogotá. With a pressurized double hull and a high-tech navigation system, the submarine was designed for deep-sea use and would have been very difficult to detect. Colombian navy Captain Fidel Azula, a former submarine captain who examined the submarine, said even the Colombian navy lacked the knowledge to build such a vessel. "This is unmistakably of superb naval construction," he said.[30] Indications were that Russian engineers were involved in the sub's design and construction. Police were led to the find by suspicious area residents who had seen Americans hanging around the warehouse, located in a cow pasture off of a highway.

Recent large seizures of cocaine include 2.7 metric tons discovered hidden in canvas bags amidst a shipment of coffee beans imported into Miami, and seven metric tons discovered aboard the fishing vessel *Don Celso* and seized by

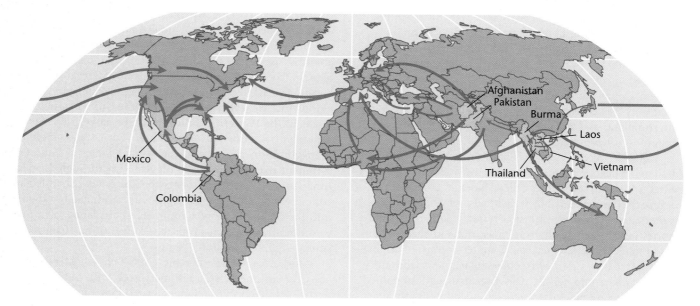

■ **FIGURE 13-6** GLOBAL HEROIN TRAFFICKING: MAJOR COUNTRIES OF ORIGIN AND ROUTES OF TRANSPORTATION.
Source: Adapted from Office of National Drug Control Policy, *The National Drug Control Strategy: 2000 Annual Report* (Washington, D.C.: U.S. Government Printing Office, 2000), p. 81.

Ecuadorian authorities at the Port of Esmeraldes.[31] In 1998, U.S. Customs Service agents in Laredo, Texas, discovered more than two tons of cocaine concealed in a double-walled cooking grease tanker attempting to enter the United States. Based on a street value for cocaine of up to $45,000 per pound, the seizure had an estimated street value of $196 million. Agents were alerted when a narcotic detector dog alerted positively to the rear wheel area of the tanker truck.[32] The most cocaine ever seized at one time, 47,554 pounds, was found in Sylmar, California, on September 29, 1989.[33]

Some trafficking methods are highly creative. As a DEA report states, "Unusual methods of concealment [include] cocaine concealed in a shipment of beach towels, inside spools of industrial thread, inside cans of lard, sealed within quartz crystals, in drums of fruit pulp, in fish meal, and in avocado paste. In addition, U.S. Customs Service and U.S. Fish and Wildlife officers seized several kilograms of cocaine from within a shipment of boa constrictors. The cocaine, wrapped in condoms, had been inserted into the snakes' intestines."[34]

The DEA follows heroin trafficking through its **heroin signature program (HSP)**, which identifies the geographic source area of a heroin sample through the laboratory detection of specific chemical characteristics in the sample which are peculiar to that area. The signature program employs special chemical analyses to identify and measure chemical constituents of a sample of seized heroin. Results of the HSP show that 62% of heroin in the United States originates in South America, 17% in Southeast Asia, 16% in Southwest Asia, and 5% in Mexico. According to the DEA, most heroin originating in Southeast Asia is produced in the Golden Triangle area, which encompasses Burma, Laos, and Thailand. Shipments are "controlled by ethnic Chinese criminal groups . . . while U.S.-based ethnic Chinese traffickers with links to these international criminal groups [are] the most prolific importers and distributors of Southeast Asian heroin" within the United States.[35] HSP data were based on examination of over 800 random samples, including some obtained through undercover purchases, domestic seizures, and seizures made at U.S. ports of entry. Learn more about the Drug Enforcement Administration and the Heroin Signature Program at Web Extra! 13-5.

Web Extra! 13-5 at crimtoday.com

DRUGS AND CRIME

While the manufacture, sale, transportation, and use of controlled substances is itself criminal, drugs and crime are also linked in other ways. The addict who is so habituated to the use of illegal drugs that he steals to support his "habit," the drug importer who kills a rival dealer, and the offender who commits a criminal act due to the stimulation provided by drugs all provide examples of how drug abuse may be linked to other forms of criminal activity.

Recognizing these differences, the Bureau of Justice Statistics (BJS) distinguishes between drug-defined and drug-related crimes. **Drug-defined crimes** are "violations of laws prohibiting or regulating the possession, use, or distribution of illegal drugs."[36] The costs of all drug-defined crime, says BJS, is directly attributable to illegal drug use. **Drug-related crimes**. on the other hand, "are not violations of drug laws but are crimes in which drugs contribute to the offense."[37] Illegal drug use, says BJS, "is related to offenses against people and property in three major ways: (1) pharmacologically drugs can induce violent behavior, (2) the cost of drugs induces some users to commit crimes to support their drug habits, [and] (3) violence often characterizes relations among participants in the drug distribution system."[38]

According to the U.S. Department of Justice, "There is extensive evidence of the strong relationship between drug use and crime." This relationship can be summarized in the following three points, each of which, the department says, is supported "by a review of the evidence."[39]

- Drug users report greater involvement in crime and are more likely than nonusers to have criminal records.
- People with criminal records are much more likely than others to report being drug users.
- Crimes rise in number as drug use increases.

One national initiative that attempts to measure the degree to which criminal offenders use controlled substances is the **Arrestee Drug Abuse Monitoring (ADAM) Program**, run by the National Institute of Justice. The ADAM Program tracks trends in the prevalence and types of drug use among booked arrestees in urban areas. ADAM currently operates in 35 sites in 25 states and the District of Columbia. The program makes it possible to identify levels of drug use among arrestees, track changes in patterns of drug use, identify specific drugs that are abused in each jurisdiction, alert officials to trends in drug use and the availability of new drugs, provide data to help understand the drug-crime connection, and evaluate law enforcement and jail-based programs and their effects.

ADAM data consist of urinalysis results and information reported to interviewers by arrestees regarding their drug use. Urine specimens collected from arrestees are sent to a central laboratory where they are analyzed for the presence of ten drugs: cocaine, opiates, marijuana, PCP, methadone, benzodiazepines (for example, Valium), methaqualone, propoxyphene (that is, Darvon-like substances), barbiturates, and amphetamines. Tests can detect the use of most drugs within the past two to three days, and marijuana and PCP can be detected as long as three weeks after use.

In a given year, ADAM collects data from approximately 30,000 adult male and 10,000 adult female arrestees. Additionally, data are typically collected from more than 2,500 male and 400 female juvenile detainees.

In mid-2000, data gathered through the ADAM Program showed that half of the adult male arrestees in 34 reporting American cities tested positively for drug use.[40] ADAM researchers uncovered significant differences in the patterns of arrestee drug use by city. For example, the percentage of male arrestees who tested positively for any drug ranged from 50% in San Antonio to 77% in Atlanta. The range among female arrestees was even more pronounced, from a low of 22% in Laredo to 81% in New York City.[41]

As in past years, cocaine remained the drug of choice among many arrestees. More than one-third of adult male arrestees in a majority of sites tested positively for cocaine. Cocaine-positive rates for women ranged from 19% in San Antonio to 65% in New York City, and cocaine-positive rates for men ranged from 14% in San Jose to 51% in Atlanta.

The study also found that the proportion of adult male arrestees testing positively for marijuana was greater than the rate for female adult arrestees in all sites. Adult male marijuana-positive rates ranged from 28% in Las Vegas to 51% in Omaha. Adult female marijuana-positive rates ranged from 9% in Laredo to 39% in Oklahoma City.

Among juvenile detainees, marijuana was the most commonly used drug—more than six times higher than cocaine use for juvenile males and females alike. Among the sites that collect juvenile data, male detainees were more likely to test positively for the use of any drug than were female detainees. At every site, more than 40% of juvenile males and 20% of juvenile females tested positively for marijuana.

The use of opiates, such as heroin and opium, remained relatively low in 1999 compared to the prevalence of cocaine and marijuana among adult arrestees. Only 12 sites had adult opiate-positive rates of 10% or higher. The proportion of women testing positive for opiates was greater than that for men in many sites. In only three sites—Chicago, New York City, and Washington, D.C.—did more than 15% of adult male arrestees test positively for opiates. In six sites—Albuquerque, Chicago, Detroit, New York City, Portland, and Seattle—more than 15% of female adult arrestees tested positively for opiates.

Consistently high percentages of overall use among arrestees, however, may mask differences in trends for specific drugs and in specific segments of the arrestee population. Methamphetamine use among ADAM arrestees, for example, appears to be concentrated mainly in the Western part of the United States, particularly in Portland, Sacramento, Salt Lake City, San Diego, San Jose, and Spokane, where more than 20% of both the men and the women tested positively for the drug. The survey found that methamphetamine use among juvenile arrestees followed a pattern similar to that of adult arrestees in that methamphetamine was more commonly used by females and was most often de-

tected at sites in the West and Southwest. Learn more about ADAM at Web Extra! 13-6.

Web EXTRA! **Web Extra! 13-6 at** **crimtoday.com**

Other information on drug use by offenders at the time of the offense comes from the National Crime Victimization Survey (NCVS), which gathers data from victims of violent crime who are asked to report their impressions about offenders. In a recent year, for example, 33% of all victims of violent crime included in the survey reported that they believed their assailants were under the influence of drugs or alcohol at the time the crime occurred. Another 46% of victims stated that they did not know whether the offender was under the influence of drugs.

Offender self-reports collected by BJS researchers show that among jail inmates[42]

■ 44% used illegal drugs in the month before the offense for which they were arrested
■ 30% used illegal drugs daily in the month before the offense
■ 27% used illegal drugs at the time of the offense
■ Cocaine and crack cocaine were the drugs most commonly abused by jail inmates

Surveys of state prison inmates reveal much the same pattern. Of inmates in state prisons, 61% say that they or their victims were under the influence of drugs or alcohol at the time of the offense, 50% report having been under the influence of alcohol or drugs, and 30% say their victims were under the influence of alcohol or drugs.[43] Nearly 40% of youths incarcerated in long-term state-operated facilities report having been under the influence of illegal drugs at the time of their offense.[44] When self-reports of jail and state prison inmates are evaluated to determine the proportion reporting having ever used drugs, nearly 80% of adult inmates report such use, while 83% of incarcerated juveniles say they have used drugs at some point in their lives.[45]

Surveys of drug-related crime have also been conducted in recent years. Interviews with adult prison inmates, for example, revealed that 24% of female and 16% of male inmates committed their offenses to get money to buy drugs. The same surveys show that approximately 30% of all robberies, burglaries, and thefts are committed to obtain drug money, while 5% of murders result from such criminal activities.[46]

Illegal Drugs and Official Corruption

Sometimes the corrupting influence of drugs and drug money extends beyond street crime and street criminals. Lucrative drug profits have the potential to corrupt official

The vast amounts of money associated with the illegal drug trade have the potential to corrupt public officials and agents of control. How can that potential be reduced? *Steve Starr, Saba Press Photos, Inc.*

agents of control, as the recent Mollen Commission study of police corruption in New York City found. The Mollen Commission, headed by former Judge Milton Mollen, made its report on July 6, 1994, and found that the severity of police corruption in New York City had worsened drastically since previous investigations into the subject. According to the report, "Police have crossed the line into actively engaging in criminal activity including robbery, drug dealing and even a killing."[47] It called today's corrupt police "criminals in blue uniforms," contrasting the severity of their illegal activity with prior forms of corruption that simply involved turning a "blind eye" to crime.

Much illegal police activity was found to be drug related, with drug monies providing powerful incentives toward corruption. The report found that police officers in certain precincts banded together and regularly robbed drug dealers, sold drugs, and conducted illegal raids to confiscate additional drugs for personal gain. The commission found that "some precincts were much more prone to corruption, particularly in minority communities because of high levels of drug activity within their borders. . . . Unlike 20 years ago, when an officer took bribes it was to turn his head away from crime. This time these (bad) cops are the criminals," Judge Mollen said, commenting on the commission's report.[48]

It is not only police officers who face the threat of corruption from the lucrative monetary rewards to be reaped from dealing drugs. In the mid-1990s, for example, 20 District of Columbia corrections officers and employees were given stiff prison sentences after being convicted of drug-smuggling activities. Even with those convictions, however, few believed that corruption in the District's prisons had been ended. U.S. District Judge Royce Lamberth, who sen-

tenced the former officers, observed that "even as the latest prison guard drug ring was being shut down . . . corruption continues today as I sit in this courtroom."[49]

SOCIAL POLICY AND DRUG ABUSE

The history of drug-control policy in the United States is as interesting as it is diverse. Prior to 1907, any and all drugs could be bought and sold in the United States without restriction. Manufacturers and distributors were not regulated and were not even required to disclose the contents of their products. Patent medicines of the time were trade secrets whose names were patented although their ingredients were known only to the manufacturers. The era of patent medicines came to an end with enactment of the federal Food and Drug Act of 1906. The law required manufacturers to list their ingredients and specifically targeted mood-changing chemicals. "For purposes of this Act," the law read, "an article shall . . . be deemed misbranded . . . if the package fails to bear a statement on the label of the quantity or proportion of any alcohol, morphine, opium, cocaine, heroin, alpha or beta eucaine, chloroform, cannabis, chloral hydrate, or acetanilide." Although the law required disclosure of the chemical composition of marketed substances, it did not outlaw them.

The Harrison Act, passed by Congress in 1914, was the first major piece of federal antidrug legislation. The Harrison Act required anyone dealing in opium, morphine, heroin, or cocaine or their derivatives to register with the federal government and to pay a tax of $1.00 per year. The act, however, only authorized the registration of physicians, pharmacists, and other medical professionals, effectively outlawing street use of these drugs. However, by 1920, court rulings severely curtailed the use of heroin for medical purposes, saying its prescribed use only prolonged addiction. Hence the beginning of complete federal prohibition over at least one major drug can be traced to that time.

In 1919, the Eighteenth Amendment to the U.S. Constitution, which prohibited the manufacture, sale, and transportation of alcoholic beverages, was ratified. The Volsted Act, passed by Congress in 1919 over President Wilson's veto, mandated Prohibition and defined "intoxicating liquors" as those containing more than 0.5% alcohol. Support for Prohibition began to wane not long after the amendment was enacted. Objections to Prohibition included the claim that it gave the government too much power over people's personal lives, that it was impossible to enforce, that it corrupted agents of enforcement, and that it made many bootleggers wealthy. The coming of the Great Depression, which began in 1929, magnified the effect of lost alcohol tax revenues on the federal government, and in 1933 Congress proposed and the states ratified the Twenty-first Amendment, which repealed Prohibition.

In 1937, passage of the Marijuana Tax Act effectively outlawed marijuana, a federal stance that was reinforced by the Boggs Act of 1951. The Boggs Act also mandated deletion of heroin from the list of medically useful substances and required its complete removal from all medicines. The 1956 Narcotic Control Act increased penalties for drug traffickers and made the sale of heroin to anyone under age 18 a capital offense.

The most comprehensive federal legislation to address controlled substances to date is the 1970 Comprehensive Drug Abuse Prevention and Control Act. Title 2 of that act is referred to as the Controlled Substances Act (CSA). It established five schedules that classify psychoactive drugs according to their medical use, degree of psychoactivity, and adjudged potential for abuse. Table 13-4 outlines the various drug schedules under federal law. Penalties under

TABLE 13-4 ■ Scheduled Drugs Under Federal Law

SCHEDULE	ABUSE POTENTIAL	EXAMPLES OF DRUGS COVERED	SOME EFFECTS	MEDICAL USE
I	Highest	Heroin, LSD, hashish, marijuana, designer drugs, methaqualone	Unpredictable effects, severe psychological or physical dependence, or death	No accepted use; some are legal for limited research use only
II	High	Morphine, PCP, codeine, cocaine, methadone, Demerol, Benzedrine, Dexedrine	May lead to severe psychological or physical dependence	Accepted use with restrictions
III	Medium	Codeine with aspirin or Tylenol, some amphetamines, anabolic steroids	May lead to moderate or low physical dependence or high psychological dependence	Accepted use
IV	Low	Darvon, Talwin, phenobarbital, Equanil, miltown, Librium, diazepam	May lead to limited physical or psychological dependence	Accepted use
V	Lowest	Over-the-counter or prescription compounds with codeine, Lomatil, Robitussin A–C	May lead to limited physical or psychological dependence	Accepted use

Source: Adapted from Drug Enforcement Administration, *Drugs of Abuse, 2000.* Web posted at http://www.usdoj.gov/dea/pubs/abuse/contents.htm.

THEORY VERSUS REALITY
Drug Courts and Public Policy

Since the 1980s, the drug epidemic in the United States and the adoption of tougher drug policies by lawmakers and officials have contributed to an abundance of drug cases on judicial dockets in many U.S. jurisdictions. About 20 years ago, in response to the ever-growing number of drug cases and the cycle of recidivism common among drug offenders, some state and local jurisdictions began experimenting with a new type of judicial proceeding known as "drug courts." Drug courts, which are generally used for nonviolent drug offenders, seek to identify eligible participants early in case processing.

Drug court programs, which may divert offenders from further handling by other official agencies, feature supervised treatment and periodic drug testing. Their purpose is to use the authority of the court to reduce crime by changing defendants' drug-using behavior. Defendants are typically diverted to drug court programs in

exchange for the possibility of dismissed charges or reduced sentences.

Judges who preside over drug court proceedings monitor the progress of defendants through frequent status hearings, and they prescribe sanctions and rewards in collaboration with prosecutors, defense attorneys, treatment providers, and others. Treatment options are determined by the judge, who holds the offender personally and publicly accountable for treatment progress.

In exchange for the defendant's successfully completing treatment, the court may dismiss the original charge, reduce or set aside a previously imposed sentence, impose a lesser penalty, or dispense any combination of these options. Although some basic elements are common to many drug court programs, the programs vary in terms of their approaches, participant eligibility, program requirements, type of treatment provided, sanctions and rewards, and other practices.

Title V of the Violent Crime Control and Law Enforcement Act of 1994 (P.L. 103-322) specifically authorizes the awarding of federal grants for drug court programs that include court-supervised drug treatment. In 1995, the federal Drug Courts Program Office was established to implement and support provisions of the act and has since funded the development and establishment of drug courts across the country.

DISCUSSION QUESTIONS

1. What is the purpose of drug courts? What do you think will be their future?
2. Do you think drug courts are a good idea? Why or why not?

Sources: Richard S. Gebelein, *Rebirth of Rehabilitation: Promise and Perils of Drug Courts* (Washington, D.C.: Department of Justice, 2000); Ken Wallentine, "Drug Courts: A Change in Tactics," *Police*, Vol. 24, No. 4 (April 2000), pp. 54–56; and U.S. General Accounting Office, *Drug Courts: Overview of Growth, Characteristics, and Results* (Washington, D.C., GAO, 1997).

federal law are generally more severe for possession of higher category substances (Schedule I being the highest), but they vary by amount possessed, the purpose of possession (for sale or personal use), and the offender's criminal history.

Another federal initiative, the 1988 Anti-Drug Abuse Act, proclaimed the goal of a "drug-free America by 1995." Although many of the act's provisions, like the preamble that contained the "drug-free" phrase, were more rhetoric than substance, the act substantially increased penalties for recreational drug users and made weapons purchases by suspected drug dealers more difficult. The law also denied federal benefits—ranging from loans (such as federal student loans) to contracts and licenses—to federal drug convicts.

In 1991, steroids were added to the list of Schedule III controlled substances by congressional action, and in 1996, the Drug-Induced Rape Prevention Act[50] increased penalties for trafficking in the drug Rohypnol®, which is known as the "date rape drug" because of its growing use by "young men [who] put doses of the drug in women's drinks without

their consent in order to lower their inhibitions."[51] Rohypnol (whose generic name is flunitrazepam) is a powerful sedative manufactured by Hoffmann-LaRoche Pharmaceuticals. A member of the benzodiazepine family of depressants, it is legally prescribed in 64 countries for insomnia and as a preoperative anesthetic. Seven to ten times more powerful than Valium®, Rohypnol is easily available on the black market. It dissolves easily in drinks and can leave anyone who unknowingly consumes it unconscious for hours, making them vulnerable to sexual assault. The drug is variously known as "roples," "roche," "ruffles," "roofies," and "rophies" on the street.

Another date rape drug, GHB (gammahydroxybutyrate) has effects similar to Rohypnol. GHB, a central nervous system depressant, was once sold in health food stores as a performance enhancer for use by bodybuilders. Rumors that GHB stimulates muscle growth were never proved. The intoxicating effects of GHB, however, soon became obvious. In 1990, the FDA banned the use of GHB except under the supervision of a physician.

Recent Legislation

Recent drug control legislation of note includes the Comprehensive Methamphetamine Control Act (CMCA) of 1996 and relevant portions of the Violent Crime Control and Law Enforcement Act of 1994. The CMCA (1) contains provisions for the forfeiture and seizure of chemicals used in the manufacture of methamphetamine, (2) added iodine to the list of chemicals controlled under the Chemical Diversion and Trafficking Act of 1988 and the Domestic Chemical Diversion Control Act of 1993, (3) created new reporting requirements for distributors of combination products containing ephedrine, pseudoephedrine, and phenylpropanolamine, and (4) increased penalties for the manufacture and possession of equipment used to make controlled substances.

The far-reaching Violent Crime Control and Law Enforcement Act of 1994 included a number of drug-related provisions. Specifically, the act

- Authorized $1 billion in Edward Byrne Memorial Formula Grant Program monies to reduce or prevent juvenile drug- and gang-related activity in federally assisted, low-income housing areas
- Authorized $1.6 billion for direct funding to localities around the country for anticrime efforts, such as drug treatment, education, and jobs, through a legislative subsection known as the Local Partnership Act
- Allocated other drug-treatment monies for the creation of state and federal programs to treat drug-addicted prisoners. The act also created a treatment schedule for all drug-addicted federal prisoners and requires drug testing of federal prisoners upon release.
- Provided $1 billion for drug court programs for non-violent offenders with substance-abuse problems. Participants will be intensively supervised, given drug treatment, and subjected to graduated sanctions—ultimately including prison terms—for failing random drug tests.
- Provided stiff new penalties for drug crimes committed by gang members, and tripled penalties for using children to deal drugs near schools and playgrounds
- Established "drug-free zones" by increasing penalties for drug dealing in areas near playgrounds, school yards, video arcades, and youth centers
- Increased penalties for drug dealing near public housing projects
- Expanded the federal death penalty to include large-scale drug trafficking, and mandated life imprisonment for criminals convicted of three drug-related felonies
- Created special penalties for drug use and drug trafficking in prison

Drug-Control Strategies

Throughout the years, major policy initiatives in the battle against illicit drugs have included (1) antidrug legislation and strict enforcement, (2) interdiction, (3) crop control, (4) forfeiture, and (5) antidrug education and drug treatment.[52] Current policy is in keeping with calls for the strict enforcement of anti-drug-abuse laws, although much enforcement emphasis in recent years has shifted from targeting users to the arrest, prosecution, and incarceration of the distributors of controlled substances. Similar shifts have occurred among employers, some of whom no longer wait for drug-influenced behavioral problems to arise but instead require routine drug testing as a condition of employment and retention.

In 1999, nearly 1.5 million people were arrested for drug-law violations throughout the United States.[53] The 1999 arrest total was 2% lower than in 1998, 7% higher than the 1995 level, and 36% higher than in 1990.[54] Enforcement activities within the United States also include the seizure and destruction of illegal drugs and clandestine drug laboratories. In 1999, for example, DEA agents destroyed 2,155 methamphetamine laboratories across the nation.[55]

Interdiction is an international drug-control policy that aims to stop drugs from entering the country illegally. In fiscal year 2000, for example, U.S. Customs agents seized 1,442,778 pounds of marijuana, cocaine, and heroin—a 10.1% increase over seizures in fiscal year 1999. More than half of all cocaine and much of the heroin, marijuana, and methamphetamine in the United States is thought to enter the country from Mexico. In 1999 alone, U.S. Border Patrol personnel, Customs agents, and Coast Guard officials oversaw the legal entry of 293 million people, 89 million cars, 4.5 million trucks, and 572,000 railroad cars into the United States from Mexico. Difficult terrain and oceans make southwestern borders especially hard to police. Drugs cross the desert in armed pack trains as well as on the backs of human "mules." They are tossed over border fences and whisked away on foot or by vehicle.[56] Operators of ships find gaps in U.S./Mexican interdiction coverage and position drugs close to the border for eventual transfer to the United States. Small boats in the Gulf of Mexico and eastern Pacific deliver drugs directly into the United States, and instances of corruption in U.S. border agencies contribute to the difficulty in interdiction enforcement.

According to the Federal-wide Drug Seizure System (FDSS), more than 1,290 metric tons of marijuana were seized by federal law enforcement agencies throughout the United States in 2000. FDSS statistics show the seizure of 112 metric tons of cocaine in 2000, along with the seizure of 1.16 metric tons of heroin and 3.51 metric tons of methamphetamine.[57]

A third strategy, crop control, has both international and domestic aspects. During 1999, for example, the DEA's

Domestic Cannabis Eradication and Suppression Program was responsible for the eradication of 3,413,083 cultivated outdoor marijuana plants and 208,027 indoor marijuana plants in the United States. In addition, the same program was responsible for 11,922 arrests, and agents seized 3,707 weapons and $26,911,262 in assets.[58] In 2000, two DEA operations code-named Conquistador and Columbus resulted in the eradication of coca plants in Panama, Colombia, Venezuela, Bolivia, Ecuador, and other Latin American countries with a production potential of 25,790 kilograms.[59] Learn more about specific DEA domestic and overseas operations and task forces at Web Extra! 13-7.

Web EXTRA! Web Extra! 13-7 at crimtoday.com

Forfeiture, or asset forfeiture, is another strategy in the battle against illegal drugs. Forfeiture is a legal procedure that authorizes judicial representatives to seize "all moneys, negotiable instruments, securities, or other things of value furnished or intended to be furnished by any person in exchange for a controlled substance . . . [and] all proceeds traceable to such an exchange."[60] Unfortunately, asset forfeiture laws have at times been abused by enforcement agencies. As one writer explains, "There have, in the past, been cases where innocent parties have had property seized and had to spend a considerable amount on lawyers' fees to get it back. Parents have had homes confiscated because children sold drugs there. Farms have been taken even though the owners were acquitted of growing marijuana on an isolated part of the property."[61] Recent U.S. Supreme Court decisions, however, now require that property owners be given notice of any pending seizures and be allowed the opportunity to respond to government charges.[62] The Court has also acted to restrain seizures of property far more valuable than the proceeds of the underlying crime with which the property owner has been charged.[63]

Antidrug education and drug treatment have gained significant popularity over the past decade. Those favoring educational attacks on the problem of drug abuse are quick to claim that other measures have not been effective in reducing the incidence of abuse. Antidrug education programs often reach targeted individuals through schools, corporations, and media campaigns. A short TV commercial of a few years ago, for example, recited the lines, "This is your brain. This is your brain on drugs," while showing an egg, followed by an egg sizzling in a frying pan. School-based programs are numerous, with many being built on the principles developed by Project D.A.R.E. (Drug Abuse Resistance Education), which began as a joint effort of the Los Angeles Police Department and the Los Angeles Unified School District in 1983. D.A.R.E. uses uniformed police officers and other "experts" to explain issues of drug abuse to school-aged chil-

dren and attempts to build resistance to what might otherwise be perceived by youths as attractive drug-related activities. D.A.R.E. focuses on developing competent decision-making skills, combating negative forms of peer pressure, and providing meaningful alternatives to drug use. Unfortunately for advocates of such programs, however, a number of recent studies have questioned the effectiveness of D.A.R.E.-type interventions, finding—after repeated evaluations—that its "effects on drug use, except for tobacco use, are nonsignificant."[64]

The National Drug-Control Policy

In 1988, with passage of the Anti-Drug Abuse Act, Congress established the Office of National Drug Control Policy and endorsed as a national policy goal the creation of a drug-free America. The director of ONDCP is a member of the president's Cabinet and is the principal national spokesperson on illicit drug use and related issues.

The ONDCP mission is to establish policies, priorities, and objectives for the nation's drug-control program. The stated goals of that program are to reduce illicit drug use, manufacturing, and trafficking; to reduce drug-related crime and violence; and to ameliorate drug-related health consequences. To achieve these goals, the director of ONDCP is charged with producing and publishing a national drug-control strategy. That strategy directs the nation's antidrug efforts and establishes a program, a budget, and guidelines for cooperation among federal, state, and local entities. Prior to 2000, Congress required the president to submit a national drug control strategy each year. Public Law 105-277 now requires the President to submit to Congress only an annual report on the progress in implementing the strategy.

Houston police remove 600 pounds of marijuana found in the false tops of trucks brought from Mexico. Are our borders adequately patrolled? *Gregg Smith, Saba Press Photos, Inc.*

CRIME IN THE NEWS
Customs Chief Calls for New Drug Strategy

America's "war on drugs" needs to be refocused to increase resources for prevention and addiction treatment, the U.S. Customs Service chief told APBnews.com.

Commissioner Ray Kelly said national policies that rely instead on interdiction and incarceration as a means to stem the flow of drugs into this country or punish those involved in the buying and selling of narcotics have not worked as effectively as hoped.

"I don't know of any thinking person in law enforcement who doesn't say we need more prevention and treatment," Kelly said.

Of the billions of dollars spent each year by the government to fight the drug problem, not enough goes to drug rehabilitation and education, he said. The national drug strategy is rooted in politics, which historically has stoked the public desire to be tough on drugs.

"I've been in this game a long time, and the emphasis has always been on interdiction," Kelly said. "It sells politically."

NEED TO REDUCE DEMAND

Intercepting drug shipments by air, land and sea will always be necessary, he predicted, but reducing the demand is also an effective way to counter the drug problem. Another useful weapon in the fight is intelligence on drug shipments bound for the United States.

In spite of the efforts of several agencies, including the Drug Enforcement Administration, the National Security Agency and the CIA to gather intelligence, Kelly said there are information "gaps" that technologically savvy drug smugglers take advantage of. They use wireless Internet, satellite telecommunications and encryption to conceal their illegal activities, making it difficult to track them, he said.

NEW CHALLENGES FOR AGENCY

During Kelly's two-year tenure as head of an agency with a $3 billion annual budget, intercepting terrorists at the borders has been a new challenge for agents entrusted with looking for contraband smuggled into or out of the country.

But the primary focus of Customs is not enforcement; it is to collect duties on imported goods. Established by congressional legislation signed by President George Washington in 1789, Customs today employs 20,000 and collected $27 billion in tariffs last year.

CREDITED WITH REFORMS

Kelly, 58, does not look like a typical government official. The stocky former Marine who sports hand-tailored wool suits carries a tough-guy swagger that is more Hell's Kitchen than Georgetown.

He is credited with many reforms at Customs. When asked about his proudest accomplishments since taking the helm, he said he brought focus to an organization that was fragmented by its many satellite offices and deficiencies in employee accountability.

The organization has since become "professionalized" in the past two years, Kelly said, with a beefed up internal affairs unit and standards set by the naming of the first director of training in 110 years.

MORALE PROBLEM?

But some veteran agents are not convinced. Morale among agents is low, sources told APBnews.com, and many are leaving Customs.

Kelly said he isn't convinced Customs has a morale problem at any level and denied that the attrition rate has increased during his leadership.

"Any objective analysis of morale in this organization would show that it has significantly improved," he said . . .

SELF-DESCRIBED "ADVENTURER"

He recalled his many commands, from service with the Marines in Vietnam to 25 different command posts in a long career with the New York Police Department.

Perhaps most unusual was his role as commander of a unit that monitored Haitian police after the U.S. intervention in 1994. A photo hanging in Kelly's office shows Kelly and a U.S. peacekeeper carrying a bloodied victim of fighting in the Caribbean nation.

"I like to think of myself as an adventurer," the commissioner said. "I'm looking for excitement."

Source: James Gordon Meek, "Customs Chief Calls for New Drug Strategy," APB News, December 29, 2000. Reprinted with permission.

The national drug-control strategy currently takes a long-term view of the nation's drug problem and focuses on prevention, treatment, research, law enforcement, protection of U.S. borders, drug-supply reduction, and international cooperation. The national strategy seeks to achieve a 50% decrease in drug use and availability and at least a 25% decrease in the consequences of drug abuse by 2007.

The strategy focuses on young people, seeking to educate them about the dangers of illegal drugs, alcohol, and tobacco. It also stresses the need to protect borders from drug incursion and to cut drug supply more effectively in domestic communities. It emphasizes initiatives to share intelligence and make use of the latest technology in these efforts. As a major gateway for the entry of illegal drugs into the United States, the Southwest border receives considerable attention within the strategy. Resources have also been allocated to close other avenues of drug entry into the United States, including the Virgin Islands, Puerto Rico, the

Canadian border, and all airports and seaports. The strategy also seeks to curtail illegal drug trafficking in the transit zone between source countries, and U.S.-led multinational efforts in the Caribbean, Central America, Europe, and the Far East are coordinated under the strategy in an effort to exert maximum pressure on drug traffickers. The strategy's stated goals, reprinted here along with official policy narrative, are as follows:[65]

Goal 1: Educate and enable America's youth to reject illegal drugs as well as alcohol and tobacco. Drug use is preventable. If children reach adulthood without using illegal drugs, alcohol, or tobacco, they are unlikely to develop a chemical-dependency problem. To this end, the *Strategy* fosters initiatives to educate children about the dangers associated with drugs. ONDCP involves parents, coaches, mentors, teachers, clergy, and other role models in a broad prevention campaign. ONDCP encourages businesses, communities, schools, the entertainment industry, universities, and sports organizations to join these national antidrug efforts.

Goal 2: Increase the safety of America's citizens by substantially reducing drug-related crime and violence. Researchers have identified important factors that place youth at risk for drug abuse or protect them against such behavior. Risk factors are associated with greater potential for drug problems while protective factors reduce the chances of drug problems. Risk factors include a chaotic home environment, ineffective parenting, anti-social behavior, drug-using peers, general approval of drug use, and the misperception that the overwhelming majority of one's peers are substance users. Protective factors include parental involvement; success in school; strong bonds with family, school, and religious organizations; knowledge of dangers posed by drug use; and the recognition by young people that substance use is unacceptable.

Goal 3: Reduce health and social costs to the public of illegal drug use. Drug addiction is a chronic, relapsing disorder that exacts an enormous cost on individuals, families, businesses, communities, and nations. Addicted individuals frequently engage in self-destructive and criminal behavior. Treatment programs can reduce the consequences of addiction on the rest of society. The ultimate goal of treatment is to enable a patient to become abstinent and to improve functioning through sustained recovery. On the way to that goal, reduction of drug use, improvement of the addict's ability to function in society, and addressing the medical needs of the addicted are useful interim outcomes. Providing treatment for America's chronic drug abusers is both compassionate public policy and a sound investment.

Goal 4: Shield America's air, land, and sea frontiers from the drug threat. The United States is obligated to protect its citizens from the threats posed by illegal drugs crossing our borders. Interdiction in the transit and arrival zones disrupts drug flow, increases risks to traffickers, drives them to less efficient routes and methods, and prevents significant quantities of drugs from reaching the United States. Interdiction operations also produce information that can be used by domestic law-enforcement agencies against trafficking organizations.

Goal 5: Break foreign and domestic drug sources of supply. The rule of law, human rights, and democratic institutions are threatened by drug trafficking and consumption. International supply-reduction programs not only reduce the volume of illegal drugs reaching our shores, they also attack international criminal organizations, strengthen democratic institutions, and honor our international drug control commitments. The U.S. supply-reduction strategy seeks to: (1) eliminate illegal drug cultivation and production, (2) destroy drug-trafficking organizations, (3) interdict drug shipments, (4) encourage international cooperation, and (5) safeguard democracy and human rights.

The United States continues to focus international drug control efforts on source countries. International drug-trafficking organizations and their production and trafficking infrastructures are most concentrated, detectable, and vulnerable to effective law-enforcement action in source countries. In addition, cultivation of coca and opium poppy and production of cocaine and heroin are labor intensive. For these reasons, cultivation and processing are relatively easier to disrupt than other aspects of the trade. The international drug control strategy seeks to bolster source-country resources, capabilities, and political will to reduce cultivation, attack production, interdict drug shipments, and disrupt and dismantle trafficking organizations, including their command and control structure and financial underpinnings.

Visit the Office of National Drug Control Policy via Web Extra! 13-8.

Web EXTRA! Web Extra! 13-8 at crimtoday.com

Policy Consequences

There can be little doubt that the "war on drugs" has been a costly one. In fiscal year 2000 alone, the federal government's drug-control budget exceeded $18.8 billion.[66] The fiscal year 2000 appropriations represent an increase of $6.9 billion, or 58%, over the fiscal year 1992 budget of $11.9 billion.[67] Broken down by goals within ONDCP's national drug-control strategy, Goal 1 funding (to reduce youth drug use) totaled $2.166 billion; Goal 2 funding (to reduce drug-related crime) totaled $7.569 billion; Goal 3 funding (to reduce health-related and social costs) totaled $3.539 billion; Goal 4 funding (to shield air, land, and sea frontiers) totaled $2.243 billion; and Goal 5 funding (to reduce sources of supply) totaled $1.983 billion. Seen another way, domestic law enforcement activities (that is, federal law enforcement programs within the nation's borders) accounted for the lion's share of federal antidrug expenditures (49%), while demand reduction programs (that is, educational activities) absorbed 32% of the antidrug budget. Interdiction at the nation's borders, a separate expenditure category, accounted for 10% of the total budget, and international efforts took 3.2% of the total allocation.[68] Figure 13-7 provides a breakdown of federal drug-control spending by functional area for the years 1992 to 2000. When state monies spent on the control of illegal drugs and the enforcement of drug laws are added to funds spent on antidrug abuse education, and when the personal and social costs of drug abuse, identified earlier, are added in, the total cost of the war on drugs has been enormous.

The drug war has been costly in other ways as well. University of Delaware Professor James A. Inciardi describes the current situation this way: "As an outgrowth of the U.S. 'war on drugs' during the 1980s and early 1990s, all phases of the criminal justice process have become 'drug driven.' "[69] The same could be said of the nation's system of civil justice. "Although at first blush it may seem unrelated," says writer J. Michael McWilliams, "the 'war on drugs' has had a major impact on the civil justice system at both the state and federal levels. Our courts, like all of government and commerce, are institutions of limited resources. To the extent that court resources must be diverted to deal with the enormous influx of drug prosecutions, these resources are not available to resolve civil matters. . . . In some jurisdictions, drug cases account for as much as two-thirds of the criminal case filings. America's major cities have been especially affected."[70] In Los Angeles, for example, three-quarters of all criminal prosecutions are for drug charges or drug-related crimes.[71]

Strict enforcement has combined with a lock-'em-up philosophy to produce astonishingly high rates of imprisonment for drug offenders. The proportion of federal prisoners who are drug offenders rose from 38% in 1986 to 53% in 1990 and, according to the Bureau of Prisons, is 58% today.[72]

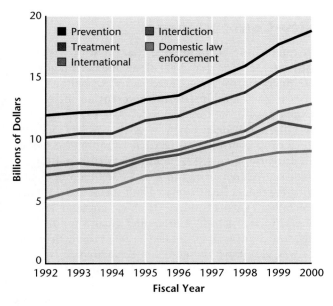

■ FIGURE 13-7 BREAKDOWN OF FEDERAL DRUG-CONTROL SPENDING BY FUNCTIONAL AREA, 1992–2000.
Source: Office of National Drug Control Policy, *The National Drug Control Strategy: 2001 Annual Report* (Washington, D.C.: U.S. Government Printing Office, 2001), p. 117.

Part of the increase is due to congressional action that, beginning in 1986, required high mandatory minimum sentences in drug cases so that even first-time offenders were sentenced to long prison terms instead of probation. Approximately 70% of all first-time offenders in federal prisons are serving drug sentences. This is also true of 85% of illegal immigrants who are federal prisoners and 66% of female federal prisoners.[73]

Alternative Drug Policies

A number of alternative drug-control policies have been tried at both state and local levels. Primary among them have been decriminalization and legalization. Both strategies are "based on the assumption that drug abuse will never be eliminated."[74] Whereas **decriminalization** typically reduces criminal penalties associated with the personal possession of a controlled substance, **legalization** eliminates "the laws and associated criminal penalties that prohibit its production, sale, distribution, and possession."[75] Decriminalization enhances personal freedoms in the face of state control, whereas legalization "is aimed," in part, "at reducing the control that criminals have over the drug trade."[76] Other arguments in favor of legalization include the following notions:

- In a free society, people should be permitted to do what they want, as long as they don't harm others. Drug use is considered by many to be a "victimless crime" that harms no one other than the user. Existing drug laws, say advocates of legalization, make criminals out of otherwise law-abiding individuals.
- Keeping drugs illegal means that they will continue to be high priced. Legalizing them could greatly lower the price. The expense of illicit drugs, kept artificially high by their illegal status, encourages the commission of many drug-related crimes, such as robbery and burglary, by users seeking to feed their habits. Legalize drugs, some argue, and many other forms of crime will decline.
- Legalizing drugs would also reduce other forms of "vice," such as prostitution, pornography, and gambling, because many such offenses are also committed in an effort to obtain money to purchase high-priced drugs.
- Legalizing drugs would reduce the influence of criminal cartels now closely involved in the production, transportation, and sale of controlled substances.
- The illegal status and associated high cost of drugs indirectly victimizes others, such as the family members of drug abusers, property owners in drug-infested areas, and taxpayers who must foot the enforcement bill. Legalization would end these forms of victimization.
- Drug legalization would dramatically reduce the opportunity for official corruption, which is now fre-

quently associated with the illicit drug trade. Enforcement agents, politicians, correctional officers, and representatives of the judiciary would cease to be subject to corrupting influences dependent upon the vast financial resources available to drug-trafficking cartels.

■ The legalization of drugs would result in increased tax revenues because drugs could be taxed just as alcohol and cigarettes are today.

■ The legalization of drugs would allow for better control over public health issues related to drug use. The spread of AIDS, for example, caused in large part by the use of dirty needles in heroin injection, could be better controlled if sterilized needles were made legally available. Similarly, drug quality and potency could be monitored and ensured, resulting in fewer overdoses and emergency room visits by drug users, who are now uncertain of the chemical composition of the substances they consume.

Were controlled substances to be legalized, they might still be dispensed under controlled conditions (as in liquor stores), and penalties might still accrue to those who used them injudiciously (as while driving a car).

In 1996, California and Arizona voters passed resolutions legalizing the medical use of marijuana under certain circumstances. The thrust of California's Proposition 215, which the voters approved, is contained in the following language taken from the proposition: "(A) To ensure that seriously ill Californians have the right to obtain and use marijuana for medical purposes where that medical use is deemed appropriate and has been recommended by a physician who has determined that the person's health would benefit from the use of marijuana in the treatment of cancer, anorexia, AIDS, chronic pain, spasticity, glaucoma, arthritis, migraine, or any other illness for which marijuana provides relief. (B) To ensure that patients and their primary caregivers who obtain and use marijuana for medical purposes upon the recommendation of a physician are not subject to criminal prosecution or sanction."

Although the California law permits possession of marijuana for valid medicinal purposes, buying and selling the drug remain illegal, meaning that legitimate users may have to grow their own supply or buy it on the black market. Arizona law requires prescribing physicians to write a scientific opinion explaining why the drug is appropriate for a specific patient, and a supportive second opinion is required before the drug can be legally used.

In 1999, Maine voters passed a referendum permitting some sick people to use small amounts of marijuana, and 26 other states and the District of Columbia have passed various laws and resolutions allowing therapeutic research programs involving the use of marijuana or asking the federal government to lift its ban on medical use of the drug.[77] Federal law enforcement agencies, however, have pointedly announced that they will continue to enforce federal antidrug laws prohibiting marijuana possession by citizens of *all* states. The agencies' stance spotlights an emerging policy issue—that is, who controls America's drug policy, the

Visitors to a cannabis festival in Amsterdam sample marijuana from a "bong." What are the advantages and disadvantages of drug legalization in the United States? *Sjoerd Van Delden, AP/Wide World Photos*

states or the federal government? In May 2001, the U.S. Supreme Court prohibited California marijuana-growing clubs from distributing the drug to those who are ill or in pain.[78] The ruling effectively prohibits the use of medical marijuana in virtually all situations.

Opponents of drug legalization argue that

- Reducing official control over psychoactive substances is immoral and socially irresponsible and would result in heightened costs to society from drug abuse.
- Drug legalization would simply increase the types of problems now associated with alcohol abuse, such as

lost time from work, drug-induced criminality (especially violence), the loss of personal self-control, and the severing of important social relationships.

- Drug laws are enforceable; we are winning the war against drugs; and because laws are not *easily* enforceable is no reason to eliminate them. (Laws against murder and rape, for example, have not entirely eliminated such crimes, and there is no conclusive evidence that laws seriously reduce the numbers of crimes committed in any category in which intense needs or emotions are involved as motivating factors.)

SUMMARY

Drug abuse has a long and varied history in American society. Policy responses to abuse have been equally diverse. Although recent statistics on drug use show some decline, a hard-core population of illicit drug users remains. Strategies to reduce the flow of illegal drugs into this country, while meeting with some success, are being increasingly supplemented with programs of education and treatment intended to reduce the demand for con-

trolled substances. In the meantime, the potential for official corruption in the face of a lucrative drug trade remains high. Drug traffickers are now in control of vast amounts of money, leading some to suggest that only legalization can solve the secondary problems of drug-related crime, official corruption, and drug-related public health concerns.

DISCUSSION QUESTIONS

1. This book emphasizes a social problems versus social responsibility theme. Which of the social policy approaches to controlling drug abuse discussed in this chapter (if any) appear to be predicated upon a social problems approach? Which (if any) are predicated upon a social responsibility approach? Explain the nature of the relationship.
2. What are some of the costs of illicit drug use in the United States today? Which costs can be more easily reduced than others? How would you reduce the costs of illegal drug use?

3. What is the difference between decriminalization and legalization? Should drug use remain illegal? What do you think of the arguments in favor of legalization? Those against?
4. What is the difference between drug-defined and drug-related crime? Which form of crime is more difficult to address? Why?
5. What is asset forfeiture? How has asset forfeiture been used in the fight against illegal drugs? How have recent U.S. Supreme Court decisions limited federal asset seizures? Do you agree that such limitations were necessary? Why or why not?

WEB QUEST!

Visit the federal Office of National Drug Control Policy on the World Wide Web (http://www.whitehousedrugpolicy.gov), and read the *National Drug Control Strategy* posted there. What topics are covered in the document? Who wrote the foreword? What message was that person trying to communicate? Summarize the information that the document

provides about each major drug category, and briefly describe the main points of the drug-control program that it outlines. Which of the strategy's stated goals do you think deserves the most attention? Why? Submit your work to your instructor if asked to do so.

LIBRARY EXTRAS!

The Library Extras! listed here complement the Web Extras! found throughout this chapter. Library Extras! may be accessed on the Web at crimtoday.com.

Library Extra! 13-1.   Arrestee Drug Abuse Monitoring Program, *ADAM Annual Report on Drug Use among Adult and Juvenile Arrestees* (Washington, D.C.: National Institute of Justice, 2000).

Library Extra! 13-2.   Drug Enforcement Administration, *National Narcotics Intelligence Consumers Committee (NNICC) Report: The Supply of Illicit Drugs to the United States* (Washington, D.C.: U.S. Government Printing Office, 1998).

Library Extra! 13-3.   Drug Enforcement Administration, *Drugs of Abuse* (online document, no date).

Library Extra! 13-4.   Drug Enforcement Administration, *DEA Briefing Book* (online document, 2000).

Library Extra! 13-5.   U.S. Code, Section 1308, *Schedule of Controlled Substances.*

Library Extra! 13-6.   National Institute on Drug Abuse, *Monitoring the Future Survey* (online document, 2000).

Library Extra! 13-7.   Office of National Drug Control Policy, *Annual Report* (online document, 2000).

Library Extra! 13-8.   Substance Abuse and Mental Health Services Administration, *National Household Survey on Drug Abuse* (online document, 2001).

NOTES

[1] Melanie Goodfellow, "INTERPOL Head Says Drugs a Threat to Democracy," Reuters wire service, October 4, 1994.

[2] "Presidential Commission Presents Recommendation on Drug Control," United Press International wire service, Northern Edition, December 13, 1993.

[3] Address to the nation with President Ronald Reagan, September 14, 1986.

[4] Address to the Federal Bar Association, Miami, November 1991. Web posted at http://www.conservativeforum.org/authquot.asp?ID=777. Accessed January 5, 2001.

[5] The information in this section comes from Niko Price, "Drug Lord's Body Hangs in Limbo," Associated Press wire service, July 6, 1997; and Michael J. Sniffen, "DEA Eyes Drug Death Aftermath," Associated Press wire service, July 7, 1997.

[6] "Did U.S. Anti-Narcotics Agents Kill the Lord of the Skies?" *Independent* (London). Via Simon & Schuster NewsLink, July 12, 1997.

[7] Ibid.

[8] Paul Savoy, "When Criminal Rights Go Wrong: Forget Liberal. Forget Conservative. Think Common Sense," *Washington Monthly,* Vol. 21, No. 11 (December 1989), p. 36.

[9] Web posted at http://librearts.com/wsn8439.html.

[10] Data in this section are derived from Substance Abuse and Mental Health Services Administration, *National Household Survey on Drug Abuse, 1999* (Washington, D.C.: U.S. Government Printing Office, 2000).

[11] Drug Enforcement Administration, *Overview of Drug Use in the United States.* Web posted at http://www.dea.gov/stats/overview.htm. Accessed April 8, 2001.

[12] Bureau of Justice Statistics, *Drug and Crime Facts, 1993* (Washington, D.C.: U.S. Department of Justice, August 1994), p. 25.

[13] Information in this section comes from "2000 Monitoring the Future Survey Released: Moderating Trend among Teen Drug Use Continues," *HHS News* (U.S. Department of Health and Human Services), December 14, 2000. Web posted at http://www.nida.nih.gov/MedAdv/00/HHS12-14.html. Accessed January 9, 2001.

[14] Office of National Drug Control Policy, *National Drug Control Strategy: 2001 Annual Report* (Washington, D.C.: U.S. Government Printing Office, 2001), p. 30.

[15] Ibid., p. 31.

[16] Mike Cooper, "CDC Charts Impact of AIDS among Blacks, Hispanics," Reuters wire service, September 8, 1994.

[17] ONDCP, *National Drug Control Strategy: 2001 Annual Report,* p. 31.

[18] National Institute on Drug Abuse and National Institute on Alcohol Abuse and Alcoholism, *The Economic Costs of Alcohol and Drug Abuse in the United States, 1992* (Washington, D.C.: U.S. Government Printing Office, 1998).

[19] National Narcotics Intelligence Consumers Committee, *The NNICC Report, 1996: The Supply of Illicit Drugs to the United States* (Arlington, VA: Drug Enforcement Administration, 1997), p. 69.

[20] Most of the information in the paragraphs that follow is taken from ibid. and from the Office of National

Drug Control Policy, *Pulse Check: Trends in Drug Abuse, January–June 1998* (Washington, D.C.: ONDCP, 1998).

21 Much of the information in this section comes from the National Institute on Drug Abuse's Web site at http://www.nida.nih.gov, accessed January 6, 2001; and from the Office of National Drug Control Policy, *Pulse Check: Special Report; Methamphetamine Trends in Five Western States and Hawaii* (Washington, D.C.: ONDCP, 1997).

22 James A. Inciardi, *The War on Drugs II* (Mountain View, CA: Mayfield, 1992), p. 69.

23 Michael D. Lyman and Gary W. Potter, *Drugs in Society: Causes, Concepts and Control* (Cincinnati: Anderson, 1991), p. 45.

24 National Inhalant Prevention Coalition Web site, www.inhalants.org. Accessed January 6, 2001.

25 Ibid.

26 Sherry Green, *Preventing Illegal Diversion of Chemicals: A Model Statute* (Washington, D.C.: National Institute of Justice, November 1993), p. 2.

27 Ibid., p. 79.

28 The provisions of the Domestic Chemical Diversion Control Act of 1993 became effective April 16, 1994.

29 As defined by federal law and precedent.

30 "Colombian Drug Smugglers' Submarine an Evolutionary Step," Associated Press wire service, September 8, 2000.

31 NNICC, *The NNICC Report, 1996.*

32 "Not So Slick: Customs Fishes Two Tons of Cocaine Out of Cooking Grease Tanker in Laredo," *U.S. Customs Service News,* May 14, 1998.

33 Drug Enforcement Administration, "Record Drug Seizures." Web posted at http://www.dea.gov/major/seizures.htm. Accessed January 8, 2001.

34 National Narcotics Intelligence Consumers Committee, *The NNICC Report, 1993* (Washington, D.C.: U.S. Government Printing Office, 1994).

35 Ibid., p. 35.

36 Bureau of Justice Statistics, *Drugs, Crime and the Justice System* (Washington, D.C.: U.S. Government Printing Office, 1992), p. 2.

37 Ibid.

38 Ibid., p. 126.

39 Ibid., p. 2.

40 National Institute of Justice, *Arrestee Drug Abuse Monitoring (ADAM) Program: 1999 Annual Report on Drug Use among Adult and Juvenile Arrestees* (Washington, D.C.: NIJ, 2000).

41 Much of the material in this section is adapted from National Institute of Justice, Office of Justice Programs, "Study Shows Substantial Levels of Drug Use among Arrestees across the Nation," *OJP News,* July 20, 2000.

42 BJS, *Drug and Crime Facts, 1993,* pp. 4–5.

43 Ibid., p. 6.

44 Ibid.

45 Ibid., p. 7.

46 Ibid., p. 8.

47 "Study: Bad NYC Cops 'Criminals in Blue,'" United Press International wire service, Northeastern Edition, July 7, 1994.

48 Ibid.

49 "Judgment on Corrections," *Washington Post* wire service, July 5, 1994.

50 Public Law 104-305.

51 "'Rophies' Reported Spreading Quickly throughout the South," *Drug Enforcement Report,* June 23, 1995, pp. 1–5.

52 For an excellent overview of policy initiatives in the area of drug control, see Doris Layton MacKenzie and Craig D. Uchida, *Drugs and Crime: Evaluating Public Policy Initiatives* (Thousand Oaks, CA: Sage, 1994).

53 Federal Bureau of Investigation, *Crime in the United States, 1999* (Washington, D.C.: U.S. Government Printing Office, 2000), p. 211.

54 Ibid.

55 Drug Enforcement Administration, "Drug Statistics." Web posted at http://www.usdoj.gov/dea/stats/drugstats.htm#meth. Accessed January 7, 2001.

56 ONDCP, *National Drug Control Strategy: 2001 Annual Report,* p. 89.

57 Ibid., pp. 18–20.

58 Drug Enforcement Administration, "Marijuana Eradication." Web posted at http://www.usdoj.gov/dea/programs/marijuana.htm. Accessed January 7, 2001.

59 Drug Enforcement Administration, "Operations Conquistador and Columbus." Web posted at http://www.dea.gov/major/conquistador.htm. Accessed January 8, 2001.

60 21 U.S.C., section 881(a)(6).

61 "Notice, Hearing and Seizure," *Washington Post* online, December 16, 1994.

62 *United States* v. *James Daniel Good Real Property,* 114 S. Ct. 492, 126 L. Ed. 2d 490 (1993).

63 *Austin* v. *U.S.,* 113 S. Ct. 2801, 15 L. Ed. 2d 448 (1993).

64 Fox Butterfield, no headline, *New York Times* news service online, 7:06 EST, April 16, 1997, citing Office of Justice Programs, *Preventing Crime: What Works, What Doesn't, What's Promising* (Washington, D.C.: U.S. Department of Justice, 1997).

65 ONDCP, *National Drug Control Strategy: 2001 Annual Report.*

66 Office of National Drug Control Policy, *National Drug Control Strategy, 1997: FY 1998 Budget Summary* (Washington, D.C.: ONDCP, 1997). Web posted at http://ncjrs.org/htm/tables.htm#table1. Accessed January 20, 1999.

67 Much of the information in this section comes from Office of National Drug Control Policy, *National Drug Control Strategy: Budget Summary* (Washington, D.C.:

ONDCP, February 2000). Web posted at http://www.whitehousedrugpolicy.gov/policy/budget00/exec_summ.html. Accessed January 6, 2001.

[68] Ibid.

[69] James A. Inciardi, *Criminal Justice* (Orlando; FL: Harcourt Brace Jovanovich, 1993), p. v.

[70] J. Michael McWilliams, "Setting the Record Straight: Facts about Litigation Costs and Delay," *Business Economics,* Vol. 27, No. 4 (October 1992), p. 19.

[71] Ibid.

[72] Bureau of Justice Statistics, *Prisoners in 1999* (Washington, D.C.: U.S. Department of Justice, August 2000).

[73] "Who Is in Federal Prison?" *Washington Post,* October 3, 1994.

[74] Lyman and Potter, *Drugs in Society,* p. 316.

[75] Inciardi, *The War on Drugs II,* p. 239, note d.

[76] Lyman and Potter, *Drugs in Society,* p. 316.

[77] *Newsweek,* February 3, 1997, pp. 20–23.

[78] *U.S. v. Oakland Cannabis Buyers, Cooperative,* U.S. Supreme Court, No. 00–151 (May 2001).

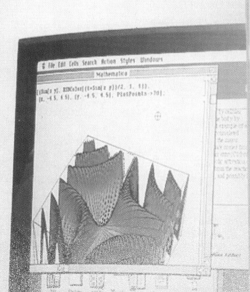

The rise of a new kind of economy, never before known, threatening to many, demanding rapid changes in work, life style, and habits, hurls large populations—terrified of the future—into spasms of diehard reaction. It opens cleavages that fanatics rush to fill. It arms all those dangerous minorities who live for crisis in the hopes of catapulting themselves onto the national or global stage and transporting us all into a new Dark Age.

—Alvin Toffler[1]

We need to take the fight against computer crime to the next level. Federal law enforcement agencies need new tools, and we need to make state and local law enforcement agencies more a part of this team effort. We also need to authorize investigative techniques to uncover the culprits behind these crimes, even when the culprits are overseas.

—Senator Patrick Leahy, Senate Judiciary Committee[2]

ONDCP, February 2000). Web posted at http://www.whitehousedrugpolicy.gov/policy/budget00/exec_summ.html. Accessed January 6, 2001.

68 Ibid.

69 James A. Inciardi, *Criminal Justice* (Orlando; FL: Harcourt Brace Jovanovich, 1993), p. v.

70 J. Michael McWilliams, "Setting the Record Straight: Facts about Litigation Costs and Delay," *Business Economics,* Vol. 27, No. 4 (October 1992), p. 19.

71 Ibid.

72 Bureau of Justice Statistics, *Prisoners in 1999* (Washington, D.C.: U.S. Department of Justice, August 2000).

73 "Who Is in Federal Prison?" *Washington Post,* October 3, 1994.

74 Lyman and Potter, *Drugs in Society,* p. 316.

75 Inciardi, *The War on Drugs II,* p. 239, note d.

76 Lyman and Potter, *Drugs in Society,* p. 316.

77 *Newsweek,* February 3, 1997, pp. 20–23.

78 *U.S. v. Oakland Cannabis Buyers, Cooperative,* U.S. Supreme Court, No. 00–151 (May 2001).

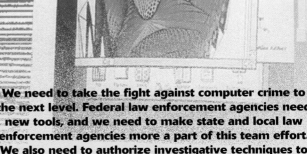

The rise of a new kind of economy, never before known, threatening to many, demanding rapid changes in work, life style, and habits, hurls large populations—terrified of the future—into spasms of diehard reaction. It opens cleavages that fanatics rush to fill. It arms all those dangerous minorities who live for crisis in the hopes of catapulting themselves onto the national or global stage and transporting us all into a new Dark Age.

—Alvin Toffler[1]

We need to take the fight against computer crime to the next level. Federal law enforcement agencies need new tools, and we need to make state and local law enforcement agencies more a part of this team effort. We also need to authorize investigative techniques to uncover the culprits behind these crimes, even when the culprits are overseas.

—Senator Patrick Leahy, Senate Judiciary Committee[2]

technology and crime

CHAPTER 14

> The world isn't run by weapons anymore, or energy, or money. It's run by ones and zeros—little bits of data—it's all electrons. . . . There's a war out there, a world war. It's not about who has the most bullets. It's about who controls the information—what we see and hear, how we work, what we think. It's all about information.
>
> —*Sneakers*[3]

> Crime is not static. Existing patterns get displaced by new ones.
>
> —Georgette Bennett[4]

KEY CONCEPTS

IMPORTANT TERMS

audit trail
Carnivore
Communications Decency Act
 (CDA)
computer abuse
computer crime
computer-related crime
computer virus
cybercrime

cyberspace
data encryption
Daubert standard
Digital Theft Deterrence and
 Copyright Damages
 Improvement Act
DNA fingerprinting
DNA profiling
expert systems

hackers
identity theft
Internet
No Electric Theft Act
phone phreaks
software piracy
TEMPEST
threat analysis

IMPORTANT CASES

Daubert v. *Merrell Dow
 Pharmaceuticals, Inc.*

Frye v. *United States*

Reno v. *ACLU*

OUTCOMES

LEARNING

After reading this chapter, you should be able to
- Describe the nature of high-technology and computer crime
- Describe some high-technology crime countermeasures
- Explain various computer-security techniques, including data encryption
- Discuss the nature of a threat analysis, and explain how one might be conducted
- Explain the nature and potential usefulness of DNA fingerprinting

Hear the author discuss this chapter at *crimtoday.com*

INTRODUCTION

In March 2000, 48-year-old Florida resident David Pugh was sentenced to a 30-month prison term for dealing in stolen property and grand theft.[5] Pugh had been arrested a year earlier, and a search of his Atlantic Beach home revealed multiple copies of more than 1,000 illegally pirated software applications. Investigators determined that Pugh's sole source of income for the past 12 years had been derived from the sale of pirated software. Pugh sold the software to customers in the United States and around the world via the Internet. Pugh also received a two-year term of probation and was ordered to pay court costs. As a condition of his probation, Pugh is not permitted to own computers or to have them in his place of residence.

CRIME AND TECHNOLOGY

Technology and criminology have always been closely linked. Early forms of technology, including the telegraph, the telephone, and the automobile, were embraced by agents of law enforcement as soon as they became available. Evidence derived from fingerprint and ballistics analysis is routinely employed by prosecutors, and emerging technologies promise to keep criminologists and law enforcement agents in step with high-tech offenders.

Technology, of course, can be employed by both crime fighters and lawbreakers. The con artist using telephones in a financial scam, the robber who uses a firearm and drives a getaway car, even the murderer who wields a knife—all employ at least rudimentary forms of technology in the crimes they commit.

Technology that is taken for granted today was at one time almost unthinkable. Telephones, for example, were invented scarcely a century ago, and mass-produced automobiles are newer still. Even firearms are of relatively recent origin if one considers the entire history of humankind, and the manufacture of contemporary cutting instruments would be impossible were it not for an accumulation of technological expertise beginning with the progress in metallurgy during the Iron Age.

As technology advances, it facilitates new forms of behavior. Just as we can be sure that everyday life in the future will be substantially different from life today, so too can we be certain that tomorrow's crimes will differ from those of today. In the future, personal crimes of violence and traditional property crimes will undoubtedly continue to occur, but advancing technology will create new and as yet unimaginable opportunities for criminals positioned to take advantage of it and of the power such technology will afford.

A frightening preview of such possibilities can be had in events surrounding the collapse of the Soviet Union more than a decade ago. The resulting social disorganization in that part of the world made the acquisition of fissionable materials, stolen from former Soviet stockpiles, simple for even relatively small outlaw organizations. In what has since become a nightmare for authorities throughout the world, Middle Eastern terrorist groups are known to be making forceful efforts to acquire former Soviet nuclear weapons and the raw materials necessary to manufacture their own bombs. Some evidence also suggests that nuclear weapons parts may have already been sold to wealthy international drug cartels and organized criminal groups, who may now be hoarding them to use as bargaining chips against possible government prosecution. Speaking before the House of Representatives Foreign Affairs Committee in the mid-1990s, then-CIA Director James Woolsey warned of the possibility "that Russian organized crime groups will be able to obtain and sell nuclear weapons or weapons-grade materials as a target of opportunity. We should not rule out the prospect that organized crime could be used as an avenue for terrorists to acquire weapons of mass destruction."[6] Recently, Russian Defense Minister Igor Rodionov issued a similar warning. Rodionov said his country's cash-starved armed forces are in such a perilous state that nuclear missiles and weapons systems might not be controllable in the near future.[7]

HIGH TECHNOLOGY AND CRIMINAL OPPORTUNITY

The twenty-first century has been described by some as the epitome of the postindustrial information age. Information, as many now recognize, is vital to the success of any endeavor, and certain forms of information hold nearly incalculable value. Patents on new products, the chemical composition of innovative and effective drugs, corporate marketing strategies, and the financial resources of competing corporations are all forms of information whose illegitimate access might bestow unfair advantages upon unscrupulous competitors. Imagine, for example, the financial wealth and market share which would accrue to the first pharmaceutical company to patent an effective AIDS cure. Imagine, as well, the potential profitability inherent in the information describing the chemical composition of that drug—especially to a competitor who might beat the legitimate originator of the substance to the patent desk or who might use stolen information in a later bid to challenge patents already issued.

Such a scenario is not far-fetched. In 1995, for example, the huge pharmaceutical manufacturer Merck filed a request with the federal government and the regulatory agencies of 27 other countries for permission to market its new medicine, Fosamax.[8] Fosamax, a drug intended to reverse the effects of osteoporosis in postmenopausal women, was described as the centerpiece in Merck's plan to ensure its leadership position among pharmaceutical manufacturers worldwide. The introduction of Fosamax to the pharmaceutical marketplace, along with ongoing clinical trials, was announced only after years of guarded negotiations and developmental research. The carefully crafted introduction was intended to ensure Merck's clear claim to ownership of the chemical compound in Fosamax, which should prove highly profitable for the company. Merck officials estimated the osteoporosis health care market in the United States alone at $10 billion annually.

High-tech criminals seeking illegitimate access to computerized information and to the databases that contain it have taken a number of routes. One is the path of direct access, by which office workers or corporate spies, planted as seemingly innocuous employees, violate positions of trust and use otherwise legitimate work-related entry to a company's computer resources to acquire wanted information. Such interlopers typically steal data during business hours under the guise of normal work routines.

Another path of illegal access, called "computer trespass," involves remote access to targeted machines. Anyone equipped with a home computer and a modicum of knowledge about computer modems, telecommunications, and log-on procedures has easy access to numerous computer systems across the country. Many such systems have few, if any, security procedures in place to thwart would-be invaders. In one recent case, for example, a Silicon Valley software company learned that a fired software developer had been using her telephone to enter the company's computers.[9] By the time she was caught, she had copied several million dollars' worth of the company's programs. It was later learned that the stolen software had been slated for illicit transmission to collaborators in Taiwan. Had the scheme succeeded, many thousands of "pirated" copies of the software would have been distributed at great financial loss to the legitimate copyright owners. In a similar scenario, a Florida television news editor was recently arrested after moving to a new job with a different station for allegedly entering his former employer's computer via telephone and copying researched stories.[10]

More exotic techniques used to steal data stored in computers extend to reading the electromagnetic radiation produced by such machines. Electromagnetic field (EMF) decoders, originally developed for military purposes, can scan radio frequency emanations generated by all types of computers. Keystroke activity, internal chip-processed computations, disk reads, and the like can all be detected and interpreted at a distance by such sophisticated devices under favorable conditions. Computers secured against such passively invasive practices are rarely found in the commercial marketplace. Those available to commercial organizations generally conform to a security standard developed by the U.S. military called **TEMPEST.** TEMPEST standards were created under a U.S. Department of Defense program which seeks to develop methods of reducing or eliminating unintended electronic emissions from computers and other electromagnetic devices.

Some criminal perpetrators intend simply to destroy or to alter data without otherwise accessing or copying the information. Disgruntled employees, mischievous computer **hackers,** business competitors, and others may all have varied degrees of interest in destroying a company's records or computer capabilities.

In 1988, in the first criminal prosecution of a person accused of creating a **computer virus,** Texas programmer Donald Gene Burleson was arrested for allegedly infecting a former employer's computer with a program designed to destroy the information it contained. Since Burleson's arrest, many imitators have taken similar paths of revenge. According to Richard Baker, author of the respected *Computer Security Handbook,* "The greatest threat to your computers and data comes from inside your company, not outside. The person most likely to invade your computer is not a gawky youngster in some other part of the country but an employee who is currently on your payroll."[11]

Technically speaking, **computer crime,** which involves a wide variety of potential activities, is any violation of a federal or state computer crime statute. Many argue that only those crimes that employ computer technology as central to their commission, and that could not be committed without it, may properly be termed "computer crimes." However, David L. Carter, a professor in the School of Criminal Justice at Michigan State University, has developed a broader classification scheme that includes four general types of computer crimes:[12] (1) crimes in which computers serve as targets—for example, crimes involving theft of intellectual property stored on a computer or techno-vandalism, (2) crimes in which computers serve as the instrumentality of the crime—for example, use of a computer to obtain account information stored in another computer, (3) crimes in which the computer is incidental to other crimes—use of computers to store illegal gambling information or a database of drug buyers, and (4) crimes associated with the prevalence of

computers—those that take advantage of the needs that computers create, such as the need for software. Another well-known typology distinguishes five types of computer crimes: (1) internal computer crimes, such as viruses, (2) telecommunications crimes, including illegal hacking, (3) support of criminal enterprises, such as databases supporting drug distribution, (4) computer-manipulation crimes, such as embezzlement, and (5) hardware and software theft.[13] Table 14-1 lists these five categories, with additional examples of each.

A recent estimate by the Computer Security Institute puts the annual cost of *reported* computer crime in the United States at around $124 million.[14] Other estimates, which include the costs of *unreported* computer crimes, run as high as $3 billion to $5 billion a year.[15] Global estimates of lost revenues due to pirated software (known as "Warez" in the computer underground) dwarf even that estimate. **Software piracy,** or the unauthorized and illegal

---

TABLE 14-1 ▪ Categories of Computer Crime

Internal Computer Crimes
Trojan horses
Logic bombs
Trapdoors
Viruses

Telecommunications Crimes
Phone phreaking
Hacking
Illegal Web sites
Misuse of telephone systems

Support of Criminal Enterprises
Databases to support drug distributions
Databases to support loan-sharking
Databases to support illegal gambling
Databases to keep records of illegal client transactions
Money laundering

Computer-Manipulation Crimes
Embezzlement
Fraud

Hardware and Software Theft
Software piracy
Thefts of computers
Thefts of microprocessor chips
Thefts of trade secrets

Source: Adapted from Catherine H. Conly and J. Thomas McEwen, "Computer Crime," *NIJ Reports,* January/February 1990, p. 3.

copying of software programs, is rampant. The Software and Information Industry Association (SIIA) distinguishes among various forms of software piracy:[16]

- *Softlifting:* purchasing a single licensed copy of software and loading the same copy onto several computers
- *Internet piracy:* making unauthorized copies of copyrighted software available to others electronically via the Internet
- *Software counterfeiting:* illegally duplicating and distributing copyrighted software in a form designed to make it appear to be legitimate
- *Original Equipment Manufacturer(OEM) unbundling:* selling as stand-alone software programs that were intended to be bundled with specific accompanying hardware
- *Hard disk loading:* installing unauthorized copies of software onto the hard disks of personal computers, often as an incentive for the end user to buy the hardware from that particular hardware vendor
- *Renting:* unauthorized rental of software for temporary installation, use, or copying

According to SIIA, global losses from software piracy totaled $12.2 billion in 1999.[17] North America (at $3.631 billion), Asia ($2.792 billion), and Western Europe ($3.63 billion) accounted for the vast majority (83%) of worldwide revenue losses. Some countries have especially high rates of illegal use. Of all the computer software in use in Vietnam, for example, it is estimated that 99% has been illegally copied. Learn more about software piracy from the Software and Information Industry Association via Web Extra! 14-1.

Web Extra! 14-1 at crimtoday.com

According to some experts, losses like these may be just the beginning. As one technological visionary observes, "Our society is about to feel the impact of the first generation of children who have grown up using computers. The increasing sophistication of hackers suggests that computer crime will soon soar, as members of this new generation are tempted to commit more serious offenses."[18]

While the theft or damage of information represents one area of illegitimate criminal activity, the use of technology in direct furtherance of criminal enterprise constitutes another. Illegal activity based on advanced technologies is as varied as the technologies themselves. Nuclear blackmail may represent the extreme technologically based criminal threat, whereas telephone fraud and phone "phreaking" are examples of low-end crimes that depend on modern technology for their commission. Some authors prefer the term **cybercrime** to distinguish crimes that involve the use of computers or the manipulation of digital data from other technologically sophisticated crimes.

Phone phreaks are a category of cybercriminals who use special dial-up access codes and other restricted technical information to avoid long-distance charges. Some are able to place calls from pay phones, while others fool telephone equipment into billing other callers. As a top telecommunications security expert explains, "Many or-

Coincidence or espionage? Before the dissolution of the Soviet Union, Eastern bloc scientists succeeded in building a copy of the American space shuttle, pictured here. Experts suspected that the Soviet model would not have been possible without information stolen from U.S. research archives. Why is technology difficult to protect? *(left) Phil Sandlin-Canapress Photo Service, AP/Wide World Photos; (right) Terry Renna-Canapress Photo Service, AP/Wide World Photos*

ganizations discover they have been victims of telephone fraud only after their telephone bill arrives in a carton instead of an envelope."[19]

As some companies have been surprised to learn, the responsibility for payment of stolen telephone time may rest with them. A few years ago, for example, a U.S. district court ordered Jiffy Lube International, Inc., to pay AT&T $55,727 for long-distance calls made by computer hackers who had stolen the company's access codes. Judge Frank Kaufman said the law "squarely places responsibility upon a customer, such as Jiffy Lube, for all calls whether or not authorized."[20] In effect, Judge Kaufman sent a message to corporations nationwide that they can be held responsible for ensuring the security of their own telephone services.

A new form of phone phreaking emerged about five years ago. It involves the electronic theft of cellular telephone numbers and access codes. Thieves armed with simple mail-order scanners and low-end computers can "literally grab a caller's phone number and identification number out of the air."[21] Say experts, "Those numbers are [then] used to program computer chips, which are placed inside other cellular phones—or 'clones'—so the long-distance calls appear on the victim's bill."[22] Such high-profile figures as New York Mayor Rudolph Giuliani and his police commissioner have been among recent victims of cellular phone piracy.

Other types of crime may be perpetrated using the telephone. The federal Violent Crime Control and Law Enforcement Act of 1994, for example, made it illegal to use interstate telephone lines in furtherance of telemarketing fraud and expanded federal jurisdiction to cover cases of insurance fraud and frauds committed against the elderly, even when such crimes do not involve use of the mail or telephone. Learn more about telemarketing fraud and Internet-based fraud at the National Fraud Information Center via Web Extra! 14-2.

Web EXTRA! Web Extra! 14-2 at crimtoday.com

Technology and Criminal Mischief

Not all computer crime is committed for financial gain. Some types of computer crime, including the creation and transmission of destructive computer viruses, "worms," and other malicious forms of programming code, might better be classified as "criminal mischief." Perhaps not surprisingly, these types of activities are typically associated with young technologically sophisticated male miscreants seeking a kind of clandestine recognition from their computer-savvy peers. Computer crimes committed by youthful and idealistic offenders may represent a new form of juvenile delinquency—one aimed at expressing dissatisfaction with the status quo.

Viruses have already shown signs of becoming effective terroristlike tools in the hands of young, disaffected "technonerds" intent on attacking or destroying existing social institutions. A computer virus is simply a computer program

that is designed to secretly invade computer systems and either to modify the way in which they operate or to alter the information they store.[23] Other types of destructive programs are logic bombs, worms, and Trojan horse routines. Distinctions between these programs are based either on the way in which they infect targeted machines or on the way in which they behave once they have managed to find their way into a computer. Figure 14-1 shows the prevalence of some of the most widespread computer viruses.

Viruses may spread from one machine to another via modem or high speed cable and DSL connections (when files are downloaded), through networks or direct links (such as that provided by popular programs like LapLink Pro or the Windows™ "Direct Connection" option), and through the exchange of floppy disks, CD-ROMs, or magnetic backup media. Most viruses hide inside executable computer software, or in the so-called boot sectors of floppy or hard disks. Recently, however, rogue codes known as "Macro viruses" have been secreted into text documents. The most famous of these, the Concept virus, affects users of Microsoft's Word software. Similarly, HTML files, which form the backbone of the World Wide Web, may be infected with viruses lurking inside Java script or Macromedia Shockwave®–generated code. Some users also worry that "cookies," or small programs sent to users' machines by servers on the Web, may spread viruses.

Viruses don't infect only desktop and laptop machines. Some viruses have been written that can interfere with the operation of popular handheld devices, including personal digital assistants (PDAs) and mobile phones. In 2000, for example, a Swedish software developer accidentally released Liberty Crack—a disabling software code that enters handheld devices like the Palm® and Handspring® products.[24]

Perhaps the most insidious forms of destructive programming making the rounds of the computer world today are polymorphic viruses. A polymorphic virus is one that uses advanced encryption techniques to assemble varied (yet entirely operational) clones of itself. Hence polymorphic viruses have the ability to alter themselves once they have in-

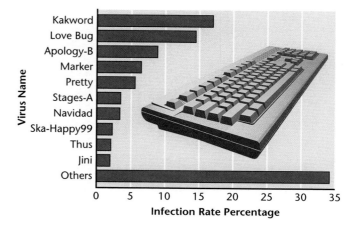

■ **FIGURE 14-1** TOP TEN PC VIRUSES IN 2000.
Source: "Damage Done," *PC Magazine,* February 6, 2001, p. 78.

fected a computer. This strategy is effective in circumventing most security devices that depend on scanning techniques to recognize viral signatures. Simply put, when viruses change, they can no longer be recognized. In typical leapfrog fashion, when crime-fighting techniques are overtaken and surpassed by new technologies favoring lawbreakers and then later regain ascendancy, polymorphic viruses have—over the last few years—largely rendered signature-based antivirus scanning technologies obsolete. Unfortunately, although many hardware devices and software products now on the market offer some degree of virus protection to individual and commercial users, new viruses are constantly being created which may soon have the ability to circumvent all security procedures now in place. The only fully effective technique for avoiding viral contamination is the complete and total isolation of computer equipment—a strategy as unlikely to be maintained as it is to be implemented. Learn more about computer viruses at Web Extra! 14-3.

Web Extra! 14-3 at crimtoday.com

Computer Crime and the Law

In late 2000, the Justice Department of the Philippines dismissed criminal charges against Onel de Guzman.[25] De Guzman, a former student at the Philippines AMA Computer College, admitted that he had unleashed the ILOVEYOU (or Love Bug) virus on the Internet on May 4, 2000, but refused to say whether he had authored it. The virus replicated rapidly throughout the world, gathering passwords from infected computers and sending them to several e-mail accounts in the Philippines. By the time the virus had run its course, official estimates were that it had caused over $10 billion in damages.[26] Because the Philippines had no law against computer crime, however, de Guzman was originally charged with theft and violation of an access device. Those laws, prosecutors finally decided, were not applicable to de Guzman's activities, and the charges were dropped. Although President Joseph Estrada signed a new law covering electronic commerce and computer hacking in June 2000, it could not be applied retroactively to the Love Bug case.

In the early years of computer-based information systems, most U.S. jurisdictions, like the Philippines, often tried to prosecute unauthorized computer access under preexisting property crime statutes, including burglary and larceny laws. Unfortunately, because the actual carrying off of a computer is quite different from simply copying or altering some of the information it contains, juries frequently could not understand the applicability of such laws to high-tech crimes, and computer criminals were often exonerated. As a result, all states and the federal government developed computer-crime statutes specifically applicable to invasive activities aimed at illegally accessing stored information. Federal statutes of relevance to crimes committed with or against computer equipment and software include (1) the

Digital Theft Deterrence and Copyright Damages Improvement Act of 1999,[27] (2) the No Electronic Theft Act of 1997,[28] (3) the Communications Decency Act, (4) the Computer Fraud and Abuse Act of 1984 and its amendments—especially Section 290001 of Title 29 of the Violent Crime Control and Law Enforcement Act of 1994, which is known as the Computer Abuse Amendments Act of 1994, (5) the Electronic Communications Privacy Act of 1986, (6) the National Stolen Property Act,[29] (7) the Federally Protected Property Act, and (8) the Federal Wiretap Act of 1968.

For the most part, federal laws protect equipment owned by the federal government or a financial institution or computers that are accessed across state lines without prior authorization.[30] The U.S. Criminal Code, Title 18, Section 1030(a), defines as criminal the intentional unauthorized access to a computer used exclusively by the federal government or any other computer used by the government when such conduct affects the government's use. The same statute also defines as criminal the intentional and unauthorized access to two or more computers in different states and conduct that alters or destroys information and causes loss to one or more parties in excess of $1,000.[31] Punishment specified under federal law is a maximum sentence of five years and a fine of up to $250,000 upon conviction. The Computer Abuse Amendments Act of 1994, however, adds the provision that "any person who suffers damage or loss by reason of a violation of [this] section . . . may maintain a civil action against the violator to obtain compensatory damages and injunctive relief or other equitable relief." The 1994 provision is intended to support civil actions in federal court against computer criminals by those suffering monetary losses as a result of computer crimes.

The **Digital Theft Deterrence and Copyright Damages Improvement Act** of 1999 amended section 504(c) of the Copyright Act and increased the amount of damages that could be awarded in cases of copyright infringement—a crime which is intimately associated with software piracy. Enacted in 1997, the **No Electronic Theft Act** (NETA, or NETAct) criminalizes the willful infringement of copyrighted works, including by electronic means, even when the infringing party derives no direct financial benefit from the infringement (such as when pirated software is freely distributed online). In keeping with requirements of the NETA, the U.S. Sentencing Commission enacted amendments to its guidelines on April 6, 2000, to increase penalties associated with electronic theft.

In 1996, President Bill Clinton signed the **Communications Decency Act (CDA)** into law. The CDA, which is Title 5 of the Telecommunications Act of 1996,[32] sought to protect minors from harmful material on the Internet. A portion of the CDA criminalized the knowing transmission of obscene or indecent messages to any recipient under 18 years of age. Another section prohibited the knowing sending, or displaying to a person under 18 any message "that, in context, depicts or describes, in terms patently offensive as measured by contemporary community standards, sexual or excretory activities or organs." The law provided acceptable defenses for those who took "good faith . . . effective . . . actions" to restrict access by minors to prohibited communications, and to those who restricted such access by requiring certain designated forms of age proof, such as a verified credit card or an adult identification number.

Shortly after the law was passed, however, the American Civil Liberties Union (ACLU) and a number of other plaintiffs filed suit against the federal government, challenging the constitutionality of the law's two provisions relating to the transmission of obscene materials to minors. In 1996, a three-judge federal district court entered a preliminary injunction against enforcement of both challenged provisions, ruling that they contravened First Amendment guarantees of free speech. The government then appealed to the U.S. Supreme Court. The Court's 1997 decision, *Reno v. ACLU*,[33] upheld the lower court's ruling and found that the CDA's "indecent transmission" and "patently offensive display" provisions abridge "the freedom of speech" protected by the First Amendment. Justice John Paul Stevens wrote for the majority, "It is true that we have repeatedly recognized the governmental interest in protecting children from harmful materials. But that interest does not justify an unnecessarily broad suppression of speech addressed to adults."

CDA supporters have worked to draft a new version of the law that can pass constitutional muster. Many doubt, however, that they can succeed, acknowledging that the Court has placed the Internet in the same category as newspapers and other print media, where almost no regulation is permitted.

The computer-crime laws of individual states are rarely modeled after federal legislation. As a result, they contain great variation. Texas law, for example, criminalizes "breach of computer security." A breach of security occurs when an individual "knowingly accesses a computer, computer network, or computer system without the effective consent of the owner" or when someone "intentionally or knowingly gives a password, identifying code, personal identification number, debit card number, bank account number, or other confidential information about a computer security system to another person without the effective consent of the person employing the computer security system to restrict access to a computer, computer network, computer system, or data."[34]

In contrast to Texas, the state of Virginia specifically defines *computer crime* according to the following categories: "theft of computer services, computer invasion of privacy, computer trespass, computer fraud, [and] personal trespass by computer" (via which physical injury accrues to someone by virtue of unauthorized access to a computer, as may happen in the case of disruption of utility services).[35] The laws of two other states, Wisconsin and Colorado, are shown in Theory versus Reality boxes in this chapter. The Colorado statute, as can be easily seen, is rather succinct, whereas Wisconsin's is quite detailed.

Ambiguities in existing computer-crime laws, complicated by rapid changes in technology, can make it difficult even to tell when a crime has occurred. In 1995, for example, 20-year-old University of Michigan student Jacob Alkhabaz (AKA Jake A. Baker) became the first person ever indicted for writing something on the Internet when he was arrested by the Federal Bureau of Investigation (FBI) and charged with five counts of interstate transmission of threats.[36] Alkhabaz had posted a series of stories on the Internet about his fantasy of torturing, raping, and murdering a female classmate. One of his messages contained the phrase, "Just thinking about it anymore doesn't do the trick. I need to do it." Another note read, "Torture is foreplay, rape is romance, snuff (killing) is climax."[37]

Although Alkhabaz might have been punished by a sentence of up to five years in prison, Detroit U.S. District Judge Avern Cohn threw out the charges after Alkhabaz had spent 29 days in jail.[38] Cohn ruled that Alkhabaz's violent-sounding Internet writings were protected under the free speech clause of the U.S. Constitution. Notably, Alkhabaz had been charged with communicating threats rather than computer crime because his activities were not specifically covered under federal computer-crime laws. Had they been, a different verdict might have resulted.

Such cases illustrate how certain, as of yet unimaginable, future illegitimate activities employing computer equipment may not be adequately covered by existing law. On the other hand, some crimes committed with the use of a computer may be more appropriately prosecuted under "traditional" laws. For that reason, some experts distinguish among computer crime (defined earlier), computer-related crime, and computer abuse. **Computer-related crime** is "any illegal act for which knowledge of computer technology is involved for its investigation, perpetration, or prosecution," whereas **computer abuse** is said to be "any incident without color of right associated with computer technology in which a victim suffered or could have suffered loss and/or a perpetrator by intention made or could have made gain."[39] Learn more about digital crime of all kinds from the Computer Crime and Intellectual Property Section (CCIPS) of the Criminal Division of the U.S. Department of Justice via Web Extra! 14-4.

Web Extra! 14-4 at crimtoday.com

A PROFILE OF COMPUTER CRIMINALS

In 1997, FBI agents arrested Adam Quinn Pletcher, 21, and charged him with trying to extort $5.25 million from Microsoft founder and chairman Bill Gates.[40] Pletcher, a loner from Illinois who spent hour after hour in front of his computer, allegedly sent several letters to Gates demanding the money and threatening to kill him or his wife, Melinda, if Gates did not respond to an America Online service known

THEORY VERSUS REALITY
Wisconsin Defines Computer Crime

THE WISCONSIN COMPUTER-CRIME LAW

A considerable difference exists between the physical theft of computer equipment and the theft through copying of information stored in computers. The Wisconsin computer-crime statute, which makes a good attempt at distinguishing between these two types of offenses, is excerpted here. The statute is also notable for the fact that it recognizes a wide range of activities as possible forms of computer crime.

State of Wisconsin
Criminal Statutes
Chapter 293, Laws of 1981
943.70 Computer crimes.
(2) Offenses Against Computer Data and Programs.
(a) Whoever willfully, knowingly and without authorization does any of the following may be penalized as provided in paragraph (b):
 1. Modifies data, computer programs or supporting documentation.
 2. Destroys data, computer programs or supporting documentation.
 3. Accesses data, computer programs or supporting documentation.
 4. Takes possession of data, computer programs or supporting documentation.
 5. Copies data, computer programs or supporting documentation.
 6. Discloses restricted access codes or other restricted access information to unauthorized person.
(b) Whoever violates this subsection is guilty of:
 1. A Class A misdemeanor unless sub. 2, 3 or 4 applies.

2. A Class E felony if the offense is committed to defraud or to obtain property.
3. A Class D felony if the damage is greater than $2,500 or if it causes an interruption or impairment of governmental operations or public communication, of transportation or of a supply of water, gas or other public service.
4. A Class C felony if the offense creates a situation of unreasonable risk and high probability of death or great bodily harm to another.
(3) Offenses Against Computers, Computer Equipment or Supplies.
(a) Whoever willingly, knowingly and without authorization does any of the following may be penalized as provided in paragraph (b):
 1. Modifies computer equipment or supplies that are used or intended to be used in a computer, computer system or computer network.
 2. Destroys, uses, takes or damages a computer, computer system, computer, network or equipment or supplies used or intended to be used in a computer, computer system, or computer network.
(b) Whoever violates this subsection is guilty of:
 1. A Class A misdemeanor unless sub. 2, 3 or 4 applies.
 2. A Class E felony if the offense is committed to defraud or obtain property.
 3. A Class D felony if the damage to the computer, computer system, computer network, equipment or supplies is greater than $2,500.
 4. A Class C felony if the offense creates a situation of unreasonable risk and high probability of death or great bodily harm to another.

PENALTIES FOR INFRACTIONS

939.50(3) Penalties for felonies are as follows:
(a) For a Class A felony, life imprisonment.
(b) For a Class B felony, imprisonment not to exceed 20 years.
(c) For a Class C felony, a fine not to exceed $10,000 or imprisonment not to exceed 10 years, or both.
(d) For a Class D felony, a fine not to exceed $10,000 or imprisonment not to exceed 5 years, or both.
(e) For a Class E felony, a fine not to exceed $10,000 or imprisonment not to exceed 2 years, or both.
939.51(3) Penalties for misdemeanors are as follows:
(a) For a Class A misdemeanor, a fine not to exceed $10,000 or imprisonment not to exceed 9 months, or both.
(b) For a Class B misdemeanor, a fine not to exceed $1,000 or imprisonment not to exceed 90 days, or both.
(c) For a Class C misdemeanor, a fine not to exceed $500 or imprisonment not to exceed 30 days, or both.

DISCUSSION QUESTIONS

1. Does the Wisconsin statute shown in this box potentially criminalize any forms of computer-related activity which, in your opinion, should not be illegal? If so, what might they be?
2. Is the Wisconsin statute sufficiently comprehensive in scope? Would you want to add any other forms of computer crime to the statute? If so, what might they be?

as "NetGirl." The service, an online dating forum, was to serve as a secure medium for the exchange of messages between Gates and the extortionist. FBI agents nabbed Pletcher after he sent a disk to Gates which held erased files containing the names of Pletcher's parents. Some months earlier, Pletcher had made headlines in Chicago when he was accused of running scams on his Internet Web page, including offering fake driver's licenses for sale, telling people he could

get them cars at bargain prices and then pocketing their money, running an illegal raffle that offered $10 chances to win an expensive automobile, and offering "free" pagers that cost more than $50 in service charges. By all accounts, Pletcher was a hacker—a technologically sophisticated loner.

It is from hacker subculture that computer criminals tend to come. Hackers and hacker identities are a product of **cyberspace,** that etheric realm where computer technology

THEORY VERSUS REALITY
Colorado Defines Computer Crime

THE COLORADO COMPUTER CRIME LAW

Like Wisconsin's computer crime law shown in an earlier box in this chapter, Colorado's computer crime law attempts to define computer crime by specifically prohibiting certain activities.

State of Colorado
TITLE 18. Criminal Code
ARTICLE 5.5. Computer Crime
C.R.S. 18-5.5-102 (July 1, 2000)
18-5.5-102. Computer crime

(1) A person commits computer crime if the person knowingly:

(a) Accesses a computer, computer network, or computer system or any part thereof without authorization; exceeds authorized access to a computer, computer network, or computer system or any part thereof; or uses a computer, computer network, or computer system or any part thereof without authorization or in excess of authorized access; or

(b) Accesses any computer, computer network, or computer system, or

any part thereof for the purpose of devising or executing any scheme or artifice to defraud; or

(c) Accesses any computer, computer network, or computer system, or any part thereof to obtain, by means of false or fraudulent pretenses, representations, or promises, money; property; services; passwords or similar information through which a computer, computer network, or computer system or any part thereof may be accessed; or other thing of value; or

(d) Accesses any computer, computer network, or computer system, or any part thereof to commit theft; or

(e) Without authorization or in excess of authorized access alters, damages, interrupts, or causes the interruption or impairment of the proper functioning of, or causes any damage to, any computer, computer network, computer system, computer software, program, application, documentation, or data contained in such computer, computer network, or computer system or any part thereof; or

(f) Causes the transmission of a computer program, software, information, code, data, or command by means of a computer, computer network, or computer system or any part thereof with the intent to cause damage to or to cause the interruption or impairment of the proper functioning of or that actually causes damage to or the interruption or impairment of the proper functioning of any computer, computer network, computer system, or part thereof.

DISCUSSION QUESTIONS

1. In what ways does Colorado's computer crime law differ from Wisconsin's statute defining offenses against computer data and programs.
2. Which law seems more comprehensive? Why?
3. If you were a Colorado legislator would you consider modifying the law shown in this box. If so, in what way? If not, why not?

and human psychology meet. Cyberspace exists only within electronic networks and is the place where computers and human beings interact with one another. For many hackers, cyberspace provides the opportunity for impersonal interpersonal contact, technological challenges, and game playing. Fantasy role-playing games are popular among hackers and may engross many "wave riders," who appear to prefer what in technological parlance is called "virtual reality" to the external physical and social worlds that surround them. As one writer states, "Cyberspace is hacker heaven."[41]

Literature that glorifies cyberspace and the people who inhabit it is called "cyberpunk," and hackers are sometimes called "cyberpunks." An understanding of cyberpunk literature is crucial for those wanting to gain an appreciation for how hackers think. According to Paul Saffo of the Institute for the Future in Menlo Park, California, "Anyone trying to make sense of [contemporary] computing . . . should add some cyberpunk books to their reading lists." Says Saffo, "Cyberpunk may become the counterculture movement" of the future. He adds that "the cyberpunk trend is likely to be matched by an increase in the number of cyber-outlaws pen-

etrating networks for criminal ends."[42] Young, idealistic, and immature, hackers of this genre typically take on pseudonyms which other hackers can identify but which also provide at least the illusion of anonymity. Phiber Optik, Acid Phreak, Knight Lightning, Time Lord, Nightcrawler, and Dark Angel are only a few of the many pseudonyms that are either now in use or that have been used by hackers in recent years.

No one knows the actual identity of many of these people, but computer-security experts have come up with a rough profile of the average hacker.[43] He is a male between the ages of 16 and 25 and lives in the United States. He is a computer user, but not a programmer, who hacks with software written by others. His primary motivation is to gain access to Web sites and computer networks, not to profit financially. A psychological and social profile of today's hackers is provided in the Theory versus Reality box entitled "The Computer Hacker."

Some of the most infamous computer hackers of recent years, those composing the Atlanta-based Legion of Doom, fit the hacker profile well. A few years ago, three Legion mem-

David L. Smith, creator of the infamous Melissa e-mail computer virus. Smith pleaded guilty in December 2000 to state charges of computer theft and federal charges of sending a damaging computer program, which caused over $80 million in damages. The virus is thought to have been named for a topless dancer Smith knew when he lived in Florida. What laws criminalize the creation and dissemination of computer viruses? *Daniel Hulshizer, AP/Wide World Photos*

bers were sentenced to prison terms of 14 to 21 months and were ordered to pay $233,000 each in restitution to BellSouth Corporation for breaking into its computer systems and stealing confidential data. After serving their jail time, some Legion members found themselves sought after by high-tech employers who wanted to exploit their skills in the development of proprietary computer-security systems. Other "legionnaires" formed a company called Comsec Data Security to help provide private businesses with the expertise necessary to fend off electronic intrusions.

The History and Nature of Hacking

Some authors have suggested that computer hacking began with the creation of the interstate phone system and direct distance dialing, implemented by AT&T in the late 1950s.[44] Early switching devices used audible tones that were easily duplicated by electronics hobbyists, and "blue boxes" capable of emulating such tones quickly entered the illicit marketplace.

Although phone phreaking has been practiced for more than 40 years, a form of illegal telephone access that

has recently come to the fore is voice-mail hacking. Private voice-mail boxes used for storing verbal messages have become the targets of corporate raiders and young vandals alike. In a recent case, two teenaged New York City brothers caused an estimated $2.4 million in lost business by gaining illegal access to the New Hampshire–based International Data Group's voice-mail system. The brothers were angry at not having received a poster promised with their magazine subscription. Security experts at the company, who first thought that the mailboxes were malfunctioning, were alerted to the intentional disruptions by obscene outgoing messages planted by the brothers that greeted unsuspecting callers.[45]

Voice-mail fraud, another form of telephone crime, involves schemes in which mailbox access codes are shared in such a way that callers to toll-free numbers can leave messages for one another in voice-mail boxes, thereby avoiding personal long-distance charges.[46] Companies that provide access to voice-mail systems through toll-free numbers often learn of the need for access code security only after they have been victimized by such schemes.

Although the hacker lifestyle may have begun with phone phreaking, phone phreaks represent only one type of hacker. Hackers can be distinguished both by their purpose and by their method of operation. Such categorization, however, is merely descriptive. Other more useful distinctions can be made on the basis of personality and lifestyle. Some experts have suggested that hackers can be classified according to psychological characteristics into the following groups:[47]

- *Pioneers:* individuals who are fascinated by the evolving technology of telecommunications and explore it without knowing exactly what they are going to find. Few hard-core criminals are found among this group.
- *Scamps:* hackers with a sense of fun. They intend no overt harm.
- *Explorers:* hackers who are motivated by their delight in the discoveries associated with breaking into new computer systems. The farther away such systems are geographically from the hacker's physical location, or the more secure such systems are, the greater the excitement associated with breaking into them.
- *Game players:* those who enjoy defeating software or system copy protection and who may seek to illegally access computer systems with games to play. Hacking itself becomes a game for this sort of hacker.
- *Vandals:* malicious hackers who deliberately cause damage with no apparent gain for themselves. The 414 Gang in Milwaukee, for example, which broke into the Sloan-Kettering Cancer Institute's computers and wiped out patient records, provides an example of this type of hacker.

THEORY VERSUS REALITY
The Computer Hacker: A Psychological and Social Profile

Computer hackers generally share the following social and personal characteristics:

- Young: Often 14 to 19 years of age.
- Intelligent: IQ probably over 120, with the ability to articulate well.
- "Nerdy": Socializes poorly with peers but may have close friends among like-minded fellows.
- "WASP"-like: Likely to be white, Protestant, and from a middle- or upper-middle-class background.
- Fond of gadgets, especially computer-related hardware.
- Academic performer: Likely to perform well on individual academic assignments, such as tests and term papers. Unlikely to perform well on group assignments.
- Self-perceived hero:
  Sees self as empowering humankind via an abstract victory over the "machine." Sees self as assisting humanity via participation in the fight against

dehumanizing organizations (that is, may seek to "liberate" information in the belief that information should be freely shared by all).
- Counterculture participant: Has likely read, or is familiar with, the following books:
  William Gibson's *Neuromancer*
  John Brunner's *Shockwave Rider*
  William Gibson's *Count Zero*
  William Gibson's *Mona Lisa Overdrive*
  Clifford Stoll's *The Cuckoo's Egg*
  Melissa Scott's *Trouble and Her Friends*
- Self-descriptions include feelings of boredom and apathy.
- Favorite activities include computer games and other games emphasizing a fantasy world (for example, Dungeons and Dragons).
- Membership in a thrill-seeking subcultural group of computer hackers, usually taking on the name of a fantasy world character. Communicates with other members of the subculture via the Internet.

- Feelings experienced when accessing a secure computer system are often referred to in terms of drug taking and sexual activity ("getting high," "orgasmic," "the big thrill," and so on).

DISCUSSION QUESTIONS

1. Does the list describing the social and personal characteristics of computer hackers that is provided in this box seem adequate to describe such people? If not, what might you add? What could be dropped?
2. While some computer hackers are law abiding, quite a few are not. What kinds of laws do such people violate? What illegal activities do they undertake?

Source: Adapted with permission from Robert W. Taylor, "Computer Crime," in C. R. Swanson, N. C. Chamelin, and L. Territo, eds., *Criminal Investigation* (New York: Random House, 1991).

- *Addicts:* classic computer "nerds" who are addicted to hacking and to computer technology. They may also be addicted to illicit drugs, as some hacker bulletin board systems post information on drugs as well as on modems, passwords, and vulnerable systems.

Psychologist Percy Black argues for the existence of an underlying theme in all cases of hacking. It is, he says, "the search for a feeling of power, possibly stemming from a deep-seated sense of powerlessness."[48] Hence hacking may serve as compensation for feelings of personal inferiority. By challenging the machine and by winning against machine culture, hackers go through a kind of rite of passage into adulthood, whereby they prove themselves capable of success.

Because most hackers are young adolescent males, however, it may be important to realize that, as one expert on hackers says, "their other favorite risky business is the time-honored adolescent sport of trespassing. They insist on going where they don't belong. But then teen-age boys have been proceeding uninvited since the dawn of human

puberty. It seems hard-wired. The only innovation is in the new form of the forbidden zone and the means of getting in it."[49]

Unfortunately, however, not all computer hackers are simply kids trying their hand at beating technological challenges. As Garry M. Jenkins, Assistant Director of the U.S. Secret Service, put it around the time of Operation Sun Devil (a joint two-year undercover operation of the Secret Service, local and state law enforcement officers, and private telephone security personnel), "Recently, we have witnessed an alarming number of young people who, for a variety of sociological and psychological reasons, have become attached to their computers and are exploiting their potential in a criminal manner. Often, a progression of criminal activity occurs that involves telecommunications fraud (free long-distance phone calls), unauthorized access to other computers (whether for profit, fascination, ego, or the intellectual challenge), credit card fraud (cash advances and unauthorized purchases of goods), and then moves on to other destructive activities like computer viruses. . . .

THEORY VERSUS REALITY
Technological Attraction

The attraction computer hacking holds is captured well in this passage from Melissa Scott's cyberpunk adventure novel, *Trouble and Her Friends:*

Trouble's on the net tonight, riding the high data like a cowboy, the plains of light stark around her. The data flows and writhes like grass in the virtual wind. IC(E)—Intrusion Countermeasures (Electronic)—rises to either side, prohibiting the nodes, and the old urge returns. . . . She can almost taste what lies behind that barrier, files and codes turned to candy-color shapes good enough to eat, and remembers the sweet-sour tang, the glorious greed of gorging on the good bits, sorting them in an eye-blink by taste and smell, faster and more sure than anyone else in the business.

DISCUSSION QUESTIONS

1. What thoughts, feeling and emotions does the writer of this paragraph want to convey?

2. How did reading the paragraph affect you? Can you identify with what the writer is saying? Why or why not?

Source: Melissa Scott, *Trouble and Her Friends* (Garden City, NJ: Science Fiction Book Club, 1994).

Our experience shows that many computer hacker suspects are no longer misguided teenagers mischievously playing games with their computers in their bedrooms. Some are now high-tech computer operators using computers to engage in unlawful conduct."[50] Learn more about hackers and information security at the CERT Coordination Center, one of the best security sites on the Internet. Located at the Software Engineering Institute, a federally funded research and development center operated by Carnegie Mellon University, CERT can be reached via Web Extra! 14-5.

Web Extra! 14-5 at crimtoday.com

Not all high-tech crimes are committed using computer technology. Many technologically sophisticated professional criminals are operating today, some of whom use the diverse fruits of high technology in the furtherance of serious criminal activity. The theft of money is a major goal of such activity. Some years ago, for example, technologically sophisticated thieves in New York City rolled a fake automated teller machine (ATM) into the local Buckland Hills shopping mall. Although the machine did not dispense money, it did record the information contained on the magnetic strips of legitimate banking cards inserted by would-be customers. The personal information numbers which the customers entered were also recorded. Armed with the necessary codes for legitimate accounts, the thieves then fabricated their own cards and used them to withdraw thousands of dollars from real ATM machines across the city.

Although most people probably think of money as dollar bills, money today is really only information—information stored in a computer network, possibly located within the physical confines of a bank, but more likely existing as bits and bytes of data on service providers' machines. Typical financial customers give little thought to the fact that very little "real" money is held by their bank, brokerage house, mutual fund, or commodities dealer. Nor do they often consider the threats to their financial well-being by activities like electronic theft or the sabotage of existing accounts. Unfortunately, however, the threat is very real. Computer criminals equipped with enough information, or able to ferret out the data they need, can quickly and easily send vast amounts of money anywhere in the world.

Although billions of dollars' worth of electronic transactions occur every day, no reliable estimates exist as to the losses suffered in such transactions due to the activities of technologically adept criminal perpetrators. Accurate estimates are lacking largely because sophisticated high-tech thieves are so effective at eluding apprehension and even detection that reliable loss figures are impossible to ascertain.

World Wide Web sites can also facilitate criminal activity. A few years ago, for example, U.S. Customs Service agents involved in Operation Longarm carried out raids on child pornographers and suspected pedophiles in 18 states using names taken from a pedophile site. According to the Customs Service, the computerized transmission of illegal pornography among pedophiles is rapidly becoming more popular than smutty magazines.[51] Similarly, in 1994, Robert and Carleen Thomas were convicted of violating antiobscenity laws, on the grounds that their California online service, Amateur Action, was used to transmit obscene materials across state lines to Tennessee. On January 29, 1996, the U.S. Court of Appeals for the Sixth Circuit upheld the couple's conviction.

CRIME IN THE NEWS
Identity Theft Thrives in Cyberspace

The information superhighway has become an express lane for identity theft, according to federal law enforcement agents.

The growth of the Internet, with its gigabytes of personal information floating around in cyberspace, has given criminals a quick and easy way to ferret out or even hack into computer systems to gather enough personal information to steal someone's identity.

That was the warning Tuesday from Gregory Regan, special agent in charge of the U.S. Secret Service's Finance Crimes Division, in testimony before the Senate Judiciary Committee's Subcommittee on Technology, Terrorism and Government Information.

Identity theft occurs when someone gains access to a person's basic information, including name, addresses and credit card or Social Security numbers, and uses that information to open new charge and bank accounts, order merchandise or borrow money.

"As financial institutions and merchants become more cautious in their approach to hand-to-hand transactions, the criminals are looking for other venues to compromise," Regan said. "Today, criminals need look no further than the Internet."

NURSE WORKS TO CLEAR NAME

Maureen Mitchell, an Ohio nurse, told the committee that someone was able to steal her identity even though she and her husband do no online buying. She is still unsure how the theft occurred, even though a suspect has been arrested.

The Mitchells have devoted hundreds of hours to sorting out their finances since they learned that someone had bought two vehicles and borrowed money in their names.

"We don't know if other accounts are still outstanding. This has a huge impact on your life," Mitchell told members of the subcommittee Tuesday.

Regan said a recent case investigated by the Secret Service and other federal agencies shows how easily Internet-savvy criminals can get personal information from public sources—in this case a promotion list of high-ranking military officers on a public Web site. In the past, published lists included the officers' Social Security numbers.

AN OVER-FRIENDLY BANK

Regan said that in this particular case, the financial institution, in an effort to operate in a consumer-friendly manner, issued credit over the Internet in less than a minute.

"Approval for credit was granted after conducting a credit check for the applicant who provided a true name and matching true Social Security number," said Regan. "All other information provided, such as the date of birth, address and telephone number, which could have been used for further verification, was fraudulent. The failure of this bank to conduct a more comprehensive verification process resulted in substantial losses and more importantly a long list of high-ranking military officers who became victims of identity fraud."

Regan said the Internet offers the anonymity that criminals desire.

"In the past, fraud schemes required false identification documents and necessitated a face-to-face exchange of information and identity verification," Regan said. "Now with just a laptop and modem, criminals are capable of perpetrating a variety of financial crimes without identity documents through the use of stolen personal information."

GAUGING THE LAW'S EFFECTIVENESS

The hearing was held to gauge the effectiveness of the Identity Theft and Assumption Deterrence Act that was passed in 1998 to give law enforcement tools to stem this problem. Under the law,

a conviction for identity theft carries a maximum penalty of 15 years imprisonment, a fine, and forfeiture of any personal property used or intended to be used to commit the crime.

Jodie Bernstein, director of the Federal Trade Commission's (FTC) Bureau of Consumer Protection, told the subcommittee that a brand new, toll-free FTC hot line to take identity theft calls is already logging 400 calls a week.

Bernstein said the agency is expecting the number of calls to increase to 200,000 annually.

The General Accounting Office reported that consumer inquiries to the Trans Union credit bureau's Fraud Victim Assistance Department increased from 35,235 in 1992 to 522,922 in 1997, and the Social Security Administration's Office of the Inspector General conducted 1,153 investigations of Social Security number misuse in 1997, compared with 305 in 1996.

In 1999, the telephone hot line established by the Social Security Administration's Office of the Inspector General received reports of almost 39,000 incidents of misuse of Social Security numbers.

DETECTING FRAUD

Bernstein said that while law enforcement has been moving aggressively against the problem, there are steps that need to be taken to curtail the trend, including "bringing together creditors and credit reporting agencies to develop mechanisms for detecting such fraud and thus heading off identity theft."

She said that victims run into numerous obstacles and bureaucratic hurdles in trying to resolve problems tied to identity theft. For example, many consumers must contact and recontact creditors, credit bureaus and debt collectors, often with frustrating results.

Bernstein said that the ideal would be a system in which consumers could make a single telephone call to any of the three

(continued on the next page)

(continued from previous page)

major credit bureaus or the FTC hot line to get fraud alerts placed on all of their credit reports.

"The success of such an effort depends on the cooperation of the major credit bureaus," she said.

Sen. John Kyl, R-Ariz., the chairman of the subcommittee and the sponsor of the identity theft law, said that since the law was enacted, a report from the inspector general of the Social Security Administration found that 81 percent of misuse of

Social Security numbers relate to identity theft.

Source: David Noack, "Identity Theft Thrives in Cyberspace," APB News, March 8, 2000. Reprinted with permission.

Computer Crime as a Form of White-Collar Crime

White-collar crime is discussed in detail in Chapter 12. It is important here, however, to recognize that a number of contemporary analysts believe that computer crime may be nothing other than a new form of white-collar crime. Some suggest that it is the ultimate expression of white-collar crime.

In what may be the definitive work to date on high-tech professional crime, Donn B. Parker, author of the National Institute of Justice's *Computer Crime: Criminal Justice Research Manual,* compares white-collar criminals with computer criminals. Both share what Parker calls "common criminal behavior-related issues," such as the following:[52]

- Both types of acts are often committed through non-violent means, although certain industrial, consumer, and environment-related crimes have life-threatening consequences.
- Access to computers or computer storage media, through employment-related knowledge or technical skills, is often needed.
- These acts generally involve information manipulations that either directly or indirectly create profits or losses.
- These crimes can be committed by an individual, by several individuals working in collusion, or by organizations, with the victims in the latter case ranging from individual clients, customers, or employees to other organizations.

According to Parker, computer crime and white-collar crime also share the following similarities:

- These crimes are often difficult to detect, with discovery quite often started by accident or by customer complaint rather than as the result of direct investigation.
- The general public views many of these acts as less serious than crimes involving physical violence.
- These crimes cost individuals, organizations, and society large amounts of money and other resources.
- Prevention of these crimes requires a combination of legal, technical, managerial, security, and audit-monitoring controls.

THE INFORMATION SUPERHIGHWAY AND DATA SECURITY

As we begin the twenty-first century, America has begun to leave behind its industrial roots and is moving toward becoming a service-oriented information-rich society. John Naisbitt, author of *Megatrends,* explains it this way: "The transition from an industrial to an information society does not mean manufacturing will cease to exist or become unimportant. Did farming end with the industrial era? Ninety percent of us produced 100 percent of the food in the agricultural era; now 3 percent of us produce 100 percent.... In the information age, the focus of manufacturing will shift from the physical to more intellectual functions on which the physical depends."[53]

Although goods and materials will always need to be created, transported, and distributed, it is information that will form the lifeblood of the coming world order. Information, many pundits believe, will be the most valuable resource of the new age, comparable to—and even exceeding—the value which natural resources like oil, gas, coal, and gold held over the past few centuries. As Naisbitt states, "Information is an economic entity because it costs something to produce and because people are willing to pay for it."[54] Nations that are able to effectively manage valuable information and that can make it accessible to their citizens will receive enhanced productivity and greater wealth as a reward.

One vocal proponent of the information superhighway is former Vice President Al Gore. Following his election to the U.S. Senate in 1984, Gore worked tirelessly to ensure that a high-speed fiber-optic computer network would be built throughout the nation, providing the backbone for future information development. Before becoming vice president, Gore was chairman of the Senate's Subcommittee on Science, Technology, and Space. Almost single-handedly, he conceived of and authored the High Performance Computing Act of 1990, which laid the groundwork for federal government support of the data superhighway. During his fight to win the legislation's passage, Gore drew an effective contrast between modern telecommunications and the invention of movable type centuries ago. "Gutenberg's invention," he said, "which so empowered Jefferson and his colleagues in their fight for democracy, seems to pale before the rise of electronic communications and innovations, from the telegraph to television, to the microprocessor and the emergence of a new computerized world—an information age."[55]

The highly touted information superhighway is a visionary way of moving data quickly and of making information accessible to masses of citizens who can use it productively. Some suggest that the information superhighway already exists in the form of the Internet. The **Internet,** which is the world's largest computer network, had its beginnings a couple of decades ago with the linkage of military and scientific computer facilities already existing on the Arpnet and Milnet. Today, the Internet consists of a vast resource of tens of thousands of computers around the world that are all linked together.

The Internet provides some amazing and constantly growing capabilities—not the least of which are access to sites on the World Wide Web, electronic mail, mailing lists, newsgroups, and file transfer capability. Although Internet access was originally restricted to commercial users, researchers, and university personnel, access to the Internet is routine today. Companies like America Online offer Internet gateways, and a large number of direct Internet service providers (ISPs) furnish Internet access to anyone able to pay the monthly fee. Web browsers make it easy to search the tremendous amount of information on the Web and to interact with other Internet users.

Unfortunately, as the Internet has grown, it has been targeted by hackers and computer criminals, some of whom have introduced rogue computer programs into the network's machines. In 1988, for example, the infamous Internet "worm" written by Cornell University graduate student Robert T. Morris, Jr., circulated through computers connected to the Internet, effectively disabling many of them. Morris was later arrested and sentenced in 1990 to 400 hours of community service and three years of probation. He was also fined $10,000. Since Morris's day, many other hackers have exploited loopholes in the software and hardware supporting the Internet.

In 1996, in response to the growing threat to the nation's information systems, President Clinton created the Commission on Critical Infrastructure Protection.[56] The commission was charged with assessing threats to the nation's computer networks and recommending policies to protect them. Security issues related to information systems which control the nation's telecommunications, electric power, oil and gas, banking and finance, transportation, water supply, emergency services, and government operations were studied by the commission, which issued its report in October 1997. Among its recommendations, the commission proposed (1) establishing an Information Analysis and Warning Center to collect information on computer security breaches in industry and government, (2) creating legislation to permit private

companies to conduct special background checks when hiring computer experts for sensitive positions, (3) creating a White House office to coordinate the information security roles of government, including the departments of Commerce, Defense, Energy, Justice, Treasury, and Transportation, and (4) quadrupling research on cyberspace security to $1 billion by the year 2004.[57]

The National Infrastructure Protection Center (NIPC) was created in 1998 and is located at the FBI's headquarters in Washington, D.C. NIPC's mission is to serve as the federal government's center for threat assessment, warnings, investigation, and response for threats or attacks against the nation's critical infrastructures. Visit NIPC via Web Extra! 14-6.

Web **Extra!** **Web Extra! 14-6 at crimtoday.com**

In February 2000, the President's Working Group on Unlawful Conduct on the Internet released a report entitled *The Electronic Frontier: The Challenge of Unlawful Conduct Involving the Use of the Internet.*[58] The group reported that "similar to the technologies that have preceded it, the Internet provides a new tool for wrongdoers to commit crimes, such as fraud, the sale or distribution of child pornography, the sale of guns or drugs or other regulated substances without regulatory protections, or the unlawful distribution of computer software or other creative material protected by intellectual property rights. In the most extreme circumstances, cyberstalking and other criminal conduct involving the Internet can lead to physical violence, abductions, and molestation." Some criminal activities, the group observed, "employ both the product delivery and communications features of the Internet." Pedophiles, for example, "may use the Internet's file transfer utilities to distribute and receive child pornography, and use its communications features to make contact with children."

The group said that "although the precise extent of unlawful conduct involving the use of computers is unclear, the rapid growth of the Internet and e-commerce has made such unlawful conduct a critical priority for legislators, policymakers, industry, and law enforcement agencies." One reason is the Internet's potential to reach vast audiences easily, meaning that the potential scale of unlawful conduct is often much wider in cyberspace than in the real world.

Significantly, said the report's authors, cybercriminals are no longer hampered by the existence of national or international boundaries because information and property can be easily transmitted through communications and data networks. As a result, a criminal no longer needs to be at the actual scene of the crime (or anywhere nearby) to prey on his or her victims. A computer server running a Web page designed to defraud senior citizens, for example, might be located in Thailand, and victims of the scam could be scattered throughout the world. A child pornographer might distribute photographs or videos via e-mail making its way through the communications networks of several countries before reaching the intended recipients. Likewise, evidence of a crime can be stored at a remote location, either for the purpose of concealing the crime from law enforcement and others or simply because of the design of the network. To clarify its point about jurisdictional issues, the working group gave this example: "A cyber-stalker in Brooklyn, New York, may send a threatening e-mail to a person in Manhattan. If the stalker routes his communication through Argentina, France, and Norway before reaching his victim, the New York Police Department may have to get assistance from the Office of International Affairs at the Department of Justice in Washington, D.C., which, in turn, may have to get assistance from law enforcement in (say) Buenos Aires, Paris, and Oslo just to learn that the suspect is in New York." In this example, the working group points out, the perpetrator needs no passport and passes through no checkpoints as he commits his crime, while law enforcement agencies are burdened with cumbersome mechanisms for international cooperation—mechanisms that often derail or slow investigations. Because the gathering of information in other jurisdictions and internationally will be crucial to investigating and prosecuting cybercrimes, the President's Working Group concluded that "all levels of government will need to develop concrete and reliable mechanisms for cooperating with each other." Read the entire text of *The Electronic Frontier* via Web Extra! 14-7.

Web Extra! 14-7 at crimtoday.com

TECHNOLOGY IN THE FIGHT AGAINST CRIME

Technology is a double-edged sword. On the one hand, it arms evildoers with potent new weapons of crime commission, while on the other it provides police agencies and criminal justice personnel with powerful tools useful in the battle against crime. Law enforcement capabilities and criminally useful or evasive technologies commonly leapfrog one another. Consider, for example, the relatively simple case of traffic radar, which has gone through an elaborate technological evolution from early "always-on" units through trigger-operated radar devices to today's sophisticated laser speed-measuring apparatus. Each change was an attempt by enforcement agencies to keep a step ahead of increasingly sophisticated radar-detection devices marketed to drivers everywhere. Although cutting-edge laser speed units are invisible to most radar detectors, laser radar detectors *do* exist. Their usefulness, however, is open to debate because they generally alert the speeding driver too late. On the other hand, radar-jamming devices are

now increasingly used by people who are apparently intent on breaking speed limit laws, and laser jammers are also available. Not to be outdone, suppliers to law enforcement agencies have created radar-detector detectors which are used by authorities in states where radar detectors have been outlawed.[59]

Other than traffic radar, the most potent technology in law enforcement service today includes computer databases of known offenders (and public access to sex offender databases), machine-based expert systems, cellular communications, electronic eavesdropping, DNA analysis, and less-than-lethal weapons. Recent advances, for example, in transponder-based automated vehicle location (AVL) systems now use patrol car–based transmitters in tandem with orbiting satellites to pinpoint police vehicle locations to within 50 feet. Dispatchers making use of such information can better allocate the resources available on a given shift and are able to substantially reduce police response times in crisis situations. Similarly, chip-based transponders are now being installed in private vehicles to deter thieves and to help trace stolen automobiles.

Computer-aided dispatch (CAD) systems, representing yet another area of advanced crime-fighting technology, are becoming increasingly sophisticated. In jurisdictions where CAD systems function, police dispatchers are prompted by computers for important information which allows them to distinguish one place from another (such as the location of a particular McDonald's restaurant) within a city. CAD systems can also quickly provide information about how often officers have been called to a given site and can tell responding officers what they might expect to find based on past calls from that location. As one writer enticingly states, "Imagine this response from a 911 call-taker: 'Yes, Ms. Smith, we are aware that beer-drinking youths at the corner of Hollywood and Vine have been a problem over the past six weeks, and in fact, we've responded seven times to requests to disperse them. As soon as one of our patrol cars frees up on a robbery call, I'll be sure that it goes over to disperse the group. And by the way, we are unaware of any serious crimes that can be attributed to these youths. But please feel free to call us immediately if you observe any criminal activities.' "[60] The same software that facilitates such a response will routinely inform responding officers about police experience with the suspects, provide background checks as a matter of course, tell whether they are likely to find registered guns at the address, and relay information about outstanding warrants on anyone who lives there. It can also inform dispatchers when responding officers do not call back after a statistically determined period of time for that type of call—alerting dispatchers to potential threats to officer safety.

Other even more innovative crime-fighting technologies are on the horizon. The "Spiderman snare," for example, now being tested for its usefulness in incapacitating fleeing suspects, is a fine net 16 feet in diameter.

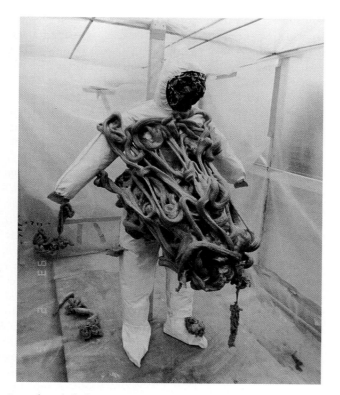

Less-than-lethal weapons are undergoing review by law enforcement agencies nationwide. Here a test dummy is encased in incapacitating polyester slime. When might such weapons be used? *Sandia National Laboratories*

Compressed into a small shotgun-like shell, the net has small weights at its circumference and is designed to wrap itself around a target when fired. The snare's impact is harmless, and test subjects report being able to watch with open eyes as the net wraps around them. Similarly, a disco-like strobe light which quickly disorients human targets is on the drawing board. The special frequency light emitted by the strobe rapidly causes intense dizziness, leaving subjects unable to resist cuffing and arrest. Operators wear special glasses designed to counter the influence of the light. Finally, a form of electronic warfare may be on the verge of being launched against speeders driving today's high-tech computer-equipped cars. Because high-speed chases pose a substantial danger to the public, scientists have developed an aimed electromagnetic pulsing device that can be used to temporarily disable a vehicle's electrical system, causing the engine to stall. The prototype is said to be safe enough to use on vehicles driven by pacemaker-equipped drivers.

As new technologies are developed, their potential usefulness in law enforcement activities is evaluated by the FBI, the National Institute of Justice (NIJ), and other agencies. NIJ's Technology Assessment Program (TAP) focuses on four areas of advancing technology: protective equipment, such as "bulletproof" vests and other body armor; forensic sciences, including the applicability of advances in DNA technology; transportation and weapons, such as electronic "stun guns" and other new less-than-lethal weapons; and communications and electronics, including computer security, electronic eavesdropping, and so on. Other groups, such as the National Computer Security Association, the American Cryptography Association, and the American Society for Industrial Security, bring more specialized high-tech expertise to the private security and public law enforcement professions.

DNA Fingerprinting

On January 16, 2001, Christopher Ochoa, 34, was released from a Texas prison after serving 13 years for a murder he did not commit.[61] Ochoa had confessed to the rape and murder of 20-year-old Nancy DePriest at a Pizza Hut in Austin in 1988. Although Ochoa later said he had been coerced by homicide detectives into confessing, no one believed him. A decade after he began serving a life sentence, however, law students at the Wisconsin Innocence Project at the University of Wisconsin–Madison took an interest in his case. They studied surviving information and concluded that DNA evidence conclusively proved that someone else killed DePriest. The students, led by their law professor, took the evidence to state District Judge Bob Perkins, who called the case "a fundamental miscarriage of justice" and ordered Ochoa set free. According to authorities, evidence of DePriest's murder now points to Texas inmate Achim Joseph Marino, who confessed to her murder in 1996 following a religious conversion. Marino, who is currently serving three life sentences for other crimes, has provided investigators with the gun and handcuffs used to commit the crime. As this book goes to press, the law students involved in the case have reportedly matched DNA samples taken from mouth swabs of Marino with the DNA found in semen taken from the victim's body. Without the technology known as **DNA profiling** (or, as it is commonly called, **DNA fingerprinting**), Ochoa would still be in prison—and DePriest's real killer would be unknown.

A person's genetic code is contained in his or her DNA (deoxyribonucleic acid), whose composition is unique to each individual, except in the case of identical twins. DNA samples can be taken from blood, hair, semen, saliva, or even small flakes of skin left at the scene of a crime. In cases of rape, for example, semen or pubic hairs left behind by the perpetrator and removed from the victim or gathered at the scene can provide the DNA evidence necessary for identifying a suspect. In cases of murder, victims sometimes fight with their attackers, retaining small bits of the killer's skin under their fingernails—thereby providing a tissue sample useful in DNA analysis.

After processing, DNA profiles appear like bar codes on film negatives. These codes can exonerate a suspect in the eyes of expert analysts—or provide nearly irrefutable evidence of guilt.

DNA evidence is long lasting; fossilized DNA is now being used to reconstruct genetic maps of long-extinct plant and animal species. Although DNA analysis is theoretically possible using only a single cell, most reputable DNA laboratories require a considerably greater quantity of material to conduct an effective analysis. That, however, may soon change. Using a technique called "polymerase chain-reaction technology," a Nobel Prize–winning technique, minute strands of DNA can be effectively amplified so that even the identity of a person taking a single puff from a cigarette can be accurately established. Although the cost and complexity of such enhancement are still prohibitive, technological advances are expected to bring the technique within the range of forensic analysts within a decade.

The National Research Council calls DNA profiling "a highly reliable forensic tool"[62] but admits that it is not infallible. Although obvious differences in scrutinized DNA samples can easily eliminate a suspect, testing provides less certainty with positive identification. Human error in conducting the tests is perhaps the greatest threat to reliable results. As of this writing, at least 20 states and the federal government generally accept DNA evidence in criminal trials. Other jurisdictions, including California, are less clear in their recognition of DNA testing, and trial judges in those states may offhandedly exclude the use of such evidence when experts disagree as to its validity.

In 1993, the U.S. Supreme Court, in the civil case of **Daubert** v. **Merrell Dow Pharmaceuticals, Inc.,**[63] revised the criteria for the admissibility of scientific evidence by rejecting a previous admissibility standard established in the 1923 case of **Frye** v. **United States.**[64] The *Daubert* Court ruled that the older *Frye* standard requiring "general acceptance" of a test or procedure by the relevant scientific community "is not a necessary precondition to the admissibility of scientific evidence." The baseline rule for the admissibility of scientific evidence, said the Court, is established by Rule 402 of the *Federal Rules of Evidence,* which was published after *Frye* and supersedes it. Rule 402 says that in a trial, "all relevant evidence is admissible, except as otherwise provided by the Constitution of the United States, by Act of Congress, by these Rules, or by other rules prescribed by the Supreme Court pursuant to statutory authority." The Court went on to say that although "the *Frye* test was displaced by the Rules of Evidence [that] does not mean . . . that the Rules themselves place no limits on the admissibility of purportedly scientific evidence. Nor is the trial judge disabled from screening such evidence. To the contrary, under the Rules the trial judge must ensure that any and all scientific testimony or evidence admitted is not only relevant, but reliable." The real test for the admissibility of scientific expert testimony, said the Court, is for the trial judge to decide "at the outset . . . whether the expert is proposing to testify to (1) scientific knowledge that (2) will assist the trier of fact to understand or determine a fact in issue." The Court concluded that the task of the trial judge is one of "ensuring

that an expert's testimony both rests on a reliable foundation and is relevant to the task at hand. Pertinent evidence based on scientifically valid principles," said the Court, "will satisfy those demands."

The plaintiffs in *Daubert* did not argue the merits of DNA testing but claimed instead that the drug Bendectin caused birth defects. Nonetheless, the **Daubert standard** eased the criteria for the introduction of scientific evidence at both civil and criminal trials—and effectively cleared the way for the use of DNA evidence in the courtroom.[65] Specifically, the *Daubert* Court found that the following factors may be used to determine whether any form of scientific evidence is reliable:

■ Whether it has been subjected to testing
■ Whether it has been subjected to peer review
■ Known or potential rates of error
■ The existence of standards controlling application of the techniques involved

One observer, discussing the general quality of DNA identification methods, notes, "The challenges today are no longer technical; instead they lie in taking the technology and building a meaningful legal infrastructure around it."[66] In other words, it appears to be only a matter of time until DNA evidence will be accepted throughout jurisdictions nationwide (and, probably, worldwide). Once that occurs, it is likely that DNA databases, similar in purpose to today's widely used fingerprint archives, will be established in individual states and at the national level. Today, a number of states and the federal government (through the FBI laboratory) have begun building digitized forensic DNA databases, and in 1998 the FBI announced that its National DNA Index System (NDIS) had begun operation.[67] NDIS enables public forensic laboratories throughout the United States to exchange and compare DNA profiles electronically, thereby linking unsolved serial violent crimes to each other and to known offenders. By June 1998, all 50 states had passed legislation requiring convicted offenders to provide samples for DNA databasing, and all states have been invited to participate in NDIS. The federal DNA Identification Act of 1994[68] authorizes the FBI to establish DNA indexes for (1) offenders convicted of crimes, (2) samples recovered from crime scenes, and (3) samples recovered from unidentified human remains. Although at this point there has been no coordination between the federally funded multibillion-dollar Human Genome Initiative and forensic DNA programs, future collaboration between the two could lead to explosive growth in the use of human DNA in criminal case processing.

In 1995, British police, operating under the aegis of a new nationwide crime bill, became the first national police force in the world to begin routine collection of DNA samples from anyone involved in a "recordable" offense (a serious crime).[69] As scientific techniques continue to be refined, it appears likely that genetic profiling will become one of the

CRIME IN THE NEWS
National DNA Database Solves Its First Crime

Police have linked a dead Florida man's DNA to eight unsolved rapes in Washington in an investigation that marks the first time police have relied solely on a new national DNA database to solve a crime.

Using the months-old National DNA Index System, sheriff's deputies from Jacksonville County, Fla., connected the DNA of Leon Dundas, 38, to serial rapes in both Washington and Jacksonville.

The FBI unveiled the National DNA Index System last October. So far, 14 states have joined the database, which holds about 180,000 DNA samples. The Dundas case represents the first "cold hit" using the new system in which police solved a crime without any other investigative leads.

Dundas was slain this past March in Jacksonville.

SUSPECT'S DEATH PROVIDES DNA SAMPLE

Police have no suspects or motives for Dundas' death. But investigators looking into the killing remembered that Dundas had been questioned last year about several rapes, said Rick Seibler, the chief of detectives for the Jacksonville County Sheriff's Department.

Last year, Dundas refused to cooperate with the rape investigation and refused to give a blood sample. But this March, with Dundas' body lying in the medical examiner's office, deputies took a blood sample and forwarded it to the Florida Department of Law Enforcement's DNA lab.

Florida investigators compared Dundas' DNA sample with DNA stored in the National DNA Index System and confirmed a match earlier this month between Dundas' DNA and DNA evidence taken from a rape victim in Washington.

The FBI, which maintains both the National DNA Index System and DNA evidence for the Washington Police Department, then entered DNA evidence from several more unsolved rapes committed in Southeast Washington.

DNA WAS THE ONLY SOLID EVIDENCE

Dundas' DNA matched genetic evidence taken from seven more attacks, all committed in late 1997 and early 1998, said Cmdr. Winston Robinson, who heads the police in the area.

Dundas' DNA also matched DNA evidence taken from three rape victims in Jacksonville.

Police in Washington said without the DNA connection they probably would never have identified Dundas, who had no history of violent crime.

"Other than the DNA, we had nothing to go on," Robinson said. "We know in some of the rapes the description given was very similar. That's all we had to go on. We had no idea it involved eight rapes."

36 STATES DON'T PARTICIPATE

The FBI is hoping the other 36 states will soon meet the mandatory lab and technology standards and join the database.

"As you see more and more states begin to participate and more profiles entered in the database, I think quite naturally, you'll see an increased number of cases being solved," said Paul Bresson, an FBI spokesman.

The promise of DNA matches from across the country has led several jurisdictions to propose expanding the pool of DNA samples. Howard Safir, the commissioner of the New York Police Department, has proposed taking DNA samples from all criminal suspects. Last year, Louisiana became the first state to pass a law mandating DNA samples from people arrested for felonies.

"GREATEST ADVENT SINCE FINGERPRINTING"

But there are still barriers to widespread genetic testing. DNA labs across the country already suffer from severe backlogs, and observers have warned that taking DNA evidence from suspects may hinder the ability of crime labs to process material taken from crime scenes.

In Washington, the FBI had processed DNA evidence from only one of the eight rape cases eventually linked to Dundas. The FBI pulled the others from a backlog of crime scene DNA waiting to be entered into the national database, Bresson said.

"The system works in two halves. You've got your offenders, which would have to include both arrestees and offenders, and your crime-scene half," said Christopher Asplen, the executive director of the National Commission on the Future of DNA Evidence. Attorney General Janet Reno has charged Asplen's group with making recommendations on the collection and use of DNA evidence.

"If your labs don't have the resources to devote to doing the crime scene, nonsuspect samples, what's the point of doing the arrestees?" Asplen added.

Still, the system that already exists is winning praise from law enforcers after the Dundas case.

"I think this is probably the greatest advent since fingerprinting," Robinson said. "This puts us right at the edge of apprehending more criminals, especially the types of criminals that commit this kind of crime."

DNA HAS HELPED BEFORE

While Dundas' case represents the first cold case using the new national databases, other cold hits have been made using DNA evidence. In one instance, luck played the part that has now been supplanted by the national database. In 1992, five prostitutes were stabbed to death in a crack house in Oklahoma City. Blood from a sixth person was noticed at the crime scene but didn't match the DNA of any known suspects in Oklahoma City.

The case would have ended there, but a chemist from the Oklahoma crime lab

(continued on the next page)

(continued from previous page)

took the DNA profile with him to California, where he was receiving training. The California state DNA lab matched the sixth person's DNA to Danny Hooks, whose DNA had been entered into California's database because of a 1988 rape conviction.

"When you don't have a suspect, you don't necessarily know where to go, but once you have a suspect, you can start building a case," said Mike Van Winkle, a spokesman for the California Department of Justice.

Hooks was arrested in San Jose, Calif., extradited to Oklahoma, and convicted and sentenced to death.

"It appears Mr. Hooks left the area after committing the homicide, so we weren't able to get a sample to match for him," said Sgt. Chris Cunningham, a spokesman for the Oklahoma City Police Department.

"But fortunately, as things evolved and things changed, people started keeping a database and keeping records, and we were able to use that," he said. "It definitely was a lot of hard work, and luck did play into it."

Source: Hans H. Chen, "National DNA Database Solves Its First Crime," APB News, July 22, 1999. Reprinted with permission.

Former football superstar O. J. Simpson. DNA evidence played a central role in Simpson's double-murder trial. What can DNA evidence tell investigators? *Los Angeles Police Department*

most significant crime-fighting technologies of the twenty-first century. In the words of one forensics expert, "Genetic profiling—the use of biotechnology to identify the unique characteristics of an individual's DNA—is about to become as prevalent as the Breathalyzer and more important than the fingerprint."[70]

In 1996, the National Institute of Justice released the most comprehensive report to date on the applicability of DNA testing to criminal case processing. The report, entitled *Convicted by Juries, Exonerated by Science,* called DNA testing "the most important technological breakthrough of twentieth-century forensic science" and provided a detailed review of 28 cases in which postconviction DNA evidence exonerated defendants who had been sentenced to lengthy prison terms.[71] The 28 cases were selected on the basis of a detailed examination of records which indicated that the convicted defendants might have actually been innocent. The men in the study had served, on average, seven years in prison, and most had been tried and sentenced prior to the widespread availability of reliable DNA testing.

The report concluded, "Momentum is growing, spurred in part by the public's education from the Simpson trial, for DNA testing in criminal cases. Juries may begin to question cases where the prosecutor does not offer 'conclusive' DNA test results if the evidence is available for testing. More defense attorneys in court-appointed cases may file motions for DNA testing and request the State to pay for the tests."[72]

Computers as Crime-Fighting Tools

The widespread use of computers and computer applications in a diversity of professions has been one of the most far-reaching social phenomena of recent years. Computers are now used to keep records of every imaginable sort, from point-of-sale contacts to inventory maintenance and production schedules. Even organized criminal groups have been known to use computers to record criminal transactions. Computers assist in the design of new technologies and aid in the assignment of resources to problem areas. Police departments, prisons, and courts now commonly employ computer software to schedule facilities and personnel; to keep track of defendants, witnesses, and cases; and to keep account of budgetary matters.

Computers also connect people. The world's largest computer network, the Internet, now contains a number of law- and law enforcement–oriented newsgroups and also provides access to United Nations and worldwide crime data through its link to the United Nations Criminal Justice Information Network. Other computer services, such as CompuServe and America Online, provide access to security information and to software useful in law enforcement administration. Specialized World Wide Web sites, such as the Society of Police Futurists International's home page, the International Association of Chiefs of Police site, and the SEARCH Group's file server, link law enforcement professionals and criminologists throughout the country.

Other innovative computer technologies facilitate the work of enforcement agents. Among them are automated fingerprint identification systems, or AFISs (often with interstate and even international links), computerized crime scene simulations and reenacts, expert systems, and online clearinghouses containing data on criminal activity and on offenders. AFIS, a technology developed some years ago by Hewlett-Packard and Cogent Systems, allows investigators to complete in a matter of minutes what would otherwise consume weeks or months of work manually matching a suspect's fingerprints against stored records. AFIS computers are able to compare and eliminate from consideration 1,200 fingerprints per second, sometimes leading to the identification of a suspect in a short time. New "Live-Scan" technology, developed jointly by IBM and Identix, allows for the easy inkless digitizing of fingerprints from live suspects. In like manner, the Bureau of Alcohol, Tobacco, and Firearms' new Bulletproof software takes a 360-degree picture of a bullet's ballistic characteristics and then compares it with others stored in a database to isolate a small universe of potential matches.

Once crime-related information or profiles of criminal offenders have been generated, they are typically stored in a database and often made accessible to law enforcement agencies at other sites. Some of today's most widely used online criminal information services are the FBI's National Crime Information Center, the Violent Criminal Apprehension Program, and METAPOL—an information-sharing network run by the Police Executive Research Forum. Other specialized database programs now track inner-city gang activity and gang membership, contain information on known sexual predators, and describe missing children.

One leader in the development of law enforcement services is the Criminal Justice Information Services Division (CJISD) of the FBI. CJISD was created in 1993 to provide state-of-the-art information services to the justice community and to assist in the future development of such services. One contemporary law enforcement–oriented software program, called COPS (for Criminal Offender Profiling System), allows for the desktop integration of digitized mug shots, videotaped images, computerized fingerprint data, and text-based information such as criminal records—all in one automated file folder.

PC radios provide another high-tech weapon in the war on crime. These devices—which are essentially combinations of laptop computers and police radios—were initially tested by the Baltimore, Maryland, police department. Mobile data terminals placed in police cars are proving useful in the apprehension of both traffic violators and other more serious offenders. Officers use PC radios to (1) obtain motor vehicle information, (2) get detailed information when answering a call, and (3) report incidents either by saving data on disk or by transmitting it to other locations, such as police headquarters. PC radios have also helped befuddle drug dealers who themselves routinely use police scanners to keep abreast of enforcement activities. The digitized transmissions of such devices consist of machine code that cannot be easily read by drug dealers or other criminals trying to outguess the police.

Forensic expert systems, representing yet another computerized law enforcement technology, deploy machine-based artificial intelligence to draw conclusions and to make recommendations to investigators and others interested in solving problems related to crime and its commission. **Expert systems**, developed by professional "knowledge engineers" who work with "knowledge bases" and computer software called "inference engines," attempt to duplicate the decision-making processes used by skilled investigators in the analysis of evidence and in the recognition of patterns which such evidence might represent. One such system is currently being perfected by the FBI's National Center for the Analysis of Violent Crime (NCAVC). The NCAVC expert system attempts to profile serial killers by matching clues left at a crime scene with individual personality characteristics. While the NCAVC system is becoming increasingly sophisticated, it has not yet replaced human investigators. As one FBI developer puts it, "There is certainly no possibility that the system we are devising will ever replace skilled human profilers. Rather, the system will function as a profiler's assistant or consultant."[73]

Finally, a number of specialized computer software programs, such as ImAger, which is produced by Face Software, Inc., and Compusketch, a product of Visatex Corporation, assist police artists in rendering composite images of suspects and missing victims.

COMBATING COMPUTER CRIME

In 1982, sales of information security products to private companies and government agencies totaled only $51 million. By 1997, expenditures exceeded $425 million. Experts predict that the world wide market for information security products will total $17 billion in 2003.[74]

Gadgets, however, are not enough. Any effective program intended to secure a company or business operation against the threat of high-tech crime must be built on a realistic threat analysis. **Threat analysis**, sometimes called "risk analysis," involves a complete and thorough assessment of the kinds of perils facing an organization. Some risks, such as floods, tornadoes, hurricanes, and earthquakes, arise from natural events and are often unpredictable. Others, including fire, electrical outages, and disruptions in public services, may be of human origin—but equally difficult to presage. Theft, employee sabotage, and terrorist attacks constitute yet another category of risk—those brought about by intentional human intervention. Responses to unpredictable threats can nonetheless be planned, and strategies for dealing with almost any kind of risk can be implemented. Unless and until an organization adequately assesses the threats to its continuing operation, however, it will be unable to formulate a plan to deal effectively with such risks. Hence threat analysis is a must for businesses and other organizations preparing to meet the many diverse challenges of today's world.

Once specific threats are identified, strategies tailored to dealing with them can be introduced. For example, one powerful tool useful in identifying instances of computer crime when they occur is the audit trail. Properly defined, an **audit trail** is "a sequential record of system activities that enables auditors to reconstruct, review, and examine the sequence of states and activities surrounding each event in one or more related transactions from inception to output of final results back to inception."[75] In other words, audit trails, which (once implemented) are recorded in some form of computer memory, trace and record the activities of computer operators and facilitate the apprehension of computer criminals.

Unfortunately, although most large companies and financial institutions have fairly extensive computer-security programs, few small businesses, schools, hospitals, and individuals have any real understanding of the need for security in the use of their computers. "What is surprising about computer crime," says computer-security expert Kenneth Rosenblatt, "is how little is being done to deter it: industry will not beef up security, the police are not equipped to catch electronic thieves, and judges do not hand down the kind of sentences that will impress would-be computer criminals. New strategies are urgently needed."[76]

Police Investigation of Computer Crime

Unfortunately, even with new laws for backup, few police departments are prepared with either the time or the qualified personnel to effectively investigate crimes committed by computer criminals. When it comes to computer-crime investigations, one technology expert concludes, "Police departments are simply unsuited to the task."[77] Although specialized computer-crime units have been created in some jurisdictions, they are often poorly funded and seriously understaffed. The cities of Los Angeles, Philadelphia, and Baltimore now have field units, as do the Illinois State Police, the Tarrant County (Texas) District Attorney's Office, the Arizona State Attorney General's Office, and the Santa Clara County (California) District Attorney's Office.

Most state and local police departments, however, have no specialized computer-crime units. Nor do they have personnel skilled in the investigation of such crimes. Most officers know little about tracing the activities of computer criminals, and some police investigators find it difficult to understand how a crime can actually have occurred when nothing at the scene appears to be missing or damaged. Horror stories of botched police investigations are plentiful. They include tales of officers standing by while high-tech offenders perform seemingly innocuous activities that destroy evidence, of seized floppy disks allowed to bake in the sun on the dashboards of police vehi-

cles, and of the loss of evidence stored on magnetic media due to exposure to police clipboards and evidence lockers containing magnets.

Police departments also sometimes intentionally avoid computer-crime investigations because they may be complex and demanding. The amount of time and money spent on computer-crime investigations, it is often felt, could better be spent elsewhere. It is not unusual for these investigations to cross state lines and to involve a number of telecommunications companies and other services. Additionally, investigators who spend a lot of time on crimes involving computers tend to not be promoted as readily as their more glamorous counterparts in the homicide and property crime divisions, and personnel who are truly skilled in computer applications are apt to take jobs with private industries where pay scales are far higher than in police work. As a consequence of these considerations and others, many police departments and the investigators who staff them frequently accord computer crime a low priority, focusing instead on highly visible offenses, such as murder and rape, and seeing computer-crime victims as too wealthy to be seriously affected by the crimes they experience.

A decade ago, one expert summed up the situation this way: "Because computer crime is too much for traditional law enforcement to handle, the bulk of computer offenses go unpunished. Probably fewer than 250 cases [were] prosecuted in the United States during the [1980s]. At this rate, prosecutions are too rare to deter computer crime. If an offender is convicted, the usual penalties are also not much of a deterrent."[78]

The situation is changing, however, thanks to federal intervention. In 1992, the FBI formed a National Computer Crime Squad (NCCS)[79] to investigate violations of the federal Computer Fraud and Abuse Act of 1984[80] and other federal computer crime laws. Since that time, most of the FBI's larger offices have established their own computer-crime squads to conduct high-tech investigations in the areas they serve. The FBI's Washington Field Office currently houses the agency's Infrastructure Protection and Computer Intrusion Squad (IPCIS). IPCIS is responsible for investigating unauthorized intrusions into major computer networks belonging to telecommunications providers, private corporations, U.S. government agencies, and public and private educational facilities.[81] The squad also investigates the illegal interception of signals (especially cable and satellite signal theft) and the infringement of copyright laws related to software. Visit IPCIS via Web Extra! 14-8.

Web Extra! 14-8 at crimtoday.com

A similar agency, the Computer Crime and Intellectual Property Section within the Criminal Division of the U.S. Department of Justice (DOJ), began in 1991 as the DOJ's

Computer Crime Unit. The CCIPS staff consists of about two dozen lawyers who focus exclusively on the issues raised by computer and intellectual property crime. CCIPS staffers work closely on computer-crime cases with Assistant U.S. Attorneys known as "computer and telecommunications co-ordinators" in U.S. Attorney's Offices around the country.[82] CCIPS attorneys take a leading role in litigating some computer crime and intellectual property investigations and a co-ordinating role in some national investigations. Section attorneys advise federal prosecutors and law enforcement agents, comment upon and propose legislation, coordinate international efforts to combat computer crime, litigate cases, and train federal law enforcement groups. Visit CCIPS via Web Extra! 14-9.

 Web Extra! 14-9 at crimtoday.com

One of the first large-scale federal computer-crime operations took place in 1997, when FBI agents raided the homes and offices of about a dozen computer bulletin board system operators and Webmasters suspected of pirating software in eight cities across the country. The operation, code-named Cyber Strike, resulted from NCCS monitoring of Internet Relay Chat channels and file transfers over the Internet.[83]

Automated monitoring of network traffic is an area of considerable interest to law enforcement officials. One network "sniffer" created by the FBI is called **Carnivore**. Carnivore (also known as "Omnivore") is a network diagnostic tool that is capable of assisting in criminal investigations by monitoring and capturing large amounts of Internet traffic. If Carnivore survives the right-to-privacy challenges now being raised, it will be installed by FBI agents in Internet service provider data centers when the need arises to monitor the electronic communications of individuals suspected of federal crimes like terrorism. Carnivore snoops essentially all data flowing through the network and saves the bits that fit a specific profile—e-mail sent or received from a particular user name, for example, or all data sent to Web sites from a particular address. Carnivore can theoretically scan millions of e-mail messages per second, processing as much as six gigabytes (6,000 megabytes) of data every hour. Although the data of many innocent people may flow through the Carnivore system, the FBI claims that their privacy will not be compromised.[84]

As this book goes to press, Justice Department officials have said that they will soon change Carnivore's name. Officials note that the name makes the program sound far more threatening to legitimate privacy interests than it actually is.[85] Keep up-to-date with the latest information on Carnivore at Web Extra! 14-10.

 Web Extra! 14-10 at crimtoday.com

Dealing with Computer Criminals

While any effective policy for dealing with computer and high-tech crime must recognize the issues associated with personal freedoms and individual rights in the information age, a second aspect of effective policy necessarily relates to crime control. How can high-tech criminals be deterred? If they succeed in committing criminal acts, how can they be reformed? Kenneth Rosenblatt, who focused on computer crimes during his work as a California district attorney, suggests three sanctions that he feels would be especially effective in deterring high-tech offenders:[86]

- Confiscating equipment used to commit a computer crime
- Limiting the offender's use of computers
- Restricting the offender's freedom to accept jobs involving computers

Such penalties, says Rosenblatt, could be supplemented by a few days or weeks in a county jail, with longer periods of incarceration applicable in serious cases. "In my experience," Rosenblatt adds, "one of the best ways to hurt computer offenders, especially young hackers, is to take away their toys."[87]

POLICY ISSUES: PERSONAL FREEDOMS IN THE INFORMATION AGE

The continued development of telecommunications resources has led not only to concerns about security and data integrity, but also to an expanding interest in privacy, free speech, and personal freedoms. While the First and Fourth Amendments of the Constitution guarantee each of us freedom of speech and security in our "persons, houses, papers, and effects, against unreasonable searches and seizures," it is understandably silent on the subject of electronic documents and advanced forms of communication facilitated by technologies which did not exist at the time of the Constitutional Convention.

Within the context of contemporary society we are left to ask, "What is speech? What are papers?" Do electronic communications qualify for protection under the First Amendment, as does the spoken word? In an era when most houses are wired for telephones and many support data links that extend well beyond voice capabilities, it becomes necessary to ask what constitutes one's "speech" or one's "home." What, exactly, is speech? Does electronic mail qualify as speech? Where does the concept of a home begin and end for purposes of constitutional guarantees? Do activities within the home that can be accessed from without (as when a computer Web site is run out of a

THEORY VERSUS REALITY
Press Release Announcing the Formation of the Electronic Frontier Foundation

In 1990, the Electronic Frontier Foundation (EFF) came into being. What follows are excerpts from the original press release announcing formation of the EFF.

FOR IMMEDIATE RELEASE

NEW FOUNDATION ESTABLISHED TO ENCOURAGE COMPUTER-BASED COMMUNICATIONS POLICIES

Washington, D.C., July 10, 1990—Mitchell D. Kapor, founder of Lotus Development Corporation and ON Technology, today announced that he, along with colleague John Perry Barlow, has established a foundation to address social and legal issues arising from the impact on society of the increasingly pervasive use of computers as a means of communication and information distribution. The Electronic Frontier Foundation (EFF) will support and engage in public education on current and future developments in computer-based and telecommunications me-

dia. In addition, it will support litigation in the public interest to preserve, protect and extend First Amendment rights within the realm of computing and telecommunications technology.

Initial funding for the Foundation comes from private contributions by Kapor and Steve Wozniak, co-founder of Apple Computer, Inc. The Foundation expects to actively raise contributions from a wide constituency.

Source: The Electronic Frontier Foundation.

home) fall under the same constitutional guarantees as a private conversation held within the physical confines of a house?

These and questions like them will be debated for years to come. In 1990, however, concerned individuals banded together to form the Electronic Frontier Foundation, a citizens' group funded by private contributions that set for itself the task of actively assisting in refining notions of privacy and legality as they relate to telecommunications and other computer-based media. In the foundation's own words, "The Electronic Frontier Foundation (EFF) was founded in July of 1990 to ensure that the principles embodied in the Constitution and the Bill of Rights are protected as new communications technologies emerge. From the beginning, EFF has worked to shape our nation's communications infrastructure and the policies that govern it in order to maintain and enhance First Amendment, privacy and other democratic values. We believe that our overriding public goal must be the creation of Electronic Democracy."[88] As Mitch Kapor, EFF cofounder and former president of Lotus Development Corporation, explained, "It is becoming increasingly obvious that the rate of technology advancement in communications is far outpacing the establishment of appropriate cultural, legal and political frameworks to handle the issues that are arising."[89]

EFF, which also supports litigation in the public interest, has been an active supporter of the public advocacy group Computer Professionals for Social Responsibility (CPSR), based in Palo Alto, California. CPSR maintains a

Computing and Civil Liberties Project much in keeping with EFF's purpose. Initial EFF litigation focused on a request for full federal government disclosure of information regarding the seizure of Jackson Games's computer equipment. Jackson Games, an Austin-based game manufacturer, was a target in the U.S. Secret Service's Operation Sun Devil. In a second action, the foundation sought *amicus curiae* (friend of the court) status in a federal case against Craig Neidorf, a 20-year-old University of Missouri student who had been editor of the electronic newsletter *Phrack World News*. EFF also supported challenges to the Communications Decency Act that resulted in the 1997 Supreme Court ruling in *Reno* v. *ACLU*, which found key provisions of the act to be unconstitutional.

WHAT THE FUTURE HOLDS

Exactly what the future holds no one knows. Of one thing we can be sure, however. New technologies will continue to give rise to new forms of crime, and novel forms of criminality will engender innovative enforcement efforts. Although it is impossible to discuss every possible answer to crimes which take advantage of high technology for their commission, data encryption can serve as an example of the types of techniques which may find widespread use in the twenty-first century and beyond. **Data encryption** is the process by which information is encoded, making it unreadable to all but its intended recipients.

When he was vice president, Al Gore described the potential held by data-encryption technologies in these words: "Encryption is a law and order issue since it can be used by criminals to thwart wiretaps and avoid detection and prosecution. It also has huge strategic value. Encryption technology and cryptoanalysis turned the tide in the Pacific and elsewhere during World War II."[90]

Many forms of encryption are now in use. Most can be "broken" through the use of supercomputers tasked with uncovering the codes upon which they are built. A few years ago, an encryption technology consisting of a hardware-software combination known as the "clipper chip" was proposed by the federal government. The clipper chip was the product of the desire to maintain a balance between the American public's right to privacy and the need for law enforcement agencies to gather information on criminal activities. Clipper (also called "key escrow encryption") is a powerful encryption technology that scrambles communications, making them unintelligible without the required decryption code. To date, clipper encryption has never been compromised, and even the most powerful supercomputers have been unable to decode clipper-encrypted documents.

The government fears, however, that criminals could also use clipper technology to render their communications unintelligible to investigators. Original plans called for government agencies, and the government alone, to hold the electronic "key" needed to decode clipper messages. Under that proposal, the key would have been separated into two pieces to avoid unauthorized snooping by government agents. The "pieces" necessary for decryption of a particular message would have been joined when enforcement agents obtained search warrants, and then they would have been used to decode communications of a suspected criminal nature.[91]

Because clipper technology is so powerful, however, and because the proposed plan only allowed government agencies to hold needed decryption keys, critics charged that abuses of the technology could easily occur. Government officials, they said, might conduct unauthorized and secretive decryptions. Moreover, important information could be kept from the public by government officials bent on secrecy—so thoroughly encrypted that its very existence might be unknown. Under such circumstances, critics argued, the Freedom of Information Act would lose its power, and government agencies could enter an electronic underground inaccessible to the public and without the need for public accounting.

In 1996, in an effort to sidestep critics, Attorney General Janet Reno withdrew the suggestion that decoding technology should be held by the federal government. Instead, Reno proposed that decryption codes be kept by third parties independent of the government.[92] Such organizations, called "escrow companies," would turn over only the information needed to decrypt specific messages, and then only when decryption was legally authorized through a court-supervised investigation. By 1998, however, industry officials and citizens' groups were largely successful in their demands that high-tech companies be allowed to hold their own decryption keys, making them available to the government only when subpoenaed and forced to do so. In any event, the battle over encryption technologies may soon become moot because well-financed criminal organizations may one day develop their own encryption technologies rivaling any of those now available.

SUMMARY

High-technology crimes could dramatically change our understanding of crime. Illegal wire transfers of huge asset stores, nuclear subterfuge, and computer crime are emerging as novel forms of criminal enterprise. Some forms of high-tech crime hold dangers never before imagined. One incident of nuclear terrorism, for example, could destroy more property and claim more human lives than decades of traditional criminal activity.

The very nature of contemporary society dictates that crimes exploiting high technology will always be with us. It can only be hoped that enforcement technologies continue to keep abreast of technologies that serve criminal purposes. Unfortunately, however, no one is able to realistically assess the current extent of high-tech crime, let alone accurately imagine the form future high-tech crimes will take.

Efforts to control high-tech crime open a Pandora's box of issues related to individual rights in the face of criminal investigation and prosecution. Such issues extend from free speech considerations to guarantees of technological privacy in the midst of digital interconnectedness. As we begin the twenty-first century, it will be necessary for our society to strike an acceptable balance between constitutional guarantees of continued freedom of access to legitimate activities based on high technology, and enforcement initiatives which can deal effectively with the massive threat high-tech crimes represent.

DISCUSSION QUESTIONS

1. This book emphasizes a social problem versus social responsibility theme. Which perspective best explains the involvement of capable individuals in criminal activity necessitating high-tech skills? What is the best way to deal with such criminals?

2. What is the difference between high-tech crime and traditional forms of criminal activity? Will the high-tech crimes of today continue to be the high-tech crimes of tomorrow? Why or why not?

3. What forms of high-tech crime can you imagine which this chapter has not discussed? Describe each briefly.

4. Do you believe that high-tech crimes will eventually surpass the abilities of enforcement agents to prevent or solve them? Why or why not?

5. What different kinds of high-tech offenders can you imagine? What is the best way to deal with each type of offender? Give reasons for your answers.

WEB QUEST!

Since 1997, the 41-nation Council of Europe (http://www.coe.fr) has been working on a treaty to standardize cybercrime laws throughout Europe. The council has been especially concerned with laws against online pornography, hacking, fraud, viruses, and other Internet-related criminal activities and has been trying to develop common methods of securing evidence to track and prosecute criminals. If the council's proposed cybercrime treaty (known as the Draft Convention on Cybercrime) is adopted by the Assembly of the Council and then approved by member nations, it will require each member country to assume responsibility for developing legislation to ensure that individual offenders can be held liable for crimes outlined in the treaty.

While the treaty is expected to be ratified shortly after this book goes to press (you can reach the council's Treaty Office at http://conventions.coe.int to check the status of the treaty), many powerful groups have objected to a number of its provisions because of concerns over individual privacy. The need to balance individual privacy with the needs of law enforcement agencies continues to be a source of concern for council members. Some interest groups are especially concerned that giving European police agencies the power to monitor communications on the Internet, as provided for in the treaty, will lead to the identification of political dissidents and the persecution of minorities.

Access the council's cybercrime treaty on the Internet (at either http://conventions.coe.int/treaty/EN/cadreprojets.htm or http://cjcentral.com/cybertreaty/Net_treaty.htm). Review the treaty, and develop a personal statement encompassing your views on the treaty's provisions. What do you like about the treaty? What do you find problematic? Why? Submit your conclusions to your instructor if asked to do so.

LIBRARY EXTRAS!

The Library Extras! listed here complement the Web Extras! found throughout this chapter. Library Extras! may be accessed on the Web at crimtoday.com.

Library Extra! 14-1. David L. Carter, *Computer Crime Categories: How Techno-Criminals Operate* (online document: National Security Institute, no date).

Library Extra! 14-2. Edward Connors et al., *Convicted by Juries, Exonerated by Science: Case Studies in the Use of DNA Evidence to Establish Innocence after Trial* (Washington, D.C.: National Institute of Justice, 1996).

Library Extra! 14-3. Federal Bureau of Investigation, *Congressional Statement on Cybercrime* (Washington, D.C.:

U.S. Senate Committee on Judiciary; Subcommittee on Technology, Terrorism, and Government Information, April, 2000).

Library Extra! 14-4. Peter Grabosky, *Computer Crime: A Criminological Overview* (online document: Australian Institute of Criminology, April 2000).

Library Extra! 14-5. National Institute of Justice, *The Future of Forensic DNA Testing: Predictions of the Research and Development Working Group* (Washington, D.C.: U.S. Government Printing Office, November 2000).

Library Extra! 14-6. Software and Information Industry Association, *Report on Global Software Piracy 2000* (online document).

Library Extra! 14-7. President's Working Group on Unlawful Conduct on the Internet, *The Electronic Frontier: The Challenge of Unlawful Conduct Involving the Use of the Internet* (Washington, D.C.: U.S. Dept. of Justice, March 2000).

Library Extra! 14-8. U.S. Information Infrastructure Task Force, *Intellectual Property and the National Information Infrastructure: Report of the Working Group on Intellectual Property Rights* (Washington, D.C.: IITF, September 1995).

NOTES

[1] Alvin Toffler, *Powershift: Knowledge, Wealth, and Violence at the Edge of the 21st Century* (New York: Bantam, 1990), p. 255.

[2] David Noack, " 'Love Bug' Damage Worldwide: $10 Billion," APB News, May 8, 2000. Web posted at http://www.apbnews.com/newscenter/internetcrime/2000/05/08/lovebug_impact0508_01.html. Accessed January 22, 2001.

[3] MCA/Universal Pictures, 1992.

[4] Georgette Bennett, Crimewarps: The Future of Crime in America (New York: Anchor, 1987), p. xiii.

[5] Business Software Alliance, "Software Pirate Receives 2 1/2 Year Jail Sentence." Web posted at http://www.bsa.org/usa/press/newsreleases/2000-03-17.193.phtml. Accessed January 8, 2001.

[6] Robert Green, "CIA Warns of Nuclear Threat from Russian Gangs," Reuters wire service, June 27, 1994.

[7] "Fears Grow Over Russia's Nuclear Arsenal," Reuters NewMedia, February 7, 1997, 10:53 A.M. EST.

[8] Merck and Co., Inc., *Interim Report for the Period Ended June 30, 1994*, p. 4.

[9] Kenneth Rosenblatt, "Deterring Computer Crime," *Technology Review*, Vol. 93, No. 2 (February/March 1990), pp. 34–41.

[10] Ibid.

[11] Richard H. Baker, *The Computer Security Handbook* (Blue Ridge Summit, PA: TAB Books, 1985).

[12] David L. Carter, "Computer Crime Categories: How Techno-criminals Operate," *FBI Law Enforcement Bulletin*. Web posted at http://nsi.org/Library/Compsec/crimecom.html. Accessed January 11, 2001.

[13] Catherine H. Conly and J. Thomas McEwen, "Computer Crime," *NIJ Reports* (January/February 1990), p. 3.

[14] Computer Security Institute, *1999 Computer Crime Security Survey*. Web posted at http://www.gocsi.com/prelea990301.htm. Accessed January 10, 2001.

[15] Rosenblatt, "Deterring Computer Crime."

[16] Software and Information Industry Association, *Report on Global Software Piracy 2000*, p. 7. Web posted at http://www.siia.net/piracy/pubs/piracy2000.pdf.

[17] Ibid.

[18] Gary H. Anthes, "Software Pirates' Booty Topped $13B, Study Finds," *Computerworld*, January 6, 1997, p. 24.

[19] Stephen R. Purdy, "Protecting Your Telephone Systems against Dial-Tone Thieves," *Infosecurity News* (July/August 1993), p. 43.

[20] "Out Slicked," *Infosecurity News* (July/August 1993), p. 11.

[21] Paul Keegan, "High Tech Pirates Collecting Phone Calls," *USA Today*, September 23, 1994, p. 4A.

[22] Ibid.

[23] This and most other definitions related to computer crime in this chapter are taken from Donn B. Parker, *Computer Crime: Criminal Justice Resource Manual* (Washington, D.C.: National Institute of Justice, 1989).

[24] "Palm, Other Handheld Devices to Face Virus Threats," Reuters wire service, August 31, 2000. Web posted at http://www.bostonherald.com/business/technology/palm08312000.htm. Accessed January 11, 2001.

[25] "New 'Love Bug' Charges Sought," Associated Press wire service, September 5, 2000. Web posted at http://www.msnbc.com/news/455702.asp. Accessed January 12, 2001.

[26] Noack, " 'Love Bug' Damage Worldwide: $10 Billion."

[27] Public Law 106-160.

[28] Public Law 105-147.

[29] And as amended by the National Information Infrastructure Protection Act of 1996; Public Law 104-294.

[30] 18 U.S.C. 1029.

[31] As described in M. Gemignani, "Viruses and Computer Law," *Communications of the ACM*, Vol. 32 (June 1989), p. 669.

[32] Public Law 104-104, 110 Stat. 56.

[33] *Reno* v. *ACLU*, 521 U.S. 844 (1997).

[34] Texas Penal Code, Section 33.01.

[35] Virginia Criminal Code, Sections 18.2-152.2 through 18.2-152.7.

[36] Brian S. Akre, "Internet-Torture," Associated Press wire service, February 10, 1995.

[37] Ibid.

[38] Jim Schaefer and Maryanne George, "Internet User's Charges Dismissed-U.S. Criticized for Pursuing U-M Case," *Detroit Free Press* on-line, June 22, 1995.

[39] Parker, *Computer Crime.*

[40] Steve Miletich, no title, *Seattle Post-Intelligencer,* via Simon & Schuster NewsLink online, May 21, 1997.

[41] Paul Saffo, "Desperately Seeking Cyberspace," *Personal Computing,* May 1989, p. 247.

[42] Ibid.

[43] John Markoff, "Cyberpunks," *New York Times Upfront,* Vol. 132, No. 15 (March 27, 2000), pp. 10–14.

[44] J. Bloombecker, "A Security Manager's Guide to Hacking," *DATAPRO Reports on Information Security,* Report IS35-450-101, 1986.

[45] Marc Robins, "Case of the Ticked-Off Teens," *Infosecurity News* (July/August 1993), p. 48.

[46] For more information, see Ronald R. Thrasher, "Voice-Mail Fraud," *FBI Law Enforcement Bulletin* (July 1994), pp. 1–4.

[47] J. Maxfield, "Computer Bulletin Boards and the Hacker Problem," *EDPACS, the Electric Data Processing Audit, Control and Security Newsletter* (Arlington, Va.: Automation Training Center, October 1985).

[48] Percy Black, personal communication, 1991. As cited in M. E. Kabay, "Computer Crime: Hackers" (undated electronic manuscript).

[49] John Perry Barlow, "Crime and Puzzlement: In Advance of the Law on the Electronic Frontier," *Whole Earth Review,* Fall 1990, p. 44.

[50] As cited in ibid.

[51] "Computer Porn," *Time,* March 15, 1993, p. 22.

[52] Parker, *Computer Crime.*

[53] John Naisbitt, *Megatrends: Ten New Directions Transforming Our Lives* (New York: Warner, 1982), p. 36.

[54] Ibid.

[55] Al Gore, "Infrastructure for the Global Village," *Scientific American,* September 1991, p. 150.

[56] Gary H. Anthes, "White House Launches Cybershield," *Computerworld,* July 22, 1996, p. 29.

[57] M. J. Zuckerman, "Clinton to Get Cyberterror Plan," *USA Today,* October 9, 1997, p. 1A.

[58] The quotations attributed to the President's Working Group in this section are from President's Working Group on Unlawful Conduct on the Internet, *The Electronic Frontier: The Challenge of Unlawful Conduct Involving the Use of the Internet* (Washington, D.C.: White House, 2000). Web posted at http://www.usdoj.gov/criminal/cybercrime/unlawful.htm. Accessed April 16, 2001.

[59] For insight into how security techniques often lag behind the abilities of criminal perpetrators in the high-technology arena, see James A. Fagin, "Computer Crime: A Technology Gap," *International Journal of Comparative and Applied Criminal Justice,* Vol. 15, Nos. 1 and 2 (spring/fall 1991), pp. 285–297.

[60] Richard Larson, "The New Crime Stoppers: State-of-the-Art Computer Technology Promises a Return to Neighborhood-Oriented Policing," *Technology Review,* Vol. 92, No. 8 (November/December 1989), p. 26.

[61] "DNA Frees Man Sentenced to Life," Associated Press wire service, January 16, 2001. Web posted at http://www.msnbc.com/news/517172.asp. Accessed January 17, 2001.

[62] Michael Schrage, "Today, It Takes a Scientist to Catch a Thief," *Washington Post* online, March 18, 1994.

[63] *Daubert* v. *Merrell Dow Pharmaceuticals, Inc.,* 113 S. Ct. 2786 (1993).

[64] *Frye* v. *United States,* 54 App. D.C. 46, 47, 293 F. 1013, 1014 (1923).

[65] For the application of *Daubert* to DNA technology, see Barry Sheck, "DNA and Daubert," *Cardozo Law Review,* Vol. 15 (1994), p. 1959.

[66] Schrage, "Today, It Takes a Scientist to Catch a Thief."

[67] See FBI press release (no title), October 13, 1998. Web posted at http://www.fbi.gov/pressrm/pressrel/pressrel98/dna.htm. Accessed January 22, 2001.

[68] 42 U.S.C. § 14132.

[69] "British Police to Use DNA to Catch Burglars," Reuters wire service, June 16, 1994.

[70] Schrage, "Today, It Takes a Scientist to Catch a Thief."

[71] Edward Connors et al., *Convicted by Juries, Exonerated by Science: Case Studies in the Use of DNA Evidence to Establish Innocence after Trial* (Washington, D.C.: National Institute of Justice, 1996).

[72] Ibid.

[73] Roland Reboussin, "An Expert System Designed to Profile Murderers," in Frank Schmalleger, ed., *Computers in Criminal Justice: Issues and Applications* (Bristol, IN: Wyndham Hall Press, 1990), p. 239.

[74] "Increased Spending for Security," *Infosecurity News* (July/August 1993), p. 11; and Stockprowler online newsletter for November 5, 2000. Web posted at http://www.stockprowler.com/previous_picks/11-5-00.shtml. Accessed April 16, 2001.

[75] Parker, *Computer Crime,* p. xiii.

[76] Kenneth Rosenblatt, "Deterring Computer Crime," *Technology Review,* Vol. 93, No. 2 (February/March 1990), pp. 34–41.

[77] Ibid.

[78] Ibid.

[79] The NCCS can be found on the World Wide Web at http://www.fbi.gov/programs/nccs/comcrim.htm.

[80] As modified in 1986, 1988, and later years.

[81] Adapted from the FBI's Washington Field Office Infrastructure Protection and Computer Intrusion Squad home page at http://www.fbi.gov/programs/ipcis/ipcis.htm.

[82] Adapted from the Computer Crime and Intellectual Property Section of the Criminal Division of the U.S. Department of Justice home page at http://www.cybercrime.gov.

[83] Wylie Wong, "FBI Targets BBS Operators, Seizes Hardware in Software Piracy Sting," *Computerworld,* February 3, 1997, p. 24.

[84] "How Powerful Is Carnivore?" Associated Press wire service, November 17, 2000. Web posted at http://www.msnbc.com/news/491454.asp. Accessed January 12, 2001.

[85] Brock N. Meeks, "Carnivore to Get New Name," MSNBC News, September 8, 2000. Web posted at http://www.msnbc.com/news/457153.asp. Accessed January 14, 2001.

[86] Rosenblatt, "Deterring Computer Crime."

[87] Ibid.

[88] EFF Statement of Purpose, from the EFF Web site. Web posted at http://eff.org/abouteff.html. Accessed April 20, 2001.

[89] S. Mace, "Kapor and Woziniak Establish Electronic Policy Foundation," *InfoWorld,* Vol. 12, No. 29 (July 16, 1990), p. 6.

[90] The White House, Office of the Vice President, "Statement of the Vice President," February 4, 1994.

[91] U.S. Department of Justice press release, "Attorney General Makes Key Escrow Encryption Announcements," February 4, 1994.

[92] Richard Cole, "Reno—Computer Security," Associated Press wire service, June 14, 1996.

responding to criminal behavior

The final section of *Criminology Today* focuses on crime control policy and possible future directions in the field of criminology. Major issues facing today's policymakers include illicit drug use and trafficking, youth and gun violence, school shootings, high rates of imprisonment, and victims' rights. Unfortunately, as Chapter 15 shows, anticrime initiatives are frequently influenced more by political exigency than by sound science.

Chapter 16 concerns itself with the future of criminology and with the future of crime control in the United States. The chapter describes some of the most effective techniques available to us today for exploring possible futures, and it discusses America's role within a rapidly changing global society.

Why is there such a wide gap between what criminologists know and what policy makers do? One reason is the failure of nerve, honesty, and seriousness among too many of our political leaders, which has ensured that there has been little serious debate in recent presidential or congressional campaigns about the roots of violent crime or the state of the criminal justice system . . .

But there is another reason for the widening gap between policy and understanding: many people are genuinely confused about what to think about the state of crime and punishment in America. And they are confused in part because they are continually bombarded with the myths, misconceptions, and half-truths that dominate public discussion, while the real story is often buried in a specialized technical literature that is increasingly difficult for most people to follow.

—Elliott Currie, University of California, Berkeley[i]

[i]Elliott Currie, *Crime and Punishment in America* (New York: Holt and Company, 1998), pp. 6–7.

CHAPTER 15
Criminology and Social Policy

CHAPTER 16
Future Directions

Criminology should be concerned with real-world applications of its research.

—Joan Petersilia, Past President of the American Society of Criminology[1]

One issue that has a major effect on research and ultimately its relationship to policymaking in the United States is the amount of attention, or more accurately, the relative *lack* of attention, accorded to criminal justice research.

—Jeremy Travis, Former Director of the National Institute of Justice[2]

criminology and social policy

CHAPTER

15

A mortal battle for the national conscience is being waged as I write and you read. The jousting . . . will determine what we, in the future, will label as "crime" and how we react to it.

—Georgette Bennett[3]

Fundamentally, our capacity to extinguish criminality and lawlessness lies in the moral training and moral stature of our people.

—President Herbert Hoover[4]

Suppose I told you that it is time to start thinking of communicable disease as a criminal and legal issue, rather than a public health issue, and . . . to recognize that "Disease is a crime."

—David B. Kopel, Colorado Attorney[5]

IMPORTANT TERMS

Anti-Drug Abuse Act (1986)	National Advisory Commission on Criminal Justice Standards and Goals	secondary victimization
Brady Handgun Violence Prevention Act (1993)		social epidemiology
		three-strikes provision
Comprehensive Crime Control Act (1984)	nurturant strategies	victim-impact statement
	Omnibus Anti-Drug Abuse Act (1988)	Victims of Crime Act (VOCA) (1984)
deterrence strategies		
habitual offender statute	Omnibus Crime Control and Safe Streets Act (1967)	victim-witness assistance programs
Hate Crimes Sentencing Enhancement Act (1994)		Violence against Women Act (VAWA) (1994)
	postcrime victimization	
Kriminalpolitik	protection/avoidance strategies	Violent Crime Control and Law Enforcement Act (1994)
Law Enforcement Assistance Administration (LEAA)	public policy	
	restitution	Wickersham Commission

OUTCOMES

LEARNING

After reading this chapter, you should be able to
- ◆ Distinguish between the social problems approach and the social responsibility approach to crime control
- ◆ Recognize and understand the different types of crime control strategies
- ◆ Relate various crime control strategies to recent American crime control policy initiatives
- ◆ Describe the history and the current state of the victims' movement in this country

Hear the author discuss this chapter at *crimtoday.com*

INTRODUCTION

In the study of crime, as in many other areas, life often imitates art. On September 7, 1996, rapper Tupac Shakur, well known for his starring role in the movie *Poetic Justice,* was gunned down after leaving a Mike Tyson fight in Las Vegas. Shakur was born in the Bronx in 1971 and was raised by a Black Panther mother. He died at a local hospital a week after being attacked. Shakur's violent past included a shooting that injured two off-duty Atlanta police officers, a conviction on sexual abuse charges in New York City,[6] and a mugging during which the rapper was shot four times. The mugging occurred in 1994 as Shakur was awaiting sentencing after being convicted of assault and battery in an attack on his former film director, Allen Hughes.[7] During his brief rise to stardom, Shakur's brand of "gangsta rap" was condemned by former Vice President Dan Quayle, who charged that Shakur's violent lyrics had led a youth to kill a Texas state trooper.

Six months after Shakur died, the Notorious B.I.G., or Biggie Smalls—another of gangsta rap's best-known

entertainers—was killed in a hail of gunfire. The 24-year-old B.I.G., whose given name was Christopher Wallace, was shot shortly after midnight on March 9, 1997, as he sat in the passenger seat of a GMC Suburban at a red light in downtown Los Angeles. He died a short time later at Cedars-Sinai Medical Center. B.I.G., a former drug dealer and street hustler from the rough Bedford-Stuyvesant section of Brooklyn, New York, had burst on the gangsta rap scene in 1994 with his million-selling album, *Ready to Die.*

About the time B.I.G. died, another infamous rapper, Snoop Doggy Dogg, and his bodyguard, McKinley Lee, were acquitted of murder charges in the 1993 slaying of Phillip Woldermariam. Woldermariam, a member of the Venice Shoreline Crips, had been shot twice in the back after meeting with Snoop. Snoop, whose birth name is Calvin Broadus, was born in Long Beach, California, in 1971. Others like Snoop have profited mightily by selling images of urban violence to mainstream youth. As a result of highly lucrative album sales, Snoop had no problem posting a $2 million bond following his arrest.[8] A $25 million wrongful death suit filed by Woldermariam's family was settled out of court in late 1996 for an undisclosed sum.

There are many more examples of the violent exploits of gangsta rappers. A few years before Shakur died, Flavor Flav (William Drayton), a singer with the group Public Enemy, was arrested for firing a .38-caliber pistol at a neighbor. Around the time of Flav's arrest, Ice-T's song "Cop Killer" was blamed in the 1992 shooting deaths of two Las Vegas police officers who were ambushed and killed by four juveniles. The juveniles continued to sing "Cop Killer" lyrics following their arrest.[9] *Body Count,* the Time-Warner album on which "Cop Killer" appears, was shipped to stores in a miniature body bag.

A year later, rapper Dr. Dre (Andre Young) directed an 18-minute video of a Snoop performance called *Murder Was the Case.* Dre said he wanted to package the video with Oliver Stone's *Natural Born Killers.*[10] *Murder* and *Killers* were both quickly criticized by law enforcement organizations, parents' groups, and black leaders decrying the lyrics of gangsta music.[11] The Reverend Arthur L. Cribbs, Jr., a black minister writing in a national editorial, called gangsta rap "nothing but modern-day violence and vulgarity wrapped and packaged in blackface." Cribbs claimed the music "would not be widespread if white megarecord companies did not put filth on sale for big dollars."[12] Soon, radio stations began banning violent rap music. WBLS-FM in New York and KACE-FM in Los Angeles announced that they would no longer play rap songs that encouraged violence, KPWR-FM in Los Angeles masked offensive words, and WCKZ-FM in Charlotte limited gangsta rap to late-night hours.

Gangsta rap and "hip-hop" music have been condemned by many who claim that their lyrics promote antisocial and violent behavior. But it is less than clear whether gangsta rap is indeed a cause of crime or merely a quasi-poetic rendering of the social conditions characteristic of many inner-city American communities today. The real problems, some claim, are outside rap music, not within it. Gangsta rap supporters suggest that rap may be the wake-up call needed to end black-on-black violence, which now seems out of control, and that by raising public awareness, it may do more to reduce violence than any government-sponsored program.

Whatever the verdict on gangsta rap will eventually turn out to be, the issue of media-fed violence is only one of the concerns facing today's crime control policymakers. Drug trafficking, illicit drug use, gun violence, youth violence, school shootings, overcrowded prisons, high imprisonment rates, and victims' rights are among the topics occupying today's policymakers. This chapter reviews many of these issues but begins with an outline of the historical development of American crime control policy.

FEDERAL ANTICRIME INITIATIVES

Some understanding of how public policy—especially crime control policy—is created is essential in the study of criminology. Before we trace the development of public policies in the crime control area, however, a definition of the term *public policy* is in order. **Public policy,** also called "social policy," is "a course of action that government takes in an effort to solve a problem or to achieve an end."[13] Analysts of public policy have observed that policies undergo five stages in their development:[14]

- Identification of the problem
- Agenda setting, or the prioritization of problems
- Policy formation
- Program implementation
- Program evaluation and reassessment

As Jeff Ferrell, a professor of criminal justice at Northern Arizona University, points out, however, "As all criminologists

The car in which "gangsta rapper" Biggie Smalls, known as the Notorious B.I.G., was shot and killed in 1997. Some claim that violent themes in "ghetto rap" lead to crime. What do you think? *Mike Meadows, AP/Wide World Photos*

know, criminality is decided as much by legal and political authorities, and by their strategies of criminalization, enforcement, and control, as by criminals themselves."[15] One could easily add that crime-fighting policies are probably more the result of politics than they are the direct outcome of social science research and data. As Nancy E. Marion, a leading figure in the public policy arena, observes, "Presidential and congressional initiatives have been largely symbolic gestures rather than coherent attempts to deal effectively with crime."[16] The Massachusetts Institute for a New Commonwealth (MassINC), which is especially interested in issues of crime control, puts it equally succinctly. The institute asserts, "Opportunities to reduce crime are systematically neglected, as policy making is dominated by the need to appease the public's justifiable fear and anger and by a wide variety of organizational and professional interests and ideological postures. The simple question, 'What policies would minimize crime?' is rarely raised, and even more rarely debated on its merits. There is little careful analysis of which actions by police, courts, prosecutors, and corrections authorities would most reduce crime, and even less serious attention to the contributions of non-criminal justice agencies and policies to crime control."[17] Visit MassINC via Web Extra! 15-1.

Web Extra! 15-1 at crimtoday.com

The Hoover Administration

Although the development of policies to combat crime and the conditions that cause it has traditionally been the responsibility of state and local governments, crime control became a part of the federal approach to social problems in the United States more than half a century ago. In the foreword to James D. Calder's *Origins and Development of Federal Crime Control Policy,* George H. Nash writes, "While all complicated social policies and institutional arrangements have many roots . . . the decisive movement in the development of comprehensive federal crime control was the period between 1929 and 1933, the presidency of Herbert Hoover."[18] Calder puts it even more succinctly: "The administration of Herbert Clark Hoover, thirty-first president of the United States, marks the origins of federal crime-control policy."[19] Calder argues that a trio of factors combined to usher in an era of federal crime control policies: (1) "the proliferating stress on the judicial system" associated mostly with Prohibition; (2) "the emergence of new perspectives in law, sociology, and criminology, and the rise of academically-trained social scientists eager to apply their knowledge to reform of the legal system"; and (3) "the election in 1928 of a president committed to reform and receptive to the approaches of the activist social scientists."[20] Other events of the era—including the sensational kidnapping of young Charles Augustus Lindbergh, Jr., better known as "the Lindbergh baby"; the rapid rise in influence of organized crime; the visibility of gang warfare; media coverage of notorious criminals; and the

effects of the Great Depression on crime rates everywhere—necessitated serious and decisive anticrime action by the Hoover administration.

In 1929, Max Lowenthal, a Hoover administration insider, called crime and its control "the dominant issue before the American people."[21] The opening words of Hoover's inaugural address focused the first order of business for the new administration upon "the failure of our system of criminal justice." Hoover observed that "crime had increased . . . and confidence in the system of criminal justice had decreased."[22] When Hoover assumed office, Calder observes, "the popular belief was that crime had increased and governments at all levels had become less able to control its growth."[23] During his campaign for the presidency, Hoover promised to initiate a scientific study of crime and law enforcement. The promise was fulfilled with the 1929 appointment of George Woodard Wickersham to chair Hoover's Commission on Law Observance and Enforcement. Wickersham, a lawyer with an outstanding professional reputation, had been U.S. attorney general during the Taft administration. Wickersham's views coincided with Hoover's in many policy areas, and the two men were in constant communication during the **Wickersham Commission** hearings.

The Hoover administration developed policy initiatives in the areas of police, courts, and corrections. Interest centered on[24]

- Developing "objectives to improve justice system practices and to reinstate law's role in civilized governance" (which was the mandate of the Wickersham Commission)
- Exploring the extent to which "Prohibition was the basis for general disrespect of the law"
- Investigating the extent to which deadly force was a necessary or reasonable law enforcement tool (an issue which arose after a number of innocent citizens were killed by federal and state enforcement agents determined to stop fleeing Prohibition law violators)
- Controlling the illegal manufacture, sale, and importation of heroin, morphine, and opium
- Developing a system of reliable information gathering, including crime statistics, which could be used in the further development of crime-fighting policies
- Codifying federal law enforcement activities, including the elimination of overlapping law enforcement activities by different agencies
- Increasing professionalism among the federal judiciary, especially through the removal and replacement of incompetent or corrupt government prosecutors
- Streamlining the federal court system, improving court procedures, and ending the massive congestion then found in federal courtrooms across the country
- Combating organized crime and reducing its influence throughout America
- Reforming the system of federal prisons so that they might not only punish, but reform and provide a visi-

ble sense of deterrence to others contemplating criminal activity
- Eliminating abusive and unprofessional prison management
- Reducing prison overcrowding and decreasing idleness among prisoners

Federal criminal justice policy during the Hoover administration era was developed with assistance from the best experts in the country—men and women like August Vollmer, a former chief of police in Berkeley, California; Roscoe Pound, Dean of the Harvard Law School; Henry W. Anderson, President of the Virginia Bar Association; Ada L. Comstock, President of Radcliffe College; Mabel Willebrandt, a highly visible Prohibition supporter; Sanford Bates, Director of the Federal Bureau of Prisons; and Frank J. Loesch, a judge and Chicago antigang leader.

Unfortunately, however, policy-making groups, most notably the Wickersham Commission, did not include a broad representation of blacks or other racial and ethnic minorities. Although some citizens expressed concerns that "blacks had endured more than a century of police abuse, rigged court rooms, and harsh prison treatment and that they were overrepresented in crime statistics for reasons that demanded inquiry,"[25] Hoover decided that the appointment of ethnic minorities to policy-making groups solely for the purpose of including them "would violate his principle of having no special interests represented"[26] and might produce less-than-objective results.

Nonetheless, the Hoover era set the tone for federal criminal justice policies that were to follow—a tone already identified in the October 1929 preliminary report of the Wickersham Commission, which said, "We found that with huge investments in plant and personnel and with great operating costs, the country has been proceeding largely in a haphazard manner, without any inventory of the available facts, without commensurate research for checking a great social evil, without the application of the principles that have been so successful in some of the professions, in many businesses and in the social sciences."[27]

Many Hoover-era reforms eventually proved themselves effective. As Calder observes, "Hoover's administration was the first to give formal policy attention to federal prisons and prisoners. Under his leadership, prison administration, historically ignored, was transformed from an antiquated and rawly inadequate collection of penitentiaries into a model system."[28] Other reforms were also well received. Prison expansion got under way, activities of the federal parole board were streamlined and centralized, and new federal district court standards were introduced, reducing the high cost of repeated and redundant appeals, which had been clogging the nation's courts.

Federal Policy Following World War II

By the end of World War II, the nation basked in the glow of economic expansion as industrial production, greatly en-

hanced by the demands of war, turned to peaceful purposes. Unfortunately, however, domestic tranquillity was about to be disrupted by the baby-boomer generation, which was an offshoot of the enthusiasm which accompanied the end of the war. Baby boomers, born in the decade following 1945, contributed significantly to rising crime rates around 1960 as they began to reach their early teen years. Rising rates made crime and its control an important political issue during the presidency of John F. Kennedy (1961–1963). The Kennedy administration expanded federal crime control policies to address juvenile crime and the rights of indigent defendants to be afforded counsel. Under the direction of Robert Kennedy, U.S. Attorney General during his brother's administration, federal anticrime efforts also focused on combating organized crime, which was seen as a crime control issue that transcended state boundaries.

After John F. Kennedy was assassinated in 1963, Lyndon Baines Johnson was sworn in as the thirty-sixth president of the United States; he served until 1969. Although candidate Barry Goldwater had highlighted issues of crime and violence during the 1964 presidential campaign, Johnson capitalized on them, playing to the rising crime fears identified by pollsters. Johnson established the President's Commission on Law Enforcement and Administration of Justice, and it formed part of his drive toward building what he called "The Great Society." Johnson's charge to the commission included these words: "The problem of crime brings us together. Even as we join in common action, we know there can be no instant victory. Ancient evils do not yield to easy conquest. We cannot limit our efforts to enemies we can see. We must, with equal resolve, seek out new knowledge, new techniques, and new understanding."[29]

The commission's report, *The Challenge of Crime in a Free Society,* which was published in February 1967, laid the groundwork for many anticrime initiatives which were to follow. True to its Democratic roots, the commission saw crime as the inevitable result of poverty, unemployment, poor educational, and other social and economic disadvantages. It proposed legislation, passed in the form of the **Omnibus Crime Control and Safe Streets Act** of 1967, to "eliminate the social conditions that bring about crime." Title 1 of the Safe Streets Act established the **Law Enforcement Assistance Administration** (**LEAA**), with the mandate of providing technical and financial assistance to the states for the purpose of improving and strengthening law enforcement activities at the local level. The LEAA spent hundreds of millions of dollars before it was disbanded.

At the time of the commission's 1967 report, crime was far less a reality than it is today. Although the fear of crime was widespread in the late 1960s, the crime rate was less than a third of what it is now. Carjackings, crack cocaine, drive-by shootings, metal detectors in schools, mass murder, drug cartels, and gang warfare with automatic weapons were unfamiliar. Even so, as the crime rate rose, personal security became a major concern of the American public. It was during this period that the nation's "war on crime" took on its modern tenor.

Although the true cause of rising crime rates that characterized the period from 1960 to 1975 may never be known, many possibilities have been suggested, ranging from maturing baby boomers (discussed earlier) to the dissolution of institutions of social control, such as the family, churches, and schools. Whatever the reason, it soon became clear that federal crime control policies were no match for the underlying social forces fueling the rapid rise in crime.

When Richard Milhous Nixon became president of the United States in 1969, federal efforts at crime control took on a decidedly Republican cast. Nixon "sought all out war on crime, frequently with little concern for the accused. In his efforts to get criminals out of circulation, Nixon advocated mandatory minimum sentences, fewer pretrial releases for multiple offenders, generally heavier penalties, and selection of judges who were strict on crime."[30] As the nation's law enforcers, courts, and correctional systems became hopelessly overworked, high rates of recidivism were cited as the basis for an emerging new "lock-'em-up" policy which emphasized retribution and deterrence by example. The war on crime turned increasingly conservative, and calls for swift and certain penalties, accompanied by increased punishments, including the reduction or abolition of parole and early release, were made into law. Nixon also established the **National Advisory Commission on Criminal Justice Standards and Goals** in 1971. In its reports, the commission called for improved police-community relations and enhanced communications between criminal justice agencies.

As some writers have observed, the first phase of the federal war on crime was based on a social philosophy that attempted to address underlying cultural and social conditions which fed crime. Unfortunately, however, even as massive federal funding infused social welfare programs, crime continued to rise. Social programs themselves faced growing criticism that they tended to perpetuate the very problems they were intended to address.

The Reagan and Bush Years

The first phase in the war on crime ended around 1980 with the election of President Ronald Reagan. During the Reagan administration (1981–1989), two new fronts in the war on crime emerged. One, which some writers have called a "war on criminals," meant that less attention would be paid to the root causes of crime, and more attention would be devoted to holding individual offenders responsible for their crimes. In support of this first front, Congress passed the **Comprehensive Crime Control Act** of 1984, a far-reaching law that mandated new sentencing guidelines, eliminated parole at the federal level, limited the use of the insanity defense, and increased penalties associated with drug dealing. Typical of Republican approaches to the problem of crime, Reagan insisted that "choosing a career in crime is not the result of poverty or of an unhappy childhood or of a misunderstood adolescence; it's the result of a conscious, willful, selfish choice made by some who consider themselves above

the law, who seek to exploit the hard work and, sometimes, the very lives of their fellow citizens."[31]

The second front in the Reagan administration's war on crime focused on drugs and their relationship to criminal activity. Some analysts claim that drug control provided the single most important issue on Reagan's crime control agenda. Reagan believed that drugs contributed, both directly and indirectly, to much of the nation's crime problem. He was strongly opposed to the legalization or decriminalization of controlled substances, and in 1985, he persuaded Congress to pass legislation criminalizing the manufacture, distribution, and possession of designer drugs. Under Reagan's leadership, Congress passed both the **Anti-Drug Abuse Act** of 1986,[32] which enacted new federal mandatory minimums for drug offenses, and the **Omnibus Anti-Drug Abuse Act** of 1988,[33] which substantially increased penalties for recreational drug users and which created a new cabinet-level position to coordinate the drug-fighting efforts of the federal government. The position, dubbed by the press the "Drug Czar," was initially filled by William Bennett (a Bush appointee), who brought federal antidrug efforts to national attention when he declared Washington, D.C., a "drug zone" in 1989. The "drug zone" designation made the city, and others like it, eligible for federal drug-fighting assistance.

George Bush assumed the presidency in 1989, and the war on drugs was well supported throughout the early 1990s by federal and state tax dollars. In 1991 alone, government agencies nationwide spent nearly $24 billion to fight the drug war,[34] with most of the money going to criminal justice efforts and very little to rehabilitation or counseling initiatives outside the system. Of all of the money spent to combat drugs that year, 79% went to criminal justice agencies, and only 21% reached agencies focused on rehabilitation and educational activities. State and local governments spent a total of $15.9 billion on criminal justice activities like incarcerating prisoners and paying for police, according to a report by the Office of National Drug Control Policy. States paid $6.8 billion in 1991 to support their prisons and local jails, with an additional $4.2 billion in state monies going to fund police services. Judicial and legal services cost states $1.5 billion. Spending on antidrug efforts varied greatly, ranging from only $13 per citizen per year in South Dakota to over $154 per person per year in Alaska. Average per capita spending by state and local governments was $63.08. Even with the aid of such massive expenditures, the war on drugs had little immediate result other than grossly overworked criminal justice agencies and intolerably overcrowded jails and prisons.

Clinton Administration Initiatives

When President William Jefferson Clinton took office in January 1993, a number of crime control initiatives were already in motion, giving the president the opportunity to influence their development. In 1993, Clinton signed the **Brady Handgun Violence Prevention Act** into law.[35] The law, which is described in greater detail later in this chapter, called for the initiation of a national background checking system for all potential gun purchasers. In August 1994, Clinton won a victory when Congress passed the **Violent Crime Control and Law Enforcement Act**,[36] a bill that he supported. The law, which is described in detail later in this chapter, became the hallmark of Clinton-era crime control policy. It called for spending billions of dollars on crime prevention, law enforcement, and prison construction. It also outlawed the sale of certain types of assault weapons and enhanced federal death penalty provisions. President Clinton was a strong backer of the **Violence against Women Act** (**VAWA**) of 1994,[37] which is a part of the Violent Crime Control and Law Enforcement Act. It, too, will be described in more detail shortly.

In 1994, the **Hate Crimes Sentencing Enhancement Act**[38]—another component of the Violent Crime Control and Law Enforcement Act—became law. The provision required the U.S. Sentencing Commission to increase the penalties for crimes in which the victim was selected "because of . . . actual or perceived race, color, religion, national origin, ethnicity, gender, disability, or sexual orientation." The measure applies specifically to attacks and vandalism that occur in national parks and on federal property or that occur while the victim is engaged in certain specified federally protected activities, such as serving on a jury, voting, or attending public school.

Gun Control Legislation

In the area of gun control, the Clinton Administration strengthened federal penalties for those who use guns during the commission of a crime. In November 1998, President Clinton signed a law that applies to all violent criminals and drug felons who commit gun crimes.[39] The law mandates that violent criminals and drug felons who *possess* a firearm during the commission of a federal crime are to be sentenced to five years in prison—in *addition* to any penalties that apply for the underlying violent or drug crime. Under the law, offenders receive a mandatory minimum sentence of at least seven years for *brandishing* a firearm and of at least ten years if the firearm is *discharged*.

Somewhat earlier, in 1994, President Clinton signed into law the Youth Handgun Safety Act,[40] which banned the possession of handguns or handgun ammunition by juveniles under the age of 18 and which made it a federal offense for adults to transfer handguns to juveniles, with limited exceptions.

In 1998, the Treasury Department concluded that modified semiautomatic assault rifles that accept large-capacity military magazines (known as LCMM rifles) are not "particularly suitable for or readily adaptable to sporting purposes" and should not be imported. Consequently, President Clinton announced a general ban on the importation of more than 50 nonrecreational, modified assault weapons. The firearms affected by the decision were modified versions of military assault weapons that were banned by the Bush administration in 1989 and by the assault weapons ban of 1994.

On March 17, 2000, President Clinton announced a voluntary partnership between the government and gun manufacturer Smith and Wesson, the largest handgun maker in the nation. The partnership was intended to bring about meaningful reforms in the way guns are designed, distributed, and marketed. The agreement included provisions for new design standards to make guns safer and to prevent accidental shootings and gun deaths, as well as sales and distribution controls to help keep guns out of the hands of criminals.

The centerpiece of the Clinton administration's gun control legislation, however, was the Brady Handgun Violence Prevention Act of 1993. The Brady law, which was mentioned earlier in this chapter, was the last act passed by Congress in 1993. The law was named after former President Ronald Reagan's White House press secretary, Jim Brady, who was shot in the head during John Hinckley's 1981 attempted assassination of Reagan. Brady, although seriously injured and impaired for life, survived.

The purpose of the Brady law was to "provide for a waiting period before the purchase of a handgun and [to establish] a national instant criminal background check system, to be contacted by firearms dealers before the transfer of any firearm."[41] Under the law, firearms dealers must register with the federal government and are required to notify law enforcement officials of all handgun purchase applications. Federal officials will then check a potential buyer's background.[42] Purchases of handguns may be disapproved for (1) individuals under indictment for, or convicted in any court of, a crime punishable by imprisonment for a term exceeding one year; (2) fugitives from justice; (3) unlawful users of or those addicted to any controlled substance; (4) people who have been adjudicated as mentally defective or who have been committed to a mental institution; (5) illegal aliens or those who are in the United States unlawfully; (6) former military personnel who were not discharged from the armed forces under honorable conditions; and (7) "a person who, having been a citizen of the United States, has renounced such citizenship." Gun dealers not abiding by the provisions of the law may have their licenses suspended or revoked and may be fined up to $5,000 per illegal transaction. Twenty-seven states and territories must comply with the law, but the District of Columbia and 23 states are exempt from the law's provisions because they have more stringent laws already in effect. The five-day waiting period for handgun purchases, called Instacheck, was phased out after the national system became fully operational.

In an effort to reduce firearm theft, especially during the interstate shipment of weapons, the Brady law also requires that "no common or contract carrier shall require or cause any label, tag, or other written notice to be placed on the outside of any package, luggage, or other container that such package, luggage, or other container contains a firearm."

Proponents of the Brady law believed that the widespread and ready availability of guns throughout the United States was a significant factor contributing to the crime problem. Statistics seem to support that view. Recent reports by the Bureau of Justice Statistics (BJS), for example, found that approximately 1.3 million crimes are committed annually in the United States with handguns.[43] Handguns are used in an ever-growing percentage of violent crimes, and overall handgun use is up—at the same time that the crime rate is dropping. According to the BJS, 92% of crimes committed with handguns are nonfatal. Handguns are used, however, in 55.6% of the nation's murders, and offenders armed with handguns commit one in every eight nonfatal violent crimes, including rape, robbery, and assault. The BJS also found that young black males comprise the group most victimized by handgun crime. Annually, approximately 40 handgun victimizations occur for every 1,000 black males aged 16 to 19 in the U.S. population—four times the rate for young white males. Other findings show that offenders fired their weapons in 17% of all nonfatal handgun crimes, missing the victim four of five times, and that approximately 21,000 victims are wounded by handguns each year. The BJS also reports that, on average, 340,000 firearms are stolen yearly.

Many dislike the Brady law, however, believing that it has not reduced crime. The strongest and most vocal opposition to handgun control comes from the National Rifle Association (NRA), which claims that the Brady law and other measures like it are unconstitutional.

In January 1994, Philip Toth, 25, became the first person formally accused of violating the Brady law.[44] Toth was charged in U.S. District Court in Cedar Rapids, Iowa, with stealing guns from a licensed firearms dealer, which is now a federal offense under the law. In April of that same year, John Arnold, a Fort Walton Beach, Florida, gun dealer, became the first person convicted under the law.[45] He was charged with stealing five guns from the Gulf Breeze, Florida, Pistol Parlor in January 1994.

As of March 2000, The National Instant Check System (NICS) had conducted over 10 million background checks on gun purchasers and had prevented an estimated 179,000 illegal gun sales.[46] Learn more about the Brady law at Web Extra! 15-2.

Web Extra! 15-2 at crimtoday.com

Gun Control Strategies

According to recent public opinion polls, Americans believe that some form of gun control is needed, and they support a wide variety of gun control measures. In a 1999 poll conducted shortly after the Columbine High School shootings, almost two-thirds of those surveyed favored stricter gun control laws.[47] Most of the remainder of the respondents favored keeping gun control laws the same, and very few of those polled wanted less restrictive laws.

Policymakers have a variety of gun control strategies at their disposal. Albert Reiss, Jr., and Jeffrey A. Roth, citing the work of the Panel on the Understanding and Control of Violent Behavior of the National Research Council, recognize four fundamental intervention strategies:[48]

- Reducing the number of guns in society. This strategy might work through restrictions on ownership, licensing, and importation.
- Reducing the destructiveness of guns. Banning dangerous ammunition (such as hollow-point or Teflon-coated rounds), reducing the caliber of guns sold, limiting the size of magazines available with semiautomatic weapons, and so on, would all contribute to the effectiveness of this type of strategy.
- Changing gun allocation. This strategy might be implemented through licensing restrictions (for example, no weapons could be licensed to convicted drug

Handgun victim James Brady sits to the right of President Bill Clinton as the Brady Bill is signed into law in 1993. Much recent anticrime policy in the United States has focused on gun control. Does the government have the right to restrict gun ownership?
Gary Hershorn, Reuters, Corbis

THEORY VERSUS REALITY
Gun Control

An important policy issue facing lawmakers across the United States today is gun control. It is difficult to know just how many firearms are held privately in this country. One international survey conducted in 17 industrialized countries between 1989 and 1992 found that 48% of U.S. households reported gun ownership.[1] The U.S. rate was more than twice that of most of the countries included in the survey. In contrast to the United States, fewer than 1% of households in Scotland, England, and Wales reported having any kind of firearm. Differences in handgun ownership—also measured by the survey—were even more striking. Twenty-eight percent of U.S. households reported handgun ownership, more than three times the rate of most other countries.

Recent surveys indicate that the rate of gun ownership in the United States may have declined. Gallup polls show that the proportion of adults reporting guns in their homes hit 51% in 1993 but declined to 36% by 1999.[2] Gallup found that in 1999, 47% of males owned guns versus 27% of females. More whites (40%) than blacks (19%) reported gun ownership, and the highest rates of gun ownership were found in the South (46% of all households). Reasons for gun ownership vary, with approximately 74% of gun owners citing hunting, 65% personal protection, 40% target shooting, and 21% gun collecting as their reasons for owning firearms.

According to the recent National Survey of Private Ownership of Firearms (NSPOF), approximately 192 million firearms are in private hands throughout the United States, with 44 million of those weapons classified as handguns.[3] NSPOF findings show that 25% of adults own firearms, with 74% of those people having two or more.

While gun ownership rates may have dropped during the 1990s, deaths and injuries caused by handguns are quite high in the United States. According to a study of three cities (Memphis, Tennessee; Seattle, Washington; and Galveston, Texas), the likelihood of being shot is highest among young black males (1,708 per 100,000) and lowest among older white females (where rates, in most parts of the country, are too low to be meaningful).[4] The likelihood of being shot varies across the nation, and the study found annual rates ranging from around 54 per 100,000 in Seattle to 223 per 100,000 in Memphis.

Although many policymakers are convinced that high levels of gun ownership produce gun violence, others emphasize the defensive aspect of ownership. Studies like the National Crime Victimization Survey (NCVS) show between 82,500 and 108,000 defensive uses (in which guns are used to prevent robberies, assaults, thefts, and household

(continued on the next page)

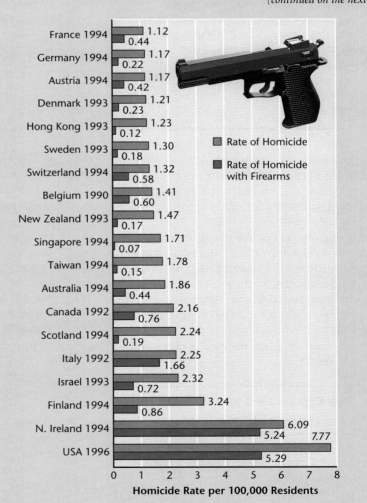

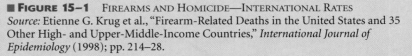

■ FIGURE 15–1 FIREARMS AND HOMICIDE—INTERNATIONAL RATES
Source: Etienne G. Krug et al., "Firearm-Related Deaths in the United States and 35 Other High- and Upper-Middle-Income Countries," *International Journal of Epidemiology* (1998); pp. 214–28.

(continued from previous page)

burglaries) per year. Florida State criminologist Gary Kleck maintains that guns actually prevent more crime and violence than they cause.[5] Kleck feels that the number of times guns are used defensively may be in the millions annually—far higher than official statistics show. Kleck points to the fact that surveys like the NCVS do not directly ask about the use of guns for self-protection, and he says that even direct questions may not get at the issue since people may be reluctant to report gun use, fearing that it might get them into trouble. Another dimension of gun protection that has not been adequately studied, says Kleck, stems from the fact that guns deter some people from even attempting crimes because they fear being shot. Kleck concludes that "the hypothesis that general gun availability causes increases in rates of homicide and other violent crime is not supported. The policy implication is that nothing appears to be gained from reducing the general gun ownership level."[6]

Many criminologists disagree with Kleck, pointing to the financial and social costs associated with widespread gun ownership. The financial cost, for example, of treating the nation's gunshot victims in a recent year was $2.3 billion, and the government paid half the bill because many victims had little or no insurance.[7] Even if what Kleck says about deterrence is true, however, many question the impact that living in an armed society has on the minds and well-being of citizens. The fear of gun-laden confrontations might keep many from asserting their legitimate rights, say Richard D. Alba and Steven F. Messner. "We wonder ... about the quality of life in the kind of society where routine social order depends upon the massive armament of the citizenry," they write.[8]

DISCUSSION QUESTIONS

1. Does gun ownership contribute to or prevent violence? Why?

2. What gun control strategies do you think might be the most effective in the United States? Why?

1. Martin Killias, "Gun Ownership, Suicide, and Homicide: An International Perspective," in Anna Alvazzi del Frate et al., eds., *Understanding Crime: Experiences of Crime and Crime Control* (Rome: U.N. Interregional Crime and Justice Research Institute, 1993).
2. The Gallup Organization, "U.S. Gun Ownership Continues Broad Decline," *Poll Releases*, April 6, 1999.
3. Philip J. Cook and Jens Ludwig, "Guns in America: National Survey on Private Ownership and Use of Firearms," *NIJ Research in Brief*, May 1997. Web posted at http://www.ncjrs.org/txtfiles/165476.txt. Accessed January 17, 2001.
4. Arthur L. Kellermann et al., "Gun Ownership as a Risk Factor for Homicide in the Home," *New England Journal of Medicine*, Vol. 329, no. 15 (1993), pp. 1048–91.
5. Gary Kleck, *Targeting Guns: Firearms and Their Control* (New York: Aldine, 1997).
6. Ibid., p. 258.
7. "Study: Gun Injuries Cost $2.3B in Year," Associated Press wire service, August 4, 1999.
8. Richard D. Alba and Steven F. Messner, "Point Blank against Itself: Evidence and Inference about Guns, Crime, and Gun Control," *Journal of Quantitative Criminology*, Vol. 11 (1995), pp. 408–409.

users), extending existing restrictions (for example, to new jurisdictions or to other categories of offenders), lengthening the waiting period for gun purchases, requiring safety and locking mechanisms on all guns sold, and so on.

- Altering the uses or the storage of guns. Techniques might involve increasing criminal sentences for gun use, restricting the carrying of guns, enhancing civil penalties associated with gun-related damage, making guns more traceable and identifiable, and educating the public about the dangers of firearms.

Learn more about the issues involved in gun control at Web Extras! 15-3 and 15-4.

Web Extras! 15-3 and 15-4 at crimtoday.com

The Violent Crime Control and Law Enforcement Act of 1994

The centerpiece of Clinton administration crime control legislation was the Violent Crime Control and Law Enforcement Act of 1994. The act was passed by Congress in response to increasingly hard-nosed voter sentiment about crime. Conservative critics of the law, however, which was passed by a Democratic-controlled Congress under the leadership of a Democratic president, claimed that it was really a liberal agenda in disguise—one that funded a significant number of social programs in the fight against crime.

The 1994 law, one of the most sweeping pieces of federal anticrime legislation of all time, provided massive funding for increased law enforcement and correctional resources, including $30.2 billion over six years for crime-reduction efforts through the Violent Crime Reduction Trust Fund. Savings from the president's reductions in the federal workforce, as calculated by the Congressional Budget Office and locked in by reductions in federal budget caps, were expected to fund the more than $30 billion in crime bill initiatives.

Under the act—through whose auspices funding continues to flow—state and local law enforcement agencies were slated to receive $10.8 billion, including (1) $8.8 billion to put 100,000 police officers on the streets in community-policing programs, (2) $245 million for rural anticrime and antidrug efforts, (3) $130 million for technical automation grants for law enforcement agencies, and (4) $200 million for college scholarships for students who agree to serve as police officers and for scholarships for in-service officers. A new federal office, Community Oriented Policing Services (COPS), was established within the U.S. Department of Justice to help funnel federal expenditures intended to put new officers on America's streets. On May 12, 1999, COPS announced that it had achieved its goal of putting 100,000 new police officers to work. Visit the COPS office via Web Extra! 15-5.

Web Extra! 15-5 at crimtoday.com

Another $2.6 billion of funding under the law was slated to go to enhance the activities of federal enforcement agencies, including $250 million to the Federal Bureau of Investigation, $150 million to the Drug Enforcement Administration, $1.2 billion to the Immigration and Naturalization Service and Border Patrol, $50 million to U.S. Attorneys, $550 million to the Treasury Department, $200 million to the Justice Department, and $200 million to federal courts.

Prisons across the nation received $9.7 billion, including (1) $7.9 billion in grants to the states to build and operate prisons and incarceration alternatives, such as boot camps, to ensure that additional prison cells would be available to put—and keep—violent offenders behind bars and (2) $1.8 billion to states for the costs of incarcerating criminal illegal aliens.

Another $6.1 billion was earmarked for crime prevention efforts, including (1) $90 million to create an interagency Ounce of Prevention Council to coordinate new and existing crime prevention programs; (2) $567 million for after-school, weekend, and summer "safe haven" programs to provide children with positive activities and alternatives; (3) $243 million to provide in-school assistance to at-risk children, including education, mentoring, and other programs; (4) $1.6 billion to fight violence against women; (5) $1.6 billion for direct funding to localities around the country for anticrime efforts, such as drug treatment, education, and jobs under a portion of the bill called the Local Partnership Act; (6) $626 million for model crime prevention programs targeted at high-crime neighborhoods; (7) $270 million for lines of credit to community development corporations to stimulate business and employment opportunities for low-income, unemployed, and underemployed individuals; and (8) $383 million for drug-treatment programs for state ($270 million) and federal ($113 million) prisoners.

Another $377 million was earmarked for a new Local Crime Prevention Block Grant program to be distributed to local governments to be used as local needs dictate for, among other things, (1) antigang programs, (2) midnight sports leagues to give at-risk youth nightly alternatives to the streets, (3) the establishment of boys and girls clubs in low-income housing communities and the encouraging of police officers to live in those communities, (4) partnerships between senior citizen groups and law enforcement to combat crimes against elderly Americans, (5) partnerships between law enforcement and social service agencies to fight crimes against children, and (6) supervised centers for divorced or separated parents to visit their children in "safe havens" when a history of risk of physical or sexual abuse is indicated. Drug courts (discussed in Chapter 13) that target

nonviolent offenders with substance-abuse problems received $1 billion in funding.

The act also increased control over firearms by (1) banning the manufacture of 19 military-style assault weapons; (2) prohibiting gun sales to, and possession by, people subject to family violence restraining orders; (3) strengthening federal licensing standards for firearms dealers; and, as mentioned earlier, (4) prohibiting the sale or transfer of a gun to a juvenile and the possession of a gun by a juvenile.

The law also (1) created drug-free zones by increasing penalties for drug dealing near playgrounds, schoolyards, public housing projects, video arcades, and youth centers; (2) authorized adult treatment of 13-year-olds charged with the most violent of crimes (murder, attempted murder, aggravated assault, armed robbery, and rape); (3) enhanced federal penalties for acts of terrorism; (4) expanded the federal death penalty to cover about 60 offenses, including terrorism, murdering a law enforcement officer, large-scale drug trafficking, drive-by shootings, and carjacking in which death occurs; (5) mandated life imprisonment for criminals convicted of three violent felonies or drug offenses (the famous "three strikes and you're out" provision); and (6) increased or created new penalties for over 70 criminal offenses, primarily covering violent crimes, drug trafficking, and gun crimes, such as drive-by shootings, the use of semi-automatic weapons, drug use and drug trafficking in prison, the possession of guns and explosives by convicts, sex offenses and assaults against children, crimes against the elderly, interstate gun trafficking, aggravated sexual abuse, gun smuggling, arson, hate crimes, and drunk driving.

In response to the complaints of state governments that the federal government was not taking seriously its responsibility to oversee the nation's borders and to stem the flow of illegal immigrants, the law designated $1.2 billion for immigration enforcement, including (1) a summary procedure to speed deportation of aliens who have been convicted of crimes, (2) increased penalties for smuggling aliens and for document fraud, and (3) monies to hire new border patrol agents, asylum reform, and other immigration enforcement activities.

In the area of victims' rights, the bill (1) allowed victims of violent and sex crimes to speak at the sentencing of their assailants, (2) required sex offenders and child molesters to pay restitution to their victims, and (3) prohibited diversion of victims' funds to other federal programs.

Finally, the 1994 legislation increased federal criminal penalties for various types of fraud, including (1) telemarketing fraud targeted at senior citizens and multiple victims, (2) computer crime offenses, (3) major fraud by insurance companies against their policyholders (a new federal offense), and (4) credit card offenses.

For all its complexity, there are those who suspect that the Violent Crime Control and Law Enforcement Act of 1994 was primarily a political product, intended to appease a variety of constituencies. As noted criminologist Alfred Blumstein explains, "The legislative amalgam . . . contained an astonishing array of programs and provisions costing 30 billion dollars. Some were intended to satisfy doves (e.g., prevention programs, drug courts), many more were directed at satisfying the hawks (e.g., major subsidies for prisons, three-strikes law, capital punishment), but very few were directed at satisfying the owls, those who would like to substitute more rationality for the ideology that dominates crime-control policy."[49] Read the text of the entire Violent Crime Control and Law Enforcement Act of 1994 at Web Extra! 15-6.

Web Extra! 15-6 at crimtoday.com

The Violence against Women Act

An important component of the Violent Crime Control and Law Enforcement Act of 1994 is the Violence against Women Act. The original VAWA legislation aimed to improve the interstate enforcement of protection orders, provide effective training for court personnel involved with women's issues, and improve the training and collaboration of police and prosecutors with victim-service providers. The VAWA also covers several other initiatives related to strengthening law enforcement efforts to reduce violence against women and efforts to increase services to victims of violence. President Clinton signed the reauthorization of this legislation, the Violence against Women Act of 2000, into law on October 28, 2000. For more information on the VAWA, including the legislation in its entirety, visit the Violence against Women Office via Web Extra! 15-7.

Web Extra! 15-7 at crimtoday.com

The full VAWA text is also available at Web Extra! 15-8.

Web Extra! 15-8 at crimtoday.com

Three-Strikes Legislation

One interesting and controversial aspect of the 1994 Violent Crime Control and Law Enforcement Act is its three-strikes provision. The **three-strikes provision** reads as follows:

Mandatory life imprisonment:
   Notwithstanding any other provision of law, a person who is convicted in a court of the United States of a serious violent felony shall be sentenced to life imprisonment if—
   (A) the person has been convicted (and those convictions have become final) on separate prior occasions in a court of the United States or of a State of—
      (i) 2 or more serious violent felonies; or
      (ii) one or more serious violent felonies and one or more serious drug offenses; and
   (B) each serious violent felony or serious drug offense used as a basis for sentencing under this subsection, other than the first, was committed after the defen-

dant's conviction of the preceding serious violent felony or serious drug offense.

On August 14, 1995, Thomas Lee Farmer, 43, of Des Moines, Iowa, became the first person sentenced under the federal three-strikes law.[50] Farmer, who had three previous convictions for murder, robbery, and conspiracy to commit murder dating back to 1971, was convicted of trying to rob a Waterloo, Iowa, grocery store at gunpoint. Farmer received a mandatory life prison term.

Three-strikes laws are part of a relatively new nationwide initiative intended to keep repeat offenders behind bars.[51] Nationally, many states are in the process of adopting three-strikes laws, which are a kind of **habitual offender statute**. Such laws generally require that offenders who are convicted of three or more serious crimes be sentenced to a lengthy prison term (often life behind bars) following their third conviction. Although three-strikes laws may be new, habitual offender statutes are not, and 35 states already have some form of habitual offender statute on the books. One of the first states to pass a habitual offender statute was Illinois. The Illinois law, which was enacted in 1978, covers only violent offenses. It sounds, however, like a three-strikes law because it mandates a life sentence without parole for people convicted of their third so-called class X felony. Fewer than a hundred offenders are currently serving sentences under the Illinois habitual offender statute.

Other states have since joined the "get tough on crime" bandwagon. In the spring of 1994, for example, California legislators passed the state's now-famous "three strikes and you're out" bill. Amid much fanfare, Governor Pete Wilson signed the three-strikes measure into law, calling it "the toughest and most sweeping crime bill in California history." California's law, which is retroactive (in that it counts offenses committed before the date the legislation was signed), requires a 25-year-to-life sentence for three-time felons with convictions for two or more serious or violent prior offenses. Criminal offenders facing a "second strike" can receive up to double the normal sentence for their most recent offense. Under the law, parole consideration is not available until at least 80% of an offender's sentence has been served. In 1996, however, the California Supreme Court, in the case of *People* v. *Superior Court of San Diego—Romero*,[52] cast the future of the three-strikes law in California into doubt. The court ruled that, regardless of the law, California judges retain the discretion to reduce three-strikes sentences and to avoid counting previous convictions at sentencing "in furtherance of justice." Efforts to modify California's three-strikes law ensued.

By mid-1997, 22 states had passed three-strikes legislation, and other states were considering the same. Some states enacted even tougher laws. Georgia, for example, passed a two-strikes law. Georgia's law, one of the stiffest in the nation, requires that murderers and offenders convicted of a second violent felony be sentenced to life in prison without parole.

Unfortunately, get-tough policies may not provide the solution those who advocate them seek. In an excellent analysis of crime control policy, Bryan Vila presents research findings which tend to show that nurturant strategies—those that attempt to get at the root causes of crime and that address child welfare needs—are more effective than others in the long run.[53] "We know full well that the most serious and intractable types of crime have their roots in the very child welfare problems that are neglected as we trash through one ineffective war on crime after another," says Vila. "Political support for nurturant programs might be obtainable," he says, "if we could reverse the vicious cycle of media sensationalism, short-sighted policy, and public impatience that encourages ineffective 'quick fixes' for crime."[54] Learn more about crime control policy at the Center for Law and Social Policy via Web Extra! 15-9.

Web Extra! 15-9 at crimtoday.com

Youth Violence Initiatives

During the Clinton administration, youth violence became a special concern. The 1994 Violent Crime Control and Law Enforcement Act targeted gangs and youth violence by (1) providing new, stiff penalties for violent and drug crimes committed by gangs, (2) tripling penalties for using children to deal drugs near schools and playgrounds, and (3) enhancing penalties for all crimes using children and for recruiting and encouraging children to commit a crime.

Four years later, in 1998, the administration created a national Safe Schools/Healthy Students Initiative. The initiative was a joint effort involving the Departments of Education, Justice, and Health and Human Services to help communities design and implement a comprehensive approach, including educational, mental health, social service, and law enforcement services to help combat youth violence. The program provided $146 million to 77 local education authorities for the establishment of formal partnerships with local mental health and law enforcement agencies. In 1999, President Clinton created the White House Council on Youth Violence to coordinate youth violence research and programs throughout the federal government and to make information derived from the federal government's efforts more accessible to the public. The Clinton administration also attempted to engage the private sector in youth violence prevention through the creation, in 1999, of a National Campaign against Youth Violence. The campaign developed antiviolence activities, including media campaigns, concerts, town hall meetings, and in-school and after-school programs, and highlighted effective youth violence initiatives in cities across the country. Learn more about youth violence and what can be done to stop it at the Center on Juvenile and Criminal Justice at Web Extra! 15-10.

Web Extra! 15-10 at crimtoday.com

The Administration of George W. Bush

As this book goes to press, President George W. Bush is serving his first year in office. Although it is too early to tell what crime control policies might emerge from the new administration, President Bush has committed himself to a number of identifiable positions. In policy statements, Bush has[55]

- said that he supports executions as a criminal deterrent and has voiced support for the death penalty for criminals as young as 17
- expressed displeasure with parole and appears to favor its elimination in most jurisdictions (something already being done in the federal system)
- supported mandatory sentences for repeat criminals
- supported two-strikes legislation and registration for sexual criminals
- advocated victim-notification laws
- favored antistalking laws
- said that he favors giving judges and juries more discretion in sentencing criminals

In the five years that President Bush served as governor of Texas, he signed warrants permitting the execution of 112 men and woman—far more than any other governor in recent times. While governor, Bush repeatedly spoke out in support of the death penalty and said on record, "I support the death penalty because I believe, if administered swiftly and justly, capital punishment is a deterrent against future violence and will save other innocent lives. Some advocates of life will challenge why I oppose abortion yet support the death penalty; to me, it's the difference between innocence and guilt."[56]

CRIME CONTROL PHILOSOPHIES TODAY

In a recent article, eminent criminologist Elliott Currie reflects on crime and criminology at the start of the twenty-first century. Currie cites the "emergence of a new kind of *triumphalism* about crime, and the capacity of the criminal justice system to control it."[57] In other words, Currie is concerned that Americans are becoming complacent about crime because statistics seem to show that the "crime problem" has somehow been solved. According to Currie, "There is a sense that we've got it 'fixed' here in the United States—that we possess the secret of how to organize your economy and society successfully, and that everyone else in the world ought to learn to do things the way we do."[58]

Unfortunately, Currie says, this kind of thinking has led to a dearth of debate at the national level over the most critical issues of crime control policy today. He identifies those issues as "the swelling of the correctional complex, the chronic revelations of terrible abuses in our prisons, jails, and juvenile facilities, the increasing resort to the death penalty in

CRIME IN THE NEWS
Should We Arm the Teachers?

everal weeks before the April 20 shooting at Columbine High School, an economist and a law professor announced that getting more guns on the street might help solve the plague of school shootings. On Thursday, as Littleton buried the last of its dead, the men stood firm in their controversial position.

In a study released earlier this month, John Lott Jr., a University of Chicago economist, and William Landes, a University of Chicago law professor, found that states with concealed-handgun laws suffered fewer cases of multiple-victim shooting rampages. Any shootings these states did suffer tended to have fewer casualties.

The two men studied 396 multiple-victim shootings between 1977 and 1995 and came up with a simple, cost-benefit analysis explaining the positive effects of concealed-weapons laws.

RAISING THE PRICE OF AN ATTACK

"If you can take away the warped benefits that [shooters] get from this so they say 'It may not be worth me doing this crime because the number of people I'm going to be able to kill is going to be small relative to the cost I have to pay—because I'm likely to be killed too,' some of these guys just might not decide to do their crimes," Lott said.

To illustrate their point, Lott and Landes described a pair of recent school shootings.

In the October 1997 school shooting in Pearl, Miss., Luke Woodham, 16, shot nine students and killed two. An assistant principal then got his own gun from his office but ended up tackling and immobilizing Woodham before the assailant could kill anyone else.

SCHOOL ATTACK STOPPED BY SHOTGUN

Last April, in Endinboro, Pa., Andrew Wurst, 15, allegedly entered his school and killed a teacher before a storeowner armed with a shotgun convinced Wurst to give up his handgun.

According to Lott, keeping a gun under the office counter may hold the answer to fewer or less lethal school rampages in the future.

"Maybe you just want a couple of administrators [with guns]," Lott said. "In general, you find big, beneficial effects from just a small percentage of the population having permits."

CONTROVERSIAL CONCEPT

Lott's conclusions have generated considerable criticism.

"His research is completely spurious because these incidents happen so infrequently," said Susan Glick, a health policy researcher at the Violence Policy Institute, a think tank that has called for harsh handgun controls. "They happen so infrequently that to say that these laws have any effect on mass shootings—that's ludicrous."

"I don't think the answer to school violence is to put more guns in school," said Nancy Hwa, a spokeswoman for the Center to Prevent Gun Violence, a leading gun-control group. "I don't think any normal human being will say that's the answer."

Lott has come under fire for his work on concealed weapons before. In 1997, Lott and another University of Chicago colleague named David Mustard published a study that showed a 10 percent reduction in murder rates for states that passed concealed-weapons laws. These states also enjoyed a decline in robberies and rapes, Lott wrote. In 1998, Lott published his findings as a book titled *More Guns, Less Crime.*

OUTDATED STATISTICAL MODELS?

Other academics accused Lott of using outdated statistical models or of improperly lumping together states with widely varying concealed-weapons laws. And because most murders involve a victim and killer who know each other, one critic wrote, the presence of a concealed weapon worn to prevent random street crime becomes irrelevant.

"We and others find numerous errors in Lott and Mustard's study which bias their findings, and little support for their conclusions that RTC [right-to-carry] laws reduce violent crime," wrote Daniel Webster, a researcher with the Johns Hopkins Center for Gun Policy and Research, in a rebuttal distributed to gun-policy researchers around the country. "Previous research finds no deterrent effects from right-to-carry laws and suggests that the laws may actually increase homicide rates."

But even if Lott's conclusions prove true, armed citizens might not even matter in some mass shooting cases. A day after the Columbine shootings, Charlton Heston, the National Rifle Association's president, said publicly that Eric Harris and Dylan Klebold could have been stopped if someone at the school had been armed.

In fact, an armed sheriff's deputy had been patrolling the grounds when the shooting began, and exchanged fire with the two student gunmen. But overwhelmed by their firepower, the deputy retreated and called for backup. In the meantime, Harris and Klebold murdered 13 classmates and then killed themselves.

"How many armed guards do we need?" Glick asked. "What type of guns do we need? Should we be arming the students?"

Source: Hans H. Chen, "Should We Arm the Teachers?," APB News, April 30, 1999. Reprinted with permission.

the face of the opposite trend in every other Western democracy, [and] the increasing use of the penal system as a substitute for more constructive approaches to the structural social ills of American society."[59]

While much of what Currie says is true, the relative lack of debate over crime and justice in America today does not mean that our society lacks policies for dealing with those issues. It means, simply, that many of today's policies are predicated upon taken-for-granted (and, as Currie says, largely unquestioned) assumptions about what works.

Analysts generally say that today's policy approach to crime control has two prongs.[60] One prong, that of crime control, defines crime as an issue of individual responsibility. The other, which is being cast in the guise of a public health agenda, sees criminals as victims of a kind of rampant social pathology that has turned them into offenders. In Chapter 1, the first prong was termed the "social responsibility perspective," and the second approach was called the "social problems perspective."

Those who portray crime as the result of poor social conditions stress the need for improvements in the American infrastructure and continue to battle for an expansion of educational and employment opportunities for the disenfranchised. One new aspect of the social problems approach is its recasting in terms of social epidemiology. In terminology akin to the old social pathology approach of the Chicago School, some contemporary politicians and criminologists now view crime and the conditions that create it in terms of a disease model.[61] The word *epidemiology* refers to the study of epidemics and diseases, and the term **social epidemiology** has come to mean the study of social epidemics and diseases of the social order. Hence the social epidemiological approach holds that crime arises from festering conditions which promote social ills and that individuals caught in an environment within which crime may be communicated display symptoms of this disease and suffer from its maladies. Crime becomes an illness, a social malady, but one which can be cured if the necessary resources could be dedicated to its treatment and eradication. Recognizing that crime and violence have reached epidemic proportions, such thinkers advance solutions based on what is, in effect, a public health model. Crime as a disease becomes a new kind of social problem—one which shifts responsibility for law violations away from individuals "afflicted" with criminality and toward the society that is ultimately responsible for their control.

On January 17, 2001, U.S. Surgeon General David Satcher released a report on youth violence in America. Excerpts from that report, which emphasized a public health approach to understanding and preventing youth violence, are reproduced in the Theory versus Reality box entitled "Youth Violence and Social Policy." According to the surgeon general, "The public health approach can help reduce the number of injuries and deaths caused by violence just as it reduced the number of traffic fatalities and deaths attributed to tobacco use." Satcher says that the public health approach "offers a practical, goal-oriented, and community-based strategy for promoting and maintaining health."[62] To identify problems and develop solutions for entire population groups, Satcher says, the public health approach

- Defines the problem, using surveillance processes designed to gather data that establish the nature of the problem and the trends in its incidence and prevalence
- Identifies potential causes, through epidemiological analyses that identify risk and protective factors associated with the problem
- Designs, develops, and evaluates the effectiveness and generalizability of interventions
- Disseminates successful models as part of a coordinated effort to educate and reach out to the public

Which crime control policies work? This is the subject of considerable debate. Here, mediators affiliated with Maharishi International University work to lower crime in Washington, D.C. Later research showed a statistically significant reduction in D.C.-area crime rates during the meditative session. Do you think the observed effect was "real"? *Courtesy Maharishi International University*

THEORY VERSUS REALITY
Youth Violence and Social Policy

On January 17, 2001, U.S. Surgeon General David Satcher released a report on youth violence in America. The report consisted of a study ordered by Congress and the president after the April 20, 1999, Columbine High School shootings in Colorado in which 15 people died and 20 were injured. The report—the first Surgeon General's report on youth violence—reviewed a massive body of research on where, when, and how much youth violence occurs, what causes it, and which of today's many preventive strategies are genuinely effective. The report also reviewed existing knowledge in an effort to provide scientifically derived bases for policy development. Edited excerpts from the executive summary accompanying the surgeon general's report are reproduced in this box.

Youth violence is a high-visibility, high-priority concern in every sector of U.S. society. No community, whether affluent or poor, urban, suburban, or rural, is immune from its devastating effects. In the decade extending from roughly 1983 to 1993, an epidemic of violent, often lethal behavior broke out in this country, forcing millions of young people and their families to cope with injury, disability, and death. This epidemic left lasting scars on victims, perpetrators, and their families and friends. It also wounded entire communities and, in ways not yet fully understood, the United States as a whole.

Since 1993, when the epidemic peaked, youth violence has declined significantly nationwide, as signaled by downward trends in arrest records, victimization data, and hospital emergency room records. But the problem has not been resolved. Another key indicator of violence—youths' confidential reports about their violent behavior—reveals no change since 1993 in the proportion of young people who have committed physically injurious and potentially lethal acts. Moreover, arrests for aggravated assault have declined

only slightly and in 1999 remained nearly 70% higher than preepidemic levels. In 1999, there were 104,000 arrests of people under age 18 for a serious violent crime—robbery, forcible rape, aggravated assault, or homicide. Of these, 1,400 were for homicides committed by adolescents and, on occasion, even younger children. But viewing homicide arrests as a barometer of all youth violence is quite misleading, as is judging the success of violence prevention efforts solely on the basis of reductions in homicides.

Arrest records give only a partial picture of youth violence. For every youth arrested in any given year in the late 1990s, at least ten were engaged in some form of violent behavior that could have seriously injured or killed another person, according to the several national research surveys in which youths report on their own behavior. Thus despite reductions in the lethality of violence and consequent arrests, the number of adolescents involved in violent behavior remains disconcertingly high, underscoring the urgency of this report.

The epidemic of lethal violence that swept the United States from 1983 to 1993 was fueled in large part by easy access to weapons, notably firearms. If the sizable numbers of youths still involved in violence today begin carrying and using weapons as they did a decade ago, this country may see a resurgence of the lethal violence that characterized the violence epidemic.

THE DEVELOPMENTAL PERSPECTIVE

This report views violence from a developmental perspective. To understand why some young people become involved in violence and some do not, it examines how youths' personal characteristics interact over time with the social contexts in which they live. This perspective considers a range of risks over the life course, from prenatal factors to factors influencing whether patterns of violent behavior in adolescence will persist into adulthood. The developmental perspective identifies two general onset trajectories of violence: one in which violent behaviors emerge before puberty, and one in which they appear after puberty.

The early-onset trajectory shows stronger links between childhood factors and persistent, even lifelong involvement in violent behavior. Identifying such pathways to violence can help researchers target interventions to the periods in development where they will be most effective.

THE PUBLIC HEALTH APPROACH

The designation of youth violence as a public health concern invites an approach that focuses more on prevention than on rehabilitation. Primary prevention identifies behavioral, environmental, and biological risk factors associated with violence and takes steps to educate individuals and communities about, and protect them from, these risks. Central to this process is the principle that health promotion is best learned, performed, and maintained when it is ingrained in individuals' and communities' daily routines and perceptions of what constitutes good health practices.

The public health perspective provides a framework for research and intervention that draws on the insights and strategies of diverse disciplines. Tapping into a rich but often fragmented knowledge base about risk factors, prevention, and public education, the public health perspective calls for critically examining and reconciling what are frequently contradictory conclusions about youth violence. Thus the approach taken in the current report, which blends offender-based research with public health concepts of prevention and intervention, constitutes an effort to bridge the gap between criminology and the social and developmental science approaches on the one hand, and the conventional public health approaches on the other.

MYTHS ABOUT YOUTH VIOLENCE

An important reason for making research findings widely available is to challenge false notions and misconceptions about youth violence. Ten myths about violence and violent youth are listed and debunked. Examples of these myths include

(continued on the next page)

(continued from previous page)

Myth: Most future offenders can be identified in early childhood.

Myth: Child abuse and neglect inevitably lead to violent behavior later in life.

Myth: African-American and Hispanic youths are more likely to become involved in violence than other racial or ethnic groups.

Myth: A new, violent breed of young superpredators threatens the United States.

Myth: Getting tough with juvenile offenders by trying them in adult criminal courts reduces the likelihood that they will commit more crimes.

Myth: Nothing works with respect to treating or preventing violent behavior.

Myth: Most violent youths will end up being arrested for a violent crime.

These false ideas are intrinsically dangerous. Assumptions that a problem does not exist or failure to recognize the true nature of a problem can obscure the need for informed policy or for interventions. An example is the conventional wisdom in many circles that the epidemic of youth violence so evident in the early 1990s is over. Alternatively, myths may trigger public fears and lead to inappropriate or misguided policies that result in inefficient or counterproductive use of scarce public resources.

An example is the current policy of waiving or transferring young offenders into adult criminal courts and prisons.

MAJOR RESEARCH FINDINGS AND CONCLUSIONS

The most important conclusion of this report is that youth violence is not an intractable problem. We now have the knowledge and tools needed to reduce or even prevent much of the most serious youth violence, with the added benefit of reducing less dangerous, but still serious problem behaviors and promoting healthy development. Scientists from many disciplines, working in a variety of settings with public and private agencies, are generating needed information and putting it to use in designing, testing, and evaluating intervention programs. However, after years of effort and massive expenditures of public and private resources, the search for solutions to the issue of youth violence remains an enormous challenge. Some traditional as well as seemingly innovative approaches to reducing and preventing youth violence have failed to deliver on their promise, and successful approaches are often eclipsed by random violent events such as the school shootings that have occurred in recent years in communities throughout the country. Thus the most urgent need is a national resolve to confront the problem of

youth violence systematically, using research-based approaches, and to correct damaging myths and stereotypes that interfere with the task at hand.

Read the surgeon general's report in its entirety at Web Extra! 15-11.

DISCUSSION QUESTIONS

1. What sparked the epidemic of youth violence during the early 1990s? How can we make sure that such an epidemic doesn't happen again?

2. Do you believe that crime and violence can be effectively portrayed as a public health issue? Why or why not?

3. What strategies to prevent youth violence are either discussed or implied in this report? How might they be implemented?

Source: U.S. Surgeon General, *Youth Violence: A Report of the Surgeon General—Executive Summary,* January 17, 2001. Web posted at http://www.surgeongeneral.gov/library/youthviolence/sgsummary/summary.htm.

The epidemiological approach is gaining in popularity among the nation's crime control policymakers. The 2001 *National Drug Control Strategy* of the Office of National Drug Control Policy (ONDCP) says, for example, "The metaphor of a 'war on drugs' is misleading. Although wars are expected to end, drug education—like all schooling—is a continuous process. The moment we believe ourselves victorious and drop our guard, drug abuse will resurface in the next generation. To reduce the demand for drugs, prevention must be ongoing. Addicted individuals should be held accountable for their actions and offered treatment to help change destructive behavior."[63]

Assuming a public health perspective, ONDCP says, "Cancer is a more appropriate metaphor for the nation's drug problem. Dealing with cancer is a long-term proposition. It requires the mobilization of support mechanisms—medical, educational, social, and financial—to check the

spread of the disease and improve the patient's prognosis. Symptoms of the illness must be managed while the root cause is attacked. The key to reducing the incidence of drug abuse and cancer is prevention coupled with treatment and accompanied by research."

Types of Crime Control Strategies

The range of effective crime control alternatives available to today's policymakers is essentially limited to three types of strategies. These three categories—identified by Bryan Vila, one of the most seminal contemporary analysts of contemporary public policy—differ in terms of "strategic focus."[64] That is, they are distinguishable from one another "by whether they attempt to block opportunities for crime, alter the outcome of conscious or unconscious decision-making that precedes a criminal act, or alter the broad strategic style with which people approach many aspects of their lives."[65] The three categories are

- Protection/avoidance strategies
- Deterrence strategies
- Nurturant strategies

Protection/avoidance strategies "attempt to reduce criminal opportunities by changing people's routine activities, increasing guardianship, or incapacitating convicted offenders."[66] Incapacitating convicted offenders via incarceration or through the use of electronic monitoring devices is an example of a protection/avoidance strategy. Target hardening through the use of architectural design, crime prevention programs like neighborhood watch, and increased policing also fit this category.

Deterrence strategies "attempt to diminish motivation for crime by increasing the perceived certainty, severity, or celerity of penalties."[67] New and tougher laws, quicker trial court processing, harsher punishments, and faster imposition of sentences are all deterrence strategies.

Nurturant strategies "attempt to forestall development of criminality by improving early life experiences and channeling child and adolescent development" into desirable directions. They "focus on prevention of criminality rather than its remediation or control."[68] Nurturant strategies include increased infant and maternal health care, child care for the working poor, training in parenting skills, enhanced public education, and better programs to reduce the number of unwanted pregnancies.

A comprehensive crime control strategy, say many criminologists, would be "a balanced mix of protection/avoidance, deterrence, and nurturant strategies."[69] Achieving the most effective balance in a politically sensitive world, however, is a difficult undertaking. Many large and influential political constituencies continue to press for crime control measures which emphasize protection/avoidance and deterrence strategies while virtually ignoring nurturant strategies. Learn more about contemporary crime control measures at the Center for Policy Alternatives via Web Extra! 15-12.

Web Extra! 15-12 at crimtoday.com

International Policies

A growing global conservatism, coupled with new concerns about crime in many nations, has led a number of countries to enact legislation designed to curb crime through the use of deterrence strategies. In 1994, for example, the British Parliament passed the Criminal Justice and Police Bill, marking a return to a get-tough English crime policy. British Home Secretary Michael Howard called the legislation "the most comprehensive attempt to tackle crime [in England] in more than three decades."[70]

The degree to which British social policy shifted with passage of the bill can be easily seen in one feature of the legisla-

tion, which removed a suspect's right to silence. According to Howard, "The right of silence, an age-old feature of Britain's justice system that has been copied in many countries, was a charter for terrorists and professional criminals."[71] Prior to the bill's passage, suspects were told that they had a right to remain silent under police questioning and that anything they might say could be taken down and be used as evidence against them. The bill mandates that suspects now be told only that failure to mention relevant information during questioning at the police station may damage their case. Another feature of the 1994 statute gives courts wide powers to sentence persistent offenders aged 12 to 14 and doubles the maximum permissible sentence in institutions for youthful offenders. Learn more about international crime control policies from the International Center for Criminal Law Reform and Criminal Justice Policy via Web Extra! 15-13.

Web Extra! 15-13 at crimtoday.com

CRIMINOLOGY AND SOCIAL POLICY

Criminologists frequently ask to what extent the discipline to which they belong actually influences crime control policy in the United States. A decade ago, as the American Society of Criminology celebrated the fiftieth anniversary of its founding, incoming president Joan Petersilia acknowledged concerns among the members that the organization has been less than successful in bringing about significant changes in government policies. Petersilia said, "Several signs indicate that our research is not influencing policy and practice the way a prolific and scholarly rigorous body of work should."[72] Among the "signs" that Petersilia identified were

- A pervasive, often-voiced feeling among criminologists that policymakers and practitioners largely ignore their findings or, worse, sometimes act counter to what the best science tells us about the [criminal justice] system
- Some policymakers' and practitioners' lack of awareness that research has influenced the system
- The scope and changing nature of research funding

Petersilia pointed out, however, that when criminologists complain that their work is not being used, they have in mind an "instrumental use model." Such a model, she said, consists of four assumptions: "1.) Here is a problem; 2.) there is a study of the problem; 3.) here is what the study says we should do about the problem; 4.) we will do it." The last assumption means that criminologists assume that policymakers will enact specific laws based on findings from specific studies.

A better way to understand the impact that criminologists have had on national policymaking, says Petersilia, can be had in a model that takes into account "conceptual use." There is evidence, she says, that the conceptual use of ideas developed through criminological research has had a broad impact on policymakers—generally influencing the *types* of provisions that have been put into place in state jurisdictions and at the national level. Learn more about the process of transforming research into action at the Center for Criminal Justice Policy Research via Web Extra! 15-14.

Web Extra! 15-14 at crimtoday.com

THE VICTIMS' MOVEMENT

One area of growing policy concern throughout the United States is for victims of crime, especially violent crime. Many supporters of the Violence against Women Act, discussed earlier in this chapter, were explicitly concerned about domestic violence, sexual brutality, and gender-motivated crimes. Similarly, hate-crimes legislation embodies the notion that certain potential victims need to have special legal protections. Support is growing for national legislation that would accord to crime victims the same kinds of procedural protections now afforded to those accused of crimes. To better understand the legal rights of victims in America today, we begin with a historical review of what is known as the "victims' movement."

A History of the Victim

In early times, victims routinely took the law into their own hands. If they were able to apprehend their victimizers, they enacted their own form of revenge and imposed some form of personal retaliation. The Code of Hammurabi (circa 1750 B.C.), one of the earliest known legal codes, required that many offenders make restitution. If the offender could not be found, however, the victim's family was duty bound to care for the needs of the victim. This early period in history has been called the Golden Age of the Victim because victims were not only well cared for, but also had considerable say in imposing punishments upon apprehended offenders.

Eventually, however, crimes came to be understood as offenses against society, and the victim was forgotten. By the late Middle Ages, the concept of the "king's peace" had emerged, wherein all offenses were seen as violations of imperial law. It became the duty of local governments to apprehend, try, and punish offenders, effectively removing the victim from any direct involvement in judicial decision making. Victims were expected only to provide evidence of a crime and to testify against those who had offended them. Society's moral responsibility toward making victims "whole again" was forgotten, and victims as a class were moved to the periphery of the justice process. Justice for the victim was forgotten, translated instead into the notion of justice for the state.

The situation remained pretty much the same until the 1960s, when renewed interest in the plight of victims led to a resurgence of positive sentiments around the world. Such sentiments were soon translated into a flurry of laws intended to provide compensation to victims of violent crimes.

Compensation for criminal injury is not unknown throughout history. More than a hundred years ago, Jeremy Bentham advocated "mandatory restitution, to be paid by a state compensation system, in cases of property crime."[73] Long before that, the Code of Hammurabi specified,

> If a man has committed robbery . . . that man shall be put to death. If the robber is not caught, the man who has been robbed shall formally declare what he has lost . . . and the city . . . shall replace whatever he has lost for him. If it is the life of the owner that is lost, the city or the mayor shall pay one maneth of silver to his kinfolk.

The first modern victim-compensation statute was adopted by New Zealand in 1963. Known as the Criminal Injuries Compensation Act, it provided an avenue for claims to be filed by victims of certain specified violent crimes. A three-member board was empowered to make awards to victims. A year later, partially in response to a movement led by social reformer Margaret Fry, Great Britain established a similar board. In 1965, the state of California passed the first piece of American legislation intended to assist victims of crime. Simultaneously, the New York City Council passed a "Good Samaritan" statute designed to pay up to $4,000 to anyone suffering physical injuries while going to the aid of others being victimized by crime. Other states soon joined the bandwagon, and today all 50 states and the District of Columbia have passed legislation providing for monetary payments to crime victims, although legislatures have rarely funded programs at the level of received requests.

All states require applicants to meet certain eligibility requirements, and most set award maximums. A number of states set minimum loss limits (similar to deductible provisions in insurance policies) and have established a "needs test," whereby only needy crime victims are eligible for compensation. Likewise, some states deny awards to family members of the offender, as in the case when a son assaults a father. In all states, payments for medical assistance, lost wages, and living expenses are commonly made. Victims who are responsible in some significant way for their own victimization are generally not reimbursed for losses under existing laws.

The concept of victim compensation rests upon at least seven philosophical underpinnings:[74]

- Strict liability theory, which claims that compensation is due victims because the social contract between victim and society (specifically, the government) has been broken by the experience of victimization. The duty of the government, says liability theory, is to safeguard its citizens, and when safeguards fail, the injured citizen is due compensation.
- Government negligence theory, a very selective approach, which holds that the negligent actions of government representatives, including law enforcement officers, jailers, correctional personnel, and the like should result in appropriate forms of compensation
- Equal protection theory, which says that compensation should serve to ameliorate imbalances in society,

including the huge variation in crime risk that citizens living in different parts of the nation face

- Humanitarian theory, which advocates compensation because of the suffering victims undergo
- Social welfare theory, similar to humanitarian theory, which says that victims should be compensated if they are in need. Social welfare approaches might exclude compensatory payments to well-heeled victims but make them available on an as-needed basis to less fortunate members of society who undergo the victimization process.
- Crime prevention theory, which holds that compensation programs will encourage more citizens to report crime, thereby resulting in more effective law enforcement programs
- Political motives theory, which says that victim compensation is in vogue with the voting public and that any politician hoping to remain in office will support the concept

Although many tout the benefits of victim-compensation programs, a recent study of the effectiveness of government-sponsored compensation programs in New York and New Jersey found that most victims had generally negative attitudes toward the programs which were supposed to help them.[75] According to the study, "Respondents were dissatisfied with delays, inconveniences, poor information, inability to participate, and the restrictive eligibility requirements. These sentiments, coupled with the large number of award applications that were denied, produced strongly negative attitudes among victims toward victim compensation."[76]

Current Directions in Victims' Rights

Victims experience many hardships extending beyond their original victimization, including the trauma of testifying, uncertainty about their role in the justice process, lost time at work, trial delays, fear of retaliation by the defendant, and a general lack of knowledge of what is expected of them as the wheels of justice grind forward. Problems which follow from initial victimization are referred to as **postcrime victimization,** or **secondary victimization.** Police, employer, and spouse insensitivity can all exacerbate the difficulties crime victims face. Even hospitals that charge high fees for medical records and social service agencies that swamp applicants in a plethora of forms can contribute to the victim's sense of continuing victimization.[77]

In recent years, a number of victims' assistance programs, designed to provide comfort and assistance to victims of crime, have been established across the nation.[78] The earliest of these programs began as grassroots movements designed to counsel victims of rape. In 1975, a national survey identified only 23 victims' assistance programs in the United States.[79] By 1986, the number had grown to over 600, and estimates today place the number of such programs at nearly 1,000. Some authors have drawn a distinction between victim-service programs, which emphasize therapeutic counseling, and victim/witness assistance programs, which provide a wide array of services.

Most **victim-witness assistance programs,** although small and often staffed by local volunteers, typically counsel victims, orient them to the justice process, and provide a variety of other services, such as transportation to court, child care during court appearances, and referrals to social service agencies when additional assistance is needed. A recent survey found that most organizations explain the court process to victims (71.2% of all organizations surveyed), make referrals to other agencies (68.4%), provide court escorts (65.2%), help victims fill out victim-compensation forms (64.1%), attempt to educate the public as to the needs of victims (60.9%), advocate with employers on behalf of victims (60.3%), and provide transportation to court (59.2%).[80]

Two large public groups, the National Organization for Victims Assistance (NOVA) and the National Victims Center, both located in the Washington, D.C., area, provide leadership in victims' education, lobby the U.S. Congress, and hold conferences and workshops designed to assist local victim-witness assistance programs.

In 1982, the President's Task Force on Victims of Crime recommended 68 strategies that could be used by federal, state, and local governments to improve the plight of crime victims. Legislation based on task force recommendations resulted in the **Victims of Crime Act** (**VOCA**), passed by Congress in 1984. VOCA established the federal Crime Victims Fund, which uses monies from fines and forfeitures collected from federal offenders to supplement state support of local victims' assistance programs and state victim-compensation programs.

Victims' advocates argue that a victims' rights amendment to the U.S. Constitution is needed to provide the same kind of fairness to victims that is routinely afforded defendants in criminal proceedings. In 1996, three senators proposed a victims' rights amendment to the U.S. Constitution. Although the proposal failed to pass Congress due to difficulties in wording, proponents of the legislation remain active as this book goes to press. A modified version of the proposal is likely to come before Congress again soon. The wording of the original proposal is reproduced in a Theory versus Reality box in this section. Learn more about crime victims and their rights at the National Center for Victims of Crime via Web Extra! 15-15.

Web EXTRA! **Web Extra! 15-15 at crimtoday.com**

Victim-Impact Statements

One consequence of the burgeoning national victims' rights movement has been a call for the use of victim-impact statements prior to the sentencing of convicted criminal defendants. A **victim-impact statement** is typically a written document which describes the losses, suffering, and trauma experienced by the crime victim or by the victim's survivors. In jurisdictions where victim-impact statements are used, judges are expected to consider them in arriving at an appropriate sanction for the offender.

Although the drive to mandate inclusion of victim-impact statements in sentencing decisions has gathered much mo-

THEORY VERSUS REALITY
A Proposed Victims' Rights Amendment to the U.S. Constitution

Senate Joint Resolution 65, introduced on September 30, 1996, by Senators Jon Kyl and Dianne Feinstein, proposed a victims' rights amendment to the U.S. Constitution. Although the proposal failed to garner the votes needed to pass Congress, supporters have continued their efforts toward passage of a victims' rights amendment. The text of the original Kyl-Feinstein resolution is reproduced here.

Proposing an amendment to the Constitution of the United States to protect the rights of crime victims. (Introduced in the Senate)

IN THE SENATE OF THE UNITED STATES

September 30, 1996

Mr. KYL (for himself, Mrs. FEINSTEIN, and Mr. EXON) introduced the following joint resolution; which was read twice and referred to the Committee on the Judiciary

JOINT RESOLUTION

Proposing an amendment to the Constitution of the United States to protect the rights of crime victims.

Resolved by the Senate and House of Representatives of the United States of America in Congress assembled (two-thirds of each House concurring therein),

That the following article is proposed as an amendment to the Constitution of the United States, which shall be valid for all intents and purposes as part of the Constitution when ratified by the legislatures of three-fourths of the several States within seven years from the date of its submission by the Congress:

Article

SECTION 1. Victims of crimes of violence and other crimes that Congress and the States may define by law pursuant to section 3, shall have the rights to notice of and not to be excluded from all public proceedings relating to the crime; to be heard if present and to submit a statement at a public pre-trial or trial proceeding to determine a release from custody, an acceptance of a negotiated plea, or a sentence; to these rights at a parole proceeding to the extent they are afforded to the convicted offender; to notice of a release pursuant to a public or parole proceeding or an escape; to a final disposition free from unreasonable delay; to an order of restitution from the convicted offender; to have the safety of the victim considered in determining a release from custody; and to notice of the rights established by this article.

SECTION 2. The victim shall have standing to assert the rights established by this article; however, nothing in this article shall provide grounds for the victim to challenge a charging decision or a conviction, obtain a stay of trial, or compel a new trial; nor shall anything in this article give rise to a claim for damages against the United States, a State, a political subdivision, or a public official; nor shall anything in this article provide grounds for the accused or convicted offender to obtain any form of relief.

SECTION 3. The Congress and the States shall have the power to enforce this article within their respective Federal and State jurisdictions by appropriate legislation, including the power to enact exceptions when required for compelling reasons of public safety.

SECTION 4. The rights established by this article shall be applicable to all proceedings occurring after ratification of this article.

SECTION 5. The rights established by this article shall apply in all Federal, State, military, and juvenile justice proceedings, and shall also apply to victims in the District of Columbia, and any commonwealth, territory, or possession of the United States.

DISCUSSION QUESTIONS

1. Would you change the proposed constitutional amendment shown in this box in any way? If so, how?
2. Do you agree with the authors of this amendment that it is time for the United States to adopt a victims' rights amendment? Why or why not?

---

mentum, their final role has yet to be decided. The President's Task Force on Victims of Crime, commissioned by then-President Reagan shortly after he took office, recommended adoption of a change to the Sixth Amendment of the U.S. Constitution. The task force specifically recommended adding these words: "Likewise, the victim, in every criminal prosecution shall have the right to be present and to be heard at all critical stages of judicial proceedings."[81] Although such a change may be long in coming, significant federal legislation has already been passed. The 1982 Victim and Witness Protection Act[82] requires victim-impact statements to be considered at federal sentencing hearings and places the responsibility for their creation on federal probation officers.

Some states have gone the federal government one better. In 1984, the state of California, for example, passed legislation to allow victims a right to attend and participate in sentencing and parole hearings.[83] Approximately 20 states now have laws mandating citizen involvement in sentencing. When written victim-impact statements are not available, courts may invite the victim to testify directly at sentencing.

Victim Restitution

The victims' movement has also spawned a rebirth of the concept of restitution. **Restitution** is punishment through imposed responsibility—in particular, the payment of compensation to the victim. Restitution encompasses the notion that criminal offenders should shoulder at least a portion of the financial obligations required to make the victim whole again. Not only does restitution help the victim heal, it places responsibility for the process back upon the offender who caused the harm initially. Advocates of restitution, which works through court-imposed fines and garnishments, claim that, as a sentence, it benefits society by leading to an

A child's grief expressed through art. "The man will be kill for killing my dad. . . . The man was not caught," the young artist writes. How might the experience of criminal victimization influence a child's development? *Illustration by Pilar Martin*

increased sense of social and individual responsibility on the part of convicted offenders.

Stephen Schafer, who wrote the book *The Victim and His Criminal* in 1968, is commonly credited with repopularizing the concept of restitution.[84] Schafer discussed three forms of restitution: (1) compensatory fines, which are imposed in addition to other court-ordered punishments and which compensate the victim for the actual amount of loss; (2) double or treble damages, in which offenders are required, as punishment, to pay the victim back more than the amount of the original injury; and (3) restitution in lieu of other punishment, where the offender discharges any criminal responsibility by compensating the victim. In the last form of restitution, no other criminal penalties are imposed if the offender meets the restitution obligations.

The 1982 President's Task Force on Victims of Crime recognized the inequitable financial consequences that often follow criminal victimization: "It is simply unfair that victims should have to liquidate their assets, mortgage their homes, or sacrifice their health or education or that of their children while the offender escapes responsibility for the financial hardship he has imposed. It is unjust that a victim should have to sell his car to pay bills while the offender drives to his probation appointments. The victim may be placed in a financial crisis that will last a lifetime. If one of the two must go into debt, the offender should do so."[85] The report went so far as to recommend that legislation be passed requiring restitution in all criminal cases and that mandates be established requiring judges to order restitution in cases where victims have suffered financially, unless compelling reasons to the contrary could be demonstrated.

A year later, in 1983, the American Bar Association, in its *Guidelines for Fair Treatment of Crime Victims and Witnesses*, recommended that "victims of a crime involving economic loss, loss of earnings, or earning capacity should be able to expect the sentencing body to give priority consideration to restitution as a condition of probation."[86]

According to Susan Hillenbrand, Director of Special Projects with the American Bar Association, the change in perspective which the American system of justice underwent in the 1970s and 1980s meant that restitution was no longer seen "solely as a punitive or rehabilitative measure," but came to be understood "as a matter of justice to crime victims."[87] Recently, however, Hillenbrand says, efforts to evaluate restitution programs "have largely assessed outcomes in terms of correctional objectives rather than in terms of benefits to victims."[88] Nonetheless, Hillenbrand offers, "restitution need not be viewed as an all or nothing proposition for either victims or defendants in order to benefit both. The fact that the criminal justice system has goals other than restoration of crime victims should not be of concern to victims as long as their own needs are included among the goals of the system."[89]

Today, restitution is widely operative in sentencing practice. Texas is one of a growing number of states that utilize restitution as a major component of its statewide alternatives to prison. The Texas Residential Restitution Program operates numerous community-based centers, housing selected nonviolent felony offenders who work at regular jobs in the community, pay for their support and for the support of their families, and make restitution to their victims. On the national level, the Office of Juvenile Justice and Delinquency Prevention has developed a monetary and direct victim-service program for juvenile courts called the Restitution, Education, Specialized Training, and Technical Assistance (RESTTA) Program. RESTTA provides local juvenile courts with the information needed to make restitution a meaningful part of the disposition process for juvenile offenders. You can reach the national directory of RESTTA programs via Web Extra! 15-16.

Web Extra! 15-16 at crimtoday.com

Contemporary restitution programs, although typically well intended, are often mired in a number of problems. Chief among them are the difficulties associated with actually collecting restitution. Offenders are typically poor, lower class, and ill-motivated to participate meaningfully in restitution programs. Overworked courts often order restitution and then do little to remedy the situation when offenders do not make their payments. In the words of Thomas C. Castellano, who conducted a 1992 survey of restitution studies, "The extant studies indicate room for concern and very little suggestion that adult restitution, particularly the mere imposition of a restitution order, achieves its desired effect on offender behavior."[90]

CAN WE SOLVE THE PROBLEM OF CRIME?

In 1956, European writer Hermanus Bianchi[91] emphasized what he saw as the difference between criminology and what he termed *Kriminalpolitik*.[91] Criminology, said Bianchi, should be considered a "metascience" or "a science of wider scope [than that of criminal law, jurisprudence, criminal justice, or corrections] whose terminology can be used to clarify the conceptions of its subdisciplines. Far from being a mere auxiliary to the criminal law," said Bianchi, "it is therefore superior to it."[92]

For Bianchi and other writers of the time, the concept of *Kriminalpolitik* referred to the political handling of crime, or—as we might say today—a criminology-based social policy. Bianchi believed that if criminology were to remain pure, it could not afford to sully its hands, so to speak, with political concerns. Today, however, the image esteemed by criminologists and the expectations they hold for their discipline are quite different than they were in Bianchi's time. Many criminologists expect to work hand in hand with politicians and policymakers, forging crime control agendas based on scientific knowledge and criminological theorizing. Some would say that this change in attitude represents a maturation of the discipline of criminology.

Whether effective crime control policies can ever be implemented, however, is another question. A number of critics argue that only drastic policy-level changes can address the real issues that underlie high rates of crime and criminal activity. Drug legalization, the elimination of guns throughout America, nightly curfews, and close control of media violence, say such reformers, may be necessary before crime can be

curbed. "Reforms that substantially will lower the crime rate are unlikely because of cultural taboos," says Lawrence Friedman, a Stanford University law professor and author of the book *Crime and Punishment in American History*. According to Friedman, "If you add up all the taboos we have—against legalization of drugs, real gun control, paying taxes for social programs we might at least try—it's hard not to come to the conclusion that there isn't much we can do about crime." Many existing taboos, say such thinkers, are rooted in citizens' demands for individual freedoms. "At one time in South Korea," says Friedman, "they had an absolute curfew between midnight and 5 A.M. The police kept everyone off the streets. It was as hard on burglars as other citizens and very effective at squelching crime. But most Americans would consider that an unacceptable inroad on their personal lives."[93]

Complicating the picture further is the fact that numerous interest groups, each with its own agenda, are clamoring to be heard by policymakers. As Robert D. Pursley, a professor of criminal justice at Buffalo State College, states, "Our nation's efforts to deal with crime remind us that crime, among other things, is a highly political issue that has been transformed into a racially volatile subject. This issue provides an excellent window into political policymaking. Opposing ideological lines have divided our efforts to develop comprehensive anticrime programs. Deep fissures in our social fabric have contributed to conflicting attitudes about crime and its control."[94]

Racial divisiveness has created one of those fissures. Pursley writes, "Our anticrime programs and studies of traditional street crimes, especially those involving violence, show that such crimes are disproportionately the acts of young African-American males. So long as black men commit violent crimes at a rate that is six to eight times higher than that found among whites and three to four times higher than that among Latino males, race and crime will be threads of the same cloth. These facts have become unpopular and certainly not politically correct to discuss in certain circles, but they remain facts. No attempt to silence those who raise such issues by denouncing them as 'racists' can conceal these statistics."[95]

Pursley is telling us, in effect, that for some groups in some locales, violations of the criminal law are simply part of the landscape. Among certain segments of the American population, crime may be an accepted way of doing business, and criminal activity, even when discovered, might not necessarily be stigmatizing. Moreover, those who commit crimes may hold positions of prestige or highly visible public offices when their constituencies fail to condemn illicit behavior. Ultimately, they may even serve as role models to youngsters—albeit dubious role models. Although such a perspective is undoubtedly a minority point of view, it seriously impacts the ability of policymakers to establish consistent policies in the battle against crime.

Symbolism and Public Policy

When all the political crime-fighting rhetoric has ended and all the dollars have been spent, some expect that crime will still be with us. Many analysts of the contemporary scene see all crime control policies, especially those at the federal level, as largely symbolic. As Nancy E. Marion, a professor of political science at the University of Akron, explained a few years ago, "No one could effectively argue that the federal government under any modern president has successfully reduced the amount of criminal activity in the United States. The FBI reports yearly that crime has not gone down, but only continues to increase [Marion was writing in 1993]. Further, the number of people using drugs has not gone down. Therefore, it can be said that the federal government is not making any progress in their fight against crime."[96]

Why is this so? Marion states it is because "many of the policies supported by the federal government may in actuality be symbolic gestures to appease the public rather than attempts to reduce crime. One reason for the presence of symbolic policies . . . is simply that the federal government cannot reduce crime—it is not within the government's capacity to do so."[97] Marion says that congressional power is fragmented through the influence of special interest groups, and as a result, the potential of crime control initiatives is effectively dispersed by the time any legislation is enacted. In addition, says Marion, the American political system is decidedly shortsighted, focusing only on issues that are likely to win elections. Similarly, due to changes in incumbents (often every two to four years), it is impossible to establish consistent crime control policies. Whereas a Democratic president may hold office for four years, for example, it is likely that a Republican president will take office with the next election—and in the meantime, a nearly continuous shuffling of cabinet members, senators, representatives, U.S. Supreme Court justices, agency heads, federal judges, and so on is occurring. Similar changes at the state level ensure constant modification of laws, enforcement practices, and criminal sanctions. Without a consistent, long-term, national, and interstate approach to crime fighting, Marion suggests, crime can never be effectively reduced.

Even consistent policies may be inaccurately targeted. As Marion explains, "One reason we cannot stop crime in the United States is because many elements of the crime problem we believe to be true simply are not. Because of the way crime is presented in the media, crime events 'become distorted and are given unprecedented social consideration.' These myths help to sustain our views of crime, criminals, and the system as a whole."[98] Part of the mythology of crime, some claim, is belief in criminological theories of limited usefulness. Another problem flows from our inability to effectively conceptualize crime itself. Laws may merely reflect moral conceptions of the political majority. Both morality and law are subject to change, making it difficult to accurately define crime. A final difficulty is one of accurately measuring the extent of crime. Although exhaustive efforts have been made toward achieving accuracy in measurement, experts are still unable to ascertain the true rate of crime in the United States. Hence as critics of contemporary crime-fighting policies indicate, if we do not fully understand what crime is or what causes it, how can we create an effective policy for controlling it?

Some people, like Alfred Blumstein of Carnegie-Mellon University, say the answer is possibly found in increased expenditures on criminological research. According to Blumstein, "That we are in this confused state is not surprising when we recognize that the nation spends less than $25 million per year for research at the National Institute of Justice on the problem that seems to be the nation's greatest concern. Contrast this with $11 billion for health research at the National Institutes of Health, $600 million on mental health, and $165 million for dental research. With so small a research effort, it is not surprising that we reach out for programs with little ability to assess the impact that they might have on the intended objective, and that we operate in a pre-Galilean mode when we debate crime policy."[99]

SUMMARY

Although crime has always been a part of American society, comprehensive efforts at crime control, at least at the federal level, originated during the Depression years of the twentieth century. Efforts to reduce crime, however, although well intentioned, are fraught with political uncertainties resting largely upon fundamental disagreements within American society itself as to the sources of crime and the most appropriate means for combating it. Bryan Vila, whose work is cited throughout this chapter, summarizes the contemporary situation this way: "Lack of a unified criminological framework has fostered shortsighted, inconsistent, and ineffective crime-control policies. Theoretical ambiguity made it easier for policymakers to base their decisions on politics rather than science. Lacking a reasonable complete and coherent explanation of the causes of crime, they have been free to shift the focus of crime-control efforts back and

forth from individual-level to macro-level causes as the political pendulum swung from right to left. This erratic approach hindered crime-control efforts and fed the desperate belief that the problem of crime is intractable."[100]

Although answers to the long-term problem of crime appear to face formidable obstacles, all may not be lost. Fundamental social changes—including the development of high moral values through education, the elimination or significant reduction of poverty, increased opportunities for success at all levels, and decriminalization of certain offenses—may all be combined some day into a workable strategy for the management of criminal activity within the United States. In any event, durable advances cannot be made until American society, and especially those parts of it which are now accepting of criminal activity and the conditions that produce it, undergoes a fundamental change in orientation.

DISCUSSION QUESTIONS

1. This book emphasizes a social problems versus social responsibility theme. What types of anticrime social policies might be based on the social responsibility perspective? The social problems approach? Explain.
2. What are the major differences between the social problems and the social responsibility approaches? With which do you most closely identify? Why?
3. What are the three types of crime control strategies that this chapter describes? Which comes closest to your own philosophy? Why?
4. Explain the social epidemiological approach to reducing crime. In your opinion, is the approach worthwhile? Why or why not?
5. If you were in charge of government crime reduction efforts, what steps would you take to control crime in the United States? Why would you choose those particular approaches?

WEB QUEST!

In this chapter, we discussed crime control policies, noting that fundamental philosophical differences in policy orientation reflect the distinction we made in Chapter 1 between the social problems and the social responsibility perspectives. To explore this dichotomy further, this Web Quest! requires that you visit a number of policy-oriented sites on the World Wide Web. Explore each site to determine the kind of orientation it embodies. Then classify each site you've visited according to which perspective it represents. Make a note of sites that don't seem to represent either the social problems or the social responsibility perspective. Although you can always search for others, here are some sites to get you started:

■ Campaign for an Effective Crime Policy (http://crime-policy.org)

■ Center for Criminal Justice Policy Research (http://www.dac.neu.edu/cj/ccjpr2.htm)
■ Center for Law and Social Policy (http://www.clasp.org)
■ Center for Policy Alternatives (http://www.cfpa.org)
■ Center for Rational Correctional Policy (http://pierce.simplenet.com/prisonerresources.html)
■ Center on Juvenile and Criminal Justice (http://www.cjcj.org)
■ Criminal Justice Policy Coalition (http://cjpc.org)
■ Criminal Justice Policy Foundation (http://www.cjpf.org)
■ International Center for Criminal Law Reform and Criminal Justice Policy (http://www.icclr.law.ubc.ca)
■ Violence Policy Center (http://www.vpc.org)

LIBRARY EXTRAS!

The Library Extras! listed here complement the Web Extras! found throughout this chapter. Library Extras! may be accessed on the Web at crimtoday.com.

Library Extra! 15-1. American Society of Criminology, *Critical Criminal Justice Issues: Task Force Reports from the American Society of Criminology* (Washington, D.C.: National Institute of Justice, 1996).

Library Extra! 15-2. Stevens H. Clarke, "Firearms and Violence: Interpreting the Connection," *Popular Government,* Vol. 65, No. 2 (Winter 2000), pp. 2–17.

Library Extra! 15-3. David B. Kopel, *Trust the People: The Case against Gun Control.*

Library Extra! 15-4. David Satcher, *Youth Violence: A Report of the Surgeon General* (Washington, D.C.: U.S. Government Printing Office, January 2001).

Library Extra! 15-5. Jeremy Travis, "Plenary Presentation to the American Society of Criminology," Washington, D.C., November 12, 1998.

NOTES

1. Joan Petersilia, "Policy Relevance and the Future of Criminology—The American Society of Criminology, 1990 Presidential Address," *Criminology,* Vol. 29, No. 1 (1991), pp. 1–15.

2. Jeremy Travis, "Criminal Justice Research and Public Policy in the United States," speech delivered at the Ninth U.N. Congress on the Prevention of Crime and the Treatment of Offenders, Cairo, Egypt, May 2, 1995. Web

posted at http://register.aspensys.com/nij/speeches/ unspeech.htm. Accessed January 22, 2001.

[3] Georgette Bennett, *Crimewarps: The Future of Crime in America* (Garden City, NY: Anchor/Doubleday, 1987), p. xix.

[4] James D. Calder, *The Origins and Development of Federal Crime Control Policy* (Westport, CT: Praeger, 1993), p. 211.

[5] David B. Kopel, "Guns, Germs, and Science," *Journal of the Medical Association of Georgia,* Vol. 84 (June 1995), p. 269.

[6] Although charged with sodomy, Shakur was convicted on three lesser counts of sexual abuse. See Samuel Maull, "Shakur Trial," Associated Press wire service, December 2, 1994.

[7] James T. Jones IV, "Real-Life Woes Beset Actor/Rapper," *USA Today,* February 11, 1994, p. 2A.

[8] $1 million for himself and another $1 million for his bodyguard. See "Prosecutors Mull Second Trial for Rapper," Reuters wire service, February 23, 1996.

[9] Dennis R. Martin, "The Music of Murder," *ACJS Today* (November/December 1993), pp. 1, 3, 20.

[10] Kendall Hamilton and Allison Samuels, "Dr. Dre's New 'Hood: Hollywood," *Newsweek,* August 22, 1994, p. 45.

[11] See, for example, Elizabeth Snead, "Dogg's 'Murder' Video Has Plenty of Bite," *USA Today,* October 13, 1994.

[12] Arthur L. Cribbs, Jr., "Gangsta Rappers Sing White Racists' Tune," *USA Today,* December 27, 1993, p. 9A.

[13] James E. Anderson, *Public Policymaking: An Introduction* (Boston: Houghton Mifflin, 1990).

[14] Nancy E. Marion, *A History of Federal Crime Control Initiatives,* 1960–1993 (Westport, CT: Praeger, 1994), p. 3. For a more detailed analysis of the process by which crime control policies are created, see Paul Rock, "The Opening Stages of Criminal Justice Policy Making," *British Journal of Criminology,* Vol. 35, No. 1 (winter 1995), pp. 1–16.

[15] Jeff Ferrell, "Criminological Verstehen: Inside the Immediacy of Crime," *Justice Quarterly,* Vol. 14, No. 1 (1997), p. 16.

[16] Marion, *A History of Federal Crime Control Initiatives,* 1960–1993 abstract.

[17] The Massachusetts Institute for a New Commonwealth, "Criminal Justice in Massachusetts: Executive Summary," July 7, 1997. Web posted at http://www.massinc.org/ reports/cjim/exec.html. Accessed April 15, 2001.

[18] Calder, *The Origins and Development of Federal Crime Control Policy.*

[19] Ibid., p. 1.

[20] Ibid., pp. ix–x.

[21] Ibid., p. 85.

[22] Ibid., p. 5.

[23] Ibid., p. 6.

[24] Ibid., various pages.

[25] Ibid., p. 83.

[26] Ibid.

[27] Ibid., p. 102, citing the commission.

[28] Ibid., p. 157.

[29] President's Commission on Law Enforcement and Administration of Justice, *The Challenge of Crime in a Free Society* (Washington, D.C.: U.S. Government Printing Office, 1967), p. xii.

[30] Steven A. Shull, *Domestic Policy Formation: Presidential-Congressional Partnership?* (Westport, CT: Greenwood Press, 1983), p. 41.

[31] "Remarks at the Annual Conference of the National Sheriff's Association in Hartford, Connecticut," June 20, 1984, *Public Papers of the President,* pp. 884–888.

[32] Pub. L. No. 99-570 (1986).

[33] Pub. L. No. 100-690 (1988).

[34] Carolyn Skorneck, "Anti-Drug Spending," Associated Press wire service, December 2, 1993.

[35] Pub. L. No. 103-159. The law became effective on February 28, 1994.

[36] Pub. L. No. 103-322.

[37] Title IV of the Violent Crime Control and Law Enforcement Act of 1994 (Pub. L. No. 103-322).

[38] 28 U.S.C. 994.

[39] Senate Bill 191.

[40] Subtitle B of the 1994 Crime Bill.

[41] 103rd Congress, H.R. 1025 ("The Brady Bill"), January 5, 1993, p. 1.

[42] The portion of the Brady Handgun Violence Prevention Act requiring the "chief law enforcement officer" of each local jurisdiction to conduct background checks and perform related tasks on an interim basis until a national checking system became operative was struck down by the U.S. Supreme Court as unconstitutional in 1997. The Court, in *Printz* v. *U.S.* (1997) and *Mack* v. *U.S.* (1997), held that the constitutional principle of "dual sovereignty" prohibited direct federal control over state officers.

[43] Marianne W. Zawitz, *Guns Used in Crime: Firearms, Crime, and Criminal Justice* (Annapolis Junction, MD: Bureau of Justice Statistics, July 1995); and Michael R. Rand, *Guns and Crime: Handgun Victimization, Firearm Self-Defense, and Firearm Theft* (Annapolis Junction, MD: Bureau of Justice Statistics, April 1994).

[44] "Iowa Man Believed First to Be Charged under Brady Bill," United Press International wire service, Northern Edition, January 11, 1994.

[45] "Brady—First Conviction," Associated Press wire service, Northern Edition, April 14, 1994.

[46] Office of the Press Secretary, "Keeping Guns away from Youth and Criminals: The Clinton-Gore Administration Record," White House press release, April 11, 2000.

[47] Frank Newport, "Americans Support Wide Variety of Gun Control Measures," Gallup News Service, June 16, 1999. Web posted at http://www.gallup.com/poll/ releases/pr990616.asp. Accessed January 22, 2001.

[48] Albert Reiss, Jr., and Jeffrey A. Roth, *Understanding and Preventing Violence* (Washington, D.C.: National Academy Press, 1993).

[49] Alfred Blumstein, "Seeking the Connection between Crime and Punishment," *Jobs and Capital* (Santa Monica, CA: Milken Institute for Job and Capital Formation), Vol. 4, Winter 1995.

50 National Association of Criminal Defense Lawyers, "Three Strikes Laws: Absurd and Unnecessary," November 1, 1997. Web posted at http://www.criminaljustice.org/media/pr000005.htm. Accessed June 2, 1999.

51 For an excellent overview of the issues in the area, see David Shichor and Dale K. Sechrest, *Three Strikes and You're Out* (Thousand Oaks, CA: Sage, 1996).

52 *People* v. *Superior Court of San Diego—Romero,* 917 P.2d 628 (California Supreme Court, 1996).

53 Bryan Vila, "Could We Break the Crime Control Paradox?" paper presented at the annual meeting of the American Society of Criminology, Miami, November 1994.

54 Ibid., abstract.

55 "Candidates and Crime," APB News. Web posted at http://www.apbnews.com/newscenter/indepth/candidates/bush_cig.html. Accessed January 20, 2001.

56 George W. Bush, *A Charge to Keep* (New York: Morrow, 1999).

57 Elliott Currie, "Reflections on Crime and Criminology at the Millennium," *Western Criminology Review,* Vol. 2, No. 1 (1999).

58 Ibid.

59 Ibid.

60 For an excellent overview of historical initiatives as well as contemporary suggestions for crime-control strategies, see James Q. Wilson and Joan Petersilia, *Crime: Twenty-Eight Leading Experts Look at the Most Pressing Problem of Our Time* (San Francisco: Institute for Contemporary Studies Press, 1995).

61 See Arthur L. Kellermann, "Understanding and Preventing Violence: A Public Health Perspective," National Institute of Justice, June 1996.

62 The Virtual Office of the Surgeon General, *Youth Violence: A Report of the Surgeon General, Executive Summary.* Web posted at http://www.surgeongeneral.gov/library/youthviolence/sgsummary/summary.htm. Accessed January 22, 2001.

63 Office of National Drug Control Policy, *National Drug Control Strategy: 2001 Annual Report* (Washington, D.C.: ONDCP, 2001), p. 7.

64 Bryan Vila, "A General Paradigm for Understanding Criminal Behavior: Extending Evolutionary Ecological Theory," *Criminology,* Vol. 32, No. 3 (August 1994), pp. 311–359.

65 Vila, "Could We Break the Crime Control Paradox?"

66 Bryan Vila, "Human Nature and Crime Control: Improving the Feasibility of Nurturant Strategies," *Politics and the Life Sciences,* March 1997, pp. 3–21.

67 Vila, "A General Paradigm for Understanding Criminal Behavior."

68 Vila, "Human Nature and Crime Control," p. 10.

69 Ibid., p. 11.

70 "Right of Silence to Go in New British Crime Bill," Reuters wire service, December 17, 1993.

71 Ibid.

72 Petersilia, "Policy Relevance and the Future of Criminology."

73 Steven Rathgeb Smith and Susan Freinkel, *Adjusting the Balance: Federal Policy and Victim Services* (Westport, CT: Greenwood Press, 1988), p. 13.

74 Robert Elias, *Victims of the System: Crime Victims and Compensation in American Politics and Criminal Justice* (New Brunswick, NJ: Transaction, 1983), pp. 24–26.

75 Ibid.

76 Ibid., p. 245.

77 For a good review of the issues involved, see Robert C. Davis, Arthur J. Lurigio, and Wesley G. Skogan, *Victims of Crime,* 2nd ed. (Thousand Oaks, CA: Sage, 1997).

78 See Davis, Lurigio, and Skogan, *Victims of Crime;* and Leslie Sebba, *Third Parties: Victims and the Criminal Justice System* (Columbus: Ohio State University Press, 1996).

79 Albert R. Roberts, *Helping Crime Victims* (Newbury Park, CA: Sage, 1990).

80 Ibid., p. 31. See also "Victim Assistance Programs: Whom They Service, What They Offer," *National Institute of Justice Update* (May 1995).

81 President's Task Force on Victims of Crime, *Final Report* (Washington, D.C.: U.S. Government Printing Office, 1982).

82 Pub. L. No. 97-291.

83 Proposition 8, "California's Victims' Bill of Rights."

84 Stephen Schafer, *The Victim and His Criminal: A Study in Functional Responsibility* (New York: Random House, 1968).

85 President's Task Force, *Final Report.*

86 American Bar Association, *Guidelines for Fair Treatment of Crime Victims and Witnesses* (Chicago: ABA, 1983), p. 22.

87 Susan Hillenbrand, "Restitution and Victim Rights in the 1980s," in Arthur J. Lurigio, Wesley G. Skogan, and Robert C. Davis, eds., *Victims of Crime: Problems, Policies, and Programs* (Newbury Park, CA: Sage, 1990), p. 192.

88 Ibid., p. 196.

89 Ibid.

90 Thomas C. Castellano, "Assessing Restitution's Impact on Recidivism: A Review of the Evaluative Literature," in Viano, ed., *Critical Issues in Victimology: International Perspectives,* (New York: Springer, 1992) p. 240.

91 Hermanus Bianchi, *Position and Subject-Matter of Criminology* (Amsterdam: North-Holland, 1956).

92 Hermann Mannheim, *Comparative Criminology* (New York: Houghton Mifflin, 1965), p. 18.

93 "Can Anything Really Be Done?" *USA Today* magazine, Vol. 122, No. 2587 (April 1994), p. 6.

94 Robert D. Pursley, *Introduction to Criminal Justice,* 6th ed. (New York: Macmillan, 1991), p. 677.

95 Ibid.

96 Marion, *A History of Federal Crime Control Initiatives,* 1960–1993, p. 250.

97 Ibid., p. 244.

98 Ibid., p. 249.

99 Blumstein, "Seeking the Connection between Crime and Punishment."

100 Vila, "Could We Break the Crime Control Paradox?" p. 3.

As surely as the future will bring new forms of technology, it will bring new forms of crime.

—Cynthia Manson and Charles Ardai[1]

The rise of a new kind of economy, never before known, threatening to many, demanding rapid changes in work, life style, and habits, hurls large populations—terrified of the future—into spasms of diehard reaction. It opens cleavages that fanatics rush to fill. It arms all those dangerous minorities who live for crisis in the hopes of catapulting themselves onto the national or global stage and transporting us all into a new Dark Age.

—Alvin Toffler[2]

future directions

CHAPTER 16

I seriously doubt that this country has the will to address . . . its crime problems. . . . We could in theory make justice swifter and more certain, but we will not. We could vastly improve the way in which our streets are policed, but some of us won't pay for it and the rest of us won't tolerate it. . . . We could alter the way in which at-risk children experience the first few years of life, but the opponents of this . . . are numerous and the bureaucratic problems enormous. Meanwhile, just beyond the horizon, there lurks a cloud that the winds will soon bring over us. By the end of this decade there will be a million more people between the ages of fourteen and seventeen. . . . This extra million will be half male. Six percent of them will become high rate, repeat offenders—thirty thousand more young muggers, killers and thieves than we have now. Get ready.

—James Q. Wilson[3]

He who controls the past, controls the future.

He who controls the future, controls the past.

—George Orwell[4]

KEY CONCEPTS

IMPORTANT TERMS

comparative criminologists	environmental scanning	metatheories
comparative criminology	future criminology	scenario writing
cross-impact analysis	futures research	strategic assessment
Delphi Method	futurists	trend extrapolation

IMPORTANT NAMES

Georgette Bennett	Richter H. Moore, Jr.	William L. Tafoya
Bernard Levin	Gene Stephens	

OUTCOMES

LEARNING

After reading this chapter, you should be able to
◆ Discuss future crimes and future studies
◆ Identify some techniques for assessing the future
◆ Describe the role of the criminological futurist in social policy development
◆ Recognize the significance of an integrated theory of crime causation
◆ Describe the advantages of a comparative approach to the study of crime and criminals

Hear the author discuss this chapter at *crimtoday.com*

INTRODUCTION

Canadian criminologist Gwynn Nettler once told a story of two people passing on a street in New York City.[5] One carried a pint of whiskey; the other had $100 in gold coins. In March 1933, near the end of the Prohibition era, the person with the alcohol would have been committing a crime, but the person carrying the gold would have been regarded as law-abiding. A year later, however, the same two people passing on the street would have occupied exactly the opposite legal positions. The repeal of Prohibition legalized carrying whiskey in most places, but gold hoarding became a federal crime in 1934, and remained so until 1974.

It is easy to look back in time and assess the legal standing of people like those in Nettler's story, but predicting what crimes the future will bring is far more difficult. Those who study the future are called **futurists**. Futurist criminologists try to imagine how crime will appear in both the near and distant future. **Future criminology** is the study of likely futures as they relate to crime and its control.

The future is an abstract concept through which human beings bring symbolic order to the present and meaning to past endeavors.[6] From our present point of view, multiple futures exist, each of which is more or less probable, and each of which may or may not come to pass. In other words, the future contains an almost limitless number of possibilities, any of which might unfold but only a few of which actually will. The task of the futurist is to effectively distinguish between these impending possibilities, assessing the likelihood of each and making more or less realistic forecasts based on such assessments.

Some assumptions about the future, such as estimates of future world populations, can be based on existing and highly credible public or private statistics and mathematical analyses of trends. Others, however, are more intuitive and result from the integration of a wide range of diverse materials derived from many different sources. As one futurist explains, "Before we can plan the future, we must make some assumptions about what that future will be like. . . . Assumptions about the future are not like assumptions in a geometry exercise. They are not abstract statements from which consequences can be derived with mathematical precision. But we need to make some assumptions about the future in order to plan it, prepare for it, and prevent undesired events from happening."[7]

Best known among groups that study the future is the World Future Society, which publishes *The Futurist,* a journal of well-considered essays about probable futures. Individual futurists who have become well known to the general public include Alvin Toffler, author of the trilogy of futurist titles *Future Shock,*[8] *Powershift,* and *The Third Wave;*[9] John Naisbitt, author of *Megatrends: Ten New Directions Transforming Our Lives;*[10] and Peter F. Drucker, who has written many books with futuristic themes, among them *Management Challenges for the 21st Century*[11] and *Post-Capitalist Society.*[12] Within criminology, the Society of Police Futurists International (PFI) represents the cutting edge of research into future crime control policy. PFI evolved from a conference of approximately 250 educators and practitioners representing most states and 20 different nations that was held at the FBI National Academy in Quantico, Virginia, in 1991. The society's Millennium Conference was held at the National Academy in July 2000. PFI members apply the principles of futures research to gain an understanding of the world as it is likely to be in the future.[13] Learn more about the society at the PFI Web site via Web Extra! 16-1.

Web EXTRA! Web Extra! 16-1 at crimtoday.com

Another group actively attempting to discern the future is the United Kingdom's government-led Foresight program, which "brings people, knowledge and ideas together to look ahead and prepare for the future."[14] Foresight's Crime Prevention Panel released a report in 2001 entitled *Just around the Corner,* focusing on the year 2020.[15] The report provides a summation of the views of 60 experts given three tasks: to describe crimes of the near future, to identify methods to reduce and detect those crimes, and to decide what role science and technology will play in future criminality and crime prevention. According to Foresight's Crime Prevention Panel, a number of social characteristics will affect future crimes in Great Britain and throughout the world. One of these is what the panel calls "individuality and independence." The panel believes that greater individuality and personal independence will arise as traditional family forms decline over the next decade or two. Once traditional families no longer provide the "foundation" of society and more people find themselves living in single-person households, says the panel, "there will be more self-centered, self-indulgent and hedonistic psychologies." Traditional limits on antisocial behavior will erode, the panel predicts, as individuals gravitate toward membership in like-minded groups, many of which "may reinforce rather than challenge anti-social views."

A second social characteristic that will affect crime in the future, says the panel, is what it terms "Information Communication Technology (ICT) usage." The panel predicts that crimes like electronic theft and fraud will occur with increasing rapidity, reducing the likelihood that offenders can be caught. Web sites are predicted to become highly targeted properties, and sites written in English will be the hardest hit. Such attacks will raise the need for increased acceptability of digital evidence in courts and will require jurors, judges, and attorneys to be educated in relevant technologies.

Technology is also leading to the growth of an impersonal society, says the panel, in which people meet and interact in virtual space rather than in physical society. As a consequence, the panel fears, physical space may become an increasingly hostile and dangerous place—"a dehumanized environment" in which "people may become less 'real' to one another leading to more extreme reactions, interactions and the reluctance to intervene in conflicts."

A third social characteristic relevant to understanding and predicting future forms of criminality, according to the panel, is globalization. Globalization, which refers to the increasingly international character of social life, is having an impact on much of society, including technology, commerce, communication, and crime. "Already," says the panel, "crimes on the internet, drug dealing, and smuggling show the power of global crime and the difficulties it poses for local level law enforcement." Local crimes and small-time perpetrators will be replaced or supplemented by crimes and criminal groups with global scope, the panel predicts.

The panel notes that criminal organizations, like organizations everywhere, "are adapting to the opportunities offered by the flexibility of the internet." However, says the panel, modern technology offers individuals new opportunities to commit crimes that may be virtually unsolvable: "The clear danger is being at the mercy of a small technologically knowledgeable elite." At the same time, the panel warns, large numbers of people either won't have the op-

William L. Tafoya, founder of the Society of Police Futurists International (PFI). Regarded by many in the field as a visionary, Dr. Tafoya is a retired FBI special agent, teaching at Governors State University in Illinois. *Courtesy Dr. William Tafoya*

portunity to acquire advanced technological skills or will be unable to learn them. The consequence will be a technologically disenfranchised underclass whose existence will "further fuel crime and reduce the opportunities for access to mainstream society."

The panel plans to release its full report soon. For more details about Foresight and for access to the complete report of Foresight's Crime Prevention Panel when it becomes available, visit Web Extra! 16-2.

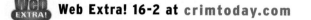

Web Extra! 16-2 at crimtoday.com

Globalization

On a global scale, there appears to be a shared agreement that society is experiencing a period of unprecedented change. Both the substance and the pace of change are fundamentally different from what has occurred in past decades and centuries. No longer are sequences of events occurring in relative isolation or over longer spans of time. No longer are discrete groups of people affected by each change; rather, there is greater simultaneity of occurrence, swifter interpenetration, and increased feedback of one set of changes upon another.[16]

Globalization, as already discussed, is making it impossible for U.S. policymakers to ignore criminal activity in other countries, especially where that crime is perpetrated by transnational criminal organizations. *Transnational crime,* or *transnational organized crime,* refers to unlawful activity undertaken and supported by organized criminal groups operating across national boundaries. Transnational crime and the internationally organized criminal groups that support it have emerged as one of the most pressing challenges of the early twenty-first century.

The globalization of crime has necessitated the enhanced coordination of law enforcement efforts in different parts of the world and the expansion of American law enforcement activities beyond national borders. The globalization of crime has also led to a resurgence in interest in **comparative criminology**, or the cross-national study of crime. Criminologists who study crime on a cross-national level are referred to as **comparative criminologists**, and comparative criminal justice is being increasingly valued for the insights it provides. By comparing crime patterns in one country with those in another, theories and policies that have been taken for granted in one place can be reevaluated in the light of world experience. As some noted comparative criminologists have observed, "The challenge for comparative criminologists is to develop theories with increased specificity while managing to construct them in such a way that they can be applied across more than one culture or nation-state. This eventually must demand that theories be developed to conceptualize societies as totalities and that theories that manage to provide a world context in which total societies behave be further constructed."[17] Some have

used the term *globalization of knowledge* to describe the increase in understanding that results from a sharing of information between cultures. The globalization of knowledge is beginning to play a significant role in both the process of theory formation within criminology and in the development of American crime control policies.

In the United States today, policies concerning crime and justice typically emerge after a highly complex and adversarial process of political exchange and bureaucratic procedure. Most policies originate from issues or problems that occur within our borders, although exceptions can be found in drug trafficking and other kinds of transnational crime. The enormous and rapidly growing availability of criminal justice information on an international level, however, holds the power to significantly influence future policy decisions. According to some, "Globalization will make it increasingly difficult for nation-states to ignore the criminal justice information of other countries. Politicians and influential bureaucrats increasingly will be forced to answer as to why their country displays crime rates, prosecution rates, incarceration rates, or rates of violence or gun ownership that are strikingly different from similar countries."[18] A wealth of international information on crime and justice can be found in the *World Factbook of Criminal Justice Systems,* available via Web Extra! 16-3.

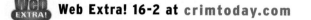

Web Extra! 16-3 at crimtoday.com

Techniques of Futures Research

Futures research has been described as "a multidisciplinary branch of operations research" whose principal aim "is to facilitate long-range planning based on (1) forecasting from the past supported by mathematical models, (2) cross-disciplinary treatment of its subject matter, (3) systematic use of expert judgment, and (4) a systems-analytical approach to its problems."[19] In the words of PFI founder **William L. Tafoya**, "Futures research offers both the philosophy and the methodological tools to analyze, forecast, and plan in ways rarely seen" in crime control planning. "Guided by insight, imagination, and innovation, a new perspective awaits criminal justice professionals willing to attempt creative new approaches to dealing with crime and criminals."[20]

Central to futures research is a futurist perspective, which some authors say is built around five principles:[21]

- The future is determined by a combination of factors, not the least of which is human choice. In other words, what we decide today will have a significant effect tomorrow.
- There are alternative futures. Hence a range of decision and planning choices is always available in the present.
- We operate within an interdependent, interrelated system. Hence any major decision, development, or force

CRIME IN THE NEWS
Technology Changing Organized Crime

In the next decade, the world's crime fighters say they will fight international organized crime on several fronts, battling financial fraud, corruption, the sale of human beings for sex and labor and the trafficking of weapons of mass destruction.

The focus of a three-day crime-fighting conference [held in Germany] sponsored by the FBI and the joint U.S.-German military George C. Marshall European Center for Security Studies was touted in advance as an assessment of organized crime's impact on national security in the next 10 years. But the meeting of American, European and Eurasian top brass ended today with little open discussion of such forecasts.

Organizers admitted the conference fell short of that objective during its many panel discussions and speeches, but said other goals had been achieved beyond their expectations, namely the forging of new East-West relationships between lawmen.

One senior U.S. law enforcement official involved in planning the event told APBnews.com it was difficult to get officials from the former Soviet republics to open up and discuss their problems and worries over the future fight against mobsters operating in their fledgling democracies.

"This is the first major meeting of its kind," the official said, comparing it almost to a warm-up act. "There will need to be more conferences like this. The first step was to get them here to meet with us. The next time they'll open up more."

RUSSIAN OFFICIAL TO MEET WITH FBI

On Wednesday, former Russian Interior Minister Gen. Anatoly Kulikov said he was coming to Washington in mid-September for high-level meetings with U.S. officials to discuss the growing relationship between his country's law enforcement apparatuses and America's. FBI officials said he will meet with Director Louis Freeh, and also said the bureau views Kulikov as a potentially major player in police matters in the administration that follows Russian President Boris Yeltsin.

Kulikov is presently running for the Russian Duma, or parliament.

Privately, many participants expressed disappointment that there wasn't more gazing into a crystal ball at this unusual gathering of security analysts, academics and senior government law enforcement officials from more than 20 nations, but confessed it is hard to guess the future.

"In 1980, could you have predicted the changes in the world and consequently the changes in organized crime?" said Gwen McClure, an FBI special agent who is chief of the organized-crime branch at Interpol in Lyon, France.

Nevertheless, McClure and other attendees offered their predictions to APBnews.com for the coming years, painting a portrait of organized crime that is potentially more sophisticated and well-funded than previously believed, thanks to the opportunity to compare notes with other countries.

NO MORE TYPICAL DON CORLEONE

Indiana's Wayne State University author and criminologist Joseph Albini said he estimates that as early as 2000, more than 90 percent of those involved in organized crime will be computer literate on some level.

"The conception of Don Corleone [from the *Godfather* movies] smoking a cigar is better seen as Don Corleone behind a laptop," he said.

It is the access to mass media information and the technology boom that are changing the face of mobsters from thugs to super-criminals, Albini said.

Kulikov echoed that view. "We are at the threshold of a new millennium. We have to be prepared for the emergence of new types of criminal activity," including technological, he said.

VIRTUAL REALITY NARCOTICS

The retired Russian general clicked off a number of examples, including trafficking illegal genetically engineered human organs and crop seeds.

A senior intelligence officer from Great Britain who specializes in organized-crime analysis said tomorrow's gangsters almost certainly will be consumed with electronic commerce, particularly online gambling, credit card fraud and virtual banking, where a financial institution exists solely in cyberspace.

Another possibility, he said, is the theoretical notion of virtual reality narcotics, which assumes it is possible to transmit a digital "stimulant" or hallucinogen across the Internet, creating a new form of addiction.

"Biotechnology and information technology are the two biggest revolutions of this century, and we should look at each of them and see where the potential for money is from the criminal point of view," the source told APBnews.com, requesting anonymity.

"Organized crime will become more sophisticated and more networked, and it is the challenge of law enforcement to look where those networks may spin in the future."

OLD INVESTIGATORS, OLD TRICKS

The biggest obstacle for investigators trying to keep up with syndicates on the electronic cutting edge may be age, said Louise Shelley, an American University professor for 22 years and an expert on international organized crime.

"We have mostly middle-aged law enforcement officials. This is not the age group that's thinking high-tech," said Shelley.

Brig. Gen. Laszlo Salgo, a security official attached to the Hungarian delegation to the Hague, Netherlands, said this is true.

(continued on the next page)

(continued from previous page)

"Hungarian police don't know much about computing, but they all have PCs," he observed, noting his classical education precluded him from mastering even e-mail.

RUSSIANS POSE A THREAT

Another serious problem facing international crime fighters is nation-building itself, threatened by the influence of mobster money in emerging democracies.

FBI Organized Crime Section Chief Thomas Fuentes told APBnews.com he thinks the No. 1 threat from international organized crime is the expansion of Russian-speaking crime groups in emerging democracies.

"They have a global reach and are very sophisticated in world financial markets. That's our most immediate and pressing threat."

Throughout the Garmisch conference, repeated emphasis was put on corruption of government and law enforcement officials. There was almost no dissent on this point, that corruption is the greatest threat to U.S., European and Eurasian national security.

FIGHTING CORRUPTION WITHIN INTERPOL

To McClure, whose international police agency is funded by member nations of Interpol, fighting corruption is particularly acute, she said, because the crooks have seemingly unlimited cash reserves and law enforcement entities in developing nations simply do not have unlimited resources for cash.

There is no evidence organized-crime syndicates are waiting for the next millennium to buy police officers. Requesting anonymity, a source said the former communist republic Ukraine is fighting broad corruption in its Interpol force.

Phil Williams of the University of Pittsburgh said there also will be a growing connection in the future between traditional profit-driven mobs and ideologically oriented terrorists, who he said already see how each can lend criminal expertise to the other without blurring the lines of their disparate motivations.

"There's a blurring of the line, but they're still going to be very different."

"AMERICANS ANGRY AT THE . . . GOVERNMENT"

The biggest danger to nations, Albini said, is that the mobs will control many markets, both major and minor. "Democracies had better start paying attention because these people will be able to *own* them."

He cited the former Soviet republics Nigeria, Rwanda, Colombia, Iraq and Iran as the countries at highest risk of becoming dominated by governments controlled by organized crime.

While various officials present from East and West insisted there was no evidence of serious smuggling of weapons of mass destruction (WMDs)—either nuclear or biological—Albini predicted it is almost inevitable that mobsters will hire "mercenary terrorists" to activate a WMD device in the future, which will create a "power profile to be used as a blackmail procedure."

"These people are not playing around. You have foreigners who are angry at the American government. There are Americans angry at the American government," he said.

TERRORIST GROUPS BECOME LEGITIMATE

Albini theorized the breakdown of syndicates like the Japanese Yakuza and Chinese triads, which he said are learning from the dysfunction of the Italian La Cosa Nostra, hampered by its Old World traditions and cultural loyalties.

Both organized crime and terrorist cells will eventually resemble legitimate businesses, Albini said, citing the increasing legitimization of Middle East terrorist groups such as Hamas and the Palestine Liberation Organization.

One speaker from a Eurasian country described some syndicates as even having political structures, with "governors" and "presidents."

ACADEMICS: CONFERENCE TOO ACADEMIC

As the rhetorical events here drew to a close tonight, attendees complained openly that the conference was dominated by academics—even the academic presenters made that complaint. The first two days the law enforcement officials—mostly from East-European countries—kept a low profile, as did the FBI.

FBI officials admitted that the nature of their business is secretive and they are not accustomed to sharing information and intelligence with great comfort. They said this is a stumbling block as they look to the years ahead, when they will have no choice but to cooperate more with foreign law enforcement in order to stop transnational organized crime.

An official said he hoped future conferences would encourage all to match the organized-crime syndicates, which sometimes makes law enforcement agencies worldwide look like deaf mutes, unable to communicate effectively with one another.

Source: James Gordon Meek, "Technology Changing Organized Crime," APB News, September 2, 1999. Reprinted with permission.

that affects any part of the system is likely to affect the entire system.

- Tomorrow's problems are developing today. Minor problems ignored today may have catastrophic consequences even a few years from now. Hence distinct trends and developments and even gradual changes cannot be ignored.
- We should regularly develop possible responses to potential changes. We should monitor trends and developments and not hesitate to use our collective creativity and judgment to develop forecasts, projections, and predictions—or to take action.

The techniques of futures research include trend extrapolation, cross-impact analysis, the Delphi Method, simulations and models, environmental scanning, scenario writing, and strategic assessment. **Trend extrapolation**, perhaps the simplest of the techniques listed here, makes future predictions based on the projection of existing trends. **Cross-impact analysis** attempts to analyze one trend or event in

THEORY VERSUS REALITY
Crime and Justice Policy Challenges of the Near Future

In September 2000, the U.S. Department of Justice issued a Strategic Plan for the Office of the Attorney General. The plan noted that "globalization and scientific and technological advances are overarching trends that will affect virtually every aspect of the Department's work in the years ahead." It went on to identify seven specific crime control issues on which the department intends to focus. Those issues, as described by the plan, are

- *Terrorism.* Although terrorist incidents within the United States have been rare, the bombings of the World Trade Center in New York City and the Murrah Federal Building in Oklahoma City demonstrate the nation's vulnerability to such crimes. In the coming years, the terrorist threat is likely to increase. Improved transportation and telecommunications technologies and rapid advances in the miniaturization of electrical and mechanical devices make it easier for both amateurs and sophisticated organizations to plan and carry out attacks on people and property. At the same time, possible attacks on information infrastructures and the emerging threats of chemical, biological, radiological, and nuclear weapons make the potential consequences of terrorism more dire.
- *Worldwide drug trafficking.* The supply and trafficking of illegal drugs into the United States continue to be fueled by a number of international and transnational drug trafficking organizations, many of which have amassed vast financial resources, are well organized and extremely sophisticated, and use deadly violence to further their criminal aims. Despite successes against the Cali and Medellín cartels, a diverse group of smaller, more specialized, and entrepreneurial Colombian drug rings and Mexican and Caribbean transportation organizations has emerged to fill the void left by their collapse.
- *Violence.* Violence is still far too prevalent in American communities.

Young people are especially at risk, both as potential victims and as perpetrators of violent acts. American Indians are twice as likely as other U.S. residents to be victims of violent crime. Firearms are used in about one-fourth of all violent crimes—and 65% of all homicides. About 30% of all female murder victims are killed by their intimate partners.
- *White-collar/economic crimes.* With the information technology revolution, opportunities for white-collar crime increase. White-collar crime inflicts both financial and social costs. Health care fraud, for example, not only siphons off billions of dollars paid out for fraudulent claims, but also may disguise inadequate and improper treatment of patients, which poses a threat to the health and safety of Americans, including the most vulnerable members of our society. Antitrust violations harm American consumers, and environmental crimes threaten our natural world, including the air we breathe and the water we drink.
- *Substance abuse and crime.* Research suggests that there is a clear nexus between substance abuse and crime. In 1997, three-quarters of state and federal prison inmates reported being involved with alcohol or drug abuse in the time leading up to their arrest. More than 36% of all convicted adult offenders under the jurisdiction of probation authorities, prisons, jails, or parole agencies in 1996 had been drinking at the time of their offense. Of special concern for the future is the continuing and regular use of drugs by a minority of "hard-core" users who are criminally involved. For the many offenders likely to be returning to their communities in the coming years, breaking the cycle between substance abuse and crime is critical to increasing their chances of successful reintegration.

- *Immigration.* The increasing ease of worldwide transportation and communications and the globalization of the economy are adding to immigration pressures. Whether to work, study, seek refuge from persecution, or simply visit, more and more people will enter this country lawfully. Providing high-quality customer service to these many lawful immigrants will be a significant challenge. At the same time, we can expect that many others will enter the United States illegally. Controlling our borders, thwarting organized alien smuggling rings, and identifying and deporting those here illegally, especially those who commit crimes, will be priorities.
- *Civil rights/hate crimes.* The increasing racial, cultural, and ethnic diversity of our society makes it all the more critical that the civil rights of all Americans are protected. This includes combating those crimes that are motivated by hatred against a particular group, promoting mutual tolerance, and ensuring that the institutions of justice are themselves fair, impartial, and free of bias.

Read the entire Strategic Plan at Web Extra! 16-4.

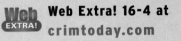

Web Extra! 16-4 at crimtoday.com

DISCUSSION QUESTIONS

1. What is globalization? What impact has it had on criminal justice practices in the United States? How are its effects recognized by the issues identified by the attorney general in this box?
2. What other important issues might you add to the ones listed here? Why?

Source: Office of the U.S. Attorney General, *Strategic Plan: Fiscal Years 2000–2005* (Washington, D.C.: U.S. Department of Justice, September 2000), pp. 14–15.

light of the occurrence or nonoccurrence of a series of related events.[22] The social consequences of the aging of the baby-boomer population, for example, will be intimately affected by the future economic health of the U.S. economy, along with the availability of medical and social programs to care for geriatric segments of the population.

The **Delphi Method**, developed at RAND by Olaf Helmer and Norman Dalkey, involves a number of steps designed to elicit expert opinion until a general consensus is reached. The steps involved include (1) problem identification, (2) development of an expert panel, (3) questions directed at the panel, and (4) the collection and synthesis of responses. The Delphi Method does not stop with one iteration of this sequence, however, but provides feedback to the experts and allows them to refine their responses.

Simulations and models attempt to replicate the system under study by reproducing its conditions in a form that can be readily manipulated to assess possible outcomes. A wind tunnel, for example, provides an environment in which models of airplanes can be tested. Many of today's simulations, of course, are based upon mathematical models and make use of computer technology in an effort to create simulated environments, and this is true of demographic and economic models which are sometimes used to predict future criminality.

Environmental scanning is a targeted effort to collect as much information as possible in "a systematic effort to identify in an elemental way future developments (trends or events) that could plausibly occur over the time horizon of interest"[23] and that might affect one's area of concern. In other words, it is impossible to predict the future without having an informed sense of what is happening now, especially where important trends are concerned. **Scenario writing** builds upon environmental scanning by attempting to assess the likelihood of a variety of possible outcomes once important trends have been identified. Scenario writing develops a list of possible futures and assigns each a degree of probability or likelihood. While not necessarily predicting a specific future, scenario writers tend to highlight a range of possible outcomes. **Strategic assessment** provides an appreciation of the risks and opportunities facing those who plan for the future.

A comprehensive futures research approach, for example, might identify an important trend that shows affluent middle- and upper-class citizens fleeing cities and suburbs for the safety of enclosed residential enclaves surrounded by secure perimeters and patrolled by paid private security personnel. Many likely scenarios could then be envisioned, including a further decline in America's cities as the moneyed classes abandon them, continued growth of street and property crimes in metropolitan areas, and rampant victimization of the urban working poor. Although crime control strategies might be developed to counter the imagined threat to cities, many risks must be considered in any planning. A serious decline in the value of the dollar, for example, as recently experienced, could cause gated communities to unravel and could create a shortfall of the tax dollars that would be needed to pay for enhanced policing in cities. The influx of new and

large immigrant populations, likely to add to the burgeoning number of inner-city dwellers, could add another new dimension to overall crime control planning.

Whatever techniques a futurist employs, however, it is important to remember that these techniques are no better than the data they use. Futurists who have made their mark on criminology include Georgette Bennett, **Bernard Levin**, Richter H. Moore, Jr., Allen Sapp, Gene Stephens, and William Tafoya. Their work, other emerging theoretical explanations for crime, and new suggestions for crime control policy are discussed in this chapter. Learn more via Web Extra! 16-5.

Web EXTRA!   Web Extra! 16-5 at crimtoday.com

FUTURE CRIMES

Murder, rape, robbery, and other types of "everyday" crime which have become mainstays of contemporary criminological analysis will continue to occur in the future, to be sure, but other new and emergent forms of criminality will grow in frequency and number. Recently, for example, Joseph F. Coates, president of the future-oriented think tank of Coates & Jarratt, predicted that by the year 2025, "socially significant crime—that is, the crimes that have the widest negative effects—in the advanced nations will be increasingly economic and computer based. Examples include disruption of business, theft, introduction of maliciously false information, and tampering with medical records, air traffic control, or national-security systems."[24] Another futurist predicts that "the top guns of twenty-first-century criminal organizations will be educated, highly sophisticated, computer-literate individuals who can wield state-of-the-art information technology to the best advantage—for themselves and for their organizations."[25]

In a wide-ranging overview of future crimes, **Richter H. Moore, Jr.**, paints a picture of future criminality that includes many dimensions. Already present are elements of what Moore predicts: "Computer hackers are changing bank records, credit accounts and reports, criminal-history files, and educational, medical, and even military records."[26] Identity manipulation, says Moore, will be a nexus of future criminality. "By the twenty-first century," he writes, "genetic-based records will include a birth-to-death dossier of a person and will be the method of criminal identification." As the Human Genome Project proceeds apace, the complete mapping of human DNA comes closer to reality. Already the U.S. military is using genetic testing to assign unique identification codes to each of its soldiers. In the event of war, such codes will allow for the identification of human remains from as little as a single cell. DNA coding, unique to each of us, may soon form the basis for nearly foolproof identification technologies which will take the science of personal identification far beyond fingerprinting, blood-type matching, or photography. The science of bioengineering, however, which is now undergoing clinical trials in the treatment of various forms of disease, may soon be clandestinely employed for the illegal modification of human DNA, with the goal of effectively altering a person's identity. It is but one more step by which the theft of computer-based genetic identification records could make it possible for one person to effectively imitate another in our future society.

Moore describes many other crimes of the future. Within a few decades, he says, "criminal organizations will be able to afford their own satellites." Drug trafficking and money-laundering operations could be coordinated via satellite communications, couriers and shipments could be tracked, and satellite surveillance could provide alerts of enforcement activity. Likewise, says Moore, "prostitution rings will use modern technology to coordinate global activities," and children and fetuses may "become subject to unlawful trafficking." The illegal disposal of toxic materials, an activity which organized crime has already explored, may become even more profitable for criminal entrepreneurs as many more hazardous substances are produced in the face of ever-tighter controls. The supply of nuclear materials and military-quality armaments to "private armies . . . terrorists, hate groups, questionable regimes, independent crime groups, and individual criminals" will be a fact of life in the next century, as will the infiltration of governments and financial institutions by sophisticated criminals whose activities are supported by large, illegally acquired fortunes.

Another writer, **Georgette Bennett**, whose seminal book *Crimewarps* was published in 1987 and helped establish the study of criminal futures as a purposeful endeavor, says that American society is about to experience major changes in both what society considers criminal and in who future offenders will be. Some areas of coming change that Bennett predicts are[27]

- A decline in street crime, such as robbery and assault
- An increase in white-collar crimes, especially high-technology crimes
- An increase in the involvement of women in crime
- An increase in crime commission among the elderly
- A shift in high crime rates from the Frost Belt to the Sun Belt
- Safer cities, with increasing criminal activity in small towns and rural areas

THE NEW CRIMINOLOGIES

Along with futures research, new and emerging criminological theories provide a picture of what criminology will be like in the years and decades to come. In an intriguing article entitled "Explaining Crime in the Year 2010," L. Edward Wells suggests that "when it comes to explaining crime, we seem to have an embarrassment of riches but a poverty of results."[28] In other words, although many explanations for criminal behavior have come and gone, "none has proven noticeably more effective in explaining, predicting, or controlling crime."[29] That may be about to change, says Wells. Contemporary criminological theorizing is interdisciplinary

and conservative in its approach to crime causation, and major changes in the premises upon which criminological theories are built are unlikely without significant ideological shifts or changes in basic components of the social structure, such as the economy, the political system, or the family. Significant social change, however, can bring about the need for new theoretical formulations, says Wells. "Legal events in the 1960s and 1970s," for example, "changed abortion from a criminal act to a routine medical procedure."[30] Similarly, an aversion to even minor forms of physical force may now be leading to a redefinition of crimes like child abuse, spousal abuse, elder abuse, and sexual aggression. Hence our basic understanding of criminal violence may be undergoing a fundamental modification that will require a concomitant change in our attempts to theorize about its causes.

Wells sees similar possibilities for theoretical change about to be introduced by advances in scientific knowledge. Should the Human Genome Project, for example, yield definitive evidence that some forms of aggression and violence are biologically grounded, it will provide the basis for an entirely new and emergent group of biological explanations for at least certain forms of criminal activity.

Wells makes a number of specific predictions about the future of criminological theorizing. He predicts that future explanations of crime will be[31]

- More eclectic than past theories and less tied to a single theoretical tradition or discipline
- More comparative and less confined to a single society or single dominant group within society
- Predominantly *individualistic* rather than collective, and *voluntaristic* rather than deterministic
- More applied and pragmatic in orientation
- More oriented toward explaining white-collar crime
- Reflective of a renewed appreciation for the biological foundations of human behavior, assigning more theoretical substance to biological and medical factors

Unfortunately, from approximately 1960 until 1985, criminology suffered through a few "black decades" in which theory building fell by the wayside as a generation of criminologists trained in quantitative analysis repeatedly tested existing ideas at the expense of developing new ones. In the mid-1980s, however, a new and dynamic era of theory building was unleashed. Frank P. Williams III and Marilyn D. McShane explain, "As if the restraints on theory building had created a pent-up demand, criminologists began exploring new theoretical constructs during the 1980s. Slowly at first, and then with great rapidity, theoretical efforts began to emerge."[32]

A number of these new approaches, including postmodernism, feminist criminology, and peacemaking criminology, were discussed in previous chapters. One perspective which deserves special attention, however, is what David P. Farrington terms the "risk factor prevention paradigm."[33] Farrington identified the paradigm during his 1999 presidential address to the

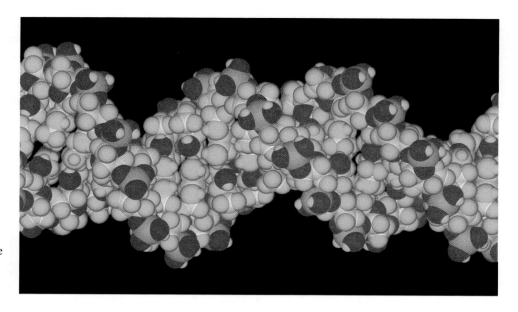

An understanding of DNA within the human genome holds great promise for the understanding of human traits. Might criminality be one of them? *Alfred Pasieka, Science Photo Library, Photo Researchers, Inc.*

American Society of Criminology. As Farrington explained, "The basic idea of the paradigm is very simple: Identify the key risk factors for offending and implement prevention methods designed to counteract them." Farrington said that the risk factor prevention paradigm has experienced "an enormous increase in influence in criminology" during the 1990s. The paradigm is especially important because of the potential it holds for guiding criminological research, crime control policy, and theoretical development well into the twenty-first century. The main challenges for the paradigm, Farrington said, "are to determine which risk factors are causes, to establish what are protective factors, to identify the active ingredients of multiple component interventions, to evaluate the effectiveness of area-based intervention programs, and to assess the monetary costs and benefits of interventions."

Theory Integration

The field of criminology today is rife with various theoretical explanations. Some are old; others are new. Many are complex, while a few are straightforward. Each theoretical approach is limited, although it may provide part of the explanation for why crime occurs, or it may offer a portion of the answer to the question of how to control crime. It may apply to only a certain type of offender, it may explain only a particular form of crime, or it may derive from only one philosophical or theoretical base.

Some have used the old fable of many blind men trying to understand an elephant to describe the contemporary situation in theoretical criminology. In the fable, each man "sees" only a small part of the overall picture. An emphasis on theory integration, with the ultimate goal of developing a unified theory of crime causation and prevention, began to emerge in the 1980s. Advocates of theory integration suggest that initial attempts at blending the propositions of different perspectives should begin at the level characteristic of those

theories. In other words, theoretical approaches concerned with analyzing crime at the individual level (often called "microlevel theories") might be integrated at the same time that sociological, political, and economic explanations (called "macrolevel theories") are woven together. Finally, cross-level integration might be attempted.[34]

Other criminologists have developed rudimentary **metatheories**, or theories about theories and the theorizing process, which they suggest may help to meld existing theories. Some metatheoreticians, however, have expressed the concern that we may integrate theories without first properly examining their worth and that, as a consequence, we may be left with highly elaborate integrated theories that are worthless.[35]

Unfortunately for advocates of integration, however, there seems "to be a consensus that there are too many problems for successful integration to take place."[36] The reasons why successful integration can never occur, say Williams and McShane, are (1) "crime is a very complex phenomenon," often determined and defined by whimsical legislative action and powerful interests; (2) "theories attempt to explain different pieces of the crime puzzle" and cannot be made to address all of its aspects; and (3) theories are "embedded in the assumptions we make about human nature and the way the world functions," and we all make different assumptions.[37]

Werner Einstadter and Stuart Henry summarize efforts at theoretical integration in criminology with these words: "The plain fact is that integrated theorizing does not lead to a more comprehensive understanding of crime or criminal etiology. Not only does the approach leave gaps between integrated theories, through which vital nuggets of the total reality of criminological explanation slip, but by presenting a range of theories as an integrated package, it tricks us into believing that a comprehensive coverage of criminological theory has been achieved."[38]

"Vital nuggets" of the reality of crime and justice can be found in such approaches as feminist criminology and black criminology, and advocates of theoretical integration are hard put to counter the ongoing development of such focused approaches. Some forms of feminist criminology, for example, even though they offer instructive insights, represent exclusive viewpoints which actively seek dismissal of much existing criminological thought—not integration with it. Similarly, other authors have advocated development of a black criminology to represent the experiences and felt needs of African-Americans and black criminologists.[39] Facing these developments, some feel that fragmentation of criminological theory, not integration, is the rule today.

Such critiques, however, may be overly harsh. One mistake made by advocates of theoretical integration is to assume that *all* existing theories must somehow be embraced and subsumed under one encompassing theoretical umbrella. A better strategy may be to work toward a multiple-theory approach that seeks the integration of only a few theories at a time. Multiple-theory formulations may provide the building blocks of larger and more comprehensive integrated theories of the future.

Sometimes a single organizing concept can help blend multiple perspectives. A few years ago, for example, Francis T. Cullen, in his address as incoming President of the Academy of Criminal Justice Sciences, identified the concept of social support as a potential "organizing concept for criminology."[40] "In short," said Cullen, "my thesis is that both across nations and across communities, crime rates vary inversely with the level of social support. America has higher rates of serious crime than other industrialized nations because it is a less supportive society." The idea of social support, said Cullen, is inherent in many criminological perspectives, even though few theorists use the term directly. Cullen pointed to the ecological theories of the Chicago School, in which gangs were said to replace ineffectual families, as early examples of the social support thesis. Other research, including that on child abuse,[41] ethnographic studies of the "truly disadvantaged," and studies of welfare which show that "governmental assistance to the poor tends to lessen violent crime," adds credence to the social support thesis, said Cullen. Because the concept of social support is capable of linking so many studies and so many other perspectives, it may truly hold value as an organizing or integrative concept in the field of criminology.

Cullen suggested that a "social support paradigm"—one which holds that "social support [whether] delivered through government social programs, communities, social networks, families, interpersonal relations, or agents of the criminal justice system . . . reduces criminal involvement"—can serve not only as a useful integrative tool, but also "can provide grounds for creating a more supportive 'Good Society.' " Specifically, Cullen maintained, "the provision of social supports reduces criminogenic strains, fosters effective parenting and a nurturing family life, supplies the human and social capital needed to desist from crime, creates opportunities for prosocial modeling, strengthens efforts at informal and formal control, and reduces opportunities for victimization."

Nonetheless, Cullen admits that an integrative theory of social support is a long way off. "Research must discern which of these hunches have merit," he says, "and to what degree."

Theory integration was also on Margaret A. Zahn's mind as she assumed the office of President of the American Society of Criminology in 1998. During her inaugural speech, Zahn told members of the society, "We will be strengthened . . . in the next century, by a greater emphasis on theoretical development, including testing our theories in new contexts, incorporating historical as well as biological data, and further inclusion of practitioners', victims', and offenders' perspectives."[42] The field of criminology has not yet realized the full promise of theoretical integration, but as Zahn and others have noted, work in the area has just begun.

POLICIES OF THE FUTURE

Recently, eminent criminologist George F. Cole raised the question, "How can lawmakers, police, courts, and corrections begin to plan for the eventualities that lie ahead?" Cole concluded that "it is essential that policy makers be given the best evidence as to prospects for future developments pertaining to the justice system and the broader socioeconomic and political context within which it will operate. Not all uncertainties about the future can be removed, but systematic and insightful exploration of the range of possibilities can provide a sounder basis for planning and a useful perspective on priorities for innovation." Cole identified a number of "drivers," or significant changes likely to occur in the near future, which he says "are likely to impact the crime and justice environment by the year 2010."[43] The list he created is shown in Table 16-1.

The significance of many of the factors listed in Table 16-1 for crime control planners can be clearly seen in the writings of **Gene Stephens**. Stephens, one of the best-known futurists of the past decade or two to focus on crime, observes that "crime is increasing worldwide, and there is every reason to believe the trend will continue . . . into the early years of the twenty-first century."[44] In particular, observes Stephens, street crimes are escalating in formerly communist countries throughout Eastern Europe and in other European nations, such as those in Scandinavia and the United Kingdom. According to Stephens, although a number of official measures show that crime is currently on the decline in the United States, America was one of the first nations to experience a rapid rise in criminality because it was the most advanced nation on the globe. The United States is a highly diverse, multicultural, industrialized, and democratic society which strongly supports individual freedoms and has fostered a strong sense of personal independence among its citizens.

Multiculturalism and heterogeneity, says Stephens, increase anomie, and previously isolated and homogeneous societies like Japan, Denmark, China, and Greece are now facing a growing cultural diversity due to international migration, the expansion of new social ideals, and an increase in foreign commerce. "Heterogeneity in societies will be the rule

TABLE 16-1   ■   Drivers Likely to Affect the Crime and Justice Environment by the Year 2010

Demography

1. Overall U.S. population increases to 300 million.
2. Proportion of Americans older than age 40 grows from 37% to 45%.
3. Minorities increase to 26% of the population.
4. The flow of legal immigrants, increasingly from Latin America and Asia, continues at a rate of about 750,000 per year.
5. Advancing technology and a changing economy result in a disproportionate impact on less skilled members of lower socioeconomic groups.

Economics

1. Restructuring of the economy continues with disruptions in some mature industrial sectors, rapid growth in the high-technology and service fields, and some outflow of jobs and capital to other nations.
2. The federal budget deficit improves, but only slowly, so funding for domestic programs remains tight.
3. The economies of the nations of the former Soviet Union remain unstable.
4. Checks and credit cards assume a larger portion of consumer monetary transactions.
5. Real growth in output and income generally is slow but steady.

Technology

1. Copying technologies advance rapidly.
2. The automation of financial transactions increases.
3. The miniaturization of computers gives patrol officers instant access to crime information files.
4. Scientists discover a chemical that has the ability to break the physical dependence on drugs from which addicts suffer.
5. Gains in laser and fiber-optic technologies revolutionize organizations.

Crime Factors

1. The war on drugs of the 1990s is cut back as cocaine use declines and law enforcement proves costly.
2. The participation of women in criminal activity increases as their societal role is redefined.
3. Handguns continue to be owned by a significant portion of the population.
4. Incarceration rates stabilize as construction of costly new prisons declines. There is an expansion of the use of probation and intermediate sanctions.
5. The disposal of nuclear and toxic wastes becomes a major organized crime activity.

Source: George F. Cole, "Criminal Justice in the Twenty-first Century: The Role of Futures Research," in John Klofas and Stan Stojkovic, eds., *Crime and Justice in the Year 2010* (Belmont, CA: Wadsworth, 1995), pp. 4–5. Copyright © 1995, Wadsworth Publishing Company, an imprint of the Wadsworth Group, a division of Thomson Learning. Reprinted with permission. Fax (800) 730-2215.

in the twenty-first century," says Stephens, "and failure to recognize and plan for such diversity can lead to serious crime problems, especially in emerging multicultural societies." Stephens's thesis is best summarized in this passage from his work: "The connection between crime and culture cannot be overemphasized: There are high-crime and low-crime cultures around the world. In the years ahead, many low-crime cultures may become high-crime cultures because of changing world demographics and politicoeconomic systems. In general, heterogeneous populations in which people have lots of political freedom (democracy) and lots of economic choice (capitalism) are prime candidates for crime unless a good socialization system is created and maintained."

Homogeneous nations—in which citizens share similar backgrounds, life experiences, and values—produce citizens who are generally capable of complying with the wishes of the majority and who can legislate controls over behavior, which are not difficult for most citizens to respect. In such societies, a tradition of discipline, a belief in the laws, and an acceptance of personal responsibility are typically the norm.

Diverse societies, on the other hand, suffer from constant internal conflict, with much of that conflict focused on acceptable ways of living and working. Heterogeneous societies tend to place a strong emphasis on individualism, and disagreement about the law and social norms is rife. Characteristic of such cultures is the fact that lawbreakers tend to deny responsibility and go to great lengths to avoid capture and conviction. To highlight the difference between homogeneous and heterogeneous societies, Stephens points out that in some highly homogeneous cultures, such as Japan, those who break norms will often punish themselves, even if their transgressions are not publicly discovered. Such self-punishing behavior would be almost unthinkable in an advanced heterogeneous society like the United States. As Stephens explains, "Some nations, such as the United States, face pervasive *anomie* due to their lack of restraints on human desires."

Heterogeneity can arise in numerous ways, even within a society that had previously been relatively homogeneous. One source of increasing and important differences in American society today, for example, has been the growth of a technological culture which has produced two separate and

An LAPD officer helps a suspect into a police vehicle. How will law enforcement technology change during the twenty-first century? *Axel Koester, Corbis/Sygma*

distinct groups: the technologically capable and those who are incapable of utilizing modern technology. To these two groups we might add a third: the technologically aware, or those who realize the importance of technology but who, for whatever reason—be it age, lack of education, poverty, or other life circumstances—have not yet acquired the skills necessary to participate fully in what our highly technological society has to offer. In Stephens's words: "More people are turning to street crime and violence because they find themselves unprepared, educationally or emotionally, to cope with the requirements for success in the new era."

Another reason why crime rates are high—and growing— in increasingly heterogeneous societies, according to Stephens, is that such societies often display a lack of consistent child-care philosophies and child-rearing methods. "In some societies," says Stephens, "parents are seen as primarily responsible for their children, but all citizens share in that responsibility, since everyone's welfare is affected by the proper socialization of each child." In others, children are viewed as the parents' property, and little is expected of parents other than that they be biologically capable of reproducing. No requirements are set in such societies for parental knowledge, skills, income, education, and so on. Stephens describes child-rearing practices in such societies as "helter-skelter, catch-as-catch-can child care." Lacking child-rearing standards in which the majority of members of society can meaningfully participate, heterogeneous societies tend to produce adults who are irresponsible and who do not adhere to legal or other standards of behavior.

According to Stephens, future crimes will be plentiful, with countries around the world experiencing explosive growth in their crime rates. "The United States," he says, "was the first industrialized, democratic, heterogeneous nation and thus the first to face the crime problems associated with *anomie*." Now, however, other nations are undergoing increased modernization, with many entering the postmodern era previously occupied solely by the United States. "We can theorize," says Stephens, "that crime will be a growth industry in many countries as they find themselves gripped by the same social forces that have long affected the United States."

Other authors have similarly attempted to describe crime control issues that may face future policymakers.[45] Richter H. Moore, Jr., for example, identifies the following seven issues that are likely to concern crime control planners in the near future:[46]

- *New criminal groups.* According to Moore, "Groups such as Colombian drug cartels, Jamaican posses, Vietnamese gangs, various Chinese groups, and Los Angeles black street gangs are now a much bigger concern than the Mafia," and the criminal activity and influence of these new groups are growing rapidly. Traditional law enforcement responses, such as those developed to deal with Italian-American Mafia organizations, may be inappropriate in the face of the new challenges these groups represent.
- *Language barriers.* According to Moore, "U.S. law-enforcement officials now find themselves hampered by a lack of understanding about the language and culture of some of the new criminal groups" operating in America. Cuban, Mexican, Colombian, Japanese, and Chinese criminals and criminal organizations are becoming commonplace, and such groups are increasingly involved in international communications and travel.
- *Distrust by ethnic communities.* Recent immigrant groups have been slow to assimilate into American culture and society. As a consequence, many of these groups hold strongly to native identities, distancing themselves from formal agencies of social control, such as the police. As Moore points out, "In many of their countries of origin, new immigrants see police as corrupt, self-serving individuals, a viewpoint often not without foundation." A distrust of police and government representatives is nearly instinctual for members of such groups, making the work of law enforcement within the context of immigrant communities challenging and often difficult.
- *Greater reliance on community involvement.* Moore observes that "due to the increasing costs of electronic surveillance, informant programs, undercover operations, and witness-protection programs, police are now encouraging community members to become more involved in their own security." The involvement of private citizens in the battle against crime may be the only realistic solution to the problem. Neighborhood watch groups, the use of community volunteers within criminal justice organizations, and other neighborhood self-help programs, such as school- and church-based education, all suggest the future of neighborhood-based crime control policy.

The parents of Cherica Adams embrace after former Carolina Panther professional football player Rae Carruth was found guilty of conspiracy in arranging her murder. Carruth had dated Adams and she was carrying his unborn child at the time of her death. Prosecutors argued that Carruth was trying to avoid having to pay child support. Are crimes of violence likely to decline in the future? *Jeff Siner, AP/Wide World Photos*

■ *Regulating the marketplace.* Moore advises that decriminalization and legalization will become of increasingly greater concern to future legislators who will focus on "regulating the marketplace" for criminal activities like gambling, drug trafficking, and prostitution.

■ *Reducing public demand.* Similarly, according to Moore, future crime control policies will aim to reduce involvement in criminal activity "through better education" and other policies that will, over the long term, lower the demand for drugs and other illegal services.

■ *Increased treatment.* Although in contrast with many of today's get-tough policies, Moore sees a greater emphasis in the future on the treatment of all forms of criminality, including drug abuse, gambling, rape, and other lawbreaking behaviors.

SUMMARY

For all but the most astute, the future is difficult to presage. It is safe to assume, however, that the future will differ from the past. Futures research, as this chapter has attempted to show, can at least point policymakers and criminologists in what should be reasonable directions.

Emerging theories of criminality are likely to be multilevel and interactional approaches, with the goal of theory integration occupying criminologists well into the twenty-first century. At the same time, additional research evaluations will be necessary to identify the most promising theoretical developments and to craft crime control policies based upon the best scientific knowledge available.

DISCUSSION QUESTIONS

1. This book emphasizes a social problems versus social responsibility theme. Which perspective do you think will be dominant in twenty-first-century crime control planning? Why?

2. Do you believe it is possible to know the future? What techniques are identified in this chapter for assessing possible futures? Which of these do you think holds the most promise? Why?

3. What is meant by "theory integration"? How might theory integration be achieved in the field of criminology?

4. What is comparative criminology? What are the advantages of a comparative perspective? Are there any disadvantages? If so, what are they?

WEB QUEST!

Visit the World Future Society on the Web at http://www. wfs.org. The society's Web site offers several moderated forums that permit you to share ideas with futurists around the world. Forums include

- The Social Innovation Forum, which presents papers outlining ideas for urban development, social reform, and other proposals for improving life in the future
- The Opportunity Forum, which offers ideas to improve your personal and professional life in the new millennium
- The Wisdom of the World Forum, in which British scholar Bruce Lloyd has collected quotes containing

wisdom essential for humanity in the new millennium. You can submit your own quotes for possible posting.
- The Methodology Forum, in which professional futurists, planners, and forecasters share tips and useful tools for futuring

This Web Quest! requires you to search through the forums to identify topics, posted papers, or contributed comments dealing with criminology, crime, and criminal justice. Identify such materials, summarize each, and submit them to your instructor if asked to do so.

LIBRARY EXTRAS!

The Library Extras! listed here complement the Web Extras! found throughout this chapter. Library Extras! may be accessed on the Web at crimtoday.com.

Library Extra! 16-1. Gregory J. Howard, Graeme Newman, and William Alex Pridemore, "Theory, Method, and Data in Comparative Criminology," in David Duffee, Ed., *Criminal Justice 2000: Volume IV—Measurement and Analysis of Criminal Justice* (Washington, D.C.: National Institute of Justice, 2000).

Library Extra! 16-2. Gary LaFree et al., "The Changing Nature of Crime in America." In Gary LaFree, Ed., *Criminal Justice 2000: Volume IV—The Nature of Crime—Continuity and Change* (Washington, D.C.: National Institute of Justice, 2000).

Library Extra! 16-3. Bernard H. Levin, "A Future of Criminal Justice, with a Focus on Policing," paper presented

at the West Virginia Criminal Justice Education Association, Summersville, WV, April 12, 1997.

Library Extra! 16-4. Office of the U.S. Attorney General, *Strategic Plan: Fiscal Years 2000–2005* (Washington, D.C.: U.S. Department of Justice, September 2000).

Library Extra! 16-5. Darlene E. Weingand, "Futures Research Methodologies: Linking Today's Decisions with Tomorrow's Possibilities," paper presented at the 61st International Federation of Library Associations and Institutions, August 20, 1995.

Library Extra! 16-6. World Future Society, *The Study of the Future* (online document).

NOTES

[1] Cynthia Manson and Charles Ardai, eds., *Future Crime: An Anthology of the Shape of Crime to Come* (New York: Donald I. Fine, 1992), p. ix.

[2] Alvin Toffler, *Powershift: Knowledge, Wealth, and Violence at the Edge of the Twenty-first Century* (New York: Bantam, 1990), p. 255.

[3] James Q. Wilson, "Crime and Public Policy," in James Q. Wilson and Joan Petersilia, eds., *Crime* (San Francisco: Institute for Contemporary Studies, 1995), p. 507.

[4] George Orwell, *1984* (New York: New American Library Classics, 1990).

[5] This story is adapted from Gary LaFree et al., "The Changing Nature of Crime in America," in Gary LaFree, ed., *Criminal Justice 2000: Volume III—The Nature of Crime—Continuity and Change* (Washington, D.C.: National Institute of Justice, 2000).

[6] Darlene E. Weingand, "Futures Research Methodologies: Linking Today's Decisions with Tomorrow's Possibilities," paper presented at the Sixty-first International Federation of Library Associations and Institutions annual conference, August 20, 1995. Web posted at http://www.ifla.org/IV/ifla61/61-weid.htm. Accessed June 16, 1998.

[7] Joseph F. Coates, "The Highly Probable Future: 83 Assumptions about the Year 2025," *Futurist,* Vol. 28, No. 4 (July/August 1994), p. 51.

[8] Alvin Toffler, *Future Shock* (New York: Random House, 1970).

[9] Alvin Toffler, *The Third Wave* (New York: Bantam, 1981).

[10] John Naisbitt, *Megatrends: Ten New Directions Transforming Our Lives* (New York: Warner, 1982).

[11] Peter F. Drucker, *Management Challenges for the 21st Century* (New York: Harper, 1999).

[12] Peter F. Drucker, *Post-Capitalist Society* (New York: Harper, 1994).

[13] Although this chapter cannot cover all future aspects of the criminal justice system, readers are referred to C. J. Swank, "Police in the Twenty-first Century: Hypotheses for the Future," *International Journal of Comparative and Applied Criminal Justice,* Vol. 17, Nos. 1 and 2 (spring/fall 1993), pp. 107–120, for an excellent analysis of policing in the future.

[14] The Foresight Web site, http://www.foresight.gov.uk. Accessed March 22, 2001.

[15] The quotations attributed to the panel in this section are from Foresight Crime Prevention Panel, *Just Around the Corner: A Consultation Document.* Web posted at http://www.foresight.gov.uk/servlet/DocViewer/docnoredirect=883. Accessed January 22, 2001.

[16] Adapted from John McHale, "Futures Critical: A Review," in *Human Futures: Needs, Societies, Technologies* (Guildford, Surrey, UK: IPC Business Press Limited, 1974), p. 13.

[17] Gregory J. Howard, Graeme Newman, and William Alex Pridemore, "Theory, Method, and Data in Comparative Criminology," in David Duffee, ed., *Criminal Justice 2000: Volume IV—Measurement and Analysis of Criminal Justice.* (Washington, D.C.: National Institute of Justice, 2000), p. 189.

[18] Ibid.

[19] Society of Police Futurists International, *PFI: The Future of Policing* (brochure), no date.

[20] William L. Tafoya, "Futures Research: Implications for Criminal Investigations," in James N. Gilbert, ed., *Criminal Investigation: Essays and Cases* (Columbus, OH: Charles E. Merrill, 1990), p. 214.

[21] Frederick R. Brodzinski, "The Futurist Perspective and the Managerial Process," *Utilizing Futures Research,* No. 6 (1979), pp. 8–19.

[22] Weingand, "Futures Research Methodologies."

[23] George F. Cole, "Criminal Justice in the Twenty-first Century: The Role of Futures Research," in John Klofas and Stan Stojkovic, eds., *Crime and Justice in the Year 2010* (Belmont, CA: Wadsworth, 1995).

[24] Joseph F. Coates, et al., *2025: Scenarios of U.S. and Global Society Reshaped by Science and Technology* (Winchester, VA: Oakhill Press, 1997).

[25] Richter H. Moore, Jr., "Wiseguys: Smarter Criminals and Smarter Crime in the Twenty-first Century," *Futurist,* Vol. 28, No. 5 (September/October 1994), p. 33.

[26] The quotations attributed to Moore in this section are from ibid, pp. 33–37.

[27] Georgette Bennett, *Crimewarps: The Future of Crime in America* (Garden City, NY: Anchor/Doubleday, 1987).

[28] L. Edward Wells, "Explaining Crime in the Year 2010," in John Klofas and Stan Stojkovic, eds., *Crime and Justice in the Year 2010,* (Belmont, CA: Wadsworth, 1995), pp. 36–61.

[29] Ibid.

[30] Ibid., pp. 48–49.

[31] Ibid., pp. 54–57.

[32] Frank P. Williams III and Marilyn D. McShane, *Criminological Theory,* 2nd ed. (Englewood Cliffs, NJ: Prentice Hall, 1994), p. 257.

[33] The quotations attributed to Farrington in this section are from David P. Farrington, "Explaining and Preventing Crime: The Globalization of Knowledge, *Criminology,* Vol. 38, No. 1 (February 2000), pp. 1–24.

[34] For a more detailed discussion of theory integration, see Stephen F. Messner, Marvin D. Krohn, and Allan A. Liska, eds., *Theoretical Integration in the Study of Deviance and Crime: Problems and Prospects* (Albany: State University of New York Press, 1989).

[35] Joan McCord, "Theory, Pseudotheory, and Metatheory," in W. S. Laufer and F. Adler, eds., *Advances in Criminological Theory,* Vol. 1 (New Brunswick, NJ: Transaction, 1989), pp. 127–145.

[36] Williams and McShane, *Criminological Theory,* p. 265.

[37] Ibid., pp. 266–267.

[38] Werner Einstadter and Stuart Henry, *Criminological Theory: An Analysis of Its Underlying Assumptions* (Fort Worth, TX: Harcourt, Brace, 1995), p. 309.

[39] See, for example, Katheryn K. Russell, "Development of a Black Criminology and the Role of the Black Criminologist," *Justice Quarterly,* Vol. 9, No. 4 (December 1992), pp. 668–683.

[40] The quotations attributed to Cullen in this section are from Francis T. Cullen, "Social Support as an Organizing Concept for Criminology: Presidential Address to the Academy of Criminal Justice Sciences," *Justice Quarterly,* Vol. 11, No. 4 (December 1994), pp. 527–559.

[41] See, for example, Carolyn Smith and Terence P. Thornberry, "The Relationship between Childhood Maltreatment and Adolescent Involvement in Delinquency," *Criminology,* Vol. 33, No. 4 (1995), pp. 451–477.

[42] Margaret A. Zahn, "Thoughts on the Future of Criminology: The American Society of Criminology 1998 Presidential Address," *Criminology,* Vol. 37, No. 1 (1999), p. 1.

[43] Cole, "Criminal Justice in the Twenty-first Century," pp. 4–5.

[44] The quotations attributed to Stephens in this section are from Gene Stephens, "The Global Crime Wave," *Futurist,* Vol. 28, No. 4 (July/August 1994), pp. 22–29.

[45] For an interesting and alternative view of the future—one that evaluates what might happen if the insight provided by feminist perspectives on crime were implemented— see M. Kay Harris, "Moving into the New Millennium: Toward a Feminist Vision of Justice," in Barry W. Hancock and Paul M. Sharp, eds., *Public Policy, Crime, and Criminal Justice,* 2nd ed. (Upper Saddle River, NJ: Prentice Hall, 2000), pp. 407–419.

[46] Moore, "Wiseguys," p. 33.

Glossary

Numbers appearing in parentheses after each term and its associated definition refer to the chapter in which that term appears.

acquaintance rape Rape characterized by a prior social, though not necessarily intimate or familial, relationship between the victim and the perpetrator. (10)

administrative law Law that regulates many daily business activities. Violations of these regulations generally result in warnings or fines, depending on their adjudged severity.

Age of Reason See **Enlightenment.**

aggravated assault (UCR) An unlawful attack by one person upon another for the purpose of inflicting severe or aggravated bodily injury. See also **simple assault.** (2)

alloplastic adaptation A form of adjustment which results from changes in the environment surrounding an individual. (6)

androcentricity A single-sex perspective; as in the case of criminologists who study only the criminality of males. (9)

anomie A social condition in which norms are uncertain or lacking. (7)

anomie theory See **strain theory.**

Anti-Drug Abuse Act A federal law (Public Law 99-570) enacted in 1986 that established new federal mandatory minimum sentences for drug offenses. (15)

antisocial personality A term used to describe individuals who are basically unsocialized and whose behavior pattern brings them repeatedly into conflict with society. Also called *asocial personality.* (6)

antisocial personality disorder A psychological condition exhibited by "individuals who are basically unsocialized and whose behavior pattern brings them repeatedly into conflicts with society."[1] (6)

applied research Scientific inquiry that is designed and carried out with practical applications in mind. (3)

Arrestee Drug Abuse Monitoring (ADAM) Program A National Institute of Justice program that tracks trends in the prevalence and types of drug use among booked arrestees in urban areas. (13)

arson The willful or malicious burning or attempt to burn, with or without intent to defraud, of a dwelling house, public building, motor vehicle or aircraft, personal property of another, and so on. (2)

asocial personality See **antisocial personality.**

assault See **aggravated assault; simple assault.**

asset forfeiture The authorized seizure of money, negotiable instruments, securities, or other things of value. In federal antidrug laws; the authorization of judicial representatives to seize all monies, negotiable instruments, securities, or other things of value furnished or intended to be furnished by any person in exchange for a controlled substance, and all proceeds traceable to such an exchange. (12)

atavism A term used by Cesare Lombroso to suggest that criminals are physiological throwbacks to earlier stages of human evolution. The term is derived from the Latin term *atavus,* which means "ancestor." (5)

attachment theory A social-psychological perspective on delinquent and criminal behavior which holds that the successful development of secure attachment between a child and his or her primary caregiver provides the basic foundation for all future psychological development. (6)

audit trail A sequential record of computer system activities that enables auditors to reconstruct, review, and examine the sequence of states and activities surrounding each event in one or more related transactions from inception to output of final results back to inception. (14)

autoplastic adaptation A form of adjustment which results from changes within an individual. (6)

behavioral genetics The study of genetic and environmental contributions to individual variations in human behavior. (5)

behavior theory A psychological perspective which posits that individual behavior which is rewarded will increase in frequency, while that which is punished will decrease. (6)

bias crime See **hate crime.**

biological theory (of criminology) A theory that maintains that the basic determinants of human behavior, including criminality, are constitutionally or physiologically based and often inherited. (5)

booster A frequent shoplifter. (11)

born criminal An individual who is born with a genetic predilection toward criminality. (5)

bourgeoisie In Marxist theory, the class of people who own the means of production. (9)

Brady Handgun Violence Prevention Act A federal law (Public Law 103-159) enacted in 1993 and which initiated a national background checking system for all potential gun purchasers. (15)

***Brawner* rule** A somewhat vague rule for determining insanity that was created in the federal court case of *U.S.* v. *Brawner* (471 F.2d 969) and in which the jury is asked to decide whether the defendant could be *justly* held responsible for the criminal act with which he or she stands charged, in the face of any claims of insanity or mental incapacity. (6)

broken windows thesis A perspective on crime causation which holds that physical deterioration in an area leads to increased concerns for personal safety among area residents and to higher crime rates in that area. (7)

bulletin board system (BBS) A computer accessible by telephone and used like a bulletin board to leave messages and files for other users. Also called *computer bulletin board.* (14)

burglary By the narrowest and oldest definition, the trespassory breaking and entering of the dwelling house of another in the nighttime with the intent to commit a felony. Also, the unlawful entry of a structure to commit a felony or a theft. (2)

burglary (UCR) The unlawful entry of any fixed structure, vehicle, or vessel used for regular residence, industry, or business, with or without force, with intent to commit a felony or a larceny. (2)

Cambridge Study in Delinquent Development A longitudinal (life course) study of crime and delinquency tracking a cohort of 411 boys born in London in 1953. (8)

capable guardian One who effectively discourages crime. (4)

capital punishment The legal imposition of a sentence of death upon a convicted offender. Also called *death penalty.* (4)

carjacking The stealing of a car while it is occupied. (2)

Carnivore A network diagnostic tool that is capable of assisting in criminal investigations by monitoring and capturing large amounts of Internet traffic. Also called *Omnivore.* (14)

Chicago Area Project A program focusing on urban ecology, and originating at the University of Chicago during the 1930s, which attempted to reduce delinquency, crime, and social disorganization in transitional neighborhoods. (7)

Chicago School of criminology See **ecological theory.**

civil law The body of law that regulates arrangements between individuals, such as contracts and claims to property.

Classical School A criminological perspective of the late 1700s and early 1800s that had its roots in the Enlightenment and that held that humans are rational beings, that crime is the result of the exercise of free will, and that punishment can be effective in reducing the incidence of crime, as it negates the pleasure to be derived from crime commission. (4)

clearance rate The proportion of reported or discovered crimes within a given offense category that are solved. (2)

Code of Hammurabi An early set of laws established by the Babylonian king Hammurabi, who ruled the ancient city from 1792 to 1750 B.C. (4)

cohort A group of individuals having certain significant social characteristics in common, such as gender and date and place of birth. (2)

cohort analysis A social scientific technique which studies over time a population that shares common characteristics. Cohort analysis usually begins at birth and traces the development of cohort members until they reach a certain age. (8)

Commission on Law Observance and Enforcement See **Wickersham Commission.**

common law Law originating from usage and custom rather than from written statutes. The term refers to nonstatutory customs, traditions, and precedents that help guide judicial decision making. (4)

Communications Decency Act A federal statute signed into law in 1996, the CDA is Title 5 of the federal Telecommunications Act of 1996 (Public Law 104-104, 110 Stat. 56). The law sought to protect minors from harmful material on the Internet and a portion of the CDA criminalized the knowing transmission of obscene or indecent messages to any recipient under 18 years of age. In 1997, however, in the case of *Reno* v. *ACLU* (521 US 844), the U.S. Supreme Court found the bulk of the CDA to be unconstitutional, ruling that it contravenes First Amendment free speech guarantees. (14)

comparative criminologist A criminologist involved in the cross-national study of crime. (16)

comparative criminology The cross-national study of crime. (16)

Comprehensive Crime Control Act A far-reaching federal law (Public Law 98–473) enacted in 1984 that mandated new federal sentencing guidelines, eliminated parole at the federal level, limited the use of the insanity defense in federal criminal courts, and increased federal penalties associated with drug dealing. (15)

computer abuse Any unlawful incident associated with computer technology in which a victim suffered or could have suffered loss or in which a perpetrator by intention made or could have made gain.[2] (14)

computer bulletin board See **bulletin board system (BBS).**

computer crime Any violation of a federal or state computer crime statute. See also **cybercrime.** (14)

computer-related crime Any illegal act for which knowledge of computer technology is involved for its perpetration, investigation, or prosecution. (14)

computer virus A set of computer instructions that propagates copies or versions of itself into computer programs or data when it is executed. (14)

conditioning A psychological principle which holds that the frequency of any behavior can be increased or decreased through reward, punishment, or association with other stimuli. (6)

conduct norms A shared expectation of a social group relative to personal conduct. (7)

confidentiality See **data confidentiality.**

conflict perspective An analytical perspective on social organization which holds that conflict is a fundamental aspect of social life itself and can never be fully resolved. (9)

confounding effects A rival explanation, or competing hypothesis, which is a threat to the internal or external validity of a research design. (3)

consensus model An analytical perspective on social organization which holds that most members of society agree about what is right and what is wrong and that the various elements of society work together in unison toward a common and shared vision of the greater good. (9)

constitutional theory A theory that explains criminality by reference to offenders' body types, inheritance, genetics, or external observable physical characteristics. (5)

constitutive criminology The study of the process by which human beings create an ideology of crime that sustains the notion of crime as a concrete reality. (9)

containment Aspects of the social bond which act to prevent individuals from committing crimes and which keep them from engaging in deviance. (8)

containment theory A form of control theory which suggests that a series of both internal and external factors contributes to law-abiding behavior. (8)

control group A group of experimental subjects which, although the subject of measurement and observation, is not exposed to the experimental intervention. (3)

controlled experiment An experiment that attempts to hold conditions (other than the intentionally introduced experimental intervention) constant. (3)

control ratio The amount of control to which a person is subject versus the amount of control that person exerts over others. (8)

control theory See **social control theory.**

corporate crime A violation of a criminal statute either by a corporate entity or by its executives, employees, or agents acting on behalf of and for the benefit of the corporation, partnership, or other form of business entity.[3] (12)

correctional psychology The branch of forensic psychology concerned with the diagnosis and classification of offenders, the treatment of correctional populations, and the rehabilitation of inmates and other law violators. (6)

correlation A causal, complementary, or reciprocal relationship between two measurable variables. See also **statistical correlation.** (2)

Cosa Nostra Literally, "our thing." A criminal organization of Sicilian origin. Also call *the Mafia, the Outfit, the Mob, the syndicate,* or simply *the organization.* (12)

crime Human conduct in violation of the criminal laws of a state, the federal government, or a local jurisdiction that has the power to make such laws. (1)

crime typology A classification of crimes along a particular dimension, such as legal categories, offender motivation, victim behavior, or the characteristics of individual offenders. (10)

criminal anthropology The scientific study of the relationship between human physical characteristics and criminality. (5)

criminal career The longitudinal sequence of crimes committed by an individual offender. (8)

criminal homicide The illegal killing of one human being by another. (2)

criminal homicide (UCR) The UCR category which includes and is limited to all offenses of causing the death of another person without justification or excuse. (2)

criminalist A specialist in the collection and examination of the physical evidence of crime. (1)

criminality A behavioral predisposition that disproportionately favors criminal activity. (1)

criminality index The actual extent of the crime problem in a society. The criminality index is computed by adding the actual crime rate and the latent crime rate. (2)

criminalize To make illegal. (1)

criminal justice The scientific study of crime, the criminal law, and components of the criminal justice system, including the police, courts, and corrections. (1)

criminal justice system The various agencies of justice, especially the police, courts, and corrections, whose goal it is to apprehend, convict, punish, and rehabilitate law violators. (1)

criminal law The body of law that regulates actions which have the potential to harm the interests of the state or the federal government.

criminaloids A term used by Cesare Lombroso to describe occasional criminals who were pulled into criminality primarily by environmental influences. (5)

criminal psychology See **forensic psychology.**

criminal receiver See **fence.**

criminologist One who is trained in the field of criminology. Also, one who studies crime, criminals, and criminal behavior. (1)

criminology An interdisciplinary profession built around the scientific study of crime and criminal behavior, including their forms, causes, legal aspects, and control. (1)

criminology of place See **environmental criminology.**

critical criminology See **radical criminology.**

cross-impact analysis A technique of futures research that attempts to analyze one trend or event in light of the occurrence or nonoccurrence of a series of related events. (16)

cultural transmission The transmission of delinquency through successive generations of people living in the same area through a process of social communication. (7)

culture conflict theory A sociological perspective on crime which suggests that the root cause of criminality can be found in a clash of values between variously socialized groups over what is acceptable or proper behavior. (7)

cybercrime Crime committed with the use of computers or via the manipulation of digital forms of data. See also **computer crime.** (14)

cyberspace The computer-created matrix of virtual possibilities, including online services, wherein human beings interact with one another and with the technology itself. (14)

cyberstalking An array of activities in which an offender may engage to harass or "follow" individuals, including e-mail and the Internet. (10)

cycloid A term developed by Ernst Kretschmer to describe a particular relationship between body build and personality type. The cycloid personality, which was associated with a heavyset, soft type of body, was said to vacillate between normality and abnormality. (5)

dangerous drug A term used by the Drug Enforcement Administration to refer to "broad categories or classes of controlled substances other than cocaine, opiates, and cannabis products." Amphetamines, methamphetamines, PCP (phencyclidine), LSD, methcathinone, and "designer drugs" are all considered to be dangerous drugs. (13)

dangerousness The likelihood that a given individual will later harm society or others. Dangerousness is often measured in terms of recidivism, or the likelihood of new crime commission or rearrest for a new crime within a five-year period following arrest or release from confinement. (4)

dark figure of crime The numerical total of unreported crimes that are not reflected in official crime statistics. (2)

data confidentiality The ethical requirement of social scientific research to protect the confidentiality of individual research participants, while simultaneously preserving justified research access to the information participants provide. (3)

data encryption The process by which information is encoded, making it unreadable to all but its intended recipients. (14)

date rape Unlawful forced sexual intercourse with a woman against her will which occurs within the context of a dating relationship. (2)

***Daubert* standard** A test of scientific acceptability applicable to the gathering of evidence in criminal cases. (14)

death penalty See **capital punishment.**

deconstructionist theory A postmodern perspective that challenges existing criminological theories in order to debunk them and that works toward replacing traditional ideas with concepts seen as more appropriate to the postmodern era. (9)

decriminalization (of drugs) The reduction of criminal penalties associated with the personal possession of a controlled substance. (13)

defensible space The range of mechanisms that combine to bring an environment under the control of its residents. (7)

Delphi Method A technique of futures research that uses repetitive questioning of experts to refine predictions. (16)

demographics The characteristics of population groups, usually expressed in statistical fashion. (2)

demography The study of the characteristics of population groups.

descriptive statistics Statistics that describe, summarize, or highlight the relationships within data which have been gathered. (3)

designer drugs One of the "new substances designed by slightly altering the chemical makeup of other illegal or tightly controlled drugs."[4] (12)

desistance The cessation of criminal activity or the termination of a period of involvement in offending behavior. (8)

desistance phenomenon The observable decrease in crime rates that is invariably associated with age. (2)

determinate sentencing A criminal punishment strategy that mandates a specified and fixed amount of time to be served for every offense category. Under the strategy, for example, all offenders convicted of the same degree of burglary would be sentenced to the same length of time behind bars. Also called *fixed sentencing.* (4)

deterrence The prevention of crime. See also **general deterrence; specific deterrence.** (4)

deterrence strategy A crime control strategy that attempts "to diminish motivation for crime by increasing the perceived certainty, severity, or celerity of penalties."[5] (15)

deviant behavior Behavior that violates social norms or is statistically different from the "average." (1)

differential association The sociological thesis that criminality, like any other form of behavior, is learned through a process of association with others who communicate criminal values. (8)

differential identification theory An explanation for crime and deviance which holds that people pursue criminal or deviant behavior to the extent that they identify themselves with real or imaginary people from whose perspective their criminal or deviant behavior seems acceptable. (8)

Digital Theft Deterrence and Copyright Damages Improvement Act Passed in 1999, this federal law (Public Law 106-160) attempted to combat software piracy and other forms of digital theft by amending Section 504(c) of the Copyright Act, thereby increasing the amount of damages that could potentially be awarded in cases of copyright infringement. (14)

disclosure (of research methods) The provision of information to potential subjects informing them of the nature of the research methods to be used by the social scientific study in which their involvement is planned. (3)

discrediting information Information that is inconsistent with the managed impressions being communicated in a given situation. (8)

displacement A shift of criminal activity from one location to another. (4)

displastic A mixed group of offenders described by constitutional theorist Ernst Kretschmer as highly emotional and often unable to control themselves. They were thought to commit mostly sexual offenses and other crimes of passion. The term is largely of historical interest.

distributive justice The rightful, equitable, and just distribution of rewards within a society. (7)

DNA fingerprinting The use of biological residue found at the scene of a crime for genetic comparisons in aiding the identification of criminal suspects. Also called *DNA profiling.* (14)

DNA profiling See **DNA fingerprinting.**

dramaturgical perspective A theoretical point of view that depicts human behavior as centered around the purposeful management of interpersonal impressions. Also called *dramaturgy.* (8)

dramaturgy See **dramaturgical perspective.**

drug-defined crime A violation of the laws prohibiting or regulating the possession, use, or distribution of illegal drugs. (13)

drug-related crime A crime in which drugs contribute to the offense (excluding violations of drug laws). (13)

drug trafficking Manufacturing, distributing, dispensing, importing, and exporting (or possession with intent to do the same) a controlled substance or a counterfeit substance.[6] (13)

***Durham* rule** A standard for judging legal insanity which holds that an accused is not criminally responsible if his unlawful act was the product of mental disease or mental defect. (6)

ecological theory A type of sociological approach which emphasizes demographics (the characteristics of population groups) and geographics (the mapped location of such groups relative to one another) and which sees the social disorganization that characterizes delinquency areas as a major cause of criminality and victimization. Also called *Chicago School of criminology.* (7)

ectomorph A body type originally described as thin and fragile, with long, slender, poorly muscled extremities and delicate bones. (5)

ego The reality-testing part of the personality. Also called the *reality principle*. More formally, the personality component that is conscious, most immediately controls behavior, and is most in touch with external reality.[7] (6)

electroencephalogram (EEG) The electrical measurement of brain wave activity. (6)

encryption See data encryption.

endomorph A body type originally described as soft and round or overweight. (5)

Enlightenment A social movement that arose during the eighteenth century and that built upon ideas like empiricism, rationality, free will, humanism, and natural law. Also called *Age of Reason*. (4)

environmental crime A violation of the criminal law which, although typically committed by businesses or by business officials, may also be committed by other people or by organizational entities and which damages some protected or otherwise significant aspect of the natural environment. (12)

environmental criminology An emerging perspective which emphasizes the importance of geographic location and architectural features as they are associated with the prevalence of criminal victimization. (Note: As the term has been understood to date, environmental criminology is not the study of environmental crime, but rather a perspective that stresses how crime varies from place to place.) Also called *criminology of place*. (7)

environmental scanning "A systematic effort to identify in an elemental way future developments (trends or events) that could plausibly occur over the time horizon of interest"[8] and that might affect one's area of concern. (16)

ethnic succession The continuing process whereby one immigrant or ethnic group succeeds another by assuming its position in society. (12)

eugenic criminology A perspective which holds that the root causes of criminality are passed from generation to generation in the form of "bad genes." (5)

eugenics The study of hereditary improvement by genetic control. (5)

evolutionary ecology An approach to understanding crime that draws attention to the ways people develop over the course of their lives. (8)

experiment See controlled experiment; quasi-experimental design.

expert systems Computer hardware and software that attempt to duplicate the decision-making processes used by skilled investigators in the analysis of evidence and in the recognition of patterns which such evidence might represent. (14)

exposure-reduction theory A theory of intimate homicide which claims that a decline in domesticity, accompanied by an improvement in the economic status of women and a growth in domestic violence resources, explains observed decreases in intimate-partner homicide. (10)

expressive crime A criminal offense that results from acts of interpersonal hostility, such as jealousy, revenge, romantic triangles, and quarrels. (10)

external validity The ability to generalize research findings to other settings. (3)

felony A serious criminal offense, specifically one punishable by death or by incarceration in a prison facility for a year or more.

felony murder A special class of criminal homicide in which an offender may be charged with first-degree murder when that person's criminal activity results in another person's death. (2)

feminist criminology A self-conscious corrective model intended to redirect the thinking of mainstream criminologists to include gender awareness. (9)

fence An individual or group involved in the buying, selling, and distribution of stolen goods. Also called *criminal receiver*. (11)

first-degree murder Criminal homicide that is planned or involves premeditation. (2)

focal concern A key value of any culture, especially a key value of a delinquent subculture. (7)

folkways A time-honored custom. Although folkways carry the force of tradition, their violation is unlikely to threaten the survival of the group. See also **mores**. (4)

forcible rape (UCR) The carnal knowledge of a female forcibly and against her will. Assaults or attempts to commit rape by force or threat of force are also included in the UCR definition; however, statutory rape (without force) and other sex offenses are excluded. (2)

forensic psychiatry A branch of psychiatry having to do with the study of crime and criminality. (6)

forensic psychology The application of the science and profession of psychology to questions and issues relating to law and the legal system. (6)

forfeiture See asset forfeiture.

frustration-aggression theory A theory that holds that frustration, which is a natural consequence of living, is a root cause of crime. Criminal behavior can be a form of adaptation when it results in stress reduction. (6)

future criminology The study of likely futures as they impinge on crime and its control. (16)

futures research "A multidisciplinary branch of operations research" whose principal aim "is to facilitate long-range planning based on (1) forecasting from the past supported by mathematical models, (2) cross-disciplinary treatment of its subject matter, (3) systematic use of expert judgment, and (4) a systems-analytical approach to its problems."[9] (16)

futurist One who studies the future. (16)

gateway offense An offense, usually fairly minor in nature, that leads to more serious offenses. Shoplifting, for example, may be a gateway offense to more serious property crimes. (11)

gender gap The observed differences between male and female rates of criminal offending in a given society, such as the United States. (9)

general deterrence A goal of criminal sentencing which seeks to prevent others from committing crimes similar to the one for which a particular offender is being sentenced. (4)

general theory A theory that attempts to explain all (or at least most) forms of criminal conduct through a single, overarching approach. (1)

genetic determinism The belief that genes are the major determining factor in human behavior. (5)

guilty but mentally ill (GBMI) A finding that offenders are guilty of the criminal offense with which they are charged, but because of their prevailing mental condition, they are generally sent to psychiatric hospitals for treatment rather than to prison. Once they have been declared cured, however, such offenders can be transferred to correctional facilities to serve out their sentences. (6)

habitual offender statute A law intended to keep repeat criminal offenders behind bars. These laws sometimes come under the "three strikes and you're out" rubric. (15)

hacker A person who uses computers for exploration and exploitation. (14)

hard determinism The belief that crime results from forces that are beyond the control of the individual. (4)

hate crime A criminal offense in which the motive is hatred, bias, or prejudice based on the actual or perceived race, color, religion, national origin, ethnicity, gender, or sexual orientation of another individual or group of individuals. Also called *bias crime*. (2)

Hate Crimes Sentencing Enhancement Act A federal law (28 U.S.C 994) enacted in 1994 as part of the Violent Crime Control and Law Enforcement Act, that required the U.S. Sentencing Commission to increase the penalties for crimes in which the victim was selected "because of [their] actual or perceived race, color, religion, national origin, ethnicity, gender, disability, or sexual orientation." (15)

hedonistic calculus The belief, first proposed by Jeremy Bentham, that behavior holds value to any individual undertaking it according to the amount of pleasure or pain that it can be expected to produce for that person. Also called *utilitarianism*. (4)

heritability A statistical construct that estimates the amount of variation in a population that is attributable to genetic factors. (3)

heroin signature program (HSP) A Drug Enforcement Administration program that identifies the geographic source of a heroin sample through the detection of specific chemical characteristics in the sample peculiar to the source area. (13)

homicide The killing of one human being by another. (2)

household crime (NCVS) An attempted or completed crime that does not involve confrontation, such as burglary, motor vehicle theft, and household larceny. (2)

human development The relationship between the maturing individual and his or her changing environment, as well as the social processes that the relationship entails. (8)

hypoglycemia A medical condition characterized by low blood sugar. (5)

hypothesis An explanation that accounts for a set of facts and that can be tested by further investigation. Also, something that is taken to be true for the purpose of argument or investigation.[10] (3)

id The aspect of the personality from which drives, wishes, urges, and desires emanate. More formally, the division of the psyche associated with instinctual impulses and demands for immediate satisfaction of primitive needs.[11] (6)

identity theft The unauthorized use of another individual's personal identity to fraudulently obtain money, goods, or services, to avoid the payment of debt, or to avoid criminal prosecution. (14)

illegitimate opportunity structure Subcultural pathways to success which the wider society disapproves of. (7)

impression management The intentional enactment of practiced behavior which is intended to convey to others one's desirable personal characteristics and social qualities. (8)

incapacitation The use of imprisonment or other means to reduce the likelihood that an offender will be capable of committing future offenses. (4)

individual rights advocate One who seeks to protect personal freedoms in the face of criminal prosecution. (4)

inferential statistics Statistics that specify how likely findings are to be true for other populations or in other locales. (3)

informed consent The ethical requirement of social scientific research that research subjects be informed as to the nature of the research about to be conducted, their anticipated role in it, and the uses to which the data they provide will be put. (3)

insanity (legal) A legally established inability to understand right from wrong or to conform one's behavior to the requirements of the law. (6)

insanity (psychological) Persistent mental disorder or derangement.[12] (6)

institutional robbery Robbery that occurs in commercial settings, such as convenience stores, gas stations, and banks. (10)

instrumental crime A goal-directed offense that involves some degree of planning by the offender. (10)

instrumental Marxism A perspective which holds that those in power intentionally create laws and social institutions that serve their own interests and that keep others from becoming powerful. (9)

integrated theory An explanatory perspective that merges (or attempts to merge) concepts drawn from different sources. (1)

interactionist perspective See **social process theory.**

interdiction An international drug control policy that aims to stop drugs from entering the country illegally. (13)

internal validity The certainty that experimental interventions did indeed cause the changes observed in the study group. Also, the control over confounding factors which tend to invalidate the results of an experiment. (3)

Internet The world's largest computer network. (14)

intersubjectivity A scientific principle which requires that independent observers see the same thing under the same circumstances for observations to be regarded as valid. (3)

intimate-partner assault A gender-neutral term used to characterize assaultive behavior that takes place between individuals involved in an intimate relationship. (10)

irresistible-impulse test A standard for judging legal insanity which holds that a defendant is not guilty of a criminal offense if the person, by virtue of his or her mental state or psychological condition, was not able to resist committing the crime. (6)

jockey A professional car thief involved regularly in calculated, steal-to-order car thefts. (11)

joyriding An opportunistic car theft, often committed by a teenager seeking fun or thrills. (11)

Juke family A well-known "criminal family" studied by Richard L. Dugdale. (5)

just deserts model The notion that criminal offenders deserve the punishment they receive at the hands of the law and that punishments should be appropriate to the type and severity of crime committed. (4)

justice model A contemporary model of imprisonment in which the principle of just deserts forms the underlying social philosophy. (9)

Kallikak family A well-known "criminal family" studied by Henry H. Goddard. (5)

Kefauver Committee The popular name for the federal Special Committee to Investigate Originated Crime in Interstate Commerce, formed in 1951. (12)

Kriminalpolitik The political handling of crime. Also, a criminology-based social policy. (15)

labeling An interactionist perspective which sees continued crime as a consequence of limited opportunities for acceptable behavior which follow from the negative responses of society to those defined as offenders. Also, the process by which a negative or deviant label is imposed. (8)

La Cosa Nostra See **Cosa Nostra.**

larceny The unlawful taking or attempted taking of property (other than a motor vehicle) from the possession of another, by stealth, without force or deceit, with intent to permanently deprive the owner of the property. (2)

larceny-theft (UCR) The unlawful taking, carrying, leading, or riding away of property (other than a motor vehicle) from the possession or constructive possession of another. Attempts are included. (2)

latent crime rate A rate of crime calculated on the basis of crimes that would likely be committed by those who are in prison or jail or who are otherwise incapacitated by the justice system. (2)

law and order advocate One who suggests that under certain circumstances involving criminal threats to public safety, the interests of society should take precedence over individual rights. (4)

Law Enforcement Assistance Administration (LEAA) A federal program, established under Title 1 of the Omnibus Crime Control and Safe Streets Act of 1967, designed to provide assistance to police agencies. (15)

learning theory (sociology) A perspective that places primary emphasis upon the role of communication and socialization in the acquisition of learned patterns of criminal behavior and the values that support that behavior. (8)

left realism A conflict perspective that insists on a pragmatic assessment of crime and its associated problems. Also called *realist criminology.* (9)

left-realist criminology See **left-realism.**

legalization (of drugs) Elimination of the laws and associated criminal penalties that prohibit the production, sale, distribution, and possession of a controlled substance. (13)

liberal feminism A perspective which holds that the concerns of women can be incorporated within existing social institutions through conventional means and without the need to drastical-

ly restructure society. Criminal laws, such as the Violence Against Women Act, for example, have been enacted in order to change the legal structure in such a way that it becomes responsive to women's issues. (9)

life course Pathways through the age-differentiated life span. Also, the course of a person's life over time. (8)

lifestyle theory See **routine activities theory.**

mafia See **Cosa Nostra.**

mala in se Acts that are thought to be wrong in and of themselves. (4)

mala prohibita Acts that are wrong only because they are prohibited. (4)

Marxist criminology See **radical criminology.**

masculinity hypothesis (1) A belief (from the late 1800s), that criminal women typically exhibited masculine features and mannerisms. (2) In the late 1900s, the belief that, over time, men and women will commit crimes that are increasingly similar in nature, seriousness and frequency. Increasing similarity in crime commission is predicted to result from changes in the social status of women (for example, better economic position, gender role convergence, socialization practices that are increasingly similar for both males and females, and so on). (5)

mass murder The illegal killing of four or more victims at one location within one event. (2)

mesomorph A body type described as athletic and muscular. (5)

meta-analysis A study of other studies about a particular topic of interest. (3)

metatheory A theory about theories and the theorizing process. (16)

misdemeanor A criminal offense which is less serious than a felony and is punishable by incarceration, usually in a local confinement facility, typically for a year or less.

M'Naughten rule A standard for judging legal insanity which requires that offenders not know what they were doing, or if they did, that they not know it was wrong. (6)

modeling theory A form of social learning theory which asserts that people learn how to act by observing others. (6)

money laundering The process of converting illegally earned assets, originating as cash, to one or more alternative forms to conceal such incriminating factors as illegal origin and true ownership.[13] (12)

Monitoring the Future A national self-report survey on drug use that has been conducted since 1975. (2)

monozygotic (MZ) twins Twins that develop from the same egg and that carry virtually the same genetic material. (5)

moral enterprise The efforts made by an interest group to have its sense of moral or ethical propriety enacted into law. (8)

more A behavioral proscription covering potentially serious violations of a group's values. Examples include strictures against murder, rape, and robbery. See also **folkway.** (4)

motor vehicle theft (UCR) The theft or attempted theft of a motor vehicle. According to the Federal Bureau of Investigation, this offense category includes the stealing of automobiles, trucks, buses, motorcycles, motorscooters, and snowmobiles. (2)

murder An unlawful homicide. (2)

National Advisory Commission on Criminal Justice Standards and Goals A federal body commissioned in 1971 by President Richard Nixon to examine the nation's criminal justice system and to set standards and goals to direct the development of the nation's criminal justice agencies. (15)

National Crime Victimization Survey (NCVS) A survey conducted annually by the Bureau of Justice Statistics that provides data on surveyed households that report they were affected by crime. (2)

National Household Survey on Drug Abuse (NHSDA) A national survey of illicit drug use among people 12 years of age and older that is conducted annually by the Substance Abuse and Mental Health Services Administration. (13)

National Incident-Based Reporting System (NIBRS) A new and enhanced statistical reporting system that will collect data on each single incident and arrest within 22 crime categories. (2)

National Violence against Women (NVAW) Survey A national survey of the extent and nature of violence against women conducted between November 1995 and May 1996 and funded through grants from the National Institute of Justice and the U.S. Department of Health and Human Services' National Center for Injury Prevention and Control. (10)

National Youth Survey (NYS) A longitudinal panel study of a national sample of 1,725 individuals that measured self-reports of delinquency and other types of behavior. (2)

natural law The philosophical perspective that certain immutable laws are fundamental to human nature and can be readily ascertained through reason. Human-made laws, in contrast, are said to derive from human experience and history—both of which are subject to continual change. (4)

natural rights The rights which, according to natural law theorists, individuals retain in the face of government action and interests. (4)

negligent homicide The act of causing the death of another person by recklessness or gross negligence. (2)

neoclassical criminology A contemporary version of classical criminology which emphasizes deterrence and retribution, with reduced emphasis on rehabilitation. (4)

neurosis Functional disorders of the mind or of the emotions involving anxiety, phobia, or other abnormal behavior. (6)

No Electronic Theft Act (NETA/NETAct) A 1997 federal law (Public Law 105-147) that criminalizes the willful infringement of copyrighted works, including by electronic means, even when the infringing party derives no direct financial benefit from the infringement (such as when pirated software is freely distributed online). In keeping with requirements of the NETA, the U.S. Sentencing Commission enacted amendments to its guidelines on April 6, 2000, to increase penalties associated with electronic theft. (14)

nonprimary homicide Murder which involves victims and offenders who have no prior relationship and which usually occurs during the course of another crime such as robbery. (10)

nothing-works doctrine The belief, popularized by Robert Martinson in the 1970s, that correctional treatment programs have little success in rehabilitating offenders. (4)

nurturant strategy A crime control strategy that attempts "to forestall development of criminality by improving early life experiences and channeling child and adolescent development" in desirable directions.[14] (15)

occasional offender A criminal offender whose offending patterns are guided primarily by opportunity. (11)

occupational crime Any act punishable by law which is committed through opportunity created in the course of an occupation that is legal.[15] (12)

offense A violation of the criminal law or, in some jurisdictions, a minor crime, such as jaywalking, sometimes described as "ticketable."

offense specialization A preference for engaging in a certain type of offense to the exclusion of others. (11)

Office of Juvenile Justice and Delinquency Prevention (OJJDP) A national office that provides monetary assistance and direct victim-service programs for juvenile courts. (8)

Office of National Drug Control Policy (ONDCP) A national office charged by Congress with establishing policies, priorities, and objectives for the nation's drug-control program. ONDCP is responsible for developing and disseminating the *National Drug-Control Strategy.* (13)

omerta The informal, unwritten code of organized crime which demands silence and loyalty, among other things, of family members. (12)

Omnibus Anti-Drug Abuse Act A federal law (Public Law 100-690) enacted in 1988 which substantially increased federal penalties for recreational drug users and created a new cabinet-level position (known unofficially as the Drug Czar) to coordinate the drug-fighting efforts of the federal government. (15)

Omnibus Crime Control and Safe Streets Act A federal law enacted in 1967 to eliminate the social conditions that create crime and which funded many anticrime initiatives nationwide. (15)

omnivore See carnivore.

operant behavior Behavior that affects the environment in such a way as to produce responses or further behavioral cues. (6)

operationalization The process by which concepts are made measurable. (3)

opportunity structure A path to success. Opportunity structures may be of two types: legitimate and illegitimate. (7)

organized crime The unlawful activities of the members of a highly organized, disciplined association engaged in supplying illegal goods and services, including gambling, prostitution, loan-sharking, narcotics, and labor racketeering.[16] (12)

panopticon A prison designed by Jeremy Bentham which was to be a circular building with cells along the circumference, each clearly visible from a central location staffed by guards. (4)

paradigm An example, model, or theory. (5)

paranoid schizophrenic A schizophrenic individual who suffers from delusions and hallucinations. (6)

Part I offense Any of a group of offenses, also called "major offenses" or "index offenses," for which the UCR publishes counts of reported instances. Part I offenses consist of murder, rape, robbery, aggravated assault, burglary, larceny, auto theft, and arson. (2)

Part II offense Any of a set of UCR categories used to report data concerning arrests for less serious offenses. (2)

participant observation A strategy in data gathering in which the researcher observes a group by participating, to varying degrees, in the activities of the group.[17] (3)

participatory justice A relatively informal type of criminal justice case processing which makes use of local community resources rather than requiring traditional forms of official intervention. (9)

patriarchy The tradition of male dominance. (9)

peacemaking criminology A perspective which holds that crime control agencies and the citizens they serve should work together to alleviate social problems and human suffering and thus reduce crime. (9)

peace model An approach to crime control which focuses on effective ways for developing a shared consensus on critical issues which could seriously affect the quality of life. (9)

penal couple A term that describes the relationship between offender and victim. Also, the two individuals most involved in the criminal act: the offender and the victim.

persistence Continuity in crime. Also, continual involvement in offending. (8)

persistent thief One who continues in common-law property crimes despite no better than an ordinary level of success. (11)

personal robbery Robbery that occurs on the highway or street or in a public place (and which is often referred to as "mugging") and robbery that occurs in residences. (10)

pharmaceutical diversion The process by which legitimately manufactured controlled substances are diverted for illicit use. (13)

phenomenological criminology The study of crime as a social phenomenon that is created through a process of social interaction.

phenomenology The study of the contents of human consciousness without regard to external conventions or prior assumptions.

phone phreak A person who uses switched, dialed-access telephone services for exploration and exploitation. (14)

phrenology The study of the shape of the head to determine anatomical correlates of human behavior. (5)

piracy See **software piracy.**

pluralist perspective An analytical approach to social organization which holds that a multiplicity of values and beliefs exists in any complex society but that most social actors agree on the usefulness of law as a formal means of dispute resolution. (9)

positivism The application of scientific techniques to the study of crime and criminals. (4)

postcrime victimization Problems which tend to follow from initial victimization. Also called *secondary victimization.* (15)

postmodern criminology A brand of criminology that developed following World War II and that builds on the tenets inherent in postmodern social thought. (9)

power-control theory A perspective which holds that the distribution of crime and delinquency within society is to some degree founded upon the consequences which power relationships within the wider society hold for domestic settings and for the everyday relationships between men, women, and children within the context of family life. (9)

primary deviance Initial deviance often undertaken to deal with transient problems in living. (8)

primary homicide Murder involving family members, friends, and acquaintances. (10)

primary research Research characterized by original and direct investigation. (3)

professional criminal A criminal offender who makes a living from criminal pursuits, is recognized by other offenders as professional, and engages in offending that is planned and calculated. (11)

Project on Human Development in Chicago Neighborhoods (PHDCN) An intensive study of Chicago neighborhoods employing longitudinal evaluations to examine the changing circumstances of people's lives in an effort to identify personal characteristics that may lead toward or away from antisocial behavior. (8)

proletariat In Marxist theory, the working class. (9)

protection/avoidance strategy A crime control strategy that attempts to reduce criminal opportunities by changing people's routine activities, by increasing guardianship, or by incapacitating convicted offenders.[18] (15)

psychiatric criminology Theories derived from the medical sciences, including neurology, and which, like other psychological theories, focus on the individual as the unit of analysis. Psychiatric theories form the basis of psychiatric criminology. See also **forensic psychiatry.** (6)

psychiatric theory A theory derived from the medical sciences, including neurology, and which, like other psychological theories, focuses on the individual as the unit of analysis. (6)

psychoactive substance A substance that affects the mind, mental processes, or emotions. (13)

psychoanalysis The theory of human psychology founded by Sigmund Freud on the concepts of the unconscious, resistance, repression, sexuality, and the Oedipus complex.[19] (6)

psychoanalytic criminology A psychiatric approach developed by Sigmund Freud which emphasizes the role of personality in human behavior and which sees deviant behavior as the result of dysfunctional personalities. (6)

psychological profiling The attempt to categorize, understand, and predict the behavior of certain types of offenders based on behavioral clues they provide. (6)

psychological theory A theory derived from the behavioral sciences which focuses on the individual as the unit of analysis. Psychological theories place the locus of crime causation within the personality of the individual offender. (6)

psychopath An individual with a personality disorder, especially one manifested in aggressively antisocial behavior, which is often said to be the result of a poorly developed superego. Also called *sociopath.* (6)

psychopathology The study of pathological mental conditions—that is, mental illness. (6)

psychosis A form of mental illness in which sufferers are said to be out of touch with reality. (6)

psychotherapy A form of psychiatric treatment based on psychoanalytical principles and techniques. (6)

public policy A course of action that government takes in an effort to solve a problem or to achieve an end. (15)

punishment An undesirable behavioral consequence likely to decrease the frequency of occurrence of that behavior. (6)

pure research Research undertaken simply for the sake of advancing scientific knowledge. (3)

qualitative method A research technique that produces subjective results, or results that are difficult to quantify. (3)

quantitative method A research technique that produces measurable results. (3)

quasi-experimental design An approach to research which, although less powerful than experimental designs, is deemed worthy of use when better designs are not feasible. (3)

Racketeer Influenced and Corrupt Organizations (RICO) A statute which was part of the federal Organized Crime Control Act of 1970, and which is intended to combat criminal conspiracies. (12)

radical criminology A perspective which holds that the causes of crime are rooted in social conditions which empower the wealthy and the politically well organized but disenfranchise the less fortunate. Also called *critical criminology; Marxist criminology.* (9)

radical feminism A perspective which holds that any significant change in the social status of women can be accomplished only through substantial changes in social institutions such as the family, law, medicine, and so on. Radical feminism argues, for example, that the structure of current legal thinking involves what is fundamentally a male perspective, which should be changed to incorporate women's social experiences and points of view. (9)

randomization The process whereby individuals are assigned to study groups without biases or differences resulting from selection. (3)

rape (NCVS) Carnal knowledge through the use of force or the threat of force, including attempts. Statutory rape (without force) is excluded. Both heterosexual and homosexual rape are included. (2)

rape (UCR) See **forcible rape.**

rape myth A false assumption about rape such as, "When a woman says no, she really means yes." Rape myths characterize much of the discourse surrounding sexual violence. (10)

rape shield law A statute providing for the protection of rape victims by ensuring that defendants do not introduce irrelevant facts about the victim's sexual history into evidence. (10)

rational choice theory A perspective which holds that criminality is the result of conscious choice and which predicts that individuals choose to commit crime when the benefits outweigh the costs of disobeying the law. (4)

reaction formation The process by which a person openly rejects that which he or she wants or aspires to but cannot obtain or achieve. (7)

realist criminology See **left-realism.**

recidivism The repetition of criminal behavior. (4)

recidivism rate The percentage of convicted offenders who have been released from prison and who are later rearrested for a new crime, generally within five years following release. See also **dangerousness.** (4)

reintegrative shaming A form of shaming, imposed as a sanction by the criminal justice system, that is thought to strengthen the moral bond between the offender and the community. (8)

relative deprivation A sense of social or economic inequality experienced by those who are unable, for whatever reason, to achieve legitimate success within the surrounding society. (7)

replicability (experimental) A scientific principle which holds that valid observations made at one time can be made again later if all other conditions are the same. (3)

research The use of standardized, systematic procedures in the search for knowledge.[20] (3)

research design The logic and structure inherent in an approach to data gathering. (3)

restitution A criminal sanction, in particular the payment of compensation by the offender to the victim. (15)

restorative justice A postmodern perspective which stresses "remedies and restoration rather than prison, punishment and victim neglect."[21] (9)

retribution The act of taking revenge upon a criminal perpetrator. (4)

reward A desirable behavioral consequence likely to increase the frequency of occurrence of that behavior. (6)

risk analysis See **threat analysis.**

robbery (UCR) The taking or attempting to take anything of value from the care, custody, or control of a person or persons by force or threat of force or violence or by putting the victim in fear. (2)

routine activities theory A brand of rational choice theory which suggests that lifestyles contribute significantly to both the volume and type of crime found in any society. Also called *lifestyle theory.* (4)

scenario writing A technique, intended to predict future outcomes, which builds upon environmental scanning by attempting to assess the likelihood of a variety of possible outcomes once important trends have been identified. (16)

schizoid A person characterized by schizoid personality disorder. Such disordered personalities appear to be aloof, withdrawn, unresponsive, humorless, dull and solitary to an abnormal degree. (6)

schizophrenic A mentally ill individual who is out of touch with reality and who suffers from disjointed thinking. (6)

secondary deviance Deviant behavior which results from official labeling and from association with others who have been so labeled. (8)

secondary research New evaluations of existing information which had been collected by other researchers. (3)

secondary victimization See **postcrime victimization.**

second-degree murder Criminal homicide that is unplanned and that is often described as "a crime of passion." (2)

selective disinhibition A loss of self-control due to the characteristics of the social setting, drugs or alcohol, or a combination of both. (10)

selective incapacitation A social policy which seeks to protect society by incarcerating the individuals deemed to be the most dangerous. (6)

self-control A person's ability to alter his or her own states and responses.[22] (6)

self-report survey A survey in which anonymous respondents, without fear of disclosure or arrest, are asked to confidentially report any violations of the criminal law that they have committed. (2)

separation assault Violence inflicted by partners on significant others who attempt to leave an intimate relationship. (10)

serial murder Criminal homicide which involves the killing of several victims in three or more separate events. (2)

sibling offense An offense or incident that culminates in homicide. The offense or incident may be a crime, such as robbery, or an incident that meets a less stringent criminal definition, such as a lover's quarrel involving assault or battery. (10)

simple assault (NCVS) An attack without a weapon resulting either in minor injury or in undetermined injury requiring less than two days of hospitalization. See also **aggravated assault.** (2)

situational choice theory A brand of rational choice theory which views criminal behavior "as a function of choices and decisions made within a context of situational constraints and opportunities."[23] (4)

situational crime prevention A social policy approach that looks to develop greater understanding of crime and more effective crime prevention strategies through concern with the physical, organizational, and social environments that make crime possible.[24] (4)

snitch An amateur shoplifter. (11)

social bond The link, created through socialization, between individuals and the society of which they are a part. (8)

social capital The degree of positive relationships with others and with social institutions that individuals build up over the course of their lives. (8)

social class Distinctions made between individuals on the basis of important defining social characteristics. (9)

social contract The Enlightenment-era concept that human beings abandon their natural state of individual freedom to join together and form society. In the process of forming a social contract, individuals surrender some freedoms to society as a whole, and government, once formed, is obligated to assume responsibilities toward its citizens and to provide for their protection and welfare. (4)

social control theory A perspective which predicts that when social constraints on antisocial behavior are weakened or absent, delinquent behavior emerges. Rather than stressing causative factors in criminal behavior, control theory asks why people actually obey rules instead of breaking them. (8)

social development perspective An integrated view of human development that examines multiple levels of maturation simultaneously, including the psychological, biological, familial, interpersonal, cultural, societal, and ecological levels. (8)

social disorganization A condition said to exist when a group is faced with social change, uneven development of culture, maladaptiveness, disharmony, conflict, and lack of consensus. (7)

social disorganization theory A perspective on crime and deviance which sees society as a kind of organism and crime and deviance as a kind of disease or social pathology. Theories of social disorganization are often associated with the perspective of social ecology and with the Chicago School of criminology which developed during the 1920s and 1930s. (7)

social ecology An approach to criminological theorizing that attempts to link the structure and organization of human community to interactions with its localized environment. (7)

social epidemiology The study of social epidemics and diseases of the social order. (15)

socialist feminism A perspective which examines social roles and the gender-based division of labor within the family, seeing both as a significant source of women's subordination within society. This perspective calls for a redefinition of gender-related job status, compensation for women who work within the home, and equal pay for equal work regardless of gender. (9)

socialization The lifelong process of social experience whereby individuals acquire the cultural patterns of their society. (1)

social learning theory A psychological perspective that says that people learn how to behave by modeling themselves after others whom they have the opportunity to observe. (8)

social life The ongoing and (typically) structured interaction that occurs between persons in a society, including socialization and social behavior in general. (7)

social pathology A concept that compares society to a physical organism and that sees criminality as an illness. (7)

social policy A government initiative, program, or plan intended to address problems in society. The "war on crime," for example, is a kind of generic (large-scale) social policy—one consisting of many smaller programs. (1)

social problems perspective The belief that crime is a manifestation of underlying social problems, such as poverty, discrimination, pervasive family violence, inadequate socialization practices, and the breakdown of traditional social institutions. (1)

social process The interaction between and among social institutions, individuals, and groups. (7)

social process theory A theory that asserts that criminal behavior is learned in interaction with others and that socialization processes that occur as the result of group membership are the primary route through which learning occurs. Also called the *interactionist perspective.* (8)

social relativity The notion that social events are differently interpreted according to the cultural experiences and personal interests of the initiator, the observer, or the recipient of that behavior. (1)

social responsibility perspective The belief that individuals are fundamentally responsible for their own behavior and that they choose crime over other, more law-abiding, courses of action. (1)

social structure The pattern of social organization and the interrelationships between institutions characteristic of a society. (7)

social structure theory A theory that explains crime by reference to some aspect of the social fabric. These theories emphasize relationships between social institutions and describe the types of behavior which tend to characterize groups of people rather than individuals. (7)

sociobiology "The systematic study of the biological basis of all social behavior."[25] (5)

sociological theory A perspective that focuses on the nature of the power relationships that exist between social groups, and on the influences that various social phenomena bring to bear on the types of behaviors that tend to characterize groups of people. (7)

sociopath See **psychopath.**

soft determinism The belief that human behavior is the result of choices and decisions made within a context of situational constraints and opportunities. (4)

software piracy The unauthorized and illegal copying of software programs. (14)

somatotyping The classification of human beings into types according to body build and other physical characteristics. (5)

specific deterrence A goal of criminal sentencing which seeks to prevent a particular offender from engaging in repeat criminality. (4)

spousal rape The rape of one spouse by the other. The term usually refers to the rape of a woman by her husband. (10)

stalking A course of conduct directed at a specific person that involves repeated visual or physical proximity; nonconsensual communication; verbal, written, or implied threats; or a combination thereof, which would cause a reasonable person fear. (10)

state-organized crime Acts defined by law as criminal and committed by state officials in the pursuit of their work as representatives of the state.[26] (12)

statistical correlation The simultaneous increase or decrease in value of two numerically valued random variables.[27] (3)

statistical school A criminological perspective with roots in the early 1800s which seeks to uncover correlations between crime rates and other types of demographic data. (2)

statute A formal written enactment of a legislative body.[28] (1)

statutory law Law in the form of statutes or formal written strictures made by a legislature or governing body with the power to make law. (1)

stigmatic shaming A form of shaming, imposed as a sanction by the criminal justice system, that is thought to destroy the moral bond between the offender and the community. (8)

strain theory A sociological approach which posits a disjuncture between socially and subculturally sanctioned means and goals as the cause of criminal behavior. Also called *anomie theory.* (7)

strategic assessment A technique that assesses the risks and opportunities facing those who plan for the future. (16)

structural Marxism A perspective which holds that the structural institutions of society influence the behavior of individuals and groups by virtue of the type of relationships created. The criminal law, for example, reflects class relationships and serves to reinforce those relationships. (9)

subcultural theory A sociological perspective that emphasizes the contribution made by variously socialized cultural groups to the phenomenon of crime. (7)

subculture A collection of values and preferences which is communicated to subcultural participants through a process of socialization. (7)

sublimation The psychological process whereby one aspect of consciousness comes to be symbolically substituted for another. (6)

substantial-capacity test A standard for judging legal insanity which requires that a person lack the mental capacity needed to understand the wrongfulness of his act, or to conform his behavior to the requirements of the law. (6)

superego The moral aspect of the personality; much like the conscience. More formally, the division of the psyche that develops by the incorporation of the perceived moral standards of the community, is mainly unconscious, and includes the conscience.[29] (6)

supermale A male individual displaying the XYY chromosome structure. (5)

superpredator One of a new generation of juveniles "who are coming of age in actual and 'moral poverty' without the benefits of parents, teachers, coaches and clergy to teach them right from wrong and show them 'unconditional love.'"[30] The term is often applied to inner-city youths who meet the criteria it sets forth. (2)

survey research A social science data-gathering technique which involves the use of questionnaires. (3)

tagging The process whereby an individual is negatively defined by agencies of justice. Also called *labeling.* (8)

target hardening The reduction in criminal opportunity for a particular location, generally through the use of physical barriers, architectural design, and enhanced security measures. (4)

technique of neutralization A culturally available justification which can provide criminal offenders with the means to disavow responsibility for their behavior. (7)

TEMPEST A standard developed by the U.S. government that requires that electromagnetic emanations from computers designated as "secure" be below levels that would allow radio receiving equipment to "read" the data being computed. (14)

terrorism A violent act or an act dangerous to human life in violation of the criminal laws of the United States or of any state to intimidate or coerce a government, the civilian population, or any segment thereof, in furtherance of political or social objectives.[31] (10)

test of significance A statistical technique intended to provide researchers with confidence that their results are in fact true and not the result of sampling error. (3)

testosterone The primary male sex hormone. Produced in the testes, its function is to control secondary sex characteristics and sexual drive. (5)

thanatos A death wish. (6)

theory A series of interrelated propositions that attempt to describe, explain, predict, and ultimately control some class of events. A theory gains explanatory power from inherent logical consistency and is "tested" by how well it describes and predicts reality. (1; 3)

threat analysis A complete and thorough assessment of the kinds of perils facing an organization. Also called *risk analysis.* (14)

three-strikes provision A provision of some criminal statutes which mandates life imprisonment for criminals convicted of three violent felonies or serious drug offenses. (15)

total institution A facility from which individuals can rarely come and go and in which communal life is intense and circumscribed. Individuals in total institutions tend to eat, sleep, play, learn, and worship (if at all) together. (6)

transnational organized crime Unlawful activity undertaken and supported by organized criminal groups operating across national boundaries. (12)

trend extrapolation A technique of futures research that makes future predictions based on the projection of existing trends. (16)

trephination A form of surgery typically involving bone, especially the skull. Early instances of cranial trephination have been taken as evidence for primitive beliefs in spirit possession. (4)

truth in sentencing A close correspondence between the sentence imposed upon those sent to prison and the time actually served prior to prison release.[32] (4)

Twelve Tables Early Roman laws written circa 450 B.C. which regulated family, religious, and economic life. (4)

unicausal Having one cause. Unicausal theories posit only one source for all that they attempt to explain. (1)

Uniform Crime Reporting Program A Federal Bureau of Investigation summation of crime statistics tallied annually, and consisting primarily of data on crimes reported to the police and of arrests. (2)

utilitarianism See **hedonistic calculus.**

variable A concept that can undergo measurable changes. (3)

verstehen The kind of subjective understanding that can be achieved by criminologists who immerse themselves in the everyday world of the criminals they study. (3)

victim-impact statement A written document which describes the losses, suffering, and trauma experienced by the crime victim or by the victim's survivors. In jurisdictions where victim-impact statements are used, judges are expected to consider them in arriving at an appropriate sentence for the offender. (15)

victimization rate (NCVS) A measure of the occurrence of victimizations among a specified population group. For personal crimes, the rate is based on the number of victimizations per 1,000 residents aged 12 or older. For household crimes, the victimization rates are calculated using the number of incidents per 1,000 households. (2)

victimogenesis The contributory background of a victim as a result of which he or she becomes prone to victimization.

victimology The study of victims and their contributory role, if any, in crime causation.

victim-precipitated homicide A killing in which the victim was the first to commence the interaction or was the first to resort to physical violence.

victim precipitation Contributions made by the victim to the criminal event, especially those that led to its initiation. (10)

victim proneness An individual's likelihood of victimization.

Victims of Crime Act (VOCA) A federal law enacted in 1984 that established the federal Crime Victims Fund. The fund uses monies from fines and forfeitures collected from federal offenders to supplement state support of local victims' assistance programs and state victim compensation programs. (15)

victim-witness assistance program A program that counsels victims, orients them to the justice process, and provides a variety of other services, such as transportation to court, child care during court appearances, and referrals to social service agencies. (15)

Violence against Women Act (VAWA) A federal law enacted as a component of the 1994 Violent Crime Control and Law Enforcement Act and which was intended to address concerns about violence against women. The law focused on improving the interstate enforcement of protection orders, providing effective training for court personnel involved with women's issues, improving the training and collaboration of police and prosecutors with victim service providers, strengthening law enforcement efforts to reduce violence against women, and on efforts to increase services to victims of violence. President Clinton signed the reauthorization of this legislation, known as the Violence against Women Act 2000, into law on October 28, 2000. (15)

Violent Crime Control and Law Enforcement Act A federal law (Public Law 103-322) enacted in 1994 that authorized spending billions of dollars on crime prevention, law enforcement, and prison construction. It also outlawed the sale of certain types of assault weapons and enhanced federal death penalty provisions. (15)

Violent Criminal Apprehension Program (VICAP) Program of the Federal Bureau of Investigation focusing on serial murder investigation and the apprehension of serial killers. (10)

virus See **computer virus.**

white-collar crime Violations of the criminal law committed by a person of respectability and high social status in the course of his or her occupation. (12)

Wickersham Commission Created by President Herbert Hoover in 1931, and officially known as the *Commission on Law Observance and Enforcement,* the mandate of this commission was to develop "objectives to improve justice system practices and to reinstate law's role in civilized governance." The Commission made recommendations concerning the nation's police forces, and described how to improve policing throughout America. (15)

NOTES

[1] American Board of Forensic Psychology, World Wide Web site. Web posted at http://www.abfp.com/brochure.html. Accessed November 22, 2000.
[2] This and other computer crime–related terms are adapted from Donn B. Parker, *Computer Crime: Criminal Justice*

Resource Manual (Washington, D.C.: National Institute of Justice, 1989).
[3] Michael L. Benson, Francis T. Cullen, and William J. Maakestad, *Local Prosecutors and Corporate Crime* (Washington, D.C.: National Institute of Justice, 1993).

[4]James A. Inciardi, *The War on Drugs II* (Mountain View, CA: Mayfield), 1992, p. 79.

[5]Bryan Vila, "A General Paradigm for Understanding Criminal Behavior: Extending Evolutionary Ecological Theory," *Criminology*, Vol. 32, No. 3 (August 1994), pp. 311–359.

[6]Bureau of Justice Statistics, *Drugs, Crime and the Justice System* (Washington, D.C.: U.S. Department of Justice, December 1992).

[7]*American Heritage Dictionary and Electronic Thesaurus* (Boston: Houghton Mifflin, 1987).

[8]George F. Cole, "Criminal Justice in the Twenty-first Century: The Role of Futures Research," in John Klofas and Stan Stojkovic, eds., *Crime and Justice in the Year 2010* (Belmont, CA: Wadsworth, 1995).

[9]Society of Police Futurists International, *PFI: The Future of Policing* (brochure), no date.

[10]*American Heritage Dictionary and Electronic Thesaurus.*

[11]Ibid.

[12]Ibid.

[13]Clifford Karchmer and Douglas Ruch, "State and Local Money Laundering Control Strategies," *NIJ Research in Brief* (Washington, D.C.: National Institute of Justice, 1992), p. 1.

[14]Vila, "A General Paradigm for Understanding Criminal Behavior."

[15]Gary S. Green, *Occupational Crime* (Chicago: Nelson-Hall, 1990), p. 12.

[16]The Omnibus Crime Control Act of 1970.

[17]Frank E. Hagan, *Research Methods in Criminal Justice and Criminology* (New York: Macmillan, 1993), p. 103.

[18]Bryan Vila, "Human Nature and Crime Control: Improving the Feasibility of Nurturant Strategies," *Politics and the Life Sciences* (March 1997), pp. 3–21.

[19]*American Heritage Dictionary and Electronic Thesaurus.*

[20]Abraham Kaplan, *The Conduct of Inquiry: Methodology for Behavioral Science* (San Francisco: Chandler, 1964), p. 71.

[21]Fay Honey Knopp, "Community Solutions to Sexual Violence: Feminist-Abolitionist Perspectives," in Harold Pepinsky and Richard Quinney, eds., *Criminology as Peacemaking* (Bloomington: Indiana University Press, 1991), p. 183.

[22]Roy F. Baumeister and Julie Juola Exline, "Self-control, Morality, and Human Strength," *Journal of Social & Clinical Psychology*, Vol. 19, No. 1 (April 2000), p. 29-42.

[23]Ronald V. Clarke and Derek B. Cornish, eds., *Crime Control in Britain: A Review of Police and Research* (Albany: State University of New York Press), p. 8.

[24]David Weisburd, "Reorienting Crime Prevention Research and Policy: From the Causes of Criminality to the Context of Crime," *NIJ Research Report* (Washington, D.C.: National Institute of Justice, June 1997).

[25]Edward O. Wilson, *Sociobiology: The New Synthesis* (Cambridge: Harvard University Press, Belknop Press, 1975).

[26]William J. Chambliss, "State-Organized Crime—The American Society of Criminology, 1988 Presidential Address," *Criminology*, Vol. 27, No. 2 (1989), pp. 183–208.

[27]*American Heritage Dictionary and Electronic Thesaurus.*

[28]Henry Campbell Black, *Black's Law Dictionary*, 6th ed. (St. Paul: West, 1990), p. 1410.

[29]*American Heritage Dictionary and Electronic Thesaurus.*

[30]See John J. DiIulio, Jr., "The Question of Black Crime," *Public Interest*, fall 1994, pp. 3–12. The term *superpredator* is generally attributed to DiIulio.

[31]Federal Bureau of Investigation, Counterterrorism Section, *Terrorism in the United States, 1987* (Washington, D.C.: FBI, December 1987).

[32]Lawrence A. Greenfeld, "Prison Sentences and Time Served for Violence," *Bureau of Justice Statistics Selected Findings*, No. 4, April 1995.

Index

natural selection, 305
natural surveillance, 121, 123
Navajo Peacemaker Court, 279
negligent homicide, 51, 52, 500
Neidorf, Craig, 441
neo-Nazis, 319
neoclassical criminology, 119–124, 131, 500
net effects, 90
neurosis, 179, 500
neuroticism, 175
neutralization, 205, 214, 504
Nevada State Athletic Commission, 54
New Afrikan Independence Movement, 96
New Age movement, 278
New Police (London, England), 118
New York City Police Department, Taxi Livery Task Force, 308
New York Times, 260, 261
Newsletter (Marxist Section, American Sociological Association), 281
Newton's Law of Criminology, 49
NGRI ("not guilty by reason of insanity"), 188, 190
Nichols, Terry, 318
NIJ (National Institute of Justice), 12, 67, 74, 98, 401–402, 434, 472
Nirvana (musical group), 395
Nixon, Richard M., 454, 500
NNICC Report (National Narcotics Intelligence Consumers Committee), 390
No Electronic Theft Act (NETA/NETAct), 423, 500
nonprimary homicide, 290, 500
Northeastern Association of Criminal Justice Sciences, 29
"not guilty by reason of insanity" (NGRI), 188, 190
nothing-works doctrine, 120, 500
Notorious B.I.G., 5, 450, 451
nurturant strategies, 252, 466, 500

O

oaths in a court of law, 117
Obasi, Myra, 85
Observance and Enforcement of Prohibition (National Commission on Law Observance and Enforcement), 370
observation, 93
Obsession (Douglas), 193
occasional criminals, 142, 144, 495
occasional offender, 332, 500
occupational crime, 362, 500
Occupational Crime (Green), 362
Ochoa, Christopher, 434
offender, psychotic, 179–180
offender deflection, 121, 123
offender self-report, 61–62, 502
offense, 500
offense specialization, 331–332, 500
Office for Victims of Crime, 74
Office of Justice Programs, 74
Office of Juvenile Justice and Delinquency Prevention (OJJDP), 74, 240–241, 252, 253, 470–471, 500
Office of National Drug Control Policy (ONDCP), 74, 407–409, 412, 500
Office of Postsecondary Education, 61
Ohlin, Lloyd E., 205
OJJDP (Office of Juvenile Justice and Delinquency Prevention), 74, 240–241, 252, 253, 470–471, 500
Oklahoma City bombing, 296, 318, 319, 483
Old Testament, 125

Oliver, Wilford, 218
Olliff, R. Hudson, 35
Olympics bombing, 317
omerta, 371–372, 374–375, 500
Omnibus Anti-Drug Abuse Act of 1988, 128, 405, 407, 454, 500
Omnibus Crime Control and Safe Streets Act, 453, 500
Omnivore (network diagnostic tool), 440, 494
On Aggression (Lorenz), 140–141
ONDCP (Office of National Drug Control Policy), 74, 407–409, 412, 500
Ong, Teng Cheong, 124
Ono, Yoko, 24
Ontario Provincial Police, 87
operant behavior, 185, 500
operant conditioning, 230, 231
Operation Longarm, 429
Operation Padlock, 208
Operation Sun Devil, 428, 441
operationalization, 88, 101, 500
opiates, 402
opium den, 389
opportunity structure, 122–123, 341, 345, 347, 500
organizational occupational crime, 362
organized crime
    activities, 372–374
    code of conduct, 371–372, 374–375, 500
    definition, 500
    families, 372
    future, 485
    history in U.S., 366, 368–372
    and Hoover administration, 452
    and the law, 377–379
    non-Mafia groups, 375–376
    policy issues, 379–381
    and technology, 481–482
    transnational, 376–377, 480, 483
Organized Crime (Abadinsky), 366
Organized Crime Control Act, 377
Ounce of Prevention Council, 459
Outsiders (Becker), 237
Over the Hill Gang (film), 65
overt pathway, 249

P

Pagans (group), 375
Paine, Thomas, 115
Palermo, Vincent "Vinny Ocean," 381
Palestine Liberation Organization (PLO), 482
Panopticon, 118, 119, 124, 500
paradigm, 158, 500
paranoid schizophrenic, 180, 500
parents
    of at-risk children, 241–242
    as prisoners, 232
Park, Robert, 205, 206
Parliament (Britain), 466
Part I offense, 37–38, 65, 66, 500
Part II offense, 60–61, 64, 500
participant observation, 91–92, 95, 96, 97–98, 500
participatory justice, 279, 501
Patriarca, Ray, Jr., 372
Patriarca crime family, 381
patriarchy, 272, 303, 304, 501
Paul, David, 360
Pavlov, Ivan, 173
pawnshops, 348
Pax Romana, 113
PC radios, 438
peace model, 278–279, 501

peacemaking criminology, 265, 277–280, 485, 501
pecuniary punishment, 118
Peel, Sir Robert, 118, 188
penal couple, 501
penitential punishment, 118
Penthouse magazine, 260, 261
People v. *Superior Court of San Diego—Romero,* 460
Pepinsky, Harold E., 265
persistence, 244, 246, 501
persistent thief, 331, 501
personal freedoms, 440–441
Personal Responsibility and Work Opportunity Reconciliation Act, 220
personal robbery, 307, 501
personality and crime, 95, 175–177
Petrosino, Joseph, 366
"phantom banks," 360
pharmaceutical diversion, 399, 501
phenomenological criminology, 501
phenomenology, 501
pheromones, 189
Philip Augustus, King of France, 113
phone phreaks, 421–422, 427, 501
Phrack World News, 441
phrenology, 141–143, 501
physical abnormalities, 145–146
physiological features, 145
Pierce, William, 319
pink color and aggression, 149–150
piracy, 418, 420–421, 440, 504
Pittsburgh Youth Study, 249
Plastic Surgery Education Foundation, 363
Pletcher, Adam Quinn, 424–425
pluralist perspective, 11–12, 263–264, 501
Pointer, Sam, 362–363
police bias, 221
Police Executive Research Forum, 37, 438
Police Foundation, 37
police misconduct, 275
Police (National Commission on Law Observance and Enforcement), 370
police officers, women, 275
Polish Peasant in Europe and America (Thomas and Znaniecki), 205
poor, 269, 270, 271
Porgrebeshski, Alexander, 317
pornography, 303–304, 305, 307
positive law, 115
positivism, 119–120, 142, 143–144, 501
Post-Capitalist Society (Drucker), 479
postcrime criminology, 501
postcrime victimization, 468, 501
postmodern criminology, 96–97, 276–277, 280, 485
Pound, Roscoe, 453
poverty, 210, 220, 221
    and crime, 305
    and homicide, 290, 291
"poverty of affect," 173–174
power-control theory, 265, 273, 501
Powershift (Toffler), 479
prediction of behavior, 191, 222, 233, 236
premeditated murder, 51, 52, 53, 497
premenstrual syndrome (PMS), 142, 151
prenatal alcohol exposure, 150
prenatal marijuana exposure, 150
prenatal smoking, 150
Preparing for the Drug Free Years, 241
Presentation of Self in Everyday Life (Goffman), 239
President's Commission on Law Enforcement and Administration of Justice, 453
primary conflict, 212

NAME INDEX

A

Abadinsky, Howard, 113, 134, 366, 370, 375, 380, 384, 385
Abrahamse, Allan, 199, 308, 325
Abrahamsen, David, 169, 173, 177, 197, 198
Abrams, Jim, 78
Academy of Criminal Justice Sciences, 29, 97, 99, 104, 105, 487
Adams, Mike S., 238, 255
Adler, Freda, 30, 33, 75, 100, 105, 157, 167, 197, 272, 283, 492
Ageton, Suzanne S., 62, 77, 79, 225
Agnew, Robert, 211, 224
Ainsworth, Mary D. Salter, 198
Akers, Ronald L., 29, 231, 233, 254, 283
Akre, Brian S., 444
Alarid, Leanne Fiftal, 78, 167
Alba, Richard D., 458
Albini, Joseph, 481, 482
Allan, Emile Anderson, 283
Alleman, Ted, 77, 283
Allen, Leana C., 256
Allen, Mary Lee, 291
Allport, Gordon W., 169, 196
Alm, P. O., 166
Alova, Natasha, 281
American Academy of Child and Adolescent Psychiatry, 18
American Academy of Forensic Psychology, 172
American Academy of Pediatrics, 18
American Academy of Psychiatry and the Law, 197
American Association for the Advancement of Science, 95
American Bar Association, 127, 135, 470, 475
American Board of Forensic Psychology, 197, 505
American Civil Liberties Union, 133
American College of Forensic Examiners, 29
American Dietetic Association, 148
American Housing Survey, 71
American Law Institute, 190
American Medical Association, 18
American Psychiatric Association, 174, 197
American Psychological Association, 18, 103, 106, 160
    Task Force on Violence Against Women, 298
American Society of Criminology (ASC), 97, 99, 104, 105, 133, 155, 473, 485–486, 487
    Critical Criminology Division, 281
American Sociological Association, 103
    Marxist Section, 281
American Sociological Society, 359, 361
American Statistical Association, 95
Amnesty International, 133
Analytical Center for Social and Economic Policies, 376
Anderson, James E., 474
Anderson, Margaret, 221, 225
Andrews, D. A., 166, 192, 197, 199
Angelo, Bonnie, 385
Anguilo, Gennaro, 285
Anthes, Gary H., 444, 445
Anti-Defamation League, 42
"Antoine" (Crip member), 201
Ardai, Charles, 477, 491
Aristotle, 141, 142
Arizona Board of Regents, 228
Arrestee Drug Abuse Monitoring (ADAM) Program, 390, 402, 413
Arseneault, L., 145–146, 164

Art Theft Recovery Project, 351
ASC. *See* American Society of Criminology (ASC)
Asma, David, 254
Asplen, Christopher, 436
Asseo, Laurie, 385
Association of State UCR Programs, 75
Attachment Research Center, 186
Attorney General (U.S.), 320, 483, 491
Auerhahn, Kathleen, 294, 322
Austin, W. Timothy, 131, 135, 256
Austin v. *U.S.*, 414
Australian National University, 238
Avary, D'Aunn Wester, 343, 354, 355
Azula, Fidel, 400

B

Bachman, Jerald G., 77
Bachman, Ronet, 76, 182, 198
Baer, Deborah, 368
Bagnell, Paul, 383
Baily, W. C., 135
Baker, Katharine K., 324
Baker, Richard H., 420, 444
Ball, Richard A., 225
Balliestri, James, 336, 353
Bandura, Albert, 180, 184, 185, 198
Barak, Gregg, 14, 17, 30, 77, 283
Barlow, John Perry, 445
Barnes, Geoffrey, 255
Baron, Larry, 304, 305, 324
Barr, R., 135
Barry, David, 352
Bartol, Curt R., 172, 197
Bartollas, Clemens, 14, 16, 278, 284
Barzini, Luigi, 384
Baskin, Deborah R., 283
Baumeister, Roy F., 198, 505
Baumer, Eric, 346, 354
Bazelon, David, 189
Beccaria, Cesare, 108, 116, 117, 134
Bechara, Antoine, 163
Bechhofer, Laurie, 323
Bechtel, R., 166
Beck, Allen, 48, 49
Becker, Howard, 237, 238, 255
Beckstrom, John H., 159, 167
Bedau, Hugo Adam, 133
Beer, J. E., 284
Behar, Richard, 384, 385
Beirne, Piers, 10, 30, 104, 272, 282
Belknap, Joanne, 283
Benetton (clothing manufacturer), 129
Bennett, Georgette, 417, 444, 449, 474, 485, 492
Bennett, Thomas, 332, 352
Benson, Michael L., 383, 506
Bentham, Jeremy, 108, 117, 118, 119, 134, 467, 498, 500
Bentham Project, 119
Berger, Ronald J., 323
Bernard, J. L., 326
Bernard, M. L., 326
Bernard, Thomas J., 2, 29, 167
Bernat, Frances P., 323
Bernhardt, Paul C., 150, 165
Bernstein, Jodie, 430–431
Beystehner, Kristen M., 196
Bianchi, Hermanus, 471, 475
Birkbeck, Christopher, 134
Bishop, Terry, 340
BJS. *See* Bureau of Justice Statistics (BJS)
Black, Henry Cambell, 506
Black, Percy, 428, 445

Blackmun, Harry A., 379
Blake, Kevin, 352
Blau, Judith, 211, 224
Blau, Peter, 211, 224
Block, Carolyn Rebecca, 292, 321
Block, Richard, 292, 321
Bloombecker, J., 445
Blum, Kenneth, 156, 166
Blumberg, Abraham S., 383, 384
Blumstein, Alfred, 18, 31, 48, 64, 76, 77, 78, 244, 256, 459–460, 472, 474, 475
Bohm, Robert M., 99, 105
Bohmer, Carol, 323
Bokun, Branko, 286, 321
Bolen, Rebecca M., 323
Bolton, J.A., 255
Bonger, Willem, 264, 281
Bonta, James, 166, 192, 197, 199
Boomsma, Dorret I., 166
Boostrom, R., 30
Booth, Alan, 150, 165
Bowlby, John, 186, 198
Bradish, Jay K., 350
Bragden, Mike, 254
Braiker, Harriet B., 199, 325
Braithwaite, John, 72, 79, 238, 255, 364–365, 381, 383
Brantingham, P., 135
Braswell, Michael, 278, 284
Bratton, William, 48
Bray, Timothy M., 322
Breggin, Peter, 139
Brennan, P.A., 167
Bresson, Paul, 436
Bretherton, Inge, 196
Bridges, George S., 254
Bridges, John Henry, 164
Brinkley, Chad A., 197
Brinton, Crane, 134
British Crime Survey, 335, 341
British Forensic Science Society, 29
Brodsky, Sascha, 327
Brodzinski, Frederick R., 492
Bronfenbrenner, U., 256
Brown, D., 282
Brown, Stephen E., 78
Browning, Katharine, 257
Brownlee, Ken, 349, 355
Brownmiller, Susan, 298, 299, 304, 324
Brunner, Han, 154
Brunton, M., 166
Bryant, Robert, 335
Buchanan, Edna, 78
Buck v. *Bell*, 166, 167
Buckley, R. E., 164
Buerger, Michael E., 135, 224
Bullock, Alan, 223
Bureau of Census (U.S.), 69
    Population Estimates Program, 78
Bureau of Justice Assistance (U.S.), 76, 232
Bureau of Justice Statistics (BJS), 42, 47, 48, 52, 55, 65, 71, 72, 73, 75, 76, 77, 78, 91, 104, 126, 291, 320, 322, 323, 326, 343, 351, 352, 354, 394, 401, 402, 413, 414, 415, 456, 474, 500, 506
Burgess, Ann Wolbert, 305, 324
Burgess, Ernest W., 206, 207, 223
Burgess, Robert, 231, 254
Burney, Melanie, 31
Burns, Edward McNall, 134
Bursik, Robert J., 225
Burt, Martha R., 299, 323
Bush, George W., 20, 475
Business Software Alliance, 444
Butler, Frank, 254, 256

CRIMINOLOGY TODAY

INTERDISCIPLINARY in its approach, while simultaneously acknowledging the strong influence of the sociological perspective in studying crime and criminal activity.

UP-TO-DATE. It addresses the latest social issues and discusses innovative criminological perspectives within a well-grounded and traditional theoretical framework.

SOCIALLY RELEVANT. It contrasts contemporary issues of crime and social order with existing and proposed crime-control policies.

POLICY ORIENTED. Unlike most existing texts, Criminology Today stresses the consequences of criminological thought for social policy, and describes the practical issues associated with understanding and controlling crime.

THEMATIC. It builds upon the divergence between the social problems viewpoint and the social responsibility perspective. In so doing, it highlights the central issue facing criminologists today, whether crime should be addressed as a matter of individual responsibility and accountability, or treated as a symptom of a dysfunctional society.

INTERESTING AND EASY-TO-READ. It is written for today's student and makes use of attention-getting stories, news briefs, images, and graphical outlines to capture student attention.